Best Books for Junior High Readers

Best Books for Junior High Readers™

John T. Gillespie

EDITOR

R. R. BOWKER
New Providence, New Jersey

3853

R.A

Published by R. R. Bowker a division of Reed Publishing (U.S.A.) Inc.
Copyright © 1991 by Reed Publishing (U.S.A.) Inc.
All rights reserved
Printed and bound in the United States of America

Library of Congress Cataloging-in-Publication Data

Best books for junior high readers / John T. Gillespie, editor.
p.   cm.
Includes bibliographical references and indexes.
ISBN 0-8352-3020-1
1.Bibliography—Best books—Children's literature.   2. Junior
high school students—Books and reading.   3. Junior high school
libraries—Book lists.   4. Children's literature—Bibliography.
I. Gillespie, John Thomas, 1928–
Z1037.B546   1991
[PN1009.A1]
011.6275—dc20   91-13521
CIP

ISBN 0 - 8352 - 3020 - 1

9 780835 230209

Contents

CONTENTS

Literary History and Criticism

Language and Communication

Religion

Society and the Individual

Guidance and Personal Development

CONTENTS

CONTENTS

CONTENTS

Major Subjects Arranged Alphabetically

Preface

"Get them while they're still young," is the response of librarians and teachers when asked how to transform America into a nation of readers. Yet despite much publicity and a few federal and state incentives, concrete government support for the literacy effort has not measurably increased. After all the campaign slogans and buzzwords and T-shirts, real progress in reading and learning rests with the parents, educators, and the quality of our educational resources.

The Best Books series was established to help librarians and media specialists meet curricular needs and the personal interests of their students. *Best Books for Junior High Readers* is the second title in the trilogy, covering recommended material for readers in grades seven through nine, or roughly, ages 12 through 15. The other two titles are *Best Books for Children* (R. R. Bowker, 4th edition, 1990) aimed at preschool through sixth-grade readers, and *Best Books for Senior High Readers* (R. R. Bowker, 1991) for students in grades ten through twelve. In view of society's intellectual concerns at large, we hope the selection and arrangement of materials in all three volumes will help users:

Respond to changes within the juvenile population. Today's child is different from yesterday's, just as tomorrow's student will be different from today's. As you are no doubt aware, the proportion of school-age children who are members of minority groups, fall below the poverty line, and live in single-parent homes is expanding dramatically. Moreover, the preteen and teenaged reader boast experience and awareness levels unthinkable even ten years ago. In recent years, publishers *have* produced more books on problematic themes as well as titles geared to readers from a variety of cultural and socioeconomic backgrounds.

Support new trends in education. In view of our global society, more attention is being devoted to geography and foreign languages.

Science instruction is less textbook-oriented, and more inclined to embrace experimentation, field trips, and tradebooks. Finally, as libraries and schools have assumed a greater responsibility for the development of America's youth, information on family life, sex education, abuse, and other realities of twentieth-century life must be made available.

Serve the interests of individuals. As important as cooperative planning and societal concerns may be, it is personal attention that inspires the love and habit of reading.

Title Selection and Overlap in the Best Books Series

To make maximum use of space in each of the three "Best Books" bibliographies, we tried to avoid duplication of titles. Thus, except for a few classics such as *Huckleberry Finn* and some basic nonfiction works such as the Golden Press (Western Publishing) field guides, a title will appear in only one of the volumes. To maintain this policy, we were forced to make many difficult decisions regarding the most appropriate placement of titles. *Best Books for Children* therefore contains titles for beginning junior high readers *as well as* elementary school readers. These are designated as IJ in the Subject/Grade Level Index and in the main entries by suitable grade levels, such as 5–7. Similarly, in *Best Books for Senior High Readers,* books suitable for more advanced junior high readers are designated as JS in the Subject/Grade Level Index and by a grade level notation in the main entry, such as 9–12.

A substantial percentage of libraries serving junior high students carry material of an advanced nature, much of which was originally written for an adult audience. In *Best Books for Junior High Readers* we have therefore included a list of selected basic titles suitable for advanced junior high students, compiled from *Best Books for Senior High Readers.* This list, divided into fiction and nonfiction, appears in the Appendix. These entries contain only author, title, and publisher information. For more complete bibliographic information, annotations, and additional advanced-level titles, the user should consult *Best Books for Senior High Readers.*

General Scope and Criteria for Inclusion

Of the 6,848 titles listed in *Best Books for Junior High Readers,* 5,674 are individually numbered entries and 743 appear in the Appendix. The remaining 431 titles are those cited within annotations as additional recommended titles by the same author. These related titles are listed with publication date and—if the publisher differs from that cited for the main entry title—with the publisher's name. In some cases where there are a large number of titles in a series, additional entries have been used. Also, some series are so extensive that, due to space limitations, only representative titles are included.

Excluded from this bibliography are general reference works, such as dictionaries and encyclopedias, professional books for librarians and teachers, and mass market series books such as Nancy Drew and Hardy Boy books.

For most fiction and nonfiction, at least two recommendations were required from the sources consulted for a title to be considered for listing. All titles had to have a verifiable in-print status as of 1990. Additional criteria included such obvious considerations as availability, up-to-dateness, accuracy, usefulness, and relevance.

Sources Used

In compiling this annotated bibliography, several retrospective sources were reviewed, including *The Junior High School Catalog* (H.W. Wilson), issues of *Your Reading* from the National Council of Teachers of English, the author's *Junior High School Paperback Collection* (American Library Association, 1985), and copies of the annual *Books for the Teen Age* (New York Public Library).

Current book reviewing media were also consulted. The primary sources were *Booklist, The Book Report, School Library Journal,* and *VOYA (Voice of Youth Advocates).* Reviews were tabulated and drawn from journal issues beginning in January 1985 through September 1990, when coverage of this book ends.

Uses of This Book

Best Books for Junior High Readers was designed to help librarians and media specialists with four vital tasks: (1) to evaluate the adequacy of existing collections; (2) to build new collections or strengthen existing holdings; (3) to provide reading guidance to young adults; and (4) to prepare bibliographies and reading lists. To increase the book's usefulness, particularly when it comes to bibliographies and suggested reading, titles are arranged under broad areas of interest, or in the case of nonfiction works, by curriculum-oriented subjects rather than the Dewey Decimal classifications (suggested Dewey classification numbers are nevertheless provided within nonfiction entries).

Subject Arrangement

To help users integrate material from all volumes in the set, we have categorized books under the same subject headings whenever possible. The junior and senior high volumes feature virtually identical headings. These also correspond to many of the subjects used in *Best Books for Children*. Since a large part of *Best Books for Children* is devoted to picture books, complete uniformity was not possible.

Some arbitrary decisions were made concerning placement of books under specific subjects. For example, books of mathematical puzzles will be found in the Mathematics section rather than with puzzles, and books of science experiments and projects (though often dealing with a particular branch of science) are grouped under General Science—Experiments and Projects.

Arrangement

In the table of contents, subjects are arranged by the order in which they appear in the book. After the table of contents, users will find a second, alphabetical listing of subjects, which provides entry numbers as well as page numbers for easy access. Following the main body of text, there is an appendix of titles recommended for advanced readers and the book's three indexes. The Author Index cites authors, titles, and entry numbers (joint authors are listed separately). The Title Index gives the text's entry number. Works of fiction in both of these indexes are indicated by (F) following the title. Finally, an extensive Subject/Grade Level Index lists entry numbers under thousands of subject headings and specifies grade-level suitability for each entry. The following codes are used to identify general grade levels:

IJ (Intermediate-Junior High) grades 6–8
J (Junior High) grades 7–9
JS (Junior-Senior High) grades 8 to 10 or higher

Entries

A typical entry contains the following information where applicable: (1) author, joint author, or editor; (2) title and subtitle; (3) specific grade levels given in parentheses; (4) adapter or translator; (5) indication of illustrations; (6) publication date; (7) publisher and price of hardbound edition (LB = library binding); (8) International Standard Book Number (ISBN) of hardbound edition; (9) paperback publisher (paper) and price (if no publisher is listed, it is the same as the hardbound edition); (10) ISBN of paperback edition; (11) annotation;

(12) review citations; (13) Dewey Decimal classification number. Bibliographic information and prices were verified in *Books in Print 1989–1990* and some publishers' catalogs.

Review Citations

Review citations are given for books published and reviewed from 1985 through mid-1990. These review citations will give librarians sources from which to find more detailed information about each of the books listed. The four sources identified are:

Booklist (BL)
The Book Report (BR)
School Library Journal (SLJ)
VOYA (Voice of Youth Advocates) (VOYA)

The citing of only one review does not necessarily mean that the book received only a single recommendation. It might easily also have been listed in one or more of the other bibliographies consulted. A single negative review does not preclude inclusion of a title if the other reviews are positive. Books without review citations are pre-1985 imprints or reprints of older recommended books recently brought back into print (the original publication date is indicated within the annotation whenever available).

Acknowledgments

Many people were involved in the preparation of this bibliography. I am particularly indebted to Christine Gilbert for her support and help and especially to Marion Sader, Publisher, R.R. Bowker, who inspired this book, as well as Nancy Bucenec, Bowker Production Editor, whose diligent efforts brought this title to print. I thank them for their suggestions, assistance, and, above all, patience.

Literary Forms

Fiction

Adventure and Survival Stories

1 Aaron, Chester. *Lackawanna* (6–9). 1986, Harper LB $11.89 (0-397-32058-2). In Depression New York, a gang of kids called the Lackawanna gang sets out to find a member who has been kidnapped. (Rev: BL 2/15/86; BR 9–10/86; SLJ 4/86; VOYA 6/86)

2 Aaron, Chester. *Out of Sight, Out of Mind* (6–9). 1985, Harper $11.89 (0-397-32100-7). Twins with psychic powers are being pursued by foreign agents who want their secret. (Rev: BR 3–4/86; VOYA 12/85)

3 Aiken, Joan. *Midnight Is a Place* (7–10). 1974, Viking $9.95 (0-670-47483-5); Dell paper $3.50 (0-440-45634-7). In Victorian England 2 young waifs are cast adrift in a hostile town when their guardian's house burns.

4 Alexander, Lloyd. *The Drackenberg Adventure* (6–9). 1988, Dutton $12.95 (0-525-44389-4). Vesper Holly and her bumbling guardian Brinnie once again confront the evil Dr. Helvitius, this time in the Grand Duchy of Drackenberg. (Rev: BL 5/1/88; BR 11–12/88; SLJ 6–7/88; VOYA 10/88)

5 Alexander, Lloyd. *The El Dorado Adventure* (6–9). 1987, Dutton $12.95 (0-525-44313-4); Dell paper $2.95 (0-440-40298-0). Vesper Holly and her sidekick Brinnie find adventure in a Central American country. (Rev: BL 4/1/87; BR 3–4/88; SLJ 5/87; VOYA 2/88)

6 Alexander, Lloyd. *The Illyrian Adventure* (6–9). 1986, Dutton $12.95 (0-525-44250-2); Dell paper $3.50 (0-440-40297-2). Vesper Holly and her companion Brinnie get involved in an archaeological expedition and unforeseen adventure in this, the first of a series. (Rev: BL 4/1/86; BR 11–12/86; SLJ 5/86; VOYA 12/86)

7 Alexander, Lloyd. *The Jedera Adventure* (7–10). 1989, Dutton $12.95 (0-525-44481-5). In this, the fourth Vesper Holly adventure, our heroine finds adventure in North Africa. (Rev: BL 6/1/89; SLJ 5/89; VOYA 8/89)

8 Alexander, Lloyd. *The Marvelous Misadventures of Sebastian* (6–8). 1973, Dutton $14.95 (0-525-34739-9). Sebastian loses his job as one of the many court violinists and then his troubles begin.

9 Alexander, Lloyd. *The Philadelphia Adventure* (6–9). 1990, Dutton $12.95 (0-525-44564-1). President Grant asks Vesper Holly to help solve a mysterious kidnapping. (Rev: BL 3/1/90; SLJ 3/90; VOYA 4/90)

10 Alexander, Lloyd. *Westmark* (7–10). 1981, Dutton $14.95 (0-525-42335-4); Dell paper $2.95 (0-440-99731-3). In this first of 3 volumes, Theo, in the imaginary kingdom of Westmark, joins revolutionaries intent on establishing a democracy. Others in this series are: *The Kestrel* (1982); *The Beggar Queen* (1984).

11 Ashley, Bernard. *Break in the Sun* (6–9). Illus. 1980, Phillips $16.95 (0-87599-299-3). Patsy Bleigh runs away on a ship belonging to a theatrical company.

12 Ashley, Bernard. *A Kind of Wild Justice* (6–9). Illus. 1978, Phillips $16.95 (0-87599-229-3). Ronnie is threatened by the same gang that made his father a criminal.

13 Baird, Thomas. *Finding Fever* (6–8). 1982, Harper $12.70 (0-06-020353-6). Kidnappers make off with Benny's sister's dog, and so Benny sets out to investigate.

14 Baird, Thomas. *Walk Out a Brother* (7–9). 1983, Harper LB $12.89 (0-06-020356-0). On a backpacking trip, Keith meets a mysterious stranger.

15 Baird, Thomas. *Where Time Ends* (7–10). 1988, Harper LB $13.89 (0-06-020360-9). A group of teenagers in a futile bid for survival after war is declared between the United States and the Soviet Union. (Rev: BL 11/1/88; BR 5–6/89; SLJ 1/89; VOYA 12/88)

16 Bawden, Nina. *Rebel on a Rock* (6–8). 1978, Harper $13.89 (0-397-32140-6). Jo reluctantly believes that her stepfather is a spy for a cruel dictator.

17 Bennett, George, ed. *Great Tales of Action and Adventure* (7–10). 1978, Dell paper $2.75 (0-440-93202-5). A fine collection of fast-moving stories by such masters as Jack London and Arthur Conan Doyle.

18 Blackwood, Gary L. *Wild Timothy* (5–9). 1987, Macmillan LB $12.95 (0-689-31352-7). Timothy gets lost in the woods and must survive on his own. (Rev: SLJ 10/87)

19 Blades, Ann. *A Boy of Tache* (6–9). 1973, Tundra $7.95 (0-88776-023-6); paper $5.95 (0-88776-034-1). A Canadian novel of a boy's trek through the wilderness to save his grandfather's life.

20 Blair, Cynthia. *The Pink Lemonade Charade* (7–9). 1988, Fawcett paper $2.95 (0-449-70258-8). Twins Susan and Christine find adventure in Washington when they encounter a Russian girl who wants to defect. Others in this series are *Marshmallow Masquerade* (1987), *The Pumpkin Principle* (1986), and *Strawberry Summer* (1986). (Rev: VOYA 4/89)

21 Bowkett, Stephen. *Catch and Other Stories* (7–12). 1990, David & Charles $17.95 (0-575-04399-7). Nine weird stories dealing with the outer fringes of behavior including contacts with aliens. (Rev: SLJ 8/90)

22 Brand, Max. *Dan Barry's Daughter* (7–12). 1976, Berkley paper $2.75 (0-425-10190-8). Harry is an accused murderer who, though innocent, is forced to hide. One of many recommended westerns by the prolific author whose work also includes *The Long Chase* (1981).

23 Budbill, David. *Snowshoe Trek to Otter River* (6–9). Illus. 1876, Bantam paper $2.25 (0-553-15469-9). Three stories about 2 boys camping out in the North Woods.

24 Bunting, Eve. *Someone Is Hiding on Alcatraz Island* (7–9). 1984, Clarion $12.95 (0-89919-219-X); Berkley paper $2.75 (0-425-10294-7). A young boy is trapped by a ruthless gang of hoodlums when he seeks shelter on Alcatraz Island.

25 Burroughs, Edgar Rice. *Tarzan of the Apes* (7–12). 1984, Ballantine paper $1.95 (0-345-31977-X). The first in a long series of tales about an English lord who becomes king of the jungle.

26 Butler, William. *The Butterfly Revolution* (7–12). 1961, Ballantine paper $3.50 (0-345-33182-6). A frightening story of problems in a boy's camp told in diary form by one of the campers.

27 Carr, Roger Vaughan. *The Clinker* (6–9). 1989, Houghton $14.95 (0-395-51737-0). A suspense story set in Australia about a boy and *The Clinker*, a skiff built by his great-grandfather. (Rev: BR 5–6/90; VOYA 2/90)

28 Cazzola, Gus. *To Touch the Deer* (6–8). 1981, Westminster $9.95 (0-664-32684-6). A runaway from his stepfather learns to survive in the wilderness.

29 Chester, Deborah. *The Sign of the Owl* (7–9). 1981, Macmillan $12.95 (0-02-718140-5). A 15-year-old boy discovers a plot against his father and he must foil it by using the sacred sword.

30 Clements, Bruce. *The Treasure of Plunderell Manor* (6–9). 1987, Farrar $12.95 (0-374-37746-4). A girl becomes a maid to a virtual prisoner of a wicked aunt and uncle in a tale of buried treasure and Dickensian derring-do. (Rev: BL 1/15/88; SLJ 3/88; VOYA 4/88)

31 Collier, James Lincoln. *When the Stars Begin to Fall* (7–10). 1986, Delacorte $14.95 (0-385-29516-2). Harry discovers no one in town wants to challenge the owners of the carpet factory that is polluting a local river because the economy of the town would be at stake. (Rev: BR 3–4/87; SLJ 11/86; VOYA 2/87)

32 Cool, Joyce. *The Kidnapping of Courtney Van Allan and What's Her Name* (7–9). 1982, Harcourt $9.95 (0-395-32557-9). A frequently humorous adventure story about the kidnapping of 2 girls visiting New York City.

33 Corbin, William. *A Dog Worth Stealing* (7–10). 1987, Watts LB $12.99 (0-531-08312-8). In this survival story, Jud finds a marijuana plantation in the wilderness and rescues a German shepherd. (Rev: BL 9/1/87; BR 1–2/88; SLJ 9/87)

34 Cormier, Robert. *After the First Death* (7–12). 1979, Pantheon LB $10.99 (0-394-94122-5). A busload of schoolchildren become the victims of a terrorist plot.

35 Cross, Gillian. *Born of the Sun* (7–10). 1984, Holiday $11.95 (0-8234-0528-1); Dell paper $2.95 (0-440-90710-1). On an expedition in Peru with her archaeologist father, Paula finds the glamour gone and her relationship with her father changing. (Rev: BL 2/15/85)

36 Cunningham, Julia. *Dorp Dead* (6–8). Illus. 1965, Pantheon LB $6.99 (0-394-91089-3); Knopf paper $2.95 (0-317-58791-9). Gilly seeks freedom as an apprentice of Kobalt and finds instead he's a prisoner.

J FIC

37 Dekkers, Midas. *Arctic Adventure* (7–9). 1987, Watts LB $12.99 (0-531-08304-7). A novel about 2 boys and how they save a whale in the Arctic with the help of Greenpeace. (Rev: BL 12/1/87; BR 5–6/88; SLJ 3/88; VOYA 2/88)

38 Dickinson, Peter. *Annerton Pit* (7–9). 1977, Little $14.95 (0-316-18430-6). Two boys, one of whom is blind, try to free their grandfather who is being held by revolutionaries.

39 Dickinson, Peter. *Healer* (7–10). 1987, Dell paper $2.95 (0-440-93377-3). Many people believe that Pinky can work miracle cures—or is she just being used by exploiters? (Rev: BL 3/1/85; BR 9–10/85; SLJ 4/85; VOYA 6/85)

YAPB at PO, CE minis

40 Dillon, Eilis. *The Island of Ghosts* (6–9). 1989, Macmillan $13.95 (0-684-19107-5). A thoughtful adventure story about the kidnapping of 2 boys by a man who wants to found a perfect society. (Rev: BL 10/15/89; BR 3–4/90; SLJ 12/89; VOYA 2/90)

JFIC at PO, CE

41 Downing, Warwick. *Kid Curry's Last Ride* (6–9). 1989, Watts LB $12.99 (0-531-08402-7). While spending a summer in Wyoming in 1935, 12-year-old Alex becomes involved with an old man who claims to be a bank-robbing ex-member of Butch Cassidy's gang. (Rev: BL 4/1/89; BR 11–12/89; SLJ 2/89; VOYA 4/89)

JFIC at PO, CE

42 Dygard, Thomas J. *Wilderness Peril* (7–12). 1985, Morrow $12.95 (0-688-04146-9). Two teenage campers find money hidden by a hijacker and soon find they are being trailed by him. (Rev: BL 4/15/85; SLJ 8/85)

JPB at PO, CE

43 East, Ben, and Jerolyn Nentl. *Danger in the Air* (6–8). Illus. 1979, Crestwood LB $9.95 (0-89686-047-7). Les is afraid that danger and trouble await him on his next deep-sea dive. Another in this series is *Trapped in Devil's Hole* (1979).

44 Fleischman, Sid. *The Ghost in the Noonday Sun* (6–8). 1989, Greenwillow $11.95 (0-688-08140-9). In this reissue of a 1965 title, Oliver is kidnapped by the pirate Captain Scratch. (Rev: VOYA 8/89)

JPB at PO, CE, minis

45 Fleming, Susan. *Countdown at 37 Pinecrest Drive* (6–8). Illus. 1982, Westminster $9.95 (0-664-32694-3). Joel, who dreams of becoming an astronaut, uncovers a real-life adventure in his home town.

46 Forman, James D. *Cry Havoc* (7–10). 1988, Macmillan $12.95 (0-684-18838-4). Killer dogs get loose in what was a quiet suburban area. (Rev: BL 7/88; BR 9–10/88; SLJ 6–7/88; VOYA 10/88)

47 Fox, Paula. *How Many Miles to Babylon?* (5–8). 1980, Bradbury $11.95 (0-02-735590-X). James is kidnapped by older boys to help their dog-stealing racket.

JFIC at CE, PO

48 French, Michael. *Circle of Revenge* (7–10). 1988, Bantam $13.95 (0-553-05495-3). Robbie agrees to participate in a scientific experiment not realizing that it involves brainwashing and international intrigue. (Rev: BL 10/1/88; BR 5–6/89; SLJ 10/88; VOYA 12/88)

49 French, Michael. *Pursuit* (6–9). 1982, Delacorte $9.95 (0-385-28781-X); Dell paper $2.95 (0-440-96665-5). In a mountainous wilderness, Gordy is being pursued by a man he knows is a murderer.

50 Garfield, Leon. *The Strange Affair of Adelaide Harris* (7–10). 1988, Dell paper $3.95 (0-440-40057-0). Though only a baby, Adelaide has many adventures that turn the town upside down.

JPB at CE, PO

51 George, Jean Craighead. *Julie of the Wolves* (6–9). Illus. 1972, Harper LB $12.89 (0-06-021944-0); paper $2.95 (0-06-440058-1). An Eskimo girl travels across Alaska alone to find a new life. Newbery Medal, 1973.

JPB

52 George, Jean Craighead. *My Side of the Mountain* (6–9). 1959, Dutton $12.95 (0-525-44392-4); paper $4.95 (0-525-44395-9). In this survival story, young Sam Gribley decides to spend a year alone in the Catskill Mountains.

JPB + JFIC

53 George, Jean Craighead. *One Day in the Alpine Tundra* (6–8). Illus. 1984, Harper $12.89 (0-690-04326-0). A boy spends a day examining the life in a tundra region of the Wyoming Tetons.

J 574, 52644

54 George, Jean Craighead. *Shark beneath the Reef* (7–9). 1989, Harper LB $11.89 (0-06-021993-9). The story of a young Mexican boy who is torn between becoming a shark fisherman like his father or going to college to be a marine biologist. (Rev: BL 6/1/89; BR 11–12/89; SLJ 6/89; VOYA 6/89)

55 George, Jean Craighead. *The Talking Earth* (6–9). 1983, Harper LB $12.89 (0-06-021976-9); paper $2.95 (0-06-440212-6). A Seminole girl is forced to survive alone in the Everglades.

JPB + JFIC at CE, PO

56 George, Jean Craighead. *Water Sky* (6–8). 1987, Harper LB $11.89 (0-06-022199-2); paper $3.95 (0-06-440202-9). A boy is sent by his father

YAPB at PO, CE, minis

5

to an Eskimo whaling camp to learn survival techniques. (Rev: BL 2/1/87; BR 9–10/87)

57 Gibbons, Faye. *King Shoes and Clown Pockets* (6–10). 1989, Morrow $12.95 (0-688-06592-9). The story of the adventures and friendship between 2 boys in a town in Alabama. (Rev: VOYA 2/90)

58 Godfrey, Martyn. *Fire! Fire!* (7–12). Illus. 1986, EMC paper $14.95 (0-8219-0233-4). An easily read adventure story about the problems of a 17-year-old female firefighter. (Rev: BL 2/1/87)

59 Hallman, Ruth. *Panic Five* (7–12). Illus. 1986, Dodd $8.95 (0-396-08788-4). While on a 5-day survival course a young navy man learns the true meaning of teamwork. (Rev: BL 5/15/86; SLJ 5/86)

60 Hallman, Ruth. *Search without Fear* (7–10). 1987, Putnam $10.95 (0-396-08924-0). An easily read thriller involving an orphan girl, a gang of criminals, and a kidnapping. (Rev: BL 10/1/87; SLJ 1/88)

61 Halvorson, Marilyn. *Hold On, Geronimo* (7–10). 1988, Delacorte $14.95 (0-385-29665-7). After a plane crash, 3 teenagers struggle to survive in a hostile Canadian wilderness. (Rev: BR 5–6/88; VOYA 8/88)

62 Hammer, Charles. *Me, the Beef and the Bum* (6–9). 1984, Farrar $12.95 (0-374-34903-7). Rosie decides to run away with her steer George to save him from the butcher block.

63 Hammer, Charles. *Wrong-Way Ragsdale* (6–9). 1987, Farrar $12.95 (0-374-38657-9). Unable to land the airplane he has stolen, 13-year-old Emmett is forced into a crash in the mountains. (Rev: VOYA 4/88)

64 Hardcastle, Michael. *Quake* (5–8). 1988, Faber $11.95 (0-571-14698-8). The dramatic story of a girl separated from the family she is going to visit by a disasterous earthquake. (Rev: SLJ 12/88)

65 Hawks, Robert. *The Stranger, My Father* (7–10). 1988, Houghton $13.95 (0-395-44089-0). Patty learns that her father is actually a convicted spy trying to escape his past. (Rev: BL 5/1/88; BR 11–12/88; SLJ 3/88; VOYA 8/88)

66 Hildick, E. W. *The Ghost Squad and the Prowling Hermits* (6–8). 1987, Dutton $12.95 (0-525-44330-4). The fifth adventure of this band of crime fighters—some mortal, others not. This time they crush a plot to implant evil ghosts into living bodies. Also use: *The Ghost Squad Flies Concorde* (1985). (Rev: BL 12/15/87; SLJ 12/87)

67 Hinton, S. E. *The Outsiders* (7–10). 1967, Viking LB $10.95 (0-670-53257-6); Dell paper $2.50 (0-440-96769-4). Two rival gangs—the "haves" and "have-nots"—fight it out on the streets of an Oklahoma city.

68 Hinton, S. E. *Rumble Fish* (7–10). 1975, Delacorte $13.95 (0-385-28675-9); Dell paper $2.50 (0-440-97534-4). Rusty-James loses everything he loves most including his brother.

69 Hinton, S. E. *Tex* (7–10). 1979, Delacorte $13.95 (0-385-29020-9); Dell paper $2.50 (0-440-97850-5). Tex and his 17-year-old older brother encounter problems with family, sex, and drugs.

70 Hinton, S. E. *That Was Then, This Is Now* (7–10). 1971, Viking $10.95 (0-670-69798-2); Dell paper $2.50 (0-440-98652-4). Bryon discovers that his "brother' Mark is a drug pusher.

71 Holland, Isabelle. *The Unfrightened Dark* (7–10). 1990, Little $13.95 (0-316-37173-4). A blind girl is the victim of a deranged person who kidnaps her guide dog. (Rev: BR 5–6/90)

72 Holman, Felice. *Slake's Limbo* (7–9). 1974, Macmillan $12.95 (0-684-13926-X); paper $3.95 (0-689-71066-6). A 13-year-old boy escapes to New York City's subways, which he learns to call his home.

73 Hoobler, Thomas. *Dr. Chill's Project* (7–10). 1987, Putnam $13.95 (0-399-21480-1). Allie and her friends, all residents in a clinic to develop ESP abilities, join forces when one of them is kidnapped. (Rev: BL 11/1/87; SLJ 1/88; VOYA 10/87)

74 Hostetler, Marian. *African Adventure* (6–8). Illus. 1976, Herald Pr. paper $2.95 (0-87311-329-2). Denise's father moves the family to Chad in Africa where he hopes to help the natives.

75 Hostetler, Marian. *Fear in Algeria* (6–8). Illus. 1979, Herald Pr. paper $3.95 (0-8361-1905). Zena finds danger awaits her when she visits Algeria.

76 Houston, James. *Frozen Fire: A Tale of Courage* (6–9). Illus. 1977, Macmillan $12.95 (0-689-50083-1). An Eskimo boy, Kayak, and his white friend set out to find Kayak's father, a prospector who has disappeared. A sequel is: *Black Diamonds* (1982).

77 Houston, James. *Ice Swords: An Undersea Adventure* (6–9). Illus. 1985, Macmillan $11.95 (0-689-50333-4). Matt and his Inuit friend, Kayak, become part of an Arctic expedition to study narwhals, an unusual aquatic animal. Other adventures featuring these 2 friends are: *Frozen Fire* (1978) and *Black Diamonds* (1980). (Rev: BL 12/15/85; SLJ 11/85)

6

78 Houston, James. *River Runners: A Tale of Hardship and Bravery* (6–8). Illus. 1979, Macmillan $11.95 (0-689-50151-X). A 15-year-old apprentice and an Indian boy set out to found a fur trading outpost in the Far North.

79 Jackson, Steve, and Ian Livingstone. *Demons of the Deep* (6–9). Illus. 1987, Dell paper $2.50 (0-400-91843-X). A participation adventure in which you are thrown overboard by pirates. (Rev: SLJ 10/87)

80 Jeffries, Roderic. *Trapped* (6–9). 1972, Harper paper $3.50 (0-06-440035-2). Two boys on a hunting trip become trapped in a snowstorm.

81 Johnson, Annabel, and Edgar Johnson. *Gamebuster* (7–10). 1990, Dutton $13.95 (0-525-65033-4). A well-paced novel about a boy who overhears a terrorist plot. (Rev: VOYA 6/90)

82 Johnston, Norma. *Whisper of the Cat* (7–12). 1988, Bantam paper $2.95 (0-553-26947-X). Tracy visits her father and stepmother on an island in Georgia and stumbles on a drug-dealing operation. (Rev: VOYA 10/88)

83 Kästner, Erich. *The Little Man* (5–8). 1980, Avon paper $1.95 (0-380-51185-1). For young readers, an adventure story about a 2-inch-tall boy who is kidnapped.

84 Klaveness, Jan O'Donnell. *Ghost Island* (7–10). 1985, Macmillan $12.95 (0-02-730740-8). Delia, her mother, and new stepfather encounter both family trauma and a murder involving poachers when they vacation on a remote Canadian lake. (Rev: BL 5/15/85; BR 11–12/85; SLJ 9/85; VOYA 2/86)

85 Klein, Norma. *Bizou* (7–9). 1987, Fawcett paper $2.50 (0-449-70252-9). A French girl finds herself alone on her first trip to the United States.

86 Konigsburg, E. L. *From the Mixed-Up Files of Mrs. Basil E. Frankweiler* (6–8). 1967, Macmillan $12.95 (0-689-20586-4); Dell paper $3.25 (0-440-93180-0). Two resourceful kids live for a week in the Metropolitan Museum of Art.

87 Kropp, Paul. *Take Off* (7–12). Illus. 1986, EMC paper $3.95 (0-8219-0231-8). Two teenage boys find that running away can be a sordid and dangerous experience. (Rev: BL 2/1/87)

88 Lasenby, Jack. *The Lake* (7–9). 1989, Oxford Univ. Pr. $14.95 (0-19-558162-8). In this story set in New Zealand, a young girl runs away from home and must survive in the wilderness. (Rev: VOYA 2/90)

89 Lasenby, Jack. *The Mangrove Summer* (6–10). 1989, Oxford Univ. Pr. $14.95 (0-19-558194-6). In New Zealand during World War II, a group of youngsters decide to run away and survive in the bush. (Rev: VOYA 4/90)

90 L'Engle, Madeleine. *The Arm of the Starfish* (7–10). 1965, Farrar $13.95 (0-374-30396-7); Dell paper $3.25 (0-440-90183-9). A young scientist becomes involved in intrigue and the disappearance of Polly O'Keefe in this tale of danger.

91 L'Engle, Madeleine. *The Young Unicorns* (7–10). 1968, Farrar $14.95 (0-374-38778-8); Dell paper $3.25 (0-440-99919-7). In this novel set in New York City and involving the Austin family, a young gang threatens the lives of an ex-member and a blind musician.

92 LeRoy, Gen. *Cold Feet* (7–9). 1986, Dell paper $1.95 (0-440-91336-5). Geneva masquerades as a boy to get a job in a local arcade where she discovers that gamblers hang out.

93 Levy, Elizabeth. *The Dani Trap* (6–8). 1984, Morrow $11.95 (0-688-03867-0). Dani becomes an undercover agent for a special squad out to get stores selling liquor to minors.

94 Lewitt, S. N. *U.S.S.A. : Book 4* (7–12). 1987, Avon paper $2.95 (0-380-75183-6). A group of teenagers devise a kidnapping plan to foil the new hated government. (Rev: BL 10/1/87; SLJ 6–7/87)

95 Luger, Harriett. *The Elephant Tree* (7–9). 1986, Dell paper $2.25 (0-440-92394-8). A survival story about 2 boys who dislike one another and their problems when stranded in a desert.

96 Major, Kevin. *Far from Shore* (7–9). 1981, Delacorte $12.95 (0-385-28266-4); Dell paper $2.95 (0-440-92585-1). An adventure story with Newfoundland as its setting.

97 Major, Kevin. *Hold Fast* (8–10). 1980, Delacorte $9.95 (0-440-03506-6); Dell paper $2.95 (0-440-93756-6). An orphaned 14-year-old boy and his cousin run away to the wilderness to try to live off the land.

98 Martin, Guenn. *Forty Miles from Nowhere: A Winter Adventure in Alaska* (5–9). 1986, Herald Pr. paper $4.95 (0-8361-3417-6). A 13-year-old girl learns self-reliance when she, her family, and their animals spend a winter on Gresham Island in Alaska. (Rev: SLJ 10/86)

99 Martin, Les. *Raiders of the Lost Ark: The Storybook Based on the Movie* (6–9). 1981, Random LB $6.99 (0-394-94802-5); paper $5.95 (0-394-84802-0). Based on the screenplay by George Lucas, this is the story of the hit movie with many accompanying movie stills.

100 Mathieson, David. *Trial by Wilderness* (7–10). 1985, Houghton $11.95 (0-395-37697-1).

When her small plane crashes in an isolated part of British Columbia, Elena must put her survival instincts into practice. (Rev: BL 6/15/85; BR 11–12/85; SLJ 5/85; VOYA 8/85)

101 Mazer, Harry. *Snow Bound* (7–10). 1975, Dell paper $2.95 (0-440-96134-3). A boy and girl survive for several days after being trapped in a snow storm. Also use *The Dollar Man* (1988).

102 Mazer, Harry, and Norma Fox Mazer. *The Solid Gold Kid* (7–10). 1978, Dell paper $1.95 (0-440-98080-1). A millionaire's son and 4 other teenagers are kidnapped.

103 Meyer, Carolyn. *Wild Rover* (7–10). 1989, Macmillan $13.95 (0-689-50475-6). An escaped convict and his daughter, a street-wise punk, set off on an odyssey to hide from the police. (Rev: BL 9/15/89; BR 3–4/90; SLJ 11/89; VOYA 10/89)

104 Miklowitz, Gloria D. *After the Bomb* (7–12). 1985, Scholastic paper $2.25 (0-590-33287-2). This novel describes the experiences of a group of young people after an atomic bomb falls on Los Angeles. Also use *After the Bomb: Week One* (1987). (Rev: BL 6/15/86; SLJ 9/85; VOYA 8/85)

105 Miller, Frances A. *The Truth Trap* (7–10). 1986, Fawcett paper $2.50 (0-449-70247-2). When Matt's parents are killed in a car accident, he leaves town only to be accused of a murder. Followed by *Aren't You the One Who . . .* (1983) and *Losers and Winners* (1986).

106 Milton, Joyce. *Save the Loonies* (6–8). 1983, Macmillan $11.95 (0-02-766950-5). A camping trip in New Hampshire for Jenny involves locating her friend's missing brother and helping wildlife rangers.

107 Moeri, Louise. *Downwind* (7–9). 1984, Dutton $13.95 (0-525-44096-8); Dell paper $2.75 (0-440-92132-5). Ephraim and his family flee a possible nuclear disaster and encounter other kinds of danger.

108 Moeri, Louise. *The Forty-third War* (6–10). 1989, Houghton $13.95 (0-395-50215-2). Set in an imaginary Central American country, this is the harrowing story of the effects of revolution on a 12-year-old boy. (Rev: BL 10/15/89; BR 3–4/90; SLJ 10/89; VOYA 12/89)

109 Moore, Ruth Nulton. *Danger in the Pines* (7–9). Illus. 1983, Herald Pr. $7.95 (0-8361-3313-7); paper $4.95 (0-8361-3314-5). A hike in the Pinelands of New Jersey becomes dangerous for Jeff and his friends when a forest fire threatens them.

110 Morey, Walt. *Angry Waters* (6–9). 1990, Blue Heron paper $6.95 (0-936085-10-X). A hos-

tile 15-year-old boy is unwillingly paroled to a family farm, where he comes to terms with himself. (Rev: VOYA 8/90)

111 Morey, Walt. *The Lemon Meringue Dog* (6–8). 1980, Dutton $13.95 (0-525-33455-6). Coast Guardsman Chris and his dog Mike become involved in a drug smuggling operation.

112 Morpurgo, Michael. *King of the Cloud Forests* (6–9). 1988, Viking $11.95 (0-670-82069-5). At age 14, Ashley Anderson flees China for India when the Japanese invade. (Rev: BL 7/88; BR 3–4/89; SLJ 9/88)

113 Morrison, Dorothy Nafus. *Whisper Again* (6–8). 1987, Macmillan $12.95 (0-689-31348-9); Troll paper $2.95 (0-8167-1307-3). Stacey is unhappy when her family has to rent part of their ranch land to a summer camp. This is a sequel to *Whisper Goodbye* (1985). (Rev: BL 9/15/87; SLJ 12/87; VOYA 10/87)

114 Mowat, Farley. *Lost in the Barrens* (7–9). 1956, Little $14.95 (0-316-58638-2). Two boys lost in the wilderness of Northern Canada must fight for survival.

115 Murphy, Jim. *Death Run* (7–10). 1982, Clarion $12.95 (0-89919-065-0). Four teenage boys try to escape from the police after they have accidentally caused the death of a fellow student.

116 Myers, Walter Dean. *Adventure in Granada* (5–9). 1985, Penguin paper $3.95 (0-14-032011-3). While in Spain, 2 teenage brothers try to clear a friend of charges of stealing a relic. Another adventure featuring Chris and Ken is *The Hidden Shrine* (1985). (Rev: BL 4/15/86; SLJ 4/86)

117 Myers, Walter Dean. *The Mouse Trap* (6–8). 1990, Harper LB $12.89 (0-06-024344-9). A group of boys in Harlem form a gang to explore a deserted building they believe contains hidden loot. (Rev: BL 4/15/90; SLJ 7/90; VOYA 6/90)

118 Myers, Walter Dean. *The Nicholas Factor* (7–10). 1983, Viking $11.50 (0-670-51055-6). A college freshman infiltrates a secret organization to secure information for the government.

119 Nelson, Theresa. *Devil Storm* (6–8). 1987, Watts LB $12.99 (0-531-08311-X). Walter and his family come to rely on an old tramp during the terrible hurricane that hit Galveston in 1900. (Rev: BL 12/1/87; BR 1–2/88; SLJ 6–7/87; VOYA 2/88)

120 Ney, John. *Ox and the Prime-Time Kid* (7–10). 1985, Pineapple $10.95 (0-910923-23-X). Seventeen-year-old Ox and his friend Mark set out on an odyssey to locate Mark's mother. (Rev: BR 3–4/86; SLJ 2/86)

121 Nichols, James. *Boundary Waters* (7–10). 1986, Holiday $12.95 (0-8234-0616-4). In this wilderness adventure, a 16-year-old boy and a World War II pilot try to foil a plot to steal a hijacker's money. (Rev: BL 12/1/86; SLJ 11/86)

122 Nolan, Lucy A. *Secret at Summerhaven* (5–8). 1987, Macmillan LB $12.95 (0-689-31336-5). Three cousins accidentally film a drug sale and find themselves targets for drug smugglers. (Rev: SLJ 4/87; VOYA 6/87)

123 O'Dell, Scott. *Alexandra* (7–9). 1984, Houghton $12.95 (0-395-35571-0); Fawcett paper $2.25 (0-449-70135-2). When her father dies, Alexandra must learn his sponge-diving occupation.

124 O'Dell, Scott. *The Black Pearl* (7–9). 1967, Houghton $13.95 (0-395-06961-0). Young Ramon dives into a forbidden cave to collect a fabulous black pearl that in time seems to bring a curse to his family.

125 O'Dell, Scott. *Black Star, Bright Dawn* (5–9). 1988, Houghton $14.95 (0-395-47778-6). An Eskimo girl faces alone the challenge of running the famous Alaskan dog race, the Iditarod. (Rev: BL 4/1/88; BR 9–10/88; SLJ 5/88; VOYA 6/88)

126 O'Dell, Scott. *Island of the Blue Dolphins* (6–9). 1960, Houghton $12.95 (0-395-06962-9); Dell paper $3.25 (0-440-43988-4). Karana must fend for herself when she is left on a remote California island. Newbery Medal, 1961. Continued in *Zia* (1976).

127 Oleksy, Walter. *The Pirates of Deadman's Cay* (7–9). 1982, Westminster $9.95 (0-664-32693-5). In this easily read adventure a boy and his father encounter pirates on a Caribbean island.

128 Paige, Harry W. *Shadow on the Sun* (7–9). 1984, Warne $9.95 (0-7232-6258-6). The son of Billy the Kid sets out to avenge his father's death.

129 Paulsen, Gary. *Canyons* (7–10). 1990, Delacorte $14.95 (0-385-30153-7). Blennan becomes obsessed with the story of a young Indian boy murdered by white men 100 years before. (Rev: SLJ 9/90)

130 Paulsen, Gary. *Dogsong* (8–10). 1985, Bradbury $11.95 (0-02-770180-8); Penguin paper $3.95 (0-14-032235-3). An Eskimo youth faces hardship and danger when he ventures alone by dogsled into the wilderness. (Rev: BL 4/1/85; SLJ 4/85; VOYA 12/85)

131 Paulsen, Gary. *Hatchet* (6–9). 1987, Macmillan $12.95 (0-02-770130-1). Teenage Brian survives a plane crash in the Canadian wilderness but then must fend for himself. (Rev: BL 11/15/87; SLJ 12/87; VOYA 2/88)

132 Paulsen, Gary. *The Voyage of the Frog* (6–8). 1989, Watts LB $12.99 (0-531-08405-1). Alone on a 22-foot sailboat, a 14-year-old boy survives a 9-day sea ordeal. (Rev: BL 3/1/89; BR 9–10/89; SLJ 1/89; VOYA 2/89)

133 Peck, Richard. *Secrets of the Shopping Mall* (7–10). 1979, Delacorte $14.95 (0-440-07664-1); Dell paper $2.95 (0-440-40270-0). Two eighth graders find they are not alone when they take up residence in a shopping mall.

134 Petersen, P. J. *The Boll Weevil Express* (7–9). 1984, Dell paper $2.95 (0-440-91040-4). Three young people decide to run away to San Francisco.

135 Petersen, P. J. *Going for the Big One* (5–9). 1986, Delacorte $14.95 (0-385-29453-0); Dell paper $2.95 (0-440-93158-4). After being abandoned by their stepmother, the 3 teenage Bates kids decide to hike the Sierras to find their father. (Rev: BL 9/1/86; BR 9–10/86; SLJ 9/86; VOYA 6/86)

136 Petersen, P. J. *How Can You Hijack a Cave?* (6–9). 1988, Doubleday $14.95 (0-440-50063-X). Curt and his fellow tour guide Lori try to rescue a millionaire's daughter who has been kidnapped and held in one of the caverns. (Rev: BL 3/1/89; BR 1–2/89; SLJ 10/88; VOYA 2/89)

137 Petersen, P. J. *Nobody Else Can Walk It for You* (7–10). 1982, Delacorte $12.95 (0-385-28730-5); Dell paper $2.95 (0-440-96733-3). A group of backpackers are terrorized by 3 motorcyclists.

138 Phillips, Tony. *Full Throttle* (6–9). 1989, Ballantine paper $2.95 (0-345-35123-1). In this novel 5 boys from ages 12 to 15 find adventure on dirt bikes in the Mojave Desert after a nuclear war. Two other titles in this series are *Jump Start* (1988) and *Spin Out* (1989). (Rev: BL 4/15/89)

139 Phipson, Joan. *The Cats* (6–8). 1989, Macmillan paper $3.95 (0-02-044653-5). Jim and Willy are kidnapped after their parents win a lottery.

140 Phipson, Joan. *Hit and Run* (7–10). 1985, Macmillan $12.95 (0-689-50362-8); paper $3.95 (0-02-044665-9). After being involved in a hit-and-run accident, a pampered Australian boy escapes into the bushland. (Rev: BL 9/1/85; SLJ 10/85; VOYA 4/85)

141 Phleger, Marjorie. *Pilot Down, Presumed Dead* (7–9). 1988, Harper paper $3.95 (0-06-440067-0). A survival story involving a pilot whose plane crashes off the Baja California coast. A reissue.

142 Randall, Florence Engel. *All the Sky Together* (7–9). 1983, Scholastic paper $2.50 (0-590-33256-2). Cassie finds unexpected danger when she becomes friendly with a rich, spoiled brother and sister.

143 Rardin, Susan Lowry. *Captives in a Foreign Land* (7–10). 1984, Houghton $12.95 (0-395-36216-4). Two teenage brothers are captured by an Islamic terrorist group.

144 Reilly, Pat. *Kidnap in San Juan* (6–9). 1984, Dell paper $2.50 (0-440-94460-0). While in Puerto Rico, Marie's younger sister is kidnapped.

145 Roberts, Willo Davis. *Megan's Island* (6–8). 1988, Macmillan $12.95 (0-689-31397-7). Two children are the victims of a custody battle that involves an attempted kidnapping. (Rev: BR 9–10/88; VOYA 6/88)

146 Roberts, Willo Davis. *What Could Go Wrong?* (6–9). 1989, Macmillan $12.95 (0-689-31438-8). A seemingly innocent plane trip from Seattle to San Francisco leads 3 cousins into danger and a confrontation with a gang of money launderers. (Rev: BL 4/15/89; SLJ 3/89; VOYA 8/89)

147 Rodgers, Raboo. *Island of Peril* (7–10). 1987, Houghton $12.95 (0-395-43082-8). Two teenagers on a Caribbean island uncover a plot to steal Mayan artifacts. (Rev: BL 7/87; SLJ 6–7/87; VOYA 8–9/87)

148 Rodgers, Raboo. *The Rainbow Factor* (7–9). 1985, Houghton $11.95 (0-395-35643-1). In this sequel to *Magnum Fault* (1984), Cody Burke and a college student named Audry find adventure in the Caribbean when they search for a cache of hidden Nazi gold. (Rev: BL 9/15/85; BR 1–2/86; SLJ 8/85)

149 Roos, Stephen. *My Favorite Ghost* (6–8). 1988, Macmillan $12.95 (0-689-31301-2). Derek persuades his friends to give him money to free a ghost from the spirit world. (Rev: BR 9–10/88)

150 Rosen, Billi. *Andi's War* (6–8). 1989, Dutton $13.95 (0-525-44473-4). Against her will, young Andi gets involved in the Greek Civil War when she finds a cache of arms in a deserted cave. (Rev: SLJ 7/89; VOYA 8/89)

151 Ross, Rhea Beth. *The Bet's On, Lizzie Bingman!* (6–9). 1988, Houghton $12.95 (0-385-44472-1). A 14-year-old girl vows to remain completely independent for one summer. (Rev: BL 6/1/88; BR 9–10/88; SLJ 4/88)

152 Roth, Arthur. *Avalanche* (7–9). 1989, Scholastic paper $2.50 (0-590-42267-7). While trapped in an avalanche for 7 days, Chris must come to terms with himself and sort out his life. A reissue.

153 Roth, Arthur. *The Iceberg Hermit* (7–9). 1976, Scholastic paper $2.25 (0-590-01582-6). In 1757 Allan Gordon survives a ship sinking that leaves him alone in the Arctic wilds.

154 Rubinstein, Robert E. *When Sirens Scream* (7–9). 1981, Dodd $8.95 (0-396-07937-7). A nuclear accident occurs in the town where Ned lives.

155 Rubinstein, Robert E. *Who Wants to Be a Hero!* (6–8). 1985, Putnam paper $3.50 (0-396-08636-5). Jason becomes the target for Jimmy's gang when he foils their attack on a school janitor.

156 Ruckman, Ivy. *Night of the Twisters* (6–8). 1984, Harper $12.95 (0-690-04408-9); paper $3.50 (0-06-440176-6). An account based on fact about children who survive a devastating series of tornadoes.

157 Ruckman, Ivy. *No Way Out* (7–10). 1988, Harper LB $11.89 (0-690-04671-5). A flash flood traps a group of teenagers in a canyon. (Rev: BL 6/1/88; SLJ 8/88; VOYA 10/88)

158 Salassi, Otto R. *And Nobody Knew They Were There* (7–9). 1984, Greenwillow LB $9.50 (0-688-00940-9). Two boys follow the tracks of 9 missing U.S. Marines.

159 Salassi, Otto R. *Jimmy D., Sidewinder, and Me* (7–9). 1987, Greenwillow $11.75 (0-688-05237-1). The "Me" in the title is Dumas Monk, an orphan who has been taught to shoot pool and gamble by his mentor Jimmy D. (Rev: BL 9/15/87; BR 3–4/88; SLJ 1/88; VOYA 2/88)

160 Savage, Deborah. *A Rumour of Otters* (7–9). 1986, Houghton $12.95 (0-395-41186-6). A teenage girl in New Zealand enters the wilderness to find otters who are reportedly in the area. (Rev: BL 7/86; SLJ 8/86)

161 Schaefer, Jack. *Shane* (7–10). Illus. 1954, Houghton $13.95 (0-395-07090-2). A drifter changes the life of a frontier family, particularly that of the 14-year-old son.

162 Schami, Rafik. *A Hand Full of Stars* (7–10). Trans. by Rika Lesser. 1990, Dutton $14.95 (0-525-44535-8). An Arab teenage boy growing up in Damascus becomes involved in a resistance movement. (Rev: BL 2/15/90; SLJ 3/90)

163 Schellie, Don. *Maybe Next Summer* (7–9). 1980, Macmillan $12.95 (0-02-781460-2). A 17-

year-old apprentice newspaperman discovers a scheme to smuggle aliens into this country.

164 Shusterman, Neal. *Dissidents* (7–10). 1989, Little $13.95 (0-316-78904-6). A teenage boy joins his mother, the American ambassador in Moscow, and becomes involved in a spy caper. (Rev: BL 8/89; BR 11–12/89; SLJ 10/89)

165 Shyer, Marlene Fanta. *Me & Joey Pinstripe, the King of Rock* (6–8). 1988, Macmillan LB $12.95 (0-684-18941-0). In her attempts to impress a rock star who has moved into her building, Mary Kate becomes involved with some sinister characters who are pushing drugs. (Rev: BR 3–4/89; SLJ 12/88; VOYA 2/89)

166 Skipper, David. *Runners* (7–10). 1988, Viking $11.95 (0-670-81994-8). Jim Taylor and his friend Casey run afoul of the Collective, a drug syndicate. (Rev: BR 9–10/88; SLJ 4/88)

167 Smith, Kay. *Skeeter* (7–12). 1989, Houghton $13.95 (0-395-49603-9). An old black man takes 2 young white boys on his last hunting trip. (Rev: BR 3–4/90; VOYA 6/89)

168 Snyder, Zilpha K. *Blair's Nightmare* (6–8). 1984, Macmillan $12.95 (0-689-31022-6); Dell paper $3.25 (0-440-40915-2). In this easily read adventure, David finds danger when he tries to find his younger brother who has wandered off in search of a phantom dog.

169 Southall, Ivan. *Rachel* (6–9). 1986, Farrar $11.95 (0-374-36163-0). Rachel and Eddie get lost in a deserted mining area in this novel set in rural Australia. (Rev: VOYA 4/87)

170 Steele, Mary Q. *Journey Outside* (6–8). 1984, Peter Smith $14.75 (0-8446-6169-4); Puffin paper $3.98 (0-14-030588-2). Dilar and his family are following an underground river looking for a better place to live.

171 Stevenson, William. *The Bushbabies* (6–8). 1984, Peter Smith $16.00 (0-8446-6167-8). An English girl and her friend, an African tribesman, trek through the wilderness of Kenya.

172 Stewart, A. C. *Ossian House* (6–8). 1976, Phillips LB $16.95 (0-87599-219-6). An 11-year-old boy inherits a mansion in Scotland and sets out alone to live there for the summer.

173 Strieber, Whitley. *Wolf of Shadows* (6–8). 1985, Knopf LB $9.99 (0-394-97224-4); Fawcett paper $3.95 (0-449-21089-8). A pack of wolves and a mother and daughter develop a relationship of trust after a nuclear war. (Rev: BL 1/1/86; SLJ 10/85; VOYA 4/86)

174 Sutton, Larry. *Taildraggers High* (6–8). 1985, Farrar $11.95 (0-374-37372-8). Although her family discourages 12-year-old Jessie from

flying, in a time of stress this skill helps save the family's orchard from freezing. (Rev: BL 11/15/85; SLJ 12/85)

175 Taylor, Theodore. *The Cay* (6–9). 1969, Doubleday $13.95 (0-385-07906-0). A blinded boy and an old black sailor are shipwrecked on a coral island.

176 Taylor, Theodore. *The Hostage* (6–9). 1988, Delacorte $14.95 (0-385-29576-6). Fourteen-year-old Jamie and his father capture a killer whale but face the wrath of environmentalists who want it freed. The novel is set in British Columbia, Canada. (Rev: BL 2/15/88; VOYA 4/88)

177 Taylor, Theodore. *The Odyssey of Ben O'Neal* (6–8). Illus. 1984, Camelot paper $1.50 (0-380-43240-4). In 1999, a 13-year-old orphaned boy sets out to search for his older brother. Preceded by *Teetoncy and Ben O'Neal* (1976).

178 Taylor, Theodore. *Sniper* (7–10). 1989, Harcourt $14.95 (0-15-276420-8). A 15-year-old boy who is running an animal preserve while his parents are away discovers a sniper is loose and killing the big cats. (Rev: BL 9/15/89; SLJ 11/89)

179 Thiele, Colin. *Shadow Shark* (6–8). 1988, Harper LB $12.89 (0-06-026179-X). Scarface, a huge shark, threatens a bayside community in South Australia. (Rev: BL 6/15/88)

180 Townsend, John Rowe. *The Islanders* (7–10). 1981, Harper $11.70 (0-397-31940-1). Two strangers washed up on a remote island are regarded as enemies by the inhabitants.

181 Townsend, John Rowe. *Kate and the Revolution* (7–10). 1983, Harper LB $12.89 (0-397-32016-7). A 17-year-old girl is attracted to a visiting prince and then the adventure begins.

182 Townsend, Tom. *Queen of the Wind* (7–12). 1989, Eakin $12.95 (0-89015-715-4). A championship sailor thinks she has found love with the owner of a sailing school. (Rev: BL 1/15/90)

183 Trivelpiece, Laurel. *Just a Little Bit Lost* (6–8). 1988, Scholastic paper $2.50 (0-590-41465-8). A romance that involves 2 hikers who become lost and separated from the rest of the party. (Rev: SLJ 3/89)

184 Ullman, James R. *Banner in the Sky* (7–9). 1988, Harper LB $12.98 (0-397-30264-9); paper $2.95 (0-694-05623-5). The thrilling story of a boy's determination to conquer a challenging Swiss mountain. (Rev: SLJ 2/88)

185 Voigt, Cynthia. *On Fortune's Wheel* (7–12). 1990, Macmillan $15.95 (0-689-31636-4). In this historical adventure, a young runaway couple are captured by pirates and sold into slavery. (Rev: BL 2/15/90; SLJ 3/90; VOYA 4/90)

186 Wells, Rosemary. *Through the Hidden Door* (5–9). Illus. 1987, Dial $14.95 (0-8037-0276-0); Scholastic paper $2.75 (0-590-41786-X). Two boys with personal problems discover the remains of a miniature civilization in a cave. (Rev: BL 4/15/87; BR 1–2/88; SLJ 4/87; VOYA 2/88)

187 Wibberley, Leonard. *Perilous Gold* (7–9). 1978, Farrar $11.95 (0-374-35824-9). A teenager conquers his fears to help his father free a disabled 2-man submarine.

188 Wisler, G. Clifton. *The Wolf's Tooth* (5–9). 1987, Lodestar $12.95 (0-525-67197-8). Elias and his family move to an Indian reservation in Texas where his father is a teacher. (Rev: SLJ 6–7/87)

189 Wood, Phyllis Anderson. *Pass Me a Pine Cone* (7–9). 1982, Westminster $11.95 (0-664-32692-7). Sam discovers that being the son of the new high school principal is not easy when his family moves to a town in the Sierras.

190 Wuorio, Eva-Lis. *Detour to Danger* (7–9). 1981, Delacorte $12.95 (0-385-282060). While on a trip to Spain, Nando and his friend uncover a terrorist's plot.

Animal Stories

191 Adler, C. S. *Carly's Buck* (7–9). 1987, Clarion $12.95 (0-89919-480-X). While still recovering from the death of her father, Carly tries to save some deer during hunting season. (Rev: BL 4/1/87; BR 5–6/87; SLJ 5/87; VOYA 6/87)

192 Ames, Mildred. *Who Will Speak for the Lamb?* (7–10). 1989, Harper LB $13.89 (0-06-020112-6). A novel that has as its focus the fight against cruelty toward animals. (Rev: BL 3/15/89; SLJ 3/89; VOYA 6/89)

193 Bagnold, Enid. *National Velvet* (7–10). 1985, Morrow $15.95 (0-688-05788-8); Pocket paper $2.75 (0-671-63889-0). The now-classic story of Heather Brown and her struggle to ride in the Grand National. A reissue.

194 Brenner, Barbara. *The Gorilla Signs Love* (8–10). 1984, Lothrop $11.00 (0-688-00995-6). Naomi is an intelligent gorilla and Maggie is trying to save her from a breeding farm.

195 Burnford, Sheila. *Bel Ria* (7–12). 1978, Bantam $12.95 (0-316-11718-8). Set in France during World War II, this is a novel about a poodle's amazing adventures.

196 Burnford, Sheila. *Incredible Journey* (7–12). 1961, Little $14.95 (0-316-11714-5); Bantam paper $2.95 (0-553-26218-1). A survival story set in Northern Canada involving 3 animals—2 dogs and a cat—and their lonely trek back to their original home.

197 Campbell, Barbara. *A Girl Called Bob and a Horse Called Yoki* (6–8). 1982, Dial LB $11.89 (0-8037-3150-7). Bob has a difficult time saving a dray horse from the glue factory.

198 Cavanna, Betty. *Banner Year* (6–9). 1987, Morrow $12.95 (0-688-05779-9). Though 16, Cindy is more interested in horses than in boys. (Rev: BL 4/15/87; BR 5–6/87; SLJ 4/87; VOYA 6/87)

199 Cavanna, Betty. *Going on Sixteen* (6–9). 1985, Morrow $11.95 (0-688-05892-2). This story of a shy girl's love for her dog has become a young adult classic. (Rev: BL 12/15/85; BR 1–2/86)

200 Cavanna, Betty. *Wanted: A Girl for the Horses* (7–9). 1984, Morrow $12.95 (0-688-02757-1). Charlotte finds both adventure and love when she accepts a job grooming horses.

201 Chambers, John W. *The Colonel and Me* (7–9). 1985, Macmillan $11.95 (0-689-31087-0). After a difficult beginning, Gussie masters horse riding with the help of Colonel Meslenko. (Rev: BL 4/1/85)

202 Collura, Mary-Ellen Lang. *Winners* (6–9). 1986, Dial $10.95 (0-8037-0011-3). An orphaned boy goes to live with his grandfather on a reservation where he learns to race horses. (Rev: BL 1/15/87; SLJ 1/87)

203 Corcoran, Barbara. *A Horse Named Sky* (6–8). 1986, Macmillan $12.95 (0-689-31193-1). In exchange for doing housework, Georgia fulfills her strongest wish—to have a horse of her own. (Rev: BL 4/15/86; SLJ 10/86)

204 Coville, Bruce. *Herds of Thunder, Manes of Gold: A Collection of Horse Stories and Poems* (5–10). Illus. 1989, Doubleday LB $14.95 (0-385-24642-0). A collection by well-known authors of poems, stories, and book excerpts about horses. (Rev: SLJ 12/89)

205 Diggs, Lucy. *Everyday Friends* (6–8). 1986, Troll paper $2.95 (0-8167-1047-3). A bond between 2 girls is strengthened by their mutual love of horses. (Rev: BL 6/1/86; SLJ 8/86; VOYA 8–10/86)

206 Diggs, Lucy. *Moon in the Water* (6–9). 1988, Macmillan $13.95 (0-689-31337-3). JoBob tries to forget his troubles at home by training a pinto named Blue. (Rev: BL 3/15/88; BR 9–10/88; SLJ 4/88; VOYA 8/88)

207 Donovan, John. *Family* (7–10). 1986, Harper LB $11.89 (0-06-021722-7). An unusual novel about a group of apes kept at a university for observation. (Rev: SLJ 8/86)

208 Doty, Jean Slaughter. *Yesterday's Horses* (5–9). 1985, Macmillan $9.95 (0-02-733040-0). Kelly's unusual pony holds the secret of immunity against an epidemic destroying the horse population. (Rev: BR 11–12/85)

209 Draper, Cena C. *The Worst Hound Around* (5–8). 1979, Westminster $8.95 (0-664-32643-9). Jorie and his 3 girl cousins try to turn his hound dog into a true hunter.

210 Eckert, Allan W. *Incident at Hawk's Hill* (6–10). Illus. 1971, Little $14.95 (0-316-20866-3). A 6-year-old boy is brought up by a badger.

211 Erickson, John R. *The Original Adventures of Hank the Cowdog* (7–10). Illus. 1988, Texas Monthly paper $3.95 (0-87719-102-6). The often hilarious adventures of a dog in charge of security on a ranch in the Texas panhandle. Also use: *The Further Adventures of Hank the Cowdog* and *Hank the Cowdog and It's a Dog's Life* (both 1988). (Rev: SLJ 9/88)

212 Farley, Walter. *The Black Stallion* (5–8). 1977, Random LB $10.99 (0-394-90601-2); paper $2.95 (0-394-83609-X). First published in 1941, this is the first of a lengthy series of horse stories by this author.

213 Farley, Walter. *The Black Stallion Legend* (6–8). 1983, Random $8.95 (0-394-86026-8); paper $2.95 (0-394-87500-1). Alex and his black stallion hold the lives of an Indian tribe in their hands. Part of a lengthy, recommended series.

214 Farley, Walter. *The Great Dane Thor* (6–8). 1980, Dell paper $1.75 (0-440-93095-2). Lars must conquer his fear of a beautiful Great Dane and also improve his relations with his father.

215 Farley, Walter, and Steven Farley. *The Young Black Stallion* (5–9). 1989, Random LB $11.99 (0-394-49562-X). In this sequel to *The Black Stallion,* the reader learns about the early life of Shêtân. (Rev: BR 5–6/90; SLJ 12/89)

216 Fleming, Susan. *The Pig at 37 Pinecrest Drive* (6–8). Illus. 1981, Westminster $9.95 (0-664-32676-5). Terry wants to be captain of the baseball team but a pig named Cadillac spoils everything.

217 Gauch, Patricia Lee. *Kate Alone* (7–9). 1980, Putnam $7.95 (0-399-20738-4). A teenage girl begins to distrust her pet dog when he returns from obedience school.

218 George, Jean Craighead. *Summer of the Falcon* (7–9). 1979, Harper paper $3.95 (0-06-440095-6). A young woman matures as she traces 3 years in the life of a falcon.

219 Gipson, Fred. *Old Yeller* (6–10). Illus. 1956, Harper LB $13.89 (0-06-011546-7). A boy and his dog in Texas of 1860. A sequel is *Savage Sam* (1976).

220 Graeber, Charlotte Towner. *Grey Cloud* (6–8). Illus. 1979, Macmillan $8.95 (0-02-736690-2). Tom and Orville become friends when they train pigeons for a big race.

221 Griffith, Helen V. *Foxy* (6–8). 1984, Greenwillow $11.95 (0-688-02567-6). Jeff doesn't like outdoor life but finding a homeless dog helps him fit in.

222 Griffiths, Helen. *Dancing Horses* (6–8). 1982, Holiday $9.95 (0-8234-0437-4). In post-Civil War Spain, Francisco gets a job taking care of a horse.

223 Griffiths, Helen. *Grip: A Dog Story* (7–9). Illus. 1978, Holiday $9.95 (0-8234-0335-1). Dudley's cruel father demands that he destroy his pet dog, Grip.

224 Gulley, Judie. *Rodeo Summer* (6–9). 1984, Houghton $11.95 (0-395-36174-5). A girl who considers herself a loser tries to train a horse for the local rodeo. (Rev: BL 1/15/85)

225 Haas, Jessie. *The Sixth Sense and Other Stories* (7–10). 1988, Greenwillow $11.95 (0-688-08129-0). A series of stories about the bonds between man and animals. (Rev: BL 11/15/88; BR 11–12/88; SLJ 11/88)

226 Hall, Lynn. *Danger Dog* (7–9). 1986, Macmillan $11.95 (0-684-18680-2). David tries in vain to reprogram a trained attack dog. (Rev: SLJ 12/86; VOYA 12/86)

227 Hall, Lynn. *Danza!* (7–9). 1981, Macmillan $12.95 (0-684-17158-9); paper $3.95 (0-689-71289-8). When he sees the stallion Danza on his grandfather's farm, Paulo discovers his true love for horses.

228 Hall, Lynn. *Half the Battle* (6–9). 1982, Macmillan $10.95 (0-684-17348-4). Jealous of his blind brother, Loren decides to enter a grueling horseback endurance test.

229 Hall, Lynn. *Halsey's Pride* (6–8). 1990, Macmillan $12.95 (0-684-19155-5). A teenage epileptic girl is sent to live with her father, who operates a kennel. (Rev: BL 4/90; SLJ 4/90)

230 Hall, Lynn. *The Horse Trader* (7–9). 1981, Macmillan $9.95 (0-684-16852-9). Karen has a secret crush on the trainer who has sold her a horse.

231 Hall, Lynn. *Uphill All the Way* (7–10). 1984, Macmillan $11.95 (0-684-18066-9). Callie's plans to become a horseshoer are going smoothly until she meets a troubled boy named Truman.

232 Hallstead, William F. *Tundra* (5–9). 1984, Crown $8.95 (0-517-55266-3). A Siberian husky named Tundra wanders away from his home and has many adventures before being reunited with his 15-year-old mistress. (Rev: BL 1/15/85)

233 Henry, Marguerite. *Mustang: Wild Spirit of the West* (6–8). 1966, Macmillan $8.95 (0-528-82327-2); paper $2.95 (0-02-688760-6). Annie Johnston's crusade is to stop the killing of the wild mustangs of the West. One of many fine horse stories by this author.

234 Holland, Isabelle. *Toby the Splendid* (6–8). 1987, Walker $12.95 (0-8027-6674-9). An intense argument arises between mother and daughter when young Janet buys a horse and wants to start riding. (Rev: BL 4/1/87; BR 9–10/87; SLJ 4/87; VOYA 8–9/89)

235 Hoppe, Joanne. *Pretty Penny Farm* (6–9). 1987, Morrow $12.95 (0-688-07201-1); Troll paper $2.50 (0-8167-1326-X). A bad-tempered 15-year-old girl learns values when she spends a summer on a farm in New Hampshire taking care of a horse. (Rev: BL 8/87; BR 9–10/87; SLJ 6–7/87; VOYA 6/87)

236 Howard, Jean G. *Half a Cage* (6–8). Illus. 1978, Tidal Pr. $3.50 (0-930954-07-6). Ann's pet monkey causes so many problems she wonders if she should give it away.

237 James, Will. *Smoky the Cow Horse* (7–12). 1926, Macmillan $12.95 (0-684-12875-6); paper $5.95 (0-684-17145-7). One of the first winners of the Newbery Medal, this is the now-classic story of a ranch horse in the Old West.

238 Jones, Adrienne. *The Hawks of Chelney* (7–9). Illus. 1978, Harper $13.95 (0-06-023057-6). A young outcast and his girlfriend try to understand the hawks and their habits.

239 Kjelgaard, James A. *Big Red* (6–9). 1956, Holiday $14.95 (0-8234-0007-7); Bantam paper $2.95 (0-553-15434-6). This is the perennial favorite about Danny and his Irish setter. Continued in *Irish Red* (1951) and *Outlaw Red* (1953).

240 Kjelgaard, James A. *Desert Dog* (6–8). 1975, Bantam paper $2.75 (0-553-15491-5). The story of how a young racing greyhound survives alone in the Arizona desert.

241 Kjelgaard, James A. *Haunt Fox* (6–8). 1981, Bantam paper $2.50 (0-553-15547-4). The story of how a young fox manages to survive the traps, hounds, and hunters.

242 Kjelgaard, James A. *Lion Hound* (6–8). 1983, Bantam paper $2.95 (0-553-15427-3). A dangerous mountain lion is tracked down by a boy and his hound.

243 Kjelgaard, James A. *Snow Dog* (6–8). 1980, Bantam paper $2.95 (0-553-15365-X). In the wilderness, a snow dog fights for survival. A sequel is: *Wild Trek* (1981).

244 Kjelgaard, James A. *Stormy* (6–8). 1983, Bantam paper $2.95 (0-553-15468-0). Alan is helped to accept his father's being sent to prison through love for a retriever named Stormy.

245 Knight, Eric. *Lassie Come Home* (6–9). 1978, Henry Holt $12.95 (0-8050-0721-0); Dell paper $4.95 (0-440-40136-4). The classic story of how a faithful collie returns to the boy who was his first master.

246 Koehler, William. *A Dog Called Lucky Tide* (6–8). 1988, Scholastic paper $2.50 (0-590-41710-X). A rescued dog amply repays its new owner in a crisis involving the family's land. (Rev: BL 2/15/89)

247 Lippincott, Joseph W. *Wilderness Champion* (7–9). 1944, Harper $11.70 (0-397-30099-9). This novel, now almost 50 years old, tells about a most unusual hound dog.

248 McHargue, Georgess. *The Horseman's Word* (7–9). 1981, Delacorte $19.95 (0-385-28472-1); Dell paper $2.95 (0-440-20126-8). Leigh uses her friendship with Rob to secure admission to a secret ceremony involving horses, with unfortunate results.

249 Manley, Seon. *A Present for Charles Dickens* (6–8). 1983, Westminster $12.95 (0-664-32706-0). A mischievous raven is left at the doorstep of the author Charles Dickens.

250 Morey, Walt. *Gentle Ben* (5–8). Illus. 1976, Dutton $11.95 (0-525-30429-0). Mark befriends a captive brown bear but eventually he must give him up.

251 Morey, Walt. *Kavik the Wolf Dog* (7–9). 1977, Dutton $12.95 (0-525-33093-3). This is a story of survival and courage set in the Far North.

252 Morey, Walt. *The Year of the Black Pony* (6–8). 1976, Blue Heron paper $5.95 (0-936085-14-2). Christopher's love for the black stallion turns to tragedy and bitterness.

253 Mukerji, Dhan Gopal. *Gay-Neck: The Story of a Pigeon* (6–8). Illus. 1968, Dutton $13.95 (0-525-30400-2). Gay-Neck, a carrier pigeon, is selected to perform dangerous missions during World War I.

254 North, Sterling. *The Wolfling* (7–9). 1980, Scholastic paper $2.25 (0-590-30254-X). In this story involving a 13-year-old boy, the reader discovers the problems and rewards of raising a wolf pup.

255 O'Hara, Mary. *My Friend Flicka* (7–10). Illus. 1973, Harper $15.45 (0-397-00981-X); paper $2.95 (0-06-080902-7). A 10-year-old boy gets a colt of his own. Followed by *Thunderhead* (1943). A reissue.

256 Peck, Robert Newton. *The Horse Hunters* (7–10). 1988, Random $15.95 (0-394-56980-6). A 15-year-old boy reaches manhood through capturing a white stallion in this novel set in Florida of the 1930s. (Rev: BL 2/15/89; BR 5–6/89; VOYA 6/89)

257 Peyton, K. M. *The Team* (7–9). Illus. 1976, Harper $12.70 (0-690-01083-4). Ruth is determined to own the special show pony that is for sale.

258 Rand, Gloria. *Salty Dog* (6–9). Illus. 1989, Henry Holt $13.95 (0-8050-0837-3). A dog and his young master are the central characters in this story about the construction of a sailboat. (Rev: BL 3/1/89)

259 Rawlings, Marjorie Kinnan. *The Yearling* (6–9). Illus. 1983, Macmillan paper $4.95 (0-02-044931-3). The classic story of Joss and the orphaned fawn he adopts.

260 Rawls, Wilson. *Summer of the Monkeys* (6–9). 1976, Doubleday $14.95 (0-385-13004-X); Dell paper $3.25 (0-440-98175-1). A 14-year-old boy tries to recapture 29 escaped monkeys.

261 Rawls, Wilson. *Where the Red Fern Grows* (6–9). 1961, Doubleday LB $13.95 (0-385-02059-7). A boy receives 2 coon dogs during his childhood in the Ozarks.

262 Rounds, Glen. *Wild Appaloosa* (6–9). Illus. 1983, Holiday $13.95 (0-8234-0482-X). A wild horse is gradually tamed by a young boy.

263 Rylant, Cynthia. *Every Living Thing* (6–9). Illus. 1985, Bradbury $10.95 (0-02-777200-4). In each of these 12 stories, the lives of humans change because of their relationship with animals. (Rev: SLJ 12/85; VOYA 4/86)

264 St. John, Chris. *A Horse of Her Own* (6–9). 1989, Ballantine paper $2.95 (0-449-13451-2). The story of 3 girls and their interest in horseback riding. Followed by *Riding High* (1989). (Rev: BL 7/89; SLJ 2/90)

265 Savitt, Sam. *A Horse to Remember* (7–9). 1984, Viking $11.95 (0-670-37920-4); Penguin paper $3.95 (0-14-032029-6). Mike tries to train his horse, a former racehorse, back to its former glory.

266 Sewell, Anna. *Black Beauty* (7–9). 1974, Airmont paper $1.50 (0-8049-0023-X). The classic sentimental story about the cruelty and kindness experienced by a horse in Victorian England.

267 Shachtman, Tom. *Wavebender: A Story of Daniel au Fond* (8–10). Illus. 1989, Henry Holt $14.95 (0-8050-0840-3). A novel about the day-to-day struggle for survival of a sea lion named Daniel au Fond. (Rev: SLJ 8/89)

268 Springer, Nancy. *A Horse to Love* (4–8). 1987, Harper LB $11.89 (0-060-25825-X). Erin's parents buy her a horse hoping that this will help cure her shyness. (Rev: SLJ 3/87)

269 Steinbeck, John. *The Red Pony* (7–12). Illus. 1959, Viking LB $11.95 (0-670-59184-X); Bantam paper $2.50 (0-553-26444-3). Jody is growing up on a California ranch where he has his first horse.

270 Stoneley, Jack. *Scruffy* (7–9). 1988, Knopf paper $2.95 (0-394-82039-8). The story of the problems faced by an unwanted dog growing up in London. A reissue.

271 Taylor, Theodore. *The Trouble with Tuck* (5–8). 1989, Doubleday $13.95 (0-385-17774-7); Avon paper $2.95 (0-380-62711-6). An easily read story about a girl's concern about her dog who is going blind.

272 Terhune, Albert Payson. *Lad: A Dog* (7–9). 1978, NAL paper $2.50 (0-451-14626-3). The classic story of a beautiful collie. The beginning of a lengthy series now all out of print.

273 Thomas, Allison. *Benji* (6–8). 1980, Jove paper $1.75 (0-515-05749-3). The adventures of a lovable dog. The basis of a successful motion picture.

274 Thomas, Joyce Carol. *The Golden Pasture* (7–10). 1986, Scholastic $11.95 (0-590-33681-9). The story of a half Indian–half black boy, his relations with his black father and grandfather, and his love for a beautiful horse. (Rev: SLJ 8/86; VOYA 10/86)

275 Vail, Virginia. *Pets Are for Keeps* (6–8). 1986, Scholastic paper $2.50 (0-590-40181-5). In this novel a veterinarian's daughter takes in a worn-out show horse. (Rev: BL 12/15/86)

276 Wallace, Bill. *A Dog Called Kitty* (7–9). 1980, Holiday $12.95 (0-8234-0376-9); paper

$2.50 (0-671-63969-2). On an Oklahoma farm a young boy adopts an abandoned puppy.

277 Wallin, Marie-Louise. *Tangles* (7–9). 1980, Dell paper $1.75 (0-440-99055-6). In this Swedish story a new friendship and love help a young girl with many problems.

278 Westall, Robert. *Blitzcat* (8–12). 1989, Scholastic $12.95 (0-590-42770-9). In World War II England, a cat named Lord Gort sets out to find her master. (Rev: BL 12/15/89; BR 1–2/90; SLJ 11/89; VOYA 2/90)

279 Wilson, A. N. *Stray* (6–10). 1989, Watts LB $15.99 (0-531-08440-X). An old stray cat tells his life story to his grandson to warn him about humans. (Rev: BL 1/1/90; BR 1–2/90; SLJ 10/89; VOYA 12/89)

280 Wrightson, Patricia. *Moon Dark* (7–10). 1988, Macmillan $13.95 (0-689-50451-9). A novel seen through the eyes of a wild dog about the effect humans have on the environment. (Rev: VOYA 6/88)

Classics

Europe

GENERAL

281 Cervantes, Miguel de. *The Adventures of Don Quixote de la Mancha* (8–12). 1983, Dent $15.00 (0-460-05024-9). One of several editions of this classic story of the misadventures of a knight enamored of chivalry.

282 Dumas, Alexandre. *The Count of Monte Cristo* (8–12). 1981, Bantam paper $3.95 (0-553-21187-0). The classic French novel about false imprisonment, escape, and revenge.

283 Dumas, Alexandre. *The Three Musketeers* (8–12). 1984, Dodd $14.95 (0-396-08355-2); paper $4.95 (0-553-21337-7). A novel of daring and intrigue in France. A sequel is *The Man in the Iron Mask* (available in various editions).

284 Maupassant, Guy de. *The Best Short Stories of Guy de Maupassant* (7–12). 1968, Airmont paper $2.75 (0-8049-0161-9). The French master is represented by 19 tales including "The Diamond Necklace."

285 Verne, Jules. *Around the World in Eighty Days* (7–12). 1974, Dent $11.00 (0-460-05082-6); Dell paper $2.95 (0-440-90285-1). Phileas Fogg and servant Passepartout leave on a world trip, in this 1873 classic adventure.

286 Verne, Jules. *A Journey to the Centre of the Earth* (7–12). Illus. 1984, Dodd $12.95 (0-396-08429-X); Penguin paper $3.95 (0-14-002265-1). A group of adverturers enter the earth through a volcano in Iceland. First published in French in 1864.

287 Verne, Jules. *Twenty Thousand Leagues under the Sea* (7–12). 1976, Dent $11.00 (0-460-05071-0); Airmont paper $1.95 (0-8049-0182-1). Evil Captain Nemo captures a group of underwater explorers. First published in 1869. A sequel is: *The Mysterious Island* (1988 Macmillan).

288 Wyss, Johann. *The Swiss Family Robinson* (6–9). 1964, Airmont paper $1.95 (0-8049-0013-2). One of many editions of the classic survival story, first published in 1814, of a family marooned on a deserted island.

GREAT BRITAIN AND IRELAND

289 Barrie, J. M. *Peter Pan* (5–8). Illus. 1980, Macmillan $18.95 (0-684-16611-9). The classic tale of the boy who wouldn't grow up and of his adventures with the Darling children.

290 Brontë, Charlotte. *Jane Eyre* (8–12). 1964, Airmont paper $2.95 (0-8049-0017-5). Jane finds terror and romance when she becomes a governess for Mr. Rochester.

291 Brontë, Emily. *Wuthering Heights* (9–12). 1959, Signet paper $2.50 (0-451-52338-5). The love between Catherine and Heathcliff that even death cannot destroy.

292 Burnett, Frances Hodgson. *The Secret Garden* (5–8). 1971, Harper $12.70 (0-397-30632-6); Dell paper $4.95 (0-440-47709-3). An easily read classic about a spoiled girl relocated to England and of the unusual friendship she finds there.

293 Cohen, Barbara. *Canterbury Tales* (5–9). Illus. 1988, Lothrop $17.95 (0-688-06201-6). Several of the popular stories are retold with handsome illustrations by Trina Schart Hyman. (Rev: BL 9/1/88) [821.1]

294 Defoe, Daniel. *Robinson Crusoe* (7–12). Illus. 1983, Macmillan $22.50 (0-684-17946-6); NAL paper $2.25 (0-451-52236-2). The classic survival story with illustrations by N. C. Wyeth.

295 Dickens, Charles. *A Christmas Carol* (7–12). 1983, Messner LB $11.97 (0-671-47646-7); Pocket paper $2.95 (0-671-47369-7). Scrooge through some trying experiences discovers the true meaning of Christmas.

296 Dickens, Charles. *David Copperfield* (7–12). 1966, Penguin paper $2.95 (0-14-043008-3). A lengthy, partly autobiographical novel about growing up in Victorian England.

297 Dickens, Charles. *Great Expectations* (8–12). 1985, Dodd $14.95 (0-396-08687-4); Bantam paper $2.95 (0-553-21342-3). The story of Pip and his slow journey to maturity and fortune.

298 Dickens, Charles. *Oliver Twist* (7–12). 1961, NAL paper $2.95 (0-451-52351-2). In probably the most accessible of Dickens' works, readers meet such immortals as Fagin, Nancy, and Oliver himself.

299 Dickens, Charles. *Tale of Two Cities* (7–12). 1985, Dodd $11.95 (0-395-08535-0); NAL paper $2.50 (0-451-52301-6). The classic novel of sacrifice during the French Revolution. A reissue.

300 Doyle, Arthur Conan. *Sherlock Holmes: The Complete Novels and Stories* (8–12). 2 vols. 1986, Bantam paper $4.95 each (vol. 1: 0-553-21241-9; vol. 2: 0-553-21242-7). A handy collection in 2 volumes of all the writings about Holmes and Watson. (Rev: BL 3/15/87)

301 Eliot, George. *Silas Marner* (8–12). 1960, NAL paper $1.95 (0-451-52108-0). The love of an old man for a young child brings redemption in this classic English novel.

302 Hastings, Selina. *The Canterbury Tales by Geoffrey Chaucer: A Selection* (6–10). Illus. 1988, Henry Holt $17.95 (0-8050-0904-3). Seven of the most popular tales are retold with charming illustrations by Reg Cartwright. (Rev: BL 12/1/88) [821.1]

303 Kipling, Rudyard. *Captains Courageous* (7–10). 1964, Airmont paper $1.75 (0-8049-0027-2). The story of a spoiled teenager who learns about life from common fishermen who save him when he falls overboard from an ocean liner.

304 Kipling, Rudyard. *Kim* (7–12). n.d., Airmont paper $1.95 (0-8049-0075-2). An outcast boy in British India becomes a member of the Secret Service.

305 Shelley, Mary Wollstonecraft. *Frankenstein* (8–12). 1964, Dell paper $1.95 (0-440-92717-X). The classic novel about a scientific experiment to create a man-made human.

306 Stevenson, Robert Louis. *Dr. Jekyll and Mr. Hyde* (7–12). 1979, Dodd $10.95 (0-396-67758-7); paper $1.95 (0-553-21087-4). This 1886 classic of horror involves a drug-induced change of personality. One of several editions.

307 Stevenson, Robert Louis. *Kidnapped* (7–12). Illus. 1886, Putnam $11.95 (0-448-06015-9); NAL paper $1.95 (0-451-51754-7). David Balfour escapes death to claim his inheritance. One of several editions. A sequel is *Master of Ballantrae* (1914).

308 Stevenson, Robert Louis. *Treasure Island* (6–9). 1956, Macmillan $20.95 (0-684-17160-0); NAL paper $1.95 (0-451-51729-6). Jim Hawkins and Long John Silver on the trail of treasure. One of several recommended editions. First published in 1882.

309 Swift, Jonathan. *Gulliver's Travels* (7–12). 1975, Dent $11.00 (0-460-05018-4); NAL paper $2.95 (0-451-52219-2). The 4 fantastic voyages of Lemuel Gulliver. First published in 1726.

310 Tennyson, Alfred. *The Lady of Shalott* (8–12). Illus. 1986, Oxford Univ. Pr. $11.95 (0-19-276057-2). Tennyson's famous poem brought to life with lavish illustrations by Charles Keeping in an oversize book. (Rev: BL 11/1/86; SLJ 2/87) [821]

311 Wilde, Oscar. *The Canterville Ghost* (7–10). Illus. 1986, Alphabet Pr. $14.95 (0-88708-027-8). A new edition with charming illustrations of the classic story of the American family who encounter a ghost in England. (Rev: SLJ 1/87)

United States

312 Alcott, Louisa May. *Little Women* (6–10). 1947, Putnam $14.95 (0-448-06019-1); Airmont paper $2.95 (0-8049-0106-6). The beginning of the story of the March family and their 4 daughters—Jo, Amy, Beth, and Meg. Also use sequels *Good Wives, Little Men,* and *Jo's Boys* (available in many editions).

313 Cooper, James Fenimore. *The Last of the Mohicans* (8–12). 1986, Macmillan $22.95 (0-684-18711-6); Bantam paper $2.95 (0-553-21329-6). This is the second of the classic Leatherstocking Tales. The others are *The Pioneers, The Prairie, The Pathfinder,* and *The Deerslayer* (all available in various editions).

314 Crane, Stephen. *The Red Badge of Courage* (8–12). 1940, Random $6.95 (0-394-60493-5); Bantam paper $1.50 (0-553-21011-4). The classic novel of a young man who explored the meanings of courage during the Civil War.

315 Hale, E. E. *The Man without a Country and Other Stories* (7–10). 1982, Airmont paper $1.75 (0-02-671980-0). A man is doomed to wander the world because he has denied his country. Five other stories are included in this volume.

316 Henry, O. *The Gift of the Magi* (5–10). Illus. 1988, Simon & Schuster $12.95 (0-671-64706-7). A beautifully illustrated edition of this classic story of Christmas and true love. (Rev: BL 12/15/88)

317 Irving, Washington. *The Legend of Sleepy Hollow and Other Selections* (7–12). 1963, Washington Square Pr. paper $3.95 (0-671-46211-3). The story of Icnabod Crane, the ill-fated schoolteacher, and his encounter with the headless horseman.

318 London, Jack. *The Call of the Wild* (7–12). Illus. 1963, Macmillan $11.95 (0-02-759510-2); NAL paper $2.50 (0-451-52390-3). In this 1903 classic, the dog Buck becomes leader of a pack of wolves.

319 London, Jack. *The Sea-Wolf* (7–12). 1958, Macmillan $15.95 (0-02-574630-8); Bantam paper $1.95 (0-553-21161-7). Wolf Larsen helps a ne'er-do-well and a female poet find their destinies in the classic that was originally published in 1904.

320 London, Jack. *White Fang* (7–12). 1972, Scholastic paper $2.50 (0-590-40523-3). A dog sacrifices himself to save his master in the classic that was first published in 1906.

321 Poe, Edgar Allan. *The Complete Tales and Poems of Edgar Allan Poe* (7–12). 1975, Vintage paper $10.95 (0-394-71678-7). One of the many editions of the macabre writings of this genius. [818]

322 Poe, Edgar Allan. *Tales of Terror* (7–12). Illus. 1985, Prentice $11.95 (0-13-884214-0). This is a collection of Poe's most famous stories illustrated by Neil Waldman. (Rev: BL 6/15/85; SLJ 9/85)

323 Sandburg, Carl. *The Sandburg Treasury: Prose and Poetry for Young People* (7–10). Illus. 1970, Harcourt $24.95 (0-15-270180-X). A collection of all of the books that Sandburg wrote for young people. [818]

324 Twain, Mark. *The Adventures of Huckleberry Finn* (7–12). 1959, NAL paper $1.75 (0-451-51912-4). The classic 1885 story of Huck and Jim on the Mississippi.

325 Twain, Mark. *The Adventures of Tom Sawyer* (7–12). 1982, Messner LB $14.79 (0-671-45647-4); Penguin paper $2.25 (0-14-035003-9). The story of Tom, Aunt Polly, Becky Thatcher, and the villainous Injun Joe. First published in 1876.

326 Twain, Mark. *A Connecticut Yankee in King Arthur's Court* (7–12). 1988, Morrow $19.95 (0-688-06346-2); Bantam paper $1.95 (0-553-21143-9). Through a time travel fantasy, a swaggering Yankee is plummeted into the age of chivalry. First published in 1889.

327 Twain, Mark. *The Prince and the Pauper* (7–12). n.d., Harper LB $11.89 (0-06-104406-8); Penguin paper $2.25 (0-14-035017-9). A king and a poor boy switch places in sixteenth-century England. First published in 1881.

328 Twain, Mark. *Pudd'nhead Wilson* (7–12). (0-8049-0124-4); 1966, Airmont paper $1.75. In the Midwest of over 100 years ago, a black servant switches her baby with a white couple's child to ensure that he gets a fair chance at life.

329 Twain, Mark. *Tom Sawyer Abroad [and] Tom Sawyer, Detective* (7–12). n.d., Airmont paper $1.50 (0-8049-0126-0). Two sequels to *The Adventures of Tom Sawyer,* both involving Tom and Huck.

Contemporary Life and Problems

Ethnic Groups and Problems

330 Angell, Judie. *One-Way to Ansonia* (7–10). 1985, Bradbury $11.95 (0-02-705860-3). In novel format this is the story of a young Russian girl's experience in this country around the turn of the century. (Rev: BL 1/1/86; SLJ 12/85; VOYA 2/86)

331 Armstrong, William H. *Sounder* (6–10). Illus. 1969, Harper LB $12.89 (0-06-020144-4); paper $2.95 (0-06-440020-4). The moving story of a black sharecropper, his family, and his devoted coon dog, Sounder. A sequel is *Sour Land* (1971).

332 Arrick, Fran. *Chernowitz!* (7–10). 1981, Bradbury $9.95 (0-02-705720-8). An anti-Semitic situation brings the victim, Bobby Cherno, to a point where he wants revenge.

333 Bargar, Gary W. *Life.Is.Not.Fair* (6–8). 1984, Houghton LB $13.95 (0-89919-218-1). Louis faces social pressure because of his friendship with DeWitt, a black boy who has moved in next door. A sequel to: *What Happened to Mr. Forster?* (1981).

334 Betancourt, Jeanne. *More Than Meets the Eye* (7–10). 1990, Bantam $14.95 (0-553-05871-1). Liz's attachment to a Chinese American boy brings out latent bigotry and prejudice in a number of friends and acquaintances. (Rev: BL 6/1/90; SLJ 8/90)

335 Bethancourt, T. Ernesto. *The Me Inside of Me* (7–10). 1985, Lerner $10.95 (0-8225-0728-5). A Mexican American boy who has received unexpected money encounters prejudice when he enters a fashionable prep school. (Rev: BL 1/15/86; SLJ 3/86; VOYA 8–10/86)

336 Blair, Cynthia. *Crazy in Love* (7–12). 1988, Ballantine paper $2.95 (0-449-70189-1). An upper-middle-class Jewish girl falls in love with a poor Puerto Rican boy and causes great family opposition. (Rev: BL 12/1/88; SLJ 1/89; VOYA 10/88)

337 Bosse, Malcolm. *Ganesh* (7–9). 1981, Harper LB $11.89 (0-690-04103-9). A young boy from India has difficulty fitting into the American Midwest and its ways.

338 Bush, Lawrence. *Rooftop Secrets: And Other Stories of Anti-Semitism* (6–9). Illus. 1986, American Hebrew Cong. paper $7.95 (0-8074-0314-8). In each of these 8 short stories, some form of anti-Semitism is encountered by a young person. (Rev: SLJ 11/86)

339 Cave, Hugh B. *Conquering Kilmarnie* (5–8). 1989, Macmillan $13.95 (0-02-717781-5). A novel set in Jamaica about the friendship of 2 boys—one black, one white. (Rev: BL 7/89; BR 11–12/89; VOYA 8/89)

340 Childress, Alice. *A Hero Ain't Nothin' but a Sandwich* (7–10). 1973, Avon paper $2.95 (0-380-00132-2). Benjie's life in Harlem, told from many viewpoints, involves drugs and rejection.

341 Childress, Alice. *Rainbow Jordan* (7–10). 1981, Putnam $9.95 (0-698-20531-6). Rainbow is growing up alternately in a foster home and with a mother who is too preoccupied to care for her.

342 Crew, Linda. *Children of the River* (7–10). 1989, Doubleday $14.95 (0-440-50122-9). The Americanization of a young Cambodian teenager who, together with her aunt's family, has relocated to Oregon. (Rev: BL 3/1/89; BR 9–10/89; SLJ 3/89; VOYA 6/89)

343 Dyer, T. A. *The Whipman Is Watching* (7–9). 1979, Houghton $7.95 (0-395-28581-X). Angie is ashamed of her Native American roots and tries to deny her heritage.

344 Fiedler, Jean. *The Year the World Was Out of Step with Jancy Fried* (6–8). 1981, Harcourt $9.95 (0-15-299818-7). In America of 1936, young Jancy suddenly becomes aware of what it means to be Jewish.

345 Gordon, Sheila. *Waiting for the Rain: A Novel of South Africa* (7–12). 1987, Watts LB $12.99 (0-531-08326-8); Bantam paper $2.95 (0-553-27911-4). The story of the friendship between a black boy and a white boy in apartheid-ridden South Africa. (Rev: BL 8/87; SLJ 8/87; VOYA 12/87)

346 Guy, Rosa. *The Friends* (7–10). 1973, Holt LB $10.95 (0-03-007876-8); Bantam paper $2.95

(0-553-26519-9). Phyllisia, a newcomer to Harlem, finds a friend in the unusual Edith Jackson.

347 Guy, Rosa. *The Ups and Downs of Carl Davis III* (6–8). 1989, Delacorte $13.95 (0-385-29724-6). A brilliant 12-year-old black boy is sent to live with his grandmother in South Carolina. (Rev: BL 5/1/89; BR 11–12/89; SLJ 6/89)

348 Hale, Janet Campbell. *The Owl's Song* (7–9). 1976, Avon paper $2.50 (0-380-00605-7). A 14-year-old American Indian boy and his sister leave their reservation to begin a new life in California.

349 Hamanaka, Sheila. *The Journey* (5–9). Illus. 1990, Watts LB $18.99 (0-531-08449-3). A picture book with text that deals with the injustices suffered by Japanese Americans at the beginning of World War II. (Rev: BL 3/15/90; VOYA 6/90)

350 Hamilton, Virginia. *Arilla Sundown* (7–9). 1976, Greenwillow $12.88 (0-688-84058-2). Arilla is part Indian and part black and growing up in a unique family situation.

351 Hamilton, Virginia. *Zeely* (6–9). 1967, Macmillan $12.95 (0-02-742470-7); Dell paper $1.95 (0-689-71110-7). A beautiful, statuesque woman enters Geeder's life and he is convinced she is an African queen.

352 Hassler, Jon. *Jemmy* (7–10). 1980, Macmillan $8.95 (0-689-50130-7). A half-Indian girl is ordered by her father to quit school when her mother dies.

353 Henderson, Lois T. *The Blessing Deer* (7–9). 1980, Cook paper $2.95 (0-89191-244-4). A girl learns about racial prejudice from her black friend Clarisse.

354 Herlihy, Dirlie. *Ludie's Song* (6–8). 1988, Dial $14.95 (0-8037-0533-6). A young white girl growing up in the South of the 1950s realizes the injustices of segregation. (Rev: BL 12/1/88; SLJ 9/88; VOYA 12/88)

355 Hernández, Irene Beltrán. *Across the Great River* (7–10). 1989, Arte Publico paper $8.50 (0-934770-96-4). The harrowing story of a young Mexican girl and her family who illegally enter the United States. (Rev: BL 8/89)

356 Hobbs, Will. *Bearstone* (7–10). 1989, Macmillan $12.95 (0-689-31496-5). A hostile, resentful Indian teenager is sent to live with a rancher in Colorado. (Rev: BL 11/1/89; BR 3–4/90; SLJ 9/89; VOYA 12/89)

357 Hooks, William H. *Circle of Fire* (6–8). 1982, Macmillan $12.95 (0-689-50241-9). In rural North Carolina of 1936, a white boy wonders if his father is a member of the Ku Klux Klan.

358 Hunter, Kristin. *The Soul Brothers and Sister Lou* (6–8). 1975, Avon paper $2.25 (0-380-00686-3). In a big city ghetto, Lou and 5 other black friends form a singing group.

359 Irwin, Hadley. *Kim/Kimi* (7–10). 1987, Macmillan $12.95 (0-689-50428-4); Penguin paper $3.95 (0-14-032593-X). A half-Japanese teenager brought up in an all-white small town sets out to explore her Oriental roots. (Rev: BL 3/15/87; SLJ 5/87; VOYA 6/87)

360 Lester, Julius. *This Strange New Feeling* (7–9). 1982, Dial $14.95 (0-8037-8491-0); Scholastic paper $2.50 (0-590-41061-X). Three stories about black couples and the meaning of freedom.

361 Lipsyte, Robert. *The Contender* (7–10). 1967, Harper $12.89 (0-06-023920-4); paper $2.50 (0-06-447039-3). A black Harlem youth tries to find release from his pressures via boxing.

362 Lord, Bette Bao. *In the Year of the Boar and Jackie Robinson* (6–8). Illus. 1984, Harper LB $12.89 (0-06-024004-0); paper $3.50 (0-06-440175-8). A young Chinese girl finds that the world of baseball helps her adjust to her new home in America.

363 MacKinnon, Bernie. *The Meantime* (7–9). 1984, Houghton $11.95 (0-395-35387-4). Luke and his family can't escape racial prejudice when they move from a black ghetto to the suburbs.

364 Marzollo, Jean. *Do You Love Me, Harvey Burns?* (7–9). 1983, Dial $12.95 (0-8037-1668-0); Scholastic paper $2.25 (0-590-33192-2). Lisa works on a science project with a Jewish boy named Harvey and discovers problems with anti-Semitism.

365 Meyer, Carolyn. *Denny's Tapes* (8–10). 1987, Macmillan $11.95 (0-689-50413-6). Denny, a high school graduate and son of a white mother and black father, sets out on a transcontinental trip to find his father. (Rev: BL 11/1/87; SLJ 12/87; VOYA 12/87)

366 Miklowitz, Gloria D. *The War between the Classes* (7–10). 1986, Dell paper $2.95 (0-440-99406-3). A Japanese American girl finds that hidden prejudices and bigotry emerge when students in school are divided into 4 socioeconomic groups. (Rev: BL 4/15/85; SLJ 8/85; VOYA 6/85)

367 Mohr, Nicholasa. *El Bronx Remembered: A Novella and Stories* (7–9). 1975, Harper $13.89 (0-06-024314-7). These 12 stories set in the Bronx reflect the general Puerto Rican experience in New York.

368 Mohr, Nicholasa. *Felita* (7–9). 1979, Dial LB $12.89 (0-8037-3144-2); Bantam paper $2.75 (0-553-15792-2). Felita, a Puerto Rican girl, encounters problems when her family moves to a non-Spanish speaking neighborhood.

369 Mohr, Nicholasa. *Going Home* (6–8). 1986, Dial LB $11.89 (0-8037-0338-4). The young heroine finds a boyfriend and spends a summer in her family's home in Puerto Rico in this sequel to *Felita* (1979). (Rev: BL 7/86; SLJ 8/86)

370 Mohr, Nicholasa. *Nilda* (7–9). 1973, Harper LB $13.89 (0-06-024332-5). The story of a 12-year-old Puerto Rican girl growing up in the New York barrio.

371 Myers, Walter Dean. *Fast Sam, Cool Clyde, and Stuff* (7–10). 1975, Viking $12.95 (0-670-30874-9); Penguin paper $3.95 (0-317-69635-1). Three male friends in Harlem join forces to found the 116th Street Good People.

372 Myers, Walter Dean. *Motown and Didi: A Love Story* (7–9). 1984, Viking $12.95 (0-670-49062-8); Dell paper $3.25 (0-440-95762-1). In the midst of trouble and despair in Harlem, this is a tender love story.

373 Myers, Walter Dean. *Scorpions* (7–9). 1988, Harper LB $12.89 (0-06-024365-1). Gang warfare, death, and despair are the elements of this story set in present-day Harlem. (Rev: BL 9/1/88; BR 11–12/88; SLJ 9/88; VOYA 8/88)

374 Myers, Walter Dean. *The Young Landlords* (7–10). 1979, Viking $11.50 (0-670-79454-6); Penguin paper $3.95 (0-14-034244-3). A group of black teenagers take over a slum building in Harlem.

375 Neufeld, John. *Edgar Allan* (6–8). 1968, Phillips $16.95 (0-87599-149-1). Michael's family adopts a 3-year-old black boy and the signs of bigotry begin.

376 Neville, Emily C. *Berries Goodman* (6–8). 1965, Harper paper $3.50 (0-06-440072-7). In his new home in the suburbs, Berries encounters anti-Semitism directed against one of his new friends.

377 Nichols, Joan Kane. *All but the Right Folks* (5–8). 1985, Stemmer $11.95 (0-88045-065-7). A novel in which a black boy spends a summer with his white grandmother. (Rev: SLJ 11/85)

378 Pfeffer, Susan Beth. *Turning Thirteen* (6–9). 1988, Scholastic $12.95 (0-590-40764-3). Two Jewish girls find that their bat mitzvahs produce unforeseen problems. (Rev: BL 11/1/88; BR 1–2/89; SLJ 11/88; VOYA 4/89)

379 Rowlands, Avril. *Milk and Honey* (6–10). 1990, Oxford Univ. Pr. $14.95 (0-19-271627-1).

An account of the difficulties faced by a Jamaican family in present-day London. (Rev: BL 6/1/90; SLJ 8/90; VOYA 8/90)

380 Ruby, Lois. *Two Truths in My Pocket* (7–9). 1982, Viking $9.95 (0-670-73724-0). Stories about Jewish young people and problems they face while growing up.

381 Sacks, Margaret. *Beyond Safe Boundaries* (7–12). 1989, Dutton $13.95 (0-525-67281-8). Growing up comfortably in a white Jewish family in the South Africa of the 1960s, Elizabeth knows little about apartheid but this soon changes. (Rev: BL 5/15/89; BR 11–12/89; SLJ 7/89; VOYA 8/89)

382 Sebestyen, Ouida. *Words by Heart* (7–10). 1979, Little $13.95 (0-316-77931-8); Bantam paper $2.95 (0-553-27179-2). In a 1910 Southwestern town, a young black girl causes problems when she defeats a white boy in a spelling contest.

383 Singer, Isaac Bashevis. *The Power of Light: Eight Stories for Hanukkah* (7–10). Illus. 1980, Farrar $13.95 (0-374-36099-5); Avon paper $2.50 (0-380-60103-6). Eight stories of the Festival of Lights that span centuries of Jewish history.

384 Singer, Marilyn. *Several Kinds of Silence* (7–10). 1988, Harper LB $13.88 (0-06-025628-1). Franny's family problems are complicated by her affection for a Japanese American boy. (Rev: BL 12/1/88; BR 1–2/89; SLJ 10/88; VOYA 2/89)

385 Smith, Rukshana. *Sumitra's Story* (7–10). 1983, Putnam $9.95 (0-698-20579-0). Sumitra finds a world of problems in England where things are different from her East Indian home.

386 Spinelli, Jerry. *Maniac Magee* (6–10). 1990, Little $13.45 (0-316-80722-2). A white boy runs away from home and suddenly becomes aware of the racism in his town. (Rev: SLJ 6/90)

387 Tate, Eleanora E. *The Secret of Gumbo Grove* (6–9). 1987, Watts LB $12.90 (0-531-10298-X); Bantam paper $2.95 (0-553-27226-8). A young girl and an older woman prove to the community that blacks have contributed a great deal to the history of their community. (Rev: BR 9–10/87; SLJ 3/87; VOYA 8–9/87)

388 Taylor, Mildred D. *The Road to Memphis* (7–12). 1990, Dial $14.95 (0-8037-0340-6). Set in 1941, this is a continuation of the story of the Logans, a poor black southern family who were previously featured in *Roll of Thunder, Hear My Cry* (1976) and *Let the Circle Be Unbroken* (1981). (Rev: BL 5/15/90; SLJ 1/90; VOYA 8/90)

389 Thomas, Joyce Carol. *Marked by Fire* (9–12). 1982, Avon paper $2.95 (0-380-79327-X). A young black girl experiences pain and anguish during her adolescence.

390 Uchida, Yoshiko. *The Happiest Ending* (6–8). 1985, Macmillan $11.95 (0-689-50326-1). There is a clash of cultures in this story of Japanese American families and an arranged marriage. By the author of *The Best Bad Thing* (1983). (Rev: BL 11/1/85)

391 Uchida, Yoshiko. *A Jar of Dreams* (6–8). 1981, Macmillan $11.95 (0-689-50210-9); paper $3.95 (0-689-71041-0). In California of Depression days, a young Japanese girl encounters prejudice.

392 Uchida, Yoshiko. *Journey Home* (7–9). Illus. 1978, Macmillan $12.95 (0-689-50126-9); paper $2.95 (0-689-70755-X). A Japanese American family return to their ordinary life after being relocated during World War II.

393 Voigt, Cynthia. *Come a Stranger* (6–9). 1986, Macmillan $14.95 (0-689-31289-X); Fawcett paper $2.95 (0-449-70246-2). Mina Smiths, a young black girl introduced in *Dicey's Song*, has trouble achieving her identity as an individual and is helped by a young minister, Tamer Shipp (from *The Runner*). (Rev: BL 9/15/86; SLJ 10/86; VOYA 4/87)

394 Wallin, Luke. *Ceremony of the Panther* (7–10). 1987, Macmillan $11.95 (0-02-792310-X). A young Indian boy leaves his parents' home to live with his grandmother and to understand his roots. (Rev: BL 8/87; BR 9–10/87; SLJ 6–7/87; VOYA 10/87)

395 Wilkinson, Brenda. *Ludell* (7–9). 1975, Harper LB $12.89 (0-06-026492-6). Three years in the life of a black girl growing up in rural Georgia. Followed by *Ludell & Willie* (1977).

396 Wilkinson, Brenda. *Not Separate, Not Equal* (6–10). 1987, Harper LB $12.89 (0-06-026482-9). Seventeen-year-old Malene finds that she is one of 6 black students in a white school in Georgia. (Rev: BR 3–4/88; SLJ 4/88)

397 Yarbrough, Camille. *The Shimmershine Queens* (6–8). 1989, Putnam $13.95 (0-399-21465-8). A young black girl faces problems in her inner-city school but is still determined to succeed. (Rev: BL 4/1/89; SLJ 2/89; VOYA 6/89)

398 Yep, Laurence. *Child of the Owl* (6–9). 1977, Harper LB $12.89 (0-06-026743-7); Dell paper $3.25 (0-440-91230-X). A young girl goes to live with her grandmother in San Francisco's Chinatown.

399 Yep, Laurence. *Dragonwings* (7–9). 1975, Harper LB $12.95 (0-06-026738-0); paper $3.50 (0-06-440085-9). At the turn of the century, a young Chinese boy in San Francisco becomes an aviation pioneer.

Family Life and Problems

400 Adler, C. S. *Ghost Brother* (6–8). 1990, Clarion $13.95 (0-395-52592-6). Visits from his dead brother help Wally adjust to his death and to the presence of Aunt Flo, who has come to take care of him. (Rev: VOYA 8/90)

401 Adler, C. S. *If You Need Me* (6–8). 1988, Macmillan $12.95 (0-02-700420-1). Lyn finds her father is becoming attracted to Mrs. Maclean, their next-door neighbor. (Rev: BL 4/15/88; SLJ 5/88; VOYA 8/88)

402 Adler, C. S. *In Our House Scott Is My Brother* (6–9). 1980, Macmillan LB $10.95 (0-02-700140-7). Jodi's father remarries and she finds herself with a new stepmother and a stepbrother both of whom have problems.

403 Adler, C. S. *The Shell Lady's Daughter* (7–10). 1983, Coward $10.95 (0-698-20580-4). Kelly's mother has emotional problems and attempts suicide.

404 Alcock, Vivien. *The Cuckoo Sister* (6–9). 1986, Delacorte $14.95 (0-385-29467-0); Dell paper $2.95 (0-440-40101-1). A tough street waif appears at the Setons' door in London and claims to be the older daughter kidnapped many years before. (Rev: BL 8/86; SLJ 4/86; VOYA 8–10/86)

405 Amoss, Berthe. *Secret Lives* (6–9). 1988, Dell paper $2.95 (0-440-47904-5). Addie decides to learn the truth about her dead mother who everyone says was perfect.

406 Anderson, Margaret J. *The Journey of the Shadow Bairns* (6–8). 1980, Knopf LB $8.99 (0-394-94511-5). An easily read story about 2 Scottish youngsters who travel alone to Canada.

407 Anderson, Mary. *Catch Me, I'm Falling in Love* (7–10). 1987, Dell paper $2.50 (0-440-91122-2). Sixteen-year-old Amelia must cope with caring for a sick family and handling a crush she has on her chiropractor. (Rev: BL 9/1/85)

408 Anderson, Rachel. *The War Orphan* (6–9). 1986, Oxford $13.95 (0-19-271496-1). When Simon's family decides to adopt Ha, a Vietnamese war orphan, they do not realize he is mentally handicapped. (Rev: BL 9/1/86; BR 9–10/86; SLJ 10/86)

409 Andrews, Kristi. *Typecast* (7–12). 1988, Bantam paper $2.50 (0-553-26569-5). Soap opera star Katie and her younger sister always seem to be at odds with one another. (Rev: SLJ 4/88)

410 Angell, Judie. *Dear Lola, or How to Build Your Own Family* (7–9). 1986, Dell paper $1.95 (0-440-91787-5). Led by 17-year-old Lola, 7 runaways from an orphanage try to establish a new home.

411 Angell, Judie. *Tina Gogo* (7–9). 1980, Dell paper $1.75 (0-440-98738-5). Sarajane becomes friends with a lonely girl whose mother has suddenly reappeared offering to make a home for her.

412 Angell, Judie. *What's Best for You* (7–9). 1981, Bradbury $9.95 (0-02-705760-7). After her parents split up, Lee decides to spend a summer with her father.

413 Arrick, Fran. *Nice Girl from Good Home* (7–10). 1984, Bradbury $11.95 (0-02-705840-9); Dell paper $2.75 (0-440-96358-3). Dory's family seems to be falling apart and she thinks the situation is out of control.

414 Asher, Sandy. *Missing Pieces* (7–10). 1984, Delacorte $12.95 (0-385-29318-6); paper $2.50 (0-440-95716-8). Heather finds a new relationship with her mother after her father dies.

415 Avi. *Sometimes I Think I Hear My Name* (6–9). 1982, Pantheon LB $9.99 (0-394-95048-8). A young boy disobeys his guardians to visit New York and find his parents.

416 Bacon, Katharine Jay. *Shadow and Light* (6–9). 1987, Macmillan $12.89 (0-689-50431-4). Emma is shocked to learn that her beloved grandmother is dying in this sequel to *Pip and Emma* (1986). (Rev: BR 11–12/87; SLJ 4/87; VOYA 6/87)

417 Baehr, Patricia. *Falling Scales* (7–10). 1987, Morrow $11.75 (0-688-07208-9). Theo, a ninth-grader, faces family problems and finds escape in music and a close friendship. (Rev: BL 1/15/88; BR 10–11/87; SLJ 11/87; VOYA 10/87)

418 Bawden, Nina. *The Finding* (6–8). 1985, Lothrop $11.95 (0-688-04979-6); Dell paper $2.95 (0-440-40004-4). Alex is so upset at receiving an inheritance he doesn't deserve that he runs away. (Rev: BL 8/85; VOYA 8/85)

419 Bawden, Nina. *Kept in the Dark* (6–9). 1982, Lothrop $12.95 (0-688-00900-X). Three children are sent to visit their grandparents in rural England.

420 Bawden, Nina. *The Outside Child* (6–8). 1989, Lothrop $12.95 (0-688-08965-8). Jane discovers that her absent father remarried years ago and has a family she would like to meet. (Rev: BL 9/1/89; BR 3–4/90; SLJ 10/89; VOYA 12/89)

421 Berry, James. *A Thief in the Village and Other Stories* (7–12). 1988, Watts LB $12.99 (0-531-08345-4); Penguin paper $3.95 (0-14-034357-1). Nine stories about a teenager in Jamaica and everyday life on this Caribbean island. (Rev: BL 4/15/88; BR 9–10/88)

422 Bess, Clayton. *Story for a Black Night* (6–8). 1982, Houghton $12.95 (0-395-31857-2). In an African village, a baby with smallpox has been abandoned and a family must decide whether or not to care for it.

423 Betancourt, Jeanne. *Home Sweet Home* (7–10). 1988, Bantam $13.95 (0-553-05469-4). A narrative of a 16-year-old girl, her happy family, and her friendship with a visiting Russian teenager. (Rev: BL 1/15/88; SLJ 2/88)

424 Birdseye, Tom. *Tucker* (5–8). 1990, Holiday $13.95 (0-8234-0813-2). A story set in rural Kentucky of a young boy reunited with his younger sister after 7 years of separation caused by divorce. (Rev: SLJ 6/90)

425 Blume, Judy. *It's Not the End of the World* (6–8). 1972, Bradbury $12.95 (0-02-711050-8); Dell paper $3.25 (0-440-44158-7). Karen cannot believe that her parents are heading for a divorce.

426 Bond, Nancy. *Country of Broken Stone* (7–9). 1980, Macmillan $12.95 (0-689-50163-3). Pennie and her family move to rural England where she must come to terms with herself and her family situation.

427 Boutis, Victoria. *Looking Out* (7–9). 1988, Macmillan $11.95 (0-02-711830-4). This novel set in 1953 explores the problems faced by a girl whose parents are Communists. (Rev: VOYA 8/88)

428 Brancato, Robin F. *Sweet Bells Jangles Out of Tune* (7–10). 1983, Scholastic paper $2.50 (0-590-40459-8). Ellen's grandmother has become a bag lady and her family is ashamed of her.

429 Bridgers, Sue Ellen. *All Together Now* (7–10). 1979, Knopf LB $13.99 (0-394-94098-9); Bantam paper $2.75 (0-553-26845-7). Twelve-year-old Casey must spend a summer with her grandparents in a small southern town.

430 Bridgers, Sue Ellen. *Home Before Dark* (7–10). 1976, Knopf $10.95 (0-394-83299-X); Bantam paper $2.50 (0-553-26432-X). A migrant worker and his family settle down in a permanent home.

431 Bridgers, Sue Ellen. *Notes for Another Life* (7–12). 1981, Knopf LB $13.99 (0-394-94885-0); Bantam paper $2.95 (0-553-27185-7). A brother and sister cope with a frequently absent mother and a mentally ill father.

432 Brooks, Bruce. *Midnight Hour Encores* (7–10). 1986, Harper LB $13.89 (0-06-020710-8); paper $2.95 (0-06-447021-0). Cello-playing Sib and her father Taxi take a transcontinental trip to meet Sib's mother, who left after her birth. (Rev: BL 9/15/86; SLJ 9/86; VOYA 12/86)

433 Brown, Irene Bennett. *Answer Me, Answer Me* (7–12). 1985, Macmillan $13.95 (0-689-31114-1); Fawcett paper $2.50 (0-449-70185-9). After her grandmother dies, 18-year-old Bryn sets out to find her remaining family. (Rev: BL 9/1/85; SLJ 10/85; VOYA 4/86)

434 Bunting, Eve. *A Sudden Silence* (7-12). 1988, Harcourt $13.95 (0-15-282058-2). Jesse sets out to find the hit-and-run driver who killed his brother. (Rev: BL 4/15/88; SLJ 5/88)

435 Burns, Peggy. *Nothing Ever Stays the Same* (6–8). 1989, Lion paper $3.95 (0-7459-1249-4). Sandie learns that her father isn't perfect. (Rev: BL 7/89)

436 Byars, Betsy. *The Glory Girl* (6–8). 1983, Viking $11.95 (0-670-34261-0); Penguin paper $3.95 (0-14-03-1785-6). Anna, part of a family of gospel singers, teams up with an uncle fresh from prison to help in a family crisis.

437 Calvert, Patricia. *When Morning Comes* (7–12). 1989, Macmillan $12.95 (0-684-19105-9). A runaway encounters problems in adjusting to her new home even though her foster mother is kind and understanding. (Rev: BL 12/15/89; BR 3-4/90; SLJ 2/90; VOYA 2/90)

438 Calvert, Patricia. *Yesterday's Daughter* (7–10). 1986, Macmillan $11.95 (0-684-18746-9). Raised by her grandparents near a Carolina swamp, 16-year-old Leenie is visited by a mother she doesn't know. (Rev: BL 11/1/86; SLJ 11/86; VOYA 12/86)

439 Cameron, Eleanor. *To the Green Mountains* (7–9). 1975, Dutton $9.95 (0-525-41355-3). Kath's family relations reach a crisis point in their drab hotel in Ohio.

440 Carey, Mary. *A Place for Allie* (6–8). 1985, Dodd $12.95 (0-396-08583-0). When their father is killed, the Hughes family including 2 young girls are forced to move to Boston. (Rev: BL 1/1/86; SLJ 2/86)

441 Carter, Alden R. *Up Country* (8–12). 1989, Putnam $15.95 (0-399-21583-2). A 15-year-old boy who repairs stolen radios to get spending money is suddenly sent away to live with conventional relatives in the country. (Rev: BL 7/89; BR 11–12/89; SLJ 6/89; VOYA 8/89)

442 Cave, Hugh B. *The Voyage* (6–8). 1988, Macmillan $13.95 (0-02-717780-7). An 11-year-old boy is torn between leaving with his father who has just escaped from prison or remaining with his mother. (Rev: VOYA 6/88)

443 Christian, Mary Blount. *Growin' Pains* (6–8). 1985, Macmillan $11.95 (0-02-718490-0); Penguin paper $3.95 (0-317-63785-1). With the help of a disabled neighbor, Ginny Ruth continues to develop her writing talent in spite of her mother's objections. (Rev: BL 2/1/86; BR 5–6/86)

444 Christiansen, C. B. *A Small Pleasure* (7–10). 1988, Macmillan $12.95 (0-689-31369-1). A young high school girl hides her grief over her father's fatal cancer by becoming the most popular girl in school. (Rev: BL 4/1/88; BR 9–10/88; SLJ 3/88; VOYA 6/88)

445 Cleary, Beverly. *Sister of the Bride* (7–9). 1963, Morrow LB $13.88 (0-688-31742-1); Dell paper $3.25 (0-440-48256-9). A young girl becomes too involved with the plans for her sister's wedding.

446 Cleaver, Vera. *Sweetly Sings the Donkey* (6–9). Illus. 1985, Harper LB $12.89 (0-397-32157-0); paper $2.95 (0-06-440233-9). Fourteen-year-old Lily Snow and her family hope that their inheritance in Florida will help them financially but this is not to be. (Rev: BL 10/1/85)

447 Cleaver, Vera, and Bill Cleaver. *Dust of the Earth* (7–9). 1975, Harper $13.70 (0-397-31650-X). Fern and her family face problems when they move to a farm in South Dakota.

448 Cleaver, Vera, and Bill Cleaver. *Queen of Hearts* (7–9). 1978, Harper $12.70 (0-397-31771-9); paper $2.95 (0-06-440196-0). Wilma must take care of her grandmother whom she really dislikes.

449 Cleaver, Vera, and Bill Cleaver. *Where the Lilies Bloom* (6–10). Illus. 1969, Harper $12.70 (0-397-31111-7). When her father dies, Mary Call must take care of her 2 siblings and keep the family together. A sequel is: *Trial Valley* (1977).

450 Clements, Bruce. *Anywhere Else but Here* (7–9). 1980, Farrar $11.95 (0-374-30371-2). Mollie's father faces poverty until he discovers the value in a dollhouse.

451 Clymer, Eleanor. *My Brother Stevie* (6–8). 1989, Dell paper $2.75 (0-440-40125-9). Annie tries to care for a younger brother who needs special attention.

452 Collier, James Lincoln. *Outside Looking In* (6–8). 1987, Macmillan $12.95 (0-02-723100-3). Fergie and his sister hate the nomadic life their parents lead and long to settle down. (Rev: BL 4/1/87; BR 9–10/87; SLJ 5/87; VOYA 10/87)

453 Colman, Hila. *Diary of a Frantic Kid Sister* (6–8). 1975, Archway paper $2.50 (0-671-61926-8). In diary format, Sarah tells of the frustrations of growing up in the shadow of a glamorous older sister.

454 Colman, Hila. *Forgotten Girl* (7–9). 1990, Crown LB $13.99 (0-517-57592-2). Kelly is saddled with an overachieving mother and an older brother who can do no wrong. (Rev: SLJ 3/90)

455 Colman, Hila. *Just the Two of Us* (7–9). 1984, Scholastic paper $2.25 (0-590-32512-4). Since her mother's death, Sammy and her father have been doing well but now he is talking of remarrying.

456 Colman, Hila. *Nobody Told Me What I Need to Know* (7–10). 1984, Morrow $11.95 (0-688-03869-7); Fawcett paper $2.95 (0-449-70136-0). Coming from a conventional family, Alix is drawn to Nick and the carefree existence he lives. Also use *A Fragile Love* (Pocket, 1985).

457 Colman, Hila. *Rich and Famous Like My Mom* (6–9). 1988, Crown $12.95 (0-517-56836-5). Cassandra is growing up in the shadow of her mother, a world-famous rock star. (Rev: BL 6/15/88)

458 Colman, Hila. *Sometimes I Don't Love My Mother* (7–10). 1979, Scholastic paper $2.25 (0-590-33736-X). Dallas discovers that, after her father's death, her mother becomes too dependent on her.

459 Colman, Hila. *Weekend Sisters* (7–9). 1985, Morrow $11.95 (0-688-05785-3). When Amanda's father remarries she gains a stepsister whom she finds difficult to like. (Rev: BL 12/1/85; BR 1–2/86; SLJ 12/85; VOYA 2/86)

460 Conrad, Pam. *Holding Me Here* (7–9). 1986, Harper LB $11.89 (0-06-021339-6). Robin attempts to help a divorced woman who is hiding from her abusive former husband and fails tragically. (Rev: BL 3/15/86; BR 11–12/86; SLJ 3/86; VOYA 6/86)

461 Conrad, Pam. *My Daniel* (6–9). 1989, Harper LB $12.89 (0-06-021314-0). A grandmother's trip to a science museum unlocks memories of her own childhood. (Rev: BL 4/15/89; BR 11–12/89; SLJ 4/89; VOYA 6/89)

462 Conrad, Pam. *Taking the Ferry Home* (7–12). 1988, Harper LB $11.89 (0-06-021318-3). Two very different teenage girls describe the course of their friendship. (Rev: BL 6/1/88; BR 11–12/88; SLJ 6–7/88; VOYA 8/88)

463 Cooney, Caroline B. *The Face on the Milk Carton* (7–10). 1990, Bantam $14.95 (0-553-05853-3). Jane wonders if the face of the missing girl on the milk carton is actually herself as a child. (Rev: BL 2/15/90; SLJ 2/90)

464 Corcoran, Barbara. *I Am the Universe* (6–8). 1986, Macmillan $12.95 (0-689-31208-3). With an indifferent father at home and her mother seriously ill in the hospital, Katherine and her older brother take care of the house. (Rev: BL 10/1/86; SLJ 10/86; VOYA 12/86)

465 Corcoran, Barbara. *The Potato Kid* (6–8). 1989, Macmillan $13.95 (0-689-31589-9). The Ellis family decides to help a 10-year-old child from a poor Maine family and then the problems begin. (Rev: BL 11/15/89; SLJ 10/89; VOYA 2/90)

466 Cormier, Robert. *Eight Plus One* (7–10). 1980, Pantheon $7.99 (0-394-94596-6); Bantam paper $2.75 (0-553-26815-5). Nine stories by this famous author, each dealing with a family situation and each with a special introduction.

467 Cresswell, Helen. *Dear Shrink* (7–9). 1982, Macmillan $12.95 (0-02-725560-3). Two English teenage brothers and younger sister are sent to foster homes when their elderly nanny dies.

468 Cross, Gillian. *Chartbreaker* (8–12). 1987, Holiday $13.95 (0-8234-0647-4); Dell paper $2.95 (0-440-20312-0). Janis, a lead singer with a British rock group, tells her story. (Rev: BL 3/1/87; SLJ 4/87; VOYA 8–9/87)

469 Curry, Jane Louise. *The Lotus Cup* (7–12). 1986, Macmillan $12.95 (0-689-50384-9). Corry gains self-fulfillment and confidence in her continued interest in pottery making. (Rev: BL 5/15/86; SLJ 5/86; VOYA 8–10/86)

470 Danziger, Paula. *The Divorce Express* (6–9). 1982, Delacorte $12.95 (0-385-28217-6); Dell paper $2.95 (0-440-92062-0). A 14-year-old girl divides time between her divorced parents.

471 Danziger, Paula. *It's an Aardvark-Eat-Turtle World* (6–9). 1985, Delacorte $13.95 (0-385-29371-2); Dell paper $2.95 (0-440-94028-1). When Rosie's father and the mother of her best friend move in together, complications begin. (Rev: BL 3/1/85; BR 9–10/85; SLJ 4/85; VOYA 6/85)

472 Danziger, Paula. *The Pistachio Prescription* (6–9). 1978, Delacorte $12.95 (0-385-28784-4); Dell paper $2.95 (0-440-96895-X). Cassie, 13 years old, faces many family and personal problems including a compulsive need for pistachio nuts.

473 Davis, Jenny. *Good-bye and Keep Cold* (8–12). 1987, Watts LB $12.99 (0-531-08315-2); Dell paper $2.95 (0-440-20481-X). A novel that covers the childhood and adolescence of a girl growing up in a mining community in Kentucky. (Rev: BL 8/87; BR 9–10/88; SLJ 8/87; VOYA 10/87)

474 Deaver, Julie Reece. *First Wedding, Once Removed* (7–10). 1990, Harper LB $13.89 (0-06-021427-9). Teenager Pokie is upset when her beloved brother becomes engaged. (Rev: SLJ 8/90)

475 DeClements, Barthe. *Monkey See, Monkey Do* (5–9). 1990, Delacorte LB $13.95 (0-385-30158-8). Jerry's father gets into trouble while on parole and his mother is suing for divorce in this novel about a young boy caught in family conflicts. This is a sequel to *Five-Finger Discount* (1989). (Rev: BL 9/15/90)

476 Dickerson, Kate. *Step Monsters* (6–9). 1989, Willowisp paper $2.50 (0-87406-375-2). An eighth-grade girl must cope with a new stepfather and 3 stepbrothers. (Rev: SLJ 1/90)

477 Donovan, John. *Remove Protective Coating a Little at a Time* (7–9). 1973, Harper LB $12.89 (0-06-021720-0). Harry seems to be losing touch with his parents and then he meets 70-year-old Amelia.

478 Douglass, Barbara. *Sizzle Wheels* (6–8). Illus. 1981, Westminster $9.95 (0-664-32680-3). More than anything Tori wants her father to be proud of her, but fate always seems to get in the way.

479 Easton, Patricia Harrison. *Summer's Chance* (6–9). 1988, Harcourt $13.95 (0-15-200591-9). Elizabeth adjusts to life with her grandmother in a story with harness racing as an important ingredient. (Rev: BL 3/15/88; SLJ 4/88)

480 Ellis, Ella Thorp. *Riptide* (7–9). 1973, Macmillan paper $0.95 (0-689-70361-9). Mike's family problems reach a crisis over his need for a car.

481 Ellis, Sarah. *A Family Project* (5–9). 1988, Macmillan $11.95 (0-689-50444-6). The story of a loving family whose happiness is shattered by a crib death tragedy. (Rev: BL 5/15/88; BR 11–12/88)

482 Evernden, Margery. *The Dream Keeper* (5–8). 1985, Lothrop $11.95 (0-688-04638-X). Through tapes found in an attic, Becka is able to re-create her grandmother's early life in Russia. (Rev: BR 11–12/85; SLJ 12/85)

483 Farish, Terry. *Why I'm Already Blue* (6–8). 1989, Greenwillow $11.95 (0-688-09096-6). Though he is confined to a wheelchair, young

Gus is able to help a neighbor girl sort out her own problems. (Rev: BL 10/1/89; BR 1–2/90)

484 Fenton, Edward. *Duffy's Rocks* (6–8). 1989, Dell paper $3.25 (0-440-20242-6). Thirteen-year-old Timothy sets out to find the father that has deserted his family.

485 Fine, Anne. *My War with Goggle-Eyes* (6–9). 1989, Little $13.95 (0-316-28314-2). Kitty tells her friend Helen about her troubles with her mother's new boyfriend whom Kitty has nicknamed Goggle-Eyes. (Rev: BL 4/15/89; SLJ 5/89) [F]

486 Fitzhugh, Louise. *Nobody's Family Is Going to Change* (6–8). 1974, Farrar $13.95 (0-374-35539-8); Dell paper $1.75 (0-440-46454-4). The children in a black middle-class family have growing-up problems.

487 Fleischman, Paul. *Rear-View Mirrors* (7–10). 1986, Harper LB $10.89 (0-06-021867-3). After her father's death, Olivia relives through memory a summer when she and her estranged father had reconciled. (Rev: BL 3/1/86; BR 11–12/86; SLJ 5/86; VOYA 8/86)

488 Foley, June. *Falling in Love Is No Snap* (7–10). 1986, Delacorte $14.95 (0-385-29490-5); Dell paper $2.95 (0-440-20349-X). Both Alexandra and friend Heracles have one thing in common—neither is happy with the future their parents have mapped out for them. (Rev: BL 9/15/86; BR 5–6/87; VOYA 12/86)

489 Forbes, Kathryn. *Mama's Bank Account* (7–10). 1968, Harcourt paper $5.95 (0-15-656377-0). The story told in vignettes of a loving Norwegian family and of Mama's mythical bank account.

490 Forman, James D. *The Pumpkin Shell* (7–9). 1981, Farrar $10.95 (0-374-36159-2). Robin's life collapses after his mother dies and his father remarries.

491 Fosburgh, Liza. *Cruise Control* (7–9). 1988, Bantam $13.95 (0-553-05491-6); paper $3.50 (0-553-28441-X). Gussie, younger sister Annie, and brother Jimbo are having difficulties growing up with an alcoholic mother and a frequently absent father. (Rev: VOYA 12/88)

492 Fosburgh, Liza. *Summer Lion* (6–8). 1987, Morrow $12.95 (0-688-06979-7). While being a companion to the ancient Mr. Baines, Leo learns a lot about the wealthy Baines clan and most of it is not good. (Rev: SLJ 11/87)

493 Fox, Paula. *Blowfish Live in the Sea* (6–8). 1970, Aladdin paper $3.95 (0-689-71092-5). Ben and Carrie go to Boston to see the father they haven't seen for years.

494 Fox, Paula. *The Moonlight Man* (8–12). 1986, Bradbury $12.95 (0-02-735480-6). During a stay together in a house in Nova Scotia, teenager Catherine learns more about her adored alcoholic father than she wants to. (Rev: BL 4/15/86; SLJ 4/86; VOYA 8–10/86)

495 Fox, Paula. *The Village by the Sea* (6–8). 1988, Watts LB $13.99 (0-531-08388-8). A 10-year-old girl is sent to live with an aunt whom she grows to despise. (Rev: BL 9/1/88; VOYA 10/88)

496 Gardiner, Judy. *Come Back Soon* (6–9). 1985, Viking $11.95 (0-670-80150-X); Penguin paper $3.95 (0-14-032017-2). In this English novel, a teenage girl's relations with the rest of her family change dramatically when her mother runs away. (Rev: BL 2/1/86; BR 5–6/86; SLJ 3/86)

497 Gates, Doris. *Blue Willow* (5–8). 1940, Viking $13.95 (0-670-17557-9); Penguin paper $3.95 (0-14-030924-1). An easily read novel about a poor girl and the china plate that belonged to her mother.

498 Geller, Mark. *Raymond* (6–9). 1988, Harper LB $10.89 (0-06-022207-7). Raymond persuades his mother that the 2 should run away from his abusive father. (Rev: BR 11–12/88; SLJ 9/88)

499 Gibbons, Faye. *Mighty Close to Heaven* (6–8). 1985, Morrow $11.95 (0-688-04147-7). Convinced that his grandparents don't love him, Dave runs away to find his absent father. (Rev: BL 9/1/85; SLJ 8/85)

500 Giff, Patricia Reilly. *The Gift of the Pirate Queen* (7–9). Illus. 1982, Delacorte LB $9.89 (0-440-02972-4). Grace's problems, which include taking care of a father and a diabetic sister, are reduced with the arrival of an Irish cousin.

501 Gioffre, Marisa. *Starstruck* (6–8). 1985, Scholastic paper $2.25 (0-590-33797-1). Alicia wants to be a singer at a local coffee house but her mother insists she take a regular paying job. (Rev: BL 3/1/86)

502 Gleeson, Libby. *I Am Susannah* (5–9). 1989, Holiday $12.95 (0-8234-0742-X). A coming-of-age novel about a young Australian teenager and her journey to self-realization. (Rev: SLJ 6/89)

503 Graber, Richard. *Doc* (7–12). 1986, Harper LB $13.89 (0-06-022094-5). Brad cannot come to terms with the fact that his beloved grandfather, once a fine doctor, is suffering from Alzheimer's disease. (Rev: BL 10/1/86; BR 3–4/87; SLJ 12/86; VOYA 12/86)

504 Green, Connie Jordan. *The War at Home* (5–8). 1989, Macmillan $12.95 (0-689-50470-5). Mattie has problems dealing with her cousin

Virgil who has come to live with her family. (Rev: BL 6/1/89; BR 9–10/89; VOYA 8/89)

505 Green, Phyllis. *It's Me, Christy* (7–9). 1983, Scholastic paper $2.50 (0-590-40651-5). After she is caught shoplifting, Christy is sent to her grandmother to get straightened out.

506 Greene, Constance C. *The Un-Making of Rabbit* (6–8). 1972, Viking $11.95 (0-670-74136-1). Paul fantasizes about being reunited with his divorced mother and then his dream comes true.

507 Guernsey, JoAnn Bren. *Journey to Almost There* (7–9). 1985, Clarion $11.95 (0-89919-338-2). Alison with her ailing grandfather takes a trip halfway across the country to find her father. (Rev: BL 12/15/85; BR 9–10/86; SLJ 11/85; VOYA 10/85)

508 Guest, Elissa Haden. *Over the Moon* (7–12). 1986, Morrow $12.95 (0-688-04148-5). Even though she has not heard from her older sister for 4 years, Kate cannot escape her influence and the feelings of rivalry. (Rev: BL 6/15/86; BR 9–10/86; SLJ 5/86)

509 Hall, Barbara. *Dixie Storms* (7–12). 1990, Harcourt $14.95 (0-15-223825-5). Dutch's troubled relationships within her family worsen when counsin Norma comes to stay. (Rev: BL 5/1/90; SLJ 9/90)

510 Hall, Lynn. *Letting Go* (6–9). 1987, Macmillan $11.95 (0-684-18781-7). Casey faces several crises with her mother in this novel that uses dog shows as a backdrop. (Rev: BL 4/15/87; SLJ 5/87; VOYA 6/87)

511 Halvorson, Marilyn. *Let It Go* (6–9). 1986, Dell paper $2.95 (0-440-20053-9). Jared is dismayed to see his friend Lance get involved with drugs because of parental problems. (Rev: BL 10/1/86; SLJ 11/86; VOYA 12/86)

512 Hamilton, Dorothy. *Amanda Fair* (6–8). 1981, Herald Pr. paper $3.95 (0-8361-1943-6). After her parents' divorce, Amanda discovers that her sister has become a shoplifter. Also use: *Eric's Discovery* and *Ken's Hideout* (both 1979).

513 Hamilton, Dorothy. *Bittersweet Days* (7–9). Illus. 1978, Herald Pr. paper $3.95 (0-8361-1846-4). Kathy has a problem getting out of the "in" group at school.

514 Hamilton, Dorothy. *Kerry* (7–9). 1973, Herald Pr. paper $3.95 (0-8361-1690-9). Kerry struggles with her need for independence and her close attachment to her family.

515 Hamilton, Dorothy. *Mari's Mountain* (7–9). Illus. 1978, Herald Pr. paper $3.95 (0-8361-1869-3). A teenager runs away from an alcoholic father only to discover an array of new problems.

Also use: *Rosalie at Eleven* (1980) and *Straight Mark* (1976).

516 Hamilton, Virginia. *M.C. Higgins, the Great* (6–10). 1974, Macmillan $14.95 (0-02-742480-4); paper $3.95 (0-02-043490-1). A young black boy growing up in Appalachia uses the strength of his family's past to ensure its future. Newbery Medal 1975.

517 Hamilton, Virginia. *Willie Bea and the Time the Martians Landed* (6–9). 1983, Macmillan $14.00 (0-688-02390-8); paper $3.95 (0-689-71328-2). Willie Bea and her family hear the 1938 radio broadcast of how Martians have landed on earth.

518 Harris, Mark Jonathan. *Come the Morning* (5–9). 1989, Bradbury $13.95 (0-02-742750-1). A mother with her family sets out to find her husband and ends up homeless on the streets of Los Angeles. (Rev: BL 6/1/89; BR 9–10/89; SLJ 3/89; VOYA 6/89)

519 Hest, Amy. *Pete and Lily* (6–8). 1986, Clarion $11.95 (0-89919-354-4). Pete finds that her mother and the father of her best friend are seeing one another. (Rev: BL 3/15/86)

520 Hill, Margaret. *Turn the Page, Wendy* (7–9). 1981, Abingdon $9.50 (0-687-42700-2). A neglected teenager must decide whether to hunt for a mother she doesn't know or live in a good foster home.

521 Hinton, S. E. *Taming the Star Runner* (7–12). 1988, Doubleday $14.95 (0-440-50058-3). A tough delinquent is sent to his uncle's ranch to be straightened out and there he falls in love with Casey, who is trying to tame a wild horse named Star Runner. (Rev: BL 10/15/88; BR 11–12/88; SLJ 10/88; VOYA 12/88)

522 Holl, Kristi. *Patchwork Summer* (6–8). 1987, Macmillan $12.95 (0-689-31347-0). Randi resents her mother's return home after deserting her family a year before. (Rev: SLJ 9/87)

523 Holland, Isabelle. *God, Mrs. Muskrat and Aunt Dot* (6–8). Illus. 1983, Westminster $10.00 (0-664-32703-6). An orphan girl finds a friend to comfort her in soft, furry Mrs. Muskrat who lives in the forest.

524 Holland, Isabelle. *Now Is Not Too Late* (6–8). 1980, Lothrop $12.95 (0-688-41937-2); Bantam paper $2.75 (0-553-15548-2). Cathy cannot believe how much the woman she has just met resembles her deceased mother.

525 Hopkins, Lee Bennett. *Mama* (7–9). 1978, Dell paper $2.50 (0-440-96174-2). Mama loves her 2 fatherless sons so much that she steals to give them what they want.

526 Hopper, Nancy J. *Carrie's Games* (7–10). 1987, Dutton $11.95 (0-525-67186-2). To divert her father, Carrie decides to date a boy of whom he does not approve. (Rev: BL 2/1/87; BR 5–6/87; SLJ 1/87; VOYA 6/87)

527 Howard, Ellen. *Her Own Song* (5–9). 1988, Macmillan LB $12.95 (0-689-31444-2). Mellie, an adopted girl, is anxious to find out about her past and if it is connected to a Chinese laundryman whom her friends ridicule. (Rev: SLJ 9/88)

528 Howker, Janni. *Isaac Campion* (6–8). 1987, Greenwillow $10.25 (0-688-06658-5); Dell paper $2.95 (0-440-40280-8). A young English boy tries to escape the cruel domination of his father. (Rev: BL 7/87; SLJ 6–7/87; VOYA 6/87)

529 Howker, Janni. *The Nature of the Beast* (8–10). 1985, Greenwillow $10.25 (0-688-04233-3); Penguin paper $4.95 (0-14-032254-X). A teenager describes the effects on his family when a plant in northern England where his father and grandfather work closes down. (Rev: BL 10/15/85; BR 11–12/85; SLJ 11/85; VOYA 2/86)

530 Hunt, Irene. *William* (6–8). 1977, Macmillan $11.95 (0-684-14902-8). A 16-year-old girl plus 8-year-old William and his 2 sisters try to form a family unit.

531 Hunter, Jana Novotny. *It's a Terrible Age to Be* (5–9). 1989, Worthington paper $2.25 (0-87406-388-4). A 14-year-old girl discovers that her beloved widowed father is going to remarry. (Rev: SLJ 2/90)

532 Irwin, Hadley. *Bring to a Boil and Separate* (7–9). 1981, NAL paper $2.50 (0-451-14825-8). Thirteen-year-old Katie faces problems about her parents' divorce and her best friend Marti.

533 Janeczko, Paul B. *Bridges to Cross* (6–9). 1986, Macmillan $11.95 (0-02-747940-4). James is in constant conflict with his mother about his conduct at a private Catholic school. (Rev: BL 8/86; SLJ 8/86; VOYA 8–10/86)

534 Johnston, Norma. *Carlisle's Hope* (7–9). 1986, Bantam paper $2.50 (0-553-25467-7). In this first in the Carlisle Chronicles series, Jess uses a school project and some documents her aunt left her to track down some interesting family history. Followed by *Carlisles All* and *To Jess, with Love and Memories* (both 1986). (Rev: BL 7/86; SLJ 8/86)

535 Johnston, Norma. *The Potter's Wheel* (7–12). 1988, Morrow $11.95 (0-688-06463-9). Three generations of women from teenage girl to domineering grandmother interact in this family novel. (Rev: BL 5/15/88; BR 5–6/88; SLJ 3/88; VOYA 6/88)

536 Jones, Adrienne. *A Matter of Spunk* (7–9). 1983, Harper LB $13.89 (0-06-023054-1). A mother and her 2 children move during the 1920s to a religious community outside of Los Angeles in this sequel to *Whistle Down a Dark Lane* (1982).

537 Joosse, Barbara M. *Pieces of the Picture* (6–8). 1989, Harper LB $12.89 (0-397-32343-3). After her father's death, Emily and her mother move to try to earn a livelihood running an inn. (Rev: BL 6/1/89; BR 11–12/89)

538 Klass, David. *Breakaway Run* (8–12). 1987, Dutton $13.95 (0-525-67190-0). Tony, a teenager whose parents are divorcing, spends 5 months as an exchange student in Japan. (Rev: BL 8/87; BR 1–2/88; SLJ 8/87; VOYA 2/88)

539 Klass, Sheila Solomon. *The Bennington Stitch* (7–10). 1985, Macmillan $12.95 (0-684-18436-2); Bantam paper $2.50 (0-553-26049-9). Two high school seniors clash with their respective parents over their plans for the future. (Rev: BL 9/15/85; SLJ 10/85; VOYA 4/86)

540 Klass, Sheila Solomon. *Page Four* (7–10). 1986, Macmillan $12.95 (0-684-18745-0); Bantam paper $2.95 (0-553-26901-1). David goes into a tailspin when his father deserts his family and runs off with his young secretary. (Rev: BL 1/1/87; SLJ 2/87)

541 Klein, Norma. *Angel Face* (7–9). 1984, Viking $13.95 (0-670-12517-2); Fawcett paper $2.95 (0-449-70282-0). Jason is facing many problems including living with an eccentric mother and adjusting to the absence of his father.

542 Klein, Norma. *Breaking Up* (7–10). 1980, Pantheon LB $9.99 (0-394-9445-3). While visiting her divorced father in California, Alison falls in love with her best friend's brother.

543 Klein, Norma. *Mom, the Wolfman and Me* (6–8). 1972, Pantheon LB $9.99 (0-394-92470-3). Brett's mother is single but the Wolfman is becoming more than a steady boyfriend.

544 Klein, Norma. *Now That I Know* (6–10). 1988, Bantam $13.95 (0-553-05472-4). Nina discovers that her divorced father is gay. (Rev: BL 4/1/88; BR 5–6/88; SLJ 6–7/88; VOYA 6/88)

545 Klein, Norma. *Robbie and the Leap Year Blues* (6–8). 1983, Pocket paper $2.50 (0-671-61930-6). A novel with touches of humor about the joint custody problems Robbie faces.

546 Klein, Norma. *What It's All About* (7–9). 1989, Knopf paper $2.95 (0-394-82302-8). Bernie's love for her mother helps her solve some of her problems. A reissue.

547 Konigsburg, E. L. *Father's Arcane Daughter* (7–9). 1976, Macmillan $11.95 (0-689-30524-9). After a 17-year absence Caroline appears—or is it Caroline?

548 Konigsburg, E. L. *Journey to an 800 Number* (7–9). 1982, Macmillan LB $12.95 (0-689-30901-5); Dell paper $2.95 (0-440-44264-8). Max feels superior to the father with whom he now must live.

549 Kropp, Paul. *Jo's Search* (7–9). Illus. 1989, Macmillan paper $2.95 (0-02-041794-2). In this easily read novel, a young adopted girl sets out to find her natural mother. (Rev: SLJ 6/89)

550 Laird, Elizabeth. *Loving Ben* (5–9). 1989, Delacorte $14.95 (0-385-29810-2). As seen through the experiences of Anna, this is the story of the life and death of her younger brother who was born hydrocephalic. (Rev: SLJ 9/89; VOYA 12/89)

551 Landis, J. D. *The Sisters Impossible* (7–9). 1981, Bantam paper $2.50 (0-553-26013-8). The world of ballet is the center of this story of sibling rivalry.

552 Lasky, Kathryn. *Prank* (7–9). 1984, Macmillan $12.95 (0-02-751690-3); Dell paper $2.75 (0-440-97144-6). Trying to find escape from a series of family problems, Birdie hopes that her new department store job will help.

553 Lelchuk, Alan. *On Home Ground* (7–10). Illus. 1987, Harcourt $9.95 (0-15-200560-9). Aaron seems to have nothing in common with his father, a Russian immigrant. (Rev: SLJ 12/87; VOYA 4/88)

554 L'Engle, Madeleine. *Meet the Austins* (6–9). 1981, Dell paper $3.25 (0-440-95777-X). The Austin family—a tightly knit loving group with 4 children—is disrupted when a young orphan girl comes to live with them.

555 L'Engle, Madeleine. *The Moon by Night* (7–10). 1963, Farrar $13.95 (0-374-35049-3); Dell paper $3.25 (0-440-95776-1). In this novel about the Austins, the family takes a cross-country camping trip and Vicki finds she is attracted to the wealthy, irresponsible Zachery Gray.

556 Leroe, Ellen. *Personal Business* (6–8). 1987, Bantam paper $2.95 (0-553-26652-7). Danny decides he will help his divorced mother find a new man. (Rev: SLJ 1/88)

557 Levin, Betty. *The Trouble with Gramary* (6–8). 1988, Greenwillow $11.95 (0-688-07372-7). A young girl's aged grandmother takes on the city father in a struggle for her property in this novel set in Maine. (Rev: BL 4/1/88; BR 9–10/88; VOYA 8/88)

558 Levinson, Marilyn. *A Place to Start* (7–10). 1987, Macmillan $12.95 (0-689-31325-X). Grant's adjustment to his parents' divorce brings him closer to girlfriend Samantha. (Rev: BL 11/15/87; SLJ 10/87; VOYA 12/87)

559 Levitin, Sonia. *A Season for Unicorns* (7–10). 1986, Macmillan $13.95 (0-689-31113-3); Fawcett paper $2.50 (0-317-57397-7). Ingrid, a teenager who suffers a fear of heights, finds that her father is having affairs with women. (Rev: BL 4/1/86; SLJ 4/86; VOYA 8–10/86)

560 Levy, Marilyn. *Touching* (7–10). 1988, Ballantine paper $2.95 (0-449-70267-7). A young girl must cope with living with an alcoholic father after her mother leaves. (Rev: BL 10/15/88; VOYA 10/88)

561 Lifton, Betty Jean. *I'm Still Me* (6–8). 1981, Knopf LB $9.99 (0-394-94783-5). An adopted girl sets out to find her biological parents.

562 Lowry, Lois. *Autumn Street* (7–9). 1980, Houghton $13.95 (0-395-27812-0); Dell paper $2.95 (0-440-40344-8). With her father away, Elizabeth with her mother and older sister move in with grandmother.

563 Lowry, Lois. *Find a Stranger, Say Goodbye* (7–10). 1978, Houghton $10.95 (0-395-26459-6); Archway paper $2.50 (0-671-62116-5). A college-bound girl decides to find her natural mother.

564 Lowry, Lois. *Rabble Starkey* (6–9). 1987, Houghton $12.95 (0-395-43607-9); Dell paper $3.25 (0-440-40056-2). The story of a friendship between 2 girls (Rabble and Veronica), their sixth-grade year, and their many experiences with family and friends. (Rev: BL 3/15/87; BR 9–10/87; VOYA 4/87)

565 Lowry, Lois. *Us and Uncle Fraud* (6–9). 1984, Houghton $10.95 (0-395-36833-X); Dell paper $2.95 (0-440-49185-1). Uncle Claude visits his sister's family with her 4 children and an experience in human relations begins.

566 Lutz, Norma Jean. *Oklahoma Summer* (6–8). 1987, Cook paper $2.95 (1-55513-028-3). Marcia is coping with such problems as adjusting to her mother's death, training for a horse show, and the selling of her grandparents' ranch. (Rev: BL 6/15/87; SLJ 9/87)

567 Lyle, Katie Letcher. *Dark but Full of Diamonds* (8–10). 1981, Putnam $9.95 (0-698-20517-0). Scott and his father are both attracted to Hilah Brown.

568 Lyon, George Ella. *Borrowed Children* (6–9). 1988, Watts LB $12.99 (0-531-08351-0). A 12-year-old girl growing up in Depression Kentucky is sent to live with her grandparents in Memphis. (Rev: BL 2/15/88)

569 McDonnell, Christine. *Count Me In* (6–9). 1986, Viking $11.95 (0-670-80417-7); Penguin paper $3.95 (0-14-031856-9). Maddie finds it difficult to adjust to her new stepfather, but several experiences during the summer before high school help her accept her situation. (Rev: BL 5/15/86; BR 11–12/86; SLJ 9/86)

570 Mace, Elisabeth. *Under Siege* (7–9). 1990, Watts $13.95 (0-531-05871-9). Beset by family problems, 16-year-old Morris finds a magical realm in his reclusive uncle's game room. (Rev: BL 6/15/90; SLJ 3/90; VOYA 6/90)

571 McGraw, Eloise. *Hideaway* (6–8). 1983, Macmillan paper $3.95 (0-02-044482-6). A 12-year-old boy arrives at his grandmother's house for a stay but finds her gone and a 16-year-old girl acting as housekeeper.

572 McHugh, Elisabet. *Karen and Vicki* (7–9). 1984, Greenwillow LB $10.25 (0-688-02543-9). The stepmother of Karen, a Korean orphan, marries and the young girl inherits a new family. Previous volumes include *Raising a Mother Isn't Easy* and *Karen's Sister* (both 1983).

573 MacLeod, Charlotte. *Maid of Honor* (7–9). 1984, Fawcett paper $2.50 (0-449-70124-7). Persis's family is so involved in preparations for their older daughter's wedding that she feels completely neglected.

574 Martin, Ann M. *With You and without You* (5–8). 1986, Holiday LB $13.95 (0-8234-0601-6); Scholastic paper $2.50 (0-590-40589-6). The O'Hara family pass through the final illness and death of their father and manage to weather the grieving process. (Rev: SLJ 8/86; VOYA 10/86)

575 Mazer, Harry. *Guy Lenny* (7–9). 1989, Peter Smith $15.00 (0-8446-6369-7); Dell paper $2.95 (0-440-93311-0). Growing up in a broken home, 12-year-old Guy is torn between loyalty toward his father and his mother.

576 Mazer, Harry. *Someone's Mother Is Missing* (7–12). 1990, Delacorte $14.95 (0-385-30161-8). After being deserted by their widowed mother, Lisa and Robin must go to live with their cousin Sam's family. (Rev: SLJ 9/90)

577 Mazer, Norma Fox. *After the Rain* (7–10). 1987, Morrow $11.75 (0-688-06867-7); Avon paper $2.95 (0-380-75025-2). Rachel gradually develops a warm relationship with her terminally ill grandfather who is noted for his bad temper. (Rev: BL 5/1/87; BR 5–6/87; SLJ 5/87; VOYA 6/87)

578 Mazer, Norma Fox. *Babyface* (7–10). 1990, Morrow $12.95 (0-688-08752-3). Toni's perfect world falls apart when her best friend moves away and her father has a heart attack. (Rev: BL 9/15/90)

579 Mazer, Norma Fox. *Downtown* (7–10). 1984, Morrow $11.95 (0-688-03859-X); Avon paper $2.50 (0-380-88534-4). Pete, 15 and the son of anti-war demonstrators who are in hiding, faces problems when his mother reappears and wants to be part of his life.

580 Mazer, Norma Fox. *A Figure of Speech* (7–10). 1989, Dell paper $2.95 (0-440-94374-4). A girl tries to help her unwanted grandfather who is only tolerated by her family. A reissue.

581 Mazer, Norma Fox. *I, Trissy* (6–8). 1972, Dell paper $2.95 (0-440-44109-9). Trissy becomes increasingly hard to control when she feels increased insecurity concerning her parents' divorce.

582 Mazer, Norma Fox. *Mrs. Fish, Ape, and Me, the Dump Queen* (7–9). 1981, Avon paper $2.95 (0-380-69153-1). Joyce has been hurt by supposed friends but somehow she trusts the school custodian, Mrs. Fish.

583 Mazer, Norma Fox. *Taking Terri Mueller* (7–10). 1983, Morrow $12.95 (0-688-01732-0); Avon paper $2.75 (0-380-79004-1). Terri realizes that her beloved father has actually kidnapped her to keep her from her mother.

584 Mazer, Norma Fox. *Three Sisters* (7–12). 1986, Scholastic $12.95 (0-590-33774-2). A 15-year-old youngest sister feels left out and unworthy. (Rev: BL 2/15/86; SLJ 3/86; VOYA 6/86)

585 Miklowitz, Gloria D. *Suddenly Super Rich* (7–10). 1989, Bantam $13.95 (0-553-05845-2). The dream of winning a lottery turns into a nightmare for Danielle and her family. (Rev: BL 10/1/89; SLJ 11/89; VOYA 12/89)

586 Miles, Betty. *Just the Beginning* (6–8). 1976, Knopf LB $10.99 (0-394-93226-9); Avon paper $2.50 (0-380-01913-2). An eighth-grader has a "perfect" older sister and a mother who has become a cleaning lady.

587 Montgomery, Lucy Maud. *Anne of Green Gables* (7–9). 1983, Putnam $12.95 (0-448-06030-0); Bantam paper $2.95 (0-553-24295-4). This is a reissue of the classic Canadian story of Anne and how she was gradually accepted in a foster home. Her story continued in *Anne of Avonlea, Anne of the Island, Anne of Windy Poplars, Anne's House of Dreams,* and *Anne of Ingleside* (all 1976).

588 Montgomery, Lucy Maud. *Emily of New Moon* (7–9). 1986, Bantam paper $3.50 (0-553-23370-X). Beginning when Emily is only 11 this trilogy continues in *Emily Climbs* and *Emily's Quest* (both 1986) and tells about the making of a writer. These are reissues.

589 Moore, Emily. *Something to Count On* (6–8). 1980, Dutton $9.95 (0-525-39595-4). Lorraine feels that her absent father really doesn't love her.

590 Morpurgo, Michael. *Mr. Nobody's Eyes* (6–8). 1990, Viking $12.95 (0-670-83022-4). Harry finds life with his stepfather unbearable and decides to run away with his pet monkey. (Rev: BL 5/1/90)

591 Murray, Marguerite. *Like Seabirds Flying Home* (7–12). 1988, Macmillan $12.95 (0-689-31459-0). Shelley's problems with her parents become exacerbated with the death of her father. (Rev: BL 12/1/88; BR 3–4/89; SLJ 9/88; VOYA 2/89)

592 Naughton, Jim. *My Brother Stealing Second* (7–10). 1989, Harper LB $13.89 (0-06-024375-9). Bobby's grief over his brother's death leads him to a friendship with Annie and finally back to playing baseball. (Rev: BL 4/1/89; BR 1–2/90; SLJ 4/89; VOYA 6/89)

593 Naylor, Phyllis Reynolds. *The Solomon System* (7–9). 1983, Macmillan $12.95 (0-689-30991-0). Two brothers who are also great friends face their parents' divorce.

594 Nelson, Carol. *Dear Angie, Your Family's Getting a Divorce* (6–8). 1980, Chariot paper $2.95 (0-89191-246-0). Reluctantly, Angie must face the fact that her quarreling parents are headed for divorce.

595 Neufeld, John. *Sunday Father* (7–9). 1977, Signet paper $1.50 (0-451-07292-8). Tessa's hopes that her parents will reunite are dashed when her father says he plans to remarry.

596 Nixon, Joan Lowery. *Overnight Sensation* (7–10). 1990, Bantam $14.95 (0-553-05865-7). The second installment of the show-business trilogy about Abby Grant, superstar. Preceded by *Star Baby* (1989). (Rev: BL 5/1/90; SLJ 5/90)

597 O'Connor, Jane. *Just Good Friends* (7–9). 1983, Harper $12.89 (0-06-024591-3). Joss knows her father is having an affair and doesn't know who to talk to about it.

598 O'Dell, Scott. *The Spanish Smile* (7–10). 1982, Houghton $12.95 (0-395-32867-5). Lucinda lives an isolated life with her father until Christopher arrives and some horrible truths are re-

vealed. By this author also use *The Amethyst Ring* and *The Castle in the Sea* (both 1983).

599 Osborne, Mary Pope. *Last One Home* (6–8). 1986, Dial $13.95 (0-8037-0219-1). Bailey does everything possible to prevent her father's remarriage. (Rev: BL 8/86; SLJ 5/86; VOYA 8–10/86)

600 Osborne, Mary Pope. *Love Always, Blue* (7–9). 1984, Dutton $12.95 (0-8037-0031-8). Blue's life seems shattered when her parents break up and her beloved father moves out.

601 Pascal, Francine. *The Hand-Me-Down Kid* (6–8). 1980, Viking $12.95 (0-670-35969-6); Dell paper $2.95 (0-440-43499-1). An easily read book about a young girl who must lie to her family about her involvement with a stolen bicycle.

602 Paterson, Katherine. *Come Sing, Jimmy Jo* (6–10). 1985, Dutton $12.95 (0-525-67167-6); Avon paper $2.95 (0-380-70052-2). When 11-year-old James joins his family of musicians as a performer, a new life begins. (Rev: BL 5/1/85; SLJ 4/85)

603 Paterson, Katherine. *Park's Quest* (6–9). 1988, Dutton $12.95 (0-525-67258-3). Park wants to learn more about his father who was killed in the Vietnam War. (Rev: BL 5/1/88; SLJ 5/88)

604 Paulsen, Gary. *The Winter Room* (6–8). 1989, Watts LB $11.99 (0-531-08439-6). A quiet novel about an 11-year-old boy growing up on a farm in Minnesota. (Rev: BL 11/1/89; BR 5–6/90; SLJ 10/89; VOYA 12/89)

605 Pearson, Gayle. *Fish Friday* (6–8). 1986, Macmillan paper $3.95 (0-689-71324-X). Jamie doesn't know whether to stay in the small town with her father or accompany her mother to New York. (Rev: BL 6/15/86; SLJ 5/86; VOYA 8–10/86)

606 Peck, Richard. *Father Figure* (7–10). 1978, Viking $11.50 (0-670-30930-3); Dell paper $2.95 (0-440-20095-5). Jim and his younger brother are sent to live in Florida with a father they scarcely know.

607 Peck, Robert Newton. *Arly* (5–8). 1989, Walker $16.95 (0-8027-6856-3). A teacher changes the life of a young boy in a migrant camp in Florida in 1927. (Rev: BL 7/89; BR 9–10/89; VOYA 8/89)

608 Peck, Robert Newton. *A Day No Pigs Would Die* (7–9). 1973, Knopf $15.95 (0-394-48235-2); Dell paper $2.95 (0-440-92083-3). A Shaker farm boy in Vermont must give up his pet pig to help his family.

609 Peck, Robert Newton. *Justice Lion* (7–9). 1981, Little $13.95 (0-316-69658-7). Two families find their friendship strained over a court case.

610 Peck, Robert Newton. *Spanish Hoof* (7–9). 1985, Knopf $11.95 (0-394-97261-9). A girl named Harry takes over responsibilities when her mother becomes ill on their Florida cattle ranch. (Rev: BR 9–10/85)

611 Pendergraft, Patricia. *Miracle at Clement's Pond* (6–8). 1987, Putnam $13.95 (0-399-21438-0); Scholastic paper $2.50 (0-590-41458-5). Three children think they are doing a good deed when they deposit a baby they have found on a spinster's porch. (Rev: BL 8/87; SLJ 8/87; VOYA 8–9/87)

612 Pevsner, Stella. *How Could You Do It, Diane?* (6–8). 1989, Clarion $13.95 (0-395-51041-4). A family copes with the devastating death of a stepchild by suicide. (Rev: BL 11/15/89; BR 1–2/90; SLJ 10/89; VOYA 2/90)

613 Pevsner, Stella. *Sister of the Quints* (6–8). 1987, Clarion $12.95 (0-89919-498-2); Pocket paper $2.75 (0-671-65973-1). Natalie is tired of baby-sitting for her half-sisters the quints and so she asks her divorced mother in Colorado if she can come there to live. (Rev: BL 3/15/87; BR 9–10/87; VOYA 6/87)

614 Pevsner, Stella. *A Smart Kid Like You* (7–9). 1979, Houghton $13.95 (0-395-28876-2). Vera discovers that her new stepmother is also her new math teacher.

615 Pfeffer, Susan Beth. *Claire at Sixteen* (7–10). 1989, Bantam $13.95 (0-553-05819-3). Claire Sebastian blackmails relatives to pay her sister Sybil's medical bills. Continued in *Sybil at Sixteen* (1989). (Rev: BL 9/15/89; BR 9–10/89; SLJ 8/89; VOYA 6/89)

616 Pfeffer, Susan Beth. *Meg at Sixteen* (8–12). 1990, Bantam $13.95 (0-553-05854-1). In this part of the ongoing series, the mother of the girls featured in the other books tells about her young adulthood. (Rev: BL 3/1/90; SLJ 8/90; VOYA 4/90)

617 Pfeffer, Susan Beth. *Thea at Sixteen* (7–10). 1988, Bantam $13.95 (0-553-05498-8). Thea, second of the Sebastian sisters, becomes involved with a dying girl and her family. (Rev: BL 11/1/88; BR 1–2/89; SLJ 11/88; VOYA 2/89)

618 Pfeffer, Susan Beth. *The Year without Michael* (7–12). 1987, Bantam $13.95 (0-553-05430-9). When Jody's brother Michael, a high school freshman, disappears, the solidarity of her family is shattered. (Rev: BL 10/1/87; BR 5–6/88; SLJ 11/87; VOYA 10/87)

619 Pople, Maureen. *The Other Side of the Family* (6–10). 1988, Henry Holt $13.95 (0-8050-0758-X). Kate leaves World War II England to live with her grandmother in a remote part of Australia. (Rev: BL 6/15/88; SLJ 6–7/88)

620 Porte, Barbara Ann. *I Only Made Up the Roses* (8–12). 1987, Greenwillow $10.25 (0-688-05126-9). An episodic novel about an interracial family as seen through the eyes of a 17-year-old girl. (Rev: BL 5/1/87; SLJ 5/87; VOYA 6/87)

621 Provost, Gary, and Gail Levine-Provost. *David and Max* (6–8). 1988, Jewish Publication Soc. $12.95 (0-8276-0315-0). David and his grandfather Max, a survivor of the Holocaust, try to locate another survivor who was Max's childhood friend. (Rev: BL 1/1/89)

622 Reading, J. P. *The Summer of Sassy Jo* (6–8). 1989, Houghton $13.95 (0-395-48950-4). Sara Jo is reunited for a summer with a mother who abandoned her years ago. (Rev: SLJ 3/89; VOYA 6/89)

623 Reed, Kit. *The Ballad of T. Rantula* (7–9). 1981, Fawcett paper $1.95 (0-449-70003-8). Freddy relies on his friends to help him when his parents break up.

624 Roberts, Nadine. *With Love, from Sam and Me* (7–9). 1990, Fawcett paper $2.95 (0-449-70368-1). A teenage girl flees with her foster baby brother from a stepfather who enjoys beating them. (Rev: VOYA 8/90)

625 Rodowsky, Colby. *Julie's Daughter* (8–10). 1985, Farrar $13.95 (0-374-33963-5). Seventeen-year-old Slug (Mary Rose) and her mother are strangers thrown together by the death of Slug's grandmother. (Rev: BL 7/85; SLJ 9/85; VOYA 4/86)

626 Rosofsky, Iris. *Miriam* (7–10). 1988, Harper LB $11.89 (0-06-024854-8). Being a member of an American Orthodox Jewish family causes some problems for Miriam. (Rev: BL 8/88; BR 1–2/89; SLJ 9/88; VOYA 8/88)

627 Ruby, Lois. *Pig-Out Inn* (7–9). 1987, Houghton $12.95 (0-395-42714-2); Fawcett paper $2.95 (0-449-70306-1). Dovi renames the pink truck-stop restaurant her mother has decided to operate—the Pig-Out Inn. (Rev: BR 9–10/87; VOYA 6/87)

628 Ruby, Lois. *This Old Man* (7–9). 1984, Houghton $11.95 (0-395-36563-5); Fawcett paper $2.50 (0-449-70152-2). In a home for wayward girls, Greta gets help from her friend, Wing.

629 Ruckman, Ivy. *Who Invited the Undertaker?* (6–8). 1989, Harper LB $12.89 (0-690-04834-3). Dale, a seventh-grader, tries to help his mother who feels lonely after her husband's death. (Rev: SLJ 9/89)

630 Rylant, Cynthia. *A Blue-Eyed Daisy* (6–8). 1985, Bradbury $11.95 (0-02-777960-2); Dell paper $2.50 (0-440-40927-6). There are 14 interrelated stories in this book about an 11-year-old girl growing up in West Virginia. (Rev: BL 6/15/85; SLJ 4/85)

631 Rylant, Cynthia. *A Kindness* (7–12). 1988, Watts LB $13.99 (0-531-05767-4); Dell paper $3.25 (0-440-20579-4). A high school sophomore learns that his single-parent mother has become pregnant and wants to keep the child. (Rev: BL 9/15/88; SLJ 9/88; VOYA 10/88)

632 Saal, Jocelyn. *On Thin Ice* (7–9). 1983, Bantam paper $1.95 (0-553-17070-8). Ellen is always overshadowed by her older sister who is a skating champion.

633 Sachs, Marilyn. *Baby Sister* (7–10). 1986, Dutton $13.95 (0-525-44213-8); Avon paper $2.95 (0-380-70358-0). Penny is torn between her admiration for her older sister and the realization that she is really selfish. (Rev: BL 2/15/86; BR 5–6/86; SLJ 8/86; VOYA 8–10/86)

634 Sachs, Marilyn. *Just Like a Friend* (6–9). 1989, Dutton $12.95 (0-525-44524-2). The friendship between a mother and a daughter falls apart when father has a heart attack. (Rev: BL 10/15/89; BR 3–4/90; SLJ 12/89; VOYA 12/89)

635 Sachs, Marilyn. *The Truth about Mary Rose* (6–8). 1987, Scholastic paper $2.50 (0-590-40402-4). The first Mary Rose died at age 11 saving lives in a fire, but her modern counterpart learns the truth about her.

636 Sargent, Sarah. *Secret Lies* (7–9). 1981, Crown $8.95 (0-517-54291-9); paper $2.95 (0-517-56927-2). Elvira's fantasies about the father she has never known are shattered by the truth.

637 Sauer, Jim. *Hank* (7–10). 1990, Delacorte $14.95 (0-385-30034-4). The story of 2 brothers—one 16 and the other 9—and of their growing up together. (Rev: BL 7/90; SLJ 8/90; VOYA 8/90)

638 Sebestyen, Ouida. *Far from Home* (7–10). 1980, Little $14.95 (0-316-77932-6); Dell paper $2.95 (0-440-92640-8). An orphaned boy is taken in by a couple who run a boardinghouse and there he uncovers secrets about his family's past.

639 Shreve, Susan. *The Masquerade* (7–10). 1981, Knopf LB $7.99 (0-394-94142-0); Dell paper $1.95 (0-440-95396-0). The 4 Walker children are confused and angry when their father is accused of embezzlement.

640 Shyer, Marlene Fanta. *My Brother, the Thief* (6–8). 1980, Macmillan $10.95 (0-684-16434-5). Carolyn wonders how far she will go to protect her brother whom she knows is a thief.

641 Silsbee, Peter. *The Big Way Out* (7–9). 1984, Bradbury $11.95 (0-02-782670-8); Dell paper $2.75 (0-440-90499-4). Paul and his mother flee his abusive father but they know he is pursuing them.

642 Sirof, Harriet. *The Real World* (6–9). 1985, Watts $11.90 (0-531-10080-4). A girl who has been raised with a feminist mother goes to live with her father and his conventional family. (Rev: BL 2/1/86; BR 5–6/86; SLJ 4/86)

643 Slepian, Jan. *Getting On with It* (7–9). 1985, Macmillan $11.95 (0-02-782930-8). Berry tries to hide the hurt she feels at her parents' divorce by making new friends when she goes to visit her grandmother. (Rev: BL 12/1/85; BR 9–10/86; SLJ 12/85)

644 Smith, Anne Warren. *Sister in the Shadow* (7–10). 1986, Macmillan $11.95 (0-689-31185-0); Avon paper $2.50 (0-380-70378-5). In competition with her successful younger sister, Sharon becomes a live-in baby-sitter with unhappy results. (Rev: BL 5/1/86; SLJ 5/86; VOYA 8–10/86)

645 Snyder, Anne, and Louis Pelletier. *The Best That Money Can Buy* (7–10). 1983, Signet paper $2.50 (0-451-13593-8). Angie's family is thrown into a crisis when their father is accused of fraud.

646 Snyder, Carol. *Leave Me Alone, Ma* (6–9). 1987, Bantam $13.95 (0-553-05442-2). Jamie misses her parents when her live-in grandmother takes over. (Rev: BL 1/1/88; BR 11–12/87; SLJ 12/87; VOYA 12/87)

647 Snyder, Carol. *Memo To: Myself When I Have a Teenage Kid* (7–9). 1984, Putnam paper $2.25 (0-399-21087-3). Karen and her mother have difficulty understanding and accepting each other.

648 Snyder, Zilpha K. *The Birds of Summer* (7–9). 1984, Dell paper $2.95 (0-440-20154-3). A 15-year-old girl who lives in a trailer with her mother and younger sister hopes through becoming a housekeeper she can change her life.

649 Stiles, Martha Bennett. *Kate of Still Waters* (6–10). 1990, Macmillan $15.95 (0-02-788395-7). Young Kate tries to help as her family struggles hard to maintain their Kentucky farm. (Rev: BL 9/15/90)

650 Stolz, Mary. *What Time of Night Is It?* (6–8). 1981, Harper LB $12.89 (0-06-026062-9). A 14-year-old girl and her brothers are taken care of by an inflexible grandmother in this sequel to *Go and Catch a Flying Fish* (1979).

651 Stretton, Barbara. *You Never Lose* (7–10). 1982, Knopf LB $9.99 (0-394-95230-8). Jim finds out that his father, with whom he has not been close, has inoperable cancer.

652 Sweeney, Joyce. *The Dream Collector* (7–12). 1989, Delacorte $14.95 (0-385-29813-7). Becky wishes for Christmas presents for her family, and what she wants most for herself are the attentions of her neighbor John. (Rev: BL 12/15/89; BR 3–4/90; SLJ 11/89; VOYA 2/90)

653 Swindells, Robert. *A Serpent's Tooth* (7–9). 1989, Holiday $13.95 (0-8234-0743-8). In this English novel, a young girl faces the pangs of growing up with the added dimension of possessing second sight. (Rev: BL 7/89; SLJ 4/89; VOYA 8/89)

654 Talbert, Marc. *Toby* (6–8). 1987, Dial $13.95 (0-8037-0441-0). Some misguided do-gooders want to sent Toby away from his illiterate parents to a foster home. (Rev: SLJ 1/88)

655 Tapp, Kathy Kennedy. *Smoke from the Chimney* (6–8). 1986, Macmillan $11.95 (0-689-50389-X). Erin has difficulty coping with her father's alcoholism. (Rev: BL 6/1/86; SLJ 9/86)

656 Taylor, William. *Paradise Lane* (8–10). 1987, Scholastic $12.95 (0-590-41013-X); paper $2.75 (0-590-41014-8). Teenage Rosie comes from a troubled home but finds hope and friendship with a neighborhood boy, Michael. (Rev: BL 12/1/87; SLJ 12/87; VOYA 12/87)

657 Terris, Susan. *Baby-Snatcher* (6–9). 1985, Farrar $11.95 (0-374-30473-4); Scholastic paper $2.50 (0-590-40241-2). Laurel discovers that the child she takes care of is both deaf and the victim of being taken from her rightful mother. (Rev: BL 3/1/85; SLJ 3/85)

658 Terris, Susan. *No Scarlet Ribbons* (7–9). 1981, Farrar $11.95 (0-374-35532-0). Two different families are joined by marriage and 14-year-old Rachel feels she is in the middle.

659 Thesman, Jean. *The Last April Dancers* (7–10). 1987, Houghton $13.95 (0-395-43024-0); Avon paper $2.75 (0-380-70614-8). Catherine tries to recover from the guilt caused by her father's suicide through friendship and love of a neighboring boy. (Rev: BL 9/15/87; SLJ 10/87; VOYA 10/87)

660 Tolan, Stephanie S. *A Good Courage* (6–9). 1988, Morrow $11.95 (0-688-07446-4). Fourteen-year-old Ty and his mother move into Kingdom, a cult community led by charismatic Brother Daniel. (Rev: BL 3/1/88; BR 5–6/88; SLJ 3/88; VOYA 6/88)

661 Towne, Mary. *Their House* (6–8). 1990, Macmillan $14.95 (0-689-31562-7). Molly gets to know an elderly couple who live in part of the house that her parents have bought and helps them with some important personal problems. (Rev: BL 3/1/90; SLJ 3/90)

662 Ure, Jean. *The Most Important Thing* (6–8). Illus. 1986, Morrow $12.95 (0-688-05859-0). Nicola has second thoughts when she is accepted at Kendra Hall, a fashionable ballet school. (Rev: BL 6/15/86; SLJ 5/86)

663 Voigt, Cynthia. *Dicey's Song* (6–9). 1982, Macmillan $12.95 (0-689-30944-9). Homeless Dicey and his younger siblings arrive at their grandmother's home. Newbery Medal, 1983. The story of their journey is told in *Homecoming* (1981).

664 Voigt, Cynthia. *Seventeen against the Dealer* (7–12). 1989, Macmillan $13.95 (0-689-31497-3). In this, the last of the Tillerman cycle, Dicey, now 21, decides to earn her living building boats. (Rev: BL 3/15/89; BR 9–10/89; SLJ 2/89; VOYA 4/89)

665 Voigt, Cynthia. *A Solitary Blue* (7–9). 1983, Macmillan $12.95 (0-689-31008-0). Jeff is invited to spend a summer with his divorced mother.

666 Voigt, Cynthia. *Sons from Afar* (6–10). 1987, Macmillan $13.95 (0-689-31349-7); Fawcett paper $3.95 (0-449-70293-6). In this part of the Tillerman family story sons James and Sammy set out to see a father they have never known. (Rev: BL 9/15/87; SLJ 9/87; VOYA 10/87)

667 Voigt, Cynthia. *Tree by Leaf* (6–8). 1988, Macmillan $13.95 (0-689-31403-5). Clothilde's father returns to Maine from World War I to find his family impoverished and himself a bitter, disfigured outcast. (Rev: BL 4/1/88; BR 9–10/88; SLJ 5/88; VOYA 8/88)

668 Wallace-Brodeur, Ruth. *Steps in Time* (7–12). 1986, Macmillan $11.95 (0-689-50399-7). A girl and her grandmother become close when they spend a summer together on an island in Maine. (Rev: BL 4/15/86; SLJ 3/87; VOYA 12/86)

669 Wallin, Luke. *The Redneck Poacher's Son* (7–10). 1981, Bradbury $12.95 (0-02-792480-7). Jesse is convinced that his ignorant Paw killed his mother and now he wants revenge.

670 Weissenberg, Fran. *The Streets Are Paved with Gold* (7–9). 1990, Harbinger paper $5.95 (0-943173-51-5). Debbie is from a poor immigrant

Jewish family and she is ashamed to bring her friends home. (Rev: BL 8/90; SLJ 8/90)

671 Wersba, Barbara. *Crazy Vanilla* (8–10). 1986, Harper LB $11.89 (0-06-026369-5). Tyler has a lot of problems—a mother who drinks, a father he can't talk to, and a brother who has just come out of the closet as gay. (Rev: BL 11/1/86; SLJ 11/86; VOYA 12/86)

672 Whelan, Gloria. *The Secret Keeper* (7–10). 1990, Knopf LB $13.99 (0-679-90572-3). While recovering from her own parents' divorce, Annie takes a job caring for a young boy who is also the product of a broken home. (Rev: BL 2/15/90; SLJ 5/90; VOYA 8/90)

673 White, Alana. *Come Next Spring* (6–9). 1990, Clarion $13.95 (0-395-52593-4). A story of family life, friendship, and growing up in the Tennessee mountains during 1949. (Rev: BL 4/1/90; SLJ 5/90)

674 White, Ellen Emerson. *White House Autumn* (7–10). 1985, Avon paper $2.95 (0-380-89780-6). The daughter of the first female president of the United States feels her family is coming apart after an assassination attempt on her mother. (Rev: BL 11/1/85; SLJ 2/86; VOYA 4/86)

675 White, Ruth. *Sweet Creek Holler* (6–8). 1988, Farrar $13.95 (0-374-37360-4). A girl's experiences growing up poor in Appalachia during the 1950s. (Rev: BL 10/1/88; BR 3–4/89; SLJ 10/88; VOYA 12/88)

676 Williams, Barbara. *Beheaded, Survived* (7–10). 1987, Watts LB $12.90 (0-531-10403-6). Two unusual American teenagers fall in love during a tour of England. (Rev: BL 12/1/87; BR 1–2/88; SLJ 12/87; VOYA 2/88)

677 Wilson, Johnniece Marshall. *Oh, Brother* (7–9). 1988, Scholastic $10.95 (0-590-41363-5). Andy is responsible for causing the theft of his younger brother's bicycle. (Rev: BR 9–10/88)

678 Wolitzer, Hilma. *Toby Lived Here* (7–9). 1978, Farrar $11.95 (0-374-37625-5); paper $3.45 (0-374-47924-0). Toby and her younger sister face problems when they go to live with foster parents.

679 Wolitzer, Hilma. *Wish You Were Here* (7–9). 1984, Farrar $11.95 (0-374-38456-8); paper $3.45 (0-374-48412-0). Bernie decides to move out when his new stepfather moves in.

680 Wolkoff, Judie. *Happily Ever After . . . Almost* (7–9). 1982, Bradbury $10.95 (0-02-793340-7); Dell paper $2.95 (0-440-43366-5). New families are created instantly when Kitty's and Sarah's parents remarry.

681 Wolkoff, Judie. *Where the Elf King Sings* (7–10). 1980, Macmillan $11.95 (0-02-793360-1). Marcie's father, a Vietnam veteran, first turns to alcohol and then leaves the family.

682 Wood, Phyllis Anderson. *Get a Little Lost, Tia* (6–8). 1978, Westminster $8.95 (0-664-32636-6). Jason often wishes that the sister he takes care of would get lost—and then she does.

683 Wood, Phyllis Anderson. *Then I'll Be Home Free* (7–10). 1986, Putnam $12.95 (0-396-08766-3); NAL paper $2.75 (0-451-15373-1). After her grandmother dies and her grandfather attempts suicide, Rosemary turns to her friend Arthur for help. (Rev: BL 3/1/86; SLJ 3/86)

Physical and Emotional Problems

684 Adler, C. S. *Eddie's Blue-Winged Dragon* (6–8). 1988, Putnam $13.95 (0-399-21535-2). An 11-year-old victim of cerebral palsy wants to get even with the school bully. (Rev: BL 12/15/88)

685 Ames, Mildred. *The Silver Link, the Silken Tie* (7–10). 1986, Scholastic paper $2.25 (0-590-33557-X). Two emotionally disturbed youngsters are drawn together in their need for help.

686 Arrick, Fran. *God's Radar* (7–10). 1983, Bradbury $12.95 (0-02-705710-0); paper $2.95 (0-440-92960-1). Roxie faces tough decisions when her parents join a fundamentalist church.

687 Arrick, Fran. *Steffie Can't Come Out to Play* (7–10). 1978, Dell paper $2.50 (0-440-97635-9). Steffie runs away to New York City and is dragged into the nightmare world of prostitution.

688 Arrick, Fran. *Tunnel Vision* (7–10). 1980, Dell paper $2.95 (0-440-98579-X). Friends and family examine their past behavior after 15-year-old Anthony commits suicide.

689 Barr, Linda. *The Wrong Way Out* (6–9). 1990, Willowisp paper $2.95 (0-87406-475-9). A teenage girl turns to alcohol to forget her problems at home. (Rev: SLJ 8/90)

690 Blume, Judy. *Deenie* (6–8). 1973, Bradbury $12.95 (0-02-711020-6); Dell paper $2.75 (0-440-93259-9). Beautiful young Deenie, intent on a modeling career, finds out she has curvature of the spine and must wear a back brace.

691 Blume, Judy. *Tiger Eyes* (7–10). 1981, Bradbury $13.95 (0-02-711080-X); Dell paper $3.25 (0-440-98469-6). The painful adjustment a girl must make to her father's death.

692 Bonham, Frank. *Gimme an H, Gimme an E, Gimme an L, Gimme a P* (7–9). 1982, Scholastic paper $2.25 (0-590-40057-6). Dana likes his girlfriend but finds she suffers bouts of depression and has suicidal thoughts.

693 Borich, Michael. *A Different Kind of Love* (7–10). 1987, NAL paper $2.50 (0-451-14718-9). A 15-year-old suffers sexual abuse from her 25-year-old uncle. (Rev: BL 4/1/85; BR 11–12/85; SLJ 10/85)

694 Brancato, Robin F. *Winning* (7–9). 1977, Knopf LB $12.99 (0-394-93581-0); Bantam paper $2.95 (0-553-26597-0). A boy must adjust to paralysis that was the result of a football accident.

695 Buchan, Stuart. *Love and Lucy Bloom* (7–9). 1988, Crosswinds paper $2.25 (0-373-98022-1). Lucy has difficulty understanding adult behavior, particularly after her parents' divorce. (Rev: VOYA 10/88)

696 Buchan, Stuart. *When We Lived with Pete* (6–8). 1986, Dell paper $2.95 (0-440-49483-4). Tommy's loneliness leads him to explore an abandoned mansion and find new friends.

697 Bunting, Eve. *Surrogate Sister* (7–10). 1984, Harper LB $13.89 (0-397-32099-X). 16-year-old girl copes with a pregnant mother who has offered to be a surrogate mother for a childless couple. Published in paperback under the title *Mother, How Could You!*

698 Burch, Robert. *Ida Early Comes over the Mountain* (5–8). 1980, Viking $12.95 (0-670-39169-7); Avon paper $2.50 (0-380-57091-2). The 4 Sutton kids find a new and most unusual housekeeper in Ida.

699 Busselle, Rebecca. *Bathing Ugly* (6–8). 1989, Watts LB $12.99 (0-531-08401-9). Twelve-year-old Betsy, who has weight problems, attends summer camp and finds losing pounds is not her only problem. (Rev: BL 5/15/89; SLJ 1/89; VOYA 4/89)

700 Butler, Beverly. *Light a Single Candle* (7–10). 1962, Putnam $11.95 (0-396-04709-2); Archway paper $1.95 (0-671-67712-8). Kathy, though only 14, must adjust to the onset of blindness.

701 Butterworth, W. E. *Under the Influence* (7–10). 1979, Macmillan $9.95 (0-02-716240-0). Keith has a drinking problem that even his friend Allan can't cope with.

702 Cameron, Eleanor. *Beyond Silence* (7–9). 1980, Dutton $9.95 (0-525-26463-9). Fifteen-year-old Andrew is taken by his father to Scotland to adjust to the death of his brother.

703 Cassedy, Sylvia. *M. E. and Morton* (6–8). 1987, Harper LB $12.89 (0-690-04562-X); paper $3.95 (0-06-440306-8). A novel dealing with the relationship between a gifted young girl and her retarded brother. (Rev: BL 9/1/87; SLJ 6–7/87; VOYA 6/87)

704 Cavallaro, Ann. *Blimp* (7–9). 1983, Dutton $11.95 (0-525-67139-0). An extremely overweight girl is flattered when a handsome new boy in school pays attention to her.

705 Cleaver, Vera, and Bill Cleaver. *Me Too* (7–9). 1973, Harper $13.95 (0-397-313485-X); paper $2.95 (0-06-440161-8). Linda is convinced that she can make her slightly retarded sister normal.

706 Clifford, Eth. *The Killer Swan* (7–9). 1980, Houghton $6.95 (0-395-29742-7). Adjusting to both the death of his father and a new home seems almost too much for Lex.

707 Cohen, Barbara. *People Like Us* (7–10). 1987, Bantam $13.95 (0-553-05441-4); paper $2.95 (0-553-27445-7). A Jewish girl, Dinah Adler, faces the consequences with her family when she dates a gentile boy. (Rev: BL 9/15/87; BR 11–12/87; SLJ 11/87; VOYA 10/87)

708 Cole, Barbara S. *Don't Tell a Soul* (7–9). 1987, Rosen $12.95 (0-8239-0701-5). The story of the aftermath of the disclosure of a girl's sexual molestation by her stepfather and how this changed a mother-daughter relationship. (Rev: BR 9–10/87; SLJ 8/87)

709 Colman, Hila. *Happily Ever After* (7–10). 1986, Scholastic paper $2.25 (0-590-33551-0). Melanie gradually realizes that her boyfriend Paul is gay. (Rev: BL 7/86; SLJ 12/86; VOYA 8-10/86)

710 Conford, Ellen. *To All My Fans, with Love, from Sylvie* (7–9). 1982, Little $14.95 (0-316-15312-5); Archway paper $2.25 (0-686-44321-7). Fifteen-year-old Sylvie runs away from home when her stepfather makes sexual advances.

711 Cook, Marjorie. *To Walk on Two Feet* (7–9). 1978, Westminster $8.95 (0-664-32628-5). A crippled girl risks her life by reporting a crime she has seen committed.

712 Corcoran, Barbara. *Annie's Monster* (6–8). 1990, Macmillan $13.95 (0-689-31632-1). Annie and her friends try to find a place for a mentally ill homeless person whom Annie has found in a park. (Rev: BL 9/1/90)

713 Cormier, Robert. *The Bumblebee Flies Anyway* (7–12). 1983, Pantheon LB $10.99 (0-394-96120-X); Dell paper $3.25 (0-440-90871-X). A terminally ill boy and his gradual realization of his situation.

714 Crawford, Charles. *Split Time* (8–10). 1987, Harper LB $12.89 (0-06-021380-9). A 15-year-old boy trying to adjust to his parents' divorce has an affair with an emotional, unstable older woman. (Rev: BL 10/1/87; BR 3–4/88; SLJ 10/87; VOYA 12/87)

715 Cunningham, Julia. *The Silent Voice* (6–8). 1981, Dutton $11.95 (0-525-39295-5). In this novel set in Paris, a 14-year-old mute is helped by a famous mime and teacher.

716 Dacquino, V. T. *Kiss the Candy Days Good-Bye* (7–9). 1982, Delacorte $11.95 (0-385-28532-9); Dell paper $2.25 (0-440-44369-5). A would-be captain of the wrestling team finds he has diabetes.

717 Dana, Barbara. *Crazy Eights* (7–10). 1978, Harper LB $12.89 (0-06-021389-2). A 14-year-old girl's chronicle of her fight with mental illness.

718 Davidson, Mary S. *A Superstar Called Sweetpea* (7–9). 1980, Viking $11.50 (0-670-68478-3). A teenager who dreams of stardom lies to her family when she accepts a job in a nightclub.

719 Davies, Andrew. *Conrad's War* (7–9). 1986, Dell paper $2.25 (0-440-91452-3). Conrad's obsession with war leads him to believe he has fought in World War II. A reissue.

720 Diezeno, Patricia. *Why Me? The Story of Jenny* (7–10). 1976, Avon paper $2.50 (0-380-00563-8). A young rape victim doesn't know how to cope.

721 Dixon, Jeanne. *The Tempered Wind* (7–12). 1987, Macmillan $13.95 (0-689-31339-X). A young humpbacked dwarf fights prejudices and cruelty to find a place for herself in a life that affords dignity and a livelihood. (Rev: BL 12/1/87; SLJ 12/87; VOYA 10/87)

722 Ethridge, Kenneth E. *Toothpick* (7–10). 1985, Holiday $12.95 (0-8234-0585-0); Troll paper $2.50 (0-8167-1316-2). A friendship between Jamie, an outsider who is unsure of himself, and Janice, a terminally ill girl, gives him the confidence he needs. (Rev: BL 11/15/85; SLJ 12/85; VOYA 4/86)

723 Evernden, Margery. *The Kite Song* (7–9). Illus. 1984, Lothrop $11.95 (0-688-01200-0). An emotionally disturbed 11-year-old boy finds some help in a new home.

724 Eyerly, Jeannette. *Someone to Love Me* (7–10). 1987, Harper LB $11.89 (0-397-32206-2). An unpopular high school girl is seduced by the school's glamor boy and decides, when she finds she is pregnant, to keep the child. (Rev: BL 2/1/87; BR 9–10/87; SLJ 4/87; VOYA 4/87)

725 Ferris, Jean. *Looking for Home* (7–10). 1989, Farrar $12.95 (0-374-34649-6). A pregnant teenager moves to the city to have her baby.

(Rev: BL 6/15/89; BR 1–2/90; SLJ 8/89; VOYA 10/89)

726 Ferris, Jean. *The Stainless Steel Rule* (8–10). 1986, Farrar $13.95 (0-374-37212-8). The close friendship between 3 girls is tested when one of them who has diabetes becomes dominated by her boyfriend who suggests a miracle cure. (Rev: BL 4/15/86; BR 9–10/86; SLJ 5/86; VOYA 12/86)

727 Forman, James D. *The Big Bang* (7–10). 1989, Macmillan LB $13.95 (0-684-19004-4). A novel told in journal form about the effects of deaths caused by drunken driving. (Rev: BR 3–4/90; SLJ 11/89; VOYA 12/89)

728 Fox, Paula. *The Stone-Faced Boy* (6–8). 1968, Bradbury $11.95 (0-02-735570-5); Aladdin paper $3.95 (0-689-71127-1). In his family Gus gets the reputation of being stone-faced because he cannot express emotion.

729 Franco, Marjorie. *Love in a Different Key* (7–10). 1983, Houghton $9.95 (0-395-34827-7). Neenah remains loyal to her boyfriend after he suffers a mental breakdown.

730 Froehlich, Margaret Walden. *Hide Crawford Quick* (7–9). 1983, Houghton $9.95 (0-395-33884-9). A family's first boy is born with a physical handicap.

731 Gabhart, Ann. *A Kindred Spirit* (7–9). 1987, Crosswinds paper $2.25 (0-373-98013-2). Even at 16, Erin has an imaginary playmate whom she claims is alive. (Rev: VOYA 4/88)

732 Garden, Nancy. *Annie on My Mind* (8–10). 1982, Farrar $11.95 (0-374-30366-5). Two girls find that they love one another but are afraid to tell anyone of their love. For mature readers.

733 Garrigue, Shelia. *Between Friends* (7–9). 1978, Bradbury $12.95 (0-02-736620-0); Scholastic paper $2.50 (0-590-40773-2). Jill, a newcomer in town, makes friends with a retarded girl.

734 Girion, Barbara. *A Handful of Stars* (7–10). 1981, Dell paper $2.95 (0-440-93642-X). In her high school sophomore year, Julie Ann learns she has epilepsy.

735 Girion, Barbara. *A Tangle of Roots* (7–10). 1979, Putnam paper $2.25 (0-448-47747-5). A 16-year-old high school girl cannot believe that her beloved mother has died.

736 Godden, Rumer. *The Diddakoi* (6–8). 1988, Penguin paper $3.95 (0-317-69637-8). When her grandmother dies, a young gypsy girl must adjust to a new life.

737 Godden, Rumer. *Thursday's Children* (6–8). 1984, Dell paper $3.25 (0-440-98790-3). A boy discovers he has talent at ballet but hides it from his father and brothers.

738 Gould, Marilyn. *The Twelfth of June* (5–8). 1986, Harper LB $11.89 (0-397-32131-7). Janis, who suffers from cerebral palsy, is suffering the first pangs of adolescence and is still fighting the battle to be treated like other girls her age, in this sequel to *Golden Daffodils* (1982). (Rev: SLJ 11/86; VOYA 12/86)

739 Grant, Cynthia D. *Hard Love* (7–9). 1980, Fawcett paper $2.25 (0-317-13274-1). Stephen's neighbor shows suicidal signs and he doesn't know how to help him.

740 Greenberg, Jan. *No Dragons to Slay* (7–10). 1983, Farrar $11.95 (0-374-35528-2); paper $3.50 (0-374-45509-0). A high school senior discovers he has hip cancer.

741 Greenberg, Jan. *The Pig-Out Blues* (7–10). 1982, Farrar $11.95 (0-374-35937-7). Jodie's being overweight and unhappy causes problems with her mother.

742 Greenberg, Jan. *A Season In-Between* (7–9). 1979, Farrar $11.95 (0-374-36564-4). Carrie's father comes home to die of cancer.

743 Greene, Bette. *The Summer of My German Soldier* (7–10). 1973, Dial $14.95 (0-8037-8321-3); Bantam paper $2.95 (0-553-27247-0). An unhappy teenager growing up in a southern town during World War II finds fulfillment when she hides an excaped German prisoner of war.

744 Greene, Shep. *The Boy Who Drank Too Much* (7–9). 1979, Penguin $11.50 (0-670-18381-4); Dell paper $2.95 (0-440-90493-5). At one time Buff's main concern was sports, now it's alcohol.

745 Grove, Vicki. *The Fastest Friend in the West* (5–8). 1990, Putnam $14.95 (0-399-22184-0). An overweight girl becomes friendly with Vern, the scruffy daughter of homeless parents who live out of a car. (Rev: BL 7/90)

746 Guccione, Leslie Davis. *Tell Me How the Wind Sounds* (7–10). 1989, Scholastic $12.95 (0-590-42615-X). On an isolated island where she is spending the summer, Amanda tries to become friendly with an attractive deaf boy. (Rev: BL 12/1/89; SLJ 10/89; VOYA 12/89)

747 Hall, Lynn. *The Boy in the Off-White Hat* (7–9). 1984, Macmillan $11.95 (0-684-18224-6). A teenage girl who is taking care of a young boy for the summer realizes that her charge is being sexually molested by an older man.

748 Hall, Lynn. *The Giver* (7–10). 1985, Macmillan $11.95 (0-684-18312-9); paper $3.95 (0-02-043290-9). The crush a high school girl has on her

homeroom teacher is returned with affection in this novel that explores pupil-teacher relationships. (Rev: BL 3/15/85; SLJ 8/85)

749 Hall, Lynn. *Just One Friend* (7–12). 1985, Macmillan $11.95 (0-684-18471-0); paper $2.95 (0-02-043311-5). The painful story of a slow student and her trauma when she is mainstreamed into a regular school. (Rev: BL 9/15/85; SLJ 12/85; VOYA 4/86)

750 Hallman, Ruth. *Breakaway* (7–9). 1981, Westminster $8.95 (0-664-32677-3). Kate and her boyfriend Rob, who is struggling with his deafness, run away to Georgia.

751 Hamilton, Dorothy. *Last One Chosen* (6–8). Illus. 1982, Herald Pr. paper $3.95 (0-8361-3306-4). A young boy must adjust to having one leg shorter than the other because of a farm accident.

752 Hamilton, Virginia. *The Planet of Junior Brown* (7–9). 1971, Macmillan $14.95 (0-02-742510-X); paper $3.95 (0-02-043540-1). A 300-pound misfit is taken care of by his friends.

753 Harlan, Elizabeth. *Watershed* (8–10). 1986, Viking $12.95 (0-670-80824-5). A brother feels guilt after the suicide of a younger brother. (Rev: BL 5/1/86; BR 11–12/86; SLJ 5/86)

754 Hautzig, Deborah. *Second Star to the Right* (7–9). 1981, Greenwillow $11.75 (0-688-00498-9); Knopf paper $2.95 (0-394-82028-2). Leslie's dieting craze turns into anorexia nervosa.

755 Heide, Florence Parry. *Growing Anyway Up* (6–8). 1976, Harper $11.70 (0-397-31657-7). Florence is shy when confronted with new situations but an aunt helps her conquer her fears.

756 Hermes, Patricia. *Nobody's Fault* (6–8). 1983, Dell paper $2.50 (0-440-46523-0). Emily feels guilty that she didn't treat her brother better when he was alive.

757 Hermes, Patricia. *What If They Knew?* (6–8). 1980, Harcourt $10.95 (0-15-295317-5); Dell paper $2.25 (0-440-49515-6). Jeremy tries to keep the fact that she is an epileptic a secret.

758 Holland, Isabelle. *Dinah and the Green Fat Kingdom* (7–9). 1978, Harper $13.90 (0-397-31818-9); Dell paper $1.75 (0-440-91918-5). Dinah faces all sorts of problems because of her weight including a nagging mother who insists she go on a diet.

759 Hopper, Nancy J. *Wake Me When the Band Starts Playing* (7–10). 1988, Dutton $12.95 (0-525-67244-3). Mike tackles his weight problem by practicing with the swim team. (Rev: BL 7/88; SLJ 5/88; VOYA 10/88)

760 Horwitz, Joshua. *Only Birds & Angels Fly* (8–11). 1985, Harper LB $12.89 (0-06-022599-8). The story of a friendship between 2 boys and the gradual, tragic deterioration of one through the use of drugs. (Rev: BL 9/15/85; BR 3/b24/86; SLJ 11/85; VOYA 2/86)

761 Hughes, Dean. *Family Pose* (6–8). 1989, Macmillan $12.95 (0-689-31396-9). An 11-year-old runaway finds a home in a Seattle hotel where the employees shelter him. (Rev: BL 4/1/89; BR 9–10/89; VOYA 8/89)

762 Hughes, Monica. *Hunter in the Dark* (7–10). 1983, Macmillan $12.95 (0-689-30959-7); Avon paper $2.50 (0-380-67702-4). In spite of his leukemia, Mike goes on a secret hunting trip.

763 Hyland, Betty. *The Girl with the Crazy Brother* (7–10). 1987, Watts $12.90 (0-531-10345-5). Dana has problems adjusting to her older brother's slide into schizophrenia. (Rev: BL 5/1/87; BR 5–6/87; SLJ 6–7/87; VOYA 6/87)

764 Jacoby, Alice. *My Mother's Boyfriend and Me* (8–10). 1987, Dial $13.95 (0-8037-0200-0). Laurie is being sexually molested by her mother's boyfriend but her mother refuses to believe her. (Rev: BL 6/15/87; SLJ 4/87; VOYA 2/88)

765 Jensen, Kathryn. *Pocket Change* (7–11). 1989, Macmillan $13.95 (0-02-747731-2). Josie finds that her beloved father is suffering from post-traumatic stress disorder caused by his experiences in the Vietnam War. (Rev: BL 4/15/89; BR 9–10/89; SLJ 3/89; VOYA 6/89)

766 Kent, Deborah. *Belonging* (7–9). 1978, Ace paper $2.25 (0-448-05385-3). A blind 15-year-old girl is mainstreamed into a regular high school.

767 Kent, Deborah. *Taking the Lead* (6–10). 1987, Bantam paper $2.95 (0-553-26528-8). A 15-year-old girl must adjust to sudden blindness and return to her former high school. (Rev: BL 10/15/87; SLJ 10/87)

768 Kingman, Lee. *Head over Wheels* (7–9). 1985, Dell paper $2.25 (0-440-93129-0). An automobile accident makes one of 2 twin brothers a cripple and both must adjust. A reissue.

769 Konigsburg, E. L. *(George)* (6–8). 1974, Macmillan $11.75 (0-689-20604-6); Dell paper $2.95 (0-440-42847-5). An 11-year-old boy discovers he has another boy named George living inside him.

770 Lee, Joanna, and T. S. Cook. *Mary Jane Harper Cried Last Night* (7–10). 1978, NAL paper $2.95 (0-451-13980-1). Mary Jane is the silent victim of her mother's physical abuse.

771 Lee, Mildred. *The Skating Rink* (7–10). 1969, Houghton $10.95 (0-395-28912-2). Tuck overcomes a speech impediment through love and success at roller skating.

772 Levinson, Nancy Smiler. *Annie's World* (7–12). 1990, Gallaudet Univ. Pr. paper $2.95 (0-930323-65-3). An almost-totally deaf girl must leave the shelter of her special school and be mainstreamed into a regular high school. (Rev: BL 9/1/90)

773 Levoy, Myron. *Alan and Naomi* (7–9). 1977, Harper LB $12.89 (0-06-023800-3); paper $2.95 (0-06-440209-6). Alan tries to reach Naomi whose mind has been warped by memories of the Holocaust.

774 Levoy, Myron. *Pictures of Adam* (6–9). 1986, Harper $12.89 (0-06-023829-1). Lisa befriends a boy who has severe emotional problems because of his father's physical abuse. (Rev: BL 7/86; BR 11–12/86; SLJ 5/86; VOYA 8–10/86)

775 Levy, Elizabeth. *Come Out Smiling* (7–10). 1981, Delacorte $8.95 (0-440-01378-X). Jenny is shocked and confused to find out about the relationship between the camp counselor, Peggy, and her assistant, Ann.

776 Levy, Marilyn. *The Girl in the Plastic Cage* (7–9). 1982, Ballantine paper $2.95 (0-449-70277-4). A budding gymnast discovers she has scoliosis and must wear a body brace.

777 Little, Jean. *Mama's Going to Buy You a Mockingbird* (6–8). 1985, Viking $12.95 (0-670-80346-4); Penguin paper $3.95 (0-14-031737-6). This novel tells of the death of Adrian's father from cancer and how the boy gradually adjusts to this terrible loss. (Rev: BL 9/1/85)

778 Lowry, Lois. *A Summer to Die* (7–10). Illus. 1977, Houghton $13.95 (0-395-25338-1); Bantam paper $2.95 (0-553-26297-1). Meg is confused and dismayed by her older sister's death.

779 Luger, Harriett. *Lauren* (8–10). 1981, Dell paper $1.50 (0-440-94700-6). Lauren, who is 17 and pregnant, leaves home to make some decisions about her life.

780 McCuaig, Sandra. *Blindfold* (7–10). 1990, Holiday $13.95 (0-8234-0811-6). The suicide of 2 brothers involves their feelings about Sally O'Leary, and she must cope with her guilt after their deaths. (Rev: BL 6/1/90; SLJ 5/90)

781 McDaniel, Lurlene. *Too Young to Die* (7–9). 1989, Bantam paper $2.95 (0-553-28008-2). Melissa discovers that she has leukemia and must learn to cope with this tragedy. Also use: *Goodbye Doesn't Mean Forever* (1989). (Rev: SLJ 8/89; VOYA 12/89)

782 McNair, Joseph. *Commander Coatrack Returns* (6–9). 1989, Houghton $13.95 (0-395-48295-X). Feeling alone after her retarded brother is sent to school, Lisa becomes friends with an emotionally disturbed boy who constantly changes identities. (Rev: BL 6/1/89; BR 3–4/90; SLJ 6/89; VOYA 8/89)

783 Madison, Winifred. *A Portrait of Myself* (7–10). 1979, Random LB $7.99 (0-394-94021-0). When her art teacher, whom she idolizes, rebuffs her, Catherine thinks of suicide.

784 Magorian, Michelle. *Good Night, Mr. Tom* (7–9). 1981, Harper LB $13.89 (0-06-024079-2); paper $3.95 (0-06-440174-X). A quiet recluse takes in an abused 8-year-old who has been evacuated from World War II London.

785 Mango, Karin N. *Just for the Summer* (7–12). 1990, Harper LB $13.95 (0-06-024039-3). Jenny is attracted to the handsome, strangely aloof boy who lives next door. (Rev: BL 4/1/90; SLJ 5/90; VOYA 6/90)

786 Mann, Peggy. *There Are Two Kinds of Terrible* (6–8). 1979, Avon paper $1.50 (0-380-45823-3). Robbie thinks breaking an arm is terrible; then he discovers that his mother has terminal cancer.

787 Marsden, John. *So Much to Tell You . . .* (6–10). 1989, Little $13.95 (0-316-54877-4). Based on a true event, this is, in diary form, the story of a girl who has been accidentally disfigured facially by her father. A prize-winning Australian novel. (Rev: BL 7/89; BR 11–12/89; SLJ 5/89; VOYA 2/90)

788 Martin, Katherine. *Night Riding* (7–9). 1989, Knopf LB $13.99 (0-679-90064-0). A disturbing novel about child abuse and incest set in Tennessee of 1958. (Rev: BL 12/1/89; SLJ 9/89)

789 Mathis, Sharon. *Teacup Full of Roses* (7–12). 1987, Penguin paper $3.95 (0-14-032238-7). For mature teens, a novel about the devastating effects of drugs on a black family.

790 Mayne, William. *Gideon Ahoy!* (6–10). 1989, Delacorte $13.95 (0-385-29702-5). A 17-year-old brain-damaged boy and his family as seen through the artistic insights of Eva, age 12. For better readers. (Rev: BL 5/1/89; SLJ 9/89; VOYA 6/89)

791 Mazer, Harry. *When the Phone Rang* (7–12). 1985, Scholastic $11.95 (0-590-32167-6); paper $2.50 (0-590-40383-4). Three youngsters in New York City decide to try life on their own after their parents are killed in an airplane crash. (Rev: BL 10/1/85; SLJ 11/85; VOYA 8/85)

792 Mazer, Norma Fox. *Silver* (6–9). 1988, Morrow $11.95 (0-688-06865-0). Sarabeth moves to a posh school and finds that her best friend there is being sexually abused. (Rev: BL 11/1/88; BR 11–12/88; SLJ 11/88; VOYA 2/89)

793 Miklowitz, Gloria D. *Anything to Win* (7–12). 1989, Delacorte $14.95 (0-385-29750-5). A high school football player takes steroids in order to get a chance at a college scholarship. (Rev: BL 7/89; BR 11–12/89; SLJ 11/89; VOYA 10/89)

794 Miklowitz, Gloria D. *Close to the Edge* (7–10). 1984, Dell paper $2.95 (0-440-91381-0). Jenny has difficulty putting her friend's suicide into perspective.

795 Miklowitz, Gloria D. *Did You Hear What Happened to Andrea?* (7–10). 1979, Delacorte $7.95 (0-440-01923-0); Dell paper $2.25 (0-440-91853-7). A 15-year-old girl is raped at gunpoint.

796 Miklowitz, Gloria D. *Good-bye Tomorrow* (7–12). 1987, Delacorte $13.95 (0-385-29562-6); Dell paper $3.25 (0-440-20081-4). Misunderstanding and hatred develop when Alex is diagnosed as being an AIDS carrier as a result of a blood transfusion. (Rev: BL 5/1/87; BR 9–10/87; SLJ 6–7/87; VOYA 6/87)

797 Minshull, Evelyn White. *But I Thought You Really Loved Me* (7–10). 1976, Westminster $7.25 (0-664-32600-5). An unwed teenager spends the last months of her pregnancy in a church-sponsored residence.

798 Moeri, Louise. *The Girl Who Lived on the Ferris Wheel* (7–10). 1979, Dutton $10.95 (0-525-30659-5); Avon paper $2.25 (0-380-52506-2). Til's parents are divorced and she is forced to live with her physically abusive mother.

799 Moore, Ruth Nulton. *In Search of Liberty* (7–9). Illus. 1983, Herald Pr. paper $4.95 (0-8361-3340-4). Jon hopes that the gift of a lucky penny will help him through the dangerous surgery he faces.

800 Morris, Winifred. *Dancer in the Mirror* (8–10). 1987, Macmillan $13.95 (0-689-31322-5); Fawcett paper $4.95 (0-449-70285-5). Carole is disturbed by her parents' divorce and turns to a free-spirited girl in her class for friendship. (Rev: BL 3/1/87; BR 11–12/87; SLJ 3/88; VOYA 6/87)

801 Mulford, Philippa Greene. *The World Is My Eggshell* (7–12). 1986, Delacorte $14.95 (0-385-29432-8); Dell paper $2.95 (0-440-20243-4). Adjusting to the death of her father and a move to a new home is not easy for high-schooler Abbey. (Rev: SLJ 5/86; VOYA 6/86)

802 Nathanson, Laura. *The Trouble with Wednesdays* (6–8). 1986, Putnam $13.95 (0-448-47775-

0); Bantam paper $2.95 (0-553-26337-4). When Becky needs dental work, the relative she is sent to turns out to be a child molester. (Rev: BL 7/86; VOYA 6/86)

803 Naylor, Phyllis Reynolds. *The Keeper* (6–10). 1986, Macmillan $13.95 (0-689-31204-0). Nick and his mother agonize over whether or not to have Nick's father institutionalized for the mentally ill. (Rev: BL 4/1/86; SLJ 5/86; VOYA 2/87)

804 Neufeld, John. *Lisa, Bright and Dark* (7–9). 1969, Phillips $16.95 (0-87599-149-1); NAL paper $2.95 (0-451-16093-2). Her friend notices that Lisa is gradually sinking into mental illness but her parents seem indifferent.

805 Neufeld, John. *Twink* (7–9). 1971, NAL paper $2.95 (0-451-15955-1). Twink faces the future courageously though she is blind and suffering from cerebral palsy.

806 Oneal, Zibby. *A Formal Feeling* (7–10). 1982, Viking $12.95 (0-670-32488-4). Anne tries hard to remember her dead mother and also accept her new stepmother.

807 Oneal, Zibby. *The Language of Goldfish* (7–10). 1980, Viking $13.95 (0-670-41785-8). Carrie appears to be slowly sinking into mental illness and seems unable to help herself.

808 Park, Barbara. *Beanpole* (7–9). 1983, Knopf LB $10.99 (0-394-95811-X); Avon paper $2.95 (0-380-69840-4). On her thirteenth birthday Lillian, who is extra tall for her age, makes 3 wishes and they seem to be coming true.

809 Paulsen, Gary. *The Crossing* (8–10). 1987, Watts LB $11.99 (0-531-08309-8); Dell paper $3.25 (0-440-20582-4). An alcoholic American soldier and a homeless street waif become friends in a Mexican border town. (Rev: BL 10/15/87; BR 1–2/88; SLJ 11/87; VOYA 10/87)

810 Peck, Richard. *Are You in the House Alone?* (7–10). 1976, Viking $12.95 (0-670-13241-1). Gail is raped by a classmate while she is on a baby-sitting assignment.

811 Peck, Richard. *Remembering the Good Times* (7–10). 1985, Delacorte $14.95 (0-385-29396-8); Dell, $2.95 (0-440-20206-X). A strong friendship between 2 boys and a girl is destroyed when one of them commits suicide. (Rev: BL 3/1/85; BR 9–10/85)

812 Pershall, Mary K. *You Take the High Road* (7–10). 1990, Dial $14.95 (0-8037-0700-2). Samantha's joy turns to grief and guilt when her newborn brother dies. (Rev: BL 4/15/90; SLJ 2/90; VOYA 2/90)

813 Pfeffer, Susan Beth. *Just between Us* (6–8). Illus. 1980, Delacorte $9.89 (0-385-28594-9); Dell paper $2.25 (0-440-44194-3). Even when her mother bribes her to keep secrets, Cass has trouble.

814 Pfeffer, Susan Beth. *What Do You Do When Your Mouth Won't Open?* (6–8). 1982, Dell paper $2.75 (0-440-49320-X). Reesa is petrified at the thought of facing an audience of 500 to read her prize-winning essay.

815 Pinsker, Judith. *A Lot Like You* (7–10). 1988, Bantam $13.95 (0-553-05445-7). An overweight teenager shares a common weight problem with her boyfriend. (Rev: BL 1/15/88; SLJ 2/88; VOYA 4/88)

816 Platt, Kin. *The Ape inside Me* (6–8). 1979, Harper LB $11.89 (0-397-31823-4); Bantam paper $2.25 (0-553-24581-3). Eddie and Debbie work together to try and curb their terrible tempers.

817 Potter, Dan. *Crazy Moon Zoo* (7–12). 1985, Watts $12.40 (0-531-10076-6). Seventeen-year-old Jory seems unable to care about anything except his older brother whom he alternately loves and hates. (Rev: BL 10/15/85; BR 5–6/86; SLJ 12/85)

818 Radley, Gail. *CF in His Corner* (7–9). 1984, Macmillan $11.95 (0-590-07901-8). Jeff must spend the summer taking care of his young brother who has cystic fibrosis.

819 Rhue, Morton. *The Wave* (7–10). 1981, Delacorte $10.95 (0-440-09822-X); Dell paper $2.95 (0-440-99371-7). A high school experiment to test social interaction backfires when an elitist group is formed.

820 Richmond, Sandra. *Wheels for Walking* (7–12). 1985, Little $13.95 (0-87113-041-6); NAL paper $2.50 (0-451-15235-2). Sally almost loses her boyfriend due to her inability to accept her physical handicap. (Rev: BL 10/1/85; BR 9–10/86; SLJ 12/85; VOYA 4/86)

821 Riley, Jocelyn. *Crazy Quilt* (7–9). 1984, Bantam paper $2.50 (0-553-25640-8). Thirteen-year-old Merle and her brother and sister are living with their grandmother because of their mother's mental illness in this sequel to *Only My Mouth Is Smiling* (1982).

822 Rodowsky, Colby. *P.S. Write Soon* (7–9). 1987, Farrar paper $3.50 (0-374-46032-9). A physically handicapped girl pours out her secret thoughts to her pen pal. A reissue.

823 Rodowsky, Colby. *What about Me?* (7–9). 1989, Farrar paper $3.50 (0-374-48316-7). A teenage girl begins to resent the attention her younger brother gets because he has Down's syndrome. A reissue.

824 Roos, Stephen. *You'll Miss Me When I'm Gone* (7–10). 1988, Doubleday $13.95 (0-385-29633-9). A 16-year-old boy in a fashionable private school tries to hide his drinking problem. (Rev: BL 9/1/88; BR 9–10/88; SLJ 3/88; VOYA 4/88)

825 Rosen, Lillian. *Just Like Everybody Else* (7–8). 1981, Harcourt $12.95 (0-15-241652-8). Jenny finds the courage to accept her deafness, which was caused by a bus accident.

826 Ruckman, Ivy. *The Hunger Scream* (7–10). 1983, Walker $13.95 (0-8027-6514-9). Lily starves herself to become a popular member of the in-crowd.

827 Sallis, Susan. *Only Love* (7–10). 1980, Harper LB $12.89 (0-06-025175-1). A physically handicapped girl finds she has a male admirer.

828 Sallis, Susan. *Secret Places of the Stairs* (7–10). 1984, Harper LB $12.89 (0-06-025147-6). Cass discovers she has a physically handicapped younger sister who is dying.

829 Samuels, Gertrude. *Yours, Brett* (7–10). 1988, Dutton $13.95 (0-525-67255-9). The story of Brett, an abused child, and Brett's fight for happiness. (Rev: BL 9/15/88; SLJ 9/88; VOYA 12/88)

830 Schwartz, Sheila. *Bigger Is Better* (6–8). 1987, Crosswinds paper $2.25 (0-373-98009-4). Sheila is in conflict with her actress mother who demands that she lose weight. (Rev: SLJ 3/88)

831 Scoppettone, Sandra. *Long Time between Kisses* (7–10). 1982, Harper $12.70 (0-06-025229-4). A 16-year-old brings together a victim of multiple sclerosis and his fiancee.

832 Scott, Virginia M. *Belonging* (7–9). Illus. 1986, Gallaudet $9.95 (0-930323-14-9). Gustie slowly rebuilds her life when her hearing is lost after a bout with meningitis at age 15. (Rev: BL 8/86; SLJ 5/86)

833 Seidler, Tor. *The Tar Pit* (6–9). 1987, Farrar $11.95 (0-374-37383-3). A painfully shy boy achieves fame when he discovers some fossils. (Rev: BL 8/87; VOYA 10/87)

834 Shyer, Marlene Fanta. *Welcome Home, Jellybean* (6–8). 1978, Macmillan LB $10.85 (0-8027-6464-9); paper $3.95 (0-689-71213-8). A 12-year-old boy tells about the return home of his older retarded sister.

835 Slepian, Jan. *Lester's Turn* (7–9). 1981, Macmillan LB $8.95 (0-02-782940-5). A boy suffering

from cerebral palsy tries to help a mentally retarded friend.

836 Smith, Doris Buchanan. *Return to Bitter Creek* (6–8). 1986, Viking $12.95 (0-670-80783-4); Penguin paper $3.95 (0-14-032223-X). In spite of grandma's hostility, Lacey and her mother journey back home to North Carolina to rejoin mother's lover David. (Rev: BL 7/86; SLJ 9/86)

837 Snyder, Anne. *First Step* (7–9). 1975, NAL paper $2.95 (0-451-15742-7). Through Alateen, Cindy is able to cope with her mother's alcoholism.

838 Snyder, Anne. *My Name Is Davy: I'm an Alcoholic* (7–10). 1978, NAL paper $2.50 (0-451-14976-9). Davy has become so dependent on alcohol that he steals to feed his habit.

839 Snyder, Carol. *Dear Mom & Dad, Don't Worry* (6–8). 1989, Bantam $13.95 (0-553-05801-0). A fall from a hammock incapacitates a young girl and she must adjust to this handicap. (Rev: SLJ 11/89; VOYA 12/89)

840 Strasser, Todd. *Angel Dust Blues* (7–9). 1979, Putnam $9.95 (0-698-20485-9); Dell paper $2.75 (0-440-90952-X). In his unhappiness and loneliness, a high school student turns to alcohol.

841 Strasser, Todd. *Friends Till the End* (7–9). 1982, Dell paper $2.75 (0-440-92625-4). David befriends a newcomer to the neighborhood who has leukemia.

842 Stren, Patti. *I Was a 15-Year-Old Blimp* (6–10). 1985, Harper LB $11.89 (0-06-026058-0). A severely overweight girl tries purging as a solution but luckily her parents realize the problem in time. (Rev: BL 9/15/85; BR 3–4/86; SLJ 11/85; VOYA 12/85)

843 Sweeney, Joyce. *Right Behind the Rain* (7–10). 1987, Delacorte $14.95 (0-385-29551-0). A high school junior realizes that her older talented brother is suicidal. (Rev: BL 7/87; BR 9–10/87; SLJ 6–7/87; VOYA 6/87)

844 Talbert, Marc. *Dead Birds Singing* (7–10). 1985, Little $13.95 (0-316-83125-5); Dell paper $2.95 (0-440-20036-9). This sensitively written novel deals with a seventh grader's grieving process after family deaths caused by a drunk driver. (Rev: BL 6/1/85; BR 9–10/85; SLJ 8/85; VOYA 8/85)

845 Talbert, Marc. *The Paper Knife* (5–9). 1988, Dial $14.95 (0-8037-0571-9). Jeremy and his mother flee her boyfriend's abuse but the mental trauma suffered by Jeremy cannot be forgotten. (Rev: BL 3/1/89; SLJ 10/88; VOYA 12/88)

846 Tapp, Kathy Kennedy. *The Sacred Circle of the Hula Hoop* (6–9). 1989, Macmillan $13.95 (0-689-50461-6). After her sister attempts suicide, 13-year-old Robin tries to understand why this could have happened. (Rev: BL 4/1/89; BR 9–10/89; SLJ 3/89; VOYA 8/89)

847 Ure, Jean. *After Thursday* (7–12). 1987, Delacorte $14.95 (0-385-29548-0). Seventeen-year-old Marianne tries to become less dependent emotionally on blind Abe Shonfield, in this sequel to *See You Thursday* (1983). (Rev: BL 6/1/87; BR 11–12/87; VOYA 6/87)

848 Ure, Jean. *One Green Leaf* (7–12). 1989, Delacorte $14.95 (0-440-50144-X). Robyn tells about her reactions to her friend David's fatal bout with cancer. (Rev: BL 7/89; SLJ 5/89; VOYA 10/89)

849 Van Leeuwen, Jean. *Seems Like This Road Goes on Forever* (7–10). 1979, Dial $8.95 (0-8037-7687-X). After shoplifting a sweater, Mary Alice is in a terrible car accident and the truth comes out.

850 Veglahn, Nancy J. *Fellowship of the Seven Stars* (7–9). 1981, Abingdon $8.75 (0-687-12927-3). Mazie wants out of the cult that now controls her every waking moment.

851 Voigt, Cynthia. *Izzy, Willy-Nilly* (7–12). 1986, Macmillan $14.95 (0-689-31202-4). A 15-year-old girl's life changes dramatically when she has a leg amputated. (Rev: BL 5/1/86; SLJ 4/86; VOYA 12/86)

852 Wallace-Brodeur, Ruth. *One April Vacation* (6–8). 1981, Macmillan $9.95 (0-689-50211-7). In her wild imagination, Kate thinks she has only one week to live and plans to make the best of it.

853 Wartski, Maureen Crane. *The Lake Is on Fire* (7–9). 1981, Westminster $9.95 (0-664-32687-0). A blind boy and his dog are alone when their cabin catches fire.

854 Wartski, Maureen Crane. *My Brother Is Special* (7–10). 1979, Westminster $8.95 (0-664-32644-7); NAL paper $2.95 (0-451-15856-3). Noni is determined that her retarded brother Kip will win at the Special Olympics.

855 Willey, Margaret. *The Bigger Book of Lydia* (7–9). 1983, Harper LB $12.89 (0-06-026486-1). The story of a friendship in which one of the girls suffers from anorexia nervosa.

856 Windsor, M. A. *Pretty Saro* (6–8). 1986, Macmillian $13.95 (0-689-31277-6). A girl with hearing problems lives without close friends on a horse farm until she meets the daughter of a family new to the area. (Rev: BL 11/15/86; BL 1/1/87; SLJ 12/86; VOYA 12/86)

857 Wojciechowska, Maia. *How God Got Christian into Trouble* (6–8). 1984, Westminster $10.95 (0-664-32717-6). Christian believes that God has become a Puerto Rican child to help him.

858 Wojciechowska, Maia. *Shadow of a Bull* (6–8). 1973, Macmillan $12.95 (0-689-30042-5); Aladdin paper $3.95 (0-689-71132-8). In this Newbery Award winner, Manolo, the son of a famous bullfighter, discovers there are many kinds of courage.

859 Wojciechowska, Maia. *Tuned Out* (7–9). 1968, Harper LB $11.89 (0-06-026577-9); Dell paper $1.50 (0-440-99139-0). A boy discovers that his older brother, whom he worships, is heavily into drugs.

860 Wolff, Virginia Euwer. *Probably Still Nick Swansen* (7–12). 1988, Henry Holt $13.95 (0-8050-0701-6). Nick, a 16-year-old victim of slight brain dysfunction, tells his story of rejection and separation. (Rev: BL 11/15/88; BR 5–6/89; SLJ 12/88; VOYA 6/89)

861 Woolverton, Linda. *Running before the Wind* (6–8). 1987, Houghton $12.95 (0-395-42116-0). A teenage girl takes up the sport of running in part to forget the abuse heaped on her by her father. (Rev: BL 4/1/87; BR 9–10/87; SLJ 4/87; VOYA 6/87)

Personal Problems and Growing into Maturity

862 Adler, C. S. *Binding Ties* (7–10). 1987, Dell paper $3.50 (0-440-20413-5). Anne's strong feelings for her boyfriend come in conflict with her family in this companion book to *Footsteps on the Stairs* (1982). (Rev: BL 3/1/85)

863 Adler, C. S. *Kiss the Clown* (7–10). 1986, Clarion $12.95 (0-89919-419-2). A newly arrived girl from Guatemala has some problems adjusting to her new school and making new friends. (Rev: BL 3/15/86; BR 3–4/87; SLJ 4/86; VOYA 6/86)

864 Adler, C. S. *Roadside Valentine* (7–10). 1983, Macmillan $11.95 (0-02-700350-7). Jamie has problems getting along with his father and with the girl who doesn't love him back.

865 Adler, C. S. *With Westie and the Tin Man* (7–9). 1985, Macmillan $12.95 (0-02-700360-4). After a year in a correctional institution, Greg comes home to many new problems. (Rev: BR 9–10/85)

866 Alcock, Vivien. *The Trial of Anna Cotman* (6–8). 1990, Delacorte $13.95 (0-385-29981-8). Anna has difficulty handling peer pressure at the new school she is attending. (Rev: BL 1/1/90; BR 5–6/90; SLJ 2/90)

867 Anderson, Mary. *Do You Call That a Dream Date?* (7–9). 1987, Delacorte $14.95 (0-385-29488-3). Tired of being classified as ordinary, Jenny copies her sister's essay to win a date with a rock star. (Rev: BR 5–6 87; SLJ 2/87)

868 Anderson, Mary. *Tune in Tomorrow* (7–9). 1985, Avon paper $2.50 (0-390-68970-6). Jo is fixated on 2 soap opera characters whom she later meets in real life.

869 Anderson, Mary. *Who Says Nobody's Perfect?* (7–10). 1987, Delacorte $14.95 (0-385-29582-0). Jenny becomes jealous of the popularity of the exchange student who comes to her house to live. (Rev: BL 12/15/87; BR 11–12/87; SLJ 11/87; VOYA 12/87)

870 Angell, Judie. *The Buffalo Nickel Blues Band* (7–10). 1982, Bradbury $11.95 (0-02-705580-9). Some friends form a band and are sent on the road.

871 Angell, Judie. *Don't Rent My Room!* (6–9). 1990, Bantam $13.95 (0-553-07023-1). Lucy must decide whether to stay and help her parents operate their country inn or go to her grandmother's in New York to attend school. (Rev: BL 9/1/90; SLJ 9/90)

872 Angell, Judie. *In Summertime It's Tuffy* (6–8). 1979, Dell paper $2.25 (0-440-94051-6). Tuffy, at summer camp with some friends, decides to get even with an unfair camp counselor.

873 Angell, Judie. *Ronnie and Rosie* (6–8). 1979, Dell paper $2.25 (0-440-97491-7). Eighth-grader Ronnie feels alone until she forms a friendship with Robert Rose.

874 Asher, Sandy. *Everything Is Not Enough* (7–10). 1987, Delacorte $14.95 (0-385-29530-8); Dell paper $2.75 (0-440-20002-4). Michael, anxious to leave his pampered affluent life, takes a job as a bus boy. (Rev: BL 4/1/87; BR 9–10/87; SLJ 8/87; VOYA 6/87)

875 Asher, Sandy. *Just Like Jenny* (7–9). 1982, Delacorte $12.95 (0-385-28496-9); Dell paper $2.50 (0-440-94289-6). Stephie's friendship with ballet classmate Jenny seems doomed when Stephie seems unable to progress at the same rate as Jenny.

876 Ashley, Bernard. *All My Men* (7–9). 1978, Phillips $16.95 (0-87599-228-5). In this English story, Paul pays a heavy price to be part of the "in" crowd.

877 Ashley, Bernard. *Terry on the Fence* (6–8). Illus. 1977, Phillips $14.95 (0-87599-222-6). Unhappy at home, Terry unwillingly becomes a member of a street gang.

878 Avi. *A Place Called Ugly* (6–9). 1981, Pantheon LB $8.99 (0-394-94755-X). A 14-year-old boy protests the tearing down of a beach cottage to build a hotel.

879 Baehr, Patricia. *Louisa Eclipsed* (6–9). 1988, Morrow $11.95 (0-688-07682-3). Louisa is spending the summer on her grandfather's farm but is too rigid to adjust to this new situation. (Rev: BL 2/1/89; BR 3–4/89; VOYA 12/88)

880 Barrett, Peter A., ed. *To Break the Silence: Thirteen Short Stories for Young Readers* (6–9). 1986, Dell paper $3.25 (0-440-98807-1). A collection of stories by such authors as Katherine Paterson, Penelope Lively, and Shirley Jackson that feature young people and their problems. (Rev: BL 6/15/86)

881 Bates, Betty. *Ask Me Tomorrow* (5–8). 1987, Holiday $12.95 (0-8234-0659-8). In this story set in Maine, a 15-year-old boy finds he is ostracized when he befriends a strange 13-year-old girl. (Rev: BL 12/1/87; SLJ 9/87; VOYA 2/88)

882 Bates, Betty. *The Great Male Conspiracy* (7–10). 1986, Holiday LB $12.95 (0-8234-0629-6). Based on her limited experience, 12-year-old Maggie decides that all men are worthless. (Rev: SLJ 12/86)

883 Bauer, Marion Dane. *Like Mother, Like Daughter* (6–9). 1985, Clarion $12.95 (0-89919-356-0). Rejecting her mother as a role model, Leslie turns to Ms. Perl, her journalism teacher. (Rev: BR 9–10/86; SLJ 1/86; VOYA 12/85)

884 Bauer, Marion Dane. *Shelter from the Wind* (7–10). 1979, Houghton $13.95 (0-395-28890-8). On the Oklahoma panhandle, a runaway girl learns about life from a reclusive woman.

885 Bawden, Nina. *The Peppermint Pig* (6–8). 1975, Harper LB $12.89 (0-397-31618-6); Dell paper $4.95 (0-440-40122-4). A brother and sister save a pig that they soon regard as a pet but they find something terrible is going to happen to it.

886 Bawden, Nina. *The Robbers* (6–8). 1979, Lothrop $12.95 (0-688-41902-X); Dell paper $3.25 (0-440-40316-2). In this novel set in contemporary London, impressionable Philip is influenced by a street-wise kid.

887 Beckman, Delores. *My Own Private Sky* (6–8). 1980, Dutton $9.95 (0-525-35510-3). At first, Arthur has problems getting used to his eccentric baby-sitter.

888 Beckman, Delores. *Who Loves Sam Grant?* (7–9). 1983, Dutton $10.95 (0-525-44055-0). Sam is facing 2 problems—she has lost her boyfriend and she is wrongfully accused of a theft.

889 Bess, Clayton. *Big Man and the Burn-out* (7–9). 1985, Houghton $12.95 (0-395-36173-7). Jess reaches out to Meechum, the class tough guy, for the friendship and confidence he sorely needs. (Rev: BL 11/15/85; BR 3–4/86; SLJ 12/85; VOYA 4/86)

890 Betancourt, Jeanne. *Not Just Party Girls* (7–10). 1989, Bantam $13.95 (0-553-05497-X). Three girls who run a children's party service each faces her own personal problems. (Rev: BL 1/15/89; SLJ 1/89; VOYA 2/89)

891 Blair, Cynthia. *The Banana Split Affair* (7–10). 1985, Fawcett paper $1.95 (0-449-70033-X). Identical twins with different personalities switch identities for 2 weeks. Part of a recommended series. (Rev: VOYA 8/85)

892 Blume, Judy. *Just as Long as We're Together* (6–8). 1987, Watts LB $12.99 (0-531-08329-2); Dell paper $3.50 (0-440-40075-9). An entering junior high student faces problems involving weight, friendships, and a family that is disintegrating. (Rev: BL 8/87; BR 1–2/88; VOYA 2/88)

893 Blume, Judy. *Then Again, Maybe I Won't* (6–8). 1971, Bradbury $12.95 (0-02-711090-7); Dell paper $3.25 (0-440-48659-9). Thirteen-year-old Tony faces many problems when his family relocates to suburban Long Island.

894 Bond, Nancy. *The Best of Enemies* (6–8). 1978, Macmillan $13.95 (0-689-50108-0). Charlotte becomes involved with some elderly citizens when she helps with the Patriot's Day celebration.

895 Bond, Nancy. *A Place to Come Back To* (7–9). 1984, Macmillan $13.95 (0-689-50302-4). Charlotte, now 15, must help friend Oliver adjust to the death of his guardian, in this sequel to *The Best of Enemies* (1978).

896 Bonham, Frank. *Durango Street* (7–10). 1965, Dutton $12.95 (0-525-28950-X). Teenage black gangs in an inner city and the problems of a teenager trying to avoid them.

897 Borntrager, Mary Christner. *Rebecca* (7–12). 1989, Herald Pr. paper $5.95 (0-8361-3500-8). A coming-of-age novel about an Amish girl and her attraction to a Mennonite young man. (Rev: SLJ 11/89)

898 Bottner, Barbara. *Nothing in Common* (7–10). 1986, Harper LB $12.89 (0-06-020605-5). When Mrs. Gregori dies both her daughter and Melissa Warren, a teenager in the household where Mrs. Gregori worked, enter a period of grief. (Rev: VOYA 2/87)

899 Boyd, Candy Dawson. *Breadsticks and Blessing Places* (6–9). 1985, Macmillan $11.95 (0-02-709290-9). A black girl from a middle-class family faces the usual pangs of adolescence. (Rev: SLJ 9/85)

900 Bradford, Richard. *Red Sky at Morning* (7–12). 1986, Harper paper $7.95 (0-06-091361-4). A boy whose family relocates to New Mexico during World War II has some humorous and poignant experiences adjusting. A reissue.

901 Brancato, Robin F. *Come Alive at 505* (7–10). 1980, Knopf LB $8.99 (0-394-94294-9). A teenage would-be disc jockey faces maturation problems.

902 Brancato, Robin F. *Something Left to Lose* (7–9). 1976, Knopf paper $6.95 (0-394-83183-7). Three girls share the problems and rewards of their friendship.

903 Brancato, Robin F. *Uneasy Money* (7–10). 1986, Knopf LB $11.99 (0-394-96954-5). A high school senior finds that winning the lottery can bring a fresh set of problems. (Rev: BL 1/1/87; BR 3–4/87; SLJ 12/86)

904 Branscum, Robbie. *The Girl* (7–10). 1986, Harper LB $10.89 (0-06-020703-5). The story of an unhappy girl and her siblings who are forced to live with sadistic grandparents. (Rev: SLJ 10/86; VOYA 12/86)

905 Branscum, Robbie. *Johnny May Grows Up* (6–8). Illus. 1987, Harper LB $11.89 (0-06-020607-1). Johnny May, the spunky mountain girl of *The Adventures of Johnny May* (1985), has no money to continue her schooling after eighth grade. (Rev: BL 10/1/87; BR 3–4/88)

906 Brenner, Barbara. *A Killing Season* (7–9). 1981, Macmillan $12.95 (0-02-712310-3). By developing outside interests, 16-year-old Allie is able to gain confidence and come to terms with her parents' deaths.

907 Bridgers, Sue Ellen. *Permanent Connections* (8–12). 1987, Harper LB $12.89 (0-06-020712-4); paper $3.50 (0-06-447020-2). When Rob's behavior gets out of control, the teenager is sent to his uncle's farm to cool off. (Rev: BL 2/15/87; BR 9–10/87; SLJ 3/87; VOYA 4/87)

908 Brink, Carol. *The Bad Times of Irma Baumlein* (5–8). 1974, Macmillan $14.95 (0-02-714220-5); paper $3.95 (0-02-041900-7). Irma, unhappy living with a strict great-uncle, gets caught in a terrible lie.

909 Brown, Irene Bennett. *I Loved You, Logan McGee!* (6–8). 1987, Macmillan $11.95 (0-689-

31295-4); Penguin paper $3.95 (0-14-032701-0). Calla falls apart emotionally when her boyfriend tells her he no longer wants to go steady. (Rev: BL 3/1/87; SLJ 4/87; VOYA 6/87)

910 Brown, Kay. *Willy's Summer Dream* (6–9). 1989, Harcourt $13.95 (0-15-200645-1). Willy lacks confidence because he is a slow learner. (Rev: BL 2/1/90; SLJ 12/89)

911 Bunting, Eve. *If I Asked You, Would You Stay?* (8–10). 1984, Harper $12.89 (0-397-32066-3); paper $2.95 (0-06-447023-7). Two lonely people find comfort in love for each other.

912 Burch, Robert. *Queenie Peavy* (6–8). 1987, Penguin paper $3.95 (0-14-032305-8). Queenie, whose father is in prison, is growing up a defiant, disobedient girl in rural Georgia.

913 Busselle, Rebecca. *A Frog's-Eye View* (8–12). 1990, Watts LB $14.99 (0-531-08507-4). Neela knows she is losing her boyfriend but she tries frantically and unsuccessfully to keep him. (Rev: BL 8/90; SLJ 9/90)

914 Butterworth, W. E. *LeRoy and the Old Man* (7–10). 1980, Scholastic paper $2.50 (0-590-40573-X). A young boy, fearful of cooperating with the police, flees to his grandfather's home in Mississippi.

915 Byars, Betsy. *Bingo Brown and the Language of Love* (5–9). 1989, Viking $11.95 (0-670-82791-6). Bingo Brown's girlfriend has moved out of town but other problems beset him and his family in this sequel to *The Burning Questions of Bingo Brown* (1988). (Rev: BL 6/1/89; SLJ 7/89)

916 Callan, Jamie. *Over the Hill at Fourteen* (7–9). 1982, NAL paper $1.95 (0-451-13090-1). A successful young model is torn with fears about the future.

917 Calvert, Patricia. *The Stone Pony* (7–9). 1983, NAL paper $2.50 (0-451-13729-9). In this touching novel, Jo Beth must adjust to the death of her older sister.

918 Calvert, Patricia. *Stranger, You & I* (8–10). 1987, Macmillan $12.95 (0-684-18896-1). High-schooler Hughie finds out that his friend Zee is pregnant by a rich boy who will take no responsibility. (Rev: BL 12/1/87; SLJ 1/88)

919 Cameron, Eleanor. *The Private Worlds of Julia Redfern* (6–10). 1988, Dutton $12.95 (0-525-44394-0). Julia, at age 15, is well on her way to becoming an author. (Rev: BL 5/15/88; BR 11-12/88; SLJ 5/88)

920 Cameron, Eleanor. *A Room Made of Windows* (6–9). Illus. 1971, Little $15.75 (0-316-12523-7). A sensitive young girl is troubled by the problems facing her mother and friends.

921 Cannon, A. E. *Cal Cameron by Day, Spider-Man by Night* (7–10). 1988, Delacorte $13.95 (0-385-29635-5). Cal, an average kid, is uneasy about his friendship with a new girl in school who is a nonconformist. (Rev: BL 4/1/88; BR 5-6/88; SLJ 4/88; VOYA 6/88)

922 Cannon, A. E. *The Shadow Brothers* (7–12). 1990, Delacorte $14.95 (0-384-29982-6). Two foster brothers, one an American Indian, gradually grow apart under the strain of outside pressures. (Rev: BL 5/1/90; BR 5-6/90; SLJ 6/90)

923 Carkeet, David. *The Silent Treatment* (7–10). 1988, Harper LB $13.89 (0-06-020979-8). Ricky learns to be more self-assertive partly through a friendship of which his parents do not approve. (Rev: BL 7/88; BR 1-2/89; SLJ 6-7/88; VOYA 8/88)

924 Cate, Dick. *Flames* (7–10). Illus. 1989, Gollancz $17.95 (0-575-04501-9). A young boy from a working class family faces problems of growing up in a northern England mining town. (Rev: SLJ 2/90)

925 Cavanna, Betty. *Storm in Her Heart* (7–9). 1983, Westminster $9.95 (0-664-32700-1). Anne's year with her grandmother in Florida turns into an adventure when a hurricane strikes.

926 Cavanna, Betty. *The Surfer and the City Girl* (7–9). 1981, Westminster $8.95 (0-664-32679-X). Anne's problems with an alcoholic grandmother are helped by a surfer named Swifty.

927 Chaikin, Miriam. *Finders Weepers* (6–8). Illus. 1982, Harper LB $12.89 (0-06-021177-6). Molly finds a lovely ring but when she finds its owner she can't get it off her finger.

928 Chambers, Aidan. *Dance on My Grave* (7–10). 1982, Harper LB $13.89 (0-06-021254-3). The tragic story of 2 boys' ill-fated homosexual relationship.

929 Chambers, Aidan. *The Present Takers* (6–8). 1983, Harper LB $12.89 (0-06-021252-7). Lucy and her friends oppose the power of a junior high protection racket.

930 Christian, Mary Blount. *Singin' Somebody Else's Song* (7–10). 1988, Macmillan $13.95 (0-02-718500-1). Seventeen-year-old Gideon grieves for his songwriting buddy, Gere, who killed himself. (Rev: BL 12/1/88; BR 3-4/89; SLJ 12/88)

931 Cleaver, Vera, and Bill Cleaver. *Ellen Grae* (6–8). 1986, NAL paper $2.25 (0-451-14830-4). Ellen Grae, an imaginative girl, finds it impossible to assimilate the story of the death of her friend Ira's parents. Included in this volume is the sequel: *Lady Ellen Grae*.

932 Cleaver, Vera, and Bill Cleaver. *Grover* (7–9). 1987, Harper $12.90 (0-397-31118-4). The death of his beloved mother seems more than Grover can handle. A reissue.

933 Cleaver, Vera, and Bill Cleaver. *Hazel Rye* (6–9). 1983, Harper LB $12.89 (0-397-31952-5); paper $2.95 (0-06-44156-1). Eleven-year-old Hazel rents the Poole family a small house in a citrus grove.

934 Cleaver, Vera, and Bill Cleaver. *The Kissimmee Kid* (7–9). 1981, Lothrop LB $12.88 (0-688-51992-X). Evelyn discovers that her beloved brother-in-law is really a cattle rustler.

935 Cleaver, Vera, and Bill Cleaver. *Sugar Blue* (7–9). Illus. 1984, Lothrop $13.00 (0-688-02720-2); Dell paper $2.95 (0-440-48422-7). Amy, age 13, is saddled with caring for a 4-year-old niece, Ella.

936 Clements, Bruce. *Coming About* (6–9). 1984, Farrar $11.95 (0-374-31457-8). High school newcomer Bob Royle forms a friendship with the class weirdo, Carl Reimer.

937 Clifford, Eth. *The Rocking Chair Rebellion* (6–9). 1978, Houghton $13.95 (0-395-27163-0). Opie gets involved in a power struggle involving a group of elderly people.

938 Cohen, Barbara. *Tell Us Your Secret* (7–10). 1989, Bantam $13.95 (0-553-05810-X). Eve, her boyfriend, and their friends are highlighted in this novel about interpersonal relations. (Rev: BL 5/15/89; BR 11–12/89; SLJ 5/89)

939 Cohen, Miriam. *Robert and Dawn Marie 4Ever* (6–9). 1986, Harper $12.70 (0-06-021396-5). Robert, a street waif, finds a new home and forms a friendship with Dawn Marie, a young girl whose mother disapproves of Robert. (Rev: BL 11/1/86; SLJ 12/86; VOYA 12/86)

940 Cole, Brock. *Celine* (8–10). 1989, Farrar $13.95 (0-374-31234-6). A Chicago high school junior is trying to distinguish between the real and the phony in her life. (Rev: BL 10/15/89; BR 3–4/90; SLJ 11/89; VOYA 2/90)

941 Cole, Brock. *The Goats* (6–9). 1987, Farrar $14.95 (0-374-32678-9); paper $3.50 (0-374-42575-2). Two misfits at summer camp find inner strength and self-knowledge when they are cruelly marooned on an island by fellow campers. (Rev: BL 11/15/87; SLJ 11/87; VOYA 4/88)

942 Collier, James Lincoln. *The Winchesters* (6–9). 1988, Macmillan $12.95 (0-02-722831-2). Chris Winchester is divided in his loyalty to the wealthy family that controls the town in which he lives and the townspeople who are organizing a strike for better wages. (Rev: BR 3–4/89; SLJ 1/89; VOYA 12/88)

943 Colman, Hila. *The Double Life of Angela Jones* (7–10). 1988, Morrow $11.95 (0-688-06781-6). A girl from a poor area comes to a classy private school and discovers that she, too, can be a snob. (Rev: BL 7/88; BR 9–10/88; SLJ 9/88)

944 Colman, Hila. *Not for Love* (7–9). 1984, Morrow $11.95 (0-688-02419-X); Fawcett paper $2.25 (0-449-70100-4). Jill discovers that even very moral people must sometimes compromise.

945 Colman, Hila. *Suddenly* (7–10). 1987, Morrow $12.95 (0-688-05865-5); Fawcett paper $2.95 (0-449-70321-5). A fatal automobile accident brings sorrow to a number of people and a maturing experience for Emily. (Rev: BL 5/1/87; BR 9–10/87; SLJ 9/87; VOYA 6/87)

946 Conford, Ellen. *You Never Can Tell* (7–9). 1984, Little $14.95 (0-316-15267-6); Archway paper $2.75 (0-671-66182-5). Katie's soap opera heartthrob enters her high school.

947 Conrad, Pam. *What I Did for Roman* (7–12). 1987, Harper LB $12.89 (0-06-021332-9). Darcie, a troubled lonely teenager, is attracted to Roman, a vibrant attractive animal keeper. (Rev: BL 2/15/87; BR 9–10/87; SLJ 3/87; VOYA 10/87)

948 Cooney, Caroline B. *Among Friends* (7–10). 1987, Bantam $13.95 (0-553-05446-5). Six high school seniors keep diaries that reveal much about themselves, family, and friends. Also use: *Last Dance* (Scholastic, 1987). (Rev: BL 11/15/87; BR 11–12/87; SLJ 3/88; VOYA 12/87)

949 Cooney, Linda A. *Freshman* (7–10). 1987, Scholastic paper $2.50 (0-590-40348-6). Five friends—3 girls and 2 boys—enter high school together. (Rev: SLJ 10/87)

950 Corcoran, Barbara. *You Put Up with Me, I'll Put Up with You* (6–8). 1987, Macmillan $12.95 (0-689-32305-5); Avon paper $2.50 (0-380-70558-3). A somewhat self-centered girl moves with her mother to a new community and has problems adjusting. (Rev: BL 3/15/87; BR 11–12/87; SLJ 3/87; VOYA 4/87)

951 Cormier, Robert. *Beyond the Chocolate War* (9–12). 1985, Knopf LB $11.99 (0-394-97343-7); Dell paper $3.25 (0-440-90580-X). The misuse of power at Trinity High by Brother Leon and the secret society of Vigils is again explored in this sequel to *The Chocolate War* (1974). (Rev: BL 3/15/85; BR 9–10/85; SLJ 4/85)

952 Cormier, Robert. *The Chocolate War* (7–12). 1974, Pantheon $17.95 (0-394-82805-4); Dell paper $3.25. A chocolate sale in a boys' private school creates power struggles. Followed by: *Beyond the Chocolate War* (1985).

953 Cormier, Robert. *I Am the Cheese* (7–12). 1977, Pantheon $12.95 (0-394-83462-3). A multilevel novel about a boy's life after his parents are forced to go underground.

954 Coryell, Susan. *Eaglebait* (6–9). 1989, Harcourt $14.95 (0-15-200442-4). An unpopular teenage nerd thinks he has found a friend in a new science teacher. (Rev: BL 11/1/89; SLJ 6/90)

955 Cossi, Olga. *The Magic Box* (7–9). 1990, Pelican $10.95 (0-88289-748-9). Mara cannot seem to give up smoking until her mother, a former smoker, develops throat cancer. (Rev: VOYA 8/90)

956 Crawford, Charles. *Letter Perfect* (7–9). 1977, Dutton $9.95 (0-525-33635-4). Chad and 2 friends blackmail their English teacher.

957 Crew, Linda. *Someday I'll Laugh about This* (6–8). 1990, Delacorte $14.95 (0-385-30083-2). The twelfth summer of Shelby is beset with problems, many of which involve her cousin Kirsten. (Rev: BL 6/1/90; BR 5–6/90; SLJ 5/90; VOYA 6/90)

958 Cross, Gillian. *A Map of Nowhere* (8–12). 1989, Holiday $13.95 (0-8234-0741-1). Nick feels that he is being exploited by his brother's street gang but he likes the sense of status and importance from being accepted by an older group. (Rev: BL 3/1/89; SLJ 6/89; VOYA 8/89)

959 Cunningham, Julia. *Flight of the Sparrow* (6–8). 1980, Pantheon $6.95 (0-394-84501-3). Little Cigarette is indebted to Mago for giving her a home but once again she is alone.

960 Cuyler, Margery. *The Trouble with Soap* (6–8). 1982, Dutton $9.95 (0-525-45111-0). Laurie must decide between the company of new friends and loyalty to her old buddy, Soap.

961 Daneman, Meredith. *Francie and the Boys* (7–9). 1989, Doubleday $14.95 (0-440-50137-7). An English story about a girl who blossoms when she accepts a part in a school play. (Rev: BL 2/15/89; BR 5–6/89; SLJ 2/89; VOYA 6/89)

962 Danziger, Paula. *Can You Sue Your Parents for Malpractice?* (6–9). 1979, Delacorte $13.95 (0-385-28112-9); Dell paper $2.25 (0-440-91066-8). Lauren, 14 years old, faces a variety of problems both at home and at school.

963 Danziger, Paula. *The Cat Ate My Gymsuit* (6–9). 1974, Delacorte LB $14.95 (0-385-28194-3); Dell paper $2.95 (0-440-41612-4). Marcy hates gym but finds in her school a supportive teacher. A sequel is *There's a Bat in Bunk Five* (1980).

964 Danziger, Paula. *Remember Me to Harold Square* (6–9). Illus. 1987, Delacorte $13.95 (0-385-29610-X); Dell paper $3.25 (0-440-20153-5). Kendra gets to know attractive Frank when they participate in scavenger hunts in New York City. (Rev: BL 10/1/87; BR 11–12/87; SLJ 11/87; VOYA 12/87)

965 Deaver, Julie Reece. *Say Goodnight, Gracie* (8–12). 1988, Harper LB $12.89 (0-06-021419-8). Morgan must adjust to the death of her dear friend Jimmy in this poignant first novel. (Rev: BL 4/1/88; BR 9–10/88; SLJ 2/88; VOYA 4/88)

966 DeClements, Barthe. *How Do You Lose Those Ninth Grade Blues?* (7–9). 1983, Scholastic paper $2.50 (0-590-33195-7). Elsie is being pursued by Craddoc but lacks the confidence to respond.

967 DeClements, Barthe. *Seventeen & In-Between* (7–10). 1984, Viking $12.95 (0-670-63615-0); Scholastic paper $2.50 (0-590-41115-2). Elsie Edwards, the heroine of *How Do You Lose Those Ninth Grade Blues?* (1983) confronts more problems, like the possibility of her first sexual experience.

968 Derby, Pat. *Goodbye Emily, Hello* (6–9). 1989, Farrar $12.95 (0-374-32744-0). In the ninth grade, a friendship between 2 girls becomes strained until one gets into trouble and seeks the other's help. (Rev: BL 7/89; SLJ 8/89; VOYA 12/89)

969 Derby, Pat. *Visiting Miss Pierce* (6–8). 1986, Farrar $11.95 (0-374-38162-3); paper $3.50 (0-374-48156-3). A high school freshman finds new meaning in his life when he visits a senile woman in a nursing home. (Rev: BL 8/86; BR 11–12/86; SLJ 8/86)

970 Dines, Carol. *Best Friends Tell the Best Lies* (7–10). 1989, Delacorte $14.95 (0-385-50131-8). Two girlfriends react differently to their parents' divorces. (Rev: BR 5–6/89; SLJ 4/89; VOYA 4/89)

971 Doherty, Berlie. *White Peak Farm* (6–12). 1990, Watts LB $12.99 (0-531-08467-1). A collection of stories involving hope, betrayal, and love—all set in present-day north of England. (Rev: BL 4/1/90; SLJ 3/90)

972 Donovan, John. *I'll Get There, It Better Be Worth the Trip* (7–9). 1969, Harper LB $12.89 (0-06-021718-9). Davy learns about life in his mother's cramped Greenwich Village apartment in New York City.

973 Draper, C. G. *A Holiday Year* (6–9). 1988, Little $12.95 (0-316-19203-1). The joys and sorrows of a teenage boy as seen through happenings on various holidays. (Rev: BL 7/88)

974 Dunlop, Beverley. *The Poetry Girl* (6–8). 1989, Houghton $13.95 (0-395-49679-9). In this novel set in New Zealand, a young girl takes refuge from an unhappy home and school life in reading poetry. (Rev: BR 1–2/90; SLJ 5/89; VOYA 6/89)

975 Eige, Lillian. *Cady* (6–9). Illus. 1987, Harper LB $11.89 (0-06-021793-6). A runaway boy finds a home and security with a secretive woman whose past intrigues him. (Rev: BL 7/87; SLJ 5/87)

976 Ethridge, Kenneth E. *Viola, Furgy, Bobbi, and Me* (7–9). 1989, Holiday $13.95 (0-8234-0746-2). Four teenagers befriend a 78-year-old woman who is being mistreated by her daughters. (Rev: VOYA 10/89)

977 Eyerly, Jeannette. *He's My Baby, Now* (7–10). 1977, Harper paper $2.25 (0-671-55269-4). Charles, fearful that his high school girlfriend is going to put their baby up for adoption, plans to kidnap him.

978 Eyerly, Jeannette. *If I Love You Wednesday* (7–10). 1980, Harper LB $11.89 (0-397-31914-2). An unpopular boy fantasizes about his substitute English teacher.

979 Facklam, Margery. *The Trouble with Mothers* (6–8). 1989, Clarion $13.95 (0-89919-773-6). Troy is incensed when the town censors target his mother's historical novel. (Rev: BL 3/1/89; SLJ 5/89; VOYA 6/89)

980 Ferris, Jean. *Amen, Moses Gardenia* (7–9). 1983, Farrar $12.95 (0-374-30252-9). A poor little rich girl finds a friend in the housekeeper.

981 Filichia, Peter. *What's in a Name?* (7–12). 1988, Avon paper $2.75 (0-380-75536-X). Rose is so unhappy with her foreign-sounding last name that she decides to change it. (Rev: BL 3/1/89; VOYA 4/89)

982 First, Julia. *The Absolute, Ultimate End* (6–8). 1985, Watts $12.90 (0-531-10075-8). When Maggie learns that school board funds for such programs as reading to the blind are being cut, she organizes a protest. (Rev: BL 2/15/86; BR 3–4/86; SLJ 2/86; VOYA 4/86)

983 Fitzhugh, Louise. *Harriet the Spy* (6–8). 1964, Harper LB $12.89 (0-06-021911-4); Dell paper $3.50 (0-440-43447-5). The story of a girl whose passion for honesty gets her into trouble. Followed by *The Long Secret* (1965).

984 Fox, Paula. *One-Eyed Cat* (6–9). 1984, Bradbury $11.95 (0-02-735540-3); Dell paper $3.50 (0-440-46641-5). A boy growing up in upstate New York during the 1930s confronts his own guilt when he secretly disobeys his father.

985 Fox, Paula. *A Place Apart* (7–9). 1980, Farrar $12.95 (0-374-35985-7); NAL paper $2.95 (0-451-14338-8). In a small town where she and her mother have moved after her father's death, Victoria meets the unusual Hugh Todd.

986 Franklin, Lance. *Takedown* (7–10). 1987, Bantam paper $2.50 (0-553-26209-2). Beset with personal problems, Kevin tries alcohol to help him with wrestling. (Rev: BL 8/87)

987 Gaeddert, LouAnn. *Daffodils in the Snow* (7–10). 1984, Dutton $11.95 (0-525-44150-6). Overly protected Marianne becomes pregnant and claims it is God's child.

988 Gallo, Donald R., ed. *Connections: Short Stories by Outstanding Writers for Young Adults* (7–10). 1989, Delacorte $14.95 (0-385-29815-3). A fresh collection of stories, many dealing with the problems boys have when growing up. (Rev: BL 12/15/89; BR 3–4/90; SLJ 10/89; VOYA 2/90)

989 Gallo, Donald R., ed. *Sixteen: Short Stories by Outstanding Writers for Young Adults* (7–12). 1984, Delacorte $16.95 (0-385-29346-1); Dell paper $3.25 (0-440-97757-6). Some of the finest young adult writers such as M. E. Kerr and Richard Peck have contributed to this collection.

990 Gallo, Donald R., ed. *Visions: Nineteen Short Stories by Outstanding Writers for Young Adults* (7–10). 1987, Delacorte $16.95 (0-385-29588-X). An excellent collection of stories for young adults by such writers as Fran Arrick, Ouida Sebestyen, and Walter Dean Myers. (Rev: BL 12/15/87; BR 11–12/87; SLJ 1/88; VOYA 2/88)

991 Garden, Nancy. *Peace, O River* (7–10). 1986, Farrar $12.95 (0-374-35763-3). Kate tries to stop the senseless feuding between 2 elements in her community but the violence gets worse. (Rev: BL 3/1/86; SLJ 4/86)

992 Gauch, Patricia Lee. *Night Talks* (7–9). 1983, Putnam $10.95 (0-399-20911-5). Three privileged girls at summer camp share their tent with a poor girl.

993 Gauch, Patricia Lee. *The Year the Summer Died* (7–9). 1985, Putnam $13.95 (0-399-21114-4). Erin tries to hold onto her friendship with older Laurie while trying to tame and ride a horse. (Rev: BL 2/15/86; SLJ 3/86; VOYA 8–10/86)

994 Geller, Mark. *My Life in the Seventh Grade* (6–8). 1986, Harper LB $10.89 (0-06-021982-3); paper $3.50 (0-06-440276-2). A first-person narrative about such occurrences as making friends, mastering difficult subjects, and having a crush. (Rev: BL 6/15/86; BR 11–12/86; VOYA 8–10/86)

995 Geller, Mark. *The Strange Case of the Reluctant Partners* (6–8). 1990, Harper LB $13.89 (0-06-021973-4). Two seventh-graders—a boy and a girl—get to know one another very well as a result of a school biography project. (Rev: BL 9/15/90)

996 Gerber, Merrill Joan. *Also Known as Sadzia! The Belly Dancer* (6–9). 1987, Harper LB $12.89 (0-06-022163-1). To lose weight and annoy her possessive mother, Sandy takes up belly dancing. (Rev: SLJ 3/87; VOYA 4/87)

997 Gerber, Merrill Joan. *Even Pretty Girls Cry at Night* (7–10). 1988, Crosswinds paper $2.25 (0-373-98017-5). Faye comes out of her shell through the help of a 17-year-old boy. (Rev: BL 8/88; SLJ 6–7/88)

998 Gerber, Merrill Joan. *I'd Rather Think about Robby* (6–9). 1989, Harper LB $11.89 (0-06-022284-0). A seventh-grader in the beginning stages of puberty develops a crush on a popular classmate. (Rev: BL 3/15/89)

999 Gerson, Corinne. *Passing Through* (7–9). 1980, Dell paper $1.50 (0-440-96958-1). Liz feels numb after the suicide death of her brother.

1000 Godden, Rumer. *An Episode of Sparrows* (7–10). 1989, Penguin paper $4.95 (0-14-034024-6). In postwar London 2 waifs try to grow a secret garden. (Rev: SLJ 6/89)

1001 Gold, Robert, ed. *Stepping Stones: Seventeen Stories of Growing Up* (7–10). 1981, Dell paper $3.25 (0-440-98269-3). A collection of stories about growing up and adolescence. Also use *Point of Departure* (1981).

1002 Grant, Cynthia D. *Kumquat May, I'll Always Love You* (7–10). 1986, Macmillan $13.95 (0-689-31198-2); Bantam paper $2.95 (0-553-26416-8). Liv keeps the fact that she is living alone a secret except from only her girlfriend Rosetta and a boyfriend who proves to be untrustworthy. (Rev: BL 4/15/86; SLJ 5/86; VOYA 8–10/86)

1003 Greenberg, Jan. *Bye, Bye, Miss American Pie* (7–10). 1985, Farrar $11.95 (0-374-31012-2); Pocket paper $2.50 (0-671-62186-6). A nice girl interested in art becomes involved with an emotionally troubled boy. (Rev: BL 6/15/85; BR 9–10/86; SLJ 9/85; VOYA 4/86)

1004 Greenberg, Jan. *Exercises of the Heart* (7–10). 1986, Farrar $11.95 (0-374-32237-6). Roxie has problems with her partially disabled mother and a friend, Glo, who refuses to accept responsibility for her actions. (Rev: BL 9/15/86; BR 11–12/86; SLJ 11/86; VOYA 12/86)

1005 Greenberg, Jan. *The Iceberg and Its Shadow* (6–8). 1982, Farrar $10.95 (0-374-33624-5). Mindy has already spoiled Anabeth and Rachel's friendship and now she turns on Anabeth.

1006 Greenberg, Jan. *Just the Two of Us* (6–8). 1988, Farrar LB $12.95 (0-374-36198-3). Holly tries every way possible not to move from New York City with her mother. (Rev: BR 3–4/89; SLJ 12/88)

1007 Greene, Bette. *Them That Glitter and Them That Don't* (7–10). 1983, Knopf LB $10.99 (0-394-94692-8). A half-gypsy girl whose parents are irresponsible must help care for the family's two younger children.

1008 Greene, Constance C. *Just Plain Al* (6–8). 1986, Viking $12.95 (0-670-81250-1); Dell paper $2.95 (0-440-40073-2). Al(exandra), now 14 and wishing she wasn't so ordinary and dull, has a chance to do something useful. Part of a series that includes *A Girl Called Al* (1980) and *Al(exandra) the Great* (1982). (Rev: BL 9/15/86; BR 3–4/87)

1009 Greene, Constance C. *Monday I Love You* (7–10). 1988, Harper LB $11.89 (0-06-022205-0). An overdeveloped bust is just one of the problems faced by 15-year-old Grace. (Rev: BL 7/88; VOYA 8/88)

1010 Greene, Constance C. *Star Shine* (6–9). 1985, Viking $11.95 (0-670-80772-9); Dell paper $2.75 (0-440-47920-7). When a movie company in town needs extras, Jenny tries out with surprising success. (Rev: BL 10/15/85; SLJ 1/67)

1011 Greene, Constance C. *Your Old Pal, Al* (6–8). 1979, Viking $13.95 (0-670-79575-5); Dell paper $2.95 (0-440-49862-7). Al has problems with her father, a boy she recently met, and her best friend. Part of a series.

1012 Grove, Vicki. *Junglerama* (5–9). 1989, Putnam $13.95 (0-399-21624-3). Three boys beset with personal problems try to create a wild-life exhibit. (Rev: SLJ 7/89)

1013 Guy, Rosa. *Mirror of Her Own* (7–10). 1981, Delacorte $8.95 (0-385-28636-8). Mary's seventeenth summer brings romance and conflicts with her beautiful older sister.

1014 Hahn, Mary Downing. *Daphne's Book* (6–8). 1983, Clarion $12.95 (0-89919-183-5); Bantam paper $2.50 (0-553-15360-9). A seventh-grader conscious of her social position is paired for an assignment with an outsider.

1015 Hahn, Mary Downing. *December Stillness* (7–9). 1988, Clarion $13.95 (0-89919-758-2). Kathy, a ninth-grader, befriends a homeless man and indirectly causes his death. (Rev: BL 9/1/88; SLJ 10/89; VOYA 4/89)

1016 Hahn, Mary Downing. *The Time of the Witch* (6–8). 1982, Clarion $12.95 (0-89919-115-0). Laura consults a witch in an effort to prevent her parents' divorce.

1017 Hall, Lynn. *The Leaving* (7–10). 1980, Macmillan $11.95 (0-684-16716-6). An 18-year-old girl leaves her parents' farm to find a new life in the big city.

1018 Hall, Lynn. *Where Have All the Tigers Gone?* (7–12). 1989, Macmillan $12.95 (0-684-19003-6). A 50-year-old woman at her class re-union recalls her school years. (Rev: BL 4/15/89; BR 9–10/89; SLJ 5/89; VOYA 8/89)

1019 Hallman, Ruth. *Tough Is Not Enough* (7–9). 1981, Hiway Books $9.95 (0-664-32686-2). An easily read book about a tough kid who has to seek the help of others when he runs away.

1020 Halvorson, Marilyn. *Cowboys Don't Cry* (6–8). 1986, Dell paper $2.95 (0-440-91303-9). While drunk, Shane's father was involved in an accident in which his wife was killed and Shane cannot forgive him for the death of his mother. (Rev: SLJ 9/85; VOYA 6/85)

1021 Hamilton, Dorothy. *Jason* (7–10). 1974, Herald Pr. paper $3.95 (0-8361-1728-X). Jason, a high school senior, wants a vocational education, but his father wants him to go to college.

1022 Hamilton, Virginia. *A Little Love* (7–10). 1984, Putnam $12.95 (0-399-21046-6). An over-weight girl leaves home with her boyfriend to find her father who left her years before.

1023 Harrell, Janice. *Easy Answers* (6–9). 1990, Pocket paper $2.95 (0-671-68571-6). A West Mount High story about several believable characters and their social problems. (Rev: SLJ 6/90)

1024 Harris, Mark Jonathan. *Confessions of a Prime Time Kid* (6–9). 1985, Lothrop $11.95 (0-688-03979-0). A novel about the life of a child star and of the problems fame brings, particularly when one has a demanding stage mother. (Rev: VOYA 8/85)

1025 Hautzig, Deborah. *Hey, Dollface* (7–10). 1978, Greenwillow LB $11.88 (0-688-84170-8); Knopf paper $2.95 (0-394-82046-0). The story of a deep friendship between two girls and the concern of one that it might become a physical relationship.

1026 Haven, Susan. *Is It Them or Is It Me?* (6–9). 1990, Putnam $14.95 (0-399-21916-1). This novel about a freshman in high school deals with some of Kathy's problems growing up. (Rev: BL 6/15/90; SLJ 6/90; VOYA 8/90)

1027 Haven, Susan. *Maybe I'll Move to the Lost & Found* (6–9). 1988, Putnam $13.95 (0-399-21509-3). In this novel set in New York City, 14-year-old Gilly is torn between 2 friendships. (Rev: BL 6/1/88; BR 1–2/89; SLJ 5/88; VOYA 8/88)

1028 Hawks, Robert. *The Twenty-Six Minutes* (6–10). 1988, Square One paper $4.95 (0-938961-03-9). Two teenage misfits join an anti-nuclear protest group. (Rev: SLJ 11/88; VOYA 4/89)

1029 Hayes, Sheila. *Me and My Mona Lisa Smile* (7–9). 1981, Lodestar $10.95 (0-525-66731-8). Rowena blossoms under the attention of a new English teacher but realizes that old friends are still important.

1030 Hayes, Sheila. *No Autographs, Please* (5–9). 1986, Berkley paper $2.50 (0-425-08859-6). Cici has a difficult time convincing others that she is destined for a life in the theater. (Rev: BR 5–6/86)

1031 Haynes, Betsy. *The Popularity Trap* (6–8). 1988, Bantam paper $2.75 (0-553-15634-9). Christie runs for class president and finds it impossible to please everyone. Others in this Fabulous Five series are: *Seventh-Grade Rumors* and *The Trouble with Flirting* (both 1988). (Rev: BL 2/15/89)

1032 Haynes, Mary. *Catch the Sea* (6–8). 1989, Bradbury $12.95 (0-02-743451-6). Left alone for a time by her artist father, Lily tries her hand at painting. (Rev: BL 6/1/89; SLJ 5/89; VOYA 6/89)

1033 Head, Ann. *Mr. and Mrs. Bo Jo Jones* (7–12). 1973, NAL paper $2.75 (0-451-15734-6). The perennial favorite about 2 teenagers madly in love but unprepared for the responsibilities of parenthood.

1034 Helldorfer, M. C. *Almost Home* (6–8). 1987, Bradbury $12.95 (0-02-743512-1). Jessie unwillingly spends a summer on a Maine island with her grandfather but while there forms a friendship with an unusual girl. (Rev: VOYA 12/87)

1035 Hentoff, Nat. *Does This School Have Capital Punishment?* (7–10). 1981, Dell paper $2.95 (0-440-92070-1). Sam is framed by a schoolmate on charges of drug use in this sequel to *This School Is Driving Me Crazy* (1976).

1036 Hentoff, Nat. *Jazz Country* (7–9). 1965, Harper LB $12.89 (0-06-022306-5); Dell paper $2.25 (0-440-94203-9). A young white boy tries to live in the black world of jazz.

1037 Hermes, Patricia. *Be Still My Heart* (7–10). 1989, Putnam $14.95 (0-399-21917-X). Allie and the boy she hopes will pay attention to her unite to help a teacher whose husband has AIDS. (Rev: BL 12/15/89; SLJ 12/89)

1038 Hermes, Patricia. *You Shouldn't Have to Say Goodbye* (7–9). 1982, Harcourt $11.95 (0-15-299944-2); Scholastic paper $2.50 (0-590-41359-7). A moving novel about a girl who must cope with her mother's death from cancer.

1039 Herzig, Alison. *Shadows on the Pond* (6–9). 1985, Little $14.95 (0-316-35895-9). A romance develops between Jill and Migan while they are trying to save some beavers in a pond. (Rev: BR 3–4/86)

1040 Hirsch, Linda. *You're Going Out There a Kid but You're Coming Back a Star* (6–8). 1984, Bantam paper $2.95 (0-553-15272-6). Ten-year-old Margaret wants to create a new self-image.

1041 Holl, Kristi. *Hidden in the Fog* (7–9). 1989, Macmillan $12.95 (0-689-31494-9). Nikki assumes adult responsibilities when her family faces financial problems that may cause them to sell their Mississippi river boat. (Rev: BR 9–10/89; VOYA 6/89)

1042 Holl, Kristi. *No Strings Attached* (6–8). 1988, Macmillan $12.95 (0-689-31399-3). A seventh-grader and her mother move in to take care of an old man who does not want to live in a retirement home. (Rev: BR 9–10/88)

1043 Holland, Isabelle. *The Man without A Face* (7–10). 1972, Harper $12.70 (0-397-31211-3); paper $2.95 (0-06-447028-8). Charles's close relations with his reclusive tutor leads to a physical experience.

1044 Hopper, Nancy J. *Lies* (7–9). 1984, Dutton $10.95 (0-525-67148-X). In order to attract a boyfriend, Allison begins lying about herself and her family.

1045 Hopper, Nancy J. *Rivals* (7–9). 1985, Dutton $10.95 (0-525-67171-4). Cousin Kate moves in and takes over not only Joni's boyfriends but also the boyfriends of Joni's friends. (Rev: BR 5–6/86)

1046 Hopper, Nancy J. *The Seven ½ Sins of Stacey Kendall* (7–9). 1982, Dutton $9.95 (0-525-45115-3); Dell paper $2.75 (0-440-47736-0). Stacey finds out the true meaning of beauty when she goes into the ear-piercing business.

1047 Howe, Norma. *The Game of Life* (7–10). 1989, Crown $13.95 (0-517-57197-8). Cairo copes with her sister's proposed marriage, falling in love, and the death of her dog in this novel about growing up. (Rev: BL 10/15/89; SLJ 10/89)

1048 Howe, Norma. *God, the Universe, and Hot Fudge Sundaes* (7–10). 1984, Houghton $11.95 (0-395-35488-8). A 16-year-old girl would like to share her mother's born-again faith but can't.

1049 Howe, Norma. *In with the Out Crowd* (7–10). 1986, Houghton $12.95 (0-395-40490-8). Robin tries to make other friends when she is ostracized by the in-crowd. (Rev: BL 11/1/86; BR 1–2/87; SLJ 1/87; VOYA 12/86)

1050 Howker, Janni. *Badger on the Barge: And Other Stories* (7–12). 1985, Greenwillow $11.95 (0-688-04215-5); Penguin paper $4.95 (0-14-032253-1). Five stories set in the north of England in which young people get help and insights from encounters with the elderly. (Rev: BL 6/1/85; BR 5–6/85; SLJ 5/85; VOYA 6/85)

1051 Hunt, Irene. *Up a Road Slowly* (6–9). 1987, Berkley paper $2.75 (0-425-10003-0). The girlhood of Julie Trelling—from her mother's death when she was a child to her high school graduation. Newbery Medal, 1967.

1052 Hunter, Mollie. *Cat, Herself* (7–10). 1986, Harper LB $12.89 (0-06-022635-8). Cat's life as part of an itinerant Scottish family is well described as is their fierce independence and hardships. (Rev: BL 6/1/86; SLJ 5/86; VOYA 6/86)

1053 Hunter, Mollie. *A Sound of Chariots* (6–10). 1972, Harper LB $12.89 (0-06-022669-2); paper $3.95 (0-06-440235-5). In post-World War I Scotland, Bridie's happy childhood ends when her father dies. A sequel is *Hold on to Love* (1983).

1054 Hurmence, Belinda. *The Nightwalker* (6–8). 1988, Clarion $12.95 (0-89919-732-9). A year-round resident of the fishing banks in South Carolina against her family's wishes befriends one of the "summer people." (Rev: BL 9/15/88)

1055 Irwin, Hadley. *The Lilith Summer* (6–8). 1979, Feminist Pr. $8.95 (0-912670-51-7). Ellen is taking care of a 77-year-old woman for the summer and learns a lot from the experience.

1056 Irwin, Hadley. *Moon and Me* (7–8). 1982, Macmillan $10.95 (0-689-50194-3). Fourteen-year-old E.J. is looking for romance but 12-year-old Moon, though helpful, doesn't seem to be the answer.

1057 Jacobs, Anita. *Where Has Deedie Wooster Been All These Years?* (7–9). 1981, Delacorte $9.95 (0-385-29133-7); Dell paper $2.25 (0-440-98955-8). Deedie writes about her problems, which include poor grades at school, lack of popularity, and adjusting to a brother's death.

1058 Johnston, Norma. *The Time of the Cranes* (7–10). 1990, Macmillan $13.95 (0-02-747713-4). A girl filled with self-doubt about her abilities receives an unexpected inheritance. (Rev: BL 4/1/90; SLJ 5/90; VOYA 6/88)

1059 Jones, Robin. *No Shakespeare Allowed* (7–12). 1989, Macmillan $12.95 (0-689-31488-4). Portia's parents would like her to follow them in a stage career but she would like to try other things. (Rev: BR 3–4/90; VOYA 12/89)

1060 Jordan, Hope Dahle. *Haunted Summer* (7–9). 1967, Lothrop $11.95 (0-688-41638-1). Rilla suffers pangs of conscience after she leaves the scene of an accident.

1061 Kassem, Lou. *Middle School Blues* (6–8). 1986, Houghton $12.95 (0-395-39499-6). Cindy finds that in her first year in middle school the pleasures and accomplishments outweigh the problems. (Rev: BL 8/86; SLJ 8/86)

1062 Kassem, Lou. *Secret Wishes* (6–8). 1989, Avon paper $2.50 (0-380-75544-0). A girl summons up her resources to try to lose weight to be a cheerleader. (Rev: SLJ 4/89)

1063 Kaufman, Stephen. *Does Anyone Here Know the Way to Thirteen?* (6–8). 1985, Houghton $11.95 (0-395-35974-0). Myron Saltz has 2 concerns, his upcoming bar mitzvah and his ineptitude at baseball. (Rev: BL 10/1/85; SLJ 8/85)

1064 Kaye, Marilyn. *Cassie* (6–9). 1987, Harcourt LB $13.95 (0-15-20042101); paper $4.95 (0-15-200422-X). A shoplifting incident forces Cassie to examine her values. A companion volume is *Lydia* (1987), about Cassie's older sister. (Rev: SLJ 12/87)

1065 Kemp, Gene. *Charlie Lewis Plays for Time* (7–9). Illus. 1984, Faber $11.95 (571-13248-0). When a favorite teacher is replaced by unpopular Mr. Carter, troubles begin for Charlie in this English novel.

1066 Kennedy, M. L. *Junior High Jitters* (6–8). 1986, Scholastic paper $2.25 (0-590-40342-7). Nora is afraid that newcomer Denise will take her best friend Jennifer away from her. (Rev: BL 12/15/86; SLJ 1/87)

1067 Kerr, M. E. *Dinky Hocker Shoots Smack!* (7–9). 1972, Harper LB $12.89 (0-06-023151-3). Overweight and underloved Dinky finds a unique way to gain her parents' attention.

1068 Kerr, M. E. *Gentlehands* (7–10). 1978, Harper LB $12.89 (0-06-023176-9). Could Buddy's beloved grandfather be a Nazi war criminal?

1069 Kerr, M. E. *Him She Loves?* (7–10). 1984, Harper LB $12.89 (0-06-023239-0); Putnam paper $2.25 (0-448-47732-7). Henry Schiller sets out to win Valerie, daughter of a famous comedian.

1070 Kerr, M. E. *I Stay Near You* (7–10). 1985, Harper LB $11.89 (0-06-023105-X); Berkley paper $2.50 (0-425-08870-7). These 3 stories of love and self-acceptance span 3 generations in a small town. (Rev: BL 4/15/85; BR 1–2/86; SLJ 4/85; VOYA 6/85)

1071 Kerr, M. E. *If I Love You, Am I Trapped Forever?* (7–10). 1973, Harper LB $12.89 (0-06-023749-1); paper $2.95 (0-06-447032-6). In spite of the fact that Alan Bennett has everything going for him including good looks, he still loses his girlfriend.

1072 Kerr, M. E. *I'll Love You When You're More Like Me* (7–10). 1977, Harper LB $12.89 (0-06-023137-8); paper $3.50 (0-06-447004-0). Wally's life changes when he meets Sabra St. Amour, teenage soap-opera queen.

1073 Kerr, M. E. *Is That You, Miss Blue?* (7–10). 1975, Harper LB $12.89 (0-06-023145-9); paper $2.95 (0-06-447033-4). A year at a private school seen through the eyes of a newcomer, Flanders Brown.

1074 Kerr, M. E. *Love Is a Missing Person* (7–10). 1975, Harper LB $13.89 (0-06-023162-9); paper $2.95 (0-06-447034-2). As a keen observer of human nature, Susan Slade is amazed at the effects that love has on people.

1075 Kerr, M. E. *The Son of Someone Famous* (7–10). 1974, Harper LB $12.89 (0-06-023147-5). In chapters alternately written by each, 2 teenagers in rural Vermont write about their friendship and their problems.

1076 Kerr, M. E. *What I Really Think of You* (7–10). 1982, Harper LB $12.89 (0-06-023189-0). The meeting of 2 teenagers who represent 2 kinds of religion—the evangelical mission and the TV pulpit.

1077 Kidd, Ronald. *Dunker* (7–9). 1984, Bantam paper $2.50 (0-553-26431-1). A star of a commercial for "Dunker Delights" wants to be accepted by his peers.

1078 King, Buzz. *Silicon Songs* (7–10). 1990, Delacorte $14.95 (0-385-30087-5). A homeless boy who is a computer whiz must confront the oncoming death of a beloved uncle. (Rev: BL 6/15/90; SLJ 6/90; VOYA 4/90)

1079 Kingman, Lee. *Break a Leg Betsy Maybe!* (7–10). 1979, Dell paper $1.95 (0-440-90794-2). Betsy matures quickly because of her experiences during her last year of high school.

1080 Kirshenbaum, Binnie. *Short Subject* (7–10). 1989, Watts LB $13.99 (0-531-08436-1). An underdeveloped teenager with many problems escapes into the glamorous world of movie-star daydreams. (Rev: BL 11/15/89; BR 1–2/90; SLJ 10/89; VOYA 12/89)

1081 Klass, David. *Wrestling with Honor* (7–12). 1988, Dutton $15.95 (0-525-67268-0). In an apparant mistake, Ron, captain of the wrestling team, tests positive in a drug test and his life begins to fall apart. (Rev: BL 11/15/88; SLJ 10/88; VOYA 12/88)

1082 Klass, Sheila Solomon. *Alive and Starting Over* (7–9). 1983, Macmillan $11.95 (0-684-17987-3). Jessica seems surrounded by other people's problems that she feels she must solve.

1083 Klass, Sheila Solomon. *Credit-Card Carole* (7–10). 1987, Macmillan $12.95 (0-684-18889-9); Bantam paper $2.50 (0-553-27355-8). When family finances get tough, Carole must change her spending ways and this in turn affects her social life. (Rev: BL 9/15/87; SLJ 10/87; VOYA 10/87)

1084 Klein, Norma. *Snapshots* (7–9). 1984, Dutton $12.95 (0-8037-0129-2); Fawcett paper $2.50 (0-449-70157-3). Two boys get in trouble when some photographs they take are considered pornographic.

1085 Klein, Norma. *Sunshine* (7–10). 1976, Avon paper $3.50 (0-380-00049-0). Based on fact, this is the story of a young woman's battle with a fatal disease.

1086 Klein, Robin. *Laurie Loved Me Best* (6–9). 1988, Viking $11.95 (0-670-82211-6). Two classmates find that they are infatuated with the same boy. (Rev: BL 3/1/89; SLJ 1/89)

1087 Klevin, Jill Ross. *The Best of Friends* (7–9). 1981, Scholastic paper $2.25 (0-590-33782-3). Two girls with serious differences show how friendship can develop.

1088 Klevin, Jill Ross. *The Turtle Street Trading Co.* (7–9). Illus. 1982, Delacorte LB $11.95 (0-385-29043-8). To make money to go to Disneyland, a group of teenagers become entrepreneurs. Followed by *Turtles Together Forever!* (1982).

1089 Konigsburg, E. L. *Jennifer, Hecate, Macbeth, William McKinley, and Me, Elizabeth* (6–8). 1967, Macmillan $12.95 (0-689-30007-7); Dell paper $2.75 (0-440-44162-5). Elizabeth finds a new friend in Jennifer, an unusual girl who is interested in witchcraft.

1090 Konigsburg, E. L. *Throwing Shadows* (7–10). 1988, Macmillan paper $3.95 (0-02-044140-1). Five short stories about teenagers learning about themselves and their emotions.

1091 Kroll, Steven. *Breaking Camp* (7–10). 1985, Macmillan $11.95 (0-02-751170-7). A new boy at summer camp rebells against the misuse of power by a fellow camper. (Rev: SLJ 1/86)

1092 Kropp, Paul. *Death Ride* (7–9). Illus. 1989, Macmillan paper $2.95 (0-02-041793-4). Tim must live with the guilt of causing a fatal car accident when under the influence of liquor and drugs. Easy reading. (Rev: SLJ 6/89; VOYA 12/89)

1093 Kropp, Paul. *Moonkid and Liberty* (6–9). 1990, Little $13.95 (0-316-50485-8). The teenage son and daughter of 2 hippies try to sort out their lives and plan for their future. (Rev: BL 6/15/90; SLJ 4/90; VOYA 6/90)

1094 Krumgold, Joseph. *Onion John* (6–8). 1959, Harper LB $12.89 (0-690-04698-7); paper $2.95 (0-06-440144-8). In this Newbery Medal winner, Andy is torn between 2 relationships—one with his father and the other with an old immigrant.

1095 Larimer, Tamela. *Buck* (7–10). 1986, Avon paper $2.50 (0-380-75172-0). The friendship between runaway Buck and Rich is threatened when Buck becomes friendly with Rich's girlfriend. (Rev: SLJ 6–7/87; VOYA 4/87)

1096 Lasky, Kathryn. *Pageant* (7–10). 1986, Macmillan $12.95 (0-02-751720-9); Dell paper $3.95 (0-440-20161-6). In the 1960s Sarah Benjamin, who is from a liberal Jewish background, has problems fitting into the WASP-ish private school she attends. (Rev: BL 11/15/86; BR 5–6/87; SLJ 12/86)

1097 Lawrence, Louise. *The Dram Road* (7–9). 1983, Harper LB $13.89 (0-06-023747-3). An English inner-city boy finds friendship while trying to avoid the police.

1098 Le Guin, Ursula K. *Very Far Away from Anywhere Else* (7–10). 1976, Macmillan $10.95 (0-689-30525-7). In his friendship for Natalie, Owen finds the fulfillment he yearns for.

1099 Lehrman, Robert. *Juggling* (7–10). 1984, Putnam paper $2.25 (0-399-21105-5). Howie is suffering with the strain of managing school, soccer, and a girlfriend all requiring his time.

1100 L'Engle, Madeleine. *Camilla* (7–10). 1982, Dell paper $3.25 (0-440-91171-0). Camilla becomes disillusioned with her parents and looks to her love Frank for support.

1101 L'Engle, Madeleine. *A House Like a Lotus* (7–12). 1984, Farrar $13.95 (0-374-33385-8); Dell paper $3.50 (0-440-93685-3). Polly O'Keefe, of previous L'Engle novels, is now 17 and encounters both lesbianism and a heterosexual romance in this probing novel.

1102 L'Engle, Madeleine. *A Ring of Endless Light* (7–10). 1980, Farrar $14.95 (0-374-36299-8); Dell paper $3.25 (0-440-97232-9). The Austin family are again central characters in this novel in which Vicki must adjust to her grandfather's death while exploring her telepathic powers with dolphins.

1103 Leroe, Ellen. *Confessions of a Teenage TV Addict* (7–9). 1983, Dutton $10.95 (0-525-66909-4); Berkley paper $2.50 (0-425-10252-1). When Jennifer transfers to a new school her life takes on the characteristics of a TV "soap."

1104 LeVert, John. *The Flight of the Cassowary* (8–10). 1986, Little $14.95 (0-316-52196-5); Bantam paper $2.95 (0-553-27389-2). John so identifies with animals and their behavior that he often feels he is an animal. (Rev: BL 4/1/86; BR 5–6/86; SLJ 5/86; VOYA 6/86)

1105 Levinson, Nancy Smiler. *The Ruthie Green Show* (6–9). 1985, Lodestar $11.95 (0-525-67172-2). A young girl beset with teen problems gets a chance to help on a TV show. (Rev: BR 9–10/86; SLJ 1/86)

1106 Levitin, Sonia. *Smile Like a Plastic Daisy* (7–9). 1984, Macmillan $12.95 (0-689-31024-2). Claudia's conversion to feminism causes trouble.

1107 Levoy, Myron. *A Shadow Like a Leopard* (7–9). 1981, Harper LB $12.89 (0-06-023817-8). The story of an unlikely friendship between a street-wise Puerto Rican punk and a wheelchair-ridden artist.

1108 Levoy, Myron. *Three Friends* (7–9). 1984, Harper LB $12.89 (0-06-023827-5). Three outsiders gain strength from their friendship.

1109 Lewis, Linda. *Is There Life After Boys?* (6–9). 1987, Archway paper $2.70 (0-671-63966-8). When Linda transfers to an all-girl school she finds the social change unbearable. (Rev: SLJ 2/88)

1110 Lipsyte, Robert. *One Fat Summer* (7–10). 1977, Harper $12.89 (0-06-023896-8). Bobby Marks at 14 loses weight and gains self-esteem in an eventful summer. Bobby is 16 in *Summer Rules* (1981) and 18 in *The Summer Boy* (1982).

1111 Lisle, Janet Taylor. *Sirens and Spies* (7–10). 1985, Macmillan $12.95 (0-02-759150-6). Elsie discovers that her beloved music teacher originally from France was an accused collaborator who had a child by a German soldier. (Rev: BL 5/15/85; SLJ 8/85; VOYA 12/85)

1112 Littke, Lael. *Loydene in Love* (8–10). 1986, Harcourt $13.95 (0-15-249888-5). A high school junior from a small town gets a different view of life when she visits Los Angeles for the summer. (Rev: BL 2/15/87; SLJ 3/87)

1113 Littke, Lael. *Shanny on Her Own* (6–9). 1985, Harcourt $12.95 (0-15-273531-3); Pocket paper $2.50 (0-691-62699-X). Shanny is sent to live with an aunt in rural Idaho to counteract her developing punkiness. (Rev: BL 1/1/86; SLJ 12/85; VOYA 4/86)

1114 Little, Jean. *Hey World, Here I Am!* (6–9). Illus. 1989, Harper LB $10.89 (0-06-024006-7). Kate, of *Look Through My Window* (1970), has a book of her own devoted to her poems, stories, and thoughts about life. (Rev: BL 7/89; SLJ 7/89)

1115 Little, Jean. *One to Grow On* (6–8). 1988, Little paper $4.95 (0-316-52793-9). Through a number of rather unpleasant experiences, Janie gains confidence in herself.

1116 Lovelace, Maude Hart. *Betsy Was a Junior* (6–9). 1947, Harper $14.70 (0-690-13946-2). In this book, which is part of a long series, Betsy is a junior in high school.

1117 Lowry, Lois. *Taking Care of Terrific* (7–9). 1983, Houghton $12.95 (0-395-34070-5); Dell paper $2.95 (0-440-48494-4). A baby-sitting job leads to all sorts of hectic adventures for 14-year-old Enid.

1118 Lyon, George Ella. *Red Rover, Red Rover* (6–8). 1989, Watts LB $12.99 (0-531-08432-9). Poised to enter the teen years, Sumi encounters many problems, including the death of her grandfather and the moving of her best friend. (Rev: BL 9/1/89; BR 1–2/90; SLJ 11/89; VOYA 12/89)

1119 McCall, Dan. *Jack the Bear* (7–9). 1981, Fawcett paper $1.95 (0-449-70009-7). After the death of his wife, a father has difficulty relating to his son.

1120 McCall, Edith. *Better Than a Brother* (6–9). 1988, Walker LB $14.85 (0-8027-6783-4). Hughie turns to her friend Jerry for help when she loses her new gold locket. (Rev: BR 9–10/88; SLJ 5/88)

1121 McCaughrean, Geraldine. *A Pack of Lies* (7–12). 1989, Oxford Univ. Pr. $14.95 (0-19-271612-3). Ailsa and her mother take in a homeless man who tells extremely unusual stories. (Rev: SLJ 5/89)

1122 McCutcheon, Elsie. *Storm Bird* (6–8). 1987, Farrar $11.95 (0-374-37269-1). In turn-of-century England, Jenny is sent to live in a coastal town with a mysterious aunt. (Rev: BL 10/1/87; SLJ 12/87)

1123 McDonnell, Christine. *Friends First* (6–8). 1990, Viking $11.95 (0-670-81923-9). The years-old friendship of Miranda and Gus becomes strained with the pressures of adolescence. (Rev: BL 6/15/90; SLJ 6/90)

1124 McDonnell, Margot. *My Own Worst Enemy* (7–9). 1984, Pacer $11.95 (0-399-21102-0); paper $2.50 (0-425-08425-6). After a bitter, hostile beginning the friendship between Todd and Robbie gradually develops.

1125 McFann, Jane. *One More Chance* (6–9). 1988, Avon paper $2.50 (0-380-75466-5). Cath works out a number of problems such as what to do with an old boyfriend and whether she should go to live with her father abroad. (Rev: VOYA 2/89)

1126 McHargue, Georgess. *See You Later, Crocodile* (6–8). 1988, Doubleday $14.95 (0-440-50052-4). Young Johanna befriends a cranky old lady and her 15 cats. (Rev: BL 1/1/89; SLJ 12/88; VOYA 12/88)

1127 McKay, Robert. *The Troublemaker* (7–10). 1972, Dell paper $1.50 (0-440-99122-6). A new boy in Garfield High School comes with a bad reputation he finds difficult to live down.

1128 MacLachlan, Patricia. *Unclaimed Treasures* (6–8). 1984, Harper $11.95 (0-06-024093-8); paper $2.95 (0-06-440189-8). Wila and her twin brother plus friend Horace spend an unusual and productive summer.

1129 McLean, Susan. *Pennies for the Piper* (7–9). 1981, Farrar $10.95 (0-374-35791-9). A teenage girl faces the problem of living after her mother has died.

1130 Madison, Winifred. *Growing Up in a Hurry* (7–10). 1975, Archway paper $1.95 (0-671-44238-4). Karen, alienated from her family, discovers she must turn to them when she finds she is pregnant.

1131 Maguire, Jesse. *Nowhere High* (6–9). 1990, Ivy paper $2.95 (0-8041-0444-1). T.J. is new to a high school in a depressed Pennsylvania mill town and has some problems adjusting. (Rev: SLJ 6/90; VOYA 6/90)

1132 Mahoney, Mary Reeves. *The Hurry-Up Summer* (5–8). 1987, Putnam LB $13.95 (0-399-21430-5). Twelve-year-old Letty decides, when the family housekeeper leaves, to grow up quickly to prove to her father that she is independent and does not need someone to look after her. (Rev: SLJ 1/88)

1133 Mahy, Margaret. *The Catalogue of the Universe* (8–12). 1986, Macmillan $12.95 (0-689-50391-1); Scholastic paper $2.50 (0-590-40450-4). Through their friendship Angela who longs to meet her absent father and Tycho who believes

he is physically ugly find tenderness and compassion. (Rev: BL 3/15/86; SLJ 4/86; VOYA 12/86)

1134 Major, Kevin. *Dear Bruce Springsteen* (6–9). 1988, Delacorte $14.95 (0-385-29584-7). In a series of letters to his idol, a 14-year-old boy writes about his problems and his dream of becoming a guitarist. (Rev: BL 2/15/88; SLJ 5/88)

1135 Makris, Kathryn. *A Different Way* (7–10). 1989, Avon paper $2.95 (0-380-75728-1). A newcomer in a Texas high school wonders if acceptance by the in crowd is worth the effort. (Rev: BL 10/15/89)

1136 Malmgren, Dallin. *The Ninth Issue* (7–12). 1989, Doubleday $14.95 (0-440-50124-5). Eight high school students and their teacher decide to breathe new life into the school newspaper. (Rev: BL 3/1/89; BR 9–10/89; SLJ 3/89; VOYA 6/89)

1137 Manes, Stephen. *The Obnoxious Jerks* (7–10). 1988, Bantam $13.95 (0-553-05488-0). A school club, the Jerks, engage in some strange behavior to prove their points. (Rev: BL 8/88; BR 9–10/88; SLJ 8/88; VOYA 10/88)

1138 Manes, Stephen. *Video War* (7–9). 1983, Avon paper $2.25 (0-380-83303-4). A group of teenagers fight to save their video arcade after there is a threat of it being closed.

1139 Mango, Karin N. *Somewhere Green* (7–12). 1987, Macmillan $13.95 (0-02-762270-3). When their parents leave for Brazil, 2 sisters and a brother try to live independently in their new home in Brooklyn. (Rev: BL 12/15/87; VOYA 12/87)

1140 Mark, Jan. *Handles* (6–8). 1985, Macmillan $12.95 (0-689-31140-0); Penguin paper $3.50 (0-14-031587-X). To help pass a tedious summer at her aunt's home, Erica begins helping at a local motorcycle repair shop. (Rev: BL 7/85; SLJ 8/85)

1141 Mark, Jan. *Thunder and Lightnings* (6–9). Illus. 1976, Harper $11.70 (0-690-03901-8). Andrew slowly develops an interest in airplanes through his friendship with Victor, who is considered a slow learner.

1142 Martin, Ann M. *Bummer Summer* (7–9). 1983, Holiday $13.95 (0-8234-0483-8); Scholastic paper $2.50 (0-590-41308-2). While her stepmother is moving in, a young girl is sent to spend a summer at Camp Arrowhead.

1143 Martin, Ann M. *The Slam Book* (6–9). 1987, Holiday $12.95 (0-0834-0666-0). Revealing the contents of a notebook in which students write freely about each other leads to broken friendships and a suicide. (Rev: SLJ 12/87; VOYA 2/88)

1144 Martin, Ann M. *Stage Fright* (6–9). Illus. 1984, Holiday $13.95 (0-8234-0541-9); Scholastic paper $2.50 (0-590-40874-7). A fourth-grade girl must conquer her fear of facing an audience when she must perform before the entire school.

1145 Martin, Guenn. *Remember the Eagle Day* (7–9). 1984, Herald Pr. paper $4.95 (0-8361-3351-X). On a remote Alaskan island, Melanie finds friendship with an ill-tempered hermit named Long Jake.

1146 Matthews, Phoebe. *Switchstance* (7–10). 1989, Avon paper $3.50 (0-380-75729-X). After her parents' divorce, Elvy moves in with her grandmother and forms friendships with 2 very different boys. (Rev: VOYA 2/90)

1147 Mauser, Pat Rhoads. *Rip-Off* (6–9). 1985, Macmillan $11.95 (0-689-31134-6). In an effort to be accepted at her new school, Ginger gets involved with some kids who shoplift and she is caught. (Rev: BL 12/1/85; SLJ 12/85; VOYA 4/86)

1148 Maxwell, Edith. *Just Dial a Number* (7–9). 1988, Archway paper $2.75 (0-671-67422-6). A prank call has serious results for 4 teenagers. A reissue.

1149 Mayhar, Ardath. *Carrots and Miggle* (6–8). 1986, Macmillan $12.95 (0-689-31184-2). Slowly Carrots and her cousin from Hungary nicknamed Miggle become friends in this novel set on an east Texas dairy farm. (Rev: BL 7/86; SLJ 5/86)

1150 Mazer, Harry. *Hey, Kid! Does She Love Me?* (7–12). 1984, Harper LB $12.89 (0-690-04276-0). Stage-struck Jeff falls in love with a woman who was once an aspiring actress in this romance that contains some sexually explicit language.

1151 Mazer, Harry. *The Island Keeper* (7–10). 1981, Delacorte $11.95 (0-385-28446-2); Dell paper $2.95 (0-440-94774-X). Feeling completely alone in this world, Cleo decides to run away to a desolate island that her father owns.

1152 Mazer, Harry. *The War on Villa Street* (7–9). 1988, Dell paper $2.95 (0-440-99062-9). Willie is trying to survive an alcoholic father at home and cruel bullies at school. A reissue.

1153 Mazer, Norma Fox. *A, My Name Is Ami* (6–8). 1986, Scholastic paper $2.25 (0-590-40054-1). Ami's friendship with Mia helps her overcome the problem of her parents' separation. (Rev: BL 9/15/86; SLJ 12/86; VOYA 12/86)

1154 Mazer, Norma Fox. *B, My Name Is Bunny* (6–8). 1987, Scholastic $12.95 (0-590-40930-1); paper $2.50 (0-590-40930-X). The story of the friendship between Bunny, a lively 13 year old,

and Emily, a quiet one. (Rev: BL 3/1/87; SLJ 3/87; VOYA 6/87)

1155 Mazer, Norma Fox. *Someone to Love* (7–12). 1983, Delacorte $13.95 (0-440-08311-7); Dell paper $3.25 (0-440-98062-3). A lonely college student moves in with her boyfriend, a dropout.

1156 Mazer, Norma Fox. *Summer Girls, Love Boys and Other Short Stories* (7–10). 1982, Delacorte $11.95 (0-385-28930-8); Dell paper $2.95 (0-440-98375-4). Stories about love and growing up, all set in the same neighborhood.

1157 Mazer, Norma Fox. *When We First Met* (7–10). 1984, Scholastic paper $2.50 (0-590-40359-1). At school Jenny tries to avoid the son of the woman who was responsible for her sister's death.

1158 Medearis, Mary. *Big Doc's Girl* (7–10). 1985, August House paper $6.95 (0-935304-87-8). The novel that originally appeared in 1942 about love and a young girl's reaction to her father's death. (Rev: SLJ 2/86)

1159 Meyer, Carolyn. *Elliott & Win* (8–10). 1986, Macmillan $12.95 (0-689-50368-7); paper $3.95 (0-02-044702-7). Win, a typical teenager, is paired with a well-meaning but effete adult named Elliott Deerfield in the local Big Brother program. (Rev: BL 4/15/86; SLJ 3/86; VOYA 8–10/86)

1160 Miklowitz, Gloria D. *The Emerson High Vigilantes* (7–12). 1988, Delacorte $14.95 (0-385-29637-1). Paul, the editor of the school newspaper, is manipulated by a candidate for the school presidency. (Rev: BL 3/15/88; BR 5–6/88; SLJ 5/88; VOYA 6/88)

1161 Miklowitz, Gloria D. *The Love Bombers* (7–10). 1980, Delacorte paper $8.95 (0-385-28545-0). With the help of Rick, Jenna tries to save her brother from a religious cult.

1162 Miles, Betty. *Looking On* (6–8). 1979, Knopf LB $6.95 (0-394-83582-4); Avon paper $2.50 (0-380-70061-1). An unhappy 14-year-old adopts a young married couple next door but finds they, too, have problems.

1163 Miles, Betty. *The Real Me* (6–8). 1975, Knopf LB $7.99 (0-394-92838-5); Avon paper $2.75 (0-380-00347-3). Barbara rebels against all the restrictions placed on her life because she is a girl.

1164 Miles, Betty. *The Trouble with Thirteen* (6–9). 1979, Knopf LB $10.99 (0-394-93930-1); paper $2.95 (0-394-82043-6). Divorce and death among other changes make 2 friends realize that they are growing up.

1165 Miller, Jim Wayne. *Newfound* (7–12). 1989, Watts LB $13.99 (0-531-08445-0). A boy's life from sixth grade to college while growing up in a divided Appalachian family. (Rev: BL 12/1/89; BR 5–6/90; SLJ 10/89; VOYA 12/89)

1166 Morey, Walt. *Run Far, Run Fast* (6–8). 1984, Avon paper $1.50 (0-380-43356-7). Nick, a 16-year-old runaway, becomes involved with a family in the Pacific Northwest. Also use *Sandy and the Rock Star* (1979).

1167 Mueller, Amelia. *Sissy Kid Brother* (6–8). Illus. 1975, Herald Pr. paper $4.95 (0-8361-1754-9). A 14-year-old boy gains maturity when he works with his older brothers.

1168 Mulford, Philippa Greene. *If It's Not Funny, Why Am I Laughing?* (8–10). 1982, Delacorte $10.95 (0-385-28441-1). Mimi has many things to adjust to: her mother's new career, father's remarriage, and boyfriend Lars who wants more than holding hands.

1169 Myers, Walter Dean. *It Ain't All for Nothin'* (7–10). 1978, Avon paper $1.75 (0-380-47621-5). Taken from his sick grandmother in Harlem to live with his father, Tippy learns about the harsh realities of life.

1170 Myers, Walter Dean. *Won't Know Till I Get There* (7–10). 1982, Viking $11.95 (0-670-77862-1); Penguin paper $3.95 (0-14-032612-X). A young subway graffiti artist is sentenced to help out in a senior citizens' home.

1171 Namovicz, Gene Inyart. *To Talk in Time* (6–9). 1987, Macmillan $11.95 (0-02-768170-X). Luke, a painfully shy boy, must take the responsibility of locating a stranger who might accidentally have contracted rabies. (Rev: BR 11–12/87; SLJ 3/87)

1172 Naylor, Phyllis Reynolds. *A String of Chances* (7–9). 1983, Fawcett paper $2.25 (0-449-70075-5). Evie faces maturation problems including the death of a cousin's baby and questioning his own religious faith.

1173 Neville, Emily C. *It's Like This, Cat* (7–9). Illus. 1963, Harper LB $12.89 (0-06-024391-0); paper $2.95 (0-06-440073-5). A New York City 14-year-old boy has more in common with his cat than his father. Newberry Medal, 1964.

1174 Neville, Emily C. *The Seventeenth-Street Gang* (6–8). 1966, Harper paper $2.95 (0-06-440019-0). Minnow and her group decide not to make friends with the new boy in the neighborhood, Hillis.

1175 Newton, Suzanne. *I Will Call It Georgie's Blues* (7–9). 1983, Viking $12.95 (0-670-39131-X); Dell paper $2.75 (0-440-94090-7). Neal and

his family must cope with a bullying, rigid father who is a Baptist minister.

1176 Newton, Suzanne. *M.V. Sexton Speaking* (7–9). 1981, Viking $9.95 (0-670-44505-3); Fawcett paper $2.25 (0-449-70049-6). An orphaned girl gains friends and a sense of self-worth through her job at a bakery.

1177 Newton, Suzanne. *A Place Between* (6–8). 1986, Viking $12.95 (0-670-80778-8). Arden has problems adjusting when she and her family move from her hometown in this sequel to *An End to Perfect* (1984). (Rev: BL 10/1/86; SLJ 11/86)

1178 Newton, Suzanne. *Reubella and the Old Focus Home* (6–8). 1978, Westminster $7.95 (0-664-32635-8). Her friendship with 3 strange elderly women changes Reubella's life forever.

1179 Nielsen, Shelly. *Just Victoria* (6–9). 1986, Cook paper $3.95 (0-89191-609-1). The thoughts and feelings of a junior high school girl are explored in this account which is continued in *Only Kidding, Victoria* and *Take a Bow, Victoria* (both 1986). (Rev: SLJ 2/87)

1180 Nixon, Joan Lowery. *Maggie Forevermore* (5–8). 1987, Harcourt LB $13.95 (0-15-250345-5); Dell paper $2.95 (0-440-40211-5). In this sequel to *Maggie, Too* (1985) and *And Maggie Makes Three* (1986), 13-year-old Maggie resents spending Christmas with her father and his new wife in California. (Rev: SLJ 3/87)

1181 O'Connor, Jane. *Yours Till Niagara Falls, Abby* (7–9). Illus. 1979, Scholastic paper $2.50 (0-590-41119-5). Only after her missing roommate arrives at Camp Pinecrest does Abby try to fit in.

1182 O'Dell, Scott. *Kathleen, Please Come Home* (7–10). 1978, Houghton $12.95 (0-395-26453-7); Dell paper $2.25 (0-440-94283-7). Kathleen's mother is pleading for the return of her runaway daughter.

1183 Offit, Sidney. *What Kind of Guy Do You Think I Am?* (7–10). 1979, Dell paper $1.75 (0-440-99455-1). Hilary and Ted decide to continue seeing each other in spite of family objections.

1184 Okimoto, Jean Davies. *Jason's Women* (7–10). 1986, Atlantic Monthly $13.95 (0-87113-061-0). Jason's life changes when he answers 2 want ads—one to meet a dark-eyed beauty and the other to work for an old lady. (Rev: BL 5/1/86; BR 9–10/86; SLJ 8/86; VOYA 6/86)

1185 Oppenheimer, Joan. *A Clown Like Me* (6–9). 1985, Harper LB $12.89 (0-690-04284-1). Shelly, a natural comic, believes she will blossom at a 4-H clowning class. (Rev: BL 6/1/85; BR 9–10/85; SLJ 8/85; VOYA 6/85)

1186 Oppenheimer, Joan. *Working on It* (7–9). 1980, Dell paper $2.25 (0-440-99514-0). Tracy is a klutz until she joins a drama class.

1187 Orden, J. Hannah. *In Real Life* (7–10). 1990, Viking $12.95 (0-670-82679-0). Marty must choose between steady loyal Ron and the troubled Brent. (Rev: BL 4/15/90; SLJ 4/90)

1188 Pasnak, William. *Exit Stage Left* (6–9). 1987, Scholastic paper $2.50 (0-590-41478-X). There is great excitement at Degrassi Junior High because the school play is being presented. Part of a series. (Rev: VOYA 10/88)

1189 Paterson, Katherine. *Jacob Have I Loved* (7–10). 1980, Harper LB $12.89 (0-690-04079-2); Avon paper $2.95 (0-380-56499-8). Louise resents her twin sister's beauty and accomplishments in this novel set in the Chesapeake Bay area.

1190 Paulsen, Gary. *The Boy Who Owned the School* (6–9). 1990, Watts LB $11.99 (0-531-08465-5). Jacob's main object in life is to be as invisible as possible and to avoid trouble. (Rev: BL 4/1/90; SLJ 4/90; VOYA 6/90)

1191 Paulsen, Gary. *Dancing Carl* (7–9). 1983, Bradbury $10.95 (0-02-770210-3). A young boy recalls his friendship with Carl, a troubled man who is an expert ice skater.

1192 Paulsen, Gary. *The Island* (7–10). 1988, Watts LB $13.99 (0-531-08349-7). A 15-year-old boy finds peace and a meaning to life when he explores his own private island. (Rev: BL 3/15/88; BR 9–10/88; SLJ 5/88; VOYA 6/88)

1193 Paulsen, Gary. *Tracker* (7–9). 1984, Bradbury $10.95 (0-02-770220-0); paper $3.95 (0-317-62280-3). John's encounters with nature help him accept the approaching death of his grandfather.

1194 Pearson, Kit. *The Daring Game* (5–8). 1986, Viking $11.95 (0-670-80751-6). Eliza gets into trouble at her new boarding school when she follows the lead of a mischievous classmate. (Rev: SLJ 2/87)

1195 Peck, Richard. *Close Enough to Touch* (7–10). 1981, Delacorte $13.95 (0-384-28145-5); Dell paper $2.25 (0-440-91282-2). Through his friendship with Margaret, Matt is able to come to terms concerning the death of Dory, his girlfriend.

1196 Peck, Richard. *Princess Ashley* (7–12). 1987, Delacorte $14.95 (0-385-29561-8); Dell paper $2.95 (0-440-20206-X). Chelsea wonders how much it is worth to be accepted by the in-crowd.

(Rev: BL 5/15/87; BR 9–10/87; SLJ 8/87; VOYA 6/87)

1197 Peck, Richard. *Representing Super Doll* (7–9). 1982, Dell paper $2.95 (0-440-97362-7). A behind-the-scenes look at teen beauty contests and their consequences.

1198 Pendergraft, Patricia. *Brushy Mountain* (6–8). 1989, Putnam $14.95 (0-399-21610-3). Young Arney at first finds it almost impossible to like old Tice Hooker in this novel set in rural America. (Rev: BL 4/15/89; BR 11–12/89; SLJ 6/89; VOYA 6/89)

1199 Pendergraft, Patricia. *Hear the Wind Blow* (6–9). 1988, Putnam $14.95 (0-399-21528-X). Isadora, age 12 and growing up in a poor community, dreams one day of being a famous dancer like her namesake. (Rev: VOYA 8/88)

1200 Perl, Lila. *Fat Glenda's Summer Romance* (6–8). 1986, Clarion $12.95 (0-89919-447-8); Pocket paper $2.50 (0-671-64857-8). When Glenda, who had a weight problem, gets a summer job as a waitress, she must be sure to stay slim. Others in this series are *Me and Fat Glenda* (1979) and *Hey, Remember Fat Glenda* (1981). (Rev: BL 9/1/86; BR 9–10/87)

1201 Perl, Lila. *The Secret Diary of Katie Dinkerhoff* (6–8). 1987, Scholastic $11.95 (0-590-41131-4); paper $2.50 (0-590-41132-2). Katie writes in her diary a day in advance and finds she is able to foretell some events. (Rev: BL 10/15/87; SLJ 10/87; VOYA 12/87)

1202 Petersen, P. J. *Corky and the Brothers Cool* (6–8). 1985, Delacorte $14.95 (0-385-29377-1); Dell paper $2.75 (0-440-91624-0). Tim's new friendship with Corky is tested when Corky's true nature emerges. (Rev: BL 5/1/85)

1203 Petersen, P. J. *Good-bye to Good Ol' Charlie* (7–10). 1987, Delacorte $14.95 (0-385-29483-2). A 16-year-old boy uses the opportunity of moving to another town to experiment with a change of self-image. (Rev: BL 1/15/87; SLJ 2/87; VOYA 4/87)

1204 Petersen, P. J. *Would You Settle for Improbable?* (7–10). 1981, Delacorte LB $8.44 (0-440-09672-3); Dell paper $3.25 (0-440-99733-X). Three junior high chums try to accomplish the impossible task of rehabilitating a confirmed juvenile delinquent. Followed by *Here's to the Sophomores* (1984).

1205 Pevsner, Stella. *And You Give Me a Pain, Elaine* (7–9). 1978, Clarion $12.95 (0-395-28877-0); Archway paper $2.75 (0-671-68838-3). Andrea is in conflict with her older sister, Elaine, age 16.

1206 Pevsner, Stella. *Call Me Heller, That's My Name* (7–9). 1973, Clarion $7.95 (0-395-28874-6). Hildegard, alias Heller, finally calms down and admits she is a girl.

1207 Pevsner, Stella. *Cute Is a Four-Letter Word* (7–9). 1980, Houghton $13.95 (0-395-29106-2); Archway paper $2.75 (0-671-68845-6). The best-laid plans of Clara go awry.

1208 Pevsner, Stella. *I'll Always Remember You . . . Maybe* (7–10). 1981, Clarion $12.95 (0-395-31024-5). Darien remembers her senior year at high school and her 2 loves.

1209 Pfeffer, Susan Beth. *About David* (7–10). 1980, Delacorte $11.95 (0-385-28013-0); Dell paper $2.25 (0-440-90022-0). David kills his parents and himself—and his friends must sort out the pieces.

1210 Pfeffer, Susan Beth. *Getting Even* (7–10). 1986, Putnam $13.95 (0-448-47777-7). Annie Powell, first seen in *Fantasy Summer* (1986), begins an eventful senior year in a high school in Boston. (Rev: BR 11–12/86; SLJ 11/86)

1211 Pfeffer, Susan Beth. *Kid Power* (6–9). Illus. 1977, Watts LB $12.90 (0-531-00123-7); Scholastic paper $2.50 (0-590-41003-2). A group of younsters join together to do jobs for money.

1212 Pfeffer, Susan Beth. *Paperdolls* (7–9). 1984, Dell paper $2.25 (0-440-96777-5). Laurie must choose between her average suburban life and one of fashion and glamour.

1213 Pfeffer, Susan Beth. *Starring Peter and Leigh* (7–9). 1978, Delacorte $7.95 (0-440-08226-9). In spite of all the glamour and attention, 16-year-old TV star Leigh longs for a quieter life.

1214 Pfeffer, Susan Beth. *Starting with Melodie* (6–9). 1982, Scholastic paper $2.50 (0-590-41213-2). Elaine envies her friend Melodie and her wealth until Melodie's parents begin divorce proceedings.

1215 Pfeffer, Susan Beth. *Truth or Dare* (6–8). 1983, Scholastic paper $2.50 (0-590-41104-7). In this easily read story, Cathy thinks she has a friend in sophisticated Jessica but learns differently later.

1216 Phipson, Joan. *Bianca* (7–10). 1988, Macmillan $12.95 (0-689-50448-9). Seventeen-year-old Hubert and his younger sister become involved with a strange, reclusive girl named Bianca. (Rev: BL 9/1/88; SLJ 11/88; VOYA 4/89)

1217 Pilling, Ann. *The Big Pink* (6–9). 1988, Viking $11.95 (0-670-81156-4). In this English novel, teenage Angela tries to gain acceptance at her new boarding school. (Rev: BL 6/15/88; BR 1–2/89; SLJ 4/88)

1218 Platt, Kin. *Crocker* (7–10). 1983, Harper $11.70 (0-397-32025-6). Dorothy is attracted to a new boy in school.

1219 Pollock, Penny. *Summer Captive* (6–9). 1987, Shoe Tree $14.95 (0-936915-06-4). Thirteen-year-old Jesse faces the problem of helping his difficult father when his mother is seriously injured. (Rev: BL 2/15/88; SLJ 1/88)

1220 Pople, Maureen. *A Nugget of Gold* (7–10). 1989, Henry Holt $13.95 (0-8050-0984-1). Two Australian teenagers, one modern and the other from 100 years ago, tell their stories in alternating chapters. (Rev: BL 4/1/89; BR 9–10/89; SLJ 4/89; VOYA 10/89)

1221 Poynter, Margaret. *A Time Too Swift* (7–10). 1990, Macmillan $12.95 (0-689-31146-X). The effects of World War II on a 15-year-old girl and her circle of friends. (Rev: BL 2/1/90; SLJ 3/90; VOYA 4/90)

1222 Quin-Harkin, Janet. *Big Sister* (7–10). 1988, Ballantine paper $2.95 (0-8041-0081-0). Chrissy and her young brother Will come to terms with each other. Also use in the same series: *Out in the Cold* (1988). (Rev: SLJ 10/88)

1223 Reit, Ann. *I Thought You Were My Best Friend* (6–9). 1988, Scholastic paper $2.50 (0-590-40445-8). Can their mutual attraction for Quent Younger destroy the close friendship that Eve and Phoebe share? (Rev: SLJ 7/89)

1224 Riddell, Ruth. *Haunted Journey* (6–10). 1988, Macmillan $13.95 (0-689-31429-9). A young boy assumes financial responsibilities for his family while also trying to develop his own talents. (Rev: BL 12/1/88; BR 5–6/89; SLJ 10/88; VOYA 2/89)

1225 Rinaldi, Ann. *The Good Side of My Heart* (8–10). 1987, Holiday $13.95 (0-8234-0648-2). In this sequel to *But in the Fall I'm Leaving* (1987), 16-year-old Brie falls in love with a boy whom her parents forbid her to see. (Rev: SLJ 8/87; VOYA 8–9/87)

1226 Roberts, Rachel Sherwood. *Crisis at Pemberton Dike* (6–8). 1984, Herald Pr. paper $4.95 (0-8361-3350-1). While helping victims of a severe flood, teenager Carol is able to sort out some of her own personal problems.

1227 Robinson, Nancy K. *Wendy and the Bullies* (6–8). Illus. 1980, Hastings LB $9.89 (0-8038-9302-7); Scholastic paper $2.50 (0-590-32975-8). Wendy has to face Stanley, the biggest bully, all by herself.

1228 Rodowsky, Colby. *Sydney, Herself* (7–12). 1989, Farrar $12.95 (0-374-30649-4). In her fantasies, an Australian teenager invents a new identity for herself. (Rev: BL 8/89; SLJ 7/89; VOYA 10/89)

1229 Roe, Elaine Corbeil. *Circle of Light* (7–9). 1989, Harper LB $13.89 (0-06-025079-8). An eighth-grade girl accepts the challenge to enter a school scholarship competition in this novel set in French Canada. (Rev: BL 9/15/89; SLJ 11/89; VOYA 6/90)

1230 Roos, Stephen. *Confessions of a Wayward Preppie* (7–10). 1986, Delacorte $13.95 (0-385-29454-9); Dell paper $2.75 (0-440-91586-4). Through an unusual bequest, Cary is able to attend a classy prep school but there his troubles begin. (Rev: BL 6/1/86; BR 9–10/86; SLJ 5/86; VOYA 8–10/86)

1231 Roos, Stephen. *Thirteenth Summer* (6–8). Illus. 1987, Macmillan $12.95 (0-689-31299-7). Pink must decide whether to work in his family's boatyard or attend a fashionable prep school with his friend. (Rev: BL 10/15/87; VOYA 10/87)

1232 Roth, Arthur. *The Caretaker* (7–10). 1981, Fawcett paper $1.95 (0-449-70013-5). Though only 17, Mark has shouldered adult responsibilities.

1233 Ruckman, Ivy. *What's an Average Kid Like Me Doing Way up Here?* (6–8). 1983, Delacorte LB $11.95 (0-385-29251-1); Dell paper $2.75 (0-440-49448-6). A group of seventh graders fight the closing of their middle school.

1234 Rue, Nancy N. *The Janis Project* (7–10). 1988, Good News paper $7.95 (0-89107-486-4). A shy girl finds confidence in succeeding at track and through the friendship of a minister's son. (Rev: BL 1/1/89; SLJ 1/89; VOYA 6/89)

1235 Ryan, Mary E. *I'd Rather Be Dancing* (7–10). 1989, Doubleday $14.95 (0-440-50121-0). Katie Kusik spends a stimulating summer in New York at a dance conservatory in this sequel to *Dance a Little Closer* (1988). (Rev: BL 1/15/89; BR 3–4/89; SLJ 2/89; VOYA 4/89)

1236 Rylant, Cynthia. *A Fine White Dust* (6–8). 1986, Bradbury $11.95 (0-02-777240-3); Dell paper $2.75 (0-440-42499-2). A 13-year-old boy falls under the spell of a traveling preacher with tragic results. (Rev: BL 9/1/86; BR 3–4/87; SLJ 9/86)

1237 Sachs, Marilyn. *Almost Fifteen* (6–8). 1987, Dutton $12.95 (0-525-44285-5); Avon paper $2.95 (0-380-10357-1). A lightweight story of a practical girl, her boyfriends, and her impractical parents. (Rev: BL 6/15/87; SLJ 5/87)

1238 Sachs, Marilyn. *Beach Towels* (7–9). 1982, Dutton $11.95 (0-525-44003-8). The chronicle of a friendship between 2 teenage girls.

1239 Sachs, Marilyn. *Bus Ride* (6–9). Illus. 1980, Dutton $10.95 (0-525-27325-5). Two seeming losers, Judy and Ernie, form a friendship during their many bus rides to school.

1240 Sachs, Marilyn. *Class Pictures* (7–9). 1980, Dutton LB $13.95 (0-525-27985-7); Avon paper $2.95 (0-380-61408-1). The friendship from kindergarten through high school between 2 girls is recalled through old class pictures.

1241 Sachs, Marilyn. *The Fat Girl* (7–10). 1984, Dutton $13.95 (0-525-44076-3); Dell paper $2.75 (0-440-02468-5). Jeff decides to transform Ellen, the very fat girl in his ceramics class.

1242 Sachs, Marilyn. *Fourteen* (7–9). 1983, Dutton $10.95 (0-525-44044-5); Avon paper $2.50 (0-380-69842-0). First love comes to Rebecca by way of a new neighbor.

1243 Sachs, Marilyn. *Peter and Veronica* (7–9). 1987, Scholastic paper $2.50 (0-590-40404-0). Peter's friendship with non-Jewish Veronica faces a crisis over his bar mitzvah.

1244 Sachs, Marilyn. *A Secret Friend* (7–9). 1978, Scholastic paper $2.50 (0-590-40403-2). Jessica thinks she has lost her best friend until she begins to receive mysterious friendly notes.

1245 Sachs, Marilyn. *A Summer's Lease* (7–9). 1979, Dutton $9.25 (0-525-40480-5). Gloria is unhappy about sharing the editorship of the school's literary magazine with Jerry Lieberman.

1246 St. George, Judith. *What's Happening to My Junior Year?* (7–10). 1986, Putnam $13.95 (0-399-21316-3). When Stephanie's do-gooder mother invites some local troubled teenagers to use their newly installed pool table, Stephanie becomes exposed to a different slice of life. (Rev: BL 12/15/86; SLJ 2/87; VOYA 2/87)

1247 Samuels, Gertrude. *Run, Shelly, Run* (7–10). 1974, Harper $12.70 (0-690-00295-5); NAL paper $2.50 (0-451-13987-9). A harrowing story about a 16-year-old runaway and her experiences.

1248 Savage, Deborah. *Flight of the Albatross* (7–10). 1989, Houghton $14.95 (0-395-45711-4). A shy girl spending a summer in New Zealand grows emotionally from her friendship with a Maori youth and caring for an injured albatross. (Rev: BL 9/1/89; BR 1–2/90; SLJ 6/89; VOYA 6/89)

1249 Say, Allen. *The Inn-Keeper's Apprentice* (7–9). 1979, Harper LB $12.89 (0-06-025209-X). A Japanese adolescent faces the pangs of growing up.

1250 Schwandt, Stephen. *Holding Steady* (7–10). 1988, Henry Holt $13.95 (0-8050-0575-7). Friendship with a sympathetic girl helps Michael adjust to the death of his father. (Rev: BL 6/15/88; SLJ 6–7/88; VOYA 12/88)

1251 Schwartz, Joel L. *Best Friends Don't Come in Threes* (6–9). Illus. 1985, Dell paper $2.75 (0-440-40603-X). Friends in the ninth grade face one predicament after another. This is a sequel to *Upchuck Summer* (1982). (Rev: SLJ 3/86)

1252 Schwartz, Joel L. *Shrink* (6–8). 1986, Dell paper $2.75 (0-440-47687-9). At first Mike is ashamed to be seeing a psychiatrist but soon realizes its value. (Rev: BL 12/15/86; SLJ 3/87)

1253 Scoppettone, Sandra. *Trying Hard to Hear You* (7–10). 1974, Harper LB $13.89 (0-06-025246-4). Two boys who are lovers face the problems of acceptance by their friends.

1254 Scott, Carol J. *Kentucky Daughter* (7–9). 1985, Clarion $12.95 (0-89919-330-7); Fawcett paper $2.50 (0-449-70196-4). To attend a better junior high school, Mary Fred goes to live with her aunt and uncle but even there the school causes many problems. (Rev: BL 6/15/85; SLJ 8/85)

1255 Scott, Elaine. *Choices* (7–10). 1989, Morrow $12.95 (0-688-07230-5). School rivalry gets out of hand and Beth is arrested for her part in the antics. (Rev: BL 4/15/89; BR 9–10/89; SLJ 4/89; VOYA 6/89)

1256 Sebestyen, Ouida. *IOU's* (7–9). 1982, Little $14.95 (0-316-77933-4); Dell paper $2.75 (0-440-93986-0). The thirteenth summer of Stowe Garrett when he ceases to be a child and becomes a young man.

1257 Sebestyen, Ouida. *On Fire* (6–9). 1985, Little $12.45 (0-87113-010-6); Bantam paper $2.95 (0-553-26862-7). Tater leaves home with his brother Sammy and takes a mining job where he confronts labor problems in this sequel to the author's powerful *Words by Heart* (1979). (Rev: BL 5/15/85; SLJ 4/85; VOYA 8/85)

1258 Sefton, Catherine. *Island of the Strangers* (7–9). 1985, Harcourt $12.95 (0-15-239100-2). City kids from Belfast clash with town toughs in this novel set on an island off Northern Ireland. (Rev: BL 1/1/86; SLJ 1/86)

1259 Segel, Elizabeth, sel. *Short Takes: A Short Story Collection for Young Readers* (6–9). Illus. 1986, Lothrop LB $12.95 (0-688-06092-7). Nine short stories for young people by writers such as Konigsburg, Springstubb, and Lowry. (Rev: SLJ 10/86)

1260 Semel, Nava. *Becoming Gershona* (6–10). 1990, Viking $11.95 (0-670-83105-0). A delicate story of a girl reaching maturity and self-acceptance in her native country, Israel. (Rev: BL 9/1/90)

1261 Service, Pamela F. *Vision Quest* (7–9). 1989, Macmillan $12.95 (0-689-31498-1). This novel blends Indian magic with the story of a girl growing up in Nevada and adjusting to her father's death. (Rev: BR 9–10/89; SLJ 3/89)

1262 Sharmat, Marjorie. *Snobs, Beware!* (7–10). 1986, Dell paper $2.50 (0-440-98092-5). Kim and friends decide to form a democratic sorority called the Pack. (Rev: SLJ 9/86)

1263 Shreve, Susan. *The Revolution of Mary Leary* (7–9). 1982, Knopf $9.95 (0-394-84776-8). A 16-year-old girl leaves her family to become a mother's helper for a pro-choice advocate.

1264 Shusterman, Neal. *The Shadow Club* (6–8). 1988, Little $12.95 (0-316-77540-1). Seven boys form a club to avenge themselves on their enemies. (Rev: BL 7/88; SLJ 5/88; VOYA 6/88)

1265 Slepian, Jan. *The Alfred Summer* (7–9). 1980, Macmillan $11.95 (0-02-782920-0); Scholastic paper $2.50 (0-590-40983-2). The story of how 4 misfits join forces to build a boat.

1266 Slepian, Jan. *The Broccoli Tapes* (6–8). 1989, Putnam $13.95 (0-399-21712-6). Sara and her older brother Sam spend time in Hawaii in this novel that explores family relationships. (Rev: BL 4/15/89; VOYA 6/89)

1267 Slepian, Jan. *Something beyond Paradise* (8–10). 1987, Putnam $13.95 (0-399-21425-9). Franny is torn between leaving her Hawaiian home to study dance in New York and remaining behind with her family. (Rev: BL 4/1/87; SLJ 4/87; VOYA 6/87)

1268 Smith, Doris Buchanan. *Dreams and Drummers* (7–9). 1978, Harper LB $12.89 (0-690-03843-7). Stephanie faces many problems: a boyfriend in the school band, a runaway brother, and a difficult friend.

1269 Snyder, Carol. *The Great Condominium Rebellion* (6–8). Illus. 1981, Delacorte LB $11.95 (0-385-28352-0). The condominium complex where Stacy and Marc are visiting their grandparents has hundreds of rules to prevent them from having a good time.

1270 Snyder, Zilpha K. *And Condors Danced* (6–8). 1987, Delacorte $14.95 (0-385-29575-8); Dell paper $3.25 (0-440-40153-4). An 11-year-old girl faces family problems while growing up on a ranch in turn-of-the-century California. (Rev: BL 10/1/87; BR 1–2/88; VOYA 12/87)

1271 Soto, Gary. *Baseball in April and Other Stories* (5–9). 1990, Harcourt $14.95 (0-15-205720-X). A group of stories about young Hispanics growing up in Southern California. (Rev: BL 3/1/90; VOYA 8/90)

1272 Southall, Ivan. *Blackbird* (6–8). 1988, Farrar $12.95 (0-374-30783-0). For better readers, this is an introspective look at the character formation of a young boy. (Rev: BL 2/1/89; SLJ 1/89; VOYA 2/89)

1273 Southall, Ivan. *Josh* (6–8). 1988, Macmillan $12.95 (0-02-786280-1). Josh encounters hostile boys when he visits his aunt's home in rural Australia. A reissue. (Rev: SLJ 2/88; VOYA 2/89)

1274 Spinelli, Jerry. *Jason and Marceline* (7–10). 1986, Little $12.95 (0-316-80719-2); Dell paper $3.25 (0-440-20166-7). Jason, now in the ninth grade, sorts out his feelings toward girls in general and Marceline in particular. Preceded by *Space Station Seventh Grade* (1982). (Rev: BL 1/1/87; SLJ 2/87)

1275 Spinelli, Jerry. *Space Station Seventh Grade* (6–8). 1982, Little $14.95 (0-316-80709-5); Dell paper $2.95 (0-440-96165-3). Jason has many adventures, mostly hilarious, during his seventh grade year.

1276 Springstubb, Tricia. *Eunice Gottlieb and the Unwhitewashed Truth about Life* (6–8). 1987, Delacorte $14.95 (0-385-29552-9). Two friends, Eunice and Joy, start a cake-baking business in this continuation of *Which Way to the Nearest Wilderness?* (1984). (Rev: BL 8/87; BR 9–10/87; VOYA 8–9/87)

1277 Stanek, Lou Willett. *Gleanings* (7–9). 1985, Harper LB $12.89 (0-06-025809-8). A feisty girl moves from California to a Long Island suburb and decides that shy Frankie Banning will help her fit in. (Rev: BL 1/1/86; BR 3–4/86; SLJ 10/85; VOYA 12/85)

1278 Stanek, Lou Willett. *Megan's Beat* (7–9). 1983, Dial $12.95 (0-8037-5201-6); Putnam paper $2.25 (0-399-21174-8). In high school, Megan tries to get into the "in" crowd by writing for the school newspaper.

1279 Steiner, Barbara. *Is There a Cure for Sophomore Year?* (7–10). 1986, Signet paper $2.25 (0-451-14057-5). When Maggie stays at her friend's house for a week she sees a totally different way of life. (Rev: SLJ 4/86)

1280 Steiner, Barbara. *Tessa* (7–9). 1988, Morrow $11.95 (0-688-07232-1). A 14-year-old girl faces problems when her mother decides on a divorce and wants to move her daughter to the big city. (Rev: BR 5–6/88; SLJ 3/88; VOYA 6/88)

1281 Strasser, Todd. *Rock 'n' Roll Nights* (7–9). 1982, Delacorte $10.95 (0-385-28855-7); Dell paper $2.95 (0-440-97318-X). Gary Specter, a high school student, promotes his rock group. Sequels are *Turn It Up!* (1985) and *Wildlife* (1987).

1282 Stretton, Barbara. *The Truth of the Matter* (7–10). 1983, Knopf LB $10.99 (0-394-96144-7); Putnam paper $2.25 (0-399-21147-0). Jenny is persuaded to join her boyfriend in a campaign to smear a teacher's reputation.

1283 Sutton, Jane. *Definitely Not Sexy* (7–9). 1988, Little $12.95 (0-316-82325-2). Ninth-grader Diana, who is a bright student, would prefer to be sexy. (Rev: BL 3/15/89; BR 3–4/89; SLJ 3/89; VOYA 2/89)

1284 Swallow, Pamela Curtis. *Leave It to Christy* (6–8). 1987, Putnam $13.95 (0-399-21482-8); Scholastic paper $2.50 (0-590-41666-9). In seventh grade, Christy sets out to help fellow classmate Michael. (Rev: BL 12/15/87; VOYA 2/88)

1285 Sweeney, Joyce. *Face the Dragon* (7–10). 1990, Delacorte $14.95 (0-385-30164-2). Two close friends find their friendship is tested when they enter high school together and when Melanie enters their lives. (Rev: BL 9/15/90)

1286 Talbert, Marc. *Rabbit in the Rock* (5–9). 1989, Dial $14.95 (0-8037-0693-6). A 16-year-old girl growing up on the family's dude ranch gradually develops a sense of self-worth. (Rev: BL 11/15/89; SLJ 1/90; VOYA 12/89)

1287 Talbert, Marc. *Thin Ice* (5–8). 1986, Little LB $13.95 (0-316-83133-6). A fifth-grade boy adjusts to his parents' divorce. (Rev: SLJ 1/87; VOYA 2/87)

1288 Tamar, Erika. *High Cheekbones* (7–9). 1990, Viking $12.95 (0-670-82843-2). A 14-year-old girl begins to lose sight of her ideals when she is caught up in the fashion world. (Rev: BL 2/1/90; SLJ 8/90)

1289 Tamar, Erika. *It Happened at Cecilia's* (6–9). 1989, Macmillan $12.95 (0-689-31478-7). Growing up in Greenwich Village has some problems for ninth-grader Andy, particularly when the mob tries to muscle in on his father's restaurant. (Rev: BL 3/15/89; BR 9–10/89; SLJ 3/89; VOYA 6/89)

1290 Tchudi, Stephen. *The Burg-O-Rama Man* (7–10). 1983, Delacorte paper $13.95 (0-385-29239-2). A fast-food chain offers a chance for Crawford High School students to appear in its commercials—a situation that eventually causes great stress and pain.

1291 Terris, Susan. *Stage Brat* (7–9). 1980, Macmillan $12.95 (0-02-789170-4). Young Linnet gets a starring role in *Peter Pan* and runs afoul of the leading lady.

1292 Thesman, Jean. *Couldn't I Start Over?* (7–10). 1989, Avon paper $2.95 (0-380-75717-6). Growing up in a caring family situation, teenager Shiloh still faces many problems in her coming of age. (Rev: BL 11/15/89; VOYA 2/90)

1293 Thomas, Karen. *Changing of the Guard* (7–10). 1986, Harper LB $11.89 (0-06-026164-1). Caroline and Maddy, 2 high school students, form a bond of friendship based on need for comfort during the grieving process. (Rev: BL 3/15/86; SLJ 4/86; VOYA 8–10/86)

1294 Thompson, Julian F. *Facing It* (7–9). 1989, Avon paper $2.95 (0-380-84491-5). An accident ruins the baseball chances of the star at Camp Raycroft. A reissue.

1295 Tilly, Nancy. *Golden Girl* (6–9). 1985, Farrar $12.95 (0-374-32694-0); Dell paper $2.95 (0-440-20095-4). Penny resents the wealth her friends have but gradually realizes her family is best. (Rev: BL 2/15/86; SLJ 3/86; VOYA 6/86)

1296 Tolan, Stephanie S. *Pride of the Peacock* (7–9). 1985, Macmillan $13.95 (0-684-18489-3). A teenage girl becomes obsessed with the fear of a nuclear war in this perceptive novel. (Rev: BL 1/15/86; SLJ 1/87; VOYA 2/87)

1297 Townsend, John Rowe. *Cloudy-Bright* (7–10). 1984, Harper LB $13.89 (0-397-32090-6). Sam borrows a camera from Jenny and their relationship begins.

1298 Ure, Jean. *What If They Saw Me Now?* (7–9). 1984, Delacorte $13.95 (0-385-29317-8). Jamie takes ballet classes in spite of his macho repugnance to the idea.

1299 Van Raven, Pieter. *The Great Man's Secret* (7–10). 1989, Macmillan $13.95 (0-684-19041-9). Jerry, a teenage reporter for the school newspaper, forms a friendship with a reclusive, difficult, but world-famous writer. (Rev: BL 9/1/89; BR 9–10/89; SLJ 6/89; VOYA 6/89)

1300 Van Raven, Pieter. *Pickle and Price* (7–10). 1990, Macmillan $13.95 (0-684-19162-8). A 20-year-old black and his friend, an illiterate 13-year-old white boy, travel across country in a rusty old truck during the 1950s. (Rev: BL 6/15/90; SLJ 5/90; VOYA 6/90)

1301 Voigt, Cynthia. *Tell Me If the Lovers Are Losers* (7–10). 1982, Macmillan $13.95 (0-689-30911-2). Three college roommates clash until they find a common interest in volleyball.

1302 Walker, Mary Alexander. *Brad's Box* (6–9). 1988, Macmillan $12.95 (0-689-31426-4). Gradually 14-year-old Rose grows to like 17-year-old Brad, an outsider who comes to stay with her family. (Rev: BL 10/1/88; BR 5–6/89; SLJ 9/88; VOYA 12/88)

1303 Walter, Mildred Pitts. *Trouble's Child* (7–9). 1985, Lothrop $11.95 (0-688-04214-7). A 14-year-old black girl summons up the courage to leave her island home to further her schooling. (Rev: BL 11/15/85; BR 1–2/86; SLJ 10/85; VOYA 2/86)

1304 Wartski, Maureen Crane. *My Name Is Nobody* (7–10). 1988, Walker $15.95 (0-8027-6770-2). A victim of child abuse survives a suicide attempt and is given a second chance by a tough ex-cop. (Rev: BL 2/1/88; BR 9–10/88; SLJ 3/88; VOYA 4/88)

1305 Webster, Elizabeth. *Johnnie Alone* (5–9). 1988, St. Martin's $15.95 (0-312-01780-4). Johnnie flees an abusive alcoholic stepfather and finally finds a home where he is loved. (Rev: SLJ 9/88)

1306 Wells, Rosemary. *Leave Well Enough Alone* (7–9). 1977, Dial $8.95 (0-8037-4754-3). While helping an unusual family, a girl faces unexpected problems.

1307 Wersba, Barbara. *The Carnival in My Mind* (7–10). 1982, Harper LB $12.89 (0-06-026410-1). A short 14-year-old boy falls for a 6 foot 20-year-old girl.

1308 Wersba, Barbara. *Just Be Gorgeous* (7–12). 1988, Harper LB $11.89 (0-06-026360-1). Heidi Rosenbloom, a lonely teenager, falls in love with a streetwise boy who is gay. (Rev: BL 9/1/88; SLJ 11/88; VOYA 12/88)

1309 White, Ellen Emerson. *Life without Friends* (7–10). 1987, Scholastic $12.95 (0-590-33781-5); paper $2.75 (0-590-33829-3). Beverly agonizes over her role in a series of drug-related murders in this sequel to *Friends for Life* (Avon, 1983). (Rev: BL 2/1/87; SLJ 4/87; VOYA 4/87)

1310 Willey, Margaret. *Finding David Dolores* (6–9). 1986, Harper LB $10.89 (0-06-026484-5). Arly, only 13 years old, develops a hopeless crush on David Dolores whom she views from afar. (Rev: BL 3/1/86; BR 11–12/86; SLJ 4/86)

1311 Willey, Margaret. *If Not For You* (7–10). 1988, Harper LB $11.89 (0-06-026499-3). A young girl discovers the differences between romance and love when she becomes involved with a young couple who have married too soon. (Rev: BL 9/1/88; BR 5–6/89; SLJ 9/88; VOYA 12/88)

1312 Windsor, Patricia. *The Summer Before* (7–10). 1974, Dell paper $2.50 (0-440-98382-7). Sandy has a breakdown after her friend Bradley dies.

1313 Wojciechowski, Susan. *Patty Dillman of Hot Dog Fame* (7–9). 1989, Watts LB $13.99 (0-531-08410-8). Life in a Catholic private school as seen by Patty Dillman, an adolescent who is still trying to find time to spend with her boyfriend Tim. This is a sequel to *And the Other Is Gold* (1987). (Rev: BL 5/15/89; BR 9–10/89; SLJ 7/89; VOYA 8/89)

1314 Wolff, Ferida. *Pink Slippers, Bat Mitzvah Blues* (6–8). 1989, Jewish Publication Soc. $13.95 (0-8276-0332-0). A young Jewish girl is torn between ballet classes or devoting time to her religious studies. (Rev: BL 11/1/89; BR 3–4/90; SLJ 7/89)

1315 Wolitzer, Hilma. *Out of Love* (7–9). 1976, Farrar $11.95 (0-374-35675-0). Teddy is unhappy with the way her adolescence is developing.

1316 Wood, Phyllis Anderson. *A Five-Color Buick and a Blue-Eyed Cat* (7–9). 1977, Westminster $7.95 (0-664-32562-9). Two boys become friends while transporting pets as a summer job.

1317 Wright, Betty Ren. *The Summer of Mrs. MacGregor* (6–8). 1986, Holiday $12.95 (0-8234-0628-8); Scholastic paper $2.50 (0-590-41052-0). Meeting an exotic teenager who calls herself Mrs. Lillina MacGregor helps Linda solve her problem of jealousy toward her older sister. (Rev: BL 11/1/86; SLJ 11/86; VOYA 4/87)

1318 Zalben, Jane Breskin. *Here's Looking at You, Kid* (7–9). 1984, Farrar $11.95 (0-374-33055-7); Dell paper $2.50 (0-440-93573-3). Enid feels she can't win Eric and therefore promotes a relationship for him with attractive Kimberly Wright.

1319 Zalben, Jane Breskin. *Water from the Moon* (8–10). 1987, Farrar $12.95 (0-374-38238-7). Nicky Berstein, a high school sophomore, tries too hard to make friends and is hurt in the process. (Rev: BL 5/15/87; SLJ 5/87; VOYA 8–9/87)

1320 Zindel, Bonnie, and Paul Zindel. *A Star for the Latecomer* (7–10). 1980, Harper $12.70 (0-06-026847-6); Bantam paper $2.50 (0-553-25578-9). When her mother dies, Brooke is freed of the need to pursue a dancing career.

1321 Zindel, Paul. *A Begonia for Miss Applebaum* (7–12). 1989, Harper LB $12.89 (0-06-026878-6). Two unconventional teens take under their wings a favorite teacher who is dying of cancer. (Rev: BL 3/15/89; BR 11–12/89; SLJ 4/89)

1322 Zindel, Paul. *Confessions of a Teenage Baboon* (7–9). 1977, Harper LB $12.89 (0-06-026844-1). Chris has difficulty adjusting to his mother's employer, a somewhat bitter loner.

1323 Zindel, Paul. *I Never Loved Your Mind* (8–12). 1970, Harper LB $12.89 (0-06-026822-0); Bantam paper $2.95 (0-553-27323-X). Two dropouts working in a hospital together suffer the pangs of love and loss.

1324 Zindel, Paul. *My Darling, My Hamburger* (8–12). 1969, Harper LB $12.89 (0-06-026824-7); Bantam paper $2.95 (0-553-27324-8). Two young couples each in love face life's complications including one girl's abortion.

1325 Zindel, Paul. *The Pigman* (7–10). 1968, Harper LB $13.89 (0-06-026828-X). Two misfit teenagers befriend a lonely old man. Followed by *The Pigman's Legacy* (1980, Bantam).

1326 Zolotow, Charlotte, ed. *Early Sorrow: Ten Stories of Youth* (8–12). 1986, Harper LB $12.89 (0-06-025937-5). This excellent collection of 12 adult stories about growing up is a companion piece to *An Overpraised Season*, another anthology about adolescence that was reissued in 1987. (Rev: BL 10/1/86; BR 3–4/87; SLJ 1/87; VOYA 2/87)

World Affairs and Contemporary Problems

1327 Ballard, John. *Monsoon: A Novel to End World Hunger* (7–10). Illus. 1986, Classroom Classics paper $9.95 (0-932279-03-1). A troubled New York teenager travels to India to meet the child she has "adopted." (Rev: SLJ 10/85)

1328 Bennett, Jack. *The Voyage of the Lucky Dragon* (6–9). 1982, Prentice $9.95 (0-13-944165-4). The saga of a Vietnamese family's escape to Australia.

1329 Bergman, Tamar. *The Boy from Over There* (7–9). 1988, Houghton $12.95 (0-395-43077-1). Avramik, a young Jewish boy who survived the Holocaust, is sent to live on a kibbutz in Palestine. (Rev: VOYA 12/88)

1330 Bograd, Larry. *The Kolokol Papers* (7–9). 1981, Farrar $11.95 (0-374-34277-6). Living under oppression in the Soviet Union, Lev decides to write his story for publication in the West.

1331 Burchard, Peter. *Sea Change* (7–9). 1984, Farrar $10.95 (0-374-36460-5). Three generations of women and their daughters face crises caused by war.

1332 Carter, Peter. *Bury the Dead* (8–12). 1987, Farrar $14.95 (0-374-31011-4). A girl from East Berlin who is proficient in high jumping discovers that her brother is a Nazi war criminal. (Rev: BL 3/1/87; SLJ 8/87)

1333 de Jenkins, Lyll Becerra. *The Honorable Prison* (7–12). 1988, Dutton $14.95 (0-525-67238-9); Penguin paper $3.95 (0-14-032952-8). A teenage girl lives through the horror of life in a Latin American police state. (Rev: BL 3/15/88; VOYA 10/88)

1334 Fenton, Edward. *The Morning of the Gods* (6–8). 1987, Delacorte $14.95 (0-385-29550-2). After the death of her mother, Carla is sent to Greece to stay with her mother's aunt and uncle. (Rev: BL 7/87; BR 9–10/87; SLJ 8/87; VOYA 6/87)

1335 Fox, Paula. *Lily and the Lost Boy* (6–9). 1987, Watts LB $12.99 (0-531-08320-9). Using the tiny island of Thasos in Greece as a setting the author tells a story of the maturation of a 12-year-old American girl and her older brother. (Rev: BL 7/87; BR 1–2/88; VOYA 2/88)

1336 Gilmore, Kate. *Remembrance of the Sun* (7–12). 1986, Houghton $12.95 (0-395-41101-1). Jill's love for a talented Iranian student is destroyed by the revolution that convulsed Iran in the late 1970s. (Rev: BL 12/1/86; BR 1–2/87; SLJ 11/86; VOYA 12/86)

1337 Hall, Lynn. *If Winter Comes* (7–10). 1986, Macmillan $12.95 (0-684-18575-X). Two teenagers spend what they believe to be their last weekend on earth because of the imminent threat of a nuclear war. (Rev: BL 6/1/86; SLJ 9/86; VOYA 8–10/86)

1338 Hentoff, Nat. *The Day They Came to Arrest the Book* (7–10). 1983, Dell paper $2.95 (0-440-91814-6). Some students at Geoge Mason High think *Huckleberry Finn* is a racist book.

1339 Ho, Minfong. *Rice without Rain* (7–12). 1990, Lothrop $11.95 (0-688-06355-1). Jinda, a 17-year-old girl, experiences personal tragedy and the awakening of love in this novel set during revolutionary times in Thailand during the 1970s. (Rev: BL 7/90; SLJ 9/90)

1340 Holman, Felice. *Secret City, U. S. A.* (7–10). 1990, Macmillan LB $14.95 (0-684-19168-7). Two boys find a deserted house in a deserted city neighborhood and decide to clean it up for homeless youngsters. (Rev: SLJ 4/90; VOYA 6/90)

1341 Langton, Jane. *The Fragile Flag* (7–9). 1984, Harper LB $12.89 (0-06-023699-X). A group of children march on Washington, D.C., to protest the building of a lethal weapon.

1342 Levitin, Sonia. *The Return* (6–10). 1987, Macmillan $12.95 (0-689-31309-8); Fawcett paper $2.95 (0-449-70280-4). Seen from the viewpoint of a teenage girl, this is the story of a group of African Jews who journey from Ethiopia to

the Sudan to escape persecution. (Rev: BL 4/15/87; BR 11–12/87; SLJ 5/87; VOYA 6/87)

1343 Linfield, Esther. *The Secret of the Mountain* (6–9). 1986, Greenwillow $10.25 (0-688-05992-9). The son of an African tribal chieftain reaches maturity through a number of experiences that test his manhood. (Rev: BL 3/15/86)

1344 Lipsyte, Robert. *Jock and Jill* (7–9). 1977, Harper LB $12.89 (0-06-023900-X). Two teenagers tackle City Hall with the problem of drugs in sports.

1345 Lukas, Cynthia K. *Center Stage Summer* (7–9). 1988, Square One paper $4.95 (0-938961-02-0). A teenage girl learns to stand up for her beliefs concerning nuclear power in spite of the consequences. (Rev: VOYA 2/89)

1346 Miles, Betty. *Maudie and Me and the Dirty Book* (5–8). 1980, Knopf LB $10.99 (0-394-94343-0); paper $2.95 (0-394-82595-0). Kate causes a community furor when she presents a picture book to first-graders about a dog having pups.

1347 Naidoo, Beverley. *Chain of Fire* (6–12). Illus. 1990, Harper LB $12.89 (0-397-32427-8). A harrowing but inspiring story about forced relocation of blacks in South Africa and the young people who have helped in the resistance movement. (Rev: BL 3/15/90; SLJ 5/90; VOYA 6/90)

1348 Pfeffer, Susan Beth. *A Matter of Principle* (7–10). 1982, Delacorte $11.95 (0-385-28649-X). A group of high school students are suspended for publishing an underground newspaper.

1349 Sherman, Eileen Bluestone. *Monday in Odessa* (5–9). 1986, Jewish Publication Soc. LB $10.95 (0-8276-0262-6). A Jewish girl in Russia faces problems when her parents want to emmigrate. (Rev: SLJ 1/87)

1350 Southall, Ivan. *The Long Night Watch* (7–10). 1984, Farrar $11.95 (0-374-34644-5). Believing the world is about to end, 100 people in Australia flee to a deserted island.

1351 Staples, Suzanne Fisher. *Shabanu: Daughter of the Wind* (7–10). 1989, Knopf LB $13.99 (0-394-94815-7). The story of a young girl coming-of-age in a family living in a desert region of Pakistan. (Rev: BL 10/1/89; SLJ 11/89; VOYA 4/90)

1352 Tchudi, Stephen. *The Green Machine and the Frog Crusade* (7–10). 1987, Delacorte $14.95 (0-385-29529-4). A young high school student and 2 others try to block the construction of a shopping mall on a swamp. (Rev: VOYA 4/87)

1353 Wartski, Maureen Crane. *A Boat to Nowhere* (7–9). 1980, Westminster $9.95 (0-664-

32661-7). A harrowing story of survival and courage about a group of Vietnamese boat people and their flight to freedom. A sequel is: *A Long Way from Home* (1980).

1354 Wiseman, David. *A Tie to the Past* (6–8). 1989, Houghton $13.95 (0-395-51135-6). From a stolen box of papers, Mary relives the suffragette movement in England. Rev: BL 9/15/89; SLJ 9/89; VOYA 12/89)

1355 Yolen, Jane. *Children of the Wolf* (6–8). 1984, Viking $11.95 (0-670-21763-8). Based on fact, this is the story of a Christian minister in India who finds 2 children who have been reared in the wild.

Fantasy

1356 Adams, Richard. *Watership Down* (7–12). 1974, Macmillan $24.95 (0-02-700030-3). In this fantasy, a small group of male rabbits sets out to find a new home.

1357 Adkins, Jan. *A Storm without Rain* (7–9). Illus. 1983, Little $14.95 (0-316-01084-7). In this time warp story, Jack meets his own grandfather in Cape Cod of 1904.

1358 Aiken, Joan. *The Shadow Guests* (7–10). 1980, Delacorte $11.95 (0-440-07746-X); Dell paper $2.95 (0-440-40037-6). A young boy adjusting to the loss of his mother and brother encounters ghosts who reveal family secrets.

1359 Aiken, Joan. *The Stolen Lake* (6–8). 1981, Delacorte $10.95 (0-385-28982-0); Dell paper $3.25 (0-440-40037-6). Dido aboard the ship *Thrush* must help a queen who claims her lake has been stolen.

1360 Aiken, Joan. *Up the Chimney Down, and Other Stories* (7–9). 1984, Harper LB $12.89 (0-06-020037-5). Eleven short stories, many of which contain elements of magic and fantasy.

1361 Alexander, Lloyd. *The First Two Lives of Lukas-Kasha* (6–9). 1978, Dutton $14.95 (0-525-29748-0); Dell paper $2.25 (0-440-42784-3). Lukas-Kasha, because of a showman's tricks, finds himself king of the land of Abadan.

1362 Alexander, Lloyd. *The Foundling and Other Tales of Prydain* (6–8). 1982, Dell paper $2.95 (0-440-42536-0). Six stories of Alexander's enchanted land of Prydain.

1363 Alexander, Lloyd. *The Wizard in the Tree* (5–8). Illus. 1975, Dutton $9.95 (0-525-43128-4); Dell paper $3.25 (0-440-49556-3). Mallory finds a wizard in a tree and must help him when he is accused of murder.

1364 Anderson, Margaret J. *The Druid's Gift* (6–8). 1989, Knopf LB $13.99 (0-394-91936-X). A fantasy involving a young girl and her encounters with Druids' beliefs in ancient Scotland. (Rev: BL 8/89; SLJ 3/89)

1365 Anderson, Margaret J. *In the Circle of Time* (5–8). 1979, Knopf LB $6.99 (0-394-94029-6). Robert and Jennifer travel in time as a result of finding a magic circle of stones. J Fic PO/CE

1366 Angell, Judie. *The Weird Disappearance of Jordan Hall* (7–10). 1987, Watts LB $11.99 (0-531-08327-6). Jordan enters a magical box that makes him disappear. (Rev: BL 9/1/87; BR 1–2/88; SLJ 11/87)

1367 Avi. *Bright Shadow* (5–8). 1985, Bradbury $11.95 (0-02-707750-0); Macmillan paper $3.95 (0-689-71256-1). At the death of the great wizard, Morenna finds she possesses the last 5 wishes in the world. (Rev: SLJ 12/85)

1368 Avi. *The Man Who Was Poe* (7–10). 1989, Watts LB $13.99 (0-531-08433-7). When Edmund goes out to search for his missing mother and sister, he encounters Edgar Allan Poe in disguise as his detective Auguste Dupin. (Rev: BL 10/1/89; BR 5–6/90; SLJ 9/89; VOYA 2/90)

1369 Babbitt, Natalie. *Herbert Rowbarge* (7–10). 1984, Farrar paper $3.95 (0-374-51852-1). A fantasy about twins who are drawn to each other in a mysterious way.

1370 Beagle, Peter S. *The Last Unicorn* (7–10). 1988, Ballantine paper $3.75 (0-345-35367-6). The haunting story about a unicorn's search for her lost fellows.

1371 Becker, Eve. *Thirteen Means Magic* (6–8). 1989, Bantam paper $2.75 (0-553-15730-2). Dawn who has just turned 13 discovers she can change events through her magical powers. (Rev: SLJ 11/89)

1372 Bedard, Michael. *A Darker Magic* (6–8). 1987, Macmillan $13.95 (0-689-31342-X); Avon paper $2.95 (0-380-70611-3). An intricate fantasy about the strange effects of a magic show run by Professor Mephisto. (Rev: BL 9/1/87; SLJ 9/87)

1373 Belden, Wilanne Schneider. *Mind-Hold* (6–9). 1987, Harcourt $14.95 (0-15-254280-9). After a violent earthquake, Carson and his sister, who has the gift of ESP, move into the desert hoping to find new friends. (Rev: BL 2/15/87; SLJ 3/87)

1374 Bell, Clare. *Ratha and Thistle-Chaser* (7–12). 1990, Macmillan $14.95 (0-689-50462-4). Further adventures of the clan of intelligent cats and their search for new land in this continuation of *Ratha's Creature* (1983) and *Clan Ground* (1984). (Rev: BL 2/1/90; SLJ 6/90; VOYA 6/90)

1375 Bell, Clare. *Tomorrow's Sphinx* (7–12). 1986, Macmillan $14.95 (0-689-50402-0); Dell paper $3.25 (0-440-20124-1). After humankind has left Egypt, a surviving female cheetah finds a strange male counterpart who lived with King Tut. (Rev: BL 10/15/86; SLJ 11/86)

1376 Berry, James. *Magicians of Erianne* (7–10). 1988, Harper LB $13.89 (0-06-020557-1). Ronan arrives in the mythical land of Erianne with magical powers but no memory of his past. (Rev: BL 6/15/88; BR 1–2/89; SLJ 8/88; VOYA 6/88)

1377 Bethancourt, T. Ernesto. *The Dog Days of Arthur Cane* (6–9). 1976, Holiday $13.95 (0-8234-0286-X). Arthur literally lives a dog's life when an amazing transformation takes place.

1378 Bond, Nancy. *A String in the Harp* (6–8). 1978, Macmillan $12.95 (0-689-50036-X); Penguin paper $5.95 (0-14-032376-7). In Wales the Morgan children find a magic harp-tuning key that takes them back in time.

1379 Bosse, Malcolm. *Cave Beyond Time* (7–9). 1980, Harper LB $12.89 (0-690-04076-8). Ben adjusts better to his parents' death after he travels back in time as a result of a rattlesnake bite.

1380 Bowkett, Stephen. *Gameplayers* (7–10). 1989, Gollancz $16.95 (0-575-03932-9). In this English novel, high school student John Warner is so overcome with personal problems that he spends too much time in his fantasy world. (Rev: BL 3/1/89; SLJ 3/89)

1381 Brittain, Bill. *The Fantastic Freshman* (6–9). 1988, Harper LB $11.89 (0-06-020719-1). Stanley's dreams of glory to excel in everything come true with unexpected but humorous results. (Rev: BL 9/1/88; BR 5–6/89; SLJ 9/88; VOYA 12/88)

1382 Buffie, Margaret. *The Haunting of Frances Rain* (7–10). 1989, Scholastic $12.95 (0-590-42834-9). Through a pair of magic spectacles, Lizzie is able to see events that occurred more than 50 years ago. (Rev: BL 10/1/89; SLJ 9/89)

1383 Charnas, Suzy McKee. *The Bronze King* (6–8). 1985, Houghton LB $12.95 (0-395-38394-3); Bantam paper $2.95 (0-553-15493-1). Tina and her friends do battle against an evil sea monster that has invaded New York City. (Rev: SLJ 11/85)

1384 Charnas, Suzy McKee. *The Golden Thread* (7–9). 1989, Bantam $13.95 (0-553-05821-5). Val is asked to use her magical powers to locate people from another world. (Rev: SLJ 8/89)

1385 Cheetham, Ann. *The Pit* (6–8). 1990, Henry Holt $14.95 (0-8050-1142-0). A contemporary English boy is drawn into the past of London during the time of the Great Plague. (Rev: BL 6/1/90; SLJ 6/90)

1386 Chetwin, Grace. *The Crystal Stair: From Tales of Gom in the Legends of Ulm* (6–8). 1988, Macmillan $13.95 (0-02-718311-4). Young Gom sets out to find a wizard who will teach him magic in this sequel to *The Riddle and the Rune* (1987). (Rev: BL 4/1/88)

1387 Chetwin, Grace. *The Riddle and the Rune: From Tales of Gom in the Legends of Ulm* (6–8). 1987, Macmillan $13.95 (0-02-718312-2); Dell paper $3.50 (0-440-20581-6). Gom sets out with a mysterious stone around his neck to find his mother, who disappeared after his birth. Part of a series about Gom. (Rev: BL 10/1/87; SLJ 12/87; VOYA 12/87)

1388 Chetwin, Grace. *The Starstone* (6–8). 1989, Bradbury $13.95 (0-02-718315-7). This third book in the Gom series finds our hero with his animal friends battling against the evil Katak. This book continues where *Gom on Windy Mountain* (1986) and *The Crystal Stair* (1988) left off. (Rev: BL 4/1/89; BR 9–10/89; SLJ 6/89; VOYA 10/89)

1389 Christopher, John. *The Fireball* (7–9). 1981, Dutton $11.95 (0-525-29735-3). Two English cousins are transported back in time to Roman Britain.

1390 Conford, Ellen. *And This Is Laura* (7–9). 1977, Little $14.95 (0-316-15300-1); Pocket paper $2.75 (0-671-67879-5). When Laura discovers she can see into the future, problems begin.

1391 Cooper, Susan. *Over Sea, Under Stone* (6–9). Illus. 1966, Harcourt $14.95 (0-15-259034-X); paper $2.95 (0-02-042785-9). Three contemporary children enter the world of King Arthur in this the first volume of The Dark Is Rising series. Followed by: *The Dark Is Rising* (1973); *Greenwitch* (1974); *The Grey King* (1975); and *Silver on the Tree* (1977).

1392 Cooper, Susan. *Seaward* (6–9). 1983, Macmillan $10.95 (0-689-50275-3); paper $3.95 (0-02-042190-7). Two youngsters embark on a fantastic voyage to find their parents.

1393 Corbett, W. J. *The Song of Pentecost* (7–9). Illus. 1983, Dutton $10.95 (0-525-44051-8). A colony of mice led by Pentecost set out to find Utopia.

1394 Cunningham, Julia. *Wolf Roland* (6–8). 1983, Pantheon LB $9.99 (0-394-85892-1). A bitter old man makes a wolf take the place of his dead donkey.

1395 Dank, Gloria Rand. *The Forest of App* (7–9). 1983, Greenwillow $10.25 (0-688-02315-0); Putnam paper $2.25 (0-399-21142-X). A trio consisting of an elf, a witch, and a dwarf adopt a crippled boy.

1396 Davies, Valentine. *Miracle on 34th Street* (6–9). Illus. 1984, Harcourt $16.95 (0-15-254526-3). Kris Kringle, living in an old folks home, plays Santa at Macy's in this 1947 fantasy.

1397 DeClements, Barthe, and Christopher Greimes. *Double Trouble* (6–9). 1987, Viking $11.95 (0-670-81567-5). Twins separated after the death of their parents discover they each have ESP. (Rev: BL 6/1/87; BR 3–4/88; SLJ 8/87)

1398 DeFelice, Cynthia. *The Strange Night Writing of Jessamine Colter* (6–9). 1988, Macmillan $12.95 (0-02-726451-3). A short tender novel about a woman who has the gift of seeing into the future. (Rev: VOYA 4/89)

1399 Dexter, Catherine. *The Oracle Doll* (6–8). 1985, Macmillan $11.95 (0-02-709810-9); Dell paper $2.95 (0-440-40114-3). Lucy receives as a present a talking doll that can foresee the future. (Rev: BL 11/1/85)

1400 Dickinson, Peter. *The Devil's Children* (6–8). 1988, Dell paper $2.95 (0-440-20082-2). Merlin the Magician comes back to life in this first volume of the Changes trilogy that is followed by *Heartease* and *The Weathermonger* (both 1986). (Rev: VOYA 12/86)

1401 Dickinson, Peter. *Merlin Dreams* (6–12). Illus. 1988, Doubleday $19.95 (0-440-50067-2). Eight short fantasies set in Arthurian times and involving the dreams of the wizard Merlin. (Rev: BL 2/1/89; BR 1–2/89; SLJ 12/88; VOYA 2/89)

1402 Downer, Ann. *The Spellkey* (8–12). 1987, Macmillan $13.95 (0-689-31329-2). Two unusual characters, a girl named Caitlin and a boy named Badger, set out on a quest that pits good versus evil. (Rev: BL 10/15/87; SLJ 9/87)

1403 Duane, Diane. *So You Want to Be a Wizard* (7–9). 1983, Delacorte $14.95 (0-385-29305-4); Dell paper $2.75 (0-440-98252-9). Nita and another wizard-in-training embark on a journey to find the key to goodness. Also use its sequel *Deep Wizardry* (1985).

1404 Estes, Rose. *The Name of the Game* (7–9). 1988, TSR paper $3.95 (0-88038-614-2). Mike comes to Perrenland in search of the princess of his dreams and finds the country attacked by an army of mythical creatures. (Rev: VOYA 2/89)

1405 Farjeon, Eleanor. *The Glass Slipper* (6–9). 1986, Harper LB $11.89 (0-397-32181-3). A ro-

mantic retelling in prose of the Cinderella story. (Rev: BL 10/15/86)

1406 Fisher, Leonard Everett. *Noonan: A Novel about Baseball, ESP, and Time Warps* (7–9). Illus. 1978, Avon paper $1.95 (0-380-53355-3). A teenage baseball enthusiast of the late nineteenth century is transported into the late twentieth century.

1407 Fleischman, Paul. *The Half-a-Moon Inn* (6–8). 1980, Harper LB $12.89 (0-06-021918-1). While searching for his mother, Aaron is captured by a witch.

1408 Fletcher, Susan. *Dragon's Milk* (5–9). 1989, Macmillan $14.95 (0-689-31579-1). To save her brother, Kaeldra embarks on a quest to find dragon's milk. (Rev: BR 3–4/90; SLJ 11/89; VOYA 12/89)

1409 Gabhart, Ann. *The Gifting* (6–8). 1987, Simon & Schuster paper $2.25 (0-373-98008-6). Ginny, in the midst of a first romance, is granted healing powers by a lonely old woman. (Rev: BL 12/15/87; VOYA 12/87)

1410 Garden, Nancy. *The Door Between* (6–8). 1987, Farrar $13.95 (0-374-31833-6). In this third of a 4-volume series, Melissa enters the Otherworld to confront an evil hermit. The first 2 were: *Fours Crossing* (1981) and *Watersmeet* (1983). (Rev: BL 11/1/87; SLJ 12/87)

1411 Gates, Susan. *The Burnhope Wheel* (7–9). 1989, Holiday $12.95 (0-8234-0767-5). Two young people fall under the spell of a revolving wheel that draws them into the possible repetition of a century-old tragedy in this English fantasy. (Rev: BL 12/1/89; SLJ 12/89; VOYA 4/90)

1412 Gilden, Mel. *Harry Newberry and the Raiders of the Red Drink* (5–9). 1989, Henry Holt LB $14.45 (0-8050-0698-2). Harry is convinced that his favorite comic characters are real in this zany fantasy. (Rev: SLJ 5/89; VOYA 10/89)

1413 Gilmore, Kate. *Enter Three Witches* (6–10). 1990, Houghton $13.95 (0-395-50213-6). Bren's mother and grandmother are witches causing problems for the boy's social life. (Rev: BL 3/15/90; SLJ 3/90; VOYA 4/90)

1414 Gloss, Molly. *Outside the Gates* (6–9). 1986, Macmillan $13.95 (0-689-31275-X). Because of his powers of ESP, Vren is exiled from his village. (Rev: VOYA 4/87)

1415 Goodwin, Marie D. *Where the Towers Pierce the Sky* (6–8). 1989, Macmillan $13.95 (0-02-736871-8). A 13-year-old girl time-travels to the days of Joan of Arc. (Rev: BL 12/1/89; BR 5–6/90; SLJ 11/89; VOYA 12/89)

1416 Gorog, Judith. *Three Dreams and a Nightmare: And Other Tales of the Dark* (6–9). 1988, Putnam $13.95 (0-399-21578-6). Fourteen more stories by a master of the fantastic. This is a companion to *A Taste for Quiet* (1983) and *No Swimming in Dark Pond* (1987). (Rev: BL 10/1/88; SLJ 11/88; VOYA 4/89)

1417 Goudge, Eileen. *Woodstock Magic* (7–9). 1986, Avon paper $2.50 (0-380-75129-1). Louise time-travels back to the Woodstock Festival because she wishes she could have lived in the 1960s. (Rev: VOYA 2/87)

1418 Green, Roger J. *They Watched Him Die* (6–8). 1988, Oxford Univ. Pr. $13.95 (0-19-271573-9). This is the last of a 4-book cycle for better readers about the power of a stone used for evil magic. The others are: *The Fear of Samuel Walton; The Devil Finds Work;* and *The Lengthening Shadow* (all 1987). (Rev: BL 2/15/89)

1419 Halam, Ann. *Transformations* (7–9). 1988, Watts LB $13.99 (0-531-08366-7). The heroine Zanne of Garth travels to an unusual land where she finds the people are prisoners of a strange secret, in a sequel to *The Daymaker* (1987). (Rev: BL 1/15/89; SLJ 12/88)

1420 Hamilton, Virginia. *Justice and Her Brothers* (7–10). 1978, Greenwillow LB $12.88 (0-688-84182-1). Four children with supernatural powers move in time in this complex novel. Sequels are *Dustland* and *The Gathering* (both 1980).

1421 Hamley, Dennis. *Blood Line* (7–9). 1990, Trafalgar paper $7.95 (0-233-98445-3). A television program comes to life in Rory's own home. (Rev: SLJ 9/90)

1422 Harris, Geraldine. *Prince of the Godborn* (7–9). 1983, Greenwillow $10.25 (0-688-01792-4); Dell paper $2.50 (0-440-95407-X). In the first part of the Seven Citadels series, 2 half-brothers set out to find 7 magic keys. Continued in *The Children of the Wind* (1987), *The Dead Kingdom* (1987), and *The Seventh Gate* (1984).

1423 Helakisa, Karina. *The Journey of Pietari and His Wolf* (7–10). Trans. by Michael Rollerson. Illus. 1985, Green Tiger $14.95 (0-88138-043-1). An innocent young child travels to a land of fear and greed to fight the power of evil. (Rev: SLJ 10/85)

1424 Heuck, Sigrid. *The Hideout* (7–10). 1988, Dutton $13.95 (0-525-44343-6). Rebecca, an unhappy waif, is comforted by her new friend Sami, who takes her into a fantasy world. (Rev: VOYA 10/88)

1425 Hilgartner, Beth. *Colors in the Dreamweaver's Loom* (6–10). 1989, Houghton $14.95 (0-395-50214-4). A 16-year-old girl walks through the woods into a different world inhabited by gentle people who are threatened from the outside. (Rev: BL 9/1/89; BR 5–6/90; SLJ 10/89; VOYA 10/89)

1426 Horowitz, Anthony. *The Night of the Scorpion* (6–9). 1985, Putnam $12.95 (0-448-47751-3). Martin and his friend Richard travel to Peru to try to prevent the evil Old Ones from returning to Earth, in this sequel to *The Devil's Doorbell* (1984). (Rev: BR 1–2/85; SLJ 5/85)

1427 Houghton, Eric. *Gates of Glass* (6–8). 1987, Oxford Univ. Pr. $13.95 (0-19-271566-6). The story of an underground world made of glass and the young girl who is drawn into it by her mirror. (Rev: SLJ 1/88)

1428 Howe, Imogen. *Vicious Circle* (7–9). 1983, Dell paper $1.95 (0-440-99318-0). Two teenagers become involved in the mysterious disappearance of 2 other young people.

1429 Hughes, Monica. *Sandwriter* (6–9). 1988, Henry Holt $12.95 (0-8050-0617-6). A spoiled young princess visits a desertlike kingdom where she believes she is to be married. (Rev: BL 3/15/88; SLJ 3/88)

1430 Hunter, Mollie. *The Mermaid Summer* (5–8). 1988, Harper LB $12.89 (0-06-022628-5). Two children challenge the power of a mermaid who threatens to destroy their village. (Rev: BL 6/1/88; BR 1–2/89)

1431 Hunter, Mollie. *A Stranger Came Ashore* (7–9). 1975, Harper LB $12.89 (0-06-022652-8); paper $3.50 (0-06-44082-4). In this fantasy set in the Shetland Islands, a bull seal takes human form and comes ashore.

1432 Jacques, Brian. *Mattimeo* (5–8). 1990, Putnam $16.95 (0-399-21741-X). The evil fox kidnaps the animal children of Redwall Abbey in this continuation of *Mossflower* (1988) and *Redwall* (1987). (Rev: SLJ 9/90; VOYA 8/90)

1433 Jones, Diana Wynne. *Archer's Goon* (7–9). 1984, Greenwillow $12.25 (0-688-02582-4). Seven wizards cause problems for a small-town family.

1434 Jones, Diana Wynne. *Dogsbody* (7–10). 1988, Morrow LB $11.95 (0-688-08191-6). The Dogstar, Sirius, is sent to Earth in the form of a dog to fulfill a dangerous mission. (Rev: BR 11–12/88; VOYA 2/89)

1435 Jones, Diana Wynne. *Eight Days of Luke* (7–9). 1988, Greenwillow $11.95 (0-688-08006-5). David utters a curse and inadvertently releases a boy named Luke from an unusual prison. (Rev: BL 10/1/88; BR 11–12/88; SLJ 9/88; VOYA 2/89)

1436 Jones, Diana Wynne. *Fire and Hemlock* (7–9). 1984, Greenwillow $13.00 (0-688-02963-9). At 19, Polly seems to live in 2 worlds—one, real and the other not.

1437 Jones, Diana Wynne, ed. *Hidden Turnings: A Collection of Stories through Time and Space* (7–12). 1990, Greenwillow $12.95 (0-688-09163-6). A collection of 12 original fantasies by some of the best writers in this field. (Rev: BL 5/1/90; SLJ 8/90)

1438 Jones, Diana Wynne. *Howl's Moving Castle* (7–12). 1986, Greenwillow $10.25 (0-688-06233-4). A fearful young girl is changed into an old woman and in that disguise moves into the castle of Wizard Howl. (Rev: BL 6/1/86; SLJ 8/86; VOYA 8–10/86)

1439 Jones, Diana Wynne. *The Lives of Christopher Chant* (5–9). 1988, Greenwillow LB $11.95 (0-688-07806-0). At night Christopher can leave his body and travel from London to other worlds. (Rev: BR 5–6/88; SLJ 5/88; VOYA 6/88)

1440 Jones, Diana Wynne. *The Magicians of Capronia* (6–9). 1980, Ace paper $2.25 (0-441-51556-8). In this fantasy set in mythical Italy, the old spells are wearing out and something must be done.

1441 Jones, Diana Wynne. *The Ogre Downstairs* (6–9). 1990, Greenwillow $11.95 (0-688-09195-4). Five youngsters conduct experiments with chemistry sets that allow them to fly, shrink, and change bodies. (Rev: VOYA 6/90)

1442 Jones, Diana Wynne. *Warlock at the Wheel: And Other Stories* (6–8). 1985, Greenwillow $10.25 (0-688-04305-4). Eight intriguing stories by this master of fantasy—each entertaining, some humorous. (Rev: BL 4/15/85; BR 5–6/85; SLJ 4/85; VOYA 6/85)

1443 Karl, Jean E. *Beloved Benjamin Is Waiting* (6–8). 1978, Dutton $10.75 (0-525-26372-1). Lucinda confides in an iron statue that seems to respond to her.

1444 Katz, Welwyn Wilton. *False Face* (6–9). 1988, Macmillan $12.95 (0-689-50456-X). Two Iroquois masks emit a strange power over an already troubled family. (Rev: BL 10/15/88; SLJ 11/88)

1445 Katz, Welwyn Wilton. *The Third Magic* (8–12). 1989, Macmillan $14.95 (0-689-50480-2). Modern Cornwall, Arthurian England, and an ancient kingdom called Nwm are the 3 intertwining settings in this fantasy. (Rev: BL 3/15/89; BR 9–10/89; VOYA 6/89)

1446 Kehret, Peg. *Sisters, Long Ago* (6–8). 1990, Dutton $13.95 (0-525-65021-0). Willow is rescued from drowning by a girl who was her sister in a previous life. (Rev: BL 2/15/90; VOYA 4/90)

1447 Kelleher, Victor. *The Red King* (6–9). 1990, Dial $13.95 (0-8037-0758-4). In this fantasy a young acrobat tries to unseat the Red King so that she can gain her freedom from slavery. (Rev: BL 4/1/90; SLJ 7/90; VOYA 6/90)

1448 Key, Alexander. *Escape to Witch Mountain* (6–9). 1968, Westminster $10.95 (0-664-32417-7). Tony and Tia become targets of an evil conspiracy because they possess unusual powers. A sequel is *Return to Witch Mountain* (1984).

1449 Kipling, Rudyard. *The Jungle Books* (6–9). 1961, NAL paper $3.95 (0-451-52340-7). The complete 15 stories that make up the original 2 volumes of jungle books.

1450 Kittleman, Laurence R. *Canyons beyond the Sky* (6–8). 1985, Macmillan $13.95 (0-689-31138-0). While helping a father he barely knows on an archaeological dig, Evan travels back in time. (Rev: BL 2/1/86)

1451 Koff, Richard M. *Christopher* (7–9). 1981, Celestial Arts $8.95 (0-89742-050-0); Bantam paper $2.25 (0-553-15363-3). Christopher tries to develop his mental powers so that he can perform such wonders as shrinking and becoming invisible.

1452 Konigsburg, E. L. *Up from Jericho Tel* (6–9). 1986, Macmillan $13.95 (0-689-31194-X); Dell paper $2.95 (0-440-49142-8). The ghost of a dead actress named Tallulah makes Jeanmarie and friend Malcolm invisible to accomplish the search for a necklace. (Rev: BL 5/1/86; SLJ 5/86; VOYA 12/86)

1453 Konwicki, Tadeusz. *The Anthropos-Specter-Beast* (7–9). Trans. by George and Audrey Korwin-Rodziszewski. 1977, S. G. Phillips $14.95 (0-87599-218-8). Peter is transported to a remote place by the talking dog Sebastian.

1454 Kushner, Donn. *A Book Dragon* (7–10). Illus. 1988, Henry Holt $14.95 (0-8050-0759-8). The story of a dragon from his birth in the fourteenth century to his appearance in present-day Canada. (Rev: BL 7/88; SLJ 6–7/88)

1455 Lasky, Kathryn. *Home Free* (8–10). 1988, Dell paper $2.95 (0-440-20038-5). Sam and friend Gus and an autistic girl travel via eagle back in time. (Rev: BL 1/15/86; VOYA 8–10/86)

1456 Lawrence, Louise. *The Earth Witch* (7–10). 1981, Harper LB $12.89 (0-06-023752-X). When the spring comes an old hag becomes a beautiful young girl in this fantasy set in Wales.

1457 Le Guin, Ursula K. *Tehanu: The Last Book of Earthsea* (7–10). 1990, Macmillan $15.95 (0-

689-31595-3). In the fourth and last of the Earthsea books, Tenar is summoned by a dying mage or wise one to teach a child the spells and magic that give the power to lead. (Rev: BL 3/1/90; SLJ 4/90; VOYA 6/90)

1458 Le Guin, Ursula K. *A Wizard of Earthsea* (8–11). Illus. 1968, Parnassus $13.95 (0-395-27653-5). An apprentice wizard accidentally unleashes an evil power onto the land of Earthsea. Followed by *The Tombs of Atuan* (1971) and *The Farthest Shore* (1972).

1459 L'Engle, Madeleine. *An Acceptable Time* (8–12). 1989, Farrar $13.95 (0-374-30027-5). Polly O'Keefe time travels (like her parents did years before in the Time trilogy) but this time to visit a civilization of Druids that lived 3,000 years ago. (Rev: BL 1/1/90; BR 5–6/90; SLJ 1/90; VOYA 4/90)

1460 Levin, Betty. *The Ice Bear* (6–8). 1986, Greenwillow $10.95 (0-688-06431-0). A strange, silent girl and a bakeshop boy flee to the Forest of Lythe to help save the white Ice Bear. (Rev: BR 5–6/87; SLJ 10/86; VOYA 12/86)

1461 Levin, Betty. *The Keeping Room* (6–10). 1981, Greenwillow $11.95 (0-688-80300-8). Hal reads the journal of a girl who disappeared over 100 years ago and is determined to solve the mystery of her disappearance.

1462 Lewis, C. S. *The Lion, the Witch and the Wardrobe* (5–8). Illus. 1988, Macmillan $12.95 (0-02-758120-9); paper $5.95 (0-02-758550-6). Four children enter the kingdom of Narnia through the back of an old wardrobe. The other 6 volumes in this series are *Prince Caspian* (1988); *The Voyage of the Dawn Treader* (1986); *The Silver Chair* (1986); *The Horse and His Boy* (1988); *The Magician's Nephew* (1985); *The Last Battle* (1988).

1463 Lillington, Kenneth. *Jonah's Mirror* (6–10). 1988, Faber $11.95 (0-571-14961-8). Jonah Sprockett moves into a world of fantasy through a magical mirror he has invented. (Rev: SLJ 10/88)

1464 Luenn, Nancy. *Arctic Unicorn* (5–9). 1986, Macmillan LB $14.95 (0-689-31278-4). A young Eskimo girl discovers she has the power to turn herself into an animal or a bird. (Rev: SLJ 10/86)

J Fie **1465** Lunn, Janet. *The Root Cellar* (5–8). 1985, Penguin paper $3.95 (0-14-031835-6). A girl travels back in time to the turmoil of the Civil War. (Rev: BL 6/1/85)

1466 McGowen, Tom. *The Magician's Challenge* (5–9). 1989, Lodestar $13.95 (0-525-67289-3). Tigg and Armindor continue their battle against the evil Reen in this, the concluding volume of

the trilogy that included *The Magician's Apprentice* (1987) and *The Magician's Company* (1988). (Rev: SLJ 11/89)

1467 McHargue, Georgess. *Stoneflight* (6–9). Illus. 1976, Avon paper $1.25 (0-380-00632-4). Jamie awakens a stone griffin who helps her solve her family problems.

1468 McKenzie, Ellen Kindt. *Kashka* (6–8). 1987, Henry Holt $14.45 (0-8050-0327-4). A young princess and her cousin devise a plan to save a prince from the control of the wicked Lady Ysene. (Rev: BL 12/1/87; BR 3–4/88; SLJ 3/88)

1469 McKillip, Patricia A. *The Changeling Sea* (7–9). 1988, Macmillan $12.95 (0-689-31436-1). An unhappy young girl causes a giant monster to rise from the sea. (Rev: BL 9/15/88; BR 1–2/89; SLJ 11/88; VOYA 12/88)

1470 McKillip, Patricia A. *The Moon and the Face* (8–10). 1985, Macmillan $12.95 (0-689-31158-3). The hero and heroine of the author's earlier *Moon-Flash* (1984) have separate adventures but are at last reunited. (Rev: BL 10/15/85; SLJ 10/85; VOYA 2/86)

1471 McKinley, Robin. *Beauty: A Retelling of the Story of Beauty and the Beast* (7–10). 1978, Harper LB $13.89 (0-06-024150-0). An enchanting reworking of the Beauty and the Beast story.

1472 McKinley, Robin. *The Blue Sword* (7–10). 1982, Greenwillow LB $13.95 (0-688-00938-7). The king of Damar kidnaps a girl to help in his war against the Northerners. A prequel to *The Hero and the Crown* (1985). Newbery Medal 1985.

1473 McKinley, Robin. *The Door in the Hedge* (7–9). 1981, Greenwillow $11.75 (0-688-00312-5). Four tales, 2 of which originated in the folklore of the Grimm Brothers.

1474 Mahy, Margaret. *Aliens in the Family* (6–8). 1986, Scholastic $12.95 (0-590-40320-6); paper $2.50 (0-590-40321-4). Two quarreling stepsisters form a bond when they rescue and help an alien. (Rev: BL 10/1/86; SLJ 11/86; VOYA 12/86)

1475 Mayhar, Ardath. *Lords of the Triple Moons* (7–10). 1984, Ace paper $2.50 (0-441-49246-0). Two teenagers escape from their captors and hope to free their land of the tyrants that control it.

1476 Mazer, Norma Fox. *Saturday, the Twelfth of October* (7–9). 1989, Dell paper $3.25 (0-440-99592-2). Through time travel Zan goes back to prehistoric times and is taken in by cave dwellers. A reissue.

1477 Melling, O. R. *The Singing Stone* (7–10). Illus. 1987, Viking $13.95 (0-670-80817-2). In Ireland 2 young women must undergo a quest to establish their identities. (Rev: BL 9/15/87; SLJ 9/87)

1478 Morpurgo, Michael. *Little Foxes* (6–9). 1987, David & Charles $15.95 (0-7182-3972-5). Two orphans—a boy and a fox—are helped by a swan in this magical story. (Rev: BR 1–2/88)

1479 Murphy, Shirley Rousseau. *Nightpool* (7–10). 1985, Harper LB $11.89 (0-06-024361-9); paper $2.95 (0-06-447041-5). In this first volume of a trilogy, Teb escapes from the castle where his father was murdered and is nurtured by a band of intelligent otters. Continued in *The Ivory Lyre* (1987) and *The Dragonbards* (1988). (Rev: BL 9/1/85; BR 3–4/86; SLJ 12/85; VOYA 12/85)

1480 Myers, Walter Dean. *The Legend of Tarik* (6–9). 1982, Scholastic paper $2.50 (0-590-41211-6). Tarik a black teenager in Africa of years ago acquires a magic sword.

1481 Nimmo, Jenny. *Orchard of the Crescent Moon* (5–9). 1989, Dutton $13.95 (0-525-44438-6). Nia, the middle child in a Welsh family, must save her friend Emlyn from the spirit world in this sequel to *The Snow Spider* (1987). (Rev: SLJ 8/89; VOYA 10/89)

1482 Norton, Andre. *Here Abide Monsters* (7–9). 1985, Tor paper $2.95 (0-8125-4732-2). Trapped in a time warp, Nick and Linda visit Arthurian England.

1483 Norton, Andre. *Red Hart Magic* (7–9). Illus. 1976, Harper $14.70 (0-690-01147-4). Chris and his stepsister travel back to the time of King James I.

1484 O'Shea, Pat. *The Hounds of the Morrigan* (6–8). 1986, Holiday $15.95 (0-8234-0595-8); Dell paper $3.95 (0-440-20001-6). The forces of good and evil in Irish mythology battle over 2 children who are on a quest for a magic pebble. (Rev: BL 4/1/86)

J FiC **1485** Park, Ruth. *Playing Beatie Bow* (6–8). 1982, Macmillan $13.95 (0-689-30889-2); Penguin paper $3.95 (0-14-031460-1). A modern-day Australian girl travels back to the nineteenth century.

J PB polCE **1486** Pascal, Francine. *Hangin' out with Cici* (6–9). 1977, Viking $12.95 (0-670-36045-7); Dell paper $2.95 (0-440-93364-1). Victoria's bump on the head takes her back to 1944 when her mother was a teenager.

1487 Pearson, Kit. *A Handful of Time* (6–8). 1988, Viking $11.95 (0-670-81532-2). Through a trip back in time, a 12-year-old girl is able to understand better her mother and her parents' impending divorce. (Rev: BL 6/1/88)

1488 Peck, Richard. *Voices after Midnight* (6–9). 1989, Delacorte $14.95 (0-385-29779-3). A 14-year-old boy and his family move to a brownstone in Manhattan and soon become involved with events and people of 100 years ago. (Rev: BL 10/1/89; BR 11–12/89; SLJ 9/89; VOYA 2/90)

1489 Pendergraft, Patricia. *The Legend of Daisy Flowerdew* (6–9). 1990, Putnam $14.95 (0-399-22176-X). In this fantasy a girl escapes a cruel stepfather by entering a disastrous marriage. (Rev: BL 5/1/90)

1490 Pfeffer, Susan Beth. *Rewind to Yesterday* (6–9). 1988, Delacorte $13.95 (0-440-50048-6). A fast-paced tale about a girl who can travel back in time via a VCR. (Rev: BR 11–12/88; VOYA 12/88)

1491 Phillips, Ann. *The Oak King and the Ash Queen* (6–8). 1985, Oxford Univ. Pr. $12.95 (0-19-271495-3). In this fantasy, the twins Dan and Daisy take different sides when they join opposite sides in a war of the trees. (Rev: BL 9/1/85; SLJ 11/85)

1492 Phipson, Joan. *The Watcher in the Garden* (7–9). 1982, Macmillan $10.95 (0-689-50246-X). Three different people are drawn to a garden for different reasons.

1493 Pierce, Meredith Ann. *Birth of the Firebringer* (7–10). 1985, Macmillan $12.95 (0-02-774610-0); Scholastic paper $2.50 (0-590-40280-3). Through a terrible ordeal, Jan discovers he is the one appointed to bring his people back to their ancestral home. (Rev: BL 2/15/86; SLJ 1/86)

1494 Pierce, Meredith Ann. *The Pearl of the Soul of the World* (7–12). 1990, Little $15.95 (0-316-70743-0). In this, the conclusion of the Darkangel trilogy, Aeriel and Irrylath try to conquer the evil white witch who wants to destroy the world. Preceded by *The Darkangel* (1982) and *A Gathering of Gargoyles* (1984). (Rev: BL 1/15/90; SLJ 4/90)

1495 Pierce, Meredith Ann. *The Woman Who Loved Reindeer* (8–10). 1985, Little $14.95 (0-87113-042-4); Tor paper $3.95 (0-8125-0305-8). A young girl with unusual powers loves a reindeer who is able to turn himself into a man. (Rev: BL 10/15/85; BR 5–6/86; SLJ 12/85; VOYA 4/86)

1496 Pierce, Tamora. *Lioness Rampant: The Song of the Lioness Book Four* (7–9). 1988, Macmillan $13.95 (0-689-31116-8). In this fourth and last of the Song of the Lioness series, Alanna sets out to secure the Dominion Jewel and capture its power. (Rev: BL 9/15/88; SLJ 12/88; VOYA 12/88)

1497 Pierce, Tamora. *The Woman Who Rides Like a Man* (8–10). 1986, Macmillan $14.95 (0-689-31117-6). In this third Song of the Lioness series, the female knight Alanna becomes shaman of her tribe and encounters some love problems. (Rev: BL 6/15/86; SLJ 8/86)

1498 Poole, Josephine. *The Visitor: A Story of Suspense* (6–9). 1972, Harper LB $11.89 (0-06-624769-X). Mr. Bogle, Harry's new tutor, seems to possess an unearthly power.

1499 Pratchett, Terry. *Truckers* (6–9). 1990, Delacorte $14.95 (0-385-29984-2). A fantasy about very little people who have taken refuge in a department store. (Rev: BL 3/15/90)

1500 Purtill, Richard. *Enchantment at Delphi* (6–9). 1986, Harcourt $14.95 (0-15-200447-5). On a trip to Delphi, Alice finds herself transported back in time to the days of Apollo and other Greek gods. (Rev: SLJ 11/86)

1501 Reynolds, Alfred. *Kiteman of Karanga* (7–10). 1985, Knopf LB $11.99 (0-394-96347-4); Bantam paper $2.75 (0-553-26036-7). Karl is able to prove his courage by helping a group of shepherds gain their freedom. The paperback edition is called *Kiteman*. (Rev: BL 10/1/85; SLJ 11/85)

1502 Roberts, John Maddox. *Conan the Bold* (7–9). 1989, Tor paper $3.95 (0-812-55210-5). Conan sets out to avenge the deaths of the people with whom he was staying. (Rev: VOYA 10/89)

1503 Rodowsky, Colby. *Keeping Time* (7–9). 1983, Farrar $11.95 (0-374-34061-7). Drew is mysteriously transported to Elizabethan London where he forms new friendships.

1504 St. George, Judith. *Who's Scared? Not Me!* (7–10). 1987, Putnam $13.95 (0-399-31481-X). Time travel, a mysterious bag lady, and a budding romance are 3 ingredients in this novel. (Rev: BL 11/15/87; SLJ 12/87; VOYA 2/88)

1505 Saint-Exupery, Antoine de. *The Little Prince* (5–9). Trans. by Katherine Woods. 1943, Harcourt $9.95 (0-15-246503-0); paper $6.95 (0-15-646511-6). An airplane pilot crashes in a desert and encounters a little prince who seeks harmony for his planet.

1506 Sargent, Sarah. *Lure of the Dark* (7–9). 1985, Scholastic paper $2.25 (0-590-33565-0). Good versus evil in this fantasy set in present-day Wisconsin.

1507 Sargent, Sarah. *Watermusic* (6–8). 1986, Clarion $11.95 (0-89919-436-2). Through a magic flute, Laura is able to bring strange beasts to life. (Rev: BL 3/15/86; BR 11–12/86; SLJ 5/86)

1508 Service, Pamela F. *The Reluctant God* (7–10). 1988, Macmillan $13.95 (0-689-31404-3). While visiting Egypt with her archaeologist father, Lorna encounters a pharaoh's son who lived 4,000 years ago. (Rev: BR 9–10/88; VOYA 6/88)

1509 Service, Pamela F. *Tomorrow's Magic* (6–9). 1987, Macmillan $12.95 (0-689-31320-9); Fawcett paper $2.95 (0-449-70305-3). In a post-nuclear holocaust world, King Arthur and his friends return to try to once again unite Britain. This is a sequel to *Winter of Magic's Return* (1987). (Rev: BL 10/15/87; SLJ 9/87)

1510 Silverstein, Herma. *Mad, Mad Monday* (6–8). 1988, Dutton $12.95 (0-525-67239-7). Miranda encounters the ghost of a teenager nicknamed Monday who supposedly died 30 years ago. (Rev: BL 4/1/88; VOYA 10/88)

1511 Singer, Marilyn. *Ghost Host* (6–9). 1987, Harper LB $11.89 (0-06-025624-9); Scholastic paper $2.50 (0-590-41547-6). Bart Hawkins has everything going for him until he discovers a poltergeist in his home. (Rev: VOYA 6/87)

1512 Singer, Marilyn. *Horsemaster* (7–9). 1985, Macmillan $13.95 (0-689-31102-8). A 14-year-old girl enters a new world where there is a struggle between good and evil elements. (Rev: BL 6/1/85; SLJ 9/85; VOYA 8/85)

1513 Sleator, William. *The Green Futures of Tycho* (6–9). 1981, Dutton $14.95 (0-525-31007-X). Tycho discovers an object that allows him to time travel. Also use: *Among the Dolls* (1975).

1514 Smith, Stephanie A. *The Boy Who Was Thrown Away* (6–9). 1987, Macmillan $13.95 (0-689-31343-8). A gifted boy is kidnapped and sold to a group of hereditary cantors. (Rev: SLJ 12/87)

1515 Smith, Stephanie A. *Snow-Eyes* (7–9). 1985, Macmillan $13.95 (0-689-31129-X). Snow-Eyes learns from her mother that she has been born with special powers that she must develop under her mother's guidance. (Rev: VOYA 4/86)

1516 Sobol, Donald J. *The Amazing Power of Ashur Fine* (5–8). 1986, Macmillan $11.95 (0-02-786270-4). Sixteen-year-old Ashur gains supernatural powers from an African elephant. (Rev: BR 5–6/87)

1517 Spicer, Dorothy. *The Humming Top* (6–8). 1968, Phillips $14.95 (0-87599-147-5). An orphan finds she is able to predict future events.

1518 Springer, Nancy. *Red Wizard* (6–8). 1990, Macmillan $12.95 (0-689-31485-X). Ryan is called into another world by an inept wizard and must find the secret of the Deep Magic of colors before he can return. (Rev: VOYA 4/90)

1519 Stolz, Mary. *Cat in the Mirror* (6–9). 1978, Dell paper $1.95 (0-440-91123-0). An outsider travels in time to ancient Egypt.

1520 Strauss, Victoria. *Worldstone* (7–12). 1985, Macmillan $14.95 (0-02-788380-9). Alexina finds that she has the power to link minds with people from other worlds. (Rev: BL 11/1/85; BR 5–6/86; SLJ 1/89)

1521 Sykes, Pamela. *Mirror of Danger* (7–9). 1976, Archway paper $1.95 (0-671-42892-6). Lucy finds a new friend in Alice but this new acquaintance brings with her days of terror.

1522 Tannen, Mary. *The Wizard Children of Finn* (5–8). Illus. 1981, Avon paper $2.25 (0-380-57661-9). Two children and an enchanted boy travel back in time to the early days of Ireland's history. A sequel is *The Lost Legend of Finn* (1982).

1523 Townsend, John Rowe. *The Fortunate Isles* (7–12). 1989, Harper LB $13.89 (0-397-32366-2). Eleni and her friend Andreas seek the living god in this novel set in a mythical land. (Rev: BL 10/15/89; SLJ 10/89)

1524 Voigt, Cynthia. *Building Blocks* (7–10). 1984, Macmillan $11.95 (0-689-31035-8). A boy travels back in time to witness his father's childhood.

1525 Walsh, Jill Paton. *A Chance Child* (7–9). 1978, Avon paper $1.95 (0-380-48561-3). In this English novel, a young boy who has been a prisoner all his life suddenly travels back in time.

1526 Walsh, Jill Paton. *Torch* (6–10). 1988, Farrar $12.95 (0-374-37684-0). Dio and Cal carry a magical torch on a quest that exposes them to forces of good and evil. (Rev: BL 4/15/88; SLJ 5/88)

1527 Wangerin, Walter, Jr. *The Book of the Dun Cow* (7–10). 1978, Harper LB $12.89 (0-06-026347-4). A farmyard fable with talking animals that retells the story of Chanticleer the Rooster.

1528 Westall, Robert. *The Devil on the Road* (7–10). 1979, Greenwillow LB $11.88 (0-688-84227-5). An abandoned barn becomes the central point for John's travels back in time. Two others fantasies by this author: *The Cats of Seroster* and *Futuretrack Five* (both 1984).

1529 Westall, Robert. *The Scarecrows* (6–9). 1981, Greenwillow LB $11.75 (0-688-00612-4). A hostile young boy believes that the 3 scarecrows in the yard have come to life.

1530 White, T. H. *The Sword in the Stone* (7–12). 1978, Dell paper $3.50 (0-440-98445-9). The first part of the retelling of the Arthurian story which ends with Wart removing the sword from the stone.

1531 Wibberley, Leonard. *The Crime of Martin Coverly* (6–9). 1980, Farrar $11.95 (0-374-31656-2). Nick's ancestor takes him back in time for a pirate adventure.

1532 Wiseman, David. *Adam's Common* (7–9). 1984, Houghton $11.95 (0-395-35976-7). A 14-year-old English girl travels through time to save the park she has grown to love.

1533 Wrightson, Patricia. *A Little Fear* (7–9). 1983, Macmillan $12.95 (0-689-50291-5). In this Australian novel an old lady battles the powers of a gnome.

1534 Wrightson, Patricia. *The Nargun and the Stars* (6–8). 1986, Macmillan $10.95 (0-689-50403-9); Penguin paper $3.95 (0-14-030780-X). In the wilderness of northern Australia, Simon encounters a wicked monster, the Nargun. A reissue. (Rev: BL 11/1/86; VOYA 2/87)

1535 Yep, Laurence. *Dragon Steel* (6–8). 1985, Harper LB $12.89 (0-06-026751-8). The dragon princess Shimmer tries to save her clan who are forced to work in an undersea volcano in this sequel to *Dragon of the Lost Sea* (1982). (Rev: BL 5/15/85; SLJ 9/85; VOYA 8/85)

1536 Yolen, Jane. *The Devil's Arithmetic* (7–12). 1988, Viking $11.95 (0-670-81027-4). At Passover service the prophet Elijah takes 12-year-old Hannah back to 1942 and the Holocaust concentration camps. (Rev: BL 9/1/88; BR 1–2/89)

1537 Yolen, Jane, et al., eds. *Dragons & Dreams* (6–10). 1986, Harper $12.50 (0-06-026792-5). A collection of 10 fantasy and some science fiction stories that can be a fine introduction to these genres. (Rev: BR 11–12/86; VOYA 6/86)

1538 Yolen, Jane. *Dream Weaver* (6–8). 1989, Putnam $15.95 (0-399-22152-2). A collection of 7 contemporary fairy tales written by a master of fantasy. A reissue. (Rev: BL 1/15/90)

1539 Yolen, Jane. *The Faery Flag: Stories and Poems of Fantasy and the Supernatural* (4–9). Illus. 1989, Watts LB $14.99 (0-531-08438-8). Using various settings and subjects, this is a collection of 9 stories and 5 poems that all use the elements of fantasy. (Rev: SLJ 9/89; VOYA 10/89)

1540 Yolen, Jane. *A Sending of Dragons* (7–12). 1987, Delacorte $14.95 (0-385-29587-1); Dell paper $3.25 (0-440-20309-0). In this concluding volume of the Pit Dragon trilogy, hero and heroine,

Jakkin and Akki, are captured by primitive people who live underground. Previous volumes are *Dragon's Blood* (1982) and *Heart's Blood* (1984). (Rev: BL 11/1/87; BR 11–12/87; SLJ 1/88)

1541 Zettner, Pat. *The Shadow Warrior* (7–10). 1990, Macmillan $13.95 (0-689-31486-8). Llyndreth sets out to find her brother, who is absent fighting goblins. (Rev: BL 6/1/90; SLJ 5/90)

Historical Fiction

Prehistory

1542 Garcia, Ann O'Neal. *Spirit on the Wall* (7–9). 1982, Holiday $9.95 (0-8234-0447-1). Three misfits of ancient times join forces to find a life of their own.

1543 Turnbull, Ann. *Maroo of the Winter Caves* (6–8). 1984, Clarion $13.95 (0-89919-304-8). In this novel set during the last Ice Age, a young girl and her family race against time to reach their cave before winter comes. (Rev: BL 1/15/85)

Ancient and Medieval History

GENERAL AND MISCELLANEOUS

1544 Carter, Dorothy Sharp. *His Majesty, Queen Hatshepsut* (6–9). 1987, Harper LB $13.89 (0-397-32179-1). A fictionalized biography of Queen Hatshepsut, daughter of Thutmose I and the only female pharaoh of Egypt. (Rev: BR 3–4/88; SLJ 10/87; VOYA 12/87)

1545 Morgan, Alison. *The Eyes of the Blind* (6–10). 1987, Oxford Univ. Pr. $13.95 (0-19-271542-9). An historical novel set in the turbulent days of ancient Palestine and involving the grandson of the prophet Isaiah. (Rev: SLJ 2/88)

1546 Speare, Elizabeth George. *The Bronze Bow* (7–10). 1961, Houghton $13.95 (0-395-07113-5); paper $7.95 (0-395-13719-5). The Newbery Award winner about a boy growing up in Roman-occupied Galilee at the time of Jesus.

1547 Stolz, Mary. *Pangur Ban* (6–9). Illus. 1988, Harper LB $13.89 (0-06-025862-4). In this historical novel set in ninth-century Ireland, a young lad enters a monastery and becomes a famous illuminator of manuscripts. (Rev: BL 11/1/88; BR 5–6/89; SLJ 11/88)

GREECE AND ROME

1548 Keaney, Brian. *No Need for Heroes* (6–8). 1989, Oxford Univ. Pr. $14.95 (0-19-271610-7). A clever retelling of the Ariadne-Theseus-Minotaur story. (Rev: SLJ 7/89)

1549 Sutcliff, Rosemary. *The Eagle of the Ninth* (7–12). 1986, Oxford Univ. Pr. $13.95 (0-19-271037-0). A reissue of the historical novel about the Roman legion that went to battle and disappeared. (Rev: BR 1–2/87)

MIDDLE AGES

1550 McCaughrean, Geraldine. *A Little Lower Than the Angels* (6–9). 1987, Oxford Univ. Pr. $13.95 (0-19-271561-5). The adventures of a young man who joins a theater troupe touring in Medieval Europe. (Rev: BL 1/1/88; SLJ 4/88)

1551 Norton, Andre. *Huon of the Horn* (7–9). 1987, Ballantine paper $2.95 (0-345-34126-0). Part of the Charlemagne legend retold with fanciful trappings.

1552 O'Dell, Scott. *The Road to Damietta* (7–10). 1985, Houghton $14.95 (0-395-38923-2). A novel set in thirteenth-century Italy and involving St. Francis of Assisi. (Rev: SLJ 12/85; VOYA 2/86)

1553 Phillips, Ann. *The Peace Child* (6–9). 1988, Oxford Univ. Pr. $13.95 (0-19-271560-7). Set in the fourteenth century at the time of the Black Death, this novel tells the story of a girl switched at birth to be brought up by a rival clan. (Rev: BL 12/1/88)

1554 Voigt, Cynthia. *Jackaroo* (8–10). 1985, Macmillan $14.95 (0-689-31123-0). In this novel set in the Middle Ages, a 16-year-old girl assumes the identity of a Robin Hood-like character named Jackaroo. (Rev: BL 9/15/85; SLJ 12/85)

Asia and the Pacific

1555 Buck, Pearl S. *The Good Earth* (7–12). 1965, Harper $16.45 (0-381-98033-2); Pocket paper $3.95 (0-671-50086-4). The epic story of the rise from poverty of Wang Lung and his family in nineteenth-century China.

1556 Els, Betty Vander. *Leaving Point* (7–10). 1987, Farrar $12.95 (0-374-34376-4). Ruth and her family of missionaries are caught in China at the time of the Maoist revolution, in this sequel to *The Bombers' Moon* (1984). (Rev: SLJ 2/88)

1557 Haugaard, Erik Christian. *The Samurai's Tale* (7–9). 1984, Houghton $12.95 (0-395-34559-

6). A Japanese orphan trains to be a samurai to fight his family's enemies.

1558 Lewis, Elizabeth Foreman. *Young Fu of the Upper Yangtze* (5–8). 1973, Henry Holt $15.95 (0-8050-0549-8). In this Newbery Medal winner set in pre-World War II China, a young boy and his mother move from the countryside to Chung King.

1559 Namioka, Lensey. *Island of Ogres* (7–10). 1989, Harper LB $13.89 (0-06-024373-2). A has-been samurai regains self-respect when he thwarts plans of a rebel invasion of a small island. (Rev: BL 5/15/89; BR 11–12/89; SLJ 3/89)

1560 Namioka, Lensey. *Valley of the Broken Cherry Trees* (6–8). 1980, Delacorte $8.95 (0-440-09325-2). An unemployed samurai and a friend investigate the mutilation of some famous cherry trees.

1561 Namioka, Lensey. *Village of the Vampire Cat* (7–10). 1981, Delacorte $9.95 (0-440-09377-5). Two samurai confront a woman-killing "Vampire Cat" in this tale set in historic Japan.

1562 Paterson, Katherine. *Rebels of the Heavenly Kingdom* (7–9). 1983, Dutton $11.95 (0-525-66911-6); Avon paper $2.95 (0-380-68304-0). In nineteenth-century China a 15-year-old boy and a young girl engage in activities to overthrow the Manchu government.

1563 Yep, Laurence. *Mountain Light* (8–11). 1985, Harper LB $12.89 (0-06-026759-3). Yep continues to explore life in nineteenth-century China through the experience of a girl, Cassia, her father and friends, and their struggle against the Manchus in this sequel to *The Serpent's Children* (1984). (Rev: BL 9/15/85; SLJ 1/87; VOYA 12/85)

Europe and the Middle East

1564 Ball, Angela. *Vixie* (6–9). 1988, Oxford Univ. Pr. $13.95 (0-19-271555-0). In England of 1908, Vixie's family faces so many problems that although she is only 11, she must become a servant in the vicar's home. (Rev: SLJ 6–7/88)

1565 Calvert, Patricia. *Hadder MacColl* (6–8). 1985, Macmillan $12.95 (0-684-18447-8); paper $3.95 (0-14-032158-6). An adventure story set in the Scotland of Bonnie Prince Charlie and featuring a spunky heroine named Hadder MacColl. (Rev: SLJ 10/85)

1566 de Trevino, Elizabeth Borton. *I, Juan de Pareja* (7–9). 1987, Farrar paper $3.45 (0-374-

43525-1). The story of the slave who became an inspiration for his master the Spanish painter, Velazquez. A Newbery Medal winner. A reissue.

1567 Fenton, Edward. *The Refugee Summer* (7–9). 1982, Delacorte $10.95 (0-385-28854-9). During 1922 in Greece, a group of youngsters become involved with a group of refugees fleeing from the Turks.

1568 Garfield, Leon. *The Apprentices* (6–9). 1988, Penguin paper $4.95 (0-14-031595-0). Twelve stories about various apprentices in nineteenth-century England.

1569 Garfield, Leon. *The December Rose* (6–9). 1987, Viking $12.95 (0-670-81054-1); Penguin paper $3.95 (0-14-032070-9). In this novel set in Victorian England, a young boy finds a trail of murder and intrigue after he overhears a criminal plot. (Rev: BL 8/87; SLJ 9/87)

1570 Garfield, Leon. *The Empty Sleeve* (6–10). 1988, Doubleday $14.95 (0-440-50049-4). The saga of twins, ghostly happenings, and spine-tingling adventure set in Victorian England. (Rev: BL 9/15/88; BR 11–12/88; SLJ 10/88)

1571 Garfield, Leon. *Footsteps* (6–9). 1980, Delacorte $12.95 (0-385-28294-X); Dell paper $3.95 (0-440-40102-X). Set in the dark streets of Victorian London, this is a novel of mystery, murder, and a young boy who wants to learn about his past. Also use: *Smith* (1987).

1572 Garfield, Leon. *Young Nick and Jubilee* (6–8). Illus. 1989, Delacorte $13.95 (0-385-39777-7). A fast-paced adventure about a 10-year-old boy and his young sister adrift on the streets of Dickensian London. (Rev: BL 8/89; BR 1–2/90)

1573 Harnett, Cynthia. *The Writing on the Hearth* (7–9). 1984, Lerner $9.95 (0-8225-0889-3). A novel of intrigue and witchcraft in England set during the fifteenth century.

1574 Haugaard, Erik Christian. *Chase Me* (7–9). 1980, Houghton $8.95 (0-395-29208-5). In pre-World War II Germany, a young Danish boy gets involved with an anti-Nazi plot.

1575 Haugaard, Erik Christian. *Leif the Unlucky* (6–8). 1982, Houghton $9.95 (0-395-32156-5). Young Leif Magnusson gets involved in a plan to help the Norwegian colony in fifteenth-century Greenland.

1576 Hendry, Frances Mary. *Quest for a Kelpie* (6–9). 1988, Holiday $12.95 (0-8234-0680-6). A 12-year-old Scottish girl growing up in eighteenth-century Scotland becomes immersed in intrigue involving Bonnie Prince Charlie. (Rev: BL 7/88; SLJ 6–7/88)

1577 Hendry, Frances Mary. *Quest for a Maid* (8–10). 1990, Farrar $13.95 (0-374-36162-2). The story of an 8-year-old princess and her maid who travel to Britain during the thirteenth century. (Rev: BL 7/90)

1578 Hilgartner, Beth. *A Murder for Her Majesty* (6–8). 1986, Houghton $12.95 (0-395-41451-2). In Elizabethan England, a young girl must disguise herself as a boy to escape her father's murderers. (Rev: BL 9/15/86; SLJ 10/86; VOYA 12/87)

1579 Holman, Felice. *The Wild Children* (7–9). 1983, Macmillan $12.95 (0-684-17970-9); Penguin paper $4.95 (0-14-031930-1). Alex joins a group of homeless children after the Russian Revolution of 1917.

1580 Horgan, Dorothy. *Then the Zeppelins Came* (5–8). 1990, Oxford Univ. Pr. $14.95 (0-19-271598-4). The story of two girls growing up in Edwardian London and of their families and minor adventures. (Rev: SLJ 7/90)

1581 Hunter, Mollie. *The Third Eye* (7–10). 1979, Harper LB $12.89 (0-06-022676-5). Jinty and her 2 sisters are growing up in the highlands of Scotland in the early 1900s.

1582 Hunter, Mollie. *You Never Knew Her As I Did!* (7–10). Illus. 1981, Harper $13.70 (0-06-022678-1). A historical novel about a plan to help the imprisoned Mary, Queen of Scots, to escape from prison.

1583 Kelly, Eric P. *The Trumpeter of Krakow* (6–9). Illus. 1966, Macmillan $13.95 (0-02-750140-X); paper $3.95 (0-02-044150-9). The celebration of a brave act and the story of a valuable jewel and its guardian in this story set in old Poland.

1584 Konigsburg, E. L. *A Proud Taste for Scarlet and Miniver* (7–9). Illus. 1973, Macmillan $12.95 (0-689-30111-1). Eleanor of Aquitaine tells her story in heaven while awaiting her second husband, Henry II.

1585 Konigsburg, E. L. *Second Mrs. Giaconda* (7–9). 1978, Macmillan paper $1.95 (0-689-70450-X). Leonardo da Vinci's valet narrates this story that tells the truth about Mona Lisa and her smile.

1586 Lasky, Kathryn. *The Night Journey* (7–9). Illus. 1986, Viking $12.95 (0-670-80935-7); Penguin paper $4.95 (0-14-032048-2). The escape of a group of Russian Jews from Tsarist cruelty told in a series of flashbacks from the present.

1587 McCaughrean, Geraldine. *El Cid* (5–9). Illus. 1989, Oxford Univ. Pr. $17.95 (0-19-276077-3). A retelling of the epic poem of Spain's national hero. (Rev: VOYA 6/90)

1588 McCutcheon, Elsie. *Summer of the Zeppelin* (6–8). 1985, Farrar $10.95 (0-374-37294-2). In England during World War I, a young girl befriends an escaped German prisoner of war. (Rev: SLJ 5/85)

1589 Magorian, Michelle. *Back Home* (7–9). 1984, Harper $14.95 (0-06-024103-9). A young English girl who returns to Britain after World War II wants to go back to her second home in the United States.

1590 Melnikoff, Pamela. *Plots and Players: The Lopez Conspiracy* (6–8). Illus. 1989, Bedrick $9.95 (0-87226-406-8). Set in Elizabethan England, this is the story of Jews who were forced to pretend to be Christians in order to stay alive. (Rev: BL 7/89; BR 9–10/89; SLJ 7/89; VOYA 10/89)

1591 Mockler, Anthony. *King Arthur and His Knights* (6–9). Illus. 1985, Oxford Univ. Pr. $14.95 (0-19-274531-X). A retelling of the story of King Arthur, the Round Table, and the exploits of the knights, with the principal focus on Sir Gawain. (Rev: SLJ 8/86)

1592 Ofek, Uriel. *Smoke over Golan* (6–8). Trans. by Israel I. Taslitt. Illus. 1979, Harper LB $10.89 (0-06-024614-6). At the beginning of the Yom Kippur War of 1973, Eita learns that the family farm is very close to the fighting.

1593 Overton, Jenny. *The Ship from Simnel Street* (6–9). 1986, Greenwillow $10.25 (0-688-06182-6). Through activities in an old English bakery, important events in nineteenth-century England are recounted. (Rev: BL 11/1/86; BR 11–12/86; SLJ 11/86; VOYA 12/86)

1594 Peyton, K. M. *Flambards* (7–12). 1989, Penguin paper $3.95 (0-14-034153-6). This novel deals with young people in the early days of flying and is set in England before and during World War I. It is followed by *The Edge of the Cloud* and *Flambards in Summer* (both 1989). A reissue. Flambards in Summer

1595 Pitt, Nancy. *Beyond the High White Wall* (6–8). 1986, Macmillan $11.95 (0-684-18663-2). In czarist Russia, Libby Kagan knows who committed a murder but is afraid that her Jewish family will emigrate to America before she can safely tell what she knows. (Rev: BL 8/86; SLJ 8/86; VOYA 12/86)

1596 Posell, Elsa. *Homecoming* (6–8). 1987, Harcourt $14.95 (0-15-235160-4). After the Russian Revolution, a Jewish family faces incredible hardships until they are able to escape to America. (Rev: BL 12/1/87; SLJ 12/87; VOYA 4/88)

1597 Pullman, Philip. *The Ruby in the Smoke* (8–10). 1987, Knopf $11.95 (0-394-88826-X); paper

$2.95 (0-394-89589-4). Sally Lockhart, alone in Dickensian London, encounters murder, opium dens, and romance in her search for her inheritance. Continued in *Shadow in the North* (1988) and *The Tiger in the Well* (1990). (Rev: BL 3/1/ 87; BR 11–12/87; SLJ 4/87; VOYA 10/87)

1598 Pyle, Howard. *Men of Iron* (7–9). 1989, Troll LB $11.89 (0-8167-1871-7); Airmont paper $1.95 (0-8049-0043-0). The days of chivalry are re-created in this tale that takes place during the reign of King Henry IV. A reissue.

1599 Singer, Isaac Bashevis. *Stories for Children* (7–9). 1984, Farrar $16.95 (0-374-37266-7); paper $7.95 (0-374-46489-8). This collection includes 36 stories most of which are fantasies about Jewish life in old Europe.

1600 Skurzynski, Gloria. *Manwolf* (7–9). 1981, Clarion $10.95 (0-395-30079-7). A diseased boy is accused of being a werewolf in fourteenth-century Poland.

1601 Stevenson, Robert Louis. *The Black Arrow* (7–12). 1963, Airmont paper $2.50 (0-8049-0020-5). Set against the War of the Roses, this is an adventure story involving a young hero, Dick Shelton. First published in 1888.

1602 Sutcliff, Rosemary. *The Best of Rosemary Sutcliff: Warrior Scarlet, The Mark of the Horse Lord, Knight's Fee* (7–10). 1989, Bedrick $13.95 (0-87226-195-6). Three novels set in Britain during the Bronze Age, Roman times, and the Middle Ages. (Rev: BR 11–12/89)

1603 Sutcliff, Rosemary. *Flame-Colored Taffeta* (6–9). 1986, Farrar $11.95 (0-374-32344-5); paper $3.50 (0-374-42341-5). Damaris and her friends help a wounded smuggler in this story set in eighteenth-century England. (Rev: BL 11/15/ 86; SLJ 2/87; VOYA 2/87)

1604 Sutcliff, Rosemary. *The Shining Company* (7–12). 1990, Farrar $13.95 (0-374-36807-4). A novel set in early Britain about a young man who with his friends confronts the enemy Saxons. (Rev: BL 6/15/90; SLJ 7/90)

1605 Von Canon, Claudia. *The Moonclock* (7–9). 1979, Houghton $6.95 (0-395-27810-4). Through a series of letters 2 couples relive their adventures during the Turkish invasion of Austria in the seventeenth century.

1606 Watson, James. *The Freedom Tree* (8–10). 1986, Gollancz $16.95 (0-575-03779-2). Will, a 16-year-old, experiences the horrors of war when he becomes a stretcher-bearer in the Republican army during the Spanish civil war. (Rev: BL 11/1/ 86; SLJ 2/87)

1607 Wheeler, Thomas Gerald. *All Men Tall* (7–9). 1969, Phillips $16.95 (0-87599-157-2). An adventurous tale set in England during the Middle Ages about a 15-year-old boy's search for security.

1608 Wheeler, Thomas Gerald. *A Fanfare for the Stalwart* (7–9). 1967, Phillips $16.95 (0-87599-152-1). An injured Frenchman is left behind when Napoleon retreats from Russia.

1609 Willard, Barbara. *The Cold Wind Blowing* (7–9). 1989, Dell paper $3.25 (0-440-20408-9). In this gripping yarn, the religious reforms of Henry VIII have disastrous effects on an English family. (Rev: VOYA 12/89)

1610 Willard, Barbara. *The Iron Lily* (7–9). 1989, Dell paper $3.25 (0-440-20434-8). In Tudor England, a 15-year-old girl tries to find out the whereabouts of her real father.

1611 Willard, Barbara. *The Sprig of Broom* (7–9). 1989, Dell paper $3.25 (0-440-20347-3). In sixteenth-century England, a 15-year-old boy sets out to find his father when his mother is killed in a witch-hunt.

Latin America and Canada

1612 Clark, Ann Nolan. *Secret of the Andes* (6–8). 1970, Viking $13.95 (0-670-62975-8); Penguin paper $3.95 (0-14-030926-8). In this Newbery Award book, a young Inca boy searches for his birthright and his identity.

1613 Howard, Ellen. *When Daylight Comes* (5–9). 1985, Macmillan LB $14.95 (0-689-31133-8). A fictionalized account of the slave uprising in the Virgin Islands in 1733 when they were under Danish control. (Rev: SLJ 11/85)

1614 Lunn, Janet. *Shadow in Hawthorn Bay* (7–9). 1987, Macmillan $12.95 (0-684-18843-0); Penguin paper $3.95 (0-14-032436-4). A Scottish girl with extrasensory perception travels to Canada during pioneer days to help her cousin Duncan. (Rev: BL 6/1/87; BR 11–12/87; SLJ 9/87; VOYA 8–9/87)

1615 Marko, Katherine McGlade. *Away to Fundy Bay* (6–9). 1985, Walker LB $12.85 (0-8027-6594-7). A novel set in the time of the American Revolution that involves a boy who runs afoul of the Tories in Nova Scotia. (Rev: BR 11–12/85; SLJ 10/85)

1616 O'Dell, Scott. *The Captive* (7–9). 1979, Houghton $9.95 (0-395-27811-2). During a voyage in the 1500s, a young Jesuit seminarian discovers that the crew of his ship plans to enslave a colony of Mayans. A sequel is *The Feathered Serpent* (1981).

1617 O'Dell, Scott. *The King's Fifth* (7–10). 1966, Houghton $14.95 (0-395-06963-7). In a story told in flashbacks, Esteban explains why he is in jail in the Mexico of the Conquistadors. Also use: *The Hawk That Dare Not Hunt by Day* (1975).

1618 O'Dell, Scott. *My Name Is Not Angelica* (6–8). 1989, Houghton $14.95 (0-395-51061-9). A novel about an African girl and her lover who are taken as slaves to the Danish Virgin Islands. (Rev: BR 3–4/90; SLJ 10/89; VOYA 12/89)

1619 Smith, T. H. *Cry to the Night Wind* (7–9). 1986, Viking $11.95 (0-670-80750-8). An adventure story set in the eighteenth century about a boy kidnapped by Indians in British Columbia. (Rev: BR 3–4/87; SLJ 2/87)

United States

INDIANS OF NORTH AMERICA

1620 Baker, Betty. *Walk the World's Rim* (7–9). 1965, Trophy LB $12.89 (0-06-020381-1). The story of an Indian boy on the doomed expedition to find Cibola, the City of Gold.

1621 Benchley, Nathaniel. *Only Earth and Sky Last Forever* (6–9). 1972, Harper paper $3.95 (0-06-440049-2). The Battle of Little Big Horn is a pivotal event in this novel of an Indian boy's journey to manhood.

1622 Borland, Hal. *When the Legends Die* (7–12). 1972, Bantam paper $2.95 (0-553-25738-2). An Indian passes from childhood to become an adult in a world that causes frustration and hostility.

1623 Doughty, Wayne Dyre. *Crimson Moccasins* (7–9). 1980, Harper paper $2.95 (0-06-440015-8). During the Revolutionary War a white boy is raised as the son of an Indian chief.

1624 Gall, Grant. *Apache: The Long Ride Home* (7–10). 1988, Sunstone paper $9.95 (0-86534-105-2). Pedro was only 9 when Apache raiders kidnapped him and renamed him Cuchillo. (Rev: BR 9–10/88)

1625 Gregory, Kristiana. *The Legend of Jimmy Spoon* (6–8). 1990, Harcourt $14.95 (0-15-200506-4). The story of a 12-year-old white boy who is adopted by the Shoshoni in 1855. (Rev: BL 7/90)

1626 Hamilton, Dorothy. *Jim Musco* (6–8). 1972, Herald Pr. paper $3.95 (0-8361-1668-2).

Jim Musco, a young Delaware Indian, is afraid he will have to leave his home when the tribe moves West.

1627 Highwater, Jamake. *Eyes of Darkness* (8–10). 1985, Lothrop $13.00 (0-688-41993-3). A fictionalized biography of Charles Alexander Eastman, an American Indian who found he could not live in either the white man's world or that of his own people. (Rev: BL 10/15/85; BR 1–2/86; SLJ 11/85)

1628 Highwater, Jamake. *Legend Days* (7–10). 1984, Harper LB $12.89 (0-06-02230-4-9). This beginning story about a young Indian girl begins a moving Ghost Horse trilogy about 3 generations of Native Americans and their fate in a white man's world. Followed by: *The Ceremony of Innocence* (1985) and *I Wear the Morning Star* (1986).

1629 Hotze, Sollace. *A Circle Unbroken* (7–10). 1988, Clarion $13.95 (0-89919-733-7). A white girl, raised by Indians, is forced at age 17 to return to her real family. (Rev: BL 9/1/88; SLJ 1/89; VOYA 2/89)

1630 Hudson, Jan. *Sweetgrass* (5–9). 1989, Putnam $13.95 (0-399-21721-5). A rich historical novel of a 15-year-old Dakota Indian girl in the 1830s who lived through a smallpox epidemic. (Rev: BL 4/1/89; BR 9–10/89; SLJ 4/89; VOYA 6/89)

1631 O'Dell, Scott. *Sing Down the Moon* (7–10). 1970, Houghton $12.95 (0-395-10919-1). A young Navaho girl sees her culture destroyed by Spanish slavers and white soldiers.

1632 Rockwood, Joyce. *To Spoil the Sun* (7–9). 1987, Henry Holt $12.95 (0-8050-0293-6). Originally published in 1977, this is the story of the destruction of an Indian village because of smallpox, a white man's disease. (Rev: BL 4/15/87)

1633 Sandoz, Mari. *The Horsecatcher* (7–9). 1957, Westminster $12.95 (0-664-30063-4); Univ. of Nebraska paper $5.95 (0-8032-9160-4). A Cheyenne youth gains stature with his tribe and gains the name of Horsecatcher.

1634 Speare, Elizabeth George. *The Sign of the Beaver* (6–9). 1983, Houghton $12.95 (0-395-33890-5); Dell paper $3.25 (0-440-47900-2). After the French and Indian wars, a young boy is raised by Indians.

1635 Wisler, G. Clifton. *Buffalo Moon* (7–9). 1984, Dutton $10.95 (0-525-67146-3). A runaway white boy survives with the help of his Comanche friend, Red Wolf.

COLONIAL PERIOD AND FRENCH AND INDIAN WARS

1636 Avi. *Night Journeys* (6–9). 1979, Pantheon $6.95 (0-384-84116-6). In the Pennsylvania of 1767, a 12-year-old orphan boy joins a hunt for escaped bondsmen. Another novel set at the same time by this author is *Encounter at Easton* (1980).

1637 Clapp, Patricia. *Constance: A Story of Early Plymouth* (7–9). 1987, Penguin paper $4.95 (0-14-032407-0). An imaginary diary kept by a young Pilgrim girl who sailed on the *Mayflower.*

1638 Clapp, Patricia. *Witches' Children: A Story of Salem* (7–10). 1987, Penguin paper $3.95 (0-14-032407-0). A novel about the Salem witchcraft trials from the standpoint of one of the 10 "afflicted girls."

1639 Collier, James Lincoln, and Christopher Collier. *The Bloody Country* (7–10). 1976, Macmillan $12.95 (0-590-07411-3); Scholastic paper $2.50 (0-590-40948-4). A pioneer story about a family that settles in the 1750s in what is now Wilkes-Barre, Pennsylvania. Also use another fine historical novel by these authors: *The Winter Hero* (1978).

1640 Fleischman, Paul. *Saturnalia* (6–9). 1990, Harper LB $12.89 (0-06-021913-0). The harshness of Colonial life is seen through the eyes of a young Indian boy who is a printer's apprentice. (Rev: BL 5/1/90; SLJ 5/90; VOYA 6/90)

1641 Greene, Jacqueline Dembar. *Out of Many Waters* (6–8). 1988, Walker $16.95 (0-8027-6811-3). A historical novel that begins in Brazil and ends with a group of Jewish settlers who, after landing in New Amsterdam, began the first synagogue in America. (Rev: BL 1/15/89; BR 1–2/89; SLJ 10/88; VOYA 12/88)

1642 Gregory, Kristiana. *Jenny of the Tetons* (6–9). 1989, Harcourt $13.95 (0-15-200480-7). An orphaned girl is brought by a trapper into his house to help care for his children in this story based on fact. (Rev: BL 7/89; SLJ 6/89; VOYA 6/90)

1643 Johnson, Mary. *To Have and to Hold* (7–12). 1961, Airmont paper $1.95 (0-8049-0160-0). The classic romantic novel set in Virginia during colonial times.

1644 Luhrmann, Winifred Bruce. *Only Brave Tomorrows* (7–10). 1989, Houghton $13.95 (0-395-47983-5). An account of an Indian massacre during King Philip's War, and of the heroic girl who is traumatized by it. (Rev: BL 7/89; BR 1–2/90; SLJ 7/89; VOYA 6/89)

1645 Moore, Ruth Nulton. *Peace Treaty* (5–8). Illus. 1977, Herald Pr. paper $3.95 (0-8361-1805-7). An easily read novel about a white boy's capture by Indians during the French and Indian War. Another novel about pioneers by this author is *Wilderness Journey* (1979).

1646 O'Dell, Scott. *The Serpent Never Sleeps: A Novel of Jamestown and Pocahontas* (6–9). Illus. 1987, Houghton $15.95 (0-395-44242-7); Fawcett paper $2.95 (0-449-70328-2). A young English girl becomes part of a settlement at Jamestown and there meets Pocahontas. (Rev: BL 11/1/87; BR 9–10/88; SLJ 9/87; VOYA 10/87)

1647 Petry, Ann. *Tituba of Salem Village* (6–9). 1964, Harper $14.89 (0-690-04766-5). Tituba, a slave in Colonial America, became an important figure in the Salem witch trials.

1648 Smith, Claude Clayton. *The Stratford Devil* (7–10). 1985, Walker $13.95 (0-8027-6544-0). A novel that uses as its background the hanging of a woman as a witch in Stratford, Connecticut, during 1651. (Rev: VOYA 8/85)

1649 Speare, Elizabeth George. *Calico Captive* (6–9). 1957, Houghton $13.95 (0-395-07112-7); Dell paper $3.25 (0-440-41156-4). In Colonial America, the Johnson family are captured by Indians and forced on a long trek.

1650 Speare, Elizabeth George. *The Witch of Blackbird Pond* (6–9). 1958, Houghton $13.95 (0-395-07114-3); Dell paper $3.25 (0-440-99577-9). Kit Tyler's wild ways lead to problems in witch conscious Colonial Connecticut.

1651 Wisler, G. Clifton. *This New Land* (6–9). 1987, Walker LB $14.85 (0-8027-6727-3). A well-researched novel about a Pilgrim boy's adventures on the *Mayflower* and in the Plymouth Rock colony. (Rev: BL 3/15/88; BR 5–6/88; SLJ 11/87)

REVOLUTIONARY PERIOD (1775–1809)

1652 Anderson, Joan. *1787* (7–10). 1987, Harcourt $14.95 (0-15-200582-X). The story of a teenager who became James Madison's aide during the 1787 Constitutional Convention in Philadelphia. (Rev: VOYA 12/87)

1653 Avi. *The Fighting Ground* (6–9). 1984, Harper LB $12.89 (0-397-32074-4); paper $3.50 (0-06-440185-5). One eventful day in the life of a 13-year-old boy during the Revolutionary War.

1654 Collier, James Lincoln, and Christopher Collier. *Jump Ship to Freedom* (7–9). 1981, Delacorte $13.95 (0-385-28484-5). A novel about slavery in Colonial Connecticut. Two other novels in this series are: *War Comes to Willy Freeman* (1983); *Who Is Carrie?* (1984).

1655 Collier, James Lincoln, and Christopher Collier. *My Brother Sam Is Dead* (7–10). 1974, Macmillan $13.95 (0-02-722980-7); Scholastic paper $2.50 (0-590-40737-6). A young boy tells of the tragic events leading up to his brother's death in the Revolutionary War.

1656 DeFord, Deborah H., and Harry S. Stout. *An Enemy Among Them* (7–9). 1987, Houghton $13.95 (0-395-44239-7). A Hessian prisoner of war and a girl who supports the Continental army meet and form a strong friendship in Revolutionary times. (Rev: BL 11/15/87; SLJ 9/87; VOYA 10/87)

1657 Fast, Howard. *April Morning* (7–10). 1961, Crown $8.95 (0-517-50681-5); Bantam paper $3.95 (0-553-27322-4). Adam Cooper changes from a boy to a man in the Battle of Lexington during the Revolutionary War.

1658 Fleischman, Paul. *Coming-and-Going Men: Four Tales* (7–10). Illus. 1985, Harper LB $12.89 (0-06-021884-3). Four short stories all set in a town in Vermont in 1800 and all dealing with traveling artisans and tradesmen. (Rev: BL 6/1/85; SLJ 8/85; VOYA 8/85)

1659 Fleischman, Paul. *Path of the Pale Horse* (7–9). 1983, Harper LB $11.89 (0-06-021905-X). Dr. Peale and his apprentice help fight a yellow fever epidemic in 1793 Philadelphia.

1660 Forbes, Esther. *Johnny Tremain* (7–9). Illus. 1943, Houghton $12.95 (0-395-06766-9); Dell paper $3.25 (0-440-94250-0). Paul Revere's apprentice during the early days of the Revolution.

1661 O'Dell, Scott. *Sarah Bishop* (7–10). 1980, Houghton $13.95 (0-395-29185-2); Scholastic paper $2.75 (0-590-42298-7). Sarah, 15 years old, tries to ignore the Revolution in her country home in Westchester, New York.

1662 Rinaldi, Ann. *Time Enough for Drums* (7–10). 1986, Holiday $12.95 (0-8234-0603-2). Jemima comes of age and finds romance and danger in this novel set during the American Revolution. (Rev: BL 5/1/86; SLJ 5/86)

1663 Wibberley, Leonard. *John Treegate's Musket* (7–9). 1959, Farrar paper $3.45 (0-374-43788-2). A novel about Peter Treegate and events immediately preceding the Revolutionary War.

NINETEENTH CENTURY TO THE CIVIL WAR (1809–1861)

1664 Avi. *The True Confessions of Charlotte Doyle* (6–9). 1990, Watts LB $14.99 (0-531-08493-0). An adventure story set in the 1850s about a 13-year-old girl and her voyage to America on a ship with a murderous crew. (Rev: BL 9/1/90; SLJ 9/90)

1665 Blos, Joan W. *A Gathering of Days: A New England Girl's Journal, 1830–32* (6–9). 1979, Macmillan $12.95 (0-684-16340-3); paper $3.95 (0-689-70750-9). In the 1830s, a young teenager faces adjusting to a new stepmother. Newbery Medal, 1980.

1666 Fox, Paula. *The Slave Dancer* (6–9). Illus. 1973, Bradbury $12.95 (0-02-735560-8); Dell paper $2.95 (0-440-96132-7). A young fifer is kidnapped and forced to play his instrument to exercise slaves on a slave ship.

1667 Harder, Janet D. *Letters from Carrie* (7–9). 1980, North Country Books $10.95 (0-932052-23-1). Carrie writes from her upstate New York home in the 1850s of how her father helped slaves escape.

1668 Lawson, John. *If Pigs Could Fly* (7–9). 1989, Houghton $13.95 (0-395-50928-9). In this humorous tale, Morgan James must deliver documents to Andrew Jackson during the War of 1812. (Rev: BL 10/15/89; SLJ 9/89)

1669 Miner, Jane Claypool. *Corey* (7–10). 1987, Scholastic paper $2.50 (0-590-40395-8). Corey is a determined girl who managed to get out of slavery and enter a Quaker school in Philadelphia. (Rev: SLJ 4/87)

1670 Miner, Jane Claypool. *Joanna* (7–10). 1984, Scholastic paper $2.95 (0-590-33241-4). Joanna, growing up in Lowell, Massachusetts in 1838, takes a job in a local textile mill to become independent.

1671 Smucker, Barbara. *Runaway to Freedom: A Story of the Underground Railway* (6–9). Illus. 1979, Harper paper $2.95 (0-06-440106-5). Two young slave girls try for freedom via the Underground Railway.

THE CIVIL WAR (1861–1865)

1672 Beatty, Patricia. *Charley Skedaddle* (6–8). 1987, Morrow $11.75 (0-688-06687-9); Troll paper $2.95 (0-8167-1317-0). A young deserter from the Union army finds out the true meaning of courage in the Virginia mountains. (Rev: BL 11/15/87; BR 11–12/87; SLJ 11/87; VOYA 12/87)

1673 Beatty, Patricia. *Turn Homeward, Hannalee* (7–9). 1984, Morrow $12.95 (0-688-03871-9). A family of mill workers—2 girls and their mother—seek employment in Indiana during the Civil War.

1674 Brenner, Barbara. *Saving the President: What If Lincoln Had Lived?* (5–8). Illus. 1987, Messner LB $9.29 (0-671-62023-1); paper $4.95 (0-671-64954-X). A novel about a courageous heroine who intervenes in the plot to kill President Lincoln. (Rev: SLJ 5/88)

1675 Clapp, Patricia. *The Tamarack Tree: A Novel of the Siege of Vicksburg* (7–10). 1986, Lothrop $11.95 (0-688-02852-7); Penguin paper $3.95 (0-14-032406-2). The siege of Vicksburg as seen through the eyes of a 17-year-old English girl who is trapped inside the city. (Rev: BL 11/15/86; BR 1–2/87; SLJ 10/86; VOYA 2/87)

1676 Cummings, Betty Sue. *Hew against the Grain* (6–9). 1978, Macmillan $6.95 (0-689-30551-6). When Mattilda is only 12, the Civil War comes bringing death to members of her family.

1677 Hansen, Joyce. *Out from This Place* (6–9). 1988, Walker LB $14.85 (0-8027-6817-2). In this volume, Easter, the companion of Obi, a slave who joined the Northern Army during the Civil War in *Which Way Freedom* (1986), tells her story and how she spent much of the war with other former slaves in the Carolina Sea Islands. (Rev: BL 1/15/89; BR 1–2/89; SLJ 12/88; VOYA 2/89)

1678 Kassem, Lou. *Listen for Rachel* (7–10). 1986, Macmillan $11.95 (0-689-50396-2). In the years after the teenage orphan Rachel arrives in the Appalachian Mountains, she gradually begins to appreciate her new home, particularly after she falls in love with a wounded Yankee soldier who wanders into her life. (Rev: BL 11/15/86; SLJ 2/87)

1679 Keith, Harold. *Rifles for Watie* (7–10). 1957, Harper $12.95 (0-690-70181-0); paper $2.95 (0-06-447030-X). Jeff, a Union soldier, learns about the realities of war when he becomes a spy. Newbery Award, 1958.

1680 Norton, Andre. *Ride Proud, Rebel!* (7–9). 1981, Fawcett paper $1.95 (0-449-70017-8). Drew Rennie, though only 15, will do anything to further the Confederate cause during the Civil War.

1681 O'Dell, Scott. *The Two Hundred Ninety* (7–9). 1976, Houghton $14.95 (0-395-24737-3). The story of a teenage boy and his involvement with the building of the *290*—a ship—for the Confederate Navy.

1682 Perez, N. A. *The Slopes of War* (7–9). 1984, Houghton $10.95 (0-395-35642-3). Young Buck Summerhill is a private during the Civil War and he with his sister experience the horror and agony of this war.

1683 Reeder, Carolyn. *Shades of Gray* (6–8). 1989, Macmillan $13.95 (0-02-775810-9). Immediately after the Civil War young Will must live with an uncle whom he considers a coward because he would not fight in the war. (Rev: VOYA 2/90)

1684 Rinaldi, Ann. *The Last Silk Dress* (7–10). 1988, Holiday $15.95 (0-8234-0690-3). A young Southern girl during the Civil War learns that slavery is evil and also uncovers an amazing family secret. (Rev: BL 6/15/88; SLJ 5/88; VOYA 12/88)

1685 Shore, Laura Jan. *The Sacred Moon Tree* (6–8). 1986, Bradbury $13.95 (0-02-782790-9). Phoebe, who is disguised as a boy, and her friend Jotham cross enemy lines to enter Virginia and save her brother during the Civil War. (Rev: BL 6/1/86; VOYA 12/86)

1686 Tolliver, Ruby C. *Muddy Banks* (5–8). Illus. 1987, Texas Christian Univ. $14.95 (0-87565-062-7). A young slave boy is torn between love for his kind mistress and sympathy for the oncoming Yankee force before the Battle of Sabine Pass in Texas during 1863. (Rev: SLJ 12/87; VOYA 4/88)

1687 Wisler, G. Clifton. *Thunder on the Tennessee* (7–10). 1983, Dutton $10.95 (0-525-67144-7). A 16-year-old Southern boy learns the value of courage and honor during the Civil War.

WESTERN EXPANSION AND PIONEER LIFE

1688 Alter, Judith MacBain. *Luke and the Van Zandt County War* (6–9). Illus. 1984, Texas Christian Univ. $10.95 (0-912646-88-8). Set in Texas after the Civil War, this novel centers on Theo, her doctor-father, and Luke, her father's apprentice.

1689 Altsheler, Joseph A. *Kentucky Frontiersman: The Adventures of Henry Ware, Hunter and Border Fighter* (6–10). Illus. 1988, Voyageur $16.95 (0-929146-01-8). A reissue of a fine frontier adventure story featuring young Henry Ware who is captured by an Indian hunting party. (Rev: BR 3–4/89; SLJ 3/89)

1690 Benchley, Nathaniel. *Gone and Back* (7–9). 1971, Harper paper $1.95 (0-06-440016-6). Obed's family moves West to take advantage of the Homestead Act and he soon finds he must assume new family responsibilities.

1691 Blos, Joan W. *Brothers of the Heart: A Story of the Old Northwest, 1837–1838* (7–9). 1985, Macmillan $12.95 (0-684-18452-4); paper $3.95 (0-689-71166-2). In the wilds of Michigan in the 1830s, a crippled young man must learn to survive. (Rev: BL 12/15/85; VOYA 4/86)

1692 Bohner, Charles. *Bold Journey: West with Lewis and Clark* (5–8). 1985, Houghton $11.95 (0-395-36691-7). A fictional account of a 17-year-old boy who accompanied Lewis and Clark on their expedition west. (Rev: BR 9–10/85; SLJ 9/85)

1693 Butler, Beverly. *My Sister's Keeper* (7–10). 1980, Putnam $8.95 (0-396-07803-6); paper $3.95 (0-396-08744-2). A self-centered teenager becomes a heroine during the terrible forest fire that devastated parts of Wisconsin in 1871.

1694 Calvert, Patricia. *The Snowbird* (7–9). 1980, Macmillan $12.95 (0-684-19120-0); NAL paper $1.95 (0-451-13353-6). Two orphans—one 14 and the other 8—are sent to the Dakota territory of 1883 to live with their uncle.

1695 Clements, Bruce. *I Tell a Lie Every So Often* (7–9). 1974, Farrar paper $3.45 (0-374-43539-1). Set on the Mississippi River during 1848, this is the story of 2 brothers, one of whom is known for stretching the truth.

1696 Conrad, Pam. *Prairie Songs* (6–9). Illus. 1985, Harper LB $12.89 (0-06-021337-X); paper $3.50 (0-06-440206-1). On the wide Nebraska prairie young Louisa forms a friendship with a doctor's wife whose hold on reality is slipping away. (Rev: BL 9/1/85; SLJ 10/85; VOYA 12/85)

1697 DeFelice, Cynthia. *Weasel* (7–9). 1990, Macmillan $12.95 (0-02-726457-2). Set in rural Ohio in 1839, this is the story of a boy's initiation into the cruel realities of life and death. (Rev: VOYA 6/90)

1698 Donahue, Marilyn Cram. *The Valley in Between* (6–9). 1987, Walker LB $15.85 (0-8027-6733-8). In a story that spans a 4-year period, a young girl comes of age in California of the 1850s. (Rev: BL 11/1/87; BR 5–6/88; SLJ 11/87; VOYA 12/87)

1699 Kherdian, David. *Bridger: The Story of a Mountain Man* (7–9). 1987, Greenwillow $11.75 (0-688-06510-4). A fictionized account of the famous mountain man who discovered the Great Salt Lake in 1824. (Rev: BR 5–6/87; SLJ 4/87; VOYA 6/87)

1700 Lasky, Kathryn. *Beyond the Divide* (7–9). 1983, Macmillan LB $13.95 (0-02-751670-9); Dell paper $3.25 (0-440-91021-8). A young girl and her father join the rush for gold in 1849.

1701 Lasky, Kathryn. *The Bone Wars* (7–10). 1988, Morrow $11.95 (0-688-07433-2). Two teenage boys are involved in the rivalries between paleontologists looking for fossils in the American West of the 1970s. (Rev: BL 11/15/88; BR 1–2/89; SLJ 11/88; VOYA 2/89)

1702 McCall, Edith. *Message from the Mountains* (6–9). 1985, Walker $11.95 (0-8027-6582-3). A fictionalized adventure on western expansion featuring Kit Carson and his friend Jim Mathews. (Rev: BR 11–12/85)

1703 McClain, Margaret S. *Bellboy: A Mule Train Journey* (6–10). Illus. 1989, New Mexico $14.95 (0-9622468-1-6). Set in California in the 1870s, this is the story of a 12-year-old boy and his first job on a mule train. (Rev: SLJ 3/90)

1704 Moeri, Louise. *Save Queen of Sheba* (6–9). 1981, Dutton $13.95 (0-525-33202-2). Two young survivors of an Indian attack set out to find their parents.

1705 Moore, Robin. *The Bread Sister of Sinking Creek* (7–10). 1990, Harper LB $12.89 (0-397-32419-7). An orphaned 14-year-old girl becomes a servant in Pennsylvania during pioneer days. (Rev: BL 7/90; SLJ 4/90; VOYA 8/90)

1706 Murrow, Liza Ketchum. *West against the Wind* (6–9). 1987, Holiday $13.95 (0-8234-0668-7). The story of a 14-year-old girl's arduous trip from Missouri to California in 1850. (Rev: BL 1/15/88; SLJ 12/87)

1707 Nixon, Joan Lowery. *In the Face of Danger* (5–8). 1988, Bantam $14.95 (0-553-05490-2); paper $2.95 (0-553-28196-8). Megan fears she will bring bad luck to her adoptive family in this story set in the prairies of Kansas. This is the third part of the Orphan Train Quartet. (Rev: BR 11–12/88; SLJ 12/88; VOYA 12/88)

1708 O'Dell, Scott. *Carlota* (7–9). 1977, Houghton $12.95 (0-395-25487-6); Dell paper $2.95 (0-440-90928-7). After the Mexican-American War some Californians continue to battle the U.S. Army.

1709 O'Dell, Scott. *Streams to the River, River to the Sea: A Novel of Sacagawea* (5–9). 1986, Houghton $14.95 (0-395-40430-4); Fawcett paper $2.95 (0-449-70244-8). A novelized life of Sacagawea that supplies details about the Lewis and Clark expedition. (Rev: BL 3/15/86; BR 9–10/86; SLJ 5/86; VOYA 6/86)

1710 Portis, Charles. *True Gift* (7–12). 1968, NAL paper $3.95 (0-451-16022-3). Mattie enlists the aid of an old U.S. marshal to avenge the death of her father.

1711 Richter, Conrad. *The Light in the Forest* (7–9). 1953, Knopf $13.95 (0-394-43314-9); Bantam paper $2.95 (0-553-26878-3). At age 15, a white boy returns to his family after living many years with Indians.

1712 Roderus, Frank. *Duster* (6–9). 1986, Texas Christian Univ. Pr. $14.95 (0-87565-055-4). A charming novel set in South Texas after the Civil War about a 16-year-old boy who suddenly has the responsibility of caring for his family. (Rev: VOYA 4/88)

1713 Sanders, Scott R. *Bad Man Ballad* (7–12). 1986, Bradbury $14.95 (0-02-778230-1). In Ohio during the War of 1812 Ely befriends a gentle, mute giant who has been accused of murder. (Rev: BL 10/1/86; BR 3–4/87; SLJ 10/86)

1714 Shura, Mary Francis. *Jessica* (7–12). 1984, Scholastic paper $2.95 (0-590-33242-2). Set in Kansas before the Civil War, this novel chronicles the rocky romance of Jessica and Will. (Rev: BL 2/15/85)

1715 Taylor, Theodore. *Walking Up a Rainbow* (6–10). 1986, Delacorte $14.95 (0-385-29435-2); Dell paper $2.95 (0-440-99326-1). Trying to make money to keep the family home, 14-year-old Susan sets off on a cross-country trek from Iowa to California to sell her sheep. (Rev: BL 6/15/86; BR 3–4/87; SLJ 8/86; VOYA 6/86)

1716 Turner, Ann. *Grasshopper Summer* (5–8). 1989, Macmillan $12.95 (0-02-789511-4). Sam and his family journey to the Dakota Territories in 1874 to begin a new life. (Rev: SLJ 5/89; VOYA 6/89)

1717 Wallin, Luke. *In the Shadow of Wind* (7–9). 1984, Macmillan $12.95 (0-02-792320-7). Caleb hides a Creek boy from the racist white settlers with whom he lives.

1718 Wilder, Laura Ingalls. *The Long Winter* (5–8). Illus. 1953, Harper LB $13.89 (0-06-026461-1). Number 6 in the Little House books. In this one the Ingalls face a terrible winter with only seed grain for food.

1719 Wisler, G. Clifton. *Piper's Ferry* (6–9). 1990, Dutton $14.95 (0-525-67303-2). This novel, set in Texas at the time of the Alamo, tells of a teenager and his participation in the revolution against Mexico. (Rev: BL 7/90; SLJ 8/90; VOYA 8/90)

1720 Wisler, G. Clifton. *The Raid* (5–9). 1985, Dutton $11.95 (0-525-67169-2). Lige, a teenage boy, sets out with a black man named Zeke to rescue Lige's brother who has been captured by Indians. (Rev: BL 2/15/86; BR 5–6/86; SLJ 12/85)

1721 Wisler, G. Clifton. *Winter of the Wolf* (7–9). 1981, Lodestar $9.95 (0-525-66716-4). In the winter of 1864, T.J. and his Comanche friend set off to hunt a mysterious wolf.

RECONSTRUCTION TO WORLD WAR I (1865–1914)

1722 Glaser, Dianne. *The Diary of Trilby Frost* (7–9). 1976, Holiday $12.95 (0-8234-0277-0). Written as a diary, this is the account of a teenager growing up in Tennessee at the turn of the century.

1723 Hurmence, Belinda. *Tancy* (6–10). 1984, Clarion $12.95 (0-89919-228-9). During Reconstruction a freed black woman sets out to find her mother.

1724 Levin, Betty. *Brother Moose* (5–8). 1990, Greenwillow $12.95 (0-688-09266-7). The story of 2 unwanted children who were shipped to Canada in the late nineteenth century and their eventual resettlement in Maine. (Rev: SLJ 7/90; VOYA 6/90)

1725 Perez, N. A. *Breaker* (6–9). 1988, Houghton $13.95 (0-395-45537-5). A teenage boy enters the mines in 1902 Pennsylvania when his father is killed in an accident. (Rev: BL 7/88; BR 11–12/88; SLJ 8/88; VOYA 10/88)

1726 Perez, N. A. *One Special Year* (7–10). 1985, Houghton $12.95 (0-395-36693-3); Penguin paper $3.95 (0-14-032202-7). Family life in a small upper New York State town in 1900 is vividly portrayed in this sensitive novel about a girl reaching maturity. (Rev: BL 6/15/85; BR 9–10/85; SLJ 8/85)

1727 Van Raven, Pieter. *Harpoon Island* (6–8). 1989, Macmillan $12.95 (0-684-19092-3). A young father encounters bigotry and prejudice when he becomes a school teacher on a Massachusetts island prior to World War I. (Rev: BR 3–4/90; SLJ 10/89; VOYA 12/89)

BETWEEN WARS AND THE GREAT DEPRESSION (1919–1948)

1728 Ames, Mildred. *The Dancing Madness* (7–9). 1980, Delacorte $8.95 (0-385-28113-7). To help her family through the Depression, Mary's sister enters a dance marathon.

1729 Bennett, Paul. *Follow the River* (6–9). 1987, Watts LB $12.99 (0-531-08314-4). Two teenagers gradually form a bond of trust and love in spite of their family differences in this novel set in Depression-era Ohio. (Rev: BL 12/15/87; BR 1–2/88; SLJ 12/87; VOYA 10/87)

1730 Cannon, Bettie. *A Bellsong for Sarah Raines* (6–9). 1987, Macmillan $12.95 (0-684-18839-2). Unable to adequately provide for his family during the Great Depression, Sarah's father kills himself and the poor girl finds it difficult to accept his death. (Rev: BL 7/87; BR 11-12/87; SLJ 6-7/87; VOYA 6/87)

1731 Corcoran, Barbara. *The Sky Is Falling* (7–10). 1988, Macmillan $13.95 (0-689-31388-8). A once-wealthy girl must cope with Depression poverty and living with a widowed aunt. (Rev: BL 9/15/88; BR 3–4/89; SLJ 9/88; VOYA 10/88)

1732 Edwards, Pat. *Nelda* (6–8). 1987, Houghton $12.95 (0-395-43021-6). In this novel set in Depression days, young Nelda has high hopes for the future though her present situation as part of a migrant worker's family is bleak. (Rev: BL 4/15/87; BR 9–10/87; SLJ 5/87; VOYA 8–9/87)

1733 Hunt, Irene. *No Promises in the Wind* (7–9). 1987, Berkley paper $2.75 (0-425-09969-5). During the Great Depression, Josh must assume responsibilities far beyond his years. A reissue.

1734 Mills, Claudia. *What about Annie?* (6–8). 1985, Walker $9.95 (0-8027-6573-4). A harrowing story of a family in Baltimore living through the Depression as seen through the eyes of a young teenage girl. (Rev: BL 9/1/85)

1735 Olsen, Violet. *View from the Pighouse Roof* (6–8). 1987, Macmillan LB $12.95 (0-689-31324-1). Thirteen-year-old Marie Carlsen is growing up with her mother on an Iowa farm during the Depression. (Rev: SLJ 5/87)

1736 Pearson, Gayle. *The Coming Home Cafe* (6–8). 1988, Macmillan $13.95 (0-689-31338-1). In Depression-bound Detroit, a young girl and her boyfriend run away to Cleveland where they hope to get jobs. (Rev: BL 2/15/89; BR 3–4/89; SLJ 10/88; VOYA 6/89)

1737 Richard, Adrienne. *Pistol* (7–10). 1989, Little $14.95 (0-316-74324-0). The story of a young boy's survival in the West during the Great Depression. (Rev: SLJ 6/89)

1738 Stolz, Mary. *Ivy Larkin* (7–9). 1986, Harcourt $13.95 (0-15-239366-8). During the Depression in New York City, 15-year-old Ivy's father loses his job and the family moves to the Lower East Side. (Rev: BL 11/1/86)

1739 Thrasher, Crystal. *A Taste of Daylight* (7–10). 1984, Macmillan $12.95 (0-689-50313-4). The story of how a midwestern family survives the Great Depression.

Twentieth Century Wars

WORLD WAR I

1740 Dank, Milton. *Khaki Wings* (7–9). 1980, Delacorte $8.95 (0-385-28523-X); Dell paper $1.95 (0-317-00572-3). A teenage boy becomes a mechanic for the air corps in France during World War I.

1741 Frank, Rudolf. *No Hero for the Kaiser* (7–10). Trans. by Patricia Crampton. Illus. 1986, Lothrop $13.00 (0-688-06093-5). The story of a 14-year-old Polish boy who acts as a scout in World War I and through the horrors of war becomes a pacifist. (Rev: BL 9/1/86; BR 11–12/86; SLJ 10/86)

1742 Hough, Richard. *Flight to Victory* (8–10). 1985, Dutton $12.95 (0-525-67159-5). An English story about a teenager who becomes a hero flying against the Germans during World War I. (Rev: BL 4/1/85; SLJ 8/85)

1743 Rostkowski, Margaret I. *After the Dancing Days* (6–9). 1986, Harper LB $13.89 (0-06-025078-X); paper $3.50 (0-06-440248-7). Annie encounters the realities of war when she helps care for wounded soldiers after World War I. (Rev: BL 10/15/86; SLJ 12/86; VOYA 4/87)

WORLD WAR II AND THE HOLOCAUST

1744 Baer, Edith. *A Frost in the Night* (6–10). 1988, Random paper $7.95 (0-8052-0857-7). A 12-year-old Jewish girl in Germany in the early 1930s gradually becomes aware of Hitler's message of hate. (Rev: BR 1–2/89)

1745 Bawden, Nina. *Carrie's War* (6–9). Illus. 1973, Harper LB $12.89 (0-397-31450-7); Dell paper $4.95 (0-440-40142-9). Carrie relives her days during World War II when she and her brothers were evacuated to Wales.

1746 Benary-Isbert, Margot. *The Ark* (6–9). 1987, Peter Smith $19.00 (0-8446-6295-X). A gripping story of a young girl caught in the turmoil in Germany immediately after the end of World War II. A reissue. (Rev: SLJ 2/88)

1747 Benchley, Nathaniel. *Bright Candles* (6–9). 1974, Harper $13.70 (0-06-020461-3). The Danish underground during World War II.

1748 Cooper, Susan. *Dawn of Fear* (7–9). 1970, Harcourt $14.95 (0-15-266201-4); Aladdin paper $3.95 (0-689-71327-4). Three boys in a London suburb become friends amid the violence of World War II.

1749 Dank, Milton. *The Dangerous Game* (7–9). 1977, Dell paper $1.50 (0-440-91765-4). As part of the resistance movement during World War II in France, a teenager on a dangerous mission is captured.

1750 Degens, T. *The Visit* (7–9). 1982, Viking $11.95 (0-670-74712-2). Kate discovers that her aunt was part of the Hitler Youth during World War II.

1751 DeJong, Meindert. *The House of Sixty Fathers* (6–9). 1956, Harper LB $13.89 (0-06-021481-3); paper $3.50 (0-06-021481-3). In war-torn China, a young boy searches for his family as the Japanese invade his country.

1752 Ferry, Charles. *Raspberry One* (7–10). 1983, Houghton $11.95 (0-395-34069-1). Friendship found on a Navy bomber during World War II.

1753 Garrigue, Sheila. *The Eternal Spring of Mr. Ito* (6–9). 1985, Bradbury $12.95 (0-02-737300-2). A novel about a girl's friendship with a Japanese Canadian family that is mistreated during World War II. (Rev: BL 12/15/85; VOYA 2/85)

1754 Gehrts, Barbara. *Don't Say a Word* (7–12). Trans. by Elizabeth D. Crawford. 1986, Macmillan $12.95 (0-689-50412-8). This is an autobiographical novel about an anti-Nazi family living in Berlin during World War II. (Rev: BL 10/1/86; SLJ 12/86; VOYA 2/87)

1755 Griese, Arnold A. *The Wind Is Not a River* (5–8). Illus. 1978, Harper LB $12.89 (0-690-03842-9). An easily read adventure about a brother and sister whose home on an island off Alaska is taken over by the Japanese during World War II.

1756 Hartling, Peter. *Crutches* (6–9). 1988, Lothrop $11.95 (0-688-07991-1). A young war refugee makes friends with a one-legged man in postwar Vienna. (Rev: VOYA 2/89)

1757 Holm, Anne. *North to Freedom* (7–9). 1974, Harcourt paper $5.95 (0-15-666100-4). A young boy wanders through war-torn Europe after escaping from a concentration camp.

1758 Kerr, Judith. *When Hitler Stole Pink Rabbit* (5–8). 1972, Putnam $8.95 (0-698-20182-5); Dell paper $3.25 (0-440-49017-0). An easily read novel of a Jewish family who leave Germany for Paris when the Nazis come to power.

1759 Laird, Christa. *Shadow of the Wall* (6–10). 1990, Greenwillow $12.95 (0-688-09336-1). The harrowing story of a teenage Jewish boy living in the Warsaw Ghetto during World War II. (Rev: BL 5/15/90; SLJ 7/90; VOYA 8/90)

1760 Levitin, Sonia. *Silver Days* (7–9). 1989, Macmillan $13.95 (0-689-31563-5). The Platt family moves to California as World War II breaks out and adjustments to the New World must be made. This is a sequel to: *Journey to America* (1986). (Rev: BL 4/1/89; BR 9–10/89; SLJ 5/89; VOYA 6/89)

1761 Lingard, Joan. *Tug of War* (7–9). 1990, Dutton $14.95 (0-525-67306-7). An historical novel about the plight of a displaced Latvian family at the end of World War II. (Rev: BL 6/15/90; SLJ 9/90)

1762 Matas, Carol. *Lisa's War* (6–9). 1989, Macmillan $12.95 (0-684-19010-9). Told in the first person, this is the story of a Jewish girl whose family must flee from their home in Denmark during the Nazi occupation. (Rev: BL 4/1/89; BR 9–10/89; SLJ 5/89)

1763 Mazer, Harry. *The Last Mission* (7–10). 1981, Dell paper $2.95 (0-440-94797-9). An underage Jewish American boy joins the Air Corps and is taken prisoner by the Germans.

1764 Miner, Jane Claypool. *Veronica* (7–12). 1986, Scholastic paper $2.95 (0-590-33933-8). A teenage girl whose father is stationed at Pearl Harbor sees her world change forever when the Japanese attack. (Rev: VOYA 12/86)

1765 Orgel, Doris. *The Devil in Vienna* (7–10). 1978, Dial $8.95 (0-8037-1920-5); Penguin paper $3.95 (0-14-032500-X). Two friends, one Jewish and the other the daughter of a Nazi, growing up in German-occupied Austria.

1766 Orlev, Uri. *The Island on Bird Street* (7–9). Trans. by Hillel Halkin. 1984, Houghton $11.95 (0-395-33887-5). An 11-year-old boy tries to survive in an empty Polish ghetto during World War II.

1767 Ossowski, Leonie. *Star without a Sky* (5–9). Trans. by Ruth Crowley. 1985, Lerner $12.95 (0-8225-0771-4). During the last days of World War II, some German teenagers find a Jewish boy in hiding. (Rev: BL 7/85; SLJ 10/85)

1768 Pearson, Kit. *The Sky Is Falling* (6–8). 1990, Viking $12.95 (0-670-82849-1). Norah and her brother Gavin face problems when, during World War II, they are evacuated to Canada. (Rev: BL 5/15/90)

1769 Serrailliers, Ian. *Escape from Warsaw* (7–9). 1972, Scholastic paper $2.50 (0-590-41176-4). Three Polish children are alone and face the dangers of being in Warsaw during World War II.

1770 Sevela, Ephraim. *We Were Not Like Other People* (8–12). Trans. by Antonia Bouis. 1989, Harper LB $12.89 (0-06-025508-0). A series of Russian stories about a young Jewish boy's struggle for survival amid the destruction of World War II. (Rev: BL 9/1/89; SLJ 12/89; VOYA 12/89)

1771 Suhl, Yuri. *Uncle Misha's Partisans* (6–8). 1988, Shapolsky Press paper $7.95 (0-933503-23-

7). A young Jewish boy joins a group of Nazi resisters and receives a dangerous assignment.

1772 Tamar, Erika. *Good-bye, Glamour Girl* (7–10). 1984, Harper LB $11.89 (0-397-32088-4). Liesl and her family flee from Hitler's Europe and Liesl must now become Americanized. (Rev: BL 1/1/85)

1773 Walsh, Jill Paton. *Fireweed* (7–10). 1988, Farrar LB $12.95 (0-374-32310-0); paper $3.50 (0-374-42316-4). A reissue of the novel about the friendship between a 15-year-old boy and a younger girl during the London blitz.

1774 Westall, Robert. *The Machine Gunners* (6–9). 1990, Knopf paper $3.50 (0-679-80130-8). A reissue of the prize-winning English novel about a boy during World War II who finds a downed German plane with a machine gun intact. (Rev: VOYA 8/90)

VIETNAM WAR

1775 Nelson, Theresa. *And One for All* (7–12). 1989, Watts LB $12.99 (0-531-08404-3). The story of the destruction of both family relationships and the friendship between 2 young men caused by the Vietnam War. (Rev: BL 3/15/89; BR 11–12/89; SLJ 2/89)

Horror Stories and the Supernatural

1776 Aiken, Joan. *Give Yourself a Fright: Thirteen Stories of the Supernatural* (7–10). 1989, Delacorte $14.95 (0-440-50120-2). Thirteen stories inhabited by ghosts, the devil, magical animals, and the occasional human. (Rev: BR 5–6/89; SLJ 4/89; VOYA 6/89)

1777 Aiken, Joan. *Return to Harken House* (6–8). 1990, Delacorte $13.95 (0-385-29975-3). For better readers, a mod piece about a girl who communicates with the dead former occupants of her father's house. (Rev: BL 1/15/90; BR 4–5/90)

1778 Aiken, Joan. *A Touch of Chill: Tales for Sleepless Nights* (7–10). 1980, Delacorte $9.95 (0-385-29310-0). Fifteen horror stories by one of the best.

1779 Aiken, Joan. *A Whisper in the Night: Tales of Terror and Suspense* (7–10). 1988, Dell paper $3.25 (0-440-20185-3). Thirteen tales of the supernatural.

1780 Alcock, Vivien. *Ghostly Companions: A Feast of Chilling Tales* (6–9). 1987, Delacorte

$13.95 (0-385-29559-6). Ten spine tingling tales of the supernatural by the author of *The Haunting of Cassie Palmer* (1982). (Rev: BL 6/15/87; BR 11–12/87; SLJ 9/87; VOYA 8–9/87)

1781 *Alfred Hitchcock's Ghostly Gallery* (7–10). 1984, Random paper $2.95 (0-394-86762-9). Eleven stories from authors like H. G. Wells, R. L. Stevenson, and Lord Dunsany.

1782 *Alfred Hitchcock's Supernatural Tales of Terror and Suspense* (7–10). Illus. 1973, Random paper $3.50 (0-394-85622-8). Horrifying tales by such masters as Patricia Highsmith and Raymond Chandler.

1783 *Alfred Hitchcock's Witch's Brew* (7–10). Illus. 1977, Random paper $2.95 (0-394-85911-1). Joan Aiken and T. H. White are 2 of the authors represented in this collection of stories about witches.

1784 Asimov, Isaac, et al., eds. *Young Ghosts* (6–9). 1985, Harper LB $12.89 (0-06-020172-8). A scary collection of ghost stories by many well-known writers whose protagonists are young. (Rev: BL 2/15/86; BR 3–4/86; SLJ 12/85)

1785 Asimov, Isaac, et al., eds. *Young Monsters* (7–9). 1985, Harper $12.89 (0-06-020169-X). Not for the weak hearted, here is a collection of grisly tales about juvenile monsters. (Rev: BL 8/85; SLJ 5/85; VOYA 8/85)

1786 Asimov, Isaac, et al., eds. *Young Witches & Warlocks* (6–9). 1987, Harper LB $11.89 (0-06-020184-3). A collection of 10 stories, most of them scary, about witches. (Rev: BL 7/87; SLJ 1/88)

1787 Avi. *Devil's Race* (7–9). 1984, Harper $12.95 (0-397-32094-9); Avon paper $2.75 (0-380-70406-4). John Proud is in constant battle with a demon who has the same name and was hanged in 1854.

1788 Bawden, Nina. *Devil by the Sea* (6–8). 1976, Harper $12.70 (1-397-31683-6). Is the strange old man Hilary sees at the beach really the devil?

1789 Bridges, Laurie, and Paul Alexander. *Swamp Witch* (7–10). 1987, Bantam paper $2.50 (0-553-26792-2). In this novel about the supernatural, the powers of voodoo are used to protect a child.

1790 Brunn, Robert. *The Initiation* (7–10). 1982, Dell paper $1.95 (0-440-94047-8). A horror story involving a vampire in a remote New England private school.

1791 Bunting, Eve. *The Ghost behind Me* (7–9). 1988, Pocket paper $2.50 (0-671-62211-0). A ghost elicits the help of a young girl so it can gain eternal rest. A reissue.

1792 Cameron, Eleanor. *The Court of the Stone Children* (6–9). 1973, Dutton $12.95 (0-525-28350-1). Nina discovers stone statues that come to life and a restless ghost in this fantasy that has its secret buried in the seventeenth century.

1793 Cervantes, Esther DeMichael, and Alex Cervantes. *Barrio Ghosts* (7–12). Illus. 1988, New Readers paper $3.75 (0-88336-315-1). Five fantastic stories feature young people in the East Los Angeles barrio. (Rev: BL 5/15/89)

1794 Chambers, Aidan, et al. *A Haunt of Ghosts* (7–12). 1987, Harper LB $12.89 (0-06-021207-1). Of the 9 ghostly tales 5 are by Chambers. Other contributors include Joan Aiken and John Gordon. (Rev: BL 9/15/87; BR 3–4/88; SLJ 11/87; VOYA 2/88)

1795 Chambers, Aidan, ed. *Shades of Dark* (7–9). 1986, Harper LB $11.89 (0-06-021248-9). Eight scary stories written by such British authors as Helen Cresswell and Vivien Alcock. (Rev: BL 12/1/86; BR 3–4/87)

1796 Charles, Steven. *Nightmare Session* (7–9). 1986, Pocket paper $2.50 (0-671-60325-6). In this supernatural story a girl at a private school finds some campus people are really werewolves. (Rev: BL 2/1/87)

1797 Cohen, Daniel, ed. *The Headless Roommate and Other Tales of Terror* (6–9). Illus. 1980, Evans $7.95 (0-87131-327-8). Nineteen stories of horror and the supernatural with many based on classic folktales.

1798 Conrad, Pam. *Stonewords: A Ghost Story* (6–9). 1990, Harper LB $12.89 (0-06-021316-7). Through the years Zoe makes friends with a girl who visits from time to time but who is actually a ghost. (Rev: VOYA 6/90)

1799 Cooney, Caroline B. *The Snow* (7–9). 1990, Scholastic paper $2.75 (0-590-41640-5). Christina is out to foil the cruel Shevvingtons and their plans to harm young girls at their school. This is part 2 of a trilogy that began with *The Fog* and ends with *The Fire* (both 1990). (Rev: VOYA 8/90)

1800 Coontz, Otto. *The Night Walkers* (7–10). 1982, Houghton $9.95 (0-395-32557-9); Pocket paper $2.25 (0-671-62739-2). A horror story about the children of Covendale and the terrible disease that is plaguing them.

1801 Coville, Bruce. *The Ghost Wore Gray* (5–8). 1988, Bantam paper $2.75 (0-553-15610-1). Nina and friend Chris investigate a haunted inn in the Catskill Mountains. (Rev: SLJ 9/88)

1802 Cross, Gilbert B. *A Witch across Time* (7–10). 1990, Macmillan $14.95 (0-689-31602-X). A sensitive girl becomes the medium for a ghost that has an unsettling story to tell. (Rev: BL 3/1/90; SLJ 3/90; VOYA 4/90)

1803 Cross, Gillian. *The Dark Behind the Curtain* (7–9). Illus. 1984, Oxford Univ. Pr. $12.95 (0-19-271457-0); Dell paper $2.95 (0-440-20207-8). Colin sees his friend Marshall turn into the character he is portraying in the school play—the demon barber Sweeney Todd.

1804 Cross, Gillian. *Roscoe's Leap* (7–9). 1987, Holiday $12.95 (0-8234-0669-5); Dell paper $2.95 (0-440-20453-4). For Stephen his family's mansion, Roscoe's Leap, holds secrets that make him relive a previous existence during the French Revolution. (Rev: BL 11/15/87; SLJ 11/87; VOYA 4/88)

1805 Duncan, Lois. *Locked in Time* (7–10). 1985, Little $12.95 (0-316-19555-3); Dell paper $2.95 (0-440-94942-4). Nore's father marries into a family that somehow never seems to age. (Rev: BL 7/85; BR 9–10/85; SLJ 11/85)

1806 Duncan, Lois. *Stranger with My Face* (7–10). 1984, Little $9.70 (0-316-19551-0); Dell paper $2.95 (0-440-98356-8). A girl encounters her evil twin who wishes to take her place.

1807 Duncan, Lois. *Summer of Fear* (7–10). 1976, Little LB $13.95 (0-316-19548-0); Dell paper $2.95 (0-440-98324-X). An orphaned cousin who comes to live with Rachel's family is really a witch.

1808 Dunlop, Eileen. *Clementina* (6–9). 1987, Holiday $12.95 (0-8234-0642-3). A British novel in which the young heroine, Daisy, finds that an acquaintance is reliving events that occurred centuries ago, and ended in a violent death. (Rev: BL 4/15/87; SLJ 5/87; VOYA 8–9/87)

1809 Dunlop, Eileen. *The House on the Hill* (6–9). 1987, Holiday $13.95 (0-8234-0658-X); Troll paper $2.95 (0-8167-1323-5). In this British mystery, Philip and his cousin Sarah investigate a mysterious light that shines from an empty room. (Rev: BL 10/15/87; SLJ 11/87)

1810 Feil, Hila. *Blue Moon* (7–10). 1990, Macmillan $13.95 (0-689-31607-0). Set on Cape Cod, this novel describes a strange friendship between Molly, a teenager, and the dead mother of the child Molly takes care of. (Rev: BL 5/15/90; SLJ 3/90; VOYA 4/90)

1811 Furlong, Monica. *Wise Child* (6–8). 1987, Knopf LB $12.99 (0-394-99105-2); paper $2.95 (0-394-82598-5). Set in ancient Scotland, this is a story of a young girl torn between the good and evil aspects of witchcraft. (Rev: BL 12/1/87; SLJ 9/87)

1812 Furman, A. L. *Ghost Stories* (6–9). 1964, Pocket paper $2.50 (0-671-62488-1). A collection of 8 easily read ghost stories.

1813 Gabhart, Ann. *Wish Come True* (7–10). 1988, Avon paper $2.50 (0-380-75653-6). Lyssie receives as a gift a mirror that grants her wishes. (Rev: VOYA 6/89)

1814 Garden, Nancy. *Prisoner of Vampires* (6–8). Illus. 1985, Farrar $12.95 (0-374-36129-0); Dell paper $2.95 (0-440-47194-X). Alexander falls under the spell of vampires who are terrorizing the neighborhood. (Rev: BL 4/1/85)

1815 Gifaldi, David. *Yours Till Forever* (7–10). 1989, Harper LB $11.89 (0-397-32356-5). In this easily read novel, a high school senior sees disturbing similarities between his friends and his dead parents. (Rev: BL 10/1/89; SLJ 11/89; VOYA 2/90)

1816 Gripe, Maria. *Agnes Cecilia* (7–10). Trans. by Rika Lesser. 1990, Harper LB $14.89 (0-06-022282-4). An orphaned Swedish girl is visited by the ghost of another lonely girl who lived earlier in the century. (Rev: BL 6/1/90; SLJ 4/90; VOYA 6/90)

1817 Hamilton, Virginia. *Sweet Whispers, Brother Rush* (7–10). 1982, Putnam $12.95 (0-399-20894-1). A 14-year-old girl, who cares for her older retarded brother, meets a charming ghost who reveals secrets of her past.

1818 Haynes, James. *Voice in the Dark* (7–10). 1982, Dell paper $1.95 (0-440-99317-2). A supernatural mystery about a mysterious horse and his ability to make wishes come true.

1819 Hoke, Helen. *Tales of Fear & Frightening Phenomena* (7–9). 1982, Lodestar $10.50 (0-525-66789-X). Eight excellent tales of horror.

1820 Hoke, Helen, and Franklin Hoke, eds. *Horrifying and Hideous Hauntings: An Anthology* (8–10). 1986, Dutton $14.95 (0-525-67179-X). A collection of tales by such well-known authors as Dorothy Sayers and Ray Bradbury. (Rev: BL 6/1/86; SLJ 9/86; VOYA 12/86)

1821 Kahn, Joan, ed. *Ready or Not: Here Come Fourteen Frightening Stories!* (7–12). 1987, Greenwillow $11.75 (0-688-07167-8). An anthology of horror stories originally written for adults and collected by the editor of *Some Things Weird and Wicked* (1976). (Rev: BL 9/1/87; SLJ 10/87; VOYA 10/87)

1822 Kahn, Joan, ed. *Some Things Strange and Sinister* (7–10). 1982, Flare Books LB $13.89 (0-06-023087-8). Fourteen sinister tales by such writers as H. G. Wells and Agatha Christie.

1823 Katz, Welwyn Wilton. *Witchery Hill* (7–9). 1984, Macmillan $12.95 (0-689-50309-1). On the island of Guernsey, Mike helps his friend Lisa fight a coven of witches to help save her father's life.

1824 Kelleher, Victor. *Baily's Bones* (6–10). 1989, Dial $13.95 (0-8037-0662-6). Two brothers discover that the inhabitants of a remote Australian valley and their retarded teenage brother are possessed by the spirits of dead aborigines. (Rev: BL 11/15/89; SLJ 11/89; VOYA 4/90)

1825 Klaveness, Jan O'Donnell. *The Griffin Legacy* (7–9). 1985, Dell paper $3.25 (0-440-43165-4). Two ghosts are laid to rest when the secret of the Griffin legacy is revealed.

1826 Kushner, Donn. *Uncle Jacob's Ghost Story* (7–10). 1986, Holt $12.95 (0-03-006502-X). Grandfather tells the story of Jacob and his 2 friends, the ghosts of Simon and Esther, who died in a typhus epidemic in old Russia. (Rev: BL 7/86; SLJ 5/86)

1827 Lonsdale, Pamela, ed. *Spooky Stories of the Supernatural* (6–8). Illus. 1985, Prentice $12.95 (0-13-835463-4). A collection of 7 really scary stories that are bound to thrill. (Rev: BL 6/15/85; SLJ 8/85)

1828 Mahy, Margaret. *The Changeover* (8–10). 1984, Macmillan $12.95 (0-689-50303-2); Scholastic paper $2.50 (0-590-41289-2). Laura must become a witch in order to destroy the evil power that is killing her brother.

1829 Marlin, J. *Getting Out the Ghost* (6–8). 1984, Putnam $11.95 (0-399-21130-6). When Joyce visits a deserted house, she sees the ghost of a girl who died in a fire there years before. (Rev: BL 1/1/85)

1830 Nixon, Joan Lowery. *Whispers from the Dead* (7–12). 1989, Delacorte $14.95 (0-385-29809-9). After being saved from drowning, Sarah is able to communicate with dead spirits. (Rev: BL 9/15/89; BR 11–12/89; SLJ 9/89; VOYA 12/89)

1831 Norton, Andre, and Phyllis Miller. *House of Shadows* (7–9). 1984, Macmillan $12.95 (0-689-50298-2). Three children encounter ghosts in their great-aunt's home.

1832 Ormondroyd, Edward. *Castaways on Long Ago* (6–8). 1983, Bantam paper $2.25 (0-553-15457-5). The ghost of a young boy lures 3 youngsters to Long Ago Island.

1833 Passey, Helen K. *Speak to the Rain* (7–10). 1989, Macmillan $12.95 (0-689-31489-2). In a family still adjusting to their mother's death, the younger daughter becomes possessed by voices that seem to come from a place where an old Indian totem pole stands. (Rev: BL 12/1/89; BR 3–4/90; SLJ 9/89; VOYA 12/89)

1834   Peck, Richard. *Blossom Culp and the Sleep of Death* (6–8). 1986, Delacorte $14.95 (0-385-29433-6). The ghost of an Egyptian princess gives Blossom Culp a difficult assignment. Other titles about this intrepid clairvoyant are: *The Ghost Belonged to Me* (1975), *Ghosts I Have Been* (1977), and *The Dreadful Future of Blossom Culp* (1983). (Rev: BL 4/15/86; SLJ 5/86; VOYA 6/86)

1835   Pope, Elizabeth Marie. *The Perilous Gard* (7–9). Illus. 1974, Houghton $13.95 (0-395-18512-2). From her castle prison in 1558, a girl encounters the supernatural.

1836   Porte, Barbara Ann. *Jesse's Ghost, and Other Stories* (7–10). 1983, Greenwillow LB $10.25 (0-688-02301-0). A total of 11 tales of ghosts and other supernatural beings.

1837   Preussler, Otfried. *The Satanic Mill* (7–10). 1985, Peter Smith $19.00 (0-8446-6196-1). A 14-year-old boy is apprenticed to a mysterious master in this tale of black magic. A reissue.

1838   Rabinowitz, Ann. *Knight on Horseback* (6–8). 1987, Macmillan $12.95 (0-02-775660-2). Eddy discovers that a cloaked man following him is really Richard III and that he also was Richard's son in a previous life. (Rev: BL 11/15/87; SLJ 10/87)

1839   Radford, Ken. *The Cellar* (6–8). 1989, Holiday $13.95 (0-8234-0744-6). In her new home in North Wales, Siân discovers the horrible secret of the room at the bottom of the stairs. (Rev: SLJ 3/89; VOYA 10/89)

1840   Richardson, Jean, ed. *Beware! Beware! : Chilling Tales* (5–9). 1989, Hamish Hamilton $11.95 (0-241-12104-3). Nine ghost stories by some excellent English writers. (Rev: BL 6/1/89; SLJ 3/89; VOYA 4/90)

1841   Riddell, Ruth. *Shadow Witch* (8–10). 1989, Macmillan $13.95 (0-689-31484-1). Drew wonders if the Shadow Witch in his mind is the result of his encounter with LSD or because of a family curse. (Rev: BL 10/15/89; BR 3–4/90; SLJ 11/89; VOYA 12/89)

1842   Roach, Marilynne K. *Encounters with the Invisible World* (6–9). 1977, Harper $12.70 (0-690-01277-2). Spooky stories about witches, demons, spells, and ghosts in New England.

1843   Roberts, Nadine. *Evil Threads* (7–10). 1988, Ballantine paper $2.95 (0-449-70303-7).

Jenny makes contact with the spirit of Sarah, who wants to use her as part of a plan for revenge. (Rev: BL 12/1/88)

1844   Rodowsky, Colby. *The Gathering Room* (6–9). 1981, Farrar $11.95 (0-374-32520-0); paper $3.45 (0-374-42520-5). A spirit befriends a young boy who lives in the caretaker's house in a cemetery.

1845   Rundle, Anne. *Moonbranches* (7–9). 1986, Macmillan $11.95 (0-02-777190-3). During a summer in Scotland, Frances finds she is in communication with the ghost of a dead young man. (Rev: BR 5–6/87)

1846   Russell, Jean, ed. *Supernatural Stories: 13 Tales of the Unexpected* (5–9). 1987, Watts $11.99 (0-531-08323-3). Thirteen creepy stories by masters such as Joan Aiken and Joan Phipson. (Rev: BL 9/1/87; SLJ 9/87; VOYA 2/88)

1847   St. George, Judith. *Haunted* (7–10). 1986, Bantam paper $2.50 (0-553-26047-2). Alex house-sits in an estate where a murder-suicide has occurred.

1848   Saul, John. *Comes the Blind Fury* (7–10). 1990, Dell paper $4.50 (0-440-11475-6). Michelle finds a doll containing the evil spirit of a dead blind girl.

1849   Service, Pamela F. *When the Night Wind Howls* (6–8). 1987, Macmillan $12.95 (0-689-31306-3); Fawcett paper $2.50 (0-449-70279-0). A 13-year-old girl discovers that an actor in her community's theater group is actually possessed by a devil. (Rev: BL 6/15/87; SLJ 4/87; VOYA 6/87)

1850   Silsbee, Peter. *The Temptation of Kate* (6–8). 1990, Bradbury $12.95 (0-02-782761-5). Kate is vulnerable to being influenced by a demon who wants her to commit suicide. (Rev: BL 9/1/90)

1851   Sleator, William. *Into the Dream* (7–9). Illus. 1979, Dutton $13.95 (0-525-32583-2); Scholastic paper $2.50 (0-590-40951-4). Two youngsters share the same strange mental power as well as the same repeated dream.

1852   Starkey, Dinah. *Ghosts and Bogles* (5–10). Illus. 1987, David & Charles $16.95 (0-434-96440-9). A collection of 16 British ghost stories, each nicely presented with illustrations. (Rev: SLJ 9/87)

1853   Storr, Catherine. *Cold Marble and Other Ghost Stories* (7–10). 1985, Faber $13.95 (0-571-13582-X). These ghost stories combine a number of elements like tenderness, humor and, of course, horror. (Rev: BL 2/15/86; SLJ 3/86)

1854 Thesman, Jean. *Appointment with a Stranger* (7–10). 1989, Houghton $13.95 (0-395-49215-7). A lonely, unhappy girl is befriended by Tom who is actually the ghost of a boy drowned many years before. (Rev: BL 5/15/89; BR 1–2/90; SLJ 2/89; VOYA 6/89)

1855 Thomas, Joyce Carol. *Journey* (8–10). 1988, Scholastic $12.95 (0-590-40627-2). Fifteen-year-old Meggie and her boyfriend find themselves in danger when they investigate a series of murders. (Rev: BL 12/1/88; BR 1–2/89; SLJ 10/88; VOYA 4/89)

1856 Westall, Robert. *Ghost Abbey* (6–9). 1989, Scholastic $12.95 (0-590-41692-8). Maggi realizes that the abbey her father is restoring seems to have a life of its own. (Rev: SLJ 3/89; VOYA 6/89)

1857 Wrightson, Patricia. *Balyet* (6–9). 1989, Macmillan $12.95 (0-689-50468-3). The malicious spirit of a dead aboriginal girl tries to possess her modern counterpart. (Rev: BL 4/1/89; BR 9–10/89; SLJ 4/89; VOYA 6/89)

1858 Yolen, Jane, and Martin H. Greenberg, eds. *Things That Go Bump in the Night: A Collection of Original Stories* (7–12). 1989, Harper LB $13.89 (0-06-026803-4). From such authors as Jane Yolen and William Sleater comes a collection of thrillers. (Rev: SLJ 10/89)

1859 Yolen, Jane, and Martin H. Greenberg, eds. *Werewolves: A Collection of Original Stories* (6–9). 1988, Harper LB $13.89 (0-06-026799-2). Fifteen mostly scary stories about all kinds of werewolves. (Rev: BL 7/88; BR 1–2/88; SLJ 9/88; VOYA 8/88)

1860 York, Carol Beach. *On That Dark Night* (5–8). 1985, Bantam paper $2.25 (0-553-25207-0). Julie discovers that she lived a previous life and had had a tragic death. (Rev: SLJ 4/86)

Humorous Stories

1861 Angell, Judie. *First the Good News* (7–9). 1984, Putnam paper $2.25 (0-399-21156-X). Five fans try to get an interview with a TV star.

1862 Angell, Judie. *Leave the Cooking to Me* (6–9). 1990, Bantam $13.95 (0-553-05849-5). A light-hearted story about a teenager who starts her own catering business without telling her mother. (Rev: BL 3/1/90; VOYA 2/90)

1863 Angell, Judie. *Suds: A New Daytime Drama* (7–10). 1983, Bradbury $10.95 (0-02-705570-1). In this takeoff on the soaps, 15-year-old Susan Sudley gets into some far-fetched situations.

1864 Avi. *Romeo and Juliet: Together (and Alive) at Last!* (6–8). 1987, Watts LB $11.99 (0-531-08321-7); Avon paper $2.50 (0-380-70525-7). Ed Sitrow decides to help true love along by casting his friends as Romeo and Juliet in a school play. Sitrow is also the "genius" behind the soccer escapades in *S.O.R. Losers* (1984). (Rev: BL 8/87; SLJ 10/87)

1865 Benedict, Rex. *Run for Your Sweet Life* (7–12). 1986, Farrar $11.95 (0-374-36359-5). A hilarious spoof on old-time westerns complete with a fine cast of zany characters. (Rev: BL 1/1/87; SLJ 12/86; VOYA 4/87)

1866 Blue, Rose. *The Secret Papers of Camp Get Around* (5–8). 1988, Signet paper $2.50 (0-451-15301-4). Marcie and her younger brother are sent to a summer camp they detest. (Rev: SLJ 10/88)

1867 Byars, Betsy. *Bingo Brown, Gypsy Lover* (6–8). 1990, Viking $11.95 (0-670-83322-3). In this installment of the Bingo Brown saga, our hero finds himself in love. (Rev: BL 5/1/90; SLJ 6/90)

1868 Callen, Larry. *Who Kidnapped the Sheriff?* (7–10). 1985, Little $14.95 (0-87113-008-4). When Deever and her con-artist father arrive in the town of Tickfaw, life changes for the inhabitants. (Rev: VOYA 4/86)

1869 Clarke, J. *The Heroic Life of Al Capsella* (7–10). 1990, Henry Holt $14.95 (0-8050-1310-5). In this humorous Australian novel, all of young Al's attempts to find stature with his peers seem thwarted. (Rev: BL 3/15/90; SLJ 7/90)

1870 Collier, James Lincoln. *The Teddy Bear Habit* (6–8). Illus. 1985, Peter Smith $15.50 (0-8446-6191-0). A 12-year-old boy cannot lose his attachment to a teddy bear. (Rev: BL 1/1/86)

1871 Conford, Ellen. *The Alfred G. Graebner Memorial High School Handbook of Rules and Regulations* (6–9). 1976, Little $14.95 (0-316-15293-5); Archway paper $2.50 (0-671-67247-9). The trials and tribulations of student life in a typical high school.

1872 Conford, Ellen. *Dear Lovey Hart: I Am Desperate* (6–9). 1975, Little $14.95 (0-316-15306-0); Scholastic paper $2.50 (0-590-40721-X). Carrie's power as a lonely hearts columnist on the school paper causes her unexpected problems. Followed by *We Interrupt This Semester for an Important Bulletin* (1979).

1873 Conford, Ellen. *Genie with the Light Blue Hair* (6–9). 1989, Bantam $13.95 (0-553-05806-

1). Jean receives a magic lamp for her birthday that brings unforeseen complications. (Rev: BL 2/15/89; BR 9–10/89; SLJ 2/89)

1874 Conford, Ellen. *Lenny Kendell, Smart Aleck* (6–9). Illus. 1983, Little $12.95 (0-316-15313-3); Archway paper $2.50 (0-671-64190-5). Lenny dreams of being a stand-up comedian but his antics often cause him problems.

1875 Conford, Ellen. *A Royal Pain* (6–9). 1986, Scholastic $11.95 (0-590-33269-4); paper $2.50 (0-590-40548-9). A typical American teenager from Kansas discovers she is really Princess Florinda of Saxony Coburn. (Rev: BL 3/1/86; SLJ 3/86; VOYA 6/86)

1876 Conford, Ellen. *Seven Days to Be a Brand-New Me* (6–9). 1981, Little $14.95 (0-316-15311-7); Scholastic paper $2.50 (0-590-40729-5). Maddy knows she will become a teenage vamp after following Dr. Dudley's program.

1877 Conford, Ellen. *Strictly for Laughs* (7–10). 1985, Putnam $12.95 (0-448-47754-8). Joey and her friend Peter both hope for a future in show business but will it be a future where they are together? (Rev: BL 10/15/85; SLJ 12/85; VOYA 4/86)

1878 Conford, Ellen. *The Things I Did for Love* (7–12). 1987, Bantam $13.95 (0-553-05431-7); paper $2.95 (0-553-27374-4). For a psychology project, Stephanie studies the mysteries of love with humorous results. (Rev: BL 9/1/87; BR 11–12/87; SLJ 1/88; VOYA 10/87)

1879 Conford, Ellen. *Why Me?* (6–9). 1985, Little $14.95 (0-316-15326-5); Pocket paper $2.75 (0-671-62841-0). G.G. Graffman has a crush on Hobie who only has eyes for Darlene who is gaga over Warren. (Rev: BL 10/15/85; BR 5–6/86; SLJ 11/85; VOYA 2/86)

1880 Cooney, Caroline B. *Family Reunion* (6–10). 1989, Bantam $13.95 (0-553-05836-3). A richly humorous novel about a family reunion where the so-called perfect relatives turn out to be something different. (Rev: BL 11/1/89; BR 11–12/89; SLJ 10/89; VOYA 12/89)

1881 Cresswell, Helen. *Bagthorpes Liberated: Being the Seventh Part of the Bagthorpe Saga* (5–8). 1989, Macmillan $13.95 (0-02-725441-0). After not finding any ghosts in Wales in *Bagthorpes Abroad* (1984) and *Bagthorpes Haunted* (1985), this zany English family is back in London and once again full of mischief. (Rev: BL 10/1/89; SLJ 11/89; VOYA 12/89)

1882 Cresswell, Helen. *Ordinary Jack* (6–9). 1977, Macmillan $12.95 (0-02-725540-9). The adventures of an eccentric English family where the only "normal" member, Jack, is considered an outsider. Followed by: *Absolute Zero* (1985); *Bagthorpes Unlimited* (1978); and *Bagthorpes vs. the World* (1979).

1883 Danziger, Paula. *This Place Has No Atmosphere* (6–9). 1986, Delacorte $14.95 (0-385-29489-1); Dell paper $2.95 (0-440-98226-1). In this humorous story set in 2057, Aurora and her family move to the moon. (Rev: BL 10/15/86; BR 3–4/87; SLJ 11/86; VOYA 2/87)

1884 Domke, Todd. *Grounded* (6–8). 1982, Knopf paper $9.95 (0-394-85163-3). Two boys decide to produce a play to make enough money to buy a glider.

1885 Fine, Anne. *Alias Madame Doubtfire* (6–9). 1988, Little $12.95 (0-316-28313-4). A divorced father disguises himself as his former wife's housekeeper to make money and be near his children. (Rev: BL 5/15/88)

1886 Gardam, Jane. *A Long Way from Verona* (7–9). 1988, Macmillan $12.95 (0-02-735781-3). An English schoolgirl has problems, many of them funny, in her attempts to grow up socially. A reissue. (Rev: VOYA 2/89)

1887 Garfield, Leon. *The Night of the Comet: A Comedy of Courtship Featuring Bostock and Harris* (7–9). 1979, Delacorte $7.95 (0-385-28753-4); Dell paper $3.25 (0-440-40070-8). Cassidy sets out to locate Mary Flatley, the girl he wants to marry.

1888 Gilson, Jamie. *Can't Catch Me, I'm the Gingerbread Man* (7–9). 1981, Lothrop $12.95 (0-688-00435-0); Pocket paper $1.95 (0-671-44835-8). Though only 12, Mitch enters a national bake-a-thon in Miami.

1889 Gilson, Jamie. *Dial Leroi Rupert, DJ* (7–9). 1979, Lothrop $11.95 (0-688-41888-0). Three friends appeal to their favorite disc jockey to help them raise thirty dollars.

1890 Greenwald, Sheila. *Blissful Joy and the SATs: A Multiple-Choice Romance* (7–10). 1982, Little $12.95 (0-316-32673-9). Bliss's poor test scores seem to preclude Vassar in her future and a stray dog that keeps following her doesn't help the situation.

1891 Greenwald, Sheila. *It All Began with Jane Eyre: Or, The Secret Life of Franny Dillman* (7–9). 1980, Little $13.95 (0-316-32671-2); Dell paper $2.25 (0-440-94136-9). Teenage trauma as depicted in novels is spoofed in this story of an imaginative 13-year-old.

1892 Hall, Lynn. *Dagmar Schultz and the Angel Edna* (6–9). 1989, Macmillan $11.95 (0-684-19097-4). Dagmar and her long dead Aunt Edna sort out some problems with the opposite sex in this humorous fantasy that was preceded by *Dagmar Schultz and the Powers of Darkness* (1989) and *The Secret Life of Dagmar Schultz* (1988). (Rev: BL 10/15/89; SLJ 9/89; VOYA 12/89)

1893 Hopper, Nancy J. *Hang On, Harvey!* (5–8). 1983, Dutton $9.95 (0-525-44045-3); Dell paper $2.25 (0-440-43371-1). Harvey's year in eighth grade is beset with such problems as a crush on a girl and a thwarted music career.

1894 Ibbitson, John. *The Wimp* (7–12). 1986, EMC paper $3.95 (0-8219-0237-7). A highly unlikely candidate enters the student council presidential election in this easy-to-read school story. (Rev: BL 2/1/87)

1895 Keller, Beverly. *Fowl Play, Desdemona* (6–8). 1989, Lothrop $11.95 (0-688-06920-7). Desdemona's friend Sherman convinces her that she should become a vegetarian. (Rev: BR 3–4/89)

1896 Kendall, Jane. *Miranda and the Movies* (6–9). Illus. 1989, Crown LB $14.99 (0-517-57357-1). Miranda and her world suddenly come alive when a movie company moves next door. (Rev: BL 10/1/89; BR 3–4/90; SLJ 10/89)

1897 Kerr, M. E. *Little Little* (7–10). 1981, Harper LB $12.89 (0-06-023185-8). The central characters in this novel are 3 dwarfs—teenager The Roach, Little Lion an evangelist, and the lovely Little Little.

1898 Kibbe, Pat. *The Hocus-Pocus Dilemma* (6–8). Illus. 1979, Knopf $12.95 Scholastic paper $2.50 (0-590-40606-X). In this easily read story a young girl with ESP tries to help her family with humorous results.

1899 Kiesel, Stanley. *The War between the Pitiful Teachers and the Splendid Kids* (7–9). 1980, Dutton $10.95 (0-525-42201-3); Avon paper $2.75 (0-380-57802-6). A humorous fantasy about a group of schoolchildren who decide to wage war on their teachers.

1900 Killien, Christi. *Fickle Fever* (6–9). 1988, Houghton $13.95 (0-395-48159-7). Skeeter bounces from boy to boy to find out what love is really all about in this humorous sequel to *Putting On an Act* (1986). (Rev: BL 1/1/89; BR 1–2/89; SLJ 12/88)

1901 Killien, Christi. *Rusty Fertlanger, Lady's Man* (7–10). 1988, Houghton $12.95 (0-395-46762-4). Fourteen-year-old Rusty is told by his wrestling coach at school that he must wrestle a girl. (Rev: BR 11–12/88; VOYA 12/88)

1902 Korman, Gordon. *Don't Care High* (7–10). 1986, Scholastic paper $2.50 (0-590-40251-8). A new student in a high school where apathy is so rife it's nicknamed Don't Care High decides to infuse some school spirit into the student body. (Rev: BL 10/15/85)

1903 Korman, Gordon. *Losing Joe's Place* (7–10). 1990, Scholastic $12.95 (0-590-42768-7). Three teenage boys take over an apartment for the summer with hilarious results. (Rev: BL 3/1/90; SLJ 5/90; VOYA 6/90)

1904 Landis, J. D. *Looks Aren't Everything* (7–10). 1990, Bantam $13.95 (0-553-05847-9). Rosie sets out to make her friend's brother fall in love with her in this humorous novel. (Rev: BL 3/15/90; SLJ 3/90; VOYA 4/90)

1905 Leonard, Laura. *Saving Damaris* (7–10). 1989, Macmillan $13.95 (0-689-31553-8). In rural Kansas of 1904, a young girl and her brother try to save their older sister Damaris from marrying the richest man in town, who is old and ugly. (Rev: BR 3–4/90; VOYA 2/90)

1906 Leroe, Ellen. *Have a Heart, Cupid Delaney* (6–10). 1986, Dutton $12.95 (0-525-67188-9). Cupid Delaney turns out to be a washout when she tries her hand at matchmaking. (Rev: BL 11/1/86; BR 3–4/87; SLJ 12/86)

1907 Leroe, Ellen. *Robot Romance* (7–10). 1985, Harper $12.89 (0-06-023746-5). Bixby, a 16-year-old human, creates havoc in a high school where all the teachers are robots. Also use *Robot Raiders* (1987). (Rev: BL 5/1/85; BR 9–10/85; SLJ 8/85)

1908 Levitin, Sonia. *The Mark of Conte* (7–9). 1987, Macmillan paper $2.95 (0-02-044191-6). Conte's high school class schedule is so confusing that he decides to become 2 people to fulfill it.

1909 Littke, Lael. *Trish for President* (6–10). 1984, Harcourt $13.95 (0-15-290512-X). Trish's political campaign for junior class president turns out to be a model of inefficiency. (Rev: BL 1/1/85)

1910 Livingston, Alan W. *Ronnie Finkelhof, Superstar* (7–10). 1988, Fawcett paper $2.95 (0-449-70134-4). Ronnie lives a double life—nerd by day, rock superstar by night. (Rev: SLJ 9/88; VOYA 6/88)

1911 Lowry, Lois. *The One Hundredth Thing about Caroline* (7–9). 1983, Houghton $10.95 (0-395-34829-3); Dell paper $2.95 (0-440-46625-3). Caroline thinks that her mother's new boyfriend looks and acts like a savage dinosaur.

1912 Lowry, Lois. *Your Move, J.P.!* (6–8). 1990, Houghton $13.95 (0-395-53639-1). J. P. Tate, a seventh-grader, is hopelessly in love with Angela. (Rev: BL 3/1/90; VOYA 4/90)

1913 McFann, Jane. *Deathtrap and Dinosaur* (7–12). 1989, Avon paper $2.75 (0-380-75624-2). An unlikely pair join forces to force the departure of a disliked history teacher. (Rev: SLJ 10/89; VOYA 10/89)

1914 McNamara, John. *Model Behavior* (7–10). 1987, Dell paper $2.75 (0-448-95569-6). A successful teen model disguises herself to attend a regular high school. (Rev: BL 10/1/85; SLJ 11/85)

1915 Merrill, Jean. *The Pushcart War* (6–12). Illus. 1964, Harper $12.70 (0-201-09313-8); Dell paper $2.95 (0-440-47147-8). Mack's truck runs down Morris's pushcart and starts a war that is humorous and also reveals many human foibles.

1916 Mooser, Stephen. *The Hitchhiking Vampire* (6–8). 1989, Delacorte $13.95 (0-385-50134-2). Two teenagers—brother and sister—are driving to Utah when they pick up a man who wants to gamble his life savings at Las Vegas. (Rev: BL 6/1/89)

1917 Murphy, Barbara Beasley, and Judie Wolkoff. *Ace Hits the Big Time* (7–9). 1982, Dell paper $2.95 (0-440-90328-9). Ace's eye patch (to cover a sty) lands him a movie role.

1918 Naylor, Phyllis Reynolds. *Alice in Rapture, Sort Of* (6–8). 1989, Macmillan $12.95 (0-689-31466-3). Our young heroine, now in seventh grade, wonders how to behave with her boyfriend, Patrick, in this sequel to *The Agonies of Alice* (1985). (Rev: BL 3/1/89; SLJ 4/89)

1919 Park, Barbara. *Buddies* (6–8). 1985, Knopf LB $9.99 (0-394-96934-0); Avon paper $2.50 (0-380-69992-3). Dinah's dreams of being popular at camp are dashed in this humorous novel because she is forever being accompanied by Fern, the camp nerd. (Rev: BL 4/15/85)

1920 Parker, Jackie. *Love Letters to My Fans* (6–9). 1986, Bantam paper $2.50 (0-553-25725-0). The son of a soap opera star begins answering his father's fan mail. (Rev: BL 9/15/86; SLJ 1/87)

1921 Pascal, Francine. *Love and Betrayal & Hold the Mayo!* (7–12). 1985, Viking $11.95 (0-670-80547-5); Dell paper $2.50 (0-440-94735-9). Victoria and Steffi are waitresses at a summer camp in this sequel to *My First Love and Other Disasters* (1979). (Rev: BL 3/15/85; SLJ 9/85)

1922 Peck, Richard. *Those Summer Girls I Never Met* (7–10). 1988, Doubleday $14.95 (0-440-50054-0). Drew and his sister accompany their grandmother, a former show biz star, on a luxury cruise to Europe. (Rev: BL 10/1/88; BR 11–12/88; SLJ 11/88; VOYA 10/88)

1923 Peck, Robert Newton. *Soup* (6–8). 1974, Knopf LB $9.99 (0-394-92700-1); Dell paper $2.75 (0-440-48186-4). The humorous story of the friendship between 2 boys growing up in a small town some years ago. The first of several engaging books about Soup and his friend.

1924 Pfeffer, Susan Beth. *Head of the Class* (7–12). 1989, Bantam paper $2.95 (0-553-28190-9). Five separate stories based on scripts from the TV sitcom. (Rev: BL 12/15/89; VOYA 4/90)

1925 Pinkwater, Jill. *Buffalo Brenda* (7–9). 1989, Macmillan $13.95 (0-02-774631-3). Brenda Tuna and her friend India Ink decide to revolutionize their high school. (Rev: BL 7/89; BR 11–12/89; SLJ 12/89; VOYA 8/89)

1926 Pinkwater, Jill. *The Disappearance of Sister Perfect* (6–8). 1987, Dutton LB $13.95 (0-525-44278-2). A humorous novel about a girl's effort to rescue her elder sister from a cult. (Rev: BR 5–6/87; SLJ 5/87)

1927 Ransom, Candice F. *Thirteen* (6–8). 1986, Scholastic paper $2.50 (0-590-40192-0). At age thirteen, Kobie thinks nothing more could go wrong with her life, but it does. (Rev: SLJ 10/87)

1928 Rodgers, Mary. *Freaky Friday* (6–9). 1972, Harper LB $12.89 (0-06-025049-6); paper $2.95 (0-06-440046-8). Annabel switches with her mother for one hilarious day. Followed by: *A Billion for Boris* (1974) and *Summer Switch* (1982).

1929 Roos, Stephen. *My Secret Admirer* (6–9). Illus. 1984, Delacorte $13.95 (0-385-29342-9); Dell paper $2.75 (0-440-45950-8). Independent Claire receives an anonymous Valentine's Day card and she wonders who her admirer is.

1930 Ryan, Mary C. *Who Says I Can't?* (7–10). 1988, Little LB $12.45 (0-316-76374-8). Tessa decides to get revenge on a boy who shows too much ardor in his romancing. (Rev: SLJ 11/88)

1931 Salassi, Otto R. *On the Ropes* (7–9). 1981, Greenwillow LB $11.25 (0-688-80313-X). Squint and Julie find their estranged Dad who turns their farm into a wrestling school.

1932 Shannon, Jacqueline. *Too Much T.J.* (7–10). 1987, Dell paper $2.95 (0-440-20222-1). When Razz's (short for Raspberry) mother remarries, she finds herself more than attracted to her new stepbrother, who is indifferent to her charms. (Rev: BL 10/15/86)

1933 Sharmat, Marjorie. *He Noticed I'm Alive . . . and Other Hopeful Signs* (7–9). 1984, Dell paper $2.25 (0-440-93809-0). Jody is attracted to the son of her father's girlfriend. A sequel is: *Two Guys Noticed Me . . . and Other Miracles* (1985).

1934 Sharmat, Marjorie. *How to Meet a Gorgeous Girl* (7–9). 1989, Dell paper $2.95 (0-440-93808-2). Mark uses a how-to manual to win the attention of an attractive girl. A companion volume is: *How to Meet a Gorgeous Boy* (1983).

1935 Sieruta, Peter D. *Heartbeats and Other Stories* (7–10). 1989, Harper LB $12.89 (0-06-025849-7). Nine stories, many humorous, about teenagers and their concerns. (Rev: BL 4/15/89; SLJ 4/89; VOYA 4/89)

1936 Smith, Alison. *Help! There's a Cat Washing in Here!* (6–8). Illus. 1981, Dutton $10.25 (0-525-31630-2). Henry is put in charge of his brother and sister for 2 weeks and the fun begins.

1937 Stone, Bruce. *Half Nelson, Full Nelson* (7–10). 1985, Harper LB $12.89 (0-06-025922-1); paper $2.25 (0-06-447047-4). To try to keep his parents together, Nelson Gato stages a fake kidnapping of his sister. (Rev: BL 8/85; SLJ 11/85; VOYA 12/85)

1938 Taha, Karen T. *Marshmallow Muscles, Banana Brainstorms* (6–8). 1988, Harcourt $13.95 (0-15-200525-0). A puny youngster tries a regime of body development through the help of his dream girl. (Rev: BL 1/1/89)

1939 Tolan, Stephanie S. *The Great Skinner Getaway* (7–10). 1987, Macmillan $12.95 (0-02-789361-8); Penguin paper $3.95 (0-14-032653-7). The Skinner family go on a hilarious vacation in a huge motor home in the sequel to *The Great Skinner Strike* (1983) and *The Great Skinner Enterprise* (1986). (Rev: BL 5/1/87; BR 9–10/87; VOYA 10/87)

1940 Tolan, Stephanie S. *The Great Skinner Homestead* (6–9). 1988, Macmillan $13.95 (0-02-789362-6). The Skinner family try their hands at roughing it à la Swiss Family Robinson. (Rev: BL 12/15/88; BR 1–2/89; VOYA 2/89)

1941 Townsend, Sue. *The Secret Diary of Adrian Mole Aged 13¾* (7–10). 1984, Avon paper $3.50 (0-380-86876-9). The diary of an English boy through darkest adolescence.

1942 Ure, Jean. *You Win Some, You Lose Some* (7–12). 1986, Delacorte $14.95 (0-385-29434-4); Dell paper $2.95 (0-440-99845-X). In *What If They Saw Me Now?* (1984), Jamie began studying ballet. In this sequel he leaves school to take up ballet seriously despite the jeers of his working-class friends. (Rev: BL 4/1/86; SLJ 8/86; VOYA 8–10/86)

1943 Weyn, Suzanne. *The Makeover Club* (7–9). 1986, Avon paper $2.50 (0-380-75007-4). Three girls decide they are going to be glamorous by forming the Makeover Club. (Rev: VOYA 12/86)

1944 Wyss, Thelma Hatch. *Here at the Scenic-Vu Motel* (7–12). 1988, Harper LB $11.89 (0-06-022251-4). Seven high school students are placed in a motel when their school board refuses to pay for bussing. (Rev: BL 6/15/88; SLJ 3/88; VOYA 4/88)

1945 Young, Alida E. *The Klutz Is Back* (6–9). 1990, Willowisp paper $2.50 (0-87406-460-0). Clumsy Megan Steele of *Megan the Klutz* (1986) enters a contest sponsored by a modeling school. (Rev: SLJ 8/90)

1946 Zable, Rona S. *Landing on Marvin Gardens* (7–10). 1989, Bantam $13.95 (0-553-05839-8). Katie and her mother must move in with crotchety Aunt Rose who has a knack for alienating everyone. (Rev: BL 11/1/89; BR 1–2/90; SLJ 11/89; VOYA 2/90)

Mystery and Detective Stories

1947 Aiken, Joan. *Died on a Rainy Sunday* (7–10). 1988, Dell paper $2.95 (0-440-20097-0). Jane's innocent act of placing her daughter in the home of the McGregors has calamitous results.

1948 Aiken, Joan. *The Teeth of the Gale* (7–9). 1988, Harper LB $14.89 (0-06-020044-8). Eighteen-year-old Felix tries to rescue 3 children who have been kidnapped. A sequel to *Go Saddle the Sea* (1977) and *Bridle the Wind* (1983). (Rev: BL 9/15/88; BR 5–6/89; SLJ 11/88; VOYA 12/88)

1949 Alcock, Vivien. *The Mysterious Mr. Ross* (6–8). 1987, Delacorte $14.95 (0-385-29581-2). Felicity saves a man from drowning and finds herself in the middle of the mystery surrounding him. (Rev: BL 11/1/87; BR 11–12/87; SLJ 10/87; VOYA 12/87)

1950 Ames, Mildred. *Conjuring Summer In* (8–10). 1986, Harper LB $12.89 (0-06-020054-5). Fourteen-year-old Bernadette frequents an occult shop and finds it is somehow connected to some mysterious murders. (Rev: BL 12/15/86; BR 3–4/87; SLJ 11/86; VOYA 12/86)

1951 Avi. *Wolf Rider: A Tale of Terror* (7–12). 1986, Macmillan $12.95 (0-02-707760-8); paper $2.95 (0-02-041511-7). In this thrilling mystery, a 15-year-old boy tries to learn the identity of a telephone caller who claims he is a murderer. (Rev: BL 11/15/86; BR 5–6/87; SLJ 12/86)

1952 Babbitt, Natalie. *Goody Hall* (6–8). 1971, Farrar $10.95 (0-374-32745-9); Sunburst paper $3.95 (0-374-42767-4). A student and his new tutor investigate the mysterious death of the boy's father.

1953 Beatty, Patricia. *The Coach That Never Came* (6–8). 1985, Morrow $11.95 (0-688-05477-3). While doing research on Colorado history, Paul unravels the mystery of a missing stagecoach that contained payroll. (Rev: BL 12/15/85)

1954 Bellairs, John. *The Lamp from the Warlock's Tomb* (6–9). 1988, Dial LB $12.89 (0-8037-0535-2). Another adventure with teenager Anthony Monday and Miss Eells, this time involving a lamp that could have caused a murder. (Rev: BL 7/88)

1955 Bennett, Jay. *The Birthday Murderer* (7–10). 1979, Dell $2.25 (0-440-90576-1). Seventeen-year-old Shan is haunted by events that occurred when he was only 5.

1956 Bennett, Jay. *The Dark Corridor* (7–12). 1988, Watts $12.95 (0-531-15090-9). Kerry believes that his girlfriend's death was not suicide but murder. (Rev: BR 3–4/89; SLJ 11/88; VOYA 2/89)

1957 Bennett, Jay. *Deathman, Do Not Follow Me* (7–10). 1986, Scholastic paper $2.50 (0-590-40525-X). Danny is convinced that the Van Gogh on exhibit at the Brooklyn Museum is a fake.

1958 Bennett, Jay. *The Haunted One* (7–12). 1987, Fawcett paper $2.95 (0-449-70314-2). Paul Barrett, an 18-year-old lifeguard, is haunted by the memory of the girl he loved, who drowned before his eyes. (Rev: BR 3–4/88; SLJ 11/87)

1959 Bennett, Jay. *The Pigeon* (7–10). 1981, Avon paper $2.50 (0-380-55848-3). A 17-year-old boy finds his girlfriend murdered and he becomes a prime suspect.

1960 Bennett, Jay. *Say Hello to the Hit Man* (7–10). 1981, Dell paper $1.95 (0-440-97618-9). A college student in New York City begins receiving life-threatening phone calls and he soon realizes the threats are real.

1961 Bennett, Jay. *Sing Me a Death Song* (7–12). 1990, Watts LB $13.40 (0-531-10853-8). Eighteen-year-old Jason wonders if his accused mother is really a murderer. (Rev: SLJ 4/90; VOYA 8/90)

1962 Bennett, Jay. *The Skeleton Man* (7–12). 1986, Watts $13.95 (0-531-15031-3). Ray receives money from his uncle just before his death—but the gambling syndicate claims it as theirs. (Rev: BL 11/1/86; BR 1–2/87; SLJ 10/86; VOYA 4/87)

1963 Bethancourt, T. Ernesto. *Doris Fein: Legacy of Terror* (6–9). 1984, Holiday $10.95 (0-8234-0506-0). In Chicago, Doris encounters danger when she investigates the last will and testament of a friend. Others in this series are: *Doris Fein: Phantom of the Casino* and *Doris Fein: The Mad Samurai* (both 1981).

1964 Blair, Cynthia. *The Double Dip Disguise* (7–10). 1988, Fawcett paper $2.95 (0-449-70256-1). Twins Susan and Chris switch places to solve a mystery. Others in this series are *The Jelly Bean Scheme* (1990), *The Apple Pie Adventure* (1989), *The Popcorn Project* (1989), and *The Candy Cane Caper* (1987). (Rev: SLJ 4/89; VOYA 6/89)

1965 Brenner, Barbara. *The Falcon Sting* (7–12). 1988, Bradbury $12.95 (0-02-712320-0). Two teenagers who are interested in falcons uncover an underground gang of bird smugglers. (Rev: BL 11/15/88; BR 5–6/89; SLJ 11/88; VOYA 12/88)

1966 Brett, Simon. *The Three Detectives and the Knight in Armor* (6–9). 1987, Macmillan $12.95 (0-684-18895-3). Three British youngsters discover a plot to steal valuable coats of armor. (Rev: BL 10/15/87; VOYA 12/87)

1967 Brett, Simon. *The Three Detectives and the Missing Superstar* (6–9). 1986, Macmillan $12.95 (0-684-18708-6). Emma and her 2 friends try to unravel the mysterious kidnapping of an English rock star. (Rev: BL 12/15/86; SLJ 1/87)

1968 Bunting, Eve. *The Haunting of Safe Keep* (7–10). 1985, Harper LB $12.89 (0-397-32113-9). In this romantic mystery, 2 college friends work out their family problems while investigating strange occurrences where they work. (Rev: BL 4/15/85; BR 11-12/85; SLJ 5/85; VOYA 8/85)

1969 Butler, Beverly. *Ghost Cat* (7–9). 1984, Dodd $10.95 (0-396-08457-5); Scholastic paper $2.50 (0-590-41837-8). A 14-year-old girl unravels a family mystery while spending time with relatives on the family farm.

1970 Cebulash, Mel. *Carly & Co.* (7–10). 1989, Ballantine paper $2.95 (0-449-14555-7). An entertaining mystery about amateur sleuth Carly and drug trafficking at a local college. (Rev: BL 1/15/90; SLJ 3/90)

1971 Cebulash, Mel. *Hot Like the Sun* (6–9). 1986, Lerner LB $9.95 (0-8225-0729-3). Terry helps Sherri solve the mystery of a missing gold coin in this easily read story. (Rev: SLJ 9/86)

1972 Chase, Emily. *Our Roommate Is Missing* (7–10). 1986, Scholastic paper $2.50 (0-590-40079-7). When their friend Shelley is kidnapped, her roommates at school try to solve the mystery in this book that is part of the Girls of Canby Hall series. (Rev: SLJ 4/86)

1973 Christie, Agatha. *Death in the Air* (7–12). 1975, Berkley paper $3.50 (0-553-26138-X). One of the many popular mysteries starring the detective Hercule Poirot.

1974 Clark, Margaret Goff. *Who Stole Kathy Young?* (6–8). 1980, Putnam $8.95 (0-396-07888-5). Meg is baffled when her friend, a wealthy deaf girl, is kidnapped.

1975 Corbett, Scott. *Witch Hunt* (6–8). 1985, Little $14.95 (0-316-15750-3). Lester and Wally of *Grave Doubts* (1982) fame solve another mystery, this one involving a murdered attorney. (Rev: BL 3/1/86; VOYA 4/86)

1976 Corcoran, Barbara. *Mystery on Ice* (6–8). 1985, Macmillan $11.95 (0-689-31089-7). Strange happenings at Camp Allegro spoil a Christmas vacation but lead to solving a mystery. (Rev: BL 4/15/85)

1977 Cross, Gillian. *On the Edge* (6–9). 1985, Holiday $13.95 (0-8234-0559-1); Dell paper $2.75 (0-440-96666-3). In rural England, Jinny discovers that a young kidnapping victim is being held in a nearby cottage. (Rev: BL 9/1/85; SLJ 8/85)

1978 Curry, Jane Louise. *The Great Flood Mystery* (6–8). Illus. 1985, Macmillan $12.95 (0-689-50306-7). Few people believe Gordy's story about encountering a burglar looking for lost treasure. (Rev: BL 10/1/85)

1979 Cusick, Richie Tankersley. *The Lifeguard* (7–10). 1988, Scholastic paper $2.50 (0-590-41549-2). After she arrives on Beverly Island, Kelsey becomes involved in mysterious happenings that eventually lead to murder. (Rev: VOYA 4/89)

1980 Cusick, Richie Tankersley. *Trick or Treat* (7–9). 1989, Scholastic paper $2.75 (0-590-42456-4). Jenny finds that mysterious events that happen to her seem to be connected to a murder that occurred some years before. (Rev: BL 2/1/90; VOYA 6/90)

1981 Davidson, Alan. *The Bewitching of Alison Allbright* (7–10). 1989, Viking $11.95 (0-670-82015-6). Alison adopts the identity of a dead girl to enjoy the wealth she had, but soon finds her new mother to be a sinister force. (Rev: BL 6/15/89; SLJ 7/89; VOYA 6/90)

1982 Davis, Leslie. *Something Out There* (7–10). 1985, Pocket paper $2.50 (0-671-54451-9). When Chips finds an unregistered boat on a deserted island, she also finds she is in the beginning of a baffling mystery. (Rev: BL 11/1/85; SLJ 1/86)

1983 Dodson, Susan. *Shadows across the Sand* (7–10). 1982, Fawcett paper $2.25 (0-317-13276-8). The residents of a small Florida town are being terrorized and 16-year-old Billie is determined to find out who is behind it.

1984 Doyle, Arthur Conan. *Adventures of Sherlock Holmes* (7–12). 1981, Avon paper $2.75 (0-380-78105-0). A collection of 12 of the most famous stories about this famous sleuth.

1985 Doyle, Arthur Conan. *The Complete Sherlock Holmes* (7–12). 1953, Doubleday $19.95 (0-385-04591-3). In 2 volumes, all the stories and novels involving Holmes and foil Watson.

1986 Doyle, Arthur Conan. *Hound of the Baskervilles* (7–12). 1986, Penguin paper $2.25 (0-14-035064-0). The classic Sherlock Holmes mystery set in the English moors. Other full-length Holmes mysteries include *A Study in Scarlet* and *The Sign of the Four* (both in many editions).

1987 Duffy, James. *The Man in the River* (5–8). 1990, Macmillan $13.95 (0-684-19161-X). Agatha Bates investigates the strange death of a reformed alcoholic in this sequel to *Missing* (1988). (Rev: BL 4/1/90; VOYA 6/90)

1988 du Maurier, Daphne. *Rebecca* (8–12). 1948, Doubleday $17.95 (0-385-04380-5); Avon paper $3.95 (0-380-00917-X). In this mystery originally published in 1938, the second wife of Max deWinter tries to find out about the death of her predecessor.

1989 Duncan, Lois. *Daughters of Eve* (7–10). 1979, Little $14.95 (0-316-19550-2); Dell paper $2.95 (0-440-91864-2). A group of girls come under the evil influence of the faculty sponsor of their club.

1990 Duncan, Lois. *Don't Look Behind You* (7–12). 1989, Delacorte $14.95 (0-385-29739-4). April and her family are on the run trying to escape from a hired hit man. (Rev: BL 5/15/89; SLJ 7/89; VOYA 8/89)

1991 Duncan, Lois. *Down a Dark Hall* (7–10). 1974, Little $13.95 (0-316-19547-2); paper $2.95 (0-440-91805-7). From the moment of arrival, Kit feels uneasy at her new boarding school.

1992 Duncan, Lois. *A Gift of Magic* (6–9). Illus. 1971, Little $14.95 (0-316-19545-6); Pocket paper $2.75 (0-671-65680-5). Twelve-year-old Kirby comes to terms with her gift of ESP.

1993 Duncan, Lois. *I Know What You Did Last Summer* (7–10). 1973, Little $13.95 (0-316-19546-4); Pocket paper $2.95 (0-671-63970-6). Four teenagers try to hide a hit-and-run accident in which they were involved.

1994 Duncan, Lois. *Killing Mr. Griffin* (7–10). 1978, Little $14.95 (0-316-19549-9); Dell paper $2.95 (0-440-94515-1). A kidnapping plot involving a disliked English teacher leads to murder.

1995 Duncan, Lois. *The Third Eye* (7–10). 1984, Little $14.95 (0-316-19553-7); Dell paper $2.95 (0-440-98720-2). Karen learns that she has mental powers that enable her to locate missing children.

1996 Duncan, Lois. *The Twisted Window* (7–10). 1987, Delacorte $14.95 (0-385-29566-9); Dell paper $3.25 (0-440-20184-5). Tracy grows to regret the fact that she has helped a young man kidnap his 2-year-old half-sister. (Rev: BL 9/1/87; BR 1–2/88; SLJ 9/87; VOYA 11/87)

1997 Ecke, Wolfgang. *The Case of the Face at the Window* (6–8). Trans. by Stella and Vernon Humphries. Illus. 1979, Prentice $9.95 (0-13-299115-2); paper $4.95 (0-13-299081-4). A group of puzzling mysteries with accompanying solutions.

1998 Ecke, Wolfgang. *The Midnight Chess Game* (6–8). Trans. by Stella and Vernon Humphries. Illus. 1985, Prentice $10.95 (0-13-582826-0). This book contains 15 short mysteries with solutions in the back. (Rev: BL 6/1/85)

1999 Ecke, Wolfgang. *The Stolen Paintings* (6–8). Trans. by Stella and Vernon Humphries. Illus. 1981, Prentice $9.95 (0-13-846865-6); paper $5.95 (0-13-846916-4). Seventeen easily read mysteries with the solutions in the back of the book.

2000 Ehrlich, Amy. *Where It Stops, Nobody Knows* (7–12). 1988, Dial $14.95 (0-8037-0575-1). When a loving daughter challenges her mother's constant moving from place to place, she uncovers a family secret. (Rev: BL 1/15/89; BR 5–6/89; SLJ 1/89; VOYA 12/88)

2001 Elfman, Blossom. *Love Me Deadly* (7–9). 1989, Fawcett paper $2.95 (0-449-70298-7). Ally and her friend Mike investigate the murder of a school secretary. (Rev: VOYA 8/89)

2002 Ellis, Carol. *My Secret Admirer* (7–9). 1989, Scholastic paper $2.75 (0-590-42515-3). An innocent scavenger hunt turns to unexplained tragedy in this thriller. (Rev: BL 2/1/90; VOYA 4/89)

2003 Evarts, Hal G. *Jay-Jay and the Peking Monster* (7–9). 1984, Peter Smith $15.25 (0-8446-6166-X). Two teenagers discover the bones of a prehistoric man and then the criminals move in.

2004 Ferguson, Alane. *Show Me the Evidence* (7–12). 1989, Bradbury $12.95 (0-02-734521-1); Avon paper $2.95 (0-380-70962-7). In this mystery story, a 17-year-old girl is fearful that her best friend might be involved in the mysterious

deaths of several children. (Rev: BL 4/1/89; BR 1–2/90; SLJ 3/89; VOYA 6/89)

2005 Fleischman, Sid. *Humbug Mountain* (6–9). Illus. 1978, Little $14.45 (0-316-28569-2); paper $4.95 (0-316-28613-3). A spoof set in the old West involving a family whose grandfather is missing.

2006 Flynn, Charlotte. *Dangerous Beat* (7–10). 1985, Pocket paper $2.25 (0-671-50783-4). Jennifer finds both romance and a life-threatening mystery when she takes a summer job on a newspaper. (Rev: BL 8/85; SLJ 9/85)

2007 French, Michael. *Us against Them* (7–12). 1987, Bantam $13.95 (0-553-05440-6); paper $2.95 (0-553-27647-6). Rivalries for leadership of a teenage gang take a serious turn when a murder is discovered. (Rev: BR 1–2/88; VOYA 2/88)

2008 Garden, Nancy. *Mystery of the Midnight Menace* (6–8). 1988, Farrar $11.95 (0-374-35203-8). Eighth-grader Brian investigates the strange deaths of creatures in Central Park. (Rev: BL 12/15/88; VOYA 2/89)

2009 Giff, Patricia Reilly. *Have You Seen Hyacinth Macaw?* (6–9). 1982, Delacorte LB $9.98 (0-440-03472-8); Dell paper $2.75 (0-440-43450-5). Two junior detectives sort out some confusing clues in their search for Hyacinth Macaw.

2010 Gorman, Carol. *Chelsey and the Green-Haired Kid* (6–8). 1987, Houghton $12.95 (0-395-41854-2). After 2 teenagers witness a murder, they find their own lives are in danger. (Rev: BL 6/1/87; BR 9–10/87; SLJ 6–7/87; VOYA 6/87)

2011 Graham, Harriet. *The Chinese Puzzle* (5–9). 1988, Houghton LB $13.95 (0-395-47689-5). In this novel set in London, the guardian of William and Flora mysteriously disappears and they set out to find him. (Rev: SLJ 10/88)

2012 Green, Roger J. *The Throttlepenny Murder* (6–9). 1989, Oxford Univ. Pr. $14.95 (0-19-271601-8). In England in 1885, a teenage girl is wrongfully accused of murder. (Rev: SLJ 7/89; VOYA 2/90)

2013 Griffiths, Helen. *The Mysterious Appearance of Agnes* (7–9). Illus. 1975, Holiday $12.95 (0-8234-0267-3). Because Agnes behaves so strangely, people think she is a witch.

2014 Guy, Rosa. *The Disappearance* (7–10). 1979, Delacorte $9.95 (0-440-92064-7); Dell paper $3.25 (0-385-28129-3). A 16-year-old black boy is accused of a kidnapping. Follow by *New Guys around the Block* (1983) and *And I Heard a Bird Sing* (1987).

2015 Hahn, Mary Downing. *The Dead Man in Indian Creek* (6–8). 1990, Clarion $13.95 (0-395-

52397-4). On a harmless camping trip, Matt and friend Parker find a body floating in Indian Creek. (Rev: BL 2/15/90)

2016 Hall, Lynn. *A Killing Freeze* (6–10). 1988, Morrow $11.95 (0-688-07867-2). A loner endangers her own life to find a murderer. (Rev: BL 8/88; BR 1–2/89; SLJ 9/88; VOYA 12/88)

2017 Hall, Lynn. *Murder at the Spaniel Show* (6–10). 1988, Macmillan $12.95 (0-684-18961-5). A young girl who works at a dog kennel gets involved in a murder that takes place during an important pet show. (Rev: BL 12/1/88; BR 5–6/89; SLJ 1/89; VOYA 4/89)

2018 Hall, Lynn. *Murder in a Pig's Eye* (7–10). 1990, Harcourt $14.95 (0-15-256268-0). In this humorous mystery a young would-be sleuth sets out to find the body of a woman he believes has been murdered. (Rev: BL 3/15/90; SLJ 5/90)

2019 Hall, Lynn. *Ride a Dark Horse* (7–10). 1987, Morrow $11.75 (0-688-07471-5); Avon paper $2.50 (0-380-75370-7). A teenage girl is fired from her job on a horse-breeding farm because she is getting too close to solving a mystery. (Rev: BL 9/15/87; BR 11–12/87; SLJ 12/87; VOYA 10/87)

2020 Hallman, Ruth. *Gimme Something, Mister!* (7–9). 1978, Westminster $8.95 (0-664-32638-2). An easily read story about a girl's exciting misadventures during Mardi Gras.

2021 Hamilton, Virginia. *The House of Dies Drear* (6–9). Illus. 1968, Macmillan $13.95 (0-02-742500-2); paper $3.95 (0-02-043520-7). The Smalls move to a new house that was formerly the home of a murdered abolitionist. A sequel is *The Mystery of Dies Drear* (1987).

2022 Hastings, Beverly. *Watcher in the Dark* (7–10). 1986, Berkley paper $2.75 (0-425-10131-2). Erin does not count on kidnapping attempts when she baby–sits 4–year-old Abby. (Rev: BL 6/15/86; SLJ 10/86)

2023 Hildick, E. W. *The Ghost Squad and the Menace of the Malevs* (6–9). 1988, Dutton $12.95 (0-525-44439-4). One of a lengthy recommended series about 2 humans and 4 ghosts who make up the Ghost Squad. In this adventure, they try to foil a psychotic murderer. (Rev: BL 2/15/89; VOYA 2/89)

2024 Hitchcock, Alfred, ed. *Spellbinders in Suspense* (7–10). 1967, Random LB $6.99 (0-394-91665-4); paper $3.95 (0-394-84900-0). A fine collection of suspenseful stories by such authors as Roald Dahl and Daphne du Maurier.

2025 Hoke, Helen, ed. *Mysterious, Menacing, and Macabre: An Anthology* (7–10). 1981, Lode-star $11.50 (0-525-66753-9). An excellent collection of 9 mystery and horror stories.

2026 Holland, Isabelle. *The Island* (7–9). 1984, Little $14.95 (0-316-36993-4); Fawcett paper $2.50 (0-449-70138-7). A teenage heroine finds her life threatened while on a visit to the Caribbean. Also use: *The Empty House* (Harper, 1983).

2027 Holland, Isabelle. *Thief* (7–9). 1989, Fawcett paper $2.95 (0-449-70269-3). Cressida, an orphan, tries to find out about her past and the parents whose death she may have caused. (Rev: SLJ 6/89; VOYA 8/89)

2028 Howard, Elizabeth. *Mystery of the Deadly Diamond* (6–9). Illus. 1987, Random $5.99 (0-394-97549-9); paper $3.95 (0-394-87549-4). A turn-of-the century novel set in Paris with a courageous 16-year-old American heroine. Others in this series: *Mystery of the Magician; Mystery of the Metro; A Scent of Murder* (all 1987). (Rev: BL 1/1/88; SLJ 1/88)

2029 Howe, James. *Dew Drop Dead* (6–8). 1990, Macmillan $13.95 (0-689-31425-6). A group of boys discover a corpse, but by the time the police arrive it has disappeared. (Rev: BL 3/1/90)

2030 Howe, James. *Stage Fright* (6–8). 1986, Macmillan $11.95 (0-689-31160-5); Avon paper $2.75 (0-380-70131-1). Thirteen-year-old Sebastian Barth, the detective of *What Eric Knew* (1985), tackles the problem of who is trying to kill a famous movie actress. (Rev: BL 5/1/86; VOYA 2/87)

2031 Johnston, Norma. *The Delphic Choice* (7–10). 1989, Macmillan $13.95 (0-02-747711-8). When her uncle is kidnapped, 17-year-old Meredith suspects some Middle East terrorists. (Rev: BL 5/1/89; SLJ 5/89; VOYA 8/89)

2032 Johnston, Norma. *Return to Morocco* (7–10). 1988, Macmillan $13.95 (0-02-747712-6). In Tangier, Texas teenager Tori and her grandmother get involved with spies and murder. (Rev: BL 11/15/88; BR 3–4/89; SLJ 9/88; VOYA 12/88)

2033 Johnston, Norma. *Shadow of a Unicorn* (7–10). 1987, Bantam paper $2.95 (0-553-26475-3). A teenager girl investigates a series of crimes on a horse farm. (Rev: BL 8/87; SLJ 10/87; VOYA 10/87)

2034 Johnston, Norma. *The Watcher in the Mist* (7–12). 1986, Bantam paper $2.95 (0-553-26032-4). Cindy's job to help convert a home into a New England inn suddenly involves arson and murder. (Rev: BL 12/15/86; VOYA 2/87)

2035 Kehret, Peg. *Deadly Stranger* (6–8). 1987, Dodd $13.95 (0-396-09039-7). Two 12-year-old girls are being stalked by a mentally deranged man. (Rev: BL 6/1/87)

2036 Kerr, M. E. *Fell* (8–12). 1987, Harper LB $12.89 (0-06-023268-4); paper $2.95 (0-06-447031-8). In a bizarre identity switch a teenager from a middle-class background enters a posh prep school. Followed by *Fell Again* (1989). (Rev: BL 6/1/87; SLJ 8/87; VOYA 10/87)

2037 Kidd, Ronald. *Second Fiddle: A Sizzle & Splat Mystery* (6–8). 1988, Dutton $12.95 (0-525-67252-4). Prudence and Arthur, better known as Sizzle and Splat, tackle the mystery of the prankster who disrupts orchestra practice. (Rev: BL 7/88; BR 3–4/89)

2038 Kidd, Ronald. *Sizzle and Splat* (7–9). 1983, Dutton $12.95 (0-525-66917-5); Dell paper $2.95 (0-440-47970-3). Two teenagers in a youth orchestra try to solve the mysterious kidnapping of their sponsor.

2039 Kilgore, Kathleen. *The Ghost-Maker* (7–9). 1984, Houghton $11.95 (0-395-35383-1). A boy learns the tricks of the trade when he becomes an assistant to a psychic.

2040 Klein, Robin. *People Might Hear You* (6–10). 1985, Viking $11.95 (0-317-62542-4); Penguin paper $3.95 (0-14-031594-2). Frances must escape her aunt's new husband and his cult-worshiping daughters before she, too, becomes brainwashed. (Rev: BL 3/1/86)

2041 Korman, Gordon. *Our Man Weston* (6–8). 1986, Scholastic paper $2.50 (0-590-40352-4). One of the Weston twins is certain that there is skullduggery afoot at the resort hotel where the twins are working. (Rev: SLJ 2/87)

2042 L'Engle, Madeleine. *Dragon in the Waters* (7–9). 1982, Farrar $13.95 (0-374-31868-9); Dell paper $3.25 (0-440-91719-0). On board an ocean liner, 13-year-old Simon encounters murder and a mystery surrounding a stolen portrait.

2043 Levin, Betty. *A Binding Spell* (7–9). 1984, Dutton $12.95 (0-525-67151-X). Strange things begin happening on the isolated farm in Maine where Wren and her brother are staying.

2044 Levitin, Sonia. *Incident at Loring Groves* (7–12). 1988, Dial $14.95 Fawcett paper $2.95 (0-449-70347-9). High school students find the body of a murdered classmate and decide to remain silent about it. (Rev: BL 9/1/88; BR 11–12/88; SLJ 6–7/88; VOYA 12/88)

2045 Levy, Elizabeth. *Cold as Ice* (6–9). 1988, Morrow $11.95 (0-688-06579-1). Two teenagers investigate strange happenings at a New York

City sports complex. (Rev: BL 12/15/88; BR 1–2/89; SLJ 12/88; VOYA 12/88)

2046 Marston, Elsa. *The Cliffs of Cairo* (7–9). 1982, NAL paper $1.75 (0-451-11530-9). Tabby slowly realizes that the men following her want the relic she bought in Cairo.

2047 Martin, Ann M. *Missing since Monday* (7–10). 1986, Holiday $12.95 (0-8234-0626-1). A graphic story of what happens to a family when one child is kidnapped. (Rev: BL 12/15/86; SLJ 11/86)

2048 Miller, Marvin. *You Be the Jury* (6–8). 1989, Scholastic paper $2.50 (0-590-40193-9). Ten mysteries (and solutions) are presented in the form of courtroom dramas. (Rev: SLJ 9/89)

2049 Moore, Ruth Nulton. *Mystery at Indian Rocks* (7–9). 1981, Herald Pr. paper $4.95 (0-8361-1944-4). Betty Jo's father is accused of robbery so she and friend Hal must find the real thief.

2050 Moore, Ruth Nulton. *Mystery of the Missing Stallions* (7–9). Illus. 1984, Herald Pr. paper $4.95 (0-8361-3376-5). Fourteen-year-old twins solve the mystery of the missing stallions. Part of a series about Sara and Sam.

2051 Murray, Marguerite. *Odin's Eye* (7–9). 1987, Macmillan $12.95 (0-689-31315-2). From the vantage point of her second cousin's rambling New England coastal house called Odin's Eye, a teenage girl investigates a number of mysterious deaths. (Rev: BL 3/1/87; BR 11–12/87; VOYA 6/87)

2052 Murrow, Liza Ketchum. *Fire in the Heart* (6–9). 1989, Holiday $14.95 (0-8234-0750-0). A teenager sets out to uncover the details of her mother's death 10 years before. (Rev: BL 3/1/89; SLJ 2/89; VOYA 10/89)

2053 Newman, Robert. *The Case of the Baker Street Irregular: A Sherlock Holmes Story* (6–8). 1984, Macmillan paper $3.95 (0-689-70766-5). Andrew becomes a Baker Street urchin who occasionally helps Sherlock Holmes or Scotland Yard inspector Peter Wyatt solve crimes. Others in this series are: *The Case of the Threatened King* (1985) and *The Case of the Vanishing Corpse* (1986).

2054 Newman, Robert. *The Case of the Indian Curse* (6–9). 1986, Macmillan $11.95 (0-689-31177-X). Andrew and Sara, 2 amateur English detectives, get involved in protecting a friend who knows a dangerous secret. (Rev: BL 9/1/86; SLJ 11/86; VOYA 2/87)

2055 Newman, Robert. *The Case of the Murdered Players* (6–8). 1985, Macmillan $12.95 (0-

689-31155-9). In Victorian England, young sleuths Andrew and Sara help Scotland Yard's Inspector Wyatt find the murderer of several actresses. (Rev: BL 9/1/85; SLJ 10/85)

2056 Newman, Robert. *The Case of the Watching Boy* (6–9). 1987, Macmillan $12.95 (0-689-31317-9). In a somewhat convoluted plot set in Victorian England, young Andrew and Sara "help" Scotland Yard solve a baffling crime. (Rev: BL 8/87; SLJ 9/87)

2057 Nixon, Joan Lowery. *Casey and the Great Idea* (6–8). Illus. 1982, Scholastic paper $2.50 (0-590-32337-7). Helping a friend in need leads to threatening phone calls for Casey.

2058 Nixon, Joan Lowery. *The Dark and Deadly Pool* (7–12). 1987, Delacorte $14.95 (0-385-29585-5). Mary Elizabeth becomes aware of strange happenings at the health club where she works. (Rev: BL 11/1/87; BR 11–12/87; SLJ 2/88; VOYA 12/87)

2059 Nixon, Joan Lowery. *The Ghosts of Now* (7–10). 1984, Dell paper $2.95 (0-440-93115-0). Angie investigates a hit-and-run accident that has left her brother in a coma.

2060 Nixon, Joan Lowery. *The Island of Dangerous Dreams* (7–12). 1989, Dell paper $2.95 (0-440-20258-2). Seventeen-year-old Andrea helps in the investigation of the murder of a judge in the Bahamas. (Rev: VOYA 8/89)

2061 Nixon, Joan Lowery. *The Kidnapping of Christina Lattimore* (7–9). 1979, Harcourt $8.95 (0-15-242657-4); Dell paper $2.75 (0-440-94520-8). Christina faces rumors that she engineered her own kidnapping.

2062 Nixon, Joan Lowery. *The Other Side of Dark* (7–10). 1986, Delacorte $14.95 (0-385-29481-6); Dell paper $2.75 (0-440-96638-8). After waking from a 4-year coma, Stacy is now the target of the man who wounded her and killed her mother. (Rev: BL 9/15/86; BR 3–4/87; SLJ 9/86; VOYA 12/86)

2063 Nixon, Joan Lowery. *The Seance* (7–10). 1980, Harcourt $12.95 (0-15-271158-8); Dell paper $2.95 (0-440-97937-4). An innocent séance leads to a double murder in this fast-paced mystery.

2064 Nixon, Joan Lowery. *Secret, Silent Screams* (7–10). 1988, Doubleday $14.95 (0-440-50059-1). Marti believes that her best friend's death was murder not suicide. (Rev: BL 9/15/88; BR 11–12/88; SLJ 11/88; VOYA 2/89)

2065 Nixon, Joan Lowery. *The Specter* (7–10). 1982, Delacorte $12.95 (0-385-28948-0).

Seventeen-year-old Dina protects a child who believes she is going to be murdered.

2066 Okimoto, Jean Davies. *Who Did It, Jenny Lake?* (6–8). 1984, Putnam paper $2.25 (0-399-21104-7). Jenny is baffled by the mysterious death of her Aunt Olivia.

2067 Orgel, Doris. *A Certain Magic* (6–8). 1976, Dial $7.95 (0-8037-5405-1). Jenny discovers an old notebook kept by her aunt that reveals secrets about the family's past.

2068 Pearce, Philippa. *The Way to Sattin Shore* (7–9). Illus. 1983, Greenwillow $10.50 (0-688-02319-3). Kate unravels the story behind her father's death.

2069 Pearce, Philippa. *Who's Afraid? And Other Strange Stories* (6–9). 1987, Greenwillow LB $10.25 (0-688-06895-2). Eleven stories that explore the disturbing dark side of life. (Rev: BR 5–6/87; SLJ 5/87)

2070 Peck, Richard. *Dreamland Lake* (7–9). 1990, Dell paper $2.50 (0-440-92079-5). The past becomes mingled with the present after 2 boys discover a skeleton in the woods. A reissue.

2071 Peck, Richard. *Through a Brief Darkness* (7–9). 1982, Dell paper $2.50 (0-440-98809-8). Karen must discover the truth about her father and hopes to find out when she visits relatives in England.

2072 Petersen, P. J. *The Freshman Detective Blues* (7–9). 1987, Delacorte $14.95 (0-385-29586-3). This intriguing mystery begins when 2 friends discover a human skeleton. (Rev: BL 1/15/88; BR 1–2/88; SLJ 10/87; VOYA 12/87)

2073 Peyton, K. M. *A Midsummer Night's Death* (7–10). 1979, Dell paper $1.75 (0-440-95615-3). In this English mystery, students wonder if the suicide of their hated teacher was really a murder.

2074 Pike, Christopher. *Gimme a Kiss* (7–12). 1988, Pocket paper $2.75 (0-671-65876-X). A girl fakes her own death in a wild plot to get revenge. (Rev: BL 10/15/88; VOYA 4/89)

2075 Pike, Christopher. *Last Act* (7–10). 1988, Pocket paper $2.75 (0-671-64980-9). The blanks in Melanie's stage pistol turn out to be real. Is she really guilty of murder? (Rev: BL 6/15/88; SLJ 11/88; VOYA 8/88)

2076 Pike, Christopher. *Slumber Party* (7–10). 1986, Scholastic paper $2.50 (0-590-33409-2). Six teenage girls stranded in a winter vacation home experience mysterious occurrences that bring terror into their lives. (Rev: SLJ 12/86)

2077 Pilling, Ann. *Henry's Leg* (6–8). 1987, Viking $10.95 (0-670-80720-6). Henry's problems begin when he finds a leg from a discarded store dummy. (Rev: BR 5–6/88)

2078 Platt, Kin. *Dracula, Go Home!* (6–8). 1981, Dell paper $1.50 (0-440-92022-1). Larry wonders if Aunt Shirley's guest isn't really Dracula.

2079 Raskin, Ellen. *The Tattooed Potato and Other Clues* (6–9). 1975, Dutton $14.95 (0-525-40805-3); Avon paper $2.25 (0-380-55558-1). An artist's apprentice encounters wild adventure, strange characters, and many mysteries in this amusing novel.

2080 Raskin, Ellen. *The Westing Game* (6–9). 1978, Dutton $14.95 (0-525-42320-6); Avon paper $2.95 (0-380-67991-4). Sixteen possible heirs try to decipher an enigmatic will. Newbery Award, 1979.

2081 Roberts, Willo Davis. *Nightmare* (7–10). 1989, Macmillan $13.95 (0-689-31551-1). After a series of unusual occurrences where 17-year-old Nick is the victim, he finds he is being followed. (Rev: BL 9/15/89; BR 3–4/90; SLJ 9/89; VOYA 12/89)

2082 Roberts, Willo Davis. *The View from the Cherry Tree* (7–9). 1975, Macmillan $14.95 (0-689-30483-8); paper $3.95 (0-689-70464-X). A boy who witnesses a murder becomes targeted as the next victim.

2083 Robinson, Nancy K. *The Phantom Film Crew* (6–8). 1986, Scholastic paper $2.25 (0-590-33593-6). On location with her filmmaker father, Tripper encounters a jewel thief. (Rev: BL 12/15/86; SLJ 1/87)

2084 St. George, Judith. *Do You See What I See?* (7–10). 1982, Putnam $9.95 (0-399-20912-3). Matt is certain he has seen violent acts committed in a Cape Cod cottage.

2085 St. John, Charlotte. *Red Hair* (6–9). 1989, Fawcett paper $2.95 (0-449-70320-7). Emily is convinced she has seen her twin who supposedly died years ago. (Rev: SLJ 3/90; VOYA 4/90)

2086 Schwandt, Stephen. *The Last Goodie* (8–10). 1985, Holt $11.95 (0-03-005182-7). Marty who is now a high school senior tries to solve the mysterious kidnapping of his baby-sitter many years before. (Rev: BL 10/1/85; BR 1–2/86; SLJ 11/85; VOYA 4/86)

2087 Shaw, Diana. *Gone Hollywood: A Carter Colborn Mystery* (7–10). 1988, Little $12.95 (0-316-78343-9). Carter solves the mystery of the disappearing teenage movie star. (Rev: BL 6/15/88; BR 11–12/88; SLJ 6–7/88; VOYA 10/88)

2088 Shaw, Diana. *Lessons in Fear* (6–9). 1987, Little $12.95 (0-316-78341-2). An unpopular teacher has a series of mysterious accidents and one of her students, Carter Colborn, decides she must investigate them. (Rev: BR 9–10/87; SLJ 10/87)

2089 Smith, Alison. *A Trap of Gold* (5–8). 1985, Dodd $10.95 (0-396-08721-3). A 14-year-old girl is certain she is being watched by a mysterious stranger. (Rev: SLJ 10/85)

2090 Stine, R. L. *The Overnight* (7–10). 1989, Pocket paper $2.75 (0-671-67687-3). While on an overnight camping trip, one of the 6 campers accidentally kills a stranger she meets in the woods. Also use: *The New Girl* (1989). (Rev: BL 12/15/89)

2091 Stine, R. L. *The Sleepwalker* (6–9). 1990, Pocket paper $2.95 (0-671-69412-X). When Mayra takes a summer job as a companion to a strange old woman, her life is suddenly in danger. (Rev: SLJ 9/90)

2092 Stine, R. L. *The Wrong Number* (5–9). 1990, Pocket paper $2.95 (0-671-69411-1). While making a crank telephone call, a teenager hears a murder being committed. (Rev: SLJ 6/90)

2093 Strasser, Todd. *The Accident* (7–10). 1988, Doubleday $14.95 (0-440-50061-3). Matt investigates a drunk driving accident in which some of his buddies are killed. (Rev: BL 10/15/88; BR 11–12/88; SLJ 11/88; VOYA 12/88)

2094 Strasser, Todd, and Dennis Freeland. *Moving Target* (6–10). 1989, Ballantine paper $2.95 (0-449-70324-X). Angelo Conti's family find that the safety they need through the Federal Witness Protection Program is not what they expected. (Rev: BL 12/1/89)

2095 Taylor, John Robert. *Hairline Cracks* (6–8). 1990, Dutton $14.95 (0-525-67304-0). Sam investigates the kidnapping of his mother in this British thriller. (Rev: BL 8/90; SLJ 9/90)

2096 Terris, Susan. *Octopus Pie* (6–8). 1983, Farrar $11.95 (0-374-35571-1). The friendship between Kristin and Mari becomes stronger when they must find out who kidnapped their pet octopus.

2097 Thesman, Jean. *Rachel Chance* (6–9). 1990, Houghton $13.95 (0-395-50934-3). Rachel's young brother has been kidnapped, but no one seems to be taking any action. (Rev: BL 5/1/90; SLJ 4/90)

2098 Towne, Mary. *Paul's Game* (7–9). 1983, Delacorte $13.95 (0-385-29248-1). Paul exerts a sinister influence over Julie through telepathy.

2099 Trease, Geoffrey. *A Flight of Angels* (6–8). 1989, Lerner $9.95 (0-8225-0731-5). An English story about a group of youngsters and a mysterious archway that has been bricked up. (Rev: BL 2/1/90)

2100 Vogt, Esther Loewen. *The Shiny Dragon* (6–8). Illus. 1983, Herald Pr. paper $3.95 (0-8361-3348-X). Brad finds that there really are strange things happening in a so-called haunted house.

2101 Voigt, Cynthia. *The Callender Papers* (7–10). 1983, Macmillan $13.95 (0-689-30971); Fawcett paper $3.50 (0-449-70184-0). A girl's life is in danger after she discovers some hidden family secrets.

2102 Walsh, Jill Paton. *Unleaving* (7–10). 1977, Avon paper $1.95 (0-380-01785-7). In this English novel, a young female university student ponders whether a cliff tragedy was really a murder.

2103 Wells, Rosemary. *The Man in the Woods* (7–9). 1984, Dial $12.95 (0-8037-0071-7); Scholastic paper $2.75 (0-590-41114-4). After she begins investigating an accident caused by a man who ran into the woods, Helen begins to receive threats.

2104 West, Tracy. *The Butterflies of Freedom* (6–9). 1988, Crosswinds paper $2.25 (0-373-98023-X). An easily read mystery involving a missing deed to valuable property. (Rev: VOYA 8/88)

2105 Whitney, Phyllis A. *Mystery of the Black Diamonds* (6–8). 1954, Westminster $7.50 (0-664-32099-6). A juvenile title by a master of the adult romantic mystery.

2106 Whitney, Phyllis A. *The Mystery of the Golden Horn* (7–10). 1990, Fawcett paper $3.95 (0-449-70363-0). In this mystery set in Turkey, young Vicky becomes involved in the disappearance of a valuable pin. (Rev: VOYA 8/90)

2107 Whitney, Phyllis A. *Secret of the Stone Face* (6–9). 1977, NAL paper $1.75 (0-451-11032-3). Jo encounters a mystery when she tries to prevent her mother's remarriage.

2108 Winfield, Julia. *Partners in Crime* (6–9). 1989, Bantam paper $2.95 (0-553-27767). Christine and Andy investigate the hunch that the school's basketball star is deliberately losing games. Also use: *Tug of Hearts* (1989). (Rev: SLJ 6/89)

2109 Wood, Marcia. *The Search for Jim McGwynn* (6–9). 1989, Macmillan $12.95 (0-689-31479-5). Jamie copes with his father's alcoholism while trying to uncover the identity of the famous mystery story writer who lives in his

town. (Rev: BL 9/15/89; BR 1–2/90; SLJ 10/89; VOYA 12/89)

2110 Woolfolk, Dorothy. *Body on the Beach and Murder in Washington* (7–10). 1982, Scholastic paper $1.95 (0-590-32000-9). Donna Rockford is up to her neck in adventure in these 2 mysteries in one volume.

2111 Yarbro, Chelsea Quinn. *Floating Illusions* (6–9). 1986, Harper LB $12.89 (0-06-026643-0). A 14-year-old girl and her aunt are on a trans-Atlantic ship when murder occurs. (Rev: BL 11/15/86; BR 3–4/87; SLJ 11/86)

2112 Yep, Laurence. *The Mark Twain Murders* (7–9). 1982, Macmillan $8.95 (0-02-793670-8). Mark Twain turns sleuth with a 15-year-old boy when they investigate a murder.

2113 York, Carol Beach. *I Will Make You Disappear* (6–8). 1974, Lodestar $6.95 (0-525-66410-6). The mystery begins when 2 girls find a secret room in a summer rental cottage.

2114 York, Carol Beach. *Remember Me When I Am Dead* (7–9). 1980, Lodestar $8.95 (0-525-66694-X). One year after their mother's death, strange occurences begin which make one think she is still alive.

2115 York, Carol Beach. *Where Evil Is* (7–10). 1987, Pocket paper $2.50 (0-671-64372-X). Marjorie wonders if her beautiful cousin's husband is not really a murderer. (Rev: BL 1/1/88; SLJ 2/88)

2116 Zindel, Paul. *The Undertaker's Gone Bananas* (7–9). 1978, Harper LB $13.89 (0-06-025846-8). Bobby and Lauri are convinced that their new neighbor is a murderer.

Romances

2117 Adler, C. S. *The Lump in the Middle* (6–10). 1989, Houghton $13.95 (0-89919-869-4). When Kelsey's father loses his job, Kelsey and her family move to Cape Cod but there she meets Gabe. (Rev: BR 1–2/90; VOYA 2/90)

2118 Althoff, Victoria M. *Key to My Heart* (7–10). 1989, Willowisp paper $2.50 (0-87406-384-1). Ginger begins dating a boy her best friend really dislikes. (Rev: SLJ 10/89)

2119 Andrews, Kristi. *Magic Time* (6–9). 1987, Bantam paper $2.50 (0-553-26342-0). Katie has a difficult time knowing whether she loves or hates her handsome TV co-star. (Rev: VOYA 10/88)

2120 Andrews, Kristi. *Upstaged* (7–10). 1988, Bantam paper $2.50 (0-553-26704-3). A young soap opera star finds her real life romance is in danger. (Rev: SLJ 10/88)

2121 Andrews, Wendy. *Vacation Fever!* (7–10). 1984, Putnam $10.95 (0-399-21084-9); paper $2.25 (0-399-21083-0). Meeting Neal becomes a pleasant incident in Mia's vacation.

2122 Angell, Judie. *Secret Selves* (7–9). 1979, Dell paper $2.25 (0-440-97716-9). Through secret telephone conversations with Rusty Parmette, Julie gets to know the other side of this snobbish boy.

2123 Barlette, Danielle. *Lovebound* (7–9). 1986, Berkley paper $2.50 (0-425-08445-0). Even though Amanda can't ski, her aunt wants her to get a product endorsement from an Olympic skier. (Rev: BL 8/86; VOYA 8–10/86)

2124 Bates, Betty. *Picking Up the Pieces* (7–10). 1982, Pocket paper $2.25 (0-671-53138-7). After her boyfriend is seriously injured in an accident, Nell wonders if the relationship will be the same.

2125 Beecham, Jahnna. *The Right Combination* (7–12). 1988, Bantam paper $2.50 (0-553-27005-2). In spite of her being pigheaded and difficult, handsome Kris still chooses Alex over an attractive cheerleader. (Rev: SLJ 4/88)

2126 Berke, Laura. *Operation Prom Date* (6–8). 1987, Ballantine paper $2.50 (0-449-70132-8). The somewhat hectic freshman year of Susie Chasen as chronicled in her journal. (Rev: BL 12/15/87; VOYA 12/87)

2127 Bischoff, David. *Some Kind of Wonderful* (7–10). 1987, Dell paper $2.50 (0-440-98042-9). Keith finds that his best friend Susan is really the girl for him after all. (Rev: BL 8/87; VOYA 8–9/87)

2128 Blake, Susan. *Crash Course* (7–12). 1987, Ballantine paper $2.50 (0-8041-0028-4). A college freshman, Stacy, who has emotional problems gets help from a local boy. By the same author of *Major Changes* (1987). (Rev: BL 10/1/87; VOYA 4/88)

2129 Blake, Susan. *Head Over Heels* (7–10). 1988, Ballantine paper $2.95 (0-8041-0234-1). Maggie chases after Adam when she should be paying attention to faithful Sam. (Rev: SLJ 10/88)

2130 Borisoff, Norman. *Bewitched and Bewildered: A Spooky Love Story* (7–9). Illus. 1982, Dell paper $1.75 (0-440-90905-8). Nicole communicates in a mysterious way with her boyfriend Michael when she is away.

2131 Bracale, Carla. *My Dream Guy* (7–10). 1989, Bantam paper $2.75 (0-553-28173-9). Kate

finds unexpected romance when she spends a week at Hidden Ranch. (Rev: SLJ 10/89)

2132 Bunn, Scott. *Just Hold On* (8–10). 1982, Delacorte paper $9.95 (0-385-28490-X). The love between 2 seniors in high school seems to be becoming so fragile it might break.

2133 Carraway, Mary. *Wendy* (7–10). 1988, Bethany House paper $3.50 (0-87123-942-6). Wendy and her boyfriend fight to save a park in a poor part of town. (Rev: SLJ 10/88)

2134 Cavanna, Betty. *Romance on Trial* (7–9). 1984, Westminster $11.95 (0-664-32715-X). Valerie goes to live in her boyfriend's home and encounters a great number of problems.

2135 Charbonneau, Eileen. *The Ghosts of Stony Clove* (7–10). 1988, Watts LB $13.99 (0-531-08339-X). A love story stretched over several years set in upstate New York and involving a young girl and her half-Indian boyfriend. (Rev: BL 5/15/88; SLJ 6–7/88; VOYA 10/88)

2136 Chase, Emily. *Keeping Secrets* (7–10). 1984, Scholastic paper $2.50 (0-590-41417-8). This is part of a series about the Girls of Canby Hall and their concerns. Others are *You're No Friend of Mine* and *Best Friends Forever* (both 1984).

2137 Chase, Emily. *The Roommate and the Cowboy* (7–10). 1988, Scholastic paper $2.50 (0-590-41390-2). The girls from Canby Hall venture to a Texas ranch. (Rev: SLJ 10/88)

2138 Chase, Emily. *Who's Got a Crush on Andy?* (7–10). 1989, Scholastic paper $2.50 (0-590-42149-2). Andy finds she has a mysterious admirer? (Rev: SLJ 10/89)

2139 Claypool, Jane. *A Love for Violet* (7–9). 1982, Westminster $8.95 (0-664-32697-8). Violet cannot believe that she has been singled out to receive the attention of Tony Dawson.

2140 Cleary, Beverly. *Fifteen* (7–9). 1956, Morrow LB $12.88 (0-688-21285-7); Dell paper $2.95 (0-440-92559-2). A young adolescent discovers that having a boyfriend isn't the answer to all her social problems.

2141 Cleary, Beverly. *Jean and Johnny* (7–9). 1959, Morrow $12.95 (0-688-21740-0). Jean is shy and uncertain of herself around handsome Johnny.

2142 Cleary, Beverly. *The Luckiest Girl* (7–9). 1958, Morrow LB $12.88 (0-688-31741-3); Dell paper $2.95 (0-440-94899-1). New social opportunities arise when a young girl spends her senior year at a school in California.

2143 Cohen, Barbara. *Lovers' Games* (7–9). 1986, Putnam paper $2.50 (0-425-08871-5). Mandy discovers being a matchmaker is a responsible position. A reissue.

2144 Cole, Brenda. *Three's a Crowd* (8–12). 1987, Crosswinds paper $2.25 (0-373-88010-3). Jodi has a steady boyfriend but is attracted to Jeff. (Rev: SLJ 1/88)

2145 Colman, Hila. *Remind Me Not to Fall in Love* (7–10). 1987, Pocket paper $2.50 (0-671-60123-7). A teenager and her divorced mother are in love with the same man. (Rev: BL 7/87)

2146 Conford, Ellen. *If This Is Love, I'll Take Spaghetti* (7–9). 1983, Macmillan $11.95 (0-02-724250-1); Scholastic paper $2.50 (0-590-41210-8). Teenage love and its frustrations form the theme of these stories.

2147 Cooney, Caroline B. *The Girl Who Invented Romance* (6–9). 1988, Bantam $13.95 (0-553-05473-2). Kelly's sociology project is a study of romance, which in time becomes a case history. (Rev: BR 5–6/88; SLJ 6–7/88; VOYA 8/88)

2148 Cooney, Linda A. *Senior* (7–12). 1989, Scholastic paper $2.50 (0-590-41678-2). In the fourth of this series, several friends face the excitement of high school graduation. (Rev: SLJ 10/89)

2149 Cooney, Linda A. *Sophomore* (7–12). 1987, Scholastic paper $2.50 (0-590-40349-4). Five friends deal with love interests and face moral dilemmas. Also use: *Junior* (1987). (Rev: SLJ 1/88)

2150 Cooper, M. E. *Changing Partners* (7–12). 1986, Scholastic paper $2.50 (0-590-40235-8). A group of high school juniors suffer the problems of first romance. (Rev: VOYA 12/86)

2151 Cooper, M. E. *Show Some Emotion* (8–12). 1987, Scholastic paper $2.50 (0-590-40424-5). Pamela's love for Matt is threatened by a scheming rival. (Rev: SLJ 4/87)

2152 Daly, Maureen. *First a Dream* (7–10). 1990, Scholastic $12.95 (0-590-40846-1). The love that Retta and Dallas feel for each other is tested during a summer when they are separated in this sequel to *Acts of Love* (1986). (Rev: BL 4/1/90; SLJ 4/90; VOYA 4/90)

2153 Daly, Maureen. *Seventeenth Summer* (6–8). 1981, Harmony LB $19.95 (0-89967-029-6); Archway paper $2.95 (0-671-61931-4). Angie experiences an idyllic summer after she meets Jack in this classic 1942 novel.

2154 deGale, Ann. *Island Encounter* (7–10). 1986, Dell paper $2.50 (0-440-94026-5). A low-key romance featuring a young girl and a Scottish boy whose families are vacationing on the island of Corfu. (Rev: SLJ 1/87)

2155 DuJardin, Rosamond. *Boy Trouble* (7–9). 1988, Harper LB $12.89 (0-397-32263-1). A harmless romance first published in the 1960s and now back in print. (Rev: SLJ 2/88)

2156 Elfman, Blossom. *First Love Lives Forever* (7–10). 1987, Ballantine paper $2.50 (0-449-70155-7). Ophelia is warned but unconvinced that her boyfriend hunky Brad is just using her. (Rev: BL 10/1/87; VOYA 10/87)

2157 Ellis, Carol. *Summer to Summer* (6–8). 1985, Ballantine paper $2.25 (0-345-31631-2). Two summers in the life of Jamie and how she finds love. (Rev: BL 4/1/85; SLJ 9/85)

2158 Ellis, Jana. *Better Than the Truth* (7–10). 1989, Troll paper $2.50 (0-8167-1362-6). Lori's lab partner Frank begins spreading vicious rumors about her. Also use *Junior Weekend* and *Never Stop Smiling* (both 1988). (Rev: SLJ 4/89)

2159 Enderle, Judith. *Secrets* (7–9). 1984, Pocket paper $1.95 (0-671-53415-7). Cara's shame that she lives in a trailer almost spoils her romance. (Rev: BL 2/1/85)

2160 Fields, Terri. *Recipe for Romance* (7–10). 1986, Scholastic paper $2.25 (0-590-33872-2). A high school senior gets a job in a college frat house on the condition that she not date any of the young men. (Rev: VOYA 12/86)

2161 Filichia, Peter. *Everything but Tuesdays and Sundays* (7–9). 1984, Fawcett paper $1.95 (0-449-70047-X). Amy's success at juggling 2 very different boyfriends can't last forever.

2162 Filichia, Peter. *Not Just Another Pretty Face* (7–10). 1988, Avon paper $2.50 (0-380-75244-1). A high school story where the course of true love does not run smoothly for Bill Richards. (Rev: BL 3/1/88; SLJ 5/88)

2163 Foley, June. *It's No Crush, I'm in Love!* (7–9). 1982, Delacorte $12.95 (0-385-28465-9). Annie doesn't understand why her ninth-grade English teacher doesn't love her as she loves him.

2164 Foley, June. *Love by Any Other Name* (7–9). 1983, Delacorte $13.95 (0-385-29245-7). Billie wonders if she really is in love with Bubba.

2165 Foster, Stephanie. *A Chance to Love* (7–12). 1988, Bantam paper $2.95 (0-553-27017-6). Diana falls for a bookish lifeguard but realizes that the boy next door is fine for her. (Rev: SLJ 4/88)

2166 Garwood, Julie. *A Girl Named Summer* (7–10). 1986, Scholastic paper $2.25 (0-590-33770-X). During an otherwise dull summer, Summer finds a heartthrob at a bingo parlor. (Rev: SLJ 9/86; VOYA 12/86)

2167 Girion, Barbara. *Front Page Exclusive: Jill's Story* (7–10). 1987, Dell paper $2.50 (0-440-92663-7). Jill finds both excitement and love when she interns on a newspaper. (Rev: BL 8/87; VOYA 12/87)

2168 Girion, Barbara. *In the Middle of a Rainbow* (7–9). 1983, Macmillan $12.95 (0-684-17885-0); Putnam paper $2.25 (0-399-21080-6). Corrie is confused about her attitudes toward her boyfriend and committing herself to a college career.

2169 Girion, Barbara. *Portfolio to Fame: Cameron's Story* (7–12). 1987, Dell paper $2.50 (0-440-97148-9). A shy girl who is a model finds romance with a photographer. Another romance by Girion is *Prescription for Success: Amanda's Story* (1987). (Rev: BL 10/1/87; SLJ 10/87)

2170 Gorman, Susan. *World Class* (7–12). 1989, Fawcett paper $2.95 (0-449-13468-7). Claire almost loses a World Class skating competition because of an infatuation. (Rev: SLJ 10/89)

2171 Goudge, Eileen. *Afraid to Love* (7–12). 1984, Dell paper $2.25 (0-440-90092-1). A senior girl in high school is afraid that people will find out that she was once overweight. Others in this series are: *Smart Enough to Know; Too Much Too Soon;* and *Winner All the Way* (all 1984). (Rev: BL 2/1/85)

2172 Goudge, Eileen. *Against the Rules* (7–9). 1986, Dell paper $2.25 (0-440-90096-4). Alex's former boyfriend comes to work at her school and the problems begin. (Rev: BL 2/1/87; SLJ 1/87)

2173 Goudge, Eileen. *Don't Say Good-Bye* (7–12). 1985, Dell paper $2.25 (0-440-92108-2). Can Roseanne's love for her boyfriend remain intact after he is crippled in an accident? Other romances by this author are: *Kiss and Make Up; Looking for Love;* and *Presenting Superhunk* (all 1986). (Rev: BL 4/15/86)

2174 Goudge, Eileen. *Night after Night* (7–12). 1986, Dell paper $2.25 (0-440-96369-9). After a plane crash, the true nature of Marcia's boyfriend emerges. Also use: *Treat Me Right* (1986). (Rev: BL 10/1/86; VOYA 12/86)

2175 Goudge, Eileen. *Sweet Talk* (7–10). 1986, Dell paper $2.25 (0-440-98411-4). Elaine's love for Carl is cooling and now she is attracted to Zack. (Rev: BL 8/86; VOYA 12/86)

2176 Goudge, Eileen. *Too Hot to Handle* (9–12). 1985, Dell paper $2.25 (0-440-98812-8). Problems begin for Elaine when her boyfriend sug-

gests they date other people. Also use: *Hands Off, He's Mine* (1989). (Rev: BL 6/1/85)

2177 Goudge, Eileen. *A Touch of Ginger* (7–12). 1985, Dell paper $2.25 (0-440-98816-0). Kit finds that her relations with boyfriend Craig change because her cousin Ginger from New York has come to visit. (Rev: BL 12/15/85)

2178 Greene, Yvonne. *Headliners* (7–12). 1986, Bantam paper $2.50 (0-553-26112-6). A charming but dangerous movie star begins noticing young Kelly. (Rev: SLJ 4/87)

2179 Gregory, Diana. *Two's a Crowd* (7–10). 1985, Bantam paper $2.25 (0-553-24992-4). Peggy finds that her business rival in a catering business is a handsome young man. (Rev: BL 10/15/85; SLJ 9/85)

2180 Guest, Elissa Haden. *The Handsome Man* (7–10). 1981, Macmillan $12.95 (0-02-741040-4); Dell paper $1.95 (0-440-93437-0). Alexandra's attraction to a good-looking stranger becomes an obsession.

2181 Hallin, Emily. *Queen Bee* (7–10). 1989, Crosswinds paper $2.25 (0-373-88039-1). During the course of this romance the heroine grows to maturity and accepts responsibilities. (Rev: SLJ 4/89)

2182 Harrell, Janice. *Love and Pizza to Go* (8–12). 1987, Crosswinds paper $2.25 (0-373-88011-1). A light romance about 4 teens who bounce back and forth from one to another. Also use: *They're Rioting in Room 32* (1987). (Rev: SLJ 1/88; VOYA 2/88)

2183 Hart, Bruce, and Carol Hart. *Waiting Games* (7–10). 1981, Avon paper $3.50 (0-380-89971-X). Jessie and Michael are in love and must make difficult decisions about sex.

2184 Haynes, Betsy. *The Great Boyfriend Trap* (6–8). 1987, Bantam paper $2.75 (0-553-15530-X). Two seventh-grade friends help each other get the boyfriends they want. (Rev: SLJ 5/88)

2185 Herrick, Ann. *The Perfect Guy* (7–10). 1989, Bantam paper $2.95 (0-553-27927-0). Fifteen-year-old Rebecca has a crush on her new stepbrother. (Rev: BL 6/15/89)

2186 Holmes, Marjorie. *Saturday Night* (7–9). 1982, Dell paper $1.95 (0-440-97645-6). Carly is flattered to be taken out by popular Danny until she learns the truth.

2187 Hooper, Mary. *Friends and Rivals* (7–10). 1986, Dell paper $2.50 (0-440-92660-2). Clare has a crush on Steve, who is attracted to Clare's cousin Angie. (Rev: SLJ 1/87; VOYA 6/86)

2188 Jones, McClure. *Fix-Up Service* (7–9). 1985, Putnam $12.95 (0-448-47756-4). Nicky gets into trouble when she begins operating a dating service at school. (Rev: BR 1–2/86; VOYA 6/85)

2189 Joyce, Rosemary. *Anything to Win!* (7–12). 1986, Pocket paper $2.50 (0-671-62110-6). Linda and Arlene are competing for John's attention. (Rev: BL 10/1/86)

2190 Kaplow, Robert. *Alessandra in Love* (8–10). 1989, Harper LB $11.89 (0-397-32282-8). Alessandra's boyfriend turns out to be a self-centered disappointment. (Rev: BL 4/15/89; SLJ 4/89; VOYA 8/89)

2191 Kaye, Marilyn. *Max in Love* (7–10). 1986, Pocket paper $2.75 (0-671-60266-7). An alien girl decides she should learn about love from an earthling. (Rev: BL 8/86; SLJ 9/86)

2192 Kent, Deborah. *Talk to Me, My Love* (7–10). 1987, Dell paper $2.75 (0-440-97810-6). In her efforts to win back Steve, Toni ignores the loyal Kenny who loves her. (Rev: VOYA 8–9/87)

2193 Killien, Christi. *All of the Above* (6–9). 1987, Houghton $12.95 (0-395-43023-2). MacBeth, a tenth-grade girl, thinks she has found the perfect boy in Blake. (Rev: BL 5/1/87; BR 9–10/87; SLJ 5/87; VOYA 6/87)

2194 Klein, Norma. *The Cheerleader* (7–9). 1985, Knopf LB $11.99 (0-394-97577-4). Two boys join the cheerleading squad to help the girls' sports teams. (Rev: BL 10/1/85; BR 3–4/86; SLJ 11/85; VOYA 4/86)

2195 Knudson, R. R. *Just Another Love Story* (7–10). 1983, Farrar $12.95 (0-374-33967-8); Avon paper $2.50 (0-380-65532-2). Dusty takes up body building to help forget the girlfriend who has spurned him.

2196 Kropp, Paul. *Getting Even* (7–10). 1986, Bantam paper $3.50 (0-7704-2112-1). Two misfits meet and fall in love in this romance told from their 2 points of view. (Rev: SLJ 10/86)

2197 Lantz, Fran. *Woodstock Magic* (7–12). 1986, Avon paper $2.50 (0-380-75129-1). In this time travel novel a teenager goes back to Woodstock days to help prevent her parents' relationship. (Rev: BL 2/1/87)

2198 L'Engle, Madeleine. *And Both Were Young* (7–10). 1983, Delacorte $14.95 (0-385-29237-6); Dell paper $3.25 (0-440-90229-0). Flip finds adjusting to her Swiss boarding school easier after she meets Paul.

2199 Levy, Elizabeth. *All Shook Up* (7–10). 1986, Scholastic paper $2.25 (0-590-33115-9). Before his rise to fame, Elvis receives advice from Amy, a high school senior, during several chance encounters. (Rev: SLJ 11/86)

2200 Levy, Marilyn. *Sounds of Silence* (7–12). 1989, Fawcett paper $2.95 (0-449-70295-2). Nikki's life becomes complicated when she falls for a deaf boy. (Rev: SLJ 10/89; VOYA 10/89)

2201 Lewis, Carrie. *Call of the Wild* (7–9). 1984, Pocket paper $1.95 (0-671-53410-6). Even though handsome David Parker is around, Annie is unenthusiastic about summer camp. (Rev: BL 2/1/85)

2202 Lewis, Linda. *All for the Love of That Boy* (7–10). 1989, Pocket paper $2.95 (0-671-68243-1). Relations between bright, attractive Linda and her somewhat dull boyfriend become strained. (Rev: BL 2/15/90; SLJ 3/90)

2203 Lewis, Linda. *My Heart Belongs to That Boy* (7–9). 1989, Pocket paper $2.75 (0-671-66604-5). Linda tries to change her first boyfriend into the image she has of him. (Rev: SLJ 3/89)

2204 Lewis, Linda. *We Love Only Older Boys* (6–8). 1988, Pocket paper $2.50 (0-671-64916-7). Thirteen-year-old Linda is out to date an older boy. (Rev: SLJ 6–7/88)

2205 McFann, Jane. *Maybe by Then I'll Understand* (7–9). 1987, Avon paper $2.50 (0-380-75221-1). Cath and Tony become a pair but Tony demands more attention and loyalty than she can give. (Rev: BL 11/15/87; SLJ 1/88; VOYA 12/87)

2206 McGill, Joyce. *Here We Go Again* (7–10). 1986, Silhouette paper $1.95 (0-373-06184-6). At an old folks' summer camp where she is helping an elderly aunt, Glynna falls for the lifeguard. (Rev: SLJ 9/86)

2207 Marlin, J. *Appeal to the Heart* (7–10). 1986, Berkley paper $2.75 (0-425-09549-5). When Sandrine becomes chief justice in a classroom trial, she suddenly gains the attention of Ted, a heartthrob who is also the defense attorney. (Rev: BL 5/1/86; SLJ 8/86)

2208 Marshall, Andrea. *Handle with Care* (7–10). 1984, Pocket paper $1.95 (0-671-53407-6). Jamie's boyfriend becomes jealous when she meets a handsome college student. (Rev: BL 2/1/85)

2209 Martin, Ann M. *Just a Summer Romance* (6–8). 1987, Holiday $13.95 (0-8234-0649-0); Scholastic paper $2.50 (0-590-41432-1). While spending a summer on Fire Island, 14-year-old Melanie becomes attracted to Justin. (Rev: BL 4/1/87; SLJ 6–7/87; VOYA 10/87)

2210 Matthews, Phoebe. *The Boy on the Cover* (6–8). 1988, Avon paper $2.50 (0-380-75407-X).

Cyndi falls in love with a boy whose picture is on the cover of a book she owns. (Rev: VOYA 2/89)

2211 Mauser, Pat Rhoads. *Love Is for the Dogs* (7–10). 1989, Avon paper $2.50 (0-380-75723-0). Janna realizes that Brian, the boy next door, can be very desirable. (Rev: SLJ 4/89)

2212 Miklowitz, Gloria D. *Love Story, Take Three* (7–12). 1987, Dell paper $2.75 (0-440-95084-8). The problems of being a television personality are explored in this novel about a teenage star who would like to live a normal life. (Rev: BL 6/15/86; BR 9–10/86; SLJ 5/86; VOYA 6/86)

2213 Miller, Sandy. *Smart Girl* (7–10). 1982, NAL paper $2.25 (0-451-11887-1). Sandy finds that some of the boys resent that she is so intelligent.

2214 Mines, Jeanette. *Risking It* (7–9). 1988, Avon paper $2.50 (0-380-75401-0). Jeannie is attracted to Trent Justin who has joined her senior class. (Rev: SLJ 1/89; VOYA 6/88)

2215 Morris, Winifred. *The Jell-O Syndrome* (7–10). 1986, Macmillan $12.95 (0-689-31190-7). A teenage feminist finds she turns to Jello-O when she meets Keith, a new student in her school. (Rev: BL 4/15/86; SLJ 4/86; VOYA 8–10/86)

2216 Nicholas, Simone. *Star Crowd* (7–12). 1987, Ballantine paper $2.50 (0-345-33243-1). Ellie finds that she and her roommate are rivals both in love and in the casting for a role in *Grease*. (Rev: BL 10/1/87)

2217 Pascal, Francine. *Bitter Rivals* (7–10). 1986, Bantam paper $2.50 (0-553-25728-5). A former wallflower returns to Sweet Valley High transformed into a beautiful young girl. (Rev: VOYA 12/86)

2218 Peyton, K. M. *The Edge of the Cloud* (7–10). 1989, Penguin paper $3.95 (0-14-030905-5). Two young people in love with each other but too young to marry find the future difficult to face.

2219 Pfeffer, Susan Beth. *Evvie at Sixteen* (7–10). 1988, Bantam $13.95 (0-553-05475-9). At the family's summer home Evvie must choose between 2 boyfriends—the socially accepted Schyler or the more stable Jewish Sam. (Rev: BR 5–6/88; VOYA 8/88)

2220 Pfeffer, Susan Beth. *Prime Time* (7–10). 1985, Putnam paper $2.25 (0-425-08400-0). In this beginning story about soap opera stars' private lives, the 6 principals get to know one another. Continued in: *Take Two and . . . Rolling!* (1985). (Rev: BL 10/15/85; SLJ 10/85)

2221 Pitt, Jane. *Secret Hearts* (7–10). 1986, Dell paper $2.50 (0-440-97722-3). Jennifer finds that a

secret her father is hiding involves the boy she loves. (Rev: BL 2/1/87)

2222 Quin-Harkin, Janet. *Dear Cousin* (7–10). 1987, Ballantine paper $2.50 (0-8041-0038-1). Chrissy becomes the new lonely hearts columnist on her school's newspaper. Also by the same author: *The Last Dance* (1987). (Rev: BL 10/1/87; SLJ 1/88)

2223 Quin-Harkin, Janet. *Flip Side* (7–12). 1987, Ballantine paper $2.95 (0-8041-0051-9). Two friends really like the other one's boyfriend more than their own. (Rev: SLJ 1/88)

2224 Quin-Harkin, Janet. *The Great Boy Chase* (7–12). 1985, Bantam paper $2.25 (0-553-25071-X). On her trip to France, Jill finds a lot of attractive boys and also gets into some very humorous situations. Also use: *101 Ways to Meet Mr. Right* and *Wanted: Date for Saturday Night* (both 1985). (Rev: BL 12/15/85; SLJ 1/86)

2225 Quin-Harkin, Janet. *One Step Too Far* (7–10). 1989, Ivy paper $2.95 (0-8041-0337-2). Caroline is attracted to a handsome prisoner when she does volunteer tutoring in a local prison. (Rev: SLJ 10/89)

2226 Quin-Harkin, Janet. *Trading Places* (7–10). 1987, Ballantine paper $2.50 (0-8041-0027-6). Naive Chrissy tries for instant sophistication to impress Hunter, scion of a wealthy family. (Rev: SLJ 10/87)

2227 Rand, Suzanne. *The Boy She Left Behind* (7–10). 1985, Bantam paper $2.25 (0-553-24890-1). Jill is torn between her summer romance and the boy she left back home. (Rev: BL 10/15/85; SLJ 9/85)

2228 Rand, Suzanne. *The Good Luck Girl* (7–12). 1986, Bantam paper $2.50 (0-553-25644-0). Tess becomes so upset about her parents' divorce that she almost loses her boyfriend. (Rev: BL 8/86)

2229 Ransom, Candice F. *Sabrina* (7–10). 1986, Scholastic paper $2.25 (0-590-33845-5). In British-occupied Charleston of 1780, Sabrina must choose between 2 loves—one a Tory and the other a rebel. (Rev: SLJ 9/86)

2230 Reit, Ann. *The First Time* (7–10). 1986, Dell paper $2.50 (0-440-92560-6). Gwen finds that the boy she loves is irresponsible. (Rev: BL 10/1/86; SLJ 1/87)

2231 Richards, Cyndi. *Go for Broke* (7–10). 1988, Fawcett paper $2.50 (0-449-70248-0). A 16-year-old girl finds romance at her father's rodeo school in California. (Rev: VOYA 6/88)

2232 Ryan, Mary C. *Frankie's Run* (6–8). 1987, Little $12.95 (0-316-76370-5). In this teen novel,

Mary Frances falls for the new boy in town but also organizes a run to aid her local library. (Rev: BR 9–10/87; SLJ 5/87)

2233 Rylant, Cynthia. *A Couple of Kooks and Other Stories about Love* (7–12). 1990, Watts LB $13.99 (0-531-08500-7). These 8 stories about love explore unexpected relationships like having a crush on a bag boy at a supermarket, or a widow finding passion at age 67. (Rev: BL 9/15/90; SLJ 9/90)

2234 Sachs, Marilyn. *Thunderbird* (7–10). Illus. 1985, Dutton $10.95 (0-525-44163-8). Two high school seniors meet and fall in love in the public library. (Rev: BL 4/15/85; SLJ 10/85)

2235 Schurfranz, Vivian. *Merrie* (7–10). 1987, Scholastic paper $2.75 (0-590-41000-8). Merrie, one of the Pilgrims, has 2 boys to choose from in this romance set in the time of the *Mayflower* landing. (Rev: SLJ 1/88)

2236 Sharmat, Marjorie. *Fighting Over Me* (7–10). 1986, Dell paper $2.50 (0-440-92530-4). Senior high student Fritzi has everything going for her, including 2 boyfriends, when the threatening notes begin to appear. (Rev: SLJ 1/87)

2237 Sharmat, Marjorie. *For Members Only* (7–10). 1986, Dell paper $2.50 (0-440-92654-8). At high school Kim is asked to join a sorority whose members are popular but not very nice. (Rev: BL 10/1/86; SLJ 9/86)

2238 Sharmat, Marjorie. *Getting Closer* (7–12). 1987, Dell paper $2.50 (0-440-92828-1). When a teen idol asks her for a date, Bridget doubts his sincerity. Also use: *I'm Going to Get Your Boyfriend* (1987). (Rev: BL 8/87; SLJ 10/87; VOYA 4/88)

2239 Sharmat, Marjorie. *Here Comes Mr. Right* (7–10). 1987, Dell paper $2.50 (0-440-93841-4). Melanie's life becomes complicated when her mother arranges a date with Norm. (Rev: VOYA 12/87)

2240 Sharmat, Marjorie. *How to Have a Gorgeous Wedding* (7–10). 1985, Dell paper $2.25 (0-440-93794-9). When attending a family wedding, 2 cousins are both attracted to the groom's son. (Rev: SLJ 9/85)

2241 Sharmat, Marjorie. *I Saw Him First* (7–9). 1983, Delacorte $12.95 (0-385-29243-0); Dell paper $2.95 (0-440-94009-5). Both Dana and friend Andrea are attracted to the same boy.

2242 Sharmat, Marjorie. *I Think I'm Falling in Love* (7–9). 1986, Dell paper $2.50 (0-440-94011-7). Tracy finds that her essay topic has been stolen by a sorority sister in this frothy romance. (Rev: BL 2/1/87; SLJ 1/87)

2243 Sharmat, Marjorie. *Nobody Knows How Scared I Am* (7–10). 1987, Dell paper $2.50 (0-440-96267-6). Teenage twins are in competition with each other for the same boy. (Rev: SLJ 10/87)

2244 Sierra, Patricia. *One-Way Romance* (7–10). 1986, Avon paper $2.50 (0-380-75107-0). A talented girl who does well with carpentry and track seems to be losing out with her boyfriend. (Rev: BL 8/86; SLJ 11/86; VOYA 12/86)

2245 Sonnenmark, Laura A. *Something's Rotten in the State of Maryland* (7–10). 1990, Scholastic $12.95 (0-590-42876-4). While rewriting the play *Hamlet,* Marie learns a lot about herself and her relations with handsome student director Simon. (Rev: BL 6/1/90; SLJ 3/90)

2246 Steiner, Barbara. *If You Love Me* (7–9). 1986, Bantam paper $2.25 (0-553-25535-5). A young tennis camp instructor finds romance with a fellow player. (Rev: VOYA 12/86)

2247 Sunshine, Tina. *An X-Rated Romance* (7–9). 1988, Avon paper $2.50 (0-380-87817-8). Two 13-year-old girls have a crush on their English teacher. A reissue.

2248 Swallow, Pamela Curtis. *No Promises* (6–9). 1989, Putnam $13.95 (0-399-21561-1). Dana is torn between her attraction to both Paul and Jared in this light romance. (Rev: BR 11–12/90; SLJ 6/89; VOYA 8/89)

2249 Thesman, Jean. *Who Said Life Is Fair?* (7–9). 1987, Avon paper $2.50 (0-380-75088-0). Teddy is trying to cope with work on the school newspaper while keeping her love life in order. (Rev: VOYA 8–9/87)

2250 Webster, Jean. *Daddy-Long-Legs* (7–9). 1982, Dell paper $4.95 (0-440-41673-6). Told in letter-format, this is the story of a girl in an orphanage and her mysterious benefactor.

2251 Weyn, Suzanne. *The Makeover Summer* (6–8). 1988, Avon paper $2.50 (0-380-75521-1). An exchange student who needs help joins three girls of the Makeover Club. Another light romance by the same author is: *Love Song* (1988). (Rev: BL 2/15/89)

2252 William, Kate. *Malibu Summer* (7–9). 1986, Bantam paper $2.95 (0-553-26050-2). Each twin takes a different summer job in Malibu and finds romance. (Rev: VOYA 2/87)

2253 Wood, Phyllis Anderson. *Song of the Shaggy Canary* (8–10). 1974, Westminster $8.95 (0-664-32543-2). Sandy, a young mother whose husband has abandoned her, hopes she has found a better man in John.

2254 York, Carol Beach. *A Likely Story* (6–9). 1985, Ballantine paper $2.25 (0-345-31635-5). Two episodes in Amy's life—one at 14 and the other at 17—show a growth to maturity. (Rev: BL 10/1/85; SLJ 9/85)

2255 Zable, Rona S. *An Almost Perfect Summer* (6–8). 1989, Bantam paper $2.95 (0-553-27967-X). A 15-year-old girl finds romance when she takes a job as a mother's helper on Cape Cod. (Rev: VOYA 8/89)

2256 Zable, Rona S. *Love at the Laundromat* (7–10). 1988, Bantam paper $2.95 (0-553-27225-X). Joanne finds romance at her mother's laundromat but not without humorous complications. (Rev: BL 7/1/88; VOYA 12/88)

2257 Zindel, Paul. *The Girl Who Wanted a Boy* (7–10). 1981, Harper LB $11.89 (0-06-066868-9); paper $2.95 (0-553-26486-9). Bright, aggressive 15-year-old Sibella decides to take aggressive measures to find herself a boy.

Science Fiction

2258 Abels, Harriette S. *Strangers on NMA-6* (6–9). 1979, Crestwood LB $7.95 (0-89686-027-2). Nine stories about space exploration and space colonies.

2259 Ames, Mildred. *Anna to the Infinite Power* (6–9). 1981, Macmillan $11.95 (0-684-16855-3); Scholastic paper $2.50 (0-599-41002-4). Twelve-year-old Anna discovers she is part of a genetic engineering project.

2260 Asimov, Isaac, et al., eds. *Caught in the Organ Draft: Biology in Science Fiction* (7–10). 1983, Farrar paper $13.95 (0-374-31228-1). Unusual aspects of biology are explored in this collection of 12 science fiction stories.

2261 Asimov, Isaac, et al., eds. *Hallucination* (7–10). 1983, Farrar $13.95 (0-374-32835-8). The mysteries of the human mind are explained in these 12 science fiction stories.

2262 Asimov, Isaac, et al., eds. *Thinking Machines* (7–9). Illus. 1981, Raintree LB $15.99 (0-8172-1727-4). Robots and other machines that think are the subjects of these 5 science fiction stories.

2263 Asimov, Isaac, et al., eds. *Young Extraterrestrials* (7–9). 1984, Harper LB $12.89 (0-06-020168-1); paper $7.95 (0-06-020167-3). Eleven stories by well-known authors about youngsters who are aliens from space.

2264 Asimov, Isaac, et al., eds. *Young Star Travelers* (7–10). 1986, Harper LB $12.89 (0-06-020179-7). A collection of 9 science fiction stories that feature young people living in space. (Rev: BL 6/15/86; BR 11–12/86; SLJ 4/86; VOYA 6/86)

2265 Asimov, Janet, and Isaac Asimov. *Norby and the Invaders* (5–8). 1985, Walker LB $10.85 (0-8027-6607-2). Jeff and his unusual robot Norby travel to a planet to help one of Norby's ancestors. Part of a series that includes *Norby's Other Secret* (1984). (Rev: BL 3/1/86)

2266 Asimov, Janet, and Isaac Asimov. *Norby and Yobo's Great Adventure* (5–8). 1989, Walker LB $14.85 (0-8027-6894-6). Norby, the robot, time travels to help Admiral Yobo of Mars to trace his family roots. Part of a series that also includes *Norby Down to Earth* (1989). (Rev: BL 10/15/89)

2267 Babbitt, Lucy Cullyford. *Children of the Maker* (8–10). 1988, Farrar $13.95 (0-374-31245-1). The 2 young rulers of Melde find that theirs is not the only colony on their planet in this sequel to *The Oval Amulet* (1985). (Rev: BL 2/1/89; BR 3–4/89; SLJ 2/89; VOYA 4/89)

2268 Baird, Thomas. *Smart Rats* (7–10). 1990, Harper LB $14.89 (0-06-020365-X). In the twenty-first century, food is so scarce that 17-year-old Laddie must be sent to a work camp. (Rev: BL 9/15/90)

2269 Belden, Wilanne Schneider. *Mind-Find* (6–9). 1988, Harcourt $14.95 (0-15-254270-1). A 13-year-old girl adjusts with difficulty to her amazing powers of ESP. (Rev: BL 2/15/88; SLJ 8/88)

2270 Bethancourt, T. Ernesto. *Instruments of Darkness* (7–9). 1979, Holiday $7.95 (0-8234-0346-7). An extraordinary 16-year-old boy tries to stop an evil man from controlling the minds of other young people.

2271 Blackwood, Gary L. *The Dying Sun* (7–10). 1989, Macmillan $13.95 (0-689-31482-5). In a future time when the earth is cooling rapidly, 2 young friends, James and Robert, try to manage a farm. (Rev: BL 6/15/89; BR 9–10/89; SLJ 5/89; VOYA 6/89)

2272 Bond, Nancy. *The Voyage Begun* (7–9). 1981, Macmillan $12.95 (0-689-50204-4). In this futuristic novel set in Cape Cod, the world is beset with problems involving climatic changes and pollution.

2273 Bonham, Frank. *The Forever Formula* (7–9). 1979, Dutton $11.95 (0-525-30025-2); Scholastic paper $1.95 (0-590-32305-9). The body of a contemporary teenager is frozen and he wakes up in the year 2164.

2274 Bonham, Frank. *The Missing Persons League* (7–9). 1983, Scholastic paper $2.25 (0-590-33847-1). In the California of 2400, Brian's parents disappear and he sets out to find them.

2275 Bradley, Marion Zimmer. *The Colors of Space* (7–10). Illus. 1988, Starblaze paper $8.95 (0-89865-191-3). A reprint of a standard science fiction novel noted for its interesting background and characters. (Rev: SLJ 2/89)

2276 Bunting, Eve. *The Cloverdale Switch* (7–9). 1979, Harper LB $10.98 (0-397-31867-7). John and Cindy encounter unusual changes in their world and find a mysterious black box.

2277 Bunting, Eve. *Strange Things Happen in the Woods* (7–9). 1984, Archway paper $1.95 (0-671-41098-9). Aliens from the planet Paca come to Earth to study humans.

2278 Burroughs, Edgar Rice. *Tarzan at the Earth's Core* (7–12). 1985, Ballantine paper $2.25 (0-345-32822-1). The author combines both his Tarzan and Pellucidar series by having the ape man visit the primitive land at the earth's core.

2279 Caraker, Mary. *The Snows of Jaspre* (6–9). 1989, Houghton $14.95 (0-395-48292-5). A novel set in the twenty-fourth century on the planet Jaspre about a dangerous journey to a city that exists under ice. (Rev: BR 5-6/90; VOYA 6/89)

2280 Carlson, Dale. *Plant People* (7–9). 1983, Dell paper $1.75 (0-440-96959-X). A mysterious fog appears that changes people into plants.

2281 Carter, Bruce. *Buzzbugs* (6–8). 1979, Avon paper $1.50 (0-380-43323-0). In this English novel, 2 youngsters discover some giant blood-sucking creatures.

2282 Chambers, Aidan. *Out of Time* (6–10). 1985, Harper LB $12.89 (0-06-021202-0). Ten science fiction stories by such well-known British writers as Louis Lawrence, Joan Aiken, and Jill Paton Walsh. (Rev: BR 3–4/86; SLJ 11/85)

2283 Chetwin, Grace. *Collidescope* (7–10). 1990, Bradbury $14.95 (0-02-718316-5). Three young people from different times and places team up in this time-travel novel. (Rev: BL 4/1/90; SLJ 5/90; VOYA 4/90)

2284 Chetwin, Grace. *Out of the Dark World* (6–9). 1985, Lothrop LB $11.95 (0-688-04272-4). In this novel set in Wales, Meg must help her cousin, whose mind is controlled by a computer maniac. (Rev: BR 1–2/86; SLJ 1/86)

2285 Christopher, John. *Dragon Dance* (7–9). 1986, Dutton $12.95 (0-525-44227-8). Two English teenage boys, Simon and Brad, time travel to the utopian land where they at last discover the secret of the fireball. They also time travel in *New Found Land* (1983). (Rev: BL 8/86; SLJ 9/86)

2286 Christopher, John. *Empty World* (7–9). 1978, Dutton $13.95 (0-525-29250-0). Neil is one of 10 survivors of a plague that has killed millions in London during the twenty-first century.

2287 Christopher, John. *The Guardians* (7–9). 1970, Macmillan paper $3.95 (0-02-042680-1). Rob, a 13 year old, is growing up in a divided England of the twenty-first century.

2288 Christopher, John. *The Lotus Caves* (7–10). 1969, Macmillan paper $4.95 (0-02-042690-9). Two young boys, part of the Earth's lunar colony, find a huge cave controlled by superintelligent plants.

2289 Christopher, John. *The Prince in Waiting* (7–10). 1970, Macmillan paper $4.95 (0-02-042400-0). This is the first exciting part of the Sword of the Spirits trilogy. The other 2 parts are *Beyond the Burning Lands* (1989) and *The Sword of the Spirits* (1986).

2290 Christopher, John. *When the Tripods Came* (6–9). 1988, Dutton $12.95 (0-525-44397-5). In this prequel to the White Mountain trilogy, the author explains how the Tripods first came to Earth. (Rev: BL 7/88; BR 5–6/89; SLJ 8/88; VOYA 8/88)

2291 Christopher, John. *The White Mountains* (7–10). 1967, Macmillan paper $3.95 (0-02-042710-2). The first of the Tripods trilogy, followed by: *The City of Gold and Lead* (1967) and *The Pool of Fire* (1968).

2292 Clarke, Arthur C. *Expedition to Earth* (7–10). 1953, Ballantine paper $2.95 (0-345-32824-8). Eleven stories about space exploration.

2293 Cooper, Clare. *Ashar of Qarius* (5–8). 1990, Harcourt $14.95 (0-15-200409-2). A teenage girl, 2 children, and their pets are left alone in a space dome and must find a way to survive. (Rev: BL 5/15/90; SLJ 7/90)

2294 Corbett, Scott. *Deadly Hoax* (6–9). 1981, Dutton $9.25 (0-525-28585-7). Aliens attempt to take over Earth and 2 young men try to stop them.

2295 Curry, Jane Louise. *Me, Myself and I: A Tale of Time Travel* (7–12). 1987, Macmillan $12.95 (0-689-50429-2). A superbright graduate student (age 16) meets himself at ages 12 and 18 when he time travels. (Rev: BL 10/15/87; SLJ 11/87)

2296 del Rey, Lester. *The Best of Lester del Rey* (7–10). 1978, Ballantine paper $3.95 (0-345-32933-3). Sixteen stories by this master of science fiction writing. Some full-length novels by del Rey are *Attack from Atlantis; Moon from Atlantis; Mysterious Planet;* and *Rocket Jockey* (all 1982).

2297 Dereske, Jo. *The Lone Sentinel* (6–10). 1989, Macmillan $13.95 (0-689-31552-X). In order to remain on the lonely planet Azure, Erik must conceal the fact that his father has died. (Rev: BL 12/15/89; SLJ 10/89; VOYA 12/89)

2298 Dickinson, Peter. *Eva* (7–12). 1989, Delacorte $14.95 (0-385-29702-5). After a terrible car accident a young girl's mind is kept alive by placing it in the body of a chimpanzee named Kelly. (Rev: BL 5/1/89; BR 5–6/89; SLJ 4/89; VOYA 6/89)

2299 Dicks, Terrance. *Doctor Who and the Genesis of the Daleks* (7–9). 1979, Amereon $12.95 (0-8488-0151-2). Based on the TV series, this is the story of an unusual Time Lord and his adventures in space.

2300 Doyle, Arthur Conan. *The Lost World & The Poison Belt* (8–12). 1989, Chronicle paper $8.95 (0-87701-620-8). Two science fiction novels by the master of the detective story. (Rev: BL 5/15/89)

2301 Engdahl, Sylvia Louise. *Enchantress from the Stars* (7–10). 1989, Macmillan paper $3.95 (0-02-043031-0). Civilizations from different worlds are in conflict in this novel. Sequels are *The Far Side of Evil* and *This Star Shall Abide* (both 1989). A reissue.

2302 Faville, Barry. *The Keeper* (7–10). 1988, Oxford Univ. Pr. $13.95 (0-19-558146-6). In this novel set in a postnuclear-war world, mankind has been reduced to a primitive life. (Rev: BL 1/1/89; SLJ 12/88)

2303 Faville, Barry. *The Return* (6–9). 1989, Oxford Univ. Pr. $14.95 (0-19-558166-0). Jonathan discovers that his new classmate is actually a space alien who is beginning to invade his mind. (Rev: BL 11/15/89; BR 5–6/90)

2304 Forman, James D. *Doomsday Plus Twelve* (7–10). 1984, Macmillan $14.95 (0-684-18221-1). After a nuclear war a group of teenagers try to build a peaceful way of life.

2305 Forrester, John. *The Forbidden Beast* (7–9). 1988, Bradbury LB $12.95 (0-02-735410-5). This final volume of the trilogy that included *Bestiary Mountain* (1985) and *The Secret of the Round Beast* (1986) concludes the struggle between the Round Beast of Old Earth and the Forbidden Beast of Luna. (Rev: BR 3–4/89; SLJ 10/88)

2306 Fradin, Dennis B. *How I Saved the World* (6–8). 1986, Dillon $10.95 (0-87518-355-7). Shelley discovers that the strange people who have moved into a deserted mining town are actually aliens. (Rev: SLJ 1/87)

2307 Gardiner, John Reynolds. *Top Secret* (6–8). Illus. 1984, Little $14.95 (0-316-30368-2); Bantam paper $2.50 (0-553-15476-1). A 9-year-old boy becomes famous when he discovers a formula for human photosynthesis and turns green as a result.

2308 Gee, Maurice. *Motherstone* (6–8). 1986, Oxford Univ. Pr. $13.95 (0-19-558130-X). Nick and Susan save the Land of O from destruction by nuclear weapons. (Rev: BR 9–10/86; SLJ 11/86)

2309 Gerrold, David. *When H.A.R.L.I.E. Was One (Release 2.0)* (7–10). 1988, Bantam paper $3.95 (0-553-26465-6). H.A.R.L.I.E. is a supercomputer that, thanks to its creator, has developed a personality. (Rev: VOYA 2/89)

2310 Gilden, Mel. *The Return of Captain Conquer* (5–9). 1986, Houghton $12.95 (0-395-40446-0). When Watson's father vanishes, he sets out from Captain Conquer's stratoship to find him. (Rev: SLJ 9/86)

2311 Godfrey, Martyn. *The Last War* (7–12). Illus. 1988, Macmillan paper $2.95 (0-02-041791-8). An easily read novel about a teenager who survives a nuclear war. (Rev: BL 5/15/89; SLJ 6/89; VOYA 12/89)

2312 Griffith, Helen V. *Journal of a Teenage Genius* (5–8). 1987, Greenwillow $11.75 (0-688-07226-7); Troll paper $2.50 (0-8167-1325-1). In diary form, a young hero tells of his encounter with a time machine. (Rev: BR 11–12/87; SLJ 10/87; VOYA 12/87)

2313 Haynes, Mary. *Raider's Sky* (6–8). 1987, Lothrop $12.95 (0-688-06455-8). In an America almost destroyed by a mysterious disease, Pokey Hughes uncovers a fiendish plot to kidnap surviving children. (Rev: BL 7/87; BR 9–10/87)

2314 Heinlein, Robert A. *Between Planets* (7–10). 1984, Ballantine paper $3.95 (0-345-32099-9). Revolt on Venus against an interplanetary alliance causes painful decisions for Don.

2315 Heinlein, Robert A. *Citizen of the Galaxy* (6–8). 1987, Macmillan $14.95 (0-684-18818-X); Ballantine paper $3.95 (0-345-34244-5). First published in 1957, this science fiction classic tells about the adventures of a young boy rescued from slavery to fulfill an unusual mission. (Rev: BL 6/1/87)

2316 Heinlein, Robert A. *Farmer in the Sky* (7–10). 1985, Ballantine paper $2.95 (0-345-32438-2). A family decides to leave Earth to find better resources on another planet. A reissue.

2317 Heinlein, Robert A. *Have Space Suit, Will Travel* (7–9). 1977, Macmillan $15.00 (0-684-14857-9); Ballantine paper $3.95 (0-345-32441-2). Kip Russell realizes his dream of visiting the moon in his own spacesuit.

2318 Heinlein, Robert A. *Red Planet* (7–10). 1981, Ballantine paper $2.95 (0-345-34039-6). A novel about the first space exploration of the planet Mars.

2319 Heinlein, Robert A. *Rocket Ship Galileo* (7–10). 1977, Macmillan $15.00 (0-684-15595-8). A pioneering novel that foretells the story of our recent space probes.

2320 Heinlein, Robert A. *The Rolling Stones* (7–10). 1985, Ballantine paper $3.50 (0-345-32451-X). The Stone family takes on the universe in this unusual science fiction adventure. A reissue.

2321 Heinlein, Robert A. *Space Cadet* (7–10). 1984, Ballantine paper $3.50 (0-345-35311-0). In the year 2075, several members of the Solar Patrol have fantastic adventures.

2322 Heinlein, Robert A. *The Star Beast* (7–10). 1977, Macmillan $15.00 (0-684-15329-7). A pet smuggled to Earth never seems to stop growing.

2323 Heinlein, Robert A. *Starman Jones* (7–10). 1985, Ballantine paper $3.50 (0-345-32811-6). Anxious for adventure, Max Jones stows away on an intergalactic spaceship. A reissue.

2324 Heinlein, Robert A. *Time for the Stars* (7–10). 1977, Macmillan $15.00 (0-684-15163-4). Interstellar communication by the use of telepathy is the subject of this novel.

2325 Heinlein, Robert A. *Tunnel in the Sky* (7–10). 1988, Macmillan $13.95 (0-684-18916-X). A standard survival test goes awry with terrible results for the participants. A reissue. Also use: *Starship Troopers* (1987).

2326 Hill, Douglas. *Alien Citadel* (7–9). 1984, Macmillan $11.95 (0-689-50281-8). Finn Ferral continues his struggle against the Slavers who dominate the Earth in this sequel to *The Huntsman* (1982) and *The Warriors of the Wasteland* (1983).

2327 Hill, Douglas. *Deathwing over Veynaa* (7–10). 1981, Dell paper $2.50 (0-440-91743-3). Keill must outwit the evil Quern to save a planet from destruction. Another story about Keill is *Day of the Starwind* (1981).

2328 Hill, Douglas. *Exiles of ColSec* (7–9). 1984, Macmillan $11.95 (0-689-50315-6). Six teenage delinquents survive the crash of their spaceship on an alien planet. Followed by: *The Caves of Klydor* and *ColSec Rebellion* (both 1985).

2329 Hill, Douglas. *Galactic Warlord* (7–9). 1987, Dell paper $2.50 (0-440-92787-0). Keil Randor wants revenge when his home planet is destroyed. A reissue.

2330 Hill, Douglas. *Master of Fiends* (6–9). 1988, Macmillan $11.95 (0-689-50419-5). Four friends attempt to rescue a wizard that has been imprisoned by the Master of Fiends. The 4 friends were first introduced in *The Blade of the Poisoner* (1987). (Rev: BL 9/15/88; BR 5–6/88; SLJ 11/88; VOYA 12/88)

2331 Hill, Douglas, ed. *Planetfall* (5–9). Illus. 1987, Oxford Univ. Pr. $13.95 (0-19-278113-8). A collection of science fiction stories, games, and art to entertain those interested in outer space. (Rev: SLJ 11/87)

2332 Hoover, H. M. *Another Heaven, Another Earth* (7–9). 1981, Viking $11.95 (0-670-12883-X). A neglected space colony is revisited by an expedition from earth.

2333 Hoover, H. M. *Away Is a Strange Place to Be* (6–8). 1990, Dutton $14.95 (0-525-44505-6). In the twenty-fourth century, 2 youngsters are kidnapped to work on a construction project in space. (Rev: BR 5–6/90)

2334 Hoover, H. M. *The Bell Tree* (7–9). 1982, Viking $11.95 (0-670-15600-0). Fifteen-year-old Jenny and her father explore the planet Tanin.

2335 Hoover, H. M. *Children of Morrow* (7–9). 1985, Penguin paper $3.95 (0-14-031873-9). Two youngsters, Tia and Rabbit, flee their village and are guided telepathically by a woman named Ashira.

2336 Hoover, H. M. *The Delikon* (7–9). 1986, Penguin paper $3.95 (0-14-032167-5). Two youngsters and their teacher are involved in the revolt against the Delikon—an alien race. A reissue.

2337 Hoover, H. M. *The Lost Star* (7–9). 1979, Viking $11.50 (0-670-44129-5); Penguin paper $3.95 (0-14-03166-7). Fifteen-year-old Lian joins an archaeological expedition on the planet Balthor.

2338 Hoover, H. M. *Orvis* (6–8). 1987, Viking $12.95 (0-670-81117-3). Toby, a 12-year-old girl, and Orvis, an outmoded robot, run away from home. (Rev: BL 6/15/87; BR 1–2/88; SLJ 6–7/87)

2339 Hoover, H. M. *Return to Earth: A Novel of the Future* (7–9). 1980, Penguin paper $3.95 (0-

14-032610-3). A religious cult is trying to enslave the world's population and Galen and Samara must help prevent this.

2340 Hoover, H. M. *The Shepherd Moon: A Novel of the Future* (7–9). 1984, Viking $11.95 (0-670-63977-X); Penguin paper $3.95 (0-14-032611-1). In the forty-eighth century, a young girl witnesses the arrival of an alien from space.

2341 Hoover, H. M. *This Time of Darkness* (7–9). 1985, Penguin paper $3.95 (0-14-031872-0). Two youngsters travel to the Outside, an area beyond the safety of their doomed city.

2342 Hughes, Monica. *The Dream Catcher* (5–9). 1987, Macmillan $11.95 (0-689-31331-4). Ruth, a misfit in her domed city, sets out with some companions on a dangerous journey, in this companion piece to *Devil on My Back* (1985). (Rev: BL 4/1/87; BR 11–12/87; SLJ 6–7/87)

2343 Hughes, Monica. *The Keeper of the Isis Light* (7–9). 1981, Macmillan LB $11.95 (0-689-30847-7). A 16-year-old girl's lonely existence on planet Isis comes to an end when settlers arrive.

2344 Hurley, Maxwell. *Max's Book* (5–9). 1985, Scholastic paper $2.25 (0-590-33203-1). Three teenagers gain supernatural powers when they touch a satellite that has fallen from the sky. (Rev: SLJ 5/86)

2345 Jacobs, Paul Samuel. *Born into Light* (7–10). 1988, Scholastic $12.95 (0-590-40710-4). Strange wild children appear in a field and are taken in by Roger Westwood's family. (Rev: BL 6/1/88; VOYA 4/88)

2346 Johnson, Annabel, and Edgar Johnson. *The Danger Quotient* (7–10). 1984, Harper $13.89 (0-06-022853-9); paper $2.95 (0-06-447029-6). Casey goes back in time to try to find out how to increase his life span.

2347 Johnson, Annabel, and Edgar Johnson. *Prisoner of Psi* (7–12). 1985, Macmillan $12.95 (0-689-31132-X). A teenager equipped with powers of extrasensory perception must rescue his father, who is being held by Libyan terrorists. (Rev: BL 10/1/85; SLJ 1/87)

2348 Jones, Diana Wynne. *The Homeward Bounders* (6–9). 1981, Greenwillow $11.75 (0-688-00678-7). Jamie is condemned by hooded figures he meets to roam as an outcast through time and space.

2349 Jones, Diana Wynne. *A Tale of Time City* (6–8). 1987, Greenwillow $11.75 (0-688-07315-8); Knopf, paper $3.95 (0-394-82030-4). Vivian is kidnapped by a young boy who takes her to a city outside the concept of time. (Rev: BL 11/15/87; SLJ 9/87; VOYA 2/88)

2350 Karl, Jean E. *But We Are Not of Earth* (7–9). 1981, Dutton $10.95 (0-525-27342-5). Four young people are sent to an isolated planet and soon begin planning their escape.

2351 Karl, Jean E. *Strange Tomorrow* (5–8). 1985, Dutton $12.95 (0-525-44162-X); Dell paper $2.95 (0-440-20052-0). There are 2 stories—one dealing with survivors when all living things are destroyed on Earth and the other about rebuilding a destroyed society—in this companion piece to *The Turning Place* (1976). (Rev: BL 5/15/85; VOYA 12/85)

2352 Key, Alexander. *The Forgotten Door* (7–9). 1986, Scholastic paper $2.50 (0-590-40398-2). An alien from another planet gets a hostile reception on Earth. A reissue.

2353 Key, Alexander. *Jagger: The Dog from Elsewhere* (7–9). 1976, Westminster $6.95 (0-664-32596-3). A giant white dog is transported to Alabama where he becomes a hunted animal.

2354 Kiesel, Stanley. *Skinny Malinky Leads the War for Kidness* (6–8). 1984, Dutton $12.95 (0-525-66918-3); Avon paper $2.50 (0-380-69875-7). Skinny is about to be captured by a powerful mutant red ant.

2355 Kruchten, Marcia H. *Skyborn* (7–9). 1989, Scholastic paper $2.75 (0-590-40279-X). Set in Atlantis, this is the story of 2 civilizations, one primitive and the other advanced. (Rev: SLJ 2/90)

2356 Lawrence, Louise. *Calling B for Butterfly* (7–9). 1982, Harper paper $3.25 (0-06-447036-9). Four youngsters and 2 children survive a tragedy aboard a spaceship.

2357 Lawrence, Louise. *Children of the Dust* (7–10). 1985, Harper LB $12.89 (0-06-023739-2). A bleak but ultimately hopeful novel about 3 generations of an English family after a nuclear holocaust. (Rev: BL 9/1/85; BR 3–4/86; SLJ 11/85)

2358 Lawrence, Louise. *Moonwind* (7–10). 1986, Harper LB $11.89 (0-06-023734-1); paper $2.95 (0-06-447037-7). An astral spirit trapped on a barren moon tries to get help from a human base on the Earth's moon. (Rev: BL 12/15/86; SLJ 12/86)

2359 Lawrence, Louise. *The Warriors of Taan* (7–10). 1988, Harper LB $12.89 (0-06-023737-6). The people of the planet Taan have conflicting ideas on how to counter the exploitation by people from Earth. (Rev: BL 2/15/88; BR 9–10/88)

2360 Lee, Robert C. *Summer of the Green Star* (6–8). 1981, Westminster $10.95 (0-664-32681-

1). David wonders if his new friend Adrienne is really a creature from outer space. More science fiction by this author in *Timequake* (1982).

2361 L'Engle, Madeleine. *Many Waters* (7–10). 1986, Farrar $12.95 (0-374-34769-4); Dell paper $3.50 (0-440-95252-2). The Murry twins, from the author's Wrinkle in Time trilogy, time travel to the Holy Land prior to the Great Flood. (Rev: BL 8/86; SLJ 11/86; VOYA 12/86)

2362 L'Engle, Madeleine. *A Wrinkle in Time* (6–9). 1962, Farrar $13.95 (0-374-38613-7); Dell paper $3.25 (0-440-49805-8). Meg and Charles Wallace Murry, with the help of Calvin O'Keefe, set out in space to find their scientist father. Newbery Award 1963. Followed by *A Wind in the Door* (1973) and *A Swiftly Tilting Planet* (1978).

2363 Lupoff, Richard A. *The Forever City* (7–10). Illus. 1987, Walker $15.95 (0-8027-6742-7). In a space colony an expedition is being prepared to search for a missing citizen who has disappeared. (Rev: BL 5/1/88; BR 9–10/88; SLJ 6–7/88; VOYA 10/88)

2364 McCaffrey, Anne. *Dragonsong* (7–12). 1976, Macmillan $14.95 (0-689-30507-9); Bantam paper $3.50 (0-553-23460-9). The first volume of the Harper Hall trilogy begins the story of Menolly, her magic harp, and the dread Thread that falls from the sky. Followed by *Dragonsinger* (1977) and *Dragondrums* (1979).

2365 Macdonald, Caroline. *The Lake at the End of the World* (7–10). 1989, Dial $12.95 (0-8037-0650-2). In a world devastated by nuclear accidents and pollution, a teenage girl finds a boy with whom she must cooperate. (Rev: BL 7/89; BR 11–12/89; SLJ 5/89; VOYA 6/89)

2366 McIntyre, Vonda. *Barbary* (6–9). 1986, Houghton $12.95 (0-395-41029-0). An orphaned girl and her pet cat travel through space looking for a new home. (Rev: BR 1–2/87; VOYA 10/86)

2367 Maguire, Gregory. *I Feel Like the Morning Star* (8–10). 1989, Harper LB $14.89 (0-06-024022-9). Three teenagers living in an underground society after a nuclear war challenge the authority of their rulers. (Rev: SLJ 5/89; VOYA 6/89)

2368 Mason, Anne. *The Stolen Law* (6–9). 1986, Harper LB $11.89 (0-06-024119-5). In this sequel to *The Dancing Meteorite* (o.p.), Kira goes on a dangerous mission to a space station where she becomes involved with an evil genius. (Rev: BL 4/15/86; BR 11–12/86; SLJ 8/86; VOYA 6/86)

2369 Mayhar, Ardath. *A Place of Silver Silence* (7–10). Illus. 1988, Walker $15.95 (0-8027-6825-3). Andraia tries to save a peaceful planet from destructive experiments while still trying to overcome her own personal problems. (Rev: BL 11/1/88; BR 3–4/89; SLJ 11/88; VOYA 2/89)

2370 Morrison, Dorothy Nafus. *Vanishing Act* (5–8). 1989, Macmillan $13.95 (0-689-31513-9). A young budding magician discovers a machine that can make her invisible. (Rev: BL 9/15/89; SLJ 11/89)

2371 Moulton, Deborah. *Children of Time* (7–10). 1989, Dial $14.95 (0-8037-0607-3). In this futuristic tale, a wicked woman plans to rule the Earth by kidnapping young people and making them her followers. (Rev: BL 12/1/89; SLJ 12/89; VOYA 2/90)

2372 Moulton, Deborah. *The First Battle of Morn* (7–10). 1988, Dial LB $14.51 (0-8037-0550-6). Torin's father breeds winged horses for the evil Teachers in this science fiction story about an unusual foal and the danger it brings to Torin. (Rev: SLJ 11/88)

2373 Murphy, Shirley Rousseau. *Caves of Fire and Ice* (7–10). 1982, Avon paper $2.95 (0-380-58081-0). Skeelie travels through time to find her friend Ramad.

2374 Nelson, O. T. *The Girl Who Owned a City* (7–9). 1977, Dell paper $2.95 (0-440-92893-1). A mysterious virus kills off Earth's population except for children under the age of 13.

2375 Norton, Andre. *The Beast Master* (7–12). 1987, Ballantine paper $2.50 (0-345-31376-3). Hosteen Storm, a Navaho Indian, survives planetary destruction and becomes a settler on another planet, Arzor.

2376 Norton, Andre. *Dread Companion* (7–12). 1972, Ballantine paper $2.50 (0-345-31556-1). A child comes under the spell of a being from another world.

2377 Norton, Andre. *Exiles of the Stars* (7–12). 1984, Ace paper $2.50 (0-441-22380-0). A forced landing on the planet Sekhmet brings terror to the space travelers.

2378 Norton, Andre. *Galactic Derelict* (7–12). 1959, Ace paper $2.95 (0-441-27234-7). A time-travel novel in which 3 adventurers encounter strange civilizations and beings.

2379 Norton, Andre. *High Sorcery* (7–12). 1971, Ace paper $2.50 (0-441-33711-2). Five short stories on how people survive in the future by using their wits.

2380 Norton, Andre. *Ice Crown* (7–12). 1971, Ace paper $2.50 (0-441-35844-6). Two girls search a forbidden planet for a great treasure—the Ice Crown.

2381 Norton, Andre. *Key Out of Time* (7–12). 1973, Ace paper $2.95 (0-441-43676-5). Two Time Agents re-create the conflict that destroyed life on the planet Hawaika.

2382 Norton, Andre. *Quest Crosstime* (7–12). 1972, Ace paper $2.50 (0-441-69685-6). Blake Walker is destined to save the planet Vroom.

2383 Norton, Andre. *The Sioux Spacemen* (7–12). 1974, Ace paper $1.95 (0-441-76804-0). A descendant of Sioux warriors, Kade Whitehawk uses his heritage to help others.

2384 Norton, Andre. *Star Gate* (7–12). 1985, Ballantine paper $2.25 (0-345-31193-0). The Star Lords travel through space looking for a place to settle. Also use: *Star Guard* (1984).

2385 Norton, Andre. *The Time Traders* (7–12). 1974, Ace paper $2.95 (0-441-81255-4). Ross Murdock becomes part of an experiment that takes him through several levels of time.

2386 Norton, Andre. *Uncharted Stars* (7–12). 1972, Ace paper $2.50 (0-441-84466-9). Murdoc and his cat Eet travel through time to find the source of a precious gem. In the same series use: *The Zero Stone* (1969).

2387 Norton, Andre. *The X Factor* (7–12). 1984, Ballantine paper $2.95 (0-345-31557-X). A space traveler meets strange beings on the unexplored planet Mimir.

2388 O'Brien, Robert C. *Z for Zachariah* (7–10). 1975, Macmillan $13.95 (0-689-30442-0); paper $3.95 (0-02-044650-0). After a nuclear holocaust, Ann believes she is the only surviving human—but is she?

2389 Payne, Bernal C., Jr. *Experiment in Terror* (5–9). 1987, Houghton $13.95 (0-395-44260-5). Steve discovers that he and his friends are actually aliens from another world. (Rev: SLJ 11/87)

2390 Payne, Bernal C., Jr. *It's about Time* (7–9). 1986, Pocket paper $2.50 (0-671-54360-1). Two teenagers traveling in time interrupt the future and their own fates are therefore sealed.

2391 Pinkwater, Daniel. *Alan Mendelsohn, the Boy from Mars* (6–10). 1979, Dutton $14.95 (0-525-25360-2). Two boys share comic adventures on the lost continent of Waka-Waka.

2392 Pinkwater, Daniel. *The Snarkout Boys & the Avocado of Death* (6–10). 1982, Lothrop $12.95 (0-688-00871-2). Two boys search for friend Rat's uncle, an unusual scientist, in this wacky adventure. A sequel is: *The Snarkout Boys & the Baconburg Horror* (1984).

2393 Richelson, Geraldine, adapt. *The Star Wars Storybook* (5–8). 1978, Random $5.95 (0-394-83785-1). An easily read book about Luke Skywalker and his battle against Darth Vader.

2394 Riding, Julia. *Space Traders Unlimited* (7–10). 1988, Macmillan $12.95 (0-689-31409-4). Teenage Streak lives a vagabond life in the subterranean passageways of Mars. (Rev: BL 3/15/88; BR 9–10/88; SLJ 8/88; VOYA 6/88)

2395 Rubinstein, Gillian. *Space Demons* (6–9). 1988, Dial $13.95 (0-8037-0534-4). A video game so absorbs a youngster that his life becomes part of a war against the game's villains, the Demons. (Rev: BL 10/1/88; SLJ 8/88; VOYA 12/88)

2396 Sanford, James E. *Nuclear War Diary* (7–12). 1989, Front Row Experience paper $5.95 (0-915256-28-2). By living in caves, 15-year-old Jessie Tienford and her family survive a nuclear war and must now rebuild their lives. (Rev: BL 11/1/89)

2397 Sargent, Pamela. *Alien Child* (8–12). 1988, Harper LB $13.89 (0-06-025203-0); paper $3.95 (0-06-447002-4). A teenage girl raised in an alien world discovers there is another human living in her complex. (Rev: BL 2/1/88; BR 9–10/88; SLJ 4/88; VOYA 8/88)

2398 Sargent, Pamela. *Earthseed* (7–9). 1983, Harper LB $10.89 (0-06-025188-3); paper $2.95 (0-06-447045-8). Zoheret and her companions prepare to populate a new planet.

2399 Service, Pamela F. *A Question of Destiny* (6–9). 1986, Macmillan LB $11.95 (0-689-31181-8); paper $2.95 (0-02-044981-X). Dan's father, a presidential candidate, discovers his adviser is from another planet. (Rev: SLJ 5/86; VOYA 10/86)

2400 Silverberg, Robert. *Project Pendulum* (7–12). Illus. 1987, Walker $15.95 (0-8027-6712-5); Bantam paper $3.95 (0-553-28001-5). Two identical twins time travel in opposite directions but are scheduled to meet at Time Zero. (Rev: BL 9/15/87; SLJ 10/87; VOYA 10/87)

2401 Sleator, William. *The Boy Who Reversed Himself* (8–12). 1986, Dutton $12.95 (0-525-44276-6). Laura travels into the fourth dimension with her gifted neighbor and literally everything in her life becomes upside down. (Rev: BL 10/15/86; BR 5–6/87; SLJ 11/86; VOYA 6/87)

2402 Sleator, William. *The Duplicate* (7–10). 1988, Dutton $12.95 (0-525-44390-8). A teenager discovers a machine that allows him the power to duplicate himself. (Rev: BL 5/15/88; SLJ 4/88; VOYA 12/88)

2403 Sleator, William. *House of Stairs* (7–10). 1974, Dutton $13.95 (0-525-32335-X). Five teenage orphans are kidnapped to become part of an experiment on aggression.

2404 Sleator, William. *Interstellar Pig* (7–10). 1984, Dutton $12.95 (0-525-44098-4); Bantam paper $2.95 (0-553-25564-9). Barney plays a strange board game with strangers who are actually aliens from space.

2405 Sleator, William. *Singularity* (7–12). 1985, Dutton $12.95 (0-525-44161-1). Twin boys discover a playhouse on the property they have inherited that contains a mystery involving monsters from space and a new dimension in time. (Rev: BL 4/1/85; SLJ 8/85)

2406 Sleator, William. *Strange Attractors* (7–12). 1989, Dutton $12.95 (0-525-44530-7). Max travels through time by using a device several people would kill to possess. (Rev: BL 1/15/90; SLJ 12/89; VOYA 2/90)

2407 Slote, Alfred. *My Robot Buddy* (5–8). Illus. 1986, Harper $12.95 (0-397-31641-0); paper $2.95 (0-06-440165-0). An easily read novel about Danny and the robot that is created for him.

2408 Smith, Cara Lockhart. *Parchment House* (6–8). 1989, Macmillan $12.95 (0-02-785845-6). In a home for orphans, Johnnie leads a revolt against their robot guardian Archibald. (Rev: BR 5–6/90; VOYA 12/89)

2409 Swindells, Robert. *Brother in the Land* (7–10). 1985, Holiday $10.95 (0-8234-0556-7). In this English novel, a teenage boy tries to survive after a nuclear war. (Rev: BL 4/1/85; SLJ 9/85; VOYA 8/85)

2410 Townsend, John Rowe. *The Creatures* (7–10). 1980, Harper $12.70 (0-397-31865-0). Earth is dominated by creatures from another planet who believe in mind over emotion.

2411 Townsend, John Rowe. *Noah's Castle* (7–10). 1975, Harper $11.70 (0-397-31654-2). In the late twentieth century in England, Norman plans for the future by hoarding food.

2412 Vardeman, Robert E. *Road to the Stars* (7–10). 1988, Harper LB $13.89 (0-06-026289-3). Clifford is on a spaceship from Earth whose mission is to find new worlds to colonize. (Rev: BL 2/15/88; BR 9–10/88; SLJ 5/88)

2413 Verne, Jules. *Master of the World* (7–10). n.d., Airmont paper $1.25 (0-8049-0073-6). A scientist who has invented an amazing machine claims it will make him master of the world.

2414 Vinge, Joan D. *Psion* (7–12). 1982, Delacorte $12.95 (0-385-28780-1); Dell paper $2.95 (0-440-97192-6). A street-smart kid becomes involved in a plot to take over a mineral rich planet.

2415 Wells, H. G. *First Men in the Moon* (7–12). n.d., Airmont paper $1.25 (0-8049-0078-7). The first men on the moon discover strange creatures living there. Also use: *The Food of the Gods; In the Days of the Comet;* and *The Island of Doctor Moreau.*

2416 Wells, H. G. *The Invisible Man* (7–12). n.d., Airmont paper $1.25 (0-8049-0040-4). One of the classic science fiction stories that begins with a stranger coming to a small English village and arousing suspicions by his actions.

2417 Wells, H. G. *Seven Science Fiction Novels* (7–12). 1950, Dover $15.00 (0-486-20264-X). This collection includes such standard titles as *The Invisible Man* and *The War of the Worlds.*

2418 Wells, H. G. *The Time Machine* (7–12). n.d., Airmont paper $1.75 (0-8049-0044-2). The classic of the first man to travel through time.

2419 Wells, H. G. *The War of the Worlds* (7–12). 1960, Random LB $5.39 (0-394-90471-0); Airmont paper $1.75 (0-8049-0045-0). Martians invade the earth in this classic science fiction novel that was first published in 1898.

2420 Westall, Robert. *Urn Burial* (7–12). 1988, Greenwillow $11.95 (0-688-07595-9). An English teenager unleashes a terrible struggle when he disturbs a mysterious grave. (Rev: BL 3/1/88; SLJ 4/88; VOYA 6/88)

2421 Windsor, Patricia. *The Hero* (7–10). 1988, Delacorte $14.95 (0-385-29624-X). Dales finds his ESP a mixed blessing when he can see into the future. (Rev: BL 4/1/88; BR 5–6/88; SLJ 5/88; VOYA 6/88)

2422 Winterfeld, Henry. *Star Girl* (6–8). Trans. by Kyrill Schabert. Illus. 1976, Avon paper $1.25 (0-380-00659-6). While in the forest Walter and his friends find a girl who is actually an alien from space.

2423 Wisler, G. Clifton. *The Seer* (6–8). 1988, Dutton $12.95 (0-525-67262-1). Scott, an alien, tries to live a normal life in small town America in this sequel to *The Antrian Messenger* (1986). (Rev: BL 10/1/88; SLJ 12/88; VOYA 12/88)

2424 Wismer, Donald. *Starluck* (6–8). 1982, Ultramarine $15.00 (0-317-54349-0). A boy with unusual powers tries to overthrow a wicked emperor.

2425 Woolverton, Linda. *Star Wind* (6–8). 1986, Houghton $12.95 (0-395-41454-7). Camden realizes that her friend WT-3 is actually working for a planet that wants to conquer the Earth. (Rev: VOYA 6/86)

2426 Yep, Laurence. *Sweetwater* (6–8). Illus. 1975, Harper LB $11.89 (0-06-026736-4); Avon paper $1.25 (0-380-00193-4). Tyree wants to keep the values and traditions of Earth from disappearing on his planet in space.

2427 Yolen, Jane, et al., eds. *Spaceships & Spells* (5–9). 1987, Harper $12.95 (0-06-026797-6). A collection of 13 original tales, mostly of science fiction but also some fantasy. (Rev: BR 3–4/88)

2428 Zebrowski, George. *The Stars Will Speak* (7–10). 1987, Harper paper $2.95 (0-06-447050-4). Lissa joins an institute on Earth investigating communications from aliens outside the solar system. (Rev: BR 3–4/86; SLJ 10/85)

2429 Zelazny, Roger. *A Dark Traveling* (7–10). Illus. 1989, Avon paper $3.50 (0-380-70567-2). A brother and sister set out to find their missing father with the help of an exchange student from another planet. (Rev: BL 4/1/87)

Sports Stories

2430 Blessing, Richard. *A Passing Season* (7–9). 1982, Little $14.95 (0-316-09957-0). Craig continues to play football primarily to please his father.

2431 Brooks, Bruce. *The Moves Make the Man* (7–9). 1984, Harper $13.95 (0-06-020679-9); paper $2.95 (0-06-447022-9). Jerome, the only black student in his high school and a star basketball player, forms an unusual friendship with Bix.

2432 Calvert, Patricia. *The Hour of the Wolf* (7–10). 1983, Macmillan $11.95 (0-684-17961-X). A boy enters a famous dogsled race in Alaska to honor his friend who committed suicide.

2433 Cate, Dick. *Foxcover* (5–9). Illus. 1989, Gollancz $17.95 (0-575-04292-3). A young English boy faces problems with his gang, his soccer playing, and his family. (Rev: SLJ 1/90)

2434 Cebulash, Mel. *Ruth Marini, World Series Star* (7–9). 1985, Lerner $8.95 (0-8225-0727-7). Ruth gets her chance to pitch a winning seventh game in the World Series. Preceded by *Ruth Marini of the Dodgers* and *Ruth Marini, Dodger Ace* (both 1983). (Rev: BL 8/85; SLJ 12/85)

2435 Christopher, Matt. *Takedown* (6–8). Illus. 1990, Little $13.95 (0-316-13930-0). A young wrestler faces problems both on and off the mat. (Rev: BL 1/15/90; BR 5–6/90)

2436 Crutcher, Chris. *The Crazy Horse Electric Game* (7–12). 1987, Greenwillow $11.75 (0-688-06683-6); Dell paper $3.25 (0-440-20094-6). A motorboat accident ends the comfortable life and budding baseball career of a teenage boy. (Rev: BL 4/15/87; BR 9–10/87; SLJ 5/87; VOYA 6/87)

2437 Crutcher, Chris. *Running Loose* (7–10). 1983, Greenwillow $12.95 (0-688-02002-X); Dell paper $2.95 (0-440-97520-0). A senior in high school faces problems when he opposes the decisions of a football coach.

2438 Crutcher, Chris. *Stotan!* (8–12). 1986, Greenwillow $10.25 (0-688-05715-2). A group of boys from different backgrounds but all close friends sign up for a brutally taxing physical program run by their school coach. (Rev: BL 3/15/86; SLJ 5/86; VOYA 4/86)

2439 Duder, Tessa. *In Lane Three, Alex Archer* (6–9). 1989, Houghton $13.95 (0-395-50927-0). A prize-winning teenage swimmer tells of her life and problems in this novel from New Zealand. (Rev: BL 11/1/89; SLJ 1/90; VOYA 2/90)

2440 Dygard, Thomas J. *Forward Pass* (7–10). Illus. 1989, Morrow $11.95 (0-688-07961-X). Safety is only one of the problems that arise when coach Gardner allows a girl to play on his football team. (Rev: BL 9/1/89; BR 3–4/90; VOYA 12/89)

2441 Dygard, Thomas J. *Halfback Tough* (7–12). 1986, Morrow $12.95 (0-688-05925-2); Penguin paper $3.95 (0-14-034113-7). Joe Atkins tries to leave his troubled past behind when he attends a new school and joins the school's football team. (Rev: BL 4/1/86; BR 9–10/86; SLJ 10/86; VOYA 6/86)

2442 Dygard, Thomas J. *Quaterback Walk-On* (7–9). 1982, Morrow $12.95 (0-688-01065-2); Penguin paper $3.95 (0-14-034115-3). A fourth-string quarterback becomes an instant star.

2443 Dygard, Thomas J. *Rebound Caper* (7–9). 1983, Morrow $12.95 (0-688-01707-X). In a fit of spite, Gary decides to join the girls' basketball team.

2444 Dygard, Thomas J. *The Rookie Arrives* (7–12). 1988, Morrow $11.95 (0-688-07598-3). Ted Bell comes of age when he becomes a major-leaguer fresh from high school. (Rev: BL 3/1/88; BR 5–6/88; SLJ 3/88)

2445 Dygard, Thomas J. *Tournament Upstart* (7–9). 1984, Morrow LB $9.50 (0-688-02761-X); Penguin paper $3.95 (0-14-034114-5). A tiny high school produces a prize-winning basketball team.

2446 Franklin, Lance. *Double Play* (7–12). 1987, Bantam paper $2.50 (0-553-26526-1). With a limited amount of free time, Tom must decide between playing with a rock group or remaining on the baseball team. (Rev: BL 10/1/87; SLJ 3/88; VOYA 12/87)

2447 French, Michael. *The Throwing Season* (7–9). 1980, Delacorte $8.95 (0-440-08600-0). A half-Indian high school junior is a champion at shot put but people want to bribe him to lose.

2448 Godfrey, Martyn. *Ice Hawk* (7–12). Illus. 1986, EMC paper $4.50 (0-8219-0235-0). An easy-to-read story about a young minor league hockey player who balks at unnecessary use of violence. (Rev: BL 2/1/87)

2449 Gutman, Bill. *Gridiron Scholar* (7–9). 1990, Queen Anne Square paper $2.95 (0-89872-304-3). Through his connection with a young oriental tutor, Bo realizes there is more to life than football. (Rev: VOYA 6/90)

2450 Hermann, Spring. *Flip City* (6–9). 1988, Watts LB $13.99 (0-531-08385-3). Each of the 4 girlfriends who work out together at improving their gymnastic skills also secretly faces a personal problem. (Rev: BL 2/15/89; SLJ 2/89; VOYA 4/89)

2451 Hoobler, Thomas. *The Revenge of Ho-Tai* (6–8). 1989, Walker $15.95 (0-8027-6870-9). A new coach takes over the basketball team at Edwards Academy and soon sparks fly. (Rev: BL 6/15/89; BR 9–10/89; SLJ 6/89; VOYA 8/89)

2452 Howe, Fanny. *Race of the Radical* (5–9). 1985, Viking $11.95 (0-670-80557-2). Alex's passion for BMX racing leads his father to design a superior bike for his son—but then it is stolen. (Rev: BL 11/15/85; SLJ 2/86)

2453 Hyde, Dayton O. *The Major, the Poacher, and the Wonderful One-Trout River* (6–10). 1985, Macmillan $12.95 (0-689-31107-9). Major Quillaine and young Plummey Pittock, 2 avid trout fishermen, are on a collision course involving catching a single wonderful trout. (Rev: BL 6/15/85; SLJ 5/85)

2454 Ibbitson, John. *The Wimp and the Jock* (7–12). Illus. 1988, Macmillan paper $2.95 (0-02-041792-6). In this easy-to-read story, the class nerd is forced to accept the consequences when under duress he says he will try out for football. (Rev: BL 5/15/89)

2455 Jorgensen, Dan. *Dawn's Diamond Defense* (6–9). 1988, Chariot paper $3.95 (1-55513-062-3). A story of girls' rivalry on and off the soccer field. (Rev: SLJ 1/89)

2456 Kaplan, Janice. *First Ride* (7–9). 1982, Avon paper $1.95 (0-380-18055-0). A female teenage rodeo star finds that many boys do not want her to compete.

2457 Klass, David. *The Atami Dragons* (7–9). 1984, Macmillan $12.95 (0-684-18223-8). Jerry's trip to Japan with his father becomes more interesting when he meets the Atami Dragons baseball team.

2458 Klass, David. *A Different Season* (7–10). 1988, Dutton $14.95 (0-525-67237-0). Jennifer joins the high school baseball team on which her boyfriend is the ace pitcher. (Rev: BL 1/1/89; BR 5–6/88; VOYA 8/88)

2459 Knudson, R. R. *Fox Running* (7–9). Illus. 1977, Avon paper $2.50 (0-380-00930-7). Kathy and an Apache Indian girl find friendship and inspiration in their mutual love of running.

2460 Knudson, R. R. *Zanballer* (7–9). 1986, Penguin paper $3.95 (0-14-032168-3). Zan Hagen loves football so much that the only way she can play is by joining the boy's team. Zan enjoys other sports in the sequels: *Zanbanger* (1977), *Zanboomer* (1978), and *Zan Hagan's Marathon* (1984). A reissue.

2461 Konigsburg, E. L. *About the B'nai Bagels* (6–8). 1973, Macmillan $13.95 (0-689-20631-3); Dell paper $2.95 (0-440-40034-1). In this easily read story, Mark is uncomfortable at the thought of his mother's being the manager of his Little League baseball team.

2462 Korman, Gordon. *The Zucchini Warriors* (6–8). 1988, Scholastic $10.95 (0-590-41335-X). Hank, a former football player, promises to build Bruno and Boots's school a recreation hall if their team has a winning season. (Rev: BR 1–2/89; VOYA 10/88)

2463 Levy, Marilyn. *Love Is a Long Shot* (7–10). 1986, Fawcett paper $2.50 (0-449-70150-6). In order to make herself visible to varsity scouts, Cass decides to play on the boy's team. (Rev: VOYA 2/87)

2464 McCrackin, Mark. *A Winning Position* (7–9). 1982, Dell paper $1.50 (0-440-99483-7). Alec is a car racer torn between winning for his coach and giving up the sport for his girlfriend.

2465 Meltzoff, Nancy. *A Sense of Balance* (7–9). 1978, Westminster $7.50 (0-664-32629-3). Gail longs for the social life but knows that it conflicts with her plan to be an Olympic gymnast.

2466 Mumma, Barbara J. *Breaking the Ice* (7–12). 1988, Fawcett paper $2.95 (0-449-13459-8). At the Lake Placid Skating School, Claire tries to juggle her training for a skating career and her feelings towards her boyfriend. (Rev: SLJ 1/89)

2467 Myers, Walter Dean. *Hoops* (7–10). 1981, Delacorte $13.95 (0-385-28142-0); Dell paper $2.95 (0-440-93884-8). Lonnie plays basketball in spite of his coach, a has-been named Cal. Followed by *The Outside Shot* (1987).

2468 Peyton, K. M. *"Who, Sir? Me, Sir?"* (7–9). 1983, Oxford Univ. Pr. $12.95 (0-19-271470-8). Four English school kids challenge a team from a private school.

2469 Platt, Kin. *Brogg's Brain* (6–9). 1981, Harper LB $11.89 (0-397-31946-0). Monty is a runner who is pushed by his father and his coach to win.

2470 Platt, Kin. *Run for Your Life* (7–9). 1979, Dell paper $1.95 (0-440-97557-3). An easily read book about a boy who wants to be a track star.

2471 Powell, Randy. *My Underrated Year* (7–10). 1988, Farrar $12.95 (0-374-35109-0). A sophomore's interest in tennis and football is distracted by falling in love with the sister of his rival. (Rev: BL 11/1/88; BR 3–4/89; SLJ 12/88; VOYA 2/89)

2472 Roberts, Nadine. *These Are the Best Years?* (7–12). 1989, Ballantine paper $2.95 (0-449-70315-0). Senior Kristin drops basketball in favor of a more challenging academic program and therefore faces disapproval from her peers. (Rev: BL 10/1/89; VOYA 12/89)

2473 Smith, Doris Buchanan. *Karate Dancer* (6–9). 1987, Putnam $13.95 (0-399-21464-X). A 14-year-old boy pursues his interest in karate while facing the problems of adolescence. (Rev: BL 1/1/88; SLJ 12/87; VOYA 2/88)

2474 Tunis, John R. *Keystone Kids* (6–9). 1990, Harcourt paper $3.95 (0-15-242388-5). A reissue of the classic 1943 baseball story about 2 exceptional brothers. Also use *Highpockets* (1948) and *World Series* (1941). (Rev: BL 4/1/90)

2475 Tunis, John R. *The Kid from Tomkinsville* (6–9). 1990, Harcourt paper $3.95 (0-15-242567-5). This novel, first published in 1940, introduces Roy Tucker and his remarkable pitching arm. It is continued in *The Kid Comes Back* (1946). Also use *Rookie of the Year* (1944). (Rev: BL 4/1/90)

2476 Wells, Rosemary. *When No One Was Looking* (7–10). 1980, Dial $14.95 (0-8037-9855-5). What is the final price one will pay to become a champion at tennis?

Short Stories and General Anthologies

2477 *Face to Face* (7–12). 1990, Putnam paper $15.95 (0-399-21951-X). A collection of 18 stories by American and Soviet writers in different genres but all aimed at young people. (Rev: BL 8/90)

2478 Fleischman, Paul. *Graven Images: Three Stories* (7–9). Illus. 1982, Harper LB $12.89 (0-06-021906-8); paper $2.95 (0-06-440186-3). Three stories that explore various aspects of human nature.

2479 Gardam, Jane. *The Hollow Land* (7–9). Illus. 1982, Greenwillow $10.25 (0-688-00873-9). A group of short stories that takes place in northern England.

2480 Paterson, Katherine, ed. *Angels and Other Strangers: Family Christmas Stories* (6–9). 1979, Harper $12.70 (0-690-03992-1); paper $3.50 (0-06-440283-5). A collection of 9 short stories that explore the true meaning of Christmas.

Plays

General and Miscellaneous Collections

2481 Bland, Joellen, adapt. *Stage Plays from the Classics* (6–9). 1987, Plays paper $13.95 (0-8238-0281-7). Fifteen plays adapted from such classics as *Oliver Twist, Dracula,* and *The Purloined Letter.* (Rev: BR 1–2/88; SLJ 3/88) [812]

2482 Latrobe, Kathy Howard, and Mildred Knight Laughlin. *Readers Theatre for Young Adults: Scripts and Script Development* (7–12). 1989, Libraries Unlimited paper $24.50 (0-87287-743-4). A collection of short scripts based on literary classics plus tips on how to do one's own adaptations. (Rev: BL 1/1/90) [808.5]

2483 Murray, John, ed. *Fifteen Plays for Today's Teen-Agers: A Collection of One-Act, Royalty-Free Comedies and Mysteries* (7–10). Rev. ed. 1985, Plays paper $10.95 (0-8238-0271-X). A collection of one-act plays of various types; for example, some are humorous, some are scary. [808.82]

2484 Nolan, Paul T. *Folk Tale Plays round the World* (6–9). 1984, Plays paper $10.95 (0-8238-0253-1). Sixteen plays like one based on Johnny Appleseed convey important folktales from many lands. [812.08]

2485 Steinhorn, Harriet. *Shadows of the Holocaust: Plays, Readings, and Program Resources* (7–9). 1983, Kar-Ben Copies paper $6.95 (0-930494-25-3). An unusual collection of plays, poems, and other pieces that can be used to commemorate the Holocaust. [812.08]

Geographical Regions

Europe

SHAKESPEARE

2486 Garfield, Leon. *Shakespeare Stories* (5–9). Illus. 1985, Schocken $18.95 (0-8052-3991-X). A modern retelling of the stories of 12 of Shakespeare's most popular plays. (Rev: BL 1/1/86) [822.3]

2487 Lamb, Charles, and Mary Lamb. *Tales from Shakespeare* (7–9). Illus. 1957, Dent $11.95 (0-460-05039-7). The famous retelling of 20 of his plays in a version first published in 1807. [822.3]

United States

2488 Davis, Ossie. *Langston: A Play* (7–12). 1982, Delacorte $11.95 (0-440-04634-3). Using a play-within-a-play technique, the author presents incidents from Hughes's life via his visit to a church drama group. [812]

2489 Jennings, Coleman A., and Gretta Berghammer, eds. *Theatre for Youth: Twelve Plays with Mature Themes* (6–9). 1986, Univ. of Texas $30.00 (0-292-78081-8); paper $15.95 (0-292-78085-0). A collection of short plays dealing with such topics as death, courage, sexuality, and moral standards. (Rev: BL 1/15/87) [812]

2490 Murray, John. *Mystery Plays for Young Actors* (6–9). 1984, Plays paper $12.95 (0-8238-0265-5). Ten one-act mysteries from *Plays* magazine with production tips. (Rev: BL 1/15/85) [812]

Poetry

General and Miscellaneous Collections

2491 Agard, John, comp. *Life Doesn't Frighten Me at All* (7–12). Illus. 1990, Henry Holt $14.95 (0-8050-1237-0). A collection of accessible contemporary poetry aimed specifically at today's young adults. (Rev: BL 6/1/90; SLJ 8/90) [821]

2492 Brewton, John E., and Lorraine A. Blackburn, eds. *They've Discovered a Head in the Box for the Bread, and Other Laughable Limericks* (6–9). Illus. 1978, Harper LB $12.89 (0-690-03883-6). A fine collection of over 200 humorous limericks. [821.08]

2493 Brewton, Sara, et al., eds. *My Tang's Tungled and Other Ridiculous Situations* (6–9). 1973, Harper $12.70 (0-690-57223-9). A wonderful collection of humorous verse. [811]

2494 Brewton, Sara, et al., eds. *Of Quarks, Quasars, and Other Quirks: Quizzical Poems for the Supersonic Age* (7–10). Illus. 1977, Harper $12.70 (0-690-01286-1). A collection of poems that make fun of modern civilization including its scientific triumphs. [821.08]

2495 Brewton, Sara, and John E. Brewton, eds. *Shrieks at Midnight: Macabre Poems, Eerie and Humorous* (7–9). Illus. 1969, Harper $13.70 (0-690-73518-9). Between the gasps there are also laughs in this unusual collection. [821.08]

2496 Chapman, Jean, comp. *Cat Will Rhyme with Hat: A Book of Poems* (5–10). Illus. 1986, Macmillan LB $12.95 (0-684-18747-7). A collection of 61 poems all about the mysterious cat. (Rev: SLJ 4/87) [808.1]

2497 Foster, John. *Spaceways: An Anthology of Space Poems* (5–8). Illus. 1987, Salem LB $10.95 (0-19-276056-4); paper $5.95 (0-19-276068-8). A collection of twentieth-century poems dealing with various aspects of space, like stars and aliens. (Rev: SLJ 5/87) [808.81]

2498 Harrison, Michael, comp. *Splinters: A Book of Very Short Poems* (5–12). Illus. 1989, Oxford Univ. Pr. $10.95 (0-19-276072-6). A collection of 103 short poems arranged by subject, most by well-known writers. (Rev: SLJ 5/89) [808.81]

2499 Hopkins, Lee Bennett, ed. *I Am the Cat* (7–9). Illus. 1981, Harcourt $10.95 (0-15-237987-8). A collection of poetry by such writers as May Swenson and T. S. Eliot about all sorts of cats and their activities. [808.81]

2500 Hopkins, Lee Bennett, ed. *My Mane Catches the Wind: Poems about Horses* (7–9). Illus. 1979, Harcourt $8.95 (0-15-256343-1). Twenty-two poems by well-known authors about horses and the great outdoors. [808.1]

2501 Janeczko, Paul B., ed. *Don't Forget to Fly: A Cycle of Modern Poets* (7–10). 1981, Bradbury $11.95 (0-02-747780-0). A collection of short modern poems that covers a large range of topics from cemeteries to love. [808.1]

2502 Janeczko, Paul B., sel. *The Place My Words Are Looking For: What Poets Say about and through Their Work* (5–9). 1990, Bradbury $13.95 (0-02-747671-5). A varied collection of poems by contemporaries who also comment on their poems. (Rev: SLJ 5/90; VOYA 6/90) [808.81]

2503 Koch, Kenneth, and Kate Farrell. *Talking to the Sun: An Illustrated Anthology of Poems for Young People* (5–9). Illus. 1985, Henry Holt

$19.95 (0-8050-0144-1). A collection of poems on many subjects illustrated by reproductions from the Metropolitan Museum of Art. (Rev: BL 1/1/86; BR 9–10/86; SLJ 1/87) [808.81]

2504 Larrick, Nancy, ed. *Piping Down the Valleys Wild: Poetry for the Young of All Ages* (6–9). Illus. 1968, Delacorte $14.95 (0-385-29429-8); Dell paper $3.95 (0-440-46952-X). A collection of favorite poems that deal with subjects related to the experience of young people. [808.81]

2505 Larrick, Nancy, ed. *Room for Me and a Mountain Lion: Poetry of Open Spaces* (7–9). Illus. 1989, Evans paper $6.95 (0-87131-569-6). A collection of poems that celebrate nature and the great outdoors. (Rev: SLJ 2/89) [808.81]

2506 Lewis, Naomi, comp. *Messages: A Book of Poems* (7–10). 1985, Faber $15.95 (0-571-13646-X); paper $5.95 (0-571-13647-8). A collection of poems that represent many cultures and many periods. (Rev: SLJ 8/86) [808.81]

2507 Lewis, Richard. *Miracles: Poems by Children of the English Speaking World* (6–9). 1966, Simon & Schuster $14.95 (0-671-50419-3). A collection of poems written by children from the English-speaking countries of the world. [811]

2508 Livingston, Myra Cohn. *Monkey Puzzle and Other Poems* (7–9). Illus. 1984, Macmillan $10.95 (0-689-50310-5). Various kinds of trees are celebrated in the collection of original poetry. [808.81]

2509 Livingston, Myra Cohn, ed. *O Frabjous Day! Poetry for Holidays and Special Occasions* (7–10). 1977, Macmillan $11.95 (0-689-50076-9). Selections that commemorate various celebrations and holidays around the world. [808.81]

2510 Livingston, Myra Cohn, ed. *Poems of Christmas* (6–9). 1980, Macmillan $12.95 (0-689-50180-3). The well-known poet has created an anthology of poetry that celebrates various subjects associated with Christmas. [808.81]

2511 Livingston, Myra Cohn, ed. *Why Am I Grown So Cold? Poems of the Unknowable* (7–10). 1982, Macmillan $14.95 (0-689-52042-7). Such unexplained mysteries of life as mermaids, forecasting the future, and devils are dealt with in this anthology. [808.81]

2512 McCullough, Frances, ed. *Love Is Like a Lion's Tooth: An Anthology of Love Poems* (7–12). 1984, Harper LB $12.89 (0-06-024139-X). A collection of love poems that span time from ancient days to the twentieth century. [808.81]

2513 Merriam, Eve. *A Word or Two with You: New Rhymes for Young Readers* (5–8). 1981, Macmillan $9.95 (0-689-30862-0). An easily read collection of poems about such subjects as parents and friends. [811]

2514 Opie, Iona, and Peter Opie, eds. *The Oxford Book of Children's Verses* (6–9). Illus. 1973, Oxford Univ. Pr. $29.95 (0-19-812140-7). Using a chronological arrangement, the editors have included 332 famous selections. [821.08]

2515 Peck, Richard, ed. *Pictures That Storm inside My Head: Poems for the Inner You* (7–10). 1976, Avon paper $2.25 (0-380-00735-5). A collection of poems about such emotions as fear, guilt, and love. [811]

2516 Plotz, Helen, ed. *Imagination's Other Place: Poems of Science and Mathematics* (7–12). Illus. 1955, Harper LB $12.89 (0-690-04700-2). Poems about different branches of science and about scientists. [808.81]

2517 Plotz, Helen, ed. *Saturday's Children: Poems of Work* (7–10). 1982, Greenwillow $11.25 (0-688-01406-2). An anthology that deals with both pleasant and unpleasant aspects of work from child labor to the joys of a job well done. [808.81]

2518 Prelutsky, Jack, ed. *The Random House Book of Poetry for Children* (6–9). Illus. 1983, Random LB $15.99 (0-394-95010-0). A selection of verse suitable for children that concentrates on light verse written recently. [821.08]

2519 Viorst, Judith. *If I Were in Charge of the World and Other Worries: Poems for Children and Their Parents* (5–8). Illus. 1984, Macmillan paper $3.95 (0-689-70770-3). This is a collection of easily read poems that is short and on topics familiar to children such as cats and spring fever. [811]

2520 Willard, Nancy. *The Ballad of Biddy Early* (4–9). Illus. 1989, Knopf LB $14.99 (0-394-88414-5). A group of poems about a most unusual Irish woman who supposedly could see into the future. (Rev: BL 12/15/89) [811]

2521 *The World's Best Poetry for Children, Volume I and Volume II* (6–9). Illus. 1986, Roth $89.99 (0-89609-260-7). Though expensive, this is a well-indexed, attractively designed collection of over 700 poems for young people. (Rev: SLJ 9/86) [808.81]

Geographical Regions

Europe

GREAT BRITAIN AND IRELAND

2522 Chaucer, Geoffrey. *The Canterbury Tales* (5–9). Adapt. by Geraldine McCaughrean. Illus. 1985, Macmillan $11.95 (0-528-82673-5). An adaptation for young readers of 13 tales that still keep the flavor and spirit of the original. (Rev: SLJ 2/86) [826]

2523 Corrin, Sara, and Stephen Corrin. *The Pied Piper of Hamelin* (6–9). Illus. 1989, Harcourt $14.95 (0-15-261596-2). A fine edition of the Browning poem with stunning illustrations by Errol Le Cain. (Rev: BL 4/1/89) [398.2]

2524 Dahl, Roald. *Rhyme Stew* (7–10). Illus. 1990, Viking $12.95 (0-670-82916-1). Lots of silly poems and parodies charmingly illustrated by Quentin Blake. (Rev: BL 5/15/90; SLJ 9/90) [821]

2525 Eliot, T. S. *Growltiger's Last Stand: And Other Poems* (6–9). Illus. 1987, Farrar $12.95 (0-374-32809-9). Shades of the musical *Cats.* Here are 3 poems, with excellent illustrations by Errol Le Cain, from Eliot's *Old Possum's Book of Practical Cats.* (Rev: SLJ 1/88) [821]

2526 Eliot, T. S. *Old Possum's Book of Practical Cats* (7–12). 1982, Harcourt $10.95 (0-15-168656-4); paper $4.95 (0-15-668568-X). Many of these whimsical poems about cats were used in the musical *Cats.* [821]

2527 Hughes, Ted. *Moon-Whales and Other Moon Poems* (7–9). Illus. 1976, Ultramarine $15.00 (0-670-48864-X). The respected English poet imagines all sorts of strange creatures that live on the moon. Also use his *Season Songs* (1976). [821]

2528 Kipling, Rudyard. *Gunga Din* (7–12). Illus. 1987, Harcourt LB $12.95 (0-15-200456-4). A splendid edition of this poem dealing with the Indian Mutiny of 1857 and the heroics of an abused water carrier. (Rev: SLJ 12/87) [821]

2529 Lear, Edward. *How Pleasant to Know Mr. Lear! Edward Lear's Selected Works* (6–9). Illus. 1982, Holiday $13.95 (0-8234-0462-5). Nonsense verse by this English master plus an introductory biographical essay. [821]

2530 Livingston, Myra Cohn, comp. *Poems of Lewis Carroll* (7–9). Illus. 1986, Harper LB $11.89 (0-690-04540-9). A complete collection of rhymes, poems, and riddles from the creator of Alice. (Rev: SLJ 8/86) [821]

2531 Millay, Edna St. Vincent. *Edna St. Vincent Millay's Poems Selected for Young People* (7–10). Illus. 1979, Harper $13.70 (0-06-024218-3). A fine selection of the poet's work illustrated with woodcuts. [811]

2532 Noyes, Alfred. *The Highwayman* (6–9). Illus. 1983, Lothrop LB $11.88 (0-688-02118-2). This edition of Noyes's mysterious narrative poem is beautifully illustrated by Charles Mikolaycak. [821]

2533 Thomas, Dylan. *A Child's Christmas in Wales* (7–12). Illus. 1980, Godine $13.95 (0-87923-337-7); paper $7.95 (0-87923-529-2). For all ages, this is a tender reminiscence with touching illustrations by Edward Ardizzone. [821]

United States

2534 Adoff, Arnold, ed. *I Am the Darker Brother: An Anthology of Modern Poems by Negro Americans* (7–12). Illus. 1968, Macmillan $10.95 (0-02-700080-X); paper $4.95 (0-02-041120-0). Twenty-eight contemporary black American poets are represented in this collection for young people. [811.08]

2535 Adoff, Arnold, ed. *My Black Me: A Beginning Book of Black Poetry* (7–10). 1974, Dutton $10.75 (0-525-35460-3). Fifty poems about black people and the joys and sorrows of being black. [811.08]

2536 Brewton, Sara, and John E. Brewton, eds. *America Forever New: A Book of Poems* (6–9). Illus. 1968, Harper LB $13.89 (0-690-04764-9). Both famous and less well-known poets are included in this book celebrating the spirit of the United States. [811.08]

2537 Brooks, Gwendolyn. *Selected Poems* (7–12). 1963, Harper $11.49 (0-06-010535-6); paper $6.95 (0-06-090989-7). A selection of this poet's work dealing principally with the place of Black America in society. [811]

2538 Cummings, e.e. *95 Poems* (7–12). 1971, Harcourt paper $4.95 (0-15-665950-6). A fine collection of this poet's works, many of which celebrate the natural, unsophisticated aspects of life. [811]

2539 Dickinson, Emily. *I'm Nobody! Who Are You?* (6–9). Illus. 1978, Stemmer $17.95 (0-916144-21-6); paper $9.95 (0-916144-22-4). A well-illustrated edition of poems that young people can appreciate. [811]

2540 Dickinson, Emily. *Poems for Youth* (7–9). 1934, Little $12.95 (0-316-18418-7). A collection

125

of poems by Emily Dickinson suitable for young readers. [811]

2541 Dunbar, Paul Laurence. *The Complete Poems of Paul Laurence Dunbar* (7–12). 1980, Dodd paper $5.95 (0-396-07895-8). The definitive collection first published in 1913 of this black poet's work. [811]

2542 Dunning, Stephen, et al., eds. *Reflections on a Gift of Watermelon Pickle . . . And Other Modern Verse* (7–12). Illus. 1967, Lothrop LB $13.88 (0-688-51231-3). Several English teachers have chosen poems for young people by 114 modern American poets. [811.08]

2543 Fleischman, Paul. *I Am Phoenix: Poems for Two Voices* (4–9). Illus. 1985, Harper LB $11.89 (0-06-021882-7). A group of love poems about birds that are designed to be read by 2 voices or groups of voices. (Rev: BL 12/1/85; BR 3–4/86) [811]

2544 Forrester, Victoria. *A Latch Against the Wind: Poems* (7–10). Illus. 1985, Macmillan $9.95 (0-689-31091-9). A series of quiet poems for young people that move from the ordinary to the abstract with illustrations by the poet. (Rev: BL 7/85; BR 1–2/86) [811]

2545 Frost, Robert. *A Swinger of Birches* (6–9). Illus. 1982, Stemmer $21.95 (0-916144-92-5); paper $14.95 (0-916144-93-3). A collection of Frost's poems suitable for young readers in a well-illustrated edition. [811]

2546 Frost, Robert. *You Come Too: Favorite Poems for Young Readers* (7–12). Illus. 1959, Henry Holt LB $9.95 (0-8050-0299-5); paper $3.95 (0-8050-0316-9). A fine introduction to this poet's works through 50 of his more accessible poems. [811]

2547 Giovanni, Nikki. *Ego-Tripping, and Other Poems for Young People* (7–12). Illus. 1973, Hill & Co. $10.00 (0-88208-020-2); paper $5.95 (0-88208-019-9). The author's own selection of her poems suitable for young people and all dealing with being black. [811]

2548 Glenn, Mel. *Class Dismissed! High School Poems* (7–12). Illus. 1982, Clarion $13.95 (0-89919-075-8). Photographs of high school students accompany poems about them and their concerns. Other successful collections by this author are: *Class Dismissed: More High School Poems, No. II* (1986); *Back to Class* (1988). [811]

2549 Hopkins, Lee Bennett, ed. *Love & Kisses* (7–10). Illus. 1983, Houghton $8.95 (0-395-34554-5); paper $3.95 (0-395-34921-4). A selection of 25 American poems celebrating various aspects of love. [811.08]

2550 Hopkins, Lee Bennett, ed. *Rainbows Are Made* (6–9). 1982, Harcourt $15.95 (0-15-265480-1). Poems by Carl Sandburg that are suitable for young readers are included in this anthology. [811]

2551 Janeczko, Paul B. *Brickyard Summer* (7–12). Illus. 1989, Watts LB $13.99 (0-531-08446-9). A collection of original poems about growing up in the big city. (Rev: BL 9/15/89; BR 11–12/89; SLJ 12/89; VOYA 2/90) [811]

2552 Janeczko, Paul B. *The Music of What Happens: Poems That Tell Stories* (7–12). 1988, Watts LB $14.99 (0-531-08357-8). An unusual collection of narrative poems all by contemporary American poets. (Rev: BL 9/1/88; BR 3–4/89; SLJ 8/88; VOYA 10/88) [811]

2553 Janeczko, Paul B., ed. *Poetspeak: In Their Work, about Their Work* (7–12). Illus. 1983, Bradbury $12.95 (0-02-74770-3). The works of 60 modern American poets are represented plus comments by the poets themselves on their work. [811.08]

2554 Janeczko, Paul B., ed. *Strings: A Gathering of Family Poems* (7–12). 1984, Bradbury $11.95 (0-02-747790-8). All kinds of family life are represented in this collection of over 100 poems. [811.08]

2555 Knudson, R. R., and May Swenson, eds. *American Sports Poems* (7–12). 1988, Watts LB $14.99 (0-531-08353-5). An excellent collection that concentrates on such popular sports as baseball, football, and swimming. (Rev: BL 8/88; BR 3–4/89; SLJ 11/88; VOYA 10/88) [811]

2556 Larrick, Nancy, ed. *On City Streets: An Anthology of Poetry* (6–9). Illus. 1968, Evans $6.95 (0-87131-551-3). A collection of poems mostly somber in tone about life in the big city. [811.08]

2557 Livingston, Myra Cohn. *No Way of Knowing: Dallas Poems* (7–9). 1981, Macmillan paper $2.79 (0-689-50179-X). In this collection of poems, the author reflects on life in Dallas from 1952 to 1964. [811]

2558 Livingston, Myra Cohn. *Sea Songs* (5–9). Illus. 1986, Holiday LB $14.95 (0-8234-0591-5). In these 15 poems, the many faces of the sea during a 24-hour period are explored. (Rev: SLJ 8/86) [808.81]

2559 Longfellow, Henry Wadsworth. *Hiawatha* (7–12). Illus. 1983, Dial $13.89 (0-8037-0014-8). The epic narrative poem about the deeds of the famous Ojibway brave. [811]

2560 Morrison, Lillian, ed. *Rhythm Road: Poems to Move You* (5–10). 1988, Lothrop $11.95

(0-688-07098-1). A collection of poems about movement involving such subjects as dancers, trains, and birds. (Rev: BL 6/1/88) [811]

2561 Nash, Ogden. *Custard and Company* (6–9). Illus. 1980, Little $12.95 (0-316-59834-8). A selection of 84 humorous poems illustrated by Quentin Blake. [811]

2562 Plotz, Helen, sel. *Poems of Emily Dickinson* (7–10). Illus. 1988, Harper LB $12.89 (0-690-63366-1). A collection of favorite poems by Emily Dickinson selected especially for a young audience. (Rev: SLJ 2/88) [811]

2563 Poe, Edgar Allan. *Annabel Lee* (5–9). Illus. 1987, Tundra $19.95 (0-88776-200-X). A haunting rendition of the Poe poem with paintings by the French Canadian artist Gilles Tibo. (Rev: BL 10/15/87; SLJ 12/87) [811]

2564 Rylant, Cynthia. *Soda Jerk* (7–12). Illus. 1990, Watts LB $14.99 (0-531-08464-7). A group of poems about the inhabitants of a small town written from the viewpoint of a teenage soda jerk. (Rev: BL 2/15/90; SLJ 4/90; VOYA 6/90) [811]

2565 Rylant, Cynthia. *Waiting to Waltz: A Childhood* (7–9). Illus. 1984, Bradbury $11.95 (0-02-778000-7). In 30 poems, the author conveys the experience of growing up in a small Appalachian town. [808.81]

2566 Sandburg, Carl. *Early Moon* (6–9). Illus. 1930, Harcourt paper $1.95 (0-15-627326-8). About 70 poems for young people illustrated by James Daugherty. [811]

2567 Silverstein, Shel. *A Light in the Attic* (6–9). Illus. 1981, Harper LB $14.89 (0-06-025674-5). Over 100 humorous poems that deal with children's interests and need for fun. Also use the author's earlier: *Where the Sidewalk Ends* (1974). [811]

2568 Strauss, Gwen. *Trail of Stones* (7–12). Illus. 1990, Knopf LB $9.99 (0-679-90582-0); paper $6.95 (0-679-80582-6). In very dark tones, the author tells in verse 12 fairy tales. (Rev: BL 3/1/90; SLJ 7/90) [811]

2569 Sullivan, Charles, ed. *Imaginary Gardens: American Poetry and Art for Young People* (6–10). Illus. 1989, Abrams $19.95 (0-8109-1130-2). A collection of well-known poems, from Ogden Nash to Walt Whitman, with accompanying illustrations that also represent a wide range of artists and styles. (Rev: BL 12/1/89) [700]

2570 Whitman, Walt. *Voyages: Poems by Walt Whitman* (7–12). Illus. 1988, Harcourt $14.95 (0-15-294495-8). After an introductory biographical sketch, there are 53 representative poems selected by Lee Bennett Hopkins. (Rev: BL 11/15/88; BR 3–4/89; SLJ 12/88; VOYA 6/89) [811.3]

Other Regions

2571 Service, Robert W. *The Cremation of Sam McGee* (5–9). Illus. 1987, Greenwillow $13.00 (0-688-06903-7). The famous gold rush poem amusingly illustrated by Ted Harrison. (Rev: BL 4/15/87; SLJ 3/87) [811]

2572 Service, Robert W. *The Shooting of Dan McGrew* (6–9). Illus. 1988, Godine $14.95 (0-87923-748-1). A bunch of the boys are still whooping it up in this nicely illustrated edition. (Rev: BL 1/1/89; SLJ 12/88) [811]

Folklore and Fairy Tales

General and Miscellaneous

2573 Harris, Rosemary, reteller. *The Lotus and the Grail: Legends from East to West* (7–10). Illus. 1985, Faber paper $7.95 (0-571-13536-6). A collection of folktales from 18 countries that covers material from a Buddhist tale to a retelling of the French account of the Holy Grail. (Rev: SLJ 3/86) [398]

2574 Haviland, Virginia. *Favorite Fairy Tales Told around the World* (6–8). Illus. 1985, Little $19.95 (0-316-35044-3). An international collection from such countries as Ireland, India, Germany, and Norway. (Rev: BR 3–4/86) [398.2]

2575 Helprin, Mark. *Swan Lake* (6–9). Illus. 1989, Houghton $19.95 (0-395-49858-9). With stunning illustrations by Chris Van Allsburg, this is a fine retelling of the story of Odette, the Prince, and evil Von Rothbart. (Rev: SLJ 12/89; VOYA 2/90) [398.2]

2576 Phelps, Ethel Johnston. *The Maid of the North: Feminist Folk Tales from around the World* (7–9). 1982, Henry Holt paper $7.95 (0-8050-0679-6). An international collection of folktales featuring many wily and clever heroines. [398]

Geographical Regions

Africa

2577 Berger, Terry. *Black Fairy Tales* (6–9). 1974, Macmillan paper $3.95 (0-689-70402-X). A collection of tales of magic that originated in Africa. [398.2]

2578 Courlander, Harold, comp. *The Crest and the Hide* (6–9). Illus. 1982, Putnam $11.95 (0-698-20536-7). Twenty intriguing tales taken from the wealth of African folk literature. [398]

2579 Green, Roger L. *Tales of Ancient Egypt* (5–9). 1972, Penguin paper $2.95 (0-14-030435-4). A collection of folktales from ancient Egypt including one about the source of the Nile. [398]

Asia and the Middle East

2580 He Liyi. *The Spring of Butterflies and Other Folktales of China's Minority Peoples* (7–12). 1986, Lothrop $13.00 (0-688-06192-3). These folktales come from such peoples as the Thais, Tibetans, Zhuangs, and Bais. (Rev: BR 11–12/86) [398]

2581 Husain, Shahrukh. *Demons, Gods & Holy Men from Indian Myths & Legends* (6–10). Illus. 1987, Schocken $16.95 (0-8052-4028-4). A generous sampling of the rich heritage of the Indian subcontinent in an illustrated oversize volume. (Rev: SLJ 12/87) [398]

2582 Kendall, Carol, reteller. *Haunting Tales from Japan* (6–9). Illus. 1985, Spencer Museum Publns. paper $6.00 (0-913689-22-X). A retelling of 6 Japanese folktales, some of which deal with murder and suicide. (Rev: SLJ 2/86) [398]

2583 Lang, Andrew. *The Arabian Nights Entertainments* (6–9). Illus. 1969, Dover paper $6.95 (0-486-22289-6). Aladdin and Sinbad are only 2 of the characters in these 26 tales taken from the 1001 nights collection. [398.2]

2584 Lewis, Naomi. *Stories from the Arabian Nights* (6–9). Illus. 1987, Henry Holt $19.95 (0-8050-0404-1). A total of 30 stories are retold through the voice of Shahrazad, master storyteller. (Rev: BL 2/1/88; SLJ 2/88) [382.2]

2585 Quayle, Eric. *The Shining Princess and Other Japanese Legends* (6–8). Illus. 1989, Arcade $15.95 (1-55970-039-4). A collection of 10 legends vividly retold. (Rev: BL 12/15/89) [398.2]

2586 Riordan, James. *Tales from the Arabian Nights* (7–9). Illus. 1985, Rand McNally $11.95 (0-528-82672-7). Among the 10 stories retold are those involving Sinbad, Ali Baba, and Aladdin. (Rev: SLJ 3/86) [398.2]

2587 Al-Saleh, Khairat. *Fabled Cities, Princes & Jinn from Arab Myths and Legends* (5–8). Illus. 1985, Schocken $15.95 (0-8052-3926-X). A collection of 40 illustrated stories from Arabian folklore that includes a few familiar ones from the *Arabian Nights*. (Rev: BL 1/15/86; SLJ 2/86) [398]

Europe

2588 Afanasiev, Alexander. *Words of Wisdom: Russian Folk Tales from Alexander Afanasiev's Collection* (5–8). Illus. 1989, Raduga $14.95 (5-05-000054-8). A wonderful cross-section of Afanasiev's collection of 42 tales; first published in English in the Soviet Union. (Rev: BL 1/15/90) [398.2]

2589 Aleichem, Sholom. *Holiday Tales of Sholom Aleichem* (7–9). Trans. by Aliza Shevrin. Illus. 1985, Macmillan paper $5.95 (0-689-71034-8). A group of often humorous stories revolving around Jewish holidays. [398.2]

2590 Andersen, Hans Christian. *Hans Andersen's Fairy Tales* (6–9). n.d., Airmont paper $1.95 (0-8049-0169-4). An inexpensive paperback collection of these standard fairy tales. A reprint of the 1898 edition. [398.2]

2591 Burkert, Nancy Ekholm. *Valentine & Orson* (5–10). Illus. 1989, Farrar $16.95 (0-374-38078-3). A stunningly illustrated retelling in verse of the old folktale of twins separated at birth, one raised in wealth and the other in poverty. (Rev: BL 9/1/89; SLJ 11/89) [843]

2592 Capek, Karel. *Nine Fairy Tales and One More Thrown in for Good Measure* (5–9). Trans. by Dagmar Herrmann. Illus. 1990, Northwestern Univ. $24.95 (0-8101-0864-X); paper $9.95 (0-8101-0865-8). A collection of 10 charming folk-

tales from Czechoslovakia. (Rev: BL 8/90) [398.2]

2593 Creswick, Paul. *Robin Hood* (7–9). Illus. 1984, Macmillan $22.50 (0-684-18162-2). A fine retelling of the stories of Robin Hood with superb illustrations by N. C. Wyeth.

2594 Crossley-Holland, Kevin, reteller. *Axe-Age, Wolf-Age: A Selection from The Norse Myths* (7–10). Illus. 1986, Dutton $11.95 (0-233-97688-4). A reprinting of 22 folktales suitable for younger readers from the 32 folktales found in the author's excellent *The Norse Myths* (Pantheon, 1981). (Rev: SLJ 2/87) [398]

2595 de France, Marie. *Proud Knight, Fair Lady: The Twelve Laïs of Marie de France* (7–10). Trans. by Naomi Lewis. Illus. 1989, Viking $19.95 (0-670-82656-1). A new translation of 12 tales that date back to the twelfth century and deal with courtly love. (Rev: BL 6/15/89; SLJ 9/89) [398.2]

2596 Green, Roger L. *Adventures of Robin Hood* (5–9). 1974, Penguin paper $2.95 (0-14-035034-9). The exploits of this folk hero of England are retold in this classic version. [398]

2597 Green, Roger L. *King Arthur and His Knights* (5–9). 1974, Penguin paper $2.95 (0-14-030073-2). The classic retelling of the deeds of this famous king and his knights. [398]

2598 Grimm Brothers. *Household Tales* (6–9). Illus. 1979, Schocken paper $4.95 (0-8052-0633-7). A collection of such folktales as *Snow White*, *Cinderella*, and *Rumpelstiltskin*. [398.2]

2599 Hastings, Selina. *Sir Gawain and the Green Knight* (7–9). Illus. 1981, Lothrop $12.95 (0-688-00592-6). Based on the epic poem of the fourteenth century, this is the tale of tests of chivalry imposed on Gawain to make him a true knight. [398.2]

2600 Jones, Gwyn, reteller. *Scandinavian Legends and Folk-Tales* (7–9). Illus. 1979, Oxford Univ. Pr. $14.95 (0-19-274124-1). A fine collection, with many involving simple people beset by trolls. [398.2]

2601 Kilgannon, Eily. *Folktales of the Yeats Country* (5–8). Illus. 1990, Mercier paper $9.95 (0-85342-861-1). Seventeen folktales that originate in County Sligo in Ireland. (Rev: BL 8/90) [398.2]

2602 Miles, Bernard. *Robin Hood: His Life and Legend* (7–9). Illus. 1979, Macmillan $11.95 (0-528-82340-X). A collection of tales about this English folk hero and his merry men. [398.2]

2603 Nye, Robert. *Beowulf: A New Telling* (7–9). 1982, Dell paper $2.50 (0-440-90560-5). A retelling in modern English of the monster Grendel and the hero Beowulf. [398.2]

2604 Pyle, Howard. *The Merry Adventures of Robin Hood of Great Renown in Nottinghamshire* (7–9). Illus. n.d., Peter Smith $15.95 (0-8446-2765-8); Dover paper $5.95 (0-486-22043-5). The classic (first published in 1883) retelling of 22 of the most famous stories. [398.2]

2605 Pyle, Howard. *The Story of King Arthur and His Knights* (7–9). Illus. n.d., Peter Smith $16.00 (0-8446-2766-6); Dover paper $6.50 (0-486-21445-1). A retelling that has been in print since its first publication in 1903. [398.2]

2606 Pyle, Howard. *The Story of Sir Launcelot and His Companions* (7–9). Illus. 1985, Macmillan $17.95 (0-684-18313-7). The story of one of Arthur's famous knights with illustrations by Howard Pyle. [398.2]

2607 Pyle, Howard. *The Story of the Champions of the Round Table* (7–9). Illus. 1984, Macmillan $17.95 (0-684-18171-1). A reissue of the 1905 book about the feats of Launcelot, Tristram, and Percival. Also reissued is: *The Story of the Grail and the Passing of Arthur* (1984). The Story of the Grail and the Passing of Arthur [398.2]

2608 Singer, Isaac Bashevis. *The Golem* (7–9). Illus. 1982, Farrar $12.95 (0-374-32741-6). The sixteenth-century Jewish tale retold about the rabbi in old Prague who brought a statue to life to help his people. [398.2]

2609 Sutcliff, Rosemary. *Dragon Slayer* (5–9). 1976, Penguin paper $3.50 (0-14-030254-9). A simple retelling of the story of Beowulf and his battle against Grendel. [398]

2610 Sutcliff, Rosemary. *The Light Beyond the Forest: The Quest for the Holy Grail* (7–9). Illus. 1979, Dutton $13.95 (0-525-33665-6). The first volume of the trilogy about the search for the Holy Grail by King Arthur and his knights. Continued in: *The Sword in the Circle* and *The Road to Camelann* (both 1981). [398.2]

2611 Vivian, E. Charles. *The Adventures of Robin Hood* (6–9). n.d., Airmont paper $1.75 (0-8049-0067-1). The principal stories about Robin Hood and his men are retold in this inexpensive edition. [398]

North America

GENERAL AND MISCELLANEOUS

2612 Haviland, Virginia, ed. *North American Legends* (7–9). Illus. 1979, Putnam $9.95 (0-399-20810-0). A collection of folktales from Indians and both black and white American settlers. [398.2]

2613 Wolkstein, Diane, comp. *The Magic Orange Tree and Other Haitian Folktales* (7–9). Illus. 1980, Schocken paper $9.95 (0-8052-0650-7). A fine collection of folktales usually told by storytellers in Haiti. [398.2]

INDIANS OF NORTH AMERICA

2614 Van Etten, Teresa. *Ways of Indian Wisdom* (7–10). 1987, Sunstone paper $10.95 (0-86534-090-0). A collection of 20 Pueblo tales that reflect the Southeastern Indians' culture and customs. (Rev: BR 1–2/88) [398.2]

UNITED STATES

2615 Cohen, Daniel. *Southern Fried Rat & Other Gruesome Tales* (7–10). Illus. 1983, Evans $9.95 (0-87131-400-2). A collection of stories based on tales about people living in urban areas today. [398.2]

2616 Hamilton, Virginia. *The People Could Fly: American Black Folk Tales* (5–9). Illus. 1985, Knopf LB $14.99 (0-394-96925-1). A retelling of 24 black folktales—some little known, others familiar like *Tar Baby*. (Rev: BL 7/85) [398.2]

2617 Highwater, Jamake. *Anpao: An American Indian Odyssey* (7–9). Illus. 1977, Harper $13.70 (0-397-31750-6). A number of Indian tradition tales are interwoven into this story of a demigod, Anpao. [398.2]

2618 Jagendorf, M. A. *Folk Stories of the South* (7–12). Illus. 1972, Vanguard $14.95 (0-8149-0000-3). A collection of pre-Civil War stories from 11 states arranged geographically. [398.2]

2619 Lester, Julius. *Further Tales of Uncle Remus* (4–9). Illus. 1990, Dial LB $14.89 (0-8037-0611-1). The third volume of Uncle Remus stories, wittily retold with illustrations by Jerry Pinkney. Preceded by *The Tales of Uncle Remus* (1987) and *More Tales of Uncle Remus* (1988). (Rev: BL 4/15/90) [398.2]

2620 Rhyne, Nancy. *More Tales of the South Carolina Low Country* (7–9). 1984, Blair paper $5.95 (0-89587-042-8). A collection of eerie and unusual folktales. [398.2]

2621 Rounds, Glen. *Ol' Paul, the Mighty Logger* (6–8). Illus. 1976, Holiday $13.95 (0-8234-0269-X); paper $4.95 (0-8234-0713-6). The colorful saga of the great tall-tale hero of American folklore. [398.2]

2622 Schwartz, Alvin. *Scary Stories to Tell in the Dark* (6–9). Illus. 1981, Harper LB $12.89 (0-

397-31927-4); paper $4.95 (0-397-31970-3). Stories about ghosts and witches that are mostly scary but often also humorous. Continued in: *More Scary Stories to Tell in the Dark* (1984). [398.2]

2623 Shepherd, Esther. *Paul Bunyan* (7–10). Illus. 1941, Harcourt $12.95 (0-15-259749-2); paper $6.95 (0-15-259755-7). The life of this lumberjack tall tale hero is well brought to life by the author and stunning illustrations by Rockwell Kent. [398.2]

2624 Steele, Phillip W. *Ozark Tales and Superstitions* (7–9). Illus. 1983, Pelican paper $4.95 (0-

88289-404-8). Twenty-six tales all from the Ozarks covering such subjects as outlaws, nature, Indians, and supernatural omens. [398.2]

South and Central America

2625 Bierhorst, John, ed. *The Hungry Woman: Myths and Legends of the Aztecs* (7–9). Illus. 1984, Morrow $11.95 (0-688-02766-0). From creation myths to the destruction of ancient Aztec culture by the Spaniards, these are the folktales of Mexico. [398.2]

Mythology

General and Miscellaneous

2626 Asimov, Isaac. *Words from the Myths* (7–10). Illus. 1961, Houghton $13.95 (0-395-06568-2); paper $2.50 (0-451-14097-4). In dictionary format explanations are given for words derived from mythology that have found their way into the English language. [292]

2627 Evslin, Bernard. *Pig's Ploughman* (7–12). Illus. 1990, Chelsea House $19.95 (1-55546-256-1). In Celtic mythology, Pig's Ploughman is the huge hog who fights Finn McCool. (Rev: BL 8/90) [398.2]

2628 Gaffron, Norma. *Unicorns* (6–8). Illus. 1989, Greenhaven $12.95 (0-89908-063-4). A history of this mythical beast, and the pros and cons about its possible existence are presented. (Rev: BL 12/15/89; SLJ 3/90) [398]

2629 Hamilton, Dorothy. *Mythology* (8–12). Illus. 1942, Little $17.95 (0-316-34114-2); NAL paper $4.50 (0-451-62702-4). An introduction to the mythology of Greece and Scandinavia plus a retelling of the principal myths. [292]

2630 Hamilton, Virginia. *In the Beginning: Creation Stories from around the World* (6–9). Illus. 1988, Harcourt $18.95 (0-15-238740-4). Twenty-five creation myths from around the world are retold with notes of the sources of each. (Rev: BL 9/15/88; SLJ 12/88; VOYA 6/89) [291.2]

2631 Kerven, Rosalind, reteller. *The Slaying of the Dragon: Tales of the Hindu Gods* (7–10). Illus. 1988, Andre Deutsch $13.45 (0-233-98037-7). A retelling of 12 popular stories from Hindu mythology. (Rev: SLJ 5/88) [291.1]

2632 Ross, Anne. *Druids, Gods and Heroes of Celtic Mythology* (6–10). Illus. 1986, Schocken $16.95 (0-8052-4014-4). An oversized book that gives detailed information on Irish and Welsh Celtic mythology as well as material on King Arthur. (Rev: SLJ 2/87) [291.1]

Classical

2633 Aesop. *Aesop's Fables* (6–9). n.d., Airmont paper $1.75 (0-8049-0081-7). An inexpensive, standard collection of these short morality tales. [291.1]

2634 Bulfinch, Thomas. *A Book of Myths: Selections from Bulfinch's Age of Fable* (7–12). Illus. 1942, Macmillan $12.95 (0-02-782280-X). From the classic collection of retellings, *Age of Fable*, 30 Greek myths have been excerpted. [292]

2635 Bulfinch, Thomas. *Bulfinch's Mythology: The Age of Fable; The Age of Chivalry; Legends of Charlemagne* 3 vols. 1922, NAL paper $3.95 (vol. 1); $4.95 (vol. 2); $4.95 (vol. 3) (vol. 1: 0-451-62444-0; vol. 2: 0-451-62252-9; vol. 3: 0-451-62659-1). These 3 volumes comprise the classic overview of world mythology first published between 1855 and 1862. [291]

2636 Connolly, Peter. *The Legend of Odysseus* (5–9). Illus. 1988, Oxford Univ. Pr. $14.95 (0-19-917065-7). A faithful retelling of the stories from the *Odyssey* and parts of the *Iliad* in modern English. (Rev: SLJ 6-7/88) [880]

2637 Coolidge, Olivia. *Greek Myths* (6–8). Illus. 1949, Houghton $13.95 (0-395-06721-9). A simplified retelling of the major Greek myths arranged by topics such as "Great Heroes." [292]

2638 Evslin, Bernard. *Amycus* (7–12). Illus. 1989, Chelsea House $19.95 (1-55546-240-5). A brilliant retelling of the myth about the mighty king who boxed against Pollux. Others in this series about mythical monsters are: *The Calydonian Boar; The Hydra;* and *Scylla and Charybdis* (all 1989). (Rev: BL 8/89; BR 1–2/90; SLJ 9/89; VOYA 10/89) [398.2]

2639 Evslin, Bernard. *Anteus* (6–9). Illus. 1988, Chelsea House $19.95 (1-55546-241-3). A retelling of the story of Hercules and his battle against the horrible giant Anteus. Also use by the same author: *Hecate* (1988). (Rev: BL 9/1/88) [292]

2640 Evslin, Bernard. *Cerberus* (6–12). Illus. 1987, Chelsea House $19.95 (1-55546-243-X). The story of the 3-headed dog in Greek mythology that guards the gates of Hell. Also in this series: *The Dragons of Boeotia* and *Geryon* (both 1987). (Rev: BL 11/15/87; SLJ 1/88) [398.2]

2641 Evslin, Bernard. *The Chimaera* (6–10). Illus. 1987, Chelsea House $19.95 (1-55546-244-8). This ugly, dangerous creature is composed of equal parts of lion, goat, and reptile. Another in the series is *The Sirens* (1987). (Rev: BL 3/1/88) [398.2]

2642 Evslin, Bernard. *The Cyclopes* (6–12). Illus. 1987, Chelsea House $19.95 (1-55546-236-7). The story of the ferocious one-eyed monster and how he was blinded by Ulysses. Others in this series about mythical monsters are: *Medusa; The Minotaur;* and *Procrustes* (all 1987). (Rev: BL 6/15/87; SLJ 8/87) [398.2]

2643 Evslin, Bernard. *The Furies* (7–12). Illus. 1989, Chelsea House $19.95 (1-55546-249-9). In Greek mythology the Furies were 3 witches. This retelling also includes the story of Circe, the famous sorceress. (Rev: BL 12/15/89) [398.21]

2644 Evslin, Bernard. *Hercules* (6–8). Illus. 1984, Morrow LB $12.95 (0-688-02748-2). The principal myths connected with this Greek hero are told in a simple, graphic way. [292]

2645 Evslin, Bernard. *Heroes, Gods and Monsters of the Greek Myths* (6–9). 1988, Scholastic paper $2.50 (0-590-41072-5). A fine retelling of some of the standard Greek myths. [291.1]

2646 Evslin, Bernard. *Jason and the Argonauts* (5–9). Illus. 1986, Morrow $13.00 (0-688-06245-8). A masterful retelling of the fantastic quest made by Jason and his valiant followers. (Rev: BL 5/1/86; SLJ 5/86) [292]

2647 Evslin, Bernard. *Ladon* (7–12). Illus. 1990, Chelsea House $19.95 (1-55546-254-5). A splen-

did retelling of the Greek myth about the sea serpent called up by Hera to fight Hercules. (Rev: BL 8/90) [398.24]

2648 Evslin, Bernard. *The Nemean Lion* (7–12). Illus. 1990, Chelsea House $19.95 (1-55546-255-3). A little-known myth filled with excitement and terror retold as part of the Monsters of Mythology series. (Rev: BL 5/15/90; SLJ 8/90) [292.1]

2649 Gates, Doris. *A Fair Wind for Troy* (6–9). Illus. 1976, Penguin paper $3.95 (0-14-031718-X). A well-known telling of the events that led up to the Trojan War. [292]

2650 Gates, Doris. *Two Queens of Heaven: Aphrodite and Demeter* (6–8). 1983, Penguin paper $3.50 (0-14-031646-9). Eight stories capture the essence of these 2 goddesses from Greek mythology. [292]

2651 Graves, Robert. *Greek Gods and Heroes* (6–8). 1973, Dell paper $2.75 (0-440-93221-1). Tales of 12 of the most important figures in Greek mythology in 27 short chapters. [292]

2652 Green, Roger L. *The Tale of Troy* (5–9). 1974, Penguin paper $3.95 (0-14-03012-8). A retelling of the story of the Trojan War and the events leading to it. [291.1]

2653 Green, Roger L. *Tales of the Greek Heroes* (5–9). 1974, Penguin paper $2.95 (0-14-030119-4). This volume includes stories about Prometheus, Dionysus, Perseus, and Heracles. [291.1]

2654 Jacobs, Joseph. *The Fables of Aesop* (7–9). Illus. n.d., Schocken $12.95 (0-8052-3068-8); paper $5.95 (0-8052-0138-6). A fine collection of 82 fables with historical notes first published in 1894. [398.2]

2655 Lang, Andrew. *Tales of Troy and Greece* (6–9). 1978, Faber paper $2.95 (0-571-08619-5). A retelling of the Trojan War story for young people. [291.1]

2656 Switzer, Ellen. *Greek Myths: Gods, Heroes, and Monsters—Their Sources, Their Stories and Their Meanings* (7–12). Illus. 1988, Macmillan $16.95 (0-689-31253-9). A collection of myths that includes 13 stories about such characters as Perseus, Odysseus, and Medusa. (Rev: BL 4/1/88; BR 1–2/89; SLJ 4/88) [292]

Scandinavian

2657 Colum, Padraic. *The Children of Odin: The Book of Northern Myths* (6–8). Illus. 1984, Macmillan $12.95 (0-02-722890-8); paper $7.95 (0-02-042100-1). A retelling of the principal Scandinavian myths including those involving Fafnir, Odin, and Baldur. [293]

2658 Evslin, Bernard. *Fafnir* (7–12). Illus. 1989, Chelsea House $19.95 (1-55546-247-2). A retelling of the Norse myth about the giant Fafnir, the god Odin, and the superhero Siegfried. (Rev: BL 12/15/89) [398.2]

Humor and Satire

2659 Keller, Charles, ed. *Growing Up Laughing: Humorists Look at American Youth* (7–10). 1981, Prentice $10.95 (0-13-367870-9). A collection of pieces by such humorists as Mark Twain and Bill Cosby. [808.7]

Speeches, Essays, and General Literary Works

2660 Hoopes, Ned E., and Richard Peck, eds. *Edge of Awareness: Twenty-five Contemporary Essays* (7–12). 1966, Dell paper $3.25 (0-440-92218-6). This anthology of essays is excellent for using in discussion groups. [808.84]

Literary History and Criticism

General and Miscellaneous

2661 Carpenter, Humphrey, and Mari Prichard. *The Oxford Companion to Children's Literature* (7–12). Illus. 1984, Oxford Univ. Pr. $35.00 (0-19-211582-0). Though intended as an adult reference work, young people can find material here on their favorite authors past and present. [809]

Fiction

2662 Gallo, Donald R., ed. *Speaking for Ourselves* (7–12). 1990, NCTE paper $12.95 (0-8141-4625-2). Short autobiographical portraits of young adult authors that explore the topics of

Plays

General and Miscellaneous

2663 Kamerman, Sylvia E., ed. *Christmas Play Favorites for Young People* (6–10). 1983, Plays paper $10.95 (0-8238-0257-4). Eighteen one-act plays that could be used in both elementary and high schools. [812.08]

2664 Kamerman, Sylvia E., ed. *On Stage for Christmas: A Collection of Royalty-Free, One-Act Christmas Plays for Young People* (6–9). 1978, Plays $13.95 (0-8238-0226-4). A collection of short plays that uses the holiday of Christmas as a subject. [808.2]

Europe

Great Britain and Ireland

SHAKESPEARE

2665 Birch, Beverley, reteller. *Shakespeare's Stories: Comedies* (5–9). Illus. 1988, Bedrick $12.95 (0-87226-191-3). This is the first of 3 volumes that retell in attractive straightforward prose the most popular of his plays. The others are: *Shakespeare's Stories: Histories* and *Shakespeare's Stories: Tragedies* (both 1988). (Rev: BL 2/15/89; BR 1–2/89; SLJ 2/89) [813]

2666 Brown, John Russell. *Shakespeare and His Theatre* (7–12). Illus. 1982, Lothrop $14.95 (0-688-00850-X). A description of Shakespeare's Globe Theatre and how it operated. [792.09]

United States

2667 Hamlett, Christina. *Humorous Plays for Teen-Agers* (7–10). 1987, Plays paper $12.00 (0-8238-0276-0). Easily read one-act plays for beginners in acting. (Rev: BL 5/1/87; BR 5–6/87; SLJ 11/87) [812]

Poetry

General and Miscellaneous

2668 Deutsch, Babette. *Poetry Handbook: A Dictionary of Terms* (7–12). 4th ed. 1981, Barnes & Noble paper $7.95 (0-06-463548-1). The standard introduction to the technical aspects of poetry through definitions of terms with examples. [808.1]

2669 Larrick, Nancy, ed. *Crazy to Be Alive in Such a Strange World: Poems about People* (7–10). 1989, Evans paper $6.95 (0-87131-566-1). A collection of poems about aspects of the human character and about some unusual characters. (Rev: SLJ 2/89) [811.08]

2670 Larrick, Nancy, ed. *Tambourines! Tambourines to Glory! Prayers and Poems* (6–8). Illus. 1982, Westminster $8.95 (0-664-32689-7). A collection of prayers in poetry form from many cultures and times. [808.81]

United States

2671 Esbensen, Barbara Juster. *Cold Stars and Fireflies: Poems of the Four Seasons* (6–8). Illus. 1984, Harper LB $12.89 (0-690-04363-5). Poems about the seasons and nature beginning with autumn. [808.1]

2672 Powell, Lawrence Clark, comp. *Poems of Walt Whitman: Leaves of Grass* (7–10). Illus. 1964, Harper LB $12.89 (0-690-64431-0). A collection of poems suitable for younger readers arranged under broad subjects. [811.08]

Language and Communication

Symbols, Words, and Languages

2673 Ashton, Christina. *Words Can Tell: A Book about Our Language* (6–9). 1989, Messner $9.79 (0-671-65223-0). A history of the English language plus information on how it is growing with numerous examples. (Rev: BL 4/1/89) [422]

2674 Crampton, William. *Flag* (5–9). Illus. 1989, Knopf LB $13.99 (0-394-92255-7). Stunning photographs and text introduce the use and nature of flags with many accompanying examples. (Rev: BL 10/15/89) [929.9]

2675 Fisher, Leonard Everett. *Alphabet Art: Thirteen ABC's from around the World* (7–9). Illus. 1978, Macmillan $14.95 (0-02-735230-7). From Arabic to Tibetan, 13 alphabets are introduced and depicted in full-page illustrations. [745.6]

2676 Hazen, Barbara Shook. *Last, First, Middle and Nick: All about Names* (7–9). Illus. 1979, Prentice $7.95 (0-13-523944-3). The stories behind personal names are given as well as an indication of their meaning. [929.8]

2677 Janeczko, Paul B. *Loads of Codes and Secret Ciphers* (7–9). Illus. 1984, Macmillan $11.95 (0-02-747810-6). An introduction to both making and breaking codes and how to transmit secret messages. [652]

2678 Lee, Mary Price, and Richard S. Lee. *Last Names First: . . . and Some First Names, Too* (5–9). Illus. 1985, Westminster $11.95 (0-664-32719-

2). A book about personal names, how they came to be, examples of some of the strangest, and how to change one's name. (Rev: BL 10/15/85; SLJ 1/86) [929.4]

2679 Meltzer, Milton. *A Book about Names* (7–9). Illus. 1984, Harper LB $13.89 (0-690-04381-3). A history of all sorts of names and where they come from. [929.4]

2680 Sarnoff, Jane, and Reynold Ruffins. *Words: A Book about the Origins of Everyday Words and Phrases* (7–9). 1981, Macmillan $11.95 (0-684-16958-4). A simple introduction to the etymology of familiar words and phrases. [422]

2681 Schwartz, Alvin, comp. *The Cats Elbow, and Other Secret Languages* (7–9). Illus. 1982, Farrar $12.95 (0-374-31224-9). Thirteen different secret languages and codes are described and explained. [410]

2682 Schwartz, Alvin. *Chin Music: Tall Talk and Other Talk* (7–9). Illus. 1979, Harper LB $9.89 (0-397-31870-7); paper $3.95 (0-397-31871-5). A collection of folk words and their meanings. [410]

2683 Swisher, Clarice. *The Beginning of Language* (6–9). Illus. 1989, Greenhaven LB $12.95 (0-89908-064-2). Many theories concerning how language originated are presented and evaluated. (Rev: SLJ 3/90) [400]

Writing and the Media

General and Miscellaneous

2684 Hackwell, W. John. *Signs, Letters, Words: Archaeology Discovers Writing* (6–9). Illus. 1987, Macmillan $13.95 (0-684-18807-4). The story of the development of writing and how this has affected civilization. (Rev: BL 8/87; SLJ 1/88; VOYA 10/87) [652]

2685 Korty, Carol. *Writing Your Own Plays: Creating, Adapting, Improvising* (7–10). 1986, Macmillan $11.95 (0-684-18470-2). A helpful guide to the basics of writing a play in a simple account that stresses adapting existing material for the stage. (Rev: BL 1/1/87; SLJ 2/87; VOYA 2/87) [808.2]

2686 Van Allsburg, Chris. *The Mysteries of Harris Burdick* (7–9). Illus. 1984, Houghton $14.95 (0-395-35393-9). Fourteen drawings and captions invite the reader to write stories that explain them. [808]

Books and Publishing

2687 Greenfeld, Howard. *Books: From Writer to Reader* (6–10). Illus. 1989, Crown $19.95 (0-517-56840-3); paper $12.95 (0-517-56841-1). Every aspect of book production from the manuscript to selling the finished product is discussed. (Rev: BL 5/15/89; SLJ 3/89; VOYA 2/90) [808]

Newspapers, Magazines, and Journalism

2688 Dubrovin, Vivian. *Running a School Newspaper* (5–9). Illus. 1985, Watts $10.40 (0-531-10046-4). A practical guide for anyone about to start a newspaper or take a position on one. (Rev: BL 2/15/86; BR 3–4/86) [371.8]

2689 English, Betty Lou. *Behind the Headlines at a Big City Paper* (6–9). Illus. 1985, Lothrop $13.00 (0-688-03936-7). By using the *New York Times* as an example, the author explains how a big city newspaper operates. (Rev: BL 3/15/86; SLJ 2/86; VOYA 6/86) [070]

2690 Fleming, Thomas. *Behind the Headlines: The Story of American Newspapers* (6–10). 1989, Walker LB $15.85 (0-8027-6891-1). A lively history of American newspapers from the Revolution on and an indication of their continued importance today. (Rev: BL 1/1/90; BR 5–6/90; SLJ 1/90; VOYA 12/90) [071.3]

2691 Jaspersohn, William. *Magazine: Behind the Scenes at Sports Illustrated* (7–10). Illus. 1983, Little $14.95 (0-316-45815-5). The story of the development and publication of one issue of *Sports Illustrated*. [070.5]

2692 Kronenwetter, Michael. *Journalism Ethics* (7–12). Illus. 1988, Watts $12.90 (0-531-10589-X). Occasions when media coverage is unethical or dangerous to national security is discussed in this unbiased account. (Rev: BL 12/1/88; BR 3–4/89; SLJ 12/88) [174]

2693 Zerman, Melvyn Bernard. *Taking on the Press: Constitutional Rights in Conflict* (8–12). Illus. 1986, Harper LB $11.89 (0-690-04302-3). By using several recent court cases, the author explores various aspects of the freedom of the press concept. (Rev: BL 4/1/86; SLJ 10/86; VOYA 12/86) [342.73]

Propaganda

2694 Klein, David, and Marymae E. Klein. *How Do You Know It's True?* (7–9). 1984, Macmillan $12.95 (0-684-18225-4). This book discusses the sources of our information and how to sort out truth from falsehoods. [303.3]

Religion

World Religions

General and Miscellaneous

2695 Bahree, Patricia. *Hinduism* (6–9). Illus. 1985, Batsford $19.95 (0-7134-3654-9). The basic beliefs and gods of Hinduism are discussed under 100 subjects arranged alphabetically. (Rev: BL 5/1/85) [294.5]

2696 Bolick, Nancy O'Keefe, and Sallie G. Randolph. *Shaker Inventions* (6–8). Illus. 1990, Walker LB $13.85 (0-8027-6934-9). This book describes the Shaker religion and explores the many contributions of the Shakers to American life, such as the clothespin and washing machine. (Rev: BL 8/90) [289]

2697 Burstein, Chaya M. *The Jewish Kids Catalog* (7–9). 1983, Jewish Publication Soc. paper $12.95 (0-8276-0215-4). All sorts of information is given on Jewish culture and history including holidays, folktales, and even some recipes. [296]

2698 Dhanjal, Beryl. *Sikhism* (7–10). Illus. 1987, David & Charles LB $19.95 (0-7134-5202-1). In alphabetical order, the major tenets, doctrines, and personages of this religion are discussed. (Rev: SLJ 9/87) [294.6]

2699 Drucker, Malka. *Celebrating Life: Jewish Rites of Passage* (7–9). Illus. 1984, Holiday LB $11.95 (0-8234-0539-7). A description of Jewish rites associated with birth, adolescence, marriage, and death. [296.4]

2700 Drucker, Malka. *Hanukkah: Eight Nights, Eight Lights* (7–9). Illus. 1980, Holiday LB $13.95 (0-8234-0377-7). An account of the origin and customs involved with the Feast of Lights. [296.4]

2701 Drucker, Malka. *Shabbat: A Peaceful Island* (7–9). Illus. 1983, Holiday LB $11.95 (0-8234-0500-1). A description of the Jewish sabbath and the observances associated with it. [296.4]

2702 Drucker, Malka. *Sukkot: A Time to Rejoice* (7–9). Illus. 1982, Holiday LB $10.95 (0-8234-0466-3). The longest and happiest holiday season of the Jewish year is described. [296.4]

2703 Holland, Isabelle. *Abbie's God Book* (6–9). Illus. 1982, Westminster $7.95 (0-664-32688-9). A young girl keeps a journal about all the thoughts and questions she has about God. [291]

2704 Johnson, Joan. *The Cult Movement* (7–10). Illus. 1984, Watts LB $12.90 (0-531-04767-9). After describing the difference between religion and cults, Johnson tells how cults control their members and talks about specific cults. [289.9]

2705 Makhlouf, Georgia. *The Rise of Major Religions* (6–8). Trans. by Walter O. Moeller. Illus. 1988, Silver Burdett $15.96 (0-382-09482-4). An oversized book that treats the beginnings of such world religions as Christianity, Islam, and Hinduism. (Rev: BL 1/1/89) [291]

2706 Metter, Bert. *Bar Mitzvah, Bat Mitzvah: How Jewish Boys and Girls Come of Age* (7–9). Illus. 1984, Clarion paper $4.95 (0-89919-292-0). The ceremonies and tradition connected with the reaching of maturity of Jewish boys and girls. [296.4]

2707 Miller, Luree. *The Black Hat Dances: Two Buddhist Boys in the Himalayas* (5–8). Illus. 1987, Dodd LB $11.95 (0-396-08835-X). The religion of Buddhism is explored through the experiences of a farm boy and a novice monk in Sikkim. (Rev: SLJ 10/87) [294.3]

2708 Moktefi, Mokhtar. *The Rise of Islam* (5–9). Illus. 1986, Silver Burdett LB $14.96 (0-382-09275-9). In addition to a history of the rise and spread of Islam, the author tells about the religion, its tenets, and its festivals. (Rev: BR 1–2/88) [297]

2709 Morgan, Peggy. *Buddhism* (7–10). Illus. 1987, David & Charles LB $19.95 (0-7134-5203-X). In a dictionary format, the major points concerning this religion and its founder are described. (Rev: SLJ 9/87) [294.3]

2710 Tames, Richard. *Islam* (8–10). Illus. 1985, David & Charles $18.95 (0-7134-3655-7). A topically arranged overview of Islam that covers such topics as marriage, mosques, festivals, and beliefs. (Rev: BL 8/85) [297]

2711 Ward, Hiley H. *My Friends' Beliefs: A Young Person's Guide to World Religions* (7–10). 1988, Walker LB $19.95 (0-8027-6793-1). An introduction to the history and beliefs of the world's great religions, plus interviews with young members. (Rev: VOYA 8/88) [200]

2712 Wood, Angela. *Being a Jew* (6–10). Illus. 1988, David & Charles $17.95 (0-7134-4668-4). This book deals with the history, religion, customs, and traditions of Jewish people around the world. (Rev: SLJ 8/88) [296]

2713 Wood, Angela. *Judaism* (6–9). Illus. 1985, David & Charles $19.95 (0-7134-3656-5). In dictionary format 70 topics related to the Jewish religion including holidays are discussed. (Rev: BL 5/1/85) [294.5]

The Bible and Bible Study

2714 Bach, Alice, and J. Cheryl Exum. *Moses' Ark: Stories from the Bible* (5–9). Illus. 1989, Delacorte $14.95 (0-385-29778-5). The retelling of 13 stories from the Old Testament involving such heroes as Saul and Solomon. (Rev: BL 11/15/89; SLJ 12/89) [222]

2715 Hagan, Lowell, and Jack Westerhof. *Theirs Is the Kingdom: The New Testament* (5–9). Illus. 1986, Eerdmans LB $16.95 (0-8028-5013-8). A collection of stories from the New Testament well illustrated by Paul Stoub. (Rev: SLJ 4/87) [220]

2716 Kite, Patricia. *Noah's Ark* (7–10). Illus. 1989, Greenhaven LB $12.95 (0-89908-073-1). The scientific evidence that proves (or disproves) the story of the Ark is presented. (Rev: BL 3/1/90) [222]

2717 Paterson, John, and Katherine Paterson. *Consider the Lilies: Plants of the Bible* (6–9). Illus. 1986, Harper LB $13.89 (0-690-04463-1). Plants mentioned in the Bible are listed, passages cited, and related stories told. Beautiful paintings of the plants by Anne Ophelia Dowden are featured. (Rev: BL 11/1/86; BR 3–4/87; SLJ 10/86; VOYA 12/86) [220.8]

Holidays and Holy Days

2718 Barth, Edna, ed. *A Christmas Feast: Poems, Sayings, Greetings, and Wishes* (6–9). Illus. 1979, Clarion $12.95 (0-395-28965-3). A collection of writing about Christmas that spans 5 centuries. [808.81]

2719 Batchelor, Mary. *Our Family Christmas Book* (7–9). 1984, Abingdon $9.95 (0-687-29587-4). A Christmas book containing stories, carols, recipes, and other ways to celebrate this holiday. [394.2]

2720 Berger, Gilda. *Easter and Other Spring Holidays* (7–9). Illus. 1983, Watts $10.40 (0-531-04547-1). An introduction to a variety of spring holidays associated with various faiths but its emphasis is on Easter. [263]

2721 Brenner, Martha. *Fireworks Tonight!* (7–9). Rev. ed. Illus. 1986, Hastings LB $13.89 (0-8038-9285-3). A general discussion of fireworks and material on when they are used and how they are made. (Rev: BL 1/15/87; SLJ 3/87) [662.1]

2722 Burnett, Bernice. *Holidays* (6–9). Rev. ed. Illus. 1983, Watts LB $10.40 (0-531-04646-X). A number of holidays from around the world are described with entries that include origins and ways of observance. [394.2]

2723 Friedhoffer, Bob, and Harriet Brown. *How to Haunt a House for Halloween* (6–10). Illus. 1988, Watts LB $11.90 (0-531-10501-6). A guide on how to convert any space into a suitably spooky locale for a Halloween party. (Rev: SLJ 9/88) [394.2]

2724 Greenberg, Judith E., and Helen H. Carey. *Jewish Holidays* (7–10). 1984, Watts $10.40 (0-531-04913-2). An introduction to the yearly cycle of Jewish holidays and the significance of each. [214]

2725 Greenfeld, Howard. *Bar Mitzvah* (6–9). Illus. 1981, Holt $7.95 (0-03-053861-0). The coming-of-age ceremonies for both Jewish boys and girls are explained. [296.4]

2726 Greenfeld, Howard. *Passover* (6–9). Illus. 1978, Holt $6.95 (0-03-039921-1). The history behind Passover and how it is celebrated today are described. [296.4]

2727 Herda, D. J. *Christmas* (7–9). Illus. 1983, Watts $10.40 (0-531-04524-2). In addition to a description of Christmas traditions around the world, this book contains recipes and gift-making suggestions. [394.2]

2728 Perl, Lila. *Piñatas and Paper Flowers: Holidays of the Americas in English and Spanish* (6–9). Illus. 1983, Harper LB $12.95 (0-89919-112-6); paper $5.95 (0-89919-155-X). The origins and customs of 8 holidays celebrated in the Americas are outlined in a bilingual text. [394.2]

2729 van Straalen, Alice. *The Book of Holidays around the World* (5–9). Illus. 1986, Dutton $14.95 (0-525-44270-7). A day-by-day listing of celebrations including birthdays and foreign holidays with a little background information for each. (Rev: BL 1/1/87) [394.2]

Society and the Individual

Government and Political Science

The United Nations and International Organizations

2730 Carroll, Raymond. *The Future of the United Nations* (6–9). Illus. 1985, Watts $12.90 (0-531-10062-6). In addition to outlining the structure and organization of the United Nations, the author outlines the many problems it is concerned with at present. (Rev: BL 12/15/85; BR 3–4/86; SLJ 1/87) [341.23]

2731 Ferrara, Peter L. *NATO: An Entangled Alliance* (7–12). Illus. 1984, Watts $12.90 (0-531-04759-8). An introduction to NATO, its history, and concerns through the early 1980s. (Rev: BL 2/15/85) [355]

2732 Ross, Stewart. *The United Nations* (7–9). Illus. 1990, Watts LB $12.90 (0-531-18295-9). An account that describes the U.N.'s present organization and concerns and also gives historical background about the League of Nations. (Rev: BL 6/1/90; SLJ 7/90) [341.23]

2733 United Nations Dept. of Public Information. *Everyone's United Nations* (7–12). 9th ed. 1979, U.N. Publns. $14.95 (92-1-100273-7); paper $9.95 (92-1-100274-5). Since its first edition in 1948, this is the standard introduction to the structure and activities of the United Nations. [341.23]

International Relations, Peace, and War

2734 Ashton, Stephen. *The Cold War* (7–10). Illus. 1990, Batsford $19.95 (0-7134-5817-8). The author traces the cold war from the end of World War II to the Cuban missile crisis of 1962 and introduces many key personages. (Rev: BL 9/1/90) [327.16]

2735 Bentley, Judith. *The Nuclear Freeze Movement* (7–10). 1984, Watts LB $11.90 (0-531-04772-5). An account that emphasizes the need to control nuclear arms buildups. [327.1]

2736 Cooney, James A. *Foreign Policy: The U.S. and the World* (7–10). 1988, Walker $14.85 (0-8027-6759-1). This introductory volume gives an overview of American foreign policy and how it evolved. (Rev: SLJ 5/88; VOYA 6/88) [327.73]

2737 Dolan, Edward F., Jr. *Panama and the United States: Their Canal, Their Stormy Years* (6–12). Illus. 1990, Watts LB $13.90 (0-531-10911-9). A history of the Canal Zone from Columbus to the arrest of Noriega. (Rev: BL 9/1/90; SLJ 9/90) [327.73]

2738 Dolan, Edward F., Jr., and Margaret M. Scariano. *Cuba and the United States* (7–9). 1987, Watts $12.90 (0-531-10327-7). An objective account of relations between Cuba and the United States that spans the years 1542 through the 1980s. (Rev: VOYA 10/87) [327.73]

2739 Feldbaum, Carl B., and Ronald J. Bee. *Looking the Tiger in the Eye: Confronting the Nuclear Threat* (7–12). Illus. 1988, Harper LB $14.89 (0-06-020415-X). A history of atomic research is given and a description of the present situation regarding various types of nuclear weapons. (Rev: BL 8/88; BR 1–2/89; SLJ 9/88; VOYA 10/88) [355]

2740 Fincher, E. B. *Mexico and the United States: Their Linked Destinies* (7–10). 1983, Harper LB $12.89 (0-690-04311-2). An historical survey of the economic and political relationships between Mexico and the United States. [327.73]

2741 Goode, Stephen. *The Foreign Policy Debate: Human Rights and American Foreign Policy* (7–10). 1984, Watts LB $12.90 (0-531-04753-9). A discussion of human rights in today's world and how they influence U.S. foreign policy. [323.4]

2742 Harbor, Bernard, and Chris Smith. *The Arms Trade* (6–8). Illus. 1988, Rourke $11.95 (0-86592-283-7). The international buying and selling of arms is discussed, plus the problems of controlling this trade. (Rev: BL 12/15/88; SLJ 5/89) [382]

2743 Mansfield, Sue, and Mary Bowen Hall. *Some Reasons for War: How Families, Myths and Warfare Are Connected* (7–12). Illus. 1988, Harper LB $13.89 (0-690-04666-9). War—its causes and consequences—in a variety of situations and cultures is explored in this account that explains why war is not a natural part of man's existence. (Rev: BL 10/1/88; BR 5–6/89; SLJ 1/89; VOYA 12/88) [303.6]

2744 Martin, Lawrence W. *Nuclear Warfare* (8–10). Illus. 1989, Lerner $9.95 (0-8225-1384-6). A somewhat technical account that covers types of weapons, their destructiveness, and the possibilities of disarmament. (Rev: BL 4/1/89) [355]

2745 Middleton, Nick. *Atlas of World Issues* (7–12). Illus. 1989, Facts on File $16.95 (0-8160-2022-1). Key problems involving many nations such as poverty and population are illustrated in charts, diagrams, and maps. (Rev: SLJ 9/89) [327]

2746 Pascoe, Elaine. *Neighbors at Odds: U.S. Policy in Latin America* (7–12). Illus. 1990, Watts LB $12.90 (0-531-10903-8). A history of U.S. relations with Latin America plus a survey of present policies. (Rev: BL 3/1/90; SLJ 5/90; VOYA 8/90) [347.73]

2747 Pimlott, John. *The Cold War* (6–9). Illus. 1987, Watts $12.90 (0-531-10320-X). An account that covers general international relations from the end of World War II through the mid-1980s. (Rev: BL 6/15/87; BR 9–10/87; SLJ 8/87) [940.55]

2748 Pringle, Laurence. *Nuclear War: From Hiroshima to Nuclear Winter* (7–12). Illus. 1985, Enslow $15.95 (0-89490-106-0). The author describes a wide range of atomic weapons and their effect should a nuclear war occur. (Rev: BL 11/15/85; BR 3–4/86; SLJ 12/85; VOYA 6/86) [355]

2749 Ribaroff, Margaret Flesher. *Mexico and the United States Today: Issues between Neighbors* (6–9). Illus. 1985, Watts $12.90 (0-531-04757-1). This account describes the sources of the major political differences between Mexico and the United States plus an appeal for cooperation and unity. (Rev: BL 8/85; SLJ 9/85) [327]

2750 Silverstein, Herma. *Spies among Us: The Truth about Modern Espionage* (7–12). Illus. 1988, Watts $12.90 (0-531-10600-4). The Englishman Kim Philby, the Walkers, and the Rosenbergs are some of the case studies referred to in this overview of spying techniques today. (Rev: BL 12/1/88; BR 3–4/89; SLJ 11/88; VOYA 4/89) [327.1]

2751 Smith, Howard E. *Disarmament: The Road to Peace* (7–10). 1986, Messner $10.79 (0-671-55495-6). Written in the mid-1980s this is a plea for ending the arms race and creating a nuclear freeze. (Rev: BL 4/1/86; SLJ 9/86) [327.1]

2752 Smoke, Richard. *Think about Nuclear Arms Control: Understanding the Arms Race* (6–8). 1988, Walker $14.85 (0-8027-6761-3). This volume explains the issues, technology, and nations involved in the present arms race. (Rev: VOYA 6/88) [355.8]

2753 Taylor, L. B., Jr. *The Nuclear Arms Race* (7–10). Illus. 1982, Watts LB $12.90 (0-531-04401-7). A history of the nuclear arms race up to and including SALT II. [355]

2754 Weiss, Ann E. *Good Neighbors? The United States and Latin America* (6–9). 1985, Houghton $12.95 (0-395-36316-0). An account of U.S. and Latin American relations that is critical of our involvement. (Rev: BR 5–6/86; SLJ 12/85; VOYA 12/85) [327.73]

2755 Weiss, Ann E. *The Nuclear Arms Race—Can We Survive It?* (7–10). Illus. 1983, Houghton $10.95 (0-395-34929-X). A chronological history of the arms race from the first atomic bomb to the early 1980s. [355]

2756 Yost, Graham. *Spies in the Sky* (8–12). Illus. 1989, Facts on File $16.95 (0-8160-1942-8). A history of aerial spying from the use of balloons to space satellite. (Rev: BL 12/15/89; VOYA 4/90) [623]

Various Forms of Government

2757 Feinberg, Barbara Silberdick. *Marx and Marxism* (7–10). 1985, Watts $12.90 (0-531-10065-0). This is a readable introduction to Marx, his ideas, and how they affected the world. (Rev: BL 1/1/86; BR 3 . . . 4/86; SLJ 8/86) [335.4]

2758 Forman, James D. *Fascism: The Meaning and Experience of Reactionary Revolution* (7–

10). 1974, Dell paper $1.75 (0-440-94707-3). An explanation of what fascism is and its formation in such countries as Germany, Italy, and Spain. [320.5]

2759 Raynor, Thomas. *Politics, Power, and People: Four Governments in Action* (7–9). 1983, Watts LB $12.90 (0-531-04662-1). A description of how 4 different governments—the United Kingdom, the United States, the Soviet Union, and Argentina—came into being and how they operated in the early 1980s. [320.3]

United States Government and Institutions

General

2760 Acheson, Patricia C. *Our Federal Government: How It Works* (7–9). 4th ed. 1984, Putnam paper $11.95 (0-396-02312-9). A general introduction to the government, its 3 branches, and major agencies. [353]

2761 Sapinsley, Barbara. *Taxes* (7–12). Illus. 1986, Watts $12.90 (0-531-10268-8). The nature of various kinds of taxes, their history, and how they are applied today are 3 of the topics discussed in this account. (Rev: BL 2/15/87; BR 3–4/87; SLJ 1/87; VOYA 4/87) [336.2]

2762 Weiss, Ann E. *God and Government: The Separation of Church and State* (7–9). 1982, Houghton $9.95 (0-395-32085-2). An objective account of the pros and cons behind the issues involved in this controversial area. [322]

The Constitution

2763 Commager, Henry Steele. *The Great Constitution: A Book for Young Americans* (7–9). Illus. 1961, Macmillan $7.50 (0-672-50299-2). A description of the framing of this document and the men behind its concepts. [342]

2764 Faber, Doris, and Harold Faber. *We the People: The Story of the United States Constitution since 1787* (7–12). Illus. 1987, Macmillan $13.95 (0-684-18753-1). A history of the framing of the Constitution and an examination of contemporary controversies that challenge it. (Rev: BL 5/15/87; SLJ 5/87) [342.73]

2765 Gerberg, Mort. *The U.S. Constitution for Everyone* (8–12). Illus. 1987, Putnam paper $4.95 (0-399-51305-1). The text of the Constitution and amendments is analyzed with many interesting asides and background information. (Rev: BL 5/1/87) [342.73]

2766 Hauptly, Denis J. *A Convention of Delegates: The Creation of the Constitution* (5–9). 1987, Macmillan $12.95 (0-689-31148-6). The story of the Constitutional Convention of 1787 and of the men that participated. (Rev: BL 3/1/87; SLJ 4/87) [342.73]

2767 Lindop, Edmund. *The Bill of Rights and Landmark Cases* (7–10). 1989, Watts LB $12.90 (0-531-10790-6). Each of the 10 amendments is analyzed and important Supreme Court cases are cited. (Rev: BL 1/1/90; BR 1–2/90; SLJ 11/89; VOYA 2/90) [342.73]

2768 Lindop, Edmund. *Birth of the Constitution* (6–10). Illus. 1987, Enslow $16.95 (0-89490-135-4). A history of the Constitution from its inception to its ratification. (Rev: BL 5/15/87; BR 5–6/87; SLJ 5/87) [347.73]

2769 Mabie, Margaret C. J. *The Constitution: Reflection of a Changing Nation* (7–12). Illus. 1987, Henry Holt $12.95 (0-8050-0335-5). A history of the Constitution, the Bill of Rights, and each of the amendments including the defeated Equal Rights Amendment. (Rev: BL 5/1/87; SLJ 9/87) [342.73]

2770 Peterson, Helen S. *The Making of the U.S. Constitution* (6–9). 1974, Garrard LB $7.12 (0-8116-6509-7). A useful survey of the U.S. Constitution and how it came into being. [342]

2771 Ritchie, Donald A. *The U.S. Constitution* (7–9). Illus. 1988, Chelsea House $16.95 (0-87754-894-3). An analysis of the Constitution and its origin in philosophy and English common law. (Rev: BL 12/1/88; SLJ 4/89; VOYA 4/89) [342.73]

2772 Sgroi, Peter. *This Constitution* (7–10). 1986, Watts $10.40 (0-531-10167-3). The act of writing the Constitution is re-created and the personalities involved are introduced. (Rev: VOYA 12/86) [342]

2773 Williams, Selma R. *Fifty-five Fathers* (7–12). Illus. 1987, Putnam $11.95 (0-396-09033-8); paper $4.95 (0-396-09037-0). A history of the Constitutional Convention, including one-paragraph biographies of each of the delegates. (Rev: BR 9–10/87) [342]

The Presidency

2774 Beard, Charles A., and Detlev Vagts. *Presidents in American History* (5–9). Illus. 1989,

Messner LB $12.98 (0-671-68574-0); paper $5.95 (0-671-68575-9). This has become a standard work on the administrations of our presidents. This revision includes the 1984 Reagan election. (Rev: BL 12/15/85; BR 1–2/90; SLJ 12/89; VOYA 4/90) [973]

2775 Bernstein, Richard B., and Jerome Agel. *The Presidency* (8–12). Illus. 1989, Walker LB $13.85 (0-8027-6831-8). A basic history of this institution with some biographical information and a final section that explores the advisability of concentrating such power in one office. (Rev: BL 5/1/89; BR 3–4/89; SLJ 1/89; VOYA 4/89) [353.03]

2776 Kronenwetter, Michael. *The Military Power of the President* (7–12). Illus. 1988, Watts $12.90 (0-531-10590-3). Using many examples from our history, the author traces this aspect of presidential power to the present and the questions that surround it in the nuclear age. (Rev: BL 2/15/89; BR 1–2/89; SLJ 12/88; VOYA 4/89) [353.03]

2777 Sullivan, George. *How the White House Really Works* (5–9). Illus. 1989, Dutton $15.95 (0-525-67266-4). A behind-the-scenes look at the presidential staff and what each member does. (Rev: BL 5/15/89; SLJ 4/89; VOYA 8/89) [975.3]

Federal Government, Its Agencies, and Public Administration

2778 Ashabranner, Melissa, and Brent Ashabranner. *Counting America: The Story of United States Census* (6–8). Illus. 1989, Putnam $14.95 (0-399-21747-9). This is the story of the purpose, the process, and the history of the U.S. Census. (Rev: VOYA 2/90) [312]

2779 Barnes-Svarney, Patricia. *The National Science Foundation* (6–10). 1989, Chelsea House $14.95 (1-55546-117-4). A readable account on this independent government agency dedicated to the advancement of scientific knowledge. (Rev: BR 5–6/89; VOYA 8/89) [353.09]

2780 Bartz, Carl F. *The Department of State* (7–9). Illus. 1988, Chelsea House $16.95 (0-877564-846-3). This introduction emphasizes today's duties of the department with an organizational flowchart. (Rev: BL 12/1/88; VOYA 4/89) [353.1]

2781 Bernstein, Richard B., and Jerome Agel. *The Congress* (7–12). Illus. 1989, Walker LB $13.85 (0-8027-6833-4). An introduction to this branch of the government with material arranged chronologically. Some coverage on recent scandals and recent decline in prestige. (Rev: BL 5/1/89; SLJ 1/89; VOYA 4/89) [328.73]

2782 Broberg, Merle. *The Department of Health and Human Services (U.S.)* (7–10). Illus. 1989, Chelsea House LB $12.95 (0-87754-840-4). A history of the department plus a rundown on current programs such as the control of AIDS. (Rev: SLJ 6/89) [353.8]

2783 Burkhardt, Robert. *The Federal Aviation Administration* (7–10). Illus. 1989, Chelsea House $14.95 (1-55546-107-7). Both a history of this agency is given plus a description of its present-day responsibilities. (Rev: BR 1–2/90; VOYA 10/89) [355.09]

2784 Clement, Fred. *The Department of the Interior* (7–10). Illus. 1989, Chelsea House LB $12.95 (0-87754-842-0). A history of this department is given and an indication of its powers and responsibilities. (Rev: SLJ 6/89) [353.3]

2785 Coffey, Wayne R. *How We Choose a Congress* (7–9). 1980, St. Martin's $10.95 (0-312-39614-7). How a person gets elected to either the Senate or House of Representatives. [328.73]

2786 Cohen, Andrew, and Beth Heinsohn. *The Department of Defense* (7–10). Illus. 1990, Chelsea House $14.95 (0-87754-837-4). An account of the history of this department and an outline of its duties in both peace and war. (Rev: BL 5/15/90) [353.6]

2787 Cutrona, Cheryl. *The Internal Revenue Service* (7–10). 1988, Chelsea House LB $12.95 (0-87754-844-7). A history of this agency is given plus material on its present structure and functions. (Rev: BR 9–10/88) [336.1]

2788 Doggett, Clinton L., and Lois T. Doggett. *The Equal Employment Opportunity Commission* (7–10). Illus. 1990, Chelsea House LB $14.95 (1-55546-106-9). The need for this agency is discussed in the context of its history and present functions. (Rev: SLJ 8/90) [351.8]

2789 Doggett, Clinton L., and Lois T. Doggett. *The U.S. Information Agency* (7–10). Illus. 1989, Chelsea House $14.95 (1-55546-124-7). A history and description of this important agency and its work interpreting America to the outside world. (Rev: BL 1/1/90) [353.5]

2790 Dolin, Eric Jay. *The U.S. Fish & Wildlife Service* (7–10). Illus. 1989, Chelsea House $14.95 (1-55546-128-X). The vital role this agency plays in maintaining the fauna of our environment is explained plus a history of its evolution. (Rev: BR 1–2/90; VOYA 8/89) [353.09]

2791 Dunn, Lynne. *The Department of Justice* (7–10). Illus. 1989, Chelsea House $14.95 (0-87754-843-9). The history, structure, and present status of this federal agency are described and pictured. (Rev: BL 1/1/90) [353.5]

2792 Ellis, Rafaela. *The Central Intelligence Agency* (7–10). Illus. 1987, Chelsea House $12.95 (0-87754-831-5). Interesting background information on origins and functions are given plus career guidance. (Rev: BL 1/1/88; SLJ 2/88) [327.1]

2793 Hopson, Glover. *The Veterans Administration* (7–10). 1988, Chelsea House LB $12.95 (1-55546-131-X). This account explains how this agency helps war veterans and why and when it was founded. (Rev: BR 9–10/88) [353]

2794 Hurt, R. Douglas. *The Department of Agriculture* (7–10). Illus. 1989, Chelsea House LB $12.95 (0-87754-833-1). Background information on the history and functions of this department are given plus material on current programs and concerns. (Rev: SLJ 6/89) [353.8]

2795 Israel, Fred L. *The FBI* (6–10). Illus. 1986, Chelsea House $14.95 (0-87754-821-8). After an explanation of the functions of the FBI, the author outlines highlights of its 50-year history. (Rev: BL 2/1/87; SLJ 12/86) [353]

2796 Kraus, Theresa L. *The Department of the Navy* (7–10). Illus. 1989, Chelsea House $14.95 (0-87754-845-5). The structure of the Navy Department is outlined with historical background and a rundown on present powers. (Rev: BL 1/1/90) [353.7]

2797 Law, Kevin. *The Environmental Protection Agency* (7–10). 1988, Chelsea House LB $12.95 (1-55546-105-0). Why this agency was founded is explained as well as its importance today in the internal affairs of our country. (Rev: BR 9–10/88; VOYA 10/88) [353]

2798 McAfee, Cheryl. *The United States Postal Service* (7–10). Illus. 1987, Chelsea House LB $12.95 (0-87754-826-9). This volume deals with the history, purpose, and development of the U.S. Postal Service. (Rev: BR 9–10/88) [393]

2799 Mackintosh, Barry. *The National Park Service* (7–10). Illus. 1987, Chelsea House $12.95 (1-55546-116-6). This account includes coverage on the history, structure, and services of this department. (Rev: BL 1/1/88) [353.0086]

2800 Matusky, Gregory, and John P. Hayes. *The U.S. Secret Service* (7–12). 1988, Chelsea House LB $12.95 (1-55546-130-1). A history of this interesting, somewhat secretive, agency is given and a description of its functions today. (Rev: BR 9–10/88) [355.3]

2801 Neal, Harry Edward. *The Secret Service in Action* (7–9). 1980, Lodestar $8.95 (0-525-66685-

6). The 125-year history of this amazing institution and how it protects public figures. [327.1]

2802 Patrick, William. *The Food & Drug Administration* (7–12). 1988, Chelsea House LB $12.95 (0-87754-822-6). This increasingly important agency is described as it first existed and as it operates today. (Rev: BR 9–10/88; VOYA 2/89) [353]

2803 Porter, Frank W. *The Bureau of Indian Affairs* (7–10). Illus. 1988, Chelsea House LB $14.95 (0-87754-828-5). As well as a history of the bureau, Porter gives an account of Indian–U.S. government relations to the present. (Rev: SLJ 12/88) [973]

2804 Ragsdale, Bruce A. *The House of Representatives* (7–9). Illus. 1988, Chelsea House $14.95 (1-55546-112-3). A history of the House, an outline of its present responsibilities, and an overview of the legislative process. (Rev: BL 12/1/88) [328.73]

2805 Rhea, John. *The Department of the Air Force* (7–10). Illus. 1989, Chelsea House $14.95 (0-87754-834-X). The powers of this department are outlined but historical information and a structural chart are included. (Rev: BL 1/1/90) [353.63]

2806 Sawyer, Kem Knapp. *The National Foundation on the Arts & Humanities* (7–10). Illus. 1989, Chelsea House $14.95 (1-55546-115-8). A history of this government agency is given plus an explanation of the vital part it plays in the artistic life of the United States. (Rev: BL 1/1/90; BR 1–2/90; SLJ 6/90; VOYA 2/90) [353.09]

2807 Simpson, Andrew L. *The Library of Congress* (7–10). Illus. 1989, Chelsea House $14.95 (1-55546-109-3). A history of the world's largest library, its present holdings, and possible future developments. (Rev: BL 8/89; BR 1–2/90; SLJ 11/89; VOYA 12/89) [027.573]

2808 Smith, Christina Rudy. *The National Archives and Records Administration* (7–10). Illus. 1989, Chelsea House $14.95 (1-55546-073-9). A behind-the-scenes glimpse into the history, operation, and collections housed in these records centers. (Rev: BR 1–2/90; SLJ 7/89; VOYA 8/89) [353.03]

2809 Sniegoski, Stephen J. *The Department of Education* (7–10). Illus. 1988, Chelsea House LB $12.95 (0-87754-838-2). An overview of this department that covers its history, functions, structure, and special programs. (Rev: SLJ 8/88) [353.8]

2810 Stefany, Wallace. *The Department of Transportation* (7–10). 1988, Chelsea House LB $12.95 (0-87754-847-1). A history of this department is given plus its present-day aims and functions. (Rev: BR 9–10/88) [353.86]

2811 Stefoff, Rebecca. *The Drug Enforcement Administration* (7–10). Illus. 1989, Chelsea House $14.95 (0-87754-849-8). This is a clear, factual profile of this important federal agency in the war on drugs. (Rev: BL 1/1/90; SLJ 6/90) [353]

2812 Tuggle, Catherine, and Gary E. Weir. *The Department of Energy* (7–10). Illus. 1989, Chelsea House $14.95 (0-87754-839-0). A description of this key agency that determines and administers the nation's energy policies. (Rev: BL 1/1/90; VOYA 2/90) [353.87]

2813 Walston, Mark. *The Department of the Treasury* (7–10). Illus. 1989, Chelsea House $14.95 (0-87754-848-X). This account describes the structures, duties, and history of this important department. (Rev: BL 1/1/90; SLJ 6/90; VOYA 4/90) [353.2]

2814 Weitsman, Madeline. *The Peace Corps* (7–10). Illus. 1989, Chelsea House $14.95 (0-87754-832-3). A history of the accomplishments of this agency is given plus details on how it is structured and administered. (Rev: BL 1/1/90; BR 1–2/90; SLJ 2/90; VOYA 2/90) [361]

2815 Yost, Graham. *The CIA* (7–12). Illus. 1989, Facts on File $16.95 (0-8160-1941-X). An overview of the history and present operation of our intelligence agency that is often critical of its covert operations. (Rev: BL 10/1/89; VOYA 12/89) [327.1]

State and Municipal Governments and Agencies

2816 Goode, Stephen. *The New Federalism: State's Rights in American History* (7–10). 1983, Watts LB $13.90 (0-531-04501-3). From the Constitutional Convention to President Reagan, a look at federalism. [353]

The Law and the Courts

2817 Bernstein, Richard B., and Jerome Agel. *The Supreme Court* (8–12). Illus. 1989, Walker LB $13.85 (0-8027-6835-0). An account that gives a history of the Supreme Court, details on landmark cases, and an outline of how it operates today. (Rev: BL 5/1/89; BR 3–4/89; SLJ 1/89; VOYA 4/89) [347]

2818 David, Andrew. *Famous Supreme Court Cases* (6–8). Illus. 1980, Lerner LB $8.95 (0-8225-1426-6). A number of cases are described including school desegregation and affirmative action. [342]

2819 Friedman, Leon. *The Supreme Court* (6–9). Illus. 1987, Chelsea House $14.95 (0-87754-825-0). A history of the U.S. Supreme Court is given plus information on its functions and key cases. (Rev: BL 6/1/87; SLJ 6–7/87) [347.37]

2820 Goode, Stephen. *The Controversial Court: Supreme Court Influences on American Life* (7–10). Illus. 1982, Messner LB $10.29 (0-671-43656-2); paper $4.95 (0-671-49496-1). The Supreme Court circa early 1980s, how it functions, and the characteristics of the Warren and Berger courts. [347]

2821 Hyde, Margaret O. *Juvenile Justice and Injustice* (7–10). Rev. ed. 1983, Watts LB $12.90 (0-531-04594-3). A description of the court procedures when young people are involved in serious crimes like rape or homocide. [345]

2822 Kolanda, Jo, and Patricia Curley. *Trial by Jury* (6–9). Illus. 1988, Watts $10.40 (0-531-10610-1). A history of the jury system from ancient Egypt to today plus information on the kinds of juries and their functions and problems. (Rev: BL 1/1/89; SLJ 11/88) [347.73]

2823 Kronenwetter, Michael. *Free Press v. Fair Trial: Television and Other Media in the Courtroom* (7–10). 1986, Watts $12.90 (0-531-10153-3). The author discusses the pros and cons of "trial by media." (Rev: BL 5/1/86; BR 9—10/86; SLJ 8/86) [345.73]

2824 Lawson, Don. *Landmark Supreme Court Cases* (6–12). Illus. 1987, Enslow $15.95 (0-89490-132-X). A discussion of the most famous Supreme Court cases each of which, like the Dred Scott case, had important social and political issues at stake. (Rev: BL 6/1/87; BR 9–10/87; SLJ 6–7/87; VOYA 10/87) [342.73]

2825 Rierden, Anne B. *Reshaping the Supreme Court: New Justices, New Directions* (8–12). 1988, Watts $11.90 (0-531-10512-1). A review of the Supreme Court and the justices' relation to the issues such as abortion that faces them. (Rev: BL 9/15/88; BR 9–10/88; SLJ 6–7/88; VOYA 2/89) [347.73]

2826 Rogers, Donald J. *Press versus Government: Constitutional Issues* (6–8). Illus. 1986, Messner LB $10.29 (0-671-61105-4). A description of several Supreme Court cases and decisions that relate to the freedom of and possible limitations on the press. (Rev: SLJ 5/87) [070]

2827 Sgroi, Peter. *The Living Constitution: Landmark Supreme Court Decisions* (7–12). 1987, Messner $10.95 (0-671-61972-1). Three Supreme Court decisions that interpreted governmental powers are analyzed including the Dred Scott and Watergate decisions. (Rev: BL 5/1/87; SLJ 6–7/87) [342.73]

2828 Weiss, Ann E. *The Supreme Court* (7–10). 1986, Enslow $14.95 (0-89490-131-1). A history of the Supreme Court which focuses on key cases and important justices. (Rev: BL 9/1/86; BR 9–10/87; SLJ 3/87) [347.73]

2829 Zerman, Melvyn Bernard. *Beyond a Reasonable Doubt: Inside the American Jury System* (7–10). Illus. 1981, Harper LB $12.89 (0-690-04095-4). A history of the jury system, its different forms, and how it functions. [345]

Politics

GENERAL

2830 Kronenwetter, Michael. *Are You a Liberal? Are You a Conservative?* (7–10). 1984, Watts $12.90 (0-531-04751-2). A history of the 2 concepts—liberal and conservative—and the role they have played in presidential administrations. [320]

2831 Kronenwetter, Michael. *Politics and the Press* (7–12). Illus. 1987, Watts $12.90 (0-531-10333-1). A discussion of the power of the press and why it must be free. (Rev: BL 5/15/87; BR 9–10/87; SLJ 9/87; VOYA 8–9/87) [302.2]

2832 Kronenwetter, Michael. *The Threat from Within: Unethical Politics and Politicians* (7–10). Illus. 1986, Watts $11.40 (0-531-10252-1). Illegal political practices such as stealing elections and bribery, as well as interest group pressures are covered. (Rev: BR 3–4/87; VOYA 2/87) [320]

2833 Meltzer, Milton. *American Politics: How It Really Works* (7–10). Illus. 1989, Morrow $12.95 (0-688-07494-2). Meltzer examines various aspects of government and political life with coverage on lobbyists, corruption, and the problems that face politicians today such as the homeless. (Rev: BL 4/15/89; BR 5–6/89; SLJ 12/89; VOYA 8/89) [320.473]

2834 Samuels, Cynthia K. *It's a Free Country! A Young Person's Guide to Politics & Elections* (6–9). Illus. 1988, Macmillan $12.95 (0-689-31416-7). An introduction to such topics as choosing candidates, different kinds of elections, and how teenagers can get involved. (Rev: BL 4/15/88) [324.973]

ELECTIONS

2835 Archer, Jules. *Winners and Losers: How Elections Work in America* (7–10). Illus. 1984, Harcourt $14.95 (0-15-297945-X). The mechanics of the election process are described with emphasis on the need to participate. [324.6]

2836 Raber, Thomas R. *Election Night* (6–9). Illus. 1988, Lerner LB $9.95 (0-8225-1751-5). Coverage in this book includes political parties, elections, and also a description of the night the candidate is elected. Also use: *Presidential Campaign* (1988). (Rev: SLJ 1/89) [324.6]

The Armed Forces

2837 Dolan, Edward F., Jr., and Margaret M. Scariano. *The Police in American Society* (7–12). Illus. 1988, Watts $13.90 (0-531-10608-X). Not simply a rundown on training and duties, this account explores the role of the police in today's society and the controversies that surround law enforcement practices today. (Rev: BL 3/1/89; BR 3–4/89; SLJ 2/89; VOYA 6/89) [363.2]

2838 Ferrell, Nancy Warren. *The U.S. Coast Guard* (6–10). Illus. 1989, Lerner LB $12.95 (0-8225-1431-1). The account gives a history of the Coast Guard, explains its functions, and tells what life is like in it. (Rev: SLJ 6/89) [355]

2839 Stefoff, Rebecca. *The U.S. Coast Guard* (7–9). Illus. 1989, Chelsea House $14.95 (1-55546-126-3). A thorough history of the Coast Guard plus firsthand accounts from 2 cadets. (Rev: BL 5/1/89; BR 1–2/90; SLJ 8/89; VOYA 8/89) [359.9]

2840 Sullivan, George. *The Thunderbirds* (5–9). Illus. 1986, Putnam $12.95 (0-396-08787-6). This book highlights the squadron of the U.S. Air Force that specializes in aerial demonstrations and stunts. (Rev: BR 11–12/86; SLJ 10/86) [355]

2841 Thum, Marcella, and Gladys Thum. *Airlift! The Story of the Military Airlift Command* (5–8). Illus. 1986, Dodd LB $12.95 (0-396-08529-6). The story of the Military Airlift Command since its beginnings in 1941 and a history of its most important exploits including the Berlin airlift. (Rev: SLJ 8/86) [355]

2842 Williams, Gene B. *Nuclear War, Nuclear Winter* (6–10). Illus. 1987, Watts $11.90 (0-531-10416-8). A history of the nuclear weapons race, its consequences, and possible alternatives are discussed. (Rev: BL 1/15/88; BR 5–6/88; SLJ 1/88; VOYA 6/88) [355.0217]

Taxes and Public Expenditure

2843 Davis, Bertha. *The National Debt* (8–12). Illus. 1987, Watts $11.90 (0-531-10415-X). Excellent background information is given to explain the current huge U.S. deficit. (Rev: BL 4/15/88; BR 1–2/88; SLJ 1/88) [336.3]

2844 Lubov, Andrea. *Taxes and Government Spending* (7–12). Illus. 1990, Lerner LB $14.95 (0-8225-1777-9). This book explores the current fiscal problems in America and the place of the national debt in the world economy. (Rev: BL 7/90; SLJ 8/90) [336.2]

Citizenship and Civil Rights

Civil and Human Rights

2845 Archer, Jules. *Who's Running Your Life? A Look at Young People's Rights* (7–9). 1979, Harcourt LB $7.95 (0-15-296058-9). A discussion of the rights of young people and the obligations associated with them. [346]

2846 Bentley, Judith. *Busing: The Continuing Controversy* (7–10). Illus. 1982, Watts LB $12.90 (0-531-04482-3). The reasons for busing, its history, and its accomplishments and failures are discussed. [370.19]

2847 Cook, Fred J. *The Ku Klux Klan: America's Recurring Nightmare* (7–10). Rev. ed. Illus. 1989, Messner LB $12.98 (0-671-68421-3). A history of the Klan from its post–Civil War origins to its present composition and activities. (Rev: BL 1/15/90; BR 5–6/90; VOYA 4/90) [322.4]

2848 Corbin, Carole Lynn. *The Right to Vote* (6–9). Illus. 1985, Watts $12.90 (0-531-04932-9). A history of how the right to vote was extended gradually during our history and of the struggles this involved. (Rev: BL 6/15/85; SLJ 8/85; VOYA 4/86) [324.6]

2849 Evans, J. Edward. *Freedom of the Press* (6–10). Illus. 1990, Lerner LB $9.95 (0-8225-1752-3). As well as a history of the struggle to keep the press free, this account discusses journalistic responsibility, censorship, and libel. (Rev: SLJ 7/90) [303.3]

2850 Freeman, Charles. *Human Rights* (6–8). Illus. 1988, Batsford $17.95 (0-7134-5543-8). A history of human rights from philosophers like Locke and our own Revolution to the present day. (Rev: BL 8/88; BR 11–12/88; SLJ 3/89) [323.4]

2851 Guggenheim, Martin, and Alan Sussman. *The Rights of Young People* (9–12). 1984, Southern Illinois Univ. paper $4.95 (0-8093-9959-8). In a question-and-answer format the authors discuss the legal rights of people under 18. [323.4]

2852 Hentoff, Nat. *American Heroes: In and Out of School* (7–12). 1987, Delacorte $14.95 (0-385-29565-0). Examples of everyday Americans—many of them students—who have stood up for civil liberties. (Rev: BL 11/1/87; BR 11–12/87; SLJ 9/87) [342.73]

2853 Holbrook, Sabra. *Fighting Back: The Struggle for Gay Rights* (7–12). 1987, Lodestar $13.95 (0-525-67187-0). The story of gay activism and the struggle of this group to fight discrimination and intolerance. (Rev: BR 11–12/87; SLJ 4/87) [323.4]

2854 King, Martin Luther, Jr. *The Words of Martin Luther King, Jr.* (7–12). Illus. 1983, Newmarket $10.95 (0-937858-28-5). A selection from the writings and speeches of Dr. King that covers a great number of topics. [323.4]

2855 Kronenwetter, Michael. *Taking a Stand against Human Rights Abuses* (6–12). Illus. 1990, Watts LB $13.40 (0-531-10921-6). An account of the worldwide oppression caused by both right- and left-wing governments. (Rev: BL 5/1/90) [323]

2856 Macdonald, Fiona. *Working for Equality* (6–9). Illus. 1988, Hampstead $11.90 (0-531-19500-7). The careers of 3 women—Millicent Fawcett from England, Rosa Parks from the United States, and Winnie Mandela from South Africa—and their struggle for equality. (Rev: BL 1/1/89; SLJ 2/89) [324.3]

2857 McKissack, Patricia, and Fredrick McKissack. *The Civil Rights Movement in Amer-*

ica from 1865 to the Present (5–9). Illus. 1987, Childrens $35.95 (0-516-00580-4). A history of the struggle by various minorities, with emphasis on black Americans, to achieve equality in America. (Rev: BL 6/1/87; SLJ 8/87) [973]

2858 Meltzer, Milton. *All Times, All Peoples: A World History of Slavery* (7–9). Illus. 1980, Harper LB $13.89 (0-06-024187-X). A history of slavery that begins with the ancient civilizations of Egypt and Rome and continues into the present. [326]

2859 Olney, Ross R., and Patricia J. Olney. *Up Against the Law: Your Legal Rights As a Minor* (7–12). 1985, Dutton $12.95 (0-525-66781-4). A clear, concise report on the legal rights of juveniles. (Rev: VOYA 12/85) [323.4]

2860 Rogers, Donald J. *Banned! Book Censorship in the Schools* (6–8). Illus. 1988, Messner $9.79 (0-671-63708-8). Interesting retelling of 9 cases of book banning in the nation's schools during the 1970s. (Rev: BL 9/1/88; SLJ 9/88; VOYA 10/88) [025.2]

2861 Selby, David. *Human Rights* (7–10). Illus. 1987, Cambridge paper $4.95 (0-521-27419-2). An exploration of the nature of civil rights, controversies surrounding their interpretation, and how they are observed throughout the world. (Rev: BL 2/15/88) [323.4]

2862 Smith, Betsy Covington. *Women Win the Vote* (6–9). Illus. 1989, Silver Burdett $16.98 (0-382-09837-4); paper $7.95 (0-382-09854-4). The story in text and illustrations of the struggle of the suffragette movement in the United States. (Rev: BL 11/1/89; BR 1–2/90) [324.6]

2863 Taylor, C. L. *Censorship* (5–8). Illus. 1986, Watts $10.90 (0-531-10211-4). After an international review of censorship, the author focuses on recent U.S. cases including one involving Judy Blume. (Rev: BL 12/1/86; SLJ 11/86; VOYA 2/87) [363.1]

2864 Totten, Samuel, and Milton Kleg. *Human Rights* (7–12). Illus. 1989, Enslow LB $16.95 (0-89490-156-7). A global look at such topics as torture, hunger, racism, treatment of prisoners, and genocide. (Rev: BL 8/89; SLJ 11/89; VOYA 10/89) [323.4]

2865 Webb, Sheyann, and Rachel West Nelson. *Selma, Lord, Selma: Girlhood Memories of the Civil-Rights Days* (7–12). Illus. 1980, Univ. of Alabama Pr. $9.95 (0-8173-0031-7). Recollections of 2 girls who, when only ages 8 and 9, participated in the Selma civil rights struggle. [323.4]

2866 Weiss, Ann E. *Who's to Know? Information, the Media, and Public Awareness* (6–9).

1990, Houghton $14.95 (0-395-49702-7). This book discusses the right to know, the importance of access to information and, on the other hand, the need for personal privacy. (Rev: BL 6/15/90; SLJ 5/90; VOYA 6/90) [363.2]

2867 Whitney, Sharon. *The Equal Rights Amendment: The History and the Movement* (7–9). 1984, Watts $12.90 (0-531-04768-7). A history of the proposed Equal Rights Amendment—what changes it would bring and why it was defeated. [324.5]

2868 Wilson, Reginald. *Our Rights: Civil Liberties and the U.S.* (7–12). Illus. 1988, Walker LB $14.85 (0-8027-6751-6). A book that explains what civil rights are, how we have these freedoms, and how to protect them. (Rev: SLJ 8/88; VOYA 8/88) [323.4]

2869 Woods, Geraldine. *Affirmative Action* (7–12). Illus. 1989, Watts $LB 12.90 (0-531-10657-8). After assessing the social and economic inequalities that exist in this country for women and racial minorities, the author describes affirmative action and the pros and cons surrounding it. (Rev: BL 6/1/89; BR 11–12/89; SLJ 7/89; VOYA 10/89) [342.73]

Immigration

2870 Ashabranner, Brent. *The New Americans: Changing Patterns in U.S. Immigration* (7–10). Illus. 1983, Putnam $14.95 (0-396-08140-1). An overview of patterns of immigration to the United States during the 1970s and early 1980s. [325.73]

2871 Bode, Janet. *New Kids on the Block: Oral Histories of Immigrant Teens* (7–10). 1989, Watts LB $12.90 (0-531-10794-9). Interviews with 11 youngsters who have come from such countries as Vietnam, El Salvador, Afghanistan, and the Philippines. (Rev: BL 9/15/89; BR 1–2/90; SLJ 10/89; VOYA 2/90) [305.2]

2872 Caroli, Betty Boyd. *Immigrants Who Returned Home* (6–10). Illus. 1990, Chelsea House $17.95 (0-87754-864-1). An account of immigrants who found life in the United States less than expected and therefore returned home to their countries. (Rev: BL 4/15/90; SLJ 8/90) [304.8]

2873 Dixon, Edward H., and Mark A. Galan. *The Immigration and Naturalization Service* (7–10). Illus. 1990, Chelsea House $14.95 (1-55546-113-1). A history of this agency with emphasis on how it operates today. (Rev: BL 5/15/90; SLJ 8/90; VOYA 8/90) [353]

2874 Freedman, Russell. *Immigrant Kids* (7–9). 1980, Dutton $13.95 (0-525-32538-7). The story of the treatment of the youngsters who came to this country in the waves of immigration 100 years ago. [973]

2875 Perrin, Linda. *Coming to America: Immigrants from the Far East* (7–9). Illus. 1980, Delacorte $9.95 (0-440-01072-1). The story of the problems faced by such groups as Japanese, Chinese, Filipinos, and Vietnamese when they come to this country. [325.73]

2876 Reimers, David M. *The Immigrant Experience* (6–9). Illus. 1989, Chelsea House $16.95 (0-87754-881-1). An overview of immigration into this country that gives details of what groups arrived and in what sequence. (Rev: BL 9/1/89; SLJ 9/89; VOYA 10/89) [325.7]

2877 Robbins, Albert. *Coming to America: Immigrants from Northern Europe* (7–9). 1982, Delacorte $9.95 (0-385-28138-2). Immigration to the United States from Scandinavia and neighboring countries is discussed in this book that also tells of the contributions these groups have made to American life. [305.8]

Ethnic Groups and Racial Prejudice

General and Miscellaneous

2878 Diamond, Arthur. *The Romanian Americans* (7–10). 1988, Chelsea House $16.95 (0-87754-898-6). This is part of a series from Chelsea House with more than 50 separate volumes called the Peoples of North America that deal with various ethnic groups. (Rev: BL 6/1/88; BR 11–12/88) [973]

2879 Gay, Kathlyn. *Bigotry* (7–12). Illus. 1989, Enslow LB $16.95 (0-89490-171-0). An account that deals primarily with the United States and explains the conditions that both produce and sustain bigotry. (Rev: BL 8/89; BR 1–2/90; SLJ 9/89; VOYA 12/89) [305.8]

2880 McKissack, Patricia, and Fredrick McKissack. *Taking a Stand against Racism and Racial Discrimination* (6–12). Illus. 1990, Watts LB $13.40 (0-531-10924-0). A fine survey of this subject plus a section on interviews with teens from various backgrounds. (Rev: BL 5/1/90) [305.8]

2881 Pascoe, Elaine. *Racial Prejudice* (7–12). Illus. 1985, Watts $12.90 (0-531-10057-X). A history of racism in the United States, its causes and consequences, and how much exists today are all covered in this book. (Rev: BL 12/15/85; BR 5–6/86; SLJ 4/86; VOYA 4/86) [305.8]

Blacks

2882 Bontemps, Arna. *100 Years of Negro Freedom* (7–12). 1961, Greenwood $24.75 (0-313-22218-5). The history of black Americans since the Civil War told primarily in terms of their leaders. [305.8]

2883 Griffin, John Howard. *Black Like Me* (7–12). 1961, Houghton $16.95 (0-395-25102-8). Griffin turned himself into a black man to experience the sting of prejudice firsthand. [323.4]

2884 Kosof, Anna. *The Civil Rights Movement and Its Legacy* (5–9). Illus. 1989, Watts LB $12.90 (0-531-10791-4). A history of the civil rights movement and its accomplishments in the past 20 years. (Rev: BL 1/1/90; SLJ 1/90) [323.1]

2885 Lester, Julius. *To Be a Slave* (7–9). Illus. 1968, Dial $13.95 (0-8037-8955-6). A powerful account of what it means to be a slave drawn largely from actual documents. [326]

2886 Meltzer, Milton, ed. *The Black Americans: A History in Their Own Words* (7–12). Illus. 1984, Harper LB $14.87 (0-690-04418-6). A history of the black people in America as told through such documents as letters, diaries, and articles. [305.8]

2887 Smead, Howard. *The Afro-Americans* (6–10). Illus. 1989, Chelsea House $16.95 (0-87754-854-4). The story of this immigrant group focusing on their treatment here in America; includes a special section on black entertainers. (Rev: BL 4/1/89; SLJ 5/89; VOYA 6/89) [973]

2888 Spangler, Earl. *Blacks in America* (6–9). 1980, Lerner $8.95 (0-8225-0207-0); paper $3.95 (0-8225-1017-0). Part of a large series of approximately 30 recommended titles each dealing with the history and contributions of a different minority group in America. [305.8]

Jews

2889 Arnold, Caroline, and Herma Silverstein. *Anti-Semitism: A Modern Perspective* (6–9). Illus. 1985, Messner LB $10.79 (0-671-49850-9). An international survey of anti-Semitism with particular focus on the United States. (Rev: BR 3–4/86; SLJ 4/85) [155.6]

2890 Brownstone, David M. *The Jewish-American Heritage* (7–12). Illus. 1988, Facts on File $15.95 (0-8160-1628-3). An account of the various waves of Jewish immigration, the integration of newcomers into American life, and a discussion of anti-Semitism. (Rev: BL 8/88; SLJ 5/88; VOYA 10/88) [973]

2891 Butwin, Frances. *The Jews in America* (6–9). 1980, Lerner $8.95 (0-8225-0217-8); paper $3.95 (0-8225-1015-4). The history of the Jewish migrations to this country is detailed plus information on the many contributions Jews have made to American life. Part of a series of approximately 30 recommended books each dealing with a different minority group. [305.8]

2892 Dolan, Edward F., Jr. *Anti-Semitism* (6–9). Illus. 1985, Watts $11.90 (0-531-10068-5). A history of the Jews, their religion, and how they have been the targets of irrational persecution through the centuries. (Rev: BL 2/15/86; BR 5–6/86; SLJ 2/86; VOYA 4/86) [305.8]

2893 Meltzer, Milton, ed. *The Jewish Americans: A History in Their Own Words* (7–12). Illus. 1982, Harper LB $13.89 (0-690-04228-0). Through the use of primary sources, the history of the Jews in America is reconstructed. [305.8]

2894 Meltzer, Milton. *The Jews in America: A Picture Album* (5–9). Illus. 1986, Jewish Publication Soc. LB $12.95 (0-8276-0246-4). In text and photographs, this book chronicles the history of the Jews in America from Colonial days in New Amsterdam to the present. (Rev: SLJ 10/86) [572]

2895 Meltzer, Milton. *World of Our Fathers: The Jews of Eastern Europe* (7–10). Illus. 1974, Farrar $13.95 (0-374-38530-0). A history of the European Jew that concentrates on the fate of those who lived in Russia. [305.8]

2896 Muggamin, Howard. *The Jewish Americans* (6–9). Illus. 1988, Chelsea House LB $16.95 (0-87754-887-0). After a brief look at Jewish history, this account covers the waves of immigration to America and the contributions of Jews to this country. This book is part of an extensive series on various ethnic and religious minorities in the United States. (Rev: BR 11–12/88; SLJ 11/88) [305.8]

2897 Patterson, Charles. *Anti-Semitism: The Road to the Holocaust and Beyond* (7–12). 1982, Walker $11.95 (0-8027-6470-3). A history of the philosophy of hate that led to the Holocaust and the problems that are still with us. [305.8]

2898 Shamir, Ilana, and Shlomo Shavit, eds. *The Young Reader's Encyclopedia of Jewish History* (5–10). Illus. 1987, Viking $15.95 (0-670-81738-4). From a home for nomadic tribes to the present, here is a history of Israel and the Jewish people in many brief chapters. (Rev: BL 3/15/88; SLJ 2/88) [909]

Indians of North America

2899 Ashabranner, Brent. *To Live in Two Worlds: American Indian Youth Today* (7–10). Illus. 1984, Putnam $13.95 (0-396-08321-8). Through text and photographs, young American Indians tell about their lives and hopes for the future. [970.004]

Hispanics

2900 Catalano, Julie. *Mexican Americans* (7–12). Illus. 1988, Chelsea House LB $16.95 (0-87754-857-9). A brief history of Mexico is given in this account that concentrates on the many contributions made by Mexican Americans. Part of an extensive series that also covers such ethnic groups as Romanian Americans, Greek Americans, and French Americans. (Rev: BR 11–12/88; VOYA 10/88) [305.8]

2901 Garver, Susan, and Paula McGuire. *Coming to North America from Mexico, Cuba, and Puerto Rico* (7–9). 1981, Dell paper $2.50 (0-317-13311-X). A brief account of why Hispanics have come to this country and of their progress here. [325.75]

2902 Gernand, Renee. *The Cuban Americans* (5–10). Illus. 1988, Chelsea House $16.95 (0-87754-869-2). An account that tells about the waves of immigration to the United States since the rise of Castro and the life of these immigrants here. Part of the extensive Peoples of North America series. (Rev: BL 2/1/89; SLJ 12/88; VOYA 4/89) [973]

2903 Harlan, Judith. *Hispanic Voters: A Voice in American Politics* (7–9). Illus. 1988, Watts $12.90 (0-531-10586-5). A history of Hispanic groups in the United States and their present political clout. (Rev: BL 12/1/88; BR 5–6/89; SLJ 12/88; VOYA 6/89) [323.1]

2904 Larsen, Ronald J. *The Puerto Ricans in America* (6–10). 1989, Lerner LB $8.95 (0-8225-0238-0); paper $3.95 (0-8225-1036-7). In addition to background material on Puerto Rico, this book supplies information on the problems and accomplishments of the Puerto Ricans who relocated in the United States. (Rev: SLJ 1/90) [973]

2905 Meltzer, Milton. *The Hispanic Americans* (7–10). Illus. 1982, Harper LB $13.89 (0-690-04111-X). The story of the various groups of Hispanics who have come to America and the problems that they have confronted. [305.8]

2906 Pinchot, Jane. *The Mexicans in America* (6–9). Rev. ed. 1979, Lerner LB $9.95 (0-8225-0222-4); paper $3.95 (0-8225-1016-2). The history of Mexican Americans is given plus a discussion of their many contributions. Part of an extensive series of about 30 recommended books each one dealing with a different minority group. [305.8]

2907 Winter, Frank H. *The Filipinos in America* (6–8). Illus. 1988, Lerner $8.95 (0-8225-0237-2); paper $3.95 (0-8225-1035-9). A brief history of the people of the Philippines, their immigrations to the United States, and their treatment and contributions in this country. (Rev: BL 12/1/88) [973]

Other Minorities

2908 Brownstone, David M. *The Chinese-American Heritage* (7–12). Illus. 1988, Facts on File $16.95 (0-8160-1627-5). A lucid, honest account of why many Chinese migrated to the United States, their treatment here, and their gradual assimilation into American life and culture. (Rev: BL 3/1/89; BR 5–6/89; VOYA 6/89) [973]

2909 Brownstone, David M. *The Irish-American Heritage* (7–12). Illus. 1989, Facts on File $16.95 (0-8160-1630-5). The story of the waves of Irish immigration and how these people became assimilated into American life. (Rev: BL 9/1/89; VOYA 2/90) [973]

2910 Cornelius, James M. *The Norwegian Americans* (5–10). Illus. 1988, Chelsea House $16.95 (0-87754-892-7). Background information is given on Norway and the contributions of Norwegians in the United States. (Rev: BL 2/1/89) [973]

2911 Costabel, Eva. *The Pennsylvania Dutch: Craftsmen and Farmers* (5–9). Illus. 1986, Macmillan LB $13.95 (0-689-31281-4). In drawings and text, this book sympathetically introduces the crafts and life-styles of the many religious groups that make up the Pennsylvania Dutch. (Rev: SLJ 10/86) [289.1]

2912 Daley, William. *The Chinese Americans* (6–9). Illus. 1987, Chelsea House $15.95 (0-87754-867-6). A nicely illustrated text that outlines the

history, culture, and customs of this group. (Rev: BL 1/1/88) [973]

2913 di Franco, J. Philip. *The Italian Americans* (6–9). Illus. 1987, Chelsea House $15.95 (0-87754-886-2). Background information on Italy, the problems faced by Italian immigrants, and their integration and contributions are outlined. (Rev: BL 1/1/88) [973]

2914 Ford, Douglas. *The Pacific Islanders* (6–10). Illus. 1989, Chelsea House $16.95 (0-87754-838-8). This account gives details on the homelands, culture, and history of these Americans from the Pacific. (Rev: BL 11/15/89; BR 5–6/90; SLJ 3/90) [973]

2915 Franck, Irene M. *The German-American Heritage* (7–12). Illus. 1988, Facts on File $16.95 (0-8160-1629-1). This book contains not only an account of the progress of Germans in this country but also a brief history of Germany. (Rev: BL 3/15/89; BR 5–6/89) [973]

2916 Franck, Irene M. *The Scandinavian-American Heritage* (7–12). Illus. 1988, Facts on File $15.95 (0-8160-1626-7). In addition to providing brief histories of Norway, Denmark, Sweden, Finland, and Iceland, the author tells of the immigration to this country from Scandinavia and of the contributions these immigrants made to American life. Part of a series of various immigrant groups. (Rev: BL 8/88; BR 11–12/88; SLJ 5/88; VOYA 10/88) [305.8]

2917 Galicich, Anne. *The German Americans* (6–10). Illus. 1989, Chelsea House $16.95 (1-55546-141-7). Material is given on the German American's homeland, but concentrates on their immigration to America and their experiences in the New World. (Rev: BL 4/1/89; VOYA 8/89) [971]

2918 Guttmacher, Peter. *The Scotch-Irish Americans* (7–10). Illus. 1988, Chelsea House LB $16.95 (0-87754-875-7). A volume devoted to the history and accomplishments of those people who came from Northern Ireland to North America. (Rev: BL 2/1/89; VOYA 4/89) [325.73]

2919 Harik, Elsa Marston. *The Lebanese in America* (6–8). Illus. 1987, Lerner LB $8.95 (0-8225-0234-8); paper $3.95 (0-8225-1032-4). This book tells about the history, geography, and culture of Lebanon and how its immigrants to this country have prospered. (Rev: SLJ 1/88) [305.8]

2920 Jones, Claire. *The Chinese in America* (6–9). 1972, Lerner $8.95 (0-8225-0223-3); paper $3.95 (0-8225-1003-0). The history and contributions of Chinese Americans are covered in this book that is part of an extensive series on minority groups in this country. [305.8]

2921 Katz, William Loren. *Black Indians: A Hidden Heritage* (7–10). 1986, Macmillan $15.95 (0-689-31196-6). A history of the group that represented a mixture of the Indian and black races and its role in opening up the West. (Rev: BL 6/15/86; SLJ 8/86) [970]

2922 Kitano, Harry. *Japanese Americans* (7–12). Illus. 1988, Chelsea House LB $17.95 (0-87754-856-0). This book covers such topics as the history, culture, and contributions of Japanese Americans. This is part of a series of over 50 books, each dealing with a different ethnic group. (Rev: BL 7/87; BR 11–12/88; SLJ 6–7/87; VOYA 10/88) [305.8]

2923 Lehrer, Brian. *The Korean Americans* (7–10). Illus. 1988, Chelsea House $16.95 (0-87754-888-9). An account that emphasizes the history and background culture of Korea. (Rev: BL 3/15/88; SLJ 4/88) [973]

2924 McGill, Allyson. *Swedish Americans* (7–12). Illus. 1988, Chelsea House LB $16.95 (1-55546-135-2). Along with information about their original homeland, this account supplies details on how Swedish Americans have prospered in this country. Also in this extensive series is a book on Danish Americans. (Rev: BR 11–12/88) [305.8]

2925 Magocsi, Paul R. *The Carpatho-Rusyn Americans* (6–10). Illus. 1989, Chelsea House $17.95 (0-87754-866-8). A narrative of the lifestyles, history, and culture of this group of immigrants from east Czechoslovakia and Poland. (Rev: BL 11/15/89; BR 5–6/90) [973]

2926 Magocsi, Paul R. *The Russian Americans* (6–9). Illus. 1989, Chelsea House LB $16.95 (0-87754-899-4). This account gives fine background information on the Russia these people left behind as well as their accomplishments in America. (Rev: SLJ 6/89) [973]

2927 Meltzer, Milton. *The Chinese Americans* (7–10). Illus. 1980, Harper LB $13.89 (0-690-04039-3). An account that covers Chinese American history from the importation of workers to help with railroad building to the present. [305.8]

2928 Naff, Alixa. *The Arab Americans* (7–10). Illus. 1988, Chelsea House $16.95 (0-87754-861-7). The homelands of the Arabs are described as well as their reasons for migrating and their contributions to American life. Part of an extensive series. (Rev: BL 3/15/88; SLJ 8/88) [973]

2929 Olsen, Victoria. *The Dutch Americans* (6–10). Illus. 1989, Chelsea House $16.95 (0-87754-873-0). The story of why the Dutch left their homeland including a section on their artwork here in America. (Rev: BL 4/1/89) [973]

2930 Osborn, Kevin. *The Ukrainian Americans* (6–9). Illus. 1989, Chelsea House LB $16.95 (1-55546-138-7). An account that tells about the culture and homeland of the Ukrainians and their reception in America. (Rev: BL 9/1/89) [973]

2931 Saxon-Ford, Stephanie. *The Czech Americans* (6–10). Illus. 1989, Chelsea House $16.95 (0-87754-870-6). In this, part of an extensive series, the contribution of Czech Americans, their homeland, and their treatment in the United States are highlighted. (Rev: BL 11/15/89; BR 11–12/89; SLJ 5/90; VOYA 12/89) [973]

2932 Shapiro, E. *The Croatian Americans* (6–9). Illus. 1989, Chelsea House $16.95 (0-87754-891-9). This book covers the native land of the Croatians and their social customs and assimilation into American life. (Rev: BL 9/1/89; BR 11–12/89) [973]

2933 Stern, Jennifer. *The Filipino Americans* (6–10). Illus. 1989, Chelsea House $16.95 (0-87754-877-3). A history of the Filipino immigrants to this country, their native culture, and how they have been treated in America. (Rev: BL 11/15/89; BR 5–6/90; SLJ 3/90) [973]

2934 Stolarik, M. Mark. *The Slovak Americans* (7–10). Illus. 1988, Chelsea House $16.95 (1-55546-134-4). The ethnic traditions and the contributions of this group are highlighted. (Rev: BL 3/15/88) [973]

2935 Toor, Rachel. *The Polish Americans* (5–10). 1988, Chelsea House $16.95 (0-87754-895-1). Why and when the great waves of Polish immigrants reached these shores are explored and their contributions to present-day American live. (Rev: BL 2/1/89) [973]

2936 Waldstreicher, David. *The Armenian Americans* (6–9). Illus. 1989, Chelsea House LB $16.95 (0-87754-862-5). The story of the immigration and gradual assimilation of these people in America plus coverage on Armenia, the land they left behind. (Rev: BL 2/1/89; SLJ 6/89) [973]

2937 Watts, J. F. *The Irish Americans* (7–12). Illus. 1988, Chelsea House LB $16.95 (0-87754-855-2). Both Irish history and the progress of the Irish in America are given in this volume that is part of an extensive series that covers the story of other immigrant groups. (Rev: BL 1/1/88; SLJ 10/88) [305.8]

Forms of Dissent

2938 Bornstein, Jerry. *The Neo-Nazis: The Threat of the Hitler Cult* (7–10). 1986, Messner $11.98 (0-671-50238-7). After a general description of Hitler's party of hate, the author describes Nazism in America and its real and possible dangers. (Rev: BL 1/15/87; SLJ 2/87) [324.273]

2939 Meltzer, Milton. *Ain't Gonna Study War No More* (7–10). Illus. 1985, Harper LB $11.89 (0-06-024200-0). From the Revolution to the Vietnam War, this is a study of the individuals and groups who have declared themselves pacifists. (Rev: BL 5/1/85; BR 1–2/86; SLJ 9/85; VOYA 8/86) [327.1]

Social Concerns and Conflicts

Environmental Problems

General

2940 Gardiner, Brian. *Energy Demands* (5–8). Illus. 1990, Gloucester LB $11.90 (0-531-17197-3). This account tells how we presently satisfy our energy needs and what the future will hold if global planning is not followed. (Rev: BL 5/15/90) [333.79]

2941 Gay, Kathlyn. *The Greenhouse Effect* (7–12). Illus. 1986, Watts $12.90 (0-531-10154-1). A discussion of why the carbon dioxide level is rising in the atmosphere, its effects, and what can be done about it. (Rev: BL 6/1/86; SLJ 8/86) [363.7]

2942 Gay, Kathlyn. *Ozone* (7–12). 1989, Watts LB $12.90 (0-531-10777-9). An account of one of our greatest environmental problems and the fight for clean air. (Rev: BL 12/15/89; BR 3–4/90; SLJ 12/89; VOYA 2/90) [363.73]

2943 Gay, Kathlyn. *Silent Killers: Radon and Other Hazards* (8–12). Illus. 1988, Watts $12.90 (0-531-10598-9). An examination of dangerous pollutants such as chemicals like Agent Orange and carbon monoxide plus radon and water pollutants. (Rev: BL 11/15/88; BR 3–4/89; SLJ 12/88; VOYA 4/89) [363.1]

2944 Gutnik, Martin J. *Ecology* (7–9). 1984, Watts $12.90 (0-531-04765-2). This book not only explains environmental problems but gives a variety of science projects involving ecology. [574.5]

2945 Johnson, Rebecca L. *The Greenhouse Effect: Life on a Warmer Planet* (6–9). Illus. 1990, Lerner LB $15.95 (0-8225-1591-1). A detailed description of the causes of the global warming

that is taking place and of its consequences. (Rev: BL 6/15/90; SLJ 8/90) [363.73]

2946 Lambert, David. *Planet Earth 2000* (6–8). Illus. 1985, Facts on File $12.95 (0-8160-1153-2). This book reviews the major problems involving ecology today including misuse of resources, pollution, depletion of energy supplies, and overpopulation. (Rev: BL 12/1/85; SLJ 2/86) [304.2]

2947 Markham, Adam. *The Environment* (6–8). Illus. 1988, Rourke $11.95 (0-86592-286-1). Such dangers to our environment as acid rain, the breakdown of the ozone layer, and the greenhouse effect are discussed. (Rev: BL 12/15/88; SLJ 5/89) [363.7]

2948 Middleton, Nick. *Atlas of Environmental Issues* (7–12). Illus. 1989, Facts on File $16.95 (0-8160-2023-X). All sorts of topics involving the environment, such as pollution, are graphically represented in diagrams and maps. (Rev: SLJ 9/89) [616.9]

2949 Miller, Christina G., and Louise A. Berry. *Wastes* (6–8). Illus. 1986, Watts $10.40 (0-531-10130-4). The problems in disposing of household wastes and garbage are the focus of this book. (Rev: BL 6/15/86; BR 9–10/86; SLJ 8/86; VOYA 6/87) [363.7]

2950 O'Connor, Karen. *Garbage* (7–10). Illus. 1989, Lucent Books LB $10.95 (1-56006-100-6). A discussion of this environmental problem and governmental action and policies. (Rev: SLJ 1/90) [628.4]

2951 Pringle, Laurence. *Restoring Our Earth* (7–10). Illus. 1987, Enslow $13.95 (0-89490-143-5). An account that tells us how we can restore Earth to roughly the same condition that it once was. (Rev: BL 9/1/87; SLJ 1/88) [333.7]

2952 Pringle, Laurence. *Throwing Things Away: From Middens to Resource Recovery* (7–10). Illus. 1986, Harper $12.95 (0-690-04420-8). The author describes the garbage we produce everyday, what happens to it, and the problems it causes. (Rev: BL 3/15/87; BR 3–4/87; SLJ 3/87; VOYA 12/86) [363.7]

2953 Taylor, Ron. *Facts on Pesticides and Fertilizers in Farming* (5–8). Illus. 1990, Watts LB $11.90 (0-531-10919-4). The author uses both text and visuals to show the dangers to our environment in the use of pesticides and some types of fertilizers in farming. Also use: *Facts on Radon and Asbestos* (1990). (Rev: BL 7/90) [668]

Pollution

2954 Brown, Joseph E. *Oil Spills: Danger in the Sea* (7–9). Illus. 1978, Putnam $8.95 (0-396-07607-6). Though dated in coverage, this account gives good background information on the causes, nature, and prevention of oil spills. [363.7]

2955 Finney, Shan. *Noise Pollution* (7–9). Illus. 1984, Watts $12.90 (0-531-04855-1). Questions such as what is the difference between noise and sound and can we be harmed by noise are answered here. [363.7]

2956 Gay, Kathlyn. *Acid Rain* (7–10). 1983, Watts LB $12.90 (0-531-04682-6). The causes, effects, and problems of this growing public problem. [363.7]

2957 Johnstone, Hugh. *Facts on Domestic Waste and Industrial Pollutants* (5–8). Illus. 1990, Watts LB $11.90 (0-531-10912-7). With the use of many visuals, the problem of pollution from personal garbage and industrial wastes is explored. Also use: *Facts on Nuclear Waste and Radioactivity* (1990). (Rev: BL 7/90; SLJ 7/90) [363.72]

2958 Kavaler, Lucy. *The Dangers of Noise* (7–9). Illus. 1978, Harper LB $12.89 (0-690-03906-9). After a discussion of sound waves and the nature of noise, Kavaler describes the problem of noise pollution. [363.7]

2959 Kiefer, Irene. *Poisoned Land: The Problem of Hazardous Waste* (7–10). Illus. 1981, Macmillan LB $12.95 (0-689-30837-X). The nature of chemical waste is explained, disasters like Love Canal are described, and possible future solutions are proposed. [363.7]

2960 Miller, Christina G., and Louise A. Berry. *Acid Rain: A Sourcebook for Young People* (6–8). Illus. 1986, Messner $10.98 (0-671-60177-6). An account that describes the origins of acid

rain, its effects, and what can be done about it. (Rev: BL 2/15/87; SLJ 1/87) [363.7]

2961 Miller, Christina G., and Louise A. Berry. *Coastal Rescue: Preserving Our Seashores* (6–9). Illus. 1989, Macmillan $12.95 (0-689-31288-1). A description of our coastlines, their ecology, and problems with pollution. (Rev: BL 6/15/89; SLJ 10/89; VOYA 6/89) [333.91]

2962 Newton, David E. *Taking a Stand against Environmental Pollution* (7–10). Illus. 1990, Watts LB $13.40 (0-531-10923-2). From the pioneering work of Thoreau and John Muir to today's environmentalists, this is an account that also stresses what every citizen can do to help. (Rev: BL 6/1/90; SLJ 7/90; VOYA 8/90) [363.7]

2963 Pringle, Laurence. *Rain of Troubles: The Science and Politics of Acid Rain* (7–12). 1988, Macmillan $13.95 (0-02-775370-0). The causes and effects of acid rain are explained as well as a number of proposed solutions. (Rev: BL 5/15/88; SLJ 4/88; VOYA 10/88) [363.7]

2964 Sandak, Cass R. *A Reference Guide to Clean Air* (7–12). 1990, Enslow LB $17.95 (0-89490-261-X). In a dictionary format, 200 words and phrases related to air pollution are defined. (Rev: BL 9/1/90) [363.73]

2965 Weiss, Malcolm E. *Toxic Waste: Clean-Up, or, Cover-Up?* (7–10). Illus. 1984, Watts LB $12.90 (0-531-04755-5). The different kinds of toxic wastes are described (e.g., PCBs) and methods of storage and disposal. [363.7]

2966 Woods, Geraldine, and Harold Woods. *Pollution* (7–10). Illus. 1985, Watts LB $9.40 (0-531-04916-7). This book describes the effects on the environment of such substances as pesticides, garbage, and toxic and nuclear wastes. (Rev: SLJ 10/85) [363.7]

Population Problems

General and Miscellaneous

2967 Becklake, John, and Sue Becklake. *The Population Explosion* (5–8). Illus. 1990, Gloucester LB $11.90 (0-531-17198-1). An account that stresses the problems an out-of-control population growth can bring and what can be done about it. (Rev: BL 5/15/90) [304.6]

2968 Fyson, Nance Lui. *Feeding the World* (6–8). Illus. 1985, Batsford $19.95 (0-7134-4264-6). This account introduces the world's increasing food problems, gives material on staple crops, and discusses production and distribution. (Rev: BL 5/15/85) [338.19]

2969 Gallant, Roy A. *The Peopling of Planet Earth: Human Population Growth through the Ages* (7–12). Illus. 1990, Macmillan $15.95 (0-02-735772-4). A history of patterns of world population, the present conditions in relation to resources, and the different future we face. (Rev: BL 3/1/90; VOYA 4/90) [304.6]

2970 Gibb, Christopher. *Food or Famine?* (5–9). Illus. 1987, Rourke LB $14.60 (0-86592-279-9). A description of world hunger, its causes, and possible solutions. (Rev: SLJ 3/88) [904]

2971 Hampton, Janie. *World Health* (6–8). Illus. 1988, Rourke $11.95 (0-86592-281-0). An international look at how basics of health care vary in their application, particularly in the Third World. (Rev: BL 12/15/88; SLJ 5/89) [362.1]

2972 Hyde, Margaret O., and Lawrence E. Hyde. *Missing Children* (7–10). Illus. 1985, Watts $12.95 (0-531-10073-1). The various kinds of missing children are described (e.g., runaways) along with measures taken to find them. (Rev: BL 10/15/85; SLJ 12/85) [362.7]

2973 McGraw, Eric. *Population Growth* (5–9). Illus. 1987, Rourke LB $14.60 (0-86592-276-4). This work gives a history of the world's population growth and special coverage on China, India, and Mexico. (Rev: SLJ 3/88) [304.6]

2974 Nam, Charles B. *Our Population: The Changing Face of America* (7–10). Illus. 1988, Walker LB $14.85 (0-8027-6753-2). An informative, well-organized book about current national demographics and trends for the future. (Rev: SLJ 6–7/88) [304.6]

Crime and Prisons

2975 Adams, Barbara Johnston. *Crime Mysteries* (6–10). Illus. 1988, Watts $11.90 (0-531-10517-2). Five famous crimes including Lizzie Borden and Judge Crater's disappearance are retold. (Rev: BL 6/1/88; SLJ 6–7/88; VOYA 8/88) [364.1]

2976 Berger, Melvin. *Police Lab* (7–9). 1976, Harper LB $12.89 (0-381-99620-4). How criminals are caught and crimes investigated using scientific methods and equipment. [363.2]

2977 Dautrich, Jack, and Vivian Huff. *Big City Detective* (6–8). Illus. 1986, Dutton $13.95 (0-525-67183-8). Using actual case histories as a focus, the authors outline the duties of a typical

urban detective. (Rev: BL 4/15/87; SLJ 3/87) [363.2]

2978 Davis, Bertha. *Instead of Prison* (7–12). Illus. 1986, Watts $12.90 (0-531-10237-8). The author describes our present prison system and discusses alternatives to incarceration. (Rev: BL 1/15/87; BR 1–2/87; SLJ 1/87; VOYA 6/87) [364.6]

2979 Landau, Elaine. *Teenage Violence* (7–12). 1990, Messner LB $11.98 (0-671-70153-3); paper $5.95 (0-671-70154-1). All kinds of violence perpetrated by young people, such as racist attacks and date rape, are examined. (Rev: BL 4/15/90; SLJ 9/90) [364.3]

2980 Loeb, Robert H., Jr. *Crime and Capital Punishment* (7–10). Illus. 1986, Watts LB $12.90 (0-531-10209-2). A history of capital punishment is given plus arguments pro and con about its justification. A revision of the 1978 title. (Rev: BL 1/1/87; BR 3–4/87; VOYA 4/87) [364.6]

2981 Solomon, Louis. *The Ma and Pa Murders and Other Perfect Crimes* (7–9). 1976, Harper $11.70 (0-397-31577-5). Here is an account of 6 unsolved crimes including the murders involving Lizzie Borden. [364]

2982 Weiss, Ann E. *Prisons: A System in Trouble* (7–12). 1988, Enslow $14.95 (0-89490-165-6). A history of penal institutions, a description of them today, and a profile of an average inmate. (Rev: BL 10/15/88; SLJ 11/88; VOYA 2/89) [365]

Illiteracy

2983 Rue, Nancy N. *Coping with an Illiterate Parent* (7–12). 1990, Rosen $12.95 (0-8239-1070-9). The causes, problems, and treatment of illiteracy as seen from a teenager's point of view. (Rev: BL 3/1/90) [306]

Poverty and Homeless People

2984 Ashabranner, Brent. *Children of the Maya: A Guatemalan Indian Odyssey* (6–9). Illus. 1986, Dodd LB $14.95 (0-396-08786-8). The story of the Mayan Indians from Guatemala who are refugees in Florida. (Rev: SLJ 8/86) [341.4]

2985 Ashabranner, Brent. *Dark Harvest: Migrant Farmworkers in America* (7–10). Illus. 1985, Dodd $14.95 (0-396-08624-1). A sobering and tragic picture of the use of migrant workers in America today and of their stilted and bleak lives. (Rev: BL 9/1/85; BR 9–10/86; SLJ 12/85) [331.5]

2986 Ashabranner, Brent, and Melissa Asha-branner. *Into a Strange Land: Unaccompanied Refugee Youth in America* (6–9). Illus. 1987, Dodd $12.95 (0-396-08841-4). A sad account of how immigrant children who are alone in the United States manage to survive. (Rev: BL 7/87; BR 11–12/87; SLJ 6-7/87; VOYA 10/87) [362.8]

2987 Coil, Suzanne M. *The Poor in America* (7–10). Illus. 1989, Messner LB $11.98 (0-671-69052-3). A history of poverty in America, starting with colonial times but with special emphasis on the present. (Rev: BL 12/1/89; BR 3–4/90; SLJ 2/90; VOYA 4/90) [362.5]

2988 Davis, Bertha. *America's Housing Crisis* (7–10). Illus. 1990, Watts LB $12.90 (0-531-10917-8). This account traces the causes of the present shortage of middle- and lower-income housing and of the plight of the homeless. (Rev: BL 6/1/90; SLJ 8/90; VOYA 8/90) [363.5]

2989 Fine, John Christopher. *The Hunger Road* (7–10). 1988, Macmillan $12.95 (0-689-31361-6). A hard-hitting account of the causes of world hunger and of the fact that fortunes are made out of human misery. (Rev: BL 1/1/89; SLJ 11/88; VOYA 12/88) [363.8]

2990 Hauser, Pierre N. *Illegal Aliens* (7–10). Illus. 1990, Chelsea House $17.95 (0-87754-889-7). A history of our immigration laws sets the stage for a discussion of the illegal aliens, particularly from Mexico, who are currently in the country. (Rev: BL 6/15/90; SLJ 8/90) [325.73]

2991 Heater, Derek. *Refugees* (6–10). Illus. 1989, Rourke LB $11.95 (0-86592-077-X). Through text, illustrations, and maps, the plight of the world's homeless is explored. (Rev: SLJ 6/89) [325]

2992 Hyde, Margaret O. *The Homeless: Profiling the Problem* (5–9). Illus. 1989, Enslow $14.95 (0-89490-159-1). The author describes the 4 million homeless in America, how they became street people, and their problems. (Rev: BL 6/15/89; SLJ 5/89) [362.5]

2993 Kosof, Anna. *Homeless in America* (7–12). Illus. 1988, Watts $11.90 (0-531-10519-9). The causes of the present situation and the heartbreaking plight of the homeless are well treated in this account. (Rev: BL 8/88; BR 11–12/88; SLJ 8/88; VOYA 12/88) [362.5]

2994 Landau, Elaine. *The Homeless* (7–12). 1987, Messner $9.79 (0-671-63492-5). The author introduces many homeless people and the reasons for their plight. (Rev: BL 1/15/88; SLJ 1/88; VOYA 12/87) [362.5]

2995 Meltzer, Milton. *Poverty in America* (6–9). Illus. 1986, Morrow $12.95 (0-688-05911-2). This is a survey of the growing problem of poverty, its causes, and a plea to redistribute some of our wealth. (Rev: BL 8/86; BR 9–10/86; SLJ 8/86; VOYA 8–10/86) [362.5]

2996 O'Connor, Karen. *Homeless Children* (5–10). Illus. 1989, Lucent Books LB $10.95 (1-56006-109-X). A short but powerful book on the causes of homelessness and the plight of children caught up in this tragedy. (Rev: BL 2/1/90; SLJ 4/90) [361.7]

Unemployment and Labor Problems

2997 Claypool, Jane. *Unemployment* (7–9). Illus. 1983, Watts LB $12.90 (0-531-04586-2). The causes and results of mass unemployment and how to avoid it. [331.1]

2998 Sproule, Anna. *Solidarity* (6–9). Illus. 1988, Watts $11.90 (0-531-19503-1). The careers of 3 female labor leaders including Mother Jones of the United States. (Rev: BL 1/1/89; SLJ 2/89) [303.4]

Public Morals

2999 Dolan, Edward F., Jr. *Gun Control: A Decision for Americans* (7–10). Rev. ed. Illus. 1982, Watts LB $12.90 (0-531-02202-1). Opposing views are given on this controversial subject plus proposed solutions. [363.3]

3000 Dolan, Edward F., Jr. *Matters of Life and Death* (7–10). 1982, Watts LB $12.90 (0-531-04497-1). Such topics as abortion, euthanasia, and birth control are discussed from the moral standpoint. [179]

3001 Francis, Dorothy B. *Vandalism: The Crime of Immaturity* (7–10). 1983, Lodestar $11.95 (0-525-66774-1). This account highlights the various kinds of vandalism, why people destroy property, and how this crime is being deterred. [364.1]

3002 Gardner, Sandra. *Street Gangs* (7–10). Illus. 1983, Watts LB $12.90 (0-531-04666-4). The nature of gang membership, their activities, and effects in the community are 3 topics covered. [364.3]

3003 Gorman, Carol. *Pornography* (8–12). Illus. 1988, Watts $11.90 (0-531-10591-1). After a general discussion of the meaning of pornography and its many kinds, the author outlines the issues involved—religious, moral, and legal. (Rev: BL 11/15/88; BR 1–2/89; SLJ 11/88; VOYA 4/89) [363.4]

3004 Langone, John. *Violence! Our Fastest-Growing Public Health Problem* (7–12). 1984, Little $14.95 (0-316-51431-4). Individual and group violence is examined with sections on who commits violence, why, and the consequences of violence. [303.6]

Sex Roles

3005 Fisher, Maxine P. *Women in the Third World* (7–12). Illus. 1989, Watts LB $13.90 (0-531-10666-7). An account of the position of women in a number of the world's poorest countries, including India and Ethiopia. (Rev: BL 7/89; BR 11–12/89; SLJ 7/89; VOYA 10/89) [305.4]

Social Change and Futurism

3006 Taylor, Paula. *The Kids' Whole Future Catalog* (6–8). 1982, Random paper $6.95 (0-394-85090-4). A project book that has a peek at life in the next century. [003]

3007 Wehmeyer, Lillian Biermann. *Futuristics* (6–8). Illus. 1986, Watts $10.40 (0-531-10116-9). A book that explains tools and techniques used to predict the future. (Rev: BL 5/15/86; BR 9–10/86; SLJ 8/86; VOYA 12/86) [303.4]

Terrorism

3008 Arnold, Terrell E., and Moorhead Kennedy. *Think about Terrorism: The New Warfare* (7–10). Illus. 1988, Walker LB $14.85 (0-8027-6757-5). Using a question-and-answer approach, this book explores the global problem of terrorism. (Rev: SLJ 9/88; VOYA 8/88) [322.4]

3009 Coker, Christopher. *Terrorism* (5–8). Illus. 1986, Gloucester $11.90 (0-531-17030-6). An account that covers international terrorism, its causes, effects, and possible solutions. (Rev: BL 11/15/86) [303.62]

3010 Coker, Christopher. *Terrorism and Civil Strife* (5–8). Illus. 1987, Watts $12.90 (0-531-

10385-4). The global problems of terrorism and possible solutions are outlined. (Rev: BL 2/15/88; SLJ 3/88) [303.62]

3011 Edwards, Richard. *International Terrorism* (6–8). Illus. 1988, Rourke $11.95 (0-86592-285-3). An overview of the causes of terrorism, the principal gangs responsible for it, and the difficulties of international control. (Rev: BL 12/15/88; SLJ 5/89) [303.6]

3012 Harris, Jonathan. *The New Terrorism: Politics of Violence* (7–10). 1983, Messner LB $9.97 (0-671-45807-8); paper $4.95 (0-671-49488-0). For better readers, an account on the roots of international terrorism. The coverage in this book ends in the early 1980s. [322.4]

3013 Meltzer, Milton. *The Terrorists* (7–10). Illus. 1983, Harper LB $12.89 (0-06-024194-2). A systematic look at terrorism at home and abroad. [303.6]

3014 Raynor, Thomas. *Terrorism: Past, Present, Future* (7–10). 1982, Watts LB $11.90 (0-531-04499-8). An account that traces the roots of terrorism from the Reign of Terror after the French Revolution to today's international conspiracies. [303.6]

3015 Taylor, L. B., Jr. *Hostage! Kidnapping and Terrorism in Our Time* (7–10). Illus. 1989, Watts $12.90 (0-531-10661-6). The use of hostage-taking as a terrorist weapon is discussed. (Rev: BL 12/15/89; BR 1–2/90; SLJ 2/90; VOYA 2/90) [364.1]

Urban and Rural Life

3016 Gay, Kathlyn. *Cities Under Stress* (6–9). 1985, Watts $12.90 (0-531-04926-4). The author explores the many problems facing American cities today, such as crime, pollution, poor sewage systems, and bad highways. (Rev: VOYA 12/85) [307.7]

3017 Haskins, James. *Street Gangs: Yesterday and Today* (7–9). Illus. 1977, Hastings paper $4.95 (0-8038-6740-9). A history of street gangs and of their present configuration. [364.3]

3018 Royston, Robert. *Cities 2000* (6–8). Illus. 1985, Facts on File $12.95 (0-8160-1154-0). This British import discusses the history of cities but concentrates on the problems that cities are facing today most of which are related to their growth. (Rev: BL 12/1/85; SLJ 1/86) [307.7]

3019 Steinberg, Barbara. *Who Keeps America Clean?* (7–9). Illus. 1977, Random paper $2.50

(0-394-83283-3). The story of urban sanitation and how it evolved. [363.7]

3020 Von Tscharner, Renata, and Ronald Lee Fleming. *New Providence: A Changing Cityscape* (5–8). Illus. 1987, Harcourt LB $10.95 (0-15-200540-4). The evolution of a small fictitious American city from 1910 to the present. (Rev: SLJ 3/87) [307.7]

3021 Webb, Margot. *Coping with Street Gangs* (7–10). Rosen, $12.95 (0-8239-1071-7). Why gangs are formed and the types of people that are in them are discussed as well as how to handle them if you are a victim, member, or friend of a member. (Rev: VOYA 8/90) [364.3]

Economics and Business

General and Miscellaneous

3022 Aaseng, Nathan. *Better Mousetraps: Product Improvements That Led to Success* (5–8). Illus. 1990, Lerner LB $10.95 (0-8225-0680-7). From Tupperware products to the Rolls Royce, the author discusses a variety of products and how creative people have improved them. (Rev: BL 3/1/90; SLJ 4/90) [658.5]

3023 Aaseng, Nathan. *Midstream Changes: People Who Started Over and Made It Work* (5–8). Illus. 1990, Lerner LB $10.95 (0-8225-0681-5). Eight accounts about such business people as Colonel Sanders and Mary Kay who turned disappointing careers into successful ones. (Rev: BL 5/15/90; SLJ 8/90) [331.7]

3024 Davies, Wendy. *The International Debt Crisis* (7–9). Illus. 1989, Rourke LB $15.93 (0-86592-076-1). A basic account that deals primarily with the troubled finances of developing countries. (Rev: BL 6/15/89; SLJ 6/89) [336.3]

3025 Kronenwetter, Michael. *Capitalism vs. Socialism: Economic Policies of the USA and the USSR* (7–9). Illus. 1986, Watts $12.90 (0-531-10152-5). This book explains the difference between the ideas of Adam Smith and Karl Marx and how their application has affected the world today. (Rev: BL 7/86; BR 11–12/86; SLJ 8/86; VOYA 12/86) [330.1]

3026 Maybury, Richard J. *Whatever Happened to Penny Candy? : For Students, Business People and Investors* (7–10). Illus. 1989, Bluestocking paper $4.95 (0-942617-03-7). The explanation of how governments make and control their currencies. (Rev: SLJ 7/89) [330]

3027 O'Toole, Thomas. *The Economic History of the United States* (7–12). Illus. 1990, Lerner LB $14.95 (0-8225-1776-0). A brief outline of the economic history of the United States that explains the influence of several key economists. (Rev: BL 7/90) [330.973]

3028 Wallace, G. David. *Money Basics* (7–9). Illus. 1984, Prentice $9.95 (0-13-600479-2). Such terms as wages, inflation, and interest rates are defined. [332.4]

Economic Systems and Institutions

General and Miscellaneous

3029 Koslow, Philip. *The Securities and Exchange Commission* (7–10). Illus. 1990, Chelsea House $14.95 (1-55546-119-0). A straightforward history of this agency with current information including the security fraud scandals. (Rev: BL 5/15/90; VOYA 8/90) [353]

3030 Lunt, Steven D. *Free Enterprise in America* (7–10). Illus. 1985, Watts $12.90 (0-531-10061-8). The relationship between private business interests and the government is explored in this discussion of American economics. (Rev: BL 12/15/85) [330.12]

3031 Taylor, Gary. *The Federal Reserve System* (7–10). Illus. 1989, Chelsea House $14.95 (1-55546-136-0). The history and present-day functions of this key regulator of the nation's finances are outlined. (Rev: BL 1/1/90; BR 1–2/90; SLJ 6/90) [332.1]

Stock Exchanges

3032 Scott, Elaine. *Stocks and Bonds, Profits and Losses: A Quick Look at Financial Markets* (7–12). Illus. 1985, Watts $11.90 (0-531-04938-8-8). An excellent overview on what is involved in making stock and bond investments geared specifically to the teenage potential investor. (Rev: BL 6/15/85; BR 11–12/85; SLJ 8/85; VOYA 12/85) [332.63]

Consumerism

3033 Schmitt, Lois. *Smart Spending: A Consumer's Guide* (6–9). 1989, Macmillan $11.95 (0-684-19035-4). A thorough account that covers such topics as advertising promotions, consumer fraud, mail-order problems, budgets, warranties, and consumerism. (Rev: BL 5/1/89; BR 11–12/89; SLJ 7/89; VOYA 12/89) [640.73]

3034 Walz, Michael K. *The Law and Economics: Your Rights As a Consumer* (7–12). Illus. 1990, Lerner LB $14.95 (0-8225-1779-5). This book explores legal concepts as they apply to such everyday matters as contracts, warranties, and security deposits. (Rev: BL 7/90) [343.794]

Employment and Jobs

3035 Berger, Gilda. *Women, Work and Wages* (7–9). Illus. 1986, Watts $12.90 (0-531-10074-X). An account of the past and present status of the American working woman. (Rev: BL 5/1/86; BR 9–10/86; SLJ 8/86) [331.4]

3036 Claypool, Jane. *The Worker in America* (6–9). Illus. 1985, Watts $12.90 (0-531-04933-7). This is a history of the labor force in America with special chapters on women, minorities, and unions. (Rev: BL 8/85; BR 11–12/85; SLJ 10/85; VOYA 12/85) [331]

Labor Unions

3037 Bornstein, Jerry. *Unions in Transition* (7–9). 1981, Messner LB $10.79 (0-671-41913-7). This account looks at labor unions today, the role they play in the American economy, and their possible future. [331.88]

3038 Flagler, John J. *The Labor Movement in the United States* (7–12). Illus. 1990, Lerner LB $14.95 (0-8225-1778-7). The story of the struggle to found labor unions, their years of power, and current decline. (Rev: BL 7/90) [331.88]

3039 Haskins, James. *The Long Struggle: The Story of American Labor* (7–9). 1976, Westminster $7.50 (0-664-32602-1). The development of the American labor union from its beginnings in the eighteenth century to the present. [331.88]

3040 McKissack, Patricia, and Fredrick McKissack. *A Long Hard Journey* (5–9). Illus. 1989, Walker LB $15.85 (0-8027-6885-7). A 150-year saga of the organization of porters into the first black American union, the Brotherhood of Sleeping Car Porters. (Rev: BL 9/15/89; SLJ 1/90; VOYA 12/89) [331]

Money and Trade

3041 Hart, William B. *The United States and World Trade* (7–12). Illus. 1985, Watts LB $12.90 (0-531-10067-7). An account that tells about world trade relationships and gives an uncritical report on the role of multinational corporations in international economics. (Rev: BR 3–4/86; SLJ 2/86) [650]

Marketing and Advertising

3042 Sullivan, George. *How Do They Package It?* (7–9). 1976, Westminster $7.50 (0-664-32601-3). A history of packaging is given as well as details on design and current disposal problems. [658]

Guidance and Personal
Development

Education and the Schools

General and Miscellaneous

3043 Dunnahoo, Terry. *How to Win a School Election* (6–9). Illus. 1989, Watts LB $11.90 (0-531-10695-0). Candidates for school office are told about campaign strategies, speech making, and the whole election process. (Rev: BL 6/1/89; BR 11–12/89; SLJ 7/89; VOYA 10/89) [373.18]

3044 Gay, Kathlyn. *Crisis in Education: Will the United States Be Ready for the Year 2000?* (7–10). Illus. 1986, Watts $11.40 (0-531-10248-3). A discussion of the major problems facing American education today with a rundown of some future trends. (Rev: BL 12/1/86; BR 3–4/87; VOYA 6/87) [370]

3045 Landau, Elaine. *Teenagers Talk about School . . . and Open Their Hearts about Their Concerns* (7–12). 1989, Messner $9.79 (0-671-64568-4). In a series of candid interviews, teenagers talk about their reactions to schools and their teachers. (Rev: BL 2/1/89; BR 9–10/89; SLJ 2/89; VOYA 12/89) [305.2]

3046 Loeper, John J. *Going to School in 1876* (7–9). Illus. 1984, Macmillan $11.95 (0-689-31015-3). The students, their schools and teachers, and the curriculum are described in this interesting account. [370.9]

3047 Loeper, John J. *Going to School in 1776* (7–9). Illus. 1973, Macmillan $13.95 (0-689-30089-1). A description of what schools were like during the late Colonial period. [370.9]

3048 Ware, Cindy. *Summer Options for Teenagers* (7–12). 1990, Prentice paper $16.95 (0-13-296443-0). A guide to over 1,000 summer programs for young people who want to study and learn in the summer. (Rev: BL 4/1/90) [371]

3049 Wirths, Claudine G., and Mary Bowman-Kruhm. *I Hate School: How to Hang In & When to Drop Out* (7–12). Illus. 1986, Harper LB $11.89 (0-690-04558-1); paper $7.95 (0-06-446054-1). A self-help book for those who are having trouble in school that emphasizes the importance of not dropping out. (Rev: BL 1/15/87; BR 3–4/87; SLJ 11/86; VOYA 12/86) [373.12]

Development of Academic Skills

Study Skills

3050 Carey, Helen H., and Judith E. Greenberg. *How to Use Primary Sources* (7–10). Illus. 1983, Watts LB $11.90 (0-531-04674-5). A guide to the use of such primary materials as interviews, diaries, documents, and on-site visits. [907]

3051 Carey, Helen H., and Deborah R. Hanka. *How to Use Your Community as a Resource* (7–9). Illus. 1983, Watts LB $11.90 (0-531-04675-3). A book that shows how the community can be used as a resource for a variety of projects. [307]

3052 James, Elizabeth, and Carol Barkin. *School Smarts: How to Succeed at Schoolwork* (5–8). 1988, Lothrop LB $12.88 (0-688-0-6799-9); paper $6.95 (0-688-06798-0). In 8 brief chapters the author covers such topics as different ways of studying, how to organize time and space, and test-taking strategies. (Rev: BR 5–6/88) [371.3]

3053 Tchudi, Stephen. *The Young Learner's Handbook* (6–9). Illus. 1987, Macmillan $13.95 (0-684-18676-4). A self-help guide for young students honing their learning, writing, and research skills. (Rev: BL 9/1/87; BR 1–2/88; SLJ 6–7/87; VOYA 12/87) [370.15]

Tests and Test Taking

3054 Gilbert, Sara. *How to Take Tests* (7–9). 1983, Morrow $11.95 (0-688-02469-6); paper $7.50 (0-688-02470-X). A handbook on study skills plus how to prepare for various kinds of tests. [371.2]

3055 Kern, Roy, and Richard Smith. *The Grade Booster Guide for Kids* (7–9). 1987, Hilton Thomas paper $7.95 (0-944162-00-2). This book covers the proper strategies and techniques to use for successful test-taking. (Rev: BR 5–6/88) [371.3]

3056 Peters, Max. *Barron's How to Prepare for High School Entrance Examinations* (7–9). Illus. 1988, Barron's paper $9.95 (0-8120-4121-6). The nature of the tests for entrance into prep schools and other secondary level schools and how to prepare to take them. [373.1]

Writing and Speaking Skills

3057 Colligan, Louise. *The A+ Guide to Book Reports* (7–9). 1984, Scholastic paper $2.25 (0-590-33313-5). This account gives plenty of useful tips on writing excellent book reports. Others in this series are: *The A+ Guide to Taking Tests* (1984); *The A+ Guide to Good Grades* (1984); *The A+ Guide to Research and Term Papers* (1984); *The A+ Guide to Good Writing* (1988); and *The A+ Guide to Studying* (1987). [411]

3058 Detz, Joan. *You Mean I Have to Stand Up and Say Something?* (7–12). 1986, Macmillan LB $12.95 (0-689-31221-0). An entertaining guide to preparation of talks and overcoming the fear of facing an audience. (Rev: SLJ 3/87) [808.5]

3059 Dubrovin, Vivian. *Creative Word Processing* (5–10). 1987, Watts $12.90 (0-531-10334-X). An introduction to word processing, its terms and commands, and how to use it for a variety of writing projects. (Rev: BL 4/15/87; BR 11–12/87; SLJ 6–7/87; VOYA 12/87) [652.5]

3060 Dunbar, Robert E. *How to Debate* Illus. 1987, Watts $12.90 (0-531-10335-8). A manual that gives good tips from the first stages to gathering material to methods of presentation and re-

buttal. (Rev: BL 4/1/87; BR 5–6/87; SLJ 9/87; VOYA 8–9/87) [808.53]

3061 Dunbar, Robert E. *Making Your Point: How to Speak and Write Persuasively* (7–10). Illus. 1990, Watts LB $12.90 (0-531-10905-4). Sound advice is given on how to develop an effective style in both writing and speaking. (Rev: BL 5/1/90; VOYA 8/90) [808]

3062 Everhart, Nancy. *So You Have to Write a Term Paper!* (7–12). 1987, Watts $11.90 (0-531-10427-3). A thorough guide to writing term papers that even includes a section on computer use. (Rev: BL 2/15/88; BR 1–2/88; SLJ 4/88; VOYA 4/88) [808]

3063 James, Elizabeth, and Carol Barkin. *How to Write a Great School Report* (7–10). Illus. 1983, Lothrop LB $11.88 (0-688-02283-9); paper $6.96 (0-688-02278-2). A basic guide to report writing from choosing the topic to preparing the final copy. [808]

3064 James, Elizabeth, and Carol Barkin. *How to Write a Term Paper* (7–12). 1980, Lothrop paper $3.95 (0-688-45025-3). A practical step-by-step approach to good report writing that uses many examples. [808]

3065 Ryan, Margaret. *So You Have to Give a Speech!* (7–12). Illus. 1987, Watts $12.90 (0-531-10337-4). A practical, step-by-step guide to the preparation and delivery of a speech. (Rev: BL 4/15/87; BR 5–6/87; SLJ 8/87; VOYA 8–9/87) [808.5]

3066 Sternberg, Patricia. *Speak Up! A Guide to Public Speaking* (7–12). 1984, Messner LB $8.79 (0-671-47371-9). All kinds of topics from preparing a speech to overcoming stage fright are well handled. [808.5]

3067 Tchudi, Susan, and Stephen Tchudi. *The Young Writer's Handbook* (6–9). 1984, Macmillan $13.95 (0-684-18090-1). This practical guide includes material on how to write journals, reports, letters, stories, and poetry. [808]

3068 Tyler, Vicki. *The A+ Guide to Grammar* (7–9). 1984, Scholastic paper $2.25 (0-590-33316-X). A handy guide to grammar and language use. Also use *The A+ Guide to Better Vocabulary* (1986). [415]

Careers and Occupational Guidance

General and Miscellaneous

3069 Alexander, Sue. *Finding Your First Job* (7–10). Illus. 1980, Dutton $10.95 (0-525-29725-1). For the first-time job hunter, plenty of tips on such topics as interviews, forms, and permits required. [650.1]

3070 Gilbert, Sara. *Lend a Hand: The How, Where, and Why of Volunteering* (7–12). 1988, Morrow $11.95 (0-688-07247-X). A guide to the pleasures of volunteer work and a directory of agencies requiring such help. (Rev: BL 6/1/88; BR 5–6/88; SLJ 5/88; VOYA 2/88) [361.7]

3071 Jones, Ilene. *Jobs for Teenagers* (7–12). 1987, Ballantine paper $2.50 (0-345-35153-3). A rundown on ways teenagers can make money working part-time. [331.1]

Careers

General and Miscellaneous

3072 Cantwell, Lois. *Modeling* (7–12). Illus. 1986, Watts $10.40 (0-531-10123-1). A book for both boys and girls about the world of modeling and how to enter it. (Rev: VOYA 2/87) [659.1]

3073 Greene, Laura. *Careers in the Computer Industry* (5–8). 1983, Watts $10.40 (0-531-04636-2). A look at the various careers available involving computers including engineers, programmers, and data processors. [001.64]

3074 Johnson, Neil. *All in a Day's Work: Twelve Americans Talk about Their Jobs* (7–10). Illus.

1989, Little $14.95 (0-316-46957-2). Twelve different occupations from musician and detective to farmer and factory worker are represented in these first-person accounts. (Rev: SLJ 5/90) [311.7]

Artists and Entertainers

3075 Busnar, Gene. *Careers in Music* (7–10). Illus. 1982, Messner LB $10.49 (0-671-42410-6). All kinds of careers—from teaching to performing in various situations—are outlined. [780.23]

3076 Edmonds, I. G., and William H. Gerhard. *Broadcasting for Beginners* (7–10). 1980, Holt $8.95 (0-03-053826-2). This is a guidebook for those who want a career in radio with emphasis on how to get started. [384.5]

3077 Hollingsworth, T. R. *Tune in to a Television Career* (7–10). Illus. 1984, Messner LB $9.29 (0-671-45581-8). A description of a number of different positions within the television industry and how to prepare for them. [384.55]

3078 Klever, Anita. *Women in Television* (7–9). 1975, Westminster $5.95 (0-664-32579-3). Thirty-seven women describe their jobs in television and how they got their start. [621.388]

3079 Lasch, Judith. *The Teen Model Book* (7–10). Illus. 1986, Messner $9.29 (0-671-52614-6). Basic information is given from the different kinds of modeling to negotiating contracts. (Rev: BL 6/15/86; SLJ 10/86) [659.1]

3080 Paige, David. *A Day in the Life of a Rock Musician* (6–9). Illus. 1980, Troll LB $10.79 (0-89375-225-8); paper $2.50 (0-89375-229-0). A day is described that includes writing music, performing, and recording. [784.5]

3081 Trainer, David. *A Day in the Life of a TV News Reporter* (6–9). Illus. 1980, Troll LB $10.79 (0-89375-228-2); paper $2.50 (0-89375-232-0). An easily read account of a typical day of a news reporter and of the backup crew. [384.55]

3082 Williamson, Walter. *Early Stages: The Professional Theater and the Young Actor* (6–9). 1986, Walker LB $12.85 (0-8027-6630-7). Through examining the careers of several young actors, tips are given on how to enter show business. (Rev: BL 7/86; BR 11–12/86; SLJ 5/86) [792]

Lawyers, Policemen, and Other Society-Oriented Careers

3083 Fenten, Barbara, and D. X. Fenten. *Tourism and Hospitality—Careers Unlimited* (7–12). 1978, Westminster $8.95 (0-664-32634-X). A career guide that covers such subjects as transportation, recreation, and food services. [910.2]

3084 Paige, David. *A Day in the Life of a Forest Ranger* (6–9). Illus. 1980, Troll LB $10.79 (0-89375-227-4); paper $2.50 (0-89375-231-2). A close look at a typical day for a forest ranger that includes both exciting and routine chores. [574.5]

3085 Poynter, Margaret. *Search and Rescue: The Team and the Missions* (7–9). Illus. 1980, Macmillan $8.95 (0-689-30756-X). A description of mountain search and rescue teams, their methods, and equipment. [363.1]

3086 Rose, Charles Jules. *Careers in Law* (7–10). 1983, Messner LB $9.29 (0-671-42128-X). A variety of positions in the legal field are described plus details on job satisfaction, pay, and possible advancement. [340]

Medical and Health Careers

3087 Lee, Mary Price. *Ms. Veterinarian* (7–9). 1976, Westminster $8.95 (0-664-32594-7). The world of the veterinarian and how women can increasingly become part of it are described. [636.089]

3088 Seide, Diane. *Careers in Health Services* (7–10). 1982, Lodestar $10.50 (0-535-66768-7). All sorts of careers in medicine are described, from nuclear medicine to podiatry. [610.69]

3089 Witty, Margot. *A Day in the Life of an Emergency Room Nurse* (7–9). Illus. 1980, Troll LB $10.79 (0-89375-226-6); paper $2.50 (0-89375-230-4). An easily read behind-the-scenes look at an emergency room and the typical day that a nurse spends there. [610]

Scientists and Engineers

3090 Jaspersohn, William. *A Day in the Life of a Marine Biologist* (6–9). 1982, Little $14.95 (0-316-45814-7). This account covers a typical workday for a marine biologist at the marine station located at Woods Hole, Massachusetts. [574.92]

3091 O'Connor, Karen. *Maybe You Belong in a Zoo! Zoo and Aquarium Careers* (7–9). Illus. 1982, Putnam $12.95 (0-396-08086-3). A variety of careers are described including training required and working conditions. [590.74]

3092 Ricciuti, Edward R. *They Work with Wildlife: Jobs for People Who Want to Work with Animals* (7–9). 1983, Harper LB $12.89 (0-06-025004-6). All kinds of jobs working with the wildlife are introduced including marine biology and field biology. [591]

3093 Williams, Barbara. *Breakthrough: Women in Archaeology* (7–9). 1981, Walker $9.95 (0-8027-6406-1). The careers of 6 women archaeologists are described with tips for those who would like to enter the field. [930.1]

Personal Finances

Money-Making Ideas

General and Miscellaneous

3094 Byers, Patricia, et al. *The Kids Money Book: Great Money Making Ideas* (7–10). 1983, Liberty paper $4.95 (0-89709-041-1). A wide variety of jobs are introduced that can be part-time and money-producing. [658.1]

Baby-sitting

3095 Dayee, Frances S. *Babysitting* (6–8). Illus. 1990, Watts LB $11.90 (0-531-10908-9). A practical manual on how to set oneself up as a babysitter and how to face situations when on the job. (Rev: BL 5/15/90; SLJ 7/90; VOYA 8/90) [649.1]

3096 James, Elizabeth, and Carol Barkin. *The Complete Babysitter's Handbook* (7–12). Illus. 1981, Messner LB $11.29 (0-671-43800-X). This book tells how to get jobs, what to do (and not do) when baby-sitting, and how to handle the children. [649]

Managing Money

3097 Kyte, Kathy S. *The Kids' Complete Guide to Money* (7–9). Illus. 1984, Knopf LB $8.99 (0-394-96672-4); paper $4.95 (0-394-86672-X). A guide to handling money wisely with many money-saving tips. [332.024]

3098 Stine, Jane, and Jovial Bob Stine. *Everything You Need to Survive: Money Problems* (7–9). 1983, Random paper $1.95 (0-394-85247-8). An amusing but practical introduction to money management. [332.024]

Health and the Human Body

General and Miscellaneous

3099 Simon, Nissa. *Don't Worry, You're Normal: A Teenager's Guide to Self-Health* (7–10). 1982, Harper LB $12.89 (0-690-04139-X). All sorts of problems associated with adolescence are explored, such as sex, drugs, and emotional concerns. [613]

3100 Taylor, Ron. *Health 2000* (6–8). Illus. 1985, Facts on File $12.95 (0-8160-1156-7). As well as citing recent advances in medicine, this account outlines problems in this area both in developed and underdeveloped countries. (Rev: BL 12/1/85; SLJ 2/86) [613]

3101 Ward, Brian R. *Body Maintenance* (6–9). Illus. 1983, Watts LB $12.40 (0-531-04457-2). A description of all of the body's support systems such as the immune and repair systems that try to keep the body healthy. [612]

3102 Weiss, Ann E. *Biofeedback: Fact or Fad?* (7–10). Illus. 1984, Watts LB $12.90 (0-531-04851-9). The study of using electrical impulses to regulate bodily functions is objectively examined. [615.8]

Aging and Death

3103 Bernstein, Joanne. *Loss and How to Cope with It* (6–8). 1981, Houghton paper $4.95 (0-395-30012-6). An introduction for survivors on how to cope with death. [128]

3104 Gaffron, Norma. *Dealing with Death* (6–12). 1989, Lucent LB $10.95 (1-56006-108-1). This account tells how various religions regard death and ways of coping with it in our present culture. (Rev: SLJ 4/90) [128]

3105 Gardner, Sandra, and Gary Rosenberg. *Teenage Suicide* (7–12). Rev. ed. 1990, Messner LB $11.98 (0-671-70200-9); paper $5.95 (0-671-70201-7). Besides giving general background material on teen suicide, this account lists danger signals and gives specifics concerning help. (Rev: SLJ 6/90) [362.2]

3106 Gravelle, Karen, and Charles Haskins. *Teenagers Face to Face with Bereavement* (7–12). 1989, Messner LB $11.88 (0-671-65856-5); paper $5.95 (0-671-65975-8). An exploration of how to cope with death and grieving that uses the words of 17 young people who have been through this experience. (Rev: BL 5/15/89; VOYA 12/89) [155.9]

3107 Hyde, Margaret O., and Lawrence E. Hyde. *Meeting Death* (5–8). 1989, Walker LB $15.85 (0-8027-6874-1). After a history of how various cultures regard death, the authors discuss this phenomenon, the concept of grieving, and how to face death. (Rev: BL 1/1/90; SLJ 11/89) [306.9]

3108 Knox, Jean McBee. *Death and Dying* (7–10). Illus. 1989, Chelsea House $18.95 (0-7910-0037-0). After a historical account of practices surrounding death, the author discusses such topics as grieving and euthanasia. (Rev: BR 11–12/89; SLJ 8/89; VOYA 10/89) [128]

3109 Landau, Elaine. *Growing Old in America* (5–8). Illus. 1985, Messner LB $9.97 (0-671-42409-2). The story of the aging of America with coverage of the sociological implications. (Rev: SLJ 9/85; VOYA 12/85) [305.2]

3110 LeShan, Eda. *Learning to Say Good-Bye: When a Parent Dies* (7–10). Illus. 1976, Macmillan $12.95 (0-02-756360-X). How to cope with the emotions caused by the death of a parent. [155.9]

3111 Pringle, Laurence. *Death Is Natural* (6–9). Illus. 1977, Macmillan $8.95 (0-590-07440-7). An explanation of death is given as it relates to the balance of nature and its necessity to ensure the future of life. [574.2]

3112 Richter, Elizabeth. *Losing Someone You Love: When a Brother or Sister Dies* (5–9). Illus. 1986, Putnam $12.95 (0-399-21243-4). Using interviews with a variety of youngsters from ages 10 to 24, the author explores the grieving processes when the death involves a brother or sister. (Rev: BL 4/15/86; SLJ 4/86; VOYA 8–10/86) [155.9]

3113 van Zwanenberg, Fiona. *Caring for the Aged* (6–9). Illus. 1989, Gloucester LB $11.90 (0-531-17190-6). The problems of old people are discussed and how young people can help. (Rev: BL 1/1/90; SLJ 4/90; VOYA 4/90) [326.6]

3114 Worth, Richard. *You'll Be Old Someday, Too* (7–10). Illus. 1986, Watts $12.90 (0-531-10158-4). Using both exposition and interviews, the author explains that old age can be a time of growth and surveys the general quality of life of the aged in America and their problems. (Rev: BL 6/1/86; SLJ 9/86; VOYA 12/86) [305.6]

Alcohol, Drugs, and Smoking

3115 Algeo, Philippa. *Acid and Hallucinogens* (5–8). Illus. 1990, Watts LB $11.90 (0-531-10932-1). This book discusses the composition and effects of such drugs as LSD, mescaline, marijuana, and angel dust. (Rev: BL 8/90) [615]

3116 Berger, Gilda. *Crack: The New Drug Epidemic!* (7–10). Illus. 1987, Watts $11.90 (0-531-10410-9). An introduction to the drug that explains why it is popular and what its dangerous side effects are. Also use by the same author: *Drug Testing* (1987). (Rev: BL 12/15/87; BR 1–2/88; SLJ 12/87; VOYA 2/88) [362.2]

3117 Berger, Gilda. *Drug Abuse: The Impact on Society* (7–12). Illus. 1988, Watts $12.90 (0-531-10579-2). This account covers the effects of drug abuse from changes in personality to physical problems. (Rev: BL 1/1/89; BR 1–2/89; VOYA 4/89) [362.2]

3118 Berger, Gilda. *Drug Testing* (7–10). Illus. 1987, Watts LB $12.90 (0-531-10411-7). After describing the "target" drugs of the testing program, the author discusses the methods used and the pros and cons of such programs. (Rev: BR 3–4/88; SLJ 2/88; VOYA 4/88) [362.2]

3119 Berger, Gilda. *Smoking Not Allowed: The Debate* (7–12). Illus. 1987, Watts $11.90 (0-531-10420-6). The pros and cons of the antismoking campaign, its history, causes, and future. (Rev: BL 1/1/88; BR 1–2/88; SLJ 1/88; VOYA 4/88) [362.2]

3120 Berger, Gilda. *Violence and Drugs* (7–12). 1989, Watts LB $12.90 (0-531-10818-X). An examination of the relationships between illicit drug manufacture, sale, and consumption and crime. (Rev: BL 4/15/90; BR 3–4/90; VOYA 2/90) [364.2]

3121 Berger, Gilda, and Melvin Berger. *Drug Abuse A-Z* (7–12). 1990, Enslow LB $16.95 (0-89490-193-1). In dictionary format of about 1,000 entries, this book is a guide to all drug-related terms. (Rev: BL 4/1/90; BR 5–6/90; SLJ 8/90; VOYA 6/90) [362.29]

3122 Chomet, Julian. *Cocaine and Crack* (5–9). Illus. 1987, Watts $11.90 (0-531-10435-4). A straightforward account of the nature and effects of these drugs. (Rev: BL 1/1/88; SLJ 2/88) [362.293]

3123 Claypool, Jane. *Alcohol and You* (7–12). Illus. 1988, Watts LB $12.90 (0-531-10566-0). A new edition of this introductory book on alcohol is objective but realistic in its coverage of the effects of alcohol and its place in the lives of teenagers. (Rev: BR 3–4/89; SLJ 3/89; VOYA 4/89) [613.8]

3124 Condon, Judith. *The Pressure to Take Drugs* (5–8). Illus. 1990, Watts LB $11.90 (0-531-10934-8). This book gives specific advice to young people on how to avoid drugs and how to respond when solicitations are made. (Rev: BL 8/90) [362.29]

3125 Dolan, Edward F., Jr. *Drugs in Sports* (7–10). Illus. 1986, Watts $12.90 (0-531-10157-6). The many different drugs used by athletes are discussed as well as their short- and long-term effects on the body. (Rev: BL 5/15/86; BR 11–12/86; SLJ 3/87; VOYA 12/86) [362.2]

3126 Dolmetsch, Paul, and Gail Mauricette, eds. *Teens Talk about Alcohol and Alcoholism* (6–9). 1987, Doubleday paper $7.95 (0-385-23084-2). Eighteen students from a junior high school in Bennington, Vermont, tell about the effects of alcohol on their lives. (Rev: BL 2/15/87) [362.2]

3127 Edwards, Gabrielle I. *Coping with Drug Abuse* (7–10). Illus. 1983, Rosen $12.95 (0-8239-1144-6). The author, a high school science teacher, discusses the effects of drugs and how they are being abused. [613.8]

3128 Gano, Lila. *Smoking* (6–10). Illus. 1989, Lucent $10.95 (1-56006-103-0). A history of tobacco, plus material on its effects and diseases related to its use. (Rev: BL 2/1/90; SLJ 5/90) [613.85]

3129 Godfrey, Martin. *Heroin* (5–9). Illus. 1987, Watts $11.90 (0-531-10436-2). A fact-filled account that deals with addiction as well as cures. (Rev: BL 1/1/88; SLJ 2/88) [362.293]

3130 Godfrey, Martin. *Marijuana* (5–9). Illus. 1987, Watts $11.90 (0-531-10437-0). An introduction to the past and present use of this drug, its effects, and dangers. (Rev: BL 1/1/88) [362.293]

3131 Graeber, Laurel. *Are You Dying for a Drink? Teenagers and Alcohol Abuse* (7–12). 1985, Messner LB $11.29 (0-671-50818-0); paper $4.95 (0-671-63180-2). Using case histories, this account explains alcoholism, the changes it produces in the body, and how to get help. (Rev: SLJ 2/86; VOYA 6/86) [616.86]

3132 Gwynne, Peter. *Who Uses Drugs?* (7–10). Illus. 1987, Chelsea House $17.95 (1-55546-223-6). An overview of different kinds of drugs and who uses them. (Rev: BL 5/1/88) [362.2]

3133 Harris, Jonathan. *Drugged Athletes: The Crisis in American Sports* (7–12). 1987, Macmillan $12.95 (0-02-742740-4). Drug abuse in both amateur and pro sports is explored in this comprehensive account. (Rev: BL 7/87; BR 11–12/87; SLJ 6–7/87; VOYA 12/87) [364.1]

3134 Harris, Neil. *Drugs and Crime* (6–10). Illus. 1989, Watts LB $11.90 (0-531-10800-7). This account traces the connection between addiction and crime from the city streets to international syndicates. (Rev: SLJ 4/90) [613.8]

3135 Hawkes, Nigel. *The International Drug Trade* (6–8). Illus. 1988, Rourke $11.95 (0-86592-280-2). An account that traces drugs from production around the world through their eventual consumption. (Rev: BL 12/15/88; SLJ 5/89) [363.4]

3136 Hoobler, Thomas, and Dorothy Hoobler. *Drugs & Crime* (7–12). Illus. 1987, Chelsea House $17.95 (1-55546-228-6). An account of how the drug traffic is fostered by layers of crime and corruption both international and local. (Rev: BL 3/15/88) [364.2]

3137 Hughes, Barbara. *Drug Related Diseases* (6–10). Illus. 1987, Watts $10.40 (0-531-10381-1). This book discusses the effects of drugs on physical, sexual, intellectual, and emotional growth. (Rev: BR 1–2/88; SLJ 3/88; VOYA 2/88) [616]

3138 Hyde, Margaret O. *Alcohol: Uses and Abuses* (6–9). Illus. 1988, Enslow LB $13.95 (0-89490-155-9). Both the social and medical problems that alcohol causes are explored in this book. (Rev: BR 1–2/89; SLJ 9/88; VOYA 2/89) [616.86]

3139 Hyde, Margaret O. *Drug Wars* (7–12). 1990, Walker LB $12.85 (0-8027-6901-2). This account discusses the violence and despair that crack cocaine has brought to America and ways in which its production and distribution can be halted. (Rev: SLJ 6/90; VOYA 6/90) [616.86]

3140 Hyde, Margaret O. *Know about Alcohol* (7–10). Illus. 1978, McGraw $9.95 (0-07-031621-X). A straightforward account of what alcohol is and how it affects the body. [613.8]

3141 Hyde, Margaret O. *Know about Drugs* (7–10). 2nd rev. ed. Illus. 1990, Walker LB $13.85 (0-8027-6923-3). A general introduction to drugs and drug abuse that includes material on alcohol, nicotine, cocaine, and marijuana. (Rev: VOYA 8/90) [616.86]

3142 Hyde, Margaret O. *Know about Smoking* (7–10). Illus. 1983, McGraw $10.95 (0-07-031671-6). The dangers of smoking are outlined plus useful tips on how to say no to the first cigarette. [613.8]

3143 Hyde, Margaret O., ed. *Mind Drugs* (7–12). 1986, Putnam $10.95 (0-396-08813-9). Experts in the field discuss such drugs as LSD, cocaine, and alcohol. (Rev: BR 3–4/87; SLJ 11/86) [613.8]

3144 Jones, Ralph. *Straight Talk: Answers to Questions Young People Ask about Alcohol* (7–9). 1989, TAB paper $4.95 (0-8306-9005-0). Fifty questions concerning alcohol and physical and psychological effects are answered in this short, straightforward book. (Rev: VOYA 12/89) [661]

3145 Keyishian, Elizabeth. *Everything You Need to Know about Smoking* (6–10). Illus. 1989, Rosen LB $12.95 (0-8239-1017-2). This book covers such topics as why people smoke, its effects, and how to quit. (Rev: SLJ 2/90) [613.8]

3146 Kittredge, Mary. *Prescription & Over-the-Counter Drugs* (7–12). 1989, Chelsea House $17.95 (0-7910-0062-1). After introducing these types of drugs, the author tells what is good and bad about them. (Rev: BR 11–12/89) [615]

3147 Knox, Jean McBee. *Drinking, Driving & Drugs* (7–10). Illus. 1988, Chelsea House $17.95

(1-55546-231-6). An overview of this national problem that focuses on teenage offenders and victims. (Rev: BL 7/88; BR 1–2/89; SLJ 9/88) [363.1]

3148 Lamberg, Lynne. *Drugs & Sleep* (8–12). Illus. 1987, Chelsea House $17.95 (1-55546-213-8). The nature of sleep is explored and the effects that drugs have on it are described. (Rev: BL 5/1/88) [616.8]

3149 Langone, John. *Bombed, Buzzed, Smashed, or . . . Sober: A Book about Alcohol* (7–12). 1976, Little $14.95 (0-316-51424-1). A well-researched account that describes the uses and effects of alcohol and how to avoid it. [613.8]

3150 McCormick, Michele. *Designer-Drug Abuse* (7–12). Illus. 1989, Watts LB $12.90 (0-531-10660-8). A book that discusses the manufacture and use of such types of drugs as amphetamines and hallucinogens. (Rev: BL 8/89; BR 9–10/89; SLJ 7/89; VOYA 10/89) [362.2]

3151 Madison, Arnold. *Drugs and You* (5–8). Rev. ed. Illus. 1990, Messner LB $10.98 (0-671-69147-3); paper $4.95 (0-671-69148-1). The author describes medicinal and nonmedicinal drugs, illegal drugs, and the consequences of addiction. (Rev: SLJ 4/90) [616.86]

3152 Madsen, Christine. *Drinking and Driving* (6–10). Illus. 1989, Watts LB $11.90 (0-531-10799-X). The effects of alcohol are outlined in relation to driving plus material on how society is penalizing drunk drivers. (Rev: SLJ 4/90) [613.8]

3153 Marshall, Eliot. *Legalization: A Debate* (7–10). Illus. 1988, Chelsea House $17.95 (1-55546-229-4). Using a trial format, this is a pro-and-con examination of the possible legalization of marijuana. (Rev: BL 6/15/88; SLJ 6–7/88) [344.73]

3154 Martin, Jo, and Kelly Clendenon. *Drugs & the Family* (7–12). Illus. 1987, Chelsea House $17.95 (1-55546-220-0). A 16-year-old and his mother discuss the boy's drug addiction and his recovery. (Rev: BL 3/1/88) [362.2]

3155 Meer, Jeff. *Drugs & Sports* (7–12). Illus. 1987, Chelsea House $18.95 (1-55546-226-X). An account that explains how various drugs affect an athlete's performance and how this abuse is being viewed by segments of the athletic world. (Rev: BL 11/1/87) [613]

3156 Miner, Jane Claypool. *Alcohol and Teens* (7–9). Illus. 1984, Messner LB $9.29 (0-671-44890-0). A description of how alcohol affects people both physically and emotionally. [362.2]

3157 Mohun, Janet. *Drugs, Steroids and Sports* (6–9). Illus. 1988, Watts $11.90 (0-531-10626-8). A description of when drugs were first used in

sports, why they are used, and their effects. (Rev: BL 2/1/89; SLJ 5/89; VOYA 4/89) [364.1]

3158 Monroe, Judy. *Stimulants & Hallucinogens* (7–12). Illus. 1988, Crestwood $10.95 (0-89686-415-4). Cocaine, crack, and caffeine are 3 of the drugs included in this account that stresses the side effects of their use. (Rev: BL 4/1/89) [362.2]

3159 Newman, Susan. *It Won't Happen to Me* (5–9). Illus. 1987, Putnam paper $8.95 (0-399-51342-6). Nine young alcoholics and drug addicts tell how they got started and the problems this caused for themselves and their families. (Rev: BL 5/15/87; SLJ 8/87) [362.2]

3160 Pownall, Mark. *Inhalants* (5–9). Illus. 1987, Watts $11.90 (0-531-10434-6). An introduction to these increasingly available drugs and the effects of their use told in straightforward terms. (Rev: BL 1/1/88; SLJ 2/88) [362.293]

3161 Rosenberg, Maxine B. *Not My Family: Sharing the Truth about Alcoholism* (5–8). 1988, Bradbury $12.95 (0-02-777911-4). Through a series of case studies the author explores alcoholism and how it affects families. (Rev: BL 1/15/89; BR 5–6/89; SLJ 11/88) [362.2]

3162 Ryan, Elizabeth A. *Straight Talk about Drugs and Alcohol* (7–12). 1989, Facts on File $14.95 (0-8160-1525-2). A straightforward account that powerfully presents the facts about drugs and alcohol; includes a directory of treatment centers. (Rev: BL 4/1/89; SLJ 5/89; VOYA 6/89) [362.2]

3163 Ryerson, Eric. *When Your Parent Drinks Too Much: A Book for Teenagers* (7–12). 1985, Facts on File $14.95 (0-8160-1259-8); Warner paper $3.95 (0-446-34692-6). A frank, realistic book of advice for young people who have alcoholic parents that includes information on Alateen. (Rev: BL 12/1/85; BR 3–4/86; SLJ 12/85; VOYA 4/86) [362.2]

3164 Schnoll, Sidney. *Getting Help: Treatments for Drug Abuse* (7–12). Illus. 1986, Chelsea House $18.95 (0-87754-775-0). This book concentrates on the many kinds of treatments available and the agencies involved in supplying this help. (Rev: BL 2/15/87) [362.2]

3165 Seixas, Judith S. *Living with a Parent Who Drinks Too Much* (7–9). 1979, Greenwillow LB $11.88 (0-688-84196-1). Ways to cope when one or both parents are alcohol abusers. [362.2]

3166 Seixas, Judith S. *Living with a Parent Who Takes Drugs* (5–9). 1989, Greenwillow $11.95 (0-688-08627-6). By using various experiences of a seventh-grade boy, the problems of a parent on drugs are explored. (Rev: SLJ 9/89; VOYA 12/89) [613.8]

3167 Shuker, Nancy. *Everything You Need to Know about an Alcoholic Parent* (7–12). Illus. 1989, Rosen $12.95 (0-8239-1011-3). After a general discussion of alcoholism, Shuker explains how it changes human relationships and how young people can cope with it. (Rev: BL 1/15/90; BR 3–4/90; VOYA 4/90) [362.29]

3168 Silverstein, Alvin, and Virginia B. Silverstein. *Alcoholism* (7–10). 1975, Harper $12.89 (0-397-31648-8); paper $3.50 (0-397-31649-6). Alcohol use and abuse are introduced, plus alcoholism and the problems it causes. [613.8]

3169 Sonnett, Sherry. *Smoking* (6–8). Illus. 1988, Watts $9.90 (0-531-10489-3). A candid explanation of the effects of tobacco on the human body. A revision of the 1977 title. (Rev: BL 3/1/88; SLJ 11/88) [613.8]

3170 Spence, Annette. *Substance Abuse* (6–10). 1989, Facts on File $18.95 (0-8160-1669-0). This volume gives good general information on the use of drugs, tobacco, and alcohol and their effects on the body. (Rev: BR 11–12/89) [613.8]

3171 Stepney, Rob. *Alcohol* (5–9). Illus. 1987, Watts $11.90 (0-531-10433-8). This account covers reasons for the drinking of alcohol, its abuse, and cure possibilities. (Rev: BL 1/1/88; BR 5–6/88) [362.292]

3172 Stepney, Rob. *Tobacco* (5–9). Illus. 1987, Watts $11.90 (0-531-10438-9). Why people smoke, the effects of tobacco, addiction, and ways to stop are topics covered. (Rev: BL 1/1/88) [362.293]

3173 Stwertka, Eve, and Albert Stwertka. *Marijuana* (7–10). Illus. 1986, Watts LB $10.40 (0-531-10122-3). A history of this drug along with material on the effects and consequences of its use are given. (Rev: SLJ 3/87; VOYA 12/86) [613.8]

3174 Taylor, L. B., Jr. *Driving High: The Hazards of Driving, Drinking, and Drugs* (7–10). Illus. 1983, Watts LB $12.90 (0-531-04663-X). With the use of case studies and background information, the author explored the dangers of driving while under the influence. [363.1]

3175 Ward, Brian R. *Smoking and Health* (5–9). Illus. 1986, Watts LB $12.40 (0-531-10180-0). This book deals primarily with the effects of tobacco smoke on smokers, nonsmokers, and unborn children. (Rev: BR 1–2/87; SLJ 2/87; VOYA 2/87) [613.8]

3176 Washton, Arnold M., and Donna Boundy. *Cocaine and Crack: What You Need to Know* (7–10). 1989, Enslow $13.95 (0-89490-162-1). Background information is given but the main focus here is on the drug, its various forms, and its terrible effects on the human body. (Rev: BL 4/1/89; BR 9–10/89; SLJ 5/89; VOYA 8/89) [362.2]

3177 Weiss, Ann E. *Over-the-Counter Drugs* (7–10). Illus. 1984, Watts LB $12.90 (0-531-04760-1). Nonprescription drugs, safety practices related to them, and labeling laws are 3 of the areas covered. [615]

3178 Woods, Geraldine. *Drug Use and Drug Abuse* (6–9). Illus. 1986, Watts LB $10.45 (0-531-10114-2). A simple introduction to many kinds of drugs and their effects. (Rev: BR 9–10/86; SLJ 5/86; VOYA 12/86) [613.8]

Bionics and Transplants

3179 Berger, Melvin. *The Artificial Heart* (7–12). Illus. 1987, Watts $11.90 (0-531-10409-5). A description of how the artificial heart was developed, how it functions, and the procedures of implanting. (Rev: BL 2/1/88; BR 1–2/88; SLJ 12/87; VOYA 4/88) [617]

3180 Facklam, Margery, and Howard Facklam. *Spare Parts for People* (7–12). Illus. 1987, Harcourt $14.95 (0-15-277410-6). A rundown on the state of bioengineering and the various transplants and implants that are now available. (Rev: BL 12/15/87; VOYA 4/88) [617]

3181 Kittredge, Mary. *Organ Transplants* (7–10). Illus. 1989, Chelsea House LB $17.95 (0-7910-0071-0). A history of transplants is given plus information on different types of operations, their risks, and the ethical questions involved. (Rev: BL 2/15/89; SLJ 2/89; VOYA 6/89) [617]

3182 Lee, Sally. *Donor Banks: Saving Lives with Organ & Tissue Transplants* (7–9). 1988, Watts LB $9.90 (0-531-10475-3). By using actual case studies, the author describes why people need transplants and the role of donor banks in supplying organs and tissues. (Rev: BR 9–10/88) [617]

3183 Leinwand, Gerald. *Transplants: Today's Medical Miracles* (7–12). 1985, Watts $11.90 (0-531-04930-2). A thorough study that gives the history, problems, progress, and moral dilemmas involved in the transplanting of organs. (Rev: BL 6/1/85; BR 3–4/86; SLJ 9/85; VOYA 12/85) [617]

3184 Metos, Thomas H. *Artificial Humans: Transplants and Bionics* (6–9). Illus. 1985, Messner LB $9.29 (0-671-44367-4). A general account that covers such areas as artificial limbs, organs, bones, skin, eyes, and ears. (Rev: SLJ 10/85) [617]

3185 Silverstein, Alvin, and Virginia B. Silverstein. *Futurelife: The Biotechnology Revolution* (7–9). Illus. 1982, Prentice $10.95 (0-13-345884-9). CAT scans, bionic parts, and DNA research are topics covered in this book on biotechnology. [610.28]

3186 Silverstein, Alvin, and Virginia B. Silverstein. *The World of Bionics* (7–9). 1979, Routledge $8.95 (0-416-30221-1). The science of creating artificial parts is introduced with material on where future developments will take place. [001.53]

Diseases and Illnesses

3187 Anderson, Madelyn Klein. *Arthritis* (5–9). Illus. 1989, Watts LB $11.90 (0-531-10801-5). This account tells about the many kinds of arthritis, present treatments available, and the research being done currently. (Rev: BR 3–4/90; SLJ 4/90; VOYA 2/90) [616.7]

3188 Anderson, Madelyn Klein. *Environmental Diseases* (6–10). Illus. 1987, Watts $10.40 (0-531-10382-X). This book discusses different kinds of environments that can cause health problems and serious diseases caused by toxic wastes. (Rev: BR 1–2/88; SLJ 3/88; VOYA 2/88) [616]

3189 Armstrong, Ewan. *The Impact of AIDS* (7–10). Illus. 1990, Gloucester LB $11.90 (0-531-17225-2). Background information on the disease is given plus coverage of how it has affected various strata of our society. (Rev: BL 5/15/90; SLJ 7/90) [362.1]

3190 Asimov, Isaac. *How Did We Find Out about Germs?* (6–8). Illus. 1973, Walker $10.85 (0-8027-6166-6). A simple history of bacteriology from Van Leeuwenhoek to the present. Others in this series explain how we have found out about blood, the brain, and vitamins. [589.9]

3191 Bevan, Nicholas. *AIDS and Drugs* (7–10). Illus. 1988, Watts LB $11.90 (0-531-10625-X). The connection between AIDS and the use of intravenous drugs is made. This book also contains a general discussion of the effects of AIDS and how AZT works. (Rev: SLJ 4/89; VOYA 4/89) [616]

3192 Brown, Fern G. *Hereditary Diseases* (6–10). Illus. 1987, Watts LB $10.40 (0-531-10386-2). After a discussion of genetics and heredity and the formation of genes, this account discusses 4 diseases in depth: diabetes, Tay-Sachs, cystic fibrosis, and sickle-cell anemia. (Rev: BR 9–10/88; SLJ 3/88) [616]

3193 Check, William A. *AIDS* (7–12). Illus. 1988, Chelsea House $17.95 (0-7910-0054-0). A concise introduction to this disease, its causes, and prevention. (Rev: BL 9/15/88; BR 9—10/88; SLJ 10/88) [362.1]

3194 Colman, Warren. *Understanding and Preventing AIDS* (7–10). Illus. 1988, Childrens LB $10.95 (0-516-00592-8); paper $6.95 (0-516-40592-6). The nature of AIDS is explained, how it is caught, and how to avoid it. (Rev: BL 7/88; SLJ 8/88) [616.9]

3195 Eagles, Douglas A. *The Menace of AIDS: A Shadow on Our Land* (6–9). Illus. 1988, Watts $10.40 (0-531-10567-9). The origins of this disease are dealt with in this thorough account, plus such topics as how the disease is transmitted and possible cures. (Rev: BL 12/15/88) [616.97]

3196 Eagles, Douglas A. *Nutritional Diseases* (6–10). Illus. 1987, Watts $10.40 (0-531-10391-9). Deficiencies in diet are discussed and their debilitating results: from diabetes and arteriosclerosis to obesity and bulimia. (Rev: BR 1–2/88; SLJ 3/88; VOYA 12/87) [616]

3197 Edelson, Edward. *Allergies* (7–12). Illus. 1989, Chelsea House $17.95 (0-7910-0055-9). Various types of allergies are described, including their effects and their treatments that have been found to help sufferers. (Rev: BL 9/1/89; BR 11–12/89; SLJ 12/89) [616.97]

3198 Edelson, Edward. *The Immune System* (7–10). Illus. 1989, Chelsea House $18.95 (0-7910-0021-4). After a general discussion of cell structure and antibodies, Edelson introduces the immune system and what happens when it fails to function. (Rev: BL 1/15/90) [616.07]

3199 Fekete, Irene, and Peter Dorrington Ward. *Disease and Medicine* (6–9). Illus. 1985, Facts on File $9.95 (0-8160-1060-9). An overview that gives a brief history of medicine and a look at how disease is being fought today. (Rev: SLJ 10/85) [616]

3200 Fine, Judylaine. *Afraid to Ask: A Book about Cancer* (7–12). 1986, Lothrop $12.88 (0-688-06195-8); paper $6.95 (0-688-06196-6). In this straightforward account about the nature, causes, and treatment of cancer, the author tries to minimize the fear and emotion surrounding the topic. (Rev: BL 3/1/86; BR 5–6/86; VOYA 8–10/86) [616.99]

3201 Frank, Julia. *Alzheimer's Disease: The Silent Epidemic* (6–8). Illus. 1985, Lerner $9.95 (0-8225-1578-4). An account of how this disease progresses and of the emotional and financial toll it takes. (Rev: BL 10/1/85) [618.97]

3202 Gravelle, Karen. *Understanding Birth Defects* (7–12). Illus. 1990, Watts $12.90 (0-531-10955-0). A clear explanation of birth defects such as Down's Syndrome, Huntington's disease, radiation disorders, and AIDS. (Rev: BL 9/15/90) [618.92]

3203 Gravelle, Karen, and Bertram A. John. *Teenagers Face to Face with Cancer* (7–12). 1986, Messner $10.95 (0-671-65856-5); paper $5.95 (0-671-65975-8). From the accounts of 16 young people ages 13 to 21, one discovers what it is like to live with cancer. (Rev: BL 1/15/87; SLJ 2/87) [618.92]

3204 Gutnik, Martin J. *Immunology: From Pasteur to the Search for an AIDS Vaccine* (7–9). Illus. 1989, Watts LB $11.90 (0-531-10672-1). A well-researched account of the search through history for vaccines and other forms of immunology and of the important breakthroughs in this science. (Rev: BL 6/15/89; BR 9–10/89; SLJ 6/89; VOYA 10/89) [616.07]

3205 Hawkes, Nigel. *AIDS* (6–9). 1987, Watts LB $11.90 (0-531-17054-3). An introduction to AIDS, its symptoms, and its current treatments. (Rev: BR 1–2/88) [616]

3206 Herda, D. J. *Cancer* (6–9). Illus. 1989, Watts LB $11.90 (0-531-10803-1). A discussion of the main types of cancers, how they form, and the current methods of treatment. (Rev: BL 12/15/89; SLJ 2/90; VOYA 6/90) [616.99]

3207 Hyde, Margaret O., and Elizabeth H. Forsyth. *AIDS: What Does It Mean to You?* (7–12). Rev. ed. 1990, Walker LB $14.85 (0-8027-6898-9). A revision of the 1987 volume with updated material, new statistics, and expanded coverage on such subjects as caring for people with AIDS and the global aspects of the disease. (Rev: BL 3/15/90; SLJ 4/90; VOYA 4/90) [616.9]

3208 Hyde, Margaret O., and Lawrence E. Hyde. *Cancer in the Young: A Sense of Hope* (6–10). 1985, Westminster $10.95 (0-664-32722-2). After a general discussion of cancer, the authors discuss specific types related to young people including leukemia. (Rev: BL 5/1/85; SLJ 11/85) [618.92]

3209 Kirby, Mona. *Asthma* (6–10). Illus. 1989, Watts LB $11.90 (0-531-10697-7). After a general discussion of the topic, the author covers subjects like what causes an attack and what happens to the body during it. (Rev: BR 3–4/90; VOYA 4/90) [616]

3210 Kittredge, Mary. *The Common Cold* (7–12). Illus. 1989, Chelsea House $18.95 (0-7910-0060-5). Although no one has found a cure for the common cold, there are effective ways of avoidance and of treatment, as this account explains. (Rev: BL 12/15/89; VOYA 4/90) [616.2]

3211 Kittredge, Mary. *Headaches* (7–10). Illus. 1989, Chelsea House $17.95 (0-7910-0064-8). A history of the treatment for headaches plus information on what causes them. (Rev: BL 6/15/89; BR 11–12/90; SLJ 8/89) [616.07]

3212 Krementz, Jill. *How It Feels to Fight for Your Life* (5–9). Illus. 1989, Little $15.95 (0-316-50364-9). Personal accounts of 14 young people who have recovered from such severe illnesses as epilepsy, cancer, and lupus. (Rev: BL 12/15/89; SLJ 10/89) [362.1]

3213 Landau, Elaine. *Alzheimer's Disease* (6–9). Illus. 1987, Watts $9.90 (0-531-10376-5). A straightforward introduction to the physical and emotional aspects of this degenerative disease. (Rev: BL 12/15/87; BR 1–2/88; SLJ 11/87) [616.8]

3214 Landau, Elaine. *Lyme Disease* (5–8). Illus. 1990, Watts LB $10.90 (0-531-10931-3). This is an account of an unusual disease, its causes, how it affects people, and its treatment. (Rev: SLJ 6/90) [616]

3215 LeShan, Eda. *When a Parent Is Very Sick* (5–9). Illus. 1986, Little $12.95 (0-87113-095-5). A guide that helps a youngster react properly when a parent is sick and needs attention. (Rev: SLJ 1/87) [362.1]

3216 McGowen, Tom. *Epilepsy* (6–10). Illus. 1989, Watts LB $11.90 (0-531-10807-4). A history of this disorder is given, plus information on its causes and treatment. (Rev: BL 12/15/89; BR 3–4/90; SLJ 5/90; VOYA 2/90) [616.8]

3217 Metos, Thomas H. *Communicable Diseases* (6–10). Illus. 1987, Watts $10.40 (0-531-10380-3). This account covers how diseases are spread, how the human body fights them, and the nature of common diseases such as influenza. (Rev: BR 1–2/88; SLJ 3/88) [616]

3218 Miller, Robyn. *Robyn's Book: A True Diary* (6–10). 1986, Scholastic paper $2.25 (0-590-33787-4). The diary of a young woman who died of cystic fibrosis at the age of 21. (Rev: BL 7/86; SLJ 9/86; VOYA 12/86) [362]

3219 Nourse, Alan E. *AIDS* (7–12). Illus. 1989, Watts LB $12.90 (0-531-10662-4). This is an update of the excellent book that first appeared in 1986. (Rev: BL 6/1/89; SLJ 7/89; VOYA 10/89) [616.97]

3220 Nourse, Alan E. *Viruses* (7–9). Rev. ed. Illus. 1983, Watts LB $10.40 (0-531-04534-X). An explanation of viruses and their importance in diseases, immunology, and vaccines. [576]

3221 Nourse, Alan E. *Your Immune System* (6–8). Rev. ed. Illus. 1989, Watts $11.90 (0-531-10817-1). The latest research on the body's immune system is conveyed plus chapters on what happens when it malfunctions including material on AIDS. (Rev: BL 11/15/89; BR 1–2/90; SLJ 9/89; VOYA 6/90) [616.07]

3222 Patent, Dorothy Hinshaw. *Germs!* (6–9). Illus. 1983, Holiday LB $12.95 (0-8234-0481-1). What germs are, how they attack the body, and how our immune system works are 3 topics covered. [616]

3223 Rodgers, Joann Ellison. *Cancer* (7–12). Illus. 1990, Chelsea House $18.95 (0-7910-0059-1). Various types of cancer are described and the strides that have been made to control it. (Rev: BL 5/1/90; SLJ 8/90; VOYA 8/90) [616.99]

3224 Shader, Laurel, and Jon Zonderman. *Mononucleosis and Other Infectious Diseases* (7–12). Illus. 1989, Chelsea House $17.95 (0-7910-0069-9). Although many diseases like syphilis and smallpox are discussed, the emphasis is on mononucleosis, a disease that often attacks teens. (Rev: BL 1/15/90; BR 11–12/89; SLJ 11/89) [616.9]

3225 Silverstein, Alvin, et al. *Lyme Disease: The Great Imitator* (6–10). Illus. 1990, Avstar $12.95 (0-9623653-8-6); paper $5.95 (0-9623653-9-4). An account that tells how the disease was discovered, how it is transmitted, and how to avoid it. (Rev: BL 5/15/90) [616.9]

3226 Silverstein, Alvin, and Virginia B. Silverstein. *Allergies* (7–10). Illus. 1977, Harper $12.70 (0-397-31758-1). The types of allergies—such as hay fever and asthma—as well as their causes, effects, and treatments, are discussed. [616.97]

3227 Silverstein, Alvin, and Virginia B. Silverstein. *Cancer: Can It Be Stopped?* (7–12). Illus. 1987, Harper LB $12.89 (0-397-32203-8). A straightforward account that emphasizes recent strides in the fight against cancer. (Rev: BL 11/15/87; BR 3–4/88; SLJ 12/87; VOYA 12/87) [616]

3228 Silverstein, Alvin, and Virginia B. Silverstein. *Headaches: All about Them* (7–10). 1984, Harper LB $12.89 (0-397-32078-7). Various types of headaches are explored along with their causes, prevention, and treatment. [616.8]

3229 Silverstein, Alvin, and Virginia B. Silverstein. *Runaway Sugar: All about Diabetes* (7–10). Illus. 1981, Harper LB $12.89 (0-397-31929-0). Among other topics, this book discusses what causes diabetes and how it can be controlled. [616.4]

3230 Stedman, Nancy. *The Common Cold and Influenza* (7–10). Illus. 1987, Messner $11.98 (0-671-60022-2). A description of the causes, symptoms, and treatments of a cold and a general discussion of the respiratory and immune systems. (Rev: SLJ 4/87) [616]

3231 Stine, Jane, and Jovial Bob Stine. *The Sick of Being Sick Book* (6–8). 1988, Scholastic paper $2.50 (0-590-41865-3). All kinds of activities are included to amuse youngsters who are sick. [362.1]

3232 Taylor, Barbara. *Everything You Need to Know about AIDS* (7–12). 1988, Rosen $11.95 (0-8239-0809-7). Basic facts are given in an easily read format. (Rev: BL 9/15/88; SLJ 10/88) [616.97]

3233 Taylor, Barbara. *Living with Diabetes* (5–8). Illus. 1989, Watts LB $11.90 (0-531-10844-9). This account tells why the pancreas fails to function, danger signs, treatments and how to cope with diabetes. (Rev: BL 2/1/90; SLJ 2/90) [362.1]

3234 Tiger, Steven. *Arthritis* (7–10). Illus. 1986, Messner $11.98 (0-671-55566-9). Different kinds of arthritis are covered, as well as a discussion of causes and progress in treatments. (Rev: SLJ 4/87) [616.7]

3235 Turck, Mary. *AIDS* (6–12). Illus. 1988, Crestwood $10.95 (0-89686-412-X). A simply written book that covers all the basic information about AIDS with many illustrations. (Rev: BL 5/15/89) [616.97]

3236 Wilson, Jonnie. *AIDS* (6–10). Illus. 1989, Lucent Books LB $10.95 (1-56006-105-7). A clear, concise account of the nature of AIDS, how it is transmitted, and how to avoid it. (Rev: BL 1/1/90; SLJ 5/90) [616.97]

Doctors, Hospitals, and Medicine

3237 Carter, Sharon, and Judy Monnig. *Coping with a Hospital Stay* (7–10). 1987, Rosen $10.97 (0-8239-0685-X). Tips for teenagers who are facing a stay in the hospital. (Rev: BL 3/15/88; SLJ 3/88) [362.1]

3238 Cosner, Shaaron. *War Nurses* (6–9). Illus. 1988, Walker LB $17.85 (0-8027-6828-8). A history of the important role nurses have played tending the wounded from our Civil War through the Vietnam conflict. (Rev: BL 12/1/88; BR 3–4/89; SLJ 12/88) [355.3]

3239 Fradin, Dennis B. *Medicine: Yesterday, Today, and Tomorrow* (5–8). Illus. 1989, Childrens

LB $30.60 (0-516-00538-3). A history of the medical profession's search to find out about the human body and the diseases that attack it, including coverage of today's challenges such as AIDS. (Rev: BL 1/15/90; SLJ 2/90) [610]

3240 Gilbo, Patrick. *The American Red Cross* (6–9). Illus. 1987, Chelsea House $14.95 (0-87754-827-7). The story of the accomplishments of this organization from its founding in the Civil War to the present AIDS epidemic. (Rev: BL 8/87; SLJ 9/87) [361.7]

3241 Gordon, James S. *Holistic Medicine* (7–10). Illus. 1988, Chelsea House LB $17.95 (O-7910-0085-0). A noncritical view of holistic medicine that is currently popular. (Rev: BR 11–12/88; SLJ 10/88; VOYA 4/88) [616]

3242 Grauer, Neil. *Medicine and the Law* (7–10). Illus. 1989, Chelsea House $18.95 (0-7910-0088-5). This book gives an overview of such issues as euthanasia, abortion, and genetic engineering. (Rev: BL 1/15/90) [614.1]

3243 Hyde, Margaret O., and Elizabeth H. Forsyth. *Medical Dilemmas* (7–10). 1990, Putnam $14.95 (0-399-21902-1). An overview of such modern medical ethical problems as experimentation on humans and a patient's right to privacy. (Rev: BL 3/15/90; SLJ 7/90; VOYA 6/90) [174.2]

3244 Jacobs, Francine. *Breakthrough: The True Story of Penicillin* (5–9). Illus. 1985, Dodd LB $10.95 (0-396-08579-2). A history of the discovery and use of this drug, which does not stop with the work of Sir Alexander Fleming. (Rev: SLJ 9/85) [615]

3245 Lee, Essie E. *A Matter of Life and Technology: Health Science Today* (6–10). Illus. 1986, Messner LB $9.79 (0-671-49847-9). A description of current health services and procedures with material on new equipment and how individual ailments are treated. (Rev: SLJ 2/87) [362.1]

3246 Monroe, Judy. *Prescription Drugs* (7–12). Illus. 1988, Crestwood $10.95 (0-89686-414-6). Familiar drugs are introduced plus material on how drugs are tested and a look at the pharmaceutical industry. (Rev: BL 4/1/89) [615]

3247 Ranahan, Demerris C. *Contributions of Women: Medicine* (7–9). 1981, Dillon LB $8.95 (0-87518-213-5). The story of the contributions of 5 important women doctors. [610]

Genetics

3248 Arnold, Caroline. *Genetics: From Mendel to Gene Splicing* (6–9). Illus. 1986, Watts LB $11.40 (0-531-10223-8). A very brief account that covers the basic history of genetics and makes some predictions for the future. (Rev: SLJ 2/87) [573.2]

3249 Asimov, Isaac. *How Did We Find Out about DNA?* (6–8). Illus. 1985, Walker LB $10.85 (0-8027-6604-8). An introduction to our knowledge about this basic genetic material. (Rev: BL 1/1/86; SLJ 2/86; VOYA 4/86) [574]

3250 Asimov, Isaac. *How Did We Find Out about Genes?* (6–9). Illus. 1983, Walker LB $10.95 (0-8027-6500-9). From Mendel on, the author traces the history of gene biology. [575.1]

3251 Bornstein, Sandy. *What Makes You What You Are: A First Look at Genetics* (6–10). 1989, Messner LB $11.98 (0-671-63711-8). This account explains how traits are inherited, the process of cell reproduction, and such concepts as DNA and RNA. (Rev: VOYA 4/90) [573.2]

3252 Bornstein, Sandy, and Jerry Bornstein. *New Frontiers in Genetics* (7–9). Illus. 1984, Messner $10.79 (0-671-45245-2). An account that tells what we have learned about life from genetics and how this knowledge can be used in the future. [573.2]

3253 Hyde, Margaret O., and Lawrence E. Hyde. *Cloning and the New Genetics* (7–10). Illus. 1984, Enslow LB $15.95 (0-89490-084-6). After a discussion of DNA and genes, the authors describe the present status of genetic engineering. [574.87]

3254 Langone, John. *Human Engineering: Marvel or Menace?* (7–9). 1978, Little $12.95 (0-316-51427-6). Such areas of science as cloning and other forms of manipulating genes are discussed as well as the many ethical questions they raise. [574.87]

3255 Oleksy, Walter. *Miracles of Genetics* (6–9). Illus. 1986, Childrens LB $17.27 (0-516-00531-6). An introduction to genetic engineering and the possible developments it might bring in the future. (Rev: SLJ 12/86) [573.2]

3256 Silverstein, Alvin, and Virginia B. Silverstein. *Genes, Medicine, and You* (7–12). Illus. 1989, Enslow LB $16.95 (0-89490-154-0). A discussion of the pros and cons of genetic engineering and how it could, if applied properly, rid us of many medical problems. (Rev: BL 10/1/89; BR 1–2/90; SLJ 9/89; VOYA 12/89) [616]

3257 Silverstein, Alvin, and Virginia B. Silverstein. *The Genetics Explosion* (7–10). Illus. 1980, Macmillan $12.95 (0-590-07517-9). After explaining the genetic code, this book deals with its applications, including cloning in plants and animals. [575.1]

3258 Snyder, Gerald S. *Test-Tube Life: Scientific Advance and Moral Dilemma* (7–10). Illus. 1982, Messner LB $10.29 (0-671-42092-5). The ethical problems associated with such genetic phenomena as test-tube babies and cloning are explored. [612]

3259 Wilcox, Frank H. *DNA: The Thread of Life* (7–10). Illus. 1988, Lerner LB $10.95 (0-8225-1584-9). The basic DNA structure is explained and material is given on what it does and what its functions are. (Rev: SLJ 6–7/88) [574.87]

Grooming, Personal Appearance, and Dress

3260 Altman, Douglas. *For Guys* (6–9). Illus. 1989, Rourke LB $9.95 (0-86625-284-3). This is a good grooming manual for boys that covers such topics as diet, exercise, clothes, and hygiene. (Rev: SLJ 6/89) [646.7]

3261 Ball, Jacqueline A. *Hygiene* (6–9). Illus. 1989, Rourke LB $9.95 (0-86625-285-1). This book is aimed at preteen and teenage girls and gives tips on care of nails, skin, hair, and so on. (Rev: SLJ 6/89) [613]

3262 Bowen-Woodward, Kathy. *Coping with a Negative Body-Image* (7–12). 1989, Rosen LB $12.95 (0-8239-0997-2). Techniques and helping agencies are given in this account to help teens adjust to their bodies. (Rev: BR 3–4/90; SLJ 11/89; VOYA 10/89) [646.7]

3263 McGrath, Judith. *Pretty Girl* (7–10). 1987, Morrow $12.88 (0-688-00694-9); paper $7.95 (0-688-00695-7). A girl's guide to good grooming that gives many beauty secrets. [646.7]

3264 Saunders, Rubie. *Good Grooming for Boys* (6–9). Rev. ed. Illus. 1989, Watts LB $12.90 (0-531-10768-X). A guide that includes material on hygiene, diet, and exercise. (Rev: BR 3–4/90; SLJ 1/90; VOYA 2/90) [646.7]

3265 Saunders, Rubie. *Good Grooming for Girls* (6–9). Rev. ed. Illus. 1989, Watts LB $12.90 (0-531-10769-8). A revision of the book that covers such topics as skin care, cleanliness, and diet. (Rev: BR 3–4/90; SLJ 1/90; VOYA 2/90) [646.7]

3266 Zeldis, Yona. *Coping with Beauty, Fitness, and Fashion: A Girl's Guide* (7–12). Illus. 1987, Rosen $12.95 (0-8239-0731-7). A practical guide covering such topics as makeup, exercise, dress and skin care. (Rev: BL 7/87; BR 11–12/87; SLJ 9/87) [646.7]

The Human Body

General and Miscellaneous

3267 Bruun, Ruth Dowling, and Bertel Bruun. *The Human Body* (6–9). Illus. 1982, Random LB $11.99 (0-394-94424-0); paper $9.95 (0-394-84424-6). The first part of this book describes the parts of the body and the second part reviews its various systems. [612]

3268 Caselli, Giovanni. *The Human Body and How It Works* (5–8). Illus. 1987, Putnam $14.95 (0-448-18997-6). The various systems of the human body are described through text and imaginative, often humorous, drawings. (Rev: BL 2/1/88; SLJ 3/88) [611]

3269 Crump, Donald J., ed. *Your Wonderful Body* (6–9). Illus. 1982, National Geographic LB $8.50 (0-87044-428-X). An attractive volume about the basic parts and functions of the human body in a question-and-answer format. [612]

3270 Donner, Carol. *The Magic Anatomy Book* (6–8). Illus. 1986, Freeman $17.95 (0-7167-1715-8). A fictionalized journey through the human body by a noted medical illustrator. (Rev: BR 11–12/86) [611]

3271 Fekete, Irene, and Peter Dorrington Ward. *Your Body* (6–9). Illus. 1984, Facts on File $12.95 (0-87196-989-0). In this oversized book, human anatomy is introduced in clear text and many color illustrations. (Rev: BL 3/15/85) [612]

3272 Herbst, Judith. *Bio Amazing: A Casebook of Unsolved Human Mysteries* (6–8). 1985, Macmillan $11.95 (0-689-31151-6). Some mysteries about the human body such as hypnosis, ESP, and near-death experiences are explored. (Rev: BL 2/1/86; SLJ 12/85) [612]

3273 Kittredge, Mary. *The Human Body: An Overview* (7–12). Illus. 1989, Chelsea House LB $17.95 (0-7910-0019-2). After a brief history of how we found out about the human body, this book explains each of the systems carefully and with several illustrations. (Rev: SLJ 3/90) [611]

3274 Seuling, Barbara. *You Can't Sneeze with Your Eyes Open* (4–8). Illus. 1986, Lodestar $10.95 (0-525-67185-4). A fascinating group of curious facts about the human body. (Rev: SLJ 2/87) [611]

3275 Silverstein, Alvin, and Virginia B. Silverstein. *Wonders of Speech* (7–10). Illus. 1988, Morrow $11.95 (0-688-06534-1). This covers a number of subjects such as the speech organs, the brain's role in speech, and such variant forms of communication as body language and computers. (Rev: BL 6/15/88; BR 5–6/88) [001.54]

3276 Walpole, Brenda. *The Julian Messner Pocket Book of the Human Body* (6–10). Illus. 1987, Messner LB $9.79 (0-671-63031-8); Wanderer paper $6.95 (0-671-62973-5). A good introduction with fine illustrations to the workings of the human body. (Rev: SLJ 6–7/87) [611]

3277 Whitfield, Philip, and Ruth Whitfield. *Why Do Our Bodies Stop Growing? Questions about Human Anatomy Answered by the Natural History Museum* (6–9). Illus. 1988, Viking $15.95 (0-670-82331-7). Such questions as "What causes goose bumps?" are answered in this book about how the human body functions. (Rev: BL 1/1/89) [611]

Brain and Nervous System

3278 Berger, Melvin. *Exploring the Mind and Brain* (7–10). Illus. 1983, Harper LB $12.89 (0-690-04252-3). A book about the functions—both normal and abnormal—of the brain. [612]

3279 Cohen, Daniel. *ESP: The New Technology* (6–8). Illus. 1986, Messner LB $9.59 (0-671-61151-8). A serious presentation of the present studies in psychic research and their findings. (Rev: BL 7/86; SLJ 10/86) [133.8]

3280 Facklam, Margery, and Howard Facklam. *The Brain: Magnificent Mind Machine* (7–12). Illus. 1982, Harcourt $12.95 (0-15-211388-6). Brain research from early times to current work on biofeedback is emphasized in this account. [612]

3281 Gallant, Roy A. *Memory: How It Works and How to Improve It* (7–9). Illus. 1980, Macmillan $11.95 (0-590-07613-2). An account of how the brain stores information and how to improve the ability to remember. [153.1]

3282 Kettelkamp, Larry. *The Human Brain* (6–10). Illus. 1986, Enslow $14.95 (0-89490-126-5). A fine overview of the composition and functions of the brain and nervous system. (Rev: BL 8/86; BR 11–12/86; SLJ 11/86; VOYA 12/86) [612]

3283 Parker, Steve. *The Brain and Nervous System* (6–8). Rev. ed. Illus. 1990, Watts LB $12.90

(0-531-14026-1). The parts of the brain and their functions are discussed plus such topics as aging and memory. (Rev: BL 5/15/90) [612.8]

3284 Silverstein, Alvin, and Virginia B. Silverstein. *Sleep and Dreams* (7–9). 1974, Harper LB $12.89 (0-397-31325-X). The research into sleep is reviewed plus a description of our sleep patterns, dreams, and what they mean. [154.6]

3285 Silverstein, Alvin, and Virginia B. Silverstein. *World of the Brain* (5–9). Illus. 1986, Morrow $12.95 (0-688-05777-2). In addition to a general discussion on the way the brain functions, this account details recent discoveries and treatments that can be used to treat disorders. (Rev: BL 8/86; SLJ 8/86; VOYA 8–10/86) [612]

3286 Stafford, Patricia. *Your Two Brains* (5–8). Illus. 1986, Macmillan LB $11.95 (0-689-31142-7). A readable, informative book that tells about the right and left brains and how they function. (Rev: SLJ 10/86) [611]

3287 Ward, Brian R. *The Brain and Nervous System* (6–9). Illus. 1981, Watts LB $12.40 (0-531-04288-X). A clear, concise guide to the nervous system in text and color diagrams. [612]

3288 Yepsen, Roger. *Smarten Up! How to Increase Your Brain Power* (5–8). Illus. 1990, Little $13.95 (0-316-96864-1). After a discussion of how the brain operates, the author explains how one can boost mental agility. (Rev: BL 7/90; SLJ 7/90) [155.42]

Circulation System

3289 Avraham, Regina. *The Circulatory System* (7–12). Illus. 1989, Chelsea House $17.95 (0-7910-0013-3). In addition to a description of the heart and circulatory system, Avraham describes various heart ailments, their treatment, and how various substances such as tobacco affect the heart. (Rev: BL 3/1/89; BR 11–12/89; SLJ 6/89; VOYA 8/89) [612.1]

3290 Dunbar, Robert E. *The Heart and Circulatory System* (7–9). Illus. 1984, Watts LB $12.95 (0-531-04766-0). In addition to a description of how the heart works, this compact volume outlines many related activities and projects. [612]

3291 McGowen, Tom. *The Circulatory System: From Harvey to the Artificial Heart* (6–8). Illus. 1988, Watts $10.40 (0-531-10574-1). From the ancient Egyptians onward, a history of what we know about the heart, its problems, and the solutions. (Rev: BL 11/15/88; SLJ 4/89) [612]

3292 Parker, Steve. *Living with Heart Disease* (5–8). Illus. 1989, Watts LB $11.90 (0-531-10845-7). The various kinds of heart disease are outlined, types of treatment, and ways to cope for the afflicted. (Rev: BL 2/1/90; SLJ 2/90) [616.1]

3293 Silverstein, Alvin, and Virginia B. Silverstein. *Heart Disease: America's #1 Killer* (7–10). Rev. ed. Illus. 1985, Harper LB $12.89 (0-397-32084-1). After a description of heart diseases, the authors present material on current treatments and preventative measures. (Rev: BR 5–6/86; SLJ 1/86) [611]

3294 Silverstein, Alvin, and Virginia B. Silverstein. *Heartbeats: Your Body, Your Heart* (7–10). Illus. 1983, Harper LB $11.89 (0-397-32038-8). Following a description of the heart and how it works, there are sections on heart disease and current research. [612]

3295 Tiger, Steven. *Heart Disease* (5–8). Illus. 1986, Messner LB $11.86 (0-671-60021-4). A fine introduction to the circulatory system, the heart, and what happens when they malfunction. (Rev: SLJ 1/87) [616.1]

3296 Ward, Brian R. *The Heart and Blood* (6–9). Illus. 1982, Watts LB $12.40 (0-531-04357-6). This is a well-organized introduction to the circulatory and lymphatic systems and to the disorders often associated with them. [612]

Digestive and Excretory Systems

3297 Avraham, Regina. *The Digestive System* (6–12). Illus. 1989, Chelsea House $17.95 (0-7910-0015-X). In a few photographs and diagrams plus text, the human digestive system is explored with a history of how we gradually accumulated knowledge about it. (Rev: BL 9/1/89; BR 11–12/89) [612]

3298 Parker, Steve. *Food and Digestion* (6–8). Rev. ed. Illus. 1990, Watts LB $12.90 (0-531-14027-X). The process of digestion is analyzed plus pointers on nutrition and good health. (Rev: BL 5/15/90) [612.3]

3299 Silverstein, Alvin, and Virginia B. Silverstein. *The Story of Your Mouth* (7–10). Illus. 1984, Putnam LB $7.99 (0-698-30742-9). The structure of the mouth, its functions, teeth, gums, and mouth problems are discussed. [612]

3300 Ward, Brian R. *Food and Digestion* (6–9). Illus. 1982, Watts LB $12.40 (0-531-04458-0). A clear, simple introduction to the digestive system. [612]

Respiratory System

3301 Kittredge, Mary. *The Respiratory System* (6–12). Illus. 1989, Chelsea House $17.95 (0-7910-0026-5). Beginning with an explanation of how animals breathe, the author describes the human breathing system and ills connected with it. (Rev: BL 3/15/89; BR 11–12/89; VOYA 8/89) [612]

3302 Ward, Brian R. *The Lungs and Breathing* (6–9). Illus. 1982, Watts LB $12.40 (0-531-04358-4). The respiratory system is introduced in a concise text with excellent graphics. [612]

Senses

3303 Churchill, E. Richard. *Optical Illusion Tricks & Toys* (6–10). Illus. 1989, Sterling $11.95 (0-8069-6868-0). A collection of over 60 optical illusions and tricks that are both fun to perform and instructive in the principles of optics. (Rev: SLJ 10/89) [152.1]

3304 Cobb, Vicki. *How to Really Fool Yourself: Illusions for All Your Senses* (7–9). Illus. 1981, Harper LB $12.89 (0-397-31908-8). A book about perception, how illusions are created, and how they are present in everyday life. [152.1]

3305 Martin, Paul D. *Messengers to the Brain: Our Fantastic Five Senses* (6–9). Illus. 1984, National Geographic LB $8.50 (0-87044-504-9). A well-illustrated introduction to the 5 senses and how they work. [612]

3306 Paraquin, Charles H. *Eye Teasers: Optical Illusion Puzzles* (7–9). Trans. by Paul Kuttner. Illus. 1978, Sterling LB $9.99 (0-8069-4539-7). A group of optical illusions that belie the adage that seeing is believing. [070.5]

3307 Rahn, Joan Elma. *Ears, Hearing, and Balance* (7–9). Illus. 1984, Macmillan $12.95 (0-689-31055-2). This account covers the sense of hearing, how it is accomplished, and what happens when it malfunctions. [617.8]

3308 Rahn, Joan Elma. *Eyes and Seeing* (7–9). Illus. 1981, Macmillan $10.95 (0-689-30828-0). After a description of the sense of sight, Rahn describes different kinds of eyes and gives some experiments involving light. [611]

3309 Silverstein, Alvin, and Virginia B. Silverstein. *Glasses and Contact Lenses: Your Guide to Eyes, Eyewear, and Eye Care* (6–9). Illus. 1989, Harper LB $12.89 (0-397-32185-6). A description of how the eye functions, disorders connected with it, and how glasses can help. (Rev:

BL 6/15/89; BR 1–2/90; SLJ 6/89; VOYA 8/89) [617.7]

3310 Silverstein, Alvin, and Virginia B. Silverstein. *The Story of Your Ear* (7–10). Illus. 1981, Putnam LB $6.99 (0-698-30704-6). Some general information on sound plus an account of how the ear functions and the problems caused when hearing is impaired. [612]

3311 Simon, Seymour. *The Optical Illusion Book* (7–9). Illus. 1984, Morrow LB $12.88 (0-688-03255-9); paper $6.95 (0-688-03254-0). How optical illusions are created and the part that the brain as well as the eye plays in their perception. [152.1]

3312 Ward, Brian R. *The Ear and Hearing* (6–9). Illus. 1981, Watts LB $12.40 (0-531-04289-8). A simple introduction with color diagrams on how the ear functions. [612]

3313 Ward, Brian R. *The Eye and Seeing* (6–9). Illus. 1981, Watts LB $12.40 (0-531-04290-1). Topics covered include the structure of the eye, how it functions, problems associated with the eyes, and how they can be corrected. [612]

3314 Ward, Brian R. *Touch, Taste and Smell* (6–9). Illus. 1982, Watts LB $12.40 (0-531-04460-2). These 3 senses are described and the organs associated with them are identified. [612]

Skeletal-Muscular System

3315 Ward, Brian R. *The Skeleton and Movement* (6–9). Illus. 1981, Watts LB $12.40 (0-531-04291-X). This book discusses bones and muscles and how, together, they promote movement. [612]

Skin and Hair

3316 Lamberg, Lynne. *Skin Disorders* (7–12). Illus. 1990, Chelsea House $18.95 (0-7910-0076-1). A discussion of how the skin functions and of malfunctions such as acne, skin cancer, and herpes. (Rev: BL 5/1/90; SLJ 8/90) [616.5]

3317 Novick, Nelson Lee. *Skin Care for Teens* (7–12). Illus. 1988, Watts $12.40 (0-531-10521-0). A no-nonsense practical guide from a well-known dermatologist. (Rev: BL 6/15/88; BR 9–10/88; SLJ 8/88; VOYA 10/88) [646.7]

3318 Riedman, Sarah R. *The Good Looks Skin Book* (7–12). Illus. 1983, Messner LB $9.29 (0-671-46744-1). A basic guide to how the skin functions and how to keep it healthy plus cover-

age on acne, freckles, cosmetics, and so on. [646.7]

3319 Silverstein, Alvin, et al. *Overcoming Acne: The How and Why of Healthy Skin Care* (7–12). 1990, Morrow $12.95 (0-688-08344-7). This should be a popular book considering that 90 percent of adolescents suffer from some form of acne and that this account is thorough and well balanced. (Rev: BL 4/15/90; SLJ 6/90) [616.5]

Teeth

3320 Rourke, A. *Teeth and Braces* (6–9). Illus. 1989, Rourke LB $9.95 (0-86625-282-7). Topics covered in this book include teeth structure, dental care, malocclusion, and gum problems. (Rev: SLJ 6/89) [617.6]

3321 Silverstein, Alvin, and Virginia B. Silverstein. *So You're Getting Braces: A Guide to Orthodontics* (6–9). 1978, Harper LB $12.89 (0-397-31786-7); paper $3.95 (0-397-31787-5). The dental specialization of orthodontics is explained as well as why braces are often needed. [617.6]

3322 Ward, Brian R. *Dental Care* (5–9). Illus. 1986, Watts LB $12.40 (0-531-10179-7). In addition to a description of the types and parts of teeth, this book tells of dental disorders and how to prevent or treat each condition. (Rev: BR 3–4/87; SLJ 2/87) [617.6]

Hygiene and Physical Fitness

3323 Bershad, Carol, and Deborah Bernick. *Bodyworks: The Kids' Guide to Food and Physical Fitness* (6–9). Illus. 1981, Random LB $8.99 (0-394-94752-5); paper $5.95 (0-394-84752-0). A serious book that handles with a humorous approach an introduction to body systems and how to keep healthy. [613]

3324 Carr, Rachel. *Wheel, Camel, Fish, and Plow: Yoga for You* (7–9). Illus. 1981, Prentice $9.95 (0-13-956045-9). An explanation of what yoga is and descriptions of 13 basic exercises. [613.7]

3325 Kettelkamp, Larry. *Modern Sports Science* (6–9). Illus. 1986, Morrow $12.95 (0-688-05494-3). An in-body look at how scientific principles are involved during exercising and sports training. (Rev: BL 11/1/86; BR 11–12/86; SLJ 12/86) [613.7]

3326 Simon, Nissa. *Good Sports: Plain Talk about Health and Fitness for Teens* (7–10). Illus. 1990, Harper LB $13.89 (0-690-04904-8). This book covers a variety of topics including nutrition, different kinds of exercise, and sports injuries. (Rev: BL 9/15/90) [613]

3327 Thompson, Trisha. *Maintaining Good Health* (7–12). Illus. 1989, Facts on File $18.95 (0-8160-1667-4). Using a question and answer format basic questions on health, exercise, and diet are discussed. (Rev: BR 9–10/89; VOYA 8/89) [613]

3328 Zeleznak, Shirley. *Jogging* (7–9). 1980, Crestwood LB $8.95 (0-89686-068-X). This popular exercise is introduced with tips on techniques, clothing, and attitudes. [796.4]

Mental Disorders and Emotional Problems

3329 Claypool, Jane, and Cheryl Diane Nelsen. *Food Trips and Traps: Coping with Eating Disorders* (7–10). Illus. 1983, Watts LB $11.90 (0-531-04664-8). Three eating disorders—bulimia, bulimarexia, and anorexia nervosa—are described. [616.8]

3330 Dick, Jean. *Mental & Emotional Disabilities* (7–10). Illus. 1988, Crestwood $10.95 (0-89686-418-9). Problems such as dyslexia, retardation, autism, and depression are investigated in this clear account. (Rev: BL 4/1/89; SLJ 2/89) [616.89]

3331 Dinner, Sherry H. *Nothing to Be Ashamed Of: Growing up with Mental Illness in Your Family* (5–10). 1989, Lothrop LB $13.00 (0-688-08482-6); paper $8.00 (0-688-08493-1). A psychologist gives good advice to those who must live with a mentally ill person. (Rev: BL 6/1/89; BR 11–12/89; SLJ 4/89; VOYA 8/89) [616.89]

3332 Epstein, Rachel. *Eating Habits and Disorders* (7–12). Illus. 1990, Chelsea House $18.95 (0-7910-0048-6). A little history on eating disorders is given, but the major focus of this book is on the kinds of eating disorders and their treatments. (Rev: BL 6/1/90; SLJ 8/90) [616.85]

3333 Erlanger, Ellen. *Eating Disorders: A Question and Answer Book about Anorexia Nervosa and Bulimia Nervosa* (6–8). Illus. 1988, Lerner $9.95 (0-8225-0038-8). Case studies are used to introduce the cases, symptoms, and treatment of these disorders. (Rev: BL 3/15/88; SLJ 4/88) [616.85]

3334 Fisher, Gary L., and Rhoda Woods Cummings. *The Survival Guide for Kids with LD (Learning Differences)* (5–8). Illus. 1990, Free Spirit paper $9.95 (0-915793-18-0). A book that explains various kinds of learning disabilities and how to cope with them. (Rev: BL 7/90; SLJ 6/90) [371.9]

3335 Francis, Dorothy B. *Suicide: A Preventable Tragedy* (7–12). 1989, Lodestar $12.95 (0-525-67279-6). This book on suicide concentrates on its causes and methods of prevention. (Rev: BR 1–2/90; SLJ 8/89; VOYA 8/89) [362.7]

3336 Hermes, Patricia. *A Time to Listen: Preventing Youth Suicide* (8–12). 1987, Harcourt $12.95 (0-15-288196-4). Through questions and answers plus many case studies, the author explores many aspects of suicidal behavior and its causes. (Rev: BL 4/1/88; SLJ 3/88; VOYA 6/88) [362.2]

3337 Hyde, Margaret O. *Is This Kid "Crazy"? Understanding Unusual Behavior* (7–10). 1983, Westminster $9.95 (0-664-32707-9). The author explores such mental problems as depression, schizophrenia, and eating disorders. [616.8]

3338 Hyde, Margaret O., and Elizabeth H. Forsyth. *Suicide: The Hidden Epidemic* (7–12). Rev. ed. 1986, Watts $12.90 (0-531-10251-3). An account that stresses an analysis of the causes of suicide. (Rev: BL 12/1/86) [362.2]

3339 Klagsbrun, Francine. *Too Young to Die: Youth and Suicide* (7–12). 3rd ed. 1984, Pocket paper $3.95 (0-671-60405-8). The reasons for teenage suicide are explained plus ways of preventing it, including crisis intervention centers. [362.7]

3340 Knox, Jean McBee. *Learning Disabilities* (7–12). Illus. 1989, Chelsea House LB $17.95 (0-7910-0049-4). An account that covers such conditions as dyslexia, dyscalculia, and hyperactivity. (Rev: BR 11–12/89; SLJ 12/89; VOYA 12/89) [153.1]

3341 Kolehmainen, Janet, and Sandra Handwerk. *Teen Suicide: A Book for Friends, Family, and Classmates* (6–8). 1986, Lerner $9.95 (0-8225-0037-X); paper $4.95 (0-8225-9514-1). A book that enumerates the kinds of suicidal behavior and what to do when one sees them in friends and classmates. (Rev: BL 1/15/87; SLJ 6–7/87; VOYA 4/87) [362.2]

3342 Landau, Elaine. *Why Are They Starving Themselves? Understanding Anorexia Nervosa and Bulimia* (7–10). 1983, Messner LB $11.29 (0-671-45582-6); paper $4.95 (0-671-49492-2). Case studies are used as a focal point for explaining these eating disorders. [616.8]

3343 Langone, John. *Dead End: A Book about Suicide* (7–12). 1986, Little $12.95 (0-316-51432-2). A general discussion of the causes of suicide and excellent coverage on suicide prevention programs. (Rev: BL 12/1/86; BR 3–4/87; SLJ 11/86; VOYA 2/87) [362.2]

3344 Lundy, Allan. *Diagnosing and Treating Mental Illness* (7–12). Illus. 1990, Chelsea House $18.95 (0-7910-0047-8). An account that explains various mental disorders and covers the work of Freud, among others. (Rev: BL 6/1/90; VOYA 8/90) [616.89]

3345 Madison, Arnold. *Suicide and Young People* (7–10). 1978, Clarion $13.95 (0-395-28913-0); paper $5.95 (0-395-30011-8). Background facts and statistics plus case histories and interviews are used to explore many aspects of this problem. [362.7]

3346 Savage, John F. *Dyslexia: Understanding Reading Problems* (6–8). Illus. 1985, Messner $9.29 (0-671-54289-3). A description of the many learning problems that collectively are called dyslexia and present-day treatment. (Rev: BL 2/1/86; SLJ 12/85) [618.92]

3347 Schleifer, Jay. *Everything You Need to Know about Teen Suicide* (7–12). Illus. 1988, Rosen $11.95 (0-8239-0812-7). Basic information is given on this sensitive subject in an easy-to-read treatment. (Rev: BL 9/15/88; SLJ 10/88; VOYA 2/89) [362.2]

3348 Stewart, Gail. *Teen Suicide* (7–10). Illus. 1988, Crestwood LB $10.95 (0-89686-413-8). A brief account that discusses the causes and preventive methods involving teenage suicide. (Rev: SLJ 3/89) [362.2]

3349 Wolhart, Dayna. *Anorexia & Bulimia* (7–12). Illus. 1988, Crestwood $10.95 (0-89686-416-2). Eating disorders are explained, possible causes are suggested, and solutions are proposed. (Rev: BL 4/1/89; SLJ 3/89) [616.85]

3350 Young, Patrick. *Mental Disturbances* (7–10). Illus. 1988, Chelsea House $17.95 (1-55546-206-5). A discussion of various forms of mental illness such as phobias and bulimia that often affect teenagers. (Rev: BL 7/88) [616.89]

Nutrition and Diet

3351 Arnold, Caroline. *Too Fat? Too Thin? Do You Have a Choice?* (7–12). 1984, Morrow LB $11.88 (0-688-02780-6); paper $5.25 (0-688-

02779-2). Such topics as heredity, diet, nutrition, and exercise are discussed. [613.2]

3352 Eagles, Douglas A. *Your Weight* (7–9). Illus. 1982, Watts LB $10.40 (0-531-04395-9). A practical book on the nature of weight loss and its advisability. [613.2]

3353 Gelinas, Paul J. *Coping with Weight Problems* (7–10). 1983, Rosen $12.95 (0-8239-0598-5). A guide to weight problems, their causes, and their solutions. [613.2]

3354 Hyman, Jane, and Barbara Posner. *The Fitness Book* (6–9). Illus. 1984, Wanderer $11.29 (0-671-46741-7); paper $3.95 (0-671-46433-7). This book not only covers exercise and nutrition but also gives extensive material on weight control. (Rev: BL 3/15/85) [613.2]

3355 Kane, June Kozak. *Coping with Diet Fads* (7–12). 1990, Rosen $12.95 (0-8239-1005-9). An account that explores the wrong and right ways to diet and also furnishes useful advice. (Rev: BL 3/15/90; VOYA 8/90) [613]

3356 Lee, Sally. *New Theories on Diet and Nutrition* (7–12). Illus. 1990, Watts LB $12.90 (0-531-10930-5). Such topics as diet, nutrition, and exercise are presented in light of current research findings. (Rev: BL 4/1/90; SLJ 6/90; VOYA 8/90) [613.2]

3357 Lukes, Bonnie L. *How to Be a Reasonably Thin Teenage Girl* (6–9). Illus. 1986, Macmillan $12.95 (0-689-31269-5). A commonsense guide that addresses the particular weight problems of young teenagers. (Rev: BL 1/1/87; SLJ 11/86; VOYA 4/87) [613.2]

3358 Peavy, Linda, and Ursula Smith. *Food, Nutrition, and You* (7–10). Illus. 1982, Macmillan $13.95 (0-684-17461-8). A discussion of digestion, food values, weight, and weight problems. [613.2]

3359 Perl, Lila. *Junk Food, Fast Food, Health Food: What America Eats and Why* (6–9). 1980, Clarion $13.95 (0-395-29108-9). A guide to food processing, convenience foods, and to some nutritious recipes. [641]

3360 Sanchez, Gail Jones, and Mary Gerbino. *Overeating: Let's Talk about It* (6–10). Illus. 1986, Dillon $9.95 (0-87518-319-0). This book explores the reasons why people overeat and suggests various solutions. (Rev: SLJ 2/87) [613.2]

3361 Spence, Annette. *Nutrition* (7–9). Illus. 1989, Facts on File $18.95 (0-8160-1670-4). After general information on nutrition, this account gives details on the use of food to improve and maintain health. (Rev: VOYA 8/89) [641.1]

3362 Thompson, Paul. *Nutrition* (6–9). Illus. 1981, Watts LB $10.40 (0-531-04328-2). A look at the digestive system and at various food groups and how each nourishes the body. [641.1]

3363 Ward, Brian R. *Diet and Nutrition* (5–8). Illus. 1987, Watts LB $12.40 (0-531-10259-9). An easily read survey that consists primarily of photographs and text about various food groups. (Rev: BR 5–6/87; SLJ 6–7/87) [641.1]

Physical Disabilities and Problems

3364 Allen, Anne. *Sports for the Handicapped* (7–9). 1981, Walker LB $10.95 (0-8027-6437-1). A description is given of sports in which handicapped people participate and organizations that help sponsor such activities. [790.1]

3365 Baron, Connie. *The Physically Disabled* (7–10). Illus. 1988, Crestwood $10.95 (0-89686-417-0). All sorts of physical handicaps from cerebral palsy to arthritis are explored. (Rev: BL 4/1/89; SLJ 3/89) [362.4]

3366 Berger, Gilda. *Speech and Language Disorders* (7–10). Illus. 1981, Watts LB $12.90 (0-531-04263-4). The origins and treatments for such speech disorders as stuttering and lisping. [616.8]

3367 Betancourt, Jeanne. *Smile! How to Cope with Braces* (6–9). Illus. 1982, Knopf LB $8.99 (0-394-94732-0); paper $5.95 (0-394-84732-6). This book explains why braces are often needed plus how to act with them in your mouth. [617.6]

3368 Costello, Elaine. *Signing: How to Speak with Your Hands* (7–9). Illus. 1983, Bantam paper $12.95 (0-553-01458-7). A simple explanation of and a guide to the use of sign language for the deaf. [001.56]

3369 Drimmer, Frederick. *Born Different: The Amazing Stories of Some Very Special People* (7–10). Illus. 1988, Macmillan $13.95 (0-689-31360-8). The lives of 7 different people—such as Tom Thumb, the Elephant Man, and the original Siamese twins—and the ways in which these people made the best of physical problems. (Rev: SLJ 1/89; VOYA 4/89) [362.4]

3370 Greene, Laura, and Eva Barash Dicker. *Sign Language* (7–9). 1981, Watts LB $11.90 (0-531-04195-6). The history of communication with the deaf by sign language is given plus a description of each format. [419]

3371 Greene, Laura, and Eva Barash Dicker. *Sign Language Talk* (5–9). Illus. 1989, Watts LB $10.90 (0-531-10597-0). A book that explains how to formulate sentences using sign language. The basics are covered in the authors' earlier *Discovering Sign Language* (1988). (Rev: BL 8/89; SLJ 8/89; VOYA 12/89) [419]

3372 Parker, Steve. *Living with Blindness* (5–8). Illus. 1989, Watts LB $11.90 (0-531-10843-0). The causes of blindness are explained plus information on how to cope with this handicap. (Rev: BL 2/1/90; SLJ 2/90) [617.7]

3373 Silverstein, Alvin, and Virginia B. Silverstein. *Epilepsy* (7–10). Illus. 1975, Harper $12.70 (0-397-31615-1). Sweeping aside all the untruths associated with this problem, the authors describe the cause and effect of seizures and their treatment. [616.8]

3374 Sullivan, Mary Beth, and Linda Bourke. *A Show of Hands: Say It in Sign Language* (7–9). Illus. 1980, Harper LB $12.70 (0-201-07456-7). A manual on sign language and how to use it. [419]

3375 Taylor, Barbara. *Living with Deafness* (5–8). Illus. 1989, Watts LB $11.90 (0-531-10842-2). In addition to a description of the causes of deafness, material is given on methods to adjust to this handicap. (Rev: BL 2/1/90) [617.8]

3376 Yates, Elizabeth. *Sound Friendships: The Story of Willa and Her Hearing Ear Dog* (5–9). 1987, Countryman paper $7.95 (0-88150-081-X). This book deals with the training of hearing aide dogs and how they are matched to their eventual owners. (Rev: SLJ 6–7/87) [362.4]

Safety, Accidents, and First Aid

3377 Berger, Melvin. *Sports Medicine: Scientists at Work* (7–10). Illus. 1982, Harper LB $12.89 (0-690-04210-8). The kinds of injuries that occur in sports and how they are treated are 2 topics discussed. [617]

3378 Edelson, Edward. *Sports Medicine* (7–10). Illus. 1988, Chelsea House $17.95 (0-7910-0030-3). A guide to the prevention, diagnosis, and treatment of all kinds of sports injuries. (Rev: BL 7/88; BR 9–10/88) [617]

3379 Ward, Brian R. *First Aid* (5–8). Illus. 1987, Watts LB $12.40 (0-531-10260-2). A simple survey that covers in text and photographs the principles of first aid. (Rev: BR 5–6/87; SLJ 6–7/87) [616.04]

Sex Education and Reproduction

3380 Ball, Jacqueline A. *Puberty* (6–9). Illus. 1989, Rourke LB $9.95 (0-86625-283-5). This account aimed at young girls covers such topics as maturation, social problems, and menstruation. (Rev: SLJ 6/89) [305.2]

3381 Bell, Ruth. *Changing Bodies, Changing Lives: A Book for Teens on Sex and Relationships* (7–12). Illus. 1980, Random $19.95 (0-394-50304-X); paper $12.95 (0-394-73632-X). Many experts combine their knowledge to discuss teenage sexuality and the emotional and physical changes that occur during adolescence. (Rev: BL 6/1/88; SLJ 6–7/88) [613.9]

3382 Berger, Gilda. *PMS: Pre-Menstrual Syndrome* (7–12). Illus. 1984, Watts LB $12.90 (0-531-04857-8). A book about the menstrual cycle and the problems it can involve. [618.1]

3383 Betancourt, Jeanne. *Am I Normal?* (7–9). Illus. 1986, Avon paper $1.95 (0-380-82040-4). For boys, this is an illustrated guide to the many changes that occur during puberty written in a reassuring style. [155.5]

3384 Cahn, Julie. *The Dating Book: A Guide to the Social Scene* (8–12). 1983, Messner LB $9.29 (0-671-46742-5); paper $3.40 (0-671-46277-6). This answers many questions girls ask including those on sex, venereal disease, and pregnancy. [306.7]

3385 Gale, Jay. *A Young Man's Guide to Sex* (8–12). Illus. 1984, Holt $14.95 (0-03-069396-9); Price/Stern/Sloan paper $7.95 (0-89586-691-9). This practical manual about young men's sexuality covers such topics as diseases, contraception, and masturbation. [613.7]

3386 Hawksley, Jane. *Teen Guide to Pregnancy, Drugs and Smoking* (7–12). Illus. 1989, Watts LB $11.90 (0-531-10835-X). The effects of drugs, including alcohol, and nicotine on the fetus are described with specific recommendations. (Rev: BL 1/1/90; SLJ 3/90) [618]

3387 Hoch, Dean, and Nancy Hoch. *The Sex Education Dictionary for Today's Teens & Pre-Teens* (7–12). Illus. 1990, Landmark paper $12.95 (0-9624209-0-5). A dictionary of 350 words related to sex, sexuality, and reproduction all given clear, concise definitions. (Rev: BL 8/90) [306.7]

3388 Hughes, Tracy. *Everything You Need to Know about Teen Pregnancy* (7–12). Illus. 1988, Rosen LB $12.95 (0-8239-0810-0). A simple unbi-ased introduction to teen pregnancy and the options available. (Rev: SLJ 4/89) [612]

3389 Hyde, Margaret O. *Teen Sex* (7–12). 1988, Westminster $9.95 (0-664-32726-5). This book concentrates on material on sexually transmitted diseases (including AIDS) and pregnancy. (Rev: BL 10/1/88; SLJ 9/88) [306.7]

3390 Jakobson, Cathryn. *Think about Teenage Pregnancy* (7–12). Illus. 1988, Walker LB $14.85 (0-8027-6768-0); paper $5.95 (0-8027-6769-9). Problems of teenagers who are pregnant. All possible options are presented plus the social issues involved. (Rev: SLJ 8/88; VOYA 10/88) [612]

3391 Johnson, Eric W. *Love & Sex & Growing Up* (5–8). Illus. 1990, Bantam $13.99 (0-553-05864-9); paper $2.95 (0-553-15800-7). A basic introduction to sex education that contains material on sexually transmitted diseases and AIDS. (Rev: SLJ 7/90; VOYA 4/90) [612]

3392 Johnson, Eric W. *Love and Sex in Plain Language* (8–12). 4th ed. 1988, Bantam paper $3.95 (0-553-27473-2). An update of this standard sex education volume that includes such topics as AIDS. (Rev: BL 1/15/89; VOYA 2/89) [613.95]

3393 Johnson, Eric W. *People, Love, Sex and Families* (7–12). Illus. 1985, Walker $13.95 (0-8027-6591-2). Johnson answers frank questions about sex and relationships posed by 1,000 pre-teens and teenagers. (Rev: BR 3–4/86) [613.9]

3394 Kitzinger, Sheila. *Being Born* (5–12). Illus. 1986, Putnam $15.95 (0-448-18990-9). Beautiful color photographs highlight this account of life from conception to birth. (Rev: BL 12/15/86) [618.2]

3395 Lieberman, E. James, and Ellen Peck. *Sex & Birth Control: A Guide for the Young* (7–12). Rev. ed. Illus. 1981, Schocken paper $4.95 (0-8052-0701-5). A basic introduction to sexual intercourse, contraception, abortion, and related topics. [613.9]

3396 McCoy, Kathy, and Charles Wibbelsman. *The Teenage Body Book* (7–12). Rev. ed. Illus. 1984, Simon & Schuster paper $9.95 (0-671-45580-X). Though basically a book on sex education, this volume also talks about grooming and health. [613]

3397 Madaras, Lynda, and Area Madaras. *The What's Happening to My Body? Book for Girls* (7–12). Illus. 1988, Newmarket paper $9.95 (0-937858-98-6). A thorough introduction for girls to puberty that, in this new edition, includes material on such subjects as pregnancy and AIDS. (Rev: VOYA 6/89) [612]

3398 Madaras, Lynda, and Dane Saavedra. *The What's Happening to My Body? Book for Boys* (7–12). Illus. 1988, Newmarket paper $9.95 (0-937858-99-4). A new edition of this fine sex education manual that now includes material on such topics as sexually transmitted diseases and AIDS. (Rev: VOYA 6/89) [612]

3399 Mahoney, Ellen Voelckers. *Now You've Got Your Period* (6–9). Illus. 1988, Rosen LB $12.95 (0-8239-0792-9). In conversational tone, this book describes the process of menstruation and gives tips on how to ease cramps, how to use sanitary protection, and so on. (Rev: SLJ 8/88; VOYA 10/88) [612]

3400 Marzollo, Jean. *Getting Your Period: A Book about Menstruation* (5–10). 1989, Dial $13.95 (0-8037-0355-4); paper $6.95 (0-8037-0356-2). A clear introduction to puberty in general and the menstrual cycle in particular. (Rev: BL 7/89; BR 1–2/90; SLJ 7/89; VOYA 8/89) [612]

3401 Mucciolo, Gary. *Everything You Need to Know about Birth Control* (7–12). Illus. 1990, Rosen LB $12.95 (0-8239-1014-8). Popular forms of birth control including abstinence are discussed with material on the effectiveness of each. (Rev: SLJ 9/90; VOYA 8/90) [613.9]

3402 Nourse, Alan E. *Menstruation* (6–9). 1987, Watts $10.40 (0-531-10308-0). A revision of the excellent, straightforward book that now contains a section on toxic shock syndrome. (Rev: BR 11–12/87; VOYA 8–9/87) [612]

3403 Nourse, Alan E. *Teen Guide to Birth Control* (7–12). Illus. 1988, Watts $11.90 (0-531-10625-X). A concise but thorough guide written in simple terms that covers the subject in both text and many illustrations. (Rev: BL 1/15/89; BR 3–4/89; SLJ 1/89; VOYA 4/89) [613.9]

3404 Packer, Kenneth. *Puberty: The Story of Growth & Change* (6–10). Illus. 1989, Watts LB $11.90 (0-531-10810-4). An overview that describes the stages of growth and changes during puberty and gives material on the fertilization process and birth. (Rev: BR 5–6/90; VOYA 2/90) [612]

3405 Pomeroy, Wardell B. *Boys and Sex* (7–12). Rev. ed. 1981, Dell paper $2.95 (0-440-90753-5). From the male's point of view, this is a basic informative account of sexual development of teenagers. A companion volume is: *Girls and Sex* (1981). [613.9]

3406 Rench, Janice E. *Teen Sexuality: Decisions and Choices* (6–9). Illus. 1988, Lerner $9.95 (0-8225-0041-8). A book that explores teenage sexuality as well as the choices and consequences this brings. (Rev: BL 10/1/88; SLJ 9/88) [306.7]

3407 Silverstein, Herma. *Teenage and Pregnant: What You Can Do* (7–12). 1988, Messner LB $11.98 (0-671-65221-4); paper $5.95 (0-671-65222-2). Options available to pregnant teens are discussed plus related material on such subjects as contraception and care for the expectant mother. (Rev: BL 3/15/89; SLJ 2/89) [306.7]

3408 Spence, Annette. *Human Sexuality* (7–12). Illus. 1989, Facts on File $18.95 (0-8160-1666-6). In a question-and-answer format, a wide range of teen concerns about sex are explored. (Rev: BR 9–10/89; VOYA 8/89) [155.3]

3409 Ward, Brian R. *Birth and Growth* (6–9). Illus. 1983, Watts LB $12.40 (0-531-04459-9). This book covers human growth from the fertilization of the egg through birth and finally old age and death. [612]

3410 Wharton, Mandy. *Abortion* (6–9). Illus. 1989, Watts LB $11.90 (0-531-17189-2). After explaining what an abortion involves, Wharton presents a clear account of the differences in the way people feel about it. (Rev: BL 1/1/90; SLJ 4/90; VOYA 4/90) [363.4]

Sex Problems [Abuse]

3411 Aho, Jennifer, and John W. Petras. *Learning about Sexual Abuse* (6–8). 1985, Enslow $14.95 (0-89490-114-1). Topics covered include tricks used by strangers intent on child abuse, the necessity of talking to a trusted adult, and a child's right to privacy. (Rev: BR 3–4/86) [364.1]

3412 Benedict, Helen. *Safe, Strong and Streetwise* (8–12). 1986, Little $14.95 (0-87113-100-5); paper $5.95 (0-87113-100-5). A sensitive and sensible book that teaches one how to avoid sexual assault. (Rev: BR 1–2/87; VOYA 2/87) [364.1]

3413 Booher, Dianna Daniels. *Rape: What Would You Do If . . . ?* (7–12). 1983, Messner $11.29 (0-671-42201-4); paper $4.95 (0-671-49485-6). This book discusses what to do if raped as well as how to prevent it with examples of many safety precautions. [364.1]

3414 Bouchard, Elizabeth. *Everything You Need to Know about Sexual Harassment* (7–10). 1990, Rosen $12.95 (0-8239-1016-4). A guide to the different kinds of sexual harassment that exist, who does the harassing, who the victims are, and what to do about it. (Rev: VOYA 8/90) [305.4]

3415 Hyde, Margaret O. *Sexual Abuse—Let's Talk about It* (7–12). 1987, Westminster LB

$8.95 (0-664-32725-7). Through a generous use of case studies the author discusses the nature of sexual abuse and how one can protect oneself. (Rev: BL 2/15/88) [362.7]

3416 Terkel, Susan N. *Abortion* (8–12). Illus. 1988, Watts $12.90 (0-531-10565-2). A history of abortion is given plus an objective assessment of the opposing viewpoints of the pro-life and freedom-of-choice movements. (Rev: BL 12/1/88; SLJ 2/89; VOYA 4/89) [363.4]

3417 Terkel, Susan N., and Janice E. Rench. *Feeling Safe, Feeling Strong: How to Avoid Sexual Abuse and What to Do If It Happens to You* (7–9). 1984, Lerner LB $9.95 (0-8225-0021-3). By using 6 different cases, various forms of sexual abuse are explored. [362.7]

Human Development and Behavior

Psychology and Human Behavior

General and Miscellaneous

3418 Berger, Gilda. *Psychology Words* (6–9). 1986, Messner LB $9.59 (0-671-54291-5). Brief entries are given for important words and concepts in psychology and for important people in the field. (Rev: SLJ 3/86) [150]

3419 Berger, Melvin. *Mind Control* (6–10). 1985, Harper $12.70 (0-690-04348-1). Various kinds of brain control are explored in this account including brainwashing, hypnosis, and behavior modification. (Rev: BL 5/15/85; BR 11–12/85; SLJ 8/85; VOYA 12/85) [155.2]

3420 Booher, Dianna Daniels. *Help! We're Moving* (6–9). 1983, Messner LB $11.29 (0-671-46057-9). A guide that stresses the positive aspects on changing homes and the adjustments this requires. [305.2]

3421 Booher, Dianna Daniels. *Making Friends with Yourself & Other Strangers* (7–9). 1982, Messner LB $11.29 (0-671-45878-7). A book about the meaning of friendship and how to make and keep friends. [155.5]

3422 Harris, Robie, and Elizabeth Levy. *Before You Were Three* (6–8). Illus. 1981, Delacorte paper $7.95 (0-440-00471-3). Early childhood development is explained in text and copious photographs. [362.7]

3423 Sternberg, Patricia. *Speak to Me: Patricia Sternberg Tells How to Put Confidence in Your Conversation* (7–10). 1984, Lothrop paper $6.50 (0-688-02722-9). The techniques of carrying on a good conversation are explained, as well as tips for special occasions. [153.6]

3424 Stwertka, Eve. *Psychoanalysis: From Freud to the Age of Therapy* (7–9). Illus. 1988, Watts $9.90 (0-531-10481-8). An explanation of psychoanalytic concepts that focuses on the life of Freud. (Rev: BL 6/1/88; BR 9–10/88; SLJ 3/88) [150.19]

3425 Varenhorst, Barbara B. *Real Friends: Becoming the Friend You'd Like to Have* (7–10). Illus. 1983, Harper paper $8.95 (0-06-250890-3). A guide to the formation of peer counseling groups to discuss the problems of adolescence. [155.5]

3426 Ward, Hiley H. *Feeling Good about Myself* (7–12). 1983, Westminster $11.95 (0-664-32704-4). Using quotes from young people ages 9 through 18, the author begins a discussion of some of the most important problems young people face today. [155.5]

Emotions and Emotional Behavior

3427 Cohen, Susan, and Daniel Cohen. *Teenage Stress* (8–12). 1984, Evans LB $10.95 (0-87131-423-1). The nature of stress, how it can be avoided, and how it can be lessened are 3 topics of discussion.

3428 Connors, Patricia. *Runaways: Coping at Home & on the Street* (7–12). 1989, Rosen $12.95 (0-8239-1019-9). Using interviews and case studies the author describes why young people run away and what usually happens to them on the streets. (Rev: BR 3–4/90; VOYA 12/89) [362.7]

3429 Eagen, Andrea Boroff. *Why Am I So Miserable If These Are the Best Years of My Life? A Survival Guide for the Young Woman* (7–10). Illus. 1976, Harper $12.70 (0-397-31655-0); Morrow paper $2.95 (0-380-75495-9). A guide for girls on how to cope with the problems of adolescence. [155.5]

3430 Galbraith, Judy. *The Gifted Kids Survival Guide* (6–9). Illus. 1983, Free Spirit paper $8.95 (0-915793-01-6). A guide to help gifted and talented youngsters cope with their special problems. [155.5]

3431 Hales, Dianne. *Depression* (7–10). Illus. 1989, Chelsea House $17.95 (0-7910-0046-X). Types of depression are outlined. Includes material on the causes, effects, and cures of depression. (Rev: BL 11/1/89; BR 11–12/89; SLJ 2/90; VOYA 2/90) [616.85]

3432 Hyde, Margaret O., and Elizabeth H. Forsyth. *Horror, Fright, and Panic* (7–12). Rev. ed. 1987, Walker LB $12.85 (0-8072-6693-5). An exploration of all types of fear, from the normal protective variety to extremes of irrational anxieties and phobias. (Rev: BL 1/1/88; BR 5–6/88; SLJ 11/87) [152.4]

3433 Laiken, Deidre S., and Alan J. Schneider. *Listen to Me, I'm Angry* (7–10). Illus. 1980, Lothrop LB $12.88 (0-688-51943-1). The causes of anger in young people and how to cope with it. [152.4]

3434 LeShan, Eda. *You and Your Feelings* (7–9). 1975, Macmillan $9.95 (0-02-757330-3). An introduction to the world of emotions and how one can control them. [155.5]

3435 Myers, Irma, and Arthur Myers. *Why You Feel Down & What You Can Do about It* (7–10). 1982, Macmillan $12.95 (0-684-17442-1). This account describes depression, its causes, and how to cope with it. [155.5]

3436 Pringle, Laurence. *Living in a Risky World* (7–9). Illus. 1989, Morrow $12.95 (0-688-04326-7). An assessment of the risks people must take in life and how to minimize the fears involved. (Rev: BL 4/15/89; SLJ 7/89; VOYA 6/89) [363.2]

3437 Silverstein, Herma. *Teenage Depression* (7–12). 1990, Watts LB $12.90 (0-531-10960-7). A comprehensive volume that concentrates on the types of depression and their causes and possible cures. (Rev: SLJ 8/90) [616.85]

3438 VanWie, Eileen Kalberg. *Teenage Stress: How to Cope in a Complex World* (7–12). 1988, Messner LB $11.29 (0-671-63824-6). The causes of stress are examined, the various types enumerated, and advice on how to lessen these tensions is given. (Rev: SLJ 11/88) [612]

Ethics and Ethical Behavior

3439 Weiss, Ann E. *Lies, Deception and Truth* (6–9). 1988, Houghton $13.95 (0-395-40486-X). The author tackles tough questions, such as should you lie to protect someone and when is it wise not to be perfectly honest, in this challenging account. (Rev: BL 1/15/89; BR 1–2/89; SLJ 5/89; VOYA 12/88) [177.3]

Etiquette and Manners

3440 Carlson, Dale, and Dan Fitzgibbon. *Manners That Matter for People under Twenty-One* (7–12). 1983, Dutton $10.95 (0-525-44008-9). Standard etiquette is covered plus how to handle particular situations concerning teenagers. [395]

3441 Hoving, Walter. *Tiffany's Table Manners for Teenagers* (7–12). Illus. 1989, Random $9.95 (0-394-82877-1). A practical guide to good table manners. (Rev: BR 9–10/89; SLJ 6/89) [395]

3442 Post, Elizabeth L., and Joan M. Coles. *Emily Post Talks with Teens about Manners and Etiquette* (7–12). Illus. 1986, Harper $16.95 (0-06-181685-X); paper $6.95 (0-06-096117-1). An up-to-date guide to manners for teenagers by the granddaughter of Emily Post. (Rev: BL 12/1/86; BR 3–4/87; SLJ 3/87) [395]

3443 Powers, David Guy. *How to Run a Meeting* (6–8). Illus. 1985, Watts LB $10.40 (0-531-04641-9). An introductory look at parliamentary procedure and how it can be applied practically. (Rev: SLJ 10/85) [060.4]

3444 Robert, Henry M. *Robert's Rules of Order* (8–12). 1989, Scott, Foresman $16.95 (0-316-38735-5); paper $8.95 (0-316-38734-7). The most authoritative guide to running meetings. [060.4]

3445 Zeldis, Yona. *Coping with Social Situations: A Handbook of Correct Behavior* (7–10). Rev. ed. 1987, Rosen $10.97 (0-8239-0767-8). A handbook on how to cope in a variety of social situations from dating to getting along with family members. (Rev: BL 5/1/88) [395]

Intelligence and Thinking

3446 Cohen, Daniel. *Intelligence—What Is It?* (7–9). Illus. 1974, Evans $10.95 (0-87131-127-5). After trying to arrive at a definition of what is intelligence, this account details methods of intelligence testing. [153]

3447 Delisle, James R., and Judy Galbraith. *The Gifted Kids Survival Guide II: A Sequel to the Original Gifted Kids Survival Guide* (7–12). Illus. 1987, Free Spirit paper $9.95 (0-915793-09-1). A revision of the 1983 title that explains what it means to be gifted and how to cope with its problems and pleasures. (Rev: BL 11/15/87; SLJ 12/87) [371.95]

Personal Guidance

3448 Adderholdt-Elliott, Miriam. *Perfectionism: What's Bad about Being Too Good?* (7–12). Illus. 1987, Free Spirit paper $8.95 (0-915793-07-5). The difference between seeking high quality in one's work and perfectionism is explored plus the debilitating aspects of the latter. (Rev: BL 10/1/87) [158]

3449 Arnold, Caroline. *Coping with Natural Disasters* (7–10). Illus. 1988, Walker LB $14.85 (0-8027-6717-6). Various natural disasters like earthquakes, hurricanes, and blizzards are discussed, with information on how to react in these emergencies. (Rev: SLJ 6–7/88; VOYA 10/88) [904]

3450 Atanasoff, Stevan E. *How to Survive as a Teen: When No One Understands* (7–12). 1989, Herald paper $6.95 (0-8361-3478-8). A practical handbook that covers such topics as friendship, sex, peer pressure, family conflicts, drugs, and suicide. (Rev: SLJ 4/89) [155.5]

3451 Blume, Judy. *Letters to Judy: What Your Kids Wish They Could Tell You* (6–9). 1986, Pocket paper $4.50 (0-671-62696-5). This collection of letters and advisory comments covers all the problems encountered by young teens such as menstruation, drugs, popularity, and divorce. (Rev: BL 6/1/86; VOYA 8–10/86) [305.2]

3452 Chaback, Elaine, and Pat Fortunato. *The Official Kids' Survival Kit: How to Do Things on Your Own* (6–9). Illus. 1981, Little $22.95 (0-316-13532-1); paper $10.95 (0-316-13531-3). A practical manual on how to cope with many situations including those that require first aid. [640]

3453 Dolan, Edward F., Jr. *Protect Your Legal Rights: A Handbook for Teenagers* (7–10). 1983, Messner $11.29 (0-671-46121-4). An introduction to the legal rights of minors. [340]

3454 Filichia, Peter. *A Boy's-Eye-View of Girls* (7–10). 1983, Scholastic paper $1.95 (0-590-32314-8). Reprinted from *Seventeen* magazine, here is a collection of questions and answers that boys ask about relationships with girls. [155.5]

3455 Fleming, Alice. *What to Say When You Don't Know What to Say* (7–10). 1982, Macmillan $11.95 (0-684-17626-2). A guide on how to cope with all sorts of anxiety-producing situations. [158]

3456 Gersh, Marvin J. *The Handbook of Adolescence: A Medical Guide for Parents and Teenagers* (7–12). 1983, Scarborough House $10.95 (0-8128-6070-5). For adults and young people, this is a guide to the problems that can occur during adolescence from acne to venereal disease. [155.5]

3457 Gilbert, Sara. *Get Help: Solving the Problems in Your Life* (7–10). 1989, Morrow $12.95 (0-688-08010-3); paper $7.95 (0-688-08928-3). Gilbert gives sound advice to teens under such topics as "Family Crises," "Sexual Health," and "Running Away." (Rev: BL 7/89; BR 5–6/89; SLJ 6/89; VOYA 6/89) [362.2]

3458 Gordon, Sol. *The Teenage Survival Book* (7–12). 1981, Times Books paper $12.95 (0-8129-0972-0). This book discusses the important concerns and worries of adolescents and gives sound practical advice. [155.5]

3459 Johnson, Eric W. *How to Live with Parents and Teachers* (7–12). 1986, Westminster LB $12.95 (0-664-21273-5). This alphabetically arranged book covers such topics as dating, sex, peer pressure, and study habits. (Rev: SLJ 4/87) [155.5]

3460 Kyte, Kathy S. *In Charge: A Complete Handbook for Kids with Working Parents* (6–9). Illus. 1983, Knopf paper $6.95 (0-394-95408-4). A guidebook for youngsters who must spend time alone at home. [640]

3461 Mabery, D. L. *Tell Me about Yourself: How to Interview Anyone from Your Friends to Famous People* (7–9). 1985, Lerner LB $9.95 (0-8225-1604-7). This book gives tips and procedures on conducting interviews, particularly with celebrities. (Rev: SLJ 3/86) [158]

3462 McCoy, Kathy, and Charles Wibbelsman. *Growing & Changing: A Handbook for Preteens* (6–8). Illus. 1987, Putnam $9.95 (0-399-51280-2). A guide to the physical, social, and emotional changes that occur during early adolescence. (Rev: BL 3/1/87) [649]

3463 Mazzenga, Isabel Burk. *Compromise or Confrontation: Dealing with the Adults in Your Life* (6–8). Illus. 1989, Watts LB $11.90 (0-531-10805-8). A guide for pre- and early teens on how to get along with parents, teachers, and other adults while still maintaining peer status. (Rev: BL 12/1/89; SLJ 11/89; VOYA 2/90) [306.874]

3464 Nida, Patricia Cooney, and Wendy M. Heller. *The Teenager's Survival Guide to Moving* (7–12). 1985, Macmillan $10.95 (0-689-31077-3). Sound, practical advice for teenagers on how to cope with the moving process, deal with separation, and make new friends. (Rev: BL 4/1/85; SLJ 5/85) [648]

3465 Powledge, Fred. *You'll Survive!* (6–8). 1986, Macmillan $11.95 (0-684-18632-2). An informal look at the problems of early adolescence as well as some good tips on how to live through it. (Rev: BL 11/1/86; SLJ 11/86; VOYA 8–10/86) [305.2]

3466 Quiri, Patricia Ryon. *Dating* (6–10). Illus. 1989, Watts LB $11.90 (0-531-10806-6). This account covers various kinds of dating, plus general points on adolescence and sex education. (Rev: BR 5–6/90; SLJ 2/90; VOYA 2/90) [306.7]

3467 Rinzler, Jane. *Teens Speak Out* (7–10). 1986, Donald I. Fine paper $7.95 (0-917657-50-0). A 16-year-old girl tries to convey what teenagers feel about such subjects as sex and drugs. (Rev: VOYA 6/86) [155.5]

3468 Rosenberg, Ellen. *Growing Up Feeling Good* (5–9). Rev. ed. Illus. 1989, Viking $19.95 (0-670-83023-2). This is the second revision of the book that tells young people how to grow up healthy in both mind and body. (Rev: BL 2/15/90) [612.6]

3469 Schneider, Meg F. *Romance! Can You Survive It? A Guide to Sticky Dating Situations* (7–10). 1984, Dell paper $2.50 (0-440-97478-X). A frank often humorous guide to dating manners. [306.7]

3470 Schneider, Meg F. *Two in a Crowd: How to Find Romance without Losing Your Friends* (6–9). 1985, Putnam paper $2.50 (0-399-21185-3). Using fictional situations, Schneider raises questions about many kinds of social relationships. (Rev: SLJ 5/85) [155.5]

3471 Schroeder, Ted. *Art of Playing Second Fiddle: Encouraging Teens Who Never Place First* (7–10). 1985, Concordia paper $4.95 (0-570-03950-9). This book gives teens advice on how to handle problems involving loneliness, shyness, parents, death, and friendships. (Rev: VOYA 4/86) [155.5]

3472 Scott, Sharon. *How to Say No and Keep Your Friends: Peer Pressure Reversal* (7–9). 1986, Human Resource Development paper $4.95 (0-87425-039-0). A practical book on how to avoid excessive influence from peers and make independent decisions. (Rev: VOYA 2/87) [155.5]

3473 Shaw, Diana. *Make the Most of a Good Thing: You!* (6–8). Illus. 1987, Little $13.95 (0-

316-78340-4); paper $6.95 (0-316-78342-0). A guidance manual for preteen girls that covers such subjects as sex, drugs, stress, and physical changes. (Rev: BL 3/15/86; BR 5–6/86; SLJ 3/86) [613]

3474 Smith, Lucinda Irwin. *Growing Up Female: New Challenges, New Choices* (6–9). Illus. 1987, Messner $11.95 (0-671-63445-3); paper $5.95 (0-671-64208-1). A book of guidance for adolescent girls to help them chart the future course of their lives. (Rev: BL 9/1/87; SLJ 9/87; VOYA 12/87) [305.2]

3475 Smith, Sandra Lee. *Coping with Decision Making* (7–12). 1989, Rosen LB $12.95 (0-8239-1000-8). A self-help book for teens on the problems of making wise decisions and accepting the consequences. (Rev: BR 9–10/89; SLJ 11/89; VOYA 10/89) [153.8]

3476 Wallace, Carol M. *Should You Shut Your Eyes When You Kiss?* (7–10). 1983, Little $13.45 (0-316-91998-5); paper $5.95 (0-316-91999-3). A guide to teenage social situations including dating. [306.7]

3477 Wesson, Carolyn McLenahan. *Teen Troubles* (7–12). 1988, Walker $17.95 (0-8027-1011-5); paper $11.95 (0-8027-7310-9). A candid sometimes humorous self-help book on teenage problems and how to face them. (Rev: VOYA 12/88) [155.5]

3478 Weston, Carol. *Girltalk: All the Stuff Your Sister Never Told You* (7–12). 1985, Harper paper $7.95 (0-06-463711-5). Solid advice is given in a non-preachy way about such topics as family, sex, drinking, friendships, and money. (Rev: VOYA 4;86) [155.5]

Social Groups

Family and Family Problems

3479 Berger, Gilda. *Violence and the Family* (7–12). 1990, Watts LB $12.90 (0-531-10906-2). Abuse to various members of the family—children, wives, the elderly—is examined along with a description of various forms of violence. (Rev: BL 4/15/90; SLJ 7/90; VOYA 8/90) [362.82]

3480 Beyer, Kay. *Coping with Teen Parenting* (7–10). 1990, Rosen $12.95 (0-8239-1155-1). This guide to baby care is an overview aimed at teenagers who need very basic information. (Rev: BL 6/15/90) [306.85]

3481 Bode, Janet. *Kids Having Kids: The Unwed Teenage Parent* (7–10). 1980, Watts LB $12.90 (0-531-02882-8). An easy-to-read account that deals with the problem of teenage pregnancies with many first-person accounts. [362.7]

3482 Booher, Dianna Daniels. *Coping . . . When Your Family Falls Apart* (6–8). 1979, Messner $9.29 (0-671-33083-7). Advice and guidance is given to youngsters whose parents are divorcing. [306.8]

3483 Check, William A. *Child Abuse* (7–12). Illus. 1989, Chelsea House $18.95 (0-7910-0043-5). A thorough treatment that covers such topics as the nature of abusers, social and economic factors that promote abuse, and the kinds of abuse and treatment. (Rev: BL 11/15/89; SLJ 5/90; VOYA 2/90) [362.7]

3484 Craven, Linda. *Stepfamilies: New Patterns of Harmony* (7–9). Illus. 1982, Messner LB $9.79 (0-671-44080-2); paper $4.95 (0-671-49478-0). Various problems and solutions associated with living in a stepfamily are discussed. [306.8]

3485 DuPrau, Jeanne. *Adoption: The Facts, Feelings, and Issues of a Double Heritage* (7–12). 1990, Messner LB $11.98 (0-671-69328-X); paper $5.95 (0-671-69329-8). A book that deals primarily with the conflicts and emotional problems related to adoption and how to get help. (Rev: BL 3/15/90; SLJ 7/90; VOYA 6/90) [362.7]

3486 Fayerweather Street School. *The Kids' Book about Parents* (6–9). 1984, Pocket paper $3.95 (0-671-55173-6). The students of the Fayerweather Street School voice their opinions about a great range of topics involving getting along with parents. [306.8]

3487 Fayerweather Street School. *The Kids' Book of Divorce: By, for, and about Kids* (6–9). Illus. 1981, Lewis $10.95 (0-86616-003-5); Random paper $7.95 (0-394-71018-5). Twenty students ages 11 to 14 talk about their experiences involving divorce. [306.8]

3488 Friedrich, Liz. *Divorce* (6–9). Illus. 1988, Watts, $11.90 (0-531-17122-1). A slim, easily read volume from Britain that discusses divorce laws, how they have changed, and the effects of divorce on various family members. (Rev: BL 12/15/88) [306.89]

3489 Friedrich, Liz. *Married Life* (6–9). Illus. 1989, Watts paper $4.95 (0-531-15209-X). This book covers such topics as how to choose a mate, problems in marriage, and secrets of success. (Rev: SLJ 3/90) [306.8]

3490 Friedrich, Liz. *Teen Guide to Married Life* (7–12). Illus. 1989, Watts LB $12.40 (0-531-10836-8). An account of the various factors that

go into making successful and unsuccessful marriages. (Rev: BL 1/1/90; BR 5–6/90; VOYA 6/90) [306.81]

3491 Gardner, Richard. *The Boys and Girls Book about Divorce* (6–9). 1971, Bantam paper $3.50 (0-553-25310-7). A helpful, sympathetic book that discusses divorce and its effects from young people's points of view. [306.8]

3492 Gardner, Richard. *The Boys and Girls Book about One-Parent Families* (6–9). 1978, Creative Therapeutics paper $3.95 (0-933812-16-7). An open discussion of the problems young people face in single-parent families. [306.8]

3493 Gardner, Richard. *The Boys and Girls Book about Stepfamilies* (6–9). 1985, Creative Therapeutics paper $3.95 (0-933812-13-2). Written from a youngster's view, this is a frank discussion of the problems that can exist in stepfamilies. [306.8]

3494 Gay, Kathlyn. *Adoption and Foster Care* (7–12). Illus. 1990, Enslow LB $17.95 (0-89490-239-3). An overview of child-rearing methods with warnings about the possible difficulties involving either adoption or foster care. (Rev: BL 8/90; SLJ 9/90) [362.7]

3495 Gay, Kathlyn. *Changing Families: Meeting Today's Challenges* (7–12). 1988, Enslow $13.95 (0-89490-139-7). The variety of family structures existing today are described plus a discussion of why some work and others do not. (Rev: BL 4/15/88; BR 9–10/88; VOYA 8/88) [306.8]

3496 Gay, Kathlyn. *The Rainbow Effect: Interracial Families* (7–12). Illus. 1987, Watts $11.90 (0-531-10343-9). An examination of interracial marriages and the problems that these sometimes cause for parents and children. (Rev: BL 6/15/87; BR 5–6/87; SLJ 5/87; VOYA 8–9/87) [306.8]

3497 Getzoff, Ann, and Carolyn McClenahan. *Stepkids: A Survival Guide for Teenagers in Stepfamilies* (6–9). 1984, Walker paper $8.95 (0-8027-7236-6). Sound advice for stepchildren on how to cope with a new family. [306.8]

3498 Gilbert, Sara. *How to Live with a Single Parent* (7–9). 1982, Lothrop LB $12.88 (0-688-00633-7). Various situations and topics important in developing good relationships in a single family situation are discussed. [306.8]

3499 Glassman, Bruce. *Everything You Need to Know about Step-Families* (5–8). Illus. 1988, Rosen LB $12.95 (0-8239-0815-1). Various kinds of stepfamilies are discussed and major problems are covered. (Rev: SLJ 4/89) [306.8]

3500 Hales, Dianne. *The Family* (7–10). Illus. 1988, Chelsea House $17.95 (0-7910-0038-9). A history of the family structure is given plus a description of the various kinds of families in America today. (Rev: BL 9/1/88; BR 11–12/88; VOYA 4/89) [306.8]

3501 Hodder, Elizabeth. *Stepfamilies* (7–10). Illus. 1990, Gloucester LB $11.90 (0-531-17226-0). Through the use of case studies, various kinds of stepfamilies are introduced and the problems many of them face. (Rev: BL 5/15/90; SLJ 7/90) [306.84]

3502 Johnson, Linda Carlson. *Everything You Need to Know about Your Parents' Divorce* (6–10). Illus. 1989, Rosen LB $12.95 (0-8239-1012-1). A book that explores the various emotional reactions to divorce and how to cope with them. (Rev: SLJ 2/90) [306.8]

3503 Jones, Charlotte Foltz. *Only Child—Clues for Coping* (5–9). 1984, Westminster $11.95 (0-664-32718-4). The problems and rewards of being an only child are described and how to adjust to not having brothers or sisters. [306.8]

3504 Kleeberg, Irene Cumming. *Latch-Key Kid* (6–9). 1985, Watts $11.90 (0-531-10052-9). This account explains how children often have to take care of themselves and how children can do it effectively. (Rev: VOYA 4/86) [306.8]

3505 Krementz, Jill. *How It Feels to Be Adopted* (6–9). Illus. 1982, Knopf $15.95 (0-394-52851-4). Nineteen adopted children—ages 8 to 16—talk about the many problems involving adoption. [362.7]

3506 Krementz, Jill. *How It Feels When Parents Divorce* (6–9). Illus. 1984, Knopf $12.95 (0-394-54079-4). Excerpts from a series of interviews with 19 young people about their parents' divorces. [306.8]

3507 Kurland, Morton. *Coping with Family Violence* (7–12). 1986, Rosen $12.95 (0-8239-0677-9). Besides exploring the causes of family violence, the author tells how to lessen it and how to seek help. (Rev: BR 1–2/87) [362.8]

3508 Landau, Elaine. *Black Market Adoption and the Sale of Children* (7–10). Illus. 1990, Watts LB $12.90 (0-531-10914-3). An account of corrupt practices in the adoption area and how these can lead to tragedy. (Rev: BL 6/15/90; SLJ 6/90; VOYA 8/90) [364.1]

3509 Landau, Elaine. *Child Abuse: An American Epidemic* (7–12). 1990, Messner LB $11.98 (0-671-68874-X); paper $5.95 (0-671-68875-8). Sexual, physical, and emotional abuse are discussed along with their causes. (Rev: SLJ 6/90; VOYA 8/90) [362.7]

3510 LeShan, Eda. *Grandparents: A Special Kind of Love* (7–9). Illus. 1984, Macmillan $11.95 (0-02-756380-4). For young people, a tribute to grandparents and tips on how to understand and get along with them. [306.8]

3511 Long, Lynette. *On My Own: The Kids' Self Care Book* (6–9). 1984, Acropolis paper $7.95 (0-87491-735-2). A self-help guide to young people in latchkey situations. [306.8]

3512 Nickman, Steven L. *The Adoption Experience: Stories and Commentaries* (8–10). 1985, Messner LB $9.79 (0-671-50817-2). Through 7 fictitious case studies, the various psychological and sociological implications of adoption are explored. (Rev: BR 9–10/86; SLJ 12/85) [362.7]

3513 Park, Angela. *Child Abuse* (6–9). Illus. 1988, Gloucester $11.90 (0-531-17121-3). An easily read introduction to this problem, its various forms, causes, and how victims can be helped. (Rev: BL 12/15/88) [362.7]

3514 Perl, Lila. *The Great Ancestor Hunt: The Fun of Finding Out Who You Are* (5–9). Illus. 1989, Clarion $15.95 (0-89919-745-0). A how-to manual on tracing your family's roots with important information on immigration to this country. (Rev: BL 11/1/89; SLJ 12/89; VOYA 2/90) [929]

3515 Powledge, Fred. *So You're Adopted* (6–9). 1982, Macmillan $11.95 (0-684-17347-6). The author, who was an adopted child, answers the questions that he wanted answered and those additional ones he feels adopted children ask today. [362.7]

3516 Rofes, Eric, ed. *The Kids' Book of Divorce: By, for and about Kids* (6–10). 1982, Random paper $5.95 (0-394-71018-5). Twenty youngsters from ages 11 to 14 who are children of divorce were asked to state their reactions and feelings. [306.8]

3517 Rosenberg, Maxine B. *Growing Up Adopted* (6–9). 1989, Bradbury $12.95 (0-02-777912-2). Interviews with 14 young people of various ages on the experience of adoptees and the emotional reactions involved. (Rev: BL 11/15/89; VOYA 2/90) [362.7]

3518 Ryan, Elizabeth A. *Straight Talk about Parents* (7–12). 1989, Facts on File $15.95 (0-8160-1526-0). A self-help manual to help teens sort out their feelings about parents. (Rev: BL 8/89; BR 11–12/89; SLJ 9/89; VOYA 2/90) [306.8]

3519 Stine, Jane, and Jovial Bob Stine. *Everything You Need to Survive: Brothers and Sisters* (6–9). 1983, Random paper $1.95 (0-394-85249-4). How to get along with older and younger siblings is discussed in this often humorous guide. [306.7]

3520 Webb, Margot. *Coping with Overprotective Parents* (7–10). 1990, Rosen $12.95 (0-8239-1088-1). Sound advice is given on how to achieve appropriate amounts of independence from one's parents. (Rev: BL 9/1/90) [306]

3521 Worth, Richard. *The American Family* (7–9). Illus. 1984, Watts $12.90 (0-531-04859-4). The traditional ideas of a typical family are examined and the realities of family structure today are given. [306.8]

Youth Groups

3522 Boy Scouts of America. *The Official Boy Scout Handbook* (7–9). 10th ed. Illus. 1990, Boy Scouts of America paper $4.95 (0-8395-3229-6). Though basically an orientation to scouting, this guide also includes much valuable material on such topics as camping, first aid, and wildlife. [369.43]

3523 Girl Scouts of the United States of America. *Girl Scout Badges and Signs* (7–9). Illus. 1980, Girl Scouts of America paper $3.00 (0-88441-326-8). A guide to how to earn various badges and insignia in the Girl Scout organization. [369.463]

3524 Girl Scouts of the United States of America. *You Make the Difference: The Handbook for Cadette and Senior Girl Scouts* (7–12). Illus. 1980, Girl Scouts of America paper $3.25 (0-88441-329-2). A description of the activities that these groups can engage in including community service and developing one's interests. [369.463]

3525 Moore, David L. *Dark Sky, Dark Land: Stories of the Hmong Boy Scouts of Troop 100* (7–10). Illus. 1989, Tessera paper $12.95 (0-9623029-0-2). A collection of stories of hardship and bravery behind Boy Scout Troop 100 in Minneapolis composed of young refugees from war-torn Laos. (Rev: BL 9/15/90) [977.6]

3526 Peterson, Robert W. *The Boy Scouts: An American Adventure* (7–12). Illus. 1984, American Heritage $24.95 (0-8281-1173-1). A nicely illustrated history of the scouting movement in America. [369.43]

The Arts and Entertainment

Architecture and Building

History of Architecture

3527 Ceserani, Gian Paolo, and Piero Ventura. *Grand Constructions* (7–12). Illus. 1983, Putnam $12.95 (0-399-20942-5). Through an introduction to famous buildings from Stonehenge to modern skyscrapers, the history of architecture is introduced. [720.9]

3528 Macaulay, David. *Castle* (7–12). Illus. 1977, Houghton $14.95 (0-395-25784-0); paper $6.95 (0-395-32920-5). In detailed line drawings, the history is traced of a thirteenth-century Welsh castle. [728.8]

3529 Macaulay, David. *Cathedral: The Story of Its Construction* (7–12). Illus. 1973, Houghton $14.95 (0-395-17513-5); paper $6.95 (0-395-31668-5). Using finely detailed line drawings, the author describes the construction of an imaginary Gothic cathedral. [726]

3530 Macaulay, David. *City: A Story of Roman Planning and Construction* (7–12). Illus. 1974, Houghton $14.95 (0-395-19492-X); paper $6.95 (0-395-34922-2). In striking illustrations, the author traces the evolution of an imaginary ancient Roman city over approximately 125 years. [711]

3531 Macaulay, David. *Pyramid* (7–12). Illus. 1975, Houghton $14.95 (0-395-21407-6); paper $6.95 (0-395-32121-2). In beautiful line drawings, the author describes how an ancient Egyptian pyramid was constructed. [726]

3532 Sancha, Sheila. *The Castle Story* (6–9). Illus. 1982, Harper LB $15.89 (0-690-04146-2). A discussion of the parts of the castle and why they were designed in the way they were. [728.8]

3533 Smith, Beth. *Castles* (6–9). Illus. 1988, Watts LB $9.90 (0-531-10511-3). A discussion of the construction of castles during the Middle Ages and of those that survive today. (Rev: BR 11–12/88) [728.8]

3534 Weeks, John. *The Pyramids* (7–12). Illus. 1977, Cambridge Univ. Pr. paper $4.95 (0-521-07240-9). An introduction to the construction of the pyramids of ancient Egypt. [726]

Art, Painting, Photography, and Sculpture

General and Miscellaneous

3535 Holme, Bryan. *Enchanted World: Pictures to Grow Up With* (7–9). 1979, Oxford Univ. Pr. $18.95 (0-19-520205-8). An introduction to art appreciation with examples from many sources, times, and cultures. [709]

3536 Horwitz, Elinor Lander. *Contemporary American Folk Artists* (7–9). Illus. 1975, Harper paper $3.95 (0-397-31627-5). An explanation of what folk art is plus samples of the products of many artists. [709]

3537 Keightley, Moy. *Investigating Art: A Practical Guide for Young People* (5–12). Illus. 1984, Facts on File $17.95 (0-87196-973-4). After an explanation of the elements of art, the author suggests a variety of interesting and imaginative projects to create one's own works of art. (Rev: BL 5/1/85) [702]

3538 Triadó, Juan-Ramón. *The Key to Painting* (7–12). Illus. 1990, Lerner LB $15.95 (0-8225-2050-8). A slim guide to art appreciation that introduces elements like color and composition. (Rev: BL 9/1/90) [750.1]

3539 Waldron, Ann. *True or False? Amazing Art Forgeries* (7–10). Illus. 1983, Hastings LB $12.95 (0-8038-7220-8). A history of art forgeries is given plus many examples in text and illustration. (Rev: SLJ 8/86) [702.8]

History of Art

3540 Bracons, José. *The Key to Gothic Art* (7–12). Illus. 1990, Lerner LB $15.95 (0-8225-2051-

6). A brief well-illustrated introduction to the art and architecture of the Middle Ages. (Rev: BL 9/1/90; SLJ 9/90) [709.02]

3541 Cirlot, Lourdes. *The Key to Modern Art of the Early 20th Century* (7–12). Illus. 1990, Lerner LB $15.95 (0-8225-2052-4). The history and characteristics of early modern art are covered plus an introduction to the major artists. (Rev: BL 9/1/90; SLJ 9/90) [709.04]

3542 De la Croix, Horst, and Richard G. Tansey. *Gardner's Art Through the Ages* (7–12). 2 vols. Illus. 1970, Harcourt paper $22.00 each (vol. 1: 0-15-503764-8; vol. 2: 0-15-503765-X). A standard adult history of art that has often been revised since its first publication in 1926. [709]

3543 Fernández Arenas, José. *The Key to Renaissance Art* (7–12). Illus. 1990, Lerner LB $15.95 (0-8225-2057-5). This slim volume covers not only painting but also sculpture, architecture, drawing, and allied arts. (Rev: BL 9/1/90; SLJ 9/90) [709.02]

3544 Gombrich, E. H. *The Story of Art* (7–12). Illus. 1985, Prentice $25.95 (0-13-850066-5). A comprehensive adult survey of the history of art that has been popular since first publication in 1950. [709]

3545 Janson, H. W. *History of Art* (8–12). 3rd ed. Illus. 1986, Abrams $49.50 (0-8109-1094-2). This standard history of art contains a time-line integrating important events in art history with those in other fields. (Rev: BL 5/1/86) [709]

3546 Janson, H. W., and Anthony F. Janson. *History of Art for Young People* (7–12). Illus. 1987, Abrams $29.95 (0-8109-1098-5). From the pyramids to op art, this readable, well-illustrated book has become a standard in the field. (Rev: BL 7/87) [709]

3547 Reyero, Carlos. *The Key to Art from Romanticism to Impressionism* (7–12). Illus. 1990, Lerner LB $15.95 (0-8225-2058-3). A solid overview with many color illustrations introduces both the style and the individual artists of this period. (Rev: BL 9/1/90; SLJ 9/90) [709.03]

3548 Triadó, Juan-Ramón. *The Key to Baroque Art* (7–12). Illus. 1990, Lerner LB $15.95 (0-8225-2056-7). The lavishness and extravagance of this period in art are captured well in text and many illustrations. (Rev: BL 9/1/90; SLJ 9/90) [709.02]

3549 Ventura, Piero. *Great Painters* (6–9). Illus. 1984, Putnam $19.95 (0-399-21115-2). An introduction to art history from ancient Greece to Picasso. [759]

Regions

Asia

3550 Anno, Mitsumasa. *The Unique World of Mitsumasa Anno: Selected Works, 1968–1977* (7–12). Trans. and adapted by Samuel Crowell Morse. Illus. 1980, Putnam $19.95 (0-399-20743-0). A collection of paintings and drawings by the Japanese artist best known for his picture books. [759.952]

North America

UNITED STATES

3551 Sufrin, Mark. *Focus on America: Profiles of Nine Photographers* (7–12). Illus. 1987, Macmillan $13.95 (0-684-18679-9). From the famous Civil War photographer Matthew Brady on, here are profiles of 9 famous photographers. (Rev: BL 4/15/87; BR 11–12/87; SLJ 6–7/87; VOYA 6/87) [770]

Decorative Arts

3552 James, Elizabeth, and Carol Barkin. *A Place of Your Own* (7–10). Illus. 1981, Dutton $9.75 (0-525-37100-1). A clear introduction on how to decorate one's own room or apartment with easily made furniture and accessories. [747]

3553 Rosenberg, Maxine B. *Artists of Handcrafted Furniture at Work* (5–12). Illus. 1988, Lothrop $14.95 (0-688-06875-8). Through the examination of the work of 4 artisans, the art of handcrafted furniture is explored. (Rev: BL 5/15/88) [749.2]

Music

General and Miscellaneous

3554 Berger, Melvin. *The Science of Music* (5–9). Illus. 1989, Harper LB $13.89 (0-690-04647-2). An introduction to such technical matters as sound and pitch plus material on musical instruments and records. (Rev: BL 5/15/89; BR 1–2/90; VOYA 12/89) [781]

3555 Fichter, George S. *American Indian Music and Musical Instruments* (7–10). Illus. 1978, Mc-Kay $8.95 (0-679-20443-1). Not only a review of the kinds of American Indian music but also directions for making their musical instruments. [781.7]

History of Music

3556 Carlin, Richard. *Man's Earliest Music* (7–12). Illus. 1987, Facts on File $15.95 (0-8160-1324-1). A volume on the kinds of music and musical instruments found in 4 cultures—the pygmies of Africa, the native Americans, the aborigines, and the Pacific Islanders. (Rev: BL 8/87; BR 9–10/87) [809]

3557 Haskins, James. *Black Music in America: A History Through Its People* (7–12). Illus. 1987, Harper LB $12.89 (0-690-04462-3). A history of the development of black music in America from its beginnings through Michael Jackson. (Rev: BL 7/87; BR 9–10/87; SLJ 6–7/87; VOYA 4/87) [781.7]

3558 Matthews, Jill. *The Lives and Loves of New Kids on the Block* (5–9). Illus. 1990, Pocket paper $3.95 (0-671-72554-8). The story behind the popular singing group and their family life. (Rev: SLJ 7/90) [780.42]

3559 Ventura, Piero. *Great Composers* (5–9). Illus. 1989, Putnam $20.95 (0-399-21746-0). From ancient times to the Beatles, this is a multicultural treatment of the topic with most emphasis on Western composers. (Rev: BL 1/15/90) [780]

Jazz, Rock, and Popular Music

3560 Berger, Gilda. *USA for Africa: Rock Aid in the Eighties* (6–9). Illus. 1987, Watts $12.90 (0-531-10299-8). The story of how rock concerts have raised money for Africa and other worthy causes and of the conditions that brought on the need for this type of fund-raising. (Rev: BL 5/1/87; BR 11–12/87; SLJ 6–7/87) [784.5]

3561 Blocher, Arlo. *Jazz* (6–8). 1976, Troll LB $9.79 (0-89375-014-X); paper $2.50 (0-89375-030-1). An easily read history of the development of jazz and of its changing characteristics. [781]

3562 Busnar, Gene. *The Rhythm and Blues Story* (6–9). Illus. 1985, Messner LB $9.79 (0-671-42145-X). A history of rhythm and blues from Africa to Michael Jackson and Bruce Springsteen. (Rev: BR 9-10/86; SLJ 3/86) [784.5]

3563 Cohen, Daniel, and Susan Cohen. *Rock Video Superstars II* (6–9). Illus. 1987, Pocket paper $2.50 (0-671-63397-X). Profiles of some of the most popular groups and individuals on the rock scene today. Preceded by *Rock and Video Superstars* (1986). (Rev: BL 2/1/87) [784.54]

3564 Crocker, Chris. *Wham!* (6–9). Illus. 1985, Messner $8.79 (0-671-60374-4); paper $3.95 (0-671-60281-0). An account of the beginnings and rise to fame of the British rock group, Wham! (Rev: BL 3/1/86; BR 5–6/86; SLJ 1/87) [784.5]

3565 Fornatale, Pete. *Story of Rock 'n' Roll* (7–12). 1987, Morrow $12.95 (0-688-06276-8); paper $7.95 (0-688-06277-6). A history that begins in the 1950s and gives an overview of the history of rock by decade into the 1980s. (Rev: BR 5–6/87; VOYA 10/87) [780.42]

3566 Griffin, Clive D. *Jazz* (6–12). Illus. 1989, Dryad $17.95 (0-85219-754-3). An examination of what jazz is, its various forms, and the careers of famous musicians. (Rev: BL 4/15/89; SLJ 5/89) [785.42]

3567 Hanmer, Trudy J. *An Album of Rock and Roll* (6–9). Illus. 1988, Watts $12.90 (0-531-10318-8). A brief overview of rock music from the early fifties through the eighties in text and photos. (Rev: BL 5/1/88) [784.5]

3568 Molina, Maria. *Menudo* (7–10). Trans. by Elizabeth Garcia. Illus. 1984, Messner LB $8.79 (0-671-50635-8). The history of the Hispanic pop group whose members must leave the group when they reach age 16. [784.5]

Opera and Musicals

3569 Headington, Christopher. *The Performing World of the Musician* (7–9). 1981, Silver Burdett $15.20 (0-382-06592-1). An introduction to the life of a musician that also supplies career information. [780.92]

3570 Ross, Beverly B., and Jean P. Durgin. *Junior Broadway: How to Produce Musicals with Children 9 to 13* (7–12). Illus. 1983, McFarland paper $13.95 (0-89950-033-1). A book useful to both youngsters and adults on how to put on musicals with amateurs. [782.81]

Orchestra and Musical Instruments

3571 Ardley, Neil. *Music* (5–9). Illus. 1989, Knopf LB $13.99 (0-394-92259-X). A profusely illustrated account that concentrates on musical instruments and their history. (Rev: BL 7/89; BR 11–12/89) [781.91]

3572 Kettelkamp, Larry. *Electronic Musical Instruments: What They Do, How They Work* (7–12). Illus. 1984, Morrow $11.95 (0-688-02781-4). This account introduces various electronic instruments and traces the development of this music into the 1980s. [789.9]

3573 Wiseman, Ann. *Making Musical Things: Improvised Instruments* (7–9). Illus. 1979, Macmillan $13.95 (0-684-16114-1). Using everyday objects, this book tells you how to make such musical instruments as chimes, drums, and horns. [781.91]

Songs and Folk Songs

3574 Berger, Melvin. *The Story of Folk Music* (7–9). 1976, S. G. Phillips LB $14.95 (0-87599-215-3). The story of the origins and characteristics of folk music with many examples. [781.7]

3575 Boy Scouts of America. *Boy Scout Songbook* (7–10). 1970, Boy Scouts of America paper $1.50 (0-8395-3224-5). Using popular melodies as a basis, this book contains the words to more than 100 scouting songs. [784]

3576 Fox, Dan. *We Wish You a Merry Christmas* (5–9). Illus. 1989, Arcade $16.95 (1-55970-043-2). A collection of 25 carols and songs associated with Christmas, illustrated with reproductions from the Metropolitan Museum of Art. (Rev: BL 11/1/89) [781.723]

3577 Glazer, Tom. *Tom Glazer's Christmas Songbook* (5–9). Illus. 1989, Doubleday $14.95 (0-385-24641-2). A wonderful sing-along collection of 39 carols and songs, each nicely illustrated. (Rev: BL 11/1/89) [781.723]

3578 Sandburg, Carl. *The American Songbag* (7–12). Illus. 1970, Harcourt paper $12.95 (0-15-605650-X). A fine collection of all kinds of American folksongs with music and background notes from Sandburg. [784.7]

The Performing Arts

Ballet and the Dance

3579 Berger, Melvin. *The World of Dance* (7–12). Illus. 1978, S. G. Phillips $18.95 (0-87599-221-8). The characteristics and history of dance is given from prehistoric times to Twyla Tharp. [792.8]

3580 Haskins, James. *Black Dance in America: A History Through Its People* (7–12). 1990, Harper LB $14.89 (0-690-04659-6). Beginning with the dances brought from Africa by the slaves, this history moves to the present with the contributions of such people as Gregory Hines and Alvin Ailey. (Rev: BL 8/90; SLJ 6/90; VOYA 6/90) [792.8]

3581 Jessel, Camilla. *Life at the Royal Ballet School* (7–9). Illus. 1979, Routledge $12.95 (0-416-86320-5). The story of student life at this ballet school from entrance auditions to first performances. [792.8]

3582 Kline, Nancy Meders. *Enjoying the Arts: Dance* (7–9). Illus. 1975, Rosen LB $10.97 (0-8239-0296-X). All kinds of dancing are introduced plus a special analysis of several examples of ballet and modern dance. [793.3]

3583 Kuklin, Susan. *Reaching for Dreams: A Ballet from Rehearsal to Opening Night* (7–12). Illus. 1987, Lothrop $12.95 (0-688-06316-0). Using the introduction of a new ballet into the Alvin Ailey dance company's repetoire as a springboard, this is the account of the pangs of creation in the ballet world. (Rev: BL 3/1/87; BR 11–12/87; SLJ 5/87; VOYA 12/87) [792.8]

3584 Royal Academy of Dancing. *Ballet Class* (7–12). Illus. 1985, Arco $14.95 (0-668-06427-7).

Behind-the-scenes information on how a ballet school operates. [792.8]

3585 Walker, Katherine Sorley, and Joan Butler. *Ballet for Boys and Girls* (7–9). Illus. 1979, Prentice $9.95 (0-13-055574-6). This dance form is analyzed, the basic steps are explained, and the different requirements for men and women are distinguished. [792.8]

Circuses, Fairs, and Parades

3586 Anderson, Norman D. *Ferris Wheels* (6–9). Illus. 1983, Pantheon LB $10.99 (0-394-95460-2). A history of the ferris wheel from the seventeenth century on, with many illustrations and photographs. [791.06]

3587 Fenten, Barbara, and D. X. Fenten. *The Team behind the Great Parades* (7–9). 1981, Westminster $9.95 (0-664-32682-X). A look at how the nation's great parades (for example, the Macy's Thanksgiving Day parade) are put together. [791]

3588 Machotka, Hana. *The Magic Ring: A Year with the Big Apple Circus* (5–10). Illus. 1988, Morrow LB $13.95 (0-688-07449-9); paper $8.95 (0-688-08222-X). A lavishly illustrated account that takes the reader behind the scenes in circus life. (Rev: SLJ 9/88) [791.3]

3589 Martin, Nancie S. *Miss America Through the Looking Glass* (7–9). Illus. 1985, Messner $9.79 (0-671-60160-1); Simon & Schuster paper $6.95 (0-671-60159-8). The story behind the Miss America beauty contest in Atlantic City and what it takes to win. (Rev: BL 4/15/86; SLJ 3/86) [305.4]

Radio and Recordings

3590 Fitzgerald, Merni Ingrassia. *The Voice of America* (6–9). Illus. 1987, Putnam $12.95 (0-396-08937-2). The story of America's international radio network from its beginnings in World War II to the present. (Rev: BL 8/87) [384.54]

3591 Hawkins, Robert. *On the Air: Radio Broadcasting* (7–9). Illus. 1984, Messner LB $9.29 (0-671-45516-8). A brief history of broadcasting is given plus a rundown on the careers available in this area. [384.54]

3592 Maie, Sondra. *The Top 40—Making a Hit Record* (7–9). Illus. 1984, Messner LB $9.79 (0-671-44275-9). A behind-the-scenes view of what goes into making a recording from both the artistic and technical standpoints. [338.4]

Television, Video, and Motion Pictures

3593 Aylesworth, Thomas G. *Monsters from the Movies* (6–9). Illus. 1972, Harper LB $12.90 (0-397-31590-2). An entertaining survey that includes Dracula and King Kong. [791.43]

3594 Aylesworth, Thomas G. *Movie Monsters* (6–9). Illus. 1975, Harper $12.70 (0-397-31639-9). Lots of photos complement this compilation of the greatest of movie monsters. [791.43]

3595 Berger, Gilda. *Violence and the Media* (9–12). 1989, Watts LB $13.40 (0-531-10808-2). An examination of violence as it exists in our society and its portrayal in the mass media. (Rev: BL 10/15/89; BR 3–4/90; SLJ 1/90; VOYA 2/90) [303.6]

3596 Cheney, Glenn Alan. *Television in American Society* (7–12). 1983, Watts LB $12.90 (0-531-04402-5). An overview that covers such topics as ratings, the place of advertising, and the influence of government controls. [302.2]

3597 Clemens, Virginia Phelps. *Behind the Filmmaking Scene* (7–9). 1982, Westminster $12.95 (0-664-32691-9). A behind-the-scenes look at how theatrical and television films are made. [791.43]

3598 Cohen, Daniel. *Horror in the Movies* (6–9). Illus. 1982, Archway paper $2.50 (0-671-62671-X). Horror movies from the silents to the present are summarized with accompanying stills. [791.43]

3599 Holliss, Richard, and Brian Sibley. *Walt Disney's Snow White and the Seven Dwarfs & the Making of the Classic Film* (4–9). Illus. 1987, Simon & Schuster $14.95 (0-671-64439-4). A behind-the-scenes look at how the first full-length animated film was made plus a full account of the movie's story. (Rev: BL 10/1/87) [791.43]

3600 Jaspersohn, William. *A Day in the Life of a Television News Reporter* (6–9). Illus. 1981, Little $14.95 (0-316-451813-9). An exciting day in the life of a Boston television reporter and his associates. [070.1]

3601 LeBaron, John, and Philip Miller. *Portable Video: A Production Guide for Young People* (7–10). Illus. 1982, Prentice paper $7.95 (0-13-686519-9). A step-by-step manual on how to create video productions, from selecting equipment to camera shots and making graphics. [778.59]

3602 Meigs, James B., and Jennifer Stern. *Make Your Own Music Video* (6–9). Illus. 1986, Watts $10.40 (0-531-10215-7). Such topics as how to choose equipment, write a script, plus shoot and edit the final product are described. (Rev: BL 1/15/87; BR 3–4/87; SLJ 11/86) [784.5]

3603 Meyer, Nicholas E. *Magic in the Dark: A Young Viewer's History of the Movies* (7–10). Illus. 1985, Facts on File $17.95 (0-8160-1256-3). A history of motion pictures from the 1880s to the 1960s with emphasis on Hollywood. (Rev: SLJ 3/86) [791]

3604 Nathan-Turner, John. *Dr. Who: The Tardis Inside Out* (6–9). Illus. 1985, Random $7.99 (0-394-97415-8); paper $6.95 (0-394-87415-3). For fans of Dr. Who, here is a backstage look at the program and stars by its television producer. Also use: *Dr. Who: The Companions* (1986). (Rev: BL 9/15/85) [791]

3605 Powers, Tom. *Horror Movies* (7–12). Illus. 1989, Lerner LB $12.95 (0-8225-1636-5). Seven horror movies are highlighted from *Frankenstein* to *Gremlins*. Also use: *Movie Monsters* (1989). (Rev: SLJ 1/90) [791.43]

3606 Rimmer, Ian. *Movies F/X* (6–9). Illus. 1988, Rourke LB $12.95 (0-86592-453-8). An introduction to the history of special effects in the movies with plenty of examples in the illustrations and text. (Rev: SLJ 5/89) [791.43]

3607 Sandler, Corey, and Tom Badgett. *Ultimate Unauthorized Nintendo Game Strategies* (6–12). Illus. 1989, Bantam $9.95 (0-553-34892-2). This is a guide to over 100 games created for the Nintendo system. (Rev: VOYA 6/90) [688.7]

3608 Schwartz, Perry. *Making Movies* (5–8). Illus. 1989, Lerner LB $12.95 (0-8225-1635-7). Various kinds of movies are introduced plus material on how they are made and distributed. (Rev: BL 1/1/90; SLJ 3/90) [791.43]

3609 Shachtman, Tom, and Harriet Shelare. *Video Power: A Complete Guide to Writing, Planning, and Shooting Videos* (7–12). Illus. 1988, Henry Holt $15.95 (0-8050-0338-X); paper $7.95 (0-8050-0414-X). From deciding on production ideas to distributing the final products, this is a complete guide to making videos. (Rev: BL 9/1/88; SLJ 6–7/88) [791.43]

3610 Smith, Dian G. *American Filmmakers Today* (7–10). 1983, Messner $9.79 (0-671-44081-0). An introduction to the early work of such directors as Coppola, Spielberg, and Lucas. [791.43]

3611 Smith, Dian G. *Great American Film Directors* (7–12). Illus. 1987, Messner $9.79 (0-671-50231-X). From D. W. Griffith to John Huston, here is a profile of 10 famous movie directors. (Rev: BL 4/15/87; SLJ 9/87; VOYA 2/88) [791.43]

3612 Weiss, Ann E. *Tune In, Tune Out: Broadcasting Regulation in the United States* (7–9). 1981, Houghton $8.95 (0-395-31610-3). The history of regulations is given plus a discussion of the kinds of regulations we have today. [384.5]

3613 Weiss, Paulette. *The Rock Video Book* (5–9). Illus. 1985, Messner LB $9.79 (0-671-55340-

2). From 38 different rock acts, about 30 trivia questions are asked. (Rev: BR 5–6/86; SLJ 12/85) [778.59]

Theater and Drama

3614 Loxton, Howard. *Theater* (5–8). Illus. 1989, Steck-Vaughn LB $15.95 (0-8114-2359-X). A brief account that covers the history of the theater, how plays are staged, and various kinds of acting styles. (Rev: BL 3/15/90) [792]

3615 McGann, Mary. *Enjoying the Arts: Theater* (7–9). Illus. 1977, Rosen LB $10.97 (0-8239-0388-5). A history of the theater as well as tips on how to enjoy it. [792]

3616 Straub, Cindie, and Matthew Straub. *Mime: Basics for Beginners* (7–12). Illus. 1984, Plays paper $12.95 (0-8238-0263-9). The fundamentals of traditional mime are explained in text, line drawings, and photographs. (Rev: BL 2/1/85) [792.3]

3617 Terry, Ellen, and Lynne Anderson. *Makeup and Masks* (7–10). Rev. ed. Illus. 1982, Rosen LB $14.95 (0-8239-0232-3). Material on how actors use makeup and how masks are made. [792]

3618 Williamson, Walter. *Behind the Scenes: The Unseen People Who Make Theater Work* (7–10). Illus. 1987, Walker LB $15.85 (0-8027-6704-4). A behind-the-scenes look at 10 careers such as a costume designer and an electrician who make their living in the theater. (Rev: BL 11/15/87; BR 5–6/88; SLJ 11/87; VOYA 12/87) [792]

Biography and True Adventure

Adventure and Exploration

Collective

3619 Crocker, Chris. *Great American Astronauts* (6–8). Illus. 1988, Watts $12.90 (0-531-10500-8). Ten biographies including John Glenn, Alan Shepard, and Sally Ride are included in this well-illustrated book. (Rev: BL 2/1/89; SLJ 1/89) [920]

3620 Hauser, Hillary. *Call to Adventure* (7–12). Illus. 1987, Bookmakers $14.95 (0-917665-18-X). Profiles of various adventurers like Jacques Cousteau and Sir Edmund Hillary who dared the unknown. (Rev: BL 4/1/88; SLJ 4/88) [920]

3621 Lomask, Milton. *Great Lives: Exploration* (6–9). Illus. 1989, Macmillan $22.95 (0-684-18511-3). An account of 25 world explorers from the ancient Greeks to the Polar expeditions of the twentieth century. (Rev: BL 3/15/89; SLJ 1/89) [910]

3622 Schwartz, Alvin. *Gold and Silver, Silver and Gold: Tales of Hidden Treasure* (6–10). Illus. 1988, Farrar LB $12.95 (0-374-32690-8). Twenty-eight short true tales of treasure around the world but chiefly in North and South America. (Rev: SLJ 2/89) [910.4]

3623 Wulffson, Don L. *Incredible True Adventures* (6–10). Illus. 1986, Dodd $8.95 (0-396-08799-X). A collection of true stories involving such villains as war, jungles, freezing cold climates, and violent seas. (Rev: BL 5/15/86) [904]

3624 Wulffson, Don L. *More Incredible True Adventures* (6–9). Illus. 1989, Dutton $12.95 (0-525-65000-8). A collection of amazing stories of men and women who lived through amazing death-defying adventures. (Rev: SLJ 11/89; VOYA 12/89) [920]

Individual

COLUMBUS, CHRISTOPHER

3625 Dolan, Sean. *Christopher Columbus: The Intrepid Mariner* (5–8). 1989, Ballantine paper $3.95 (0-449-90393-1). An easily read biography of the explorer that makes for lively reading. (Rev: BL 12/15/89; BR 3–4/90) [921]

3626 Levinson, Nancy Smiler. *Christopher Columbus: Voyager to the Unknown* (5–9). Illus. 1990, Lodestar $16.95 (0-525-67292-3). Based on current research, this is a fine profile of the explorer that supplies excellent details of his voyages. (Rev: SLJ 6/90) [921]

3627 Soule, Gardner. *Christopher Columbus on the Green Sea of Darkness* (6–9). Illus. 1988, Watts $12.90 (0-531-10577-6). Using excerpts from Columbus's log and many illustrations, this account concentrates on the diverse accomplishments of this mariner. (Rev: BL 2/1/89; SLJ 12/88; VOYA 6/89) [921]

COOK, CAPTAIN JAMES

3628 Hoobler, Dorothy, and Thomas Hoobler. *The Voyages of Captain Cook* (7–10). Illus. 1983, Putnam paper $10.95 (0-399-20975-1). A biography that concentrates on Cook's 3 long sea voyages that brought him to the coast of North America. [921]

CORTES, HERNAN

3629 Wilkes, John. *Hernan Cortes: Conquistador in Mexico* (7–9). 1977, Cambridge Univ. Pr. paper $5.25 (0-527-20424-0). The story of the Spanish adventurer who conquered the Aztecs of Mexico. [921]

DRAKE, SIR FRANCIS

3630 Macdonald, Fiona. *Drake and the Armada* (6–9). Illus. 1988, Hampstead $12.40 (0-531-19504-X). A biography of the Elizabethan seadog that focuses on the war against Spain. (Rev: SLJ 4/89) [921]

EARHART, AMELIA

3631 Leder, Jane. *Amelia Earhart* (6–9). Illus. 1990, Greenhaven LB $12.95 (0-89908-070-7). A thorough biography and good coverage of theories about Earhart's disappearance. (Rev: BL 3/1/90; SLJ 5/90) [921]

3632 Pearce, Carol A. *Amelia Earhart* (7–12). Illus. 1988, Facts on File $14.95 (0-8160-1520-1). The story of the record-breaking aviator and of her disappearance in 1937. (Rev: BL 7/88; BR 9–10/88; SLJ 5/88; VOYA 8/88) [921]

3633 Randolph, Blythe. *Amelia Earhart* (7–12). Illus. 1987, Watts $12.90 (0-531-10331-5). An examination of the events in the life of this adventurer and aviator plus a fine re-creation of her personality. (Rev: BL 5/15/87; BR 11–12/87; SLJ 6–7/87; VOYA 8–9/87) [921]

3634 Sloate, Susan. *Amelia Earhart: Challenging the Skies* (5–8). Illus. 1990, Fawcett paper $3.95 (0-449-90396-6). The aviator's life story is told along with an examination of all the theories concerning her disappearance. (Rev: SLJ 6/90) [921]

HENSON, MATTHEW

3635 Gilman, Michael. *Matthew Henson* (6–10). Illus. 1988, Chelsea House $16.95 (1-55546-590-0). The life story of the black explorer who accompanied Peary on expeditions in search of the North Pole. (Rev: BL 6/15/88; SLJ 4/88) [921]

HEYERDAHL, THOR

3636 Heyerdahl, Thor. *Kon-Tiki: Across the Pacific by Raft* (7–12). Trans. by F. H. Lyon. 1987, Pocket paper $3.95 (0-671-63789-4). The epic story of the 6-man voyage across 4,300 miles of the Pacific Ocean in an open raft. [910.4]

LEWIS AND CLARK

3637 Petersen, David, and Mark Coburn. *Meriwether Lewis and William Clark: Soldiers, Explorers, and Partners in History* (6–9). Illus. 1988, Childrens LB $10.95 (0-516-03264-X). Using original sources the authors have re-created accurately the lives of these 2 men and of their momentous journey. (Rev: SLJ 3/89) [921]

LINDBERGH, CHARLES

3638 Randolph, Blythe. *Charles Lindbergh* (6–9). Illus. 1990, Watts LB $12.90 (0-531-10918-6). A straightforward account of the man who captured the imagination of millions by his trans-Atlantic flight. (Rev: BL 2/15/90; SLJ 8/90) [921]

MAGELLAN, FERDINAND

3639 Stefoff, Rebecca. *Ferdinand Magellan and the Discovery of the World Ocean* (7–12). Illus. 1990, Chelsea House $18.95 (0-7910-1291-3). Using many quotes from original sources, this is an engrossing account of the explorer and his voyage. (Rev: BL 6/15/90) [921]

RIDE, SALLY

3640 Hurwitz, Jane, and Sue Hurwitz. *Sally Ride: Shooting for the Stars* (5–8). 1989, Ballantine paper $3.95 (0-449-90394-X). An interestingly written account in paperback format of the female space pioneer. (Rev: BL 12/15/89; BR 3–4/90; SLJ 2/90; VOYA 2/90) [921]

STANLEY, HENRY

3641 Cohen, Daniel. *Henry Stanley and the Quest for the Source of the Nile* (6–9). Illus. 1985, Evans $11.95 (0-87131-445-2). The story of the man who located Dr. Livingstone and later explored the source of the Nile River. (Rev: BL 2/15/85; SLJ 5/85) [921]

YEAGER, CHUCK

3642 Levinson, Nancy Smiler. *Chuck Yeager* (6–9). 1988, Walker LB $14.85 (0-8027-6799-0). A brief biography of the man whose life has been associated with adventure and risk-taking. (Rev: BR 9–10/88; VOYA 8/88) [921]

The Arts and Entertainment

Collective

3643 Brower, Millicent. *Young Performers: On the Stage, in Film, and on TV* (6–9). Illus. 1985, Messner $8.79 (0-671-50229-8). Profiles and interviews with 8 young show biz professionals are given. They include Matthew Broderick and Liz Callaway. (Rev: BL 5/15/85; SLJ 5/85) [920]

3644 Cohen, Daniel, and Susan Cohen. *Young and Famous* (6–8). Illus. 1987, Pocket paper $2.50 (0-671-63493-3). Brief biographies of young actors such as Tom Cruise, Lisa Bonet, and Molly Ringwald. (Rev: BL 6/15/87) [920]

3645 O'Connor, Karen. *Contributions of Women: Literature* (7–9). Illus. 1984, Dillon LB $8.95 (0-87518-234-8). Five women authors including Emily Dickinson and Maya Angelou are profiled. [920]

3646 Terkel, Studs, and Milly Hawk Daniel. *Giants of Jazz* (7–10). Rev. ed. Illus. 1975, Harper $15.70 (0-690-00998-4). Thirteen subjects are highlighted including Benny Goodman, Louis Armstrong, Bessie Smith, and Dizzy Gillespie. [920]

Artists

BOURKE-WHITE, MARGARET

3647 Daffron, Carolyn. *Margaret Bourke-White* (7–12). Illus. 1988, Chelsea House $16.95 (1-55546-644-3). The life story of this famous photographer in an account well illustrated with the artist's work. (Rev: BL 5/1/88; BR 5–6/88; SLJ 8/88) [921]

CALDER, ALEXANDER

3648 Lipman, Jean, and Margaret Aspinwall. *Alexander Calder and His Magical Mobiles* (7–9). Illus. 1981, Hudson Hills $15.00 (0-933920-17-2). A biography of the noted sculptor with many interesting incidents from his childhood. [921]

CASSATT, MARY

3649 Cain, Michael. *Mary Cassatt* (7–10). Illus. 1989, Chelsea House LB $16.95 (1-55546-647-8). A well-illustrated account of the evolution of the American artist who broke with tradition and worked with the Impressionists. (Rev: BL 5/15/89; BR 9-10/89; SLJ 6/89; VOYA 8/89) [921]

KURTZMAN, HARVEY

3650 Kurtzman, Harvey, and Howard Zimmerman. *My Life as a Cartoonist* (6–8). Illus. 1988, Pocket paper $2.75 (0-671-63453-4). The cartoonist who founded *Mad* magazine tells his story. (Rev: BL 2/15/89; SLJ 4/89; VOYA 4/89) [921]

LARSSON, CARL

3651 Rudström, Lennart. *A Family* (7–10). Illus. 1980, Putnam $10.95 (0-399-20700-7). The Swedish artist Carl Larsson used the family he loved as his subject. [921]

MORGAN, JULIA

3652 James, Cary. *Julia Morgan: Architect* (7–10). Illus. 1990, Chelsea House LB $17.95 (1-55546-669-9). The story of the outstanding female architect who now has over 700 projects to her credit. (Rev: SLJ 8/90) [921]

Authors

MOSES, GRANDMA

3653 Biracree, Tom. *Grandma Moses* (7–10). Illus. 1989, Chelsea House $16.95 (1-55546-670-2). This primitive artist's life and works are discussed, and insets are provided of some of her paintings. (Rev: BL 12/1/89; BR 3–4/90; SLJ 1/90; VOYA 2/90) [921]

NEVELSON, LOUISE

3654 Cain, Michael. *Louise Nevelson* (6–10). Illus. 1989, Chelsea House $16.95 (1-55546-671-0). The story of the famous artist and of her amazing struggle for recognition. (Rev: BL 1/15/90; BR 3-4/90; SLJ 1/90; VOYA 2/90) [921]

O'KEEFFE, GEORGIA

3655 Berry, Michael. *Georgia O'Keeffe: Painter* (7–12). Illus. 1988, Chelsea House $16.95 (1-55546-673-7). Illustrated chiefly in black and white this is the story of the artist who reached maturity painting subjects in the southwestern states. (Rev: BL 9/15/88; BR 5–6/89; SLJ 9/88; VOYA 2/89) [921]

3656 Gherman, Beverly. *Georgia O'Keeffe: The Wideness and Wonder of Her World* (7–9). Illus. 1986, Macmillan $13.95 (0-689-31164-8). This biography emphasizes the total commitment this artist felt toward her work. (Rev: BL 4/1/86; SLJ 5/86) [921]

RIVERA, DIEGO

3657 Hargrove, Jim. *Diego Rivera: Mexican Muralist* (5–9). Illus. 1990, Childrens LB $15.93 (0-516-03268-2). The world-famous painter and muralist comes to life in this brief biography illustrated with black-and-white reproductions. (Rev: BL 8/90) [921]

TURNER, MORRIE

3658 Ericsson, Mary Kentra. *Morrie Turner: Creator of "Wee Pals"* (6–8). Illus. 1986, Childrens $15.93 (0-516-03222-4). The life story of the black cartoonist who created the nationally syndicated strip "Wee Pals." (Rev: BL 8/86) [921]

ALCOTT, LOUISA MAY

3659 Burke, Kathleen. *Louisa May Alcott* (6–10). Illus. 1988, Chelsea House $16.95 (1-55546-637-0). A portrait of this remarkable strong woman who assumed unusual family responsibilities while persuing a writing career. (Rev: BL 3/1/88) [921]

3660 Meigs, Cornelia. *Invincible Louisa: The Story of the Author of Little Women* (6–9). Illus. 1968, Little $14.95 (0-316-56590-3); Scholastic paper $2.50 (0-590-41937-4). The Newbery Award-winning biography (1934) of the courageous writer of *Little Women*. [921]

BALDWIN, JAMES

3661 Rosset, Lisa. *James Baldwin* (8–10). Illus. 1989, Chelsea House $16.95 (1-55546-572-2). A biography of this important black writer plus a discussion of his work. (Rev: BL 6/15/89; BR 9–10/89; SLJ 8/89; VOYA 10/89) [921]

BLUME, JUDY

3662 Lee, Betsy. *Judy Blume's Story* (6–9). Illus. 1981, Dillon LB $8.95 (0-87518-209-7). An easily read biography of the most popular of present-day children's book writers. [921]

BRONTË FAMILY

3663 Martin, Christopher. *The Brontës* (7–12). Illus. 1989, Rourke $12.95 (0-86592-299-3). The life and works of the 3 Brontë sisters—Charlotte, Emily, and Anne—are highlighted as well as details of the society in which they lived. (Rev: BL 3/1/89) [921]

BUCK, PEARL

3664 La Farge, Ann. *Pearl Buck* (7–10). Illus. 1988, Chelsea House $16.95 (1-55546-645-1). The life of the writer who introduced pre-Revolutionary China to millions of American readers. (Rev: BL 8/88) [921]

CLEARY, BEVERLY

3665 Cleary, Beverly. *A Girl from Yamhill: A Memoir* (6–12). Illus. 1988, Morrow $14.95 (0-688-07800-1). The growing-up years in the Northwest of one of the greats of children's literature. (Rev: BL 6/1/88; BR 5–6/88; SLJ 5/88; VOYA 6/88) [921]

DAHL, ROALD

3666 Dahl, Roald. *Boy: Tales of Childhood* (7–12). Illus. 1984, Farrar $12.95 (0-374-37374-4); Penguin paper $4.95 (0-14-031890-9). The famous author's autobiography—sometimes humorous, sometimes touching—of growing up in Wales of a Norwegian family. [921]

DICKINSON, EMILY

3667 Olsen, Victoria. *Emily Dickinson* (7–12). Illus. 1990, Chelsea House $17.95 (1-55546-649-4). An illustrated biography that describes both the life of Emily Dickinson as well as her work. (Rev: BL 7/90) [921]

DUNBAR, PAUL LAURENCE

3668 Gentry, Tony. *Paul Laurence Dunbar* (7–12). Illus. 1988, Chelsea House $16.95 (1-55546-583-8). A richly illustrated biography of one of the chief poets of the Harlem Renaissance of the 1920s. (Rev: BL 2/15/89; BR 1–289; VOYA 2/89) [921]

DUNCAN, LOIS

3669 Duncan, Lois. *Chapters: My Growth as a Writer* (7–12). 1982, Little $15.95 (0-316-19552-9). The popular writer of mystery stories tells about her life as an author. [921]

ELLISON, RALPH

3670 Bishop, Jack. *Ralph Ellison: Author* (6–10). Illus. 1988, Chelsea House LB $16.95 (1-55546-585-4). A straightforward account of the black writer that includes material on the Harlem Renaissance, the Depression, and the Federal Writers Project. (Rev: SLJ 6–7/88) [921]

FRITZ, JEAN

3671 Fritz, Jean. *Homesick: My Own Story* (7–10). Illus. 1982, Putnam $12.95 (0-399-20933-6); Dell paper $2.95 (0-440-43683-4). The story of the author's childhood in China. [921]

HUGHES, LANGSTON

3672 Meltzer, Milton. *Langston Hughes: A Biography* (7–10). 1968, Harper $13.89 (0-690-48525-5). A rounded biography of the great black writer and poet who spoke with great pride of his race. [921]

3673 Rummel, Jack. *Langston Hughes* (8–10). Illus. 1988, Chelsea House LB $17.95 (1-55546-595-1). A highly readable biography of the black poet and fiction writer that is well illustrated and contains excerpts from his writings. Part of the Black Americans of Achievement series. (Rev: BL 12/1/87; BR 1–2/89; VOYA 10/88) [921]

KERR, M. E.

3674 Kerr, M. E. *Me Me Me Me Me: Not a Novel* (7–12). 1983, Harper LB $12.89 (0-06-023193-9); NAL paper $2.50 (0-451-13208-4). A fine autobiography that concentrates on humorous incidents of the author's teenage years. [921]

LAZARUS, EMMA

3675 Lefer, Diane. *Emma Lazarus* (6–10). Illus. 1988, Chelsea House $16.95 (1-55546-634-6). The life story of the famous poet who also helped the cause of Russian Jews. (Rev: BL 6/15/88) [921]

LITTLE, JEAN

3676 Little, Jean. *Little by Little: A Writer's Education* (6–9). Illus. 1988, Viking $11.95 (0-670-81649-3). The autobiography of the Canadian writer who spent her childhood in Taiwan and gained fame with such novels as *Mine for Keeps* (1962). (Rev: BL 7/88; BR 11–12/88; SLJ 6–7/88) [921]

MELTZER, MILTON

3677 Meltzer, Milton. *Starting from Home: A Writer's Beginnings* (7–12). Illus. 1988, Viking $13.95 (0-670-81604-3). The youth of the famous writer who grew up in the 1920s and 1930s, the son of Jewish immigrants. (Rev: BL 8/88; SLJ 9/88; SLJ 3–4/89) [921]

MILLAY, EDNA ST. VINCENT

3678 Daffron, Carolyn. *Edna St. Vincent Millay* (7–12). Illus. 1989, Chelsea House $17.95 (1-55546-668-0). The life and career of this noted poet with examples of her work. (Rev: BL 12/1/89; BR 3–4/90; SLJ 3/90) [921]

RYLANT, CYNTHIA

3679 Rylant, Cynthia. *But I'll Be Back Again: An Album* (6–10). 1989, Watts LB $12.99 (0-531-08406-X). The childhood and adolescence of this fine writer as seen in the context of the 1960s and earlier. (Rev: BL 5/15/89; SLJ 7/89; VOYA 6/89) [921]

SANDBURG, CARL

3680 Hacker, Jeffrey H. *Carl Sandburg* (7–10). Illus. 1984, Watts LB $12.90 (0-531-04762-8). Poet, sometime hobo, and great lover of America—this is his story illustrated with photographs by Edward Steichen. [921]

3681 Sandburg, Carl. *Prairie-Town Boy* (7–9). 1977, Harcourt paper $1.75 (0-15-673700-0). An autobiographical account of the poet's youth in a small American town. [921]

SHAKESPEARE, WILLIAM

3682 Martin, Christopher. *Shakespeare* (7–12). Illus. 1989, Rourke $12.95 (0-86592-296-9). A biography that pays particular attention to life in Elizabethan England. (Rev: BL 3/1/89) [921]

SINGER, ISAAC BASHEVIS

3683 Kresh, Paul. *Isaac Bashevis Singer: The Story of a Storyteller* (6–9). Illus. 1984, Lodestar $13.95 (0-525-67156-0). This writer's life from the ghettos of Warsaw, Poland, to the Nobel Prize for literature. [921]

3684 Singer, Isaac Bashevis. *A Day of Pleasure: Stories of a Boy Growing Up in Warsaw* (6–8). Illus. 1969, Farrar paper $3.95 (0-374-41696-6). Autobiographical anecdotes of Singer's growing up Jewish in Poland; includes photographs of the time. [921]

STEIN, GERTRUDE

3685 La Farge, Ann. *Gertrude Stein* (7–12). Illus. 1988, Chelsea House $16.95 (1-55546-678-8). The life of this controversial writer and her amazing circle of friends are well-reconstructed. (Rev: BL 5/1/88; SLJ 9/88) [921]

STEINBECK, JOHN

3686 Ferrell, Keith. *John Steinbeck: The Voice of the Land* (8–10). 1986, Evans $11.95 (0-87131-480-0). A biography with some critical commentary about the writer who identified with the poor and homeless in America. (Rev: BL 12/15/86) [921]

STOWE, HARRIET BEECHER

3687 Jakoubek, Robert E. *Harriet Beecher Stowe: Author and Abolitionist* (6–9). Illus. 1989, Chelsea House LB $16.95 (1-55546-680-X). This account is valuable not only as a biography of this famous writer but also as an insight into the horrors of slavery. (Rev: SLJ 6/89) [921]

THOREAU, HENRY DAVID

3688 Stern, Philip Van Doren. *Henry David Thoreau: Writer and Rebel* (7–12). 1972, Harper $12.70 (0-690-37715-0). A clear biography of the man who was both a great writer and naturalist. [921]

TWAIN, MARK

3689 Meltzer, Milton. *Mark Twain: A Writer's Life* (7–12). Illus. 1985, Watts $12.90 (0-531-10072-3). A fine portrait of this writer that uses many quotes from Twain himself to reveal specific points like his genius for comedy. (Rev: BL 10/1/85; SLJ 12/85) [921]

WELLS, H. G.

3690 Martin, Christopher. *H. G. Wells* (7–12). Illus. 1989, Rourke $12.95 (0-86592-297-7). The life of the English writer who rose from poverty to be a well-known author in many genres including science fiction. (Rev: BL 3/1/89) [921]

WHEATLEY, PHILLIS

3691 Richmond, Merle. *Phillis Wheatley* (7–10). Illus. 1988, Chelsea House LB $16.95 (1-55546-683-4). A heavily illustrated account of this poet who triumphed over slavery. (Rev: BL 2/15/88; SLJ 4/88) [921]

WILDER, LAURA INGALLS

3692 MacBride, Roger Lea, ed. *West from Home: Letters of Laura Ingalls Wilder, San Francisco, 1915* (7–10). 1974, Harper LB $13.89 (0-06-024111-X); paper $3.50 (0-06-440081-6). This segment of the author's life tells us about life in San Francisco in 1915. [921]

3693 Wilder, Laura Ingalls. *On the Way Home: The Diary of a Trip from South Dakota to Mansfield, Missouri, in 1894* (7–12). Illus. 1962, Harper LB $12.89 (0-06-026490-X). The diary of an arduous journey by the author of the Little House books. [921]

WRIGHT, RICHARD

3694 Urban, Joan. *Richard Wright* (7–10). Illus. 1989, Chelsea House $16.95 (1-55546-618-4). A well-illustrated biography that also tells a little about the author's work. (Rev: BL 6/15/89; BR 9–10/89; SLJ 8/89) [921]

YATES, ELIZABETH

3695 Yates, Elizabeth. *My Diary—My World* (7–9). 1981, Westminster $12.95 (0-664-32675-7). The story of the famous writer of children's books who was a teenager during World War I. [921]

Composers

ELLINGTON, DUKE

3696 Frankl, Ron. *Duke Ellington: Bandleader and Composer* (6–10). Illus. 1988, Chelsea House LB $16.95 (1-55546-584-6). The story of the evolution of a great composer and of his life in music. (Rev: BR 1–2/89; SLJ 8/88) [921]

GERSHWIN, GEORGE

3697 Kresh, Paul. *An American Rhapsody: The Story of George Gershwin* (7–10). Illus. 1988, Dutton $14.95 (0-525-67233-8). The story of a Jewish boy from Brooklyn who became one of America's favorite composers. (Rev: BL 7/88; BR 11–12/88; SLJ 3/88; VOYA 2/89) [921]

JOPLIN, SCOTT

3698 Preston, Katherine. *Scott Joplin: Composer* (7–10). Illus. 1988, Chelsea House LB $16.95 (1-55546-598-6). The story of the talented musician, composer, and performer and the legacy of ragtime music he has left us. (Rev: BL 2/1/88; SLJ 5/88) [921]

Entertainers and Performers

3699 Busnar, Gene. *Superstars of Country Music* (7–12). Illus. 1984, Messner LB $10.79 (0-671-45627-X). People such as Hank Williams, Loretta Lynn, and Willie Nelson are among the 9 musicians featured. [920]

3700 Busnar, Gene. *The Superstars of Rock: Their Lives and Their Music* (7–12). Illus. 1980, Messner LB $10.79 (0-671-32967-7). The Rolling Stones, the Beatles, Janis Joplan, Eric Clapton, and 5 others are profiled. [920]

3701 Cohen, Daniel. *Master of Horror* (7–10). Illus. 1984, Clarion LB $12.95 (0-89919-221-1). Actors, writers, and directors are featured in profiles that include Stephen King and Boris Karloff. [920]

3702 Dillon, Ann, and Cynthia Bix. *Contributions of Women: Theater* (7–9). Illus. 1978, Dillon LB $8.95 (0-87518-152-X). The sketches included are those of Minnie Maddern Fiske, Ethel Barrymore, Helen Hayes, Lillian Hellman, and Julie Harris. [920]

ANDERSON, MARIAN

3703 Patterson, Charles. *Marian Anderson* (6–12). Illus. 1988, Watts $12.90 (0-531-10568-7). A profile of the great black singer who was the first of her race to sing at the Metropolitan Opera. (Rev: BL 12/15/88; BR 3–4/89; SLJ 1/89; VOYA 4/89) [921]

3704 Tedards, Anne. *Marian Anderson* (6–10). Illus. 1987, Chelsea House $16.95 (1-55546-638-9). The life story of the great singer-artist who helped destroy many color barriers. (Rev: BL 2/1/88; SLJ 4/88) [921]

ARMSTRONG, LOUIS

3705 Collier, James Lincoln. *Louis Armstrong: An American Success Story* (6–10). 1985, Macmillan $11.95 (0-02-722830-4). This is the story of the jazz great who rose from a destitute childhood to great success. (Rev: BL 10/1/85; SLJ 10/85; VOYA 12/85) [921]

3706 Tanenhaus, Sam. *Louis Armstrong* (7–10). Illus. 1989, Chelsea House $16.95 (1-55546-571-4). The story of the black musician who rose from poverty in New Orleans to the heights of the jazz world. (Rev: BL 3/15/89) [921]

BARNUM, P. T.

3707 Tompert, Ann. *The Greatest Showman on Earth: A Biography of P.T. Barnum* (5–8). Illus. 1987, Dillon LB $11.95 (0-87518-370-0). An entertaining profile of the flamboyant showman and a discussion of his many money-making schemes. (Rev: SLJ 3/88) [921]

COSBY, BILL

3708 Haskins, James. *Bill Cosby, America's Most Famous Father* (7–10). 1988, Walker LB $14.85 (0-8027-6786-9). As well as providing biographical details, this book explores Cosby's attitudes and his personality. (Rev: VOYA 8/88) [921]

DE MILLE, AGNES

3709 Speaker-Yuan, Margaret. *Agnes de Mille* (7–12). Illus. 1990, Chelsea House $17.95 (1-55546-648-6). The life story of the famous dancer and choreographer who influenced the entire course of American dance. (Rev: BL 7/90; SLJ 8/90; VOYA 8/90) [921]

DUNCAN, ISADORA

3710 Kozodoy, Ruth. *Isadora Duncan* (5–9). Illus. 1988, Chelsea House LB $16.95 (1-55546-650-8). The story of the remarkable woman who was one of the founders of modern dance. (Rev: SLJ 11/88) [921]

DYLAN, BOB

3711 Aaseng, Nathan. *Bob Dylan: Spellbinding Songwriter* (6–8). Illus. 1987, Lerner $8.95 (0-8225-0489-8). A short biography with many photographs of this composer and singer who influenced a whole generation. (Rev: BL 9/15/87) [921]

FITZGERALD, ELLA

3712 Kliment, Bud. *Ella Fitzgerald* (7–12). Illus. 1988, Chelsea House $16.95 (1-55546-586-2). The biography of the great black singer who began singing at age 16 with Chick Webb's orchestra. (Rev: BL 12/1/88) [921]

FONDA, JANE

3713 Collins, Tom. *Jane Fonda: An American Original* (7–12). Illus. 1990, Watts LB $13.90 (0-531-10929-1). The story of the controversial screen star which emphasizes her activities in the 1960s. (Rev: BL 3/1/90; SLJ 5/90) [921]

3714 Erlanger, Ellen. *Jane Fonda, More Than a Movie Star* (7–10). Illus. 1984, Lerner LB $8.95 (0-8225-0485-5). This biography deals with the actress's professional life, political activism, and personal relations. [921]

FOX, MICHAEL J.

3715 Daly, Marsha. *Michael J. Fox: On to the Future* (5–9). Illus. 1985, St. Martin's paper $2.95 (0-312-90253-7). The life of the film idol through the first *Back to the Future*. (Rev: BL 2/15/86) [921]

GELDOF, BOB

3716 Gray, Charlotte. *Bob Geldof* (6–9). Illus. 1988, Stevens LB $12.45 (1-55532-839-3). A brief biography of the rock star who has organized many international relief concerts. (Rev: SLJ 11/88) [921]

3717 May, Chris. *Bob Geldof* (6–9). Illus. 1989, Hamish Hamilton $9.95 (0-241-12295-3). The story of the rock musician who was responsible for Band Aid. (Rev: SLJ 6/89) [921]

HAYES, HELEN

3718 Kittredge, Mary. *Helen Hayes* (7–10). Illus. 1990, Chelsea House LB $17.95 (1-55546-656-7). A straightforward biography of one of America's most beloved actresses and her life both in and out of the theater. (Rev: SLJ 9/90) [921]

HEPBURN, KATHARINE

3719 Latham, Caroline. *Katharine Hepburn* (7–12). Illus. 1987, Chelsea House $16.95 (1-55546-658-3). An interesting portrait of this fine actress and Hollywood renegade. (Rev: BL 3/15/88; SLJ 4/88) [921]

HOLIDAY, BILLIE

3720 Deveaux, Alexis. *Don't Explain: A Song of Billie Holiday* (7–12). Illus. 1980, Harper LB $12.89 (0-06-021630-1). A prose poem on the life of Lady Day, the great popular singer. [921]

HORNE, LENA

3721 Palmer, Leslie. *Lena Horne* (8–10). Illus. 1989, Chelsea House $16.95 (1-55546-594-3). A well-illustrated biography of this black singer and actress who rose from poverty to stardom. (Rev: BR 9–10/89; VOYA 8/89) [921]

HOUSTON, WHITNEY

3722 Busnar, Gene. *The Picture Life of Whitney Houston* (5–8). Illus. 1988, Watts $10.90 (0-531-10498-2). An appealing, well-illustrated biography about the singer, her family, and friends. (Rev: BL 4/15/88) [921]

IDOL, BILLY

3723 Russell, Kate. *Billy Idol* (5–9). Illus. 1985, Messner LB $8.79 (0-671-55479-4); Simon & Schuster paper $3.50 (0-671-55474-3). The life and career of this popular performer are presented in a very flattering portrait. (Rev: BR 3–4/86; SLJ 9/85) [921]

JACKSON, MAHALIA

3724 Jackson, Jesse. *Make a Joyful Noise Unto the Lord! The Life of Mahalia Jackson, Queen of Gospel Singers* (7–9). Illus. 1974, Harper $12.70 (0-690-43344-1). The biography of the great black gospel singer who was also a strong supporter of civil rights. [921]

LAUPER, CYNDI

3725 Crocker, Chris. *Cyndi Lauper* (5–9). Illus. 1985, Messner LB $8.79 (0-671-55478-6); Simon & Schuster paper $3.50 (0-671-55475-1). A flattering account of the life and career of this pop star. (Rev: BR 3–4/86; SLJ 9/85) [921]

LENNON, JOHN

3726 Corbin, Carole Lynn. *John Lennon* (7–10). Illus. 1982, Watts LB $12.90 (0-531-04478-5). A clear well-illustrated biography of the singer from his roots in Liverpool to his death in New York. [921]

3727 Wootton, Richard. *John Lennon* (7–10). Illus. 1985, Random $6.99 (0-394-97047-0); paper $4.95 (0-394-87047-6). The story with photographs of the rise of this poor Liverpool lad and his career to his tragic death in 1980. (Rev: BL 6/15/85; BR 11–12/85; SLJ 10/85) [921]

MADONNA

3728 Matthews, Gordon. *Madonna* (6–8). Illus. 1985, Messner LB $8.79 (0-671-60375-2); Simon & Schuster paper $3.50 (0-671-60280-2). A biography of this performer that ends in the mid-1980s. (Rev: BR 5–6/86; SLJ 1/86) [921]

MARLEY, BOB

3729 May, Chris. *Bob Marley* (7–9). Illus. 1985, Hamish Hamilton $8.95 (0-241-11476-4). A biography of the Jamaican reggae singer who died of cancer in 1981. (Rev: BL 4/15/86; SLJ 2/86) [921]

MILANO, ALYSSA

3730 Catalano, Grace. *Alyssa Milano: She's the Boss* (5–8). Illus. 1989, Bantam paper $2.75 (0-553-28158-5). The story of this popular teen star, with advice for other teens on dating, fashion, and so on. (Rev: BL 7/89; SLJ 11/89; VOYA 10/89) [921]

PRESLEY, ELVIS

3731 Love, Robert. *Elvis Presley* (7–10). Illus. 1986, Watts $12.90 (0-531-10239-4). A biography of this musical luminary from his humble beginnings to his reign as the King of Rock 'n' Roll. (Rev: BL 12/15/86; BR 1–2/87; SLJ 3/87) [921]

3732 Wootton, Richard. *Elvis!* (7–10). Illus. 1985, Random $6.99 (0-394-97046-2); paper $4.95 (0-394-87046-8). The rise of the poor southern boy to stardom is chronicled in a book that includes material on his drug probles. (Rev: BL 6/15/85; BR 11–12/85; SLJ 10/85) [921]

PRINCE

3733 Matthews, Gordon. *Prince* (5–9). Illus. 1985, Messner LB $8.79 (0-671-55480-8); Simon & Schuster paper $3.50 (0-671-55477-8). An uncritical look at the life and career of this singer. (Rev: BR 3–4/86; SLJ 9/85) [921]

ROBESON, PAUL

3734 Ehrlich, Scott. *Paul Robeson: Singer and Actor* (7–10). Illus. 1988, Chelsea House LB $16.95 (1-55546-608-7). A biography of this talented actor, singer, and athlete whose career suffered for his civil rights activities and Communist affiliations. (Rev: BL 2/1/88; SLJ 5/88) [921]

3735 Larsen, Rebecca. *Paul Robeson: Hero before His Time* (7–12). Illus. 1989, Watts LB $13.90 (0-531-10779-5). The life of this controversial singer, actor, and civil rights pioneer. (Rev: BL 10/15/89; BR 3–4/90; SLJ 12/89; VOYA 2/90) [921]

ROSS, DIANA

3736 Haskins, James. *I'm Gonna Make You Love Me: The Story of Diana Ross* (7–10). 1982, Dell paper $2.25 (0-440-94172-5). An easily read biography of Diana Ross that ends in the early 1980s. [921]

SALERNO-SONNENBERG, NADJA

3737 Salerno-Sonnenberg, Nadja. *Nadja: On My Way* (7–12). Illus. 1989, Crown LB $13.99 (0-517-57391-1). The autobiography of the brilliant young violinist who is also an avid baseball fan. (Rev: BL 12/1/89; BR 3–4/90; SLJ 12/89) [921]

SILLS, BEVERLY

3738 Paolucci, Bridget. *Beverly Sills* (7–12). Illus. 1990, Chelsea House $17.95 (1-55546-677-X). A flattering biography of the opera star that has inspired many newcomers in the field. (Rev: BL 3/15/90; BR 5–6/90; SLJ 4/90) [921]

STRATTON, CHARLES S.

3739 Cross, Helen Reeder. *The Real Tom Thumb* (7–9). Illus. 1980, Macmillan $8.95 (0-02-724600-0). The story of the circus entertainer who at age 5 was still only 25 inches tall. [921]

SUMMER, DONNA

3740 Haskins, James, and J. M. Stifle. *Donna Summer: An Unauthorized Biography* (7–12). Illus. 1983, Little $14.95 (0-316-35003-6). From a bit part in *Hair* to complete stardom, this account of Donna Summer's life ends in the early 1980s. [921]

3741 Kaye, Annene. *Van Halen* (5–9). 1985, Messner LB $8.79 (0-671-55032-2); Simon & Schuster paper $3.50 (0-671-55031-4). A brief account that highlights the lives of all 4 members of this rock band. (Rev: BR 3–4/86; SLJ 9/85) [921]

WALTERS, BARBARA

3742 Malone, Mary. *Barbara Walters: T.V. Superstar* (6–9). Illus. 1990, Enslow LB $15.95 (0-89490-287-3). The life story of the first woman to co-anchor a nightly television news program. (Rev: BL 6/1/90; SLJ 8/90) [921]

Miscellaneous Artists

DE MILLE, AGNES

3743 Gherman, Beverly. *Agnes de Mille: Dancing Off the Earth* (6–10). 1990, Macmillan $13.95 (0-689-31441-8). The story of the choreographer who enriched both American ballet and the

Broadway stage with her inventive, groundbreaking work. (Rev: BL 5/15/90; SLJ 6/90; VOYA 6/90) [921]

FULLER, BUCKMINSTER

3744 Aaseng, Nathan. *More with Less: The Future World of Buckminster Fuller* (6–8). Illus. 1986, Lerner $9.95 (0-8225-0498-7). The famous architect and futurist comes alive in the pages of this biography about the man who originated the geodesic dome. (Rev: BL 9/15/56; SLJ 10/86) [921]

GOLDWYN, SAMUEL

3745 Barnes, Jeremy. *Samuel Goldwyn: Movie Mogul* (6–9). Illus. 1989, Silver Burdett LB $11.98 (0-382-09586-3). A biography of the movie mogul noted for his fine films and his misuse of the English language. (Rev: BL 1/1/90; BR 3–4/90; SLJ 11/89; VOYA 4/90) [921]

SAWYER, DIANE

3746 Blue, Rose, and Joanne E. Bernstein. *Diane Sawyer: Super Newswoman* (6–9). Illus. 1990, Enslow LB $15.95 (0-89490-288-1). The story of the newswoman who spent several years as an aide to President Nixon. (Rev: BL 6/1/90; SLJ 8/90) [921]

Contemporary and Historical Americans

Collective

3747 Altman, Susan. *Extraordinary Black Americans: From Colonial to Contemporary Times* (5–9). Illus. 1989, Childrens LB $30.60 (0-516-00581-2). A collection of 85 short biographies of important black Americans from a wide variety of fields. (Rev: BL 6/15/89) [920]

3748 Ashabranner, Brent. *People Who Make a Difference* (6–10). Illus. 1989, Cobblehill $15.95 (0-525-65009-1). An account that focuses on 14 Americans whose lives show that they care for other people. (Rev: SLJ 1/90; VOYA 2/90) [920]

3749 Beard, Annie E. S. *Our Foreign-Born Citizens* (7–9). 6th ed. 1968, Harper $14.70 (0-690-60525-0). Some of the famous Americans whose lives are retold are Audubon, Pulitzer, Einstein, and Hitchcock. [920]

3750 Blassingame, Wyatt. *The Look-It-Up Book of Presidents* (6–9). Illus. 1990, Random LB $11.99 (0-679-90353-4); paper $5.95 (0-679-80358-0). The author devotes 2 to 6 pages on each president and covers all the salient facts about each. (Rev: SLJ 5/90) [920]

3751 Deur, Lynne. *Indian Chiefs* (7–9). 1978, Fearon-Pitman LB $5.95 (0-8225-0461-8). Biographies of such great Indian leaders as Crazy Horse, Geronimo, and Black Hawk. [920]

3752 Faber, Doris, and Harold Faber. *Great Lives: American Government* (6–9). Illus. 1988, Macmillan $22.95 (0-684-18521-0). Arranged chronologically, there are many thumbnail sketches of famous American statesmen from Washington to Nixon. (Rev: BL 2/1/88; SLJ 1/89) [920]

3753 Freedman, Russell. *Indian Chiefs* (6–9). Illus. 1987, Holiday $16.95 (0-8234-0625-3). Brief biographies of 6 Indian chiefs including Red Cloud, Sitting Bull, and Joseph of the Nez Perce. (Rev: BL 5/1/87; SLJ 5/87; VOYA 8–9/87) [920]

3754 Freidel, Frank. *Our Country's Presidents* (7–12). Illus. 1973, National Geographic $7.95 (0-87044-024-1). A popularly written introduction to our presidents and their contributions. [920]

3755 Healy, Diana Dixon. *America's First Ladies: Private Lives of the Presidential Wives* (8–12). Illus. 1988, Macmillan $18.95 (0-689-11873-2). Thumbnail sketches of presidential wives from Martha Washington to Nancy Reagan. (Rev: BL 5/15/88) [920]

3756 Jacobs, William Jay. *Great Lives: Human Rights* (5–8). Illus. 1990, Macmillan $22.95 (0-689-19036-2). Jacobs profiles 30 American leaders who worked for human rights that span time from the colonist Roger Smith to Martin Luther King, Jr. (Rev: BL 7/90; SLJ 9/90) [921]

3757 Lee, George. *Interesting People: Black American History Makers* (7–12). Illus. 1989, McFarland LB $15.95 (0-89950-403-5). Short biographies of over 200 famous black Americans both past and present are included in this volume. (Rev: BR 9–10/89) [920]

3758 LeVert, Suzanne. *The Doubleday Book of Famous Americans* (6–9). Illus. 1989, Doubleday $15.95 (0-385-23699-9). Biographies are included of 101 famous historical and contemporary Americans, including Susan B. Anthony, Noah Webster, and Woody Allen. (Rev: BL 12/1/89; BR 11–12/89) [920]

3759 Lindsay, Rae. *The President's First Ladies* (8–12). Illus. 1989, Watts LB $14.90 (0-531-10798-1). Biographies of the 40 first ladies categorized by such headings as spokeswomen or stand-ins. (Rev: BL 10/1/89; BR 3–4/90; SLJ 12/89; VOYA 4/90) [920]

3760 McLenighan, Valijean. *Women Who Dared* (7–9). Illus. 1979, Raintree LB $13.31 (0-8172-1375-9). The story of 6 American women (e.g., Margaret Bourke-White and Diana Nyad) who have accomplished much in different fields. [920]

3761 Morey, Janet, and Wendy Dunn. *Famous Mexican Americans* (5–8). Illus. 1989, Dutton $14.95 (0-525-65012-1). The biographies of 15 prominent Mexican Americans from various walks of life are given with accompanying photographs. (Rev: BL 11/15/89; SLJ 10/89; VOYA 12/89) [920]

3762 Peavy, Linda, and Ursula Smith. *Dreams into Deeds: Nine Women Who Dared* (6–8). Illus. 1985, Macmillan $12.95 (0-684-18484-2). This account contains biographies of 9 interesting women including Jane Addams, Margaret Mead, Juliette Low, Mother Jones, and Elizabeth Cady Stanton. (Rev: BL 11/1/85; SLJ 2/86; VOYA 6/86) [920]

3763 Peavy, Linda, and Ursula Smith. *Women Who Changed Things* (7–10). Illus. 1983, Macmillan $12.95 (0-684-17849-4). Biographies are given of 9 relatively unknown American women activists who accomplished a great deal around the turn of the century. [920]

3764 Richardson, Ben, and William A. Fahey. *Great Black Americans* (7–9). 1976, Harper $16.70 (0-690-00994-1). The lives of 31 black leaders from a number of different fields including the arts, sports, and politics. [920]

3765 Sweeney, James B. *Army Leaders of World War II* (7–10). Illus. 1984, Watts LB $10.40 (0-531-04820-9). Biographies are given on such leaders as Patton, MacArthur, Marshall, and Eisenhower. [920]

3766 Williams, Barbara. *Breakthrough: Women in Politics* (7–9). Illus. 1979, Walker $9.95 (0-8027-6366-9). Seven contemporary women from various parts of the country are highlighted. [920]

Civil Rights Leaders

ANTHONY, SUSAN B.

3767 Weisberg, Barbara. *Susan B. Anthony* (6–10). Illus. 1988, Chelsea House $16.95 (1-55546-639-7). The biography of the woman who led the early suffragette movement. (Rev: BL 12/1/88) [921]

BETHUNE, MARY MCLEOD

3768 Halasa, Malu. *Mary McLeod Bethune* (6–10). Illus. 1988, Chelsea House $16.95 (1-55546-574-9). A stirring biography of the black woman who fought for the right to a quality education for her people. (Rev: BL 3/15/89) [921]

BROWN, JOHN

3769 Scott, John Anthony. *John Brown of Harper's Ferry* (7–12). Illus. 1988, Facts on File $14.95 (0-8160-1347-0). A biography of the headstrong abolitionist that focuses on the Harper's Ferry raid. (Rev: BL 2/1/88; BR 11–12/88; SLJ 5/88; VOYA 8/88) [921]

BURNS, ANTHONY

3770 Hamilton, Virginia. *Anthony Burns: The Defeat and Triumph of a Fugitive Slave* (7–12). 1988, Knopf LB $12.99 (0-394-98185-5). Burns, who lived only 28 years, rebelled against his slave status with repercussions felt around the country. (Rev: BL 6/1/88; BR 11–12/88; SLJ 6–7/88; VOYA 10/88) [921]

CUFFE, PAUL

3771 Diamond, Arthur. *Paul Cuffe* (7–10). Illus. 1989, Chelsea House $16.95 (1-55546-579-X). The story of the freed American slave who in 1810 proposed the founding of an African colony for black Americans. (Rev: BL 11/15/89; BR 11–12/89; SLJ 1/90; VOYA 12/89) [921]

DOUGLASS, FREDERICK

3772 Miller, Douglas T. *Frederick Douglass and the Fight for Freedom* (7–12). Illus. 1988, Facts on File $15.95 (0-8160-1617-8). An engrossing biography of the self-taught former slave who led the abolitionist movement. (Rev: BL 11/1/88; BR 1–2/89; SLJ 10/88; VOYA 2/89) [921]

3773 Russell, Sharman Apt. *Frederick Douglass* (6–10). Illus. 1988, Chelsea House LB $16.95 (1-55546-580-3). This biography of the civil rights leader supplies detail in both his private and public life. (Rev: BL 2/1/88; SLJ 6–7/88) [921]

DU BOIS, W. E. B.

3774 Hamilton, Virginia. *W. E. B. Du Bois: A Biography* (7–9). Illus. 1972, Harper $13.89 (0-690-87256-9). The life story of this great teacher and civil rights leader who played an important part in black American history. [921]

3775 Stafford, Mark. *W. E. B. Du Bois* (6–9). Illus. 1989, Chelsea House $17.95 (1-55546-582-X). A fine profile of the man who was not only an important writer but also a prominent opponent of racism. (Rev: BL 12/15/89; BR 1–2/90; SLJ 5/90) [921]

GARVEY, MARCUS

3776 Lawler, Mary. *Marcus Garvey* (7–10). Illus. 1987, Chelsea House $17.95 (1-55546-587-0). The story of the black leader who preached black separation and founded the Universal Negro Improvement Association. Part of an extensive series on black Americans. (Rev: BL 12/1/87; BR 1–2/89; VOYA 10/88) [921]

JACKSON, JESSE

3777 Chaplik, Dorothy. *Up with Hope: A Biography of Jesse Jackson* (6–9). Illus. 1986, Dillon $11.95 (0-87518-347-6). A straightforward biography that covers Jackson's public and private life. (Rev: BL 1/1/87) [921]

3778 Kosof, Anna. *Jesse Jackson* (7–12). Illus. 1987, Watts $11.90 (0-531-10413-3). A clear, positive portrait of this national leader that details his roots, accomplishments, and opinions. (Rev: BL 1/1/88; BR 1–2/88; SLJ 1/88; VOYA 6/88) [921]

3779 McKissack, Patricia. *Jesse Jackson* (6–9). 1989, Scholastic $11.95 (0-590-43181-1). A complimentary biography of this civil rights leader and politician. (Rev: BL 12/1/89; VOYA 12/89) [921]

3780 Otfinoski, Steven. *Jesse Jackson: A Voice for Change* (5–8). Illus. 1990, Fawcett paper $3.95 (0-449-90402-4). Besides detailing the life story of Jesse Jackson, this book describes the civil rights movement of the 1950s and 1960s. (Rev: SLJ 6/90) [921]

KING, MARTIN LUTHER, JR.

3781 Darby, Jean. *Martin Luther King, Jr.* (6–8). Illus. 1990, Lerner $14.95 (0-8225-4902-6). An account that gives details of both King's life and the racial strife of the 1960s. (Rev: BL 7/90) [921]

3782 Faber, Doris, and Harold Faber. *Martin Luther King, Jr.* (6–8). Illus. 1986, Messner $9.79 (0-671-60175-X). A straightforward biography of the civil rights leader that uses quotations liberally from his writing and speeches. (Rev: BL 8/86; SLJ 8/86) [921]

3783 Harris, Jacqueline L. *Martin Luther King, Jr.* (7–10). Illus. 1983, Watts LB $12.90 (0-531-04588-9). A fine introduction to the life and work of this civil rights leader. [921]

3784 Haskins, James. *The Life and Death of Martin Luther King, Jr.* (7–10). Illus. 1977, Lothrop LB $12.88 (0-688-51802-8). A simple biography that focuses on the events surrounding King's death. [921]

3785 Jakoubek, Robert E. *Martin Luther King, Jr.* (6–9). Illus. 1989, Chelsea House $16.95 (1-55546-597-8). A stirring biography that also gives a good history of the nonviolent civil rights movement. (Rev: BL 12/15/89; BR 1–2/90; SLJ 3/90; VOYA 2/90) [921]

3786 Patterson, Lillie. *Martin Luther King, Jr. and the Freedom Movement* (7–12). Illus. 1989, Facts on File $16.95 (0-8160-1605-4). A biography of the civil rights leader and the movement he led. (Rev: BL 7/89; BR 11–12/89; SLJ 9/89; VOYA 12/89) [921]

3787 Peck, Ira. *The Life and Words of Martin Luther King, Jr.* (7–10). 1986, Scholastic paper $2.25 (0-590-40132-7). A fine biography of the civil rights leader that quotes liberally from his speeches and general writings. (Rev: SLJ 2/86) [921]

3788 Quayle, Louise. *Martin Luther King, Jr. : Dreams for a Nation* (5–8). Illus. 1990, Fawcett paper $3.95 (0-449-90377-X). This account gives good background information on the civil rights movement and describes the life of its leader. (Rev: SLJ 6/90) [921]

3789 Schloredt, Valerie. *Martin Luther King, Jr.* (6–9). Illus. 1988, Stevens LB $12.45 (1-55532-817-2). A quickly paced, brief biography that concentrates on the contributions of Dr. King. (Rev: SLJ 11/88) [921]

MALCOLM X

3790 Rummel, Jack. *Malcolm X* (6–9). Illus. 1989, Chelsea House $16.95 (1-55546-600-1). A heavily illustrated portrait of the black leader and his movement for civil rights for his people. (Rev: BL 5/15/89; BR 9–10/89; SLJ 6/89; VOYA 8/89) [921]

POWELL, ADAM CLAYTON, JR.

3791 Jakoubek, Robert E. *Adam Clayton Powell, Jr.* (7–12). Illus. 1988, Chelsea House $16.95 (1-55546-606-0). The story of the Harlem civil rights leader who was a congressman for over 20 years. (Rev: BL 10/1/88; VOYA 12/88) [921]

RANDOLPH, A. PHILIP

3792 Hanley, Sally. *A. Philip Randolph* (6–9). Illus. 1988, Chelsea House $16.95 (1-55545-607-9). The story of the black labor leader who founded the Brotherhood of Sleeping Car Porters. (Rev: BL 10/1/88; BR 1–2/89; VOYA 2/89) [921]

RUSSWURM, JOHN

3793 Borzendowski, Janice. *John Russwurm* (6–10). Illus. 1989, Chelsea House LB $16.95 (0-55546-610-9). Russwurm was the black American who worked for the establishment of Liberia, a colony for freed slaves. (Rev: BL 6/1/89; BR 9–10/89; VOYA 10/89) [921]

STEINEM, GLORIA

3794 Daffron, Carolyn. *Gloria Steinem* (7–12). Illus. 1988, Chelsea House LB $17.95 (1-55546-679-6). The story of the influential woman who founded *Ms.* magazine and who is also a leader in the feminist movement. (Rev: BL 11/1/87; BR 11–12/88; VOYA 2/89) [921]

3795 Henry, Sondra, and Emily Taitz. *One Woman's Power: A Biography of Gloria Steinem* (6–9). Illus. 1987, Dillon $11.95 (0-87518-346-8). The story of the feminist and founder of *Ms.* magazine told in a readable, thorough fashion. (Rev: BL 3/1/87; SLJ 9/87) [921]

TRUTH, SOJOURNER

3796 Krass, Peter. *Sojourner Truth* (7–12). Illus. 1988, Chelsea House $16.95 (1-55546-611-7). The life of a woman who began as a slave and ended as a respected abolitionist and feminist. (Rev: BL 10/1/88) [921]

3797 Ortiz, Victoria. *Sojourner Truth, a Self-Made Woman* (6–9). Illus. 1974, Harper $11.89 (0-397-31504-X). The biography of the former slave who fought against social injustice. [921]

3798 Taylor-Boyd, Susan. *Sojourner Truth* (5–8). Illus. 1990, Stevens LB $12.45 (0-8368-0101-6). The story of the famous black woman who spoke out for equality and justice by using peaceful means. (Rev: BL 6/15/90) [921]

TUBMAN, HARRIET

3799 Carlson, Judy. *Harriet Tubman: Call to Freedom* (5–8). 1989, Ballantine paper $3.95 (0-449-90376-1). A biography that is a lively account of the early fighter against slavery. (Rev: BL 12/15/89; BR 3–4/90; SLJ 2/90) [921]

3800 Petry, Ann. *Harriet Tubman: Conductor on the Underground Railroad* (7–10). 1955, Harper $14.38 (0-690-37236-1); Archway paper $2.95 (0-671-50442-8). The story of the leader of the Underground Railroad and of her religious faith. [921]

TURNER, NAT

3801 Bisson, Terry. *Nat Turner: Slave Revolt Leader* (7–10). Illus. 1988, Chelsea House $16.95 (1-55546-613-3). A biography of the courageous black man who led one of the nation's most important slave revolts. (Rev: BL 8/88; BR 1–2/89; SLJ 2/89; VOYA 2/89) [921]

VESEY, DENMARK

3802 Edwards, Lillie J. *Denmark Vesey: Slave Revolt Leader* (6–9). Illus. 1990, Chelsea House LB $17.95 (1-55546-614-1). The story of the slave who bought his freedom and was later hanged for plotting a slave rebellion. (Rev: SLJ 7/90) [921]

Presidents and Their Wives

ADAMS, JOHN

3803 Dwyer, Frank. *John Adams* (6–9). Illus. 1989, Chelsea House $16.95 (1-55546-801-2). A biography of the president who helped ensure the survival of his fledgling country. (Rev: BL 4/15/89; BR 9–10/89; VOYA 8/89) [921]

3804 Stefoff, Rebecca. *John Adams: 2nd President of the United States* (7–9). 1988, Garrett LB $12.95 (0-944483-10-0). Both the life and the times of our second president are well re-created in this account. (Rev: SLJ 9/88) [921]

BUSH, GEORGE

3805 Sullivan, George. *George Bush* (6–10). Illus. 1989, Messner LB $11.98 (0-671-64599-4); paper $5.95 (0-671-67814-0). A detailed account of the life of this president that nicely balances praise with criticism. (Rev: BR 1–2/90; SLJ 11/89; VOYA 4/90) [921]

CARTER, JIMMY

3806 Slavin, Ed. *Jimmy Carter* (7–10). 1989, Chelsea House $16.95 (1-55546-828-4). An account that covers both the highs and lows of the personal and political life of this president. (Rev: BL 7/89; BR 9–10/89; SLJ 8/89; VOYA 10/89) [921]

CLEVELAND, GROVER

3807 Collins, David R. *Grover Cleveland: 22nd and 24th President of the United States* (7–9). Illus. 1988, Garrett LB $12.95 (0-944483-01-1). A fine introduction to this president, his career, and interesting sidelights to his life that make this account interesting. (Rev: SLJ 9/88) [921]

EISENHOWER, DWIGHT D.

3808 Cannon, Marian G. *Dwight David Eisenhower: War Hero and President* (7–9). Illus. 1990, Watts LB $12.90 (0-531-10915-1). The story of the 5-star general and president who served his country throughout his entire life. (Rev: BL 7/90; SLJ 6/90) [921]

3809 Darby, Jean. *Dwight D. Eisenhower: A Man Called Ike* (6–9). Illus. 1989, Lerner LB $14.95 (0-8225-4900-X). An easily read account of the highlights in the life of this general and president. (Rev: SLJ 9/89) [921]

3810 Ellis, Rafaela. *Dwight D. Eisenhower: 34th President of the United States* (6–8). Illus. 1989, Garrett LB $12.95 (0-944483-13-5). A clearly written biography of the soldier-statesman who became our thirty-fourth president. (Rev: BR 9–10/89; SLJ 8/89) [921]

3811 Sandberg, Peter Lars. *Dwight D. Eisenhower* (7–12). Illus. 1986, Chelsea House $17.95 (0-87754-521-9). A brief biography of the president and war leader that emphasizes the human side of this historical figure. (Rev: SLJ 11/86) [921]

FORD, GERALD R.

3812 Randolph, Sallie. *Gerald R. Ford, President* (6–9). Illus. 1987, Walker LB $13.85 (0-8027-6667-6). A straightforward account of Gerald R. Ford's rise to power and of his administration. (Rev: BL 7/87; SLJ 8/87) [921]

GRANT, ULYSSES S.

3813 Falkof, Lucille. *Ulysses S. Grant: 18th President of the United States* (6–9). Illus. 1988, Garrett LB $12.95 (0-944483-02-X). The career of the soldier statesman is re-created with information about the background events of his time. (Rev: SLJ 10/88) [921]

HOOVER, HERBERT

3814 Hilton, Suzanne. *The World of Young Herbert Hoover* (4–8). Illus. 1987, Walker LB $13.85 (0-8027-6709-5). This brief biography takes Hoover through his college years and gives some indication of events to follow. (Rev: SLJ 1/88) [921]

JACKSON, ANDREW

3815 Stefoff, Rebecca. *Andrew Jackson: 7th President of the United States* (7–9). Illus. 1988, Garrett LB $12.95 (0-944483-08-9). An interesting account of this president's life plus good background material on the period in which he lived. (Rev: SLJ 9/88) [921]

JEFFERSON, THOMAS

3816 Bober, Natalie S. *Thomas Jefferson: Man on a Mountain* (7–12). 1988, Macmillan $14.95 (0-689-31154-0). A detailed biography of an amazing multitalented founding father and president. (Rev: BL 1/15/89; BR 5–6/89; SLJ 11/88; VOYA 10/88) [921]

3817 Milton, Joyce. *The Story of Thomas Jefferson: Prophet of Liberty* (5–9). Illus. 1990, Dell paper $2.95 (0-440-40265-4). A biography that brings Jefferson alive and gives fine background material on his times. (Rev: SLJ 8/90) [921]

3818 Moscow, Henry. *Thomas Jefferson and His World* (6–10). Illus. 1960, Troll LB $14.95 (0-8167-1532-7). The story of this multitalented man and his many contributions to American life. [921]

JOHNSON, LYNDON B.

3819 Falkof, Lucille. *Lyndon B. Johnson: 36th President of the United States* (6–8). Illus. 1989, Garrett LB $12.95 (0-944483-20-8). An informative biography that covers both the public and private life of this president. (Rev: BR 9–10/89; SLJ 8/89) [921]

3820 Kaye, Tony. *Lyndon B. Johnson* (6–10). Illus. 1987, Chelsea House $16.95 (0-87754-536-7). A biography of the president associated with Great Society legislation and the Vietnam War. (Rev: BL 1/15/88) [921]

3821 Lynch, Dudley. *The President from Texas: Lyndon Baines Johnson* (7–10). Illus. 1975, Harper $12.70 (0-690-00627-6). A portrait of this president that does not omit the ruthless side of his character. [921]

KENNEDY, JOHN F.

3822 Falkof, Lucille. *John F. Kennedy: 35th President of the United States* (6–9). Illus. 1988, Garrett LB $12.95 (0-944483-03-8). As well as the life and career of this president, the author gives good background material on the issues and general events of the times. (Rev: SLJ 10/88) [921]

3823 Randall, Marta. *John F. Kennedy* (6–10). Illus. 1987, Chelsea House $16.95 (0-87754-586-3). A biography of this beloved president that includes coverage of domestic and international crises. (Rev: BL 1/15/88; BR 9–10/88; VOYA 10/88) [921]

3824 Selfridge, John W. *John F. Kennedy: Courage in Crisis* (5–8). 1989, Ballantine paper $3.95 (0-449-90399-0). A simple biography of the late president that tells about his youth as well as his presidency. (Rev: BL 12/15/89; BR 3–4/90; SLJ 2/90) [921]

3825 Waggoner, Jeffrey. *The Assassination of President Kennedy* (7–10). Illus. 1989, Greenhaven LB $12.95 (0-89908-068-5). The evidence supporting various theories on the death of President Kennedy is presented in this readable account. (Rev: BL 3/1/90; SLJ 5/90) [921]

LINCOLN, ABRAHAM

3826 Freedman, Russell. *Lincoln: A Photobiography* (5–10). Illus. 1987, Clarion $15.95 (0-89919-380-3). This Newbery Award-winning title beautifully re-creates the life of this great American in text and pictures. (Rev: BL 12/15/87; SLJ 12/87) [921]

3827 Kigel, Richard. *The Frontier Years of Abe Lincoln: In the Words of His Friends and Family* (7–12). 1986, Walker $15.95 (0-8027-0921-4). A portrait of Lincoln that traces his early life from birth to entry into the Illinois legislature. (Rev: BL 3/15/87; BR 3–4/87; SLJ 1/87; VOYA 2/87) [921]

3828 Sandburg, Carl. *Abe Lincoln Grows Up* (6–9). 1975, Harcourt $16.95 (0-15-201037-8); paper $4.95 (0-15-602615-5). From the pen of one of America's great poets, this is an account of the boyhood of his great hero. [921]

3829 Sloate, Susan. *Abraham Lincoln: The Freedom President* (5–8). 1989, Ballantine paper $3.95 (0-449-90375-3). An accessible account of the president who led his country through division back to unity. (Rev: BL 12/15/89; BR 3–4/90) [921]

3830 Stefoff, Rebecca. *Abraham Lincoln: 16th President of the United States* (6–8). Illus. 1989, GEC LB $12.95 (0-944483-14-3). A serviceable biography that gives information about Lincoln's personality and his family life. (Rev: SLJ 8/89) [921]

MADISON, JAMES

3831 Banfield, Susan. *James Madison* (6–8). Illus. 1986, Watts $10.40 (0-0531-10217-3). The life of one of the shapers of the Constitution who later became the fourth president. (Rev: BL 12/1/86; SLJ 11/86) [921]

3832 Fritz, Jean. *The Great Little Madison* (5–8). Illus. 1989, Putnam $15.95 (0-399-21768-1). With wit and imagination the author captures the life of our fourth president. (Rev: BL 10/1/89; BR 3–4/90; SLJ 11/89; VOYA 12/89) [921]

3833 Leavell, J. Perry. *James Madison* (6–10). Illus. 1988, Chelsea House $16.95 (1-55546-815-2). The life of our fourth president, the man who continued to battle the British and who convened the 1787 Continental Congress. (Rev: BL 7/88; BR 9–10/88; VOYA 10/88) [921]

MONROE, JAMES

3834 Wetzel, Charles. *James Monroe* (6–10). Illus. 1989, Chelsea House $16.95 (1-55546-817-9). The life of the Revolutionary War hero, his presidency, and the foreign policy named after him. (Rev: BL 7/89; BR 9–10/89) [921]

NIXON, RICHARD M.

3835 Randolph, Sallie. *Richard M. Nixon, President* (6–9). Illus. 1989, Walker LB $15.85 (0-8027-6849-0). A straightforward account using many original sources that doesn't skirt the controversial issues. (Rev: BL 1/15/90; SLJ 12/90; VOYA 2/90) [921]

3836 Ripley, C. Peter. *Richard Nixon* (6–10). Illus. 1987, Chelsea House $16.95 (0-87754-585-5). Beginning with his 1974 resignation, Nixon's life is retraced and an assessment of his career is given. (Rev: BL 12/1/87; BR 5–6/88; SLJ 12/87) [921]

REAGAN, RONALD

3837 Fox, Mary Virginia. *Mister President: The Story of Ronald Reagan* (6–8). Rev. ed. Illus. 1986, Enslow $16.95 (0-89490-130-3). An account that covers the childhood, political career, and presidency of Ronald Reagan. (Rev: BL 11/1/86; BR 3–4/87) [921]

3838 Sullivan, George. *Ronald Reagan* (7–10). Illus. 1985, Messner LB $9.95 (0-671-60168-7). The life of our former president from birth through the 1984 election. (Rev: SLJ 1/86) [921]

ROOSEVELT, ELEANOR

3839 Jacobs, William Jay. *Eleanor Roosevelt: A Life of Happiness and Tears* (6–9). Illus. 1983, Putnam $10.95 (0-698-20585-5). A fine introduction to the life of this amazing woman who refused to live in the shadow of her husband's fame. [921]

3840 Roosevelt, Elliott. *Eleanor Roosevelt, with Love: A Centenary Remembrance* (7–9). 1984, Dutton $12.95 (0-525-67147-1). A personal tribute by the son of the beloved first lady. [921]

3841 Toor, Rachel. *Eleanor Roosevelt* (6–10). Illus. 1989, Chelsea House $16.95 (1-55546-674-5). An affectionate portrait of a first lady who was also a great humanitarian and internationalist. (Rev: BL 4/1/89; BR 5–6/89; SLJ 5/89; VOYA 8/89) [921]

ROOSEVELT, FRANKLIN D.

3842 Devaney, John. *Franklin Delano Roosevelt, President* (6–10). Illus. 1987, Walker LB $13.85 (0-8027-6713-3). An account that detailed Roosevelt's personality as well as his career. (Rev: SLJ 1/88; VOYA 12/87) [921]

3843 Greenblatt, Miriam. *Franklin D. Roosevelt: 32nd President of the United States* (6–8). Illus. 1989, GEC LB $12.95 (0-944483-06-2). A clearly written, objective biography of Roosevelt that also includes information about his family life. (Rev: SLJ 8/89) [921]

3844 Hacker, Jeffrey H. *Franklin D. Roosevelt* (7–9). 1983, Watts LB $12.90 (0-531-04487-4). The biography of the 4-term president who led America through the Depression and most of World War II. [921]

ROOSEVELT, THEODORE

3845 Stefoff, Rebecca. *Theodore Roosevelt: 26th President of the United States* (7–9). 1988, Garrett LB $12.95 (0-944483-09-7). The adventurous life of this president is re-created as well as his pioneering work in conservation. (Rev: SLJ 9/88) [921]

TRUMAN, HARRY S.

3846 Farley, Karin C. *Harry Truman: The Man from Independence* (6–9). Illus. 1989, Messner LB $11.98 (0-671-65853-0). A clearly written, objective account of Truman and the events associated with his presidency. (Rev: BR 11–12/89; SLJ 11/89; VOYA 12/89) [921]

3847 Greenberg, Morrie. *The Buck Stops Here: A Biography of Harry Truman* (5–9). Illus. 1989, Dillon LB $11.95 (0-87518-394-8). A competent retelling of the major events in Truman's life and of his importance as a U.S. president. (Rev: SLJ 4/89) [921]

3848 Leavell, J. Perry. *Harry S. Truman* (6–10). Illus. 1987, Chelsea House $16.95 (0-87754-558-8). The story of the president who faced the mountain of problems following World War II. [921]

WASHINGTON, GEORGE

3849 Bruns, Roger. *George Washington* (6–10). Illus. 1986, Chelsea House $17.95 (0-87754-584-7). A solid, readable biography of our first president. (Rev: BL 3/1/87) [921]

3850 Cunliffe, Marcus. *George Washington and the Making of a Nation* (6–10). Illus. 1966, Troll LB $14.95 (0-8167-1523-8). Not only the life story of our first president but also a good background history of the Revolutionary Period. [921]

3851 Falkof, Lucille. *George Washington: 1st President of the United States* (6–8). Illus. 1989, Garrett LB $12.95 (0-944483-19-4). An objective, readable portrait of the life and times of our first president. (Rev: BR 9–10/89; SLJ 8/89) [921]

3852 Fleming, Thomas. *First in Their Hearts: A Biography of George Washington* (7–9). Illus. 1984, Walker $11.95 (0-8027-0809-9). A highly regarded biography of the career of George Washington that was first published in 1968. (Rev: BL 4/1/85) [921]

3853 Hilton, Suzanne. *The World of Young George Washington* (5–8). 1987, Walker $12.95 (0-8027-6657-9). Washington as a youth plus detailed information on life in pre-Revolutionary America. (Rev: BR 5–6/87) [921]

3854 Meltzer, Milton. *George Washington and the Birth of Our Nation* (7–9). Illus. 1986, Watts $13.90 (0-531-10253-X). An account not only of Washington's political life but also of his personality and of the times in which he lived. (Rev: BL 11/15/86; BR 1–2/87; SLJ 12/86; VOYA 2/87) [921]

WILSON, WOODROW

3855 Collins, David R. *Woodrow Wilson: 28th President of the United States* (6–8). Illus. 1989,

Garrett LB $12.95 (0-944483-18-6). An objective account of the life of the president who brought us through World War I. (Rev: SLJ 8/89) [921]

3856 Leavell, J. Perry. *Woodrow Wilson* (6–10). Illus. 1986, Chelsea House $17.95 (0-87754-557-X). A readable, straightforward account that uses many quotes from original sources. (Rev: BL 3/1/87) [921]

Statesmen and Other Public Figures

ARNOLD, BENEDICT

3857 Fritz, Jean. *Traitor: The Case of Benedict Arnold* (7–9). Illus. 1981, Putnam $9.95 (0-399-20834-8). A biography that tries to probe the many reasons for Arnold's motives. [921]

BLY, NELLIE

3858 Ehrlich, Elizabeth. *Nellie Bly* (7–10). Illus. 1989, Chelsea House LB $16.95 (1-55546-643-5). A cursory view of this exciting journalist and reformer who worked to correct the social and economic ills of her day. (Rev: BL 6/1/89; BR 9–10/89; SLJ 7/89; VOYA 8/89) [921]

BOONE, DANIEL

3859 Lawlor, Laurie. *Daniel Boone* (5–9). Illus. 1988, Whitman LB $10.50 (0-8075-1462-4). A sound, well-researched biography that tries to separate myth from truth concerning this solitary frontiersman. (Rev: BL 2/15/89; SLJ 12/88) [921]

BRANDEIS, LOUIS D.

3860 Gross, David C. *A Justice for All the People: Louis D. Brandeis* (7–9). Illus. 1987, Dutton $14.95 (0-525-67194-3). A biography of the liberal lawyer, Supreme Court justice, and late in life supporter of Zionist causes. (Rev: BL 5/1/87; SLJ 8/89) [921]

DAVIS, JEFFERSON

3861 King, Perry Scott. *Jefferson Davis* (7–10). Illus. 1990, Chelsea House $17.95 (1-55546-806-3). With many illustrations, King recreates the life and times of the president of the Confederacy. (Rev: BL 8/90; SLJ 8/90) [921]

FRANKLIN, BENJAMIN

3862 Looby, Chris. *Benjamin Franklin* (6–10). Illus. 1990, Chelsea House $17.95 (1-55546-808-X). A well-illustrated account of the life of this complex man that also introduces many of his contemporaries. (Rev: BL 8/90; SLJ 7/90; VOYA 8/90) [921]

3863 Meltzer, Milton. *Benjamin Franklin: The New American* (7–10). Illus. 1988, Watts $14.90 (0-531-10582-2). The life of a multifaceted genius who was one of America's most influential founding fathers. (Rev: BL 2/15/89; BR 3–4/89; SLJ 1/89; VOYA 6/89) [921]

FREMONT, JESSIE BENTON

3864 Morrison, Dorothy Nafus. *Under a Strong Wind: The Adventures of Jessie Benton* (6–9). 1983, Macmillan $12.95 (0-689-31004-8). The story of the wife of John Charles Fremont and how she helped in the opening of the West and participated in the politics of the day. [921]

HAMILTON, ALEXANDER

3865 Keller, Mollie. *Alexander Hamilton* (6–10). Illus. 1986, Watts LB $10.40 (0-531-10214-9). The career of this shaper of our Constitution is traced from birth in the West Indies to his unfortunate death by dueling. (Rev: SLJ 2/87) [921]

HOUSTON, SAM

3866 Fritz, Jean. *Make Way for Sam Houston* (6–9). Illus. 1986, Putnam $12.95 (0-399-21303-1); paper $5.95 (0-399-21304-X). An authentic portrait of this colorful figure who served the state of Texas faithfully. (Rev: BL 6/1/86; VOYA 6/86) [921]

JACKSON, STONEWALL

3867 Fritz, Jean. *Stonewall* (7–10). Illus. 1979, Putnam $10.95 (0-399-20698-1). The great Confederate general portrayed realistically as the complex man he was. [921]

KISSINGER, HENRY

3868 Israel, Fred L. *Henry Kissinger* (6–10). Illus. 1986, Chelsea House $17.95 (0-87754-588-X). An objective view of the man who shaped American foreign policy through several administrations. (Rev: BL 2/1/87; SLJ 3/87) [921]

LEE, ROBERT E.

3869 Weidhorn, Manfred. *Robert E. Lee* (6–9). Illus. 1988, Macmillan $14.95 (0-689-31340-3). A sensitive portrait of one of the tragic figures of our Civil War. (Rev: BL 3/1/88; BR 9–10/88; SLJ 6–7/88; VOYA 8/88) [921]

MACARTHUR, DOUGLAS

3870 Darby, Jean. *Douglas MacArthur* (6–9). Illus. 1989, Lerner LB $14.95 (0-8225-4901-8). The career of the controversial general who led the war in the Pacific is outlined in this volume. (Rev: SLJ 9/89) [921]

3871 Finkelstein, Norman H. *The Emperor General: A Biography of Douglas MacArthur* (5–9). Illus. 1989, Dillon LB $11.95 (0-87518-396-4). The high points in the life of General MacArthur are covered in this attractive biography. (Rev: SLJ 4/89) [921]

MARSHALL, GEORGE

3872 Lubetkin, Wendy. *George Marshall* (7–10). Illus. 1989, Chelsea House $17.95 (1-55546-843-8). The story of the World War II hero who authored the revolutionary Marshall Plan, the base for European recovery after World War II. (Rev: BR 3–4/90) [921]

MARSHALL, THURGOOD

3873 Aldred, Lisa. *Thurgood Marshall* (7–10). Illus. 1990, Chelsea House $17.95 (1-55546-601-X). The story of the first black American to serve as a justice on the Supreme Court. (Rev: BL 7/90) [921]

MURROW, EDWARD R.

3874 Vonier, Sprague. *Edward R. Murrow* (6–8). Illus. 1990, Stevens LB $12.95 (0-8368-0100-8). A simple biography of the man who pioneered television newscasting and media journalism. (Rev: BL 4/1/90; SLJ 8/90) [921]

NADER, RALPH

3875 Peduzzi, Kelli. *Ralph Nader* (5–8). Illus. 1990, Stevens LB $12.45 (0-8368-0098-2). An interesting account of the life and career of this famous consumer advocate. (Rev: BL 6/15/90) [921]

O'CONNOR, SANDRA DAY

3876 Bentley, Judith. *Justice Sandra Day O'Connor* (7–10). Illus. 1983, Messner LB $9.29 (0-671-45809-4); paper $4.95 (0-671-49489-9). An informal biography that traces O'Connor's career to her early days on the Supreme Court. [921]

3877 Woods, Harold, and Geraldine Woods. *Equal Justice: A Biography of Sandra Day O'Connor* (6–8). Illus. 1985, Dillon $11.95 (0-87518-292-5). This biography of the conservative Supreme Court Justice covers her life through her first 3 years on the Court. (Rev: BL 11/1/85; BR 1–2/86) [921]

PAINE, THOMAS

3878 Vail, John. *Thomas Paine* (6–10). Illus. 1990, Chelsea House $17.95 (1-55546-819-5). The story of the outspoken radical whose writings influenced the development of the American Revolution. (Rev: BL 8/90; SLJ 6/90; VOYA 8/90) [921]

PATTON, GEORGE

3879 Peifer, Charles, Jr. *Soldier of Destiny: A Biography of George Patton* (5–9). Illus. 1989, Dillon LB $11.95 (0-87518-395-6). The story of this colorful war hero and his importance in history. (Rev: SLJ 4/89; VOYA 8/89) [921]

SANGER, MARGARET

3880 Topalian, Elyse. *Margaret Sanger* (7–10). Illus. 1984, Watts LB $12.90 (0-531-04763-6). A portrait of the feminist and advocate of safe birth control. [921]

Miscellaneous Historical Figures

ADAMS, ABIGAIL

3881 Osborne, Angela. *Abigail Adams* (6–10). Illus. 1988, Chelsea House $16.95 (1-55546-635-4). The biography of the early feminist who was a strong influence on husband John and a fine recorder of American history. (Rev: BL 12/1/88; BR 5–6/89; SLJ 1/89) [921]

ADAMS, GRIZZLY

3882 McClung, Robert M. *The True Adventures of Grizzly Adams* (6–9). Illus. 1985, Morrow $11.95 (0-688-05794-2). The stranger-than-fiction story of the mountain man who after winning and losing several fortunes went to live in Sierra Nevada. (Rev: BL 2/1/86; BR 11–12/85; SLJ 11/85; VOYA 12/85) [921]

ADDAMS, JANE

3883 Kittredge, Mary. *Jane Addams* (6–10). Illus. 1988, Chelsea House $16.95 (1-55546-636-2). Jane Addams helped immigrants by founding the first settlement house, Hull House, in Chicago. (Rev: BL 6/15/88; BR 11–12/88; SLJ 1/89) [921]

BARTON, CLARA

3884 Hamilton, Leni. *Clara Barton* (5–10). Illus. 1987, Chelsea House $17.95 (1-55546-641-9). The story of the Civil War nurse and how she prepared for the founding of the American Red Cross. (Rev: BL 11/1/87) [921]

BLACKWELL, ELIZABETH

3885 Brown, Jordan. *Elizabeth Blackwell* (7–10). Illus. 1989, Chelsea House LB $16.95 (1-55546-642-7). The life story of the first woman doctor who also organized a nursing service during the Civil War and helped provide educational opportunities for other young women. (Rev: BL 5/15/89) [921]

BOWDITCH, NATHANIEL

3886 Latham, Jean Lee. *Carry On Mr. Bowditch* (7–9). 1955, Houghton $13.95 (0-395-06881-9). The story of the man who influenced American maritime history through his work on navigation. A Newbery Medal winner. [921]

DUNANT, HENRY

3887 Brown, Pam. *Henry Dunant* (5–9). Illus. 1989, Stevens LB $12.45 (1-55532-824-5). The story of this great humanist who helped found the Red Cross. (Rev: BL 8/89) [921]

FIDLER, NOAH

3888 Wolcott, Leonard T., and Carolyn E. Wolcott. *Wilderness Rider* (6–8). 1984, Abingdon $9.95 (0-687-45570-7). The story of a traveling minister in the late 1700s who preached from Pennsylvania to Ohio. [921]

FORTUNE, AMOS

3889 Yates, Elizabeth. *Amos Fortune, Free Man* (6–9). Illus. 1950, Dutton $12.95 (0-525-25570-2). Based on fact, this Newbery Medal winner tells of the courageous slave who not only bought his own freedom but also that of several others. [921]

FRANKLIN, BENJAMIN

3890 Cousins, Margaret. *Ben Franklin of Old Philadelphia* (6–8). 1963, Random paper $3.95 (0-394-84928-0). The story of this father of America who was a master in many fields. [921]

FRAUNCES, PHOEBE

3891 Griffin, Judith Berry. *Phoebe the Spy* (7–9). 1989, Scholastic paper $2.50 (0-590-42432-7). The story of the 13-year-old black girl who saved George Washington's life from an assassination attempt. [921]

GALLAUDET, T. H.

3892 Neimark, Anne E. *A Deaf Child Listened: Thomas Gallaudet, Pioneer in American Education* (7–10). 1983, Morrow $11.95 (0-688-01719-3). The biography of the famous educator who founded the first school for the deaf in the United States. [921]

GILBRETH FAMILY

3893 Gilbreth, Frank B., Jr., and Ernestine Carey. *Cheaper by the Dozen* (7–10). 1963, Harper $15.45 (0-690-18632-0); Bantam paper $3.50 (0-553-25018-3). Father is an efficiency expert so he has 12 children in this account of the Gilbreth family continued in *Belles on Their Toes* (1965). [921]

JAMES, JESSE

3894 Ernst, John. *Jesse James* (7–9). 1976, Prentice LB $9.95 (0-13-509696-2). An objective account of the life and death of the famous outlaw. [921]

KELLER, HELEN

3895 Peare, Catherine Owens. *The Helen Keller Story* (6–9). Illus. 1959, Harper $12.70 (0-690-37520-4). A biography of the handicapped girl and her devoted therapist, Anne Sullivan Macy. [921]

3896 Sloan, Carolyn. *Helen Keller* (5–9). Illus. 1985, David & Charles $9.95 (0-241-11295-8). A brief review of the life of this woman who conquered her physical handicaps. (Rev: SLJ 5/85) [921]

3897 Wepman, Dennis. *Helen Keller* (6–10). Illus. 1987, Chelsea House $17.95 (1-55546-662-1). The inspiring story of this handicapped woman and her struggle to help people like herself. (Rev: BL 8/87; SLJ 9/87) [921]

SACAGAWEA

3898 Brown, Marion Marsh. *Sacagawea: Indian Interpreter to Lewis and Clark* (6–9). Illus. 1988, Childrens LB $10.95 (0-516-03262-3). The story of the Indian girl who traveled with Lewis and Clark and acted as both guide and interpreter. (Rev: SLJ 3/89) [921]

SAMPSON, DEBORAH

3899 McGovern, Ann. *The Secret Soldier: The Story of Deborah Sampson* (7–9). Illus. 1987, Macmillan $12.95 (0-02-765780-9); paper $2.25 (0-590-32176-5). The exciting story of the girl who disguised herself as a man to fight in the Revolutionary War. A reissue. [921]

SHREVE, HENRY MILLER

3900 McCall, Edith. *Mississippi Steamboatman: The Story of Henry Miller Shreve* (5–8). Illus. 1986, Walker $11.95 (0-8027-6597-1). The story of Henry Shreve, whose freight and passenger boats helped open up the Midwest. (Rev: BR 5–6/86; SLJ 3/86; VOYA 4/86) [921]

SQUANTO

3901 Ziner, Feenie. *Squanto* (7–10). 1988, Linnet $17.50 (0-208-02218-X). The story of the Wampanoag Indian who was kidnapped and taken to England and later returned to America with Captain John Smith. (Rev: BR 11–12/88) [921]

STRAUSS, LEVI

3902 Van Steenwyk, Elizabeth. *Levi Strauss: The Blue Jeans Man* (5–9). 1988, Walker LB $14.85 (0-8027-6796-6). A biography of the Bavarian immigrant, Levi Strauss, who became the blue jeans king of the western world. (Rev: BL 6/15/88; SLJ 10/88; VOYA 8/88) [921]

WALD, LILLIAN

3903 Siegel, Beatrice. *Lillian Wald of Henry Street* (7–12). Illus. 1983, Macmillan $12.95 (0-02-782630-9). The story of the woman who though born into affluence became a social worker with the poor in New York's Lower East Side. [921]

WOMAN CHIEF

3904 Sobol, Rose. *Woman Chief* (7–9). n.d., Dell paper $1.25 (0-440-99657-0). The story of the great woman warrior and how she led the Crow nation. [921]

Science, Medicine, Industry, and Business

Collective

3905 Bryan, Jenny. *Health and Science* (5–9). Illus. 1988, Hampstead $11.90 (0-531-19501-5). A description of the careers in science and medicine of such important women as Clara Barton and Madame Curie. (Rev: BL 1/15/89; SLJ 2/89) [920]

3906 Fox, Mary Virginia. *Women Astronauts: Aboard the Shuttle* (5–9). Illus. 1988, Messner $10.79 (0-671-64840-3); paper $5.95 (0-671-64841-1). An overview of women astronauts with a history of their contributions and their biographies. (Rev: BL 6/1/88) [629.45]

3907 Richards, Norman. *Dreamers and Doers: Inventors Who Changed Our World* (5–9). 1984, Macmillan $12.95 (0-689-30914-7). The achievements of 4 men who dreamed their dreams into inventions—Robert H. Goddard, Charles Goodyear, Thomas Edison, and George Eastman. [920]

3908 Sproule, Anna. *New Ideas in Industry* (5–9). Illus. 1988, Watts $11.90 (0-531-19502-3). Biographies of 3 women including Mary Quant of England who made it in the world of business. (Rev: BL 1/15/89; SLJ 2/89) [920]

3909 Stott, Carole. *Into the Unknown* (6–9). Illus. 1989, Hampstead LB $11.90 (0-531-19513-9). This book contains profiles of 3 American women scientists—an astronomer, a pilot, and the astronaut/physicist, Sally Ride. (Rev: SLJ 9/89) [920]

Individual

ARCHIMEDES

3910 Ipsen, D. C. *Archimedes: Greatest Scientist of the Ancient World* (5–10). 1989, Enslow $12.95 (0-89490-161-3). A biography that incorporates all the fact and fiction surrounding this important mathematician and scientist. (Rev: BL 3/15/89; BR 9–10/89; SLJ 7/89) [921]

BANNEKER, BENJAMIN

3911 Conley, Kevin. *Benjamin Banneker* (5–9). Illus. 1989, Chelsea House $17.95 (1-55546-573-0). Banneker was a remarkable black man who in the eighteenth century was able to turn to mathematics and science where he excelled. (Rev: BL 1/1/90; SLJ 5/90; VOYA 4/90) [921]

BELL, ALEXANDER GRAHAM

3912 Shippen, Katherine B. *Mr. Bell Invents the Telephone* (6–8). 1963, Random LB $8.99 (0-394-90330-7). A simple account of the life of the inventor of the telephone. [921]

CARNEGIE, ANDREW

3913 Bowman, John. *Andrew Carnegie: Steel Tycoon* (6–9). Illus. 1989, Silver Burdett LB $11.98 (0-382-09582-0). The multimillionaire who was also known for his philanthropy is profiled in this account. (Rev: BL 1/1/90; BR 3–4/90; SLJ 3/90) [921]

CARSON, RACHEL

3914 Jezer, Marty. *Rachel Carson* (6–9). 1988, Chelsea House $16.95 (1-55546-646-X). The biography of the scientist who was one of the first to warn us of our environmental problems. (Rev: BL 9/1/88; BR 11–12/88; VOYA 2/89) [921]

CARVER, GEORGE WASHINGTON

3915 Adair, Gene. *George Washington Carver* (7–10). Illus. 1989, Chelsea House $16.95 (1-55546-577-3). The story of the first black scientist to gain national prominence and of his efforts to help poor black farmers. (Rev: BL 11/15/89; BR 11–12/89; SLJ 1/90; VOYA 2/90) [921]

CURIE, MARIE

3916 Birch, Beverley. *Marie Curie* (6–9). Illus. 1988, Stevens LB $12.45 (1-55532-818-0). A brief, quickly paced biography of Madame Curie and her scientific contributions. (Rev: SLJ 11/88) [921]

3917 Keller, Mollie. *Marie Curie* (7–10). Illus. 1982, Watts LB $12.90 (0-531-00476-0). The story of the Polish scientist who discovered radium. [921]

DARWIN, CHARLES

3918 Hyndley, Kate. *The Voyage of the Beagle* (5–9). Illus. 1989, Bookwright LB $11.90 (0-531-18272-X). The story of Darwin and his 5-year voyage that gave the stimulus to the formulation of the theory of evolution. (Rev: SLJ 2/90) [921]

DREW, CHARLES

3919 Mahone-Lonesome, Robyn. *Charles Drew* (6–10). Illus. 1990, Chelsea House $17.95 (1-55546-581-1). The biography of the black American scientist who did pioneer work in blood preservation and the establishment of blood banks. (Rev: BL 2/15/90; BR 5–6/90) [921]

EDISON, THOMAS ALVA

3920 Cousins, Margaret. *Story of Thomas Alva Edison* (6–8). 1981, Random paper $3.95 (0-394-84883-7). The story of this man associated with so many important nineteenth-century inventions. [921]

3921 Mintz, Penny. *Thomas Edison: Inventing the Future* (5–8). Illus. 1990, Fawcett paper $3.95 (0-449-90378-8). A biography of the inventor that gives a good, accurate picture of his personality as well as his accomplishments. (Rev: SLJ 6/90) [921]

EINSTEIN, ALBERT

3922 Dank, Milton. *Albert Einstein* (7–10). Illus. 1983, Watts LB $12.90 (0-531-04587-0). The life of the great physicist is told with particular attention to the theory of relativity. [921]

FARADAY, MICHAEL

3923 Gutnik, Martin J. *Michael Faraday: Creative Scientist* (6–8). Illus. 1986, Childrens $13.95 (0-516-03224-0). A biography of the English physicist with emphasis on his work with electricity and magnetism. (Rev: BL 1/15/87) [921]

FORD, HENRY

3924 Harris, Jacqueline L. *Henry Ford* (7–10). Illus. 1984, Watts LB $12.90 (0-531-04754-7). The American inventor and businessman who founded the Ford Motor Company is well portrayed in this readable biography. [921]

FREUD, SIGMUND

3925 Lager, Marilyn. *Sigmund Freud: Doctor of the Mind* (6–10). 1986, Enslow $13.95 (0-89490-117-6). A view of this scientist's life and of the ideas behind psychoanalysis. (Rev: BR 11–12/86) [921]

GETTY, J. PAUL

3926 Glassman, Bruce. *J. Paul Getty: Oil Billionaire* (6–9). Illus. 1989, Silver Burdett LB $11.98 (0-382-09584-7). The fascinating career of the oil tycoon is well presented as is an introduction to the personality of this man. (Rev: BL 1/1/90; BR 3–4/90; SLJ 3/90) [921]

HEARST, WILLIAM RANDOLPH

3927 Frazier, Nancy. *William Randolph Hearst: Press Baron* (6–9). Illus. 1989, Silver Burdett LB $11.98 (0-382-09585-5). The story of the man who built a newspaper empire in this well-researched account. (Rev: BL 1/1/90) [921]

HOPPER, GRACE

3928 Billings, Charlene W. *Grace Hopper: Navy Admiral and Computer Pioneer* (7–10). Illus. 1989, Enslow LB $15.95 (0-89490-194-X). The biography of the woman who became one of the first leaders in the world of computers. (Rev: BL 10/15/89; BR 1–2/90; SLJ 3/90; VOYA 2/90) [921]

IACOCCA, LEE

3929 Haddock, Patricia. *Standing Up for America: A Biography of Lee Iacocca* (6–9). Illus. 1987, Dillon $11.95 (0-87518-362-X). The story of the man who was fired by Henry Ford and went on to fame at Chrysler Corporation. (Rev: SLJ 9/87) [921]

LAVOISIER, ANTOINE

3930 Grey, Vivian. *The Chemist Who Lost His Head: The Story of Antoine Laurent Lavoisier* (6–8). 1982, Putnam paper $9.95 (0-698-20559-6). The story of the father of chemistry, Lavoisier, who was executed during the French Revolution. [921]

MEAD, MARGARET

3931 Ludel, Jacqueline. *Margaret Mead* (7–10). 1983, Watts LB $12.90 (0-531-04590-0). The life of the anthropologist with special coverage on her South Seas expeditions. [921]

3932 Rice, Edward. *Margaret Mead: A Portrait* (7–12). Illus. 1979, Harper LB $13.89 (0-06-025002-X). A fine objective biography written by a friend that tells about her personal life as well as her accomplishments in the field. [921]

3933 Ziesk, Edra. *Margaret Mead* (6–10). Illus. 1989, Chelsea House $17.95 (1-55546-667-2). Beginning with her work in Samoa and moving backward and forward this account emphasizes the anthropologist's professional career. (Rev: BL 2/15/90; SLJ 9/90; VOYA 8/90) [921]

MUIR, JOHN

3934 Tolan, Sally. *John Muir* (5–8). Illus. 1990, Stevens LB $12.45 (0-8368-0099-0). The story of the famous environmentalist and founder of the Sierra Club. (Rev: BL 6/15/90) [921]

NEWTON, SIR ISAAC

3935 Ipsen, D. C. *Isaac Newton: Reluctant Genius* (7–10). Illus. 1985, Enslow LB $14.95 (0-89490-090-0). A readable account of Newton's life and the significance of his work. (Rev: BR 9–10/85; SLJ 5/85) [921]

NIGHTINGALE, FLORENCE

3936 Brown, Pam. *Florence Nightingale* (5–9). Illus. 1989, Stevens LB $12.45 (1-55532-860-1). The story of the nursing pioneer who became known for her work during the Crimean War. (Rev: BL 8/89) [921]

OPPENHEIMER, J. ROBERT

3937 Driemen, J. E. *Atomic Dawn: A Biography of Robert Oppenheimer* (6–9). Illus. 1989, Dillon LB $11.95 (0-87518-397-2). The story of the development of the atomic bomb and the man most responsible for it. (Rev: SLJ 4/89) [921]

3938 Larsen, Rebecca. *Oppenheimer and the Atomic Bomb* (8–10). Illus. 1988, Watts $13.90 (0-531-10607-1). A straightforward biography of the Manhattan project chief who later faced accusations about Communist affiliations. (Rev: BL 2/15/89; BR 3–4/88; SLJ 1/89; VOYA 6/89) [921]

PASTEUR, LOUIS

3939 Birch, Beverley. *Louis Pasteur* (6–8). Illus. 1990, Stevens LB $12.95 (1-55532-839-3). This easily read account tells about both Pasteur's accomplishments and his personality. (Rev: BL 4/1/90) [921]

ROCKEFELLER, JOHN D.

3940 Coffey, Ellen Greenman. *John D. Rockefeller: Empire Builder* (6–9). Illus. 1989, Silver Burdett LB $11.98 (0-382-09583-9). The story of how this self-made man made his millions and how he gave away some of his wealth. (Rev: BL 1/1/90) [921]

SAGAN, CARL

3941 Cohen, Daniel. *Carl Sagan: Superstar Scientist* (6–9). Illus. 1987, Putnam $13.95 (0-399-21702-9). The story of one of America's most famous popularizers of astronomy and how he became interested in science. (Rev: BL 8/87; BR 11–12/87; SLJ 8/87; VOYA 10/87) [921]

SCOTT, PETER MARKHAM

3942 Courtney, Julia. *Sir Peter Scott* (5–9). Illus. 1989, Stevens LB $12.45 (1-55532-819-9). The life of the great British naturalist and founder of the World Wildlife Fund. (Rev: BL 8/89) [921]

STRAUSS, LEVI

3943 Henry, Sondra, and Emily Taitz. *Everyone Wears His Name: A Biography of Levi Strauss* (5–9). Illus. 1990, Dillon LB $11.95 (0-87518-375-1). The story of the German Jew and his family who made millions making riveted denim pants. (Rev: SLJ 7/90) [921]

VON BRAUN, WERNHER

3944 Lampton, Christopher. *Wernher Von Braun* (6–9). Illus. 1988, Watts $11.90 (0-531-10606-3). The story of the space expert who began his career in Nazi Germany and continued as a driving force behind our space program. (Rev: BL 11/1/88; BR 1–2/89; SLJ 2/89; VOYA 4/89) [921]

WILLIAMS, DANIEL HALE

3945 Patterson, Lillie. *Sure Hands, Strong Heart: The Life of Daniel Hale Williams* (7–9). Illus. 1981, Abingdon $8.95 (0-687-40700-1). The story of the black surgeon who brought many of his people into the practice of medicine. [921]

WRIGHT BROTHERS

3946 Reynolds, Quentin. *The Wright Brothers* (6–8). 1963, Random $8.99 (0-394-90310-2); paper $3.95 (0-394-84700-8). An easily read account of the 2 young men and their dream of flight. [921]

3947 Taylor, Richard L. *The First Flight: The Story of the Wright Brothers* (5–8). Illus. 1990, Watts LB $10.90 (0-531-10891-0). The story of the famous brothers and the drive and determination that finally led them to Kitty Hawk. (Rev: BL 4/15/90) [921]

Sports

Collective

3948 Aaseng, Nathan. *Baseball's Ace Relief Pitchers* (7–9). Illus. 1984, Lerner LB $7.95 (0-8225-1334-X). Eight famous relief pitchers are highlighted. Also use: *Baseball's Brilliant Managers* (1982). [920]

3949 Aaseng, Nathan. *Baseball's Hottest Hitters* (7–9). Illus. 1983, Lerner LB $7.95 (0-8225-1331-5). This book features the careers of 8 batters including Pete Rose and Keith Hernandez. Also use: *Baseball's Power Hitters* (1983). [920]

3950 Aaseng, Nathan. *Football's Crushing Blockers* (7–9). Illus. 1983, Lerner LB $7.95 (0-8225-1332-3). The crucial game of each of 8 of football's important blockers is recalled. [920]

3951 Aaseng, Nathan. *World-Class Marathoners* (7–9). Illus. 1982, Lerner LB $7.95 (0-8225-1325-0). Stories that highlight the careers of 7 championship runners are retold. [920]

3952 Hollander, Phyllis, and Zander Hollander, eds. *Dan Fouts, Ken Anderson, Joe Theismann and Other All-Time Great Quarterbacks* (7–9). Illus. 1983, Random paper $2.50 (0-394-85805-0). Ten football greats are highlighted in this book of biographies. [920]

3953 Hollander, Phyllis, and Zander Hollander, eds. *Winners under 21* (7–10). Illus. 1982, Random paper $1.95 (0-394-85015-7). There are a dozen profiles of athletes who achieved fame at an early age. [920]

3954 Olney, Ross R. *Modern Speed Record Superstars* (7–9). Illus. 1982, Putnam LB $8.95 (0-396-08072-3). The life stories of 6 daredevils who have set speed records. [920]

3955 Olney, Ross R. *Super Champions of Auto Racing* (7–9). Illus. 1984, Clarion LB $11.95 (0-89919-259-9); paper $4.95 (0-89919-289-0). Biographies of 6 contemporary racing champions are given. [920]

3956 Sullivan, George. *Great Lives: Sports* (7–10). Illus. 1988, Macmillan LB $22.95 (0-684-18510-5). An alphabetically arranged series of profiles of people who have greatly contributed to a variety of sports. (Rev: SLJ 1/89) [920]

Baseball

CARLTON, STEVE

3957 Aaseng, Nathan. *Steve Carlton: Baseball's Silent Strongman* (7–10). Illus. 1984, Lerner LB $8.95 (0-8225-0491-X). The life and career of the Philadelphia Phillies pitcher. [921]

PAIGE, SATCHEL

3958 Humphrey, Kathryn Long. *Satchel Paige* (6–9). Illus. 1988, Watts $11.90 (0-531-10513-X). The story of the great black pitcher who played for years in the Negro American League and later with the Cleveland Indians. (Rev: BL 4/15/88; BR 9–10/88; VOYA 8/88) [921]

ROBINSON, JACKIE

3959 Frommer, Harvey. *Jackie Robinson* (6–12). Illus. 1984, Watts $12.90 (0-531-04858-6). This biography describes not only the career but also the personality and character of this baseball legend. (Rev: BL 1/1/85) [921]

3960 Scott, Richard. *Jackie Robinson* (5–10). Illus. 1987, Chelsea House $12.95 (1-55546-609-5). A well-researched biography giving good material on Robinson's life outside of baseball. (Rev: BL 9/1/87; SLJ 9/87) [921]

RUTH, BABE

3961 Berke, Art. *Babe Ruth* (6–8). Illus. 1988, Watts $12.90 (0-531-10472-9). The life story of the man many regard as the greatest baseball player ever. (Rev: BL 2/15/89; BR 3–4/89; SLJ 2/89; VOYA 4/89) [921]

SCHMIDT, MIKE

3962 Hochman, Stan. *Mike Schmidt: Baseball's King of Swing* (6–9). Illus. 1983, Random paper $2.50 (0-394-85806-9). A portrait that takes Schmidt from Little League to the 1982 season. [921]

Basketball

BIRD, LARRY

3963 Corn, Frederick Lynn. *Basketball's Magnificent Bird* (7–9). 1982, Random paper $1.95 (0-394-85019-4). The life and career through the early 1980s are given about this amazing basketball star. [921]

JORDAN, MICHAEL

3964 Martin, Gene L. *Michael Jordan: Gentleman Superstar* (5–9). Illus. 1987, Tudor $11.95 (0-936389-02-8); paper $5.95 (0-936389-03-6). The rise of the basketball superstar from his beginning to the NBA. (Rev: BL 8/87) [921]

Boxing

ALI, MUHAMMAD

3965 Lipsyte, Robert. *Free to Be Muhammad Ali* (7–9). 1978, Harper LB $12.89 (0-06-023902-6). A biography that tells of the youth and career of Muhammad Ali through the mid-1970s. [921]

3966 Rummel, Jack. *Muhammad Ali* (6–10). Illus. 1988, Chelsea House $16.95 (1-55546-569-2). A biography that emphasizes the boxer's professional career rather than his personal life. (Rev: BL 6/15/88) [921]

HAWKINS, DWIGHT

3967 Hawkins, Dwight, and Morrie Greenberg. *Survival in the Square* (7–10). Illus. 1989, Brooke-Richards paper $5.95 (0-9622652-0-9). A story of a black American boy who overcame a physical handicap and became a boxing champion. (Rev: BL 11/15/89; VOYA 12/89) [921]

LEONARD, SUGAR RAY

3968 Haskins, James. *Sugar Ray Leonard* (7–9). Illus. 1982, Lothrop $12.95 (0-688-01436-4). A biography of the boxer from his beginning fights throughout the early 1980s. [921]

LOUIS, JOE

3969 Jakoubek, Robert E. *Joe Louis* (6–9). Illus. 1990, Chelsea House $17.95 (1-55546-599-4). Both the professional career of Joe Louis and his often unfortunate personal life are handled in this account. (Rev: BL 5/1/90) [921]

Football

BRYANT, BEAR

3970 Lee, S. C. *Young Bear: The Legend of Bear Bryant's Boyhood* (7–9). 1983, Strode paper $6.95 (0-87397-250-3). The story of the famous football coach of the University of Alabama. [921]

DICKERSON, ERIC

3971 Dickerson, Eric, and Steve Delsohn. *On the Run* (6–9). Illus. 1986, Contemporary paper $7.95 (0-8092-4973-1). The life of this football hero including information on his early training and successes. (Rev: BL 12/1/86) [921]

JACKSON, BO

3972 Delaney, John. *Bo Jackson: A Star for All Seasons* (6–9). Illus. 1988, Walker LB $14.85 (0-8027-6819-9). The story of the star athlete who won the Heisman Trophy and was equally proficient in baseball and football. (Rev: BR 3–4/89; VOYA 2/89) [921]

MARINO, DAN

3973 Marino, Dan, and Steve Delsohn. *Marino!* (6–9). Illus. 1986, Contemporary $5.95 (0-8092-4980-4). This autobiography gives personal insights on Marino and his thoughts about the game. (Rev: BL 12/1/86) [921]

PAYTON, WALTER

3974 Sufrin, Mark. *Payton* (7–9). Illus. 1988, Macmillan $12.95 (0-684-18940-2). An admiring biography of the retired star of the Chicago Bears. (Rev: BL 2/1/89; BR 5–6/89; SLJ 1/89; VOYA 4/89) [921]

WALKER, HERSCHEL

3975 Prugh, Jeff. *Herschel Walker: From the Georgia Backwoods and the Heisman Trophy to the Pros* (7–9). 1983, Random paper $2.50 (0-394-86163-9). This biography of this amazingly talented football pro ends in the early 1980s. [921]

Gymnastics and Track and Field

OWENS, JESSE

3976 Gentry, Tony. *Jesse Owens: Champion Athlete* (6–9). Illus. 1990, Chelsea House LB $17.95 (1-55546-603-6). The story of the black American track star who upset Hitler's master race theory at the Olympics. (Rev: SLJ 7/90; VOYA 8/90) [921]

RUDOLPH, WILMA

3977 Biracree, Tom. *Wilma Rudolph* (7–12). Illus. 1987, Chelsea House $16.95 (1-55546-675-3). The inspiring story of the black athlete who conquered polio and won 3 Olympic gold medals in track in a single year. (Rev: BL 8/88) [921]

Tennis

GIBSON, ALTHEA

3978 Biracree, Tom. *Althea Gibson* (7–12). Illus. 1989, Chelsea House $17.95 (1-55546-654-0). The rags-to-riches story of the black athlete who was once the best woman tennis player in the world. (Rev: BL 2/15/90; BR 3–4/90; SLJ 2/90; VOYA 2/90) [921]

LLOYD, CHRIS EVERT

3979 Hahn, James, and Lynn Hahn. *Chris! The Sports Career of Chris Evert Lloyd* (7–9). 1981, Crestwood LB $8.95 (0-89686-131-7). The story of the early career of this headliner in tennis. [921]

Miscellaneous Sports

HAMILL, DOROTHY

3980 Hamill, Dorothy, and Elva Clairmont. *Dorothy Hamill On and Off the Ice* (7–10). Illus. 1983, Knopf LB $10.99 (0-394-95610-9). The world figure skating champion tells about her rise to the top and her life there. [921]

ZAHARIAS, BABE DIDRIKSON

3981 Knudson, R. R. *Babe Didrikson: Athlete of the Century* (5–8). 1985, Viking $10.95 (0-670-80550-5); Penguin paper $3.50 (0-14-032095-4). The life story of the amazing sportswoman who excelled in many sports, including track and golf. (Rev: SLJ 5/85; VOYA 8/85) [921]

3982 Lynn, Elizabeth A. *Babe Didrikson Zaharias* (6–10). Illus. 1988, Chelsea House $16.95 (1-55546-684-2). The story of the all-around athlete best known for her accomplishments in golf. (Rev: BL 12/1/88; BR 5–6/89) [921]

World Figures

Collective

3983 Dunn, Wendy, and Janet Morey. *Who's News! World Personalities* (6–9). Illus. 1985, Messner LB $9.79 (0-671-54436-5). Brief biographies of 49 personalities from various areas who are currently in the news. (Rev: SLJ 2/86) [920]

3984 Fradin, Dennis B. *Remarkable Children: Twenty Who Made History* (5–9). 1987, Little LB $14.95 (0-316-29126-9). A collection of 20 biographies of children who accomplished a great deal. Subjects include Mozart, Picasso, Judy Garland, and the Bedouin goatherd who discovered the Dead Sea Scrolls. (Rev: BL 12/1/87; SLJ 12/87) [920]

3985 Levite, Christine, and Julie Moline. *Princesses* (6–9). Illus. 1989, Watts LB $12.90 (0-531-10772-8). A collection of biographies of 9 living princesses including Diana, Fergie, and Caroline of Monaco. (Rev: BL 9/15/89; BR 1–2/90; SLJ 10/89; VOYA 2/90) [920]

3986 Shiels, Barbara. *Winners: Women and the Nobel Prize* (6–10). Illus. 1985, Dillon $14.95 (0-87518-293-3). A collective biography of 8 women who won the Nobel Prize for literature, science, or promoting peace. (Rev: BL 8/85; BR 11–12/85; SLJ 9/85) [920]

FERDINAND V, KING OF SPAIN

3987 Stevens, Paul. *Ferdinand and Isabella* (6–10). Illus. 1987, Chelsea House $16.95 (0-87754-523-5). The story of the 2 Spanish monarchs that brought Spain into the modern world. (Rev: BL 3/1/88) [921]

Africa

CLEOPATRA

3988 Hoobler, Dorothy, and Thomas Hoobler. *Cleopatra* (6–10). Illus. 1986, Chelsea House $17.95 (0-87754-589-8). Through recounting the story of this amazing queen, the author tells about life in ancient Egypt. (Rev: BL 2/1/87; SLJ 2/87) [921]

MANDELA, NELSON AND WINNIE

3989 Hoobler, Dorothy, and Thomas Hoobler. *Nelson and Winnie Mandela* (6–12). Illus. 1987, Watts $12.90 (0-531-10332-3). Not only a biography of these civil rights leaders but also a history of the movement in South Africa. This account ends before Mr. Mandela's release. (Rev: BL 4/15/87; BR 11–12/87; SLJ 5/87; VOYA 8–9/87) [921]

3990 Vail, John. *Nelson and Winnie Mandela* (7–12). Illus. 1988, Chelsea House $16.95 (1-55546-841-1). A biography of this courageous couple as well as a history of apartheid in South Africa. (Rev: BL 10/15/88; BR 5–6/89; SLJ 3/89; VOYA 2/89) [921]

MANDELA, NELSON

3991 Hargrove, Jim. *Nelson Mandela: South Africa's Silent Voice of Protest* (7–9). Illus. 1989, Childrens LB $10.95 (0-516-03266-6). A straightforward account of the life and political activities of Mandela that was published just before his release from prison. (Rev: SLJ 9/89) [921]

MANDELA, WINNIE

3992 Haskins, James. *Winnie Mandela: Life of Struggle* (7–10). Illus. 1988, Putnam $14.95 (0-399-21515-8). A portrait of the South African civil rights leader who has tried to follow the path her then-imprisoned husband, the revered anti-apartheid leader, would have wanted. (Rev: BL 5/1/88; SLJ 6–7/88; VOYA 8/88) [921]

NASSER, GAMAL ABDEL

3993 DeChancie, John. *Gamal Abdel Nasser* (6–10). Illus. 1987, Chelsea House $17.95 (0-87754-542-1). The story of the Egyptian leader who helped lead his country to independence after World War II. (Rev: BL 12/15/87; SLJ 2/88) [921]

NKRUMAH, KWAME

3994 Kellner, Douglas. *Kwame Nkrumah* (6–10). Illus. 1987, Chelsea House $17.95 (0-87754-546-4). The biography of the African leader who oversaw the independence of his homeland, Ghana. (Rev: BL 8/87; SLJ 9/87) [921]

QADDAFI, MUAMMAR

3995 Gottfried, Ted. *Muammar El-Qaddafi* (7–10). Illus. 1987, Chelsea House $17.95 (0-87754-598-7). This is not only the life story of this controversial leader but also a history of U.S. Libian relations through the mid-1980s. (Rev: BL 6/15/87) [921]

3996 Lawson, Don. *Libya and Qaddafi* (7–10). Illus. 1987, Watts $12.90 (0-531-10329-3). A biography of this unusual Libian leader with emphasis on his foreign relations and policies. (Rev: BL 6/15/87; BR 9–10/87; SLJ 6–7/87; VOYA 8–9/87) [921]

SADAT, ANWAR

3997 Sullivan, George. *Sadat: The Man Who Changed Mid-East History* (7–9). Illus. 1981, Walker LB $9.89 (0-8027-6435-5). A biography of the Egyptian leader that ends immediately before his death. [921]

SCHWEITZER, ALBERT

3998 Bentley, James. *Albert Schweitzer* (5–9). Illus. 1989, Stevens LB $12.45 (1-55532-823-7). A biography of the doctor/musician who became a missionary and healer in Africa. (Rev: BL 8/89) [921]

SELASSIE, HAILE

3999 Negash, Askale. *Haile Selassie* (7–10). Illus. 1989, Chelsea House $16.95 (1-55546-850-0). Illustrated with many photographs, this is the story of the former leader of Ethiopia. (Rev: BL 10/1/89; BR 11–12/89; SLJ 9/89) [921]

TUTU, DESMOND

4000 Bentley, Judith. *Archbishop Tutu of South Africa* (6–9). Illus. 1988, Enslow $13.95 (0-89490-180-X). The biography of the churchman who has become a symbol of the fight against oppression in South Africa. (Rev: BL 2/1/89; BR 1–2/89; SLJ 11/88) [921]

4001 Wepman, Dennis. *Desmond Tutu* (7–10). Illus. 1989, Watts LB $12.90 (0-531-10780-9). The story of the Nobel Prize-winning foe of oppression told in simple text and many photographs. (Rev: BL 9/1/89; BR 5–6/90; SLJ 2/90; VOYA 2/90) [921]

4002 Winner, David. *Desmond Tutu* (5–9). Illus. 1989, Stevens LB $12.45 (1-55532-822-9). A nicely illustrated biography of the South African churchman and leader against apartheid. (Rev: BL 8/89) [921]

Asia and Middle East

AARONSOHN, SARAH

4003 Cowen, Ida, and Irene Gunther. *A Spy for Freedom: The Story of Sarah Aaronsohn* (7–9). 1984, Dutton $14.95 (0-525-67150-1). The exciting life story of the Jewish woman who led a secret spy organization during World War I to free Jews from the Turks. [921]

AQUINO, CORAZON

4004 Nadel, Laurie. *Corazon Aquino: Journey to Power* (6–8). Illus. 1987, Messner $9.79 (0-671-63950-1). A profile of the Philippine leader who brought democracy to her country. (Rev: BL 9/1/87; SLJ 10/87; VOYA 2/88) [921]

ARAFAT, YASIR

4005 Stefoff, Rebecca. *Yasir Arafat* (7–10). Illus. 1988, Chelsea House $16.95 (1-55546-826-8). An impartial account of the life of the leader of the PLO. (Rev: BL 11/1/88; BR 11–12/88; SLJ 12/88) [921]

ASSAD, HAFEZ

4006 Gordon, Matthew S. *Hafez Al-Assad* (7–10). Illus. 1989, Chelsea House $16.95 (1-55546-827-6). A portrait of the controversial Syrian president and his relations with his neighboring countries. (Rev: BL 11/15/89; BR 1–2/90; VOYA 2/90) [921]

BEGIN, MENACHEM

4007 Amdur, Richard. *Menachem Begin* (6–10). Illus. 1987, Chelsea House $17.95 (0-87754-561-8). A re-creation of the colorful life of this soldier, adventurer, and Israeli politician. (Rev: BL 11/15/87) [921]

BEN-GURION, DAVID

4008 Silverstein, Herma. *David Ben-Gurion* (6–9). Illus. 1988, Watts $11.90 (0-531-10509-1). The story of Israel's first prime minister and the early days of his country. (Rev: BL 3/1/88; BR 9–10/88; SLJ 5/88; VOYA 8/88) [921]

4009 Vail, John. *David Ben-Gurion* (6–10). Illus. 1987, Chelsea House $17.95 (0-87754-509-X). A portrait of the Polish Jew who helped transform Palestine into Israel. (Rev: BL 10/15/87; BR 9–10/88; SLJ 2/88) [921]

BEN-YEHUDA, ELIEZER

4010 Drucker, Malka. *Eliezer Ben-Yehuda: The Father of Modern Hebrew* (6–9). Illus. 1987, Dutton $13.95 (0-525-67184-6). The story of the Russian Jew who later lived in then-Palestine and his efforts to make Hebrew a modern language. (Rev: BL 1/15/87; SLJ 3/87; VOYA 4/88) [921]

CHIANG KAI-SHEK

4011 Dolan, Sean. *Chiang Kai-Shek* (7–9). Illus. 1988, Chelsea House LB $16.95 (0-87754-517-0). More than just a biography, this is also a history of China in the twentieth century. (Rev: SLJ 11/88; VOYA 2/89) [921]

CHOU EN-LAI

4012 Hoobler, Dorothy, and Thomas Hoobler. *Zhou Enlai* (7–12). Illus. 1986, Chelsea House $17.95 (0-87754-516-2). A biography of the Chinese leader told in an interesting text with many illustrations. (Rev: SLJ 11/86) [921]

DENG XIAOPING

4013 Lubetkin, Wendy. *Deng Xiaoping* (7–10). Illus. 1988, Chelsea House $16.95 (1-55546-830-6). The amazing career of China's Communist leader is interestingly told. (Rev: BL 6/15/88; BR 5–6/88; SLJ 8/88) [921]

FAISAL, KING OF SAUDI ARABIA

4014 Stefoff, Rebecca. *Faisal* (7–10). Illus. 1989, Chelsea House $16.95 (1-55546-833-0). A biography of the king of Saudi Arabia who ruled from 1964 to 1975 and helped to modernize his country. (Rev: BL 11/15/89; BR 1–2/90; SLJ 2/90) [921]

GANDHI, INDIRA

4015 Currimbhoy, Nayana. *Indira Gandhi* (7–12). Illus. 1985, Watts $12.90 (0-531-10064-2). This biography of India's late prime minister outlines, in a candid style, both her accomplishments and failures. (Rev: BL 12/15/85; BR 5–6/86; SLJ 1/86) [921]

4016 Haskins, James. *India under Indira and Rajiv Gandhi* (6–9). Illus. 1989, Enslow LB $15.95 (0-89490-146-X). A history of India under the leadership of mother and then son with emphasis on Indira Gandhi. (Rev: BL 7/89; SLJ 8/89) [921]

GANDHI, MAHATMA

4017 Cheney, Glenn Alan. *Mohandas Gandhi* (7–10). Illus. 1983, Watts LB $12.90 (0-531-04600-1). Nonviolent opposition to British rule in India was spearheaded by this inspiring leader. [921]

4018 Faber, Doris, and Harold Faber. *Mahatma Gandhi* (6–9). Illus. 1986, Messner $9.79 (0-671-60176-8). A fine introduction to both the life and philosophical beliefs of this Indian leader. (Rev: BL 12/15/86) [921]

GEMAYEL FAMILY

4019 Gordon, Matthew S. *The Gemayels* (6–9). Illus. 1988, Chelsea House $16.95 (1-55546-834-9). An account of the family—father and 2 sons—who have played an important role in the history of Lebanon. (Rev: BL 8/88; BR 9–10/88; VOYA 2/89) [921]

GENGHIS KHAN

4020 Humphrey, Judy. *Genghis Khan* (6–10). Illus. 1987, Chelsea House $17.95 (0-87754-527-8). The story of the fierce warrior who shaped the Mongolian empire in the twelfth century. (Rev: BL 11/15/87; SLJ 12/87) [921]

HERZL, THEODOR

4021 Finkelstein, Norman H. *Theodor Herzl* (8–12). Illus. 1987, Watts $11.90 (0-531-10421-4). The story of the Jewish writer who devoted his life to the founding of the state of Israel. (Rev: BL 3/1/88; BR 1–2/88; SLJ 2/88; VOYA 6/88) [921]

4022 Gurko, Miriam. *Theodor Herzl: The Road to Israel* (5–8). Illus. 1988, Jewish Publication Soc. $12.95 (0-8276-0312-6). The story of the idealist whose dream was to found an independent homeland for his people, the Jews. (Rev: BL 3/15/89) [921]

HIROHITO, EMPEROR OF JAPAN

4023 Severns, Karen. *Hirohito* (6–10). Illus. 1988, Chelsea House $16.95 (1-55546-837-3). Beginning with Japan's defeat in World War II, this biography traces the life of its emperor. (Rev: BL 6/1/88) [921]

HO CHI MINH

4024 Lloyd, Dana O. *Ho Chi Minh* (6–10). Illus. 1986, Chelsea House $17.95 (0-87754-571-5). The controversial North Vietnamese leader is presented in this balanced account that stresses his activities to oust foreigners from his country. (Rev: BL 2/1/87) [921]

HUSSEIN, KING OF JORDAN

4025 Hayes, John P., and Gregory Matusky. *King Hussein* (7–10). Illus. 1987, Chelsea House LB $17.95 (0-87754-533-2). A straightforward biography of the King of Jordan that ends with 1987. (Rev: SLJ 5/87) [921]

4026 Matusky, Gregory, and John P. Hayes. *King Hussein* (6–10). Illus. 1987, Chelsea House $17.95 (0-87754-533-2). This account includes both a biography of the king and a history of Jordan that encapsulates the last 100 years. (Rev: BL 7/87) [921]

KHOMEINI, AYATOLLAH

4027 Gordon, Matthew S. *Ayatollah Khomeini* (7–10). Illus. 1987, Chelsea House $17.95 (0-87754-559-6). A biography of this controversial Iranian leader plus much background information on Islam and Iran. (Rev: BL 4/15/87; SLJ 5/87) [921]

MACCABEUS, JUDAS

4028 Fortier, E. H. *Judas Maccabeus* (7–10). Illus. 1988, Chelsea House $16.95 (0-87754-539-

1). The story of the ancient Jewish leader and his revolt against tyranny. (Rev: BL 9/15/88) [921]

MAO TSE-TUNG

4029 Garza, Hedda. *Mao Zedong* (7–10). Illus. 1987, Chelsea House $16.95 (0-87754-564-2). A portrait of the man most responsible for shaping twentieth-century China. (Rev: BL 3/15/88) [921]

4030 Poole, Frederick King. *Mao Zedong* (7–10). Illus. 1982, Watts LB $12.90 (0-531-04481-5). The story of the Chinese leader and of the 1967 Cultural Revolution. [921]

MEIR, GOLDA

4031 Keller, Mollie. *Golda Meir* (7–10). Illus. 1983, Watts LB $12.90 (0-531-04591-9). The biography of the Zionist who at age 70 became prime minister of Israel. [921]

NEHRU, JAWAHARLAL

4032 Finck, Lila, and John P. Hayes. *Jawaharlal Nehru* (6–10). 1987, Chelsea House $17.95 (0-87754-543-X). The biography of India's first prime minister after separation from Britain in 1947. (Rev: BL 6/1/87; SLJ 8/87) [921]

PAHLAVI, MOHAMMED REZA

4033 Cockcroft, James D. *Mohammed Reza Pahlavi, Shah of Iran* (7–10). Illus. 1989, Chelsea House LB $17.95 (1-55546-847-0). An objective account of the dictator of Iran who modernized his country but at a terrible price. (Rev: BR 5–6/89; SLJ 1/89; VOYA 4/89) [921]

PAUL, SAINT

4034 Arbuckle, Gwendolyne. *Paul: Adventurer for Christ* (7–9). 1984, Abingdon paper $5.50 (0-687-30487-3). This account covers the life of St. Paul from childhood through his conversion and many journeys preaching Christianity. [921]

SUKARNO

4035 Beilenson, John. *Sukarno* (8–12). Illus. 1990, Chelsea House LB $17.95 (1-55546-853-5). The story of Indonesia's fight for freedom and the man who lead them. (Rev: SLJ 6/90) [921]

SUN YAT-SEN

4036 Barlow, Jeffrey. *Sun Yat-Sen* (6–10). Illus. 1987, Chelsea House $17.95 (0-82254-441-7). The story of the Chinese leader who helped overthrow the Manchu dynasty. (Rev: BL 9/1/87; SLJ 10/87) [921]

SZOLD, HENRIETTA

4037 Krantz, Hazel. *Daughter of My People: Henrietta Szold and Hadassah* (7–10). Illus. 1987, Lodestar $14.95 (0-525-67236-2). The inspiring story of the Jewish woman who founded the Hadassah Hospital in Palestine and helped resettle refugee children in camps in Palestine during World War II. (Rev: BL 11/1/87; SLJ 1/88; VOYA 6/88) [921]

TAMERLANE

4038 Wepman, Dennis. *Tamerlane* (6–10). Illus. 1987, Chelsea House $17.95 (0-87754-442-5). The story of the barbaric Mongol chieftain who lived in the fourteenth century and was responsible for the death of millions. (Rev: BL 7/87; SLJ 8/87) [921]

TERESA, MOTHER

4039 Clucas, Joan Graff. *Mother Teresa* (8–10). Illus. 1988, Chelsea House $16.95 (1-55546-855-1). The moving story of the life and accomplishments of this amazing woman. (Rev: BL 6/15/88) [921]

WEIZMANN, CHAIM

4040 Amdur, Richard. *Chaim Weizmann* (7–10). Illus. 1988, Chelsea House $16.95 (0-87754-446-8). The life story of one of the contemporary founders of Zionism. (Rev: BL 9/15/88; BR 11–12/88) [921]

XERXES I, KING OF PERSIA

4041 Llywelyn, Morgan. *Xerxes* (6–10). Illus. 1987, Chelsea House $17.95 (0-87754-447-6). The life of the great Persian leader who was humbled by the naval defeat by the Greeks at Salamis. (Rev: BL 11/15/87; SLJ 12/87) [921]

Australia and the Pacific Islands

AQUINO, CORAZON

4042 Chua-Eoan, Howard. *Corazon Aquino* (6–10). Illus. 1987, Chelsea House $16.95 (1-55546-825-X). A portrait of the Philippine leader with coverage through early 1987. (Rev: BL 4/15/88) [921]

4043 Haskins, James. *Corazon Aquino: Leader of the Philippines* (6–10). Illus. 1988, Enslow $13.95 (0-89490-152-4). Good background information given about this leader and the Philippines. (Rev: BL 4/15/88; BR 9–10/88; SLJ 3/88) [921]

4044 Siegel, Beatrice. *Cory: Corazon Aquino and the Philippines* (6–8). Illus. 1988, Dutton $15.95 (0-525-67235-4). A story of the Philippine leader and the mantle of responsibility to her people she inherited from her husband. (Rev: BL 8/88; BR 11–12/88; VOYA 12/88) [921]

MARCOS, FERDINAND

4045 Slack, Gordy. *Ferdinand Marcos* (6–10). Illus. 1988, Chelsea House $16.95 (1-55546-842-X). A truthful biography that reveals the scandal and corruption of this dictator's reign. (Rev: BL 9/1/88; BR 11–12/88; VOYA 10/88) [921]

Europe

ALEXANDER THE GREAT

4046 Lasker, Joe. *The Great Alexander the Great* (6–9). Illus. 1983, Viking LB $13.95 (0-670-34841-4). A very readable biography that highlights the most important events in Alexander the Great's short life. [921]

ANASTASIA, NIKOLAEVNA

4047 McGuire, Leslie. *Anastasia, Czarina or Fake?* (7–10). Illus. 1990, Greenhaven LB $12.95 (0-89908-074-X). This account concentrates on the question of whether Anastasia was or was not a real member of the Russian royal family who survived the massacre of her relatives. (Rev: BL 3/1/90; SLJ 5/90) [921]

ANTONY, MARC

4048 Kittredge, Mary. *Marc Antony* (7–12). Illus. 1988, Chelsea House LB $16.95 (0-87754-505-7). The story of the noble Roman whose love for Cleopatra spelled his downfall. (Rev: BL 1/15/88; BR 11–12/88; SLJ 3/88) [921]

ATATÜRK, KEMAL

4049 Tachau, Frank. *Kemal Atatürk* (6–10). Illus. 1987, Chelsea House $16.95 (0-87754-507-3). A biography of the man who transformed Turkey and brought it into the twentieth century. (Rev: BL 1/1/88; SLJ 3/88) [921]

BAECK, LEO

4050 Neimark, Anne E. *One Man's Valor: Leo Baeck and the Holocaust* (5–9). Illus. 1986, Dutton $14.95 (0-525-67175-7). The story of the gallant German Jewish rabbi who, during the Holocaust, sacrificed himself for his people. (Rev: BL 8/86; SLJ 10/86; VOYA 12/86) [921]

BISMARCK, OTTO VON

4051 Rose, Jonathan E. *Otto von Bismarck* (6–10). Illus. 1987, Chelsea House $17.95 (0-87754-510-3). The life of the Prussian leader who helped in the unification of Germany during the nineteenth century. (Rev: BL 9/1/87; BR 5–6/88; SLJ 1/88) [921]

BORGIA, CESARE

4052 Haney, John. *Cesare Borgia* (6–10). Illus. 1987, Chelsea House $17.95 (0-87754-595-2). While supplying material on the Renaissance, Haney tells the story of this evil Italian leader and his unprincipled behavior. (Rev: BL 8/87) [921]

BRAILLE, LOUIS

4053 Birch, Beverley. *Louis Braille* (6–8). Illus. 1990, Stevens LB $12.95 (0-8368-0097-4). A brief life story of the man who changed the way deaf people could communicate. (Rev: BL 4/1/90; SLJ 8/90) [921]

CAESAR, AUGUSTUS

4054 Walworth, Nancy Zinsser. *Augustus Caesar* (6–10). Illus. 1988, Chelsea House $16.95 (1-55546-804-7). The story of Julius Caesar's adopted son who later avenged his death and led the Empire through a peaceful era. (Rev: BL 12/1/88; BR 5–6/89; SLJ 2/89; VOYA 2/89) [921]

CAESAR, JULIUS

4055 Bruns, Roger. *Julius Caesar* (6–10). Illus. 1987, Chelsea House $17.95 (0-87754-514-6). Us-

ing many sources, the author creates an accurate picture of the rise and fall of this Roman leader. (Rev: BL 11/15/87; BR 9-10/88; SLJ 12/87; VOYA 10/88) [921]

CALVIN, JOHN

4056 Stepanek, Sally. *John Calvin* (6–10). Illus. 1986, Chelsea House $17.95 (0-87754-515-4). A well-researched biography of the sixteenth-century leader of the Protestant Reformation. (Rev: BL 3/1/87; SLJ 3/87) [921]

CHARLEMAGNE

4057 Westwood, Jennifer. *Stories of Charlemagne* (7–9). 1976, Phillips $14.95 (0-87599-213-7). A biography of the famous emperor of the Holy Roman Empire who was one of the most influential men of the Middle Ages. [921]

CHURCHILL, WINSTON

4058 Keller, Mollie. *Winston Churchill* (7–10). Illus. 1984, Watts $12.90 (0-531-04752-0). The biography of the British statesman and adventurer who achieved his finest hour as leader of his people during World War II. [921]

CLEMENCEAU, GEORGES

4059 Gottfried, Ted. *Georges Clemenceau* (6–10). Illus. 1987, Chelsea House $17.95 (0-87754-518-9). A biography of the French political leader who served his country with distinction during World War I. (Rev: BL 11/15/87; SLJ 3/88) [921]

CONSTANTINE

4060 Walworth, Nancy Zinsser. *Constantine* (7–10). Illus. Chelsea House $17.95 (1-55546-805-5). A biography of the early Holy Roman Emperor and of the founding of Constantinople. (Rev: BR 1–2/90) [921]

DE VALERA, EAMON

4061 MacNamara, Desmond. *Eamon De Valera* (7–12). Illus. 1988, Chelsea House LB $16.95 (0-87754-520-0). The story of the Irish political leader who led his country after the struggle for separation from Britain. (Rev: BR 11–12/88; VOYA 4/89) [921]

DIANA, PRINCESS OF WALES

4062 Fox, Mary Virginia. *Princess Diana* (6–8). Illus. 1986, Enslow $15.95 (0-89490-129-X). This biography not only tells about Princess Diana's public life but also reveals something about her real personality. (Rev: BL 9/1/86; BR 11–12/86; SLJ 1/87; VOYA 12/86) [921]

4063 Nesnick, Victoria Gilvary. *Princess Diana: A Book of Questions and Answers* (6–8). Illus. 1988, Evans $13.95 (0-87131-558-0). A profile of the Princess of Wales organized by the questions most frequently asked about her. (Rev: BL 12/15/88) [921]

DISRAELI, BENJAMIN

4064 McGuirk, Carol. *Benjamin Disraeli* (6–10). Illus. 1987, Chelsea House $17.95 (0-87754-565-0). The story of this influential prime minister who led Britain during much of the Victorian period. (Rev: BL 8/87; SLJ 11/87) [921]

ELEANOR OF AQUITAINE, QUEEN

4065 Brooks, Polly Schoyer. *Queen Eleanor* (7–10). Illus. 1983, Harper LB $12.89 (0-397-31995-9). The story of Eleanor of Aquitaine who ruled France and, later as Henry II's wife, also England. [921]

4066 Kaplan, Zoe Coralnik. *Eleanor of Aquitaine* (6–10). Illus. 1986, Chelsea House $17.95 (0-87754-552-7). The biography of one of the most amazing women in history, who became queen of both France and England. (Rev: BL 2/1/87) [921]

ELIZABETH I, QUEEN OF ENGLAND

4067 Zamoyska, Betka. *Queen Elizabeth I* (7–10). Illus. 1981, McGraw $7.95 (0-07-07272-X). The life of Elizabeth the Great including the Armada and her relationship with Mary, Queen of Scots. [921]

FRANCO, FRANCISCO

4068 Garza, Hedda. *Francisco Franco* (6–10). Illus. 1987, Chelsea House $17.95 (0-87754-524-3). The story of the rise and career of the Spanish fascist dictator. (Rev: BL 8/87; SLJ 11/87) [921]

FRANK, ANNE

4069 Frank, Anne. *Anne Frank's Tales from the Secret Annex* (7–12). 1984, Doubleday $14.95 (0-385-18715-7); Pocket paper $2.95 (0-671-45857-4). This volume includes the diary plus material not published before. [921]

4070 Frank, Anne. *The Diary of a Young Girl* (7–12). Trans. by B. M. Mooyaart. Illus. 1967, Doubleday $18.95 (0-385-04019-9). The world-famous diary of the young Jewish girl kept while she was being hidden with her family from the Nazis. [921]

4071 Frank, Anne. *The Diary of Anne Frank: The Critical Edition* (7–12). Illus. 1989, Doubleday $30.00 (0-385-24023-6). The most complete version of the diary to appear in English plus a history of the volume. (Rev: BL 5/15/89) [921]

FREDERICK II, KING OF PRUSSIA

4072 Kittredge, Mary. *Frederick the Great* (6–10). Illus. 1987, Chelsea House $17.95 (0-87754-525-1). The life of the Prussian leader who brought his country to international prominence during the eighteenth century. (Rev: BL 11/15/87; SLJ 12/87) [921]

GARIBALDI, GIUSEPPI

4073 Viola, Herman J., and Susan P. Viola. *Giuseppi Garibaldi* (6–10). Illus. 1987, Chelsea House $17.95 (0-87754-526-X). Garibaldi was a hero, patriot, and the man who led the movement to unify his country, Italy. (Rev: BL 11/15/87; SLJ 3/88) [921]

GORBACHEV, MIKHAIL

4074 Butson, Thomas. *Mikhail Gorbachev* (6–10). Illus. 1986, Chelsea House $17.95 (1-55546-200-6). A view of the Russian leader and his hopes for a revitalized U.S.S.R. (Rev: BL 2/15/87; SLJ 2/87) [921]

4075 Oleksy, Walter. *Mikhail Gorbachev: A Leader for Soviet Change* (6–9). Illus. 1989, Childrens LB $10.95 (0-516-03265-8). A richly detailed biography of Gorbachev that uses many first-hand quotes. (Rev: SLJ 11/89) [921]

4076 Otfinoski, Steven. *Mikhail Gorbachev: The Soviet Innovator* (5–8). 1989, Ballantine paper $3.95 (0-449-90400-8). A very accessible account in paperback of this Soviet leader that includes material on his youth. (Rev: BL 12/15/89; BR 3–4/90; SLJ 2/90) [921]

4077 Sullivan, George. *Mikhail Gorbachev* (6–8). 1988, Messner LB $9.79 (0-671-63263-9); paper $5.95 (0-671-66937-0). A biography that also analyzes the differences between communist and democratic forms of government. (Rev: BR 5–6/89; SLJ 8/88) [921]

GREY, LADY JANE

4078 Smith, Anthony Charles H. *Lady Jane* (7–9). 1985, Holt $12.95 (0-03-006168-7). A biography of the ill-fated Queen of England who ruled for only 9 days in 1553. (Rev: VOYA 2/86) [921]

HAMMARSKJÖLD, DAG

4079 Sheldon, Richard N. *Dag Hammarskjöld* (6–10). Illus. 1987, Chelsea House $17.95 (0-87754-529-4). The life story of the Swedish man who served as the secretary general of the United Nations for 8 years. (Rev: BL 9/1/87; SLJ 10/87) [921]

HENRY IV, KING OF FRANCE

4080 Gross, Albert C. *Henry of Navarre* (6–10). Illus. 1988, Chelsea House $16.95 (0-87754-531-6). Henry IV was King of France from 1589 to 1610 and was noted as a man tolerant of differing religious beliefs. (Rev: BL 6/15/88) [921]

HENRY VIII, KING OF ENGLAND

4081 Dwyer, Frank. *Henry VIII* (7–12). Illus. 1988, Chelsea House LB $16.95 (0-87754-530-8). This is a fact-crammed biography with a great deal of English history given for background. (Rev: BL 1/15/88; SLJ 3/88) [921]

HINDENBURG, PAUL VON

4082 Berman, Russell A. *Paul von Hindenburg* (6–10). Illus. 1987, Chelsea House $17.95 (0-87754-532-4). The story of the German military and political leader who became famous during World War I. (Rev: BL 8/87; SLJ 11/87) [921]

HITLER, ADOLF

4083 Marrin, Albert. *Hitler* (5–9). Illus. 1987, Viking $14.95 (0-670-81546-2). A matter-of-fact account of the life of the German dictator that tries to explain how he became the man he was. (Rev: BL 7/87; BR 1–2/88; SLJ 6–7/87) [921]

4084 Rubenstein, Joshua. *Adolf Hitler* (7–10). Illus. 1982, Watts $12.90 (0-531-04477-7). An easily read introduction to the life of this hated dictator. [921]

IVAN THE TERRIBLE, CZAR OF RUSSIA

4085 Butson, Thomas. *Ivan the Terrible* (6–10). Illus. 1987, Chelsea House $17.95 (0-87754-534-0). The story of the Russian czar who accomplished much for his country but is known chiefly for his excessive cruelty and barbarism. (Rev: BL 11/15/87; SLJ 12/87) [921]

JAMES I, KING OF ENGLAND

4086 Dwyer, Frank. *James I* (6–10). Illus. 1988, Chelsea House $16.95 (1-55546-811-X). The story of the first Stuart king of both England and Scotland. (Rev: BL 6/15/88) [921]

JOAN OF ARC

4087 Brooks, Polly Schoyer. *Beyond the Myth: The Story of Joan of Arc* (6–9). 1990, Harper LB $13.89 (0-397-32423-5). An interesting, well-researched biography of the heroine who inspired her country to oust the English invaders. (Rev: BL 4/15/90; SLJ 8/90; VOYA 8/90) [921]

JOHN PAUL II, POPE

4088 Sullivan, George. *Pope John Paul II: The People's Pope* (7–9). Illus. 1984, Walker $11.95 (0-8027-6523-8). A very readable biography of this beloved pope and his activities for world peace. [921]

4089 Walch, Timothy. *Pope John Paul II* (7–10). Illus. 1989, Chelsea House $17.95 (1-55546-839-X). A biography of this active, courageous pope, who fought in the Resistance during World War II, and of his controversial stands on many of today's key issues. (Rev: BL 12/15/89; BR 1–2/90; VOYA 4/90) [921]

JOHN XXIII, POPE

4090 Walch, Timothy. *Pope John XXIII* (6–9). Illus. 1986, Chelsea House $17.95 (0-87754-535-9). An introduction to the life of the beloved modern pope who reached out to the world with his ideas. (Rev: BL 3/1/87; SLJ 3/87) [921]

KHRUSHCHEV, NIKITA

4091 Kort, Michael. *Nikita Khrushchev* (7–12). Illus. 1989, Watts LB $12.90 (0-531-10776-0). An outline of the life and career of the unpredictable, often boorish Soviet leader who fell from power in 1964. (Rev: BL 11/1/89; BR 3–4/90; SLJ 11/89) [921]

KORCZAK, JANUSZ

4092 Bernheim, Mark. *Father of the Orphans: The Life of Janusz Korczak* (6–9). Illus. 1989, Lodestar LB $14.51 (0-525-67265-6). The inspiring story of a Jewish doctor who gave his life during the Holocaust to remain with the children who lived in an orphanage he founded. (Rev: BR 1–2/90; SLJ 5/89) [921]

LAFAYETTE, MARQUIS DE

4093 Horn, Pierre. *Marquis de Lafayette* (7–12). Illus. 1988, Chelsea House $17.95 (1-55546-813-6). With many illustrations, this gives a lively account of the life of the international freedom fighter who played an important role in the American Revolution. (Rev: BR 5–6/89; SLJ 10/88; VOYA 2/89) [921]

LENIN, VLADIMIR ILICH

4094 Haney, John. *Vladimir Ilich Lenin* (6–10). Illus. 1988, Chelsea House $16.95 (0-87754-570-7). A biography of the man who led the Russia Revolution and established the U.S.S.R. (Rev: BL 4/1/88) [921]

4095 Rawcliffe, Michael. *Lenin* (7–10). Illus. 1989, David & Charles $19.95 (0-7134-5611-6). Besides supplying a biography of this Russian leader, this book evaluates Lenin's significance in history. (Rev: SLJ 5/89) [921]

LLOYD GEORGE, DAVID

4096 Shearman, Deidre. *David Lloyd George* (7–12). Illus. 1987, Chelsea House $16.95 (0-87754-581-2). The biography of the Welsh statesman who was British prime minister during World War I. (Rev: BL 1/15/88) [921]

MARY STUART, QUEEN OF SCOTS

4097 Stepanek, Sally. *Mary, Queen of Scots* (6–10). Illus. 1987, Chelsea House $16.95 (0-87754-540-5). The tragic story of this ill-fated queen, in prose and many pictures. (Rev: BL 6/1/87; SLJ 12/87) [921]

MUSSOLINI, BENITO

4098 Hartenian, Larry. *Benito Mussolini* (6–10). Illus. 1988, Chelsea House $16.95 (0-87754-572-3). A fascinating biography of the Italian Fascist leader who brought his country to defeat in World War II. (Rev: BL 6/1/88) [921]

4099 Lyttle, Richard B. *Il Duce: The Rise & Fall of Benito Mussolini* (7–12). 1987, Macmillan $15.95 (0-689-31213-X). This account focuses on the rise of this Italian Fascist dictator, his mistakes in World War II, and his execution at the end of the war. (Rev: BL 10/1/87; SLJ 1/88) [921]

NERO

4100 Powers, Elizabeth. *Nero* (6–10). Illus. 1987, Chelsea House $16.95 (0-87754-554-8). The story of the infamous Roman emperor that distinguishes fact from myth. (Rev: BL 1/15/88) [921]

NICHOLAS II, EMPEROR OF RUSSIA

4101 Vogt, George. *Nicholas II* (7–10). 1987, Chelsea House $17.95 (0-87754-545-6). A portrait of the last tsar of Russia, his family, and the monk Rasputin. (Rev: BL 5/1/87; SLJ 9/87) [921]

PERICLES

4102 King, Perry Scott. *Pericles* (7–12). Illus. 1987, Chelsea House LB $17.95 (0-87754-547-2). Besides giving a biography of this famous leader, this account provides background information on the Golden Age of Athens. (Rev: SLJ 3/88) [921]

ROBESPIERRE, MAXIMILIEN

4103 Carson, S. L. *Maximilien Robespierre* (7–12). Illus. 1987, Chelsea House $16.95 (0-8775-549-9). A biography of the French revolutionary who died a victim of his own Reign of Terror. (Rev: BL 1/15/88) [921]

SAKHAROV, ANDREI

4104 LeVert, Suzanne. *The Sakharov File: A Study in Courage* (6–8). Illus. 1986, Messner $9.79 (0-671-60070-2). The story of the famous Russian scientist and dissenter and his wife written before his death. (Rev: BL 6/15/86; SLJ 10/86) [921]

SENESH, HANNAH

4105 Atkinson, Linda. *In Kindling Flame: The Story of Hannah Senesh 1921–1944* (7–10). Illus. 1985, Lothrop LB $13.95 (0-688-02714-8). The story of the Hungarian poet who was killed in 1944 by the Germans for helping Jews to escape. (Rev: SLJ 5/85) [921]

4106 Schur, Maxine. *Hannah Szenes: A Song of Light* (5–8). 1986, Jewish Publication Soc. $10.95 (0-8275-0251-0). A brief biography of the Hungarian Jew who was executed in 1944 for helping the Resistance Movement. (Rev: SLJ 10/86) [921]

STALIN, JOSEPH

4107 Marrin, Albert. *Stalin: Russia's Man of Steel* (7–12). 1988, Viking $13.95 (0-670-82102-0). The story of how this ruthless dictator brought Russia into the twentieth century and the terrible price the country paid. (Rev: BL 12/15/88; BR 9–10/89; SLJ 11/88) [921]

THATCHER, MARGARET

4108 Hole, Dorothy. *Margaret Thatcher: Britain's Prime Minister* (7–12). Illus. 1990, Enslow LB $17.95 (0-89490-246-6). A well-rounded portrait of Britain's first female prime minister and of the many crises in her political career. (Rev: SLJ 9/90) [921]

TITO, JOSIP BROZ

4109 Schiffman, Ruth. *Josip Broz Tito* (6–10). Illus. 1987, Chelsea House $17.95 (0-87754-443-3). The story of this unusual Yugoslavian leader and of the unique Communist regime he founded. (Rev: BL 6/15/87; SLJ 8/87) [921]

WALESA, LECH

4110 Craig, Mary. *Lech Walesa* (6–8). Illus. 1990, Stevens LB $12.45 (1-55532-821-0). This biography of the Solidarity leader also gives good coverage of the political developments inside Poland since World War II. (Rev: BL 7/90) [921]

4111 Kaye, Tony. *Lech Walesa* (7–10). Illus. 1989, Chelsea House $16.95 (1-55546-856-X). Numerous illustrations complement this account of the much-admired Polish leader who helped bring his government to its knees. (Rev: BL 10/1/89; BR 11–12/89; SLJ 10/89; VOYA 12/89) [921]

WALLENBERG, RAOUL

4112 Nicholson, Michael, and David Winner. *Raoul Wallenberg* (5–9). Illus. 1989, Stevens LB $12.45 (1-55532-820-2). The life and mysterious disappearance of the Swedish man who helped many Jews escape the Holocaust in Hungary. (Rev: BL 8/89) [921]

WESLEY, JOHN

4113 McNeer, May, and Lynd Ward. *John Wesley* (6–8). Illus. 1957, Abingdon paper $3.95 (0-687-20430-5). A beautifully illustrated life story of the religious man who founded Methodism. [921]

North America (excluding United States)

DUVALIER, FRANÇOIS AND JEAN-CLAUDE

4114 Condit, Erin. *The Duvaliers* (6–9). Illus. 1989, Chelsea House LB $16.95 (1-55546-832-2). A history of modern Haiti is given as well as the

life stories of these 2 dictators. (Rev: BL 8/89; VOYA 12/89) [921]

JUAREZ, BENITO

4115 de Trevino, Elizabeth Borton. *Juarez: Man of Law* (7–9). 1974, Farrar $5.95 (0-374-33950-3). A biography of Mexico's hero and leader against injustice. [921]

4116 Wepman, Dennis. *Benito Juarez* (6–9). Illus. 1986, Chelsea House $17.95 (0-87754-537-5). The story of the Mexican Indian who rose from poverty to become president of his country. (Rev: BL 2/15/87; SLJ 2/87) [921]

L'OUVERTURE, TOUSSAINT

4117 Hoobler, Thomas, and Dorothy Hoobler. *Toussaint L'Ouverture* (7–10). Illus. 1990, Chelsea House $17.95 (1-55546-818-7). The story of the slave and the rebellion he led that brought Haiti freedom from France. (Rev: VOYA 8/90) [921]

ZAPATA, EMILIANO

4118 Ragan, John David. *Emiliano Zapata* (6–9). Illus. 1989, Chelsea House LB $16.95 (1-55546-823-3). A sympathetic portrait of the Mexican revolutionary who fought for land reforms. (Rev: BL 8/89; BR 9–10/89; SLJ 10/89; VOYA 12/89) [921]

South and Central America

ALLENDE, SALVADOR

4119 Garza, Hedda. *Salvador Allende* (7–12). Illus. 1989, Chelsea House $16.95 (1-55546-824-1). This is not only a biography of Chile's democratically elected Socialist leader but also a current history of this troubled country. (Rev: BR 9–10/89; SLJ 8/89; VOYA 8/89) [921]

GUEVARA, CHE

4120 Kellner, Douglas. *Ernesto "Che" Guevara* (7–12). Illus. 1988, Chelsea House LB $16.95 (1-55546-835-7). A fine, objective biography that gives excellent background material on the Cuban Revolution and its aftermath. (Rev: BR 9–10/90; SLJ 6/89; VOYA 2/89) [921]

4121 Neimark, Anne E. *Ché! Latin America's Legendary Guerrilla Leader* (7–10). Illus. 1989, Harper LB $13.89 (0-397-32309-3). A portrait of the Latin American revolutionary who tried to help the oppressed and poor of the nations in Spanish America. (Rev: BL 5/15/89; SLJ 5/89) [921]

PERON, JUAN

4122 DeChancie, John. *Juan Peron* (6–10). Illus. 1987, Chelsea House $17.95 (0-87754-548-0).

The story of the Argentine dictator who created a modern nation built on Fascist ideologies. (Rev: BL 11/15/87; SLJ 2/88) [921]

Miscellaneous Interesting Lives

BEDOUKIAN, KEROP

4123 Bedoukian, Kerop. *Some of Us Survived: The Story of an Armenian Boy* (6–10). Illus. 1979, Farrar $13.95 (0-374-37132-6). A biography of a boy who lived through the terrible Turkish massacres of the Armenians from 1916 to 1926. [921]

BUTTERWORTH, EMMA MACALIK

4124 Butterworth, Emma Macalik. *As the Waltz Was Ending* (7–10). 1982, Macmillan $9.95 (0-590-07835-6). Growing up in Austria before, during, and after World War II. [921]

GUNTHER, JOHN

4125 Gunther, John. *Death Be Not Proud: A Memoir* (7–12). 1989, Harper paper $4.95 (0-06-080973-6). The moving tribute to Gunther's son who died at age 17 of a brain tumor. [921]

HAUTZIG, ESTHER

4126 Hautzig, Esther. *The Endless Steppe: Growing Up in Siberia* (7–12). 1968, Harper $13.70 (0-690-26371-6); paper $2.95 (0-06-447027-X). The autobiography of the Polish girl who with her family was exiled to Siberia during World War II. [921]

HOUSTON, JEANNE WAKATSUKI

4127 Houston, Jeanne Wakatsuki, and James Houston. *Farewell to Manzanar* (7–10). 1974, Bantam paper $2.95 (0-553-27258-6). The story of a Japanese American family and their shameful treatment in the United States during World War II. [921]

HUYNH, QUANG NHUONG

4128 Huynh, Quang Nhuong. *The Land I Lost: Adventures of a Boy in Vietnam* (7–10). Illus. 1985, Harper paper $3.50 (0-06-440183-9). The story of a boy growing up in Vietnam before the war. [921]

KHERDIAN, VERON

4129 Kherdian, David. *The Road from Home: The Story of an Armenian Girl* (7–10). 1979, Greenwillow LB $12.88 (0-688-84205-4); Penguin paper $4.95 (0-14-032524-7). A portrait of the youth of the author's mother, an Armenian girl who suffered many hardships and finally arrived in America as a mail-order bride. [921]

KILLILEA, KAREN

4130 Killilea, Marie. *Karen* (6–12). 1980, Dell paper $3.25 (0-440-94376-0). The stirring biography of a young girl who would not give in to a crippling bout of cerebral palsy. For a younger group use *With Love from Karen* (1980). [921]

KOEHN, ILSE

4131 Koehn, Ilse. *Mischling, Second Degree: My Childhood in Nazi Germany* (7–10). 1977, Greenwillow LB $12.88 (0-688-84110-4). The story of a girl growing up in Nazi Germany and forced to join the Hitler Youth Movement. [921]

MERRICK, JOSEPH

4132 Drimmer, Frederick. *The Elephant Man* (6–8). Illus. 1985, Putnam $13.95 (0-399-21262-0). The story of Joseph Merrick who was severely disfigured by disease but through a doctor's efforts was able to live a comparatively happy life. (Rev: BL 1/15/86; SLJ 2/86; VOYA 4/86) [921]

PRESTON, BRUCE

4133 Bruce, Preston. *From the Door of the White House* (6–9). 1984, Lothrop $12.95 (0-688-00883-6). The story of a member of the president's personal staff from Eisenhower through Ford. [921]

REISS, JOHANNA

4134 Reiss, Johanna. *The Upstairs Room* (7–10). 1972, Harper $12.89 (0-690-85127-8); paper $2.50 (0-06-447043-1). The author's story of the years spent hiding from the Nazis in occupied Holland. Followed by: *The Journey Back* (1976). [921]

RICHTER, HANS PETER

4135 Richter, Hans Peter. *I Was There* (7–9). Trans. by Edite Kroll. 1987, Penguin paper $4.95 (0-14-032206-X). The author tells of his youth in Nazi Germany as a member of Hitler Youth and later in the army. [921]

SIEGAL, ARANKA

4136 Siegal, Aranka. *Upon the Head of the Goat: A Childhood in Hungary* (7–10). 1981, Farrar $14.95 (0-374-38059-7). A childhood in Hungary during Hitler's rise to power. [921]

SMEDLEY, AGNES

4137 Milton, Joyce. *A Friend of China* (7–9). 1980, Hastings LB $9.95 (0-8038-2388-6). The engrossing story of Agnes Smedley, the American woman who was a foreign correspondent in China during the 1950s. [921]

History and Geography

General History and Geography

Miscellaneous Works

4138 Marrin, Albert. *The Sea Rovers: Pirates, Privateers, and Buccaneers* (7–9). 1984, Macmillan $14.95 (0-689-31029-3). A history of such seafarers as Drake, Morgan, Captain Kidd, and Blackbeard. [910.4]

Atlases, Maps, and Mapmaking

4139 Baynes, John. *How Maps Are Made* (7–10). Illus. 1987, Facts on File $10.95 (0-8160-1691-7). A difficult topic well explained with many activities to make the concepts more easily understood. (Rev: SLJ 4/88) [526.8]

4140 Carey, Helen H. *How to Use Maps and Globes* (7–9). Illus. 1983, Watts LB $11.90 (0-531-04673-7). Such concepts as scale, legend, and symbols as related to maps and globes are explained and illustrated. [912]

4141 Madden, James F. *The Wonderful World of Maps* (7–9). Illus. 1982, Hammond $9.95 (0-8437-3411-6). From a famous mapmaker comes a manual on how to read and use maps. [912]

4142 Mango, Karin N. *Mapmaking* (7–9). Illus. 1984, Messner LB $9.29 (0-671-45518-4). Various kinds of maps are introduced plus their uses and how to read them. [526]

Paleontology

4143 Asimov, Isaac. *How Did We Find Out about Dinosaurs?* (6–8). 1982, Walker LB $11.85 (0-8027-6134-8). Through a history of how we found out about dinosaurs, a great deal of information is given about them. [567.9]

4144 Barnes-Svarney, Patricia. *Clocks in the Rocks: Learning about Earth's Past* (7–12). Illus. 1990, Enslow LB $13.95 (0-89490-275-X). An explanation of how fossil dating works and a description of life at different periods in the earth's history. (Rev: SLJ 4/90; VOYA 8/90) [560]

4145 Branley, Franklyn M. *Dinosaurs, Asteroids & Superstars: Why the Dinosaurs Disappeared* (7–9). Illus. 1982, Harper LB $12.89 (0-690-04212-4). A discussion of the various theories on why the dinosaur became extinct. [567.9]

4146 Charig, Alan. *A New Look at the Dinosaurs* (7–9). Illus. 1985, Facts on File paper $12.50 (0-8160-1167-2). An easy-to-read book explaining how dinosaurs were fossilized, how they are classified, and their geographic distribution. (Rev: BR 9–10/85) [567.9]

4147 Chorlton, Windsor. *Ice Ages* (7–12). Illus. 1983, Silver Burdett LB $19.94 (0-8094-4328-7). A description of the glacial periods and how life changed during them. [551.7]

4148 Crump, Donald J., ed. *Giants from the Past: The Age of Mammals* (7–10). Illus. 1983, National Geographic LB $8.50 (0-87044-429-8). A description of the first animals, like the mastodon, and how they evolved during the Ice Age. [569]

4149 Dixon, Dougal. *A Closer Look at Prehistoric Reptiles* (5–8). Illus. 1984, Watts $11.90 (0-531-03480-1). An easily read book that introduces in text and illustrations the amazing world of extinct reptiles. [560]

4150 Elting, Mary. *The Macmillan Book of Dinosaurs, and Other Prehistoric Creatures* (6–10). Illus. 1984, Macmillan $14.95 (0-02-733430-9); paper $8.95 (0-02-043000-0). The 12 time periods of Earth's history are individually described as well as the life forms that existed in each. [567.9]

4151 Lampton, Christopher. *Dinosaurs and the Age of Reptiles* (6–8). 1983, Watts $10.40 (0-531-04526-9). A fine introduction to dinosaurs, how they lived, and theories about why they disappeared. [567.9]

4152 Lampton, Christopher. *Mass Extinctions: One Theory of Why the Dinosaurs Vanished* (7–12). Illus. 1986, Watts $12.90 (0-531-10238-6). A review of the many theories past and present about the reason for the extinction of the dinosaur, focusing on a theory advanced by Lampton. (Rev: BL 12/15/86; BR 1–2/87; VOYA 2/87) [560]

4153 Lampton, Christopher. *New Theories on the Dinosaurs* (6–9). Illus. 1989, Watts LB $13.40 (0-531-10781-7). The traditional theories plus the latest thinking on the subject of why dinosaurs became extinct are lucidly explained. (Rev: BL 11/15/89; BR 1–2/90; SLJ 1/90; VOYA 2/90) [567.91]

4154 Mannetti, William. *Dinosaurs in Your Backyard* (7–9). Illus. 1982, Macmillan LB $11.95 (0-689-30906-6). A description of the characteristics of dinosaur behavior and why they died out. [567.9]

4155 Minelli, Giuseppe. *Dinosaurs & Birds* (7–12). Illus. 1988, Facts on File $12.95 (0-8160-1559-7). This book contains stunning graphics on the history and evolution of birds and dinosaurs. (Rev: BR 5–6/88) [567.9]

4156 Norman, David, and Angela Milner. *Dinosaur* (5–9). Illus. 1989, Knopf LB $13.99 (0-394-92253-0). Superb illustrations highlight this introduction to prehistoric life. (Rev: BL 10/15/89) [567.9]

4157 Rhodes, Frank H. T., et al. *Fossils: A Guide to Prehistoric Life* (7–12). Illus. 1962, Western paper $3.95 (0-307-24411-3). An account of how fossils are formed plus an illustrated guide to the most common plant and animal fossils. [560]

4158 Rosenbloom, Joseph. *Dictionary of Dinosaurs* (6–9). Illus. 1980, Messner LB $9.79 (0-671-34038-7). Information including an illustration is given for more than 80 dinosaurs. [567.9]

4159 Sattler, Helen Roney. *The Illustrated Dinosaur Dictionary* (6–9). Illus. 1983, Lothrop $17.50 (0-688-00479-2). For each entry there is a picture plus descriptive text on how the dinosaur lived and its physical characteristics. [567.9]

4160 Stidworthy, John. *Creatures from the Past* (5–9). Illus. 1987, Silver Burdett $13.96 (0-382-09488-3). A heavily illustrated account covering life's beginnings, dinosaurs, early mammals, and the beginning of mankind. (Rev: BR 1–2/88; VOYA 12/87) [560]

4161 Thompson, Ida. *The Audubon Society Field Guide to North American Fossils* (7–12). Illus. 1982, Knopf $14.45 (0-394-52412-8). An illustrated guide to the identification of North American fossils plus some background information on their formation. [560]

4162 Wallace, Joseph. *The Complete Book of the Dinosaur* (5–8). Illus. 1989, Smith $29.98 (0-8317-2362-9). An oversized compendium of knowledge about the dinosaur, extinction theories, and how and where to dig for dinosaur bones. (Rev: BL 1/15/90) [567.91]

4163 Zallinger, Peter. *Dinosaurs and Other Archosaurs* (6–10). Illus. 1986, Random paper $8.95 (0-394-84421-1). A colorful, chatty introduction to the world of the dinosaur. (Rev: VOYA 12/86) [565.9]

Anthropology and Evolution

4164 Asimov, Isaac. *How Did We Find Out about Our Human Roots?* (6–9). Illus. 1979, Walker LB $10.95 (0-8027-6361-8). A book that traces the development of man as expressed first through creationism and later modified by scientific findings. [573.2]

4165 Bell, Neill. *Only Human: Why We Are the Way We Are* (7–9). Illus. 1983, Little $14.95 (0-316-08816-1); paper $7.95 (0-316-08818-8). The evolution of human behavior is discussed as well as the development of such institutions as marriage. [573]

4166 Benton, Michael. *The Story of Life on Earth: Tracing Its Origins and Development Through Time* (6–9). Illus. 1986, Watts LB $13.90 (0-531-19019-6). This book describes how life originated and how it has evolved through geological eras. (Rev: BR 1–2/87; SLJ 1/87) [573.2]

4167 Branigan, Keith. *Prehistory* (7–9). Illus. 1984, Watts $12.40 (0-531-03745-2). A history of prehistoric people and how they lived. [573.2]

4168 de Saint-Blanquat, Henri. *The First People* (5–9). Illus. 1986, Silver Burdett LB $14.96 (0-382-09212-0). Beginning with the birth of the sun, this account traces history to the beginning of life on earth and ends with the emergence of the human species. (Rev: BR 9–10/87; SLJ 9/87) [573.2]

4169 de Saint-Blanquat, Henri. *The First Settlements* (5–9). Illus. 1986, Silver Burdett LB $14.96 (0-382-09213-9). The history of mankind from nomadic hunter to settled urban and rural community dweller. (Rev: BR 9–10/87; SLJ 9/87) [573]

4170 Fisher, Maxine P. *Recent Revolutions in Anthropology* (7–10). Illus. 1986, Watts $12.90 (0-531-10240-8). A lively account that traces advancements in various branches of anthropology plus material on the people responsible and questions that still remain unanswered. (Rev: BL 11/1/86; BR 1–2/87; SLJ 11/86; VOYA 2/87) [306]

4171 Gallant, Roy A. *From Living Cells to Dinosaurs* (5–8). Illus. 1986, Watts LB $10.40 (0-531-10207-6). A clear discussion on how life evolved up to and including the age of dinosaurs. (Rev: BR 5–6/87; SLJ 2/87) [573.2]

4172 Lampton, Christopher. *New Theories on the Origins of the Human Race* (6–9). Illus. 1989, Watts LB $13.40 (0-531-10783-3). Various theories on the origins of the human race are explained with emphasis on current thinking on the subject. (Rev: BL 11/15/89; SLJ 1/90) [573.3]

4173 Lampton, Christopher. *The Origin of the Human Race* (7–12). Illus. 1989, Watts LB $13.40 (0-531-10783-3). A clear explanation of the human family tree and how it came to be. (Rev: BR 3–4/90; VOYA 2/90) [573]

4174 Lasky, Kathryn. *Traces of Life: The Origins of Humankind* (5–8). Illus. 1990, Morrow $16.95 (0-688-07237-2). With drawings, photographs, and lively prose, Lasky re-creates the history of man with projections into the future. (Rev: BL 5/1/90; SLJ 6/90) [573.2]

4175 Merriman, Nick. *Early Humans* (5–9). Illus. 1989, Knopf LB $13.99 (0-394-92257-3). An account of prehistoric life in text and lavish pictures. (Rev: BL 7/89; BR 11–12/89) [930.1]

4176 Stein, Sara. *The Evolution Book* (6–8). Illus. 1986, Workman $12.95 (0-89480-927-X). A history of evolution that covers time from 4,000 million years ago to the present. (Rev: BL 2/15/87; BR 5–6/87; SLJ 3/87; VOYA 4/87) [508]

Archaeology

4177 Braymer, Marjorie. *Atlantis: The Biography of a Legend* (7–10). Illus. 1983, Macmillan $13.95 (0-689-50264-8). The story of the Atlantis legend and its possible connection with the present-day island of Thera. [930.1]

4178 Glubok, Shirley. *Art and Archeology* (7–10). Illus. 1966, Harper LB $12.89 (0-06-022036-8). An account of the major finds by archaeologists around the world. [930.1]

4179 Lampton, Christopher. *Undersea Archaeology* (7–10). Illus. 1988, Watts LB $9.90 (0-531-10492-3). A history of undersea archaeology is given including the work of Jacques Cousteau, plus a peek into the future. (Rev: SLJ 10/88) [930.1]

4180 Marston, Elsa. *Mysteries in American Archaeology* (6–9). Illus. 1986, Walker LB $13.85 (0-8027-6627-7). Mysteries involving early people in America such as the Hopewell Indians and the Mound Builders are introduced. (Rev: BL 8/86; BR 11–12/86; SLJ 5/86) [973.1]

World History and Geography

General

4181 Asimov, Isaac. *Words on the Map* (7–9). Illus. 1962, Houghton $9.95 (0-395-06569-0). An introduction to 1,500 place names and how they originated. [910.3]

4182 Bell, Neill. *The Book of Where; or, How to Be Naturally Geographic* (7–9). Illus. 1982, Little $13.95 (0-316-08830-7); paper $7.95 (0-316-08831-5). Starting with one's own home environment and moving outward, this is an introduction to concepts in geography. [910]

4183 Caselli, Giovanni. *Life Through the Ages* (5–8). Illus. 1987, Putnam $14.95 (0-448-18996-8). The history of Western civilization from prehistoric times is covered in this outline with many illustrations. (Rev: SLJ 3/88) [900]

4184 Chadefaud, Catherine. *The First Empires* (5–8). Trans. by Anthea Ridett. Illus. 1988, Silver Burdett $15.96 (0-382-09481-6). In an oversized volume with many illustrations, this is a description of the early empires of Asia and the Middle East. (Rev: BL 2/15/89) [939.4]

4185 Corn, Kahane, and Jacki Moline. *Madcap Men and Wacky Women from History* (6–9). Illus. 1987, Messner LB $10.98 (0-671-63398-8). Brief biographies of 39 unusual characters, including Lady Godiva, King Ludwig II, and Barbara Hutton. (Rev: SLJ 9/87) [900]

4186 De Pauw, Linda Grant. *Seafaring Women* (7–9). 1982, Houghton LB $13.95 (0-395-32434-3). An exploration of the many roles women have played as they have gone to sea from ancient times to the present. [910.4]

4187 Dixon, Dougal. *Geography* (7–10). Illus. 1984, Watts LB $11.40 (0-531-04744-X). An introduction to land masses, oceans, weather, and man's effect on the environment. [910]

4188 Giblin, James Cross. *Walls: Defenses Throughout History* (6–10). Illus. 1984, Little $14.95 (0-316-30954-0). The role of walls as a method of defense from Stone Age times to the Berlin Wall. (Rev: BL 1/15/85) [623]

4189 Lauber, Patricia. *Tales Mummies Tell* (6–8). Illus. 1985, Harper LB $11.89 (0-690-04389-9). A fascinating account of all we can learn about civilizations that used mummification to preserve bodies by examining the mummies themselves. (Rev: BL 6/15/85) [930]

4190 Lyttle, Richard B. *Land beyond the River: Europe in the Age of Migration* (6–9). Illus. 1986, Macmillan $14.95 (0-689-31199-0). The migration of such peoples as the Huns, Goths, Vikings, and Gypsies between the second and ninth centuries is discussed in this fine presentation. (Rev: BL 8/86; SLJ 4/86; VOYA 2/87) [940.1]

4191 Olliver, Jane, ed. *The Warwick Atlas of World History* (6–8). Illus. 1988, Warwick $15.50 (0-531-19037-4). All sorts of graphics, including drawings, photographs, and maps, make world geography and history come alive. (Rev: BL 11/15/88) [911]

4192 Phillips, Douglas A., and Steven C. Levi. *The Pacific Rim Region: Emerging Giant* (7–12). Illus. 1988, Enslow $14.95 (0-89490-191-5). A history and economic introduction to the regions and countries that border the Pacific Ocean. (Rev: BL 1/15/89; BR 1–2/89; SLJ 1/89; VOYA 2/89) [330.99]

4193 Rahn, Joan Elma. *Animals That Changed History* (6–9). Illus. 1986, Macmillan $11.95 (0-689-31137-0). Stories such as how the demand for beaver pelts helped open up the West abound in this account of how animals changed the fate of the world. (Rev: BL 2/1/87; SLJ 2/87) [909]

4194 Sandak, Cass R. *Explorers and Discovery* (5–8). Illus. 1983, Watts $10.40 (0-531-04537-4). A history of exploration from earliest times to the present. [910.92]

4195 Van Loon, Hendrik Willem. *The Story of Mankind* (7–9). Illus. 1985, Liveright $19.95 (0-87140-647-0). A readable introduction to world history that won the first Newbery Award in 1922. [909]

Ancient History

General and Miscellaneous

4196 Caselli, Giovanni. *The First Civilizations* (6–8). Illus. 1985, Bedrick $15.95 (0-911745-59-9). This account traces the early history of man, from the first toolmakers to the civilizations of Egypt and Greece, through the objects that were made and used. (Rev: BL 11/15/85; BR 3–4/86; SLJ 1/87) [930]

4197 Crump, Donald J., ed. *Builders of the Ancient World: Marvels of Engineering* (8–12). Illus. 1986, National Geographic LB $9.50 (0-87044-590-1). A number of important structures are discussed that represent many different cultures, from ancient Greece to China and South America. (Rev: SLJ 5/87) [930]

4198 Simon, Charnan. *Explorers of the Ancient World* (6–8). Illus. 1990, Childrens LB $23.93 (0-516-03053-1). Profiles of some of the great explorers of ancient history, such as Alexander the Great, plus a discussion of the ships, routes taken, and instruments used. (Rev: BL 8/90) [910.92]

4199 *Splendors of the Past: Lost Cities of the Ancient World* (6–9). Illus. 1981, National Geographic $19.95 (0-87044-358-5). Lost cities from 7 periods including Pompeii and Sumeria are included with fine illustrations. [930]

4200 Ventura, Piero, and Gian Paolo Ceserani. *In Search of Ancient Crete* (5–9). Trans. by Michael Shaw. Illus. 1985, Silver Burdett LB $12.96 (0-382-09117-5); paper $7.75 (0-382-09120-5). The thrill of archaeology is conveyed in this account of the exploration of the ruins of ancient Crete. (Rev: SLJ 8/86) [939]

4201 Ventura, Piero, and Gian Paolo Ceserani. *In Search of Troy* (5–9). Trans. by Pamela Swinglehurst. Illus. 1985, Silver Burdett LB $12.96 (0-382-09121-3); paper $7.75 (0-382-09118-3). The story behind the archeological findings concerning the ancient city of Troy in Asia Minor. (Rev: SLJ 8/86) [937]

Egypt and Mesopotamia

4202 Harris, Geraldine. *Ancient Egypt* (5–8). Illus. 1990, Facts on File LB $17.95 (0-8160-1971-1). This account of Egyptian history is enlivened by excellent maps, photographs, and drawings. (Rev: SLJ 8/90) [932]

4203 Katan, Norma Jean, and Barbara Mintz. *Hieroglyphs: The Writings of Ancient Egypt* (7–9). Illus. 1981, Macmillan $12.95 (0-689-50176-5). An explanation of hieroglyphics is given—how they originated and how the Rosetta Stone helped solve their mystery. [493]

4204 Payne, Elizabeth. *The Pharaohs of Ancient Egypt* (6–8). 1981, Random paper $4.95 (0-394-84699-0). Through the story of the chief rulers of Egypt, a basic history and cultural overview of ancient Egypt are given. [932]

4205 Robinson, Charles Alexander, Jr. *Ancient Egypt* (6–9). Rev. ed. Illus. 1984, Watts LB $10.40 (0-531-04819-5). A basic introduction that covers an outline of history, major construction, and daily life. [932]

4206 Scott, Joseph, and Lenore Scott. *Egyptian Hieroglyphs for Everyone: An Introduction to the Writing of Ancient Egypt* (7–9). 1968, Harper $13.70 (0-308-80223-3). A description of how the writing of ancient Egypt developed and how it can be read today. [493]

4207 Ventura, Piero, and Gian Paolo Ceserani. *In Search of Tutankhamun* (5–9). Trans. by Pamela Swinglehurst. Illus. 1985, Silver Burdett LB $12.96 (0-382-09119-1); paper $7.75 (0-382-09122-1). An account of the great archeological find of King Tut's tomb in the Valley of the Kings. (Rev: SLJ 8/86) [932]

Greece

4208 Asimov, Isaac. *The Greeks: A Great Adventure* (7–10). Illus. 1965, Houghton $14.95 (0-395-06574-7). The history of ancient Greece from 200 B.C. to the fall of Constantinople. [938]

4209 Coolidge, Olivia. *The Trojan War* (7–9). Illus. 1952, Houghton $14.95 (0-395-06731-6). The history of the origins of this war, its outcome, and the return of the Greeks. [939]

4210 Stewart, Gail. *The Trojan War* (6–9). Illus. 1989, Greenhaven LB $12.95 (0-89908-065-0). This book explores various viewpoints to sort out fact from fancy concerning the Trojan War. (Rev: SLJ 3/90) [938]

4211 Windrow, Martin. *The Greek Hoplite* (5–10). Illus. 1986, Watts $11.90 (0-531-03780-0). In addition to describing the training given to each Greek soldier, details are furnished on the battle tactics of the time. (Rev: BR 1–2/87) [938]

4212 Woodford, Susan. *The Parthenon* (7–12). Illus. 1983, Lerner LB $8.95 (0-8225-1228-9); Cambridge paper $4.95 (0-521-22629-5). A history of the famous temple in Athens and of the religion of ancient Greece. [938]

Rome

4213 Caselli, Giovanni. *The Roman Empire and the Dark Ages* (6–8). Illus. 1985, Bedrick $15.95 (0-911745-58-0). From the objects that were made and used by people, the author has recreated history from the Roman empire to medieval times. (Rev: BL 11/15/85; BR 3–4/86; SLJ 1/87) [940.1]

4214 Connolly, Peter. *Tiberius Claudius Maximus: The Legionary* (6–10). Illus. 1989, Oxford Univ. Pr. $12.95 (0-19-917105-X). In this account, the reader is both entertained and informed by the story of the rise of a Roman soldier through the ranks. (Rev: SLJ 5/89)

4215 Corbishley, Mike. *The Roman World* (7–9). Illus. 1986, Watts LB $13.90 (0-531-19018-8). In brief chapters, the history of ancient Rome is traced with some additional material on such topics as religion, education, and food. (Rev: SLJ 2/87) [937]

4216 Davis, William Stearns. *A Day in Old Rome: A Picture of Roman Life* (7–12). Illus. 1959, Biblo & Tannen $16.00 (0-8196-0106-3). The classic account, first published in 1925, about daily life of the various classes of ancient Rome. [937]

4217 Goor, Ron, and Nancy Goor. *Pompeii* (6–10). Illus. 1986, Harper $12.70 (0-690-04515-8). After a description of the eruption of Vesuvius, the daily life in Pompeii is discussed. (Rev: BR 3–4/87) [937]

4218 Windrow, Martin. *The Roman Legionary* (7–10). Illus. 1985, Watts LB $11.90 (0-531-03781-9). A look at the life and times of the common soldier during the days of the Roman Empire. (Rev: BR 3–4/86) [937]

Middle Ages through Renaissance (500–1700)

4219 *The Age of Exploration* (5–8). Illus. 1989, Marshall Cavendish LB $19.95 (0-86307-997-0). With lavish illustrations, this account details the careers of Marco Polo, Columbus, and Cortés. (Rev: SLJ 7/90) [910.92]

4220 Cairns, Conrad. *Medieval Castles* (6–9). Illus. 1989, Lerner LB $8.95 (0-8225-1235-1). A history of British castles from 650 A.D. to 1580 with many illustrations. (Rev: SLJ 8/89) [728.8]

4221 Caselli, Giovanni. *The Renaissance and the New World* (6–8). Illus. 1986, Bedrick $12.95 (0-87226-050-X). Almost 400 years of history are covered in this account that uses objects made and used by people during the period as its focus. (Rev: BL 4/15/86; SLJ 8/86) [940]

4222 Corbishley, Mike. *The Middle Ages* (6–9). Illus. 1990, Facts on File $17.95 (0-8160-1973-8). An overview of medieval Europe is given, covering history and culture with some material on stained glassmaking. (Rev: SLJ 9/90) [909]

4223 *The Italian Renaissance* (5–8). Illus. 1989, Marshall Cavendish LB $19.95 (0-86307-998-9). The accomplishments of da Vinci, Michelangelo, and Galileo are highlighted in this well-illustrated account. (Rev: SLJ 7/90) [940.2]

4224 Pierre, Michel. *The Renaissance* (7–9). Illus. 1987, Silver Burdett LB $14.96 (0-382-09295-3). This brief overview with many illustrations covers the salient movements and events from 1450 to 1550. (Rev: BR 1–2/88; SLJ 3/88) [940.2]

4225 Sabbagh, Antoine. *Europe in the Middle Ages* (5–8). Trans. by Anthea Ridett. Illus. 1988, Silver Burdett $15.96 (0-382-09484-0). An oversized volume that gives a colorful introduction to medieval society and culture. (Rev: BL 2/15/89) [940.1]

4226 Sancha, Sheila. *Walter Dragun's Town: Crafts and Trade in the Middle Ages* (5–9). Illus. 1989, Harper LB $13.89 (0-690-04806-8). A fascinating, well-illustrated glimpse of the crafts and trades of medieval England. (Rev: SLJ 12/89) [909.07]

4227 Windrow, Martin. *The Medieval Knight* (5–10). Illus. 1986, Watts $11.90 (0-531-03834-3). The stages passed through to become a knight are discussed, plus details on the battle tactics of the day. (Rev: BR 1–2/87) [940.1]

4228 Windrow, Martin. *The Viking Warrior* (7–10). Illus. 1984, Watts LB $11.90 (0-531-03816-5). More than the title might suggest, this book gives a good introduction to Viking civilization. [948]

Eighteenth through Nineteenth Centuries (1700–1900)

4229 Killingray, David. *The Transatlantic Slave Trade* (7–12). Illus. 1987, Batsford LB $19.95 (0-7134-5469-5). This book gives detailed coverage on the causes, history, and end of the international slave trade and how it has affected demographics today. (Rev: SLJ 1/88) [380.1]

The Twentieth Century

General and Miscellaneous

4230 Snow, Jon. *Atlas of Today: The World Behind the News* (6–10). Illus. 1987, Watts LB $13.90 (0-531-19028-5). An atlas illustrating current subjects such as unemployment, industry, and health. (Rev: SLJ 2/88) [912]

World War I

4231 Lawson, Don. *The United States in World War I* (7–10). Illus. 1963, Harper $12.95 (0-200-71939-4). An account that emphasizes the work of such men as Pershing, Billy Mitchell, Rickenbacker, and Alvin York. [940.4]

4232 Marrin, Albert. *The Yanks Are Coming: The United States in the First World War* (7–10). 1986, Macmillan $15.95 (0-689-31209-1). An account of the U.S. participation in World War I from 1917 to the end. (Rev: BL 10/15/86; SLJ 2/87; VOYA 6/87) [954]

4233 Pimlott, John. *The First World War* (6–9). Illus. 1986, Watts $12.90 (0-531-10234-3). The events leading up to the war are outlined plus an account of the course of the war and the participa-

tion of the United States. (Rev: BL 1/15/87; SLJ 4/87) [940.4]

4234 Ross, Stewart. *The Origins of World War I* (7–10). Illus. 1989, Bookwright LB $12.90 (0-531-18260-6). A fine account of the complex origins of this war in a profusely illustrated account. (Rev: SLJ 5/90) [940.3]

Between the Wars (1918–1939)

4235 Banyard, Peter. *The Rise of the Dictators, 1919–1939* (6–9). Illus. 1986, Watts $12.90 (0-531-10233-5). A discussion of how the unsatisfactory peace treaties after World War I lead to the rise of Hitler, Franco, and Mussolini. (Rev: BL 1/15/87; BR 3–4/87; SLJ 4/87) [940.5]

4236 Goldston, Robert. *The Road between the Wars: 1918–1941* (7–9). Illus. 1978, Dial $8.95 (0-8037-7467-2). An account that traces the roots of World War II through the aftermath of the first World War and the Great Depression. [909.82]

World War II and the Holocaust

4237 Adler, David. *We Remember the Holocaust* (6–9). Illus. 1989, Henry Holt $15.95 (0-8050-0434-3). Through actual accounts, Adler recreates the horror of the Holocaust. (Rev: BL 12/15/89; BR 3–4/90) [940.53]

4238 Altshuler, David A. *Hitler's War Against the Jews: A Young Reader's Version of The War Against the Jews, 1933–1945, by Lucy S. Dawidowicz* (7–10). Illus. 1978, Behrman $8.95 (0-87441-293-5); paper $7.95 (0-87441-222-6). The tragic story of Hitler's Final Solution and its aftermath. [940.54]

4239 Bernbaum, Israel. *My Brother's Keeper: The Holocaust Through the Eyes of an Artist* (6–9). Illus. 1985, Putnam $16.95 (0-399-21242-6). Through an examination of his 5 paintings collectively titled *Warsaw Ghetto 1943*, Bernbaum explains the true meaning of the Holocaust. (Rev: BL 9/1/85; VOYA 12/85) [759.13]

4240 Blanco, Richard L. *The Luftwaffe in World War II: The Rise and Decline of the German Air Force* (7–12). Illus. 1987, Messner $10.29 (0-671-50232-8). This account tells how the World War II German Air Force emerged and how it became an important part of Hitler's war machine. (Rev: BL 6/15/87; SLJ 8/87) [358.4]

4241 Bliven, Bruce, Jr. *From Casablanca to Berlin: The War in North Africa and Europe: 1942–1945* (7–9). Illus. 1965, Random LB $7.99 (0-394-90412-5). An easily read introduction to the war in the west roughly from the U.S. entry until victory. [940.54]

4242 Bliven, Bruce, Jr. *From Pearl Harbor to Okinawa: The War in the Pacific: 1941–1945* (7–9). Illus. 1960, Random LB $7.99 (0-394-90394-3). This account begins with Pearl Harbor and ends with V-J day. [940.54]

4243 Bliven, Bruce, Jr. *Story of D-Day, June 6, 1944* (6–8). 1963, Random LB $8.99 (0-394-90362-5); paper $2.95 (0-394-84886-1). An accurate but simple hour-by-hour account of the Allied invasion of Normandy. [940.53]

4244 Carter, Hodding. *Commandos of World War II* (6–8). 1966, Random paper $2.95 (0-394-84735-0). The exciting exploits of these British crack hit-and-run forces. [940.53]

4245 Chaikin, Miriam. *A Nightmare in History: The Holocaust 1933–1945* (7–10). Illus. 1987, Clarion $14.95 (0-89919-461-3). A harrowing account of the 12 years during which Hitler waged war on the Jews. (Rev: BR 5–6/88; SLJ 1/88; VOYA 4/88) [940.53]

4246 Dank, Milton. *D-Day* (7–10). 1984, Watts $12.90 (0-531-04863-2). A history of Operation Overlord, the code name for the invasion of Normandy by British and American troops that took place in June 1944. [940.53]

4247 Dolan, Edward F., Jr. *Victory in Europe: The Fall of Hitler's Germany* (7–10). 1988, Watts $12.90 (0-531-10522-9). An account of the last 7 months of World War II in Europe. (Rev: BL 9/1/88; BR 9–10/88; SLJ 6–7/88; VOYA 8/88) [940.54]

4248 Dudman, John. *The Division of Berlin* (6–9). Illus. 1988, Rourke LB $11.95 (0-86592-037-0). A British import that tells about the division of Berlin into 4 zones after World War II and the gradual consolidation of East and West Berlin. (Rev: SLJ 2/89) [940.53]

4249 Friedman, Ina R. *The Other Victims: First-Person Stories of Non-Jews Persecuted by the Nazis* (7–12). 1990, Houghton $14.95 (0-395-50212-8). This account deals with the other victims of the Holocaust, like Gypsies, homosexuals, dissenters, and some religious minorities. (Rev: BL 6/15/90; SLJ 4/90; VOYA 6/90) [940.53]

4250 Goldston, Robert. *Sinister Touches: The Secret War against Hitler* (7–9). 1982, Dial $11.95 (0-8037-7903-8). The history of the underground battle against the Nazis that involved many complex espionage plans. [914.053]

4251 Gordon, Sheila. *3rd September 1939* (7–12). Illus. 1988, Batsford $16.95 (0-8521-9757-8). A clear account of the events that led to Hitler's invasion of Poland and the outbreak of World War II. (Rev: SLJ 1/89) [940.53]

4252 Harris, Nathaniel. *Pearl Harbor* (7–9). Illus. 1987, David & Charles $17.95 (0-8521-9669-5). This book not only describes the events of December 7, 1941, but also gives historical background on the attack. (Rev: SLJ 9/87) [940.53]

4253 Hills, C. A. R. *The Second World War* (7–12). Illus. 1986, David & Charles $19.95 (0-7134-4531-9). A brief but comprehensive history of World War II as seen through the eyes of its leaders. (Rev: SLJ 11/86) [940.53]

4254 Hoare, Stephen. *Hiroshima* (4–8). Illus. 1987, David & Charles LB $17.95 (0-8521-9695-4). This book describes the events on the day the atomic bomb was dropped, the events that led up to it, and the postwar arms race. (Rev: BR 11–12/87; SLJ 12/87) [940.53]

4255 Hoobler, Dorothy, and Thomas Hoobler. *An Album of World War II* (7–10). Illus. 1977, Watts LB $13.90 (0-531-02911-5). With over 100 illustrations, this book provides a capsule history of World War II. [940.54]

4256 Isaacman, Clara, and Joan Adess Grossman. *Clara's Story* (6–9). 1984, Jewish Publication Soc. $11.95 (0-8276-0243-X). The story of how Clara, the author, and her Jewish family spent two and a half years in hiding during the German occupation of Belgium in World War II. (Rev: BL 3/15/85) [940.53]

4257 Küchler-Silberman, Lena. *My Hundred Children* (7–12). 1987, Dell paper $3.50 (0-440-95263-8). The memoir of a Jewish survivor of the Holocaust and how she helped a group of orphaned children who also survived. (Rev: BL 4/1/87; VOYA 6/87) [940.547]

4258 Lawson, Don. *The French Resistance* (7–10). 1984, Messner LB $8.79 (0-671-50832-6). The story of the many gallant French men and women who defied death to oppose the German forces that occupied their country. [940.53]

4259 Leckie, Robert. *The Story of World War II* (6–9). Illus. 1964, Random LB $13.99 (0-394-90295-5). From the rise of Hitler to Japan's surrender told in pictures and simple text. [940.53]

4260 McGowen, Tom. *Midway and Guadalcanal* (7–10). Illus. 1984, Watts LB $12.90 (0-531-

04866-7). The story of 2 decisive Pacific battles during 1942 and 1943. [940.54]

4261 Marrin, Albert. *The Secret Armies: Spies, Counterspies, and Saboteurs in World War II* (7–10). Illus. 1985, Macmillan $13.95 (0-689-31165-6). A fascinating account of Allied clandestine operations during World War II. (Rev: BL 10/1/85; SLJ 4/86) [940.54]

4262 Marrin, Albert. *Victory in the Pacific* (7–10). Illus. 1983, Macmillan $13.95 (0-689-30948-1). The story of the Navy and Marines during the war in the Pacific theater. [940.54]

4263 Maruki, Toshi. *Hiroshima No Pika* (7–10). Illus. 1982, Lothrop $23.00 (0-688-01297-3). One family's experiences during the day the bomb dropped on Hiroshima told in text and moving illustrations by the author. [940.54]

4264 Meltzer, Milton. *Never to Forget: The Jews of the Holocaust* (7–12). 1976, Harper $13.89 (0-06-024174-8). The story of the murder of over 6 million Jews during World War II. [940.54]

4265 Meltzer, Milton. *Rescue: The Story of How Gentiles Saved Jews in the Holocaust* (6–9). 1988, Harper LB $12.89 (0-06-024219-8). The uplifting story of those courageous few who helped save Jews from Nazi death camps. (Rev: BL 10/1/88; BR 1–2/89; SLJ 8/88; VOYA 8/88) [940.53]

4266 Messenger, Charles. *The Second World War* (6–9). Illus. 1987, Watts $12.90 (0-531-10321-8). Causes of the war, the major events in it, and its effects on the world. (Rev: BL 6/15/87; SLJ 6–7/87) [940.54]

4267 Miller, Marilyn. *D-Day* (7–10). Illus. 1986, Silver Burdett LB $14.96 (0-382-06825-4); paper $5.75 (0-382-06972-2). A brief overview of the invasion of France and the events leading up to it. (Rev: BR 9–10/87; SLJ 8/87) [940.53]

4268 Pierre, Michel, and Annette Wieviorka. *The Second World War* (6–9). Illus. 1987, Silver Burdett LB $14.96 (0-382-09298-8). An overview account that deals with the causes and principal events of World War II, and ends with Hiroshima. (Rev: BR 1–2/88; SLJ 12/87) [940.53]

4269 Pitt, Barrie. *The Battle of the Atlantic* (7–12). Illus. 1977, Time-Life $22.60 (0-8094-2467-3). The fight against the German U-boats told in text, photos, and paintings. [940.54]

4270 Prager, Arthur, and Emily Prager. *World War II Resistance Stories* (7–9). Illus. 1984, Dell paper $2.25 (0-440-99800-X). Each chapter is devoted to a single resistance fighter and his or her courageous story. [940.54]

4271 Richardson, Nigel. *The July Plot* (6–8). Illus. 1987, Dryad $15.95 (0-8521-9672-5). The story behind the plot to kill Hitler on July 20, 1944. (Rev: BL 8/87; BR 9–10/87) [364.1]

4272 Richter, Hans Peter. *Friedrich* (7–9). Trans. by Edite Kroll. 1987, Penguin paper $4.95 (0-14-032205-1). The story of a Jewish boy and his family caught in the horror of the rise of the Nazi party and the Holocaust. [940.54]

4273 Rogasky, Barbara. *Smoke and Ashes: The Story of the Holocaust* (6–12). Illus. 1988, Holiday $16.95 (0-8234-0697-0). The incredible story of the Holocaust from the first rumblings of anti-Semitism in Nazi Germany to the liberation of the death camps. (Rev: BL 6/15/88; SLJ 6–7/88; VOYA 12/88) [940.53]

4274 Rossel, Seymour. *The Holocaust: The Fire That Raged* (5–9). Illus. 1989, Watts LB $11.90 (0-531-10674-8). The story of the rise of Hitler and his systematic plan to eradicate the Jews, with warnings of how such a situation could happen again. (Rev: BL 6/1/89; BR 11–12/89; SLJ 8/89) [940.53]

4275 Roth-Hano, Renee. *Touch Wood: A Girlhood in Occupied France* (6–9). 1988, Macmillan $13.95 (0-02-777340-X). A memoir of a harrowing childhood experienced by a French Jew and her family during World War II. (Rev: BL 8/88; BR 1–2/89; SLJ 6–7/88; VOYA 8/88)

4276 Saunders, Alan. *The Invasion of Poland* (7–9). 1984, Watts $12.90 (0-531-04864-0). The story of the invasion that began World War II and of the historical background to this event. [940.53]

4277 Shapiro, William E. *Pearl Harbor* (7–10). Illus. 1984, Watts LB $12.90 (0-531-04865-9). The story of the day of infamy that brought the United States into World War II. [940.54]

4278 Snyder, Louis L. *World War II* (7–9). Rev. ed. Illus. 1981, Watts LB $10.40 (0-531-04333-9). A brief introduction in text and pictures to the causes and main events of the war. [940.53]

4279 Sweeney, James B. *Famous Aviators of World War II* (7–10). Illus. 1987, Watts LB $10.40 (0-531-10302-1). Profiles of five aviators, including Chennault and Doolittle, with emphasis on their contributions during World War II (Rev: SLJ 9/87) [940.53]

4280 Taylor, Theodore. *Air Raid—Pearl Harbor! The Story of December 7, 1941* (7–10). Illus. 1971, Harper $12.70 (0-690-05378-8). A detailed, gripping account of the raid on Pearl Harbor. [940.54]

4281 Taylor, Theodore. *Battle in the Arctic Seas: The Story of Convoy PQ 17* (7–10). Illus. 1976, Harper $12.70 (0-690-01084-2). The story of an actual convoy as it tried to carry supplies to the Russians via the Atlantic during World War II. [940.54]

4282 Taylor, Theodore. *Battle in the English Channel* (7–10). Illus. 1983, Avon paper $2.50 (0-380-85225-X). The retelling of the exciting World War II incident when Hitler tried to free 3 of his battleships from French waters. [940.54]

4283 Taylor, Theodore. *The Battle Off Midway Island* (7–10). Illus. 1981, Avon paper $2.50 (0-380-78790-3). The story of the brilliant victory of U.S. forces at Midway is excitingly retold. [940.54]

4284 Taylor, Theodore. *H.M.S. Hood vs. Bismarck: The Battleship Battle* (7–10). Illus. 1982, Avon paper $2.50 (0-380-81174-X). The subject of this book is the sinking of the battleship *Bismarck* by the English navy. [940.54]

4285 Tregaskis, Richard. *Guadalcanal Diary* (6–9). Illus. 1955, Random LB $8.99 (0-394-09355-2); paper $3.95 (0-394-86268-6). This is a simplified version of the adult book that tells of the Marine landing at Guadalcanal in 1942. [940.54]

4286 Ziemian, Joseph. *The Cigarette Sellers of Three Crosses Square* (7–10). Trans. by Janina David. 1977, Lerner LB $7.95 (0-8225-0757-9). The harrowing but inspiring story of how a group of Jewish children by their wits escaped the Holocaust in Poland. [940.53]

Modern World History (1945–)

4287 Healey, Tim. *The 1960s* (6–8). Illus. 1989, Watts LB $12.90 (0-531-10551-2). A copiously illustrated volume that covers such subjects as politics, the arts, science, and pop culture. Also use *The 1970s* (1989). (Rev: BL 5/1/89; SLJ 7/89) [909.826]

4288 Heater, Derek. *The Cold War* (7–10). Illus. 1989, Bookwright LB $12.90 (0-531-18275-4). A lavishly illustrated history of East-West relations that ends with the beginnings of Gorbachev's reforms. (Rev: SLJ 5/90; VOYA 4/90) [909.82]

Geographical Regions

Africa

General and Miscellaneous

4289 Baynham, Simon. *Africa from 1945* (6–9). Illus. 1987, Watts $12.90 (0-531-10319-6). After giving background information, this account covers internal problems in African countries and possible future developments. (Rev: BL 1/15/88; BR 1–2/88) [960.32]

4290 Chiasson, John. *African Journey* (5–9). Illus. 1987, Macmillan $16.95 (0-02-718530-3). Six different places in Africa are examined to show the relationship between man and nature on this continent. (Rev: BL 12/1/87) [306]

4291 Percefull, Aaron W. *The Nile* (6–9). Illus. 1984, Watts LB $10.40 (0-531-04828-4). The last 2 centuries of Nile history plus a rundown on current developments. [962]

4292 Timberlake, Lloyd. *Famine in Africa* (6–8). Illus. 1986, Gloucester LB $11.90 (0-531-17017-9). The causes of the famine in Africa are explored and blame placed on climate, the environment, and government policies. (Rev: SLJ 8/86) [960]

Central and Eastern Africa

4293 *Central African Republic . . . in Pictures* (6–9). Illus. 1989, Lerner $9.95 (0-8225-1858-9). An introduction to the history, geography, and people of this country in both text and pictures. Other African countries in this series are *Madagascar in Pictures, Malawi in Pictures,* and *Tanzania in Pictures* (all 1988). (Rev: SLJ 7/89) [967]

4294 Creed, Alexander. *Uganda* (6–8). Illus. 1987, Chelsea House $11.95 (1-55546-189-1). A noncontroversial treatment of this country's geography and history. (Rev: BL 2/1/88) [967.6]

4295 Hanmer, Trudy J. *Uganda* (6–10). Illus. 1989, Watts LB $11.90 (0-531-10816-3). A history of this troubled land with special emphasis on today's problems such as poverty, internal strife, AIDS, and hunger. (Rev: BL 1/15/90; BR 3–4/90; SLJ 12/89; VOYA 6/90) [967.6]

4296 *Kenya . . . in Pictures* (5–9). Illus. 1988, Lerner LB $9.95 (0-8225-1830-9). A current, concise guide to Kenya, its history, and its people. Others in this series are *Cote D'Ivoire . . . in Pictures* and *Senegal . . . in Pictures* (both 1988). (Rev: SLJ 11/88) [967.6]

4297 Maren, Michael. *The Land and People of Kenya* (6–9). Illus. 1989, Harper LB $14.89 (0-397-32335-2). The history, geography, and people of this African country are clearly presented in text and some photographs. (Rev: BL 9/15/89; BR 3–4/90; SLJ 10/89; VOYA 2/90) [916.76]

4298 Wolbers, Marian F. *Burundi* (6–8). Illus. 1989, Chelsea House $12.95 (1-55546-785-7). In text and pictures, this book offers a general introduction to the land and people of this African country. (Rev: BL 10/15/89; VOYA 2/90) [967]

North Africa

4299 Abebe, Daniel. *Ethiopia in Pictures* (5–8). Illus. 1988, Lerner $9.95 (0-8225-1836-8). Part of a lengthy series which introduces basic facts about a country through text and many photographs. Some of the other African nations covered in these books are: Tanzania, Egypt, Madagascar, Malawi, and Sudan. (Rev: BL 2/1/89) [963]

4300 *Egypt . . . in Pictures* (5–9). Rev. ed. Illus. 1988, Lerner LB $9.95 (0-8225-1840-6). A brief, current presentation of salient facts about Egypt and its people. (Rev: SLJ 5/89) [962]

4301 Fradin, Dennis B. *Ethiopia* (7–9). Illus. 1988, Childrens $22.60 (0-516-02706-9). An introduction to this country's past and present with special coverage on recent famines and political problems. (Rev: BL 2/15/89) [963]

4302 *Tunisia . . . in Pictures* (6–9). Illus. 1989, Lerner LB $9.95 (0-8225-1844-9). This account includes material on the geography, history, religion, and economy of Tunisia. Other titles in this series dealing with North Africa are: *Morocco in Pictures* and *Egypt in Pictures* (both 1988). (Rev: SLJ 9/89) [961]

South Africa

4303 Barnes-Svarney, Patricia. *Zimbabwe* (6–8). Illus. 1989, Chelsea House $12.95 (1-55546-799-7). A general account that introduces the salient facts and features of this African nation. (Rev: BL 10/15/89; BR 11–12/89) [968.91]

4304 Canesso, Claudia. *South Africa* (6–9). Illus. 1989, Chelsea House LB $12.95 (1-55546-790-3). A fine overview of the history, society, economics, and politics of this country. (Rev: SLJ 7/89; VOYA 8/89) [968]

4305 Griffiths, Ieuan. *The Crisis in South Africa* (6–9). Illus. 1988, Rourke LB $11.95 (0-86592-035-4). With generous use of photographs and brief text, this British import explains the internal situation in South Africa. (Rev: SLJ 2/89) [968]

4306 Harris, Sarah. *Timeline: South Africa* (5–9). Illus. 1988, Dryad $17.95 (0-8521-9724-1). A history of South Africa with particular emphasis on the roots of apartheid. (Rev: BL 1/15/89; BR 11–12/88; SLJ 1/89) [968]

4307 Hayward, Jean. *South Africa since 1948* (6–9). Illus. 1989, Bookwright LB $12.90 (0-531-18262-2). Reaching back to pre-1948 history, Hayward explains apartheid and present racial conditions in South Africa. (Rev: BL 1/1/90; SLJ 3/90; VOYA 4/90) [968.06]

4308 James, R. S. *Mozambique* (6–8). Illus. 1987, Chelsea House $11.95 (1-55546-194-8). A factual profile of this country that emphasizes

basic information on history, culture, and the economy. (Rev: BL 2/1/88) [967]

4309 Lawson, Don. *South Africa* (7–10). 1986, Watts $10.40 (0-551-10128-2). This book gives general information about South Africa but deals mainly with apartheid. (Rev: VOYA 12/86) [968]

4310 *Madagascar . . . in Pictures* (5–9). Rev. ed. Illus. 1988, Lerner LB $9.95 (0-8225-1841-4). This island country is well introduced in a concise text and fine illustrations. (Rev: SLJ 5/89) [959]

4311 Meyer, Carolyn. *Voices of South Africa: Growing Up in a Troubled Land* (7–10). 1986, Harcourt $14.95 (0-15-200637-0). An account based on interviews and a 5-week stay in South Africa. (Rev: BL 9/15/86; SLJ 11/86) [305.2]

4312 Pascoe, Elaine. *South Africa: Troubled Land* (7–12). Illus. 1987, Watts $11.90 (0-531-10432-X). A fine history of South Africa that traces the beginning of apartheid and other current problems. (Rev: BL 1/1/88; SLJ 2/88; VOYA 6/88) [968]

4313 Paton, Jonathan. *The Land and People of South Africa* (7–10). Illus. 1989, Harper LB $14.89 (0-397-32362-X). This account covers history, geography, and economics, but the emphasis is on the people and the tragedy of apartheid. (Rev: BL 12/15/89; SLJ 6/90; VOYA 6/90) [968]

4314 Sanders, Renfield. *Malawi* (6–8). Illus. 1987, Chelsea House $11.95 (1-55546-193-X). History, geography, ethnic makeup, and culture are discussed. (Rev: BL 2/1/88) [968.97]

4315 Stevens, Rita. *Madagascar* (6–8). Illus. 1987, Chelsea House $11.95 (1-55546-195-6). History, including slavery and colonization, is covered with geography and economics. (Rev: BL 2/1/88) [969]

4316 Stevens, Rita. *Venda* (7–12). Illus. 1989, Chelsea House LB $11.95 (1-55546-788-1). The story of one of the "homelands" set up for black South Africans by the apartheid-ridden white government. (Rev: SLJ 11/89) [968]

4317 *Zimbabwe . . . in Pictures* (5–9). Illus. 1988, Lerner LB $9.95 (0-8225-1825-2). A thorough introduction to the country formerly known as Rhodesia. (Rev: SLJ 6–7/88) [968.9]

West Africa

4318 Hathaway, Jim. *Cameroon in Pictures* (5–8). Illus. 1989, Lerner LB $11.95 (0-8225-1857-0). With many photographs, charts, and other illustrations, this is an easy introduction to this country. Many other African countries are also

286

included in this extensive series. (Rev: BL 9/15/89) [967]

4319 *Liberia . . . in Pictures* (5–9). Illus. 1988, Lerner LB $9.95 (0-8225-1837-6). An introduction to this country that describes its economic problems and political unrest. Some other African countries in this series are: *South Africa . . . in Pictures; Malawi . . . in Pictures; Tanzania . . . in Pictures* (all 1988). (Rev: SLJ 10/88) [966.6]

4320 Lutz, William. *Senegal* (6–8). Illus. 1987, Chelsea House $11.95 (1-55546-192-1). A physical description of the country is given plus other background information on history and culture. (Rev: BL 2/1/88) [966]

4321 Winslow, Zachery. *Togo* (6–8). Illus. 1987, Chelsea House $11.95 (1-55546-190-5). The information given on this coastal country includes history, physical description, culture, and problems. (Rev: BL 2/1/88) [966]

Asia

General and Miscellaneous

4322 Coblence, Jean-Michel. *Asian Civilizations* (6–8). Illus. 1988, Silver Burdett $15.96 (0-382-09483-2). An overview of the culture of Asian countries with emphasis on China, Japan, and India. (Rev: BL 1/1/89) [950]

4323 de Lee, Nigel. *Rise of the Asian Superpowers from 1945* (6–9). Illus. 1987, Watts $12.90 (0-531-10407-9). An account that chiefly outlines the post-World War II history of China and Japan. (Rev: BL 1/15/88; BR 9–10/88; SLJ 2/88) [950.42]

4324 Lightfoot, Paul. *The Mekong* (6–9). Illus. 1981, Silver Burdett $14.96 (0-382-06520-4). This important Asian river is described in terms of the lands through which it travels. [959.7]

4325 *Mysteries of the Ancient World* (6–9). Illus. 1979, National Geographic LB $9.50 (0-87044-259-7). All sorts of curiosities from ancient history are recounted and illustrated. [930]

China

4326 Bradley, John. *China: A New Revolution?* (6–9). Illus. 1990, Gloucester LB $11.90 (0-531-17203-1). A book about the recent history of China and material on the massacre in Tiananmen Square. (Rev: SLJ 6/90) [951]

4327 China Features Agency Staff. *We Live in China* (6–9). Illus. 1984, Bookwright LB $12.90 (0-531-04779-2). Through interviews with 28 people with different backgrounds, the diversity of life in China is explored. [951.05]

4328 Dures, Alan. *The Postwar World: China since 1949* (6–9). Illus. 1988, Batsford $19.95 (0-7134-5774-0). Forty years of Chinese history are covered in this concise, well-illustrated account. (Rev: SLJ 3/89) [951]

4329 Filstrup, Chris, and Janie Filstrup. *China: From Emperors to Communes* (6–8). 1983, Dillon $12.95 (0-87518-227-5). An account giving good background information on the history and people of China. [951]

4330 Fritz, Jean. *China's Long March: 6,000 Miles of Danger* (6–9). Illus. 1988, Putnam $14.95 (0-399-21512-3). A description of the legend-making 6,000-mile march of the Chinese Communists during the 1930s. (Rev: BL 3/1/88; SLJ 5/88) [951.04]

4331 Hacker, Jeffrey H. *The New China* (7–12). Illus. 1986, Watts $12.90 (0-531-10156-8). A review of the opening up of China in the mid-twentieth century from the Cultural Revolution through the mid-1980s. (Rev: BL 9/1/86; BR 11–12/86; SLJ 9/86) [951]

4332 Lawson, Don. *The Eagle and the Dragon: The History of U.S.–China Relations* (7–10). Illus. 1985, Harper LB $12.89 (0-690-04486-0). In addition to material on relations through the ages between the United States and China, this account gives a great deal of background Chinese history. (Rev: BL 11/15/85; BR 5–6/86; SLJ 12/85; VOYA 12/85) [327.5]

4333 Lawson, Don. *The Long March: Red China under Chairman Mao* (7–10). Illus. 1983, Harper LB $12.89 (0-690-04272-8). An account of the rise of communism in China and the part played by Mao. [951.04]

4334 Major, John S. *The Land and People of China* (6–9). Illus. 1989, Harper LB $14.89 (0-397-32337-9). An excellent overview of the history, geography, and culture of China in clear prose and some black-and-white photographs. (Rev: BL 9/15/89; BR 3–4/90; SLJ 10/89; VOYA 8/89) [951]

4335 Marrin, Albert. *Mao Tse-tung and His China* (7–12). Illus. 1989, Viking $14.95 (0-670-82940-4). The story of the Chinese regime that united its people under communism and then almost destroyed it with the Cultural Revolution. (Rev: BL 12/15/89; SLJ 2/90) [951.05]

4336 Murphy, Rhoads, ed. *China* (6–9). Illus. 1988, Gateway $16.95 (0-934291-26-8). A brief, simple introduction to this country, which includes history through 1987. (Rev: BL 12/1/88) [951]

4337 Newlon, Clarke. *China: The Rise to World Power* (7–10). 1983, Putnam LB $10.95 (0-396-08136-3). This account focuses on development in China from World War II onward. [951]

4338 Patent, Gregory. *Shanghai Passage* (5–8). Illus. 1990, Clarion $13.95 (0-89919-743-4). The story of the author's life in China as a youngster and of conditions in China during World War II. (Rev: BL 6/15/90) [951]

4339 Perl, Lila. *Red Star & Green Dragon: Looking at a New China* (7–10). Illus. 1983, Morrow LB $11.95 (0-688-01721-5). A history of China plus a description of life there. [951.05]

4340 Rau, Margaret. *Holding Up the Sky: Young People in China* (7–10). 1983, Dutton $12.50 (0-525-66718-0). A view of both urban and rural young people growing up in China. [951]

4341 Rau, Margaret. *The Minority Peoples of China* (7–10). Illus. 1982, Messner LB $9.29 (0-671-41545-X). A description of the 56 different minorities all living within the boundaries of present-day China. [305.8]

4342 Rau, Margaret. *Young Women in China* (7–12). Illus. 1989, Enslow LB $16.95 (0-89490-170-2). A history of the position of women in China from ancient days to the present plus interviews with over a dozen contemporary Chinese women. (Rev: BL 11/1/89; BR 3–4/90; SLJ 12/89; VOYA 4/90) [305.4]

4343 Ross, Stewart. *China since 1945* (7–12). Illus. 1989, Bookwright LB $12.90 (0-531-18220-7). An account of what caused the Communist revolution and the events in China since, ending with 1988. (Rev: BL 6/1/89; SLJ 8/89) [335.43]

4344 Rowland-Entwistle, Theodore. *Confucius and Ancient China* (4–8). Illus. 1987, Watts LB $12.40 (0-531-18104-4). After a brief biography of Confucius, the author supplies the reader with an introduction to early Chinese history. (Rev: SLJ 8/87) [951]

4345 Wolf, Bernard. *In the Year of the Tiger* (7–10). Illus. 1988, Macmillan LB $14.95 (0-02-793390-3). A photo-essay that deals with the everyday life of a Chinese peasant family in the rural southwest of the country. (Rev: SLJ 8/88; VOYA 12/88) [951]

4346 Wolff, Diane. *Chinese Writing: An Introduction* (5–9). Illus. 1975, Holt paper $2.75 (0-03-048946-6). Basic Chinese characters are illustrated and instructions are given for copying them. [652]

India

4347 *India . . . in Pictures* (6–9). Illus. 1989, Lerner LB $9.95 (0-8225-1852-X). A fine introduction to India in both text and pictures. Other recent titles in this series dealing with Asian countries are: *Sri Lanka . . . in Pictures; China . . . in Pictures;* and *Nepal . . . in Pictures* (all 1988). (Rev: SLJ 9/89) [954]

4348 Karan, P. P., ed. *India* (6–9). Illus. 1988, Gateway $16.95 (0-934291-30-6). An easily read account that covers history, resources, and how the inhabitants live. (Rev: BL 12/1/88) [954]

4349 Meyer, Carolyn. *A Voice from Japan: An Outsider Looks In* (7–12). 1988, Harcourt $14.95 (0-15-200633-8). An overview of Japan—its history, culture, traditions, religion, and social ways. (Rev: BL 11/15/88; SLJ 11/88) [952.04]

4350 Traub, James. *India: The Challenge of Change* (7–9). Rev. ed. Illus. 1985, Messner $10.29 (0-671-60460-0). A readable account that covers the history, culture, and geography of the country with material that ends at the mid-1980s. (Rev: BL 3/1/86; SLJ 2/86) [954]

Japan

4351 Davidson, Judith. *Japan: Where East Meets West* (6–9). 1983, Dillon $12.95 (0-87518-230-5). An introduction to Japan that emphasizes its history and culture. [952]

4352 *Japan in Pictures* (5–8). Illus. 1989, Lerner LB $11.95 (0-8225-1861-9). An introduction to this country through sparse text and many illustrations. This series covers many other Asian countries such as Pakistan, Taiwan, Thailand, and South Korea. (Rev: BL 9/15/89) [952]

4353 Pitts, Forrest R. *Japan* (6–9). Illus. 1988, Gateway $16.95 (0-934291-28-4). A variety of topics including history, geography, economics, and the people's life-styles are introduced in a simple text. (Rev: BL 12/1/88) [952]

4354 Roberson, John R. *Japan: From Shogun to Sony 1543–1984* (7–12). Illus. 1985, Macmillan $13.95 (0-689-31076-5). The history of Japan and its development from its first contacts with the Western world to the present. (Rev: BL 10/15/85; SLJ 12/85) [952]

4355 Stefoff, Rebecca. *Japan* (6–8). Illus. 1988, Chelsea House $11.95 (1-55546-199-9). A serviceable guide to this country, its culture, and life-styles. (Rev: BL 5/15/88) [952.04]

4356 Thurley, Elizabeth Fusae. *Through the Year in Japan* (7–12). Illus. 1986, David & Charles $19.95 (0-7134-4819-9). An exploration of how people live in Japan, with a separate chapter from each month of the year. (Rev: SLJ 2/87) [952]

Other Asian Lands

4357 Beckett, Ian. *Southeast Asia from 1945* (6–9). Illus. 1987, Watts $12.90 (0-531-10322-6). This account covers the problems that emerged after World War II and the Vietnam War as well as current areas of trouble. (Rev: BL 6/15/87) [959.053]

4358 Canesso, Claudia. *Cambodia* (6–8). Illus. 1989, Chelsea House $12.95 (1-55546-798-9). An introduction to this troubled Asian land in text and many photographs, some in color. (Rev: BL 10/15/89; VOYA 2/90) [959.6]

4359 Cole, Wendy M. *Vietnam* (6–10). Illus. 1989, Chelsea House LB $12.95 (1-55546-800-4). In addition to a history of Vietnam, this account tells about the land and its people. (Rev: VOYA 10/89) [957]

4360 Farley, Carol. *Korea: A Land Divided* (6–9). Illus. 1983, Dillon LB $12.95 (0-87518-244-5). In addition to a description of the land and culture of Korea, the reader is introduced to the 2 different regimes. [951.9]

4361 Friese, Kai. *Tenzin Gyatso, the Dalai Lama* (7–10). Illus. 1989, Chelsea House $17.95 (1-55546-836-5). This is part biography but mostly a discussion of Tibetan culture and history. (Rev: BL 2/15/90; BR 3–4/90; SLJ 3/90; VOYA 4/90) [294]

4362 Jacobs, Judy. *Indonesia: A Nation of Islands* (5–8). Illus. 1990, Dillon $12.95 (0-87518-423-5). A clear overview of the major Indonesian islands that covers history, customs, ethnic groups, economics, and life-styles. (Rev: SLJ 9/90) [959.8]

4363 McClure, Vimala. *Bangladesh: Rivers in a Crowded Land* (5–9). Illus. 1989, Dillon $12.95 (0-87518-404-9). Life in this third world country is described plus a generous introduction to its history and geography. (Rev: BL 11/1/89) [954.9]

4364 Major, John S. *The Land and People of Mongolia* (7–10). Illus. 1990, Harper LB $14.89 (0-397-32387-5). A revised, updated edition that

gives current information on the many Mongol groups and their way of life. (Rev: BL 6/15/90; SLJ 8/90; VOYA 6/90) [951.73]

4365 *Philippines in Pictures* (5–8). Illus. 1989, Lerner LB $11.95 (0-8225-1863-5). The history, geography, and people of this Pacific land are treated in text and photographs. Other lands in Asia are also included in this series, for example, *South Korea in Pictures* (1989). (Rev: BL 1/15/90) [959.9]

4366 Withington, William A. *Southeast Asia* (6–9). Illus. 1988, Gateway $16.95 (0-934291-32-2). Coverage includes material on 10 countries such as Vietnam, Laos, and the Philippines. (Rev: BL 12/1/88) [959]

4367 Wright, David K. *Vietnam* (5–9). Illus. 1989, Childrens $16.95 (0-516-02712-3). An introduction to the history of this country that begins in 1874 and stresses the Vietnam War. (Rev: SLJ 1/90) [959.7]

Australia and the Pacific Islands

4368 Ball, John. *We Live in New Zealand* (6–9). Illus. 1984, Bookwright LB $12.90 (0-531-04781-4). From over 20 interviews, a composite view of life in New Zealand emerges. [993.1]

4369 Crump, Donald J., ed. *Amazing Animals of Australia* (6–9). Illus. 1984, National Geographic LB $8.50 (0-87044-520-0). A colorful introduction to such animals as the kangaroo and platypus. [591.9]

4370 Lawson, Don. *The New Philippines* (7–10). 2nd ed. Illus. 1986, Watts $12.90 (0-531-10269-6). This account gives valuable background information on the history and geography of the Philippines as well as coverage on both Marcos and Aquino. (Rev: BL 11/15/86; BR 1–2/87) [959.9]

Europe

General and Miscellaneous

4371 Armitage, Paul. *The Common Market* (7–10). Illus. 1978, Silver Burdett LB $14.96 (0-382-06199-3). Information on the history and aims of the European Economic Community are given through the mid-1970s. [382.9]

4372 Roberts, Elizabeth. *Europe 1992: The United States of Europe?* (6–9). Illus. 1990, Gloucester LB $11.90 (0-531-17204-X). The focus of this book is a description of the 12-nation European community that is scheduled to be operating in 1992. (Rev: SLJ 6/90) [940]

Central Europe and the Balkans

4373 Barker, Peter. *Eastern Europe* (6–9). Illus. 1979, Silver Burdett LB $14.96 (0-382-06326-0). Such countries as Poland, Czechoslovakia, and those in the Balkans are described in an account now useful chiefly for background information. [947]

4374 Blackwood, Alan. *The Hungarian Uprising* (7–10). Illus. 1987, Rourke LB $10.95 (0-86952-032-X). The story of the heroic but tragic rebellion of November 1956 that sent shock waves through the Communist world. (Rev: SLJ 8/87) [943.9]

4375 Hintz, Martin. *Hungary* (7–9). Illus. 1988, Childrens $22.60 (0-516-02707-7). A good introduction to the history and geography of the country that ends before the fall of the Communist dictatorship. (Rev: BL 2/15/89) [943.9]

4376 Sharman, Tim. *The Rise of Solidarity* (7–10). Illus. 1987, Rourke LB $10.95 (0-86592-030-3). A history of the working classes in Poland after World War II, the emergence of the labor union movement, and the work of Lech Walesa are covered in this book. (Rev: SLJ 8/87) [943.8]

4377 Strom, Yale. *A Tree Still Stands: Jewish Youth in Eastern Europe Today* (6–12). Illus. 1990, Putnam $16.95 (0-399-22154-9). A photo-essay of the Jewish children from ages 7 to 20 growing up in Eastern Europe today. (Rev: BL 9/1/90) [947]

France

4378 Balerdi, Susan. *France: The Crossroads of Europe* (6–9). 1984, Dillon $12.95 (0-87518-248-8). A general introduction to the land and its people with coverage on folklore, customs, and life-styles. [944]

4379 Harris, Jonathan. *The Land and People of France* (6–9). Illus. 1989, Harper LB $14.89 (0-397-32321-2). A completely new work in an attractive format that gives up-to-date material on the history, geography, people, and culture of France. (Rev: BL 9/15/89; BR 3–4/90; SLJ 12/89; VOYA 8/89) [944]

4380 Harris, Nathaniel. *The Fall of the Bastille* (7–10). Illus. 1987, David & Charles LB $17.95 (0-8521-9670-9). A vivid account of the event that marks the beginning of the French Revolution. (Rev: SLJ 2/88) [944.04]

4381 Hills, C. A. R. *The Seine* (6–9). Illus. 1981, Silver Burdett LB $14.96 (0-382-06519-0). The course of the river through the countryside and particularly passing through Paris. [944]

4382 Luxardo, Hervé. *The French Revolution* (7–9). Illus. 1987, Silver Burdett LB $14.96 (0-382-09294-5). A brief account with many illustrations of the salient events and the consequences of the French Revolution. (Rev: BR 1–2/88; SLJ 3/88) [944.04]

4383 Sookram, Brian. *France* (5–8). Illus. 1990, Chelsea House $14.95 (0-7910-1111-9). In addition to good background information, this book discusses such contemporary problems as how France will be affected by the new trade arrangements within the European community. (Rev: BL 6/1/90; SLJ 7/90) [944]

Germany

4384 Gray, Ronald D. *Hitler and the Germans* (7–10). Illus. 1983, Lerner LB $8.95 (0-8225-1231-9). A brief illustrated account of the rise and fall of Adolf Hitler. [943.086]

4385 McKenna, David. *East Germany* (6–8). Illus. 1988, Chelsea House $11.95 (1-55546-197-2). A practical guide to the history, geography, culture, and the like, of the eastern part of Germany, written before the Berlin Wall came down. (Rev: BL 5/15/88) [943.1]

4386 Richardson, Nigel. *How and Why: The Third Reich* (7–10). 1988, David & Charles $17.95 (0-8521-9723-3). In a brief account the author describes the rise and fall of Hitler's Germany with background material that begins at World War I. (Rev: SLJ 12/88) [943]

4387 Shirer, William L. *The Rise and Fall of Adolf Hitler* (6–9). Illus. 1961, Random LB $7.99 (0-394-90547-4); paper $2.95 (0-394-86270-8). The life and times of the German dictator. [943.086]

4388 Westerfeld, Scott. *The Berlin Airlift* (6–9). Illus. 1989, Silver Burdett $16.98 (0-382-09833-1); paper $7.95 (0-382-09852-8). The story of how the United States and Western Europe overcame the East German blockade of West Berlin. (Rev: BL 11/1/89; BR 1–2/90; SLJ 12/89) [943.1]

4389 Williamson, David. *The Third Reich* (6–8). Illus. 1989, Watts LB $12.90 (0-531-18261-4). A useful brief guide to the rise and fall of Hitler's plan for a Germany that would dominate Europe. (Rev: BL 12/1/89) [943.086]

Great Britain and Ireland

4390 Andronik, Catherine M. *Quest for a King: Searching for the Real King Arthur* (6–9). Illus. 1989, Macmillan $12.95 (0-689-31411-6). A reconstruction of Anglo-Saxon history in England of the possibilities of the existence of King Arthur, Merlin, and of the famous knights. (Rev: BL 11/15/89; BR 3–4/90; SLJ 11/89; VOYA 12/89) [942.01]

4391 Atkins, Sinclair. *From Stone Age to Conquest* (7–10). Illus. 1986, Hulton paper $10.95 (0-7175-1305-X). A well-illustrated account of British history from prehistoric times to the Norman Conquest. (Rev: SLJ 4/86) [941.01]

4392 Fairclough, Chris. *We Live in Britain* (6–9). Illus. 1984, Bookwright LB $12.90 (0-531-04783-0). From interviews with 28 different people we learn about many facets of life in Britain. [941]

4393 Meek, James. *The Land and People of Scotland* (7–10). Illus. 1990, Harper LB $14.89 (0-397-32333-6). Current social, political, and economic information is given on Scotland plus background history and geography. (Rev: BL 12/15/89; SLJ 4/90) [941.1]

4394 Meyer, Carolyn. *Voices of Northern Ireland: Growing Up in a Troubled Land* (7–12). 1987, Harcourt $15.95 (0-15-200635-4). A cross-section of opinions is given about the struggle in Northern Ireland plus background history. (Rev: BL 12/1/87; SLJ 11/87; VOYA 4/88) [941]

4395 Mitchell, Graham. *The Napoleonic Wars* (5–9). Illus. 1990, Batsford $19.95 (0-7134-5729-5). This British import tells about the war chiefly from the British point of view and uses many quotes from original sources. (Rev: BR 3–4/90; SLJ 3/90) [944.05]

4396 Roop, Peter, and Connie Roop. *Stonehenge* (7–10). Illus. 1989, Greenhaven LB $12.95 (0-89908-066-9). The mystery of the Stonehenge, how it was constructed, and its significance are discussed in this account. (Rev: BL 3/1/90) [936.2]

4397 Sancha, Sheila. *The Luttrell Village: Country Life in the Middle Ages* (7–10). Illus. 1983, Harper LB $13.89 (0-690-04324-4). Life and activities in an English village of 1328 are revealed

in words and excellent drawings by the author. [942.03]

4398 *Shakespeare's England* (5–8). Illus. 1989, Marshall Cavendish LB $19.95 (0-86307-999-7). The careers of Shakespeare, Henry VIII, and Elizabeth I are highlighted in this lavishly illustrated account. (Rev: SLJ 7/90) [941]

4399 White-Thomson, Stephen. *Elizabeth I and Tudor England* (6–9). Illus. 1985, Watts LB $12.40 (0-531-18008-5). A portrait of Elizabethan England and of the monarch and the events associated with her reign. (Rev: SLJ 4/86) [941.05]

4400 Wigner, Annabel. *Timeline: Ireland* (7–10). Illus. 1989, David & Charles $19.95 (0-8521-9716-0). An explanation of how political, social, and historical factors contributed in producing the current situation in Northern Ireland. (Rev: SLJ 7/89) [941.5]

4401 Windrow, Martin. *The British Redcoat of the Napoleonic Wars* (7–10). Illus. 1986, Watts LB $11.90 (0-531-10082-0). The story of the common British soldier during the Napoleonic Wars, with some background material on the war itself. (Rev: BR 1–2/87; SLJ 11/86) [941.08]

Low Countries

4402 Ozer, Steve. *The Netherlands* (6–8). Illus. 1990, Chelsea House $14.95 (0-7910-1107-0). This account covers basic background material and also covers extensively the current living conditions in this progressive country. (Rev: BL 7/90) [949.2]

Scandinavia, Iceland, and Greenland

4403 Andersen, Ulla. *We Live in Denmark* (6–9). Illus. 1984, Bookwright LB $12.90 (0-531-04782-2). Various aspects of life in Denmark are explored through interviews with different people. [948.9]

4404 Anderson, Madelyn Klein. *Greenland: Island at the Top of the World* (7–10). Illus. 1983, Putnam LB $10.95 (0-396-08139-8). A history of this little-known country from the early Viking culture to the twentieth century. [998]

4405 Janeway, Elizabeth. *The Vikings* (6–8). 1981, Random paper $4.95 (0-394-84885-3). The exploits, explorations, and contributions of the Vikings are given. [936]

4406 Lander, Patricia, and Claudette Charbonneau. *The Land and People of Finland* (7–10). Illus. 1990, Harper LB $14.89 (0-397-32358-1). A clearly written book that covers the history, geography, culture, and people of this northern land. (Rev: BL 12/15/89; SLJ 4/90; VOYA 2/90) [948.9]

4407 Olsson, Kari. *Sweden: A Good Life for All* (6–8). 1983, Dillon $12.95 (0-87518-231-3). The country and how its people live are covered in this introduction to Sweden. [948]

Spain and Portugal

4408 Anderson, David. *The Spanish Armada* (5–9). Illus. 1988, Hampstead $11.90 (0-531-19505-8). A gripping account that gives background about Spain and England, the plan of attack, the battles, and the aftermath. (Rev: BL 1/15/89; SLJ 4/89) [942.05]

4409 Bristow, Richard. *We Live in Spain* (6–9). Illus. 1984, Bookwright LB $12.90 (0-531-04780-6). A diversity of people explain what it is like living in Spain. [946]

4410 Connatty, Mary. *The Armada* (7–12). Illus. 1988, Warwick LB $13.90 (0-531-19030-7). A well-researched account that stresses the issues and conflicts behind the actual battles. (Rev: SLJ 5/88) [946]

4411 Finkelstein, Norman H. *The Other 1492: Jewish Settlement in the New World* (6–9). Illus. 1989, Macmillan $12.95 (0-684-18913-5). The story of Spanish Jews and their expulsion in 1492 at the hands of the all-powerful Inquisition. (Rev: BL 11/1/89; SLJ 1/90; VOYA 2/90) [946]

4412 Harris, Nathaniel. *The Armada: The Decisive Battle* (7–12). Illus. 1987, David & Charles LB $17.95 (0-8521-9686-5). The account tells what happened during the sea battle involving the Armada and gives excellent background material on the cause of this war and its consequences in Europe. (Rev: BR 11–12/87; SLJ 3/88) [942.05]

4413 Katz, William Loren, and Marc Crawford. *The Lincoln Brigade: A Picture History* (7–12). Illus. 1989, Macmillan $14.95 (0-689-31406-X). A well-illustrated account of the young Americans who went to Spain as volunteers in the war against Franco. (Rev: BL 7/89; BR 11–12/89; SLJ 9/89) [946.081]

4414 Lawson, Don. *The Abraham Lincoln Brigade: Americans Fighting Fascism in the Spanish Civil War* (7–10). Illus. 1989, Harper LB $11.89 (0-690-04699-5). An account of the exploits of the Americans who went to Spain in the 1930s to fight against Franco's fascism. (Rev: BL 5/15/89; BR 11–12/89; SLJ 7/89; VOYA 10/89) [946.081]

4415 Woods, Geraldine. *Spain: A Shining New Democracy* (5–8). Illus. 1987, Dillon LB $12.95 (0-87518-340-5). An introduction to Spain that even includes some Spanish jokes and recipes. (Rev: SLJ 10/87) [946]

U.S.S.R.

4416 Anderson, Madelyn Klein. *Siberia* (6–9). Illus. 1988, Dodd $13.95 (0-396-08662-4). A description of the history and the people who live in this remote part of the Soviet Union. (Rev: BL 4/1/88; SLJ 6–7/88) [957]

4417 Baker, David. *The Soviet Air Force* (7–10). Illus. 1988, Rourke LB $11.95 (0-86625-331-9). A description of the strength of the Soviet Air Forces and the kinds of planes they have. Also use: *Soviet Forces in Space* (1988). (Rev: SLJ 3/89) [947]

4418 Feinstein, Stephen C. *Soviet Union in Pictures* (5–8). Illus. 1989, Lerner LB $11.95 (0-8225-1864-3). A brief but attractive introduction to the land and people of the Soviet Union. (Rev: BL 1/15/90) [947]

4419 Jackson, W. A. Douglas. *Soviet Union* (6–9). Illus. 1988, Gateway $16.95 (0-934291-34-9). An introduction to this massive country that gives simple information on basic topics. (Rev: BL 12/1/88) [947]

4420 Miller, David. *The Soviet Navy* (7–10). Illus. 1988, Rourke LB $11.95 (0-86652-336-X). In many photographs and text, the Soviet Navy is reviewed and its strengths assessed. Also use: *Soviet Rocket Forces* and *Soviet Submarines* (both 1988). (Rev: SLJ 3/89) [947]

4421 Resnick, Abraham. *Russia: A History to 1917* (6–9). Illus. 1983, Childrens LB $23.93 (0-516-02785-9). A basic account that covers Russian history from the ninth century to the revolution. [947]

4422 Ross, Stewart. *The Russian Revolution* (7–12). Illus. 1989, Bookwright LB $12.90 (0-531-18221-5). The causes of the revolution and its major events are outlined, and the reshaping of Russia into the U.S.S.R. by Lenin is described. (Rev: BL 6/1/89; SLJ 8/89) [947.08]

4423 Wood, Ernest. *The Soviet Army* (7–10). Illus. 1988, Rourke LB $11.95 (0-86652-334-3). The size and strength of the Soviet army is assessed in this heavily illustrated account. (Rev: SLJ 3/89) [947]

4424 Yost, Graham. *The KGB* (7–12). Illus. 1989, Facts on File $16.95 (0-8160-1940-1). An overview of U.S.-Soviet relations and a history of the Russian secret police from Stalin's time to the present. (Rev: BL 10/1/89; SLJ 11/89; VOYA 4/90) [363.3]

Middle East

General and Miscellaneous

4425 Batchelor, John, and Julie Batchelor. *The Euphrates* (6–9). Illus. 1981, Silver Burdett $14.96 (0-382-06518-2). A description of this historic river as it wends from Turkey to the Persian Gulf. [956.7]

4426 Ferrara, Peter L. *East vs. West in the Middle East* (7–9). 1983, Watts $12.90 (0-531-04543-9). An account of how the superpowers have played the power game for oil in the Middle East. [956]

4427 Messenger, Charles. *The Middle East* (7–10). 1987, Watts LB $12.90 (0-531-10539-3). An overview of the Middle East that discusses the conflicts that exist in terms of historical, economic, and social concerns. (Rev: BL 6/15/88; BR 9–10/88) [956]

4428 Osborne, Christine. *People at Work in the Middle East* (6–8). 1988, David & Charles $17.95 (0-7134-5571-3). Thirteen different occupations are discussed and brief information given on each country in this region. (Rev: BR 5–6/88) [956]

4429 Swanson, Glen. *Oil and Water: A Look at the Middle East* (7–9). Illus. 1981, Prentice $7.95 (0-13-633677-9). Though somewhat dated, this account gives good background material on the development of the Middle East. [956]

4430 Worth, Richard. *Israel and the Arab States* (7–10). 1983, Watts LB $12.90 (0-531-04545-5). This account begins with the partition of Palestine in 1948 and covers conditions until the early 1980s. [956]

Israel

4431 Ashabranner, Brent. *Gavriel and Jemal: Two Boys of Jerusalem* (6–9). Illus. 1984, Putnam $11.95 (0-396-08455-9). Two aspects of life

in Jerusalem as seen through the eyes of an Arab and a Jewish boy. [956.94]

4432 Carroll, Raymond. *The Palestine Question* (7–10). 1983, Watts LB $12.90 (0-531-04549-8). Now useful chiefly for background information, this account traces the roots of the conflict in Israel. [956]

4433 Clayton-Felt, Josh. *To Be Seventeen in Israel: Through the Eyes of an American Teenager* (7–12). Illus. 1987, Watts LB $12.90 (0-531-10249-1). The account of an American teenager's 5-week stay with a family in Israel. (Rev: SLJ 6–7/87; VOYA 8–9/87) [956.94]

4434 Harper, Paul. *The Arab-Israeli Conflict* (7–9). Illus. 1990, Watts LB $12.90 (0-531-18294-0). This account covers such topics as the birth of the Israeli state, the rise of Arab nationalism, and the present conflict. (Rev: BL 6/1/90; SLJ 5/90) [956]

4435 Rosenblum, Morris. *Heroes of Israel* (5–8). 1972, Fleet $9.50 (0-8303-0086-4). A collective set of profiles of people important in the history of Israel. [956.9]

4436 Stefoff, Rebecca. *West Bank/Gaza Strip* (5–8). Illus. 1988, Chelsea House $11.95 (1-55546-782-2). An objective look at the people, land, and history of these occupied lands. (Rev: BL 5/15/88) [956.95]

Other Middle East Lands

4437 Beaton, Margaret. *Syria* (7–9). Illus. 1988, Childrens $22.60 (0-516-02708-5). A fine introduction to this country central to the Arab-Israeli question. (Rev: BL 2/15/89) [956.91]

4438 Clifford, Mary Louise. *The Land and People of Afghanistan* (6–9). Illus. 1989, Harper LB $14.89 (0-397-32339-5). A thorough revision of the old edition with excellent new material and illustrations. (Rev: BL 9/15/89; BR 3–4/90; SLJ 9/89; VOYA 8/89) [958.1]

4439 Griffiths, John C. *The Conflict in Afghanistan* (6–9). Illus. 1988, Rourke LB $11.95 (0-86592-039-7). This well-illustrated account discusses the original reasons for Soviet intervention in Afghanistan, why they withdrew, and the results of their leaving. (Rev: SLJ 2/89) [958.1]

4440 Herda, D. J. *The Afghan Rebels: The War in Afghanistan* (7–9). Illus. 1990, Watts LB $12.90 (0-531-10897-X). A history of the 10-year struggle in Afghanistan from the invasion of the Russians to their withdrawal in 1989. (Rev: BL 8/90) [958.104]

4441 Husain, Akbar. *The Revolution in Iran* (6–9). Illus. 1988, Rourke LB $11.95 (0-86592-038-9). This book discusses the causes of the revolution, the political and religious factions inside Iran, and the events that led to the Shah's downfall. (Rev: BL 12/1/88; SLJ 2/89) [955]

4442 *Iraq in Pictures* (5–8). Illus. 1990, Lerner LB $11.95 (0-8225-1847-3). An updated glimpse through text and many photographs of this mideastern land. (Rev: BL 1/15/90) [956.7]

4443 *Jordan in Pictures* (5–8). Illus. 1988, Lerner $9.95 (0-8225-1834-1). Part of the Visual Geography series that introduces countries simply and effectively primarily through pictures. Another in this series is *Lebanon in Pictures* (1988). (Rev: BL 2/1/89) [956]

4444 *Kuwait . . . in Pictures* (6–9). Illus. 1989, Lerner LB $9.95 (0-8225-1846-5). Through text and pictures the land, people, economy, and culture of Kuwait are introduced. Other Middle Eastern lands in recent volumes from this series are: *Afghanistan in Pictures* (1988), *Lebanon in Pictures* (1989), and *Jordan in Pictures* (1988). (Rev: SLJ 9/89) [956]

4445 *Lebanon . . . in Pictures* (5–9). Rev. ed. Illus. 1988, Lerner LB $9.95 (0-8225-1832-5). Though the text is brief, this guide gives a good introduction to Lebanon, its peoples, and its problems. (Rev: SLJ 5/89) [956.9]

4446 Sanders, Renfield. *Iran* (5–8). Illus. 1990, Chelsea House $14.95 (0-7910-1104-6). As well as basic background material, this book describes Iran 10 years after the revolution and gives insights into its recent war with Iraq. (Rev: BL 6/1/90; SLJ 8/90) [955]

4447 *Saudi Arabia . . . in Pictures* (6–9). Illus. 1989, Lerner LB $9.95 (0-8225-1845-7). The most important aspects of life in this country are conveyed in text and pictures. Another Middle Eastern country in this series is: *Iran in Pictures* (1988). (Rev: SLJ 9/89) [956]

4448 Spencer, William. *The Land and People of Turkey* (7–10). Illus. 1989, Harper LB $14.89 (0-397-32364-6). The history, geography, and people of Turkey are examined with coverage of such other topics as Cyprus and the Armenian question. (Rev: BL 12/15/89; SLJ 7/90; VOYA 2/90) [956.1]

4449 *Turkey . . . in Pictures* (5–9). Illus. 1988, Lerner LB $9.95 (0-8225-1831-7). A general introduction to this mideast country that relies heavily on illustrations. Also use *Jordan . . . in Pictures* (1988). (Rev: SLJ 9/88) [956.1]

North and South America (excluding the United States)

4450 Pimlott, John. *South & Central America* (7–10). 1987, Watts LB $12.90 (0-531-10540-7). Conflicts in South and Central America involving historic, social, and economic factors. (Rev: BL 6/15/88; BR 9–10/88) [980]

General History and Geography

4451 *America's Magnificent Mountains* (7–9). Illus. 1980, National Geographic LB $9.50 (0-87044-286-4). A book that highlights the most famous mountains of North America. [917]

4452 *America's Majestic Canyons* (7–9). Illus. 1979, National Geographic LB $9.50 (0-87044-276-7). A number of North American canyons are highlighted plus their inhabitants. [917]

4453 Johnson, Raymond. *The Rio Grande* (6–9). Illus. 1981, Silver Burdett $14.96 (0-382-06521-2). A journey downstream on one of America's great rivers. [976.4]

4454 Karlowich, Robert A. *Rise Up in Anger: Latin America Today* (7–10). Illus. 1985, Messner $9.29 (0-671-46525-2). This account traces in terms of their history the roots of the social, political, and economic unrest in Central and South America today. (Rev: BL 8/85; BR 5–6/86; SLJ 9/85) [980]

4455 O'Neill, Thomas. *Lakes, Peaks, and Prairies: Discovering the United States-Canadian Border* (7–12). Illus. 1984, National Geographic LB $9.50 (0-87044-483-2). A trip across the continent that reveals much about the diversity of these regions. [973]

North America

GENERAL AND MISCELLANEOUS

4456 Barden, Renardo. *The Discovery of America* (6–9). Illus. 1990, Greenhaven LB $12.95 (0-89908-071-5). The exploits of the Vikings as well as exploits in Irish, Welsh, and African legends are retold in this search for the first discoverers of the New World. (Rev: BL 3/1/90; SLJ 5/90) [970.1]

4457 Beck, Barbara L. *The Ancient Maya* (6–9). Rev. ed. Illus. 1983, Watts LB $10.40 (0-531-04529-3). A brief history of the Mayas, their culture, downfall, and ruins still standing today. [972]

4458 Meyer, Carolyn, and Charles Gallenkamp. *The Mystery of the Ancient Maya* (7–10). Illus. 1985, Macmillan $12.95 (0-689-50319-9). In this volume the authors try to reconstruct the history, accomplishments, and way of life of the Mayas. (Rev: BL 3/15/85; SLJ 5/85) [972.81]

4459 Winks, Honor Leigh, and Robin W. Winks. *The St. Lawrence* (6–9). Illus. 1980, Silver Burdett LB $14.96 (0-382-06368-6). From the Gaspe to Niagara Falls the course of this historic river is traced. [971.4]

CANADA

4460 Anderson, Joan. *Pioneer Settlers of New France* (5–9). Illus. 1990, Dutton $15.95 (0-525-67291-5). A visit to the French settlement at Louisbourg in Nova Scotia during the early 1700s. (Rev: BL 6/1/90) [971.01]

4461 *Canada in Pictures* (5–8). Illus. 1989, Lerner LB $11.95 (0-8225-1870-8). An updated volume that covers salient features of Canada in brief text and many photographs. (Rev: BL 1/15/90) [971]

4462 Ray, Delia. *Gold! The Klondike Adventure* (6–9). Illus. 1989, Dutton $14.95 (0-525-67288-5). A well-organized account of the mass migration to the Yukon to find gold in 1897. (Rev: BL 11/15/89; VOYA 2/90) [971.9]

4463 Schultz, J. W. *Sinopah, the Indian Boy* (5–9). 1985, Confluence paper $7.95 (0-917652-42-8). The story of the Blackfeet Nation and of a boy who reached manhood in it. (Rev: BR 5–6/85) [970.004]

4464 Wartik, Nancy. *The French Canadians* (6–10). Illus. 1989, Chelsea House $16.95 (0-87754-879-X). A history of the French in Canada plus material on the status of this important minority in today's Canada. (Rev: BL 4/1/89; SLJ 6/89; VOYA 8/89) [971]

MEXICO

4465 Beck, Barbara L. *The Aztecs* (6–10). Rev. ed. Illus. 1983, Watts LB $10.40 (0-531-04522-6). A clearly written introduction to this ancient Mexican civilization. [972]

4466 Berdan, Frances F. *The Aztecs* (7–10). Illus. 1988, Chelsea House $16.95 (1-55546-692-3). An illustrated account of the rise and fall of this ancient Mexican civilization. (Rev: BL 3/1/89) [972]

4467 Epstein, Sam, and Beryl Epstein. *Mexico* (6–10). Rev. ed. Illus. 1983, Watts LB $10.40 (0-531-04530-7). An introduction to the life, history, and culture of Mexico and its peoples. [972]

4468 Marrin, Albert. *Aztecs and Spaniards: Cortes and the Conquest of Mexico* (7–10). Illus. 1986, Macmillan $12.95 (0-689-31176-1). The story of the decline and fall of the Aztec civilization and the Spanish conquistadors who caused it. (Rev: BL 4/15/86; SLJ 8/86; VOYA 2/87) [972.01]

4469 *Mexico . . . in Pictures* (7–10). Illus. 1987, Lerner LB $9.95 (0-8225-1801-5). An appealing look at Mexican geography and history as well as its people. (Rev: SLJ 8/87) [972]

4470 Millard, Anne. *The Incas* (6–9). Illus. 1980, Watts $10.95 (0-531-09171-6). Color photographs and drawings complement the text that describes the grandeur of the Inca civilization in the highlands of Peru. [980.004]

4471 Ochoa, George. *The Fall of Mexico City* (6–9). Illus. 1989, Silver Burdett LB $16.98 (0-382-09836-6); paper $7.95 (0-382-09853-6). An account of the American occupation of Mexico City during 1847 and 1848. (Rev: BL 11/1/89; BR 1–2/90; SLJ 12/89) [973]

4472 Rosenblum, Morris. *Heroes of Mexico* (5–8). 1972, Fleet $9.50 (0-8303-0082-1). A collected group of profiles of people important in the history of Mexico. [972]

4473 Smith, Eileen Latell. *Mexico: Giant of the South* (6–8). 1983, Dillon $12.95 (0-87518-242-9). This account introduces the life-styles and culture plus the history and geography of Mexico. [972]

4474 Stein, R. Conrad. *Mexico* (6–9). Illus. 1984, Childrens LB $23.93 (0-516-02772-7). A good introduction to the people and the land of Mexico. [972]

OTHER CENTRAL AMERICAN LANDS

4475 Bachelis, Faren. *The Central Americans* (6–9). Illus. 1989, Chelsea House $17.95 (1-55546-868-4). A history of modern Central America, an explanation for immigration of some residents to the United States, and a plea to change our policies toward them. (Rev: BL 2/1/90; VOYA 4/90) [972:8]

4476 Bachelis, Faren. *El Salvador* (5–8). Illus. 1990, Childrens LB $23.93 (0-516-02718-2). An introduction to the history, geography, and people of this small Central American country so frequently in the news. (Rev: BL 7/90) [972]

4477 Cheney, Glenn Alan. *El Salvador: A Country in Crisis* (7–10). Illus. 1990, Watts LB $12.90 (0-531-10916-X). Background information on the causes of the conflict in El Salvador is given and the problems as of the early 1980s. (Rev: SLJ 6/90; VOYA 8/90) [972.84]

4478 Cheney, Glenn Alan. *Revolution in Central America* (7–10). Illus. 1984, Watts LB $12.90 (0-531-04761-X). This book explores the conflicts in Central America and their status as of the early 1980s. [972.8]

4479 *Costa Rica . . . in Pictures* (7–10). Illus. 1987, Lerner LB $9.95 (0-8225-1805-8). An attractive introduction to the land, people, government, and economy of Costa Rica. Also use in this series: *El Salvador . . . in Pictures; Guatemala . . . in Pictures;* and *Honduras . . . in Pictures* (all 1987). (Rev: SLJ 6–7/87) [972.8]

4480 Gelman, Rita Golden. *Inside Nicaragua: Young People's Dreams and Fears* (7–12). Illus. 1988, Watts $13.90 (0-531-10538-5). A firsthand account of what it is like to be a teenager growing up in this troubled country. (Rev: BL 7/88; BR 11–12/88; SLJ 6–7/88) [972.85]

4481 Griffiths, John C. *The Crisis in Central America* (6–9). Illus. 1988, Rourke LB $11.95 (0-86592-034-6). In a brief, well-illustrated text, this book explains both internal conditions and American policy in Central America. (Rev: SLJ 2/89) [972.8]

4482 Jenness, Aylette, and Lisa W. Kroeber. *A Life of Their Own: An Indian Family in Latin America* (6–9). Illus. 1975, Harper $12.70 (0-690-00572-5). The life of the Hernandez family in Guatemala is described with material on how they work and live. [972.8]

4483 St. George, Judith. *Panama Canal: Gateway to the World* (5–9). 1989, Putnam $15.95 (0-399-21637-5). A vivid account of the problems and eventual triumph connected with the building of the Panama Canal. (Rev: BL 4/15/89; SLJ 4/89; VOYA 8/89) [972.87]

4484 Tessendorf, K. C. *Uncle Sam in Nicaragua* (7–10). Illus. 1987, Macmillan $12.95 (0-689-31286-5). An account of American involvement in Nicaragua and the history of the Sandinista-contra struggle. (Rev: BL 1/1/88; SLJ 12/87; VOYA 12/87) [327.7307285]

PUERTO RICO, CUBA, AND OTHER CARIBBEAN ISLANDS

4485 Anthony, Suzanne. *Haiti* (6–8). Illus. 1989, Chelsea House LB $13.95 (1-55546-796-2). A general introduction to the history, geography,

people, and problems of Haiti. (Rev: BR 11–12/89; VOYA 12/89) [972.94]

4486 *Dominican Republic in Pictures* (5–9). Illus. 1988, Lerner LB $9.95 (0-8225-1812-0). With the help of maps and many illustrations, this book gives a clear introduction to the country that shares Hispaniola with Haiti. (Rev: SLJ 4/88) [972.9]

4487 Hanmer, Trudy J. *Haiti* (5–8). Illus. 1988, Watts LB $9.90 (0-531-10479-6). A clear, objective introduction to this troubled island and its present problems. (Rev: SLJ 6–7/88) [972.9]

4488 *Puerto Rico . . . in Pictures* (7–10). Illus. 1987, Lerner LB $9.95 (0-8225-1821-X). An attractive introduction to this island that explains how it became a commonwealth. Also use in the same series: *Haiti . . . in Pictures* and *Panama . . . in Pictures* (both 1987). (Rev: SLJ 10/87) [972.9]

4489 Tuck, Jay, and Norma C. Vergara. *Heroes of Puerto Rico* (5–8). 1969, Fleet $9.50 (0-8303-0070-8). A series of profiles of famous Puerto Ricans. [972.9]

South America

4490 *Argentina . . . in Pictures* (5–9). Illus. 1988, Lerner LB $9.95 (0-8225-1807-4). An up-to-date view of this country told in brief text and many fine photographs. Also use: *Paraguay . . . in Pictures* (1988). (Rev: SLJ 5/88) [982]

4491 Beatty, Noëlle B. *Suriname* (6–8). Illus. 1987, Chelsea House $11.95 (1-55546-196-4). An account that gives straightforward information on the history and geography of this country. (Rev: BL 2/1/88) [988]

4492 Beck, Barbara L. *The Incas* (6–8). Rev. ed. 1983, Watts LB $10.40 (0-531-04528-5). A fine introduction to the interesting culture—its rise, flowering, and decline with the Spanish conquest. [985]

4493 Bender, Evelyn. *Brazil* (6–8). Illus. 1990, Chelsea House $14.95 (0-7910-1108-9). In addition to providing general background information, this account covers the economic problems of this developing country. (Rev: BL 7/90) [984]

4494 *Bolivia . . . in Pictures* (5–9). Rev. ed. Illus. 1987, Lerner $9.95 (0-8225-1808-2). A highly pictorial introduction to the history, geography, and people of Bolivia. Other Latin American countries included in these 1987 revisions in the series are: Colombia, Cuba, Nicaragua, Jamaica, and Peru. (Rev: BL 10/15/87) [984]

4495 *Brazil . . . in Pictures* (7–10). Illus. 1987, Lerner LB $9.95 (0-8225-1802-3). In color photographs and a few pages of text, Brazil and its people are introduced. (Rev: SLJ 8/87) [981]

4496 Carter, William E. *South America* (6–8). Rev. ed. 1983, Watts LB $10.40 (0-531-04531-5). Though somewhat dated, this account gives good background information on each country. [980]

4497 Cheney, Glenn Alan. *The Amazon* (6–12). Illus. 1984, Watts LB $10.40 (0-531-04818-7). The story of this mighty river and of the possible complete destruction of the rain forest it nourishes. [981]

4498 *Chile . . . in Pictures* (5–9). 1988, Lerner LB $9.95 (0-8225-1809-0). A basic introduction to the history, geography, people, and economics of Chile. (Rev: SLJ 10/88) [983]

4499 *Ecuador in Pictures* (5–9). Rev. ed. Illus. 1987, Lerner LB $9.95 (0-8225-1813-9). The land, history, people, and economy of Ecuador is pictorially presented with accompanying text. Also use: *Uruguay in Pictures* and *Venezuela in Pictures* (both 1987). (Rev: SLJ 3/88) [986.6]

4500 Fox, Geoffrey. *The Land and People of Argentina* (7–10). Illus. 1990, Harper LB $14.89 (0-397-32381-6). An extensive account dealing fully with history, economics, people, and current problems. (Rev: BL 5/1/90; VOYA 6/90) [982]

4501 Liebowitz, Sol. *Argentina* (6–8). Illus. 1990, Chelsea House $14.95 (0-7910-1106-2). A readable, illustrated account that covers basic material on the land and its people. (Rev: BL 5/1/90; VOYA 8/90) [982]

4502 Marrin, Albert. *Inca & Spaniard: Pizarro and the Conquest of Peru* (7–10). 1989, Macmillan $13.95 (0-689-31481-7). A fine introduction to the Incas, their Spanish conquerors, and the tragic struggle that ended their empire. (Rev: BL 10/15/89; BR 1–2/90; SLJ 11/89; VOYA 12/89) [985]

4503 Morrison, Marion. *Bolivia* (7–9). Illus. 1988, Childrens $22.60 (0-516-02705-0). The geography, history, culture, and economics of this country are introduced in this account that does not gloss over the poverty and illiteracy. (Rev: BL 2/15/89) [984]

4504 Peck, Robert McCracken. *Headhunters and Hummingbirds: An Expedition into Ecuador* (7–10). Illus. 1987, Walker LB $14.85 (0-8027-6646-3). An account of an ill-fated scientific expedition into the land of the Jívaro Indians in Ecuador. (Rev: SLJ 6–7/87; VOYA 8–9/87) [986]

4505 Peterson, Marge, and Rob Peterson. *Argentina: A Wild West Heritage* (5–9). Illus. 1990, Dillon LB $12.95 (0-87518-413-8). As well as information on the history, government, geography and economics of this country, the authors give good coverage of the people and how they live. (Rev: SLJ 7/90) [982]

4506 Strange, Ian J. *The Falklands: South Atlantic Islands* (6–9). Illus. 1985, Putnam $15.95 (0-396-08616-0). A history of these remote islands is given and an explanation of their present economy and problems. (Rev: BL 10/15/85; SLJ 10/85; VOYA 4/86) [997]

Polar Regions

4507 Asimov, Isaac. *How Did We Find Out about Antarctica?* (6–8). Illus. 1979, Walker LB $11.85 (0-8027-6371-5). A chronological account from early explorers like Drake to expeditions to the South Pole. [998]

4508 Osborn, Kevin. *The Peoples of the Arctic* (7–10). Illus. 1990, Chelsea House $17.95 (0-87754-876-5). This account describes the history and way of life of the Eskimos and Indians in the Arctic regions. (Rev: BL 6/15/90) [305.8]

4509 Yue, Charlotte, and David Yue. *The Igloo* (6–8). Illus. 1988, Houghton $13.95 (0-395-44613-9). This account describes the geography of the Arctic and the life led by the native Eskimos. (Rev: BR 9–10/89) [970.004]

United States

General History and Geography

4510 Andrist, Ralph K. *Steamboats on the Mississippi* (6–10). Illus. 1962, Troll LB $14.95 (0-8167-1530-0). A lavishly illustrated history of the role of the steamboat in the opening up of the middle West. [973.5]

4511 Arnold, Pauline, and Percival White. *How We Named Our States* (7–9). Illus. 1986, Harper $13.70 (0-200-71911-4). Early American history is retold in these stories behind the naming of our states and their capitals. [917.3]

4512 Crisman, Ruth. *The Mississippi* (6–9). Illus. 1984, Watts LB $10.40 (0-531-04826-8). From the headwaters in Minnesota to its mouth in the Gulf of Mexico this is the story of America's grandest river. [977]

4513 Dunnahoo, Terry. *U.S. Territories and Freely Associated States* (5–9). Illus. 1988, Watts $11.90 (0-531-10605-5). A description of those territories principally in the Caribbean and the Pacific Ocean that concentrates on the larger islands. (Rev: BL 1/15/89; BR 1–2/89; SLJ 3/89; VOYA 4/89) [973]

4514 Furlong, William Rea, and Byron Mc-Candless. *So Proudly We Hail: The History of the United States Flag* (7–12). Illus. 1981, Smithsonian Inst. paper $14.95 (0-87474-449-0). From the flags used by early settlers to today's stars and stripes, this is the evolution of our flag. [929.9]

4515 Gardner, Robert, and Dennis Shortelle. *The Future and the Past: Life 100 Years from Now and 100 Years Ago* (6–9). Illus. 1989, Messner LB $11.98 (0-671-65742-9). This volume supplies a contrast concerning American middle-class life—past, present, and future. (Rev: BR 1–2/90; SLJ 10/89; VOYA 2/90) [973]

4516 Haban, Rita D. *How Proudly They Wave: Flags of the Fifty States* (4–9). Illus. 1989, Lerner $16.95 (0-8225-1799-X). Each of the state flags is pictured, and historical background is also given. (Rev: BL 12/15/89; SLJ 3/90) [929.9]

4517 Lawson, Don. *Famous Presidential Scandals* (7–10). Illus. 1990, Enslow LB $15.95 (0-89490-247-4). The 4 scandals discussed occurred during the administrations of Grant, Harding, Nixon, and Reagan. (Rev: BL 6/15/90) [973]

4518 McCall, Edith. *Biography of a River: The Living Mississippi* (7–10). Illus. 1990, Walker LB $17.85 (0-8027-6915-2). The story of the role the Mississippi River has played in the history of the United States. (Rev: SLJ 9/90) [977]

4519 Newhouse, Elizabeth L., ed. *The Story of America: A National Geographic Picture Atlas* (5–9). Illus. 1984, National Geographic LB $21.95 (0-87044-535-9). A profusely illustrated account that also includes many maps on American history. (Rev: BL 1/15/85) [973]

4520 Parrish, Thomas. *The American Flag* (7–12). Illus. 1973, Simon & Schuster $7.95 (0-671-65204-4). The story of our flag told through illustrations and incidents that changed its composition. [929.9]

4521 Ross, Wilma. *Fabulous Facts about the Fifty States* (7–9). 1986, Scholastic paper $1.95 (0-590-33958-3). For each of the states, basic and sometimes unusual information is given. [973]

4522 Scott, John Anthony. *The Facts on File History of the American People* (7–10). 1990, Facts on File $24.95 (0-8160-1739-5). From prehistoric times to the Vietnam War, this is a clear, succinct account. (Rev: BL 4/15/90; SLJ 4/90; VOYA 8/90) [973]

4523 Shapiro, Irwin. *Story of Yankee Whaling* (6–10). Illus. 1959, Troll LB $14.95 (0-8167-1531-9). A history of the American whaling industry told in lucid text and many illustrations. [973]

4524 *Wilderness U.S.A.* (7–10). Illus. 1973, National Geographic $9.95 (0-87044-116-7). Fifteen areas in the United States that are unspoiled wilderness are described. [574.9]

4525 Williams, Earl P. *What You Should Know about the American Flag* (4–9). 1987, Maryland Historical Pr. paper $5.95 (0-917882-25-3). A history of the flag and persons connected with it plus information on how to display it properly. (Rev: BL 11/15/87) [929.9]

4526 Winks, Honor Leigh, and Robin W. Winks. *The Colorado* (6–9). Illus. 1980, Silver Burdett LB $14.96 (0-382-06372-4). An account that traces the route of the river from its beginning to the Gulf of California. [979.1]

Historical Periods

INDIANS OF NORTH AMERICA

4527 Ashabranner, Brent. *Morning Star, Black Sun: The Northern Cheyenne Indians and America's Energy Crisis* (7–10). Illus. 1982, Putnam $11.95 (0-396-08045-6). How the Northern Cheyenne Indians have fought for over 100 years to keep their land. [970.004]

4528 Baird, W. David. *The Quapaws* (6–10). Illus. 1989, Chelsea House LB $16.95 (1-55546-728-8). A history of this Indian tribe that originally lived where the Arkansas and Mississippi rivers meet that also contains information on culture, population, and present status. (Rev: VOYA 8/89) [970.004]

4529 Bee, Robert L. *The Yuma* (6–10). Illus. 1989, Chelsea House $16.95 (0-55546-737-7). A history of this tribe plus information on present problems. (Rev: BL 8/89; BR 1–2/90) [973]

4530 Bonvillain, Nancy. *The Huron* (6–9). Illus. 1989, Chelsea House $16.95 (1-55546-708-3). A study of the history of this tribe and its treatment by the invading white man. (Rev: BL 11/15/89; SLJ 3/90; VOYA 2/90) [971.3]

4531 Calloway, Colin G. *The Abenaki* (6–10). Illus. 1989, Chelsea House LB $16.95 (1-55546-687-7). In addition to a history of this tribe, the author tells about its members' life-styles and beliefs. (Rev: SLJ 11/89; VOYA 12/89) [970]

4532 Clifton, James A. *The Potawatomi* (6–9). Illus. 1987, Chelsea House $16.95 (1-55546-725-3). A history of this tribe that lived in the Upper Great Lakes with material on their present-day life-style. (Rev: BL 11/1/87; SLJ 1/88) [970]

4533 Dobyns, Henry F. *The Pima-Maricopa* (6–10). Illus. 1989, Chelsea House $16.95 (1-55546-724-5). The history, culture, and present status of these Indian tribes with several illustrations. Part of an extensive Indians of North America series. (Rev: BL 8/89; BR 1–2/90; SLJ 1/90) [979]

4534 Ehrlich, Amy, adapt. *Wounded Knee: An Indian History of the American West* (7–10). Illus. 1975, Dell paper $1.50 (0-440-95768-0). An adaptation for young readers of Dee Brown's *Bury My Heart at Wounded Knee* about the tragic wars against the Indians from 1860 to 1890. [970.004]

4535 Faulk, Odie B., and Laura E. Faulk. *The Modoc* (7–10). Illus. 1988, Chelsea House $16.95 (1-55546-716-4). The history of the Indian tribes now close to extinction whose home was in Oregon and Northern California. (Rev: BL 6/1/88) [970.004]

4536 Feest, Christian F. *The Powhatan Tribes* (7–10). Illus. 1990, Chelsea House $17.95 (1-55546-726-1). A description of the Indian federation of groups that came into being in the sixteenth century. (Rev: BL 2/1/90) [973]

4537 Fowler, Loretta. *The Arapaho* (6–10). Illus. 1989, Chelsea House $17.95 (1-55546-690-7). An account that supplies accurate background material on this tribe and how they have fared in the past and present at the hands of the white man. (Rev: BL 8/89) [973]

4538 Franklin, Robert J. *The Paiute* (6–9). Illus. 1990, Chelsea House $17.95 (1-55546-723-7). In this detailed account, both the past and the present of this Indian tribe are discussed in detail. (Rev: BL 6/15/90) [970.004]

4539 Gallant, Roy A. *Ancient Indians: The First Americans* (7–10). Illus. 1989, Enslow $13.95 (0-89490-187-7). A history of the American Indians from their arrival from Asia to the formation of tribes. (Rev: BL 7/89; SLJ 4/89) [970.01]

4540 Garbarino, Merwyn S. *The Seminole* (6–10). Illus. 1989, Chelsea House LB $16.95 (1-55546-729-6). Both the past and the present of the Seminole are covered with the inclusion of some folktales, biographical sketches, and many illustrations. (Rev: BL 12/1/88; SLJ 5/89; VOYA 4/89) [970.004]

4541 Graymont, Barbara. *The Iroquois* (6–10). Illus. 1988, Chelsea House LB $16.95 (1-55546-709-1). The story of the history and the culture of the Iroquois from about 1450 when the tribal union took place to the present day. (Rev: BL 12/1/88; SLJ 5/89; VOYA 4/89) [970.004]

4542 Grumet, Robert S. *The Lenapes* (6–9). Illus. 1989, Chelsea House $17.95 (1-55546-712-1). This tribe of the Delaware Indians is highlighted in this account that concentrates on the history, culture, and present status of this group. (Rev: BL 11/15/89; VOYA 2/90) [975.1]

4543 Harlan, Judith. *American Indians Today: Issues and Conflicts* (7–12). Illus. 1987, Watts $12.90 (0-531-10325-0). This account concentrates on the presents conditions on Indian reservations and how Indians are trying to get both independence and stature. (Rev: BL 6/1/87; BR 9–10/87; SLJ 8/87; VOYA 8–9/87) [973]

4544 Hirschfelder, Arlene. *Happily May I Walk: American Indians and Alaskan Natives Today* (6–9). Illus. 1986, Macmillan LB $13.95 (0-684-18624-1). Stereotypes of Indians and Eskimos are shattered in this account of how they live today and the problems they face. (Rev: SLJ 1/87) [970.004]

4545 Hoig, Stan. *The Cheyenne* (7–10). Illus. 1989, Chelsea House $16.95 (1-55546-696-6). In addition to a history of this Indian tribe, the book gives an account of its present-day conditions. (Rev: BL 3/1/89; VOYA 6/89) [973]

4546 Hook, Jason. *Sitting Bull and the Plains Indians* (4–8). Illus. 1987, Watts LB $12.40 (0-531-18012-2). This account not only discusses the life of Sitting Bull but also tells about the history and culture of the Plains Indians. (Rev: SLJ 8/87) [970.004]

4547 Hoover, Herbert T. *The Yankton Sioux* (7–10). Illus. 1988, Chelsea House LB $16.95 (1-55546-736-9). This account concentrates on one of the branches of the Sioux but gives a history of the entire Sioux federation. (Rev: SLJ 3/88) [970.004]

4548 Hoxie, Frederick E. *The Crow* (6–9). Illus. 1989, Chelsea House $17.95 (1-55546-704-0). This Great Plains tribe is discussed in terms of their history, life-style, and relations with the white man. (Rev: BL 11/15/89; VOYA 4/90) [971.3]

4549 Iverson, Peter. *The Navajos* (6–9). Illus. 1990, Chelsea House $17.95 (1-55546-719-9). An introduction to the history and culture of the Navajos and their relationship with the federal government. (Rev: BL 6/15/90; VOYA 8/90) [970.004]

4550 Jacobson, Daniel. *Indians of North America* (7–9). 1983, Watts $10.40 (0-531-04647-8). An alphabetically arranged book covering basic facts about Native Americans. [970]

4551 Kelly, Lawrence C. *Federal Indian Policy* (7–10). Illus. 1989, Chelsea House $17.95 (1-55546-706-7). A historical account of the often shameful treatment American Indians received from the federal government. (Rev: BL 2/1/90; SLJ 4/90; VOYA 4/90) [323.1]

4552 McKee, Jesse O. *The Choctaw* (6–9). Illus. 1989, Chelsea House $16.95 (1-55546-699-0). The story of this southern Indian tribe, their legends, and way of life as well as their status today. (Rev: BL 7/89; VOYA 10/89) [973]

4553 Melody, Michael E. *The Apache* (7–10). Illus. 1988, Chelsea House $16.95 (1-55546-689-3). Both past and present history of this tribe are given along with coverage on culture and social conditions. (Rev: BL 3/1/89) [973]

4554 Merrell, James H. *The Catawbas* (6–10). 1989, Chelsea House LB $16.95 (1-55546-694-X). The history and culture of this tribe that lived on the Atlantic side of the Appalachians are given plus its members' conversion to Mormonism and life-styles today. (Rev: VOYA 8/89) [970.004]

4555 Nabokov, Peter, ed. *Native American Testimony* (7–12). Illus. 1978, Harper paper $7.95 (0-06-131993-7). An anthology of original source materials that tells the history of the American Indian over a 400-year period. [970.004]

4556 Ourada, Patricia K. *The Menominee* (6–9). Illus. 1990, Chelsea House $17.95 (1-55548-715-6). Many photographs are used to amplify this detailed description of the history and life-style of this Indian tribe. (Rev: BL 6/15/90) [970.004]

4557 Perdue, Theda. *The Cherokee* (7–10). Illus. 1988, Chelsea House $16.95 (1-55546-695-8). An overview of the history of this tribe is given plus a glimpse of the federal regulations that now govern its existence. (Rev: BL 3/1/89) [973]

4558 Porter, Frank W. *The Coast Salish Peoples* (6–9). Illus. 1989, Chelsea House $17.95 (1-55546-701-6). The home territory of this tribe is highlighted plus information on how these Indians lived and their fate at the hands of the white man. (Rev: BL 11/15/89) [970.004]

4559 Porter, Frank W. *The Nanticoke* (6–8). Illus. 1987, Chelsea House $17.95 (1-55546-686-9). A history of the Nanticoke who originally occupied the shore regions of Maryland and Delaware. (Rev: BL 9/1/87; SLJ 6–7/87) [973]

4560 Rachlis, Eugene. *Indians of the Plains* (6–10). Illus. 1960, Troll LB $14.95 (0-8167-1524-6). A general history of the Plains Indians, their tribes, culture, and their contacts with white men. [973.5]

4561 Rollings, Willard H. *The Comanche* (6–9). Illus. 1989, Chelsea House $16.95 (1-55546-702-4). With a text supplemented by actual accounts and a number of illustrations, this book tells of the history and culture of this important tribe. Part of an extensive Indians of North American series. (Rev: BL 11/15/89; BR 1–2/90; VOYA 12/89) [973]

4562 Schuster, Helen H. *The Yakima* (6–9). Illus. 1990, Chelsea House $17.95 (1-55546-735-0). The history, culture, religion, and present condition of this northwestern tribe are discussed in detail in this account. (Rev: BL 6/15/90) [970.004]

4563 Simmons, William S. *The Narragansett* (6–10). Illus. 1989, Chelsea House LB $16.95 (1-55546-718-0). An interesting profile of this northeastern Indian tribe that supplies details about its history and culture. (Rev: SLJ 11/89; VOYA 8/89) [970]

4564 Snow, Dean R. *The Archaeology of North America* (6–12). Illus. 1989, Chelsea House $16.95 (1-55546-691-5). A comprehensive and somewhat difficult history of the first inhabitants of North America through the conquest of their land by the white man. (Rev: BL 5/1/89; SLJ 7/89; VOYA 8/89) [973]

4565 Trafzer, Clifford E. *The Chinook* (6–9). Illus. 1990, Chelsea House $17.95 (1-55546-689-2). A detailed account about this northwestern tribe, how they lived, and their conditions today. (Rev: BL 6/15/90) [970.004]

4566 Tunis, Edwin. *Indians* (7–10). Rev. ed. Illus. 1979, Harper LB $24.89 (0-690-01283-7). Nine different tribes and the way they lived are highlighted in this excellently author illustrated account. [970.004]

4567 Weinstein-Farson, Laurie. *The Wampanoag* (7–9). Illus. 1988, Chelsea House $16.95 (1-55546-733-4). A detailed account of the history and fate of the Indian tribe that first greeted the Pilgrims. (Rev: BL 12/1/88; VOYA 4/89) [973]

4568 Wilson, Terry P. *The Osage* (7–9). Illus. 1988, Chelsea House $16.95 (1-55546-722-9). The history, culture, and present status of the Indian tribe are given in this detailed account. (Rev: BL 12/1/88) [973]

4569 Wunder, John R. *The Kiowa* (6–9). Illus. 1989, Chelsea House $16.95 (1-55546-710-5). The story of the nomadic hunters of the plains, the Kiowa, and the effects of the white man's invasion of their land. (Rev: BL 7/89; VOYA 10/89) [973]

4570 Yue, Charlotte, and David Yue. *The Pueblo* (6–8). Illus. 1986, Houghton $12.95 (0-395-38350-1). A description of how a pueblo is constructed, how its design has changed, and how it is used today. (Rev: BL 7/86; VOYA 12/86) [979]

4571 Yue, David, and Charlotte Yue. *The Tipi: A Center of Native American Life* (6–8). Illus. 1984, Knopf LB $10.99 (0-394-96177-3). In simple language and many drawings the role of the tipi in the life of the Plains Indians is explained. [970.004]

DISCOVERY AND EXPLORATION

4572 Meltzer, Milton. *Columbus and the World around Him* (7–10). 1990, Watts LB $14.90 (0-531-10899-6). A handsome addition to the literature about Columbus that also deals with the culture and attitudes of the Spanish at the time. (Rev: BL 4/15/90; SLJ 7/90) [970.01]

COLONIAL PERIOD AND FRENCH AND INDIAN WARS

4573 Daugherty, James. *Landing of the Pilgrims* (6–8). 1987, Random paper $2.95 (0-394-84697-4). A history of the first 3 years of the colony at Plymouth. [974.4]

4574 Fishwick, Marshall W. *Jamestown, First English Colony* (6–10). Illus. 1965, Troll LB $14.95 (0-8167-1525-4). The life of this ill-fated colony is re-created with extraordinary illustrations and clear text. [973.2]

4575 Jackson, Shirley. *The Witchcraft of Salem Village* (6–9). Illus. 1956, Random LB $8.99 (0-394-90369-2). The causes and incidents involved in the Salem witchcraft trials of the seventeenth century. [133.4]

4576 Madison, Arnold. *How the Colonists Lived* (6–10). Illus. 1981, McKay $8.95 (0-679-20685-X). A chronological review of the different colonists and their life-styles. [973.2]

4577 Marrin, Albert. *Struggle for a Continent: The French and Indian Wars, 1690–1760* (6–9). Illus. 1987, Macmillan $13.95 (0-689-31313-6). A vivid re-creation of the events and personalities of these wars and how they helped lead to the Revolution. (Rev: BL 1/15/88; SLJ 12/87; VOYA 10/87) [973.2]

4578 Perl, Lila. *Slumps, Grunts, and Snickerdoodles: What Colonial America Ate and Why* (7–9). Illus. 1975, Clarion $13.95 (0-395-28923-8). A description of what was eaten in the various colonies plus 13 recipes from the period. [641.5]

4579 Starkey, Marion. *The Visionary Girls: Witchcraft in Salem Village* (7–9). 1973, Little $15.95 (0-316-81087-8). The story of the Salem witch hunts and of the hundreds of women who were accused of dealing with the devil. [133.4]

4580 Tunis, Edwin. *Colonial Craftsmen and the Beginnings of American Industry* (6–9). Illus. 1976, Harper $24.70 (0-690-01062-1). A variety of trades like papermaking and shipbuilding are pictured as they were practiced in Colonial times. [670]

4581 Tunis, Edwin. *Colonial Living* (7–10). Illus. 1976, Harper $24.70 (0-690-01063-X). Through detailed drawings and text, both by the author, the daily life of the colonists is explored. [973.2]

4582 Tunis, Edwin. *The Tavern at the Ferry* (7–10). Illus. 1973, Harper $24.70 (0-690-00099-5). This volume illustrates in drawing and text the growth of transportation and commerce in colonial times and continues to the onset of the Revolutionary War. [973.2]

4583 Zeinert, Karen. *The Salem Witchcraft Trials* (6–9). Illus. 1989, Watts LB $11.90 (0-531-10673-X). A vivid account of the hysteria that enveloped Salem and of the 19 people who lost their lives as a result. (Rev: BL 4/15/89; BR 9–10/89; SLJ 6/89; VOYA 10/89) [345.744]

4584 Ziner, Feenie. *Pilgrims and Plymouth Colony* (6–10). Illus. 1961, Troll LB $14.95 (0-8167-1528-9). This is a fine account of the Massachusetts colony and the people who founded it, with many illustrations and maps, many in color. [973.2]

REVOLUTIONARY PERIOD AND THE YOUNG NATION (1775–1809)

4585 Bliven, Bruce, Jr. *The American Revolution, 1760–1783* (6–9). Illus. 1958, Random LB $8.99 (0-394-90383-8); paper $2.95 (0-394-84696-6). A concise account of the causes, battles, and results of the Revolution. [973.3]

4586 Carter, Alden R. *Colonies in Revolt* (6–9). 1988, Watts LB $10.40 (0-531-10576-8). This volume covers the years before the Revolution and ends with the battles of Lexington and Concord. The end of the Revolution and the writing of the Constitution are described in *Birth of a Republic* (1988). (Rev: SLJ 11/88) [973.3]

4587 Carter, Alden R. *Darkest Hours: The American Revolution* (6–9). Illus. 1988, Watts LB $10.40 (0-531-10578-4). The story of the important battles in the American Revolution and how each battle changed the course of history. (Rev: SLJ 1/89) [973.3]

4588 Commager, Henry Steele. *The Great Declaration: A Book for Young Americans* (7–9). Illus. 1958, Bobbs-Merrill $7.50 (0-672-50301-8). A very readable account of the drafting of the Declaration of Independence. [973.3]

4589 Davis, Burke. *Black Heroes of the American Revolution* (7–9). Illus. 1976, Harcourt $13.95 (0-15-208560-2). A book that highlights the contributions of a group of black patriots who fought for freedom. [973.3]

4590 De Pauw, Linda Grant. *Founding Mothers: Women in America in the Revolutionary Era* (7–10). Illus. 1975, Houghton $13.95 (0-395-21896-9). The role of women during the Revolutionary War period. [305.4]

4591 Faber, Doris, and Harold Faber. *The Birth of a Nation: The Early Years of the United States* (6–9). Illus. 1989, Macmillan $13.95 (0-684-19007-9). This history that uses original sources extensively covers the first 8 years of the United States from 1789 to 1797. (Rev: BL 9/1/89; BR 1–2/90; SLJ 7/89; VOYA 10/89) [973.4]

4592 Hilton, Suzanne. *We the People: The Way We Were, 1783–1793* (7–9). 1981, Westminster $12.95 (0-664-32685-4). This book describes how Americans lived in the first years of independence. [973.4]

4593 Holley, Erica. *How and Why: The American Revolution* (6–9). Illus. 1987, David & Charles $19.95 (0-8521-9664-4). This British import tells about the Revolution objectively but from a different point of view. (Rev: BR 9–10/87; SLJ 8/87) [973.3]

4594 McDowell, Bart. *The Revolutionary War: America's Fight for Freedom* (7–12). Illus. 1967, National Geographic $7.95 (0-87044-047-0). In 200 illustrations, many maps, and concise text, the major events of the Revolution are re-created. [973.3]

4595 McPhillips, Martin. *The Battle of Trenton* (5–9). Illus. 1985, Silver Burdett paper $7.95 (0-382-09900-1). In addition to a description of this battle, the author gives good general background material on the entire Revolution. (Rev: SLJ 11/85) [973.3]

4596 Marrin, Albert. *The War for Independence: The Story of the American Revolution* (6–9). 1988, Macmillan $15.95 (0-689-31390-X). The great 8-year war that brought America's independence is well re-created along with the colorful characters involved in it. (Rev: BL 7/88; BR 11–12/88; SLJ 6–7/88; VOYA 6/88) [973.3]

4597 Meltzer, Milton, ed. *The American Revolutionaries: A History in Their Own Words, 1750–1800* (7–10). 1987, Harper $13.95 (0-690-04641-3). Excerpts from letters, diaries, and other first-person accounts make the Revolution and the people involved come to life. (Rev: BL 6/1/87; SLJ 6–7/87; VOYA 10/87) [973.3]

4598 Phelan, Mary Kay. *The Story of the Boston Massacre* (6–9). Illus. 1976, Harper $13.70 (0-690-00716-7). The events leading up to the massacre, the event itself, and its aftermath are described in vivid narrative. [973.3]

4599 Russell, Francis. *Lexington, Concord and Bunker Hill* (6–10). Illus. 1963, Troll LB $14.95 (0-8167-1526-2). The story of 3 of the early battles of the Revolution that also contains lavish illustrations. [973.3]

NINETEENTH CENTURY TO THE CIVIL WAR (1809–1861)

4600 Evitts, William J. *Captive Bodies, Free Spirits: The Story of Southern Slavery* (5–8). Illus. 1985, Messner $9.79 (0-671-54094-7). This is a story of slavery in the southern states and the fight against it. (Rev: BL 2/1/86; SLJ 3/86; VOYA 6/86) [305.8]

4601 Fisher, Leonard Everett. *The Alamo* (5–8). Illus. 1987, Holiday $13.95 (0-8234-0646-6). In text, photos, and drawings the author re-creates the heroic siege and fall of the Alamo in 1836. (Rev: BL 5/15/87; SLJ 6–7/87) [976.4]

4602 Freedman, Florence. *Two Tickets to Freedom: The True Story of Ellen & William Craft, Fugitive Slaves* (5–9). 1989, Bedrick $12.95 (0-87226-330-4); paper $4.95 (0-87226-221-9). The story of 2 courageous married slaves and their flight to Canada and freedom. (Rev: BR 3–4/90) [973.5]

4603 Lawson, Don. *The United States in the Mexican War* (7–9). Illus. 1976, Harper LB $12.89 (0-690-04723-1). The story of the war in which the United States gained California, Texas, and New Mexico. [973.6]

4604 Lyon, Jane D. *Clipper Ships and Captains* (6–10). Illus. 1962, Troll LB $14.95 (0-8167-1519-X). The history of the clipper ships and the men who worked on them is given in this account particularly noted for its illustrations. [973.5]

4605 Marrin, Albert. *1812: The War Nobody Won* (5–9). Illus. 1985, Macmillan $12.95 (0-689-31075-7). An account that brings both the events and the personalities involved alive. (Rev: BL 8/85; SLJ 9/85) [973.5]

4606 Remini, Robert V. *The Revolutionary Age of Andrew Jackson* (7–9). 1980, Harper LB $13.89 (0-06-024857-2). A history of the formative years of the Republic before the Civil War. [973.5]

4607 Tunis, Edwin. *The Young United States, 1783 to 1830* (7–10). Illus. 1976, Harper $24.70 (0-690-01065-6). A handsomely illustrated volume on how Americans lived in the nineteenth century prior to the Civil War. [973]

THE CIVIL WAR (1861–1865)

4608 Catton, Bruce. *Battle of Gettysburg* (6–10). Illus. 1963, Troll LB $14.95 (0-8167-1517-3). The story of this bloody battle is retold in text, paintings, maps, and photographs. [973.7]

4609 Fleming, Thomas. *Band of Brothers: West Point in the Civil War* (6–9). Illus. 1988, Walker LB $14.85 (0-8027-6741-9). The influence in the Civil War of such men as Grant and Lee, all of whom were graduates of West Point. (Rev: BL 2/1/88) [973.7]

4610 Johnson, Neil. *The Battle of Gettysburg* (5–9). Illus. 1989, Macmillan $14.95 (0-02-747831-9). An account of the battle that uses photographs of the 1988 reenactment to add graphic details. (Rev: BL 10/15/89; SLJ 12/89) [973.7]

4611 Jordan, Robert Paul. *The Civil War* (7–12). Illus. 1969, National Geographic $7.95 (0-87044-077-2). A heavily illustrated volume that covers causes, personalities, battles, and results of the Civil War. [973.7]

4612 Kantor, MacKinlay. *Gettysburg* (6–9). Illus. 1952, Random LB $8.99 (0-394-90323-4); paper $2.95 (0-394-89181-3). The story of the crucial battle of the Civil War that could have meant a total victory for the Confederacy. [973.7]

4613 Lawson, Don. *The United States in the Civil War* (7–9). Illus. 1977, Harper LB $12.89 (0-354-28665-X). A readable introduction to the major events and personalities involved in the Civil War. [973.7]

4614 Meltzer, Milton, ed. *Voices from the Civil War: A Documentary History of the Great American Conflict* (7–12). 1989, Harper LB $13.89 (0-690-04802-5). Through letters, speeches, and other primary sources from the famous and the unknown, Meltzer has created a vivid picture of the war. (Rev: BL 12/15/89; SLJ 12/89; VOYA 12/89) [973.7]

4615 Ray, Delia. *A Nation Torn: The Story of How the Civil War Began* (5–8). 1990, Lodestar $15.95 (0-525-67308-3). An introduction in clear prose to all the factors that contributed to the outbreak of the Civil War. (Rev: SLJ 9/90) [973.7]

4616 Windrow, Martin. *The Civil War Rifleman* (5–10). Illus. 1986, Watts $11.90 (0-531-10080-2). The life of a common soldier during the Civil War is described in detail, plus illustrations of uniforms and equipment. (Rev: BR 1–2/87) [973.7]

WESTWARD EXPANSION AND PIONEER LIFE

4617 Andrist, Ralph K. *California Gold Rush* (6–10). Illus. 1961, Troll LB $14.95 (0-8167-1518-1). A reissue of the beautifully illustrated account of the California gold rush. [979.4]

4618 Andrist, Ralph K. *To the Pacific with Lewis and Clark* (6–10). Illus. 1967, Troll LB $14.95 (0-8167-1533-5). The story with excellent illustrations of this historic expedition and the people involved. [973.5]

4619 Berger, Josef. *Discoverers of the New World* (6–10). Illus. 1960, Troll LB $14.95 (0-8167-1521-1). The story of the exploration of both North and South America is retold in interesting text and lavish color illustrations. [973]

4620 Blumberg, Rhoda. *The Great American Gold Rush* (6–9). Illus. 1989, Bradbury $16.95 (0-02-711681-6). The search for gold in the late 1840s and 1850s, with information on the routes the miners took, camp life, and the fate most suffered. (Rev: BL 11/15/89; SLJ 11/89; VOYA 2/90) [979.4]

4621 Blumberg, Rhoda. *The Incredible Journey of Lewis and Clark* (6–8). Illus. 1987, Lothrop $15.00 (0-688-06512-0). A gripping, well-illustrated retelling of the story of this expedition with emphasis on the feelings and relationships of those involved. (Rev: BL 1/1/88; SLJ 12/87) [917.8]

4622 Brown, Dee. *Wounded Knee* (7–9). 1975, Dell paper $1.75 (0-440-95768-0). From the Indians' point of view, this is a history of the white man's move into the American West. [970.004]

4623 Cowing, Sheila. *Searches in the American Desert* (7–10). Illus. 1989, Macmillan $14.95 (0-689-50469-1). Eight accounts about such early American explorers and adventurers as Brigham Young and John Charles Frémont. (Rev: BL 12/15/89; BR 5–6/90; VOYA 12/89) [979]

4624 Freedman, Russell. *Buffalo Hunt* (7–10). 1988, Holiday LB $16.95 (0-8234-0702-0). A history of how the buffalo were hunted from the times of the Indians to the slaughter by whites that brought on the near extinction of this animal. (Rev: SLJ 10/88) [973]

4625 Freedman, Russell. *Children of the Wild West* (6–9). Illus. 1983, Clarion $14.95 (0-89919-143-6). A look at the life of the children of pioneers. [978]

4626 Freedman, Russell. *Cowboys of the Wild West* (6–9). Illus. 1985, Clarion $14.95 (0-89919-301-3). A true portrait of the real cowboys who worked during the years that cattle roamed the open range. (Rev: BL 12/15/85; SLJ 12/85) [978]

4627 Hanmer, Trudy J. *The Advancing Frontier* (7–12). Illus. 1986, Watts $12.90 (0-531-10267-X). A history of the move west in America and the effects of this on our culture today. (Rev: BL 2/15/87; SLJ 1/87; VOYA 2/87) [973]

4628 Harris, Edward D. *John Charles Fremont and the Great Western Reconnaissance* (6–9). Illus. 1990, Chelsea House $18.95 (0-7910-1312-X). An account of the exploration of the West that concentrates on the 5 major journeys taken by Fremont. (Rev: BL 9/15/90) [973.6]

4629 Hilton, Suzanne. *Getting There: Frontier Travel without Power* (7–9). 1980, Westminster $10.95 (0-664-32657-9). This book describes all the different means of transportation used by the pioneers on their way west. [973]

4630 Jones, Evan. *Trappers and Mountain Men* (6–10). Illus. 1961, Troll LB $14.95 (0-8167-1534-3). The story behind the men who explored the West is given with brief biographies of the most important. [973.5]

4631 Katz, William Loren. *Black People Who Made the Old West* (7–10). Illus. 1977, Harper $12.70 (0-690-01253-5). Short sketches of 35 black Americans who contributed to the opening up of the West. [920]

4632 McCready, Albert L. *Railroads in the Days of Steam* (6–10). Illus. 1960, Troll LB $14.95 (0-8167-1529-7). A history of the early days of railroads and how they helped open up the American West. [973.8]

4633 McNeer, May. *California Gold Rush* (6–9). 1962, Random LB $8.99 (0-394-90306-4). An easily read account of the gold rush and its effects on the development of California. [973.4]

4634 Marrin, Albert. *War Clouds in the West: Indians and Cavalrymen, 1860–1890* (7–9). 1984, Macmillan $14.95 (0-689-31066-8). A history of the Indian Wars on the Plains that involved such

personalities as General Custer and Crazy Horse. [973.8]

4635 Matthews, Leonard J. *Cowboys* (6–9). Illus. 1988, Rourke LB $11.95 (0-86625-363-7). A glimpse of the old Wild West and the men who rode the ranges. Also use in the same series: *Gunfighters* (1989). (Rev: SLJ 6/89) [975.5]

4636 Matthews, Leonard J. *Indians* (6–9). Illus. 1988, Rourke LB $11.95 (0-86625-364-5). An overview of how Indians lived during the days of the Wild West. (Rev: SLJ 6/89) [970.004]

4637 Matthews, Leonard J. *Pioneers* (6–9). Illus. 1988, Rourke LB $11.95 (0-86625-362-9). A tribute to the homesteaders who risked their lives to find a new home in the West. Also use in the same series: *Railroaders* and *Soldiers* (both 1989). (Rev: SLJ 6/89) [973.5]

4638 Perl, Lila. *Hunter's Stew and Hangtown Fry: What Pioneer America Ate and Why* (7–9). Illus. 1977, Clarion $13.95 (0-395-28922-X). Twenty recipes are included along with much information on what nineteenth-century pioneers ate. [641.5]

4639 Place, Marian T. *Westward on the Oregon Trail* (6–10). Illus. 1962, Troll LB $14.95 (0-8167-1535-1). The days of pioneers and wagon trains are re-created in text and many illustrations. [973.5]

4640 Platt, Rutherford. *Adventures in the Wilderness* (6–10). Illus. 1963, Troll LB $14.95 (0-8167-1516-5). The story of the settling of the West is told in this account noted for its many fine illustrations. [973.5]

4641 Reynolds, Quentin. *Custer's Last Stand* (6–8). 1987, Random $8.99 (0-394-90320-X); paper $2.95 (0-394-89178-3). The story of General Custer, the campaign against the Indians, and the battle of Little Big Horn. A reissue. [973.8]

4642 Surge, Frank. *Western Lawmen* (7–9). 1978, Lerner LB $5.95 (0-8225-0451-0). A history of how the law was administered during the opening up of the American West. [973.5]

4643 Tunis, Edwin. *Frontier Living* (7–10). Illus. 1976, Harper $24.70 (0-690-01064-8). The daily life of the pioneers told in text and drawings by the author. [978]

4644 Ward, Don. *Cowboys and Cattle Country* (6–10). 1961, Troll LB $14.95 (0-8167-1520-3). The story of the cowboy and the great days of ranching are re-created in this book that contains many stunning illustrations. [973.8]

RECONSTRUCTION TO WORLD WAR I
(1865–1917)

4645 Cable, Mary. *The Blizzard of '88* (7–10). Illus. 1988, Macmillan $19.95 (0-689-11591-1). A vivid description of the events and people in this record snowfall that covered the entire eastern seaboard. (Rev: VOYA 10/88) [973.8]

4646 Cooper, Michael. *Klondike Fever: The Famous Gold Rush of 1898* (7–10). Illus. 1989, Clarion $14.95 (0-89919-803-1). A chronological account of the gold rush that made some rich and others broken human beings. (Rev: SLJ 4/90) [979.8]

4647 Lawson, Don. *The United States in the Spanish-American War* (7–9). Illus. 1976, Harper LB $12.89 (0-200-00163-9). The causes, events, and results of the war that made the United States a world power. [973.9]

4648 Stewart, Gail. *1900s* (5–9). Illus. 1990, Crestwood LB $10.95 (0-89686-471-5). Both the serious history and the trivia associated with this decade are presented in chronological order. Also use *1910s* (1990). (Rev: SLJ 6/90) [973.9]

4649 Wilder, Laura Ingalls. *West from Home: Letters of Laura Ingalls Wilder, San Francisco 1915* (7–9). 1974, Harper LB $13.89 (0-06-024111-4); paper $3.95 (0-06-44008-6). The author describes her trip from Missouri to San Francisco in 1915. [973.9]

BETWEEN THE WARS AND THE GREAT
DEPRESSION (1918–1941)

4650 Glassman, Bruce. *The Crash of '29 and the New Deal* (6–9). Illus. 1986, Silver Burdett LB $14.96 (0-382-06831-9); paper $5.75 (0-382-06978-1). The causes of the Great Depression are dealt with in this book as well as the methods used to bring America back. (Rev: SLJ 12/86) [973.9]

4651 Harris, Nathaniel. *The Great Depression* (7–12). Illus. 1988, David & Charles $18.95 (0-7134-5658-2). This account describes the 1930s not only in the United States but also in Britain and Europe. (Rev: SLJ 1/89) [973.91]

4652 Lawson, Don. *FDR's New Deal* (7–9). 1979, Harper $12.70 (0-690-03953-0). The story of how President Roosevelt's policies helped this country out of the Great Depression. [973.91]

4653 Meltzer, Milton. *Brother, Can You Spare a Dime?* (7–12). Illus. 1977, NAL paper $3.95 (0-451-61577-8). A history of the Great Depression of the 1930s and the beginnings of the New Deal. [330.973]

4654 Scott, Lynn H. *The Covered Wagon: And Other Adventures* (6–10). Illus. 1987, Univ. of Nebraska Pr. $12.95 (0-8032-4179-8). The true story of the Scott family and its wanderings out West from 1906 through 1923. (Rev: SLJ 5/88) [973.7]

4655 Stewart, Gail. *1920s* (5–9). Illus. 1990, Crestwood LB $10.95 (0-89686-473-1). A chronological description of the Great War and its aftermath plus material on the trivia associated with this period. Also use *1930s* (1990). (Rev: SLJ 6/90) [973.9]

WORLD WAR II TO THE PRESENT (1945–)

4656 Archer, Jules. *The Incredible Sixties: The Stormy Years That Changed America* (7–12). 1986, Harcourt $16.95 (0-15-238298-4). A topically arranged overview of the events, trends, and significance of the 1960s and how they have shaped our future. (Rev: BL 5/15/86; SLJ 9/86; VOYA 4/87) [973.922]

4657 Davis, Daniel S. *Behind Barbed Wire: The Imprisonment of Japanese Americans during World War II* (7–10). Illus. 1982, Dutton $13.95 (0-525-26320-9). The story of the internment of Japanese Americans during World War II told in an objective, clear narrative. [940.54]

4658 Fyson, Nance Lui. *The 1940s* (6–9). Illus. 1990, Batsford $19.95 (0-7134-5628-0). The story of World War II and its aftermath are covered plus development in such areas as sports, the arts, science, and invention. (Rev: SLJ 7/90) [973.9]

4659 Goldstein, Toby. *Waking from the Dream: America in the Sixties* (7–12). Illus. 1988, Messner LB $10.29 (0-671-63709-6); paper $5.95 (0-671-66051-9). A clearly written history that highlights events such as the Vietnam War, the women's rights movement, and the race for space. (Rev: SLJ 1/89) [973.92]

4660 Griffiths, John C. *The Cuban Missile Crisis* (7–10). Illus. 1987, Rourke LB $10.95 (0-86592-028-1). A chronicle of the tense days during the Kennedy administration that brought a confrontation between the Soviet Union and the United States in the Western hemisphere. (Rev: SLJ 8/87) [972.91]

4661 Haskins, James, and Kathleen Benson. *The 60s Reader* (7–12). Illus. 1988, Viking $13.95 (0-670-80674-9). Excerpts from writings of the period plus thumbnail sketches of key figures highlight this account. (Rev: BL 9/1/88; BR 11–12/88; SLJ 8/88; VOYA 4/89) [973.92]

4662 Kilian, Pamela. *What Was Watergate?* (7–12). Illus. 1990, St. Martin's $14.95 (0-312-

04446-1). A factual, objective account of the break in and its aftermath. (Rev: BL 9/1/90) [973.924]

KOREAN AND VIETNAM WARS

4663 Ashabranner, Brent. *Always to Remember: The Vietnam Veterans Memorial* (6–10). Illus. 1988, Dodd $12.95 (0-396-09089-3). The story of the memorial from the dream of a single man to the moving monument it became. (Rev: BL 6/15/88; SLJ 10/88; VOYA 2/89) [957.704]

4664 Dolan, Edward F., Jr. *America after Vietnam: Legacies of a Hated War* (7–12). 1989, Watts LB $12.90 (0-531-10793-0). The account of the effects of the Vietnam War particularly on those who returned from combat. (Rev: BL 9/1/89; BR 3–4/90; SLJ 11/89; VOYA 4/90) [959.704]

4665 Dolan, Edward F., Jr. *MIA: Missing in Action—A Vietnam Drama* (7–12). Illus. 1989, Watts LB $12.90 (0-531-10665-9). After a brief history of the Vietnam War, this account explores the complex and controversial mystery surrounding the MIAs and POWs of this conflict. (Rev: BL 5/1/89; BR 1–2/90; SLJ 7/89; VOYA 10/89) [959.705]

4666 Edwards, Richard. *The Korean War* (6–9). Illus. 1988, Rourke LB $11.95 (0-86592-036-2). A brief, objective, nicely illustrated account of the war and its aftermath. (Rev: SLJ 2/89) [951.9]

4667 Edwards, Richard. *The Vietnam War* (7–10). Illus. 1987, Rourke LB $10.95 (0-86592-031-1). An overview that covers both the war in Asia and the reaction in the United States. (Rev: SLJ 8/87) [959.704]

4668 Fincher, E. B. *The Vietnam War* (7–10). Illus. 1980, Watts LB $11.90 (0-531-04112-3). An account of the 30 years of conflict and of American involvement in the climax of this war. [959.704]

4669 Griffiths, John C. *The Last Day in Saigon* (6–9). Illus. 1987, Batsford $17.95 (0-8521-9671-7). This account focuses on the last day of the Vietnam War (April 30, 1975), but also includes background material on the war. (Rev: BL 7/87; BR 9–10/87; SLJ 9/87) [959.804]

4670 Lawson, Don. *An Album of the Vietnam War* (7–12). Illus. 1986, Watts LB $13.90 (0-531-10139-8). A simple text is complemented by many fine photographs in this pictorial survey of the Vietnam War. (Rev: BR 11–12/87; SLJ 8/86) [959.704]

4671 Lawson, Don. *The United States in the Vietnam War* (7–10). Illus. 1981, Harper LB $12.89

(0-690-04105-5). In addition to major events, this account gives background information, differences in philosophies, and the politics involved. [959.704]

4672 Lawson, Don. *The War in Vietnam* (7–10). Illus. 1981, Watts LB $10.40 (0-531-04331-2). The causes of the war are explored, its tragic course, and also its aftermath. [959.704]

4673 McCloud, Bill. *What Should We Tell Our Children about Vietnam?* (7–12). 1989, Univ. of Oklahoma $17.95 (0-8061-2229-3). Over 120 individuals including President Bush and Garry Trudeau tell what they think young people should know about the war. (Rev: BL 9/15/89) [959.704]

4674 Nickelson, Harry. *Vietnam* (5–10). Illus. 1989, Lucent Books LB $10.95 (1-56006-110-3). An easily read account that traces the war from its origins before American intervention to the eventual pullout. (Rev: BL 1/15/90; SLJ 4/90) [959.9]

4675 Warren, James A. *Portrait of a Tragedy: America and the Vietnam War* (6–10). Illus. 1990, Lothrop $17.95 (0-688-07454-5). An objective account that gives good information on the background of the war and how the United States became involved. (Rev: BL 4/1/90; SLJ 6/90; VOYA 8/90) [959.704]

4676 Wills, Charles. *The Tet Offensive* (6–9). Illus. 1989, Silver Burdett $16.98 (0-382-09849-8); paper $7.95 (0-382-09855-2). The story of the 1968 campaign in Vietnam plus general material about the war and the Memorial in Washington, D.C. (Rev: BL 11/1/89; BR 1–2/90) [959.704]

4677 Wright, David K. *War in Vietnam, Book I: Eve of Battle* (5–10). 4 vols. Illus. 1989, Childrens LB $79.93 (per set) (0-516-02286-5). This is the first volume of an excellent 4-volume set. The other volumes are: *War in Vietnam, Book II: A Wider War; War in Vietnam, Book III: Vietnamization;* and *War in Vietnam, Book IV: Fall of Vietnam* (all 1989, available only as a set). (Rev: BL 6/1/89; SLJ 6/89) [959.704]

Regions

MIDWEST

4678 Darrell-Brown, Susan. *The Mississippi* (6–9). Illus. 1979, Silver Burdett LB $14.96 (0-382-06204-3). A description of the river from its source in the north to its emptying into the Gulf of Mexico. [977]

4679 Jacobson, Daniel. *The North Central States* (6–9). Illus. 1984, Watts LB $10.40 (0-531-04731-

8). A description of these states that includes material on history, industry, farming, and principal cities. [977]

MOUNTAIN STATES

4680 St. George, Judith. *The Mount Rushmore Story* (6–10). Illus. 1985, Putnam $13.95 (0-399-21117-9). This account tells about this familiar landmark and the sculptor Gutzon Borglum who was its creator. (Rev: BL 9/15/85; SLJ 10/85; VOYA 12/85) [730]

4681 Smith, Don. *The Grand Canyon: Journey through Time* (7–9). 1976, Troll LB $9.79 (0-89375-007-7); paper $2.50 (0-89375-023-9). Explains how this natural phenomenon was formed and takes us on a trip through it. [917]

4682 Taylor, L. B., Jr., and C. L. Taylor. *The Rocky Mountain States* (6–9). Illus. 1984, Watts LB $10.40 (0-531-04735-0). The 8 mountain states are introduced with material on their history, economy, and everyday life. [978]

NORTHEAST

4683 Andrist, Ralph K. *The Erie Canal* (6–10). Illus. 1964, Troll LB $14.95 (0-8167-1522-X). The story of the amazing engineering project that linked Lake Erie with New York City. [973.5]

4684 Burchard, Sue. *The Statue of Liberty: Birth to Rebirth* (7–9). Illus. 1985, Harcourt $13.95 (0-15-279969-9). After a tour of present-day Liberty Island the author describes the history behind the statue. (Rev: BL 12/1/85; SLJ 12/85) [941.7]

4685 Fradin, Dennis B. *The Connecticut Colony* (5–9). Illus. 1990, Childrens LB $23.93 (0-516-00393-3). A history of Connecticut from its first settlements to its statehood. (Rev: BL 8/90) [974.6]

4686 Gilfond, Henry. *The Northeast States* (6–9). Illus. 1984, Watts LB $10.40 (0-531-04732-6). A survey of the states from Maine to Maryland giving details on life, history, and economy. [974]

4687 Harris, Jonathan. *A Statue for America: The First 100 Years of the Statue of Liberty* (6–10). Illus. 1986, Macmillan $14.95 (0-02-742730-7). A history of the Statue of Liberty that spans the time from its original inception to its recent renovation. (Rev: BL 12/1/85; BR 11–12/86; SLJ 4/86; VOYA 8–10/86) [974.7]

4688 Mercer, Charles. *Statue of Liberty* (6–9). Illus. 1985, Putnam $12.95 (0-399-20670-1); paper $7.95 (0-399-21231-0). A history of the statue from the original idea to its dedication. (Rev: VOYA 12/85) [974.7]

4689 St. George, Judith. *The White House: Cornerstone of a Nation* (5–8). Illus. 1990, Putnam $16.95 (0-399-22186-7). A history of the White House from the late eighteenth century to the present with anecdotes from its famous residents. (Rev: BL 8/90; VOYA 6/90) [975.3]

4690 Siegel, Beatrice. *George and Martha Washington at Home in New York* (5–8). Illus. 1989, Macmillan $13.95 (0-02-782721-6). A view of life in New York City years ago as experienced by the original First Family. (Rev: SLJ 8/89) [974.7]

PACIFIC STATES

4691 Brown, Joseph E., et al. *The Sierra Club Guide to the National Parks of the Pacific Southwest and Hawaii* (7–12). Illus. 1984, Stewart, Tabori & Chang paper $14.95 (0-394-72490-9). Many color photographs and maps enhance the detailed description of each park. [917.9]

4692 Cash, Judy. *Kidding Around Los Angeles: A Young Person's Guide to the City* (6–10). Illus. 1989, John Muir paper $9.95 (0-945465-34-3). Lots of information and guided tours suitable both for the young tourist and resident of Los Angeles. (Rev: SLJ 5/90) [979]

4693 Lawson, Don. *The Pacific States* (6–9). Illus. 1984, Watts LB $10.40 (0-531-04733-4). An introduction to California, Oregon, Washington, Alaska, and Hawaii that tells a little of their histories, geography, and economies. [979]

4694 Rayson, Ann. *Modern Hawaiian History* (5–9). Illus. 1984, Bess Pr. $21.95 (0-935848-24-X); paper $19.95 (0-935848-23-1). A detailed account that covers Hawaiian history from 1898 to our present-day concerns. (Rev: BL 2/1/85) [996.9]

SOUTH

4695 Berger, Gilda. *The Southeast States* (6–9). Illus. 1984, Watts LB $10.40 (0-531-04738-5). Eleven states from Virginia to Florida are described in terms of their people, economy, and history. [975]

4696 Douglas, Marjory Stoneman. *The Everglades: River of Grass* (7–10). Illus. 1988, Pineapple $17.95 (0-910923-38-8). A reissue of this work now updated to 1988 about this unique part of Florida. (Rev: SLJ 2/89) [975.9]

4697 Linn, Christopher. *The Everglades: Exploring the Unknown* (6–9). 1976, Troll LB $9.79 (0-89375-006-9); paper $2.50 (0-89375-022-0). An easily read tour of the Florida Everglades and of the flora and fauna found there. [917.3]

4698 Peacock, Howard. *The Big Thicket of Texas: America's Ecological Wonder* (7–9). Illus. 1984, Little $14.95 (0-316-69583-1). Peacock describes the amazing flora and fauna of the Big Thicket of southeast Texas. [976.4]

4699 Pedersen, Anne. *Kidding Around Atlanta: A Young Person's Guide to the City* (6–10). Illus. 1989, John Muir paper $9.95 (0-945465-35-1). Both the young tourist and the resident of Atlanta will learn from this information-packed volume. (Rev: SLJ 5/90) [975]

4700 Woods, Harold, and Geraldine Woods. *The South Central States* (6–9). Illus. 1984, Watts LB $10.40 (0-531-04737-7). A history of the region plus profiles of Texas, Arkansas, Oklahoma, and Louisiana. [976]

SOUTHWEST

4701 McCarry, Charles. *The Great Southwest* (7–12). Illus. 1980, National Geographic LB $9.50 (0-87044-288-0). In pictures and text, descriptions are given of such states as New Mexico, Colorado, and Arizona [979.1]

Physical and Applied Sciences

General and Miscellaneous

4702 Aaseng, Nathan. *The Inventors: Nobel Prizes in Chemistry, Physics, and Medicine* (6–9). Illus. 1988, Lerner LB $9.95 (0-8225-0651-3). A description of 8 inventions, such as the transistor, that won for the scientists involved the Nobel Prize. (Rev: SLJ 8/88) [608]

4703 Bleifeld, Maurice. *Experimenting with a Microscope* (5–9). Illus. 1988, Watts $11.90 (0-531-10580-6). The story of the microscope plus many experiments and projects involving its use. (Rev: BL 1/15/89; BR 3–4/89) [578]

4704 Crump, Donald J., ed. *On the Brink of Tomorrow: Frontiers of Science* (7–9). Illus. 1982, National Geographic LB $7.85 (0-87044-414-X). With many color illustrations, this account covers recent advances in such areas as physics, astronomy, and medicine. [500]

4705 Gottlieb, William P. *Science Facts You Won't Believe* (7–9). 1983, Watts LB $9.90 (0-531-02875-5). Common misconceptions such as the fact that we do not have 5 senses are explored in this myth-exploding book. [500]

4706 Grillone, Lisa, and Joseph Gennaro. *Small Worlds Close Up* (7–9). Illus. 1978, Crown $12.95 (0-517-53289-1). A number of common objects such as chalk and salt granules are seen through the electron microscope. [500]

4707 Haines, Gail Kay. *Micromysteries: Stories of Scientific Detection* (6–10). Illus. 1988, Putnam $14.95 (0-396-09000-1). A collection of true stories behind various scientific discoveries—some the work of scientific detection, others of serendipity. (Rev: SLJ 5/88) [500]

4708 Haines, Gail Kay. *Test-Tube Mysteries* (7–9). Illus. 1982, Putnam $11.95 (0-396-08075-8). Great breakthroughs in science from Pasteur's discoveries to work on Legionnaires' disease are described. [509]

4709 Paton, John, ed. *Knowledge Encyclopedia* (5–8). Illus. 1984, Arco $16.95 (0-668-06137-5). This browsing book supplies a little information on more than 2,500 topics, many of them scientific in nature. (Rev: BL 2/15/85) [032]

4710 Ross, Frank, Jr. *Oracle Bones, Stars, and Wheelbarrows: Ancient Chinese Science and Technology* (7–9). 1982, Houghton $8.95 (0-395-32083-6). A rundown is given of the many discoveries by the ancient Chinese in the areas of astronomy, medicine, mathematics, and technology. [509]

4711 Simon, Seymour. *Hidden Worlds: Pictures of the Invisible* (7–9). Illus. 1983, Morrow LB $11.88 (0-688-02465-3). A variety of photographs produced by use of the telescope, microscope, X rays, and so on, reveal a world unknown to the naked eye. [500]

Experiments and Projects

4712 Adams, Florence. *Catch a Sunbeam: A Book of Solar Study and Experiments* (7–9). Illus. 1978, Harcourt $10.95 (0-15-215197-4). With simple materials, 16 experiments using solar energy are described. [621.47]

4713 Beller, Joel. *So You Want to Do a Science Project!* (7–12). Illus. 1982, Arco LB $9.95 (0-668-04987-1). A practical step-by-step manual that starts with choosing a subject and continues to its final completion. [507]

4714 Bombaugh, Ruth. *Science Fair Success* (7–10). Illus. 1989, Enslow LB $14.95 (0-89490-197-4). A practical guide to choosing a science project, developing it, and presenting it effectively. (Rev: BR 3–4/90; SLJ 12/89) [507]

4715 Bonnet, Robert L., and G. Daniel Keen. *Botany: 49 Science Fair Projects* (6–10). Illus. 1989, TAB $16.95 (0-8306-9277-0); paper $9.95 (0-8306-3277-8). Well-explained projects involving such phenomena as photosynthesis, hydroponics, fungi, and germination. (Rev: BL 1/15/90; BR 1–2/90; VOYA 2/90) [581]

4716 Brown, Bob. *More Science for You: 112 Illustrated Experiments* (6–8). Illus. 1988, TAB paper $7.95 (0-8306-3125-9). A collection of simple experiments involving such topics as heat, sound, weight, and tricks. (Rev: VOYA 4/89) [507]

4717 Brown, Robert J. *333 Science Tricks and Experiments* (7–12). Illus. 1984, TAB $15.95 (0-8306-0825-7); paper $9.65 (0-8306-1825-0). Basic scientific principles are demonstrated in experiments and projects. [507]

4718 Brown, Vinson. *Building Your Own Nature Museum: For Study and Pleasure* (9–12). Illus. 1984, Arco $12.95 (0-668-06057-3); paper $7.95 (0-668-06061-1). A manual on how to mount and display materials and specimens plus details on associated projects. (Rev: BL 2/1/85) [069]

4719 Cobb, Vicki. *Chemically Active! Experiments You Can Do at Home* (6–9). Illus. 1985, Harper LB $12.89 (0-397-32080-9). A group of scientific experiments that demonstrate chemical principles and can be performed with common household items. (Rev: BR 9–10/86; SLJ 8/85; VOYA 12/85) [507]

4720 Cobb, Vicki. *Science Experiments You Can Eat* (7–9). Illus. 1972, Harper LB $12.89 (0-397-31179-6). Recipes for soups, ice cream dishes, gelatin, and other ordinary dishes are used to explain scientific phenomena. Continued in: *More Science Experiments You Can Eat* (1979). [507]

4721 Cobb, Vicki. *The Secret Life of Cosmetics: A Science Experiment Book* (6–8). Illus. 1985, Harper LB $13.89 (0-397-32122-8). An examination of the history and composition of cosmetics and a number of experiments to perform using these materials. (Rev: BL 3/15/86; SLJ 1/86) [668]

4722 Cobb, Vicki. *The Secret Life of Hardware: A Science Experiment Book* (7–9). Illus. 1982, Harper LB $13.89 (0-397-32000-0). A book of science activities and experiments that involve a hammer, saw, soaps, paints, and other commonly found items. [670]

4723 Gardner, Robert. *Energy Projects for Young Scientists* (8–12). Illus. 1987, Watts $11.90 (0-531-10338-2). A total of 60 projects that deal with various forms of energy. (Rev: BL 2/15/88; BR 1–2/88; SLJ 10/87; VOYA 12/87) [621.042]

4724 Gardner, Robert. *Ideas for Science Projects* (5–10). Illus. 1986, Watts $12.90 (0-531-10246-7); paper $5.95 (0-531-15125-5). Along with giving many ideas in various branches of science, the author gives tips on methodology, supplies, and reporting techniques. (Rev: BL 2/1/87; BR 1–2/87; VOYA 2/87) [507]

4725 Gardner, Robert. *Kitchen Chemistry: Science Experiments to Do at Home* (7–9). Illus. 1982, Messner LB $10.95 (0-671-42102-6); paper $4.95 (0-671-67576-1). Simple gadgets and materials found in the kitchen are used in a series of entertaining and instructive experiments. [542]

4726 Gardner, Robert. *More Ideas for Science Projects* (6–10). Illus. 1989, Watts LB $12.90 (0-531-10676-4). One hundred innovative ideas for projects from astronomy to zoology. A sequel to *Ideas for Science Projects* (1986). (Rev: BL 5/15/89; BR 11–12/89; SLJ 8/89; VOYA 10/89) [507]

4727 Goodwin, Peter H. *Engineering Projects for Young Scientists* (8–12). Illus. 1987, Watts $11.90 (0-531-10339-0). A number of projects are outlined covering such areas as force, motion, light waves, bridges, and pin-hole cameras. (Rev: BL 2/15/88; BR 1–2/88; SLJ 3/88) [620]

4728 Gutnik, Martin J. *How to Do a Science Project and Report* (7–10). Illus. 1980, Watts LB $10.90 (0-531-04129-8). An outline of the scientific method and how it can be applied to doing science projects. [507]

4729 Herbert, Don. *Mr. Wizard's Supermarket Science* (7–9). Illus. 1980, Random LB $8.99 (0-394-93800-3); paper $7.95 (0-394-83800-9). Magic tricks and experiments performed using common household objects. [507]

4730 Hussey, Lois J., and Catherine Pessino. *Collecting for the City Naturalist* (7–9). Illus. 1975, Harper $12.70 (0-690-00317-X). Science activities that can be carried out in an urban environment, such as collecting spider webs, are outlined. [500.7]

4731 MacFarlane, Ruth B. Alford. *Making Your Own Nature Museum* (5–9). 1989, Watts LB $11.90 (0-531-10809-0). A manual for young nature lovers on how to collect rock, animal, and plant specimens and how to classify and exhibit them. (Rev: BL 2/1/90; BR 3–4/90; VOYA 4/90) [508]

4732 McKay, David W., and Bruce G. Smith. *Space Science Projects for Young Scientists* (7–12). Illus. 1986, Watts $12.90 (0-531-10244-0). A series of clearly explained projects that involve possible space environments and forces such as gravity. (Rev: BL 12/15/86; BR 1–2/87; SLJ 12/86) [500.5]

4733 Markle, Sandra. *The Young Scientists Guide to Successful Science Projects* (5–9). Illus. 1990, Lothrop LB $12.88 (0-688-07217-8); paper $6.95 (0-688-09137-7). A step-by-step guide to choosing a project and carrying it out effectively. (Rev: BL 7/90; SLJ 9/90) [507.8]

4734 Mebane, Robert, and Thomas Rybolt. *Adventures with Atoms and Molecules* (6–9). 1985, Enslow $10.95 (0-89490-120-6). Thirty questions about atoms and molecules are asked and after each is a series of simple experiments using everyday objects that give the answers. This is followed by *Adventures with Atoms and Molecules Book II* (1987). (Rev: BR 5–6/86; VOYA 2/86) [507]

4735 Moeschl, Richard. *Exploring the Sky: 100 Projects for Beginning Astronomers* (7–12). Illus. 1988, Chicago Review paper $14.95 (1-55652-039-5). Not only an introduction to astonomy, this book outlines fascinating projects involving such areas as the seasons, maps, sundials, and space flight. (Rev: SLJ 1/89) [523]

4736 Rainis, Kenneth G. *Nature Projects for Young Scientists* (5–10). Illus. 1989, Watts LB $12.90 (0-531-10789-2). A fine idea book for young people needing science projects involving biology. (Rev: BL 1/15/90; BR 1–2/90; SLJ 3/90; VOYA 4/90) [508]

4737 Simon, Seymour. *How to Be a Space Scientist in Your Own Home* (7–9). Illus. 1982, Harper LB $12.89 (0-397-31991-6). A description of 23 simple experiments involving space science using easily found materials. [500.5]

4738 Smith, Norman F. *How to Do Successful Science Projects* (5–8). Rev. ed. Illus. 1990, Messner LB $10.98 (0-671-70685-3); paper $4.95 (0-671-70686-1). This guide gives many fine tips and concentrates on the applications of the scientific method. (Rev: BL 7/90) [507.8]

4739 Stangle, Jean. *The Tools of Science* (5–9). Illus. 1987, Dodd $16.95 (0-396-08965-8); paper $8.95 (0-396-08966-6). While covering basic facts in science, this book offers a series of simple experiments using common household objects. (Rev: BR 1–2/88) [507]

4740 Stone, George K. *Science Projects You Can Do* (6–8). Illus. 1963, Prentice paper $4.95 (0-13-795328-3). A book of simple projects explained clearly in text and pictures. [507]

4741 Tocci, Salvatore. *How to Do a Science Fair Project* (5–10). Illus. 1986, Watts $12.90 (0-531-10245-9); paper $5.95 (0-531-15123-9). A practical, well-organized account that follows the development of a science project from the initial idea to its completion and display. (Rev: BL 2/1/87; VOYA 2/87) [507]

4742 Walker, Ormiston H. *Experimenting with Air and Flight* (6–10). Illus. 1989, Watts LB $11.90 (0-531-10670-5). The forces of life, thrust, and gravity are demonstrated through a series of experiments and then an explanation is given on how they effect flight. (Rev: BL 5/15/89; BR 1–2/90; SLJ 7/89; VOYA 4/90) [629.13]

4743 Wallace, Diane A., and Phillip L. Hershey. *How to Master Science Labs* (6–9). Illus. 1987, Watts $11.90 (0-531-10323-4). The authors explain how to do science projects and how to feel comfortable in a lab. (Rev: BL 2/15/88; BR 1–2/88; SLJ 10/87; VOYA 12/87) [507]

4744 Webster, David. *Dissection Projects* (6–9). Illus. 1988, Watts $9.90 (0-531-10474-5). A guide to the tools and techniques of dissecting various specimens like fish, clams, and chickens. (Rev: BL 4/15/88; BR 9–10/88) [591.4]

4745 Zubrowski, Bernie. *Wheels at Work* (5–9). Illus. 1986, Morrow LB $11.88 (0-688-06348-9); paper $6.95 (0-688-06349-7). A series of projects using wheels are described, including windmills, pulleys, and water wheels. (Rev: SLJ 2/87) [507]

Astronomy and Space Science

General and Miscellaneous

4746 Asimov, Isaac. *How Did We Find Out about the Universe?* (6–9). Illus. 1983, Walker LB $10.85 (0-8027-6477-0). The discoveries of ancient and modern astronomers are outlined, including the invention of the telescope; current theories are explained simply. [523.1]

4747 Branley, Franklyn M. *Sun Dogs and Shooting Stars: A Skywatcher's Calendar* (6–9). Illus. 1980, Houghton $13.95 (0-395-29520-3). A month-by-month look at facts, myths, and projects involving the sky and stars. [523]

4748 Brown, Peter Lancaster. *Astronomy* (7–10). Illus. 1984, Facts on File $12.95 (0-87196-985-8). A well-illustrated introduction to the world of astronomy, its history, and present-day concerns. [523]

4749 Chartrand, Mark R. *Skyguide: A Field Guide for Amateur Astronomers* (7–12). Illus. 1982, Golden paper $9.95 (0-307-13667-1). A guide for sky watchers who have only binoculars or a simple telescope. [523]

4750 *Exploring Space and Atoms* (5–9). Illus. 1984, Arco $9.95 (0-668-06175-8). This introductory volume covers such topics as the structure of matter and the nature of the universe. (Rev: BL 4/1/85) [500]

4751 Fradin, Dennis B. *Astronomy* (6–9). Illus. 1987, Childrens $26.50 (0-516-00533-2). A general introduction to astronomy that covers its history, present developments, and the questions that will be answered in the future. (Rev: BL 11/1/87; SLJ 12/87) [523]

4752 Gallant, Roy A. *101 Questions & Answers about the Universe* (6–9). Illus. 1984, Macmillan $10.95 (0-02-736750-9). A group of topically arranged questions dealing with many aspects of astronomical findings about planets, the Sun, stars, black holes, and so on. (Rev: BL2/15/85) [520]

4753 Gallant, Roy A. *Rainbows, Mirages, and Sundogs: The Sky as a Source of Wonder* (6–8). Illus. 1987, Macmillan $12.95 (0-02-737010-0). All sorts of astral phenomena are explained including twinkling stars, rainbows, and northern lights. (Rev: BL 9/1/87) [551.56]

4754 Herbst, Judith. *Sky Above and Worlds Beyond* (7–9). Illus. 1983, Macmillan $14.95 (0-689-30974-0). An introduction to astronomy that includes some history, material on the solar system and stars, and a brief look at space exploration. [523]

4755 Kelsey, Larry, and Darrel Hoff. *Recent Revolutions in Astronomy* (8–10). Illus. 1987, Watts $12.90 (0-531-10340-4). The new tools and techniques used by astronomers are discussed and coverage on recent findings is given. (Rev: BL 3/1/87; BR 9–10/87; SLJ 5/87; VOYA 10/87) [520]

4756 Lampton, Christopher. *Astronomy: From Copernicus to the Space Telescope* (7–10). Illus. 1987, Watts LB $10.40 (0-531-10300-5). A general account that covers the history of astronomy with coverage of Newton, Einstein, and the modern age. (Rev: SLJ 8/87) [523]

4757 Lampton, Christopher. *Space Sciences* (7–10). Illus. 1983, Watts LB $10.40 (0-531-04539-0). In a dictionary format, terms and objects related to astronomy are described and explored. [500.5]

4758 McGowen, Tom. *Album of Astronomy* (7–9). Rev. ed. Illus. 1981, Macmillan $8.95 (0-528-82048-6); paper $4.95 (0-02-688501-8). From the solar system to the universe, this is a general introduction to astronomy. [523]

4759 Mayall, Newton, et al. *The Sky Observer's Guide* (7–10). Illus. 1985, Western paper $3.95 (0-307-34009-2). A basic guide to sky watching illustrated with many color diagrams. [523]

4760 Mayer, Ben. *Starwatch* (7–9). Illus. 1984, Putnam paper $9.95 (0-399-51009-5). Information on common constellations and how to view them are 2 topics covered. [523]

4761 Moche, Dinah L. *Astronomy Today* (7–10). Illus. 1982, Random LB $11.99 (0-394-84423-8); paper $9.95 (0-394-94423-2). A history is given of our discoveries in astronomy plus material on space exploration and our ideas of the universe today. [523]

4762 Nourse, Alan E. *Radio Astronomy* (5–10). 1989, Watts LB $11.90 (0-531-10811-2). An account that covers the history of telescopes and the development of the radio telescope and its many accomplishments. (Rev: BL 1/15/90; BR 3–4/90; SLJ 11/89) [522]

4763 Ridpath, Ian. *The Young Astronomer's Handbook* (7–12). Illus. 1984, Arco $9.95 (0-668-06046-8). A general astronomy text with good elementary material on history plus the most common stars and constellations found in the sky. [523]

4764 Simon, Seymour. *Look to the Night Sky: An Introduction to Star Watching* (7–9). Illus. 1977, Penguin paper $5.95 (0-14-049185-6). A simple, well-organized introduction to star gazing with many diagrams. [523]

4765 Vbrova, Zuza. *Space and Astronomy* (6–8). Illus. 1989, Gloucester LB $12.40 (0-531-17143-4). Space exploration and an introduction to the solar system and stars are the major thrusts of this brief account. (Rev: BL 5/15/89) [520]

Astronautics and Space Exploration

4766 Apfel, Necia H. *Space Law* (6–8). Illus. 1988, Watts LB $10.40 (0-531-10599-7). This account discusses the present regulations involving space and the needs in this area for future peaceful development. (Rev: SLJ 11/88) [341.4]

4767 Apfel, Necia H. *Space Station* (5–8). Illus. 1987, Watts $10.40 (0-531-10394-3). An overview of progress made in space exploration that in-cludes coverage of the *Challenger* accident. (Rev: BL 1–2/88) [629.44]

4768 Asimov, Isaac. *How Did We Find Out about Outer Space?* (6–9). Illus. 1977, Walker LB $11.85 (0-8027-6284-0). A history from the ancients' first dreams of flying to the spaceships of today. [629.4]

4769 Asimov, Isaac, and Frank White. *Think about Space: Where Have We Been and Where Are We Going?* (7–10). Illus. 1989, Walker $14.85 (0-8027-6766-4); paper $5.95 (0-8027-6767-2). A history of space exploration and a discussion of possible future developments. (Rev: BL 10/1/89; BR 5–6/90; SLJ 11/89) [500.5]

4770 Berger, Melvin. *Space Shots, Shuttles, and Satellites* (7–9). Illus. 1984, Putnam $7.99 (0-399-61210-6). A brief history of space flight, explanations of space shuttles and satellites, and how one becomes an astronaut are 3 topics explored. [629.4]

4771 Branley, Franklyn M. *Mysteries of Life on Earth and Beyond* (5–9). Illus. 1987, Dutton $11.95 (0-525-67195-1). This book explores the fascinating topic of whether or not intelligent life exists in our galaxy. (Rev: BL 7/87) [574.999]

4772 Branley, Franklyn M. *Space Colony: Frontier of the 21st Century* (7–10). Illus. 1982, Elsevier $10.95 (0-525-66741-5). The present status of space colonies and the possible developments in the future are discussed. [629.44]

4773 Cohen, Daniel, and Susan Cohen. *Heroes of the Challenger* (5–8). Illus. 1986, Archway paper $2.50 (0-671-62948-4). Biographies of each of the astronauts on the *Challenger* are given, plus details of the tragedy and of space exploration in general. (Rev: SLJ 9/86) [629.47]

4774 Collins, Michael. *Flying to the Moon, and Other Strange Places* (7–10). Illus. 1976, Farrar paper $3.45 (0-374-42355-5). An account that describes how it was to train and be part of the flight to the moon. [629.45]

4775 Crouch, Tom D. *The National Aeronautics and Space Administration* (7–10). Illus. 1990, Chelsea House $14.95 (1-55546-120-4). A history of the government's involvement in flight since the Wright brothers and a rundown on present activities. (Rev: BL 5/15/90) [353]

4776 Dwiggins, Don. *Flying the Frontiers of Space* (7–9). Illus. 1982, Putnam LB $10.95 (0-396-08041-3). A description of the aircraft that led to the development of the space shuttle. [629.1]

4777 Fichter, George S. *The Space Shuttle* (7–9). Illus. 1981, Watts LB $10.40 (0-531-04354-1).

Good background information is given on the early attempts and successes to launch space shuttles. [629.44]

4778 Hawkes, Nigel. *Space Shuttle* (7–9). Illus. 1983, Watts LB $12.40 (0-531-04583-8). Large color illustrations highlight this book about the first space shuttles. [629.44]

4779 Herda, D. J. *Research Satellites* (5–9). Illus. 1987, Watts $10.40 (0-531-10311-0). A history of data-gathering space instruments plus how this development has helped in weather forecasting and other areas. (Rev: BR 1–2/88; SLJ 5/87) [629.44]

4780 Irvine, Mat. *Satellites and Computers* (7–9). 1984, Watts $11.90 (0-531-04817-9). An explanation of the role of computers in space satellites and the many functions satellites perform. [629.4]

4781 Lampton, Christopher. *Rocketry* (6–10). 1988, Watts LB $9.90 (0-531-10483-4). After giving a history of rockets, the author explains how they are used in space exploration. (Rev: BR 9–10/88) [629.133]

4782 Long, Kim. *The Astronaut Training Book for Kids* (6–9). Illus. 1990, Lodestar $15.95 (0-525-67296-6). After a historic overview of manned space flight, this account tells about the elements of training necessary to prepare for a variety of missions. (Rev: VOYA 8/90) [629.4]

4783 McDonough, Thomas R. *The Search for Extraterrestrial Intelligence: Listening for Life in the Cosmos* (9–12). Illus. 1987, Wiley $19.95 (0-471-84684-8). In nontechnical language, the author describes the projects and future possibilities in the search for extraterrestrial intelligence. (Rev: SLJ 6–7/87) [574.999]

4784 McPhee, Penelope, and Raymond McPhee. *Your Future in Space: The U.S. Space Camp Training Program* (6–8). Illus. 1986, Crown paper $14.95 (0-517-56418-1). A description of the U.S. Space Camp that takes youngsters from grades 5 through 10 for training. (Rev: SLJ 12/86) [629]

4785 Newton, David E. *U.S. and Soviet Space Programs* (7–10). Illus. 1988, Watts $12.40 (0-531-10515-6). An examination of the similarities and differences in the purposes and achievements of American and Russian space programs from Sputnik on. (Rev: BL 10/1/88; BR 9–10/88; SLJ 6–7/88; VOYA 10/88) [387.8]

4786 O'Connor, Karen. *Sally Ride and the New Astronauts: Scientists in Space* (7–10). Illus. 1983, Watts LB $11.90 (0-531-04602-8). A description of the careers of women astronauts, particularly Sally Ride. [629.45]

4787 Poynter, Margaret, and Michael J. Klein. *Cosmic Quest: Searching for Intelligent Life among the Stars* (6–9). 1984, Macmillan $11.95 (0-689-31068-4). This account tells of the SETI (Search for Extraterrestrial Intelligence) Project, which was founded by a group of international scientists. [574.999]

4788 Schulke, Flip, et al. *Your Future in Space: The U.S. Space Camp Training Program* (6–10). Illus. 1986, Crown paper $14.95 (0-517-56418-1). A clear account on the training of astronauts and how they use these skills in flight. (Rev: BL 1/1/87) [629.4]

4789 Smith, Howard E. *Daring the Unknown: A History of NASA* (6–9). Illus. 1987, Harcourt $14.95 (0-15-200435-1). An account that concentrates on the history of NASA, its accomplishments, and the important people involved. (Rev: BL 1/15/88; SLJ 1/88) [353.0087]

4790 Spangenburg, Ray, and Diane Moser. *Living and Working in Space* (7–10). Illus. 1989, Facts on File $22.95 (0-8160-1849-9). An account of the problems posed by the use of space shuttles and by the creation of space stations. For a rundown of the people involved in our space program use *Space People from A–Z* (1990). (Rev: BL 4/15/90; BR 5–6/90; VOYA 6/90) [639.4]

4791 Stern, Alan. *The U.S. Space Program after Challenger: Where Are We Going?* (7–12). Illus. 1987, Watts $11.90 (0-531-10412-5). An outline of our space program since Sputnik plus an examination of the alternatives after the Challenger disaster. (Rev: BL 2/15/88; SLJ 3/88; VOYA 6/88) [387.8]

4792 Taylor, L. B., Jr. *Commercialization of Space* (7–12). Illus. 1987, Watts $11.90 (0-531-10236-X). The use of space for profit in such areas as satellites, mining, and energy production is discussed. (Rev: BL 5/15/87; BR 9–10/87; SLJ 6–7/87; VOYA 8–9/87) [338]

4793 Taylor, L. B., Jr. *Gifts from Space: How Space Technology Is Improving Life on Earth* (7–9). 1977, Harper $12.70 (0-381-90056-8). This book tells how by-products of space research such as computer chips and electronic implants have affected our lives. [629]

4794 Taylor, L. B., Jr. *Space: Battleground of the Future?* (7–10). Illus. 1988, Watts $11.90 (0-531-10514-8). An update of the 1983 edition with extensive coverage on Reagan's Star Wars initiative. (Rev: BL 6/15/88; BR 11–12/88; SLJ 8/88; VOYA 10/88) [358]

4795 Taylor, L. B., Jr. *Space Shuttle* (7–9). 1979, Harper $12.70 (0-690-03897-6). Though somewhat dated this is a description of NASA's space shuttle program and its benefits for us. [629.47]

4796 Trefil, James S. *Living in Space* (7–10). Illus. 1981, Macmillan $10.95 (0-684-17171-6). The possible nature of space colonies and how they might come to be are discussed. [629.44]

4797 Vogt, Gregory. *The Space Shuttle* (7–10). Illus. 1983, Watts LB $12.90 (0-531-04669-9). An explanation of the workings of a space shuttle and how young scientists can get space aboard for their own experiments. [500.5]

4798 Vogt, Gregory. *A Twenty-fifth Anniversary Album of NASA* (7–10). 1983, Watts $12.95 (0-531-04655-9). This account traces the history and accomplishments of the National Aeronautics and Space Administration. [629.4]

4799 White, Jack R. *Satellites of Today and Tomorrow* (6–8). 1985, Dodd $10.95 (0-396-08514-8). This account covers how satellites are made, how they are placed in space, and how they are used. (Rev: VOYA 4/86) [629.44]

Comets, Meteors, and Asteroids

4800 Anderson, Norman D., and Walter R. Brown. *Halley's Comet* (7–9). Illus. 1981, Dodd LB $9.95 (0-396-07974-1). An account written before the comet's appearance in 1985–1986 that tells about its history and previous visits. [523.6]

4801 Asimov, Isaac. *How Did We Find Out about Comets?* (6–9). Illus. 1975, Walker $10.95 (0-8027-6204-2). After introducing comets, this volume outlines our knowledge and attitudes about comets from ancient times to today. [523.6]

4802 Berger, Melvin. *Comets, Meteors and Asteroids* (7–9). Illus. 1981, Putnam LB $6.99 (0-399-61148-7). A rundown on the composition and origin of these bodies and present-day knowledge about them. [523.6]

4803 Branley, Franklyn M. *Halley: Comet 1986* (7–9). Illus. 1982, Lodestar $10.95 (0-525-66780-6). Using the life of Halley and his discoveries as a beginning, the author gives general information about comets and their strange behavior. [523.6]

4804 Branley, Franklyn M. *Mysteries of the Satellites* (6–8). Illus. 1986, Dutton $11.95 (0-525-67176-5). Branley tries to explain some of the mysteries of the orbiting bodies—where they came from, their composition, and where they travel. (Rev: BL 11/1/86; SLJ 11/86) [523.9]

4805 Couper, Heather. *Comets and Meteors* (5–9). Illus. 1985, Watts LB $11.90 (0-531-10000-6). With excellent illustrations, this is an introduction to the group of smaller heavenly bodies. (Rev: SLJ 2/86) [523.6]

4806 Donnelly, Judy, and Sydelle Kramer. *Space Junk: Pollution beyond the Earth* (6–9). Illus. 1990, Morrow LB $12.88 (0-688-08679-9). This book tells how we are polluting space with such objects as used satellites and parts of rockets. (Rev: SLJ 9/90) [629.4]

4807 Fichter, George S. *Comets and Meteors* (7–9). Illus. 1982, Watts LB $10.40 (0-531-04382-7). After explaining what comets and meteors are, this account tells how to spot them. [523.6]

4808 Moskin, Marietta. *Sky Dragons and Flaming Swords* (7–10). Illus. 1985, Walker $12.95 (0-8027-6575-0). An up-to-date account of such phenomena as comets, eclipses, and meteors. (Rev: BR 5–6/86) [523.6]

4809 Winter, Frank H. *Comet Watch: The Return of Halley's Comet* (6–9). Illus. 1986, Lerner LB $9.95 (0-8225-1579-2). A history of comets is given plus theories about their existence and good background material on Halley's Comet. (Rev: SLJ 4/86) [523.6]

Earth and the Moon

4810 Blumberg, Rhoda. *The First Travel Guide to the Moon: What to Pack, How to Go, and What to See When You Get There* (7–9). 1980, Macmillan $9.95 (0-02-711680-8). Everything one would need for a successful tour of the moon. [523.3]

4811 Couper, Heather, and Nigel Henbest. *The Moon* (7–10). Illus. 1987, Watts LB $11.90 (0-531-10266-1). The story of the moon, its origin, eclipses, and exploration. (Rev: BR 9–10/87; SLJ 4/87) [523.3]

Sun and the Solar System

4812 Asimov, Isaac. *Venus, Near Neighbor of the Sun* (6–9). Illus. 1981, Lothrop LB $12.95 (0-688-51976-8). Information about Venus and Mercury plus comets and asteroids. [523.4]

4813 Branley, Franklyn M. *Jupiter: King of the Gods, Giant of the Planets* (6–9). Illus. 1981,

Lodestar $12.95 (0-525-66739-3). Information about Jupiter and its satellites using information from the *Voyager* probe. [523.4]

4814 Branley, Franklyn M. *Mysteries of the Planets* (6–9). Illus. 1988, Dutton $11.95 (0-525-67240-0). Data are given on each of the planets including material on temperature, size, and satellites. (Rev: BL 11/1/88) [523.4]

4815 Branley, Franklyn M. *Saturn: The Spectacular Planet* (6–9). Illus. 1983, Harper LB $12.95 (0-690-04214-0); paper $4.95 (0-06-446056-8). An introduction to this planet and the theories concerning its rings. [523.4]

4816 Couper, Heather, and Nigel Henbest. *The Sun* (5–8). Illus. 1986, Watts LB $11.90 (0-531-10055-3). In addition to material on the composition of the sun and its functions, this account covers such topics as sunspots and eclipses. (Rev: SLJ 3/87) [523.7]

4817 Darling, David J. *The Planets: The Next Frontier* (6–9). Illus. 1984, Dillon LB $10.95 (0-87518-263-1). Descriptions in text and photographs of the planets are given plus hints on how they can be observed. [523.4]

4818 Gallant, Roy A. *The Planets: Exploring the Solar System* (6–9). Illus. 1982, Macmillan $15.95 (0-02-736930-7). A straightforward tour of the solar system with stops at each of the planets. [523.2]

4819 Kelch, Joseph W. *Small Worlds: Exploring the 60 Moons of Our Solar System* (5–8). Illus. 1990, Messner LB $16.98 (0-671-70013-8). A guided tour of the 60 moons that we know exist in the solar sytem with a short history of space exploration. (Rev: BL 8/90; SLJ 9/90) [523.9]

4820 Lampton, Christopher. *The Sun* (6–9). Illus. 1982, Watts LB $10.40 (0-531-04390-8). What we once thought of the sun and what we currently know are the 2 principal topics covered in this volume. [523.7]

4821 Lauber, Patricia. *Journey to the Planets* (7–9). 1982, Crown $13.95 (0-517-54477-6). The characteristics of each of the planets in the solar system are described. [523.4]

4822 Nourse, Alan E. *The Giant Planets* (6–10). Rev. ed. Illus. 1982, Watts LB $10.40 (0-531-00816-9). Introductory information on Jupiter, Saturn, Uranus, Neptune, and Pluto. [523.4]

4823 Spangenburg, Ray, and Diane Moser. *Exploring the Reaches of the Solar System* (7–10). Illus. 1990, Facts on File $22.95 (0-8160-1850-2). This is a fine summary of what the space probes have told us about the solar system. For histori-

cal information use *Opening the Space Frontier* (1989). (Rev: BL 4/15/90) [639]

4824 Vogt, Gregory. *Mars and the Inner Planets* (6–10). Illus. 1982, Watts LB $10.40 (0-531-04384-3). An introduction to Mars plus reports on Venus and Mercury. [523.4]

Stars

4825 Asimov, Isaac. *How Did We Find Out about Black Holes?* (6–9). Illus. 1978, Walker LB $12.95 (0-8027-6337-5). The research that lead to our ideas about collapsed stars and present thoughts on the subject is presented simply. [523.8]

4826 Berger, Melvin. *Bright Stars, Red Giants and White Dwarfs* (7–9). Illus. 1983, Putnam LB $6.99 (0-399-61209-2). The life cycle of stars is discussed and the current theories concerning this topic are presented. [523.8]

4827 Couper, Heather, and Nigel Henbest. *Galaxies and Quasars* (7–10). Illus. 1987, Watts LB $11.90 (0-531-10265-3). This oversized book looks at many galaxies (chiefly the Milky Way), the universe, and how it is expanding. (Rev: BR 9–10/87; SLJ 4/87) [523.8]

4828 Gallant, Roy A. *Private Lives of the Stars* (6–8). Illus. 1986, Macmillan $13.95 (0-02-737350-9). An account of how stars are formed, of the various stages in their lives, and the various types in existence. (Rev: BL 2/1/87; BR 5–6/87; SLJ 12/86) [523.8]

4829 Lampton, Christopher. *Supernova!* (6–10). Illus. 1988, Watts $12.90 (0-531-10602-0). The story of the occurrence of the first observed supernova in 1987 and its impact on our theories of the universe. (Rev: BL 12/1/88; BR 3–4/89; SLJ 2/89; VOYA 4/89) [523.8]

4830 Muirden, James. *About Stars and Planets* (5–8). Illus. 1987, Watts $11.90 (0-531-19023-4). A broad outline that covers topics such as stars, galaxies, the universe, and our solar system. (Rev: SLJ 5/87) [523.8]

4831 Zim, Herbert, and Robert Baker. *Stars* (7–12). 1985, Western paper $3.95 (0-307-24493-8). A fine little paperback guide to stars and the solar system. [523.8]

Universe

4832 Branley, Franklyn M. *Mysteries of Outer Space* (6–8). Illus. 1985, Dutton $11.95 (0-525-67149-8). Through a series of questions, the nature of outer space is described and the possibility of life there is explored. (Rev: BL 4/15/85; SLJ 8/85) [500.5]

4833 Branley, Franklyn M. *Mysteries of the Universe* (6–9). Illus. 1984, Lodestar $10.95 (0-525-66914-0). While explaining such concepts as black holes and pulsars, this account also mentions theories on the creation and possible future of the universe. [523.1]

4834 Fisher, David E. *The Origin and Evolution of Our Own Particular Universe* (7–12). 1988, Macmillan $14.95 (0-689-32368-3). An introduction to what we believe about the beginnings of our universe that introduces such concepts as

relativity, black holes, and the big bang theory. (Rev: BL 1/1/89; SLJ 1/89; VOYA 2/89) [523.1]

4835 Friedman, Herbert. *The Amazing Universe* (7–10). Illus. 1975, National Geographic LB $9.50 (0-87044-184-1). A well-illustrated account that gives general information and theories related to the universe and its components. [523.1]

4836 Jacobs, Francine. *Cosmic Countdown: What Astronomers Have Learned about the Life of the Universe* (7–9). Illus. 1983, Evans $9.95 (0-87131-404-5). The big bang theory, the life of stars, and radio astronomy are 3 topics covered here. [523.1]

4837 Lampton, Christopher. *New Theories on the Birth of the Universe* (6–9). Illus. 1989, Watts LB $13.40 (0-531-10782-5). An up-to-date account that explores various theories on the origin of the universe and the latest beliefs of scientists on the subject. (Rev: BL 11/15/89; BR 3–4/90; VOYA 6/90) [523.1]

Biological Sciences

■■■■

General and Miscellaneous

4838 Asimov, Isaac. *How Did We Find Out about the Beginning of Life?* (6–9). Illus. 1982, Walker LB $10.85 (0-8027-6448-7). A history of various theories on the origin of life concluding with present-day thoughts on the subject. [577]

4839 Corrick, James A. *Recent Revolutions in Biology* (8–12). Illus. 1987, Watts $12.95 (0-531-10341-2). From recent discoveries in evolution to the latest in genetic engineering this is a fine account of the present frontiers in biology. (Rev: BL 3/1/87; BR 9–10/87; SLJ 8/87; VOYA 8-9/87) [574]

4840 Evans, Ifor. *Biology* (6–8). Illus. 1984, Watts $12.40 (0-531-04743-1). A general introduction to biology covering such topics as cells, reproduction, growth, and evolution. [574]

4841 Fichter, George S. *Cells* (6–8). Illus. 1986, Watts $10.40 (0-531-10210-6). This introductory account covers such subjects as the kinds, structure, and reproduction of cells, and genetic engineering. (Rev: BL 12/15/86; SLJ 2/87) [574.87]

4842 *Our Continent: A Natural History of North America* (7–12). Illus. 1976, National Geographic $14.95 (0-87044-153-1). The plant and animal life on this continent are described over a 4-billion-year time span. [574.9]

4843 *Patterns of Life on Earth* (5–9). Illus. 1984, Arco $9.95 (0-668-06182-0). This book is a well-illustrated introduction to biology and its various divisions. (Rev: BL 4/1/85) [574]

4844 Raham, R. Gary. *Dinosaurs in the Garden: An Evolutionary Guide to Backyard Biology* (6–10). Illus. 1988, Plexus $22.95 (0-937548-10-3). The author uses common creatures to explain how they fit into the scheme of nature and overall patterns of evolution. (Rev: BL 12/1/88) [575]

Botany

General and Miscellaneous

4845 Lambert, David. *Vegetation* (6–8). 1984, Watts $11.40 (0-531-03804-1). A volume that introduces the variety of plant life found on our planet and the various ways plant life manages to survive and adapt. [581]

Foods

4846 Penner, Lucille Recht. *The Honey Book* (7–9). Illus. 1980, Hastings $10.95 (0-8038-3054-8). An account that describes the history of honey plus a compilation of 50 recipes using it. [638]

4847 Tchudi, Stephen. *Soda Poppery: The History of Soft Drinks in America* (5–9). 1986, Macmillan $13.95 (0-684-18488-5). Americans once believed that soda pop was good for general well-being. This and many other facts are included in this history of soft drinks. (Rev: BL 5/15/86; SLJ 9/86) [338.4]

Fungi

4848 Johnson, Sylvia A. *Mushrooms* (6–9). Illus. 1982, Lerner LB $12.95 (0-8225-1473-7). A stunning look at mushrooms and how they grow, shown in photographs and lucid text. [589.2]

4849 Lincoff, Gary. *The Audubon Society Field Guide to North American Mushrooms* (7–12). Illus. 1981, Knopf LB $14.45 (0-394-51992-2). Over 700 species are introduced and pictured in color photographs. [589.2]

Forestry and Trees

4850 Brockman, C. Frank. *Trees of North America* (7–12). Illus. 1968, Golden paper $9.95 (0-307-63658-5). This handy guide identifies 594 different trees that grow north of Mexico. [582.16]

4851 Burnie, David. *Tree* (6–8). Illus. 1988, Knopf LB $13.99 (0-394-99617-8). In a series of short, lushly illustrated chapters such topics as bark, leaves, cones, and tree diseases are introduced. (Rev: SLJ 12/88) [582.12]

4852 Line, Les, et al. *The Audubon Society Book of Trees* (7–12). Illus. 1981, Abrams $35.00 (0-8109-0673-2). Using various environments as chapter headings (for example, tropical rain forest), this is a worldwide introduction to trees. [582.16]

4853 Little, Elbert L. *The Audubon Society Field Guide to North American Trees: Eastern Region* (7–12). Illus. 1980, Knopf $14.45 (0-394-50760-6). This volume describes through text and pictures of leaves, needles, and so on, the trees found east of the Rocky Mountains. [582.16]

4854 Little, Elbert L. *The Audubon Society Field Guide to North American Trees: Western Region* (7–12). Illus. 1980, Knopf $14.45 (0-394-50761-4). Trees west of the Rockies are identified and pictured in photos and drawings. [582.16]

4855 Mabey, Richard. *Oak and Company* (7–9). Illus. 1983, Greenwillow $11.75 (0-688-01993-5). The story of a 200-year-old oak tree and how it grew and helped sustain life around it. [583]

4856 Petrides, George A. *A Field Guide to Trees and Shrubs* (7–12). 2nd ed. Illus. 1972, Houghton paper $13.95 (0-395-17579-8). A total of 646 varieties found in northern United States and southern Canada are described and illustrated. [582.1]

4857 Selsam, Millicent E. *Tree Flowers* (6–9). Illus. 1984, Morrow LB $12.88 (0-688-02769-5).

Flowering trees are identified and in 12 cases, like the magnolia and apple tree, watercolors are used to illustrate their beauty. [582.16]

4858 Whipple, Jane B. *Forest Resources* (5–8). 1985, Watts LB $10.40 (0-531-04909-4). This book includes material on types of forests found in the United States, today's logging industry, and the part played by forests in our history. (Rev: SLJ 12/85) [574.5]

4859 Zim, Herbert, and Alexander C. Martin. *Trees* (7–12). 1952, Western paper $3.95 (0-307-24056-8). A description of 143 species of North American trees. [582.16]

Plants and Flowers

4860 Asimov, Isaac. *How Did We Find Out about Photosynthesis?* (6–8). Illus. 1989, Walker LB $11.85 (0-8027-6886-5). The process of how plants turn sunlight into food is explored along with the unanswered questions about this phenomenon that scientists are still trying to understand. (Rev: BL 1/15/90; VOYA 4/90) [581.1]

4861 Burnie, David. *Plant* (5–9). Illus. 1989, Knopf LB $13.99 (0-394-92252-2). Extraordinary photographs and clear text are used to introduce the plant world. (Rev: BL 10/15/89) [581]

4862 Busch, Phyllis B. *Wildflowers and the Stories behind Their Names* (7–9). Illus. 1977, Macmillan $10.00 (0-684-14820-X). In this compact volume, 60 wildflowers are identified and pictured. [582.13]

4863 Crowell, Robert L. *The Lore & Legends of Flowers* (7–9). Illus. 1982, Harper LB $14.89 (0-690-04035-0). The origins and characteristics of 10 different common flowers such as irises and dandelions are given. [582.13]

4864 Dowden, Anne Ophelia. *The Clover & the Bee: A Book of Pollination* (5–10). Illus. 1990, Harper LB $17.89 (0-690-04679-0). An account that introduces the parts of flowers, the need for pollination, and how it is accomplished. (Rev: BL 5/15/90; SLJ 7/90; VOYA 6/90) [582]

4865 Dowden, Anne Ophelia. *From Flower to Fruit* (6–9). Illus. 1984, Harper $14.70 (0-690-04402-X). A description of seeds, how they are scattered, and how fruit is produced. [582]

4866 Dowden, Anne Ophelia. *State Flowers* (6–9). Illus. 1978, Harper LB $13.89 (0-690-03884-4). Each state's flower is introduced alphabetically and pictured in realistic drawings. [582.13]

4867 Eshleman, Alan. *Poison Plants* (7–9). Illus. 1970, Houghton $12.95 (0-395-25298-9). A description of all kinds of poisonous plants (for example, some types of fungi) and how to identify them. [581.6]

4868 Fichter, George S. *Wildflowers of North America* (5–8). 1982, Random paper $5.95 (0-394-84770-9). For the beginning naturalists, a basic identification guide to common wildflowers. [582.13]

4869 Holmes, Anita. *Cactus: The All-American Plant* (6–9). Illus. 1982, Macmillan $14.95 (0-590-07402-4). A discussion of cacti, specifically, but also of general desert flora and fauna. [635.9]

4870 Janulewicz, Mike. *Plants* (6–9). Illus. 1984, Watts LB $12.40 (0-531-03477-1). An examination of the different kinds of plants and of their various parts. [581]

4871 Kavaler, Lucy. *Green Magic: Algae Rediscovered* (7–9). Illus. 1983, Harper $12.70 (0-690-04221-3). This unusual class of plants is highlighted with coverage on how in the future they might be an important source of food. [589.3]

4872 Lerner, Carol. *Dumb Cane and Daffodils: Poisonous Plants in the House and Garden* (5–9). Illus. 1990, Morrow LB $13.88 (0-688-08796-5). A fascinating glimpse at common garden plants such as narcissus bulbs and delphiniums that are poisonous. (Rev: BL 2/15/90) [581.6]

4873 Lerner, Carol. *Pitcher Plants* (7–9). Illus. 1983, Morrow LB $12.88 (0-688-01718-5). Various species of these mysterious plants are highlighted in words and pictures. [583]

4874 Martin, Alexander C. *Weeds* (7–12). 1973, Western paper $3.95 (0-307-24353-2). A compact guide to many different varieties of weeds, how to identify them, and their characteristics. [632]

4875 Martin, Alexander C., and Herbert Zim. *Flowers* (7–12). 1987, Western paper $3.95 (0-307-24054-1). An introduction to many flowers with material on how to identify and grow them. [582.13]

4876 Niehaus, Theodore F. *A Field Guide to Pacific States Wildflowers* (7–12). Illus. 1976, Houghton paper $12.95 (0-395-31662-6). About 1,500 wildflowers from the Pacific States are highlighted in this volume of the Peterson Field Guide series. [582.13]

4877 Overbeck, Cynthia. *Carnivorous Plants* (7–9). Illus. 1982, Lerner LB $12.95 (0-8225-1470-2). An explanation of how these plants evolved plus examples in text and pictures. [581.5]

4878 Peterson, Roger Tory, and Margaret McKenny. *A Field Guide to Wildflowers of Northeastern and North-Central North America* (7–12). Illus. 1968, Houghton $17.95 (0-395-08086-X);

paper $12.95 (0-395-18325-1). Approximately 1,300 wildflowers are described in this Peterson Field Guide to the flowers of our northern, central, and eastern states. [582.13]

4879 Pringle, Laurence. *Wild Foods* (7–9). Illus. 1978, Macmillan $12.95 (0-590-07511-X). Pringle describes in text and pictures 19 edible plants and gives recipes for their tasty preparation. [581.6]

4880 Rahn, Joan Elma. *More Plants That Changed History* (6–9). Illus. 1985, Macmillan $11.95 (0-689-31099-4). In this account the author traces the impact of papyrus, rubber, tea, and opium on world history and cultural development. (Rev: BL 5/15/85; SLJ 10/85) [581]

4881 Venning, Frank D. *Wildflowers of North America* (7–12). Illus. 1984, Western paper $3.95 (0-307-13664-7). A concise guide that describes in text and illustrations hundreds of wildflowers that grow in North America. [582.13]

4882 Woods, Sylvia. *Plant Facts and Fancies* (6–9). Illus. 1985, Faber $10.95 (0-571-13436-X). A survey of plant life that covers such topics as their history and uses, and unusual facts about them. (Rev: SLJ 11/85) [581]

Zoology

General and Miscellaneous

4883 Chinery, Michael, ed. *Dictionary of Animals* (6–9). Illus. 1984, Arco $17.95 (0-668-06155-3). In dictionary format, this handbook contains pictures and descriptions of about 2,000 different animals. (Rev: BL 4/1/85) [591]

4884 Curtis, Patricia. *Animal Rights: Stories of People Who Defend the Rights of Animals* (7–9). 1980, Macmillan $9.95 (0-02-725580-8). From experimental laboratories to factory farms, this is an account of the various ways animals are abused and the dedicated people who fight for animal rights. [179]

4885 Dolan, Edward F., Jr. *Animal Rights* (7–10). Illus. 1986, Watts $12.90 (0-531-10247-5). A searing account of how animals are mistreated today from experimentation to circus use and what young people can do about it. (Rev: BL 10/15/86; BR 9–10/87; SLJ 1/87) [346]

4886 Freedman, Russell. *Animal Superstars: Biggest, Strongest, Fastest, Smartest* (7–9). 1984, Prentice paper $5.95 (0-13-037615-9). A Guinness-type book of records from the animal kingdom. [591]

4887 Gallant, Roy A. *The Rise of Mammals* (5–8). Illus. 1986, Watts $10.40 (0-531-10206-8). An account that stretches from the emergence of mammals to today's problems with population growth. (Rev: BR 5–6/87) [559]

4888 Hiller, Ilo. *Introducing Mammals to Young Naturalists* (5–9). Illus. 1990, Texas A & M $21.50 (0-89096-427-0); paper $12.95 (0-89096-428-9). An introduction to a number of mammals; most, like the squirrels, are common while others, like the armadillo, are more exotic. (Rev: BL 7/90) [599]

4889 Hoffmeister, Donald, and Herbert Zim. *Mammals* (7–12). 1987, Western paper $3.95 (0-307-24058-4). This book identifies 218 species and gives details on the habitats of each. [559]

4890 Hutchins, Ross E. *Nature Invented It First* (7–9). Illus. 1980, Dodd LB $6.95 (0-396-07788-9). An introduction to specific animal behavior and adjustments that have their counterparts in the modern world (for example, air-conditioning). [591]

4891 Poynter, Margaret. *Too Few Happy Endings: The Dilemma of the Humane Societies* (7–9). 1981, Macmillan $9.95 (0-689-30864-7). The activities inside a humane society are described, and some of the unusual stories behind its caring for animals are presented. [179]

4892 Pringle, Laurence. *The Animal Rights Controversy* (7–12). Illus. 1989, Harcourt $15.95 (0-15-203559-1). A book about the way animals are abused and misused that covers topics such as factory farming, experimentation, and zoos. (Rev: BL 1/15/90; SLJ 5/90; VOYA 4/90) [197]

4893 Seddon, Tony. *Animal Vision* (5–8). Illus. 1988, Facts on File $13.95 (0-8160-1652-6). With accompanying photographs, this book explores the many types and uses of eyes in the animal kingdom. (Rev: SLJ 1/89) [591.51]

4894 Weber, William J. *Wild Orphan Babies: Mammals and Birds* (7–9). Illus. Holt, $9.95 (0-03-044976-6); paper $5.95 (0-03-056821-8). This account describes how to care for orphaned or injured wild animals and how to release them back to the wild. [590]

Amphibians and Reptiles

GENERAL AND MISCELLANEOUS

4895 Conant, Roger. *A Field Guide to Reptiles and Amphibians of Eastern and Central North America* (7–12). 2nd ed. Illus. 1975, Houghton $17.95 (0-395-19979-4); paper $12.95 (0-395-

19977-8). Another authoritative volume in the Peterson Field Guide series. This one identifies hundreds of turtles, snakes, frogs, crocodiles, and other amphibians and reptiles. A companion volume is: *A Field Guide to Western Reptiles and Amphibians* (1985). [597.6]

4896 Fichter, George S. *Reptiles and Amphibians of North America* (5–8). 1982, Random paper $5.95 (0-384-84769-5). A simple introduction to the identification of many common reptiles and amphibians. [597.9]

4897 Smith, Hobart M., and Edmund Brodie Jr. *Reptiles of North America* (7–10). Illus. 1982, Western $9.95 (0-307-13666-3). This book identifies many reptiles, gives pictures of them, and describes their habitats. [597.9]

4898 Smith, Hobart M., and Herbert Zim. *Reptiles and Amphibians* (7–12). Illus. 1987, Western paper $3.95 (0-307-24057-6). A concise well-illustrated guide to 212 American species. [597.9]

4899 Stidworthy, John. *Reptiles and Amphibians* (5–9). Illus. 1989, Facts on File $17.95 (0-8160-1965-7). Excellent photographs and a concise text highlight this very attractive introduction to these species. (Rev: BL 1/15/90; BR 5–6/90) [597.6]

FROGS AND TOADS

4900 Mattison, Chris. *Frogs & Toads of the World* (8–12). Illus. 1987, Facts on File $22.95 (0-8160-1602-X). An overview of these amphibians under such topics as physiology, feeding, and reproduction. (Rev: BL 4/15/88; BR 3–4/88; VOYA 10/88) [597.8]

SNAKES AND LIZARDS

4901 Fichter, George S. *Poisonous Snakes* (7–9). Illus. 1982, Watts LB $10.40 (0-531-04349-5). Such snakes as cobras and vipers are pictured and described. [597.9]

4902 Griehl, Klaus. *Snakes* (6–8). 1984, Barron's paper $4.95 (0-8120-2813-9). As well as identifying many snakes, this book tells how to take care of them in a terrarium. [597.96]

4903 Roever, J. M. *Snake Secrets* (6–9). 1979, Walker LB $11.85 (0-8027-6333-2). An in-depth look at snakes, their behavior, and how people react to them. [597.96]

4904 Simon, Seymour. *Poisonous Snakes* (6–9). Illus. 1981, Macmillan $13.95 (0-590-07513-6). An explanation of venom and fangs is given and an introduction to the world's most famous poisonous snakes. [597.9]

Animal Behavior

GENERAL AND MISCELLANEOUS

4905 Arnosky, Jim. *Secrets of a Wildlife Watcher* (7–9). Illus. 1983, Lothrop LB $11.88 (0-688-02081-X). A guide to successful finding and viewing such wildlife as deer, squirrels, and rabbits. [591.5]

4906 Crump, Donald J., ed. *How Animals Behave: A New Look at Wildlife* (6–9). Illus. 1984, National Geographic LB $8.50 (0-87044-505-7). A general, colorful introduction to why and how animals perform such functions as courting, living together, and caring for their young. [591.5]

4907 Freedman, Russell. *Can Bears Predict Earthquakes? Unsolved Mysteries of Animal Behavior* (7–9). 1982, Prentice $10.95 (0-13-114009-4). This book answers such questions about animal behavior as how smart are dolphins and are there really elephant "burial" grounds. [591.51]

4908 Hughey, Pat. *Scavengers and Decomposers: The Cleanup Crew* (7–9). Illus. 1984, Macmillan $13.95 (0-689-31032-3). Nature's garbage collectors—animals, birds, and plants—are highlighted. [591.5]

4909 Kohl, Judith, and Herbert Kohl. *Pack, Band, and Colony: The World of Social Animals* (7–9). Illus. 1983, Farrar $13.95 (0-374-35694-7). Termites and wolves are 2 of the social animals described here. [591.5]

4910 Kohl, Judith, and Herbert Kohl. *The View from the Oak* (6–8). 1988, Little $13.95 (0-316-50137-9). An exploration of the senses of various different animals. [591.51]

4911 Parker, Steve. *Mammal* (5–9). Illus. 1989, Knopf LB $13.99 (0-394-92258-1). In text and full-color photographs, animal evolution is explained and a variety of mammals are introduced. (Rev: BL 9/15/89; BR 11–12/89) [599]

4912 Patent, Dorothy Hinshaw. *How Smart Are Animals?* (7–12). 1990, Harcourt $16.95 (0-15-236770-5). The controversy involving instinct versus thought in animal behavior is well explored with many examples to support both points of view. (Rev: BL 3/15/90; SLJ 6/90; VOYA 8/90) [591.5]

4913 Pringle, Laurence. *Animals at Play* (6–8). Illus. 1985, Harcourt $12.95 (0-15-203554-0). The author looks at the role of play behavior in a number of species of animals to find a relationship to human activities. (Rev: BL 5/1/86; SLJ 2/86)

4914 Pringle, Laurence. *Feral: Tame Animals Gone Wild* (7–10). Illus. 1983, Macmillan LB $11.95 (0-02-775420-0). What happens when dogs, pigs, cats, horses, and other domesticated animals run wild. [591.5]

4915 Rahn, Joan Elma. *Keeping Warm, Keeping Cool* (7–9). Illus. 1983, Macmillan $12.95 (0-689-30995-3). How animals adjust to changes in temperature. [591.19]

4916 Sattler, Helen Roney. *Fish Facts & Bird Brains: Animal Intelligence* (7–9). Illus. 1984, Lodestar $12.95 (0-525-66915-9). An exploration of animal intelligence starting with the lowly worm and ending with language training for primates. [591.5]

4917 Simon, Hilda. *Sight and Seeing: A World of Light and Color* (6–9). Illus. 1983, Putnam $12.95 (0-399-20929-8). The importance of vision in animals is highlighted and how eyes develop in various species. [591.1]

4918 Wilcox, Tamara. *Bats, Cats, and Sacred Cows* (7–9). 1977, Raintree LB $14.65 (0-8172-1026-1). This account describes some unusual animal behavior and how it has affected humans. [591.5]

CAMOUFLAGE

4919 Bailey, Jill. *Mimicry and Camouflage* (5–8). Illus. 1988, Facts on File $13.95 (0-8160-1657-7). In lavish photographs, this book explores the amazing ways nature uses camouflage—whether to hide, attract, or warn. (Rev: SLJ 1/89) [591.57]

COMMUNICATION

4920 Gravelle, Karen, and Anne Squire. *Animal Talk* (6–8). Illus. 1988, Messner $9.79 (0-671-63726-6). How and why animals communicate with one another and the methods used to do so. (Rev: BL 10/15/88) [591.59]

REPRODUCTION AND BABIES

4921 McClung, Robert M. *The Amazing Egg* (6–9). Illus. 1980, Dutton $15.95 (0-525-25480-3). All kinds of eggs, from those of the jellyfish to those of birds, are introduced with accompanying drawings. [591.1]

TRACKS

4922 Murie, Olaus J. *A Field Guide to Animal Tracks* (7–12). 2nd ed. Illus. 1974, Houghton $17.95 (0-395-19978-6); paper $12.95 (0-395-18323-5). This important volume in the Peterson

Field Guide series first appeared in 1954 and now has become a classic in the area of identifying animal tracks and droppings. [591.5]

Animal Species

GENERAL AND MISCELLANEOUS

4923 Alden, Peter. *Peterson First Guide to Mammals of North America* (8–12). Illus. 1987, Houghton paper $3.95 (0-395-42767-3). An uncluttered basic guide to mammal identification with many illustrations and useful background material. (Rev: BL 5/15/87) [599]

4924 Blassingame, Wyatt. *The Strange Armadillo* (7–9). Illus. 1983, Putnam LB $8.95 (0-396-08190-0). The nature and characteristics of the armadillo are discussed plus information on the sloth and anteater. [599.3]

4925 Bramwell, Martyn, and Steve Parker. *Mammals: The Small Plant-Eaters* (6–10). Illus. 1989, Facts on File $17.95 (0-8160-1958-4). An introduction to each animal is given in text and outstanding illustrations. (Rev: VOYA 12/89) [559]

4926 Burt, William Henry. *A Field Guide to the Mammals* (7–12). 3rd ed. Illus. 1976, Houghton $17.95 (0-395-24082-4); paper $12.95 (0-395-24084-0). Part of the Peterson Field Guide series, this volume describes almost 400 species found north of Mexico. [599]

4927 Davidson, Margaret. *Wild Animal Families* (7–9). Illus. 1980, Hastings $8.95 (0-8038-8098-7). A variety of mammals are introduced as are their different ways of rearing families. [591.51]

4928 Facklam, Margery. *Wild Animals, Gentle Women* (7–9). Illus. 1978, Harcourt $5.95 (0-15-296987-X). The stories of 11 different women such as Jane Goodall and their careers with animals. [591.51]

4929 Kerrod, Robin. *Mammals: Primates, Insect-Eaters and Baleen Whales* (6–10). Illus. 1989, Facts on File $17.95 (0-8160-1961-4). Complete with superb photographs, this account introduces various animals and explains the living habits of each. (Rev: VOYA 12/89) [559]

4930 MacClintock, Dorcas. *A Natural History of Raccoons* (7–9). Illus. 1981, Macmillan $11.95 (0-684-16619-4). A portrait of these animals noted for both their curiosity and intelligence. [590]

4931 MacClintock, Dorcas. *A Natural History of Zebras* (7–9). Illus. 1976, Macmillan $2.95 (0-684-14621-9). An account that reveals the unusual habits and social behavior of the zebra. [590]

4932 Minelli, Giuseppe. *Mammals* (7–12). Illus. 1988, Facts on File $12.95 (0-8160-1560-0). This account of the evolution of mammals is particularly strong on illustrations. (Rev: BR 5–6/88) [599]

4933 North, Sterling. *Rascal: A Memoir of a Better Era* (7–12). Illus. 1963, Dutton $13.95 (0-525-18839-8); Avon paper $2.75 (0-380-01518-8). Remembrances of growing up in Wisconsin in 1918 and of the joys and problems of owning a pet raccoon. [599.74]

4934 O'Toole, Christopher, and John Stidworthy. *Mammals: The Hunters* (6–10). Illus. 1989, Facts on File $17.95 (0-8160-1959-2). Basic facts about each animal are given including habitats, complemented by amazing illustrations. (Rev: VOYA 12/89) [559]

4935 Stidworthy, John. *Mammals: The Large Plant-Eaters* (6–10). Illus. 1989, Facts on File $17.95 (0-8160-1960-6). Drawings and photographs are used effectively in this introduction to such animals as deer, elk, and moose. (Rev: VOYA 12/89) [559]

4936 Whitaker, John O., Jr. *The Audubon Society Field Guide to North American Mammals* (7–12). Illus. 1980, Knopf $14.45 (0-394-50762-2). This excellent guide contains almost 200 pages of color photographs. [599]

4937 *Wild Animals of North America* (7–12). Illus. 1979, National Geographic $19.95 (0-87044-294-5). A superbly illustrated guide to the common species of animals found on our continent. [599]

APE FAMILY

4938 McClung, Robert M. *Gorilla* (7–9). Illus. 1984, Morrow LB $12.88 (0-688-03876-X). The life cycle of gorillas is portrayed and efforts to preserve them are described. [599.88]

BEARS

4939 Calabro, Marian. *Operation Grizzly Bear* (5–8). Illus. 1989, Macmillan $12.95 (0-02-716241-9). An account by 2 naturalists on a 12-year study of silvertip bears in Yellowstone Park. (Rev: BL 3/15/90; VOYA 4/90) [599.74]

4940 Domico, Terry, and Mark Newman. *Bears of the World* (7–12). Illus. 1988, Facts on File $29.95 (0-8160-1536-8). An oversized volume containing more than 150 color photographs that surveys the various species of bears. (Rev: BL 2/15/89) [599.74]

4941 Ford, Barbara. *Black Bear: The Spirit of the Wilderness* (7–9). Illus. 1981, Houghton $8.95 (0-395-30444-X). A description of the behavior and habitats of this wilderness animal. [599.74]

4942 Graham, Ada, and Frank Graham. *Bears in the Wild* (7–9). Illus. 1981, Delacorte LB $8.44 (0-440-00538-8); Dell paper $2.25 (0-440-40897-0). The life cycle and habits of bears around the world are described. [599.74]

BIG CATS

4943 Hunt, Patricia. *Tigers* (7–9). Illus. 1981, Putnam LB $8.85 (0-396-07932-6). A description in text and black-and-white photographs of the largest member of the cat family. [599.74]

4944 Ryden, Hope. *Bobcat* (7–9). Illus. 1983, Putnam $10.95 (0-399-20976-X). This interesting member of the cat family—its characteristics and its evolution—is described in text and the author's photographs. [599.74]

DEER FAMILY

4945 Scott, Jack Denton. *Moose* (7–9). Illus. 1981, Putnam $9.95 (0-399-20721-X). This creature of the far north is described in words and beautiful photographs. [599.73]

MARSUPIALS

4946 Rue, Leonard Lee, III. *Meet the Opossum* (7–9). Illus. 1983, Putnam LB $8.95 (0-396-08221-1). A thorough and entertaining introduction to this common animal about which much legend exists. [599.2]

PANDAS

4947 Schlein, Miriam. *Project Panda Watch* (7–9). Illus. 1984, Macmillan $11.95 (0-689-31071-4). The efforts that are being made to save the giant panda from extinction are described. [599.74]

RODENTS

4948 Bare, Colleen Stanley. *Tree Squirrels* (7–9). Illus. 1983, Putnam LB $10.95 (0-396-08208-4). Lots of information on this exotic animal plus 48 of the author's own photographs. [599.32]

4949 Leen, Nina. *The Bat* (7–9). 1976, Holt $7.50 (0-03-015881-9). An account of how these unique mammals live and of their many benefits to people. [599.4]

4950 Silverstein, Alvin, and Virginia B. Silverstein. *Mice: All about Them* (6–9). Illus. 1980,

Harper LB $12.89 (0-397-31923-1). The physical characteristics and survival patterns of mice are described as well as some advice on keeping them as pets. [599.32]

Birds

GENERAL AND MISCELLANEOUS

4951 Austin, Oliver L., Jr. *Families of Birds* (7–12). Illus. 1971, Golden LB $9.95 (0-307-13669-8). This handy guide identifies over 200 bird families and gives many full-color illustrations. [598]

4952 Bailey, Jill, and Steve Parker. *Birds: The Plant- and Seed-Eaters* (5–9). Illus. 1989, Facts on File $17.95 (0-8160-1964-9). Stunning photography and a well-organized text highlight this description of many of our common birds. (Rev: BL 1/15/90; BR 5–6/90) [598.2]

4953 Blassingame, Wyatt. *Wonders of Egrets, Bitterns, and Herons* (6–9). Illus. 1982, Putnam LB $10.95 (0-396-08033-2). Thirteen different wading birds found in North America are introduced and their life cycles discussed. [598]

4954 Callahan, Philip S. *Birds and How They Function* (7–9). Illus. 1979, Holiday $8.95 (0-8234-0363-7). A book about the evolution, structure, and behavior of birds. [598]

4955 Dewey, Jennifer Owings. *Clem: The Story of a Raven* (7–10). Illus. 1986, Dodd $11.95 (0-396-08728-0). A delightful account of the Dewey family and of the raven they adopt. (Rev: BL 7/86; VOYA 8–10/86) [636.6]

4956 Haley, Neale. *Birds for Pets and Pleasure* (6–9). Illus. 1981, Delacorte LB $8.95 (0-385-28053-X); paper $4.95 (0-440-00475-6). The selection and care of such caged birds as canaries and budgies are discussed [636.6]

4957 Peterson, Roger Tory. *A Field Guide to the Birds* (7–12). 4th ed. rev. Illus. 1980, Houghton $17.95 (0-395-26621-1); paper $12.95 (0-395-26619-X). An exhaustive guide to the birds found east of the Rockies. A companion volume, also part of the Peterson Field Guide series, is: *A Field Guide to Western Birds* (1961). [598]

4958 Robbins, Chandler S., et al., eds. *Birds of North America* (7–12). Rev. ed. Illus. 1983, Western $12.95 (0-307-37002-X); paper $9.95 (0-307-33656-5). A handy compact guide arranged into 2 main sections—water birds and land birds. [598]

4959 Scott, Jack Denton. *Discovering the American Stork* (7–9). Illus. 1976, Harcourt $6.50 (0-

15-223580-9). The habitats of the stork are identified and an account of their habits is given. [598]

4960 Scott, Jack Denton. *Discovering the Mysterious Egret* (7–9). Illus. 1978, Harcourt $7.95 (0-15-223593-0). The habitats and habits of this graceful water bird are discussed and illustrated with photographs. [598]

4961 Scott, Jack Denton. *Orphans from the Sea* (6–9). Illus. 1982, Putnam $10.95 (0-399-20858-5). A description of the founding of the Suncoast Seabird Sanctuary in Florida and of its many activities to save wildlife. [639.9]

4962 Scott, Shirley L., ed. *Field Guide to the Birds of North America* (7–12). Illus. 1983, National Geographic paper $14.95 (0-87044-472-7). A guide to over 800 species (each with a color print) arranged by families. [598]

4963 Weissinger, John. *Birds—Right Before Your Eyes* (7–12). 1988, Enslow LB $12.95 (0-89490-167-2). A fascinating compendium of birds and bird lore that answers such questions as "Why do some birds migrate?" (Rev: BR 5–6/88) [598]

4964 *The Wonder of Birds* (7–9). Illus. 1983, National Geographic $29.95 (0-87044-470-0). This guide to 800 species of North American birds also comes with a recording of bird sounds. [598]

4965 Zim, Herbert, and Ira Gabrielson. *Birds* (7–12). 1956, Western paper $3.95 (0-307-24053-3). A handy field guide to the identification of about 120 common birds. [598]

BEHAVIOR

4966 Johnson, Sylvia A. *Inside an Egg* (7–9). Illus. 1982, Lerner LB $12.95 (0-8225-1472-9); paper $4.95 (0-8225-9522-2). An excellently illustrated account tracing the growth of a chicken in an egg until it is hatched. [598]

DUCKS AND GEESE

4967 Kerrod, Robin. *Birds: The Waterbirds* (5–9). Illus. 1989, Facts on File $17.95 (0-8160-1962-2). Ducks and geese are only 2 of the species described and pictured in this attractive volume. (Rev: BL 1/15/90; BR 5–6/90) [598.29]

EAGLES, HAWKS, AND OTHER BIRDS OF PREY

4968 Bailey, Jill. *Birds of Prey* (5–8). Illus. 1988, Facts on File $13.95 (0-8160-1655-0). In brief, lavishly illustrated chapters, various characteristics of birds of prey are explored and the most

important types are described. (Rev: SLJ 1/89) [598]

4969 Bramwell, Martyn. *Birds: The Aerial Hunters* (5–9). Illus. 1989, Facts on File $17.95 (0-8160-1963-0). Eagles, hawks, and condors are only 3 of the many predators described and pictured in lavish photographs. (Rev: BL 1/15/90; BR 5–6/90) [598.91]

4970 Parnall, Peter. *The Daywatchers* (7–10). Illus. 1984, Macmillan $18.95 (0-02-770190-5). A highly personal account about such birds of prey as falcons and hawks based on the author's experiences. (Rev: BL 3/1/85) [598]

4971 Ryden, Hope. *America's Bald Eagle* (5–9). Illus. 1985, Putnam $11.95 (0-399-21181-0). The physical characteristics, habitat, and behavior of our national bird are described in text and black-and-white photographs. (Rev: BL 7/85) [598]

4972 Sattler, Helen Roney. *The Book of Eagles* (6–10). Illus. 1989, Lothrop LB $14.88 (0-688-07022-1). This book tells about the habits and the history of the eagle and about its modern enemies including man. (Rev: VOYA 2/90) [598]

OWLS

4973 Mowat, Farley. *Owls in the Family* (7–9). 1962, Little $14.95 (0-316-58641-2). Two seemingly harmless owls turn a household upside down when they are adopted as pets. [598]

PENGUINS

4974 Strange, Ian J. *Penguin World* (7–9). Illus. 1981, Putnam LB $8.95 (0-396-08000-6). A report on 5 different kinds of penguins that breed on a remote Falkland Island. [598]

4975 Todd, Frank S. *The Sea World Book of Penguins* (7–9). Illus. 1981, Harcourt $12.95 (0-15-271949-0). This account describes where and how this wingless bird lives. [598]

Conservation and Endangered Species

4976 Banks, Martin. *Endangered Wildlife* (6–8). Illus. 1988, Rourke $11.95 (0-86592-284-5). A global look at how man's expanding environment has endangered the continued existence of many species. (Rev: BL 12/15/88; SLJ 5/89) [333.95]

4977 Bloyd, Sunni. *Endangered Species* (6–12). Illus. 1989, Lucent LB $10.95 (1-56006-106-5). A book that highlights several of the endangered species and explains why they are now facing possible extinction. (Rev: SLJ 4/90) [574]

4978 Grove, Noel. *Wild Lands for Wildlife: America's National Refuges* (9–12). Illus. 1984, National Geographic LB $9.50 (0-87044-482-4). A guide to the national wildlife refuges and how they help save endangered species. (Rev: BL 3/15/85) [333.95]

4979 Lampton, Christopher. *Endangered Species* (6–10). 1988, Watts LB $10.90 (0-531-10510-5). Lampton discusses the causes of extinction of a species and various ways one can prevent it. (Rev: BL 5/15/88; BR 9–10/88; SLJ 8/88) [591]

4980 Pringle, Laurence. *Saving Our Wildlife* (7–10). 1990, Enslow $13.95 (0-89490-204-0). This account explains how animals become extinct and outlines many projects that have been undertaken to stop this process. (Rev: BL 3/15/90; VOYA 6/90) [639.9]

Farms and Ranches

GENERAL AND MISCELLANEOUS

4981 Ashabranner, Brent. *Born to the Land: An American Portrait* (5–9). Illus. 1989, Putnam $14.95 (0-399-21716-9). Through photographs and text, ranch and farm life in southwestern New Mexico and the people who live in this area are introduced. (Rev: BL 5/15/89; SLJ 8/89) [978.9]

4982 Fichter, George S. *Underwater Farming* (7–10). 1988, Pineapple $14.95 (0-910923-48-5). This book explores the advantages and disadvantages of raising both fish and plants for food underwater. (Rev: BR 9–10/89; SLJ 4/89) [639]

4983 Gorman, Carol. *America's Farm Crisis* (7–12). Illus. 1987, Watts $12.90 (0-531-10408-7). An overview of the many problems facing America's farmers today including surpluses, subsidies, and corporation takeovers. (Rev: BL 10/15/87; BR 1–2/88; SLJ 11/87; VOYA 2/88) [338.1]

4984 Murphy, Wendy, et al. *The Future World of Agriculture* (5–9). Illus. 1985, Watts $12.90 (0-531-04880-2). This book deals with the challenge of feeding the world's population and possible new solutions in the future and includes a chapter devoted to Disney's EPCOT Center science exhibits. (Rev: BL 6/1/85; SLJ 9/85) [630]

ANIMALS AND CROPS

4985 Giblin, James Cross. *Milk: The Fight for Purity* (5–8). Illus. 1986, Harper LB $12.89 (0-690-04574-3). After a general discussion of the importance of milk as a food, this book deals

with the way it has been purified both in the past and present. (Rev: SLJ 2/87) [637]

4986 Hopf, Alice L. *Chickens and Their Wild Relatives* (6–9). Illus. 1982, Putnam $10.95 (0-396-08085-5). The domestic chicken is introduced plus some of its relatives like the grouse and pheasant. [636.5]

4987 Lavine, Sigmund A., and Vincent Scuro. *Wonders of Turkeys* (6–9). Illus. 1984, Putnam LB $10.95 (0-396-08333-1). The history of turkeys in this country is explained plus material on how they are raised today. [636.5]

Insects

GENERAL AND MISCELLANEOUS

4988 Burton, Maurice. *Insects and Their Relatives* (6–9). Illus. 1984, Facts on File $12.95 (0-87196-986-6). In a large format the world of insects is introduced, their body parts and lives are discussed, and a rundown on several specific species is given. [595.7]

4989 Cottam, Clarence, and Herbert Zim. *Insects* (7–12). 1987, Western paper $3.95 (0-307-24055-X). A handy field guide that gives identification material on 218 common species. [595.7]

4990 Dallinger, Jane. *Grasshoppers* (6–9). Illus. 1981, Lerner LB $12.95 (0-8225-1455-9). The life cycle of the grasshopper in photographs and words. [595.7]

4991 Fichter, George S. *Insect Pests* (7–12). 1966, Western paper $3.95 (0-307-24016-9). A handy field guide to 350 insect pests found in North America. [595.7]

4992 Hellman, Hal. *Deadly Bugs and Killer Insects* (7–9). 1978, Evans $6.95 (0-87131-269-7). Killer bees, fire ants, and the common housefly are only 3 of the potentially dangerous insects described. [595.7]

4993 Horton, Casey. *Insects* (6–9). Illus. 1984, Watts LB $12.40 (0-531-03476-3). The major kinds of insects are described (for example, bees, ants, and moths) and their habits are introduced. [595.7]

4994 Johnson, Sylvia A. *Ladybugs* (6–9). Illus. 1983, Lerner LB $12.95 (0-8225-1481-8). Lavish illustrations are used to give the life story and contributions of the ladybug. [595.7]

4995 Lavies, Bianca. *Backyard Hunter: The Praying Mantis* (5–8). Illus. 1990, Dutton $13.95 (0-525-44547-1). A stunning photo essay on the life of the praying mantis. (Rev: BL 3/15/90) [595.7]

4996 Leahy, Christopher. *Peterson First Guide to Insects of North America* (8–12). Illus. 1987, Houghton paper $3.95 (0-395-35640-7). This simplified guide supplies basics on identification, anatomy, and life stages. (Rev: BL 5/15/87) [599]

4997 Milne, Lorus J., and Margery Milne. *The Audubon Society Field Guide to North American Insects and Spiders* (7–12). Illus. 1980, Knopf $14.45 (0-394-50763-0). An extensive use of color photographs makes this a fine guide for identifying insects. [595.7]

4998 Moulton, Robert R. *First to Fly* (7–9). Illus. 1983, Lerner LB $12.95 (0-8225-1576-8). This "insects in flight" experiment by a high school student was chosen to be performed on the space shuttle. [595.7]

BEES AND WASPS

4999 Pringle, Laurence. *Here Come the Killer Bees* (5–8). Illus. 1986, Morrow LB $11.88 (0-688-04631-2). An account of the Brazilian honeybee, its travels, and the danger it can cause particularly to crops. (Rev: BL 11/15/86; SLJ 11/86) [595.79]

BEETLES

5000 Milne, Lorus J., and Margery Milne. *Nature's Clean-Up Crew: The Burying Beetles* (6–9). Illus. 1982, Putnam LB $8.95 (0-396-08038-3). Dead animals and birds are the particular target of these natural garbage collectors. [595.7]

5001 Patent, Dorothy Hinshaw, and Paul C. Schroeder. *Beetles and How They Live* (7–9). 1978, Holiday $7.95 (0-8234-0332-7). Descriptions are given of the various kinds of beetles including ladybugs and fireflies. [595.7]

BUTTERFLIES, MOTHS, AND CATERPILLARS

5002 Mitchell, Robert T., and Herbert Zim. *Butterflies and Moths* (7–12). 1964, Western paper $3.95 (0-307-24052-5). This compact guide identifies and describes hundreds of varieties of butterflies and moths. [595.7]

5003 Pyle, Robert Michael. *The Audubon Society Field Guide to North American Butterflies* (7–12). Illus. 1981, Knopf $14.45 (0-394-51914-0). An introduction to over 600 species of butterflies in about 1,000 color photographs and text. [595.7]

5004 Whalley, Paul. *Butterfly & Moth* (6–8). Illus. 1988, Knopf LB $13.99 (0-394-99618-6). Short chapters are used to describe the characteristics of moths and butterflies, the various spe-

cies, and their life cycles. (Rev: SLJ 12/88) [595.7]

SPIDERS

5005 Levi, Herbert, and Lorna R. Levi. *Spiders and Their Kin* (7–12). Illus. 1969, Western paper $3.95 (0-307-24021-5). A handy identification guide to many kinds of spiders with illustrations for each. [595.4]

5006 Patent, Dorothy Hinshaw. *The Lives of Spiders* (6–9). Illus. 1980, Holiday $12.95 (0-8234-0418-8). Such subjects as web spinning, reproduction, and social habits are described. [595.4]

Land Invertebrates

5007 Halton, Cheryl. *Those Amazing Leeches* (6–10). Illus. 1989, Dillon $12.95 (0-87518-408-1). A well-illustrated account that explains what leeches are, their habits, and their uses in medicine. (Rev: BR 1–2/90) [595.1]

Marine and Freshwater Life

GENERAL AND MISCELLANEOUS

5008 Boschung, Herbert T., Jr., et al. *The Audubon Society Field Guide to North American Fishes, Whales, and Dolphins* (7–12). Illus. 1983, Knopf $14.45 (0-394-53405-0). Color photos of about 600 sea creatures are followed by an explanatory text. [597]

5009 Parker, Steve. *Pond & River* (6–8). Illus. 1988, Knopf LB $13.99 (0-394-99615-1). In 28 short, lavishly illustrated chapters, various aspects of pond and river ecology are explored. (Rev: SLJ 12/88) [551.48]

5010 Reid, George K. *Pond Life: A Guide to Common Plants and Animals of North America Ponds and Lakes* (7–12). Illus. 1967, Western paper $3.95 (0-307-24017-7). Text and illustrations present the plants, animals, fish, and insects found in and around ponds. [574.92]

CORALS AND JELLYFISH

5011 Johnson, Sylvia A. *Coral Reefs* (7–9). Illus. 1984, Lerner LB $12.95 (0-8225-1451-6). Through many illustrations and concise text, the reader is introduced to coral reefs and the life they help support. [574.92]

FISH

5012 Eschmeyer, William N., and Earl S. Herald. *A Field Guide to Pacific Coast Fishes of North America: From the Gulf of Alaska to Baja California* (7–12). Illus. 1983, Houghton $19.95 (0-395-26873-7); paper $12.95 (0-395-33188-9). In this volume in the Peterson Field Guide series, about 500 fish are described and illustrated. [597]

5013 Filisky, Michael. *Peterson First Guide to Fishes of North America* (7–12). Illus. 1989, Houghton paper $4.95 (0-395-50219-5). This is a concise version of the parent Peterson guide. This one gives basic material on common fish with less detail. (Rev: BL 6/1/89) [597]

5014 Parker, Steve. *Fish* (5–9). Illus. 1990, Knopf LB $14.99 (0-679-90439-5). A general introduction to fish, their physiology, and the main fish groups. (Rev: BL 7/90; SLJ 9/90) [597]

5015 Shoemaker, Hurst, and Herbert Zim. *Fishes* (7–12). Illus. 1987, Western paper $3.95 (0-307-24059-2). A compact, colorfully illustrated guide to 278 of the most common fish of North America. [597]

SHARKS

5016 Blassingame, Wyatt. *Wonders of Sharks* (6–9). Illus. 1984, Putnam LB $10.95 (0-396-08463-X). The life cycle, appearance, and habits of these formidable creatures are examined. [597]

5017 Coupe, Sheena M. *Sharks* (5–8). Illus. 1990, Facts on File $17.95 (0-8160-2270-4). An oversized book that contains a well-organized text and many illustrations. (Rev: BL 4/1/90) [597]

5018 Dingerkus, Guido. *The Shark Watchers' Guide* (7–12). Illus. 1985, Messner $10.89 (0-671-50234-4); paper $5.95 (0-671-55038-1). As well as materials on 30 different varieties of sharks this book tells about shark anatomy, habits, and evolution and gives tips on how to handle a shark attack. (Rev: BL 11/15/85; SLJ 12/85) [597]

5019 McGowen, Tom. *Album of Sharks* (7–9). Illus. 1981, Rand McNally $8.95 (0-528-82023-0). An introduction to the various species of sharks and their individual habits. [597]

5020 Penzler, Otto. *Hunting the Killer Shark* (7–9). 1976, Troll LB $9.79 (0-89375-009-3); paper $2.50 (0-89375-025-5). An introduction to sharks and how they have survived for over 320 million years. [597]

5021 Reed, Don C. *Sevengill: The Shark and Me* (5–9). Illus. 1986, Knopf LB $11.99 (0-394-96926-X). A professional diver writes about his relationship with a huge broadhead sevengill shark. (Rev: SLJ 11/86) [597]

SHELLS

5022 Abbott, R. Tucker. *Seashells of North America: A Guide to Field Identification* (7–12). Illus. 1968, Golden Press paper $9.95 (0-307-13657-4). This handy volume identifies 850 species found on either or both of our coasts. [594]

5023 Abbott, R. Tucker. *Seashells of the World* (7–12). Rev. ed. Illus. 1985, Western paper $3.95 (0-307-24410-5). A concise guide that identifies in text and color pictures 850 common shells. [564]

5024 Arthur, Alex. *Shell* (5–9). Illus. 1989, Knopf LB $13.99 (0-394-92256-5). Through a series of stunning 2-page photographs, various kinds of animals with shells—like mollusks and turtles—are pictured and described in the text. (Rev: BL 9/15/89; BR 11–12/89) [594]

5025 Douglass, Jackie Leatherby. *Peterson First Guide to Shells of North America* (7–12). Illus. 1989, Houghton paper $4.95 (0-395-48297-6). This is an abridged edition of the complete field guide that is more accessible and less forbidding than the parent volume. (Rev: BL 6/1/89) [594]

5026 Morris, Percy A. *A Field Guide to Pacific Coast Shells, Including Shells of Hawaii and the Gulf of California* (7–12). 2nd rev. ed. Illus. 1966, Houghton $17.95 (0-395-08029-0); paper $12.95 (0-395-18322-7). A total of 945 species are described and illustrated in this Peterson Field Guide. A companion volume is *A Field Guide to Shells of the Atlantic and Gulf Coasts and the West Indies* (1973). [594]

5027 Rehder, Harold A. *The Audubon Society Field Guide to North American Seashells* (7–12). Illus. 1981, Knopf paper $14.45 (0-394-51913-2). Seven hundred of the most common seashells from our coasts are pictured in color photographs and described in the text. [594]

WHALES, DOLPHINS, AND OTHER SEA MAMMALS

5028 Dow, Lesley. *Whales* (5–8). 1990, Facts on File $17.95 (0-8160-2271-2). A fine introduction to this endangered animal—its species and living habits—as well as information on legends concerning the whale. (Rev: BL 4/1/90) [599.5]

5029 Graham, Ada, and Frank Graham. *Whale Watch* (7–9). Illus. 1978, Delacorte $7.95 (0-440-09505-0); paper $6.46 (0-440-09506-9). In addition to introducing a variety of whales, the authors make a strong plea for the conservation of the sea mammal. [599.5]

5030 McCoy, J. J. *The Plight of the Whales* (7–12). Illus. 1989, Watts LB $12.90 (0-531-10778-7). McCoy describes the many ways by which the whale population has been decimated and the struggle for survival that is still facing the whale population today. (Rev: BL 11/1/89; BR 5–6/90; SLJ 10/89; VOYA 2/90) [639.9]

5031 McGowen, Tom. *Album of Whales* (7–9). Illus. 1980, Rand McNally $8.95 (0-528-82281-X). From the relatively small beluga to the gigantic blue whale, this is a rundown of various species and their habits. [599.5]

5032 Patent, Dorothy Hinshaw. *Whales: Giants of the Deep* (7–9). Illus. 1984, Holiday LB $14.95 (0-8234-0530-3). An introduction to whales and whaling and how the whales' survival is being threatened. [599.5]

5033 Scheffer, Victor B. *A Natural History of Marine Mammals* (7–9). Illus. 1976, Macmillan paper $5.95 (0-684-16952-5). An introduction to the mammals that live in the sea and how through evolution these now land-based creatures have adapted to their new environment. [599]

Microbiology and Biotechnology

5034 Gross, Cynthia S. *The New Biotechnology: Putting Microbes to Work* (6–12). Illus. 1988, Lerner $12.95 (0-8225-1583-0). After an introduction to DNA and how genes can be manipulated, there is coverage of the applications of this knowledge. (Rev: BL 4/1/88; SLJ 4/88) [660.6]

5035 Stwertka, Eve, and Albert Stwertka. *Microscope: How to Use It & Enjoy It* (6–9). Illus. 1989, Silver Burdett LB $9.29 (0-671-63705-3); paper $4.95 (0-671-67060-3). A fine introduction that covers such topics as the parts of the microscope, how they operate, techniques for use, and how to prepare slides. BR 9–10/89) [502.8]

Pets

GENERAL AND MISCELLANEOUS

5036 Blumberg, Leda. *Pets: A Reference First Book* (6–9). 1983, Watts $10.40 (0-531-04649-4). Essential facts are given on the care and choosing of a wide variety of pets. [636.08]

5037 Chrystie, Frances N. *Pets* (7–12). 3rd rev. ed. Illus. 1974, Little $15.95 (0-316-14051-1). A

standard manual (first published in 1953) so wide in scope it includes farm animals, wild birds, and horses. [636.08]

5038 Simon, Seymour. *Pets in a Jar: Collecting and Caring for Small Wild Animals* (7–10). Illus. 1975, Penguin paper $5.95 (0-14-049186-4). Valuable information is given on caring for such small pets as ants, crickets, crabs, and starfish. [639]

5039 Smith, Jack. *Cats, Dogs, and Other Strangers at My Door* (7–10). 1984, Watts $13.95 (0-531-09751-X). A wide variety of animals have found their way to the home of author Smith on Mount Washington in Los Angeles. [636.08]

5040 Weber, William J. *Care of Uncommon Pets* (7–9). Illus. 1979, Henry Holt $10.95 (0-8050-0294-4); paper $5.95 (0-8050-0320-7). A total of 12 animals are discussed, including frogs, turtles, rabbits, mice, and hamsters. [636.08]

CATS

5041 Shelley, Purcy B. *Cat-a-Log* (7–9). 1983, Putnam paper $6.95 (0-448-18959-3). A collection of cat lore and literature including poems, stories, and factual material. [599.74]

DOGS

5042 American Kennel Club. *The Complete Dog Book* (7–12). Illus. 1985, Howell $19.95 (0-87605-432-7). The standard manual for dog owners and guide to every AKC-recognized breed. The first edition appeared over 50 years ago. (Rev: BL 6/15/85) [636.7]

5043 Benjamin, Carol Lea. *Dog Training for Kids* (5–8). Rev. ed. Illus. 1988, Howell LB $12.95 (0-87605-541-2). A simple guide to dog training that emphasizes the goal of having fun with a dog you are proud of. (Rev: SLJ 4/89) [636.7]

5044 Curtis, Patricia. *Dogs on the Case: Search Dogs Who Help Save Lives and Enforce the Law* (5–9). Illus. 1989, Dutton $14.95 (0-525-67274-5). An account that shows how trained dogs can perform such services as sniffing out drugs and finding lost persons. (Rev: BL 10/1/89; BR 1–2/90; VOYA 8/89) [363.2]

5045 Mowat, Farley. *The Dog Who Wouldn't Be* (7–10). 1957, Little $16.95 (0-316-58636-6). The humorous adventures of a dog named Mutt who thought he was a person. [599.74]

5046 Paulsen, Gary. *Woodsong* (7–12). Illus. 1990, Bradbury $12.95 (0-02-770221-9). Paulsen describes his experiences with sleds and dogs and his entry into the grueling Iditarod Sled Dog Race in Alaska. (Rev: BL 8/90) [796.5]

5047 Pinkwater, Jill, and Daniel Pinkwater. *Superpuppy: How to Choose, Raise, and Train the Best Possible Dog for You* (6–9). Illus. 1977, Clarion $13.95 (0-395-28878-9). The joy and problems of owning a dog plus advice on how to overcome the problems. [636.7]

5048 Poynter, Margaret. *What's One More?* (8–10). 1985, Macmillan $11.95 (0-689-31083-8). The true story of how this author began to help unwanted dogs and soon found herself owning 15. (Rev: BL 8/85) [636.08]

5049 Silverstein, Alvin, and Virginia B. Silverstein. *Dogs: All about Them* (6–8). Illus. 1986, Lothrop $12.95 (0-688-04850-6). After a history of dogs from the Stone Age on, the authors cover such topics as breeds, uses, and care of dogs. (Rev: BL 3/1/86; SLJ 9/86; VOYA 2/86) [599.74]

FISH

5050 Halstead, Bruce W., and Bonnie L. Landa. *Tropical Fish* (7–12). Illus. 1975, Golden paper $3.95 (0-307-24361-3). A handy guide to the various species of tropical fish plus some material on caring for them. [639.3]

HORSES

5051 Brady, Irene. *America's Horses and Ponies* (7–9). 1969, Houghton $17.95 (0-395-06659-X); paper $9.95 (0-395-24050-6). Thirty-nine of the most popular breeds of horses are introduced and described. [599.72]

5052 Clemens, Virginia Phelps. *A Horse in Your Backyard?* (7–9). Illus. 1977, Westminster $8.50 (0-664-32616-1). For the new horse owner, this book is a guide to the care, feeding, and grooming of these animals. [599]

5053 Henschel, Georgie. *Horses and Riding* (5–8). Illus. 1986, Watts $8.90 (0-531-19021-8). The main topics covered here are the history of the horse and the kinds of competitions in which horses are involved today. (Rev: BR 3–4/87) [636.1]

5054 Jurmain, Suzanne. *Once upon a Horse: A History of Horses and How They Shaped Our History* (5–9). Illus. 1989, Lothrop $15.95 (0-688-05550-8). A history of the horse and how it has been domesticated and used by humans. (Rev: BL 12/15/89; BR 3–4/90; SLJ 1/90; VOYA 4/90) [636.1]

5055 Patent, Dorothy Hinshaw. *Arabian Horses* (6–9). Illus. 1982, Holiday LB $14.95 (0-8234-0451-X). One of the world's fastest and most beautiful horses is described in words and black-and-white photographs. [636.1]

5056 Patent, Dorothy Hinshaw. *Horses of America* (7–9). 1981, Holiday $14.95 (0-8234-0399-8). In addition to material on the evolution of the horse, this account emphasizes its importance to civilization and tells about the many breeds of horses. [599.72]

5057 Patent, Dorothy Hinshaw. *Thoroughbred Horses* (6–9). Illus. 1985, Holiday LB $12.95 (0-8234-0558-3). A history of horses—how their different characteristics developed and how they are scientifically bred today. (Rev: SLJ 10/85) [639.9]

5058 Sayer, Angela. *The Young Rider's Handbook* (7–10). Illus. 1984, Arco $9.95 (0-688-06044-1). Riding skills are discussed as are selecting and caring for ponies. [636.1]

Zoos, Aquariums, and Animal Care Shelters

5059 Brown, Vinson. *How to Make a Miniature Zoo* (6–10). Illus. 1987, Dodd $15.95 (0-396-09041-9); paper $7.95 (0-396-09042-7). A practical guide to the care of a variety of animals and birds and how to house them properly. (Rev: BL 1/15/88) [636.08]

5060 Curtis, Patricia. *All Wild Creatures Welcome: The Story of a Wildlife Rehabilitation Center* (5–9). Illus. 1985, Dutton $13.95 (0-525-67164-1). This is the story of a wildlife rehabilitation center in New York State that takes in abandoned, injured animals, cares for them, and eventually sets them free. (Rev: BL 10/15/85; BR 3–4/86; SLJ 9/85) [636.089]

5061 Hewett, Joan. *When You Fight the Tiger* (5–9). Illus. 1984, Little $14.95 (0-316-35956-4). A photographic account of a teenager's summer at a zoo where animals are trained for work in show business. (Rev: BL 2/1/85) [636.08]

5062 Rinard, Judith E. *Zoos without Cages* (6–9). Illus. 1981, National Geographic LB $8.50 (0-87044-340-2). A description of the new kinds of zoos which strive to reproduce the natural habitat of the enclosed animals. [590.74]

5063 Thomson, Peggy. *Keepers and Creatures at the National Zoo* (6–9). Illus. 1988, Harper LB $12.89 (0-690-04712-6). An examination of the careers of many of the men and women employed at the National Zoo in Washington. (Rev: BL 10/1/88) [590.74]

Chemistry

General and Miscellaneous

5064 Adler, Irving. *How Life Began* (7–10). Rev. ed. Illus. 1977, Harper $12.95 (0-381-99603-4). From basic chemistry the author moves to organic substances and then to the theories of the beginning of life. [577]

5065 Ardley, Neil. *The World of the Atom* (6–8). Illus. 1989, Gloucester LB $12.40 (0-531-17145-0). Such concepts as compounds, elements, and nuclear energy are introduced in a brief text. (Rev: BL 5/15/89) [541.24]

5066 Berger, Melvin. *Solids, Liquids and Gases: From Superconductors to the Ozone Layer* (6–8). 1989, Putnam $11.99 (0-399-21731-2). The concept of matter and its relation to current pollution problems are explained. (Rev: BL 12/15/89) [530.4]

5067 Corrick, James A. *Recent Revolutions in Chemistry* (7–12). Illus. 1986, Watts $12.90 (0-531-10241-6). An excellent overview that covers a variety of subjects such as plastics, computers, nuclear chemistry, pharmaceuticals, and biochemistry. (Rev: BL 12/15/86; BR 1–2/87; SLJ 12/86; VOYA 4/87) [540]

5068 McGowen, Tom. *Chemistry: The Birth of a Science* (6–12). 1989, Watts LB $13.40 (0-531-10804-X). The history of chemistry from ancient Greece and Egypt through the end of the eighteenth century. (Rev: BL 1/15/90; SLJ 12/89; VOYA 2/90) [540.9]

5069 Walters, Derek. *Chemistry* (7–9). Illus. 1982, Watts LB $11.90 (0-531-04581-1). Simple experiments and several illustrations are used to explain the science of chemistry and its branches. [540]

Geology and Geography

General and Miscellaneous

5070 Aylesworth, Thomas G. *Moving Continents: Our Changing Earth* (5–8). 1990, Enslow LB $15.95 (0-89490-273-3). A discussion of plate tectonics and how this explains such phenomena as earthquakes and volcanic eruptions. (Rev: BL 8/90; SLJ 9/90) [551.1]

5071 Bain, Ian. *Mountains and Earth Movements* (6–8). 1984, Bookwright $11.40 (0-531-03802-5). An introduction to Earth and to such topics as continental drifts, faults, earthquakes, and volcanoes. [550]

5072 Ballard, Robert D. *Exploring Our Living Planet* (7–9). Illus. 1983, National Geographic LB $21.95 (0-87044-397-6). Theories about the earth's origins are explained and such topics as the causes of earthquakes and volcanoes are covered briefly. [551.1]

5073 Gallant, Roy A. *Our Restless Earth* (5–8). Illus. 1986, Watts LB $10.40 (0-531-10205-X). Theories about how Earth was formed are explained with additional material on how our earth is still changing. (Rev: BR 5–6/87; SLJ 2/87) [550]

5074 Kiefer, Irene. *Global Jigsaw Puzzle: The Story of Continental Drift* (7–10). Illus. 1978, Macmillan $8.95 (0-689-30621-0). Plate tectonics and continental drift are explored and the formation of the earth's continents is explained. [551.1]

5075 O'Neill, Catherine. *Natural Wonders of North America* (7–12). Illus. 1984, National Geographic LB $8.50 (0-87044-519-7). Excellent color photographs complement the text and maps that describe such natural wonders as tun-dra regions, volcanoes, glaciers, and the Badlands of South Dakota. [557]

5076 Rhodes, Frank H. T. *Geology* (7–12). Illus. 1972, Western paper $3.95 (0-307-24349-4). A well-illustrated introduction to such topics as the earth's composition, earthquakes, oceans, winds, and the formation of mountains. [551]

5077 Rossbacher, Lisa. *Recent Revolutions in Geology* (7–9). Illus. 1986, Watts $12.90 (0-531-10242-4). Recent discoveries in plate tectonics and oceanography are 2 of the areas reported on. (Rev: SLJ 12/86; VOYA 4/87) [550]

Earth and Geology

5078 Dixon, Dougal. *The Planet Earth* (6–8). Illus. 1989, Gloucester LB $12.40 (0-531-17142-6). Earth's origins, its makeup, and how humankind is interrupting its equilibrium are discussed. (Rev: BL 5/15/89) [551]

5079 *Earth, Sea and Sky* (5–9). Illus. 1984, Arco $9.95 (0-668-06181-2). An attractive volume that introduces the earth, its atmospheres, and geography. (Rev: BL 4/1/85) [551]

5080 Fodor, R. V. *Chiseling the Earth: How Erosion Shapes the Land* (7–9). Illus. 1983, Enslow LB $14.95 (0-89490-074-9). A description of how the earth surface is being changed, often dramatically, by the force of erosion. [551.3]

5081 Rapp, George F., and Laura L. Erickson. *Earth's Chemical Clues: The Story of Geochemistry* (7–12). Illus. 1990, Enslow LB $13.95 (0-89490-153-2). The chemical composition of the earth is explained and the science of geochemis-

335

try introduced. (Rev: SLJ 4/90; VOYA 6/90) [551.9]

5082 Sagan, Dorion, and Lynn Margulis. *Biospheres from Earth to Space* (7–10). Illus. 1989, Enslow LB $14.95 (0-89490-188-5). The protective layer that extends from inside the ocean to the atmosphere is described, as well as the dangers that this environment faces. (Rev: BL 6/15/89; SLJ 5/89) [335.95]

5083 Seddon, Tony, and Jill Bailey. *The Physical World* (5–9). Illus. 1987, Doubleday $12.95 (0-385-24179-8). A collection of facts about our earth that touches on geology, astronomy, meteorology, oceanography, and other sciences. (Rev: SLJ 11/87) [550]

Earthquakes and Volcanoes

5084 Asimov, Isaac. *How Did We Find Out about Earthquakes?* (6–9). Illus. 1978, Walker LB $10.85 (0-8027-6306-5). Early beliefs about earthquakes are mentioned, coverage of important earthquakes of the past is given, and an overview of our current knowledge of plate tectonics is also covered. [551.2]

5085 Asimov, Isaac. *How Did We Find Out about Volcanoes?* (6–8). 1981, Walker LB $10.85 (0-8027-6412-6). An account of what we have believed about volcanoes through history and how the truth was gradually accumulated. [551.2]

5086 Aylesworth, Thomas G., and Virginia L. Aylesworth. *The Mount St. Helens Disaster: What We've Learned* (7–10). Illus. 1983, Watts LB $12.90 (0-531-04488-2). In addition to coverage of the St. Helens eruption, coverage is included on how nature can recover from these upheavals and how they can be predicted. [551.2]

5087 Cox, James A., et al. *Our Violent Earth* (6–9). Illus. 1982, National Geographic LB $8.50 (0-87044-388-7). A discussion of such phenomena as earthquakes, volcanoes, and floods. [363.3]

5088 Golden, Frederic. *The Trembling Earth: Probing & Predicting Quakes* (7–9). Illus. 1983, Macmillan $13.95 (0-684-17884-2). As well as the phenomenon of earthquakes, this account discusses such related topics as plate tectonics. [551.2]

5089 Place, Marian T. *Mount St. Helens: A Sleeping Volcano Awakes* (7–9). Illus. 1981, Putnam $10.95 (0-396-07976-8). Using many eye-witness accounts and many photographs, this is a reconstruction of the 1980 disaster. [551.2]

5090 Vogt, Gregory. *Predicting Earthquakes* (6–9). Illus. 1989, Watts LB $11.90 (0-531-10788-4). The causes of earthquakes are mentioned and the attempts scientists have made through various methods and equipment to predict them. (Rev: BL 1/1/90; SLJ 1/90) [551.2]

5091 Vogt, Gregory. *Predicting Volcanic Eruptions* (6–9). Illus. 1989, Watts LB $11.90 (0-531-10786-8). Types of volcanoes and eruptions are introduced plus a description of the ways scientists are trying to determine new volcanic activity. (Rev: BL 1/1/90; BR 5–6/90; SLJ 1/90) [551.2]

Physical Geography

5092 Browne, Tom. *Rivers and People* (6–9). Illus. 1982, Silver Burdett LB $15.96 (0-382-06671-5). An account that describes the formation of rivers, their various kinds, and how they are used. [551.48]

5093 Carson, James. *Deserts and People* (7–9). Illus. 1982, Silver Burdett LB $15.96 (0-382-06669-3). An introduction to the climate and vegetation of deserts and the people who live there. Special emphasis is placed on the Sahara. [551.4]

5094 Cochrane, Jennifer. *Air Ecology* (5–8). Illus. 1987, Watts LB $12.40 (0-531-18151-0). In addition to a discussion of our atmosphere, this account gives many science projects to illustrate concepts introduced. Also use: *Land Ecology; Plant Ecology;* and *Water Ecology* (all 1987). (Rev: SLJ 2/88) [574.5]

5095 Cochrane, Jennifer. *Urban Ecology* (6–9). 1987, Watts LB $12.40 (0-531-18156-1). This volume describes animals and plants in an urban setting and explains how they live and adjust. (Rev: BR 9–10/88) [574.5]

5096 Hanmer, Trudy J. *Living in the Mountains* (7–12). 1988, Watts LB $11.90 (0-531-10149-5). A discussion of cultural geography as it relates to people living in such areas as the Appalachians and the Andes. (Rev: BR 9–10/88) [551.4]

5097 Lambert, Mark, and John Williams. *Animal Ecology* (5–9). 1987, Watts LB $12.40 (0-531-18155-3). This book describes where animals live, how they adjust to various climates, and their relationships with humans. (Rev: BR 9–10/88) [591]

5098 Markl, Lise. *Living in Maritime Regions* (7–12). 1988, Watts LB $11.90 (0-531-10148-7).

Such areas as places in the Netherlands and Chesapeake Bay are used to illustrate the cultural geography of marine environments. (Rev: BR 9–10/88) [551.4]

5099 Milne, Lorus J., and Margery Milne. *The Mystery of the Bog Forest* (7–9). Illus. 1984, Putnam $8.95 (0-396-08318-8). The nature of marshes and bogs and the life and the interrelationships that exist there are discussed. [574.5]

5100 Nations, James D. *Tropical Rainforests: Endangered Environment* (7–9). Illus. 1988, Watts $12.90 (0-531-10604-7). An examination of tropical rainforests, the wildlife they sustain, and why they are presently in danger. (Rev: BL 12/15/88; BR 1–2/89; SLJ 3/89; VOYA 4/89) [574.5]

5101 Robert, Leo. *Living in the Grasslands* (7–12). 1988, Watts LB $11.90 (0-531-10146-0). The ways in which living in a grassland environment affects the lives of people are discussed with examples from around the world. (Rev: BR 9–10/88) [551.4]

5102 Schoonmaker, Peter K. *The Living Forest* (6–8). Illus. 1990, Enslow LB $13.95 (0-89490-270-9). After a general introduction to forests, this book discusses specific kinds found in North America. (Rev: BL 7/90) [574.5]

5103 Watson, Jane Werner. *Deserts of the World: Future Threat or Promise?* (7–9). Illus. 1981, Putnam $13.95 (0-399-20785-6). Following a description of deserts and how they are formed, there is discussion of how life adjusts in these areas. [551.4]

Rocks, Minerals, and Soil

5104 Bates, Robert L. *Industrial Minerals: How They Are Found and Used* (6–9). Illus. 1988,

Enslow $12.95 (0-89490-174-5). Such substances as salts, clays, phosphates, diamonds, and asbestos are introduced and discussed. (Rev: BL 12/1/88; BR 1–2/89) [553.6]

5105 Chesterman, Charles W., and Kurt E. Lowe. *The Audubon Society Field Guide to North American Rocks and Minerals* (7–12). Illus. 1978, Knopf $14.45 (0-394-50269-8). A key by color arrangement plus color illustrations of each rock and mineral are 2 features of this basic guide. [549]

5106 Fichter, George S. *Rocks and Minerals* (5–8). 1982, Random paper $5.95 (0-394-84772-5). For the beginning geologist, a simple field guide from the Audubon Society. [552]

5107 McGowen, Tom. *Album of Rocks and Minerals* (7–9). Illus. 1981, Macmillan $8.95 (0-528-82400-7); paper $4.95 (0-02-688504-2). The history and value of 22 common rocks and minerals are described in text and large color illustrations. [549]

5108 Pough, Frederick H. *A Field Guide to Rocks and Minerals* (7–12). 4th ed. Illus. 1976, Houghton $17.95 (0-395-24047-6); paper $12.95 (0-395-24049-2). This volume in the Peterson Field Guide series gives photos and identifying information on 270 rocks and minerals. [549]

5109 Sorrell, Charles A. *Rocks and Minerals* (7–12). Illus. 1974, Western $9.95 (0-307-47005-9). A basic compact guide that identifies hundreds of mineral varieties with color illustrations. [552]

5110 Zim, Herbert, and Paul R. Shaffer. *Rocks and Minerals: A Guide to Familiar Minerals, Gems, Ores and Rocks* (7–12). Rev. ed. Illus. 1960, Golden paper $3.95 (0-307-24499-7). A quick identification guide to 400 rocks and minerals plus background information on formation and uses. [549]

Mathematics

General and Miscellaneous

5111 Bendick, Jeanne. *Mathematics Illustrated Dictionary: Facts, Figures & People* (7–10). Illus. 1989, Watts LB $12.90 (0-531-10664-0). An easy-to-use dictionary that explains words and terms clearly and usually with illustrations. (Rev: BR 5–6/90; VOYA 4/90) [510]

5112 Dilson, Jesse. *The Abacus: A Pocket Computer* (7–10). Illus. 1975, St. Martin's paper $6.95 (0-312-00140-1). A history of this important early calculator and how it can be built and used today. [513.028]

5113 Ecker, Michael W. *Getting Started in Problem Solving and Math Contests* (7–12). Illus. 1987, Watts $11.90 (0-531-10342-0). An entertaining guide to entering math contests with many examples and tips. (Rev: BL 3/1/88; BR 1–2/88; SLJ 2/88; VOYA 12/87) [510]

5114 Fekete, Irene, and Jasmine Denyer. *Mathematics* (6–9). Illus. 1984, Facts on File $12.95 (0-87196-990-4). Through clear text and many illustrations, the world of mathematics and its history are introduced. (Rev: BL 3/15/85) [510]

5115 Hershey, Robert L. *How to Think with Numbers* (7–9). Illus. 1982, Janson paper $7.95 (0-86576-014-4). Elementary mathematical concepts such as percentage and interest are explained through a series of puzzles and problems. [510]

5116 Stwertka, Albert. *Recent Revolutions in Mathematics* (8–12). Illus. 1987, Watts $11.90 (0-531-10418-4). In addition to reporting on recent advances in mathematics, this account stresses their practical applications and their effects on other sciences. (Rev: BL 12/15/87; BR 1–2/88; SLJ 3/88; VOYA 2/88) [510]

Algebra, Numbers, and Number Systems

5117 Fisher, Leonard Everett. *Number Art: Thirteen 1 2 3s from around the World* (6–9). Illus. 1982, Macmillan $12.95 (0-590-07810-0). Different numbering systems from around the world (for example, Chinese, Arabic) are explained and illustrated. [513]

Mathematical Games and Puzzles

5118 Burns, Marilyn. *The I Hate Mathematics! Book* (7–9). Illus. 1975, Little $14.95 (0-316-11740-4). A book of games and puzzles that present mathematical concepts. [793.7]

5119 Burns, Marilyn. *Math for Smarty Pants* (6–9). Illus. 1982, Little $13.95 (0-316-11738-2); paper $7.95 (0-316-11739-0). A series of games, puzzles, and tricks that use numbers. [513]

Metric System

5120 Ardley, Neil. *Making Metric Measurements* (6–9). Illus. 1983, Watts LB $11.90 (0-531-04615-

X). This account describes metric units and gives projects on how to use them. [389]

5121 Ross, Frank, Jr. *The Metric System: Measures for All Mankind* (7–9). 1974, Phillips $16.95 (0-87599-198-X). A simple account of the metric system and the pros and cons of America going metric. [389]

Time and Clocks

5122 Apfel, Necia H. *Calendars* (5–8). Illus. 1985, Watts LB $10.40 (0-531-10034-0). A detailed history of the various kinds of calendars and how our present one evolved. (Rev: SLJ 1/86) [529]

DC / 6A
J 529 APF

Meteorology

General and Miscellaneous

5123 Facklam, Margery, and Howard Facklam. *Changes in the Wind: Earth's Shifting Climate* (6–9). Illus. 1986, Harcourt $14.95 (0-15-216115-5). An excellent explanation of what causes climate and how and why it changes. (Rev: BL 8/86; SLJ 12/86) [551.6]

Air

5124 Smith, Henry. *Amazing Air: Step-by-Step* (7–9). Illus. 1982, Lothrop LB $11.88 (0-688-00973-5); paper $7.95 (0-688-00977-8). A variety of experiments are described that deal with such topics as the components of air, its characteristics, and uses. [507]

Storms

5125 Lee, Sally. *Predicting Violent Storms* (6–10). Illus. 1989, Watts LB $11.90 (0-531-10787-6). General weather forecasting is covered in this account as well as how we can predict the coming of tornadoes, hurricanes, and other storms. (Rev: BL 1/1/90; BR 5–6/90; SLJ 1/90; VOYA 4/90) [551.5]

Water

5126 Goldin, Augusta. *Water: Too Much, Too Little, Too Polluted?* (7–9). Illus. 1983, Harcourt $12.95 (0-15-294819-8). Facts and fables about water are given plus a description of the water cycle, and methods of water management. [333.91]

5127 Pringle, Laurence. *Water: The Next Great Resource Battle* (7–9). Illus. 1982, Macmillan $12.95 (0-02-775400-6). A description of our water resources and how we are using and misusing them. [333.91]

Weather

5128 Borland, Hal. *The Golden Circle: A Book of Months* (7–9). Illus. 1977, Harper $13.70 (0-690-03803-8). Through 12 paintings and essays, the various stages of the seasons are chronicled. [525]

5129 Dickinson, Terrence. *Exploring the Sky by Day: The Equinox Guide to Weather and the Atmosphere* (7–10). Illus. 1988, Camden House LB $12.95 (0-920656-73-0); paper $9.95 (0-920656-71-4). A book about weather that explores such subjects as types of clouds and kinds of precipitation. (Rev: SLJ 1/89) [551.6]

5130 Dolan, Edward F., Jr. *Drought: The Past, Present, and Future Enemy* (7–12). 1990, Watts LB $13.40 (0-531-10900-3). An account describing what causes drought, its effects, and its present dangers such as the greenhouse effect. (Rev: BL 8/90; VOYA 8/90) [551.57]

5131 Gallant, Roy A. *Earth's Changing Climate* (6–9). Illus. 1979, Macmillan $13.95 (0-02-736840-8). How such factors as sunspots and man's pollution are changing our weather. [551.6]

5132 Lambert, David, and Ralph Hardy. *Weather and Its Work* (7–9). Illus. 1984, Facts on File $12.95 (0-87196-987-4). Topics such as wind, drought, floods, hurricanes, and weather forecasting are explored. [551.6]

5133 Tannenbaum, Beulah, and Harold E. Tannenbaum. *Making and Using Your Own Weather Station* (6–10). Illus. 1989, Watts LB $11.90 (0-531-10675-6). A concise, easily followed guide to making such instruments as a thermometer, rain gauge, barometer, and wind vane plus background material on what they measure. (Rev: BL 5/15/89; BR 11–12/89; SLJ 9/89; VOYA 10/89) [551.6]

5134 Zim, Herbert, et al. *Weather* (7–12). Illus. 1987, Western paper $3.95 (0-307-24051-7). A nicely illustrated handy guide to all kinds of weather and what causes them. [551.6]

Oceanography

General and Miscellaneous

5135 Asimov, Isaac. *How Did We Find Out about Life in the Deep Sea?* (6–8). 1981, Walker LB $10.85 (0-8027-6428-2). A simple account of how the science of oceanography began and some of the knowledge scientists now have about the oceans. [551.46]

5136 Bramwell, Martyn. *Oceanography* (5–9). Illus. 1989, Hampstead LB $12.90 (0-531-19510-4). A look at this developing science with many photographs and drawings. (Rev: BL 6/1/89; SLJ 9/89) [551.46]

5137 Fine, John Christopher. *Oceans in Peril* (5–10). Illus. 1987, Macmillan $13.95 (0-689-31328-4). An eloquent plea to save our last great resource—the oceans—from destruction. (Rev: BL 1/1/88; SLJ 12/87; VOYA 10/87) [363.7]

5138 Lambert, David, and Anita McConnell. *Seas and Oceans* (5–9). Illus. 1985, Facts on File $12.95 (0-8160-1064-1). After a general discussion of oceans, the authors describe life in the sea and man's relationships with it through the centuries. (Rev: BL 9/1/85; SLJ 11/85) [551.46]

5139 Meyerson, A. Lee. *Seawater: A Delicate Balance* (6–9). Illus. 1988, Enslow $12.95 (0-89489-157-5). A discussion of the composition of seawater and of the present threat to oceans from pollution. (Rev: BL 12/1/88; SLJ 12/88) [551.46]

5140 National Geographic Society. *The Ocean Realm* (7–9). Illus. 1978, National Geographic LB $9.50 (0-87044-256-2). Through the adventures of individuals, such topics as coral reefs, seashores, and ocean depths are described. [551.46]

5141 Polking, Kirk. *Oceans of the World: Our Essential Resource* (7–9). 1983, Putnam paper $14.95 (0-399-20919-0). Topics such as how oceans were formed, the life that exists in them, and the energy they contain are developed. [551.46]

5142 Poynter, Margaret, and Donald Collins. *Under the High Seas: New Frontiers in Oceanography* (7–9). Illus. 1983, Macmillan $11.95 (0-689-30977-5). A history of man's relationship to the oceans and how we have collected our present knowledge about them. [551.46]

5143 Sedge, Michael H. *Commercialization of the Oceans* (6–9). 1987, Watts $12.90 (0-531-10326-9). The commercial uses of the world's oceans are explored and projections are made concerning future developments. (Rev: BL 4/15/87; BR 5–6/87; SLJ 6–7/87; VOYA 8–9/87) [331.91]

5144 Simon, Seymour. *How to Be an Ocean Scientist in Your Own Home* (6–8). Illus. 1988, Harper LB $12.89 (0-397-32292-5). A great deal of information about oceans and life in them is imparted through a series of simple experiments and activities. (Rev: BL 10/1/88) [551.46]

Seashores

5145 Arnosky, Jim. *Near the Sea: A Portfolio of Paintings* (5–10). Illus. 1990, Lothrop LB $13.88 (0-688-09327-2). A portfolio of oil paintings that explores seashore life on a Maine island. (Rev: BL 9/1/90) [759.12]

5146 Hecht, Jeff. *Shifting Shores: Rising Seas, Retreating Coastlines* (7–12). Illus. 1990, Macmillan $14.95 (0-684-19087-7). This book explores shoreline changes, the problems they are creating, and how to cope with them. (Rev: BL 6/15/90; SLJ 7/90; VOYA 6/90) [551.4]

5147 Maxwell, Gavin. *Ring of Bright Water* (7–12). Illus. 1987, Penguin paper $6.95 (0-14-003923-6). In this book, originally published in 1960, this Scottish author describes seashore life close to his cottage, with emphasis on his 2 pet otters. [574.9]

5148 Meinkoth, Norman A. *The Audubon Society Field Guide to North American Seashore Creatures* (7–12). Illus. 1981, Knopf $14.95 (0-394-51993-0). Sponges, jellyfish, and urchins are pictured, and a total of almost 700 species are described. [592]

5149 Parker, Steve. *Seashore* (5–9). Illus. 1989, Knopf LB $13.99 (0-394-92254-9). Text and stunning color photographs are used to supply much information about seashores and the life they support. (Rev: BL 10/15/89) [591.909]

5150 Zim, Herbert, and Lester Ingle. *Seashores* (7–12). 1955, Western paper $3.95 (0-307-24496-6). About 500 species of plants, shells, animals, and birds that are found on seashores are identified. [551.4]

Underwater Exploration and Sea Disasters

5151 Ballard, Robert D. *Exploring the Titanic* (5–8). Illus. 1988, Scholastic $14.95 (0-590-41953-6). The story by the underwater explorer of his expeditions to explore the sunken *Titanic*. (Rev: BL 1/15/89) [363.1]

5152 Cousteau, Jacques, and Frederic Dumas. *The Silent World* (7–12). Illus. 1987, Lyons & Burford paper $12.95 (0-941130-45-2). A description of how the aqualung was developed and how it has opened up the exploration of oceans and their sunken treasures. [551.46]

5153 Fine, John Christopher. *Sunken Ships and Treasure* (5–9). Illus. 1986, Macmillan $16.95 (0-689-31280-6). An account of some of the most daring underwater operations with good background information on equipment and techniques. (Rev: BL 2/1/87; SLJ 4/87; VOYA 6/87) [910.4]

5154 Hackwell, W. John. *Diving to the Past: Recovering Ancient Wrecks* (6–8). Illus. 1988, Macmillan $14.95 (0-684-18918-6). An introduction to the many riches contained in sunken ships and the dangers and excitement of salvaging them. (Rev: BL 3/1/88; SLJ 6–7/88) [930.1]

5155 Oleksy, Walter. *Treasures of the Deep: Adventures of Undersea Exploration* (7–9). 1984, Messner LB $9.79 (0-671-42269-3). A series of underwater quests are interestingly re-created.

5156 Sullivan, George. *Treasure Hunt: The Sixteen-Year Search for the Lost Treasure Ship Atocha* (6–9). Illus. 1987, Henry Holt $13.95 (0-8050-0569-2). The riveting story of the undersea salvage operation of the Spanish galleon lost at sea in 1622. (Rev: BL 1/15/88; BR 3–4/88; SLJ 6–7/88) [917.59]

5157 *Undersea Treasures* (7–9). Illus. 1974, National Geographic $7.95 (0-87044-147-7). A number of underwater explorers describe their adventures. [910.4]

Physics

General and Miscellaneous

5158 Apfel, Necia H. *It's All Relative: Einstein's Theory of Relativity* (5–9). 1985, Lothrop paper $7.25 (0-688-04301-1). An explanation of relativity that gives complex concepts in an interesting and understandable way. (Rev: BR 5–6/86) [530.1]

5159 Bendick, Jeanne. *How Much & How Many? The Story of Weights and Measures* (5–8). Rev. ed. Illus. 1989, Watts LB $13.90 (0-531-10679-9). A clear, basic explanation of weights and measures. (Rev: BL 7/89; SLJ 8/89) [530.8]

5160 Berger, Melvin. *Atoms, Molecules and Quarks* (6–8). Illus. 1986, Putnam $9.99 (0-399-61213-0). A lucid introduction to the world of physics and the building blocks of the earth. (Rev: BL 10/1/86; SLJ 11/86) [539.7]

5161 Fleisher, Paul. *Secrets of the Universe* (7–10). Illus. 1987, Macmillan LB $17.95 (0-689-31266-0). A discussion of the discovery of the great theories in science from Archimedes on. (Rev: BR 11–12/87; SLJ 6–7/87; VOYA 6/87) [530]

5162 Gardner, Robert. *Experimenting with Illusions* (5–10). Illus. 1990, Watts LB $11.90 (0-531-10909-7). A work about optical illusions and how to create them with mirrors and other materials. (Rev: BL 6/15/90; SLJ 8/90) [152.14]

5163 McGowen, Tom. *Radioactivity: From the Curies to the Atomic Age* (6–8). Illus. 1986, Watts $10.40 (0-531-10132-0). The work of 5 scientists (including Roentgen, the Curies, and Rutherford) and how they solved the mystery of radioactivity are the subjects dealt with in this book. (Rev: BL 7/86; BR 11–12/86; SLJ 8/86) [539.7]

5164 McGrath, Susan. *Fun with Physics* (5–9). Illus. 1986, National Geographic LB $8.50 (0-87044-581-2). An introduction to physics that uses everyday situations as examples and supplies a smattering of experiments. (Rev: SLJ 6–7/87) [530]

5165 Newton, David E. *Particle Accelerators: From the Cyclotron to the Superconducting Super Collider* Illus. 1989, Watts LB $11.90 (0-531-10671-3). A discussion of linear and circular accelerators and the Superconducting Super Collider in clear text with some photographs and diagrams. (Rev: BL 8/89; BR 11–12/89; SLJ 8/89; VOYA 10/89) [539.7]

5166 Stwertka, Albert. *Recent Revolutions in Physics* (7–12). 1986, Watts $12.96 (0-531-10066-9). Stwertka has taken some of the most difficult areas in nuclear physics and made them understandable. (Rev: BR 11–12/86) [530]

5167 Stwertka, Albert, and Eve Stwertka. *Physics: From Newton to the Big Bang* (6–8). Illus. 1986, Watts $10.40 (0-531-10224-6). A history of physics that covers the work of Newton, Einstein, and such modern concepts as the theory of an expanding universe. (Rev: BL 1/15/87; SLJ 2/87; VOYA 2/87) [530]

5168 Tauber, Gerald E. *Relativity: From Einstein to Black Holes* (7–10). Illus. 1988, Watts $11.90 (0-531-10482-6). A history of the theory of relativity from its origins with Einstein to modern applications. (Rev: BL 12/15/88; BR 1–2/89; SLJ 3/89; VOYA 4/89) [530.1]

5169 Van Fleet, Alanson A. *The Tennessee Valley Authority* (6–9). Illus. 1987, Chelsea House $14.95 (1-55546-123-9). A description of this

Depression-age project that brought both business and government together for the nation's good. (Rev: BL 9/1/87; SLJ 12/87) [353]

5170 White, Jack R. *The Hidden World of Forces* (6–9). Illus. 1987, Dodd LB $11.95 (0-396-08947-X). This book explores such topics as gravity, pressure, lift, friction, electromagnetism, and sound in a way that relates them to everyday objects. (Rev: SLJ 6–7/88) [530]

Energy and Motion

General and Miscellaneous

5171 Douglas, John H. *The Future World of Energy* (6–9). 1984, Watts $12.90 (0-531-04881-0). From the Universe of Energy exhibit at the EPCOT Center, this book explains the history of energy, its future, and its sources. [333.7]

5172 *Energy, Forces and Resources* (5–9). Illus. 1984, Arco $9.95 (0-668-06178-2). An introductory volume that discusses various types of energy, their uses, and sources. (Rev: BL 4/1/85) [621.042]

5173 Fogel, Barbara R. *Energy: Choices for the Future* (8–12). Illus. 1985, Watts LB $12.90 (0-531-10060-X). After a description of what causes energy crises, the author describes alternate sources of energy such as synfuels, natural gas, and solar energy. (Rev: BR 5–6/86; SLJ 2/86; VOYA 4/86) [333.7]

5174 Goldin, Augusta. *Geothermal Energy: A Hot Prospect* (7–9). 1981, Harcourt $11.95 (0-15-230662-5). A study of the energy resources inside our earth and how we tap them. [333.8]

5175 Goldin, Augusta. *Small Energy Sources: Choices That Work* (7–10). 1988, Harper $17.95 (0-15-276215-9). A discussion of alternate energy sources that involve the sun, wind, water, and waste products. (Rev: BL 11/1/88; SLJ 8/88) [333.79]

5176 Jacobs, Linda. *Letting Off Steam: The Story of Geothermal Energy* (7–12). Illus. 1989, Carolrhoda LB $12.95 (0-87614-300-1). A lucid account that tells about the sources and the use of geothermal energy. (Rev: SLJ 9/89) [333.8]

5177 McKie, Robin. *Energy* (5–9). Illus. 1989, Hampstead LB $12.90 (0-531-19509-0). In brief text plus many illustrations, the author introduces various kinds of power resources. (Rev: BL 6/1/89; SLJ 9/89) [621.042]

Coal, Gas, and Oil

5178 Asimov, Isaac. *How Did We Find Out about Coal?* (6–9). Illus. 1980, Walker LB $10.85 (0-8027-6401-0). A description of how coal is formed, and its many uses throughout history. There is a companion volume on oil. [553.2]

5179 Asimov, Isaac. *How Did We Find Out about Oil?* (6–9). Illus. 1980, Walker LB $10.85 (0-8027-6381-2). An introduction to origins of petroleum and why it has become the world's leading source of energy. [553.2]

5180 Brown, A. S. *Fuel Resources* (5–9). Illus. 1985, Watts $10.40 (0-531-04911-6). A book that introduces fuels and gives particulars on individual ones such as coal, petroleum, and uranium. (Rev: BR 9–10/85) [333.7]

5181 Davis, Bertha, and Susan Whitfield. *The Coal Question* (7–9). Illus. 1982, Watts LB $12.90 (0-531-04484-X). A history of the use of this source of energy and a view of its future. [662.6]

5182 Hansen, Michael C. *Coal: How It Is Found and Used* (6–9). Illus. 1990, Enslow LB $13.95 (0-89490-286-5). Various aspects of coal are explored; for example, its formation, types, mining methods, and uses. (Rev: BL 7/90) [662.6]

5183 Lynch, Michael. *How Oil Rigs Are Made* (5–9). Illus. 1985, Facts on File $10.95 (0-8160-0041-7). Detailed illustrations and clear text highlight this account of how and where oil rigs are constructed. (Rev: BL 6/15/85; SLJ 11/85) [627]

5184 Lyttle, Richard B. *Shale Oil & Tar Sands: The Promises and Pitfalls* (7–10). Illus. 1982, Watts LB $12.90 (0-531-04489-0). An objective view of the possible exploitation of this source of petroleum. [333.8]

5185 Pampe, William R. *Petroleum: How It Is Found and Used* (7–9). Illus. 1984, Enslow LB $13.95 (0-89490-100-1). How oil deposits are formed is discussed as well as how its use has resulted in an international industry. [553.2]

5186 Scott, Elaine. *Oil! Getting It, Shipping It, Selling It* (5–8). 1984, Warne $13.95 (0-7232-6260-8). This book tells how we find oil deposits and how petroleum is refined, transported, and used. [665]

Nuclear Energy

5187 Asimov, Isaac. *How Did We Find Out about Nuclear Power?* (6–9). Illus. 1976, Walker LB $10.85 (0-8027-6266-2). The story of how man has gradually accumulated the knowledge necessary to split the atom and utilize nuclear energy. [539.7]

5188 Halacy, Dan. *Nuclear Energy* (7–10). Rev. ed. Illus. 1984, Watts LB $10.40 (0-531-04829-2). Some topics covered are how nuclear plants operate, uses of nuclear power, accidents, and radioactive wastes. [621.48]

5189 Hawkes, Nigel. *Nuclear Power* (7–9). Illus. 1984, Gloucester LB $12.40 (0-531-04870-5). A concise introduction to atoms, fission, and nuclear energy uses. [539.7]

5190 Helgerson, Joel. *Nuclear Accidents* (7–12). Illus. 1988, Watts $11.90 (0-531-10330-7). A history of the use of nuclear power and its possible dangers. (Rev: BL 8/88; BR 11–12/88; SLJ 5/88; VOYA 8/88) [363.1]

5191 Kiefer, Irene. *Nuclear Energy at the Crossroads* (7–9). Illus. 1982, Macmillan $14.95 (0-689-30926-0). The peaceful uses of nuclear energy as well as their consequences are described. [333.79]

5192 Milne, Lorus J., and Margery Milne. *Understanding Radioactivity* (7–9). Illus. 1989, Macmillan $12.95 (0-689-31362-4). A concise account of the effects of radiation in the environment is preceded with an explanation of atomic theory and what causes radioactivity. (Rev: BL 5/15/89; SLJ 5/89) [539.7]

5193 Pringle, Laurence. *Nuclear Energy: Troubled Past, Uncertain Future* (6–10). Rev. ed. 1989, Macmillan $13.95 (0-02-775391-3). The nature of nuclear power and the pendulum swings involving the pros and cons of development and uses are well detailed. (Rev: BL 5/1/89; BR 5–6/90; SLJ 4/89; VOYA 12/89) [363.1]

5194 Weiss, Ann E. *The Nuclear Question* (7–9). 1981, Harcourt $10.95 (0-15-259596-0). The advantages and dangers in developing nuclear resources are explained along with useful background historical material. [621.48]

Solar Energy

5195 Asimov, Isaac. *How Did We Find Out about Solar Power?* (6–9). Illus. 1981, Walker LB $10.85 (0-8027-6423-1). An explanation is given on how the sun's energy has been used from the earliest time until today. [621.47]

5196 Cross, Wilbur. *Solar Energy* (6–8). Illus. 1984, Childrens $17.27 (0-516-00511-1). This account tells how the sun's energy has been used in

the past, how it is currently being harnessed, and plans for future use. (Rev: BL 5/1/85) [333.79]

5197 Yates, Madeleine. *Sun Power: The Story of Solar Energy* (7–9). Illus. 1982, Abingdon $9.95 (0-687-40627-7). Past and present uses of solar energy are enumerated plus hints on how this energy source might be used in the future. [621.47]

Light, Color, and Laser Science

5198 Berger, Melvin. *Light, Lenses and Lasers* (7–9). Illus. 1987, Putnam $10.99 (0-399-61214-9). Such topics as microscopes, eyeglasses, and contact lenses as well as lasers and light theories are discussed. (Rev: BL 2/1/88) [535]

5199 Billings, Charlene W. *Fiber Optics: Bright New Way to Communicate* (6–8). Illus. 1986, Putnam $9.95 (0-396-08785-X). The story of these threads of glass that carry light beams and that are currently revolutionizing the communications industry. (Rev: BL 10/1/86) [621.36]

5200 Branley, Franklyn M. *Color, from Rainbows to Lasers* (6–9). Illus. 1978, Harper LB $13.89 (0-690-03847-X). Theories about light are explained as well as a presentation of materials on such topics as the spectrum, types of colors, and color printing. [535.6]

5201 Burroughs, William. *Lasers* (7–10). Illus. 1982, Warwick LB $10.90 (0-531-09196-1). The properties of laser light are described plus its use in a variety of industries and medicine. [621.36]

5202 Filson, Brent. *Exploring with Lasers* (6–8). Illus. 1984, Messner $8.79 (0-671-50573-4). After a discussion of light in general and laser light in particular, this book discusses the applications of laser technology in such areas as medicine and communication. (Rev: BL 2/15/85) [621.36]

5203 Hecht, Jeff. *Optics: Light for a New Age* (6–10). Illus. 1987, Macmillan $14.95 (0-684-18879-1). In this general discussion of light such topics as the human eye, optical instruments, and artificial light are also described. (Rev: BL 4/1/88; SLJ 3/88) [535]

5204 Lafferty, Peter. *Energy and Light* (6–8). Illus. 1988, Gloucester LB $12.40 (0-531-17144-2). A general introduction to the subjects of energy and light plus coverage of lasers and fiber optics. (Rev: BL 5/15/89) [535]

5205 *Sight, Light and Color* (5–9). Illus. 1984, Arco $9.95 (0-668-06177-4). In addition to introducing light, color, and the science of optics, this well-illustrated book describes the human eye and how we see. (Rev: BL 4/1/85) [535]

5206 Simon, Hilda. *The Magic of Color* (6–9). Illus. 1981, Lothrop $12.95 (0-688-00619-1). The nature of color is explored, coverage is given on how color illustrations are produced, and topics such as color blindness are discussed. [535.6]

5207 White, Jack R. *The Invisible World of the Infrared* (7–10). Illus. 1984, Dodd LB $9.95 (0-396-08319-6). Infrared light is introduced and its many uses in such areas as geology, medicine, and astronomy. [535]

Magnetism and Electricity

5208 Asimov, Isaac. *How Did We Find Out about Microwaves?* (5–9). Illus. 1989, Walker LB $12.85 (0-8027-6838-5). Beginning with the discoveries of Newton, this account traces how we learned about microwaves and the uses that are made of them today. (Rev: SLJ 4/89; VOYA 6/89) [537.5]

5209 Boltz, C. L. *How Electricity Is Made* (5–9). Illus. 1985, Facts on File $10.95 (0-8160-0039-5). A nicely illustrated volume on sources of electricity and how it is generated and distributed. (Rev: BL 6/15/85; SLJ 11/85) [621.3]

5210 Branley, Franklyn M. *The Electromagnetic Spectrum: Key to the Universe* (7–10). Illus. 1979, Harper LB $12.89 (0-690-03869-0). The nature of electricity and magnetism is explained and the interrelationships between these 2 forces. [537]

5211 Gutnik, Martin J. *Electricity: From Faraday to Solar Generators* (6–10). Illus. 1986, Watts $10.40 (0-531-10222-X). This account briefly covers the developments in electricity from the ancient Greeks to television, solar generators, and other modern achievements. (Rev: BR 3–4/87; SLJ 2/87) [537]

5212 Gutnik, Martin J. *Simple Electrical Devices* (7–10). Illus. 1986, Watts LB $10.40 (0-531-10127-4). The historical development of concepts involving electromagnetism is explained and a number of projects outlined that illustrate each. (Rev: BR 11–12/86; SLJ 10/86) [537]

5213 Math, Irwin. *More Wires and Watts: Understanding and Using Electricity* (7–12). Illus. 1988, Macmillan $13.95 (0-684-18914-3). The principles and properties of electricity are explored chiefly through a series of projects. (Rev: BL 1/1/89; BR 5–6/89; SLJ 4/89) [537]

5214 Math, Irwin. *Wires and Watts: Understanding and Using Electricity* (7–9). Illus. 1981, Macmillan $13.95 (0-684-16854-5). After the principles of electricity are introduced, a number of easy projects applying these principles are given. [537]

5215 Vogt, Gregory. *Electricity and Magnetism* (5–8). 1985, Watts $10.40 (0-531-10038-3). A clear, interesting explanation that gives historical background and 11 easy experiments. (Rev: BR 5–6/86) [537]

5216 Vogt, Gregory. *Generating Electricity* (6–9). Illus. 1986, Watts $10.40 (0-531-10117-7). This account includes an explanation of electricity, the ways in which it is generated and a number of experiments. (Rev: BL 3/15/86; SLJ 5/86) [621.3]

Nuclear Physics

5217 Apfel, Necia H. *It's All Elementary: From Atoms to the Quantum World of Quarks, Leptons, and Gluons* (7–12). Illus. 1985, Lothrop $12.88 (0-688-04093-4); paper $7.25 (0-688-04092-6). Nuclear physics is introduced in a logically arranged but demanding account. (Rev: BL 2/15/86; BR 5–6/86; SLJ 3/86; VOYA 6/86) [539.7]

5218 Asimov, Isaac. *How Did We Find Out about Electricity?* (6–8). 1973, Walker LB $10.85 (0-8027-6124-0). A history of how we have accumulated knowledge about electricity from ancient times to the present. [537]

5219 Berger, Melvin. *Our Atomic World* (6–9). Illus. 1989, Watts LB $10.90 (0-531-10690-X). An up-to-date volume that covers the structure of the atom, quarks, and particle theory. (Rev: SLJ 6/89) [539]

5220 Pringle, Laurence. *Radiation: Waves and Particles/Benefits and Risks* (7–10). Illus. 1983, Enslow LB $13.95 (0-89490-054-4). After a discussion of the nature of radiation, this account explains the results of exposure to radiation from various sources. [539.2]

Simple Machines

5221 Weiss, Harvey. *Machines and How They Work* (6–9). Illus. 1983, Harper LB $12.89 (0-690-04300-7). Such simple machines as the pulley and lever are described. [621.8]

Technology and Engineering

General Works and Miscellaneous Industries

5222 Claypool, Jane. *Manufacturing* (7–9). Illus. 1984, Watts LB $10.40 (0-531-04825-X). Topics related to industry in this country such as unions, management, and competition are introduced. [338.4]

5223 Crump, Donald J., ed. *How Things Are Made* (6–9). Illus. 1981, National Geographic LB $8.50 (0-80744-339-9). An inquiry into how such objects as baseballs and light bulbs are made. [670]

5224 Crump, Donald J., ed. *How Things Work* (7–9). Illus. 1983, National Geographic LB $8.50 (0-87044-430-1). An exploration of the principles on which such common objects as alarm clocks and bicycles work. [600]

5225 Crump, Donald J., ed. *Small Inventions That Make a Big Difference* (6–9). Illus. 1984, National Geographic LB $8.50 (0-87044-503-0). A book on inventions and inventors that covers such common items as the zipper. [608]

5226 Dineen, Jacqueline. *Plastics* (5–8). Illus. 1988, Enslow LB $9.95 (0-89490-221-0). This account discusses such plastics as molded plastics, paints, adhesive foam, and glass and man-made fibers. (Rev: SLJ 4/89) [668.4]

5227 Dineen, Jacqueline. *Rubber* (5–8). Illus. 1988, Enslow LB $9.95 (0-89490-222-9). Both natural and synthetic rubber are introduced with material on how they are produced and their uses. (Rev: SLJ 4/89) [678]

5228 Evans, Peter. *Technology 2000* (6–8). Illus. 1985, Facts on File $12.95 (0-8160-1155-9). This well-illustrated book deals with recent advances in computers, transportation, communication, and medicine, and makes predictions for the future. (Rev: BL 12/1/85; SLJ 2/86) [303.4]

5229 Fisher, Trevor. *Communications* (7–9). Illus. 1985, Batsford $19.95 (0-7134-4631-5). This is a clear history of communication from the development of language to today's sophisticated telecommunications networks. (Rev: SLJ 2/86) [302.2]

5230 Gardner, Robert. *Experimenting with Inventions* (5–10). Illus. 1990, Watts LB $11.90 (0-531-10910-0). A review of the inventive process; a discussion of the inventions of da Vinci, Edison, and Buckminster Fuller; plus sets of situations that challenge one's powers of invention. (Rev: BL 6/15/90; SLJ 8/90) [609]

5231 Gay, Kathlyn. *Ergonomics: Making Products and Places Fit People* (7–12). Illus. 1986, Enslow $15.95 (0-89490-118-4). An explanation of the applied science that makes products user friendly, for example, proper designs for toothbrushes. (Rev: BL 10/1/86; BR 11–12/86; VOYA 12/86) [620.8]

5232 Grigoli, Valorie. *Service Industries* (5–8). Illus. 1984, Watts $10.40 (0-531-04832-2). A very general overview of the various kinds of service industries and their importance in today's economy. (Rev: BL 2/1/85) [338.4]

5233 Kolb, Kenneth E., and Doris K. Kolb. *Glass: Its Many Facets* (6–9). Illus. 1988, Enslow $12.95 (0-89490-150-8). The story of glass from ancient Egypt to today's uses in fiber optics and in space shuttles. (Rev: BL 10/1/88; BR 1–2/89; SLJ 10/88) [666]

5234 Lambert, Mark. *Living in the Future* (6–8). Illus. 1986, Bookwright $12.40 (0-531-18040-9).

This book covers "future" advances in such areas as communications, housing, energy, and transportation. (Rev: SLJ 11/86) [236]

5235 Lambert, Mark. *Spotlight on Plastics* (6–8). Illus. 1988, Rourke $14.60 (0-86592-269-1). The story of the manufacture, types, and uses of carbon-based plastics. (Rev: BL 12/1/88) [668.4]

5236 *Machines, Power and Transportation* (5–9). Illus. 1984, Arco $9.95 (0-668-06179-0). Types of power are described and how they are used in machines, particularly those involved in transportation. (Rev: BL 4/1/85) [620.9]

5237 Murphy, Jim. *Guess Again: More Weird & Wacky Inventions* (5–9). 1986, Bradbury $12.95 (0-02-767720-6). In this book an invention is presented and the reader must determine its purpose. (Rev: BL 7/86) [609]

5238 Paterson, Alan J. *How Glass Is Made* (5–9). Illus. 1985, Facts on File $10.95 (0-8160-0038-7). In this well-illustrated volume, a history of glass making is given with text and diagrams on the kinds of glass and the processes in existence today. (Rev: BL 6/15/85; SLJ 2/86) [666]

5239 Perrins, Lesley. *How Paper Is Made* (5–9). Illus. 1985, Facts on File $10.95 (0-8160-0036-0). In this oversized, illustrated volume, processes involved in making paper both in the past and the present are outlined. (Rev: BL 6/15/85; SLJ 2/86) [677]

5240 Rickard, Graham. *Spotlight on Diamonds* (6–8). Illus. 1988, Rourke $14.60 (0-86592-271-3). The history and uses of diamonds are treated plus information on where and how they are mined. (Rev: BL 12/1/88) [553.8]

5241 Rickard, Graham. *Spotlight on Silver* (6–8). Illus. 1988, Rourke $14.60 (0-86592-273-X). An account that tells the location of silver mines (past and present), the uses of this metal, and the possibilities of future supply and demand. (Rev: BL 12/1/88) [669]

5242 Smith, Norman F., and Douglas W. Smith. *Simulators* (6–8). 1989, Watts LB $11.90 (0-531-10812-0). An account of how devices were developed to substitute for actual experiences in such areas as aeronautics, automobile driving, and space science. (Rev: BL 2/1/90; BR 3–4/90; SLJ 4/90) [620]

5243 Taylor, Barbara. *Be an Inventor* (5–9). Illus. 1987, Harcourt $11.95 (0-15-205950-4); paper $4.95 (0-15-205951-2). A discussion of the process of invention and some examples plus coverage of entries in a Weekly Reader invention contest. (Rev: SLJ 3/88) [608]

Building and Construction

5244 Adkins, Jan. *How a House Happens* (7–9). 1983, Walker paper $3.95 (0-8027-7206-4). From land selection to the completed building, this is how a house takes shape. [728]

5245 Bates, Robert L. *Stone, Clay, Glass: How Building Materials Are Found and Used* (6–9). Illus. 1987, Enslow $13.95 (0-89490-144-3). This is a discussion of 3 basic building materials, their history, manufacture, and uses. (Rev: SLJ 5/87) [691]

5246 Giblin, James Cross. *Let There Be Light: A Book about Windows* (6–10). Illus. 1988, Harper LB $14.89 (0-690-04695-2). A stunning history of windows and their importance in civilization from ancient times to the present. (Rev: BL 11/1/88; BR 5–6/89; SLJ 11/88) [690]

5247 Kingston, Jeremy. *How Bridges Are Made* (5–9). Illus. 1985, Facts on File $10.95 (0-8160-0040-9). An oversized book with lavish illustrations that describes various kinds of bridges and how they are constructed. (Rev: BL 6/15/85; SLJ 11/85) [624.2]

5248 Macaulay, David. *Unbuilding* (7–12). Illus. 1980, Houghton $14.95 (0-395-29457-6); paper $6.95 (0-395-45360-7). In a humorous flight of fancy the author describes in drawings how the Empire State Building could be dismantled. Also use this author's spoof *Great Moments in Architecture* (1982). [690]

5249 Macaulay, David. *Underground* (7–12). Illus. 1976, Houghton $14.95 (0-395-24739-X); paper $6.95 (0-395-34065-9). The infrastructure of a large city is explored in drawings that show how building foundations and underground utility connections exist. [624]

5250 Wilson, Forrest. *What It Feels Like to Be a Building* (4–8). Illus. 1988, Preservation Pr. $15.95 (0-89133-142-5). A simple introduction to structural engineering that introduces such subjects as columns, arches, and domes. (Rev: BL 1/1/89) [690]

Clothing and Textiles

5251 Macaulay, David. *Mill* (7–12). Illus. 1983, Houghton $14.95 (0-395-34830-7). Four different Rhode Island textile mills of the nineteenth century are described in text and excellent drawings. [690]

Computers and Automation

5252 Asimov, Isaac. *How Did We Find Out about Computers?* (6–9). Illus. 1984, Walker LB $11.85 (0-8027-6533-5). An explanation of how computers work plus a history of their development. There is a companion volume on robots. [001.64]

5253 Ault, Roz. *BASIC Programming for Kids* (7–9). Illus. 1983, Houghton paper $9.95 (0-395-34920-6). A guide for the most commonly used personal computers to the techniques of simple programming. [001.64]

5254 Baldwin, Margaret, and Gary Pack. *Computer Graphics* (6–8). Illus. 1984, Watts $10.40 (0-531-04704-0). An explanation of computer illustration and how it is used in a variety of fields including the home. [001.64]

5255 Baldwin, Margaret, and Gary Pack. *Robots and Robotics* (7–10). Illus. 1984, Watts LB $10.90 (0-531-04705-9). A history of robots, how they are used at present, and possible future developments are all introduced. [629.8]

5256 Berger, Melvin. *Computers in Your Life* (6–9). 1985, Harper LB $12.89 (0-690-04101-2). A simple explanation of how computers work and their present-day uses. [001.64]

5257 Berger, Melvin. *Word Processing* (7–10). Illus. 1984, Watts LB $10.40 (0-531-04729-6). A general guide on how to use the computer to produce documents and reports. [652]

5258 Bolognese, Don, and Robert Thornton. *Drawing and Painting with the Computer* (7–10). Illus. 1983, Watts LB $10.90 (0-531-04653-2); paper $4.95 (0-531-03593-X). This book outlines techniques of using the computer to create artworks. [760]

5259 Boren, Sharon. *An Apple for Kids* (5–8). 1983, Weber paper $9.95 (0-88056-119-X). For youngsters 9 to 13, this is a guide to how an Apple computer works and how one can do simple programming. Also in this series: *An Atari for Kids* and *A Pet for Kids* (both 1984). [001.64]

5260 Cattoche, Robert J. *Computers for the Disabled* (7–9). Illus. 1986, Watts $10.40 (0-531-10212-2). A book that describes the use of computers with the disabled. (Rev: VOYA 2/87) [001.64]

5261 D'Ignazio, Fred. *Invent Your Own Computer Games* (7–9). 1983, Watts LB $10.90 (0-531-04637-0). A how-to book on creating one's own word, adventure, sports, or number games for the personal computer. [001.64]

5262 D'Ignazio, Fred. *Working Robots* (7–12). Illus. 1982, Lodestar $12.50 (0-525-66740-7). The world of robotics is introduced plus descriptions of how robots are built and used. [629.8]

5263 D'Ignazio, Fred, and Allen L. Wold. *The Science of Artificial Intelligence* (7–9). Illus. 1984, Watts LB $10.40 (0-531-04703-2). A review of the progress made in machine-made intelligence. [001.53]

5264 Duck, Mike. *Graphics: Hangman* (6–9). Illus. 1984, Gloucester $12.40 (0-531-03483-6). The game of Hangman is used to teach some computer programming using BASIC. (Rev: BL 7/85) [001.64]

5265 Fang, Irving. *The Computer Story* (6–9). 1988, Rada Pr. paper $9.95 (0-9604212-4-6). A readable history of the development of the computer up to the present-day desktop publishing capabilities. (Rev: BR 1–2/89) [001.64]

5266 Ford, Roger, and Oliver Strimpel. *Computers: An Introduction* (6–10). Illus. 1985, Facts on File $12.95 (0-8160-1061-7). A lavishly illustrated book that gives the history of computers, tells how they work, and explains peripherals. (Rev: BR 5–6/86; SLJ 1/86) [001.64]

5267 Forsyth, Richard. *Machines That Think* (7–10). Illus. 1986, Watts LB $10.90 (0-531-19017-X). An introduction to artificial intelligence, how these machines work, and what they can and cannot do. (Rev: SLJ 3/87) [001.53]

5268 Francis, Dorothy B. *Computer Crime* (7–12). 1987, Lodestar $12.95 (0-525-67192-7). A description of the various computer crimes and how they are perpetrated and detected. (Rev: BL 7/87; SLJ 9/87) [001.64]

5269 Galanter, Eugene. *Advanced Programming Handbook* (7–12). 1984, Putnam $14.95 (0-399-50975-5); paper $8.95 (0-399-50976-3). An advanced text geared to those who have mastered the basics. [001.64]

5270 Galanter, Eugene. *Elementary Programming for Kids in BASIC* (7–9). 1983, Putnam $15.95 (0-399-50976-3); paper $7.95 (0-399-50867-8). An introduction to programming with many practical applications. [001.64]

5271 Greene, Laura. *Computer Pioneers* (7–9). Illus. 1985, Watts LB $10.40 (0-531-04906-X). A history of computers and the men who devised them from the seventeenth century to the late 1970s. (Rev: SLJ 5/85) [001.64]

5272 Hawkes, Nigel. *Computers: How They Work* (6–9). Illus. 1983, Watts $11.90 (0-531-04679-6). A simple explanation of what computers can and cannot do and why. [001.64]

5273 Hawkes, Nigel. *Computers in Action* (7–10). Illus. 1983, Watts LB $11.90 (0-531-04723-7). An explanation of the variety of uses made of computers in such fields as industry, medicine, and business. [001.64]

5274 Hawkes, Nigel. *Computers in the Home* (7–10). Illus. 1984, Watts LB $11.90 (0-531-04725-3). A discussion of the many uses of home computers plus a look at their future place in everyday life. [001.64]

5275 Hawkes, Nigel. *Robots and Computers* (7–9). Illus. 1984, Watts $11.90 (0-531-04816-0). An explanation of how robots are controlled by computers and the kinds of jobs they are presently performing. [001.64]

5276 Herda, D. J. *Computer Peripherals* (6–8). Illus. 1985, Watts $10.40 (0-531-10036-7). This book introduces and explains the function of such peripherals as the printer, monitor, keyboard, and modem. (Rev: BL 4/1/86; SLJ 1/86; VOYA 4/86) [001.64]

5277 Herda, D. J. *Microcomputers* (7–10). Illus. 1984, Watts LB $10.40 (0-531-04730-X). The parts of home computers are explained, various models are introduced, and uses at home and school are explored. [001.64]

5278 Hintz, Sandy, and Martin Hintz. *Computers in Our World, Today and Tomorrow* (7–9). 1983, Watts $10.40 (0-531-04639-7). An explanation of the role that computers can play in the future in such fields as medicine, entertainment, and education. [001.64]

5279 Hyde, Margaret O. *Artificial Intelligence: A Revision of Computers That Think?* (6–8). Illus. 1986, Enslow $15.95 (0-89490-124-9). Can computers really think? This is just one of the questions explored in this volume. (Rev: BL 9/1/86; BR 11–12/86; SLJ 11/86; VOYA 12/86) [006.3]

5280 Jackson, Peter. *The Chip* (7–9). Illus. 1986, Warwick LB $11.90 (0-531-19006-4). An information-packed short book that explains what microchips are, how they work, and how they are made. (Rev: BR 9–10/86; SLJ 8/86; VOYA 4/87) [001.64]

5281 Jespersen, James, and Jane Fitz-Randolph. *RAMS, ROMS & Robots: The Inside Story of Computers* (7–9). Illus. 1984, Macmillan $13.95 (0-689-31063-3). A clear, well-organized introduction to the computer, its uses and limitations. [004]

5282 Kettelkamp, Larry. *Computer Graphics: How It Works, What It Does* (6–10). Illus. 1989, Morrow $12.95 (0-688-07504-5). After a discussion of how computer graphics work, Kettelkamp investigates such topics as their appli-

cations and the important people and programs in the field. (Rev: BL 8/89; BR 9–10/89; SLJ 12/89) [006.6]

5283 Lampton, Christopher. *Advanced BASIC* (7–10). 1984, Watts $11.90 (0-531-04848-9). For the person who has mastered the basics here are instructions on more sophisticated programs. [001.64]

5284 Lampton, Christopher. *BASIC for Beginners* (7–10). 1984, Watts LB $11.90 (0-531-04745-8). The basics are covered thoroughly with many projects outlined at each difficulty level. [001.64]

5285 Lampton, Christopher. *Computer Languages* (7–9). 1983, Watts $10.40 (0-531-04638-9). An introduction to the number languages such as BASIC and FORTRAN that are used to talk to computers. [001.64]

5286 Lampton, Christopher. *FORTRAN for Beginners* (7–10). 1984, Watts LB $11.90 (0-531-04747-4). An introduction to FORTRAN IV with a number of interesting projects. [001.64]

5287 Lampton, Christopher. *Graphics and Animation on the Apple: II, II+, IIe, and IIc* (7–12). Illus. 1986, Watts LB $12.90 (0-531-10143-6). An advanced text that explains the production of both graphics and animation on Apple computers. Companion volumes are *Graphics and Animation on the Atari: 800, 400, 1200XL, 800XL, and 600XL; Graphics and Animation on the TRS-80: Models I, III, and 4* (both 1986); and *Graphics and Animation on the Commodore 64* (1985). (Rev: SLJ 8/86) [001.64]

5288 Lampton, Christopher. *How to Create Computer Games* (7–9). 1986, Watts $10.40 (0-531-10120-7). Using BASIC, Lampton describes how to program such games as "Go Fish" and tic-tac-toe. (Rev: BR 9–10/86) [001.64]

5289 Lampton, Christopher. *The Micro Dictionary* (7–10). 1984, Watts $11.90 (0-531-04840-3). For the beginner, here is a dictionary of terms, concepts, and jargon related to the microcomputer. [001.64]

5290 Lampton, Christopher. *Programming in BASIC* (7–10). 1983, Watts $10.40 (0-531-04664-3). A guide to writing simple computer programs using BASIC. [001.64]

5291 Laron, Carl. *Computer Software Basics* (5–9). Illus. 1985, Prentice LB $9.95 (0-13-163858-0). After an introduction to computers, the author describes word processors and various kinds of software, such as data systems and spreadsheets. (Rev: SLJ 1/86) [001.64]

5292 Liptak, Karen. *Robotics Basics* (7–9). Illus. 1984, Prentice $10.95 (0-13-782087-9). An account that tells what robots are, what they presently can do, and perhaps what they might do in the future. [629.8]

5293 Madison, Arnold, and David L. Drotar. *Pocket Calculators: How to Use and Enjoy Them* (7–9). 1978, Lodestar $8.95 (0-525-66580-3). This book describes the various kinds of pocket calculators, how they work, and the different activities related to them. [651.8]

5294 Marshall, Gary. *Beginning BASIC: Space Journey* (6–9). Illus. 1984, Gloucester $12.40 (0-531-03482-8). Three simple game programs in BASIC are introduced for the Apple and Commodore. (Rev: BL 7/85) [001.64]

5295 Math, Irwin. *Bits and Pieces: Understanding and Building Computing Devices* (7–10). Illus. 1984, Macmillan $13.95 (0-684-17879-6). Both analog and digital computing devices are explained with instructions for construction. [621.3819]

5296 Milton, Marcus. *Moving Graphics: Alien Invaders* (6–9). Illus. 1985, Gloucester $12.40 (0-531-03491-7). The author teaches computer users to create alien figures in this simple guide to programming in BASIC. (Rev: BL 7/85; SLJ 8/85) [001.64]

5297 Pallas, Norvin. *Calculator Puzzles, Tricks and Games* (7–9). Illus. 1978, Sterling paper $4.95 (0-8069-7688-8). All sorts of activities—some practical, others for fun—are described using the pocket calculator. [651.8]

5298 Perry, Robert L. *Computer Crime* (5–9). 1986, Watts $10.40 (0-531-10113-4). This book explores the kinds of computer crime that exist and the moral and legal issues involved. (Rev: BR 9–10/86) [364.1]

5299 Pizzey, Steve, and Sheila Snowden. *The Computerized Society* (7–12). 1986, Bookwright $12.40 (0-531-18039-5). A book that explains how computers have revolutionized our world and what lies in the future. (Rev: VOYA 12/86) [001.64]

5300 Rodgers, Steve, and Marcus Milton. *Creating a Database: Adventure Game* (6–9). Illus. 1985, Gloucester $12.40 (0-531-03490-9). Using a game called Adventure and BASIC, some programming concepts are taught. (Rev: BL 7/85; SLJ 8/85) [001.64]

5301 Schneiderman, Ron. *Computers: From Babbage to the Fifth Generation* (6–8). Illus. 1986, Watts $10.40 (0-531-10131-2). A history of computers from the very earliest calculators to the present with a peek into the future. (Rev: BL 7/86; SLJ 8/86) [004]

5302 Schulman, Elayne Engelman, and Richard R. Page. *Spreadsheets for Beginners* (6–9). Illus. 1987, Watts $11.90 (0-531-10232-7). An account of how to produce these record-keeping devices and their various formats. (Rev: BL 2/15/87; SLJ 3/87; VOYA 12/87) [650]

5303 Silverstein, Alvin, and Virginia B. Silverstein. *The Robots Are Here* (6–9). Illus. 1983, Prentice LB $10.95 (0-13-782185-9). A survey of the world of robots including speculations as to future developments. [629.8]

5304 Slater, Don. *Information Technology* (6–9). Illus. 1986, Watts LB $11.90 (0-531-10198-3). This book discusses how informational networks are constructed and their application in such fields as business, medicine, and industry. (Rev: SLJ 3/87) [001.5]

5305 Spencer, Donald D. *What Computers Can Do* (7–10). 1982, Camelot paper $6.95 (0-89218-043-9). An informative book about the many present-day applications of computer technology. Also by the same author: *Understanding Computers* (1988) and *BASIC Programming* (1983). [001.64]

5306 Taft, David. *Computer Programming* (7–9). Illus. 1986, Warwick LB $11.90 (0-531-19007-2). Using BASIC as an example, the author explains the basics of computer programming in this compact volume. (Rev: SLJ 8/86; VOYA 10/86) [001.64]

5307 Thomas, David A. *The Math-Computer Connection* (6–9). Illus. 1986, Watts $11.90 (0-531-10231-9). Using BASIC, the author explains how various problems in mathematics can be solved. (Rev: BL 2/15/87; VOYA 2/87) [510]

5308 Wold, Allen L. *Computer Science* (7–10). Illus. 1984, Watts LB $12.90 (0-531-04764-4). A guide for students on the use of the computer in school and related projects. [001.64]

Electronics

5309 Filson, Brent. *Superconductors and Other New Breakthroughs in Science* (7–10). Illus. 1989, Messner LB $10.29 (0-671-65857-3). The story of superconductors plus developments in such areas as computers, monoclonal antibodies, and supernovas. (Rev: BL 8/89; SLJ 9/89) [500]

5310 Lampton, Christopher. *Superconductors* (7–10). Illus. 1989, Enslow LB $13.95 (0-89490-

203-2). A history of superconductors, how they work, and a rundown on present and future application. (Rev: BL 8/89; BR 1–2/90; SLJ 2/90; VOYA 2/90) [539.7]

5311 LeBlanc, Wayne J., and Alden R. Carter. *Modern Electronics* (5–8). Illus. 1986, Watts $10.40 (0-531-10218-1). A simple introduction to electronics, with many experiments, that covers such developments as compact disc players and supercomputers as well as predictions for the future. (Rev: BL 11/15/86; SLJ 2/87; VOYA 4/87) [621]

5312 Ross, Frank, Jr. *The Magic Chip: Exploring Microelectronics* (7–10). Illus. 1984, Messner LB $9.79 (0-671-49373-6). The microchip is defined and its many applications in a variety of technologies are described. [621.381]

Machinery

5313 Cooper, Chris, and Tony Osman. *How Everyday Things Work* (7–10). Illus. 1984, Facts on File $12.95 (0-87196-988-2). From bicycles and elevators to compact discs and video cameras, the inner workings are explained. [600]

5314 Siegel, Beatrice. *The Sewing Machine* (7–9). Illus. 1984, Walker LB $10.85 (0-8027-6532-7). The development of the sewing machine by such men as Isaac Singer is told and of the effect this invention had on society. [681]

5315 Weitzman, David. *Windmills, Bridges, and Old Machines: Discovering Our Industrial Past* (7–9). Illus. 1982, Macmillan $15.95 (0-684-17456-1). A history of American industry as seen through some of the old machinery that was used. [620]

Metals

5316 Cohen, Daniel. *Gold: The Fascinating Story of the Noble Metal through the Ages* (7–9). Illus. 1976, Evans $10.95 (0-87131-218-2). The story of gold from ancient times to today's uses, including its use as a monetary standard. [669]

5317 Fodor, R. V. *Gold, Copper, Iron: How Metals Are Formed, Found, and Used* (7–12). Illus. 1989, Enslow LB $13.95 (0-89490-138-9). A somewhat technical account that describes how metals are formed, where they are found,

and how they are processed and used. (Rev: BL 4/1/89; BR 9–10/89; SLJ 4/89) [546]

5318 Kerrod, Robin. *Metals* (7–9). Illus. 1982, Silver Burdett LB $14.96 (0-382-06661-8). A general introduction that includes material on mining, refining, and uses. [669]

5319 Lambert, Mark. *Spotlight on Copper* (6–8). Illus. 1988, Rourke $14.60 (0-86592-270-5). A description of where and how copper is mined and its many uses. (Rev: BL 12/1/88) [669]

5320 Lambert, Mark. *Spotlight on Iron and Steel* (6–8). Illus. 1988, Rourke $14.60 (0-86592-268-3). A history of iron plus information on mining, processing, and using this resource. (Rev: BL 12/1/88) [669]

5321 Lye, Keith. *Spotlight on Gold* (6–8). Illus. 1988, Rourke $14.60 (0-86592-272-1). A well-illustrated account of the uses of this precious mineral, its history, and how it is mined. (Rev: BL 12/1/88) [669]

Telegraph and Telephone

5322 Graham, Ian. *Communications* (5–9). Illus. 1989, Hampstead LB $12.90 (0-531-19508-2). An overview of how people communicate with special emphasis on telecommunications. (Rev: BL 6/1/89; SLJ 9/89) [001.51]

5323 Taylor, L. B., Jr. *Electronic Surveillance* (7–12). Illus. 1987, Watts $12.90 (0-531-10328-5). This book discusses how some surveillants like space satellites benefit people whereas others like bugging and telephone taps can threaten civil liberties. (Rev: BL 5/15/87; BR 9–10/87; SLJ 10/87; VOYA 8–9/87) [621.389]

Television, Motion Pictures, Radio, and Recording

5324 Ferrell, Nancy Warren. *The New World of Amateur Radio* (7–10). Illus. 1986, Watts LB $10.40 (0-531-10219-X). An introduction to amateur radio that covers such topics as licensing, practices, and theory. (Rev: SLJ 2/87; VOYA 4/87) [621.3841]

5325 Irvine, Mat. *TV & Video* (6–9). Illus. 1983, Watts LB $11.90 (0-531-04726-1). In simple terms and many diagrams the author explains how television cameras and receivers operate. [621.388]

5326 Kuslan, Richard, and Louis Kuslan. *Ham Radio: An Introduction to the World beyond CB* (7–10). 1981, Prentice $10.95 (0-13-372334-8). An easily followed introduction to the world of amateur radio and how to get started in it. [621.38]

5327 Renowden, Gareth. *Video* (5–8). 1983, Watts $12.40 (0-531-04584-6). An introduction to the world of video that covers such topics as how pictures are transmitted, home applications, videodiscs, and videocassettes. [621.388]

5328 Wicks, Keith. *Sound and Recording* (7–9). Illus. 1982, Watts LB $10.90 (0-531-09197-X). A history of sound recording from the use of drums and wires to today's hi-fi and stereo. [620.2]

5329 Young, Frank. *Radio & Radar* (7–10). Illus. 1984, Watts LB $10.90 (0-531-04724-5). This book explains what radio, sonar, and radar waves are and how they are used. [621.384]

Transportation

General and Miscellaneous

5330 Graham, Ian. *Transportation* (5–9). Illus. 1989, Hampstead LB $12.90 (0-531-19511-2). Various kinds of transportation are introduced from the most primitive to supersonic aircraft. (Rev: BL 6/1/89; SLJ 4/89) [629.04]

5331 Hilton, Suzanne. *Faster Than a Horse: Moving West with Engine Power* (7–9). 1983, Westminster $14.95 (0-664-32709-5). The story of how the steamboat, railroad, trolley, and automobile affected the history of the United States. [380.5]

5332 Moolman, Valerie. *The Future World of Transportation* (5–9). 1984, Watts $12.90 (0-531-04882-9). Based on the World of Motion exhibit at Walt Disney's EPCOT center in Florida, this book covers both the history and future of transportation. [380]

5333 Tunis, Edwin. *Wheels: A Pictorial History* (6–9). Illus. 1977, Harper $24.70 (0-690-01282-9). A pictorial history of wheels from primitive times to the automobiles and trains of today. [388.3]

Airplanes and Aeronautics

5334 Berger, Gilda. *Aviation* (5–8). 1983, Watts $9.90 (0-531-04645-1). This simple introduction to aircraft starts with the seventeenth century and ends with the supersonic Concorde. [629.1]

5335 Berliner, Don. *Research Airplanes: Testing the Boundaries of Flight* (6–9). Illus. 1988, Lerner $12.95 (0-8225-1582-2). A chapter from aviation history as well as a description of the contributions that designers of today's planes are making to research. (Rev: BL 10/1/88; SLJ 1/89) [629.1]

5336 Berliner, Don. *Unusual Airplanes* (5–9). Illus. 1986, Lerner $9.95 (0-8225-0431-6). An examination of both the successful and unsuccessful airplane designs that have incorporated unusual features. (Rev: BL 7/86) [629.133]

5337 Boyne, Walter J. *The Smithsonian Book of Flight for Young People* (7–10). Illus. 1988, Macmillan $16.95 (0-689-31422-1); Aladdin paper $9.95 (0-689-71212-X). A history of flight from balloons to modern aircraft in text and excellent photographs. (Rev: BL 3/15/89; BR 3–4/89; SLJ 1/89; VOYA 4/89) [387.7]

5338 Braybrook, Roy. *The Aircraft Encyclopedia* (7–10). Illus. 1985, Messner LB $9.79 (0-671-55338-0); Simon & Schuster paper $5.95 (0-671-55337-2). An introductory guide that includes sections on the history of airplanes, military and civilian aircraft, and a few pages of general information. (Rev: SLJ 9/86) [629.133]

5339 Briggs, Carole S. *Research Balloons: Exploring Hidden Worlds* (6–9). Illus. 1988, Lerner $12.95 (0-8225-1585-7). Past and present contributions to our knowledge of the world that we have gained by the use of balloons are outlined (Rev: BL 10/1/88; SLJ 1/89) [551.5]

5340 Coombs, Charles. *Ultralights: The Flying Featherweights* (7–12). Illus. 1984, Morrow $12.95 (0-688-02775-X). An introduction to ultralights, how they are constructed, and how to fly them. [629.133]

5341 Kaufmann, John. *Voyager: Flight Around the World* (6–10). Illus. 1989, Enslow LB $13.95 (0-89490-185-0). The inspiring story of the first nonstop around-the-world plane flight and of the people responsible for it. (Rev: SLJ 9/89; VOYA 10/89) [629.1]

5342 Lambert, Mark. *Aircraft Technology* (6–8). Illus. 1990, Bookwright LB $12.40 (0-531-18310-6). This survey covers airplane design from the 1930s to the supersonic planes of the future. (Rev: BL 7/90) [629.133]

5343 Lampton, Christopher. *Flying Safe?* (7–10). Illus. 1986, Watts $12.90 (0-531-10169-X). A discussion of air safety that includes material on weather, air traffic control, and airplane engineering. (Rev: BL 6/1/86; SLJ 10/86; VOYA 8–10/86) [363.1]

5344 Moxon, Julian. *How Jet Engines Are Made* (5–9). Illus. 1985, Facts on File $10.95 (0-8160-0037-9). A clear explanation of the history and development of the jet engine is given plus coverage on its parts and how they function. (Rev: BL 6/15/85; SLJ 2/86) [629.134]

5345 Robins, Jim. *The Story of Flight* (5–8). Illus. 1987, Watts $11.90 (0-531-19022-6). A broad introduction that covers the history of all kinds of flying craft. (Rev: SLJ 5/87) [629.132]

5346 Rosenblum, Richard. *Wings: The Early Years of Aviation* (7–9). Illus. 1980, Macmillan $8.95 (0-02-777380-9). A history of airplanes from Leonardo da Vinci to Charles Lindbergh. [629.133]

5347 Schleier, Curt. *The Team behind Your Airline Flight* (7–9). 1981, Westminster $9.95 (0-664-32678-1). From travel agent to destination, this is a rundown on all the people involved in an airplane trip. [387.7]

5348 Sullivan, George. *Famous Blimps and Airships* (5–9). Illus. 1988, Putnam $11.95 (0-396-09119-9). An account that traces the history of airships from the first zeppelins in the 1900s to the present. (Rev: BL 1/15/89) [629.133]

5349 Tessendorf, K. C. *Barnstormers and Daredevils* (6–9). Illus. 1988, Macmillan $13.95 (0-689-31346-2). The fascinating story of the fearless pioneers of flight including Lindbergh and Wiley Post. (Rev: BL 9/15/88; BR 1–2/89; SLJ 10/88) [797.5]

5350 Zisfein, Melvin B. *Flight: A Panorama of Aviation* (7–10). Illus. 1981, Pantheon LB $17.99 (0-394-94272-8). A history of the airplane from its beginnings to the world of today in text and excellent drawings. [629.13]

Automobiles and Trucks

5351 *Chilton's Auto Repair Manual* (7–12). Illus. 1989, Chilton $25.95 (0-8019-7900-5). The standard manual for do-it-yourself automobile repairs. [629.28]

5352 Dexler, Paul R. *Yesterday's Cars* (6–9). Illus. 1979, Lerner LB $8.95 (0-8225-0420-0). Various kinds of old cars are described and tips for collecting and restoring them are given. [629]

5353 Hoffman, Jeffrey. *Corvette: America's Supercar* (7–10). Illus. 1984, Messner LB $9.29 (0-671-43485-3). A history of one of America's most popular sports cars. [629.2]

5354 Knudson, Richard L., and Tom Moran. *Restoring Yesterday's Cars* (7–12). Illus. 1983, Lerner LB $9.95 (0-8225-0440-5). A basic manual on how to buy and restore old cars. [629.28]

5355 Lord, Harvey G. *Car Care for Kids and Former Kids* (7–12). Illus. 1983, Macmillan $14.95 (0-689-30975-9). Basic maintenance routines like changing oil are thoroughly described in text and illustrations. [629.28]

5356 Pizer, Vernon. *The Irrepressible Automobile: A Freewheeling Jaunt Through the Fascinating World of the Motorcar* (5–8). 1986, Putnam $10.95 (0-396-08580-6). From the invention of the wheel to modern air pollution, here is a history of the automobile, its components, and its effects on modern life. (Rev: BL 3/15/86; BR 9–10/86; SLJ 8/86; VOYA 8–10/86) [629.2]

5357 Taylor, John. *How Cars Are Made* (7–10). Illus. 1987, Facts on File $10.95 (0-8160-1689-5). A fine up-to-date overview of the topic that even covers the role of robots in automobile manufacture. (Rev: SLJ 4/88) [629.2]

5358 Trier, Mike. *Supercar* (5–8). Illus. 1988, Watts $11.90 (0-531-17098-5). An account that gives information on the design and construction of such luxury cars as the BMW 7 line of automobiles. (Rev: BL 2/1/89) [629.22]

Railroads

5359 Weitzman, David. *Superpower: The Making of a Steam Locomotive* (6–9). Illus. 1987, Godine $24.95 (0-87923-671-X). A step-by-step guide to the parts of a locomotive and how they are assembled. (Rev: SLJ 1/88) [625.2]

5360 Yepsen, Roger. *Train Talk* (7–9). Illus. 1983, Pantheon $9.95 (0-394-85750-X). An explanation of the inner systems that make a railroad work. [625.1]

Ships and Boats

5361 Boyer, Edward. *River and Canal* (5–8). Illus. 1986, Holiday LB $11.95 (0-8234-0598-2). The story of the networks of canals built in eastern United States during the early 1800s. (Rev: SLJ 9/86) [627]

5362 Huff, Barbara A. *Welcome Aboard! Travelling on an Ocean Liner* (5–8). Illus. 1987, Clarion LB $14.95 (0-89919-503-2). The reader is taken on a transatlantic trip aboard the *QE2*. (Rev: SLJ 1/88) [387.2]

Weapons, Submarines, and the Armed Forces

5363 Brett, Bernard. *The Fighting Ship* (5–8). Illus. 1988, Oxford Univ. Pr. $14.95 (0-19-273155-6). An account that shows the development of ships and submarines through text, cutaway diagrams, and drawings. (Rev: SLJ 6–7/88) [387.2]

5364 Colby, C. B. *Two Centuries of Weapons, 1776–1976* (7–10). Illus. 1975, Putnam LB $6.99 (0-698-30596-5). Weapons, from 1776, 1876, and 1976, are pictured with explanations. [623.4]

5365 Fleisher, Paul. *Understanding the Vocabulary of the Nuclear Arms Race* (6–9). Illus. 1988, Dillon $14.95 (0-87518-352-2). In often lengthy articles, terms and expressions involved in nuclear weapons are explained. (Rev: BL 3/15/88; SLJ 4/88) [355]

5366 Gibbons, Tony. *Submarines* (6–9). Illus. 1987, Lerner LB $9.95 (0-8225-1383-8). This British import explains how a submarine works and its role in modern warfare. (Rev: SLJ 3/88) [359.3]

5367 Graham, Ian. *Submarines* (5–8). Illus. 1989, Gloucester $11.90 (0-531-17153-1). An explanation of how submarines work and how maneuvers such as surfacing and diving are accomplished. (Rev: BL 4/1/89) [623.825]

5368 Hogg, Ian. *Tanks and Armored Vehicles* (7–10). Illus. 1984, Watts LB $12.90 (0-531-04868-3). Several armored vehicles are introduced with details on their construction and operation. [623.74]

5369 Lowe, Malcolm V. *Bombers* (6–9). Illus. 1987, Lerner LB $9.95 (0-8225-1381-1). In addition to discussing the designs of attack aircraft, this illustrated account tells about their use in war and the tactics of which they are capable. (Rev: SLJ 3/88) [359.4]

5370 Messenger, Charles. *Combat Aircraft* (7–10). Illus. 1984, Watts LB $12.90 (0-531-04867-5). Military airplanes are described with facts about their engines and weapons. [623.74]

5371 Pangallo, Michelle. *North American Forts and Fortifications* (5–8). 1986, Cambridge Univ. Press $9.95 (0-521-26642-4); paper $3.95 (0-521-31982-X). Thirteen forts such as those at Ticonderoga, Sumter, the Alamo, and McHenry are described. (Rev: BR 1–2/87) [623]

5372 Preston, Antony. *Aircraft Carriers* (7–10). Illus. 1984, Lerner LB $9.95 (0-8225-1377-3); paper $4.95 (0-8225-9504-4). The story of aircraft carriers from World War I on, plus an account of their importance today. [359.3]

5373 Rummel, Jack. *The U.S. Marine Corps* (7–10). Illus. 1990, Chelsea House $14.95 (1-55546-110-7). A history of the Marine Corps from the late eighteenth century to the present with emphasis on its accomplishments. (Rev: BL 3/15/90) [359.9]

5374 Sullivan, George. *Famous Air Force Bombers* (7–12). Illus. 1985, Dodd LB $9.95 (0-396-08621-7). Descriptions in text and photos of famous bombers. A companion volume is *Famous Air Force Fighters* (1985). (Rev: SLJ 5/86) [355]

5375 Sullivan, George. *Famous Navy Attack Planes* (7–9). Illus. 1986, Putnam LB $10.95 (0-396-08770-1). An illustrated history of U.S. naval attack planes from World War I to the present. A companion volume is *Famous Navy Fighter Planes* (1986). (Rev: BR 11–12/86; SLJ 2/87) [359]

5376 Sullivan, George. *Famous U.S. Spy Planes* (5–8). 1987, Putnam $10.95 (0-396-08844-9). This account covers famous spy planes used between 1916 and the present. (Rev: BR 11–12/87) [623.74]

5377 Sullivan, George. *Inside Nuclear Submarines* (7–10). Illus. 1982, Putnam LB $10.95 (0-396-08093-6). A history of the development of these submarines and the role they can play in twentieth-century defense and warfare. [359.3]

5378 Tunis, Edwin. *Weapons: A Pictorial History* (6–9). Illus. 1977, Harper $24.70 (0-690-01285-3). In this book, first published in 1954, the author illustrates through pen-and-ink drawings a history of weapons from prehistoric man to the near present. [623.4]

5379 Van Tol, Robert. *Surface Warships* (7–10). Illus. 1984, Watts LB $12.90 (0-531-04935-3). A rundown on many vessels such as destroyers, aircraft carriers, and cruisers. [623.8]

5380 Windrow, Martin, and Richard Hook. *The Footsoldier* (5–8). Illus. 1988, Oxford Univ. Pr. $14.95 (0-19-273147-5). This book shows the dress and development of the common soldier through the ages plus illustrations of weapons and gear. Also use: *The Horse Soldier* (1988). (Rev: SLJ 6–7/88) [356]

Recreation and Sports

Crafts

General and Miscellaneous

5381 Eckstein, Joan, and Joyce Gleit. *Fun with Making Things: An Activity Book for Kids* (7–9). Illus. 1979, Avon paper $1.50 (0-380-43315-X). A collection of 50 projects using such common items as tin cans and paper clips. [745.5]

5382 Ford, Marianne. *Copycats & Artifacts: 42 Creative Artisan Projects to Make* (5–10). Illus. 1986, Godine paper $14.95 (0-87923-645-0). An unusual craft book in which the projects are to duplicate a museum treasure such as a Faberge egg. (Rev: BL 2/1/87; SLJ 6–7/87) [745.5]

5383 Grainger, Sylvia. *How to Make Your Own Moccasins* (7–9). 1977, Harper $9.25 (0-397-31754-9); paper $3.95 (0-397-31755-7). Detailed instructions are given on how to make 10 different moccasin styles. [745.5]

5384 Hautzig, Esther. *Make It Special: Cards, Decorations, and Party Favors for Holidays and Other Celebrations* (5–8). Illus. 1986, Macmillan $11.95 (0-02-743370-6). A collection of crafts ideas for gifts that concentrates on greeting cards and house decorations. (Rev: SLJ 2/87) [745.5]

5385 Pettit, Florence H. *The Stamp-Pad Printing Book* (7–9). Illus. 1979, Harper $12.70 (0-490-03967-0). An introduction to this age-old art and instructions on how to make greeting cards, posters, and other objects using stamp-pad printing. [070.5]

5386 Purdy, Susan. *Christmas Gifts for You to Make* (7–9). 1976, Harper LB $12.89 (0-397-31695-X). Instructions on how to make a wide variety of gifts including puppets, note pads, and aprons. [745.5]

5387 Sattler, Helen Roney. *Recipes for Art and Craft Materials* (4–12). 1987, Lothrop $11.95 (0-688-07374-3). A collection of recipes for materials used in crafts such as colorings, crayons, and nutty putty. (Rev: BL 9/1/87; BR 1–2/88) [745.5]

5388 Simons, Robin. *Recyclopedia* (6–8). 1976, Houghton $9.95 (0-395-24380-7). A craft book showing how to use materials that are usually thrown out. [745.5]

Costume Making, Dress, and Fashion

5389 Cummings, Richard. *101 Costumes for All Ages, All Occasions* (5–9). Illus. 1987, Plays paper $10.00 (0-8238-0286-8). A variety of easily made costumes are described from Frankenstein and Captain Hook to Cleopatra and even a tube of toothpaste. (Rev: BL 1/1/88; BR 3–4/88) [792.026]

5390 Walker, Mark. *Creative Costumes for Any Occasion* (9–12). Illus. 1984, Liberty paper $5.95 (0-89709-138-8). Ideas for 35 different easily made costumes as well as instructions and lists of materials needed. (Rev: BL 3/15/85) [391]

Drawing and Painting

5391 Ames, Lee J. *Draw 50 Airplanes, Aircraft & Spacecraft* (7–10). Illus. 1977, Doubleday LB $9.95 (0-385-12236-5). Simple instruction and copious illustrations accompany each short project. Also use: *Draw 50 Animals* (1974) and *Draw 50 Buildings and Other Structures* (1980). [743]

5392 Ames, Lee J. *Draw 50 Athletes* (6–8). Illus. 1985, Doubleday LB $12.95 (0-385-19056-5). A drawing book that teaches one to sketch athletes in a number of different sports. (Rev: BL 12/15/85) [743]

5393 Ames, Lee J. *Draw 50 Beasties and Yugglies and Turnover Uglies and Things That Go Bump in the Night* (4–9). Illus. 1988, Doubleday $12.95 (0-385-24625-0). Instructions on how to draw various monsters and science fiction aliens. (Rev: BL 2/1/89) [743]

5394 Ames, Lee J. *Draw 50 Dogs* (7–10). Illus. 1981, Doubleday LB $9.95 (0-385-15687-1). Using simple shapes like ovals and squares, a wide variety of dogs can be pictured. Also use *Draw 50 Dinosaurs and Other Prehistoric Animals* (1977). [743]

5395 Ames, Lee J. *Draw 50 Famous Cartoons* (7–10). Illus. 1979, Doubleday $12.95 (0-385-13661-7). Instructions are given to re-create such cartoon characters as Popeye, Dagwood, and Scooby Doo. Part of an extensive series of "Draw 50" books. [741.5]

5396 Ames, Lee J. *Draw 50 Famous Faces* (7–10). Illus. 1978, Doubleday LB $9.95 (0-385-13218-2). All sorts of famous people from history, sports, entertainment, and so on, can be easily drawn by following these simple instructions. Also use: *Draw 50 Famous Stars* (1982). [743]

5397 Ames, Lee J. *Draw 50 Horses* (7–10). Illus. 1984, Doubleday LB $12.95 (0-385-17641-4). Different breeds of horses are drawn in a variety of situations. [743]

5398 Ames, Lee J. *Draw 50 Monsters, Creeps, Superheroes, Demons, Dragons, Nerds, Dirts, Ghouls, Giants, Vampires, Zombies, and Other Curiosa . . .* (7–10). Illus. 1983, Doubleday LB $9.95 (0-385-17638-4). A simple shape can be easily transformed into an unusual creature. Also use: *Draw 50 Vehicles* (1978). [743]

5399 Arnosky, Jim. *Drawing from Nature* (5–9). Illus. 1987, Lothrop paper $8.95 (0-688-01295-7). In basic terms with many illustrations, the author explains how to master such areas as drawing landscapes. Also use: *Drawing Life in Motion* (1987). (Rev: BL 10/15/87; BR 11–12/87; VOYA 10/87) [743]

5400 Arnosky, Jim. *Sketching Outdoors in Spring* (6–8). Illus. 1987, Morrow $12.95 (0-688-06284-9). A beautifully illustrated book on how to draw items such as trees, spring flowers, and

some animals. There are companion volumes that cover the other seasons—*Autumn, Summer,* and *Winter* (all 1985). (Rev: BR 9–10/87; SLJ 5/87) [741]

5401 Baron, Nancy. *Getting Started in Calligraphy* (7–9). 1979, Sterling $9.95 (0-8069-8840-1). How to draw letters with beauty and grace using few materials. [745.6]

5402 Bolognese, Don, and Elaine Raphael. *Drawing Fashions: Figures, Faces, and Techniques* (7–9). Illus. 1985, Watts LB $10.90 (0-531-10049-9). An introduction to fashion drawing that also covers figure drawing. (Rev: BR 5–6/86; SLJ 4/86) [741]

5403 Foster, Patience. *Guide to Drawing* (5–8). Illus. 1981, Usborne Hayes $12.96 (0-88110-025-0); paper $5.95 (0-86020-540-1). This book covers such topics as color, media, and perspective while dealing with a large number of subjects. Also use *Guide to Painting* (1981). [741]

5404 Frame, Paul. *Drawing the Big Cats* (7–10). Illus. 1981, Watts LB $10.90 (0-531-04321-5). Beginners are taught through practice to observe anatomy and perspective and eventually to draw large cats. [743]

5405 Ivenbaum, Elliott. *Drawing People* (7–10). Illus. 1980, Watts LB $10.90 (0-531-02283-8). Through text and pencil sketches, the author describes human anatomy and how to draw figures. [743]

5406 Stwertka, Eve, and Albert Stwertka. *Make It Graphic! Drawing Graphs for Science and Social Studies Projects* (6–9). Illus. 1985, Messner LB $9.29 (0-671-54287-7). An introductory volume on how to represent facts pictorially and how to draw graphs both manually and on the computer. (Rev: SLJ 10/85) [760]

5407 Zaidenberg, Arthur. *How to Draw and Compose Pictures* (7–12). Illus. 1971, Harper LB $12.89 (0-200-71772-3). Such concepts as composition, balance, and interrelationships are introduced in a variety of settings. [741]

5408 Zaidenberg, Arthur. *How to Draw Heads and Faces* (7–12). Illus. 1966, Harper LB $12.89 (0-200-71813-4). Starting with the parts of the face, the author illustrates expression, the use of light and shade, and several different media. The author has several other books on drawing basics. [743]

Paper Crafts

5409 Bottomley, Jim. *Paper Projects for Creative Kids* (6–9). 1983, Little paper $10.95 (0-316-10349-7). Clear instructions and diagrams help in explaining these clever paper projects. [731]

5410 Churchill, E. Richard. *Building with Paper* (5–9). Illus. 1990, Sterling $14.95 (0-8069-5772-7). Churchill gives instructions on how to make such items as bridges, boats, castles, forts, and a stadium, in this continuation of *Quick and Easy Paper Toys* (1988). (Rev: SLJ 9/90) [731]

5411 Fowler, Virginie. *Paperworks: Colorful Crafts from Picture Eggs to Fish Kites* Illus. 1982, Prentice $10.95 (0-13-648543-X); paper $7.95 (0-13-649551-0). Using such techniques as collage and papier mâché, one is given directions on how to make a variety of jewelry, toys, and decorations. [745.54]

Toys and Dolls

5413 Fowler, Virginie. *Folk Toys around the World: And How to Make Them* (7–10). Illus. 1984, Prentice LB $10.95 (0-13-323148-8). Thirty toys from around the world are described and directions are given on how to make them from common materials. [745.592]

5414 Zubrowski, Bernie. *Tops: Building and Experimenting with Spinning Toys* (5–9). Illus. 1989, Morrow LB $11.88 (0-688-08811-2); paper $6.95 (0-688-07561-4). As well as having a good time constructing and playing with a variety of tops, the reader learns some of the principles of rotation and optics. (Rev: SLJ 5/89) [688.7]

Sewing and Needle Crafts

5412 Cone, Ferne Geller. *Classy Knitting: A Guide to Creative Sweatering for Beginners* (7–9). Illus. 1984, Macmillan $14.95 (0-689-31062-5). An introduction to knitting that includes instruction on basic stitches and gives easy-to-follow patterns. [746.43]

Woodworking and Carpentry

5415 Brown, William F. *Wood Works: Experiments with Common Wood and Tools* (7–9). Illus. 1984, Macmillan LB $11.95 (0-689-31033-1). Several simple projects based on historical discoveries are outlined for the novice carpenter. [684]

Hobbies and Pastimes

General and Miscellaneous

5416 Billy, Christopher. *Summer Opportunities for Kids and Teenagers* (7–12). 1984, Petersons Guides paper $10.95 (0-87866-370-3). Activities such as summer camps, travel, and advanced schooling are described. [790.1]

5417 Feinman, Jeffrey, and Betty Schwartz. *Freebies for Kids* (6–9). Rev. ed. 1983, Wanderer paper $4.95 (0-671-42657-5). A number of free materials (posters, maps, pamphlets) are listed as well as their sources [011]

5418 Fujino, Alison, and Benjamin Ruhe. *The Stunt Kite Book* (6–10). Illus. 1989, Running Pr. paper $9.95 (0-39471-697-2). This book on stunt kites covers a wide range of subjects from history to common maneuvers and a chart rating various modes. (Rev: SLJ 8/89) [796.1]

Cooking

5419 Amari, Suad. *Cooking the Lebanese Way* (7–10). Illus. 1986, Lerner $9.95 (0-8225-0913-X). After a general introduction to Lebanon, this book introduces recipes for more than 20 native dishes. (Rev: BL 6/1/86) [641]

5420 Andreev, Tania. *Food in Russia* (6–9). Illus. 1989, Rourke LB $9.50 (0-86625-343-2). Both an introduction to Russia and a survey of foods and typical recipes. (Rev: SLJ 12/89) [641.5]

5421 Bacon, Josephine. *Cooking the Israeli Way* (7–10). Illus. 1986, Lerner $9.95 (0-8225-0912-

1). A brief history and geography of Israel is given followed by more than 20 tempting native recipes. One of an extensive series. (Rev: BL 6/1/86) [641]

5422 *Better Homes and Gardens Microwave Cooking for Kids* (5–8). Illus. 1984, Meredith paper $5.95 (0-696-01425-4). After a general introduction to the microwave and how to use it, a number of recipes are given for each meal. (Rev: BL 2/1/85) [641.588]

5423 Bisignano, Alphonse. *Cooking the Italian Way* (7–9). Illus. 1982, Lerner LB $9.95 (0-8225-0906-7). Like others in this extensive series on ethnic foods, this account gives recipes plus an introduction to the country and its culture. [641.5]

5424 Coronado, Rosa. *Cooking the Mexican Way* (7–9). Illus. 1982, Lerner LB $9.95 (0-8225-0907-5). Mexican culture is highlighted as well as a few basic recipes. Part of an extensive series. [641.5]

5425 *Easy Basics for Good Cooking* (7–12). Illus. 1983, Sunset-Lane paper $14.95 (0-376-02088-1). Basic cooking skills are taught through a series of recipes. [641.5]

5426 Gaspari, Claudia. *Food in Italy* (6–9). Illus. 1989, Rourke LB $9.50 (0-86625-342-4). This account introduces Italy and its food and gives some recipes. (Rev: SLJ 12/89) [641.5]

5427 George, Jean Craighead. *The Wild, Wild Cookbook: A Guide for Young Wild-Food Foragers* (7–9). Illus. 1982, Harper LB $12.89 (0-690-04315-5). Wild plants are identified and a selection of easy recipes using them is given. [641.6]

5428 Gomez, Paolo. *Food in Mexico* (6–9). Illus. 1989, Rourke LB $9.50 (0-86625-341-6). As well as some typical recipes, this account introduces

Mexico and its types of food. (Rev: SLJ 12/89) [641.5]

5429 Hautzig, Esther. *Holiday Treats* (7–9). Illus. 1983, Macmillan $11.95 (0-02-743350-1). A collection of simple recipes for 16 holidays including Halloween and Christmas. [641.5]

5430 Kaur, Sharon. *Food in India* (6–9). Illus. 1989, Rourke LB $9.50 (0-86625-339-4). This illustrated book gives recipes, and introduces the foods and dining customs of India. (Rev: SLJ 12/89) [641.5]

5431 Knox, Gerald M., ed. *Better Homes and Gardens Microwave Cooking for Kids* (6–9). Illus. 1984, Meredith paper $5.95 (0-696-01425-4). Easily followed recipes using the microwave oven are given for all meals and snack times. [641.5]

5432 Lafargue, Francoise. *French Food and Drink* (6–8). Illus. 1987, Watts $12.40 (0-531-18130-8). Far from being only a collection of recipes, this book introduces the country, its kinds of dishes, and the nature of its cuisine. Part of an extensive series. (Rev: BL 12/15/87; BR 1–2/88; SLJ 2/88) [641]

5433 Moore, Carolyn E., et al. *Young Chef's Nutrition Guide and Cookbook* (6–9). 1990, Barron's $11.95 (0-8120-5789-9). After a quick guide to diet and nutrition, this book gives 150 easy-to-follow recipes. (Rev: BL 7/90) [641.5]

5434 Nabwire, Constance, and Bertha Vining Montgomery. *Cooking the African Way* (5–10). Illus. 1988, Lerner $9.95 (0-8225-0919-9). Part of the extensive Easy Menu Ethnic Cookbook series, this volume describes the land and culture of East and West Africa and gives several recipes for native dishes. (Rev: BL 3/15/89) [394.1]

5435 Nguyen, Chi, and Judy Monroe. *Cooking the Vietnamese Way* (6–10). Illus. 1985, Lerner $9.95 (0-8225-0914-8). The authors introduce the land and people of Vietnam before giving recipes for regional dishes. Part of a lengthy series. (Rev: BL 9/15/85) [641]

5436 Perl, Lila. *The Hamburger Book: All about Hamburgers and Hamburger Cookery* (7–9). Illus. 1974, Clarion $8.95 (0-395-28921-1). A history of ground meat from thirteenth-century Russia to fast food chains plus a nice selection of recipes using ground meat. [641.6]

5437 Purdy, Susan. *Christmas Cooking around the World* (7–9). Illus. 1983, Watts LB $10.90 (0-531-04654-0); paper $4.95 (0-531-03578-6). A selection of 30 recipes, many from foreign lands, but all associated with Christmas. [641.5]

5438 Rombauer, Irma S., and Marion Rombauer Becker. *Joy of Cooking* (7–12). Illus. 1986, Macmillan $16.95 (0-02-604570-2); NAL paper $11.95 (0-452-26189-9). First published in 1931, this has through several editions become one of the standard basic American cookbooks. [641.5]

5439 Shui, Amy, and Stuart Thompson. *Chinese Food and Drink* (6–9). 1987, Watts $12.40 (0-531-18130-4). Recipes are given for characteristic dishes plus background material on the origins of Chinese cuisine and methods of food production. Part of the Food and Drink series. (Rev: BL 12/15/87; BR 1–2/88; SLJ 2/88) [641.5]

5440 Stanley, Marcia, ed. *Better Homes and Gardens Beginner's Cook Book* (7–9). Illus. 1984, Meredith paper $5.95 (0-696-01310-X). A good book on such basics as reading a recipe and the use of standard kitchen tools plus an introduction to terms and techniques. Also use *Better Homes and Gardens Junior Cook Book* (1979) and *Better Homes and Gardens Step-by-Step Kids' Cook Book* (1984). [641.5]

5441 Takeshita, Jiro. *Food in Japan* (6–9). Illus. 1989, Rourke LB $9.50 (0-86625-340-8). This book provides an introduction to Japan and its food plus supplying a few basic recipes. (Rev: SLJ 12/89) [641.5]

5442 Tan, Jennifer. *Food in China* (6–9). Illus. 1989, Rourke LB $9.50 (0-86625-338-6). Recipes are given plus general information on China, its food and eating habits. (Rev: SLJ 12/89) [641.5]

5443 Villios, Lynne W. *Cooking the Greek Way* (5–9). Illus. 1984, Lerner $9.95 (0-8225-0910-5). Along with traditional recipes, this account introduces the country and its people. [641]

5444 Warner, Margaret Brink, and Ruth Ann Hayward, comps. *What's Cooking? Favorite Recipes from around the World* (7–9). 1981, Little $15.95 (0-316-35252-7). A collection of recipes associated with various ethnic groups that have come to America. [641.5]

5445 Yu, Ling. *Cooking the Chinese Way* (7–9). Illus. 1982, Lerner LB $9.95 (0-8225-0902-4). Part of the Easy Menu Ethnic Cookbooks series, this gives information on Chinese life followed by a selection of recipes from soups to desserts. [641.5]

5446 Zamojska-Hutchins, Danuta. *Cooking the Polish Way* (7–9). Illus. 1984, Lerner LB $9.95 (0-8225-0909-1). Part of a lengthy series of ethnic cookbooks that give recipes and details about life in each individual country. [641.5]

Magic and Tricks

5447 Baker, James W. *Illusions Illustrated: A Professional Magic Show for Young Performers* (7–10). Illus. 1984, Lerner LB $10.95 (0-8225-07681-4); paper $4.95 (0-8225-9512-5). Ten baffling tricks, like making a coin disappear, are explained. [793.8]

5448 Barry, Sheila Anne. *Tricks & Stunts to Fool Your Friends* (7–9). Illus. 1984, Sterling paper $3.50 (0-8069-7856-2). Lots of simple tricks are explained. [793.8]

5449 Cobb, Vicki. *Magic . . . Naturally! Science Entertainments and Amusements* (7–9). Illus. 1976, Harper $11.70 (0-397-31631-3). Thirty magic acts are described, each involving a scientific principle. [507]

5450 Friedhoffer, Bob. *Magic Tricks, Science Facts* (5–9). Illus. 1990, Watts LB $12.90 (0-531-10902-X). Through various magic tricks, different scientific and mathematical principles are demonstrated. (Rev: BL 7/90; SLJ 7/90) [793.8]

5451 Lewis, Shari, and Abraham B. Hurwitz. *Magic for Non-Magicians* (6–9). 1977, NAL paper $3.95 (0-451-15641-2). A simple guide to 60 clever and mystifying tricks. [793.8]

5452 McGill, Ormond. *Balancing Magic and Other Tricks* (6–9). Illus. 1986, Watts $11.40 (0-531-10208-4). A group of tricks and stunts involving sleight of hand, balancing, and juggling. (Rev: VOYA 2/87) [793.8]

5453 Severn, Bill. *Magic with Rope, Ribbon and String* (7–9). 1981, McKay paper $9.95 (0-679-20813-5). A collection of tricks using only these simple household objects. [793.8]

5454 Severn, Bill. *More Magic in Your Pockets* (7–9). Illus. 1980, McKay $8.95 (0-679-20806-2). A total of 37 tricks are explained plus instructions on how to present them. [793.8]

5455 Tarr, Bill. *Now You See It, Now You Don't! Lessons in Sleight of Hand* (7–9). Illus. 1976, Random paper $9.95 (0-394-72202-7). Over 100 easy tricks to mystify one's friends. Each is graded by level of difficulty. [793.8]

Model Making

5456 Cummings, Richard. *Make Your Own Model Forts & Castles* (7–9). Illus. 1977, McKay $8.95 (0-679-20400-8). Instructions are given for making a Norman castle, a stockade, and a World War I trench. [623]

5457 Weiss, Harvey. *How to Run a Railroad: Everything You Need to Know about Model Trains* (7–9). 1977, Harper $12.70 (0-690-01304-3). A guidebook that tells the hobbyist how to make model railroads more interesting by building hills, lakes, bridges, and other articles of scenery. [625.1]

5458 Weiss, Harvey. *Model Airplanes and How to Build Them* (7–10). Illus. 1975, Harper $13.98 (0-690-00594-6). Directions are given for building various toy airplanes, some powered by battery motors, others by elastic bands. [629.133]

5459 Weiss, Harvey. *Model Buildings and How to Make Them* (7–9). Illus. 1979, Harper $13.70 (0-690-01341-8). A simple how-to book on constructing a variety of model buildings using cardboard and wood. [690]

Photography and Filmmaking

5460 Cumming, David. *Photography* (5–8). Illus. 1989, Steck-Vaughn LB $15.95 (0-8114-2360-3). A history of photography is given plus a discussion of its place in the world of art. (Rev: BL 3/15/90; SLJ 8/90) [770]

5461 Davis, Edward E. *Into the Dark* (7–10). 1979, Macmillan $9.95 (0-689-30676-8). A step-by-step guide to setting up a dark room and developing one's own photographs. [770]

5462 Smith, Peter. *The First Photography Book* (7–9). Illus. 1988, Sterling $14.95 (0-85112-846-7). In a few pages of text and many pictures, the basics of photography are explained, including the kinds of equipment and picture-taking techniques. (Rev: SLJ 4/88) [770]

5463 Van Wormer, Joe. *How to Be a Wildlife Photographer* (7–10). Illus. 1982, Lodestar $10.95 (0-525-66772-5). A useful manual on how to photograph animal life in its natural habitat. [778.9]

Stamp, Coin, and Other Types of Collecting

5464 Andrews, Charles J. *Fell's International Coin Book* (7–12). Illus. 1983, Fell $14.95 (0-8119-0594-2); paper $9.95 (0-8119-0587-X). A standard identification guide to foreign coins with information on coin collecting. [737.4]

5465 Andrews, Charles J. *Fell's United States Coin Book* (7–12). Illus. 1983, Fell $11.95 (0-8119-0595-0); paper $7.95 (0-8119-0588-8). Every coin minted in the United States is listed with material about value and the history of coins. [737.4]

5466 Hobson, Burton. *Coin Collecting as a Hobby* (6–9). Illus. 1986, Sterling LB $13.29 (0-8069-4749-7). In addition to a general introduction to this hobby, the author gives information on the history of coins and on coin manufacture. (Rev: BL 2/1/87; BR 3–4/87; SLJ 4/87) [737.407]

5467 Hobson, Burton. *Stamp Collecting as a Hobby* (6–9). Illus. 1986, Sterling LB $13.29 (0-8069-4795-0). Various stamps of the world are introduced, tips on collecting and mounting are given, as well as information on how to keep up to date in this hobby. (Rev: BL 2/1/87; BR 3–4/87; SLJ 4/87) [769.56]

5468 Reinfeld, Fred. *A Catalogue of the World's Most Popular Coins* (7–12). Illus. 1987, Sterling $29.95 (0-8069-4738-1); paper $19.95 (0-8069-4740-3). For both modern and ancient coins, histories are given plus current values. [737.4]

5469 *Scott Standard Postage Stamp Catalogue* (7–12). 4 vols. Illus. 1989, Scott paper $20.00 each (vol. 1: 0-685-70738-5; vol. 2: 0-685-70739-3; vol. 3: 0-685-70740-7; vol. 4: 0-685-70741-5). This is the most comprehensive stamp catalog in print. Volume 1 deals with stamps from the English-speaking world; the other 3 volumes cover alphabetically the other countries of the world. [769.56]

5470 Seaver, Tom, et al. *Tom Seaver's Baseball Card Book* (7–10). Illus. 1985, Messner LB $8.79 (0-671-53106-9); Simon & Schuster paper $6.95 (0-671-49525-9). A guide to cards issued from 1980 through 1985 and how to collect them. (Rev: SLJ 5/85) [796.357]

Jokes, Puzzles, Riddles, and Word Games

Jokes and Riddles

5471 Bishop, Ann. *Hello, Mr. Chips! Computer Jokes & Riddles* (6–9). Illus. 1982, Lodestar $9.95 (0-525-66775-X); paper $3.95 (0-525-66782-2). A collection of computer jokes that produce both laughs and groans. [793.7]

5472 Corbett, Scott. *Jokes to Read in the Dark* (6–9). Illus. 1980, Dutton $11.95 (0-525-32796-7). A collection guaranteed to produce groans. [808.7]

5473 Doty, Roy. *King Midas Has a Gilt Complex* (6–8). 1979, Scholastic paper $1.50 (0-590-31543-9). Lots of funny jokes with accompanying cartoons. [808.7]

5474 Kohl, Marguerite, and Frederica Young. *Jokes for Children* (5–8). 1963, Hill & Wang paper $6.95 (0-374-43832-3). A collection of over 650 riddles and jokes plus some amusing rhymes. [808.7]

5475 Rosenbloom, Joseph. *Biggest Riddle Book in the World* (6–9). Illus. 1977, Sterling LB $15.69 (0-8069-4533-8); paper $4.95 (0-8069-8884-3). Very clever riddles collected by a children's librarian. [808.7]

5476 Rosenbloom, Joseph. *Dr. Knock-Knock's Official Knock-Knock Dictionary* (6–9). Illus. 1977, Sterling $10.95 (0-8069-4536-2); paper $3.95 (0-8069-8936-X). Over 500 knock-knock jokes in this very humorous collection. [808.7]

5477 Rosenbloom, Joseph. *The Gigantic Joke Book* (6–9). 1978, Sterling LB $15.69 (0-8069-4591-5); paper $4.95 (0-8069-7514-8). A large collection of jokes that span time from King Arthur to the space age. Also use Rosenbloom's

Monster Madness: Riddles, Jokes, Fun (1980). [808.7]

5478 Rosenbloom, Joseph. *Sports Riddles* (6–9). Illus. 1982, Harcourt $8.95 (0-15-277994-9). A delightful collection of riddles involving favorite sports such as baseball and basketball. [398]

5479 Schwartz, Alvin, comp. *Flapdoodle: Pure Nonsense from American Folklore* (6–9). Illus. 1980, Harper LB $10.10 (0-397-31920-7). A collection of jokes and humorous stories from American folklore. [398]

5480 Schwartz, Alvin, comp. *Tomfoolery: Trickery and Foolery with Words* (6–9). Illus. 1973, Harper $12.70 (0-397-31466-3). A collection of jokes and riddles from folklore and from children. [398]

5481 Schwartz, Alvin, comp. *Unriddling: All Sorts of Riddles to Puzzle Your Guessery* (6–9). Illus. 1983, Harper LB $12.89 (0-397-32030-2). A collection of puzzling and amusing riddles garnered from American folklore. [398]

5482 Schwartz, Alvin, comp. *Witcracks: Jokes and Jests from American Folklore* (6–9). Illus. 1973, Harper $11.89 (0-397-31475-2). Tall tales, jokes, riddles, and humorous stories are included in this collection from our past. [398]

Puzzles

5483 Adler, Irit, and Shem Levy. *Picture Puzzles for the Super Smart* (6–9). 1985, Sterling paper $4.95 (0-8069-7952-6). There are 152 brain teasers, all using graphics, in this fascinating little book. (Rev: VOYA 12/85) [793.7]

5484 Barry, Sheila Anne. *Super-Colossal Book of Puzzles, Tricks and Games* (5–9). Illus. 1978, Sterling $6.98 (0-8069-4720-9). A huge selection of activities, games, and puzzles just made for a rainy afternoon. [793.7]

5485 Fixx, James F. *Solve It! A Perplexing Profusion of Puzzles* (7–9). 1983, Warner paper $2.95 (0-446-31080-8). A book of puzzles that require logical thinking to solve them. [793.7]

5486 Leider, Vera F. *Puzzle Pursuit* (7–12). 1986, Putnam paper $6.95 (0-399-51234-9). A collection of word and number puzzles that will challenge high school readers. (Rev: VOYA 12/86) [793.7]

Word Games

5487 Brandreth, Gyles. *The Biggest Tongue Twister Book in the World* (6–9). 1980, Sterling LB $15.29 (0-8069-4594-X); paper $3.95 (0-8069-8972-6). Hundreds of tongue twisters to amuse and try one's verbal agility. [793.7]

5488 Rosenbloom, Joseph. *Twist These on Your Tongue* (6–9). Illus. 1978, Lodestar $10.95 (0-525-66612-5). Tongue twisters are given for both the beginner and the expert. [808.88]

5489 Schwartz, Alvin, ed. *A Twister of Twists, a Tangler of Tongues: Tongue Twisters* (6–9). Illus. 1972, Harper $12.70 (0-397-31387-X). An outstanding collection of tongue twisters arranged by subject. [808.88]

Mysteries, Curiosities, Controversial and General Knowledge

5490 Aylward, Jim. *Things No One Ever Tells You* (7–9). 1981, Avon paper $2.25 (0-380-57935-9). From history and from places around the world here is a collection of most unusual facts. [133]

5491 Berger, Melvin. *UFOs, ETs & Visitors from Space* (6–8). Illus. 1988, Putnam $10.99 (0-399-61218-1). An examination of sightings, most of which Berger claims can be logically explained. (Rev: BL 10/1/88; SLJ 11/88) [001.9]

5492 Branley, Franklyn M. *Age of Aquarius: You and Astrology* (7–9). Illus. 1979, Harper LB $12.89 (0-690-03988-3). Information about your personality and fate derived from your birth date is given in this easily read book. [133]

5493 Cohen, Daniel. *Creatures from UFO's* (7–9). 1978, Putnam $8.95 (0-396-07582-7). A factual account of people who claim to have seen UFOs. [001.9]

5494 Cohen, Daniel. *The Encyclopedia of Ghosts* (7–12). Illus. 1984, Dodd $14.95 (0-396-08308-0). Four hundred years of ghost history is drawn on in this well-researched book of unusual phenomena. [133.1]

5495 Cohen, Daniel. *Ghostly Terrors* (6–9). 1981, Archway paper $1.95 (0-671-45856-6). A collection of 13 supposedly true ghost stories that are easily read. [133]

5496 Cohen, Daniel. *Real Ghosts* (7–9). 1984, Archway paper $2.50 (0-671-62670-1). Several real ghost happenings are reported on and evaluated concerning their validity. [133.1]

5497 Cohen, Daniel. *The Restless Dead: Ghostly Tales from around the World* (7–9). Illus. 1989, Pocket paper $2.50 (0-671-64373-8). A recounting of 11 ghost stories from various parts of the world. [133.1]

5498 Cohen, Daniel. *The World of UFOs* (7–10). Illus. 1978, Harper $13.70 (0-397-31780-8). Various sightings are discussed and other background information is given on this controversial subject. [001.9]

5499 Cohen, Daniel. *The World's Most Famous Ghosts* (7-9). Illus. 1989, Pocket paper $2.75 (0-671-69145-7). Accounts of many different ghosts—from Abraham Lincoln to the Flying Dutchman. [133.1]

5500 Elwood, Ann, and Carol Orsag Madigan. *The Macmillan Book of Fascinating Facts: An Almanac for Kids* (5–8). Illus. 1989, Macmillan $16.95 (0-02-733461-9). Lots of interesting facts presented in a tantalizing way. (Rev: BL 7/89; VOYA 8/89) [051]

5501 Gaffron, Norma. *Bigfoot: Opposing Viewpoints* (7–10). Illus. 1989, Greenhaven $12.95 (0-89908-058-8). The possible existence of this mysterious creature is explored objectively and from many different vantage points. (Rev: BL 3/1/89; SLJ 6/89) [001.9]

5502 Garden, Nancy. *Devils and Demons* (7–9). 1976, Harper $11.25 (0-397-31666-6). An international survey of the weird demons believed in by various cultures and peoples. [133]

5503 Hoffman, Elizabeth P. *This House Is Haunted!* (7–9). 1977, Raintree LB $14.65 (0-

8172-1033-4). A family buys a house that is supposedly haunted and finds that it really is. [133]

5504 Jagendorf, M. A. *Stories and Lore of the Zodiac* (7–9). Illus. 1977, Vanguard $10.95 (0-8149-0752-0). The stories behind the signs of the zodiac and the influence these signs supposedly have on people. [133.5]

5505 Knight, David C. *The Moving Coffins: Ghosts and Hauntings around the World* (7–9). Illus. 1987, Prentice paper $7.95 (0-13-604752-1). Supernatural occurrences from 20 different countries. [133.1]

5506 Leokum, Arkady. *The Curious Book* (7–10). 1977, NAL paper $2.25 (0-451-11944-4). That Sumo wrestlers usually weigh around 300 pounds is just one of the unusual facts in this volume. [133]

5507 McHargue, Georgess. *Meet the Werewolf* (6–9). 1976, Harper $11.95 (0-397-31662-3). A factual account that explores the evidence concerning the existence of werewolves. Also use: *Meet the Witches* (1984). [133.4]

5508 O'Connell, Margaret F. *The Magic Cauldron: Witchcraft for Good and Evil* (7–9). 1976, Phillips $17.95 (0-87599-187-4). In this history of witchcraft, the reader learns that witches can be agents of both good and evil. [133]

5509 O'Neill, Catherine. *Amazing Mysteries of the World* (7–12). Illus. 1983, National Geographic LB $8.50 (0-87044-502-2). UFOs, Bigfoot, and Easter Island are only 3 of the many mysteries explored. [001.9]

5510 Pringle, Laurence. *"The Earth Is Flat"—and Other Great Mistakes* (6–8). Illus. 1983, Morrow LB $12.88 (0-688-02467-X). A number of blunders, errors, and mistakes are explored—some funny, some tragic. [001.9]

5511 Reiff, Stephanie Ann. *Visions of the Future: Magic Numbers and Cards* (7–9). 1977,

Raintree LB $14.25 (0-8172-1027-X). Numerology and forecasting using tarot cards are 2 of the subjects discussed. [133]

5512 Risedorf, Gwen. *Born Today, Born Yesterday: Reincarnation* (7–9). 1977, Raintree LB $14.65 (0-8172-1045-8). Reincarnation is explored through case histories of people who believe they have lived before. [129]

5513 Roberts, Nancy. *Southern Ghosts* (6–9). Illus. 1979, Sandlapper paper $1.95 (0-87844-075-5). Thirteen ghostly tales from the South are retold with photographs of their locales. [133]

5514 San Souci, Robert. *The Loch Ness Monster* (7–10). Illus. 1989, Greenhaven LB $12.95 (0-89908-072-3). The evidence for and against the existence of this monster is presented in a fascinating account. (Rev: BL 3/1/90) [001.9]

5515 Scavone, Daniel C. *The Shroud of Turin: Opposing Viewpoints* (7–10). Illus. 1989, Greenhaven $12.95 (0-89908-061-8). In this nicely illustrated book, the authenticity of this artifact is debated with many different opinions expressed. (Rev: BL 3/1/89; SLJ 6/89) [232.9]

5516 Warren, William R. *The Headless Ghost: True Tales of the Unexplained* (5–9). 1986, Prentice $10.95 (0-13-384280-0). Famous unexplained mysteries such as Lincoln's ghost in the White House and the pharaohs' curses are retold. (Rev: BL 6/1/86) [031]

5517 Weiss, Ann E. *Seers and Scientists: Can the Future Be Predicted?* (7–10). Illus. 1986, Harcourt $13.95 (0-15-272850-3). The author surveys such unscientific methods of forecasting as astrology and then gives coverage on more reliable methods involving such concepts as the laws of probability. (Rev: BL 2/15/87; SLJ 2/87) [303.4]

5518 Windham, Kathryn Tucker. *Jeffrey Introduces 13 More Southern Ghosts* (7–10). 1978, Univ. of Alabama Pr. paper $9.50 (0-8173-0381-2). A total of 13 ghosts tell their weird stories.

Sports and Games

General and Miscellaneous

5519 Aaseng, Nathan. *Pro Sports' Greatest Rivalries* (7–12). Illus. 1987, Lerner LB $9.95 (0-8225-1530-X). An account of 6 famous rivalries and their outcomes is presented in chronological order. (Rev: SLJ 6–7/87) [796]

5520 Aaseng, Nathan. *Record Breakers of Pro Sports* (5–9). Illus. 1987, Lerner $8.95 (0-8225-1533-4). Records in such sports as baseball, hockey, and football are described. (Rev: BL 3/15/88) [796]

5521 Berger, Gilda. *Violence and Sports* (7–12). 1990, Watts LB $12.90 (0-531-10907-0). A sport-by-sport examination of the components in the playing, managing, and viewing that lead to violence. (Rev: BL 4/15/90; SLJ 7/90) [796]

5522 Brimner, Larry Dane. *Footbagging* (6–9). Illus. 1988, Watts $9.90 (0-531-10477-X). An introduction to a sport that is easily played and becoming very popular. (Rev: BL 3/1/88; SLJ 6–7/88) [796.33]

5523 Cooper, Michael. *Racing Sled Dogs: An Original North American Sport* (5–8). Illus. 1988, Clarion $13.95 (0-89919-499-0). A simple but fascinating account of this sport that focuses on the Iditarod Trail Race in Alaska. (Rev: BL 2/1/89) [798]

5524 Davis, Mac. *Great Sports Humor* (7–9). 1982, Putnam paper $4.95 (0-448-12327-4). This is a collection of amusing anecdotes involving a number of different sports. [796]

5525 Davis, Mac. *Strange and Incredible Sports Happenings* (6–9). 1982, Putnam paper $4.95 (0-448-12326-6). Unusual happenings in a number of sports are reported on in this anecdotal anthology. [796]

5526 Dolan, Edward F., Jr. *The Julian Messner Sports Question and Answer Book* (7–12). Illus. 1984, Messner LB $10.79 (0-671-53134-4); Wanderer paper $8.95 (0-671-47749-8). Questions and answers are given about the rules, plays, and players of many sports including tennis, baseball, and football. [796]

5527 Fichter, George S. *Karts and Karting* (7–10). Illus. 1982, Watts LB $10.40 (0-531-04394-0). Topics covered include a history of the sport plus a rundown on the various types of races involved in karting. [796.7]

5528 Finney, Shan. *Cheerleading and Baton Twirling* (7–12). Illus. 1982, Watts LB $10.40 (0-531-04391-6). A step-by-step manual on moves and routines with many illustrations. [791]

5529 Gardner, Robert. *Science and Sports* (8–10). Illus. 1988, Watts $11.90 (0-531-10593-8). An account that shows how scientific principles such as gravity and momentum are applied in the world of sports. (Rev: BL 1/1/89; BR 5–6/89; SLJ 3/89; VOYA 6/89) [796]

5530 Gay, Kathlyn. *They Don't Wash Their Socks! Sports Superstitions* (6–9). Illus. 1990, Walker LB $14.85 (0-8027-6917-9). A compendium of myths and superstitions that helps explain some of the unusual behavior of players and coaches. (Rev: VOYA 8/90) [796]

5531 Gryski, Camilla. *Super String Games* (6–8). Illus. 1988, Morrow LB $10.88 (0-688-07685-8); paper $6.95 (0-688-07684-8). Directions for 26 string games from around the world are given in text and diagrams. (Rev: BR 5–6/88) [793]

5532 Gutman, Bill. *Great Sports Upsets* (7–10). Illus. 1988, Archway paper $2.50 (0-671-66699-1). Ten thrilling sports episodes are reported of the underdog becoming the unexpected winner. (Rev: VOYA 6/89) [796]

5533 Hollander, Zander, and David Schulz. *Sports Teasers: A Book of Games and Puzzles* (7–9). Illus. 1982, Random paper $1.95 (0-394-85014-9). A fun book of sports questions plus games with solutions. [796]

5534 Lipsyte, Robert. *Assignment: Sports* (7–10). Rev. ed. 1984, Harper LB $12.89 (0-06-023908-5). A professional sportswriter recalls some of the highlights of his career. [796]

5535 Liss, Howard. *The Giant Book of More Strange but True Sports Stories* (7–9). Illus. 1983, Random paper $7.95 (0-394-85633-3). A collection of 150 unusual occurrences in a dozen different sports. [796]

5536 Murphy, Joseph E. *Adventure beyond the Clouds: How We Climbed China's Highest Mountain—and Survived!* (7–12). Illus. 1986, Dillon LB $12.95 (0-87518-330-1). The adventure of climbing Gongga Shan in China by a 7-member American climbing team. (Rev: SLJ 9/86; VOYA 12/86) [796.5]

5537 Myers, Gail. *FunSports for Everyone* (5–9). Illus. 1985, Westminster $12.95 (0-664-32720-6). A number of sports activities such as canoeing, biking, karate, and frisbee throwing are introduced. (Rev: BL 7/85; SLJ 5/85) [796]

5538 Myers, Gail. *A World of Sports for Girls* (7–10). 1981, Westminster $10.95 (0-664-32683-8). A book that gives lots of information for women trying to succeed in sports including such topics as training, finding coaches, and getting college scholarships. [796.7]

5539 Reiser, Howard. *Skateboarding* (5–9). Rev. ed. 1989, Watts LB $11.90 (0-531-10813-9). Topics covered include a history of the sport, equipment, terms, famous skateboarders, and kinds of tricks. (Rev: BR 3–4/90; VOYA 2/90) [796.2]

5540 Sullivan, George. *Better Roller Skating for Boys and Girls* (7–9). Illus. 1980, Putnam LB $9.95 (0-396-07784-6); paper $2.95 (0-396-08291-2). Lots of background material on history and equipment, plus practical pointers on becoming a good roller skater. [796.2]

5541 Vecchione, Glen. *The World's Best Street & Yard Games* (5–8). Illus. 1989, Sterling $11.95 (0-8069-6900-8). About 100 street games such as tag and rough-house are described with rules and special requirements. (Rev: BL 7/89) [796]

Air Games and Sports

5542 Adler, Irene. *Ballooning: High and Wild* (6–9). 1976, Troll LB $9.79 (0-89375-001-8); paper $2.50 (0-89375-017-4). A book that introduces you to the excitement and danger involved in hot-air ballooning. [797.5]

5543 Benson, Rolf. *Skydiving* (7–10). Illus. 1979, Lerner LB $9.95 (0-8225-0425-1). A brief introduction to this sport with material on training, skills, equipment, and techniques. [797.5]

5544 Dean, Anabel. *Wind Sports* (7–12). Illus. 1982, Westminster $12.95 (0-664-32696-X). This book introduces such sports as hang gliding, parachute jumping, iceboating, and sailboarding. [797.5]

5545 Nentl, Jerolyn. *Skydiving* (7–9). 1978, Crestwood LB $8.95 (0-913940-87-9). This sport is described in terms of the thrills it affords and the safety measures that are necessary. [797.5]

5546 Penzler, Otto. *Hang Gliding: Riding the Wind* (6–9). Illus. 1976, Troll LB $9.79 (0-89375-008-5); paper $2.50 (0-89375-024-7). An easily read book that explains the fundamentals of hang gliding through text and pictures. [797.5]

Automobile Racing

5547 Gregory, Stephen. *Racing to Win: The Salt Flats* (6–9). 1976, Troll LB $9.79 (0-89375-010-7); paper $2.50 (0-89375-026-3). An easily read account of the racing that is conducted on the salt flats at Bonneville, Utah. [796.7]

5548 Knudson, Richard L. *Racing Yesterday's Cars* (5–9). Illus. 1986, Lerner $9.95 (0-8225-0512-6). An introduction to the sport of vintage car racing plus information on clubs and how to restore old automobiles. (Rev: BL 4/1/86) [796.7]

Baseball

5549 Aaseng, Nathan. *Baseball, It's Your Team* (6–10). Illus. 1985, Lerner LB $8.95 (0-8225-1558-X); Dell paper $2.50 (0-440-90507-9). The reader is given several choices from real-life situations to build a fine baseball team. (Rev: SLJ 11/85) [769.357]

5550 Aaseng, Nathan. *You Are the Manager: Baseball* (7–9). 1984, Dell paper $1.95 (0-440-99829-8). Readers must make important decisions when they become managers of baseball clubs. [796.357]

5551 Alvarez, Mark. *The Official Baseball Hall of Fame Answer Book* (6–10). Illus. 1989, Simon & Schuster paper $6.95 (0-671-67377-7). The history, statistics, and unusual happenings involved with this sport are told in an easy-going question-and-answer style. (Rev: BL 6/1/89) [796.357]

5552 Benagh, Jim. *Baseball: Startling Stories Behind the Records* (5–9). Illus. 1987, Sterling $11.95 (0-8069-6402-2); paper $4.95 (0-8069-6788-9). A collection of short pieces concerning unusual facts about baseball. (Rev: BL 8/87; BR 11–12/87) [796.357]

5553 Durant, John. *The Story of Baseball* (7–12). Illus. 1973, Hastings $10.95 (0-8038-6715-8). An excellent history of baseball in words and pictures. [796.357]

5554 Forker, Dom. *Baseball Brain Teasers* (7–12). 1986, Sterling paper $4.95 (0-8069-6284-4). A baseball trivia book in which baseball situations are described and questions are asked about them. (Rev: BR 11–12/86; SLJ 12/86) [796.357]

5555 Frommer, Harvey. *Baseball's Hall of Fame* (6–10). 1985, Watts LB $10.40 (0-531-04904-3). A history of the Hall of Fame in Cooperstown, New York, and a membership list from 1936 through 1985. (Rev: BR 3–4/86) [796.357]

5556 Frommer, Harvey. *A Hundred and Fiftieth Anniversary Album of Baseball* (7–12). Illus. 1988, Watts LB $13.90 (0-531-10588-1). In brief text and 145 photographs the history of baseball is covered. (Rev: SLJ 1/89) [796.357]

5557 Gergen, Joe. *World Series Heroes and Goats: The Men Who Made History in America's October Classic* (7–12). Illus. 1982, Random paper $1.95 (0-394-85018-1). In reverse chronological order Gergen covers nearly 40 World Series games from 1905 through 1981. [796.357]

5558 Gutman, Bill. *Baseball's Hot New Stars* (7–9). 1988, Archway paper $2.50 (0-671-65971-5). Profiles of some of the younger baseball stars like Don Mattingly, Roger Clemens, and Darryl Strawberry. (Rev: VOYA 10/88) [796.357]

5559 Hollander, Zander. *The Baseball Book* (7–9). 1983, Random $8.99 (0-394-94296-5); paper $6.95 (0-394-84296-0). A fine background book that explains the game, the rules, and the positions as well as giving some baseball history. [796.357]

5560 Nash, Bruce, and Allan Zullo. *The Baseball Hall of Shame: Young Fans Edition* (5–8). Illus. 1990, Pocket paper $2.95 (0-671-69354-9). For younger readers, here is an edition of the authors' collection of baseball's worst moments. (Rev: SLJ 7/90) [796.357]

5561 Nelson, Don. *Baseball's Home Run Hitters: The Sultans of Swat* (6–9). Illus. 1984, Leisure paper $9.95 (0-88011-220-4). Outstanding batters in the history of baseball are highlighted with accompanying statistics. [796.357]

5562 Nuwer, Hank. *Strategies of the Great Baseball Managers* (7–12). Illus. 1988, Watts $13.90 (0-531-10601-2). Profiles of 12 of the most famous managers in baseball history with details of the styles and techniques of each. (Rev: BL 1/1/89; SLJ 1/89; VOYA 4/89) [796.357]

5563 Reichler, Joseph L., ed. *The Baseball Encyclopedia: The Complete and Official Record of Major League Baseball* (7–12). 6th ed. 1985, Macmillan $39.95 (0-02-601930-2). This has become the standard reference work on baseball and contains information through 1984. (Rev: BL 8/85) [796.357]

5564 Ritter, Lawrence S. *The Story of Baseball* (5–9). Illus. 1990, Morrow $13.95 (0-688-09056-7); paper $8.95 (0-688-09057-5). A revision of the 1983 edition that supplies an interesting, readable introduction to this sport and how it is played. (Rev: BL 7/90; SLJ 9/90) [796.357]

5565 Solomon, Abbot N. *Secrets of the Super Athletes: Baseball* (7–9). 1982, Dell paper $1.95 (0-440-97979-X). Some of the best give tips on the fine art of baseball. [796.357]

5566 Sullivan, George. *Baseball Backstage* (5–9). 1986, Holt $11.95 (0-03-000758-5). This book gives an introduction to such careers in behind-the-scenes baseball as managers, scouts, public relations personnel, and reporters. (Rev: BL 4/1/86; BR 9–10/86; SLJ 5/86) [796.357]

5567 Sullivan, George. *Better Baseball for Boys* (7–10). Rev. ed. Illus. 1981, Putnam LB $9.95 (0-396-07912-1); paper $2.95 (0-396-08288-2). Good general advice followed by specifics for each position and for batters. [796.357]

5568 Weber, Bruce. *Inside Baseball 1989* (6–12). Illus. 1989, Scholastic paper $2.25 (0-590-42449-1). A collection of team profiles that also highlights individual players. (Rev: VOYA 8/89) [796.357]

Basketball

5569 Aaseng, Nathan. *Basketball's Power Players* (6–9). Illus. 1985, Lerner LB $7.95 (0-8225-1342-0). Profiles of the careers of 8 of the powerhouses of basketball. (Rev: SLJ 5/85) [796.32]

5570 Anderson, Dave. *The Story of Basketball* (5–9). Illus. 1988, Morrow $12.95 (0-688-06748-4); paper $8.95 (0-688-06749-2). The first part of this book describes the history of this sport and the second, its fundamentals. (Rev: BL 1/15/89; SLJ 2/89) [796.32]

5571 Antonacci, Robert J., and Jene Barr. *Basketball for Young Champions* (7–9). 2nd ed. Illus. 1979, McGraw $10.95 (0-07-002141-4). Pointers are given on each of the important moves like dribbling, shooting, and passing. [796.32]

5572 Boyd, Brendan, and Robert Garrett. *Hoops: Behind the Scenes with the Boston Celtics* (4–10). Illus. 1989, Little $15.95 (0-316-37319-2); paper $7.95 (0-316-37309-5). A candid look at this top basketball team and its players. (Rev: BL 6/1/89; BR 9–10/89) [796.323]

5573 Clark, Steve. *Illustrated Basketball Dictionary for Young People* (7–9). Illus. 1978, Prentice paper $2.50 (0-13-450940-4). In easily understood prose and diagrams, the terms, playing positions, and strategies connected with basketball are explained. [796.32]

5574 Jarrett, William S. *Timetables of Sports History: Basketball* (7–12). Illus. 1990, Facts on File $17.95 (0-8160-1920-7). From 1890 through 1989, here is a chronologically arranged history of basketball highlights. (Rev: BL 3/1/90) [796.323]

5575 Jones, Ron. *B-Ball: The Team That Never Lost a Game* (7–12). 1990, Bantam $14.95 (0-553-05867-3). An inspiring story of the San Francisco Special Olympics basketball team, written by the man who coached them for years. (Rev: BL 7/90; VOYA 6/90) [796.323]

5576 Morris, Greggory. *Basketball Basics* (7–9). Illus. 1976, Treehouse $6.95 (0-13-072256-1); Prentice paper $2.50 (0-13-072223-5). A fine book for the beginner that explains basic moves, shots, and skills. [796.32]

5577 Sullivan, George. *Better Basketball for Boys* (7–9). Rev. ed. Illus. 1980, Putnam LB $9.95 (0-396-07857-5); paper $2.95 (0-396-08242-4). Black-and-white photos and drawings help illustrate basic moves and skills. [796.32]

5578 Sullivan, George. *Better Basketball for Girls* (7–10). Illus. 1978, Putnam LB $9.95 (0-396-07580-0); paper $2.95 (0-396-08243-2). Basic skills and conditioning exercises are covered plus a history of women's participation in the game. [796.32]

5579 *Youth League Basketball: Coaching and Playing* (7–10). Illus. 1983, Athletic Inst. paper $7.95 (0-87670-092-X). Offensive tactics, defensive tactics, and coaching information are 3 areas covered. [796.32]

Bicycles and Cycling

5580 Coombs, Charles. *All-Terrain Bicycling* (6–10). Illus. 1987, Henry Holt $13.95 (0-8050-0204-9). After an introduction to various kinds of bicycles and their parts, Coombs gives tips that emphasize safety in all kinds of biking. (Rev: BL 3/15/87; BR 11–12/87; SLJ 8/87; VOYA 8-9/87) [796.6]

5581 Coombs, Charles. *BMX: A Guide to Bicycle Motocross* (7–12). Illus. 1983, Morrow $12.95 (0-688-01867-X). How to choose and care for a bike are covered plus techniques and a history of the sport. [796.6]

5582 Grant, Richard, and Nigel Thomas. *BMX Action Bike Book* (7–12). Illus. 1985, Arco paper $3.95 (0-668-06372-6). A brief overview of techniques, jargon, and various competitions involving bicycle motocross. [796.6]

5583 Sullivan, George. *Better Bicycling for Boys and Girls* (6–8). 1984, Putnam paper $2.95 (0-396-08479-6). A collection of useful tips that stresses safety. [796.6]

5584 Sullivan, George. *Better BMX Riding and Racing for Boys and Girls* (7–10). Illus. 1984, Putnam LB $9.95 (0-396-08331-5); paper $3.95 (0-396-08376-5). A book for the beginner that covers topics such as equipment selection, basic riding skills, bicycle maintenance, and what an average meet is like. [796.6]

Bodybuilding

5585 Columbu, Franco, and Dick Tyler. *Weight Training and Bodybuilding: A Complete Guide for Young Athletes* (7–12). Illus. 1979, Wanderer paper $6.95 (0-671-33006-3). Sane, moderate advice for both beginning and advanced students from a former Mr. Universe. [796.4]

5586 Jarrell, Steve. *Working Out with Weights* (7–12). Illus. 1978, Arco paper $5.95 (0-668-04221-4). A basic book written for teens stressing moderate and practical exercise programs. [796.4]

5587 Smith, Tim. *Junior Weight Training and Strength Training* (6–9). Illus. 1985, Athletic Inst. $11.95 (0-87670-097-0); paper $7.95 (0-87670-098-9). A straightforward, well-organized book that gives safe advice for beginning weight trainers of both sexes. (Rev: BR 11–12/85; SLJ 11/85) [796.4]

Boxing and Wrestling

5588 Bernstein, Al. *Boxing for Beginners* (7–10). Illus. 1978, Contemporary paper $7.95 (0-8092-7757-3). This volume gives a good introduction to boxing, its fundamentals, details on a training program, and kinds of punches and strategies. [796.8]

5589 Cohen, Daniel, and Susan Cohen. *Wrestling Superstars* (5–9). Illus. 1985, Pocket paper $2.50 (0-671-60648-4). Thirty different wrestling stars such as Hulk Hogan are introduced along with their techniques. (Rev: BL 10/1/85; SLJ 2/86; VOYA 2/86) [796.812]

5590 Gutman, Bill. *Strange & Amazing Wrestling Stories* (5–9). Illus. 1986, Pocket paper $2.50 (0-671-61134-8). A collection of stories involving 30 years of wrestling history with emphasis on today's stars. (Rev: BL 7/86; VOYA 12/86) [796.812]

5591 Jarman, Tom, and Reid Hanley. *Wrestling for Beginners* (7–12). Illus. 1983, Contemporary paper $8.95 (0-8092-5656-8). From a history of wrestling, this book moves on to skills, strategies, moves, and holds. [796.8]

5592 Ricciuti, Edward R. *How to Box: A Guide for Beginners* (7–10). Illus. 1982, Harper LB $12.89 (0-690-04181-0). This book covers a history of boxing, its stances, punches, footwork, and training programs. [796.8]

Camping, Hiking, and Backpacking

5593 Boy Scouts of America. *Fieldbook* (5–9). Illus. 1985, Boy Scouts of America paper $7.95 (0-8395-3200-8). Though written specifically for the Boy Scouts this is a fine guide for the outdoor person interested in camping, hiking, or related activities. (Rev: BL 8/85) [369]

5594 Elman, Robert, and Clair Rees. *The Hiker's Bible* (7–12). Rev. ed. Illus. 1982, Doubleday paper $4.95 (0-385-17505-1). A comprehensive guide to hiking and backpacking. [796.5]

5595 Stine, Jane, and Jovial Bob Stine. *The Cool Kids' Guide to Summer Camp* (6–9). 1984, Scholastic paper $2.25 (0-590-40302-8). Tips are given on how to survive and even enjoy the summer camp experience. [796.54]

5596 *Wilderness Challenge* (7–10). Illus. 1980, National Geographic LB $8.50 (0-87044-338-0). Color photographs add to this series of outdoor adventures in various parts of the United States. [796.5]

5597 Zeleznak, Shirley. *Backpacking* (7–9). 1980, Crestwood LB $8.95 (0-89686-069-8). Equipment, routes, clothing, food, and walking techniques are only a few of the subjects introduced. [795.5]

Chess, Checkers, and Other Board and Card Games

5598 Carroll, David. *Make Your Own Chess Set* (7–10). 1975, Prentice paper $2.95 (0-13-547786-7). In addition to giving a history of each piece, instructions are given for making 23 different chess sets. [794.1]

5599 Keene, Raymond. *The Simon & Schuster Pocket Book of Chess* (6–8). Illus. 1989, Simon & Schuster $12.95 (0-671-67923-6); paper $7.95 (0-671-67924-4). An introduction to this game plus the mastery of more complicated moves are given through text, diagrams, and attractive photographs. (Rev: BL 6/1/89; BR 11–12/90; VOYA 12/89) [794.1]

5600 Pandolfini, Bruce. *Let's Play Chess! A Step-by-Step Guide for Beginners* (7–12). Illus. 1980, Messner LB $9.29 (0-671-34054-9). An expert teacher of chess explains the basics. [794.1]

Fishing and Hunting

5601 Arnosky, Jim. *Flies in the Water, Fish in the Air: A Personal Introduction to Fly Fishing* (5–

9). Illus. 1986, Lothrop $12.95 (0-688-05834-5). An explanation of fly fishing that elevates it to an art form. (Rev: BL 7/86; SLJ 8/86) [799.1]

5602 Arnosky, Jim. *Freshwater Fish and Fishing* (7–9). Illus. 1982, Macmillan $9.95 (0-02-705850-6). Various kinds of fish are introduced and information on how to fish for them and the equipment necessary is provided. [799.1]

5603 Evanoff, Vlad. *A Complete Guide to Fishing* (7–10). Rev. ed. Illus. 1981, Harper LB $12.89 (0-690-04091-1). In addition to equipment and techniques, this account tells about types of fish and fresh and saltwater fishing. [799.1]

5604 Fichter, George S., and Phil Frances. *Fishing* (7–12). 1987, Western paper $3.95 (0-307-24050-9). This guide not only identifies many fish but also tells how they can be caught. [799.1]

5605 Roberts, Charles P., and George F. Roberts. *Fishing for Fun: A Freshwater Guide* (7–12). Illus. 1984, Dillon paper $5.95 (0-87518-279-8). A practical introduction to fishing skills and equipment that even tells you how to clean your catch. [799.1]

Football

5606 Aaseng, Nathan. *College Football's Hottest Rivalries* (5–9). Illus. 1987, Lerner $8.95 (0-8225-1531-8). Six traditionally tight contests (e.g., Army vs. Navy) are described. Also use: *Football's Incredible Bulks* (1987). (Rev: BL 3/15/88) [796.322]

5607 Aaseng, Nathan. *Football's Super Bowl Champions, I–XVI* (7–10). 2 vols. Illus. 1982, Lerner LB $7.95 ea. (vol. 1: 0-8225-1072-3; vol. 2: 0-8225-1333-1). Team-by-team coverage of the first 26 Super Bowl games in two illustrated volumes. [796.332]

5608 Aaseng, Nathan. *You Are the Coach: Football* (7–9). 1983, Dell paper $2.50 (0-440-99136-6). The outcome of the game is determined by the answers to situations given by the reader. [796.332]

5609 Anderson, Dave. *The Story of Football* (5–10). Illus. 1985, Morrow $12.95 (0-688-05634-2); paper $8.95 (0-688-05635-0). As well as important personalities in the history of football, this account deals with the development of rules, techniques, and various teams and leagues. (Rev: BL 10/1/85; BR 5–6/86; SLJ 10/85; VOYA 2/86) [796.332]

5610 Benagh, Jim. *Football: Startling Stories Behind the Records* (5–9). Illus. 1987, Sterling LB $12.49 (0-8069-6619-X). Stories culled from both collegiate and professional football that reveal unusual facts about its history. (Rev: BL 4/15/88) [796.332]

5611 Berger, Melvin. *The Photo Dictionary of Football* (7–9). Illus. 1980, Routledge $9.95 (0-416-30131-2). The language of football is explained in words and many photographs. [796.332]

5612 Brenner, Richard J. *The Complete Super Bowl Story: Games I–XXIII* (5–8). Illus. 1990, Lerner LB $9.95 (0-8225-1503-2). A detailed look at the first 23 Super Bowl games. (Rev: BL 2/1/90) [796.332]

5613 Bryce, James, and Bill Polick. *Power Basics of Football* (7–9). Illus. 1985, Prentice paper $5.95 (0-13-688318-4). Well-known stars are used to demonstrate basic and intermediate football skills. (Rev: BL 10/1/85) [796.332]

5614 Devaney, John. *Winners of the Heisman Trophy* (5–8). Rev. ed. Illus. 1990, Walker LB $15.85 (0-8027-6907-1). A history of the award is given, plus profiles of 15 past winners. (Rev: SLJ 6/90) [796.332]

5615 Gutman, Bill. *Sports Illustrated: Pro Football's Record Breakers* (5–9). 1987, Pocket paper $2.50 (0-671-64375-4). From the earliest days of football to the present, here is a rundown of the records and record breakers. (Rev: BL 9/1/87) [796.332]

5616 Hollander, Phyllis, and Zander Hollander, eds. *Touchdown! Football's Most Dramatic Scoring Feats* (6–9). Illus. 1982, Random paper $1.95 (0-394-85020-3). Fifty unusual touchdowns of this century are described. [796.332]

5617 Lorimer, Lawrence T., and John Devaney. *The Football Book* (7–9). Illus. 1977, Random $7.99 (0-394-93574-8); paper $5.95 (0-394-83574-3). An illustrated guide that explains rules, teams, and strategies and identifies famous players. [796.332]

5618 Nuwer, Hank. *Strategies of the Great Football Coaches* (7–10). Illus. 1988, Watts $12.40 (0-531-10518-0). Tips and biographical information by and about 12 great football coaches past and present. (Rev: BL 7/88; BR 9–10/88; SLJ 8/88; VOYA 8/88) [796.332]

5619 Olgin, Joseph. *Illustrated Football Dictionary for Young People* (7–9). Illus. 1978, Prentice paper $2.50 (0-13-450874-2). In an alphabetical arrangement entries are given for rules, terms, plays, and signals. [796.332]

5620 Solomon, Abbot N. *Secrets of the Super Athletes: Football* (7–9). 1982, Dell paper $1.95 (0-440-97979-X). The great stars of football reveal their professional secrets. [797.332]

5621 Sullivan, George. *Better Football for Boys* (7–10). Rev. ed. Illus. 1980, Putnam $9.95 (0-396-07843-5); paper $2.95 (0-396-08241-6). The basic skills in football are introduced with tips on how to master them. [796.332]

Gymnastics

5622 Murdock, Tony, and Nik Stuart. *Gymnastics: A Practical Guide for Beginners* (7–12). Rev. ed. Illus. 1989, Watts LB $13.40 (0-531-10770-1). A basic book for both boys and girls that not only covers skills but also such topics as equipment and warm-ups. (Rev: BR 3–4/90; SLJ 3/90; VOYA 4/90) [796.4]

5623 Sullivan, George. *Better Gymnastics for Girls* (7–10). Illus. 1977, Putnam LB $9.95 (0-396-07453-7); paper $3.95 (0-396-08292-0). Various sequences are carefully pictured with accompanying text. [796.4]

5624 Traetta, John, and Mary Jean Traetta. *Gymnastics Basics* (7–10). Illus. 1979, Prentice paper $3.95 (0-13-371740-2). In addition to pointers on choosing the right gymnastics program there is specialized information on 7 different events such as working on the parallel bars and the rings. [796.4]

Horsemanship

5625 Pervier, Evelyn. *Horsemanship* (7–12). 3 vols. Illus. 1984, Messner LB $9.29 each (vol. 1: 0-671-45519-2; vol. 2: 0-671-45520-6; vol. 3: 0-671-45521-4); paper $5.95 each (vol. 1: 0-688-05935-4; vol. 2: 0-688-05942-7; vol. 3: 0-688-05950-8). The 3 volumes in this set are *Basics for Beginners; Basics for Intermediate Riders;* and *Basics for More Advanced Riders.* [798.2]

5626 Philp, Candice Tillis. *Rodeo Horses* (6–9). Illus. 1983, Crestwood LB $9.95 (0-89686-302-5). A history of rodeos is given, a description of the events, and a rundown on the types of horses used. [798.2]

5627 Roth, Harold. *A Day at the Races* (6–9). Illus. 1983, Pantheon $10.95 (0-394-85814-X).

Behind the scenes during a typical day at the racetrack. [798.4]

Ice Hockey

5628 MacLean, Norman. *Hockey Basics* (6–9). Illus. 1983, Prentice LB $10.95 (0-13-392506-4). All kinds of plays and strategies are outlined plus material on the history of the sport, its rules, and the equipment necessary. [796.96]

Ice Skating

5629 MacLean, Norman. *Ice Skating Basics* (6–9). Illus. 1984, Prentice $10.95 (0-13-448762-1). Equipment, training, and techniques are 3 topics covered. [796.91]

5630 Sullivan, George. *Better Ice Skating for Boys and Girls* (7–10). Illus. 1976, Putnam LB $9.95 (0-396-07339-5); paper $3.95 (0-396-08475-3). The 3 types of ice skating—figure, power, and speed—are introduced. [796.91]

5631 Young, Stephanie, and Bruce Curtis. *Peggy Fleming: Portrait of an Ice Skater* (7–12). Illus. 1984, Avon paper $2.25 (0-380-85720-0). This is a do-it-yourself manual on figure skating as demonstrated by the Olympic winner. [796.91]

Kite Making and Flying

5632 Schmitz, Dorothy Childers. *Kite Flying* (7–9). 1978, Crestwood LB $8.95 (0-913940-92-5). A history of kites is given and instructions on how to make and fly a variety of models. [796.1]

Martial Arts

5633 Kozuki, Russell. *Junior Karate* (7–9). Illus. 1971, Sterling LB $14.49 (0-8069-4447-1). The basics of karate are explained simply in text; many illustrations. [796.8]

5634 Kozuki, Russell. *Karate for Young People* (7–10). Illus. 1974, Sterling LB $14.49 (0-8069-4075-1); paper $4.95 (0-8069-7560-1). All sorts of strikes, punches, and blocks are pictured and described in the text. [796.8]

5635 Nardi, Thomas J. *Karate Basics* (6–9). Illus. 1984, Prentice $10.95 (0-13-514548-1). The history of this sport and basic techniques are introduced. [796.8]

5636 Neff, Fred. *Lessons from the Art of Kempo: Subtle and Effective Self-Defense* (5–9). Illus. 1987, Lerner LB $9.95 (0-8225-1160-6); paper $4.95 (0-8225-9532-X). This account gives detailed information on stances, punches, kicks, blocks, and other movements. Also use: *Lessons from the Samurai: Ancient Self-Defense Strategies and Techniques* (1987). (Rev: SLJ 1/88) [796.8]

5637 Neff, Fred. *Lessons from the Western Warriors: Dynamic Self-Defense Techniques* (5–8). Illus. 1987, Lerner LB $9.95 (0-8225-1159-2). Using western forms of self-defense such as boxing and street fighting a type of occidental martial art is described. (Rev: SLJ 10/87) [796.8]

5638 Parulski, George R., Jr. *Action Karate* (6–8). Illus. 1987, Sterling LB $16.79 (0-8069-6269-0). A general introduction that explains basic moves and gives a history and the ranking system in this sport. (Rev: SLJ 3/87) [796.8]

5639 Parulski, George R., Jr., et al. *Karate Power! Learning the Art of the Empty Hand* (5–8). Illus. 1985, Contemporary paper $5.95 (0-8092-5295-3). A very basic, easy-to-read introduction to Japanese karate. (Rev: SLJ 2/86) [796.8]

5640 Ribner, Susan, and Richard Chin. *The Martial Arts* (7–10). Illus. 1978, Harper LB $12.89 (0-06-025000-3). This is not a manual but a thoughtful introduction to the history and philosophy behind the martial arts. [796.8]

5641 Yates, Keith D., and H. Bryan Robbins. *Korean Karate* (6–8). Illus. 1987, Sterling LB $14.49 (0-8069-6459-6); paper $4.95 (0-8069-6836-2). This text introduces and explains the Korean martial art of the *tae kwon do*. (Rev: SLJ 10/87) [796.8]

Motor Bikes and Motorcycles

5642 Armitage, Barry. *Motorcycles!* (5–8). Illus. 1988, Sterling $10.95 (0-8069-6892-3). Various types of motorcycles and famous races are described in this exciting illustrated book. (Rev: BL 2/15/89) [629.2]

5643 Jennings, Gordon. *Minibikes* (7–9). Illus. 1979, Prentice paper $1.50 (0-13-583849-5).

Small bikes are introduced plus pointers on buying them and maintaining them. [629.2]

5644 Kerrod, Robin. *Motorcycles* (5–8). Illus. 1989, Gloucester $11.90 (0-531-17152-3). The various types and parts of motorcycles are pictured and explained in the text; includes a short history of the vehicle. (Rev: BL 4/1/89) [629.227]

5645 Naden, C. J. *Rough Rider: The Challenge of Moto-Cross* (6–9). 1980, Troll LB $9.79 (0-89375-250-9); paper $2.50 (0-89375-251-7). An easily read introduction to this form of motorcycling with coverage on equipment and safety precautions. [629.227]

Olympic Games

5646 Frommer, Harvey. *Olympic Controversies* (6–10). Illus. 1987, Watts $11.90 (0-531-10417-6). An account of the problems—political, personal, commercial—that have beset the Olympic Games through the ages. (Rev: BL 1/15/88; BR 1–2/88; SLJ 1/88; VOYA 2/88) [796.4]

5647 Glubok, Shirley, and Alfred Tamarin. *Olympic Games in Ancient Greece* (7–10). 1976, Harper LB $13.89 (0-06-022048-1). History and legend are combined in this account of the first Olympics. [796.4]

Sailing and Boating

5648 Burchard, Peter. *Venturing: An Introduction to Sailing* (7–12). Illus. 1986, Little $17.95 (0-316-11613-0). A well-organized introduction to sailing that explains terms and describes important maneuvers. (Rev: SLJ 10/86) [797.1]

5649 Slocombe, Lorna. *Sailing Basics* (7–10). Illus. 1982, Prentice $9.95 (0-13-786053-6). Techniques on how to master both wind and water are described and water traffic rules are included. [797.1]

Skateboarding

5650 Cassorla, Albert. *The Ultimate Skateboard Book* (5–9). Illus. 1989, Running Press paper $8.95 (0-89471-564-X). In addition to coverage on techniques, this book gives a history of the sport, material on types of skateboards, and how to prepare for participation. (Rev: BL 3/15/89; SLJ 6/89) [796.2]

Skiing

5651 Nentl, Jerolyn. *Freestyle Skiing* (7–10). 1978, Crestwood LB $8.95 (0-913940-90-9). This specialized style of skiing that starts when the conventional form ends is well described in terms of the many techniques it involves. [796.93]

Soccer

5652 Gardner, James B. *Illustrated Soccer Dictionary for Young People* (7–9). Illus. 1978, Prentice paper $2.50 (0-13-451146-8). The jargon, plays, and techniques associated with soccer are defined in words and pictures. [796.334]

5653 Jackson, C. Paul. *How to Play Better Soccer* (7–12). Illus. 1978, Harper LB $12.89 (0-690-03838-3). A history of the game is followed by explanations of the rules, positions, and team techniques. [796.334]

5654 Kowet, Don. *The Soccer Book* (7–9). Illus. 1978, Random paper $5.95 (0-394-83250-7). The rules, techniques, equipment, and stars of this sport are introduced. [796.334]

5655 Laitin, Ken, et al. *The World's #1 Best-Selling Soccer Book* (7–9). Illus. 1979, Soccer for Americans paper $7.95 (0-916802-13-2). A good introduction to the sport that covers the rules and strategies and includes a glossary of terms. [796.335]

5656 Sullivan, George. *Better Soccer for Boys and Girls* (7–10). Illus. 1978, Putnam $9.95 (0-396-07533-9); paper $3.95 (0-396-08246-7). Expert advice is given on how to play each position and develop winning tactics at each stage of the game. [796.334]

5657 Yannis, Alex. *Soccer Basics* (7–10). Illus. 1982, Prentice $9.95 (0-13-815290-X). A clear, concise handling of such skills as kicking, trapping, passing, and shooting. [796.334]

Surfing, Water Skiing, and Other Water Sports

5658 Smith, Don. *Surfing, the Big Wave* (6–9). 1976, Troll LB $9.79 (0-89375-011-5); paper $2.50 (0-89375-027-1). The basic techniques and jargon of surfing are introduced in this easily read book. [797.1]

5659 Wallace, Don. *Watersports Basics* (6–10). Illus. 1985, Prentice LB $9.95 (0-13-945957-X). This is a fine introduction to surfing, waterskiing, and windsurfing. (Rev: SLJ 11/85) [797]

Swimming and Diving

5660 Orr, C. Rob, and Jane B. Tyler. *Swimming Basics* (7–10). Illus. 1980, Prentice paper $4.95 (0-13-879594-0). In addition to an introduction to the 4 basic strokes (e.g., backstroke, breaststroke), there are instructions on turns, water safety, and so on. [797.2]

5661 Sullivan, George. *Better Swimming for Boys and Girls* (6–8). Illus. 1985, Dodd $9.95 (0-396-08071-5). An introductory volume that describes basic techniques and strokes in text and illustrations. [797.2]

Tennis and Other Raquet Games

5662 Goffi, Carlos. *Tournament Tough* (7–10). Illus. 1985, Holt $13.45 (0-03-071598-9). How to prepare for tennis tournaments plus tips on how to improve one's game. (Rev: SLJ 5/85) [796.342]

5663 LaMarche, Robert J. *Tennis Basics* (6–9). Illus. 1983, Prentice LB $9.95 (0-13-903237-1). In only a few pages, LaMarche introduces the game and its rules and covers such skills as serving, volleying, and developing court strategies. [796.342]

5664 Lorimer, Lawrence T. *The Tennis Book* (7–9). 1980, Random paper $6.95 (0-394-83806-8). A comprehensive guide that includes terms, rules, grips, famous players, and techniques. [796.342]

5665 Sullivan, George. *Better Tennis for Boys and Girls* (6–8). 1987, Putnam $10.99 (0-399-

61264-5). A basic guide to playing this increasingly popular sport. [796.342]

Track and Field

5666 Aaseng, Nathan. *Ultramarathons: The World's Most Punishing Races* (5–9). Illus. 1987, Lerner $8.95 (0-8225-1534-2). A description of 8 marathon courses noted for their adverse conditions. (Rev: BL 3/15/88) [796.4]

5667 Alford, Jim. *Track Athletics* (6–9). Illus. 1984, Batsford $19.50 (0-7134-3412-X). This book gives general material on such topics as exercise as well as pointers for each track event. (Rev: BL 1/1/85) [796.4]

5668 McMane, Fred. *Track & Field Basics* (7–10). Illus. 1983, Prentice LB $9.95 (0-13-925966-X). Various events, training exercises, and rules are all introduced in this handy volume. [796.4]

5669 Sullivan, George. *Better Cross-Country Running for Boys and Girls* (7–10). Illus. 1983, Putnam LB $9.95 (0-396-08172-X); paper $2.95 (0-396-08474-5). Equipment, training, and tips on how to improve one's performance are 3 topics covered. [796.4]

5670 Sullivan, George. *Better Field Events for Girls* (6–8). 1982, Putnam paper $9.95 (0-396-08030-8). An easily read introduction to track and field events for girls with tips on how to succeed in each. Also use: *Better Field Hockey for Girls* (1981). [796.4]

5671 Sullivan, George. *Better Track for Boys* (5–9). Illus. 1985, Putnam $9.95 (0-396-08604-7); paper $3.50 (0-396-08628-4). General information is given on such topics as equipment and warm-ups, but specific material is also introduced on such events as sprints, hurdling, and relays. (Rev: BL 7/85; SLJ 12/85) [796.4]

5672 Sullivan, George. *Better Track for Girls* (7–10). Illus. 1981, Dodd LB $9.95 (0-396-07911-3); paper $2.95 (0-396-08244-0). Track events and hurdle running are 2 subjects covered from a woman athlete's point of view. [796.4]

5673 Sullivan, George. *Marathon: The Longest Race* (7–10). Illus. 1980, Westminster LB $9.95 (0-664-32671-4). From the first marathon in ancient Greece to the present day this is a history of the event plus listings of record holders. [796.4]

Volleyball

5674 Rosenthal, Gary. *Volleyball: The Game & How to Play It* (7–12). Illus. 1983, Macmillan paper $9.95 (0-684-17908-3). The basic skills in volleyball are explained plus training and conditioning tips. [796.32]

Appendix: For Advanced Students

These titles for advanced junior high students have been selected from *Best Books for Senior High Readers* (R.R. Bowker, 1991). Nonfiction titles follow the fiction titles.

Fiction

Adams, Douglas. *The Hitchhiker's Guide to the Galaxy* (Crown; Pocket)
Restaurant at the End of the Universe (Crown)
So Long and Thanks for All the Fish (Pocket)
Allman, Paul. *The Knot* (Rosen)
Arnold, Elliott. *Blood Brother* (Univ. of Nebraska Pr.)
Asimov, Isaac. *Caves of Steel* (Ballantine)
Fantastic Voyage (Houghton; Bantam)
Fantastic Voyage II: Destination Brain (Bantam)
Foundation (Ballantine)
Foundation and Empire (Ballantine)
Foundation Trilogy (Doubleday; Ballantine)
Foundation's Edge (Ballantine)
Nine Tomorrow (Ballantine)
The Robots of Dawn (Ballantine)
Second Foundation (Ballantine)
Austen, Jane. *Pride and Prejudice* (Putnam)
Bach, Richard. *Jonathan Livingston Seagull* (Macmillan; Avon)
Baklanov, Grigory. *Forever Nineteen* (Harper)
Banks, Lynne Reid. *Melusine* (Harper)
Barrett, William E. *The Lilies of the Field* (Doubleday)
Beagle, Peter S. *A Fine and Private Place* (Ballantine)
The Last Unicorn (Ballantine)
Betancourt, Jeanne. *Sweet Sixteen and Never* (Bantam)
Blair, Alison. *Love by the Book* (Ivy)
Bond, Nancy. *Another Shore* (Macmillan)
Bosse, Malcolm. *Captives of Time* (Delacorte)
Boulle, Pierre. *The Bridge over the River Kwai* (Amereon; Bantam)
Planet of the Apes (Vanguard; NAL)
Bradbury, Ray. *Dandelion Wine* (Knopf; Bantam)
Fahrenheit 451 (Ballantine)

The Halloween Tree (Knopf)
R Is for Rocket (Bantam)
Something Wicked This Way Comes (Knopf; Bantam)
The Stories of Ray Bradbury (Knopf)
Braithwaite, E. R. *To Sir, with Love* (Jove)
Brooks, Bruce. *No Kidding* (Harper)
Buck, Pearl. *The Good Earth* (Buccaneer; Oxford Univ. Pr.)
Bunting, Eve. *Will You Be My Posslq?* (Harcourt)
Burroughs, Edgar Rice. *At the Earth's Core* (Peter Smith)
A Princess of Mars (Ballantine)
Tarzan of the Apes (Crown; NAL)
Cather, Willa. *My Antonia* (Amereon; Houghton)
Christie, Agatha. *Miss Marple: The Complete Short Stories* (Putnam)
Witness for the Prosecution (Dell)
Clark, Mary Higgins. *The Cradle Will Fall* (Dell)
A Cry in the Night (Dell)
A Stranger Is Watching (Dell)
Weep No More, My Lady (Simon & Schuster)
Where Are the Children? (Dell)
While My Pretty One Sleeps (Simon & Schuster)
Clarke, Arthur C. *Childhood's End* (Harcourt; Ballantine)
Dolphin Island (Ace)
Rendezvous with Rama (Ballantine)
2001: A Space Odyssey (Ballantine)
2010: Odyssey Two (Ballantine)
2061: Odyssey Three (Ballantine)
Clarke, Arthur C., and Gentry Lee. *Rama II* (Bantam)
Conroy, Pat. *The Water Is Wide* (Bantam)
Cooney, Linda A. *Change of Hearts* (Scholastic)
Cormier, Robert. *Fade* (Doubleday)
Craven, Margaret. *I Heard the Owl Call My Name* (Dell)
Walk Gently This Good Earth (Dell)

Crichton, Michael. *The Andromeda Strain* (Knopf; Dell)
The Terminal Man (Ballantine)
Cronin, A. J. *The Citadel* (Little)
The Keys of the Kingdom (Little)
Cussler, Clive. *Raise the Titanic* (Bantam)
Dana, Barbara. *Necessary Parties* (Harper)
Dann, Jack, and Gardner Dozois, eds. *Bestiary!* (Ace)
Magicats! (Ace)
Unicorns! (Ace)
Davidson, Linda. *On the Edge* (Ivy)
Davidson, Nicole. *Crash Course* (Avon)
Deighton, Len. *The Ipcress File* (Ballantine)
Deuker, Carl. *On the Devil's Court* (Little)
Doherty, Berlie. *Granny Was a Buffer Girl* (Watts)
Downer, Ann. *The Glass Salamander* (Macmillan)
DuMaurier, Daphne. *Jamaica Inn* (Buccaneer; Avon)
Falkner, J. Meade. *Moonfleet* (Windrush)
Fast, Howard. *The Immigrants* (Dell)
Ferber, Edna. *Show Boat* (A M S Press)
Feuer, Elizabeth. *Paper Doll* (Farrar)
Forester, C. S. *Admiral Hornblower in the West Indies* (Little)
Mr. Midshipman Hornblower (Little)
Forshay-Lunsford, Cin. *Walk through Cold Fire* (Dell)
Forsyth, Frederick. *The Day of the Jackal* (Bantam)
Frank, Elizabeth Bales. *Cooder Cutlas* (Harper)
Freedman, Benedict, and Nancy Freedman. *Mrs. Mike* (Berkley)
French, Michael. *Soldier Boy* (Berkley)
Gaines, Ernest J. *The Autobiography of Miss Jane Pittman* (Bantam)
Gallico, Paul. *Thomasina* (Avon)
Garfield, Leon. *The Wedding Ghost* (Oxford Univ. Pr.)
Gerber, Merrill Joan. *Handsome as Anything* (Scholastic)
Gilman, Dorothy. *Mrs. Pollifax and the Golden Triangle* (Doubleday)
Mrs. Pollifax and the Hong Kong Buddha (Fawcett)
Mrs. Pollifax and the Whirling Dervish (Doubleday)
Gordon, Ruth, sel. *Under All Silences: Shades of Love* (Harper)
Green, Richard Lancelyn, ed. *The Further Adventures of Sherlock Holmes, after Sir Arthur Conan Doyle* (Penguin)
Greene, Constance C. *The Love Letters of J. Timothy Owen* (Harper)
Greenwood, L. B. *Sherlock Holmes and the Case of the Raleigh Legacy* (Macmillan)

Grey, Zane. *Riders of the Purple Sage* (Penguin; Pocket)
Guthrie, A. B., Jr. *The Big Sky* (Bantam)
Haggard, H. Rider. *King Solomon's Mines* (Penguin)
Hall, Lynn. *The Solitary* (Macmillan)
Hamilton, Virginia. *A White Romance* (Putnam)
Hardy, Jon. *Biker* (Oxford Univ. Pr.)
Harrell, Janice. *So Long, Senior Year* (Crosswinds)
Harris, Mark. *Bang the Drum Slowly* (Univ. of Nebraska Pr.)
Heggen, Thomas. *Mister Roberts* (Amereon)
Heinlein, Robert A. *Between Planets* (Ballantine)
Revolt in 2100 (Baen)
Stranger in a Strange Land (Baen)
Time for the Stars (Baen)
Herbert, Frank. *Dune* (Putnam; Berkley)
Hilton, James. *Goodbye, Mr. Chips* (Bantam)
Lost Horizon (Buccaneer; Pocket)
Hobbs, Will. *Changes in Latitudes* (Macmillan)
Hobson, Laura. *Gentlemen's Agreement* (Cherokee)
Holt, Victoria. *The Captive* (Doubleday)
The Demon Lover (Fawcett)
The Devil on Horseback (Fawcett)
House of a Thousand Lanterns (Fawcett)
The Judas Kiss (Fawcett)
Kirkland Revels (Fawcett)
On the Night of the Seventh Moon (Fawcett)
Shivering Sands (Fawcett)
The Time of the Hunter's Moon (Fawcett)
Huxley, Aldous. *Brave New World* (Buccaneer; Harper)
Innes, Hammond. *The Wreck of the Mary Deare* (Carroll & Graf)
Irving, Washington. *The Legend of Sleepy Hollow* (Greenwillow; Pocket)
Irwin, Hadley. *Abby, My Love* (Macmillan)
So Long at the Fair (Macmillan)
Jackson, Helen Hunt. *Ramona* (Avon)
Jackson, Shirley. *The Haunting of Hill House* (Penguin)
We Have Always Lived in the Castle (Penguin)
Jacobs, Barbara. *Stolen Kisses* (Dell)
James, Betsy. *Long Night Dance* (Dutton)
Jones, Adrienne. *Street Family* (Harper)
Kaufman, Bel. *Up the Down Staircase* (Avon)
Kerr, M. E. *Night Kites* (Harper)
Korman, Gordon. *A Semester in the Life of a Garbage Bag* (Scholastic)
La Farge, Oliver. *Laughing Boy* (Harmony-Raine; NAL)
Lanier, Sterling E. *Hiero's Journey* (Ballantine)
Lee, Harper. *To Kill a Mockingbird* (Harper)
Leonard, Alison. *Tina's Chance* (Viking)
Lichtman, Wendy. *Telling Secrets* (Harper)
Lillington, Kenneth. *Full Moon* (Faber)

Lyons, Pam. *Love Around the Corner* (Dell)

Macaulay, David. *Baaa* (Houghton)

McCaffrey, Anne. *Dinosaur Planet* (Ballantine)
Dinosaur Planet Survivors (Ballantine)
Dragonflight (Ballantine)
Dragonlady of Pern (Ultramarine; Ballantine)
Dragonsdawn (Ballantine)
The Renegades of Pern (Ballantine)
The White Dragon (Ballantine)

McCullers, Carson. *The Member of the Wedding* (Bantam)

McKinley, Robin, ed. *Imaginary Lands* (Greenwillow)

MacLean, Alistair. *Force 10 from Navarone* (Fawcett)
Goodbye California (Amereon)
The Guns of Navarone (Fawcett)
Ice Station Zebra (Fawcett)
Night without End (Fawcett)
Partisans (Fawcett)
San Andreas (Doubleday)
Santorini (Doubleday; Fawcett)

MacLean, John. *Mac* (Houghton)

Mahy, Margaret. *Memory* (Macmillan)
The Tricksters (Macmillan)

Marshall, Catherine. *Christy* (Avon)
Julie (Avon)

Maugham, W. Somerset. *Of Human Bondage* (Doubleday; Penguin)

Mazer, Norma Fox, and Harry Mazer. *Heartbeat* (Bantam)

Miklowitz, Gloria. *Secrets Not Meant to Be Kept* (Dell)

Miller, Frances A. *Losers and Winners* (Fawcett)

Mitchell, Margaret. *Gone with the Wind* (Avon)

Myers, Walter Dean. *Crystal* (Viking)
Fallen Angels (Scholastic)

Naylor, Phyllis Reynolds. *The Dark of the Tunnel* (Macmillan)
The Year of the Gopher (Macmillan; Bantam)

Nixon, Joan Lowery. *The Stalker* (Delacorte)

Norton, Andre. *Knave of Dreams* (Ace)
Witch World (Ace)

Oaks, Tina. *That Cheating Sister* (Scholastic)

O'Har, George M. *Psychic Fair* (Pocket)

Oneal, Zibby. *In Summer Light* (Viking)

Orczy, Baroness. *The Scarlet Pimpernel* (Buccaneer; NAL)

Paulsen, Gary. *Sentries* (Bradbury)

Pei, Lowry. *Family Resemblances* (Random)

Pike, Christopher. *Chain Letter* (Avon)

Plaidy, Jean. *Passage to Pontefract* (Fawcett)
The Star of Lancaster (Putnam)
The Vow of the Heron (Fawcett)

Portis, Charles. *True Grit* (NAL)

Potok, Chaim. *My Name Is Asher Lev* (Knopf; Fawcett)
The Promise (Fawcett)

Pullman, Philip. *Ruby in the Smoke* (Knopf)
Shadow in the North (Knopf)
The Tiger in the Well (Knopf)

Quin-Harkin, Janet. *The Great Boy Chase* (Bantam)

Rabinowitz, Ann. *Bethie* (Macmillan)

Raymond, Patrick. *Daniel and Esther* (Macmillan)

Remarque, Erich Maria. *All Quiet on the Western Front* (Buccaneer; Fawcett)

Rochman, Hazel, ed. *Somehow Tenderness Survives: Stories of Southern Africa* (Harper)

Rolvaag, O. E. *Giants in the Earth* (Harper)

Ross, Leonard Q. *The Education of H*Y*M*A*N K*A*P*L*A*N* (Harcourt)

Rostkowski, Margaret I. *The Best of Friends* (Harper)

Rue, Nancy. *Row This Boat Ashore* (Crossway)
Stop in the Name of Love (Rosen)

Saki (Hector Hugh Munro). *The Best of Saki* (Penguin)

Saroyan, William. *The Human Comedy* (Harcourt; Dell)

Schaefer, Jack. *Shane* (Bantam)

Schwandt, Stephen. *Holding Steady* (Henry Holt)
A Risky Game (Henry Holt)

Schwartz, Betty Ann, ed. *Great Ghost Stories* (Simon & Schuster)

Scoppettone, Sandra. *Playing Murder* (Harper)

Shannon, George. *Unlived Affections* (Harper)

Shelley, Mary. *Frankenstein* (Penguin)

Shute, Nevil. *On the Beach* (Morrow; Ballantine)

Siegal, Aranka. *Grace in the Wilderness: After the Liberation, 1945–1948* (Farrar)

Smith, Betty. *Joy in the Morning* (Harper)
Tomorrow Will Be Better (Harper)
A Tree Grows in Brooklyn (Harper)

Speare, M. Edmund, ed. *The Pocket Book of Short Stories* (Washington Square Pr.)

Steinbeck, John. *The Pearl* (Bantam)
The Red Pony (Bantam)

Stewart, Mary. *The Crystal Cave* (Fawcett)
The Hollow Hills (Fawcett)
The Last Enchantment (Fawcett)
My Brother Michael (Fawcett)
Touch Not the Cat (Fawcett)
The Wicked Day (Fawcett)

Stoker, Bram. *Dracula* (Oxford Univ. Pr.; NAL)

Stone, Bruce. *Been Clever Forever* (Harper)

Stone, Irving. *Love Is Eternal* (NAL)
The President's Lady (NAL)

Stowe, Harriet Beecher. *Uncle Tom's Cabin* (Houghton; Bantam)

Swarthout, Glendon. *Bless the Beasts and Children* (Pocket)

Tolkien, J. R. R. *Fellowship of the Ring* (Ballantine)

Tryon, Thomas. *The Other* (Dell)

Twain, Mark. *Complete Short Stories* (Bantam)
The Mysterious Stranger and Other Stories (NAL)

Uris, Leon. *Battle Cry* (Bantam)
Exodus (Bantam)

Verne, Jules. *Michael Strogoff* (Amereon; Airmont)

Vidal, Gore. *Burr* (Ballantine)
1876 (Ballantine)
Lincoln (Ballantine)
Washington, D.C. (Ballantine)

Vinge, Joan D. *Psion* (Delacorte)

Voight, Cynthia. *The Runner* (Macmillan)

Walker, Margaret. *Jubilee* (Bantam)

West, Jessamyn. *The Friendly Persuasion* (Buccaneer; Harcourt)

White, T. H. *The Once and Future King* (Berkley)

Whitney, Phyllis. *Black Amber* (Fawcett)
Blue Fire (Fawcett)
Rainsong (Fawcett)
Seven Tears for Apollo (Fawcett)
Silversword (Doubleday; Fawcett)
The Singing Stones (Doubleday)
Snowfire (Fawcett)
Spindrift (Fawcett)
The Stone Bull (Fawcett)
The Trembling Hills (Fawcett)
Window on the Square (Fawcett)

Wibberley, Leonard. *The Mouse That Roared* (Bantam)

Windsor, Patricia. *The Sandman's Eyes* (Delacorte)

Yep, Laurence. *Shadow Lord* (Pocket)

Zindel, Paul. *The Amazing and Death-Defying Diary of Eugene Dingman* (Harper; Bantam)

Nonfiction

Abrahams, Roger D., ed. *Afro-American Folktales: Stories from Black Traditions in the New World* (Pantheon)

Abrams, Kathleen S. *Guide to Careers without College* (Watts)

Adamson, Joy. *Born Free: A Lioness of Two Worlds* (Pantheon)

Allen, Frederick Lewis. *The Big Change: America Transforms Itself 1900–1959* (Greenwood; Harper)

Allen, Oliver E. *Atmosphere* (Silver Burdett)
The Windjammers (Time-Life)

American Kennel Club Staff. *The Complete Dog Book* (Howell Book House)

America's Seashore Wonderlands (National Geographic)

Andrews, Elaine K. *Civil Defense in the Nuclear Age* (Watts)

Appelbaum, Diana Karter. *The Glorious Fourth: An American Holiday, an American History* (Facts on File)

Aquila, Richard. *That Old Time Rock & Roll: A Chronicle of an Era, 1954–1963* (Schirmer)

Archer, Jules. *Winners and Losers: How Elections Work in America* (Harcourt)

Asimov, Isaac. *Prelude to Foundation* (Doubleday)
Robots and Empire (Doubleday)
Words from the Myths (NAL)

Associated Press, eds. *World War II: A 50th Anniversary History* (Henry Holt)

Astor, Gerald, et al. *The Baseball Hall of Fame 50th Anniversary Book* (Prentice)

Attenborough, David. *Life on Earth: A Natural History* (Little)

Avraham, Regina. *The Downside of Drugs* (Chelsea House)
Substance Abuse (Chelsea House)

Bailey, Ronald H. *The Air War in Europe* (Silver Burdett)
The Bloodiest Day: The Battle of Antietam (Silver Burdett)
The Home Front: U.S.A. (Silver Burdett)
Prisoners of War (Silver Burdett)

Balanchine, George, and Francis Mason. *101 Stories of the Great Ballets* (Doubleday)

Barker, Ralph. *The RAF at War* (Silver Burdett)

Benedict, Helen. *Safe, Strong, and Streetwise* (Little)

Benton, Barbara. *Ellis Island: A Pictorial History* (Facts on File)

Bergreen, Gary. *Coping with Difficult Teachers* (Rosen)

Berlitz, Charles. *The Bermuda Triangle* (Avon)
The Lost Ship of Noah: In Search of the Ark at Ararat (Putnam)

Bernstein, Carl, and Bob Woodward. *All the President's Men* (Simon & Schuster)

Berry, R. J., and A. Hallam, eds. *The Encyclopedia of Animal Evolution* (Facts on File)
The Best of Life (Crown)

Bethell, Nicolas. *Russia Besieged* (Silver Burdett)
Better Homes and Gardens New Garden Book (Meredith)
Betty Crocker's Cookbook (Western)
Betty Crocker's Step-by-Step Cookbook (Prentice)

Biscardi, Cyrus Henry. *The Storybook of Opera* (Learning Pubs.)

Bishop, Jim. *The Day Christ Died* (Harper)
The Day Lincoln Was Shot (Harper)

Blood-Patterson, Peter, ed. *Rise Up Singing* (Sing Out)

Blum, Arlene. *Annapurna, a Woman's Place* (Sierra)

Blumenson, Martin. *Liberation* (Silver Burdett)

Bode, Janet. *Different Worlds: Interracial and Cross-Cultural Dating* (Watts)

Bohn, Thomas W., and Richard L. Stromgren. *Light and Shadows: A History of Motion Pictures* (Mayfield)

Bombeck, Erma. *At Wit's End* (Fawcett)

The Grass Is Always Greener over the Septic Tank (Fawcett)

I Lost Everything in the Post-Natal Depression (Fawcett)

If Life Is a Bowl of Cherries, What Am I Doing in the Pits? (McGraw)

Just Wait Till You Have Children of Your Own (Fawcett)

Motherhood: The Second Oldest Profession (Dell)

Boston Children's Hospital. *What Teenagers Want to Know about Sex: Questions and Answers* (Little)

Botkin, B. A., ed. *A Treasury of American Folklore: Stories, Ballads, and Traditions of the People* (Bonanza)

Botting, Douglas. *The Giant Airships* (Silver Burdett)

The Second Front (Silver Burdett)

Bouvier, Leon F. *Immigration: Diversity in the U.S.* (Walker)

Bowe-Gutman, Sonia. *Teen Pregnancy* (Lerner)

Boyne, Walter J. *The Smithsonian Book of Flight* (Smithsonian Inst.)

Brondino, Jeanne, et al. *Raising Each Other* (Hunter House)

Brother against Brother: Time-Life Books History of the Civil War (Prentice)

Burgess, Alan. *The Longest Tunnel: The True Story of World War II's Great Escape* (Weidenfeld)

Burton, Jane, and Michael Allaby. *A Dog's Life* (Howell Book House)

Byrde, Penelope. *A Visual History of Costume: The Twentieth Century* (Batsford)

Cahn, Julie. *The Dating Book: A Guide to the Social Scene* (Messner; Simon & Schuster)

Callaham, Steven. *Adrift: Seventy-six Days Lost at Sea* (Houghton; Ballantine)

Campbell, Stu, et al. *The Way to Ski!* (HP Books)

Capotosto, Rosario. *Woodworking Projects for the Home Workshop* (Sterling)

Capps, Benjamin. *The Great Chiefs* (Silver Burdett)

The Indians (Silver Burdett)

Caras, Roger, ed. *Harper's Illustrated Handbook of Cats* (Harper)

Harper's Illustrated Handbook of Dogs (Harper)

Carey, Helen H., and Deborah R. Hankar. *How to Use Your Community as a Resource* (Watts)

Carlin, Richard. *Rock and Roll: 1955–1970* (Facts on File)

Carlson, Dale, and Dan Fitzgibbon. *Manners That Matter for People under 21* (Dutton)

Carson, Rachel. *The Edge of the Sea* (Houghton)

The Sea Around Us (Oxford Univ. Pr.)

Catton, Bruce. *This Hallowed Ground: The Story of the Union Side of the Civil War* (Doubleday; Pocket)

Chaback, Elaine, and Pat Fortunato. *The Official Kids' Survival Kit: How to Do Things on Your Own* (Little)

Chaple, Glenn. *Exploring with a Telescope* (Watts)

Charlton, Jim, and Maria Robbins. *A Christmas Companion: Recipes, Traditions and Customs from around the World* (Putnam)

Chase, Deborah. *The New Medically Based No-Nonsense Beauty Book* (Henry Holt)

Check, William A. *Alzheimer's Disease* (Chelsea House)

Christie, Agatha. *The Mousetrap and Other Plays* (Bantam)

Chute, Marchette. *Shakespeare of London* (Dutton)

Stories from Shakespeare (NAL)

Claypool, Jane. *Unemployment* (Watts)

Clifford, Mike, comp. *The Harmony Illustrated Encyclopedia of Rock* (Harmony)

Cline, Don. *Alias Billy the Kid, the Man Behind the Legend* (Sunstone)

Clurman, Harold, ed. *Famous American Plays of the 1930s* (Dell)

Famous American Plays of the 1960s (Dell)

Coffey, Wayne. *Straight Talk about Drinking: Teenagers Speak Out about Alcohol* (NAL)

Cohen, Shari. *Coping with Being Adopted* (Rosen)

Coping with Failure (Rosen)

Coping with Sibling Rivalry (Rosen)

Cohen, Susan, and Daniel Cohen. *Teenage Stress* (Evans)

Collier, Richard. *War in the Desert* (Silver Burdett)

Collins, Larry, and Dominique Lapierre. *Freedom at Midnight* (Avon)

The Complete Book of Needlecrafts (Chilton)

The Complete Manual of Fitness and Well-Being (Reader's Digest)

Constable, George, ed. *Arabian Peninsula* (Time-Life Books)

Mexico (Time-Life Books)

Consumer Guide Automobile Book: All New 1990 Edition (NAL)

Cook, Roy J., comp. *One Hundred and One Famous Poems* (Contemporary)

Coombs, H. Samm. *Teenage Survival Manual* (Discovery)

Corson, Richard. *Stage Makeup* (Prentice)

Cosby, Bill, et al. *You Are Somebody Special* (McGraw)

Cotterell, Arthur. *The Macmillan Illustrated Encyclopedia of Myths & Legends* (Macmillan)

Cousteau, Jacques, and Alexis Sivirine. *Jacques Cousteau's Calypso* (Abrams)

Crook, Marion. *Teenagers Talk about Suicide* (NC Pr.)

Cross, Milton. *The New Milton Cross' Complete Stories of the Great Operas* (Doubleday)

Crow, Tatu, and Kevin Crow. *Championship Soccer* (Contemporary)

Cunningham, Marion. *The Fannie Farmer Cookbook* (Knopf)

Curtis, Robert H. *Mind and Mood: Understanding and Controlling Your Emotions* (Macmillan)

Dahl, Roald. *Going Solo* (Farrar; Penguin)

Davis, Bertha. *Crisis in Industry: Can America Compete?* (Watts)

Davis, Franklin M., Jr. *Across the Rhine* (Silver Burdett)

Davis, Kenneth C. *Don't Know Much about History: Everything You Need to Know about American History but Never Learned* (Crown)

Day, Carol Olsen, and Edmund Day. *The New Immigrants* (Watts)

DeBarr, Candice M., and Jack A. Bonkowske. *Saga of the American Flag: An Illustrated History* (Harbinger)

Dellar, Fred, and Alan Cackett, eds. *The Harmony Illustrated Encyclopedia of Country Music* (Harmony)

Devaney, John. *Where Are They Today? Great Sport Stars of Yesteryear* (Crown)

Diagram Group. *A Field Guide to Dinosaurs* (Avon)

Dolan, Edward F. *International Drug Traffic* (Watts)

Duncan, David. *Pedaling to the Ends of the Earth* (Simon & Schuster)

Dunkling, Leslie. *Guinness Book of Names* (Sterling)

Ebony Magazine, eds. *Ebony Pictorial History of Black Americans* (Johnson)

Egbert, Barbara. *Action Cheerleading* (Sterling)

Einstein, Charles, ed. *The Fireside Book of Baseball* (Simon & Schuster)

Elson, Robert T. *Prelude to War* (Silver Burdett)

Elting, John R. *Battles for Scandinavia* (Silver Burdett)

Emmens, Carol A. *The Abortion Controversy* (Messner)

Ephron, Della. *Teenage Romance, or How to Die of Embarrassment* (Ballantine)

Erickson, Jon. *Exploring Earth from Space* (TAB)

Fast, Howard. *The Jews: Story of a People* (Dell)

Fiedler, Jean, and Hal Fiedler. *Be Smart about Sex: Facts for Young People* (Enslow)

Fisher, Trevor. *The 1960s* (Batsford)

Fishman, Ross. *Alcohol and Alcoholism* (Chelsea House)

Football Register (Sporting News)

Foster, John, comp. *Let's Celebrate: Festival Poems* (Oxford Univ. Pr.)

Foster, Rory C. *Dr. Wildlife* (Watts)

   I Never Met an Animal I Didn't Like (Watts)

Franck, Irene M., and David M. Brownstone.
   Artists and Artisans (Facts on File)
   Builders (Facts on File)
   Clothiers (Facts on File)
   Communicators (Facts on File)
   Financiers and Traders (Facts on File)
   Harvesters (Facts on File)
   Healers (Facts on File)
   Helpers and Aides (Facts on File)
   Leaders and Lawyers (Facts on File)
   Manufacturers and Miners (Facts on File)
   Performers and Players (Facts on File)
   Restaurateurs and Innkeepers (Facts on File)
   Scholars and Priests (Facts on File)
   Scientists and Technologists (Facts on File)
   Warriors & Adventurers (Facts on File)

Frankel, Marvin E. *Out of the Shadows of Night: The Struggle for International Human Rights* (Delacorte)

Fritz, Jean. *China Homecoming* (Putnam)

Fuller, John. *Prescription for Better Home Video Movies: How to Avoid the Most Common Mistakes* (Price/Stern/Sloan)

Gall, Meredith D., and Joyce P. Gall. *Study for Success* (Damien)

Gallo, Donald R., ed. *Center Stage: One-Act Plays for Teenage Readers & Actors* (Harper)

Garber, Angus. *End Zone: A Photographic Celebration of Football* (Henry Holt)

Gardner, Robert. *The Young Athlete's Manual* (Messner)

Garraty, John A. *1,001 Things Everyone Should Know about American History* (Doubleday)

Gelinas, Paul J. *Coping with Shyness* (Rosen)

George, M. B. *Basic Sailing* (Morrow)

Gersh, Marvin J. *The Handbook of Adolescence: A Medical Guide for Parents and Teenagers* (Scarborough House)

Gibson, William. *The Miracle Worker* (Knopf; Bantam)

Gies, Miep, and Alison Leslie Gold. *Anne Frank Remembered: The Story of the Woman Who Helped to Hide the Frank Family* (Simon & Schuster)

Gilbert, Richard J. *Caffeine: The Most Popular Stimulant* (Chelsea House)

Glenn, Mel. *Back to Class* (Clarion)
   Class Dismissed (Clarion)
   Class Dismissed II (Clarion)

Glossbrenner, Alfred. *The Complete Handbook*

of Personal Computer Communications (St. Martin's)

Goldston, Robert. *The Sword of the Prophet* (Dial)

The Good Housekeeping Illustrated Cookbook (Hearst)

Graeber, Laurel. *Are You Dying for a Drink?* (Messner)

Gragg, Rod. *The Civil War Quiz and Fact Book* (Harper)

The Old West Quiz and Fact Book (Harper)

Grant, Richard, and Nigel Thomas. *BMX Action Bike Book* (Arco)

Greenberg, Martin H., and Mark J. Sabljak. *Who's Who in the Super Bowls* (Dembner Books)

Greenberg, Stan. *The Guinness Book of Olympics Records* (Bantam)

Greenfeld, Howard. *Books: From Writer to Reader* (Crown)

Greenwald, Dorothy. *Coping with Moving* (Rosen)

Griffin, John Howard. *Black Like Me* (NAL)

Grosshandler, Janet. *Coping with Verbal Abuse* (Rosen)

Guinness Sports Record Book, 1989–90 (Sterling)

Gunston, Bill, et al. *Guinness Book of Speed Facts and Feats* (Sterling)

Gunther, John. *Death Be Not Proud* (Harper)

Gunther, Marc, and Bill Carter. *Monday Night Mayhem: The Inside Story of ABC's Monday Night Football* (Morrow)

Haley, Alex. *Roots* (Doubleday; Dell)

Hammerslough, Jane. *Everything You Need to Know about Teen Motherhood* (Rosen)

Hanmer, Trudy. *The Growth of Cities* (Watts)

Hansberry, Lorraine. *A Raisin in the Sun: A Drama in Three Acts* (Random)

Hargrove, Hondon. *Buffalo Soldiers in Italy: Black Americans in World War II* (McFarland)

Hart, William B. *The United States and World Trade* (Watts)

Heckman, Philip. *The Magic of Holography* (Macmillan)

Heinonen, Janet. *Sports Illustrated Running for Women* (NAL)

Heintze, Carl. *Medical Ethics* (Watts)

Herbst, Dan. *Sports Illustrated Soccer* (NAL)

Herriot, James. *James Herriot's Dog Stories* (St. Martin's)

Herzstein, Robert Edwin. *The Nazis* (Silver Burdett)

Hobson, Burton. *Stamp Collecting for Beginners* (Wilshire)

Hocken, Sheila. *Emma and I* (Dutton)

Honig, Donald. *The World Series: An Illustrated History from 1903 to the Present* (Crown)

Hoose, Philip M. *Hoosiers: The Fabulous Basketball Life of Indiana* (Random)

Hoppel, Joe. *The Series: An Illustrated History of Baseball's Postseason Showcase* (Sporting News)

Horn, Huston. *The Pioneers* (Silver Burdett)

House, Tom. *The Winning Pitcher: Baseball's Top Pitchers Demonstrate What It Takes to Be an Ace* (Contemporary)

Howarth, David. *The Voyage of the Armada* (Penguin)

Hyde, Margaret O., and Elizabeth H. Forsyth. *AIDS: What Does It Mean to You?* (Walker)

Terrorism: A Special Kind of Violence (Dodd)

Ignoffo, Matthew. *Coping with Your Inner Critic* (Rosen)

Images of America: A Panorama of History in Photographs (Smithsonian Inst.)

Iritz, Maxine Haren. *Science Fair: Developing a Successful and Fun Project* (TAB)

Jackson, Donald Dale. *The Aeronauts* (Silver Burdett)

Underground Worlds (Silver Burdett)

Jackson, Michael. *Moonwalk* (Doubleday)

Janeczko, Paul B., ed. *Don't Forget to Fly: A Cycle of Modern Poems* (Bradbury)

Going Over to Your Place: Poems for Each Other (Macmillan)

Janson, H. W., and Anthony F. Janson. *History of Art for Young People* (Abrams)

Jarrett, William. *Timelines of Sports History: Baseball* (Facts on File)

Timelines of Sports History: Football (Facts on File)

Javna, John. *Cult TV: A Viewer's Guide to the Shows America Can't Live Without!* (St. Martin's)

Johanson, Chris-Ellyn. *Cocaine: A New Epidemic* (Chelsea House)

Johnson, Linda Carlson. *Responsibility* (Rosen)

Johnson, William Weber. *The Forty-niners* (Silver Burdett)

Jones, Constance. *Karen Horney* (Chelsea House)

Jones, Dick. *Spider* (Facts on File)

Jordan, Pat. *Sports Illustrated Pitching* (NAL)

Jorgensen, Donald G., Jr., and June A. Jorgensen. *Secrets Told by Children of Alcoholics* (TAB)

Jussim, Daniel. *Drug Tests and Polygraphs: Essential Tools or Violations of Privacy?* (Messner)

Katakis, Michael. *The Vietnam Veterans Memorial* (Crown)

Katz, William Loren. *The Black West* (Open Hand)

Keller, Helen. *The Story of My Life* (Doubleday; Airmont)

Kerr, Jean. *Please Don't Eat the Daisies* (Fawcett)

Ketels, Hank, and Jack McDowell. *Sports Illustrated Scuba Diving* (NAL)

Kindall, Jerry. *Sports Illustrated Baseball* (NAL)

King, Martin Luther, Jr. *Why We Can't Wait* (NAL)

Kliment, Bud. *Billie Holiday* (Chelsea House)

Kolodny, Nancy J. *When Food's a Foe: How to Confront and Conquer Eating Disorders* (Little)

Kosof, Anna. *Incest: Families in Crisis* (Watts)
Why Me? Coping with Family Illness (Watts)

Kronenwetter, Michael. *Managing Toxic Wastes* (Messner)

Laiken, Deidre S., and Alan J. Schneider. *Listen to Me, I'm Angry* (Lothrop)

Lambert, David. *A Field Guide to Dinosaurs* (Avon)

Lamm, Kathryn. *10,000 Ideas for Term Papers, Projects, and Reports* (Arco)

Lampton, Christopher. *CD ROMs* (Watts)
Predicting Nuclear and Other Technological Disasters (Watts)

Landon, Margaret. *Anna and the King of Siam* (Harper)

LeBaron, John, and Philip Miller. *Portable Video: A Production Guide for Young People* (Prentice)

Leder, Jane Mersky. *Dead Serious: A Book for Teenagers about Teenage Suicide* (Macmillan)

Lee, Essie E., and Richard Wortman. *Down Is Not Out: Teenagers and Depression* (Messner)

Leeds, Robert X. *All the Comforts of Home: The Story of the First Pet Motel* (Dodd)

Lenburg, Jeff. *Baseball's All-Star Game: A Game-by-Game Guide* (McFarland)

Lens, Sidney. *Strikemakers & Strikebreakers* (Dutton)

Lerner, Alan Jay. *My Fair Lady* (NAL)

Leroi-Gourhan, Andre. *The Hunters of Prehistory* (Macmillan)

Levine, Mel. *Keeping a Head in School: A Student's Book about Learning Abilities and Learning Disorders* (Educators Publ.)

Levine, Saul, and Kathleen Wilcox. *Dear Doctor* (Lothrop)

Life Goes to War: A Picture History of World War II (Pocket)

Lindsay, Jeanne Warren. *Teenage Marriage: Coping with Reality* (Morning Glory Pr.)

Lord, Walter. *Day of Infamy* (Bantam)
The Miracle of Dunkirk (Penguin)
A Night to Remember (Bantam)
A Time to Stand (Univ. of Nebraska Pr.)

Macaulay, David. *The Way Things Work* (Houghton)

McCoy, Kathleen. *Coping with Teenage Depression* (NAL)

McCoy, Kathleen, and Charles Wibbelsman. *The New Teenage Body Book* (HP Books)

McCuen, Gary E. *The International Drug Trade* (GEM)
Militarizing Space (GEM)
Religion and Politics: Issues in Religious Liberty (GEM)
The Religious Right (GEM)

McFarland, Rhoda. *Coping through Self-Esteem* (Rosen)
Coping with Substance Abuse (Rosen)

McGee, Dorothy H. *Framers of the Constitution* (Putnam)

McGuire, Paula. *Putting It Together: Teenagers Talk about Family Breakups* (Delacorte)

McGurn, James. *On Your Bicycle: An Illustrated History of Cycling* (Facts on File)

Mackay, James. *The Guinness Book of Stamps, Facts and Feats* (Guinness)

McWhirter, Norris, et al., eds. *Guinness Book of World Records* (Sterling)

Maddocks, Melvin. *The Atlantic Crossing* (Silver Burdett)

Manning, Harvey. *Backpacking One Step at a Time* (Random)

Margulies, Alice. *Compassion* (Rosen)

Marks, Lillian S. *Touch Typing Made Simple* (Doubleday)

Martin, Pol. *Easy Cooking for Today* (Brimar)

Mast, Gerald. *A Short History of the Movies* (Macmillan)

Mathews, Jay. *Escalante: The Best Teacher in America* (Henry Holt)

Mazer, Norma Fox, and Marjorie Lewis, eds. *Waltzing on Water* (Dell)

Meltzer, Milton. *Bread and Roses: The Struggle of American Labor* (Facts on File)
Brother, Can You Spare a Dime? (Facts on File)
The Landscape of Memory (Viking)
The Truth about the Ku Klux Klan (Watts)

Mendheim, Beverly. *Ritchie Valens: The First Latino Rocker* (Bilingual Pr.)

Meyer, Nicholas E. *Magic in the Dark: A Young Viewer's History of the Movies* (Facts on File)

Miles, Bernard. *Favorite Tales from Shakespeare* (Macmillan)

Miller, Arthur. *The Crucible* (Penguin)

Miller, Johnny, and Desmond Tolhurst. *Johnny Miller's Golf for Juniors* (Doubleday)

Miller, Robert M. *Most of My Patients Are Animals* (Eriksson)

Miller, Russell. *The Commandos* (Silver Burdett)

Monk, Lorraine. *Photographs That Changed the World* (Doubleday)

Moore, Patrick. *The Guinness Book of Astronomy* (Sterling)

More Joy of Photography (Addison-Wesley)

Morris, Desmond. *Catlore* (Crown)
  Catwatching (Crown)
  Dogwatching (Crown)

Morris, Jeannie. *Brian Piccolo: A Short Season* (Dell)

Mosley, Leonard. *Battle of Britain* (Silver Burdett)

Mowat, Farley. *The Boat Who Wouldn't Float* (Bantam)
  Grey Seas Under (Bantam)
  Never Cry Wolf (Bantam)
  The People of the Deer (Bantam)
  A Whale for the Killing (Bantam)

Murrells, Joseph. *Million Selling Records from the 1900s to the 1980s* (Arco)

Namath, Joe. *Football for Young Players and Parents* (Simon & Schuster)

Nash, Ogden. *The Pocket Book of Ogden Nash* (Pocket)

National Board of Review of Motion Pictures, eds. *The 500 Best American Films to Buy, Rent, or Videotape* (Morrow)

Neil, Randy L., and Elaine Hart. *The All-New Official Cheerleader's Handbook* (Simon & Schuster)

Nevin, David. *Architects of Air Power* (Silver Burdett)
  The Expressmen (Silver Burdett)
  The Mexican War (Silver Burdett)
  The Pathfinders (Silver Burdett)
  The Soldiers (Silver Burdett)

Newton, David E. *Science Ethics* (Watts)

Nourse, Alan E. *Birth Control* (Watts)
  Herpes (Watts)

Nye, Peter. *Hearts of Lions: The History of American Bicycle Racing* (Norton)

Obojski, Robert. *Baseball's Strangest Moments* (Sterling)

O'Neil, Paul. *The Frontiersmen* (Silver Burdett)

Osborn, Bob. *The Complete Book of BMX* (Harper)

Page, Jake. *Arid Lands* (Silver Burdett)

Palmer, E. Laurence. *Fieldbook of Natural History* (McGraw)

Papashvily, George, and Helen Papashvily. *Anything Can Happen* (St. Martin's)

Pareles, Jon, and Patricia Romanowski, eds. *The Rolling Stone Encyclopedia of Rock & Roll* (Summit)

Parks-McKay, Jane. *The Make-Over: A Teen's Guide to Looking & Feeling Beautiful* (Morrow)

Pascoe, Elaine. *Racial Prejudice* (Watts)

Peary, Danny, ed. *Cult Baseball Players: The Greats, the Flakes, the Weird, and the Wonderful* (Simon & Schuster)

Peck, Richard E. *Something for Joey* (Bantam)

Pellant, Chris, and Roger Phillips. *Rocks, Minerals & Fossils of the World* (Little)

Petrick, Tim. *Sports Illustrated Skiing* (Harper)

Pezzano, Chuck, and Herm Weiskopf. *Sports Illustrated Bowling* (NAL)

Phillips, Carolyn E. *Michelle* (NAL)

Pinsent, John. *Greek Mythology* (Bedrick)

Pogue, William R. *How Do You Go to the Bathroom in Space?* (Tor)

Poole, Robert M., ed. *The Incredible Machine* (National Geographic)
  Nature's Wonderlands: National Parks of the World (National Geographic)

Porter, Martin. *The Complete Guide to Making Home Video Movies* (Pocket)

Prendergast, Curtis. *The First Aviators* (Silver Burdett)

Raynor, Thomas. *Terrorism: Past, Present, Future* (Watts)

Reader's Digest ABC's of the Human Body: A Family Answer Book (Reader's Digest)

Reader's Digest America's Historic Places (Reader's Digest)

The Reader's Digest Illustrated Book of Dogs (Reader's Digest)

Reader's Digest Illustrated Guide to Gardening (Reader's Digest)

The Reader's Digest Illustrated History of World War II: The World at Arms (Reader's Digest)

Reader's Digest, eds. *Our National Parks* (Reader's Digest)

Reisfeld, Randi. *So You Want to Be a Star: A Teenager's Guide to Breaking into Show Business* (Pocket)

Remarkable Animals: A Unique Encyclopedia of Wildlife Wonders (Guinness)

Reynolds, Barbara. *And Still We Rise: Interviews with 50 Black Role Models* (USA Today Books)

Richards, Arlene Kramer, and Irene Willis. *Boy Friends, Girl Friends, Just Friends* (Macmillan)

Riehm, Sarah. *The Teenage Entrepreneur's Guide: 50 Money-Making Business Ideas* (Surrey Books)

Rinzler, Jane. *Teens Speak Out* (Donald I. Fine)

Riva, Peter, comp. *Sightseeing: A Space Panorama* (Knopf)

Robert, Henry M. III. *The Scott, Foresman Robert's Rules of Order* (Scott, Foresman)

Robertson, Dougal. *Survive the Savage Sea* (Sheridan)

Robertson, James I., Jr. *Tenting Tonight: The Soldier's Life* (Silver Burdett)

Robertson, Patrick. *Guinness Film Facts and Feats* (Guinness)

Rodgers, Joann Ellison. *Drugs & Sexual Behavior* (Chelsea House)

Ronan, Colin, and Storm Dunlop. *The Skywatcher's Handbook* (Random)

Rooney, Andy. *A Few Minutes with Andy Rooney* (Warner)

Rosenberg, Stephen N. *The Johnson & Johnson First Aid Book* (Warner)

Rosenfeld, Arthur. *Exotic Animals as Pets* (Simon & Schuster)

Rovin, Jeff. *The Encyclopedia of Monsters* (Facts on File)

Rowe, Peter. *American Football: The Records* (Sterling)

Sabbagh, Karl. *Skyscraper* (Viking)

Sagan, Carl. *Cosmos* (Random; Ballantine)

Salinger, Margaretta. *Masterpieces of American Painting in the Metropolitan Museum of Art* (Metropolitan Museum of Art)

Sandoz, Mari. *Cheyenne Autumn* (Avon)

Santos, Jim, and Ken Shannon. *Sports Illustrated Trace: Championship Field Events* (NAL)

Sarrantonio, Al, ed. *Fireside Treasury of Great Humor* (Simon & Schuster)

Schaffer, Moselle. *Camel Lot: The True Story of a Zoo-Illogical Farm* (Viking)

Scott, Robert L. *God Is My Co-Pilot* (Ballantine)

Segal, Lore. *The Book of Adam to Moses* (Random)

Severn, Bill. *Bill Severn's Best Magic: 50 Top Tricks to Entertain and Amaze Your Friends on All Occasions* (Stackpole)

Sheahan, Casey. *Sports Illustrated Cross-Country Skiing* (NAL)

Shelley, Purrey B. *Cat-a-Log* (Putnam)

Shenkman, Richard. *Legends, Lies, and Cherished Myths of American History* (Morrow)

Shields, Brooke. *On Your Own* (Random)

Shipman, David. *A Pictorial History of Science Fiction Films* (Salem House)

Shuker-Haines, Frances. *Everything you Should Know about Date Rape* (Rosen)

Simon, Neil. *Broadway Bound* (Random)

Simonides, Carol, and Diane Gage. *I'll Never Walk Alone: The Inspiring Story of a Teenager's Struggle Against Cancer* (Jove)

Simons, Gerald. *Victory in Europe* (Silver Burdett)

Simpson, Carolyn. *Coping with an Unplanned Pregnancy* (Rosen)

Slater, Peter J., ed. *The Encyclopedia of Animal Behavior* (Facts on File)

Smith, Susan Rogerson. *Cheerleader-Baton Twirler* (Tor)

Spangenburg, Ray, and Diane Moser. *Opening the Space Frontier* (Facts on File)

Specht, Robert. *Tisha* (Bantam)

Spence, Annette. *Exercise* (Facts on File)
Stress & Mental Health (Facts on File)

Sperling, Abraham, and Monroe Stuart. *Mathematics Made Simple* (Doubleday)

Steinberg, Rafael. *Island Fighting* (Silver Burdett)
Return to the Philippines (Silver Burdett)

Steltzer, Ulli. *The New Americans: Immigrant Life in Southern California* (NewSage)

Stokes, Donald, and Lillian Stokes. *The Bird Feeder Book* (Little)

Story of the Great American West (Reader's Digest)

Strauss, Linda L. *Coping When a Parent Has Cancer* (Rosen)

Stuart, Jesse. *The Thread That Runs So True* (Macmillan)

Stwertka, Eve, and Albert Stwertka. *Genetic Engineering* (Watts)

Sullivan, Tom. *If You Could See What I Hear* (NAL)

Tanner, Ogden. *The Canadians* (Silver Burdett)
The Ranchers (Silver Burdett)

Taylor, David. *You & Your Cat* (Knopf)

Taylor, David, and Peter Scott. *You & Your Dog* (Knopf)

Taylor, L. B., and C. L. Taylor. *Chemical and Biological Warfare* (Watts)

Ten Boom, Corrie, and John Sherrill. *The Hiding Place* (Bantam)

Thapar, Valmik. *Tiger: Portrait of a Predator* (Facts on File)

Thompson, Ernest. *On Golden Pond* (NAL)

Thubron, Colin. *The Ancient Mariners* (Time-Life)

The Time-Life Book of Christmas (Prentice)

Time-Life Books, eds. *Canada* (Silver Burdett)
China (Silver Burdett)
Christmas in America (Silver Burdett)
Dragons (Silver Burdett)
East Africa (Silver Burdett)
France (Silver Burdett)
Ghosts (Silver Burdett)
Japan at War (Silver Burdett)
Lee Takes Command: From Seven Days to Second Bull Run (Silver Burdett)
The Loggers (Silver Burdett)
The Railroaders (Silver Burdett)
Southeast Asia (Silver Burdett)
The Soviet Union (Silver Burdett)
The Spanish West (Silver Burdett)
The United States (Silver Burdett)
Volcano (Silver Burdett)
The Women (Silver Burdett)

Tinkle, Lon. *The Alamo* (NAL)

Trapp, Maria Augusta. *The Story of the Trapp Family Singers* (Doubleday)

Valens, E. G. *The Other Side of the Mountain* (Harper)

Van der Plas, Rob. *The Bicycle Repair Book* (Bicycle Books)

Van Devanter, Lynda. *Home before Morning* (Warner)

Vaughan, Andrew. *Who's Who in New Country Music* (St. Martin's)

Vedral, Joyce L. *My Parents Are Driving Me Crazy* (Ballantine)

Voss, Jacqueline, and Jay Gale. *A Young Woman's Guide to Sex* (Henry Holt)

Walker, Bryce. *The Armada* (Time-Life)
Earthquake (Silver Burdett)

Wallace, Robert. *The Miners* (Silver Burdett)

Wallechinsky, David. *The Complete Book of the Olympics* (Viking; Penguin)

Ward, Ed, et al., comps. *Rock of Ages: The Rolling Stone History of Rock & Roll* (Summit)

Weber, Jack. *Computers: The Next Generation* (Arco)

Weiss, Ann E. *Bioethics: Dilemmas in Modern Medicine* (Enslow)

Wernick, Robert. *Blitzkrieg* (Silver Burdett)

Weston, Carol. *Girltalk about Guys* (Harper)

Wheeler, Keith. *The Alaskans* (Silver Burdett)
The Scouts (Silver Burdett)
The Townsmen (Silver Burdett)

Whipple, A. B. C. *The Clipper Ships* (Silver Burdett)
Fighting Sail (Time-Life)
Restless Oceans (Silver Burdett)

Whitfield, Philip, ed. *The Macmillan Illustrated Encyclopedia of Birds: A Visual Who's Who in the World of Birds* (Macmillan)

Whitney, Sharon, and Tom Raynor. *Women in Politics* (Watts)

Whittingham, Richard, ed. *Life in Sports: A Pictorial History of Sports* (Harper)

Wilder, Thornton. *Three Plays by Thornton Wilder* (Harper)

Williams, Tennessee. *My Glass Menagerie* (NAL)

Wiswell, Phil. *Kids' Games: Traditional Indoor and Outdoor Activities for Children* (Doubleday)

Wood, Gerald L. *Guinness Book of Pet Records* (Sterling)

Woods, Samuel G. *Everything You Need to Know about Sexually Transmitted Disease* (Rosen)

WW II: Time-Life Books History of the Second World War (Silver Burdett)

Worth, Fred L. *Rock Facts* (Facts on File)

Yenne, Bill, and Susan Garratt. *Pictorial History of the North American Indian* (Exeter)

Ying, Mildred, et al., eds. *The New Good Housekeeping Cookbook* (Hearst)

Yolen, Jane, ed. *Favorite Folktales from Around the World* (Pantheon)

Your United Nations: The Official Guidebook. (United Nations Pubs.)

Zich, Arthur. *The Rising Sun* (Silver Burdett)

Zindel, Paul. *The Effect of Gamma Rays on Man-in-the-Moon Marigolds* (Harper; Bantam)

Author Index

Authors are arranged alphabetically by last name. Authors' and joint authors' names are followed by book titles—which are also arranged alphabetically—and the text entry number. Book titles may refer to those that appear as a main entry or as an internal entry in the text. All fiction titles are indicated by (F), following the entry number.

Aaron, Chester. *Lackawanna*, 1(F)
Out of Sight, Out of Mind, 2(F)
Aaseng, Nathan. *Baseball, It's Your Team*, 5549
Baseball's Ace Relief Pitchers, 3948
Baseball's Brilliant Managers, 3948
Baseball's Hottest Hitters, 3949
Baseball's Power Hitters, 3949
Basketball's Power Players, 5569
Better Mousetraps, 3022
Bob Dylan, 3711
College Football's Hottest Rivalries, 5606
Football's Crushing Blockers, 3950
Football's Incredible Bulks, 5606
Football's Super Bowl Champions, I–XVI, 5607
The Inventors, 4702
Midstream Changes, 3023
More with Less, 3744
Pro Sports' Greatest Rivalries, 5519
Record Breakers of Pro Sports, 5520
Steve Carlton, 3957
Ultramarathons, 5666
World-Class Marathoners, 3951
You Are the Coach, 5608
You Are the Manager, 5550
Abbott, R. Tucker. *Seashells of North America*, 5022
Seashells of the World, 5023
Abebe, Daniel. *Ethiopia in Pictures*, 4299
Abels, Harriette S. *Strangers on NMA-6*, 2258(F)
Acheson, Patricia C. *Our Federal Government*, 2760
Adair, Gene. *George Washington Carver*, 3915
Adams, Barbara Johnston. *Crime Mysteries*, 2975
Adams, Florence. *Catch a Sunbeam*, 4712
Adams, Richard. *Watership Down*, 1356(F)
Adderholdt-Elliott, Miriam. *Perfectionism*, 3448
Adkins, Jan. *How a House Happens*, 5244
A Storm without Rain, 1357(F)

Adler, C. S. *Binding Ties*, 862(F)
Carly's Buck, 191(F)
Eddie's Blue-Winged Dragon, 684(F)
Footsteps on the Stairs, 862(F)
Ghost Brother, 400(F)
If You Need Me, 401(F)
In Our House Scott Is My Brother, 402(F)
Kiss the Clown, 863(F)
The Lump in the Middle, 2117(F)
Roadside Valentine, 864(F)
The Shell Lady's Daughter, 403(F)
With Westie and the Tin Man, 865(F)
Adler, David. *We Remember the Holocaust*, 4237
Adler, Irene. *Ballooning*, 5542
Adler, Irit. *Picture Puzzles for the Super Smart*, 5483
Adler, Irving. *How Life Began*, 5064
Adoff, Arnold, ed. *I Am the Darker Brother*, 2534
My Black Me, 2535
Aesop. *Aesop's Fables*, 2633
Afanasiev, Alexander. *Words of Wisdom*, 2588
Agard, John, comp. *Life Doesn't Frighten Me at All*, 2491
Agel, Jerome (jt. author). *The Congress*, 2781
The Presidency, 2775
The Supreme Court, 2817
Aho, Jennifer. *Learning about Sexual Abuse*, 3411
Aiken, Joan. *Bridle the Wind*, 1948(F)
Died on a Rainy Sunday, 1947(F)
Give Yourself a Fright, 1776(F)
Go Saddle the Sea, 1948(F)
Midnight Is a Place, 3(F)
Return to Harken House, 1777(F)
The Shadow Guests, 1358(F)
The Stolen Lake, 1359(F)
The Teeth of the Gale, 1948(F)
A Touch of Chill, 1778(F)

Cole, Wendy M. *Vietnam,* 4359
Coles, Joan M. (jt. author). *Emily Post Talks with Teens about Manners and Etiquette,* 3442
Collier, Christopher (jt. author). *The Bloody Country,* 1639(F)
Jump Ship to Freedom, 1654(F)
My Brother Sam Is Dead, 1655(F)
War Comes to Willy Freeman, 1654(F)
Who Is Carrie? 1654(F)
The Winter Hero, 1639(F)
Collier, James Lincoln. *The Bloody Country,* 1639(F)
Jump Ship to Freedom, 1654(F)
Louis Armstrong, 3705
My Brother Sam Is Dead, 1655(F)
Outside Looking In, 452(F)
The Teddy Bear Habit, 1870(F)
War Comes to Willy Freeman, 1654(F)
When the Stars Begin to Fall, 31(F)
Who Is Carrie? 1654(F)
The Winchesters, 942(F)
The Winter Hero, 1639(F)
Colligan, Louise. *The A+ Guide to Book Reports,* 3057
The A+ Guide to Good Grades, 3057
The A+ Guide to Good Writing, 3057
The A+ Guide to Research and Term Papers, 3057
The A+ Guide to Studying, 3057
The A+ Guide to Taking Tests, 3057
Collins, David R. *Grover Cleveland,* 3807
Woodrow Wilson, 3855
Collins, Donald (jt. author). *Under the High Seas,* 5142
Collins, Michael. *Flying to the Moon, and Other Strange Places,* 4774
Collins, Tom. *Jane Fonda,* 3713
Collura, Mary-Ellen Lang. *Winners,* 202(F)
Colman, Hila. *Diary of a Frantic Kid Sister,* 453(F)
The Double Life of Angela Jones, 943(F)
Forgotten Girl, 454(F)
A Fragile Love, 456(F)
Happily Ever After, 709(F)
Just the Two of Us, 455(F)
Nobody Told Me What I Need to Know, 456(F)
Not for Love, 944(F)
Remind Me Not to Fall in Love, 2145(F)
Rich and Famous Like My Mom, 457(F)
Sometimes I Don't Love My Mother, 458(F)
Suddenly, 945(F)
Weekend Sisters, 459(F)
Colman, Warren. *Understanding and Preventing AIDS,* 3194
Colum, Padraic. *The Children of Odin,* 2657
Columbu, Franco. *Weight Training and Bodybuilding,* 5585

Commager, Henry Steele. *The Great Constitution,* 2763
The Great Declaration, 4588
Conant, Roger. *A Field Guide to Reptiles and Amphibians of Eastern and Central North America,* 4895
A Field Guide to Western Reptiles and Amphibians, 4895
Condit, Erin. *The Duvaliers,* 4114
Condon, Judith. *The Pressure to Take Drugs,* 3124
Cone, Ferne Geller. *Classy Knitting,* 5412
Conford, Ellen. *The Alfred G. Graebner Memorial High School Handbook of Rules and Regulations,* 1871(F)
And This Is Laura, 1390(F)
Dear Lovey Hart, 1872(F)
Genie with the Light Blue Hair, 1873(F)
If This Is Love, I'll Take Spaghetti, 2146(F)
Lenny Kendell, Smart Aleck, 1874(F)
A Royal Pain, 1875(F)
Seven Days to Be a Brand-New Me, 1876(F)
Strictly for Laughs, 1877(F)
The Things I Did for Love, 1878(F)
To All My Fans, with Love, from Sylvie, 710(F)
We Interrupt This Semester for an Important Bulletin, 1872(F)
Why Me? 1879(F)
You Never Can Tell, 946(F)
Conley, Kevin. *Benjamin Banneker,* 3911
Connatty, Mary. *The Armada,* 4410
Connolly, Peter. *The Legend of Odysseus,* 2636
Tiberius Claudius Maximus, 4214(F)
Connors, Patricia. *Runaways,* 3428
Conrad, Pam. *Holding Me Here,* 460(F)
My Daniel, 461(F)
Prairie Songs, 1696(F)
Stonewords, 1798(F)
Taking the Ferry Home, 462(F)
What I Did for Roman, 947(F)
Cook, Fred J. *The Ku Klux Klan,* 2847
Cook, Marjorie. *To Walk on Two Feet,* 711(F)
Cook, T. S. (jt. author). *Mary Jane Harper Cried Last Night,* 770(F)
Cool, Joyce. *The Kidnapping of Courtney Van Allan and What's Her Name,* 32(F)
Coolidge, Olivia. *Greek Myths,* 2637
The Trojan War, 4209
Coombs, Charles. *All-Terrain Bicycling,* 5580
BMX, 5581
Ultralights, 5340
Cooney, Caroline B. *Among Friends,* 948(F)
The Face on the Milk Carton, 463(F)
Family Reunion, 1880(F)
The Fire, 1799(F)
The Fog, 1799(F)
The Girl Who Invented Romance, 2147(F)
Last Dance, 948(F)
The Snow, 1799(F)

Quin-Harkin, Janet. *Big Sister,* 1222(F)
Dear Cousin, 2222(F)
Flip Side, 2223(F)
The Great Boy Chase, 2224(F)
The Last Dance, 2222(F)
101 Ways to Meet Mr. Right, 2224(F)
One Step Too Far, 2225(F)
Out in the Cold, 1222(F)
Trading Places, 2226(F)
Wanted, 2224(F)
Quiri, Patricia Ryon. *Dating,* 3466

Raber, Thomas R. *Election Night,* 2836
Presidential Campaign, 2836
Rabinowitz, Ann. *Knight on Horseback,* 1838(F)
Rachlis, Eugene. *Indians of the Plains,* 4560
Radford, Ken. *The Cellar,* 1839(F)
Radley, Gail. *CF in His Corner,* 818(F)
Ragan, John David. *Emiliano Zapata,* 4118
Ragsdale, Bruce A. *The House of Representatives,* 2804
Raham, R. Gary. *Dinosaurs in the Garden,* 4844
Rahn, Joan Elma. *Animals That Changed History,* 4193
Ears, Hearing, and Balance, 3307
Eyes and Seeing, 3308
Keeping Warm, Keeping Cool, 4915
More Plants That Changed History, 4880
Rainis, Kenneth G. *Nature Projects for Young Scientists,* 4736
Ranahan, Demerris C. *Contributions of Women,* 3247
Rand, Gloria. *Salty Dog,* 258(F)
Rand, Suzanne. *The Boy She Left Behind,* 2227(F)
The Good Luck Girl, 2228(F)
Randall, Florence Engel. *All the Sky Together,* 142(F)
Randall, Marta. *John F. Kennedy,* 3823
Randolph, Blythe. *Amelia Earhart,* 3633
Charles Lindbergh, 3638
Randolph, Sallie. *Gerald R. Ford, President,* 3812
Richard M. Nixon, President, 3835
Randolph, Sallie G. (jt. author). *Shaker Inventions,* 2696
Ransom, Candice F. *Sabrina,* 2229(F)
Thirteen, 1927(F)
Raphael, Elaine (jt. author). *Drawing Fashions,* 5402
Rapp, George F. *Earth's Chemical Clues,* 5081
Rardin, Susan Lowry. *Captives in a Foreign Land,* 143(F)
Raskin, Ellen. *The Tattooed Potato and Other Clues,* 2079(F)
The Westing Game, 2080(F)
Rau, Margaret. *Holding Up the Sky,* 4340
The Minority Peoples of China, 4341

Young Women in China, 4342
Rawcliffe, Michael. *Lenin,* 4095
Rawlings, Marjorie Kinnan. *The Yearling,* 259(F)
Rawls, Wilson. *Summer of the Monkeys,* 260(F)
Where the Red Fern Grows, 261(F)
Ray, Delia. *Gold! The Klondike Adventure,* 4462
A Nation Torn, 4615
Raynor, Thomas. *Politics, Power, and People,* 2759
Terrorism, 3014
Rayson, Ann. *Modern Hawaiian History,* 4694
Reading, J. P. *The Summer of Sassy Jo,* 622(F)
Reed, Don C. *Sevengill,* 5021
Reed, Kit. *The Ballad of T. Rantula,* 623(F)
Reeder, Carolyn. *Shades of Gray,* 1683(F)
Rees, Clair (jt. author). *The Hiker's Bible,* 5594
Rehder, Harold A. *The Audubon Society Field Guide to North American Seashells,* 5027
Reichler, Joseph L., ed. *The Baseball Encyclopedia,* 5563
Reid, George K. *Pond Life,* 5010
Reiff, Stephanie Ann. *Visions of the Future,* 5511
Reilly, Pat. *Kidnap in San Juan,* 144(F)
Reimers, David M. *The Immigrant Experience,* 2876
Reinfeld, Fred. *A Catalogue of the World's Most Popular Coins,* 5468
Reiser, Howard. *Skateboarding,* 5539
Reiss, Johanna. *The Journey Back,* 4134
The Upstairs Room, 4134
Reit, Ann. *The First Time,* 2230(F)
I Thought You Were My Best Friend, 1223(F)
Remini, Robert V. *The Revolutionary Age of Andrew Jackson,* 4606
Rench, Janice E. *Teen Sexuality,* 3406
Rench, Janice E. (jt. author). *Feeling Safe, Feeling Strong,* 3417
Renowden, Gareth. *Video,* 5327
Resnick, Abraham. *Russia,* 4421
Reyero, Carlos. *The Key to Art from Romanticism to Impressionism,* 3547
Reynolds, Alfred. *Kiteman,* 1501(F)
Kiteman of Karanga, 1501(F)
Reynolds, Quentin. *Custer's Last Stand,* 4641
The Wright Brothers, 3946
Rhea, John. *The Department of the Air Force,* 2805
Rhodes, Frank H. T. *Geology,* 5076
Rhodes, Frank H. T., et al. *Fossils,* 4157
Rhue, Morton. *The Wave,* 819(F)
Rhyne, Nancy. *More Tales of the South Carolina Low Country,* 2620
Ribaroff, Margaret Flesher. *Mexico and the United States Today,* 2749
Ribner, Susan. *The Martial Arts,* 5640
Ricciuti, Edward R. *How to Box,* 5592
They Work with Wildlife, 3092
Rice, Edward. *Margaret Mead,* 3932

Sniegoski, Stephen J. *The Department of Education,* 2809

Snow, Dean R. *The Archaeology of North America,* 4564

Snow, Jon. *Atlas of Today,* 4230

Snowden, Sheila (jt. author). *The Computerized Society,* 5299

Snyder, Anne. *The Best That Money Can Buy,* 645(F)

First Step, 837(F)

My Name Is Davy, 838(F)

Snyder, Carol. *Dear Mom & Dad, Don't Worry,* 839(F)

The Great Condominium Rebellion, 1269(F)

Leave Me Alone, Ma, 646(F)

Memo To, 647(F)

Snyder, Gerald S. *Test-Tube Life,* 3258

Snyder, Louis L. *World War II,* 4278

Snyder, Zilpha K. *And Condors Danced,* 1270(F)

The Birds of Summer, 648(F)

Blair's Nightmare, 168(F)

Sobol, Donald J. *The Amazing Power of Ashur Fine,* 1516(F)

Sobol, Rose. *Woman Chief,* 3904

Solomon, Abbot N. *Secrets of the Super Athletes,* 5565, 5620

Solomon, Louis. *The Ma and Pa Murders and Other Perfect Crimes,* 2981

Sonnenmark, Laura A. *Something's Rotten in the State of Maryland,* 2245(F)

Sonnett, Sherry. *Smoking,* 3169

Sookram, Brian. *France,* 4383

Sorrell, Charles A. *Rocks and Minerals,* 5109

Soto, Gary. *Baseball in April and Other Stories,* 1271(F)

Soule, Gardner. *Christopher Columbus on the Green Sea of Darkness,* 3627

Southall, Ivan. *Blackbird,* 1272(F)

Josh, 1273(F)

The Long Night Watch, 1350(F)

Rachel, 169(F)

Spangenburg, Ray. *Exploring the Reaches of the Solar System,* 4823

Living and Working in Space, 4790

Opening the Space Frontier, 4823

Space People from A–Z, 4790

Spangler, Earl. *Blacks in America,* 2888

Speaker-Yuan, Margaret. *Agnes de Mille,* 3709

Speare, Elizabeth George. *The Bronze Bow,* 1546(F)

Calico Captive, 1649(F)

The Sign of the Beaver, 1634(F)

The Witch of Blackbird Pond, 1650(F)

Spence, Annette. *Human Sexuality,* 3408

Nutrition, 3361

Substance Abuse, 3170

Spencer, Donald D. *BASIC Programming,* 5305

Understanding Computers, 5305

What Computers Can Do, 5305

Spencer, William. *The Land and People of Turkey,* 4448

Spicer, Dorothy. *The Humming Top,* 1517(F)

Spinelli, Jerry. *Jason and Marceline,* 1274(F)

Maniac Magee, 386(F)

Space Station Seventh Grade, 1275(F)

Springer, Nancy. *A Horse to Love,* 268(F)

Red Wizard, 1518(F)

Springstubb, Tricia. *Eunice Gottlieb and the Unwhitewashed Truth about Life,* 1276(F)

Which Way to the Nearest Wilderness? 1276(F)

Sproule, Anna. *New Ideas in Industry,* 3908

Solidarity, 2998

Squire, Anne (jt. author). *Animal Talk,* 4920

Stafford, Mark. *W. E. B. Du Bois,* 3775

Stafford, Patricia. *Your Two Brains,* 3286

Stanek, Lou Willett. *Gleanings,* 1277(F)

Megan's Beat, 1278(F)

Stangle, Jean. *The Tools of Science,* 4739

Stanley, Marcia, ed. *Better Homes and Gardens Beginner's Cook Book,* 5440

Better Homes and Gardens Junior Cook Book, 5440

Better Homes and Gardens Step-by-Step Kids' Cook Book, 5440

Staples, Suzanne Fisher. *Shabanu,* 1351(F)

Starkey, Dinah. *Ghosts and Bogles,* 1852(F)

Starkey, Marion. *The Visionary Girls,* 4579

Stedman, Nancy. *The Common Cold and Influenza,* 3230

Steele, Mary Q. *Journey Outside,* 170(F)

Steele, Phillip W. *Ozark Tales and Superstitions,* 2624

Stefany, Wallace. *The Department of Transportation,* 2810

Stefoff, Rebecca. *Abraham Lincoln,* 3830

Andrew Jackson, 3815

The Drug Enforcement Administration, 2811

Faisal, 4014

Ferdinand Magellan and the Discovery of the World Ocean, 3639

Japan, 4355

John Adams, 3804

Theodore Roosevelt, 3845

The U.S. Coast Guard, 2839

West Bank/Gaza Strip, 4436

Yasir Arafat, 4005

Stein, R. Conrad. *Mexico,* 4474

Stein, Sara. *The Evolution Book,* 4176

Steinbeck, John. *The Red Pony,* 269(F)

Steinberg, Barbara. *Who Keeps America Clean?* 3019

Steiner, Barbara. *If You Love Me,* 2246(F)

Is There a Cure for Sophomore Year? 1279(F)

Tessa, 1280(F)

Steinhorn, Harriet. *Shadows of the Holocaust,* 2485

Stepanek, Sally. *John Calvin,* 4056

Mary, Queen of Scots, 4097

Trainer, David. *A Day in the Life of a TV News Reporter,* 3081

Traub, James. *India,* 4350

Trease, Geoffrey. *A Flight of Angels,* 2099(F)

Trefil, James S. *Living in Space,* 4796

Tregaskis, Richard. *Guadalcanal Diary,* 4285

Triadó, Juan-Ramón. *The Key to Baroque Art,* 3548

The Key to Painting, 3538

Trier, Mike. *Supercar,* 5358

Trivelpiece, Laurel. *Just a Little Bit Lost,* 183(F)

Tuck, Jay. *Heroes of Puerto Rico,* 4489

Tuggle, Catherine. *The Department of Energy,* 2812

Tunis, Edwin. *Colonial Craftsmen and the Beginnings of American Industry,* 4580

Colonial Living, 4581

Frontier Living, 4643

Indians, 4566

The Tavern at the Ferry, 4582

Weapons, 5378

Wheels, 5333

The Young United States, 1783 to 1830, 4607

Tunis, John R. *Highpockets,* 2474(F)

Keystone Kids, 2474(F)

The Kid Comes Back, 2475(F)

The Kid from Tomkinsville, 2475(F)

Rookie of the Year, 2475(F)

World Series, 2474(F)

Turck, Mary. *AIDS,* 3235

Turnbull, Ann. *Maroo of the Winter Caves,* 1543(F)

Turner, Ann. *Grasshopper Summer,* 1716(F)

Twain, Mark. *The Adventures of Huckleberry Finn,* 324(F)

The Adventures of Tom Sawyer, 325(F)

A Connecticut Yankee in King Arthur's Court, 326(F)

The Prince and the Pauper, 327(F)

Pudd'nhead Wilson, 328(F)

Tom Sawyer Abroad [and] Tom Sawyer, Detective, 329(F)

Tyler, Dick (jt. author). *Weight Training and Bodybuilding,* 5585

Tyler, Jane B. (jt. author). *Swimming Basics,* 5660

Tyler, Vicki. *The A+ Guide to Better Vocabulary,* 3068

The A+ Guide to Grammar, 3068

Uchida, Yoshiko. *The Best Bad Thing,* 390(F)

The Happiest Ending, 390(F)

A Jar of Dreams, 391(F)

Journey Home, 392(F)

Ullman, James R. *Banner in the Sky,* 184(F)

United Nations Dept. of Public Information. *Everyone's United Nations,* 2733

Urban, Joan. *Richard Wright,* 3694

Ure, Jean. *After Thursday,* 847(F)

The Most Important Thing, 662(F)

One Green Leaf, 848(F)

See You Thursday, 847(F)

What If They Saw Me Now? 1298(F)

You Win Some, You Lose Some, 1942(F)

Vagts, Detlev (jt. author). *Presidents in American History,* 2774

Vail, John. *David Ben-Gurion,* 4009

Nelson and Winnie Mandela, 3990

Thomas Paine, 3878

Vail, Virginia. *Pets Are for Keeps,* 275(F)

Van Allsburg, Chris. *The Mysteries of Harris Burdick,* 2686

Van Etten, Teresa. *Ways of Indian Wisdom,* 2614

Van Fleet, Alanson A. *The Tennessee Valley Authority,* 5169

Van Leeuwen, Jean. *Seems Like This Road Goes on Forever,* 849(F)

Van Loon, Hendrik Willem. *The Story of Mankind,* 4195

Van Raven, Pieter. *The Great Man's Secret,* 1299(F)

Harpoon Island, 1727(F)

Pickle and Price, 1300(F)

Van Steenwyk, Elizabeth. *Levi Strauss,* 3902

van Straalen, Alice. *The Book of Holidays around the World,* 2729

Van Tol, Robert. *Surface Warships,* 5379

VanWie, Eileen Kalberg. *Teenage Stress,* 3438

Van Wormer, Joe. *How to Be a Wildlife Photographer,* 5463

van Zwanenberg, Fiona. *Caring for the Aged,* 3113

Vardeman, Robert E. *Road to the Stars,* 2412(F)

Varenhorst, Barbara B. *Real Friends,* 3425

Vbrova, Zuza. *Space and Astronomy,* 4765

Vecchione, Glen. *The World's Best Street & Yard Games,* 5541

Veglahn, Nancy J. *Fellowship of the Seven Stars,* 850(F)

Venning, Frank D. *Wildflowers of North America,* 4881

Ventura, Piero. *Great Composers,* 3559

Great Painters, 3549

In Search of Ancient Crete, 4200

In Search of Troy, 4201

In Search of Tutankhamun, 4207

Ventura, Piero (jt. author). *Grand Constructions,* 3527

Vergara, Norma C. (jt. author). *Heroes of Puerto Rico,* 4489

Verne, Jules. *Around the World in Eighty Days,* 285(F)

A Journey to the Centre of the Earth, 286(F)

Master of the World, 2413(F)

The Mysterious Island, 287(F)

458

Title Index

This index contains both main entry titles and internal titles cited in the entries. References are to entry numbers, not page numbers. All fiction titles are indicated by (F), following the entry number.

Human Rights, 2850, 2861, 2864
Human Sexuality, 3408
Humbug Mountain, 2005(F)
The Humming Top, 1517(F)
Humorous Plays for Teen-Agers, 2667
A Hundred and Fiftieth Anniversary Album of Baseball, 5556
The Hungarian Uprising, 4374
Hungary, 4375
The Hunger Road, 2989
The Hunger Scream, 826(F)
The Hungry Woman: Myths and Legends of the Aztecs, 2625
Hunter in the Dark, 762(F)
Hunter's Stew and Hangtown Fry: What Pioneer America Ate and Why, 4638
Hunting the Killer Shark, 5020
The Huntsman, 2326(F)
Huon of the Horn, 1551(F)
The Huron, 4530
The Hurry-Up Summer, 1132(F)
The Hydra, 2638
Hygiene, 3261

I Am Phoenix: Poems for Two Voices, 2543
I Am Susannah, 502(F)
I Am the Cat, 2499
I Am the Cheese, 953(F)
I Am the Darker Brother: An Anthology of Modern Poems by Negro Americans, 2534
I Am the Universe, 464(F)
I Feel Like the Morning Star, 2367(F)
The I Hate Mathematics! Book, 5118
I Hate School: How to Hang In & When to Drop Out, 3049
I, Juan de Pareja, 1566(F)
I Know What You Did Last Summer, 1993(F)
I Loved You, Logan McGee! 909(F)
I Never Loved Your Mind, 1323(F)
I Only Made Up the Roses, 620(F)
I Saw Him First, 2241(F)
I Stay Near You, 1070(F)

I Tell a Lie Every So Often, 1695(F)
I Think I'm Falling in Love, 2242(F)
I Thought You Were My Best Friend, 1223(F)
I, Trissy, 581(F)
I Was a 15-Year-Old Blimp, 842(F)
I Was There, 4135
I Wear the Morning Star, 1628(F)
I Will Call It Georgie's Blues, 1175(F)
I Will Make You Disappear, 2113(F)
Ice Ages, 4147
The Ice Bear, 1460(F)
Ice Crown, 2380(F)
Ice Hawk, 2448(F)
Ice Skating Basics, 5629
Ice Swords: An Undersea Adventure, 77(F)
The Iceberg and Its Shadow, 1005(F)
The Iceberg Hermit, 153(F)
I'd Rather Be Dancing, 1235(F)
I'd Rather Think about Robby, 998(F)
Ida Early Comes over the Mountain, 698(F)
Ideas for Science Projects, 4724, 4726
If I Asked You, Would You Stay? 911(F)
If I Love You, Am I Trapped Forever? 1071(F)
If I Love You Wednesday, 978(F)
If I Were in Charge of the World and Other Worries: Poems for Children and Their Parents, 2519
If It's Not Funny, Why Am I Laughing? 1168(F)
If Not For You, 1311(F)
If Pigs Could Fly, 1668(F)
If This Is Love, I'll Take Spaghetti, 2146(F)
If Winter Comes, 1337(F)
If You Love Me, 2246(F)
If You Need Me, 401(F)
The Igloo, 4509
Il Duce: The Rise & Fall of Benito Mussolini, 4099
I'll Always Remember You . . . Maybe, 1208(F)

I'll Get There, It Better Be Worth the Trip, 972(F)
I'll Love You When You're More Like Me, 1072(F)
Illegal Aliens, 2990
Illusions Illustrated: A Professional Magic Show for Young Performers, 5447
Illustrated Basketball Dictionary for Young People, 5573
The Illustrated Dinosaur Dictionary, 4159
Illustrated Football Dictionary for Young People, 5619
Illustrated Soccer Dictionary for Young People, 5652
The Illyrian Adventure, 6(F)
I'm Going to Get Your Boyfriend, 2238(F)
I'm Gonna Make You Love Me: The Story of Diana Ross, 3736
I'm Nobody! Who Are You? 2539
I'm Still Me, 561(F)
Imaginary Gardens: American Poetry and Art for Young People, 2569
Imagination's Other Place: Poems of Science and Mathematics, 2516
The Immigrant Experience, 2876
Immigrant Kids, 2874
Immigrants Who Returned Home, 2872
The Immigration and Naturalization Service, 2873
The Immune System, 3198
Immunology: From Pasteur to the Search for an AIDS Vaccine, 3204
The Impact of AIDS, 3189
In Charge: A Complete Handbook for Kids with Working Parents, 3460
In Kindling Flame: The Story of Hannah Senesh 1921–1944, 4105
In Lane Three, Alex Archer, 2439(F)
In Our House Scott Is My Brother, 402(F)
In Real Life, 1187(F)
In Search of Ancient Crete, 4200
In Search of Liberty, 799(F)
In Search of Troy, 4201

509

Subject/Grade Level Index

All entries are listed within specific subjects and then according to grade level suitability (see the key at the foot of pages for grade level designations). Subjects are arranged alphabetically and subject heads may be subdivided into nonfiction (e.g., "Adoption") and fiction (e.g., "Adoption–Fiction"). Reference to entries are by entry numbers, not pages.

A

Aaronsohn, Sarah
J: 4003

Abacus
JS: 5112

Abenaki Indians
JS: 4531

Abortion
IJ: 3410
JS: 3000, 3242, 3395, 3416

Abortion–Fiction
J: 1263
JS: 1324

Academic skills, 3050–3068

Accidents–Fiction
IJ: 63, 751
J: 141, 768, 825, 1060, 1092, 1219, 1725, 2103
JS: 105, 727, 849, 945, 1993, 2093, 2124, 2173–74, 2298

Acid rain
IJ: 2960
JS: 2956, 2963

Acne
JS: 3316, 3318–19

Acting
IJ: 3082

Acting–Fiction
IJ: 1024, 1188
J: 1186

Actors
IJ: 3643–44
JS: 3701

Actors–Biography
IJ: 3715
JS: 3708

Actors–Fiction
IJ: 11, 1849
J: 1291
JS: 596

Actresses–Biography
IJ: 3730
J: 3702
JS: 3713–14, 3718–19

Actresses–Fiction
IJ: 1030, 1452, 2030
JS: 1059

Adams, Abigail
J: 3881

Adams, Grizzly
IJ: 3882

Adams, John
IJ: 3803
J: 3804

Addams, Jane
J: 3883

Adolescence
IJ: 3462, 3465
JS: 3099, 3381, 3425, 3429, 3456, 3458, 3477

Adolescence–Fiction
IJ: 738, 899, 998, 1026, 1123, 1132, 1335, 1927, 2254
J: 218, 1249, 1256, 1315, 2473
JS: 389, 988, 1001, 1047, 1156,

1260, 1292, 1326, 1726, 1941, 2181

Adolescence–Poetry
JS: 2548

Adolescence–Problems–Fiction
862–1326

Adoption
IJ: 3505, 3515, 3517
JS: 3485, 3494, 3508, 3512

Adoption–Fiction
IJ: 375, 408, 527, 561, 1707
J: 549
JS: 563

Adventure and survival stories–Fiction, 1–190

Adventure stories–Fiction
IJ: 1–2, 4–6, 8, 11–13, 16, 18–19, 23, 27–28, 36, 40–41, 43–45, 47, 49, 51–53, 57, 63–64, 66, 74–75, 78–80, 83, 86, 93, 98–99, 106, 110, 112, 119, 122, 125–26, 131–32, 136, 138–39, 144, 146, 149–50, 155, 165, 168–73, 177, 179, 212, 216, 232, 242, 253, 288, 308, 941, 1166, 1377, 1531, 1565, 1572, 1575, 1664, 1672, 1685, 1702, 1755, 1884
J: 9, 14, 20, 24, 29–30, 32, 37, 50, 65, 76, 85, 92, 95–96, 107, 109, 114, 123–24, 127, 134, 142, 148, 151–54, 156, 158–59, 163, 187, 190, 1353, 1361, 1573, 1616, 1619, 1749
JS: 3, 7, 10, 15, 17, 21, 25–26, 31, 33, 35, 38, 42, 46, 48, 58–61, 71, 73, 77, 81–82, 84, 87, 90–91, 94, 97, 100–3, 105, 115, 118, 120–21, 129, 137, 143, 147, 157, 162,

IJ = Intermediate–Junior High; J = Junior High; JS = Junior–Senior High

Amphibians
IJ: 4896, 4899
JS: 4895, 4898, 4900

Amphibians and reptiles, 4895–4904

Amputations–Fiction
JS: 851

Anastasia, Nikolaevna
JS: 4047

Ancient history
IJ: 2652, 2655, 4046, 4196, 4198–99, 4201–2, 4204, 4210–11, 4325
J: 2858, 4100, 4203
JS: 3534, 3988, 4102, 4197, 4218

Ancient history–Historical fiction, 1544–1554

Ancient world
See also Egypt; Greece; Rome
IJ: 4325

Andersen, Hans Christian
IJ: 2590

Anderson, Marian
J: 3704
JS: 3703

Angel dust (drug)
IJ: 3115

Anger
JS: 3433

Anger–Fiction
IJ: 110, 816

Animal abuse
J: 4884
JS: 4885, 4892

Animal care
IJ: 5059–60
J: 4884, 4891, 4894, 5052
JS: 4885, 4892

Animal care–Fiction
JS: 192

Animal intelligence
J: 4916
JS: 4912

Animal species, 4923–4975

Animal stories–Fiction, 191–280

Animal tracks
JS: 4922

Animals
IJ: 4925
J: 4924, 4945
JS: 5037, 5463

Animals–Australia
IJ: 4369

Animals–Behavior
IJ: 4906, 4910
J: 4890, 4905, 4907–9, 4915–16, 4918
JS: 4912, 4914

Animals–Behavior–Fiction
IJ: 4913
JS: 1104

Animals–Camouflage
IJ: 4919

Animals–Communication
IJ: 4920

Animals–Families
J: 4927

Animals–Field guides
JS: 4923, 4926, 4936–37

Animals–General
IJ: 4193, 4883, 4929, 5061–62, 5097
J: 4886, 4928
JS: 4937, 5039

Animals–Homes
IJ: 5024

Animals–Reproduction
IJ: 4921

Animals–Vision
IJ: 4893, 4917

Anorexia
J: 3333
JS: 3329, 3342, 3349

Anorexia–Fiction
J: 754, 855
JS: 826

Antarctic
IJ: 4507

Anthony, Susan B.
JS: 3767

Anthropology
IJ: 4169, 4174–75
J: 4165
JS: 3931–33, 4170, 4173

Anti-Semitism
IJ: 2889, 2892
JS: 2890, 2897, 4245, 4273

Anti-Semitism–Fiction
IJ: 338, 376
J: 364
JS: 332

Antique automobiles
IJ: 5352, 5548
JS: 5354

Antony, Marc
JS: 4048

Ants–Fiction
IJ: 2354

Anxieties
JS: 3432

Apache Indians
JS: 4553

Apache Indians–Fiction
J: 2459
JS: 1624

Apartheid
IJ: 4000, 4002, 4306–7
JS: 3992, 4001, 4309, 4311–13, 4316

Apartheid–Fiction
JS: 345, 381, 1347

Apartments–Fiction
JS: 1903

Apes–Fiction
JS: 207

Appalachia–Fiction
IJ: 516, 675
JS: 1165

Appalachia–Poetry
J: 2565

Appalachian Mountains–Fiction
JS: 1678

Aquaculture
JS: 4982

Aqualung
JS: 5152

Aquariums
J: 3091
JS: 5050

Aquino, Corazon
IJ: 4004, 4042–44

Arab Americans
J: 2928

Arabia–Folklore
IJ: 2583–84, 2587
J: 2586

Arabs
J: 4005

Arabs–Fiction
JS: 162

Arafat, Yasir
J: 4005

Arapaho Indians
JS: 4537

Archaeology
IJ: 2684, 4180, 4200–1, 4207
J: 3093
JS: 4177–79, 4564

IJ = Intermediate–Junior High; J = Junior High; JS = Junior–Senior High

IJ = Intermediate–Junior High; J = Junior High; JS = Junior–Senior High

Australia–Fiction
IJ: 27, 169, 179, 502, 1273, 1485, 1534, 1824, 1857
J: 619, 1350, 1533
JS: 140, 787, 1220, 1228, 1869

Austria–Fiction
J: 1605
JS: 1765

Austria–History
JS: 4124

Authors–Biography, 3659–3695

Autism–Fiction
JS: 1455

Automation, 5252–5308

Automobile racing
IJ: 5547–48
J: 3955

Automobile racing–Fiction
J: 2464

Automobiles
IJ: 3929, 5358
J: 5331
JS: 3924, 5353, 5357

Automobiles–History
IJ: 5356

Automobiles–Repairs
IJ: 5352, 5548
JS: 5351, 5354–55

Avalanches–Fiction
J: 152

Aviation
IJ: 3631, 3634, 3638, 3642, 5334
JS: 3633, 4279, 5350

Aviation–Fiction
J: 399

Aztec Indians
IJ: 4465
J: 2625, 3629
JS: 4466, 4468

B

Babies–Fiction
IJ: 611
J: 50
JS: 812

Baby care
JS: 3480

Baby-sitting
IJ: 3095
JS: 3096

Baby-sitting–Fiction
IJ: 887
J: 1117
JS: 644, 810, 2022, 2086

Backpacking
J: 5597
JS: 5594

Backpacking–Fiction
J: 14
JS: 137

Bacteriology
IJ: 3190

Badgers–Fiction
IJ: 210

Baeck, Leo
IJ: 4050

Bahamas–Fiction
JS: 2060

Baldwin, James
JS: 3661

Ballet
J: 3581–82, 3585
JS: 3579, 3583–84, 3709, 3743

Ballet–Fiction
IJ: 662, 737, 1314
J: 551, 875, 1298
JS: 1235, 1942

Ballooning
IJ: 5339, 5542

Baltimore–Fiction
IJ: 1734

Bangladesh
IJ: 4363

Banneker, Benjamin
IJ: 3911

Bar mitzvah
IJ: 2725
J: 2706

Bar mitzvah–Fiction
IJ: 1063
J: 1243

Barnum, P. T.
IJ: 3707

Baroque art
JS: 3548

Barton, Clara
IJ: 3884

Baseball
IJ: 3958, 3960–62, 5549, 5551–52, 5555, 5560–61, 5564, 5566
J: 3948–49, 5550, 5558–59, 5565
JS: 3957, 3959, 5553–54, 5556–57, 5562–63, 5567–68

Baseball–Fiction
IJ: 362, 1063, 2461, 2474–75
J: 1294, 1406, 2434, 2457
JS: 592, 2436, 2444, 2446, 2458

Baseball cards
JS: 5470

BASIC (computer language)
IJ: 5264, 5294, 5296, 5300, 5307
J: 5253, 5284, 5306
JS: 5283, 5290

Basketball
IJ: 3964, 5569–70, 5572
J: 3963, 5571, 5573, 5576–77
JS: 5574–75, 5578–79

Basketball–Fiction
IJ: 2451
J: 2108, 2431, 2443, 2445
JS: 2463, 2467, 2472

Bastille (Paris)
JS: 4380

Bat mitzvah
J: 2706

Bat mitzvah–Fiction
IJ: 1314
J: 378

Baton twirling
JS: 5528

Bats
J: 4949

Battered women
JS: 3479

Battered women–Fiction
J: 460

Battle of Trenton
IJ: 4595

Bears
IJ: 4939
J: 4941–42
JS: 4940

Bears–Fiction
IJ: 250

Beauty care
JS: 3266

Beauty contests
J: 3589

Beauty contests–Fiction
J: 1197

Beavers–Fiction
IJ: 1039

Bedoukian, Kerop
JS: 4123

Bees
IJ: 4999

IJ = Intermediate–Junior High; J = Junior High; JS = Junior–Senior High

Beetles
IJ: 5000
J: 5001

Begin, Menachem
IJ: 4007

Behavior
See Human behavior

Bell, Alexander Graham
IJ: 3912

Ben-Gurion, David
IJ: 4009
J: 4008

Ben-Yehuda, Eliezer
IJ: 4010

Berlin–History
IJ: 4248, 4388

Bethune, Mary McLeod
JS: 3768

Bible and bible study
IJ: 2714–15, 2717
JS: 2716

Bicycle motocross
JS: 5582

Bicycle motocross–Fiction
IJ: 2452

Bicycles
IJ: 5583
J: 5643
JS: 5580–81, 5584

Bigfoot
JS: 5501

Bill of Rights
JS: 2767, 2769

Billy the Kid–Fiction
J: 128

Biofeedback
J: 3280
JS: 3102

Biography, 3619–4137

Biological sciences, 4838–5063

Biology
IJ: 4736, 4840–41, 4843
J: 4844
JS: 4839, 5064

Biology–Fiction
JS: 2260

Bionics
IJ: 3184
J: 3186

Biosphere
JS: 5082

Biotechnology
J: 3185
JS: 3258, 5034

Bird, Larry
J: 3963

Birds
IJ: 4952–53, 4956, 4961, 4968–69,
4971–72
J: 4954, 4959–60
JS: 4155, 4951, 4955, 4963, 4970

Birds–Fiction
IJ: 249

Birds–Field guides
JS: 4957–58, 4962, 4964–65

Birds–Poetry
IJ: 2543

Birds of prey
IJ: 4969, 4971–72
JS: 4970

Birth control
JS: 3000, 3395, 3401, 3403, 3407,
3880

Bismarck, Otto von
JS: 4051

Black Americans, 2882–2888

Black Americans–Biography
IJ: 3658, 3696, 3722, 3747, 3775,
3777, 3779–82, 3785, 3788–90,
3792, 3797–99, 3802, 3889, 3911,
3958, 3960, 3964, 3969, 3976
J: 3635, 3704, 3724, 3764, 3773–
74, 3891, 3945, 3965–66, 3968
JS: 2488, 3661, 3668, 3670, 3672–
73, 3691, 3694, 3703, 3705–6,
3708, 3712, 3720–21, 3734–36,
3757, 3768, 3770–72, 3776, 3778,
3783–84, 3786–87, 3791, 3793,
3796, 3800–1, 3873, 3915, 3919,
3959, 3967, 3977–78

Black Americans–Dance
JS: 3580

Black Americans–Fiction
IJ: 117, 175, 333, 351, 354, 357–
58, 375, 377, 387, 393, 397, 486,
516–17, 899, 910, 1677
J: 347, 350, 353, 360, 363, 372–73,
395, 1036, 1303, 1667, 2431
JS: 167, 274, 328, 331, 340–41,
346, 361, 365, 371, 374, 382,
388–89, 396, 620, 789, 896,
1022, 1169, 1300, 1669, 1723,
1817, 1855, 2014, 2021, 2467

Black Americans–Folklore
IJ: 2616, 2619

Black Americans–History
IJ: 2857, 2884, 2888, 3040, 4602

J: 2885, 4589, 4631
JS: 2865, 2882, 2886–87, 2921

Black Americans–Music
JS: 3557

Black Americans–Poetry
JS: 2534–35, 2537, 2541, 2547

Black children–Fiction
IJ: 486

Black holes
IJ: 4825

Blackfeet Indians
IJ: 4463

Blackwell, Elizabeth
JS: 3885

Blind
IJ: 3372, 3895–96
JS: 3897

Blind–Fiction
IJ: 175, 271, 982
J: 228, 766, 805, 853
JS: 38, 71, 91, 700, 767, 847, 1848

Blizzards
JS: 4645

Blood
See also Circulatory system;
Heart
IJ: 3296

Blues (music)
IJ: 3562

Blume, Judy
IJ: 3662

Bly, Nellie
JS: 3858

Boat People–Fiction
J: 1353

Bobcats
J: 4944

Bodybuilding
IJ: 5587
JS: 5585–86

Bodybuilding–Fiction
IJ: 1938
JS: 2195

Bolivia
IJ: 4494
J: 4503

Bombers
IJ: 5369
JS: 5374

Bones
IJ: 3315

Books and publishing
JS: 2687, 2691

IJ = Intermediate–Junior High; J = Junior High; JS = Junior–Senior High

Boone, Daniel
IJ: 3859

Borgia, Cesare
JS: 4052

Borglum, Gutzon
IJ: 4680

Boston—Fiction
IJ: 440, 493
JS: 1210

Boston Massacre
IJ: 4598

Botany, 4845–4882

Bourke-White, Margaret
JS: 3647

Bowditch, Nathaniel
J: 3886

Boxing
IJ: 3969
J: 3965–66, 3968
JS: 3967, 5588, 5592

Boxing—Fiction
JS: 361

Boy Scouts of America
IJ: 5593
J: 3522
JS: 3525–26, 3575

Boyfriends—Fiction
IJ: 543, 909, 1125, 1237, 1918,
2117, 2184
J: 750, 888, 1044–45, 1911, 2130,
2134, 2139–40, 2161, 2172, 2203,
2241
JS: 336, 709, 729, 820, 862, 913,
938, 1002, 1155, 1282, 2118,
2124, 2129, 2133, 2144, 2156,
2173–77, 2190, 2202, 2208, 2219,
2223, 2228, 2236, 2244, 2458

Boys—Grooming
IJ: 3260, 3264

Boys—Puberty
J: 3383
JS: 3398, 3405

Braces
IJ: 3320–21, 3367

Braille, Louis
IJ: 4053

Brain and nervous system
IJ: 3282–83, 3285–88
J: 3280–81
JS: 3278

Brandeis, Louis D.
J: 3860

Brazil
IJ: 4493
JS: 4495

Bridger, Jim—Fiction
J: 1699

Bridges
IJ: 5247

Broadcasting
J: 3612

Brontë family
JS: 3663

Brown, John
JS: 3769

Bryant, Bear
J: 3970

Buck, Pearl
J: 3664

Buddhism
IJ: 2707
JS: 2709, 4361

Buffalo
JS: 4624

Building and construction
IJ: 5245, 5250
J: 5244
JS: 3530, 5248–49

Building materials
IJ: 5245

Buildings (model)
J: 5459

Bulfinch's *Age of Fable*
JS: 2634–35

Bulimia
J: 3333
JS: 3342, 3349–50

Bulimia—Fiction
JS: 842

Bullfighting—Fiction
IJ: 858

Bullies—Fiction
JS: 2454

Bureau of Indian Affairs (U.S.)
JS: 2803

Burns, Anthony
JS: 3770

Burundi
IJ: 4298

Bush, George
JS: 3805

Business
See Economics and business

Businessmen
IJ: 3926, 3940, 3943

Busing
JS: 2846

Butterflies and moths
IJ: 5004
JS: 5002–3

Butterworth, Emma Macalik
JS: 4124

C

Cactus
IJ: 4869

Caesar, Augustus
JS: 4054

Caesar, Julius
IJ: 4055

Calculating machines
J: 5293, 5297

Calder, Alexander
J: 3648

Calendars
IJ: 5122

California
JS: 4692

California—Fiction
IJ: 126, 518, 1180, 1270–71, 1698,
1715
J: 141, 348, 536, 1706, 1708, 1760,
2142, 2252, 2274
JS: 104, 269, 1112, 1703, 2231

California—History
IJ: 4620, 4633
JS: 4617

Calligraphy
J: 2675, 5401

Calligraphy—Chinese
IJ: 4346

Calvin, John
JS: 4056

Cambodia
IJ: 4358

Cambodian Americans—Fiction
JS: 342

Cameroon
IJ: 4318

Camouflage
IJ: 4919

Camping—Fiction
IJ: 23, 106, 2015
JS: 555, 2090

IJ = Intermediate–Junior High; J = Junior High; JS = Junior–Senior High

Camps
IJ: 5595
JS: 5416

Camps–Fiction
IJ: 113, 699, 872, 941, 1181, 1866,
1919
J: 992, 1142, 1294, 2201, 2246
JS: 26, 775, 1091, 1921, 2206

Canada
IJ: 4459, 4461
JS: 4455, 4464

Canada–Fiction
IJ: 19, 131, 176, 406, 1614–15,
1768
J: 114, 587, 1229, 1454, 1619
JS: 61, 84, 100, 196

Canada–Historical fiction,
1612–1619

Canada–History and geogra-
phy, 4460–4464

Canals
IJ: 4483, 5361
JS: 4683

Cancer
IJ: 3206, 3208
JS: 3200, 3203, 3223, 3227, 4125

Cancer–Fiction
IJ: 777, 786
J: 444, 742, 955
JS: 651, 740, 848, 1321

Canyons
J: 4452

Cape Cod–Fiction
IJ: 2117, 2255
J: 1357, 2272
JS: 1810, 2084

Capital punishment
JS: 2980

Capitalism
J: 3025
JS: 3030

Careers
IJ: 3073, 3080–82, 3084, 3089–90,
5232, 5566
J: 3078, 3087, 3091–93, 3569,
3591, 3766, 5063
JS: 2792, 3069, 3074–77, 3083,
3086, 3088, 3094, 3618

Caribbean Islands
IJ: 4485–87, 4489
JS: 4117, 4121, 4488

Caribbean Islands–Fiction
IJ: 339, 1613, 1618
J: 127, 148, 2026, 2613
JS: 147, 421

Caribbean Islands–History
and geography, 4485–4489

Carlton, Steve
JS: 3957

Carnegie, Andrew
IJ: 3913

Carnivorous plants
J: 4873, 4877

Carols
IJ: 3576–77

Carpentry
J: 5415

Carroll, Lewis
J: 2530

Carson, Kit–Fiction
IJ: 1702

Carson, Rachel
IJ: 3914

Carter, Jimmy
IJ: 3806

Cartography
JS: 4139

Cartoonists
IJ: 3650

Cartoons
IJ: 3658
JS: 5395

Carver, George Washington
JS: 3915

Cassatt, Mary
JS: 3649

Castles
IJ: 3532–33, 4220
JS: 3528

Catawba Indians
JS: 4554

Cathedrals
JS: 3529

Catholocism
IJ: 4090
J: 4088
JS: 4089

Cats
JS: 5404

Cats–Fiction
IJ: 279, 1126
J: 1173, 1969
JS: 196, 278, 1374

Cats–Lore
J: 5041

Cats–Poetry
IJ: 2496

J: 2499
JS: 2526

Catskill Mountains–Fiction
IJ: 52, 1801

Cattle–Fiction
J: 62

Caves–Fiction
IJ: 136, 186

Cells
IJ: 4841

Celts–Mythology
JS: 2627, 2632

Cemeteries–Fiction
IJ: 1844

Censorship
IJ: 2826, 2860, 2863, 2866
JS: 2849

Censorship–Fiction
IJ: 979, 1346
JS: 1338, 1348

Census
IJ: 2778

Central African Republic
IJ: 4293

Central America
IJ: 4457, 4475–76, 4481–82
JS: 4450, 4458, 4477–80

Central America–Fiction
IJ: 5, 108

Central America–Folklore,
2625

Central America–History and
geography, 4454, 4465–4484

Central Intelligence Agency
(U.S.)
JS: 2792, 2815

Cerebral palsy
JS: 4130

Cerebral palsy–Fiction
IJ: 684, 738
J: 805, 835

Challenger (space shuttle)
IJ: 4773

Charlemagne
J: 4057

Charlemagne–Fiction
J: 1551

Chaucer–Adaptations
IJ: 293, 2522
J: 302

Cheerleading
JS: 5528

IJ = Intermediate–Junior High; J = Junior High; JS = Junior–Senior High

IJ = Intermediate–Junior High; J = Junior High; JS = Junior–Senior High

IJ = Intermediate–Junior High; J = Junior High; JS = Junior–Senior High

Confucius
IJ: 4344

Congress (U.S.)
J: 2785
JS: 2781

Connecticut–Fiction
IJ: 1650
J: 1654

Connecticut–History
IJ: 4685

Conservation
IJ: 2940, 3914, 3934, 4976, 5137
J: 3845, 5127
JS: 4980

Conservation–Fiction
JS: 1455

Conservatism
JS: 2830

Constantine
JS: 4060

Constitution of the United States
IJ: 2766
J: 2763, 2770–71
JS: 2764–65, 2767–69, 2772–73, 2824

Consumerism
IJ: 3875
J: 3033
JS: 3034

Contemporary life and problems–Fiction, 330–1355

Continental drift
JS: 5074

Conversation
JS: 3423

Cook, Captain James
JS: 3628

Cookbooks
IJ: 5422, 5431, 5433
J: 4578, 4638, 4846, 4879, 5427, 5429, 5436, 5440
JS: 5425, 5438

Cookbooks–Christmas
J: 5437

Cookbooks–Ethnic
IJ: 5420, 5426, 5428, 5430, 5432, 5435, 5439, 5441–43
J: 5423–24, 5444–46
JS: 5419, 5421, 5434

Cooking, 5419–5446

Cooking–Fiction
IJ: 1276, 1862
J: 1888
JS: 2179

Copper
IJ: 5319

Coral reefs
J: 5011

Corruption
JS: 4517

Cortès, Hernan
J: 3629
JS: 4468

Cosby, Bill
JS: 3708

Cosmetics
IJ: 4721

Costa Rica
JS: 4479

Costumes
IJ: 5389
JS: 5390

Country music
JS: 3699

Country music–Fiction
IJ: 602

Courtroom trials
IJ: 2822
JS: 2821, 2823, 2829

Courtroom trials–Fiction
IJ: 2048

Courts
See Laws and legal systems

Cowboys
IJ: 4626, 4635
JS: 4644

Cowboys–Fiction
IJ: 1020
JS: 2137

Crack (drug)
IJ: 3122
JS: 3116, 3139, 3158, 3176

Crafts
IJ: 5382, 5384, 5388
J: 5381, 5383, 5385–86
JS: 5387, 5411, 5413

Creativity
IJ: 3022

Creek Indians–Fiction
J: 1717

Crete–History
IJ: 4200

Crib death–Fiction
IJ: 481

Crime and criminals
IJ: 2977
J: 2976, 2981

JS: 2975, 2978, 2980, 3120, 3134, 3136

Crime and criminals–Fiction
IJ: 12
J: 711
JS: 645, 2094

Croatian Americans
IJ: 2932

Crow Indians
IJ: 4548
J: 3904

Cruises–Fiction
JS: 1922

Cuba–History
J: 2738
JS: 4120–21, 4660

Cuban Americans
IJ: 2902

Cuban Missile Crisis
JS: 4660

Cuffe, Paul
JS: 3771

Cults
JS: 2704

Cults–Fiction
IJ: 1926, 2040
J: 660, 850, 2339
JS: 1161

Cultural Revolution (China)
JS: 4030, 4331, 4335, 4343

Cultural Revolution (China)–Fiction
JS: 1556

Curie, Marie
IJ: 3916
JS: 3917

Curiosities
IJ: 4325, 5510, 5516
J: 5490, 5506
JS: 5509

Curses–Fiction
J: 124

Custer, George Armstrong
IJ: 4641

Cystic fibrosis
JS: 3218

Cystic fibrosis–Fiction
J: 818

Czech Americans
JS: 2931

Czechoslovakia–Folklore
IJ: 2592

IJ = Intermediate–Junior High; J = Junior High; JS = Junior–Senior High

527

D

D-Day
IJ: 4243
JS: 4246, 4267

Dahl, Roald
JS: 3666

Dakota Indians–Fiction
IJ: 1630

Dakota Territory–Fiction
IJ: 1716
J: 1694

Dance
IJ: 3710
J: 3581–82, 3585
JS: 3579–80, 3583–84, 3709, 3743

Dancing–Fiction
IJ: 662, 1199
J: 875, 1298, 1728
JS: 1235, 1267, 1320, 1942

Darwin, Charles
IJ: 3918

Dating
IJ: 3466
J: 3445
JS: 3384, 3469, 3476

Dating–Fiction
J: 2188
JS: 526, 707, 2176, 2239

Davis, Jefferson
JS: 3861

Deafness
IJ: 3371, 3375–76, 4053
J: 3307, 3368, 3370, 3374
JS: 3892

Deafness–Fiction
IJ: 657, 715, 856, 1974
J: 750, 825, 832
JS: 746, 772, 2200

Death
IJ: 3103, 3107, 3111–12
JS: 3104, 3106, 3108, 3110, 4125

Death–Fiction
IJ: 400, 405, 416, 440, 481, 524,
537, 550, 566, 574, 629, 736,
756, 777, 786, 852, 931, 1118,
1164, 1334, 1730, 1952, 2052
J: 191, 444, 490, 617, 702, 706,
742, 841, 895, 906, 917, 932,
1015, 1038, 1057, 1119, 1129,
1172, 1193, 1205, 1261, 1358,
1379, 1502, 1697, 1833, 2027,
2068, 2114, 2273
JS: 115, 167, 414, 433–34, 487,
577, 591–92, 637, 651, 683, 691,

713, 735, 762, 778, 791, 801,
806, 812, 844, 848, 898, 945,
965, 1053, 1078, 1085, 1102,
1157–58, 1195, 1209, 1250, 1293,
1312, 1320–21, 1325, 1710, 2004,
2062, 2074, 2297

Debates and debating
JS: 3060

Debt (international)
J: 3024

Decision making
JS: 3475

Declaration of Independence
J: 4588

Decorative arts, 3552–3553

Deep-sea diving–Fiction
IJ: 43

Deer
JS: 3225

Deer family
IJ: 4935
J: 4945

Deer–Fiction
IJ: 259
J: 191, 1193

Defense departments
JS: 2786

Delaware Indians
IJ: 4542

Delaware Indians–Fiction
IJ: 1626

de Mille, Agnes
JS: 3709, 3743

Deng, Xiaoping
J: 4013

Denmark
IJ: 4403

Denmark–Fiction
J: 1747

Dentistry
IJ: 3320–22
JS: 3299

Dentists–Fiction
IJ: 802

Department of Agriculture (U.S.)
JS: 2794

Department of Defense (U.S.)
JS: 2786

Department of Education (U.S.)
JS: 2809

Department of Energy (U.S.)
JS: 2812

Department of Health and Human Services (U.S.)
JS: 2782

Department of Justice (U.S.)
JS: 2791

Department of the Interior (U.S.)
JS: 2784

Department of the Navy (U.S.)
JS: 2796

Department of the Treasury (U.S.)
JS: 2813

Department of Transportation (U.S.)
JS: 2810

Depression, Great
IJ: 4650
J: 4236, 4652
JS: 4651, 4653

Depression, Great–Fiction
IJ: 1, 391, 1729–30, 1732, 1734–36
J: 568, 1728, 1733, 1738
JS: 1731, 1737, 1739

Depression (mental)
J: 3435
JS: 3330, 3337, 3431, 3437

Depression (mental)–Fiction
J: 692

Deserts
IJ: 4869
J: 5093
JS: 4623, 5103

Deserts–Fiction
IJ: 138, 240
J: 95, 1429
JS: 1351

Detective stories
See Mystery and detective
stories–Fiction

Detectives
IJ: 2977

De Valera, Eamon
JS: 4061

Diabetes
IJ: 3233
JS: 3229

Diabetes–Fiction
J: 500, 716
JS: 726

Diamonds
IJ: 5240

IJ = Intermediate–Junior High; J = Junior High; JS = Junior–Senior High

Diana, Princess of Wales
IJ: 4062–63

Diaries
JS: 3050, 3218, 3693

Diaries–Fiction
IJ: 1201, 1461, 2067, 2126
JS: 948, 1941, 2396

Dickens, Charles–Fiction
IJ: 249

Dickerson, Eric
IJ: 3971

Dickinson, Emily
JS: 2562, 3667

Dictators
IJ: 4235

Dictionaries
IJ: 4158–59, 4883
J: 5573, 5611, 5619, 5652
JS: 3121, 3387, 4757, 5111, 5289

Diet
See Nutrition and diet; Obesity

Digestive and excretory systems
IJ: 3298, 3300, 3362
JS: 3297

Dinosaurs
IJ: 4143, 4150–51, 4153, 4156, 4158–60, 4162–63, 4171
J: 4145–46, 4154, 4844
JS: 4152, 4155

Dinosaurs–Fiction
IJ: 461

Disabilities
See also Dyslexia; Learning disabilities; Physical handicaps
JS: 3366

Disabilities–Computer use
J: 5260

Disabilities–Fiction
IJ: 684

Disabilities–Sports
JS: 5575

Disarmament
JS: 2735, 2751, 2753, 2755

Disc jockeys–Fiction
J: 1889
JS: 901

Discrimination
JS: 2853

Diseases and illness
See also individual diseases
IJ: 3128, 3187, 3199, 3201, 3212–

15, 3222, 3231, 3233, 3239, 3244, 3292
J: 3204, 3220
JS: 3137, 3188, 3192, 3196, 3200, 3210, 3211, 3217, 3224–25, 3227, 3229, 3234, 3237, 3245, 3293–94

Disraeli, Benjamin
JS: 4064

Dissection
J: 4744

Dissent groups, 2938–2939

Divorce
IJ: 3482, 3487–88, 3491, 3506, 3516
JS: 3502

Divorce–Fiction
IJ: 145, 424–25, 470, 506, 512, 545, 556, 581, 594, 1016, 1164, 1214, 1287, 1885
J: 412, 460, 532, 575, 593, 595, 600, 643, 665, 695, 1280, 1487
JS: 538, 542, 544, 558, 672, 714, 798, 800, 970, 1146, 1380, 2228

DNA
IJ: 3249, 3251
JS: 3253, 3259, 5034

Doctors
IJ: 3905
JS: 3885

Dogs
IJ: 3376, 5044, 5049
JS: 5042, 5048, 5394

Dogs–Fiction
IJ: 13, 111, 199, 209, 214, 219, 221, 229, 232, 239–40, 243–46, 258, 261, 271, 273, 510, 1377, 2017
J: 217, 223, 226, 247, 251, 272, 1453, 2353
JS: 33, 46, 195–96, 211, 280, 318, 320, 331, 5045

Dogs–Stories–Fiction
J: 270, 276

Dogs–Training
IJ: 5043, 5047

Dogsled racing–Fiction
JS: 2432

Dolls–Fiction
IJ: 1399

Dominican Republic
IJ: 4486

Don Quixote–Fiction
JS: 281

Douglass, Frederick
J: 3773
JS: 3772

Down's syndrome–Fiction
J: 823

Dragons–Fiction
IJ: 1535
J: 1454
JS: 1540

Drake, Sir Francis
IJ: 3630

Drawing and painting
IJ: 5392–93, 5399–400, 5403
J: 5397, 5402
JS: 5258, 5391, 5394–96, 5398, 5404–5, 5407–8

Drawing and painting–Fiction
IJ: 1032

Dreams
J: 3284

Dreams–Fiction
J: 1851

Dress
See Grooming, personal appearance, and dress

Drew, Charles
JS: 3919

Drought
JS: 5130

Drowning–Fiction
JS: 1854, 1958

Drug Enforcement Administration (U.S.)
JS: 2811

Drugs
IJ: 3115, 3122, 3124, 3129–30, 3135, 3151, 3157, 3159–60, 3166, 3170, 3178, 3451
JS: 2811, 3116–18, 3120–21, 3125, 3127, 3132–34, 3136–37, 3139, 3141, 3143, 3146–48, 3150, 3153–55, 3158, 3162, 3164, 3173–74, 3176–77, 3191, 3246, 3386, 3467, 3732

Drugs–Fiction
IJ: 111, 122, 165, 511
J: 859, 1092, 1344
JS: 33, 69–70, 82, 166, 306, 340, 760, 789, 793, 1035, 1081, 1309, 1841, 1970

Druids–Fiction
IJ: 1364

Drunk driving
JS: 3147, 3152, 3174

Drunk driving–Fiction
J: 1092
JS: 844, 2093

IJ = Intermediate–Junior High; J = Junior High; JS = Junior–Senior High

Du Bois, W. E. B.
J: 3774, 3775

Dunant, Henry
IJ: 3887

Dunbar, Paul Laurence
JS: 3668

Duncan, Isadora
IJ: 3710

Duncan, Isadora–Fiction
IJ: 1199

Duncan, Lois
JS: 3669

Dutch Americans
JS: 2929

Duvalier, François and Jean-Claude
IJ: 4114

Dwarfs–Fiction
JS: 721, 1897

Dylan, Bob
IJ: 3711

Dyslexia
See also Learning disabilities
IJ: 3334, 3346
JS: 3330, 3340

E

Eagles
IJ: 4971–72

Ear
IJ: 3312
J: 3307
JS: 3310

Earhart, Amelia
IJ: 3631, 3634
JS: 3632–33

Earth
IJ: 4150, 5073, 5078–79, 5083
J: 5080
JS: 5076, 5081

Earthquakes
IJ: 5070–71, 5084, 5087, 5090
J: 5072, 5088
JS: 5076

Earthquakes–Fiction
IJ: 64

Easter
J: 2720

Eastman, Charles Alexander–Fiction
JS: 1627

Eating disorders
J: 3333
JS: 3329, 3332, 3337, 3342, 3349, 3360

Eating disorders–Fiction
JS: 842

Eclipses
JS: 4811

Ecology
IJ: 2946, 2961, 5009, 5094–95, 5097
J: 2944
JS: 2951, 5082

Economic systems and institutions, 3029–3032

Economics and business
J: 3024–25, 3028, 3037
IJ: 3022–23
JS: 2843–44, 3026–27, 3029–30, 3041, 4192

Ecuador
IJ: 4499
JS: 4504

Edison, Thomas Alva
IJ: 3920–21

Education, 3043–3068

Eggs
IJ: 4921
J: 4966

Egrets
J: 4960

Egypt
IJ: 4300

Egypt–Fiction
IJ: 1519, 1544
J: 2046
JS: 1375, 1508

Egypt–Folklore
IJ: 2579

Egypt–History
IJ: 4189, 4202, 4204–5, 4207, 4291
J: 3997, 4203, 4206
JS: 3531, 3534, 3988, 3993

Einstein, Albert
IJ: 5158
JS: 3922

Eisenhower, Dwight D.
IJ: 3809–10
J: 3808
JS: 3811

El Cid–Fiction
IJ: 1587

El Salvador
IJ: 4476
JS: 4477

Elderly persons
IJ: 3109, 3113
JS: 3114

Elderly persons–Abuse–Fiction
J: 976

Elderly persons–Fiction
IJ: 387, 492, 650, 661, 894, 937, 969, 1042, 1055, 1094, 1126, 1178, 1409, 2091
J: 448, 477, 557, 976, 1533
JS: 428, 1050, 1170, 1184, 1325, 1438, 2206

Eleanor of Aquitaine
JS: 4065–66

Eleanor of Aquitaine–Fiction
J: 1584

Elections
IJ: 2834, 2836, 3043
JS: 2835

Electrical energy
IJ: 5169

Electricity
IJ: 3923, 5209, 5215–16, 5218
J: 5214
JS: 5211–13

Electromagnetism
JS: 5210

Electronic surveillance
JS: 5323

Electronics
IJ: 5311

Elephant Man
IJ: 4132
JS: 3369

Elephants–Fiction
IJ: 1516

Elizabeth I, Queen of England
IJ: 4398–99
JS: 4067

Elizabethan England
IJ: 4399
JS: 3682

Elizabethan England–Fiction
IJ: 1578, 1590
J: 1503, 1610

Ellington, Duke
IJ: 3696

Ellison, Ralph
JS: 3670

IJ = Intermediate–Junior High; J = Junior High; JS = Junior–Senior High

IJ = Intermediate–Junior High; J = Junior High; JS = Junior–Senior High

European Economic Community
IJ: 4372, 4383
J: 4371

Euthanasia
JS: 3000, 3108

Everglades (Florida)
IJ: 4697
JS: 4696

Everglades (Florida)–Fiction
IJ: 55

Evolution
IJ: 3918, 4164, 4166, 4168, 4171–72, 4174, 4176, 4911
J: 4844
JS: 4932

Excretory system
See Digestive and excretory systems

Exercise
IJ: 3354
JS: 3326–27

Experiments and projects, 4712–4745

Explorers
IJ: 3621, 3625–26, 3637, 4194, 4198, 4219, 4405, 4456, 4507, 4621
J: 3635
JS: 3620, 3628, 3639, 4619, 4623, 4630

Explorers–Biography, 3619–3642

Explorers–Fiction
IJ: 1692, 1709
J: 1699

Extrasensory perception (ESP)
IJ: 3272, 3279

Extrasensory perception (ESP) –Fiction
IJ: 2, 1201, 1373, 1397–99, 1414, 1517, 1614, 1898, 1992
J: 653, 1390, 2098, 2269, 2335, 2421
JS: 73, 1102, 1995, 2324, 2347

Extrasensory perception– Poetry
IJ: 2520

Extraterrestrial intelligence
JS: 4783

Extraterrestrial life
IJ: 4787, 4832

Extraterrestrial persons
IJ: 5296, 5491

Extraterrestrial persons– Fiction
IJ: 1474, 2294, 2303, 2306, 2360, 2389, 2399, 2422–23, 2425
J: 2263, 2277, 2336, 2340, 2352
JS: 21, 2191, 2378, 2387, 2397, 2404, 2410, 2415, 2419, 2428–29

Extraterrestrial persons– Poetry
IJ: 2497

Eyes
IJ: 3309, 3313, 4917
J: 3308

F

Fables
IJ: 2633
J: 2654

Fairy tales
See also Folklore and fairy tales
IJ: 1405, 1583, 2574–75, 2577, 2590, 3599
JS: 2568, 2595

Faisal, King of Saudi Arabia
JS: 4014

Faith healing–Fiction
JS: 39

Falcons–Fiction
J: 218
JS: 1965

Falkland Islands
IJ: 4506

Family
J: 3510, 3521
JS: 3500

Family life
J: 3484

Family life–Fiction
IJ: 604
J: 608
JS: 637

Family life–Poetry
JS: 2554

Family problems
IJ: 3112, 3166, 3482, 3486–88, 3491–92, 3499, 3503–4, 3517, 3519
J: 3165, 3484, 3497–98
JS: 3167, 3479, 3485, 3490, 3495–96, 3500, 3507, 3518, 3520

Family problems–Fiction
IJ: 28, 135, 145, 203, 214, 234, 390, 400, 402, 404, 418, 420, 422, 424–25, 435–36, 440, 442–43, 446, 451–53, 464, 471–72, 474–76, 478, 481, 483–85, 492–93, 495–99, 501, 504, 506, 510–11, 519, 522, 524, 527, 530–31, 533, 537, 545, 556, 561, 569, 571, 586, 589, 599, 605, 612–13, 622, 629–30, 634, 640, 642, 650, 654–57, 662–63, 666–67, 682, 689, 696, 698, 777, 836, 871, 892, 974, 1020, 1153, 1180, 1317, 1444, 1467, 1529, 1564, 1712, 1732, 1734
J: 96, 401, 403, 410–12, 415, 419, 426–27, 439, 447–50, 454–55, 457, 459, 467, 477, 479–80, 490–91, 500, 507, 515, 520, 525, 536, 541, 546, 549, 551–52, 557, 562, 568, 570, 572–73, 575, 597, 600, 610, 614, 619, 623, 627–28, 632, 636, 641, 646–48, 653, 658, 665, 670, 678–80, 695, 708, 758, 821, 837, 865, 889, 934–35, 1041, 1173, 1205, 1303, 1330, 1690, 1728
JS: 35, 97, 103, 336, 341, 384, 394, 407, 409, 413–14, 417, 428, 431–33, 437–38, 441, 456, 458, 463, 466, 468, 473, 487–88, 494, 503, 508–9, 526, 528–29, 535, 539–40, 553, 559, 563, 567, 576–80, 583–85, 591, 596, 598, 606, 615, 618, 625, 633, 638–39, 645, 651, 659, 664, 668–69, 671–72, 674, 676, 681, 686, 693, 697, 753, 764, 787, 791, 817, 828, 862, 874, 1004, 1007, 1013, 1017, 1022, 1059, 1083, 1100, 1139, 1169–70, 1224, 1267, 1726, 1937, 1968, 2000, 2145

Family reunions–Fiction
JS: 1880

Family stories–Fiction
IJ: 252, 312, 369, 377, 387, 405, 416, 461, 482, 516–17, 543, 554, 564–65, 574, 602, 621, 635, 673, 1010, 1167, 1237, 1707, 1718, 1882
J: 151, 368, 423, 445, 514, 534, 547–48, 587–88, 617, 677, 914, 1940
JS: 382, 429–30, 489, 555, 616, 620, 652, 790, 801, 919, 1102, 1165, 1292, 1739, 1880

Family violence
JS: 3507

Famine
IJ: 2970, 4292

IJ = Intermediate–Junior High; J = Junior High; JS = Junior–Senior High

IJ = Intermediate–Junior High; J = Junior High; JS = Junior–Senior High

IJ = Intermediate–Junior High; J = Junior High; JS = Junior–Senior High

1724, 1729, 1756, 1876, 1923,
1938, 2204
J: 378, 411, 423, 477, 532, 562,
582, 609, 643, 752, 773, 792,
855, 868, 870, 875–76, 889, 895,
902, 921, 956, 972, 976, 985,
992–93, 1015, 1019, 1027, 1029,
1087–88, 1097, 1107–8, 1124,
1138, 1145, 1238, 1240, 1242–45,
1265, 1302, 1316, 2098
JS: 231, 345–46, 456, 462, 676,
701, 713, 722, 726, 760, 800,
811, 848, 890, 918–19, 922–23,
938, 948–49, 965, 1004, 1025,
1037, 1043, 1095, 1098, 1121,
1133, 1146, 1159, 1204, 1234,
1250, 1262, 1285, 1293, 1299–
301, 1308, 1312, 1775, 1854,
2118, 2271

Fritz, Jean
JS: 3671

Frogs and toads
JS: 4900

Frontier life (U.S.)
IJ: 3637, 3859, 3864, 3882, 3888,
4625–26, 4628, 4635, 4637
J: 3894, 4622, 4629, 4631, 4634,
4638, 4642
JS: 3693, 3827, 4618, 4623, 4627,
4630, 4632, 4639–40, 4643–44,
4654

Frontier life (U.S.)–Fiction
IJ: 219, 1625, 1634, 1642, 1649,
1665, 1692, 1696, 1698, 1702,
1704, 1707, 1712, 1715–16,
1718–20, 1953
J: 128, 1621, 1691, 1694–95, 1697,
1699–700, 1706, 1708, 1711,
1721
JS: 161, 313, 1689, 1693, 1703,
1705, 1710, 1713–14

Fuller, Buckminster
IJ: 3744

Fund-raising
IJ: 3560

Fungi
J: 4867

Furniture
JS: 3553

Future prediction
JS: 5517

Futurism
IJ: 3006–07, 4515, 5234, 5332

G

Galaxies
JS: 4827

Gallaudet, T. H.
JS: 3892

Gambling–Fiction
IJ: 1916

Games
IJ: 5484, 5541

Gandhi, Indira
IJ: 4016
JS: 4015

Gandhi, Mahatma
IJ: 4018
JS: 4017

Gandhi, Rajiv
IJ: 4016

Gangs
J: 3017
JS: 3002, 3021

Gangs–Fiction
IJ: 117, 146, 155, 1289, 2433
J: 373, 877, 1258
JS: 67–68, 91, 896, 958, 2007

Garbage
JS: 2952

Gardens–Fiction
J: 1492

Garibaldi, Giuseppi
JS: 4073

Garvey, Marcus
JS: 3776

Gawain
J: 2599

Gaza Strip
IJ: 4436

Geldof, Bob
IJ: 3716–17

Gemayel Family
IJ: 4019

Gems
IJ: 5240

Genealogy
IJ: 3514

Genealogy–Fiction
J: 534

Genetic diseases
JS: 3202

Genetic engineering
IJ: 3255

J: 3254
JS: 3253, 3256, 5034

Genetics
IJ: 3248–51, 3255, 4841
J: 3185, 3252, 3254
JS: 3192, 3253, 3256–59

Genetics–Fiction
IJ: 2259

Genghis Khan
JS: 4020

Geochemistry
JS: 5081

Geography, 4138–4701

Geology, 5070–5110

Georgia
JS: 4699

Georgia–Fiction
IJ: 912
J: 395
JS: 396

Geothermal resources
J: 5174
JS: 5176

German Americans
JS: 2915, 2917

Germany (East)
IJ: 4385

Germany–Fiction
IJ: 1746, 1758
J: 1574, 1750
JS: 1332, 1744, 1754

Germany–Folklore
IJ: 2598

Germany–History
IJ: 4083, 4248, 4271, 4274, 4387–
89
J: 4135
JS: 2915, 4051, 4072, 4082, 4084,
4131, 4240, 4247, 4251, 4384,
4386

Germs
IJ: 3222

Gershwin, George
JS: 3697

Getty, J. Paul
IJ: 3926

Gettysburg, Battle of
IJ: 4610, 4612
JS: 4608

Ghana–History
JS: 3994

Ghosts
IJ: 2622, 5495

IJ = Intermediate–Junior High; J = Junior High; JS = Junior–Senior High

Ghosts (*cont.*)
J: 5496–97, 5499, 5503, 5505, 5513
JS: 5398, 5494

Ghosts–Fiction
IJ: 66, 149, 400, 1510–11, 1777,
  1784, 1792, 1798, 1801, 1812,
  1829, 1832, 1839–40, 1842, 1844,
  1852, 1856, 2023
J: 1358, 1791, 1795, 1825, 1831,
  1845
JS: 311, 1776, 1781, 1794, 1802,
  1816, 1826, 1836, 1853, 5518

Gibson, Althea
JS: 3978

Gifted children
IJ: 3430
JS: 3447

Gifted children–Fiction
IJ: 1514

Gilbreth Family–Fiction
JS: 3893

Girl Scouts of America
J: 3523
JS: 3524

Girlfriends
JS: 3454

Girlfriends–Fiction
IJ: 915, 2450
J: 238, 864, 2464
JS: 558, 1071, 1099, 1195, 2127,
  2195

Girls–Fiction
IJ: 312

Girls–Grooming
IJ: 3261, 3265
JS: 3263, 3266

Girls–Guidance manual
IJ: 3473–74
JS: 3478

Girls–Puberty
IJ: 3380
JS: 3397

Glasnost
JS: 4288

Glass
IJ: 5233, 5238

Glasses
IJ: 3309

Glasses–Fiction
JS: 1382

Gliding and soaring
JS: 5544

Globe Theatre
JS: 2666

Goblins–Fiction
JS: 1541

Gold
IJ: 5321
J: 5316

Gold Rush
IJ: 4620, 4633
J: 4646
JS: 4617

Gold Rush–Fiction
J: 1700

Gold Rush–Poetry
IJ: 2571

Goldwyn, Samuel
IJ: 3745

Golem
J: 2608

Golf
IJ: 3981
J: 3982

Gorbachev, Mikhail
IJ: 4075–77
JS: 4074

Gorillas
J: 4938

Gorillas–Fiction
JS: 194

Gothic art
JS: 3540

Government
J: 2759
JS: 2776

Government–United States
See United States–
  Government

Government and political science, 2730–2844

Grammar
J: 3068

Grand Canyon
J: 4681

Grandparents
J: 3510

Grandparents–Fiction
IJ: 19, 202, 377, 398, 416, 461,
  499, 879, 1269, 2005
J: 419, 448, 479, 507, 646, 821,
  926, 1193
JS: 394, 428–29, 433, 438, 503,
  580, 668, 904

Grant, Ulysses S.
IJ: 3813

Graphics
IJ: 5406

Grasshoppers
IJ: 4990

Grasslands
JS: 5101

Graves–Fiction
JS: 2420

Great Britain
See also England
IJ: 4392

Great Britain–Fiction, 289–311

Great Britain–History
IJ: 4220, 4395
JS: 4058, 4096, 4108, 4401

Great Britain–Plays, 2486–2487,
  2665–2666

Great Britain–Poetry, 2522–
  2533

Great Danes–Fiction
IJ: 214

Great Lakes
IJ: 4532

Greece–Cookbooks
IJ: 5443

Greece–Fiction
IJ: 150, 1334–35, 1500
J: 1567
JS: 2154

Greece–Historical fiction, 1548

Greece–History
IJ: 2652, 4046, 4210–11
J: 4209
JS: 4041, 4102, 4208, 4212, 5647

Greece–Mythology
IJ: 2636, 2639, 2644–46, 2649–51,
  2653, 2655
J: 2641
JS: 2629, 2634, 2637–38, 2640,
  2642–43, 2647–48, 2656

Greece–Mythology–Fiction
IJ: 1500, 1548

Greenhouse effect
IJ: 2945, 2947
JS: 2941, 5130

Greenland–Fiction
IJ: 1575

Greenland–History
J: 4404

Greeting cards
IJ: 5384

Grey, Lady Jane
J: 4078

IJ = Intermediate–Junior High; J = Junior High; JS = Junior–Senior High

IJ = Intermediate–Junior High; J = Junior High; JS = Junior–Senior High

IJ = Intermediate–Junior High; J = Junior High; JS = Junior–Senior High

Human anatomy
JS: 5405

Human behavior
J: 4165
JS: 3278, 3419, 3440, 3448

Human body
IJ: 3101, 3267–72, 3274, 3276–77,
3325
JS: 3273

**Human development and be-
havior,** 3418–3526

Human rights, 2845–2869
See also Civil rights

Humanitarians
IJ: 3748

Humor and satire–Fiction, 2659

Humorous stories
J: 2589

Humorous stories–Fiction
IJ: 963, 983, 1006, 1008, 1275,
1381, 1412, 1862, 1864, 1866–67,
1870, 1873–76, 1879, 1881–85,
1892–93, 1895–96, 1898, 1900,
1909–10, 1912, 1915–16, 1918–
20, 1923, 1926–29, 1936, 1938–
39, 1945, 2310, 2391–92, 2462
J: 1433, 1668, 1861, 1863, 1871,
1886–89, 1891, 1899, 1908, 1911,
1917, 1925, 1931, 1933–34, 1940,
1943, 2256
JS: 325, 488, 891, 1137, 1865,
1868–69, 1877–78, 1880, 1890,
1894, 1897, 1901–7, 1913–14,
1921–22, 1924, 1930, 1935, 1937,
1941–42, 1944, 1946, 2018, 2211,
2224, 2226, 2257

Hungary–History
J: 4375
JS: 4136, 4374

Hunger and starvation
IJ: 2970
JS: 2989

Hunger and starvation–Fiction
JS: 1327, 2268

Hunting–Fiction
JS: 167, 762

Huron Indians
IJ: 4530

Hurricanes–Fiction
IJ: 119
J: 925

Hussein, King of Jordan
JS: 4025–26

Huynh, Quang Nhuong
JS: 4128

Hydrocephaly–Fiction
IJ: 550

Hygiene and physical fitness,
3323–3328

Hypnosis
IJ: 3272

I

Iacocca, Lee
IJ: 3929

Ice Age–Fiction
IJ: 1543

Ice ages
JS: 4147–48

Ice hockey
IJ: 5628

Ice skating
IJ: 5629
JS: 3980, 5630–31

Ice skating–Fiction
IJ: 2045
J: 632, 1191
JS: 2170, 2466

Idaho–Fiction
IJ: 1113

Idol, Billy
IJ: 3723

Igloos
IJ: 4509

Illiteracy
JS: 2983

Illness
See Diseases and illness;
Illness–Fiction

Illness–Fiction
IJ: 574
J: 500, 507, 610, 781, 818, 1038,
2374
JS: 577–78, 615, 713, 722, 726,
734, 828, 1004, 1085

Illusions
J: 3304

Immigration
IJ: 2876, 2891, 2896, 2902, 2907,
2913, 2919, 2930, 2935–36, 2986,
3514, 4475
J: 2874–75, 2877, 2901, 2928, 3749
JS: 2870–73, 2890, 2900, 2908–9,
2916–18, 2922, 2924–25, 2933,
2937, 2990

Immigration–Fiction
IJ: 1349, 1664
J: 163
JS: 355, 553, 863, 1772

**Immigration and Naturaliza-
tion Service (U.S.)**
JS: 2873

Immune system
IJ: 3101, 3221–22
J: 3204, 3220
JS: 3198

Incas
IJ: 4470, 4492
JS: 4502

Incas–Fiction
IJ: 1612

India
IJ: 4347–48, 4363
J: 4039, 4350

India–Cookbooks
IJ: 5430

India–Fiction
J: 337
JS: 304, 385, 1327

India–Folklore
JS: 2581

India–History
IJ: 4016, 4018
JS: 4015, 4017, 4032

India–Mythology
JS: 2631

India–Poetry
JS: 2528

Indiana–Fiction
J: 1673

Indians
JS: 4458

Indians of Central America
IJ: 4482
J: 4116

Indians of North America
IJ: 4180, 4463, 4544, 4565, 4571
J: 4550
JS: 2803, 2899, 2921, 3555–56,
4508, 4543, 4566

**Indians of North America–
Biography**
IJ: 3753, 3898
J: 3751, 3904
JS: 3901

**Indians of North America–
Fiction**
IJ: 78, 188, 202, 213, 1625–26,
1630, 1634, 1640, 1642, 1645,
1649, 1704, 1720

IJ = Intermediate–Junior High; J = Junior High; JS = Junior–Senior High

J

IJ = Intermediate–Junior High; J = Junior High; JS = Junior–Senior High

Jackson, Jesse
IJ: 3777, 3779–80
JS: 3778

Jackson, Mahalia
J: 3724

Jackson, Stonewall
JS: 3867

Jamaica–Fiction
IJ: 339
JS: 421

James I, King of England
J: 4086

James, Jesse
J: 3894

Jamestown Colony
JS: 4574

Japan
IJ: 4254, 4322, 4351–53, 4355
JS: 4349, 4356

Japan–Art
JS: 3550

Japan–Cookbooks
IJ: 5441

Japan–Fiction
IJ: 1560
J: 1249, 1557, 2457
JS: 538, 1559, 1561

Japan–Folklore
IJ: 2582, 2585

Japan–History
J: 4023, 4323
JS: 4263, 4354

Japanese Americans
JS: 2922, 4127, 4657

Japanese Americans–Fiction
IJ: 349, 390–91
J: 392
JS: 359, 366, 384

Japanese Canadians–Fiction
IJ: 1753

Jazz
IJ: 3561
JS: 3566, 3646, 3698, 3705

Jazz–Fiction
J: 1036
JS: 1035

Jealousy–Fiction
JS: 869, 2208

Jefferson, Thomas
IJ: 3817
JS: 3816, 3818

Jerusalem
IJ: 4431

Jet engines
IJ: 5344

Jewels–Fiction
IJ: 2105

Jewish Americans
IJ: 2889, 2891, 2894, 2896
JS: 2890, 2893

Jewish Americans–Fiction
JS: 626, 1763

Jewish customs–Fiction
IJ: 1063

Jewish folklore
J: 2608, 2697

Jewish history
IJ: 2892, 2894, 2896, 2898, 4007,
4112, 4237, 4239, 4256, 4265,
4411, 4435
J: 4028, 4272, 4286, 4434
JS: 2893, 2895, 4238, 4245, 4257,
4264

Jewish history–Fiction
IJ: 1641, 4275
JS: 1744

Jewish history–Plays
J: 2485

Jewish holy days
IJ: 2713, 2726
J: 2697, 2700–2
JS: 2724

Jewish holy days–Fiction
JS: 383

Jewish holy days–Folklore
J: 2589

Jews
IJ: 2889
J: 2697
JS: 2712, 2897, 4377

Jews–Biography
IJ: 3683–84, 3902, 3943, 4022,
4050, 4092, 4106, 4435
J: 3675, 3860, 4003, 4040
JS: 3677, 3697, 4021, 4037, 4064,
4105

Jews–Ceremonies
IJ: 2725
J: 2699, 2706

Jews–Fiction
IJ: 338, 344, 376, 482, 621, 1314,
1349, 1590, 1595–96, 1758–59,
1762, 1767, 1771, 2461
J: 364, 378, 380, 670, 773, 1243,
1329, 1586, 1599, 1760, 1766
JS: 332, 336, 381, 626, 707, 1096,
1260, 1342, 1763, 1765, 1770,
1772, 1826, 2219

Joan of Arc
IJ: 4087

Joan of Arc–Fiction
IJ: 1415

Job hunting
JS: 3069, 3071, 3094

Jobs–Fiction
IJ: 1140, 1200, 1211, 1231, 2091,
2255
J: 92, 552, 1176, 1316
JS: 1670, 2058

Jogging
J: 3328

John Paul II, Pope
J: 4088
JS: 4089

John XXIII, Pope
IJ: 4090

Johnson, Lyndon B.
IJ: 3819
JS: 3820–21

Jokes and riddles
IJ: 5471–82

Joplin, Scott
JS: 3698

Jordan
IJ: 4443

Jordan, Michael
IJ: 3964

Jordan–History
JS: 4025–26

Journalism
IJ: 2688–90
JS: 2692

Journalism–Ethics
JS: 2693

Journalism–Fiction
IJ: 1872
J: 2249
JS: 1136, 2167

Journalists
IJ: 3874

Juarez, Benito
J: 4115–16

Judaism
IJ: 2713
JS: 2712

Jupiter (planet)
IJ: 4813

Jury
IJ: 2822
JS: 2829

IJ = Intermediate–Junior High; J = Junior High; JS = Junior–Senior High

Juvenile delinquency
JS: 2821, 2979, 3001–2

Juvenile delinquency–Fiction
J: 1097, 1107
JS: 67–70, 133, 521, 1204

K

Kai-Shek, Chiang
J: 4011

Kansas–Fiction
IJ: 1875–76
JS: 1905

Karate
IJ: 5635, 5638–39, 5641
J: 5633
JS: 5634

Karate–Fiction
J: 2473

Karting
JS: 5527

Keller, Helen
IJ: 3895–96
JS: 3897

Kennedy, John F.
IJ: 3822, 3824
J: 3823
JS: 3825

Kentucky–Fiction
IJ: 424
JS: 473, 649

Kenya
IJ: 4296–97

Kenya–Fiction
IJ: 171

Kerr, M. E.
JS: 3674

KGB (Russian secret police)
JS: 4424

Kherdian, Veron
JS: 4129

Khomeini, Ayatollah
JS: 4027

Khrushchev, Nikita
JS: 4091

Kidnapping
JS: 3015

Kidnapping–Fiction
IJ: 13, 40, 44, 47, 83, 136, 139,

144–45, 404, 1514, 1666, 1974,
1977, 2097, 2313, 2333, 2349
J: 9, 32, 1948, 2038, 2061
JS: 60, 102, 307, 583, 1472, 1937,
1972, 1994, 1996, 2014, 2022,
2031, 2047, 2086, 2371, 2403

Killer bees
IJ: 4999
J: 4992

Killilea, Karen
JS: 4130

King Arthur
See Arthur, King

King, Martin Luther, Jr.
IJ: 3781–82, 3785, 3788–89
JS: 2854, 3783–84, 3786–87

King Philip's War–Fiction
JS: 1644

Kiowa Indians
IJ: 4569

Kissinger, Henry
JS: 3868

Kites
IJ: 5418
J: 5632

Klondike Gold Rush
IJ: 4462
J: 4646

Knights
IJ: 4227, 4390
J: 2607

Knights–Fiction
IJ: 1591
J: 1598

Knights–Folklore
J: 2599

Knitting
J: 5412

Koehn, Ilse
JS: 4131

Korczak, Janusz
IJ: 4092

Korea
IJ: 4360
J: 2923

Korean Americans
J: 2923

Korean Americans–Fiction
J: 572

Korean War
IJ: 4666

Ku Klux Klan
JS: 2847

Ku Klux Klan–Fiction
IJ: 357

Kurtzman, Harvey
IJ: 3650

Kuwait
IJ: 4444

L

Labor movements–Fiction
IJ: 942

Labor problems–Fiction
IJ: 1257

Labor unions
IJ: 2998, 3040, 3792
J: 3037, 3039
JS: 3038, 4376

Laboratories
J: 4743

Ladybugs
IJ: 4994

Lafayette, Marquis de
JS: 4093

Lakes
JS: 5010

Language
IJ: 2683
J: 2681, 5229

Language and communication,
2673–2694

Larsson, Carl
JS: 3651

Las Vegas–Fiction
IJ: 1916

Lasers
IJ: 5202
J: 5198
JS: 5201

Latchkey children
IJ: 3460, 3504, 3511

Latin America
IJ: 2754, 4494
JS: 2746

Latin America–Fiction
JS: 1333

Latin America–Historical fiction, 1612–1619

Lauper, Cyndi
IJ: 3725

IJ = Intermediate–Junior High; J = Junior High; JS = Junior–Senior High

IJ = Intermediate–Junior High; J = Junior High; JS = Junior–Senior High

M

MacArthur, Douglas
IJ: 3870–71

Maccabeus, Judas
J: 4028

Machinery
IJ: 5221, 5236
J: 5315
JS: 5313

Madagascar
IJ: 4310
J: 4315

Madison, James
IJ: 3831–32
JS: 3833

Madonna
IJ: 3728

Magazines
JS: 2691

Magellan, Ferdinand
JS: 3639

Magic
IJ: 2577, 5450–52
J: 4729, 5448–49, 5453–54
JS: 5447, 5455

Magic–Fiction
IJ: 1366, 1371–72, 1418, 1440, 2370
J: 1360, 1384
JS: 1376, 1457, 1837

Magicians–Fiction
IJ: 1400

Magnetism
IJ: 5215

Maine
IJ: 5145

Maine–Fiction
IJ: 465, 667, 881, 1034, 1724
J: 2043
JS: 668

Makeup
JS: 3617

Malawi
J: 4314

Malcolm X
IJ: 3790

Mammals
IJ: 4887–88, 4911, 4925, 4929, 4934–35
J: 4930–31, 4938, 4947, 4949
JS: 4923, 4926, 4932, 4936

Mammals–extinct
JS: 4148

Mammals–Field guides
JS: 4889

Mandela, Nelson
J: 3991
JS: 3989–90

Mandela, Winnie
JS: 3989–90, 3992

Manners
J: 3445
JS: 3440–42, 3469

Manufacturing
IJ: 4580, 5223
J: 5222

Mao Tse-tung
J: 4029
JS: 4030, 4333, 4335

Maps and globes
J: 4140–42
JS: 4139

Marathon race
JS: 5673

Marco Polo
IJ: 4219

Marcos, Ferdinand
JS: 4045

Mardi Gras–Fiction
J: 2020

Marijuana
IJ: 3115, 3130
JS: 3153, 3173

Marine and freshwater life,
5008–5033

Marine biology
IJ: 3090
J: 3092

Marine Corps (U.S.)
JS: 4262, 5373

Marines–Fiction
J: 158

Marino, Dan
IJ: 3973

Maritime history
J: 3886

Maritime regions
JS: 5098

Marley, Bob
J: 3729

Marriage
IJ: 3489
JS: 3490, 3496

Mars
JS: 4824

Marshall, George
JS: 3872

Marshall Plan
JS: 3872

Marshall, Thurgood
JS: 3873

Marshes
J: 5099

Martial arts
IJ: 5636–39, 5641
J: 5633
JS: 5634, 5640

Marx, Karl
JS: 2757

Mary, Queen of Scots
JS: 4067, 4097

Mary, Queen of Scots–Fiction
JS: 1582

Masks
JS: 3617

Mass media
JS: 3595

Massachusetts–Fiction
IJ: 1727

Matchmaking–Fiction
J: 2143
JS: 1906

Mathematical puzzles
IJ: 5119
J: 5115, 5118

Mathematics
IJ: 5114, 5307
J: 5115
JS: 3935, 5113, 5116

Mathematics–Dictionaries
JS: 5111

Matter
IJ: 5066

Mayan Indians
IJ: 2984, 4457
JS: 4458

Mayan Indians–Fiction
J; 1616
JS: 147

Mayflower–Fiction
J: 1637, 1651

Mead, Margaret
JS: 3931–33

Media
See Writing and the media

IJ = Intermediate–Junior High; J = Junior High; JS = Junior–Senior High

IJ = Intermediate–Junior High; J = Junior High; JS = Junior–Senior High

IJ = Intermediate–Junior High; J = Junior High; JS = Junior–Senior High

Movie stars–Fiction
IJ: 2030
J: 2087
JS: 2178

Moving
IJ: 3420
JS: 3464

Moving–Fiction
IJ: 292, 605, 661, 893, 950, 1006,
1125, 1177, 1558, 1626
J: 189, 426, 562, 679, 706, 985,
1277, 1280
JS: 606, 801, 900, 1017, 1052,
1203, 1946, 2000

Mozambique
J: 4308

Muir, John
IJ: 3934

Multiple sclerosis–Fiction
JS: 831

Mummies
IJ: 4189

Murrow, Edward R.
IJ: 3874

Muscular system
IJ: 3315

Museums–Fiction
IJ: 86
JS: 1957

Mushrooms
IJ: 4848
JS: 4849

Music
See also Composers
IJ: 3554, 3561–62
JS: 3075, 3557

Music–Fiction
IJ: 8, 1893
JS: 417

Music–History
IJ: 3559
JS: 3556

**Music–Indians of North Amer-
ica**
JS: 3555

Musical instruments
IJ: 3571
J: 3573
JS: 3572

Musicals
JS: 3570

Musicians
J: 3569
JS: 3646

Musicians–Biography
IJ: 3711
JS: 3706, 3737

Mussolini, Benito
J: 4098
JS: 4099

Mustangs–Fiction
IJ: 233

Mysteries
JS: 2975

**Mystery and detective stories–
Fiction,** 1947–2116

Mystery stories–Fiction
IJ: 116, 635, 1372, 1452, 1560,
1569, 1571, 1834, 1949, 1952–54,
1963, 1966–67, 1971, 1974–78,
1987, 1992, 1997–99, 2005,
2008–12, 2015–17, 2023, 2029–
30, 2035, 2037, 2040–41, 2045,
2048, 2052–57, 2066–67, 2069,
2077–80, 2083, 2085, 2088–89,
2091–92, 2095–97, 2099–100,
2104–5, 2107, 2109, 2111, 2113
J: 547, 1358, 1521, 1570, 1804,
1948, 1969, 1980, 2001–3, 2013,
2020, 2026–28, 2032, 2038,
2042–43, 2046, 2049–51, 2061,
2068, 2070–72, 2082, 2087, 2103,
2108, 2112, 2115–16
JS: 105, 300, 328–29, 598, 1058,
1368, 1504, 1830, 1843, 1947,
1950–51, 1955–62, 1964–65,
1968, 1970, 1972–73, 1979,
1981–86, 1988–91, 1993–94,
1996, 2000, 2004, 2006–7, 2014,
2018–19, 2021–22, 2024–25,
2031, 2033–34, 2036, 2044, 2047,
2058–60, 2062–65, 2073–76,
2081, 2084, 2086, 2090, 2093–94,
2101–2, 2106, 2110, 2295

Mythology
IJ: 1548, 2633, 2639, 2644–46,
2649–51, 2653
J: 2630, 2641, 2654
JS: 2626–27, 2629, 2631–32, 2638,
2640, 2642–43, 2647–48, 2658

Mythology–Anthologies
IJ: 2657
JS: 2634–35, 2637, 2656

Mythology–Fiction
IJ: 1484, 1548

N

Nader, Ralph
IJ: 3875

Names
IJ: 2678
J: 2676, 2679

Nanticoke Indians
IJ: 4559

**Napoleon, Emperor of the
French**
IJ: 4395

Napoleonic Wars
IJ: 4395
JS: 4401

Narragansett Indians
JS: 4563

Narrative poems
JS: 2552, 2559

Nasser, Gamal Abdel
JS: 3993

**National Aeronautics and
Space Administration
(NASA)**
IJ: 4789
JS: 4775, 4791, 4798

**National Archives and Records
Administration (U.S.)**
JS: 2808

National debt (U.S.)
JS: 2844

**National Foundation on the
Arts and Humanities**
JS: 2806

National Park Service (U.S.)
JS: 2799

National Parks (U.S.)
JS: 4691, 4978

National Science Foundation
JS: 2779

Native Americans
See Indians of North America

Natural disasters
IJ: 5084–85, 5087, 5090–91
J: 5089
JS: 3449, 4645, 5086

Natural disasters–Fiction
J: 156
JS: 157

Natural history
IJ: 4993

IJ = Intermediate–Junior High; J = Junior High; JS = Junior–Senior High

IJ = Intermediate–Junior High; J = Junior High; JS = Junior–Senior High

Norwegian Americans
IJ: 2910

Norwegian Americans–Fiction
JS: 489

Nova Scotia
IJ: 4460

Nova Scotia–Fiction
IJ: 1615
JS: 494

Nuclear accidents–Fiction
J: 107, 154
JS: 2365

Nuclear energy
IJ: 5065, 5187
J: 5189, 5191–92, 5194
JS: 5188, 5190, 5193

Nuclear energy–Fiction
J: 1345

Nuclear physics
JS: 5166, 5217

Nuclear war
J: 2842
JS: 2735, 2739, 2744, 2748, 2776

Nuclear war–Fiction
IJ: 138, 173, 1509, 2308
J: 1296
JS: 104, 1028, 1337, 2302, 2304,
   2311, 2357, 2367, 2388, 2396,
   2409

Nuclear weapons
IJ: 2752, 5365
J: 2842
JS: 2739, 2751, 2753, 2755, 5377

Numbers
IJ: 5117

Numerology
J: 5511

Nurses
IJ: 3089, 3238, 3936

Nutrition and diet
IJ: 3298, 3323, 3354, 3357, 3359,
   3362–63, 5433
J: 3361
JS: 3327, 3355–56, 3358

Nutritional diseases
JS: 3196

O

Oak tree
J: 4855

Obesity
J: 3352
JS: 3351, 3353

Obesity–Fiction
IJ: 745, 830, 996
J: 704, 752, 758, 815, 1067, 1110
JS: 741, 842, 1022, 1241, 2171

Occult–Fiction
JS: 1950

Occupations
See Careers; Job hunting;
   Jobs–Fiction

Ocean liners
IJ: 5362

Ocean liners–Fiction
IJ: 2111
J: 2042
JS: 303, 1922

Oceanography
IJ: 5135–37, 5144
J: 5077, 5142

Oceans
IJ: 3918, 4961, 5138, 5143–44
J: 5011, 5139–42
JS: 3628, 4179, 5022–23

Oceans–Fiction
JS: 267

Oceans–Poetry
IJ: 2558

O'Connor, Sandra Day
IJ: 3877
JS: 3876

Odysseus
IJ: 2636

Ohio–Fiction
J: 439, 1697
JS: 1713

Oil
IJ: 3926, 5179–80, 5186
J: 4426, 5185
JS: 4430, 5184

Oil rigs
IJ: 5183

Oil spills
J: 2954

O'Keeffe, Georgia
J: 3656
JS: 3655

Oklahoma–Fiction
J: 276

Old age
See also Elderly persons
IJ: 3109, 3113
JS: 3114

Old age–Fiction
IJ: 937, 969

Olympic Games
J: 5646
JS: 5647

Only children
IJ: 3503

Opossums
J: 4946

Oppenheimer, J. Robert
IJ: 3937
JS: 3938

Optical illusions
IJ: 3303, 5162
J: 3306, 3311

Optics
J: 5203

Orchestras–Fiction
IJ: 2037
J: 2038

Oregon
JS: 4535

Oregon–Fiction
JS: 342

Oregon Trail
JS: 4639

Organ transplants
IJ: 3184
J: 3182
JS: 3181, 3183

Orphans–Fiction
IJ: 523, 554, 1478, 1517, 2366
J: 159, 410, 2027, 2250
JS: 60, 638

Osage Indians
J: 4568

Otters
JS: 5147

Otters–Fiction
J: 160
JS: 1479

Outdoor life
IJ: 5593
J: 3522
JS: 5046, 5596

Owens, Jesse
IJ: 3976

Owls
J: 4973

Ozark Mountains–Fiction
IJ: 261

Ozark Mountains–Folklore
J: 2624

IJ = Intermediate–Junior High; J = Junior High; JS = Junior–Senior High

Ozone layer
JS: 2942

P

Pacific Islands Americans
JS: 2914

Pacific Ocean
JS: 3636

Pacific Ocean–World War II
J: 4242

Pacific Rim
See Asia; China; Japan

Pacific States
J: 4694
IJ: 4692–93
JS: 4691, 4876

Pacifism–Fiction
JS: 1741

Pacifists
JS: 2939

Packaging
J: 3042

Pahlavi, Mohammed Reza
IJ: 4033

Paige, Satchel
IJ: 3958

Paine, Thomas
JS: 3878

Paiute Indians
IJ: 4538

Pakistan–Fiction
JS: 1351

Paleontology, 4143–4163

Paleontology–Fiction
JS: 1701

Palestine–Fiction
JS: 1545–46

Palestine Liberation Organization
J: 4005

Panama Canal
IJ: 4483
JS: 2737

Pandas
J: 4947

Paper
IJ: 5239

Paper crafts
IJ: 5409–10
JS: 5411

Parachutes
JS: 5544

Parades
J: 3587

Parapsychology
IJ: 3279

Parenting
JS: 3480

Parenting–Fiction
JS: 3893

Parents
IJ: 3166, 3215, 3486–87, 3492
J: 3165
JS: 2983, 3110, 3163, 3167, 3502, 3518, 3520

Parents–Fiction
IJ: 435, 442, 470–71, 478, 484–85, 493, 496, 510, 522, 556, 589, 622, 629, 634, 655, 803, 962, 979, 1287, 1392, 1885, 1928
J: 454, 457, 541, 560, 575, 597, 636, 647, 837, 932, 1067, 1219, 1911, 1931
JS: 120, 431, 458, 487, 539–40, 559, 576, 591, 625, 639, 669, 691, 735, 765, 953, 1007, 1053, 1250

Parents–Poetry
IJ: 2513

Paris–Fiction
J: 2028

Parliamentary practice
IJ: 3443
JS: 3444

Parthenon
JS: 4212

Particles (physics)
JS: 5165, 5217

Passover
IJ: 2726

Passover–Fiction
JS: 1536

Pasteur, Louis
IJ: 3939

Patent, Gregory
IJ: 4338

Patton, George
IJ: 3879

Paul Bunyan
JS: 2623

Paul, Saint
J: 4034

Payton, Walter
J: 3974

Peace, 2734–2756

Peace Corps
JS: 2814

Pearl Harbor
J: 4242, 4252
JS: 4277, 4280

Pearl Harbor–Fiction
JS: 1764

Peer pressure
J: 3472
JS: 3450, 3459

Peer pressure–Fiction
IJ: 866
J: 513
JS: 1049, 1196, 2472

Performing arts, 3579–3618
See also Ballet; Dance; Motion pictures; Television; Theater; Videos

Pen pals–Fiction
J: 822

Penguins
J: 4974–75

Penicillin
IJ: 3244

Pennsylvania–Fiction
IJ: 1131, 1636
J: 1725
JS: 1639, 1705

Pennsylvania Dutch
IJ: 2911

Perception
J: 3304, 3311

Perfectionism
JS: 3448

Pericles
JS: 4102

Peron, Juan
JS: 4122

Pershing, John J.
JS: 4231

Personal appearance
See Grooming, personal appearance, and dress; Hygiene and physical fitness; Skin care

IJ = Intermediate–Junior High; J = Junior High; JS = Junior–Senior High

IJ = Intermediate–Junior High; J = Junior High; JS = Junior–Senior High

IJ = Intermediate–Junior High; J = Junior High; JS = Junior–Senior High

Powhatan Indians
JS: 4536

Prayers
IJ: 2670

Praying mantis
IJ: 4995

Pregnancy
IJ: 3175
JS: 3384, 3386, 3388–90, 3394,
3407, 3481

Pregnancy–Fiction
JS: 631, 697, 724–25, 779, 797,
918, 987, 1130

Prehistoric animals
IJ: 4149–50, 4160

Prehistoric life
JS: 4157

Prehistoric man
IJ: 4164, 4168, 4172, 4175, 4196
J: 4167

Prehistoric man–Fiction
IJ: 1543
J: 1542, 2003

Prehistoric times–Fiction
J: 1476

Prejudice
JS: 2881, 2883

Prejudice–Fiction
IJ: 375–76, 1727
J: 353, 363–64
JS: 334–35, 366, 379, 385, 388,
396, 707, 721, 991, 1342

Presidency (U.S.), 2774–2777

Presidents (U.S.)
IJ: 2774, 2777, 3750, 4133
JS: 2775–76, 3754, 3838, 3849

Presidents (U.S.)–Biography
IJ: 3803, 3806, 3809–10, 3812–14,
3817, 3819, 3822, 3824, 3826,
3828–32, 3835, 3837, 3843,
3846–47, 3851, 3853, 3855
J: 3804, 3807–8, 3815, 3823, 3844–
45, 3848, 3852, 3854
JS: 3805, 3811, 3816, 3818, 3820–
21, 3825, 3827, 3833–34, 3836,
3842, 3850, 3856

Presidents (U.S.)–Fiction
JS: 674

Presidents (U.S.)–Scandals
JS: 4517

Presley, Elvis
JS: 3731–32

Presley, Elvis–Fiction
JS: 2199

Preston, Bruce
IJ: 4133

Prince Edward Island–Fiction
J: 587

Prince (singer)
IJ: 3733

Princesses
IJ: 3985

Prison
See also Crime and criminals
JS: 2978, 2982

Prison–Fiction
IJ: 110, 244, 442, 475
J: 865, 1525
JS: 103, 282, 1582, 1617, 2225

Privacy
IJ: 2866

Private schools
J: 3056

Private schools–Fiction
IJ: 533, 1194, 1231, 1313
J: 1217, 1796, 2468
JS: 824, 943, 952, 1073, 1096,
1230, 1790, 1991, 2036, 2198

Propaganda
J: 2694

Prostitution–Fiction
JS: 687

Protestantism–History
IJ: 4113

Psychoanalysis
J: 3424
JS: 3925

**Psychology and human behav-
ior,** 3418–3426

Psychotherapy–Fiction
IJ: 1252

Puberty
IJ: 3404
JS: 3456

Puberty–Boys
J: 3383
JS: 3398

Puberty–Fiction
IJ: 998

Puberty–Girls
IJ: 3380
JS: 3397

Public administration (U.S.),
2778–2815

Public speaking
JS: 3058, 3061, 3065–66

Publishing
See Books and publishing

Pueblo Indians
IJ: 4570
JS: 2614

Puerto Ricans
IJ: 2904

Puerto Ricans–Fiction
IJ: 369
J: 367–68, 370

Puerto Rico
IJ: 4489
JS: 4488

Puerto Rico–Fiction
IJ: 144

Puzzles
IJ: 5483–84
J: 3306, 5485, 5533
JS: 5486

Pyramids
JS: 3531, 3534

Q

Qaddafi, Muammar
JS: 3995–96

Quapaw Indians
JS: 4528

Quintuplets–Fiction
IJ: 613

R

Rabbits–Fiction
JS: 1356

Rabies–Fiction
IJ: 1171

Raccoons
J: 4930
JS: 4933

Racial prejudice, 2878–2937

Racism
IJ: 3775
JS: 2847, 2879–81

Racism–Fiction
IJ: 386

IJ = Intermediate–Junior High; J = Junior High; JS = Junior–Senior High

IJ = Intermediate–Junior High; J = Junior High; JS = Junior–Senior High

IJ = Intermediate–Junior High; J = Junior High; JS = Junior–Senior High

Russian Revolution–Fiction
IJ: 1596
J: 1579

Russwurm, John
JS: 3793

Ruth, Babe
IJ: 3961

Ruthenian Americans
JS: 2925

Rylant, Cynthia
JS: 3679

S

Sabbath (Jewish)
J: 2701

Sabotage
JS: 4261

Sacagawea
IJ: 3898

Sacagawea–Fiction
IJ: 1709

Sadat, Anwar
J: 3997

Safety
JS: 5343

Sagan, Carl
IJ: 3941

Sahara Desert
J: 5093

Sailboarding
JS: 5544

Sailing–Fiction
IJ: 132
J: 1265
JS: 182

Sailing and boating
JS: 5648–49

Sailing ships
JS: 4604

Sakharov, Andrei
IJ: 4104

Salem (Massachusetts)–Fiction
IJ: 1647
JS: 1638

Salerno-Sonnenberg, Nadja
JS: 3737

Sampson, Deborah
J: 3899

Samurai–Fiction
IJ: 1560
J: 1557
JS: 1559, 1561

San Francisco
JS: 3692

San Francisco–Fiction
IJ: 398
J: 24, 134, 399

Sandburg, Carl
J: 3681
JS: 3680

Sanger, Margaret
JS: 3880

Sanitation
J: 3019

Santa Claus–Fiction
JS: 1396

Satellites–Fiction
IJ: 2344

SATS–Fiction
JS: 1890

Saturn
IJ: 4815

Saudi Arabia
IJ: 4447
JS: 4014

Sawyer, Diane
IJ: 3746

Scandinavia
IJ: 4407
JS: 2924, 4406

Scandinavia–Folklore
J: 2600
JS: 2594

Scandinavia–History
IJ: 4405
JS: 2916, 4228

Scandinavia–Mythology
IJ: 2657
JS: 2629, 2658

Scandinavian Americans
J: 2877
JS: 2916

Scavengers
J: 4908

Schizophrenia–Fiction
JS: 763

Schmidt, Mike
IJ: 3962

School dropouts
JS: 3049

School dropouts–Fiction
JS: 1323

School stories–Fiction
IJ: 397, 533, 589, 866, 883, 929, 936, 954, 962–63, 982, 994, 1005, 1014, 1026, 1031, 1062, 1109, 1144, 1147, 1188, 1190, 1194, 1233, 1239, 1264, 1275, 1284, 1313, 1864, 1872, 1909, 2088, 2126, 2451
J: 614, 956, 967, 1065, 1077, 1103, 1106, 1116, 1217, 1229, 1254, 1278, 1283, 1803, 1871, 1899, 1908, 1925, 2172, 2247, 2249, 2468
JS: 748, 943, 949, 951–52, 978, 1018, 1035, 1069, 1073, 1096, 1135–37, 1160, 1196, 1210, 1218, 1230, 1255, 1282, 1290, 1890, 1894, 1902, 1906, 1924, 1944, 1989, 2036, 2136, 2148, 2207, 2217, 2437–38, 2440

School–Poetry
JS: 2548

Schools
See also Education
JS: 3045, 3048

Schools–Fiction
IJ: 1061

Schools–History
J: 3046–47

Schweitzer, Albert
IJ: 3998

Science careers, 3090–3093

Science exhibits
IJ: 4731
JS: 4718

Science fairs
IJ: 4741
JS: 4714–15

Science fiction
IJ: 1883, 2258–59, 2265–66, 2279, 2281–82, 2284, 2290, 2294, 2303, 2306–8, 2310, 2312–13, 2315, 2330, 2333, 2338, 2342, 2344, 2348–49, 2351, 2354, 2360, 2362, 2366, 2368, 2370, 2389, 2391–93, 2395, 2399, 2407–8, 2422–27
J: 2262–63, 2269–70, 2272–74, 2276–77, 2280, 2285–87, 2299, 2305, 2317, 2326, 2328–29, 2332, 2334–37, 2339–41, 2343, 2350, 2352–53, 2355–56, 2359, 2374, 2390, 2394, 2398, 2412, 2421
JS: 286–87, 305, 2191, 2260–61, 2264, 2267–68, 2271, 2275, 2278, 2283, 2288–89, 2291–93, 2295–98, 2300–2, 2304, 2309, 2311, 2314, 2316, 2318–25, 2327, 2331,

IJ = Intermediate–Junior High; J = Junior High; JS = Junior–Senior High

IJ = Intermediate–Junior High; J = Junior High; JS = Junior–Senior High

Shakers (religion)
IJ: 2696

Shakespeare, William
IJ: 2486, 2665, 4398
J: 2487
JS: 2666, 3682

Sharks
IJ: 5016–17, 5021
J: 5019–20
JS: 5018

Sharks–Fiction
IJ: 179

Shells
IJ: 5024

Sherlock Holmes–Fiction
JS: 300, 1984–86, 2300

Shetland Islands–Fiction
J: 1431

Ships and boats
IJ: 5363
JS: 5379

Ships and boats–Fiction
IJ: 258
J: 1681

Shipwrecks
IJ: 5151, 5153
J: 5155–56

Shipwrecks–Fiction
IJ: 175, 288
JS: 180, 294

Shoplifting–Fiction
IJ: 1147

Shopping malls–Fiction
JS: 133

Short stories–Fiction
IJ: 23, 263, 316, 880, 1114, 1259, 1271, 1362, 1416, 1442, 1449, 1537–39, 1568, 1780, 1784, 1786, 1797, 1827, 1846, 1859, 1997–99, 2048, 2069, 2258, 2282, 2427, 2480
J: 225, 360, 380, 1360, 1473, 1599, 1785, 1795, 1819, 2146, 2262–63, 2478–79
JS: 17, 21, 284, 300, 315, 322–23, 383, 421, 466, 971, 988–90, 1001, 1050, 1090, 1156, 1326, 1401, 1437, 1658, 1776, 1778–79, 1781–83, 1794, 1821–22, 1836, 1858, 1935, 1984–85, 2024–25, 2233, 2260–61, 2264, 2292, 2296, 2331, 2379, 2477

Shoshoni Indians–Fiction
IJ: 1625

Shreve, Henry Miller
IJ: 3900

Shroud of Turin
JS: 5515

Shrubs
JS: 4856

Shyness–Fiction
IJ: 199, 268, 833, 1171
J: 2141
JS: 1234, 1248

Siberia
J: 4416
JS: 4126

Sibling rivalry–Fiction
IJ: 1317
J: 551, 632, 823, 1205
JS: 409, 508, 644, 1013, 1189

Siblings
IJ: 3112, 3519

Siblings–Fiction
IJ: 168, 177, 451–53, 464, 474, 586, 640, 650, 663, 682, 703, 756, 834, 846, 1167, 1266, 1335, 1446, 1936
J: 142, 445, 449, 454, 467, 491, 593, 617, 677–78, 705, 859, 999, 1057
JS: 68, 143, 584, 592, 618, 633, 637, 753, 778, 780, 812, 817, 843, 854, 1161, 1216, 1222, 1581, 1828

Siegal, Aranka
JS: 4136

Sierra Club
IJ: 3934

Sight
IJ: 4917

Sign language
IJ: 3371
J: 3368, 3370, 3374

Sikhism
JS: 2698

Sikkim
IJ: 2707

Sills, Beverly
JS: 3738

Silver
IJ: 5241

Simulators
IJ: 5242

Singer, Isaac Bashevis
IJ: 3683–84

Singers
IJ: 3711
JS: 3568

Singers–Biography
IJ: 3723, 3725, 3728, 3733

J: 3724, 3729
JS: 3703, 3712, 3720–21, 3726–27, 3735–36, 3738, 3740

Singers–Fiction
IJ: 358, 501

Single parents
IJ: 3492
J: 3498

Single parents–Fiction
IJ: 519
JS: 631

Sioux Indians
JS: 4547

Sioux Indians–Fiction
JS: 2383

Sitting Bull
IJ: 4546

Skateboarding
IJ: 5539, 5650

Skeleton
IJ: 3315

Skeletons–Fiction
J: 2070, 2072

Skiing
JS: 5651

Skiing–Fiction
J: 2123

Skin
JS: 3316

Skin care
JS: 3317–19

Sky
IJ: 4753

Skydiving
J: 5545
JS: 5543

Slave trade
JS: 4229

Slavery
IJ: 3687, 3797, 3799, 3802, 3889, 4600, 4602
J: 2885, 4315
JS: 3769–72, 3793, 3800–1, 4229

Slavery–Fiction
IJ: 1613, 1618, 1666, 1671, 1677, 1686, 2315
J: 1654, 1667
JS: 324, 1631, 1669, 1684

Slavery–History
J: 2858

Sled dog racing
IJ: 5523
JS: 5046

IJ = Intermediate–Junior High; J = Junior High; JS = Junior–Senior High

IJ = Intermediate–Junior High; J = Junior High; JS = Junior–Senior High

IJ = Intermediate–Junior High; J = Junior High; JS = Junior–Senior High

IJ = Intermediate–Junior High; J = Junior High; JS = Junior–Senior High

Symbols, words, and languages, 2673–2683

Synthetic training devices
IJ: 5242

Syria
J: 4437
JS: 4006

Syria–Fiction
JS: 162

Szold, Henrietta
JS: 4037

T

Tamerlane
JS: 4038

Tanks
JS: 5368

Tarzan–Fiction
JS: 25, 2278

Taxes and taxation
JS: 2761, 2786, 2844

Teachers
JS: 3045

Teachers–Fiction
IJ: 188, 1498, 1727, 2088
J: 1065, 2163, 2247, 2336, 2449
JS: 1037, 1282, 1321, 1907, 1913

Technology and engineering,
5222–5380
IJ: 3022, 5228, 5234
J: 5224
JS: 5313

Teenage parents
JS: 3390, 3407, 3480–81

Teenage parents–Fiction
JS: 724–25, 977, 1033

Teeth
IJ: 3320–22, 3367

Telecommunications
IJ: 5322

Television
IJ: 3081, 3600, 3604, 3643, 3742,
3746, 3874, 5325, 5327
J: 3078, 3597
JS: 1072, 1076, 1924, 2120, 2212,
2220, 2823, 3077, 3596

Television–Fiction
IJ: 1105, 1920, 2119

J: 868, 946, 1077, 1103, 1213,
1421, 1861, 1863
JS: 409

Temper–Fiction
IJ: 816

Temperature
J: 4915

Tennessee–Fiction
IJ: 673
J: 1722

Tennessee Valley Authority
IJ: 5169

Tennis
IJ: 5663, 5665
J: 3979, 5664
JS: 5662

Tennis–Fiction
J: 2246, 2471
JS: 2476

Tepees
IJ: 4571

Teresa, Mother
J: 4039

Terrariums
IJ: 4902

Territories–United States
IJ: 4513

Terrorism
IJ: 3009–11
JS: 3008, 3012–15

Terrorism–Fiction
J: 190
JS: 34, 81, 143, 2031, 2347

Tests and test taking
J: 3054–56

Tet Offensive
IJ: 4676

Texas
J: 4698

Texas–Fiction
IJ: 119, 188, 219, 1149, 1686,
1688, 1712, 1719
JS: 211, 1135, 2137

Texas–History
IJ: 3866, 4601

Texas–Poetry
J: 2557

Textile mills–Fiction
JS: 1670

Textiles
JS: 5251

Thailand–Fiction
JS: 1339

Thanksgiving Day parade
J: 3587

Thatcher, Margaret
JS: 4108

Theater
IJ: 3082, 3614, 3643
J: 3615
JS: 3570, 3618

Theater–Fiction
IJ: 11, 1030, 1849
J: 1291
JS: 1059, 2075, 2216, 2245

Theaters
JS: 2666

Third World
IJ: 2971, 4363
JS: 3005

Thoreau, Henry David
JS: 3688

Tibet–History
JS: 4361

Time and clocks
IJ: 5122

Time-warp stories–Fiction
IJ: 1365, 1415, 1439, 1450, 1465,
1485–86, 1488, 1490, 1513, 1519,
1522, 2266, 2348–49
J: 1357, 1389, 1406, 1417, 1476,
1482–83, 1487, 1525, 1532, 2197,
2285, 2390
JS: 326, 1437, 1459, 1524, 1528,
2283, 2295, 2361, 2373, 2378,
2385–86, 2400, 2406, 2418

Titanic
IJ: 5151

Tito, Josip Broz
IJ: 4109

Tobacco
IJ: 3128, 3169, 3172
JS: 3119, 3142

Togo
J: 4321

Tom Thumb
J: 3739
JS: 3369

Tongue twisters
IJ: 5487–89

Tops
IJ: 5414

Tornadoes–Fiction
J: 156

Tourism
JS: 3083

IJ = Intermediate–Junior High; J = Junior High; JS = Junior–Senior High

IJ = Intermediate–Junior High; J = Junior High; JS = Junior–Senior High

IJ = Intermediate–Junior High; J = Junior High; JS = Junior–Senior High

Voodoo–Fiction
JS: 1789

Voyager (airplane)
IJ: 5341

W

Wald, Lillian
JS: 3903

Wales
JS: 3528, 3666

Wales–Fiction
IJ: 1481, 1839, 2284
J: 1745
JS: 1456

Wales–Poetry
JS: 2533

Walesa, Lech
IJ: 4110
JS: 4111

Walker, Herschel
J: 3975

Wallenberg, Raoul
IJ: 4112

Walls–History
JS: 4188

Walters, Barbara
IJ: 3742

Wampanoag Indians
J: 4567
JS: 3901

War, 2734–2756

War–Fiction
IJ: 108, 150
J: 1331, 1682
JS: 15, 34

War of 1812
IJ: 4605

War of 1812–Fiction
J: 1668
JS: 1713

War of the Roses–Fiction
JS: 1601

War veterans
JS: 2793, 4664

**Wars of the Twentieth
Century–Historical fiction,**
1740–1775

Washington, George
IJ: 3851, 3853, 4690
J: 3852, 3854
JS: 3849–50

Washington (state)–Fiction
IJ: 761

Waste and waste disposal
JS: 2952

Water
J: 5126–27

Water birds
IJ: 4967

Water sports
IJ: 5659

Watergate Affair
JS: 4662

Wealth–Fiction
IJ: 1295

Weapons
IJ: 2742, 4616, 5378, 5380
JS: 5364

Weapons control–Fiction
J: 1341

Weather
IJ: 4779, 5131
J: 5132
JS: 4187, 4645, 5125, 5129–30,
5133–34

Weddings–Fiction
J: 445, 573
JS: 2240

Weeds
JS: 4874

Weight lifting
IJ: 5587

Weight problems
IJ: 3354, 3357
J: 3352
JS: 3329, 3351, 3353, 3355, 3358,
3360

Weight problems–Fiction
IJ: 699, 745, 830, 892, 1062, 1200
J: 704, 754, 758–59, 815, 1067,
1110
JS: 741, 1009, 1080, 1241

Weights and measures
IJ: 5159

Weizmann, Chaim
J: 4040

Wells, H. G.
JS: 3690

Werewolves
IJ: 5507

Werewolves–Fiction
IJ: 1859
J: 1600, 1796

Wesley, John
IJ: 4113

West Bank (Israel)
IJ: 4436

West Point
J: 4609

West (U.S.)
IJ: 4621, 4682
JS: 4876, 4895

West (U.S.)–Fiction
IJ: 41, 53, 233, 761, 1113, 2005
J: 128, 189, 934, 1261
JS: 22, 161, 237, 342, 356, 1701,
1737, 1865

West (U.S.)–History
IJ: 3864, 3882, 4625, 4628, 4635–
37
J: 3894, 4629, 4631, 4634, 4642,
4649
JS: 2921, 4534, 4627, 4630, 4632,
4639–40, 4654

West Virginia–Fiction
IJ: 630

**Westward expansion (U.S.)–
History,** 4617–4644

Whales
IJ: 5028
J: 5029, 5031–32
JS: 5008, 5030

Whales–Fiction
IJ: 176
J: 37

Whaling–History
JS: 4523

Wheatley, Phillis
JS: 3691

Wheels
IJ: 4745

Wheels–History
IJ: 5333

**White House (Washington,
D.C.)**
IJ: 2777, 4689

Whitman, Walt
JS: 2570, 2672

Wife abuse–Fiction
J: 460

Wilder, Laura Ingalls
JS: 3692–93

IJ = Intermediate–Junior High; J = Junior High; JS = Junior–Senior High

IJ = Intermediate–Junior High; J = Junior High; JS = Junior–Senior High

IJ = Intermediate–Junior High; J = Junior High; JS = Junior–Senior High